ESSAYS

of an

INFORMATION SCIENTIST

by

EUGENE GARFIELD

with a foreword by

DEREK J. de SOLLA PRICE

VOLUME THREE **1977—1978**

3501 Market Street, University City Science Center
Philadelphia, PA 19104 U.S.A. (215)386-0100, Cable:SCINFO

Published by ISI PRESS
a division of the
Institute for Scientific Information
3501 Market Street
University City Science Center
Philadelphia, Pennsylvania 19104

Library of Congress Card Number 77–602
ISBN 0-89495-000-2 (the set)
ISBN 0-89495-009-6 (this volume)
ISBN 0-89495-001-0 (volume one)
ISBN 0-89495-002-9 (volume two)

Library of Congress Cataloging in Publication Data

Garfield, Eugene.
  Essays of an information scientist.

  Includes bibliographies and indexes.
  1. Communication in science—Collected works.
  2. Science—Abstracting and indexing—Collected works.
  3. Information Science—Collected works.   I.   Title
Z7405.C6G37   [Q223]   029′.9′5   77–602

Printed in the United States of America
at Havertown Printing, Inc.
Broomall, Pennsylvania 19008

In memory of my daughter Thea

Foreword

by
Derek J. de Solla Price

I was inoculated with Citation Fever shortly after coming to Yale and delivering the lectures that became *Science Since Babylon* (1961). In those days, the early 1960s, the National Science Foundation had a Science Information Council, which was supposed to advise and consult on policy questions concerned with funding the scientific literature. One may question how much impact we had on policy, but there is no doubt that the Council was one of the best information and education channels to which I have ever had access.

One memorable day that unforgettable character Gene Garfield appeared before the Council with a request to support the printing and distribution of the first experimental *Science Citation Index*, the data for which had been created to compile the *Genetics Citation Index*, funded by NIH. Unfortunately, NSF refused the request. Notwithstanding the refusal, I personally was immediately struck by the realization that citation links represented a radically new kind of data with far-reaching potential. Though we couldn't predict with absolute certainty how much a citation index might be used, or even to what purpose, it seemed clear to me that such an index must be developed. It also seemed clear to me that such an index would have a good chance of becoming a commercial success, instead of becoming a permanent burden on the federal budget; though a new immigrant to the land of federal fiscal matters, I was able to recognize that prospect as being nearly unique.

From that day to the present, which offers me the privilege of contributing this foreword in honor of Gene and his venture, I have found megavitamins for my intellectual diet on the cutting-room floor of ISI's computer room. Bit by bit we have begun to understand how citations work, and in the course of this, there has emerged a new sort of statistical sociology of science that has thrown light on many aspects of the authorship, refereeing, and publication of scientific research papers. The Society for Social Studies of Science (known colloquially as the 4S Group) now has an annual meeting devoted to this new method of understanding science that has grown, almost as an accidental by-product, from the indexing technology developed by the Institute for Scientific Information. Our initial intuitive perceptions have turned out to be correct.

One thing that we failed to perceive in those early years, however, was the open-ended character of the computer revolution. It was reasonably supposed at that time that the computer would soon have the capacity to do various large memory jobs, such as computer indexing, and that it would gradually do them faster and faster as well as cheaper and cheaper. What was not perceived was that the rate and magnitude of hardware advances would be such that it would become possible to do classes of jobs one year that had not even been conceptualized the previous year. It is rather like the early days of some other technologies; it would have been difficult to perceive that the typewriter would generate a new sociology of office workers, or that the automobile would invent suburbs.

What I see now with the new understanding of how citations and papers work, and with a more realistic appreciation for the technological potential of computers, is that one may use citations as a way of organizing and filing the scientific literature as an omniscient and perfectly-read scholar in the field would do. All this derives from the discovery by Henry Small and Belver Griffith that co-citation mapping can order papers in clusters that map on a two-dimensional plane. It may seem a rather abstruse finding, but I believe it to be revolutionary in its implications.

The finding suggests that there is some type of natural order in science crying out to be recognized and diagnosed. Our method of indexing papers by descriptors or other terms is almost certainly at variance with this natural order. If we can successfully define the natural order, we will have created a sort of giant atlas of the corpus of scientific papers that can be maintained in real time for classifying and monitoring developments as they occur.

I believe it will soon (in five years or so) be possible to display pages from such an atlas, showing not only the natural place of each new paper in "knowledge space" but also giving the degree and nature of the activity resulting from each contribution. As in air-traffic-controller displays, each element in the atlas display can be tagged—in this case with the nation, institution, person, and granting program associated with each paper.

The new mapping theorem has both theoretical and practical implications. On the side of pure speculative theory I suggest that *information is measured, as we well know from Shannon theory, by the order it produces out of disorder. But order of what? The answer seems to be that each piece of information has value insofar as it relates to the order of other information, and that what we see in mapping is this basic order.* That order has been invisible till now, because the structure of previous information systems has constrained information to a single dimension. When we let information spread out into a second dimension, as on a plane, the order becomes visible. I, for one, find that very challenging and provocative.

At the practical level I feel we shall be able to use the mapping theorem for indexing. At an even more elementary level, it suggests a useful condensation of printed citation indexes. We already know from cumulative-advantage theory that knowledge grows almost entirely from the small core of highly-active papers that are more than minimally cited. The co-citation mapping work demonstrates the fundamental nature of that core and raises the question of whether it is worthwhile to include anything more than that in printed citation indexes, when we know that the rest has a very low utility and creates functional and economic problems. Mightn't we produce smaller, easier to handle, and less expensive printed indexes by restricting entry to those papers cited more than once or, in annual and larger cumulations, perhaps even to those cited by three different source papers. Besides reducing the bulk and cost of the printed volumes, such a strategy would automatically exclude all the very annoying garbage that is introduced by mis-citations, bibliographic and transcription errors, and the half of all references that are scattered around as random noise. The full citation file could be maintained on-line for those unwilling to trade off unnecessary completeness for a much higher degree of relevance.

This volume of essays contains one item that touches on this very point of condensation. The one on *Project Keysave* describes a technique that has proved very useful and economical at ISI. A select file of the more highly cited papers is combed through automatically as each new reference is keyed into the system in abbreviated form. For many journals 90 percent of all references can be "recognized" at this early stage of inputting, eliminating the need for additional keying. One idea suggested by this methodology is that the contents of this file of constantly-used references would make a valuable personal possession for most publishing scientists. I suppose that if each good old standby paper in the file were issued with a social security number, future authors could cite that and avoid all the usual misidentifications.

Amongst other essays reprinted in this volume, I would like to draw the reader's special attention to those dealing with citation studies, in particular, the one on the study of the parochial character (or otherwise) of French science, "Le Nouveau Défi Américain," which drew scandalized protests from the French undoubtedly because of the special political significance they have always attached to the international civilizing mission of the French language. Similar studies of other nations, areas, and languages make an impressive and policy-provoking set of points.

I think it will be necessary one day to organize these insights in a way that makes them useful at the national-policy-making level. What should the government of Brazil do about its scientific journals, for example, in the light of this citation data? Should they publish their best work in the Portuguese language? Almost certainly not. Should they continue to claim, as they do in their national bibliography, that they publish some 3000 scientific and technical journals? It is hardly useful when one cannot find citation evidence that more than a handful of these are ever used or cited by anyone in their own country.

These essays document the peculiarly strategic role Gene Garfield and ISI play in using the computer to deepen our understanding of scientific information and the natural order of scientific knowledge. They are not just the best ballgame in town, but the only one in the sense that they are covering all of science rather than some particular fragment of it, and in the sense that they have developed, and are evolving, a perspective of the whole that is unique to the computer manipulation of information. My guess, for what it is worth, is that the continuing development of computerized information will carry their effort forward for many decades to come, and the provocative observations and useful insights collected in this volume will be followed by many more.

Derek J. de Solla Price
Department of History of Science and Medicine
Yale University
Box 2036
Yale Station
New Haven, Connecticut 06520

PREFACE

In preparation for the writing of this preface I re-examined the many published reviews of the first two volumes of my essays. I was impressed, if not annoyed, by the frequent assertions that a considerable number of my essays had little, or nothing, to do with the information sciences. Reviewers often implied that they were pleasantly surprised by this discovery. I'm surprised at their surprise.

I understand, of course, that their expectations were conditioned by the title, *Essays of an Information Scientist.* Apparently, they assumed that an information scientist would write only about information science. I suppose such an assumption may not be entirely unwarranted, but it seems to me to be based on an unduly narrow view of a human being. We are, after all, multi-dimensional creatures in an intellectual and emotional, as well as physical, sense. The first two volumes of my essays reflect some of the intellectual and emotional dimensions that, along with information science, are found in this particular information scientist. This, the third, volume continues in the same vein.

The book contains more about science in general than it does about information science in particular. For that reason, I think any scientist, whether particularly interested in information science or not, might find much of interest. One essay deals with *Citation Classics.* This weekly feature in *Current Contents* permits authors of important scientific papers to describe in their own words why and how they came about doing some of their most useful work. Other essays wander among such subjects as the role of style in scientific writing, a proposal for paying scientists to produce high quality reviews on a regular basis, a new way of looking at reprint requests, copyright practices, management of personal reprint files, chiropractic medicine, and the state-of-the-art of science journalism. Many of the essays of general scientific interest analyze the literature of various specialties, disciplines, and nations to uncover some insights into the orientation and structure of their research activity.

This subject of analyzing research activity through the literature it produces is one of my special interests and one of several recurrent themes running through the book. The study of science mainly through citation analysis is now called scientometrics, having evolved from bibliometrics. It is a field of study that has taken on new vitality in recent years, fueled by the development of several methods of citation analysis that have greatly increased its power and utility. Both ISI and I have played, and continue to play, a prominent role in this resurgence. Yet the field is dominated not by information scientists, but by sociologists and historians of science and by science administrators. Most of the support for this kind of research comes from people concerned with science policy and the administration of large science programs. These people, plus the historians and sociologists, will find a continuing record of citation analysis studies, with fat bibliographies, in this volume.

Another recurring theme in this volume has to do with the editorial practices of scientific journals. As the head of a company that produces "secondary" indexing and other information services, I have a natural interest in such things as journal design, publication schedules, and editorial conventions. As a scientist with a penchant for communication, these interests extend into matters of editorial style, the economics of publishing, and the individual and collective roles played by journals. Journal editors and others interested in scientific communication will find essays on all those subjects. Many of the citation analyses reprinted here have to do with my efforts to clearly define parts of the network of journals that serve the international scientific community.

Some of the essays are unabashedly personal. I have had the good fortune to become friends with some very special people. Some are towering figures in the world of science. Others have no scientific credentials, but are people who have won my love or respect with other strengths. Periodically, I am moved to document one of these friendships, to publicly acknowledge the way in which that person has enriched my life. Several of those acknowledgements are reprinted here.

I don't mean to imply by this discourse that I'm an information scientist who writes about everything but information science. The expectations raised in the hearts of reviewers, and maybe readers, by the title of *Essays of an Information Scientist* are at least partially fulfilled. There is more than enough on information science to keep professionals from that field from feeling the least bit slighted. Though my interests may be considered eclectic, the perspective of an information scientist lies at the core of them.

The point that I have been laboring, perhaps too hard, to make is that while this volume, as the preceding ones, reflects the perspective of an information scientist, it also reflects the interests of a person who is involved with and concerned about much more of the total scope of scientific and human activity than information science circumscribes. The result is a potpourri of essays that just won't fit very neatly into any single subject classification. About the best I can do in the way of producing a general characterization of this book is to say that it contains some of the observations and concerns that one scientist thinks he may share with others.

Eugene Garfield

Institute for Scientific Information
3501 Market Street
University City Science Center
Philadelphia, Pennsylvania 19104

January 2, 1980

Essays of an Information Scientist

TABLE OF CONTENTS

Volume 3

Contents

Contents

Contents

Contents

Contents

Contents

Essays
of an
Information Scientist

CURRENT COMMENTS

Introducing *Citation Classics:*
The Human Side of Scientific Reports

Number 1, January 3, 1977

With this first issue of 1977, we begin an experiment unique to *Current Contents®* . Immediately following this essay, you will discover a new feature entitled *Citation Classics*. Each week we will select an article that has become a classic in its field. Each *Citation Classic* will include a commentary by the author. In particular, we want to know why the paper proved to be so important, and, as a consequence, highly cited. For each paper we will provide a synopsis or digest. In this way, readers who are unfamiliar with the field can better appreciate its significance.

Citation Classics will enable the authors of these papers to discuss their work retrospectively. It is the kind of science 'reviewing' rarely seen in scientific journals. It will provide a kind of living history. Authors will discuss interesting aspects in the development of their techniques, the role played by coauthors or others, and the encouragement received from colleagues. This is the human side of science.

Undoubtedly most of these authors will not only be among the most cited, but also the most highly-qualified in their respective fields. The candidates for *Citation Classics* will be selected from a group of 500 papers most cited during the years 1961-1975. Many of these have been listed before in *Current Contents*.

Papers in this group include some of the most cited papers ever published--thus the designation of 'classics.' If one were to assume that the history of science encompasses 20 million papers, then one percent of these would constitute a large block of 200 thousand. One tenth of one percent would include a healthy 20 thousand, and .01% about 2,000 papers. Even if our estimate of the number of papers published to-date is high, 500 papers is still an incredibly small part of the history of scientific publication. It will be interesting to observe over the next ten years whether the literature doubles and how many new classics will have appeared on our lists by that time.

Despite the age of the papers (most were published during the 1940s, 50s, and 60s), many achieved their *highest* citation rates within the past four years. Predominating the list, which will be published in the future, are 'methodology' papers in the fields of molecular biology and biochemistry, clearly reflecting the high rate of activity in those areas. Addressing that point, Dr. Walter C. Schneider, of the National Cancer Institute, remarked that, ''It is not entirely surprising to me that this should be the case since methods are the backbone of all scientific research.''[1]

The authors of these classics, upon being informed of the status of their papers, expressed varying degrees of surprise and delight. Dr. Schneider wrote of his 1944 paper on phosphorus compounds in animal tissue[2] that, "It is indeed most gratifying to learn 31 years after publishing my paper that it is one of the most cited scientific papers."[1] His sentiments are echoed by Dr. Norton Nelson, of the New York University Medical Center, who commented that, "I was startled but interested at your letter notifying me that my paper, 'A photometric adaptation of the Somogyi method for the determination of glucose (1944),' [3] was still a best seller."[4]

In some cases, perhaps, these papers may have marked the beginnings of distinguished careers in the sciences. In the instance of Dr. W.E. Trevelyan, of Surrey, England, it seems that his 'classic' paper was his first published research. He comments: "Your letter...informing me that my paper on the detection of sugars on paper chromatograms[5] had attained the dignity of a citation classic caused a deal of ribald comment amongst my colleagues and may cost me a few pints [of beer]. Never mind, I am secretly very pleased-- it was my first publication, based on work done in my first research job. Moreover, I left the scientific field as an undergraduate in 1937, and came back as a self-taught biochemist ten years later, my research post being obtained on the basis of an MSc I collected for work done in a sewage laboratory with a handful of 1 ml pipettes and litre bottles."[6] (It was not our intention to cause the authors of citation classics any financial loss in order to quell the ribaldry of envious colleagues!)

In a previous editorial[7] we published a list of the all-time classics. Were we to publish a similar list today, it would have changed very little. Indeed, the 50 papers would appear in very nearly the same rank-ordered positions. But the all-time citation classic is Lowry's 1951 paper, "Protein measurement with the Folin phenol reagent,"[8] which I discussed on an earlier occasion.[9] This single paper has accumulated more citations (50,016) than the next 6 papers combined! It is worth noting, too, that Professor Lowry has authored two other papers on the list of 500 classics.[10,11] It seems fitting, that Professor Lowry's commentary on his 1951 paper should initiate our new feature page.

REFERENCES

1. **Schneider W C.** Personal communication, 10 November 1976.
2. **Schneider W C.** Phosphorus compounds in animal tissues. 1. Extraction and estimation of desoxypentose nucleic acid and of pentose nucleic acid. **J. Biol. Chem.** 161:293-303, 1945.
3. **Nelson N.** A photometric adaptation of the Somogyi method for the determination of glucose. **J. Biol. Chem.** 153:375-80, 1944.
4. **Nelson N.** Personal communication, 26 October 1976.
5. **Trevelyan W E, Proctor D P & Harrison J S.** Detection of sugars on paper chromatograms. **Nature** 166:444-45, 1950.
6. **Trevelyan W E.** Personal communication, 24 November 1976.
7. **Garfield E.** Selecting the all-time citation classics; here are the fifty most cited papers for 1961-1972. *Current Contents* (*CC®*), No. 6, 9 January 1974, p. 5-8.
8. **Lowry O H, Rosebrough N J, Farr A L & Randall R J.** Protein measurement with the Folin phenol reagent. **J. Biol. Chem.** 193:265-75, 1951.
9. **Garfield E.** Citation frequency as a measure of research activity and performance. *CC* No. 5, 31 January 1973, p. 5-7.
10. **Lowry O H, Passonneau J V, Hasselberger F X & Schulz D W.** Effects of ischemia on known substrates and cofactors of the glycolytic pathway in brain. **J. Biol. Chem.** 239:18-30, 1964.
11. **Lowry O H & Lopez J A.** The determination of inorganic phosphate in the presence of labile phosphate esters. **J. Biol. Chem.** 162:421-28, 1946.

CURRENT COMMENTS

On Style in Scientific Writing

Number 2, January 10, 1977

In the pages that follow, Steve Aaronson, the editor of our weekly *ISI Press Digest*, demonstrates his talent and style. It takes a good writer to do a good digest. So it isn't surprising that the *Press Digest* receives accolades from so many readers. I don't agree with everything Steve says and quotes. But I do like the way he says it. He's also done some creditable research.

Steve's admonitions about the stylistic value of short words and simple sentences should be taken to heart. There are people who habitually confuse us with long words and complex sentences in a misguided search for effect. But there is a place for both. A certain well-known close colleague of mine, who would find mention of his name **embarrassing**, writes with a vocabulary that must rival Shakespeare's. I love his use of rare words. Some would stump the average college graduate, as they often stump me. Would Aaronson absolutely deny me the pleasure of using a dictionary?

On the other hand, I have a running battle with my chief editor, Bob Hayne. It never satisfies him that the subject matter is interesting. The manner of its expression must also be interesting. He can, and gladly will, write gramatically perfect sentences thirty lines long. I tell him I prefer sentences of ten words or so. I am somewhat simple-minded. I prefer to have complex thoughts spelled out in brief sentences. Hayne contends this produces a staccato style that is no style at all. He wants me to write more like Henry James. But I prefer the simple style. This reminds me of the lady who asked for a gift that was "simple but expensive." Like her, I prefer elegant simplicity.

I also happen to value a sense of humor, even in science. Most science writing is unnecessarily dull. A few quips, a light touch here and there, can help the reader get through otherwise dreary deserts of data.

This topic of style in scientific writing was first proposed as something I should undertake myself, with some research and drafting help from Steve. I couldn't, with a clear conscience, have put my name to the "draft" he submitted. And, though I don't disagree with much of it, I didn't want to modify or edit it in order to justify claiming it as my own. So here is Aaronson's "draft," as it was submitted for "review." You can say I got a week's vacation. After reading what he wrote it required little work to write this introduction.

Style in Scientific Writing

by Steve Aaronson

This space is usually devoted to a macroscopic view of scientific information: the characteristics of individual papers, of journals, of aggregates of journals, and even of whole countries or scientific disciplines. This wide-angle view is useful and necessary, but it also makes it easy to lose one's sense of perspective. It is worth remembering that communication of scientific results is accomplished mainly by the written word.

Language is the starting and ending point for science. In 1789, Antoine Laurent Lavoisier wrote that, "It is impossible to dissociate language from science or science from language, because every natural science always involves three things: the sequence of phenomena on which the science is based; the abstract concepts which call these phenomena to mind; and the words in which the concepts are expressed. To call forth a concept a word is needed; to portray a phenomenon, a concept is needed. All three mirror one and the same reality."[1]

The principle by which phenomena and concepts are reduced to language is style. It is no less important in scientific writing than in poetry.

Although a sense of style is indispensable for any writer, defining exactly what is meant by the word *style* is difficult. Jonathan Swift's definition is succinct: "Proper words in proper places, make the true definition of a style."[2] But style is more than proper words in proper places. In literature, the writer may deliberately and self-consciously use style to help convey meaning. For instance, narrating an outrageously comic scene in an understated style may reinforce the satirical effect. But in science writing the best style is transparent; the reader sees through the words to the underlying phenomena and concepts. The best scientific writing is characterized by brevity, clarity, and precision.

In 1888 Ludwig Boltzmann compared scientific style to musical style. "Just as a musician recognizes Mozart, Beethoven or Schubert from the first few bars, so does a mathematician recognize his Cauchy, Gauss, Jacobi or Helmholtz from the first few pages."[3] Charles Darwin is reported to have said, "I think too much pains cannot be taken in making the style transparently clear and throwing eloquence to the dogs."[4] Even as early as 1667, Thomas Sprat implored the members of the newly formed Royal Society of London for Improving Natural Knowledge to "reject all the amplifications, digressions, and swellings of style; to return back to the primitive purity, and shortness, when men delivered so many *things,* almost in an equal number of *words.*"[5]

More recently, style has been defined statistically. Martin Robbins, a teacher of science writing at the Massachusetts Institute of Technology, has his students compute percentages of word usage in selected examples of scientific writing in order to analyze

4

and understand the writer's style.[6] He explains that this type of style analysis is similar to first-year work in a traditional art school, where students use the work of the masters for models. In this case, the "masters" include Einstein, Oppenheimer, Gardner, Hoyle, Bronowski, Asimov, Russell, Whitehead, Carson, and Krutch. The students take samples of the writing of each, and then compute the types of sentence structure and word usage. For instance, one student found that a 426-word sample from Jacob Bronowski's *The Identity of Man* had 3 paragraphs, 21 sentences averaging 20.3 words per sentence, an average of 1.8 syllables per word, an average of 2.65 prepositional phrases per sentence, and an average of 0.6 adjectives per sentence. The sentence structure was 24% simple, 48% complex, 14% compound, and 14% compound-complex.[7]

This type of statistical analysis can be extended to include paragraph strategies, transitions, vocabulary, rhetorical devices, and figures of speech. Its primary value is that it allows students to examine style without being distracted by content. Robbins feels that as a result of the assignment, the students "become aware of how much a writer's style is part of what he says."

It is an obvious but often forgotten fact that recognition—of both a discovery and its discoverer—depends on the use of language. Scientific findings must be translated into comprehensible language—which then will be published. The physicist John Rader Platt wrote,

> The failure to recognize a brilliant man is only partly due to the stupidity or stubbornness of the scientific community; it is also partly his own fault.
>
> For brilliance has an obligation not only to create but also to communicate. A scientist cannot really go 'voyaging through strange seas of thought alone.' The more penetrating eye will see him to be surrounded by a cloud of witnesses. He takes from others; he gives to others. He must address the problems of his time. He must translate his thoughts into the language of his contemporaries. He must scatter them abroad for interaction. A thought which has not penetrated to other minds will die unfruitful.
>
> As a result, the scientist can hardly be recognized posthumously, like the artist or poet. He is much less independent, much more bound to the current needs and purposes of the scientific community. His achievement of thought needs to be at the same time an achievement of communication and leadership which must be acknowledged by the group—by at least one editor ! —before its intellectual viability fades away.[8]

It is unfortunate that so many of us devote so little attention to our choice of words. Although we don't like to admit it, many scientists believe that scientists had better *sound* scientific—the more scientific the better. This often means using scientific jargon instead of plain language. The defenders of scientific jargon claim that it allows greater brevity and exactitude than ordinary language. It is true that most of those familiar with jargon find it agreeable. The cognoscenti are pleased by what they perceive as jargon's precision and aura of scientific objectivity. They are also delighted by the fact that their jargon renders their field incomprehensible to outsiders, enabling them to cultivate the impression that only they—the experts—can understand the deep mysteries involved.

Jargon can be a useful form of shorthand, especially in cases where the discovery of a new substance or property demands that new terms be coined. But even in such cases, the discoverer is often unaware of the implications of the names he chooses. For example, Platt points out,

> Without Newton himself, we might never have had 'force' or 'mass' in the equations of motion; or they might have had very different definitions and emphases. Philosophers have pulled and hauled at them for centuries; the difficulties were ineradicable, because these symbols were written from the beginning in the Newtonian equations that worked. The Father of Physics has imprinted 'force' and 'mass,' like intellectual genes, into every cell of the physical sciences today.
>
> Kepler, on the other hand, seems to have eschewed, largely on aesthetic grounds, the anthropomorphic concept of 'force' between heavenly bodies. In this question of taste, he anticipates Einstein. If history had put the Kepler mind in the Newton body, it might have delayed the discovery of universal gravitation, which would have been difficult for Kepler—but it might have accelerated the discovery of general relativity.
>
> Terminology is often chained to such initial biases. Franklin's choice of the arithmetic terms 'positive' and 'negative' to designate the two supplementary types of electricity still plagues our thinking and may have delayed who knows what happier synthesis.
>
> The idiosyncrasies of taste and choice, of abilities and workmanship, embellish and modify a discovery. The work method is determined; the style is not.[8]

But too often the jargon of scientific specialists is like political rhetoric and bureaucratic mumblespeak: ugly-sounding, difficult to understand, and clumsy. Those who use it often do so because they prefer pretentious, abstract words to simple, concrete ones. Such writers want to dignify not only the subject, but also the writer. They believe that important matters require a special vocabulary.

The limitations of scientific jargon can be illustrated by looking at another type of jargon. Consider *turn on, out of sight, uptight, rap, cop-out, busted, bummer, groove, hip, rap, out front, far out, bread,* and *freak out.* Most are vague, shallow substitutes for ordinary words—but they allow members of a particular subculture to exclude outsiders—"The establishment"—from their communications.

In the same way, vague words like *interface, operational, viable, dimension,* and *replicate* often enable scientists to obscure their meaning. "Every profession has its growing arsenal of jargon to fire at the layman and hurl him back from its walls,"[9] says William Zinsser. Consider the words *infrastructure, functional, gradualism, time-*

phase, reciprocal, systematized, and *organizational.* Such words may make what is simple appear complex.

Many words which have specific technical meanings in one context have been popularized in such a way that the original meaning is badly misrepresented. From chemistry and physics, the words *acid test, reaction, end product,* and *potentials* are often misused; from logic *dilemma, beg the question,* and *dichotomy;* from mathematics *factor, progression, to the nth, proportion, curve,* and *differential;* and from architecture *flamboyant, baroque,* and *rococo.*

Perhaps the most insidious jargon has arisen from the cult of psychoanalysis. Freudian English has given us *ambivalent, complex, ego, extrovert, father figure, fixation, id, inhibition, introvert, libido, manic, masochistic, narcissism, phobia, psyche, psychopath, repression, schizophrenic,* and *subconscious.* These words are widely used and are widely thought to be key concepts— but almost no one is quite sure what they mean.

It has been charged that some of the worst, most offensive jargon is spoken and written by sociologists. For example, Fowler asserts that, "Sociology is a new science concerning itself not with esoteric matters outside the comprehension of the layman, as the older sciences do, but with the ordinary affairs of ordinary people. This seems to engender in those who write about it a feeling that the lack of any abstruseness in their subject demands a compensatory abstruseness in their language."[10] Consider such phrases as *coherent social consciousness, situational interactors,* and *adjustment alternatives.*

Why call a slum a *depressed socioeconomic area,* a salesman a *marketing representative,* or a dumb kid an *underachiever?* Why use *facilitate* for ease, *numerous* for many, *remainder* for rest, *initial* for first, *implement* for do, *sufficient* for enough, *refer to as* for call, or *attempt* for try? Why say *utilize* for use, *perform* for do, or *chemotherapeutic agent* for drug? Why not use the plain instead of the formal; stop instead of *cease,* begin instead of *commence,* hide instead of *conceal,* stop instead of *desist,* give instead of *donate,* foresee instead of *visualize,* true instead of *veritable,* buy instead of *purchase,* find instead of *locate,* get instead of *obtain,* send instead of *transmit,* and go instead of *proceed?*

Many of us clutter our prose with unnecessary verbiage. We use a large word where a small one will suffice, or three words where one will do. This waste of words is caused by two things: a failure to understand what words mean, and the notion that an idea is more noticeable and effective if it is reinforced. Thus arise such redundant phrases as *personal friend, short minute, future prospect, solid facts, final conclusion, successful triumph, positive growth, renovated like new, defense posture, tire and fatigue, hopes and aspirations, help and assistance, prompt and speedy, mutual compromise,* and *fatal slayings*—which Edwin Newman calls "the very worst kind."[11]

Some words serve only as excess baggage; eliminating them lightens a heavy sentence without losing meaning. Examples of such words are *nature* (a tool of a useful nature = a useful tool), *factor* (the time factor), *character* (of an unpleasant character), *aspect* (has a definitive aspect), *condition* (weather conditions), and *quality* (a flaccid quality).

Writers sometimes use words merely to pad their sentences with extra syllables. Examples of such words are *render inoperative, militate against, make contact with, be subjected to, have the effect of, play a leading part in, make itself felt, exhibit a tendency to, serve the purpose of,* and *give rise to.* Simple one-syllable conjunctions are replaced by such phrases as *with respect to, the fact that, having regard to, in view of, in the interests of,* and *on the hypothesis that.*

A satirical "Glossary for Research Reports" compiled by C.D. Graham, Jr.[12] translates the familiar, rather pompous phrases "It is suggested that...", "It is believed that...", and "It may be that..." to "I think...." Instead of "It has long been known that..." he reads, "I haven't bothered to look up the original reference." For "of great theoretical and practical importance" he reads "A couple of other guys think so too." For "It is clear that much additional work will be required before a complete understanding..." he reads, "I don't understand it." Although Graham is pressing the point for the sake of humor, working scientists will recognize the essential veracity of his translations.

Consider too these examples of pseudo-scientific writing from astronomer Paul W. Merrill's satirical article, "The Principles of Poor Writing."[13]

> *Bible:* Render to Caesar the things that are Caesar's.
> *Poor:* In the case of Caesar it might well be considered appropriate from a moral or ethical point of view to render to that potentate all of those goods and materials of whatever character or quality which can be shown to have had their original source in any portion of the domain of the latter.
> *Shakespeare:* I am no orator as Brutus is.
> *Poor:* The speaker is not what might be termed an adept in the profession of public speaking, as might properly be stated of Mr. Brutus.[14]

Besides the use of jargon and nonsense words, one of the main causes of dullness in scientific and technical reports is the use of the passive voice. Apparently, many writers think that passivity is more appropriate to the dispassionate communication of objective results than the use of active verbs and straightforward sentence construction. They write, "The wave motions are caused by the wind," instead of, "The wind causes the wave motions." Unnecessary use of the passive voice makes for tedious, monotonous, lifeless prose.

Syntax, or the sequence of words within the sentence, is also crucial to style. In 1789, George Henry Lewes wrote,

> Words are not like iron and wood, coal and water, invariable in their properties, calculable in their effects. They are mutable in their powers,

deriving force and subtle variations of force from very trifling changes of position; colouring and coloured by the words which precede and succeed; significant or insignificant from the powers of rhythm and cadence. It is the writer's art to to arrange words that they shall suffer the least possible retardation from the inevitable friction of the reader's mind. The analogy of a machine is perfect. In both cases the object is to secure the maximum of disposable force, by diminishing the amount absorbed in the working.[15]

In order to demonstrate the importance of style, E.B. White has taken Thomas Paine's familiar and enduring sentence, "These are the times that try men's souls," and has tried to alter its style while preserving its meaning. He came up with these variations: "Times like these try men's souls." "How trying it is to live in times like these ! " "These are trying times for men's souls." "Soulwise, these are trying times."[16] Would any of these have endured? Obviously, each of the variations destroys the elegant simplicity of Paine's style.

Lewes proposed another illustration of the importance of economy in writing. He took his example from the Bible:

> "God said: Let there be light ! and there was light." This is a conception of power so calm and simple that it needs only to be presented in the fewest and the plainest words, and would be confused or weakened by any suggestion of accessories. Let us amplify the expression in the redundant style of miscalled eloquent writers: 'God, in the magnificent fulness of creative energy, exclaimed: Let there be light ! and lo ! the agitating fiat immediately went forth, and thus in one indivisible moment the whole universe was illumined.' We have here a sentence which I am certain many a writer would, in secret, prefer to the masterly plainness of Genesis. It is not a sentence which would have captivated critics."[15]

In 1946, George Orwell satirized pseudo-scientific jargon by composing a parody of a well-known verse from Ecclesiastes.[17] Here is Orwell's "Modern English" version:

> "Objective consideration of contemporary phenomena compels the conclusion that success or failure in competitive activities exhibits no tendency to be commensurate with innate capacity, but that a considerable element of the unpredictable must invariably be taken into account."

The original was:

> "I returned and saw under the sun, that the race is not to the swift, nor the battle to the strong, neither yet bread to the wise, nor yet riches to men of understanding, nor yet favour to men of skill; but time and chance happeneth to them all."

Orwell used this example to lament the loss of vivid, concrete images from modern prose. He said, "Modern writing at its worst does not consist in picking out words for the sake of their meaning and inventing images in order to make the meaning clearer. It consists in gumming together long strips of words which have already been set in order by someone else, and making the results presentable by sheer humbug. The attraction of this way of writing is that it is easy. It is easier—even quicker, once you have the habit— to say *In my opinion it is not an unjustifiable assumption that* than to say *I think.*"

Orwell pointed out that in the same way as words like *epic* and *historic* are used "to dignify the sordid processes of international politics," such words as *phenomenon, element, individual, objective, categorical, effective, virtual, basic, primary, promote, constitute, exhibit, exploit,* and *utilize* "are used to dress up simple statements and give an air of scientific impartiality to biased judgements." He said, "Bad writers, and especially scientific, political and sociological writers, are nearly always haunted by the notion that Latin or Greek words are grander than Saxon ones, and unnecessary words like expedite, ameliorate, predict, extraneous, deracinated, cladestine, subaqueous and hundreds of others constantly gain ground from their Anglo-Saxon opposite numbers."[17]

Scientific writers could well heed the six concise rules that Orwell set forth in his essay "Politics and the English Language":

(1)   Never use a metaphor, simile or other figure of speech
         which you are used to seeing in print.
(2)   Never use a long word where a short one will do.
(3)   If it is possible to cut a word out, always cut it out.
(4)   Never use the passive where you can use the active.
(5)   Never use a foreign phrase, a scientific word or a jargon word if
         you can think of an everyday English equivalent.
(6)   Break any of these rules sooner than say anything outright
         barbarous.[17]

Facts—whether baseball scores or historical dates or atomic numbers— are chaos until they have been selected, isolated, and combined in relation to one another. Meaning is the selection and juxtaposition of evidence. It is as futile for a TV sportscaster to try to present all the available information on a baseball game as for a scientist to try to present *all* the data on a given phenomenon. The compulsion to include everything, leaving nothing out, does not prove that one has unlimited information; it proves that one lacks discrimination.

A. N. Whitehead has asserted that the task of science "is the discovery of the relations which exist within that flux of perceptions, sensations, and emotions which forms our experience of life. The panorama yielded by sight, sound, taste, smell, touch, and by more inchoate sensible feelings, is the sole field of activity... I insist on the radically untidy, ill-adjusted character of the fields of actual experience from which science starts. To grasp this fundamental truth is the first step in wisdom, when constructing a philosophy of science. The fact is concealed by the influence of language, molded by science, which foists on us exact concepts as though they represented the immediate deliverances of experience."[18]

In a speech almost a century ago, William James discussed the problem of using language to bring order out of chaos—the function of style:

> The real world as it is given objectively at this moment is the sum total of all its being and events now. But can we think of such a sum? Can we realize for an instant what a cross-section of all existence at a definite point of time would be? While I talk and the flies buzz, a sea gull catches a fish at the mouth of the Amazon, a tree falls in the Adirondack wilderness, a man sneezes in Germany, a horse dies in Tartary, and twins are born in France. What does that mean? Does the contemporaneity of these events with one another, and with a million others disjointed, form a rational bond between them, and unite them into anything that means for us a world? Yet just such a collateral contemporaneity, and nothing else, is the real order of the world. It is an order with which we have nothing to do but to get away from it as fast as possible. As I said, we break it: we break it into histories, and we break it into arts, and we break it into sciences; and then we begin to feel at home. We make ten thousand separate serial orders of it, and on any one of these we react as though the others did not exist. We discover among its various parts relations that were never given to sense at all (mathematical relations, tangents, squares, and roots and logarithmic functions), and out of an infinite number of these we call certain ones essential and lawgiving, and ignore the rest. Essential these relations are, but only *for our purpose,* the other relations being just as real and present as they; and our purpose is to *conceive simply* and to *foresee.* Are not simple conception and prevision subjective ends pure and simple? They are the ends of what we call science; and the miracle of miracles, a miracle not yet exhaustively cleared up by any philosophy, is that the given order lends itself to the remodeling. It shows itself plastic to many of our scientific, to many of our aesthetic, to many of our practical purposes and ends."[19]

Various authors have commented on the peculiar problems of organizing and writing a scientific paper.[20,21] Robert A. Day's "How to Write a Scientific Paper"[22] is notable among recent contributions. But few of these writers bother to define style.

Ultimately, style is what gives meaning to thoughts. The sense data of commonplace experience are highly disordered. We impose order by the rigor and neatness of language. If, as Albert Einstein said, "The whole of science is nothing more than a refinement of everyday thinking,"[23] then in scientific writing style is the principle by which everyday thoughts are refined. "Science is built up with facts, as a house is with stones," said Jules Henri Poincare', "but a collection of facts is no more a science than a heap of stones is a house."[24] Style is the architect.

"The only thing that is indispensable for the possession of a good style is personal sincerity"[25] says Herbert Read. But sincerity is not enough. In order to promote the vigorous and efficient exchange of scientific information, scientific writers should be trained in rhetoric, the effective use of language. Students must be convinced that they do not *know* what they mean until they can *say* what they mean. Perhaps all undergraduate science majors should be required to take at least one college course in scientific writing.

It is well known that skills can be taught, but the essential ingredient of good style—honesty—is often thought to be innate. It is not. S. Leonard Rubinstein, director of the writing program at the Pennsylvania State University, asserts that, "If a man intends to impress someone, his work will not be clear, because he does not intend clarity: he intends to impress.... A man's intention is his instrument. He must learn that instrument. He must be honest. And to be honest, he must recognize that desire to be honest is not enough. Honesty is a skill, and the skill must be learned."[26]

One of the best definitions of style for scientists was written in 1948 by the atomic physicist J. Robert Oppenheimer. He said:

> The problem of doing justice to the implicit, the imponderable, and the unknown is of course not unique to politics. It is always with us in science, it is with us in the most trivial of personal affairs, and it is one of the great problems of writing and of all forms of art. The means by which it is solved is sometimes called style. It is style which complements affirmation with limitation and with humility; it is style which makes it possible to act effectively, but not absolutely; it is style which, in the domain of foreign policy, enables us to find a harmony between the pursuit of ends essential to us and the regard for the views, the sensibilities, and aspirations of those to whom the problem may appear in another light; it is style which is the deference that action pays to uncertainty; it is above all style through which power defers to reason.[27]

I hope that this discussion of the importance of style doesn't cause an epidemic of writer's block among its readers. Those who might take the matter of style too seriously can take comfort in Benjamin Franklin's conclusion to a letter describing his electrical experiments:

> Those thoughts, my dear friend, are many of them crude and hasty; and if I were merely ambitious of acquiring some reputation in philosophy, I ought to keep them by me, till corrected and improved by time, and farther experience. But since even short hints and imperfect experiments in any new branch of science, being communicated, have oftentimes a good effect, in exciting the attention of the ingenious to the subject, and so become the occasion of more exact disquisition, and more compleat discoveries, you are at liberty to communicate this paper to whom you please; it being of more importance that knowledge should increase, than your friend should be thought an accurate philosopher.[28]

1. **Lavoisier A L.** *Traité elementaire de chimie,* tr. J Lipetz, D E Gershenson & D A Greenberg. Quoted in : **J Bartlett,** *Familiar quotations* (Boston: Little Brown, 1968), p. 474.
2. **Swift J.** *Letter to a young clergyman,* 9 January 1720. Quoted in: **J Bartlett,** *Familiar quotations,* p. 389.
3. **Boltzmann L.** Quoted in: **R L Weber** (comp.), *A random walk in science* (New York: Crane Russak, 1973), p. 43.
4. **Darwin C.** Quoted in L V Ryan, *A science reader* (New York: Holt Rinehart & Winston, 1959), p. 11-13.
5. **Sprat T.** Quoted in L V Ryan, *A science reader,* p. 249-56.
6. **Robbins M.** Science meets style; bridging the two cultures. *Key Reporter* 40(4):1 passim, 1975.
7. **Hartman C.** *Style analysis of* The Identity of Man *by Jacob Bronowski.* Unpub. ms., 1975.
8. **Platt J R.** Style in science. *Harper's Magazine,* October 1956. Reprinted in: **L V Ryan,** *A science reader, p. 245-58.*
9. **Zinsser W.** *On writing well; an informal guide to writing nonfiction* (New York: Harper & Row, 1976), p. 15.
10. **Fowler H W.** *A dictionary of modern English usage,* 2nd ed. (New York: Oxford University Press, 1965), p. 569-70.
11. **Newman E.** A fatal slaying of the very worst kind. *Atlantic Monthly* 283(3):68-74, March 1976.
12. **Graham C D Jr.** A glossary for research reports. *Metal Progress* 71:75, 1957. Reprinted in L. Weber, *A random walk,* p. 120-21.
13. **Merrill P W.** Quoted in: L V Ryan, *A science reader,* p. 18-22.
14. **Swain P W.** Quoted in **L V Ryan,** *A science reader.*
15. **Lewes G H.** Quoted in **L V Ryan,** *A science reader,* p. 13-17.
16. **White E B & Strunk W.** *The elements of style* (New York: Macmillan, 1972).
17. **Orwell B.** Politics and the English language, in *A collection of essays by George Orwell* (Garden City: Doubleday, 1954), p. 162-76.
18. **Whitehead A N.** Quoted in: **W Gibson** (ed), The limits of language (New York: Hill & Wang, 1962), p. 10-14.
19. **James W.** Reflex action and theism. Quoted in: W. Gibson, *The limits of language,* p. 3-9.
20. **Orth M F.** Color their prose gray. *IEEE Trans. Profess. Commun.* PC-18 (2): 65-66, 1975.
21. **Clark A K.** Readability in technical writing; principles and procedures. *IEEE Trans. Profess. Commun.* PC-18(2): 67-70, 1975.
22. **Day R A.** How to write a scientific paper. *Canad. J. Med. Technol.* 38(3):B100-04, 1976.
23. **Einstein A.** *Physics and reality,* 1936. Quoted in: **J.** Bartlett, *Familiar quotations,* p. 950.
24. **Poincare J H.** La science et l'hypothese, tr. G B Halsted. Quoted in: **J Bartlett,** *Familiar quotations,* p. 829.
25. **Read H.** *English prose style* (Boston: Beacon Press, 1970), p. 115.
26. **Rubinstein S L.** Writing: a habit of mind (Dubuque, Iowa: William C. Brown, 1972).
27. **Oppenheimer J R.** Quoted in: W. Gibson, *The limits of language.*
28. **Franklin B.** Quoted in **L V Ryan,** *A science reader.*

"Current Comments"

Introducing: The Unification Church and the Reverend Moon

Number 3   January 17, 1977

In the report which follows, a member of the ISI® *Press Digest* staff has reviewed the literature on one of the most pernicious of the various religious cults that have appeared during the past decade. The scientific angle to the Moon story is the series of Unity of Science conferences which have been reported on extensively in *Science*[1,2] and elsewhere.

Since I have not been personally affected by Moon's cult and others like it, I lack the motivation common to parents who have decided to take action of one kind or another against Moon. I do have close friends, however, whose son is a convert to Scientology, and I know how it has upset them. Apart from my suspicions that Scientology, like the Unification Church, is a racket, I do not feel threatened by it.

When I hear about Rev. Moon, I cannot avoid thinking about the rise of Adolf Hitler. One can argue that Moon is no more or less successful than a Billy Graham or some other 'evangelist.' Even when I heard about Moon's visit with Richard Nixon, I didn't feel threatened. How is one to decide when a 'nothing' becomes a 'something?' It was precisely the extremism of Adolf Hitler that deluded liberals and others into thinking that he could not be acceptable to sensible people. How many must Rev. Moon convert before you and I and all of the others who simply want to be left alone decide that it is time to do something about him?

The trouble with freedom is that you must sacrifice a little of it from time to time to keep it most of the time. Why don't some of the mathematicians out there come up with a formula for calculating the critical mass of a screwball or sociopath? Maybe they can also formulate the right amount of discipline needed to produce Moon-free children. There is a strong probability that too little discipline may produce a drug addict, while too much may produce a Moon addict--or is it vice versa?

Not too long ago there was a best-seller entitled *Small is Beautiful.*[3] That's an expression I like in connection with all political and religious cults. When a religious cult becomes powerful enough to buy the Hotel New Yorker and Manhattan Center, I suspect that we are approaching a critical-mass situation. Perhaps it is too early, but some good investigative reporting is needed on Moon.

I wonder if any of the United States Congressmen who were so upset by some of the more abstruse research supported by the National Science Foundation have ever considered funding studies on the rise of religious cults in this country, and the reasons for it. Should the National Academy of Sciences create a blue-ribbon panel to tell us whether the Rev. Moon is a sincere 'evangelist' (whatever you or I think of him and his methods), or whether he is just a clever little man who's found a new way to make a fast buck.

REFERENCES

1. **Walsh J.** Meeting on the unity of science: reflections on the Rev. Moon. *Science* **189**:975-6, 1975.
2. **Holden C.** Science and values discussed at Moon-sponsored parley. *Science* **190**:1073, 1975.
3. **Schumacher E F.** *Small is beautiful: a study of economics as if people mattered.* New York: Harper & Row, 1973.

The Unification Church and the Reverend Moon

by Robert Cohen
Institute for Scientific Information
325 Chestnut Street
Philadelphia, Pennsylvania

"I am a thinker, I am your brain. When you join the effort with me, you can do everything in utter obedience to me. Because what I am doing is not done at random but what I am doing is under God's command."--Sun Myung Moon

An acquaintance of mine who was in town for the bicentennial celebration told me about a strange encounter he had. He said he was walking down a street near Independence Hall when a young man dressed in the fashion of the 18th century with knee breeches and a three-cornered hat suddenly jumped in his path and held out a flower.

"Please," the young man said with a smile, "have a flower."

My friend said that he reached out his hand and nearly accepted, but sensed a gimmick. He replied warily, "Ah, I'm not so crazy about flowers."

"Well, could you make a donation?"

"A donation to what?" asked my friend.

"For the flower."

"But I don't want it."

"Make a donation anyway," insisted the young man.

My friend reported that at this point he quickly side-stepped the young man and sought escape. But the young man caught up to him. The young man held a red flower up against my friend's shirt pocket, saying, "It would look very nice." My friend paid him no attention and continued walking and the flower-bearer eventually abandoned my friend without ever explaining who he was or what the donation was for.

Even if asked, the young man would not have said who he represented. His Church instructed him against it. If pressed to explain the destination of the money, the young man would have lied, according to Church instructions. The Church is the Unification Church, its head, the Rev. Sun Myung Moon.

Moon's followers are instructed that because of the unfavorable publicity the Church has received in the media, they should deny any personal link to Rev. Moon. Said one former member of the Church, Peter Tipograph, 23, "The Church taught that the outside world was 'satanic' and that it was all right to use lies and deceit to sell goods on the streets to support the Church."[1] For these deceitful tactics the Unification Church has been severely criticized in the media. It has also been rumored that the Church is a front organization for the government of South Korea.

To support this accusation, critics point out that some of Rev. Moon's closest advisors were once, and may still be, employed by the South Korean CIA and military establishment. U.S. federal investigators are presently involved in an inquiry into the activities of Moon's chief aide, a former military attache to Washington, Pak Bo Hi. Pak, president of the Korean Cultural and Freedom Foundation, has been accused of siphoning off funds from this tax-exempt organization and passing it along to Korean agents attempting to buy political influence.

Moon's economic empire is a conglomerate of corporations which includes, in South Korea, a weapons factory, a pharmaceutical company and a tea company. In the U.S., Moon's Unification Church has bought up valuable real estate in New York, and holds 44 percent of the total shares of stock in the Diplomat National Bank in Washington, D.C. Their 42,820 shares alone in the Diplomat National Bank are worth more than $1 million.

The Washington Post recently reported that Moon's latest business venture, the Tong Il Fishing Company, has developed a lucrative tuna business on the East Coast in Massachusetts.[2] The company exports the tuna to Japan, where a premium price is paid for the meat of giant, bluefin tuna. A major expansion of their commercial fishing operations in the U.S. is presently under consideration. A Tong Il spokesman explained that, "Rev. Moon is looking at a number of things in the ocean. It has resources that can be used for the good of people, because of protein. And he's aware that the United States fishing industry is in a state of decline."

Moon's primary concern, he says, is not for his business interests, or America's fishing industry: he is primarily concerned with the state of moral decline in America. He contends that the evil of communism is sweeping across America, and that it can be defeated by reviving the revolutionary spirit of America. America's vehicle for this revival, according to Moon's plan, will be his Bicentennial God Bless America Committee. Earlier last year in New York's Yankee Stadium, and in Washington, D.C. in September, Moon's Bicentennial God Bless America Committee sponsored "festivals" in which Moon delivered the keynote speeches. In his speech at New York, which was reprinted as a full page advertisement in newspapers across the country, Moon said that, "God anointed America with oil," and that "America must be God's champion."[3]

Moon warned, however, that, "Throughout all of America, Satan is becoming the master." This decline "will be the perfect opportunity for the evil of communism to overtake America."[3] Therefore, he has gathered together the "noble sons and daughters" of America to wage battle against this evil. The main battleground for this Armageddon will be centered, Moon asserts, in Korea, along the 38th parallel which divides communist North Korea from the South. And these forces of good and evil will be spear-headed by the Messiah and Satan.

Moon does not say directly that he is the Messiah, but his associates coyly reveal that the Messiah was born in the year 1920 in Korea and that he may already be amongst us. Unsurprisingly, Moon was born in the year 1920 in Korea.

According to Moon, he possesses an impressive list of credentials for the post of Messiah. He claims that he has had visionary chats with Moses and the Buddha, among others, and that Jesus personally called upon him in a vision to carry out his unfinished work.

This work involves the world unification of all religions and nations, and to this end Moon founded the Holy Spirit Association for the Unification of World Christianity in 1954 in Seoul, South Korea. He first gained international notoriety when he performed two mass marriage ceremonies for some 430 couples in 1968 and 777 couples in 1970. The Unification Church claims that these international weddings symbolized the creation of world brotherhood. In publicity pictures distributed by the Church, the Rev. Moon is always shown at the head of this brotherhood.

Moon has attempted to increase his popularity with the American public through an extensive media campaign. He has displayed a keen sense of opportunism in allowing himself to be photographed next to people with whom he'd like to be associated. Some years ago Moon succeeded in having his picture taken with President Dwight Eisenhower, and more recently with Hubert Humphrey, Edward Kennedy, Strom Thurmond and James Buckley, and he uses these pictures in publicity releases to associate himself with political figures.

In recent years, Moon has also waged a campaign to associate himself with members of the scientific community. Beginning in 1972 in New York, the Unification Church has sponsored the annual International Conference on the Unity of the Sciences. The second, third, and fourth annual conferences were held in Tokyo, London, and again in New York.

An article in the *New York Times Magazine* reported that for the 1975 New York conference held at the Waldorf Astoria, "The letters of invitation--offering to pay all expenses, plus $3,000 for co-chairmen--failed to mention that the affair was sponsored by the Unification Church or that Sun Moon would give the opening address. When they learned of Moon's involvement, many of those invited-- Buckminster Fuller, Norman Cousins and several others who had agreed to serve as advisors for the conference-- withdrew."[4] Another who withdrew, Amitai Etzioni, the prestigious sociologist from Columbia University, remarked that, "The conference sponsors have tried to inject Moon into everything and of course we do not share his views."[5]

However, the Conference did proceed, and Moon scheduled his fifth annual International Conference on the Unity of the Sciences for November 1976 in Washington, D.C. The conference, sponsored by a Moon front, the International Cultural Foundation, was held on the subject of "The Search for Absolute Values: Harmony Among the Sciences."[6]

Apparently, there must be a solid block of scientists and scholars who deem it important that a scientific conference be held under any sponsorship, so long as science benefits. But as Etzioni indicated, there is a question about who the real beneficiary of a Moon-sponsored science conference is-- Moon or the scientists.

In addition to scientific gatherings, Moon forces have made forays into the U.S. Congress and state legislatures in an attempt to win endorsements from elected officials. Public officials were approached by members of the Unification Church with the same ethnic character as the person they were trying to win over. The Church's political strategy is embodied in Moon's pamphlet,

"Master Speaks." In it Moon advises sending "three pretty girls" to talk to each member of the U.S. Senate. However, in politics, as in science, Moon has not encountered great success.[7]

The organization's greatest political inroads were initially made in the New York State Legislature where they received 12 endorsements in support of the group's patriotic activities. In retrospect, though, after the "patriotic" girls' motives were unmasked, many of the 12 legislators said that it was a mistake to have endorsed their activities.

However, Rev. Moon is not fazed by politicians who refuse to lend support. Moon commented that, "If we find among the Senators and Congressmen no one really usable for our purposes, we can make Senators and Congressmen out of our members."[8]

The membership of the Unification Church in America has been estimated at over 7,000 members, hardly enough to form a political base. But the membership is almost certain to rise worldwide. In Japan the Unification Church claims over 210,000 members, in West Germany 6,000, and in South Korea, Moon's home country, the Church enjoys the support not only of a large popular following, but of the government as well. The Moon organization has announced that it will next focus on Europe, where Moon intends to send hundreds of his American believers to convert Europeans. Moon anticipates a similar degree of success in Europe as he achieved in the U.S.

Until the early seventies there were only a small number of Moon converts in the U.S. However, after Moon moved to the U.S. with his wife and eight children in 1973 the organization rapidly expanded. The reason for their growth, argues Thomas Robbins of Queens College, New York, is that America was, in a sense, "ripe" for Moon.[9]

Robbins claims that there was a "deterioration in civil religiosity" in America. Possibly due to Vietnam, or Watergate, or detente, suggests Robbins, the decline of American civil religion disrupted "the whole fabric of American life." Robbins asserts that the Unification Church "represents an attempt to legitimate a secondary group ministering to communal deprivation in collectivist terms. It does so by appealing to the ideology traditionally used for legitimating social integration, the American civil religion."

It is not specifically Robbins' task to explain why the deterioration occurred. He only points out that Moon is moving into that religious vacuum with an organizational machine perfectly geared to the civil-religious foundations already layed. The Unification Church seeks to fulfill the needs of young people not only by offering religion, but by offering a special communal life-style.

Many parents assert that their children were attracted to religious cults because they needed to escape from their worries and problems. As adolescents they faced a time of major upheaval in which the thought and behavioral patterns of the child were exchanged for those of an adult in society. In short, parents contend that it is a time of vulnerability for the child, and that the structured behavioral patterns in a commune would appeal to one's need for security.

Esther Alexander of Munroe Falls, Ohio, whose husband became active in "deprogramming" cult members after their nephew joined the Children of

God sect, has noticed that college people "drift into fanatical cults most readily in periods when their lives are coming unstuck."[10]

She explained further that, "The cults get a lot of kids at exam time. I've heard this same story from young men and women over and over again. They were depressed and anxious about the exams, afraid they were flunking, so they went away with some mystical group and kind of escaped from the world. Most of these cults, the evangelist ones and also the Eastern-mystical ones, preach exactly what a troubled young person wants to hear: It isn't important to pass exams and get a good job, and so on. The only important thing is to save your soul or find peace." This same vulnerability applies, she claims, to people having painful experiences with sex or drugs.

James T. Wooten of the *New York Times* reports that for some of the cults, like the Children of God, the communal life-style is the essence of the religious experience.[11] Members of the Children of God, writes Wooten, "believe the universe is on its last legs and...have left family, friends and society behind in their retreat to isolated communes." There, they hope "to resume the ascetic, communal life style they believe to be patterned after the earliest disciples of the Christian faith." Wooten writes that the Children of God "had its origins among a small group of conservatives within the Jesus Movement, a nationwide Fundamentalist movement among youth." (Other offshoots of the Jesus Movement include the Love Family, Body of Christ, and Love Israel.)

The life-style in one of these isolated, religious communities is highly structured. In a Moon community, converts to the Unification Church are required to participate in group activities and are given no time for privacy. They are allowed only 5-6 hours of sleep at night and are awakened at 7 A.M. for calisthenics and song sessions. The daytime program includes 4-5 hours of lectures, interspersed with prayer meetings, exercise sessions, group discussions, and clean-up chores. Small, unchaperoned, conversational groups are prohibited. Newspapers from the outside world are prohibited, and anyone wishing to make a telephone call must do so in the presence of an authoritative member of the community.

Pre-marital sex is prohibited, but recruits are subjected to "love-bombing,"[12] a technique of group support and reinforcement which consists of constant smiling, friendly patting, and handholding. While the recruits are bombarded with this "love" they are being bombarded, as well, by the Unification Church ideology. Their activities are woven together by a common thread: songs are sung about the Messiah; prayers are said for his inevitable Coming; lectures are given to illuminate His purpose. Moon's book, *The Divine Principle,* is required reading.

This book specifies the rules and regulations governing all forms of interpersonal behavior, even casual social interaction. "As a result," says Robbins, "the social behavior of Moon followers has a somewhat mechanical and stereotypical quality."[9]

For some concerned parents of members, and former members themselves, Robbins' explanation for the "mechanical" behavior of Moon followers is not simply a result of obeying rules. Many have described the Moon methods as a form of brainwashing, and accused the Unification Church of practicing mind control. One former member, Mr. Paul Engel, said, "I left, but if I had stayed in the Church much longer, I know that I would have been unable to make this or any other decision myself. This was inevitable because I know my mind was brainwashed, hypnotized, and under the control of 'Reverend' Moon and the Church.... I was in the process of becoming a total obedient, non-thinking robot."[13]

Despite accusations of brainwashing and involuntary confinement charged of religious sects, no legal action can be undertaken because of the Constitution's First Amendment, which protects an individual's freedom of religion. However, Children of God, Inc., a non-profit Texas entity, was denied a Federal tax exemption as a religious institution in 1972, and some months ago, when it was reported that the Unification Church's holdings were well into the millions, the Internal Revenue Service announced that it was going to review the Unification Church's status as a tax-exempt religious institution. But nothing was ever announced about the results of that review. Presumably, they still enjoy their tax-exempt status as a religious organization.

Although the courts are powerless to act against the religious sects, the same cannot be said about the parents whose children have abandoned home, school, and their past lives to join these groups. The parents' movement grew out of a series of incidents in which parents attempted to rescue, or abduct, depending upon your point of view, members of the sects by force.

These "abduction" stories seem to revolve around the activities of Ted Patrick, a former community relations worker with Gov. Ronald Reagan. Patrick has set up a "deprogramming" operation in San Diego, California, to help parents recover children who are minors from the sects. Patrick justifies his abduction work on the ground that he is liberating people from mind-control religions. On that point, he is supported by law.

Although Patrick was brought to court in New York in 1973 on the charge of unlawful imprisonment of a person he was attempting to deprogram, the jury acquitted him. The acquittal was based "on a section of the penal law allowing parents of a minor to use physical, but not deadly, force on the off-spring if they 'reasonably' believe this is necessary to maintain discipline or promote his welfare."[14] The jury believed that Patrick, together with the parents of the complainant, were justified in seizing him because they "reasonably" believed he faced psychological harm through the indoctrination of the New Testament Missionary Fellowship, a Christian fundamentalist group.

Despite the outcome of this judicial decision, several questions remain. What exactly is a mind-control religion when the adherents voluntarily let their minds be subjected to its tenets? And does the right of free, religious worship cease when a minor chooses a faith of which the parents strongly disapprove? *Webster's Third New International*

Dictionary defines brainwashing as "the forcible application of prolonged and intensive indoctrination sometimes including mental torture in an attempt to induce someone to give up basic political, social, or religious beliefs and attitudes and to accept contrasting regimented ideas." The claim could perhaps be made that converts to the Unification Church "give up basic political, social, or religious beliefs and attitudes," but whether this occurred because of "mental torture" is a moot point. It is equally difficult to determine at what point religious education ceases and becomes "prolonged and intensive indoctrination."

Only on one point, it seems, are the supporters and critics of Moon in agreement--that Moon has some sort of master plan. Each group, however, differs as to its interpretation of Moon's plan. As viewed by Unification Church members, Moon is indeed not acting at "random," but obeying "God's command." To critics, however, Moon's plan is a devious strategy of the Unification Church to consolidate power and wealth under a religious guise.

REFERENCES

1. **Thomas T A.** Unification science parley. *New York Times* November 29, 1975, p. 25.
2. **Morgan D.** Sun Myung Moon gets into the tuna business. *Washington Post* November 1, 1976, p. A1, A6.
3. **Moon S M.** Text of keynote speech printed as a two-page, paid advertisement in *Washington Post* June 20, 1976, p. E6-7.
4. **Rice B.** The pull of Sun Moon. *New York Times Magazine* May 30, 1976, p. 8.
5. **Banner B.** In search of certitude. *New Age* 2:51-7, January 1976.
6. The Rev. Moon is back to unify the sciences. *Science & Government Report* July 1, 1976, p. 2.
7. **Friedman J.** The moonies get into state politics. *New York Post* June 25, 1976, p. 4.
8. The secret sayings of 'master' Moon. *Time* June 14, 1976, p. 49.
9. **Robbins T.** The last civil religion: Reverend Moon and the unification church. *Sociological Analysis* 37:111-25, Summer 1976.
10. **Gunther M.** Brainwashing: persuasion by propaganda. *Today's Health* February, 1976, p. 15-7, 54.
11. **Wooten J T.** Ill winds buffet communal sect. *New York Times* November 29, 1971, p. 41.
12. The darker side of Sun Moon. *Time* June 14, 1976, p. 48-50.
13. **Engel P.** The world of the cult. (Engel's address: Box 53, Westview Station, Binghamton, N.Y.)
14. **Blau E.** Patrick acquitted in seizure of youth. *New York Times* August 7, 1973, p. 24.

CURRENT COMMENTS

**Journal Citation Studies. 31.
Italian Journals.**

Number 4, January 24, 1977

In our on-going series of regional journal analyses we turn now from East Europe[1] to Italy. The 34 journals covered in this analysis are listed in Figure 1. Another eleven journals were covered by the *Science Citation Index®* (*SCI®*) in 1974. However, either no issues of them were received that year, or the issues arrived too late to be included in compilation of the *Journal Citation Reports®* , on which this study is based.[2]

Figure 1 gives for each journal its impact; the number of times it was cited in 1974; the number of times its 1972 and 1973 articles were cited in 1974; and the number of articles it published in 1972 and 1973. The journals are ranked by impact.

Only two Italian journals achieved an impact greater than the international average of 1.015.[3] One of them is *Journal of Submicroscopic Cytology* (1.184), published in English. The other is *Archives Italiennes de Biologie* (1.061), also published in English, despite its French title. Ranking third in impact (0.994) is *Nuovo Cimento*, the most *cited* of the Italian journals. This will not surprise physicists anywhere since it is an international journal.

The 34 journals constitute just about 1.4% of the 2443 journals processed for the *SCI* in 1974. They published 3016 source items that year, about 0.8% of the total 400,971 source items from all *SCI* journals. Of the more than 5.2 million references processed for the 1974 *SCI*, these 34 Italian journals produced 46,906--about 0.9% of the total.

Thus, in comparison with the 'average' journal, the Italian journals published fewer articles than the average (88 compared with 165), but the articles contained slightly more than the international number of references--about 16 instead of 13.

As I've noted in other regional studies, the regional-journal output doesn't represent the regional-research output. ISI's *Who Is Publishing in Science®* shows that in 1974 at least 5662 articles were published in which the address of the first author was Italian.[4] The 34 Italian journals accounted at most for only 53% of those research reports. The percentage must be even lower, considering that some first-class Italian journals--such as *Nuovo Cimento, Lettere al Nuovo Cimento, Tumori*--attract articles from other countries. In other words, probably as much as 50% of Italian research is published abroad.

Figure 2 shows the 50 journals most often *cited by* the Italian journals. Figure 3 shows the 50 journals that most often cited them. Both the figures have columns giving the number of references or citations made or received by each listed journal, the number of references or citations made or received by the Italian group, the number of self-citations, and columns for percentages

Figure 1. Italian journals indexed by the *Science Citation Index* in 1974. Journals are listed in descending order of impact factor. **A** = impact factor. **B** = number of times journal was cited in 1974. **C** = 1974 citations of articles published by the journal in 1972 and 1973. **D** = number of articles published by the journal in 1972 and 1973. (A = C/D).

	A		B	C	D		A		B	C	D
1.	1.184	J. Submicr. Cytol.	140	45	38	18.	0.192	Ing. Chim. Ital.	40	15	78
2.	1.061	Arch. Ital. Biol.	673	70	66	19.	0.156	Riv. Ital. Geofisica	21	17	109
3.	0.994	Nuovo Cimento	5474	999	1005	20.	0.130	Acta Genet. Med.	122	6	46
4.	0.982	Acta Diabet. Lat.	281	56	57	21.	0.120	Atti Ass. Genet. Ital.	44	10	83
5.	0.775	Lett. Nuovo Cim.	1707	929	1230	22.	0.112	Metallurgia Ital.	69	20	179
6.	0.643	Gazz. Chim. Ital.	1305	166	258	23.	0.107	Boll. Soc. Ital. Biol.	471	78	731
7.	0.540	Ital. J. Biochem.	118	27	50	24.	0.098	Ann. Geofisica	60	6	61
8.	0.466	Caryologia	362	55	118	25.	0.094	Giorn. Fis. San.	8	3	32
9.	0.390	Farmaco Ed. Prat.	104	46	118	26.	0.080	Ric. Matematica	15	2	25
10.	0.363	J. Nucl. Biol. Med.	96	29	80	27.	0.075	Giorn. Gerontol.	73	166	258
11.	0.344	Farmaco Ed. Sci.	196	64	186	28.	0.060	Riv. Met. Aeronaut.	4	3	50
12.	0.318	Acta Gerontol.	17	14	44	29.	0.049	Gaslini	3	2	41
13.	0.311	J. Cardiovasc. Surg.	349	61	196	30.	0.045	Surgery in Italy	4	3	67
14.	0.306	Acta Vitam. Enzym.	24	11	36	31.	0.044	Atti Acc. Lincei Fis.	267	18	405
15.	0.283	Annali di Chimica	910	21	100	32.	0.043	FAO Plant Protect.	30	3	69
16.	0.280	Tumori	127	21	75	33.	0.040	Energia Nucleare	59	4	100
17.	0.210	Agrochimica	108	21	100	34.	0.007	Elettrotecnica	6	1	151

that relate these counts to each other. The last column in each figure gives each journal's impact.

In 1974 the Italian journals cited 4691 different published items in their 46,906 references. The 50 journals listed in Figure 2, 1% of the total published items cited, accounted for 27% of the citations in the references of the Italian journals. Of the fifty journals only five are Italian: *Nuovo Cimento; Lettere al Nuovo Cimento; Il Farmaco, Edizione Scientifica; Gazzetta Chimica Italiana;* and *Bollettino della Societa Italiana di Biologia Serpimentale.* As a whole, the list is roughly half physics and half biochemistry and medicine. The physics journals--probably boosted by *Nuovo Cimento's* presence in the citing group-- are at the top of the list. It is interesting to note that except for the Italian journals, all the journals in Figure 2 (the

cited journals) are English-language. And only one of the five Italian journals (*Boll. Soc. Ital. Biol. Sper.*) publishes mainly in Italian. The other four are published in English or English and Italian (*Farm. Ed. Sci.*).

Figure 3 shows the 50 *SCI*-covered journals that *cited* Italian journals most. The Italian journals were cited by 1094 different *SCI* journals 12,976 times. The 50 journals in Figure 2--about 5% of the total 1094--accounted for 57% of the citations received by Italian journals-- 7,363 of the total 12,976. Only twelve of the fifty citing journals are Italian. In fact, almost 70% (5094/7363) of the citations summarized in Figure 3 come from non-Italian journals. Physics again predominates, accounting for 3/5 of the list; chemistry and medicine about equally divide the rest. There are six journals that are neither Italian nor

Figure 2. **Journals that were *cited* by Italian journals.** Journals are listed in order of their citation by the Italian group. **A** = total citations by all journals. **B** = total citations by Italian journals. **C** = self-citations. **D** = **B/A** (Italian citations in terms of total citations). **E** = **C/A** (self-citations in terms of total citations, the self-*cited* rate). **F** = **C/B** (self-citations in terms of Italian citations). **G** = impact factor.

		A	B	C	D	E	F	G
1.	Physical Rev.	50828	1291	– –	2.5	– –	– –	– –
2.	Physical Rev. Lett.	29275	933	– –	3.2	– –	– –	5.059
3.	Nuovo Cimento	5474	892	606	16.3	11.1	67.9	0.994
4.	Physical Rev. D.	9441	829	– –	8.8	– –	– –	2.723
5.	Physics Lett. B.	9958	763	– –	7.7	– –	– –	3.428
6.	Nuclear Phys. B.	6220	698	– –	11.2	– –	– –	2.646
7.	Lett. Nuovo Cimento	1707	512	320	30.0	18.7	62.5	0.755
8.	J. Amer. Chem. Soc.	98995	392	– –	0.4	– –	– –	4.383
9.	Lancet	37047	371	– –	1.0	– –	– –	6.677
10.	Physical Rev. B.	16104	277	– –	1.7	– –	– –	2.864
11.	Nuclear Phys. A.	12176	271	– –	2.2	– –	– –	2.423
12.	J. Biol. Chem.	81354	267	– –	3.3	– –	– –	5.843
13.	Nature	59206	260	– –	0.4	– –	– –	3.636
14.	Annals Physics	4347	228	– –	5.2	– –	– –	2.128
15.	J. Math. Phys.	3820	215	– –	5.6	– –	– –	1.046
16.	New Engl. J. Med.	26726	184	– –	0.7	– –	– –	8.364
17.	Prog. Theor. Physics	3864	172	– –	4.5	– –	– –	1.421
18.	J. Chem. Physics	62041	168	– –	0.3	– –	– –	2.918
19.	Farmaco. Ed. Sci.	196	167	164	85.2	83.7	98.2	0.344
20.	Biochim. Biophys. Acta	51491	160	– –	0.3	– –	– –	3.120
21.	J. Chem. Soc.	19955	155	– –	0.8	– –	– –	– –
22.	Science	47505	151	– –	0.3	– –	– –	5.412
23.	J. Cell Biol.	19103	148	– –	0.8	– –	– –	6.770
24.	J. Thor. Card. Surg.	4093	147	– –	3.6	– –	– –	1.480
25.	Gazz. Chim. Ital.	1305	145	117	11.1	9.0	80.7	0.643
26.	Brit. Med. J.	20748	144	– –	0.7	– –	– –	3.556
27.	J. Clin. Invest.	24768	138	– –	0.6	– –	– –	6.992
28.	Boll. Soc. Ital. Biol. Sper.	471	136	93	28.9	19.7	68.4	0.107
29.	J. Amer. Med. Assoc.	17211	134	– –	0.8	– –	– –	3.068
30.	Proc. Nat. Acad. Sci. USA	46917	133	– –	0.3	– –	– –	8.989
31.	Nuclear Phys.	4064	127	– –	3.1	– –	– –	– –
32.	Proc. Soc. Exp. Biol. Med.	18171	126	– –	0.7	– –	– –	1.471
33.	Physical Rev. A	9870	122	– –	1.2	– –	– –	2.613
34.	Diabetes	3952	119	– –	3.0	– –	– –	3.941
35.	Biochemical J.	31563	118	– –	0.4	– –	– –	3.627
36.	J. Exp. Med.	20699	116	– –	0.6	– –	– –	11.874
37.	J. Organ. Chem.	20539	116	– –	0.6	– –	– –	1.495
38.	J. Physiology (London)	22520	115	– –	0.5	– –	– –	4.495
39.	Proc. Roy. Soc. London A	12224	114	– –	0.9	– –	– –	2.215
40.	Circulation	14461	113	– –	0.8	– –	– –	6.834
41.	Arch. Surgery	5491	110	– –	2.0	– –	– –	1.462
42.	Rev. Mod. Physics	5186	110	– –	2.1	– –	– –	21.500
43.	J. Immunology	15826	108	– –	0.7	– –	– –	5.112
44.	Gastroenterology	8693	103	– –	1.2	– –	– –	5.394
45.	Physical Rev. C.	5410	101	– –	1.9	– –	– –	2.299
46.	Ann. Surgery	7459	100	– –	1.3	– –	– –	2.129
47.	J. Clin. Endocr. Metab.	11645	100	– –	0.9	– –	– –	5.170
48.	Surface Science	10275	100	– –	1.0	– –	– –	2.446
49.	J. Geophys. Res.	15281	96	– –	0.6	– –	– –	2.536
50.	Physics Letters	15666	92	– –	0.6	– –	– –	– –

Figure 3. **Journals that *cited* Italian journals.** Journals are listed in order of their citation of the Italian group. **A** = total citations of all journals. **B** = total citations of Italian journals. **C** = self-citations. **D** = **B/A** (Italian citations in terms of total citations). **E** = **C/A** (self-citations in terms of total citations, the self-*citing* rate). **F** = **C/B** (self-citations in terms of Italian citations). **G** = impact factor.

	A	B	C	D	E	F	G
1. Physical Rev. D.	16727	1102	– –	6.6	– –	– –	2.723
2. Nuclear Phys. B.	9617	838	– –	8.7	– –	– –	2.646
3. Nuovo Cimento	6066	794	606	13.1	10.0	76.3	0.994
4. Lett. Nuovo Cimento	4486	603	320	13.4	7.1	53.1	0.755
5. Physics Lett. B.	7860	357	– –	4.5	– –	– –	3.428
6. Nuclear Phys. A.	18463	252	– –	1.4	– –	– –	2.423
7. Prog. Theor. Phys.	5970	227	– –	3.8	– –	– –	1.421
8. Sov. J. Nucl. Phys.	5667	203	– –	3.6	– –	– –	0.549
9. Farmaco Ed. Sci.	1304	194	164	14.9	12.6	84.5	0.344
10. J. Math. Physics	3745	189	– –	5.1	– –	– –	1.046
11. Annals Physics	3029	144	– –	4.8	– –	– –	2.128
12. Physical Rev. C.	13095	130	– –	1.0	– –	– –	2.299
13. Physical Rev. Lett.	11203	130	– –	1.2	– –	– –	5.059
14. Brain Res.	19626	127	– –	0.6	– –	– –	3.104
15. Gazz. Chim. Ital.	2219	122	117	5.5	5.3	95.9	0.643
16. Boll. Soc. Ital. Biol. Sper.	1748	114	93	6.5	5.3	81.6	0.107
17. J. Physics A	3334	93	– –	2.8	– –	– –	1.195
18. Giorn. Gerontol.	1012	91	66	9.0	6.5	72.5	0.075
19. Physical Rev. B	27280	88	– –	0.3	– –	– –	2.864
20. Rev. Mod. Physics	3731	84	– –	2.3	– –	– –	21.500
21. Arch. Ital. Biol.	615	83	80	13.5	13.0	96.4	1.061
22. Physical Rev. A.	13126	77	– –	0.6	– –	– –	2.613
23. J. Cardiovasc. Surg.	1251	65	37	5.2	3.0	56.9	0.311
24. Acta Physica Austriaca	953	62	– –	6.5	– –	– –	0.546
25. Ann. Sclavo	– –	59	34	– –	– –	57.6	– –
26. Boll. Inst. Sieroter. Milan	– –	59	50	– –	– –	84.7	– –
27. J. Organ. Chem.	21976	59	– –	0.3	– –	– –	1.495
28. Tetrahedron	13059	57	– –	0.4	– –	– –	1.576
29. Phys. Stat. Sol. B.	9465	54	– –	0.6	– –	– –	1.113
30. Canadian J. Phys.	4465	51	– –	1.1	– –	– –	1.038
31. J. Organomet. Chem.	22699	49	– –	0.2	– –	– –	2.392
32. Acta Phys. Hung.	1206	48	– –	4.0	– –	– –	0.286
33. Exp. Brain Res.	3257	48	– –	1.5	– –	– –	3.596
34. Experientia	9248	48	– –	0.5	– –	– –	0.883
35. Farmaco. Ed. Prat.	832	48	33	5.8	4.0	68.8	0.390
36. J. Heterocyclic Chem.	2893	47	– –	1.6	– –	– –	0.756
37. J. Chem. Physics	33404	46	– –	0.1	– –	– –	2.918
38. Zh. Eksp. Teor. Fiz.	6043	45	– –	0.7	– –	– –	1.195
39. Zschr. Physik	5961	44	– –	0.7	– –	– –	1.340
40. Physica	4490	43	– –	1.0	– –	– –	0.969
41. Exp. Neurol.	4431	42	– –	0.9	– –	– –	1.827
42. Usp. Fiz. Nauk	5957	42	– –	0.7	– –	– –	1.514
43. EEG Clin. Neurol.	2344	40	– –	1.7	– –	– –	1.493
44. J. Chem. Soc. Perkin	20327	40	– –	0.2	– –	– –	1.348
45. Ann. Rev. Nucl. Sci.	1837	38	– –	2.1	– –	– –	3.783
46. Izv. Akad. Nauk SSSR Fiz.	4871	38	– –	0.8	– –	– –	0.440
47. J. Neurophysiology	2959	38	– –	1.3	– –	– –	4.537
48. Acta Diabetol. Latina	1012	37	36	3.7	3.6	97.3	0.982
49. Inorg. Chem.	15048	37	– –	0.2	– –	– –	2.457
50. J. Inorg. Nucl. Chem.	9026	37	– –	0.4	– –	– –	0.962

English-language: three are Russian and three German.

If you remove the few Italian journals from the lists in Figures 2 and 3, the lists would look like so many others we have published. The cited journals in Figure 2 might come from any highly cited list. Despite the heavy physics orientation, the top 25 includes such ever-present journals as *Lancet, Journal of Biological Chemistry, Nature, New England Journal of Medicine, Science, Journal of Cell Biology*. The same is true of the citing list in Figure 3. Remove the Italian journals and one is left with a list of the significant journals of physics, many of the significant journals of chemistry, and a few specialized journals like *Brain Research, Experimental Neurology, EEG and Clinical Neurology* and *Journal of Neurophysiology*. The presence of this neurological group seems to indicate a significant emphasis in Italian biomedical research.

The low impact of the Italian journals should be cause for concern. I thought it possible that publication and delivery delays might be responsible. Impact is calculated by using 1974 citations of 1972 and 1973 articles. But recalculating impact on the basis of 1974 citations of 1971 and 1972 articles makes little difference. *Nuovo Cimento's* impact drops from 0.994 to 0.929. *Gazzetta Chimica Italiana* improves slightly from 0.643 to 0.757. *Tumori* shows greater improvement--from 0.280 to 0.703. But the recalculation doesn't push any of the impacts up to the average. Perhaps the Italians, like the Latin-Americans, should consider the consolidation of journals, as suggested earlier.[5] It seems obvious that Italian journals are not attracting the best product of Italian research.

The probable advantages of consolidation should, in my opinion, be considered by the publishers of the *Minerva* series of Italian medical journals. There are about 20 in the series, but in 1974 only *two* were cited more than 100 times by all *SCI*-covered journals. *Minerva Medica* was cited 227 times, and *Minerva Pediatrica* 118 times. In neither case was this enough to put them on the list in Figure 2. In previous regional studies we've found that at least one or two 'national' medical journals turned up in such lists. The *Minervas'* fragmentation of Italian medical publication seems to me to account for the fact that in this study none did.

In a future essay we will list the most highly cited articles from the Italian journals for the period 1961-1975. However, a more important future analysis will take into account the significant Italian research published outside Italy.

1. **Garfield E.** Journal citation studies. 29. East European journals. *Current Contents®* (*CC®*) No. 45, 8 November 1976, p. 5-12.

2. ------------. *Journal citation reports; a bibliometric analysis of references processed for the 1974 Science Citation Index.* Science Citation Index 1975 Annual, vol. 9. (Philadelphia: Institute for Scientific Information® , 1976).

3. ------------. Significant journals of science. *Nature* 264:609-15, 1976.

4. *Who is publishing in science, 1975 annual; an interdisciplinary directory of scientists and scholars in the life, physical, social, and applied sciences.* (Philadelphia: Institute for Scientific Information, 1976), p. 8. -- See "Statistical summaries of author address frequency by geographical distribution".

5. **Garfield E.** Journal citation studies. 26. Latin-American journals. *CC* No. 37, 13 September 1976, p. 5-11.

CURRENT COMMENTS

New Year's Greetings
—and Other Correspondence—
Keep the Spirit Bright All Year Long!

Number 5, January 31, 1977

Letters from *Current Contents*® readers are a constant source of stimulation, frustration, joy, and sadness. Correspondence is so large that I can't possibly deal with all of it without assistance. In an average week I receive more than 100 letters. Some of them contain lengthy supporting documents. Others can be dealt with simply by referring the request to the appropriate ISI® department. But each is given individual care. Everyone at ISI knows how I feel about this.[1]

Some of the most delightful, and least enervating, correspondence arrives on the New Year holiday. Our Asian colleagues send the most creative greeting cards--many beautiful enough to frame. Our East European friends often send cards relating to themes from the history of science.

Perhaps the most original card I received this year was printed by the World Health Organization. It was sent by an old friend, a pioneer information scientist, Herb Ohlman. The theme of the WHO card, the inside pages of which are reproduced here, is the smallpox eradication program in Ethiopia. The scenes in the card, originally in color, depict Ethiopia's campaign to educate people about smallpox vaccination.

During the past year, I had a rash of letters complaining about subscription problems. During that time we converted our computer processing from a batch to an online system. This was somewhat agonizing, but the worst is over. It is significant that we can now process any new subscription order within 36 hours, and all correspondence is dealt with in a few days. If your experience is otherwise, you should not hesitate to write me.[2] If you prefer to complain by phone, contact one of our marketing representatives. In the U.S. you can also call 1-800-523-1850.

Each year over 30,000 different subscriptions must be processed. Like any other publication we lose subscribers for a variety of reasons. Obviously, it is impossible to prevent cancellation in some cases-- subscribers unfortunately die. But hundreds of cancellations are due to other causes. Retirement is not an uncommon reason. But many of our readers continue to use CC® after retirement so they can keep in touch with research.

The most significant cause of cancellation is financial. While *CC* is 'absolutely essential' even to some high school teachers of science, there are research scientists who rely on research grants to support their personal subscriptions. These have been lean years in some areas of research.

Because of tight budgets, some people have asked me to drop one feature or another in order to cut costs. Some people would gladly have us drop *Current Comments Press Digest*--anything but *their* favorite journals--if this would reduce the price. It is difficult for many individuals to accept the fact that it is the variety of customer satisfactions that makes *CC* acceptable to a large audience. What is of marginal interest to one person may be 'must' reading for the next. Greater selectivity for a smaller audience may increase the cost for that special group.

Often we hear from individuals in developing nations that the cost of a subscription represents a significant fraction of their budget. For the developing nations we have special rates for our more expensive services like *Science Citation Index®* . Perhaps we should extend this idea to *CC*. The best way to do that might be to include air service

at low cost since it is *CC*'s timeliness that makes it possible for scientists in these countries to feel closer to the world of international science! We already do this in Japan.

An increasing number of scientists write to me complaining that they need access to more than one edition of *CC*. It is not that they need access to more than 1000 journals. Rather, the mix of journals they require is peculiar to their multidisciplinary specialities. I often tell such persons to use our selective *ASCA®* weekly service. *ASCA* covers over 5000 journals. It has no subject boundaries. Considering the growth of journal coverage, the growth in the size of journals, and the inflation of the past ten years, *ASCA* is a real bargain. And for *CC* readers we have a special $50.00 *ASCA* monthly supplement.

It is surprising how many readers believe journal selection for *CC* to be a somewhat mystical process. After twenty years of producing *CC* it is surprising that there are even journal editors who have never heard of *Current Contents*. Far from being an arcane ritual it is quite simple to have their journals evaluated for coverage.

Letters often complain about some of the material we include in *Press Digest*. Many of these irate readers think that I am the author, not only of the digests, but of the original articles. As a result of this we are including in *Press Digest* a statement briefly explaining our editorial policy.

Professor Joshua Lederberg of Stanford University, who is also a member of the ISI Board of Directors, has this to say about the function of *Press Digest* and the editorial policy which guides us in the selection of items for review. "It is the function of *Press Digest* to give our readers a view of what is said about science, and in the name of science, both in the lay press and in scientific journals. Some of this material will stimulate thoughtful responses; some will be exasperating; we leave it to our readers to make their own judgments. In any event, it should be obvious that ISI takes no position on the material chosen for quotation here--not even on whether it warranted publication to begin with. Whatever their content, it is an historical fact that these selections have already appeared in print. That may be important for us all to know in understanding how science is viewed both within our own community, and by others."[3]

Many letters raise questions concerning the weekly subject indexes. The natural language of science is constantly changing. We think we do better than most in keeping up with these changes, but it is a never-ending task. If you have a better perspective on your own speciality than we do, then don't hesitate to contact us.

Frequency analysis is very useful in detecting new or better indexing terms, but there are slow moving fields where this may not be adequate. Our indexing systems are part human and part computer. They aren't completely automatic now and probably never will be. And certainly our treatment of correspondence will remain personal though aided by word-processors or any other devices we can employ or devise to make the process responsive.

While this may be a somewhat belated greeting to friends in the Western world, let me extend a Happy New Year to all on the occasion of the Chinese New Year.

REFERENCES

1. **Garfield E.** Learn to complain; the ultimate responsibility is with the individual, not the corporation. *Current Contents* No. 29, 18 July 1973, p. 5-6.
2. -------------, Don't kill us with kindness--complain! *Current Contents* No. 6, 10 February 1975, p. 5-6.
3. **Lederberg J.** Personal communication to E. Garfield, 6 January 1977.

SEASON'S GREETINGS

祝賀新年

BONNE ANNÉE

عام ســـعيد

FELICES FIESTAS

መልካም አዲስ ዓመት

СЧАСТЛИВОГО НОВОГО ГОДА

The multilingual greeting above and the illustrations on the three following pages are reproduced from a greeting card sold by the World Health Organization for the benefit of the Voluntary Fund for Health Promotion. The illustration, which constitutes a single continuous 'panel' in the original, is the work of a traditional Ethiopian artist Ato Tesfaye Taye. In it he depicts activities of the smallpox eradication program in his country. The languages from the front of the card shown above are English, Chinese, French, Arabic, Spanish, Amharic (the language also of the captions in the illustration), and Russian.

Highly Cited Articles. 34.
Articles from Italian Journals and
from Italian Laboratories.

Number 6, February 7, 1977

In a recent study we reported on the most frequently cited Italian journals.[1] As a follow-up to that study, here is a list of 50 articles from Italian journals most cited during the period 1961-1975. The list will disappoint anyone who expects to find a list of articles by Italian scientists. Therefore, we give another list of highly cited articles from *non*-Italian journals where the first author's address is Italian.

The five journals in Figure 1 account for all the articles in the Italian-journal list (Figure 4). *Nuovo Cimento* accounts for 40 of the 50! Figure 2 shows the national distribution of first-author addresses. Switzerland accounts for the most--16; Italy, for 12. The other 22 articles come from six other countries. Figure 3 shows the years in which the articles were published. Surprisingly, only eleven were published before 1960. That is fairly unusual in a list such as this. This is caused by the dominance of *Nuovo Cimento*-- a journal of nuclear physics. In this field there is relatively less dependence upon the older literature. These articles were heavily cited for short periods, but few will prove to have a long 'half-life'. Thus you will find that the 1974-1975 citation counts of these articles are on the average much lower than such counts in similar lists.

In our study of Italian journals we detected an emphasis on neurophysiologic

Figure 1. Journals that published the Italian-journal articles listed in Figure 4. A = number of articles on list. B = impact factor. C = journal title.

A	B	C
40	0.994	Nuovo Cimento
7	1.061	Arch. Ital. Biol
1	0.098	Ann. Geofiz.
1	— —	Minerva Chir.
1	— —	Ricerca Scientifica

Figure 2. First-author address country of articles listed in Figure 4. A = number of articles. B = country of origin.

A	B	A	B
16	Switzerland	4	England
12	Italy	3	Germany
6	United States	3	Soviet Union
5	France	1	Australia

Figure 3. Year of publication of articles listed in Figure 4. A = year of publication. B = number of articles.

A	B	A	B
1945	1	1962	6
1947	1	1963	8
1954	1	1964	6
1956	2	1965	4
1958	3	1966	2
1959	3	1967	2
1960	5	1968	1
1961	4	1969	1

research. This is confirmed in this list of highly cited articles. Of the ten articles not published in *Nuovo Cimento*, seven deal with neurophysiology. Most of them concern the physiology of sleep.

Article number 40 is an important surgical report on the subclavian artery. It has been and continues to be well-cited in the international literature. Of the two remaining articles, number 39 deals with earthquakes, and number 50 concerns the statistical analysis of crystalline structure data.

As previously suggested in our study of Italian journals, much of the best of Italian research is published outside Italy. To confirm that assumption, we compiled a 'special' list of such highly cited articles. Figure 5 shows the journals in which the articles were published. Figure 6 lists the articles. They are the most cited articles from Italian laboratories published during the period 1965-1970, on the basis of citation counts for the years 1967-72.

Most of the authors on this second list are Italian. Some of the addresses indicate an international organization, but most are from Italian academic institutions. The articles come from 27 different journals. Figure 5 gives their titles and the number of articles each contributed. Though physics is well represented again, it takes second place to the life sciences. On the whole these 50 articles have higher citation counts for the six-year period 1967-1972 than the articles in Figure 4 have for the fifteen-year period 1961-1975.

About 17 of the articles concern physics, chemistry, and physical chemistry. The majority have to do with molecular biology and physiology, especially genetic aspects of cellular physiology.

Reference

1. Garfield E. Journal citation studies. 30. Italian journals. *Current Contents* No. 4, 24 January 1977, p. 5-9.

Figure 4. Highly cited articles from Italian journals. A = item number. **B** = total citations 1961-1975. **C** = total citations 1974-1975. * = non-physics articles.

A	B	C	Bibliographic Data
1.	639	57	**Gell-Mann M & Levy M.** The axial vector current in beta decay. **Nuovo Cimento** 16:705-26, 1960. [*Ecole Normale Superieure, Paris*]
2.	526	112	**Amati D, Stanghellini A & Fubini S.** Theory of high-energy scattering and multiple production. **Nuovo Cimento** 26:896-954, 1962. [*CERN, Geneva*]
3.*	359	26	**Jouvet M.** Neural anatomy and reactive mechanisms in different phases of physiologic sleep. **Arch. Ital. Biol.** 100:125-206, 1962. [*Univ. Lyon*]
4.	335	32	**Gottfried K & Jackson J D.** On the connection between production mechanism and decay of resonances at high energies. **Nuovo Cimento** 33:309-30, 1964. [*CERN, Geneva*]
5.	332	33	**Jackson J D.** Remarks on the phenomenological analysis of resonances. **Nuovo Cimento** 34:1644-66, 1964. [*CERN, Geneva*]
6.	327	30	**Gottfried K & Jackson J D.** Influence of absorption due to competing processes on peripheral reactions. **Nuovo Cimento** 34:735-52, 1964. [*CERN, Geneva*]
7.	299	10	**Regge T.** Introduction to complex orbital momenta. **Nuovo Cimento** 14:951-76, 1959. [*Max-Planck-Inst. Physik Astrophysik, Munich*]
8.	243	12	**Mandelstam S.** Cuts in the angular-momentum plane.2. **Nuovo Cimento** 30:1148-62, 1963. [*Dept. Mathematical Physics, Univ. Birmingham*]

(Figure 4 continued)

9.   236   53   **Goldstone J.** Field theories with "superconductor" solutions.
               Nuovo Cimento 19:154-64, 1961. [*CERN, Geneva*]

10. 225   9   **Lehmann H.** Uber Eigenschaften von Ausbreitungsfunktionen und
               Renormierungskonstanten quantisierter Felder.
               Nuovo Cimento 11:342-57, 1954.
               [*Max-Planck-Inst. Physik, Goettingen*]

11. 219   17   **Mandelstam S.** Cuts in the angular-momentum plane. I.
               Nuovo Cimento 30:1127-47, 1963.
               [*Dept. Mathematical Physics, Univ. Birmingham*]

12. 212   10   **Lehmann H, Symanzik K & Zimmerman W.** On the formulation of
               quantitized field theories. 2. **Nuovo Cimento 1:**205, 1955.
               [*Max-Planck-Inst. Physik, Goettingen*]

13.* 200   22   **Rossi G F & Zanchetti A.** The brain stem reticular formation.
               Arch. Ital. Biol. 95:199-435, 1957. [*Inst. Fisiologia, Univ. Pisa*]

14. 191   13   **Omnes R.** On the solution of certain singular integral equations of
               quantum field theory. **Nuovo Cimento 8:**316-26, 1958. [*CERN, Geneva*]

15. 189   48   **Bertocchi L, Fubini S & Tonin M.** Integral equation for high-energy pion-pion
               scattering. **Nuovo Cimento 25:**626-54, 1962.
               [*Inst. Naz. Fisica Nucleare, Bologna*]

16. 186   7   **Regge T.** Bound states, shadow states and Mandelstam representation.
               Nuovo Cimento 18:947-56, 1960. [*Palmer Physical Laboratory, Princeton Univ.*]

17. 175   8   **Gourdin M & Salin P.** Analysis of photoproduction with an isobaric model.
               Nuovo Cimento 27:193-207, 1963. [*CERN, Geneva*]

18. 150   10   **Fubini S.** Equal-time commutators and dispersion relations.
               Nuovo Cimento 43:457-82, 1966. [*Inst. Advanced Study, Princeton*]

19. 143   6   **Jackson J D & Pilkuhn H.** On the production of vector mesons and isobars in the
               peripheral model. **Nuovo Cimento 33:**906-38, 1964. [*CERN, Geneva*]

20.* 142   15   **Eccles R M & Lundberg A.** Synaptic actions in motoneurones by afferents
               which may evoke the flexion reflex. **Arch. Ital. Biol. 97:**199-221, 1959.
               [*Inst. Physiol., Univ. Lund, Sweden; Dept. Physiology, Australian National
               University, Canberra*]

21. 140   7   **Toller M.** Three-dimensional Lorentz group and harmonic analysis of the scatter-
               ing amplitude. **Nuovo Cimento 37:**631-57, 1965. [*Inst. Naz. Fisica Nucleare,
               Univ. Roma*]

22. 137   9   **Sopkovich N J.** The annihilations NN KK and YY.
               Nuovo Cimento 26:86-89, 1962. [*Carnegie Inst. of Technol., Pittsburgh*]

23. 134   8   **Bottino A, Longoni A M & Regge T.** Potential scattering for complex energy
               and angular momentum. **Nuovo Cimento 23:**954-1004, 1962.
               [*Inst. Fisica, Univ. Torino*]

24. 132   27   **Bell J S & Jackiw R.** A PCAC puzzle: ∏ ° YY in the O-model.
               Nuovo Cimento 60:47-60, 1969. [*CERN, Geneva*]

25.* 122   7   **Batini C, Moruzzi G, Palestini M, Rossi G F & Zanchetti A.** Effects of com-
               plete pontine transections on the sleep-wakefulness rhythm; the mid-pontine pre-
               trigeminal preparation. **Arch. Ital. Biol. 97:**1-12, 1959.
               [*Inst. Fisiologia, Univ. Pisa*]

26. 114   10   **Fubini S, Furlan G & Rossetti C.** A dispersion theory of symmetry breaking.
               Nuovo Cimento 40:1171-93, 1965. [*Inst. Fisica, Torino*]

27. 114   8   **Martin A.** Geometrical restrictions on the pion-pion partial waves.
               Nuovo Cimento 47:265-80, 1967. [*CERN, Geneva*]

28. 111   11   **Foldy L L & Wallecka J D.** Muon capture in nuclei.
               Nuovo Cimento 34:1026-61, 1964. [*CERN, Geneva*]

29. 111   14   **Harting D et 17 al.** [*CERN, Geneva*]. ∏± -p and p - p elastic scattering at
               8.5, 12.4, and 18.4 GeV/c. **Nuovo Cimento 38:**60-94, 1965.

(Figure 4 continued)

30. 111 9 **Valatin J G.** Comments on the theory of superconductivity.
Nuovo Cimento 7:843-57, 1958.
[*Dept. Mathematical Physics, Univ. Birmingham*]

31. 105 1 **Bernstein J, Fubini S, Gell-Mann M & Thirring W.** On the decay rate of the charged pion. **Nuovo Cimento** 17:757-66, 1960. [*Faculte des Sciences, Orsay*]

32.* 103 16 **Brooks D C & Bizzi E.** Brain stem electrical activity during deep sleep.
Arch. Ital. Biol. 101:648-65, 1963. [*Univ. Pisa*]

33. 100 1 **Ferrari E & Selleri F.** An approach to the theory of single pion production in the nucleon-nucleon collisions. **Nuovo Cimento** 27:1450-83, 1965.
[*CERN, Geneva*]

34. 98 3 **Bowcock J, Cottingham W N & Lurie D.** Effect of a pion-pion scattering resonance on low energy pion-nucleon scattering.
Nuovo Cimento 16:918-38, 1960. [*CERN, Geneva*]

35. 97 12 **Nozieres P & Pines D.** A dielectric formulation of the many body problem; application to the free electron gas. **Nuovo Cimento** 9:470-89, 1958.
[*Lab. Physique, Ecole Normale Superieure, Paris*]

36.* 95 5 **Rossi G F, Favale E, Hara T, Giussani A & Sacco G.** Researches on the nervous mechanisms underlying deep sleep in the cat.
Arch. Ital. Biol. 99:270-92, 1961. [*Univ. Genova*]

37. 91 0 **Martin A W & Wali K C.** Meson-baryon resonances in the octet model.
Nuovo Cimento 31:1324-51, 1964. [*Argonne Nat. Lab., Argonne, Ill.*]

38. 90 16 **Martin A.** Extension of the axiomatic analyticity domain of scattering amplitudes by unitarity. I. **Nuovo Cimento** 42:930-53, 1966. [*CERN, Geneva*]

39.* 85 17 **Gutenberg B & Richter C F.** The magnitude and energy of earthquakes.
Ann. Geofis. 9:1-15, 1956. [*Calif. Inst. Technology, Pasadena*]

40.* 81 8 **Contorni L.** The collateral vertebral circulation in total excision to its source of the subclavian artery. **Minerva Chir.** 15:268-71, 1960. [*Inst. Clinica Chirurgica Generale e Terapio Chirurgica Univ. Parma*]

41. 80 5 **Erba E, Facchini U & Menichella E S.** Statistical emission in nuclear reactions and nuclear level density. **Nuovo Cimento** 22:1237-60, 1961.

42.* 78 2 **Rossi G F, Minobe K & Candia O.** An experimental study of the hypnogenic mechanisms of the brain stem. **Arch. Ital. Biol.** 101:470-92, 1963.
[*Univ. Geneva*]

43. 77 1 **Chew G F & Mandelstam S.** Theory of the low-energy pion-pion interaction. 2.
Nuovo Cimento 19:752-76, 1961. [*Lawrence Radiation Lab., Univ. Calif.*]

44. 72 14 **Logunov A A & Tavkhelidze A N.** Quasi-optical approach in quantum field theory. **Nuovo Cimento** 29:380, 1963. [*Inst. High energy Physics, Serpukhov, USSR*]

45. 69 0 **Bogolyubov N N.** On a new method in the theory of superconductivity.
Nuovo Cimento 7:794-806, 1958. [*Joint Institute for Nuclear Research, Dubna, USSR*]

46. 68 4 **Lifshitz I M.** Some problems of the dynamic theory of non-ideal crystal lattices.
Nuovo Cimento 3:716-34, 1956. [*Academy of Science of USSR, Moscow*]

47. 68 0 **Ruhl W.** A relativistic generalization of the SU_6 symmetry group.
Nuovo Cimento 37:301-18, 1965. [*CERN, Geneva*]

48. 65 5 **Gourdin M & Salin P.** Some remarks about gauge invariance in the isobaric model for photoproduction. **Nuovo Cimento** 27:309-12, 1963.
[*Lab. Physique, Orsay, France*]

49. 65 4 **Salam A.** Lagrangian theory of composite particles.
Nuovo Cimento 25:224-27, 1962. [*Imperial College, London*]

50.* 61 24 **Immirzi A.** A new computation program for refinement of crystalline structures using the method of least squares. **Ricerca Scientifica** 37:743, 1967.
[*Inst. Chimica Industriale, Centro Nazionale de Chimica Macromol.*]

Figure 5. Journals that published the articles from Italian laboratories listed in **Figure 6.** A = number of articles. B = impact factor. C = journal.

A	B	C	A	B	C
1	6.433	Adv. Enzymology	1	6.677	Lancet
1	2.129	Annals of Physics	2	3.636	Nature
2	16.795	Bacteriol. Rev.	1	8.364	New Engl. J. Med.
3	4.711	Biochemistry	1	2.518	Nuclear Physics
1	2.492	Biopolymers	3	0.994	Nuovo Cimento A
1	2.457	Inorganic Chemistry	1	9.577	Pharmacol. Rev.
1	4.383	J. Amer. Chem. Soc.	2	8.989	P. Nat. Acad. Sci. USA
1	1.558	J. Appl. Physics	2	2.133	Physics Letters
3	5.843	J. Biol. Chemistry	3	2.684	Physical Review
1	6.770	J. Cell Biology	5	5.059	Phys. Rev. Letters
1	2.919	J. Endocrinology	1	21.500	Rev. Mod. Physics
1	11.874	J. Exp. Medicine	2	5.412	Science
1	2.536	J. Geophys. Res.	1	0.149	Zschr. Krebsforsch.
7	7.502	J. Mol. Biology			

Figure 6. Articles from laboratories in Italy, published during the period 1965-1970, and highly cited during the period 1967-1972. A = item number. B = total citations 1967-1972.

A	B	Bibliographic Data
1.	344	**Bishop D H L, Claybrook J R & Spiegelman S.** Electrophoretic separation of viral nucleic acids on polyacrylamide gels. **J. Mol. Biology** 26:373, 1967. [*Internat. Lab. Genet. & Biophys., Naples*]
2.	399	**Taylor A L.** Revised linkage map of *E. coli.* **Bacteriol. Reviews** 31:332-53, 1967. [*Food & Agric. Org., UN, Rome*]
3.	312	**Edelhoch H.** Spectroscopic determination of tryptophan and tyrosine in proteins. **Biochemistry** 6:1948, 1967. [*Univ. Naples*]
4.	278	**Druckrey H & Schneider H.** Organotropic carcinogenic effects of 65 different N-nitroso compounds in BD rats. **Zschr. Krebsforsch.** 69:103-201, 1967. [*Gemeinsame Kernforsch., EURATOM, Varese*]
5.	271	**Sottocasa G L, Kuylenstierna B, Ernster L & Bergstrand A.** An electron-transport system associated with the outer membrane of liver mitochrondria; a biological and morphological study. **J. Biol. Chemistry** 32:415-38, 1967. [*Inst. Chim., Univ. Trieste*]
6.	254	**Taylor A L.** Current linkage map of *E. coli.* **Bacteriol. Reviews** 34:155-75, 1970. [*Food & Agric. Org., UN, Rome*]
7.	233	**Penman S & Vesco C.** Localization and kinetics of formation of nuclear hetero-disperse RNA, cytoplasmic heterodisperse RNA, and polyribome-associated messenger RNA in HeLa cells. **J. Mol. Biology** 34:49-69, 1968. [*Intern. Lab. Genet. & Biophys., Naples; Lab. Biol. Cellulare, Rome*]
8.	227	**DeAlfaro V, Fubini S, & Rossetti G.** Sum rules for strong interactions. **Phys. Letters** 21:576-81, 1966. [*Univ. Inst. Fisica Teor., Univ. Torino; Univ Trieste*]
9.	224	**Pople J A & Gordon M.** Molecular orbital theory of the electron structure of organic compounds. 1. Substituent effects and dipole moments. **J. Amer. Chem. Soc.** 89:4253-61, 1967. [*CNR, Lab. Neurofisiol., Pisa*]

(Figure 6 continued)

10. 194 **Kennel C F & Petschek H E.** Limit on stably trapped particle fluxes.
          J. Geophys. Res. 71:1-28, 1966. [*Int. Ctr. Theoret. Phys., Trieste*]

11. 182 **DeLucia P & Cairns J.** Isolation of an *E. coli* strain with a mutation affecting DNA
          polymerase. **Nature** 224:1164-6, 1969. [*Consiglio Naz. Ricerche, Naples*]

12. 179 **Milicemili J, Henderson J A, Dolovich M B, Trop D & Kanesko K.** Regional
          distribution of inspired gas in lung. **J. Appl. Physiology** 21:749, 1966.
          [*Inst. Fisiol., Univ. Milan*]

13. 159 **Mangiarotti G & Schlessinger D.** Polyribosome metabolism in *E. coli.* 1. Extraction
          of polyribosomes and ribosomal subunits from fragile growing *E. coli.*
          J. Mol. Biology 20:123, 1966. [*Inst. Chim. Biol., Univ. Genova*]

14. 156 **Edsall J T, Liquori A M, Flory P J, Kendrew J C, Nemethy G, Ramachandran G N
          & Scherage H A.** A proposal of standard conventions and nomenclature for descrip-
          tion of polypeptide conformations. **Biopolymers** 4:121, 1966.
          [*Centro Naz. Chim., Univ. Naples; Lab. Chim. Fisica, Univ. Rome*]

15. 151 **Mermin M D & Wagner H.** Absence of ferromagnetism or antiferromagnetism in
          one- or two-dimensional isotropic Heisenberg models.
          Phys. Rev. Letters 17:1133-36, 1966. [*Inst. Fis. G. Marconi., Univ. Rome*]

16. 141 **Fubini S & Veniziano G.** Level structure of dual-resonance models.
          Nuovo Cimento A 64:811, 1969. [*Inst. Fisica Teor. Univ. Torino*]

17. 140 **Weiss J F & Kelmers A D.** A new chromatographic system for increased resolution of
          transfer ribonucleic acids. **Biochemistry** 6:2507, 1967. [*Univ. Milano*]

18. 139 **Cool R L, Giacomelli G, Kycia T F, Leontic B A, Li K K, Lundby A &
          Teiger J.** New structure in the K + ·P and K + ·D total cross sections between 0.9
          and 2.4 GEV/c. **Phys. Rev. Letters** 17:102, 1966.
          [*Inst. Naz. Fisica Nucl., Inst. Fisica, Bologna; Fac. Sci. MFN, Univ. Pisa*]

19. 137 **Bussolati G & Pearse A G E.** Immunofluorescent localization of calcitonin in C cells of
          of pig and dog thyroid. **J. Endocrinology** 37:205, 1967.
          [*Inst. Anat. & Istol. Patol., Univ. Torino*]

20. 132 **Edsall J T, Liquori A M, Flory P J, Kendrew J C, Nemethy G, Ramachandran G N,
          & Scherage H A.** A proposal of standard conventions and nomenclature for
          description of polypeptide conformations. **J. Mol. Biology** 15:399, 1966.
          [*Centro Naz. Chim., Univ. Naples; Inst. Chim., Lab. Chim. Fisica, Univ. Rome*]

21. 132 **Muirhead H, Mazzarella L, Cox J M & Perutz M F.** Structure and function of
          hemoglobin. 3. A three-dimensional Fourier synthesis of human deoxyhemoglobin
          at 5.5 A resolution. **J. Mol. Biology** 28:117, 1967.
          [*Inst. Chim, Centro Naz. Chim., Naples; Inst. Anat., Univ. Bari*]

22. 128 **Lehninger A L, Carafoli E & Rossi C S.** Energy linked ion movements in
          mitochondrial systems. **Adv. Enzymology** 29:259-320, 1967.
          [*Inst. Pathol., Univ. Modena; Inst. Biol. Chim., Univ. Padova*]

23. 127 **Cabibbo N & Radicati L A.** Sum rule for isovector magnetic moment of nucleon.
          Phys. Letters 19:697, 1966. [*Inst. Fis., Univ. Rome*]

24. 126 **Ciampolini M & Nardi N.** 5-coordinated high-spin complexes of bivalent cobalt
          nickel and copper with TRIS (2-dimethylaminoethyl) amine.
          Inorg. Chemistry 5:41, 1966. [*Inst. Chim. Gen. Inorg., Univ. Firenze*]

25. 122 **Fubini S, Furlan G & Rossetti C.** A dispersion theory of symmetry breaking.
          Nuovo Cimento A 40:1171, 1965. [*Inst. Fisica Teor. Torino;
          Inst. Fis Teor. Univ. Trieste*]

26. 120 **Grillo M A.** Electron microscopy of sympathetic tissues.
          Pharmacol. Reviews 18:387, 1966. [*Inst. Biol. Chim., Univ. Sassari;
          Inst. Chim. Biol., Univ. Torino*]

(Figure 6 continued)

27. 120 **Pernis B, Forni L & Amante L.** Immunoglobulin spots on the surface of rabbit
          lymphocytes. **J. Exp. Med. 132:**1001-18, 1970. [*Inst. Medicina, Univ. Genova;
          Lab. Immunol., Univ. Milano*]

28. 119 **Edsall J T, Liquori A M, Flory P J, Kendrew J C, Nemethy G, Ramachandran G N
          & Scheraga H A.** A proposal of standard conventions and nomenclature for
          description of polypeptide conformation. **J. Biol. Chemistry 241:**1004, 1966.
          [*Centro Naz. Chim., Univ. Naples; Inst. Chim., Lab. Chim. Fisica, Univ. Rome*]

29. 115 **Gilat G & Raubenheimer L J.** Accurate numerical method for calculating frequency
          distribution functions in solids. **Phys. Review 144:**390-5, 1966.
          [*Comitato Naz. Energia Nucl., Varese*]

30. 114 **Fubini S.** Equal-time commutators and dispersion relations.
          Nuovo Cimento A 43:475, 1966. [*Inst. Fisica Teor., Torino*]

31. 114 **Schlessinger D, Mangiarotti G & Apirion D.** Formation and stabilization of 30S
          and 50S ribosome couples in *E. coli*. **Proc. Nat. Acad. Sci. USA 58:**1782, 1967.
          [*Inst. Chim. Biol., Univ. Genova*]

32. 110 **Corneo G, Moore C, Sanadi D R, Grossman L I & Marmur J.** Mitochondrial
          DNA in yeast and some mammalian species. **Science 151:**687, 1966.
          [*Centro Patol. Molecol., Univ. Milano*]

33. 110 **Griffiths R B.** Thermodynamic functions for fluids and ferromagnets near the
          critical point. **Phys. Review 158:**176, 1967. [*Food & Agr. Org., UN, Rome*]

34. 109 **Azzi A, Chance B, Radda G K & Lee C P.** A fluorescence probe of energy-
          dependent structure changes in fragmented membranes.
          Proc. Nat. Acad. Sci. USA 62:612, 1969. [*G. Vernoni Stud. Fis., Univ. Padova*]

35. 108 **Mangiarotti G & Schlessinger D.** Polyribosome metabolism in *E. coli.* 2. Formation
          and lifetime of messenger RNA molecules, ribosomal subunit couples, and poly-
          ribosomes. **J. Mol. Biology 29:**395, 1967. [*Inst. Chim. Biol., Univ. Genova*]

36. 104 **Mangiarotti G, Apirion G, Schlessinger D & Silengo L.** Biosynthetic procursors of
          30S and 50S ribosomal particles in *E. coli*. **Biochemistry 7:**456, 1968.
          [*Inst. Chim. Biol., Univ. Genova*]

37. 104 **Sakurai J J.** Eight ways of determining the rho-meson coupling constant.
          Phys. Rev. Letters 17:1021, 1966. [*Scuola Normale Superiore, Pisa*]

38. 103 **Bloom F E & Groppetti A.** Lesions of central norepinephrine terminals with 6-OH
          dopamine; biochemistry and fine structure. **Science 166:**1284-6, 1969.
          [*Lab. Farmaceut. Milan*]

39. 100 **Teegarden K & Baldini G.** Optical absorption spectra of alkali halides at 10 degrees K.
          Phys. Review 155:896. 1967. [*Inst. Fisica, Univ. Milan*]

40.   99 **Bellettini G, Cocconi G, Diddens A N, Lillethun E, Matthiae G, Scanlon J P &
          Wetherell A M.** Proton-nuclei cross sections at 20 GEV.
          Nucl. Physics 79:609, 1966. [*Inst. Naz. Fis. Nucl., Univ. Pisa;
          Inst. Super. Sanita, Rome*]

41.   99 **Rosenberg S A & Guidotti G G.** Protein of human erythrocyte membranes. 1.
          Preparation, solubilization, and partial characterization.
          J. Biol. Chemistry 243:1985, 1968. [*Inst. Patol. Gen., Univ. Cagliari;
          Inst. Gen. Pathol., Univ. Milano*]

42.   98 **Greaves M F, Trusi A, Torrigiani G, Zamir R, Playfair J H & Roitt I M.**
          Immunosuppressive potency and *in vitro* activity of antilymphocyte globulin.
          Lancet 1:68, 1969. [*Clin. Med. II., Univ. Bari*]

43.   96 **Cool R L, Giacomelli G, Kycia T F, Leontic B A, Li K K & Teiger J.**
          New structure in K--P and K--D total cross sections between 1.0 and 2.45
          GEV/c. **Phys. Rev. Letters 16:**1228, 1966. [*Inst. Naz. Fis. Nucl., Bologna;
          Fac. Sci., Univ. Pisa*]

44.   96 **McClusky R T, Gallo G, Vassalli P & Baldwin D S.** Immunofluorescent study
          of pathogenic mechanisms in glomular diseases. **New Engl. J. Med. 274:**695, 1966.
          [*Inst. Naz. Appl. Cal., Rome; Inst. Fisiol. Gen., Univ. Genova;
          Lab. Richerche, Lepetit SPA, Milano*]

(Figure 6 continued)

45. 96 **Oakes R J & Sakurai J J.** Spectral-function sum rules, omega-phi mixing, and lepton-pair decays of vector mesons. **Phys. Rev. Letters 19:**1266, 1967. [*Scuola Normale Superiore, Pisa*]

46. 96 **Perutz M F, Mazzarella L., Muirhead H, Crowther R A, Greer J & Kilmartin J V.** Identification of residues responsible for the alkaline Bohr effect in hemoglobin. **Nature 222:**1240, 1969. [*Inst. Chim. Centro Naz. Chim. CNR, Naples; Inst. Anat., Univ. Bari*]

47. 94 **Martinez-Carrion M, Bossa F, Chiancone E, Fasella P, Riva F, Turano C & Giartosio A.** Isolation and characterization of multiple forms of glutamate-aspartate aminotransferase from pig heart. **J. Biol. Chemistry 242:**2397, 1967. [*CNR, Ctr. Molec. Biol., Univ. Rome; Fac. Med., Cattedra Chim. Biol., Univ. Rome; Lab. Recerche Reologia, Univ. Naples; Fac. Farm., Univ. Perugia; Inst. Biol., Chim., Univ. Rome*]

48. 93 **Fubini S & Furlan G.** Dispersion theory of low-energy limits. **Ann. Physics 43:**322, 1968. [*Inst. Fis. Teor. Torino; Inst. Fis. Teor., Univ. Trieste*]

49   91 **Zylber E, Vesco C & Penman S.** Selective inhibition of the synthesis of mitochrondria-associated RNA by ethidium bromide. **J. Mol. Biology 44:**195-204, 1969. [*Intern. Lab. Genet. & Biophys., Naples; Lab. Biol. Cellulare, Rome*]

50. 91 **DiMauro S, Snyder L, Marino P, Lamberti A, Coppo A & Tocchini G P.** Rifampicin sensitivity of components of DNA-dependent RNA polymerase. **Nature 222:**533, 1969. [*Inst. Internaz. Genet., Naples.*]

ERRATUM:
In preparing Figure 6 we compiled a list of "Italian" authors. In that list a number of names were included for persons who *at one time* had been co-authors of papers published by Italian laboratories. For example, A.L. Taylor (papers #2 and #6) had been at FAO in Rome, but not when these papers were written.

During 1980 we intend to publish a revised analysis of the most-cited papers by Italian scientists. I apologize to the authors of the papers which were listed with incorrect addresses. The inclusion of these names meant that a large group of well-cited Italian authors was excluded.

CURRENT COMMENTS

Project *Keysave* ™ --ISI's New
On-Line System for Keying Citations
Corrects Errors!

Number 7, February 14, 1977

At a seminar in 1969, one of ISI®'s vice-presidents, Phil Sopinsky, overheard Derek de Solla Price conjecture that "80% to 90% of the literature cited in a current year had been cited previously." Sopinsky's systems intuition immediately recognized unnecessary redundancy. Each of those repeated citations was unnecessarily recorded in its entirety. Indeed, many citations were being keyed two, three, or more times. This involved an enormous waste of time and energy in creating ISI's data bank.

Under Phil Sopinsky's guidance, Project *Keysave*™ was launched. Citation files for the years 1966, 1967, and 1968 were merged into one large file. This file was matched against the citation file for 1969. The match rate between these two files was found to be 66%! However, to verify Price's original conjecture was one thing. To develop a means for exploiting it was another.

A great deal of work would be saved even if one continued to key the full citation, that is author, journal, volume, page and year. However, this information would now be matched against an on-line master file of citations. Whenever there was a match we could eliminate manual verification. This is a process which involves re-keying the identical information for each citation. *Keysave* eliminated verification on as many as 90% of citations depending upon the journal involved.

However, Phil Sopinsky realized that we could use our knowledge of citation redundancy to reduce the initial keying effort as well. For many years we have known that 14 characters of information is all one needs to identify most articles uniquely. By keying just these 14 characters we could identify each citation on a file containing both the 14 character code and the complete citation. Consequently, whenever a match was obtained, we would eliminate keying the remaining characters of the citation. Only in a small percentage of cases would the entire citation be keyed.

The non-*Keysave* system involved keying as many as 48 characters; 18 for the author's name; 20 for the journal title; and 4, 4, and 2 for the cited volume, page number, and year. Under the old system, if the identical article was cited by two different authors, the journals might be abbreviated differently. Authors' initials might be omitted as well. Under the *Keysave* system, however, each citation requires only 14 characters; the first four characters of the first author's last name, and the same 4, 4, and 2 for volume, page number, and year. When the computer 'recognizes' this abbreviated citation, it instantaneously informs the data-entry operator, by flashing a special symbol on the terminal screen. When the citation does *not* match the *Keysave* library a bell sounds, indicating to the operator that there is no match. Then the entire citation must be keyed and subsequently verified by another operator.

The advantages of the *Keysave*™ system are threefold: increased productivity and less boredom for the data-entry operator; decreased expense for ISI; and the greater standardization of citations. A fourth benefit is that the new procedure also corrects errors in citations--a significant qualitative improvement of *SCI*® and its related services.

Project *Keysave* was initially proposed for use at ISI in March 1972. Further studies were then conducted to determine feasibility. Two prime topics considered were the number of citations to be stored, and their chronological distribution.

A new test file was accumulated for 1964-69. The 1970 file was matched against this five-year file of approximately 8 million cited articles. A match rate of 72.5% was attained. We knew from *SCI* statistical data that about 25% of all citations are to papers published in the previous two years. So we felt confident that we could use our own source data files to augment the *Keysave* file with accurate data. Eventually, by a combination of source and citation data, we developed a file of about 5 million citations that gave us a 60% match rate. This file became operational in October 1974.

If one considers that we key over 6 million citations in a year, a match rate of 60% means we save most of the keying and complete verification of 3.5 million citations per year! However, the savings are more dramatic when individual journals are studied. For example, in keying 1,918 citations in the *Journal of Virology* during the first quarter of 1972, the match rate was 91%. Of 5,857 citations keyed from the *Journal of Bacteriology*, 89% matched. The same figure obtained for *Virology* on the basis of 2,880 citations. And 88% of the citations in the *Journal of Molecular Biology* matched in a sample of 3,974 citations.

Obviously, we get the best results with journals that have high impact since impact is based on the number of citations to articles published in the two years prior to the year studied. Journals in the social sciences produce the worse results since they involve citation of books and other non-journal material. Hopefully, we can develop *Keysave* so that it will include book references as well. In that way, for some journals we will have a 100% match rate. If present hardware prevents expansion of the *Keysave*™ disc file we can also augment the capabilities of the system by using an auxiliary tape file to correct errors in citations subsequent to keying. By using such tapes in batch-mode we can correct errors for all but the most obscure items.

For a variety of reasons it is our responsibility to take every reasonable step to assure accuracy in our files. Since there has been so much discussion about the use of citation data for research evaluation,[1] it is essential that we take every reasonable step to improve accuracy. Citation errors creep into the literature for all sorts of reasons.[2] Not the least of these is the failure to eliminate printer's errors in proofreading. This happened to me recently in the citation of my own work[3]--rather embarrassing for a citation expert. But in spite of the known errors in the literature, we should not forget that the vast majority of citations are accurate and even those which contain small errors are still recognizable with a minimum of human or computer effort.

Phil Sopinsky

Phil Sopinsky is ISI's vice-president for computer services. He has been with ISI ten years, most of them spent in the development and management of computer systems and data processing. Understandably, his position gives him a key responsibility for the accuracy and timeliness of ISI products and services.

Phil is a native of Philadelphia and came to ISI after employment with the United States Army Signal Corps, the Curtis Publishing Company, and Food Fair Stores Inc. He is a graduate of Temple University and of the United States Naval Reserve.

Phil lives in Elkins Park, a suburb of Philadelphia, with his wife, four children, and 114 clocks. The last represents a 20-year hobby of collecting and restoration--of which many ISI employees and friends have taken happy advantage.

1. **Roy R.** Comments on citation study of materials science departments. *Journal of Metals* 28(6):29-30, 1976.
2. **Garfield E.** Errors--theirs, ours and yours. *Current Contents*® No. 25, 19 June 1974, p. 5-6.
3. --------------. Significant journals of science. *Nature* 264:609-15, 1976.

CURRENT COMMENTS

Highly Cited Articles. 35.
Biochemistry Papers
Published in the 1940s.

Number 8, February 21, 1977

We recently published a list of citation classics from the life sciences published in the 1930s that were heavily cited in the period 1961-1975.[1] That list of 59 articles was predominantly composed of biochemical articles, many relating to the analysis of phosphorus and its physiologic compounds.

The number of citation classics published in the forties is too formidable to discuss in one issue. So we have broken them into three groups--biochemical, life sciences, and physical sciences. In Figure 2 we have listed the highly- cited biochemical articles. Papers dealing with phosphorus separation and determination are again prevalent since phosphorus is basic in the study of DNA, sugars, lipids, and other biochemical substances.

Dr. Steward A. Narrod of the Albert Einstein Medical Center in Philadelphia has commented on this parallel. "The work done in the late 1930s and continuing through the 40s laid the basis for biochemical research today.... A good deal of the work today is an offshoot of the work done in the 1940s.

Since much of this is a totally new branch, the papers reporting this research would refer back to the 'parent' paper of the field."[2]

For example, paper 52 by Moore and Stein (both Nobel Prize winners) reported the initial separation of proteins into amino acid components. A paper by two other Nobel winners (80), Sutherland and Cori, was the original work leading to the discovery of cyclic AMP as a mediator of hormone reactions.

There are 13 Nobelists on this list. The papers which they either authored or coauthored constitute 13.5% of the 89 articles. Axelrod (paper 12) was the recipient of the 1970 Nobel Prize in Medicine; Martin (15 and 50), 1952 in Chemistry; Kornberg (30), 1959 in Medicine; Lipmann (41 and 42), 1953 in Medicine; Synge (50), 1952 in Chemistry; Moore (52), 1972 in Chemistry; Sanger (65), 1958 in Chemistry; Sumner (79), 1946 in Chemistry; Sutherland (80), 1971 in Medicine; Cori (80), 1947 in Medicine; Huggins (81), 1966 in Medicine; and Otto

Figure 1. **Journals that published the highly cited 1940s articles** listed in Figure 2. **A** = number of articles. **B** = 1975 impact factor. (Present titles of some journals are given in parentheses.)

A	B	Journal
1	0.346	Acta Biochim. Biophys.
1	1.208	Acta Chem. Scand.
2	1.373	Amer. J. Clin. Pathology
2	2.416	Analytical Chemistry
2	2.887	Arch. Biochemistry (Arch. Biochem. Biophys.)
1	3.188	Biochim. Biophys. Acta
10	3.456	Biochemical Journal
2	3.876	Biochem. Zschr. (Eur. J. Biochemistry)
1	1.475	Chemische Berichte
1	4.700	Endocrinology
6	4.671	J. Amer. Chem. Soc.
45	6.059	J. Biol. Chemistry
1	7.418	J. Clin. Invest.
2	2.855	J. Lab. Clin. Med.
1	1.634	J. Org. Chemistry
1	3.594	J. Pharmacol. Exp. Ther.
3	3.737	Nature
1	2.602	Plant Physiology
1	1.451	Proc. Soc. Exp. Biol. Med.
1	— —	Q.J. Microsc. Sci.
2	5.605	Science
1	0.835	Soil Science
1	0.670	Stain Technology

Warburg, who died in 1970, received the Nobel Prize for Medicine in 1931.

Not by sheer coincidence, in this week's *Citation Classics* we publish the comments of Dr. Walter C. Schneider regarding his classic paper (69) on this list. This paper, as Schneider indicates, was his first as a sole author, and the first paper in a series on "Phosphorus compounds in animal tissue." Number 3 in that series also appears on this list (70). Dr. Schneider comments that it is not entirely surprising to him that so long after publishing the paper it should attain the status of a classic, since methods are the backbone of all scientific research. "What is surprising," he asserts, "is that the method should have survived this comparatively long period of time and still maintained a high citation frequency. For it is the nature of science that methods are constantly being modified and refined with the result that literature references shift from the original to modifications."[3]

In a previous *Citation Classics*[4] we published the comments of Professor Norton Nelson of the New York University Medical Center. His paper (54) was an adaptation of the Somogyi method for the determination of glucose. The presence of his paper on this list illustrates how literature references shift from an original method to modifications of it. Incidentally, Somogyi's original 1945 papers continue to be highly cited and are numbers 74 and 75 on this list. This illustrates the phenomenon of co-citations I've discussed before.

The 89 articles on this list were published in 23 different journals. These journals are listed alphabetically in Figure 1. Thirteen journals published one article apiece: six journals published two apiece. Four journals published the other 72% of the articles.

Nature published three, *Journal of the American Chemical Society* 6, *Biochemical Journal* 10, and the *Journal of Biological Chemistry* 45. The vast majority of the articles are in English (85). Three articles were published in a German-language journal, and one in French.

More than two-thirds of the articles were published in the latter half of the 1940s--65, as compared to 24 for the period from 1940 to 1944. All of the articles were cited more than 150 times during the period 1961-1975. On the average, they were each cited 650 times during those 15 years, and continue to be cited about 45 times a year.

The most frequently cited paper (26 by Gornall, Bardawill, and David) was cited 5,400 times from 1961 to 1975, and averaged 360 citations per year. Nelson's paper (54) ranked second--3,265 citations--an average of 218 over the 15 year period. Significantly, both of those articles continue to be heavily cited. The citation rate for the paper by Gornall et al. has even increased, reflecting the high interest in the measurement of serum protein.

Some of the procedures on this list are now so basic it is remarkable that they continue to be cited at all. Roe and Kuether's blood ascorbic acid determination (61); Dische's color reaction of hexuronic acids (17); Somogyi's sugar determination (74 and 75); and the Bonsnes/Taussky colorimetric determination of creatine (10)--all are still heavily cited. However, the Martin/Synge (50) chromatographic method for determining amino acids in proteins is now less cited. This is probably due to the "obliteration phenomenon."5

There can be no doubt about the significance of the articles on this list. Published nearly 30 years ago, most of these classics are still highly-cited. To de-emphasize the significance anyone may attribute to absolute citation counts we have listed the papers in alphabetic order.

REFERENCES

1. **Garfield E.** Citation classics. 2. Articles from the life sciences 1930-1939. *Current Contents*® No. 43, 25 October 1976, p. 5-10.
2. **Narrod S A.** Personal communication, 16 November 1976.
3. **Schneider W C.** Personal communication, 9 November 1976.
4. **Nelson N.** *Citation classics:* A photometric adaptation of the Somogyi method for the determination of glucose. *Current Contents* No. 3, 17 January 1976, p. 13.
5. **Garfield E.** The 'obliteration phenomenon' in science, and the advantage of being obliterated. *Current Contents* No. 51/52, 22 December 1975, p. 5-7.

Figure 2. Highly cited articles in biochemistry published in the 1940s. A = item number. **B** = total citations 1961-1975. **C** = average yearly citations 1961-1975. **D** = citations in 1974. **E** = citations in 1975. Articles are listed alphabetically by first author.

A	B	C	D	E	Bibliographic Data
1.	1105	73	56	61	Allen R J L. The estimation of phosphorus. Biochem. J. 34:858-65, 1940.
2.	263	17	16	10	Archibald R M. Determination of citrulline and allantoin and demonstration of citrulline in blood plasma. J. Biol. Chem. 156:121-42, 1944.
3.	213	14	15	10	Archibald R M. Colorimetric determination of urea. J. Biol. Chem. 157:507-18, 1945.
4.	1806	120	213	222	Arnon D I. Copper enzymes in isolated chloroplasts; polyphenoloxidase in *Beta Vulgaris*. Plant Physiology 24:1-15, 1949.
5.	412	27	19	12	Baker J R. The histochemical recognition of lipine. Q. J. Microscop. Sci. 87:441-70, 1946.
6.	2019	134	56	68	Barker S B & Summerson W H. The colorimetric determination of lactic acid in biological material. J. Biol. Chem. 138:535-54, 1941.
7.	694	46	51	59	Benesi H A & Hildebrand J H. A spectrophotometric investigation of the interaction of iodine with aromatic hydrocarbons. J. Amer. Chem. Soc. 71:2703-07, 1949.
8.	958	63	82	83	Bessey O A, Lowry O H & Brock M J. A method for the rapid determination of alkaline phosphatase with five cubic millimeters of serum. J. Biol. Chem. 164:321-29, 1946.
9.	300	20	10	20	Blix G. The determination of hexosamines according to Elson and Morgan. Acta. Chem. Scand. 2:467-73, 1948.
10.	832	55	38	50	Bonsnes R W & Taussky H H. On the colorimetric determination of creatine by the Jaffe reaction. J. Biol. Chem. 158:581-91, 1945.
11.	206	13	6	4	Brockmann H & Schodder H. Aluminiumoxyd mit abgestuftem Adsorptionsvermögen zur chromatographischen Adsorption (Aluminum oxide with stepped adsorption capacity for chromatographic adsorption). Chem. Berichte 74:73-8, 1941.
12.	191	12	21	15	Brodie B B & Axelrod J. The estimation of acetanilide and its metabolic products, aniline, n-acetyl p-aminophenol and p-aminophenol (free and total conjugated) in biological fluids and tissues. J. Pharmacol. Exp. Ther. 94:22-8, 1948.
13.	426	28	28	25	Brown A H. Determination of pentose in the presence of large quantities of glucose. Arch. Biochem. Biophys. 11:269-78, 1946.
14.	489	32	35	24	Cohn E F, Strong L E, Hughes W L Jr, Mulford D J, Ashworth J N, Melin M & Taylor H L. Preparation and properties of serum and plasma proteins. 4. A system for the separation into fractions of the protein and lipoprotein components of biological tissues and fluids. J. Amer. Chem. Soc. 68:459-75, 1946.
15.	294	19	12	6	Consden R, Gordon A H & Martin A J P. Qualitative analysis of proteins; a partition chromatographic method using paper. Biochem. J. 38:224-32, 1944.
16.	183	12	10	3	Derrien Y, Michel D & Roche J. Recherches sur la preparation et les proprietes de la thyroglobuline pure (On preparation and properties of pure thyroglobulin). Biochim. Biophys. Acta. 2:454-70, 1948.
17.	1326	88	69	70	Dische Z. A new specific color reaction of hexuronic acids. J. Biol. Chem. 167:189-98, 1947.
18.	946	63	66	50	Dische Z & Shettles L B. A specific color reaction of methylpentoses and a spectrophotometric micromethod for their determination. J. Biol. Chem. 175:595-604, 1948.
19.	191	12	10	11	Dische Z, Shettles L B & Osnos M. New specific color reactions of hexoses and spectrophotometric micromethods for their determination. Arch. Biochem. 22:169-84, 1949.
20.	314	20	27	30	Drabkin D L. Spectrophotometric studies. 14. The crystallographic and optical properties of the hemoglobin of man in comparison with those of other species. J. Biol. Chem. 164:703-23, 1946.

Figure 2 (Cont.)

21. 297 19 16 19 Fishman W H, Springer B & Brunetti R. Application of an improved glucuronidase assay method to the study of human blood β -glucuronidase. J. Biol. Chem. 173:449-56, 1948.

22. 1288 85 46 37 Friedemann T E & Haugen G E. Pyruvic acid. 2. The determination of keto acids in blood and urine. J. Biol. Chem. 147:415-42, 1943.

23. 182 12 15 10 Gilman H & Haubein A H. The quantitative analysis of alkyllithium compounds. J. Amer. Chem. Soc. 66:1515-6, 1944.

24. 514 34 28 39 Gomori G. A modification of the colorimetric phosphorus determination for use with the photoelectric colorimeter.
J. Lab. Clin. Med. 27:955-60, 1942.

25. 884 58 71 81 Goodwin T W & Morton R A. The spectrophotometric determination of tyrosine and tryptophan in proteins. Biochem. J. 40:628-32, 1946.

26. 5396 359 497 425 Gornall A G, Bardawill C J & David M M. Determination of serum proteins by means of the biuret reaction. J. Biol. Chem. 78:751-66, 1949.

27. 1339 89 57 59 Hanes C S & Isherwood F A. Separation of the phosphoric esters on the filter paper chromatogram. Nature 164:1107-12, 1949.

28. 163 10 8 4 Henderson L M & Snell E E. A uniform medium for determination of amino acids with various microorganisms.
J. Biol. Chem. 172:15-29, 1948.

29. 963 64 52 55 Hestrin S. The reaction of acetylcholine and other carboxylic acid derivatives with hydroxylamine and its analytic application.
J. Biol. Chem. 180:249-61, 1949.

30. 574 38 26 34 Horecker B L & Kornberg A. The extinction coefficients of the reduced band of pyridine nucleotides. J. Biol. Chem. 175:385-90, 1948.

31. 398 26 15 19 Hotchkiss R D. A microchemical reaction resulting in the staining of polysaccharide structures in fixed tissue preparations.
Arch. Biochem. 16:131-41, 1948.

32. 559 37 31 34 Hughes E W. The crystal structure of melamine.
J. Amer. Chem. Soc. 63:1737, 1941.

33. 301 20 2 3 Jermyn M A & Isherwood F A. Improved separation of sugars on the paper partition chromatogram. Biochem. J. 44:402-07, 1949.

34. 305 20 12 7 Johnson M J. Isolation and properties of a pure yeast polypeptidase.
J. Biol. Chem. 137:575-86, 1941.

35. 378 25 17 25 Kalckar H M. Differential spectrophotometry of purine compounds by means of specific enzymes. 1. Determination of hydroxypurine compounds. J. Biol. Chem. 167:429-43, 1947.

36. 640 42 40 50 Kalckar H M. Differential spectrophotometry of purine compounds by means of specific enzymes. 3. Studies of the enzymes of purine metabolism. J. Biol. Chem. 167:461-75, 1947.

37. 170 11 10 27 Kilmer V J & Alexander L T. Methods of making mechanical analyses of soils. Soil Science 68:15-24, 1949.

38. 216 14 17 20 Klotz I M, Walker M & Pivan R B. The binding of organic ions by proteins. J. Amer. Chem. Soc. 68:1486-90, 1946.

39. 467 31 43 24 Koelle G B & Friedenwald J S. A histochemical method for localizing cholinesterase activity. Proc. Soc. Exp. Biol. Med. 70:617-22, 1949.

40. 172 11 11 8 Kubowitz F & Ott P. Isolierung und Kristallisation eines Gärungsfermentes aus Tumoren (Isolation and crystallization of a respiratory enzyme from tumors). Biochem. Zschr. 314:94-117, 1943.

41. 753 50 35 34 Lipmann F & Tuttle L C. A specific micromethod for the determination of acyl phosphates. J. Biol. Chem. 159:21-8, 1945.

42. 209 13 14 10 Loomis W F & Lipmann F. Reversible inhibition and the coupling between phosphorylation and oxidation. J. Biol. Chem. 173:807-09, 1948.

43. 745 49 41 47 Lowry O H & Lopez J A. The determination of inorganic phosphate in the presence of labile phosphate esters. J. Biol. Chem. 162:421-8, 1946.

44. 361 24 24 21 McManus J F A. Histological demonstration of mucin after periodic acid. Nature 158:202, 1946.

45. 242 16 10 13 McManus J F A. Histological and histochemical uses of periodic acid. Stain Technol. 23:99-108, 1948.

Figure 2 (cont.)

46. 203 13 12 12 **MacFadyen D A.** Estimation of formaldehyde in biological mixtures.
J. Biol. Chem. **158**:107-33, 1945.

47. 441 29 43 38 **MacKinney G.** Absorption of light by chlorophyll solutions.
J. Biol. Chem. **140**:315-22, 1941.

48. 396 26 16 12 **Markham R.** A stream distillation apparatus suitable for micro-Kjeldahl
analysis. Biochem. J. **36**:790-91, 1942.

49. 296 19 6 3 **Markham R & Smith J D.** Chromatographic studies of nucleic acids. 1.
A technique for the identification and estimation of purine and pyrimi-
dine bases, nucleosides and related substances.
Biochem. J. **45**:294-8, 1949.

50. 245 15 11 11 **Martin A J P & Synge R L M.** A new form of chromatogram employing two liquid phases. 1. A theory of chromatography. 2. Application to
the micro-determination of the higher monoamino-acids in proteins.
Biochem. J. **35**:1358-68, 1941.

51. 382 25 22 23 **Michel H O.** An electrochemical method for the determination of red
blood cell and plasma cholinesterase activity.
J. Lab. Clin. Med. **34**:1564-8, 1949.

52. 895 59 47 47 **Moore S & Stein W H.** Photometric ninhydrin method for use in the
chromatography of amino acids. J. Biol. Chem. **176**:367-88, 1948.

53. 534 35 22 37 **Morris D L.** Quantitative determinations of carbohydrates with Dreywood's
anthrone reagent. Science **107**:254-55, 1948.

54. 3265 217 165 153 **Nelson N.** A photometric adaptation of the Somogyi method for the determination of glucose. J. Biol. Chem. **153**:375-80, 1944.

55. 767 51 54 45 **Park J T & Johnson M J.** A submicrodetermination of glucose.
J. Biol. Chem. **181**:149-51, 1949.

56. 901 60 39 24 **Partridge S M.** Aniline hydrogen phthalate as a spraying reagent for chromatography of sugars. Nature **164**:443, 1949.

57. 934 62 39 26 **Partridge S M & Westall R G.** Filter-paper partition chromatography of
sugars. 1. General description and application of the qualitative analysis
of sugars in apple juice, egg white and foetal blood of the sheep.
Biochem. J. **42**:238-50, 1948.

58. 225 15 11 21 **Racker E.** Spectrophotometric measurement of hexokinase and phospho-
hexokinase activity. J. Biol. Chem. **167**:843-54, 1947.

59. 293 19 11 9 **Remmert L F & Cohen P P.** Partial purification and properties of a proteolytic enzyme of human serum. J. Biol. Chem. **181**:431-48, 1949.

60. 564 37 27 18 **Roe J H, Epstein J H & Goldstein N P.** A photometric method for the
determination of insulin in plasma and urine.
J. Biol. Chem. **178**:839-45, 1949.

61. 537 35 31 23 **Roe J H & Kuether C A.** The determination of ascorbic acid in whole
blood and urine through the 2,4-dinitrophenylhydrazine derivative of de-
hydroascorbic acid. J. Biol. Chem. **147**:399-407, 1943.

62. 423 28 21 22 **Roe J H & Rice E W.** A photometric method for the determination of
free pentoses in animal tissues. J. Biol. Chem. **173**:507-12, 1948.

63. 346 23 11 21 **Rosenthal T B.** The effect of temperature on the pH of blood and plasma
in vitro. J. Biol. Chem. **173**:25-30, 1948.

64. 214 14 12 3 **Russell J A.** The colorimetric estimation of small amounts of ammonia by
the phenol-hypochlorite reaction. J. Biol. Chem. **156**:457-61, 1944.

65. 938 62 25 31 **Sanger F.** The free amino groups of insulin. Biochem. J. **39**:507-15, 1945.

66. 214 14 9 7 **Sayers M A, Sayers G & Woodbury L A.** The assay of adrenocorticotrophic hormone by the adrenal ascorbic acid-depletion method.
Endocrinology **42**:379-93, 1948.

67. 676 45 25 39 **Schales O & Schales S S.** A simple and accurate method for the determination of chloride in biological fluids. J. Biol. Chem. **140**:879-84, 1941.

68. 1761 117 135 86 **Schmidt G & Thannhauser S J.** A method for the determination of
desoxyribonucleic acid, ribonucleic acid, and phosphoproteins in animal
tissues. Biochem. J. **161**:83-9, 1945.

Figure 2 (cont.)

69. 1518 101 71 72 **Schneider W C.** Phosphorus compounds in animal tissues. 1. Extraction and estimation of desoxypentose nucleic acid and of pentose nucleic acid. **J. Biol. Chem. 161**:293-303, 1945.

70. 282 18 16 14 **Schneider W C.** Phosphorus compounds in animal tissues. 3. A comparison of methods for the estimation of nucleic acids. **J. Biol. Chem. 164**:747-51, 1946.

71. 738 49 32 29 **Schneider W C.** Intracellular distribution of enzymes. 3. The oxidation of octonic acid by rat liver fractions. **J. Biol. Chem. 176**:259-66, 1948.

72. 706 47 25 31 **Scholander P F.** Analyzer for accurate estimation of respiratory gases in one-half cubic centimeter scales. **J. Biol. Chem. 167**:235-50, 1947.

73. 393 26 21 14 **Sibley J A & Lehninger A L.** Determination of aldolase in animal tissues. **J. Biol. Chem. 177**:859-72, 1949.

74. 603 53 35 35 **Somogyi M.** A new reagent for the determination of sugars. **J. Biol. Chem. 160**:61-8, 1945.

75. 970 64 49 37 **Somogyi M.** Determination of blood sugar. **J. Biol. Chem. 160**:69-73, 1945.

76. 289 19 20 19 **Spies J R & Chambers D C.** Chemical determination of tryptophan; study of color-forming reactions of tryptophan p-dimethylaminobenzaldehyde, and sodium nitrite in sulfuric acid solution. **Analytical Chem. 20**:30-9, 1948.

77. 739 49 43 42 **Spies J R & Chambers D C.** Chemical determination of tryptophan in proteins. **Analytical Chem. 21**:1249-66, 1949.

78. 173 11 10 11 **Stadie W C & Riggs B C.** Microtome for the preparation of tissue slices for metabolic studies of surviving tissues *in vitro*. **J. Biol. Chem. 154**:687-90, 1944.

79. 311 20 24 17 **Sumner J B.** A method for the colorimetric determination of phosphorus. **Science 100**:413-4, 1944.

80. 330 22 17 25 **Sutherland E W, Cori C F, Haynes R & Olsen N.** Purification of the hyperglycemic-glycogenolytic factor from insulin and from gastric mucosa. **J. Biol. Chem. 180**:825-37, 1949.

81. 314 20 19 21 **Talalay P, Fishman W H & Huggins C.** Chromogenic substrates. 2. Phenolphthalein glucuronic acid as substrate for the assay of glucuronidase activity. **J. Biol. Chem. 166**:757-72, 1946.

82. 158 10 11 10 **Tipson R S.** On esters of p-toluenesolfonic acid. **J. Org. Chem. 9**:235-41, 1944.

83. 678 45 42 40 **Vandekamer J H, Ten Bokkel Huinink H & Weyers H A.** Rapid method for the determination of fat in feces. **J. Biol. Chem. 177**:347-55, 1949.

84. 294 19 7 8 **Van Slyke D D & Folch J.** Manometric carbon determination. **J. Biol. Chem. 136**:509-41, 1940.

85. 454 30 17 25 **Vosburgh W C & Cooper G R.** Complex ions. 1. The identification of complex ions in solution by spectrophotometric measurements. **J. Amer. Chem. Soc. 63**:437-42, 1941.

86. 2594 172 193 161 **Warburg O & Christian W.** Isolierung und Kristallisation des Garungsferments Enolase (Isolation and crystallisation of the enzyme enolase) **Biochem. Zschr. 310**:384-421, 1942.

87. 285 19 17 15 **Ware A G & Seegers W H.** Two-stage procedure for the quantitative determination of prothrombin concentration. **Amer. J. Clin. Pathol. 19**:471-82, 1949.

88. 181 12 4 4 **Winzler R J, Devor A W, Mehl J W & Smyth L M.** Studies on the mucoproteins of human plasma. 1. Determination and isolation. **J. Clin. Invest. 27**:609-16, 1948.

89. 187 12 9 12 **Wolfson W Q, Cohn C, Calvary E & Ichiba F.** Studies on serum proteins. 4. A rapid procedure for the estimation of total protein, true albumin, total globulin, alpha globulin, beta globulin and gamma globulin in 1.0 ml. of serum. **Amer. J. Clin. Pathol. 18**:723-30, 1948.

ISI Adds "Non-Journal" Material to the 1977 *Science Citation Index*

Number 9, February 28, 1977

Beginning in 1977 there will be a major addition to the 2,600 journals presently covered by the *Science Citation Index®* . *SCI®* will also include items from an important class of "non-journal" material: published proceedings, symposia, monographic series, and multi-authored books (thematic collections of papers).

This is a major departure for ISI® . Till now we've concentrated on the journal literature. Two factors have influenced our decision.

One is the growing tendency among researchers in recent years to seek forums outside the important journals in their fields to announce their findings. This has been due, in a large part, to the tremendous competition among authors for space in prominent journals and the resultant lag time between discovery and publication. In consequence, an increasing amount of important information is appearing in the "non-journal" literature I've described above. As I noted earlier, specialized conferences alone now account for publication of 2,500—4,000 single-volume monographs each year![1]

The other factor that influenced our expansion of *SCI's* coverage is the long-standing problem of locating material published in proceedings and other scientific books. The conference literature has always been a bibliographic nightmare. Often this is due to the time between published proceedings and the event they record.[2] It is not unusual for proceedings to appear in book form long after the conference. And then they may be disguised by a title that makes no mention of the conference. Although there are several bibliographic aids to the conference literature, most do not list the individual papers presented. Librarians and scientists alike have had no way to locate such items easily.

As a partial solution to the "non-journal" literature problem we introduced *Current Book Contents®* to *CC®* subscribers in 1972. *CBC™* not only alerts readers to new publications. It also gives a chapter-by-chapter breakdown. In this way you can scan the contents of multi-authored works the way you scan a journal contents page.

The success of *CBC* has proven to us that the non-journal literature is both important to the scientific community and inadequately retrievable--thus the need for indexing in the *Science Citation Index.*

In the first year of this program, the *SCI* will cover some 40,000 items from 1,400 non-journal publications of the kind described above. Among them will be such influential publications as the *INSERM Symposia Series, Methods in Enzymology, Science in the Practice of Clinical Medicine, Advances in Geophysics,* the *Kroc Foundation Series,* and the *Chemical Society of London's Specialist Periodical Reports.*

This material will be distributed among the same five broad disciplines and in the same percentages as represented in the *SCI*'s present journal coverage: 42% will be in the life sciences, 23% in the physical and chemical sciences, 12% in clinical practice, 12% in engineering and technology, and 11% in agriculture, biology, and environmental sciences.

It has always been possible to use the *SCI* to determine what journal articles have cited particular papers in multi-authored books. Every book that is cited in a journal article becomes an entry in the *SCI*. But with the first quarterly issue of *SCI* in 1977 you will also be able to retrieve "non-journal" material when you look up a particular item or author. This means that we will index every item cited in these chapters or papers. And we will also, as is usual with the *SCI*, index the chapter by title words, source authors, and organizations.

As with all material covered in the *SCI*, indexing will be timely. Since many publishers like Elsevier/North Holland have been able to accelerate the process of publishing conference proceedings, this gives a new significance to such information, especially for current awareness. It is not unusual today for proceedings to appear within three months after the conference.[3]

Searchers will be able to find papers delivered at recent meetings and even follow the latest developments subsequent to presentation. This will be augmented by our coverage of monographic and review series.

You will now find in the *SCI* all the bibliographic information you need to obtain any "non-journal" publication indexed. The entry for each volume covered will include: title, sub-title, all editors, publisher's name and location, publication date, number of pages, International Standard Book Number, and Library of Congress card number. Where applicable, the series title, volume, issue, and date will appear. Entries for conference proceedings will also include the conference name, location, date and sponsor. Each description will be as complete as possible.

To choose what "non-journal" publications should be covered, we have had to develop a new system of selection that markedly differs from the way we choose what journals are to be covered in the *SCI*. For example, of primary importance in selecting journals is frequency of citation and impact. But, we also have an editorial advisory board. Experts in a variety of disciplines regularly evaluate new journals. And we also reply on input from users and publishers.

Of course, we will give priority to those highly cited and well known book series which do have extended publishing histories. Unlike multi-authored serial books one-time symposia cannot have citation histories by which their value can be judged directly. However, the quality of the work can be judged as well as relevance to our users by other methods. Not only will we continue to use subscribers, advisory boards, and reference works. We can also follow indicators such as the number of particular books ordered through *CBC*.

Over time we plan to expand and perfect this selection process to insure that *SCI* users will be able to search with confidence the most significant portion of "non-journal" literature published every year.

1. **Garfield E.** Of conferences and reviews. *Current Contents*® No. 48, 1 December 1975, p. 5-9.
2. **Drubba H.** Conference documentation; general overview and survey of the present position. *Associations Internationales* 28(8-9):383-87, 1976.
3. **Verbeek J L.** Personal communication, 2 December 1975.

CURRENT COMMENTS

Highly Cited Articles. 36.
Physics, Chemistry and Mathematics Papers
Published in the 1940s

Number 10, March 7, 1977

Recently we published a list of the biochemical classics of the 1940s.[1] Here is a list of highly cited articles published in the 1940s in physics, physical and synthetic chemistry, and mathematics.

While the 101 articles on the list were published in 32 different journals, only six journals account for half of the articles. Twenty of the articles listed in Figure 1 were published in *Journal of Chemical Physics;* 14 in *Physical Review;* 12 in *Journal of the American Chemical Society;* and 5 articles each in *Bell System Technical Journal, Reviews of Modern Physics,* and *Transactions of the Faraday Society (Journal of the Chemical Society Faraday).*

Other journals which published more than one article on this list are *Proceedings of the Physical Society of London* (4 articles), *Analytical Chemistry* (3), *Journal of the Chemical Society* (3), *Journal of Physics USSR* (3), *Industrial and Engineering Chemistry Analytical Edition* (2), *Journal de Chimie Physique* (2), *Nature* (2), *Philosophical Transactions of the Royal Society A* (2), and *Proceedings of the Royal Society London A* (2). *Science* is notably absent from the list.

Most of the articles were published in English. Three were in French, two in German, and 96 in what was, as early as the 1940's, the world language of the physical sciences--English. The articles are listed alphabetically by author in Figure 2.

According to C.W. Ufford, professor emeritus of physics at the University of Pennsylvania, one-third of these articles deal with molecular and chemical structure. Eleven deal with solutions, 6 with crystals, 5 with chemical analysis, 5 with ferromagnetism, 4 with x-rays, 3 with plasmas, and 2 each with chemical bonds, dipole movement, Brownian motion, metals, and nuclear magnetic resonance. Overall, Dr. Ufford notes that the articles on the list are heavily chemical in nature.

Several of the papers on this list have amassed a remarkable number of citations. The paper by N. Bloembergen et al. (1), for example, was cited 1145 times in the period 1961-1975. It concerns nuclear magnetic resonance, a powerful tool for the study of chemical structure. Also, the paper by K. Bowden et al. (12), a methods paper in chemical preparation, was cited 1127

Figure 1. Journals that published the highly cited 1940s articles listed in Figure 2. A = number of articles. B = 1975 impact factor. (Present titles of journals are given in parentheses.)

A	B	Journal
1	1.357	Acta Crystallographica
1	– –	Acta Physicochemica URSS (disc.)
3	2.416	Analytical Chemistry
1	1.764	Annals of Mathematics
1	0.592	Annals Math. Statistics (Ann. Statistics)
1	0.641	Annalen der Physik
1	2.600	Annales de Physique
5	2.021	Bell Syst. Techn. J.
1	10.392	Chemical Reviews
1	0.465	Industr. Eng. Chem. (Chemical Technology)
2	2.416	Ind. Eng. Chem. Anal. Ed. (Analytical Chemistry)
12	4.671	J. Amer. Chem. Soc.
20	2.931	J. Chemical Physics
3	1.713	J. Chem. Soc.
2	0.780	J. Chimie Physique
1	1.881	J. Opt. Soc. America
1	2.171	J. Phys. Chemistry
3	– –	J. Physics USSR (disc.)
1	2.171	J. Phys. Colloid Chem. (J. Phys. Chemistry)
1	0.604	J. Sci. Instruments (J. Physics E Sci. Instr.)
1	0.109	Kolloid Zschr.
2	3.737	Nature
1	1.800	Philosophical Magazine
2	1.353	Phil. Trans. Roy. Soc. A
14	2.490	Physical Review
1	7.876	Proc. Nat. Acad. Sci. USA
4	1.767	Proc. Phys. Soc. London (J. Physics A, B, C, D, E, F)
2	1.737	Proc. Roy. Soc. London A
5	15.841	Rev. Mod. Physics
1	– –	Trans. Amer. Inst. Min. Engrs (Mining Engineering)
1	1.204	Trans. Electrochem. Soc. (J. Electrochem. Soc.)
5	1.720	Trans. Faraday Soc. (J. Chem. Soc. Faraday)

times in the same period. Other papers on this list with remarkable citation records include those by S. Chandrasekhar (15), J.B. Martin et al. (61), J.H. VanVleck (91)--also dealing with magnetic resonance--and A.J.C. Wilson (96).

Some of the articles listed here (numbers 8, 11, 13, 23, 27, 28, 29, 36, 37, 41, and 62) are still on the ascendency, since their citation rate in 1974 exceeds their average yearly citation rate for the years 1961-1975--and their 1975 citation rate is higher than that for 1974. It will be interesting to see if the number of citations these articles receive continues to increase in the future.

The significance of this group of articles is indicated by the fact that one fifth of them were written by Nobel Prize winners. Two fundamental papers on nuclear magnetic resonance helped F. Bloch (1) and E.M. Purcell (10), win the Nobel Prize for physics in 1952. R.P. Feynman, whose fundamental paper on quantum mechanics is on the list (27), won the Nobel Prize for physics in 1965. D. Gabor (32), who helped improve the microscope in the 1940s and later invented holography, won the Nobel for physics in 1971. W. Shockley (84), who developed the transistor, won the Nobel for physics in 1956. In recent years he has unfortunately involved himself in discussions of the genetics of intelligence. I do not agree with Shockley's theories, but I do defend at least his right to expound them.

My good friend Harold C. Urey, whose paper (90) on the thermodynamic properties of isotopic substances appears on this list, is best known for the discovery of deuterium, for which he won the Nobel Prize for chemistry in 1934. The public also knows him for his interest in the origin of the solar system. Professor Urey still serves as a member of ISI® 's board of directors.

Other Nobel winners whose names appear on this list include E.P. Wigner (7), physics in 1963; M. Calvin (13), chemistry in 1961; P. Debye (23), chemistry in 1936; L.D. Landau (25,55 and 56), physics in 1962; P.J. Flory (28), chemistry in 1974; R.S. Mulliken (65, 66, and 67), chemistry in 1966; L. Neel (68), physics in 1970; L. Onsager (70), chemistry in 1968; J. Schwinger (77), physics in 1965; and C.H. Townes (89), physics in 1964.

Of these 101 articles of the 1940s, only 30 were published in the years 1940 to 1944--6 in 1940, 8 in 1941, 9 in 1942, 2 in 1943 and 5 in 1944. The remaining 70 were published in the latter half of the decade. Six appeared in 1945, the last year of World War II. Eight were published in 1946, 11 in 1947, 24 in 1948, and 22 in 1949. This chronological distribution follows remarkably well the size of the literature during those years. An examination of the statistical data for any annual *Science Citation Index®* reflects the size of the literature for earlier years.

The data in columns D and E show the degree of current interest in the subjects represented by these papers. However, to obtain a more complete picture of what these data indicate one would have to examine the cluster maps in which these papers occur.[2]

The small number of papers in mathematics should be interpreted carefully. On average, math papers are not cited as heavily as others, because of the low average number of references in math papers.

Several of the journals in Figure 1 are no longer published or have changed title. One curiosity is the paper by L.S. Darken (21) on the interrelation of diffusion and mobility through free energy in binary metallic systems. I wonder why he published in a journal of mining engineers.

As a final personal note I was pleased to see a paper (38) by Professor Ralph Halford of Columbia University. He was one of my professors in undergraduate physical chemistry. Later when I became a graduate student, he helped me through the personal crisis that made me realize experimental physical chemistry was not my career bag.

REFERENCES

1. **Garfield E.** Highly cited articles. 35. Biochemistry papers published in the 1940s. *Current Contents®* No. 8, 21 February 1977.

2. ----------- . Clusters and classification. *Current Contents* No. 42, 20 October 1975, p. 354-65.

Figure 2. Highly cited articles in physics, physical and synthetic chemistry, and mathematics published in the 1940s. A = item number. **B** = total citations 1961-1975. **C** = average yearly citations 1961-1975. **D** = citations in 1974. **E** = citations in 1975. Articles are listed alphabetically by first author.

A	B	C	D	E	Bibliographic Data
1.	201	13	13	9	Albert A, Goldacre R & Phillips J. The strength of heterocyclic bases. **J. Chem. Soc.** p. 2240-49, 1948.
2.	347	23	31	38	Anderson P W. Pressure broadening in the microwave and infra-red regions. **Physical Review 76**:647-61, 1949.
3.	415	27	16	10	Archibald W J. A demonstration of some new methods of determining molecular weights from the data of the ultracentrifuge. **J. Phys. Coll. Chem. 51**:1204-14, 1947.
4.	256	17	24	21	Avrami M. Kinetics of phase change. 2. Transformation-time relations for random distribution of nuclei. **J. Chem. Physics 8**:212-24, 1940.
5.	174	11	21	16	Avrami M. Kinetics of phase change. 3. Granulation, phase change, and microstructure. **J. Chem. Physics 9**:177-84, 1941.
6.	201	13	13	10	Bargmann V. Irreducible unitary representations of the Lorentz group. **Annals Math. 48**:568-640, 1947.
7.	198	13	9	13	Bargmann V & Wigner E P. Group theoretical discussion of relativistic equations. **Proc. Nat. Acad. Sci. USA 34**:211-23, 1948.
8.	416	27	33	45	Bates D R & Damgaard A. The calculation of the absolute strengths of spectral lines. **Phil. Trans. Roy. Soc. A 242**:101-22, 1949.
9.	374	24	22	27	Bloch F. Nuclear induction. **Physical Review 70**:460-74, 1946.
10.	1145	76	72	68	Bloembergen N, Purcell E M & Pound R V. Relaxation effects in nuclear magnetic resonance absorption. **Physical Review 73**:679-712, 1948.
11.	203	13	19	20	Bogolyubov N N. On the theory of superfluity. **J. Physics USSR 11**:23-32, 1947.
12.	1127	75	45	63	Bowden K, Heilbron I M, Jones E R H & Weedon B C L. Researches on acetylenic compounds. 1. The preparation of acetylenic ketones by oxidation of acetylenic carbinols and glycols. **J. Chem. Soc.** p.38-45, 1946.
13.	268	17	27	37	Calvin M & Wilson K W. Stability of chelate compounds. **J. Amer. Chem. Soc. 67**:2003-07, 1945.
14.	195	13	20	14	Casimir H B G & Polder D. The influence of retardation in the London-van der Waals forces. **Physical Review 73**:360-72, 1948.
15.	876	58	97	68	Chandrasekhar S. Stochastic problems in physics and astronomy. **Rev. Mod. Physics 15**:1-89, 1943.
16.	595	39	48	37	Cole D S & Cole R H. Dispersion and absorption in dielectrics. 1. Alternating current characteristics. **J. Chem. Physics 9**:341-51, 1941.
17.	259	17	13	19	Cottrell A H & Bilby B A. Dislocation theory of yielding and strain ageing of iron. **Proc. Phys. Soc. London A 62**:49-62, 1949.
18.	207	13	13	24	Coulson C A & Longuet-Higgins H C. The electronic structure of conjugated systems. 1. General theory. **Proc. Roy. Soc. London A 191**:39-60, 1947.
19.	204	13	19	10	Coulson C A & Moffitt W E. The properties of certain strained hydrocarbons. **Philosophical Mag. 40**:1-35, 1949.
20.	384	25	7	7	Cruickshank D W J. The accuracy of electron-density maps in x-ray analysis with special reference to dibenzyl. **Acta Crystallogr. 2**:65-82, 1949.
21.	153	10	19	16	Darken L S. Diffusion, mobility and their interrelation through free energy in binary metallic systems. **Trans. Amer. Inst. Min. Eng. 175**:184-201, 1948.
22.	284	18	12	28	Darken L S & Gurry R W. The system iron-oxygen. 1. The Wustite field and related equilibria. **J. Amer. Chem. Soc. 67**:1398-1412, 1945.
23.	327	21	27	41	Debye P. Reaction rates in ionic solutions. **Trans. Electrochem. Soc. 82**:265-72, 1942.
24.	177	11	16	13	Denbigh K G. The polarisability of bonds. I. **Trans. Faraday Soc. 36**:936-48, 1940.

Figure 2 (cont.)

25.	153	10	12	19	Derjaguin B V & Landau L. Theory of the stability of strongly charged lyophobic sols and of the addition of strongly charged particles in solutions of electrolytes. Acta Physicochim. URSS 14:633-662, 1941.

25. 153 10 12 19 Derjaguin B V & Landau L. Theory of the stability of strongly charged lyophobic sols and of the addition of strongly charged particles in solutions of electrolytes. **Acta Physicochim. URSS** 14:633-662, 1941.

26. 253 16 14 10 Doub L & Vandenbelt J M. The ultraviolet absorption spectra of simple unsaturated compounds. 1. Mono- and p-disubstituted benzene derivatives. **J. Amer. Chem. Soc.** 69:2714-23, 1947.

27. 197 13 15 27 Feynman R P. Space-time approach to non-relativistic quantum mechanics. **Rev. Mod. Physics** 20:367-87, 1948.

28. 286 19 21 25 Flory P J. Thermodynamics of high polymer solutions. **J. Chem. Physics** 10:51-61, 1942.

29. 381 25 33 46 Forster T. Zwischenmolekulare Energiewanderung und Fluoreszenz (Intermolecular energy transfer and fluorescence). **Ann. Physik** 2:55-77, 1948.

30. 782 52 36 57 Frank H S & Evans M W. Free volume and entropy in condensed systems. 3. Entropy in binary liquid mixtures; partial molal entropy in dilute solutions; structure and thermodynamics in aqueous electrolytes. **J. Chem. Physics** 13:507, 1945.

31. 193 12 12 9 Gabor D. Microscopy by reconstructed wave-fronts. **Proc. Roy. Soc. London A** 197:454-87, 1949.

32. 228 15 13 12 Gabor D. A new microscopic principle. **Nature** 161:777-78, 1948.

33. 165 11 19 19 Garlick G F J & Gibson A F. The electron trap mechanism of luminescence in sulphide and silicate phosphors. **Proc. Physical Soc.** 60:574-90, 1948.

34. 178 11 19 12 Gordy W. A relationship between bond force constants, bond orders, bond lengths, and the electronegativities of the bonded atoms. **J. Chem. Physics** 14:305-20, 1946.

35. 399 26 26 21 Grahame D C. The electrical double layer theory and the theory of electrocapillarity. **Chemical Reviews** 41:441-502, 1947.

36. 299 19 22 30 Grunwald E & Winstein S. The correlation of solvolysis rates. **J. Amer. Chem. Soc.** 70:846-54, 1948.

37. 178 11 23 27 Guggenheim E A. A proposed simplification in the procedure for computing dipole movement. **Trans. Faraday Soc.** 45:714-20, 1949.

38. 266 17 13 11 Halford R S. Motions of molecules in condensed systems. 1. Selection rules, relative intensities, and orientation effects for Raman and infra-red spectra. **J. Chem. Physics** 14:8-15, 1946.

39. 488 32 29 38 Halverstadt I F & Kumler W D. Solvent polarization error and its elimination in calculating dipole moments. **J. Amer. Chem. Soc.** 64:2988-92, 1942.

40. 183 12 16 5 Herring C & Nichols M H. Thermionic emission. **Rev. Mod. Physics** 21:185-270, 1949.

41. 326 21 25 31 Holstein T. Imprisonment of resonance radiation in gases. **Physical Review** 72:1212-33, 1947.

42. 333 22 19 20 Holstein T & Primakoff B. Field dependence of the intrinsic domain magnetization of a ferromagnet. **Physical Review** 58:1098-1113, 1940.

43. 187 12 8 9 Hornig D F. The vibrational spectra of molecules and complex ions in crystals. 1. General theory. **J. Chem. Physics** 16:1063-76, 1948.

44. 365 24 12 12 Huang Min Lon A simple modification of the Wolff-Kishner reduction. **J. Amer. Chem. Soc.** 68:2487-88, 1946.

45. 215 14 20 14 Huggins M L. The viscosity of dilute solutions of long-chain molecules. 4. Dependence on concentration. **J. Amer. Chem. Soc.** 64:2716-18, 1942.

46. 205 13 4 9 Johnston J P & Ogston A G. A boundary anomaly found in the ultracentrifugal sedimentation of mixtures. **Trans. Faraday Soc.** 42:789-99, 1946.

47. 278 18 28 17 Kellermann E W. Theory on the vibrations of the sodium chloride lattice. **Phil. Trans. Roy. Soc. A** 238:513-48, 1940.

48. 174 11 11 13 Kilpatrick J E, Pitzer K S & Spitzer R. The thermodynamics and molecular structure of cyclopentane. **J. Amer. Chem. Soc.** 69:2483-88, 1947

Figure 2 (cont.)

49.	221	14	17	13	Kirkwood J G. The statistical mechanical theory of transport processes. **J. Chem. Physics 14**:180-201, 1946.
50.	277	18	28	19	Kirkwood J G & Riseman J. The intrinsic viscosities and diffusion constants of flexible macromolecules in solution. **J. Chem. Physics 16**:565-73, 1948.
51.	253	16	13	12	Kittel C. Physical theory of ferromagnetic domains. **Rev. Mod. Physics 21**:541-83, 1949.
52.	162	10	11	8	Klevens H B & Platt J R. Spectral resemblances of cata-condensed hydrocarbons. **J. Chem. Physics 17**:470-81, 1949.
53.	164	10	13	12	Kubelka P. New contributions to the optics of intensely light-scattering materials. 1. **J. Optical Soc. Amer. 38**:448-57, 1948.
54.	183	12	10	13	Kuhn W & Grün F. Beziehungen zwischen elastischen Konstanten und Dehnungsdoppelbrechung hochelastischer Stoffe (Relation between elastic constants and stress double fracture of highly elastic substances). **Kolloid Zschr. 101**:248-71, 1942.
55.	360	24	17	20	Landau L. On the vibrations of the electronic plasma. **J. Physics USSR 10**:25-34, 1946.
56.	214	14	22	18	Landau L D. The theory of superfluity of helium III. **J. Physics USSR 5**:71-90, 1941.
57.	315	21	13	10	Lewis G N & Kasha M. Phosphorescence and the triplet state. **J. Amer. Chem. Soc. 66**:2100-16, 1944.
58.	247	16	10	13	Lyddane R H, Sachs R G & Teller E. On the polar vibrations of alkali halides. **Physical Review 59**:673-6, 1941.
59.	285	19	10	11	Ma T S & Zuazaga G. Micro-Kjeldahl determination of nitrogen. **Ind. Eng. Chem. Anal. Ed. 14**:280-2, 1942.
60.	277	18	23	23	Mann H B. On a test of whether one of two random variables is stochastically larger than the other. **Annals Math. Statistics 18**:50-60, 1947.
61.	942	62	58	67	Martin J B & Doty D M. Determination of inorganic phosphate modification of isobutyl alcohol procedure. **Analytical Chem. 21**:965-67, 1949.
62.	300	20	32	34	Mayo F R & Lewis F M. Copolymerization. 1. A basis for comparing the behavior of monomers in copolymerization; the copolymerization of styrene and methyl methacrylate. **J. Amer. Chem. Soc. 66**:1594-1601, 1944.
63.	375	25	25	24	McClure D S. Triplet-singlet transitions in organic molecules; lifetime measurements of the triplet state. **J. Chem. Physics 17**:905-13, 1949.
64.	173	11	18	7	Meites L & Meites T. Removal of oxygen from gas streams. **Analytical Chem. 20**:984-85, 1948.
65.	382	25	25	15	Mulliken R S. Quelques aspects de la theories des orbitales moleculaires (On some aspects of the molecular orbital theory). **J. Chim. Physique 46**:497-542, 1949.
66.	164	10	10	9	Mulliken R S. Quelques aspects de la theorie des orbitales moleculaires. (Some aspects of the molecular orbital theory). **J. Chim. Physique 46**:675-713, 1949.
67.	580	38	27	23	Mulliken R S, Riecke C A, Orloff D & Orloff H. Formulas and numerical tables for overlap integrals. **J. Chem. Physics 17**:1248, 1949.
68.	301	20	13	20	Neel L. Proprietes magnetiques des ferrites; ferrimagnetisme et antiferromagnetisme. **Annales Physique 3**:137-95, 1948.
69.	331	22	19	10	Nelson J B & Riley D P. An experimental investigation of extrapolation methods in the derivation of accurate unit-cell dimensions of crystals. **Proc. Physical Soc. London 57**:160-77, 1945.
70.	432	28	46	35	Onsager L. Crystal statistics. 1. A two-dimensional model with an order-disorder transition. **Physical Review 65**:117-49, 1944.
71.	306	20	9	18	Pake G E. Nuclear resonance absorption in hydrated crystals; fine structure of the proton line. **J. Chem. Physics 16**:327-36, 1948.
72.	328	21	21	15	Platt J R. Classification of spectra of cata-condensed hydrocarbons. **J. Chem. Physics 17**:484-95, 1949.
73.	453	30	33	24	Racah G. Theory of complex spectra. 2. **Physical Review 62**:438-62, 1942.
74.	337	22	21	12	Racah G. Theory of complex spectra. 3. **Physical Review 63**:367-82, 1943.
75.	215	16	12	10	Racah G. Theory of complex spectra. 4. **Physical Review 76**:1352-65, 1949.

Figure 2 (cont.)

76. 175 11 11 10 **Rachinger W A.** A correction for the $\alpha_1\alpha_2$ double in the measurement of widths of x-ray diffraction lines. **J. Sci. Instruments 25:**254-56, 1948.

77. 187 12 8 14 **Rarita W & Schwinger J.** On a theory of particles with half-integral spin. **Physical Review 60:**61, 1941.

78. 236 15 19 12 **Redlich O & Kister A T.** Algebraic representation of thermodynamic properties and the classification of solutions. **Ind. Eng. Chem. Anal. Ed. 40:**345-56, 1948.

79. 399 26 18 20 **Rice S O.** Mathematical analysis of noise. 3. Statistical properties of random noise currents. **Bell Syst. Tech. J. 24:**46-156, 1945.

80. 410 27 17 20 **Rice S O.** Mathematical analysis of random noise. **Bell Syst. Tech. J. 23:**282-332, 1944.

81. 155 10 15 14 **Schomaker V & Stevenson D P.** Some revisions of the covalent radii and the additivity rule for the lengths of partially ionic single covalent bonds. **J. Amer. Chem. Soc. 63:**37-40, 1941.

82. 501 33 33 50 **Shannon C E.** A mathematical theory of communications. **Bell Systm. Tech. J. 27:**379-423, 1948.

83. 388 25 25 28 **Shannon C E.** A mathematical theory of communications. 3. Mathematical preliminaries. **Bell Syst. Tech. J. 27:**623-36, 1948.

84. 281 18 17 10 **Shockley W.** The theory of p-n junctions in semiconductors and p-n junction transistors. **Bell Syst. Tech. J. 28:**435-89, 1949.

85. 173 11 14 9 **Simha R.** The influence of Brownian movement on the viscosity of solutions. **J. Phys. Chem. 44:**25-34, 1940.

86. 260 17 14 19 **Stokes A R.** A numerical Fourier-analysis method for the correction of widths and shapes of lines on x-ray powder photographs. **Proc. Phys. Soc. London 61:**382-92, 1948.

87. 232 15 10 10 **Stull D R.** Vapor pressure of pure substances; organic compounds. **Ind. Eng. Chem 39:**517-40, 1947.

88. 188 12 11 11 **Szigeti B.** Polarisability and dielectric constant of ionic crystals. **Trans. Faraday Soc. 45:**155-66, 1949.

89. 288 19 26 21 **Townes C H & Dailey B P.** Determination of electronic structure of molecules from nuclear quadrupole effects. **J. Chem. Physics 17:**782-796, 1949.

90. 151 10 13 15 **Urey H C.** The thermodynamic properties of isotopic substances. **J. Chem. Soc.** p. 562-81, 1947.

91. 907 60 52 59 **Van Vleck J H.** The dipolar broadening of magnetic resonance in crystals. **Physical Review 74:**1168-83, 1948.

92. 366 24 13 18 **Van Vleck J H** Paramagnetic relaxation times for chromium and chrome alum. **Physical Review 57:**426-47, 1940.

93. 242 16 24 12 **Walsh A D.** The structures of ethylene oxide, cyclopropane, and related molecules. **Trans. Faraday Soc. 45:**179-90, 1949.

94. 313 20 36 27 **Wang M C & Uhlenbeck G E.** On the theory of the Brownian motion. 2. **Rev. Mod. Physics 17:**323-42, 1945.

95. 162 10 5 4 **Wheland G W.** A quantum mechanical investigation on the orientation of substituents in aromatic molecules. **J. Amer. Chem. Soc. 64:**900-08, 1942.

96. 824 54 65 81 **Wilson A J C.** Determination of absolute from relative x-ray intensity data. **Nature 150:**151-52, 1942.

97. 332 22 13 11 **Wilson E B.** Some mathematical methods for the study of molecular vibrations. **J. Chem. Physics 9:**76-84, 1941.

98. 434 28 26 27 **Yoe J H & Jones A L.** Colorimetric determination of iron with disodium-1,2-hydroxybenzene-3,5,-disulfonate. **Analytical Chem. 16:**111-15, 1944.

99. 348 23 30 21 **Zimm B H.** Apparatus and methods for measurement and interpretation of the angular variation of light scattering; preliminary results on polystyrene solutions. **J. Chem. Physics 16:**1099-1116, 1948.

100. 283 18 21 15 **Zimm B H.** The scattering of light and the radical distribution function of high polymer solutions. **J. Chem. Physics 16:**1093-99, 1948.

101. 197 13 16 14 **Zimm E H & Stockmayer E.** The dimensions of chain molecules containing branches and rings. **J. Chem. Physics 17:**1301-14, 1949.

CURRENT COMMENTS

The Vegetarian Alternative

Number 11, March 14, 1977

Despite the increasing prices, beef consumption in the United States has continued to rise. In 1940 the average beef intake per person was 55 pounds, in 1960 the average was 190 pounds, and in 1970 it was 236 pounds.[1] For the next quarter of a century, moreover, the meat industry expects this figure to increase. Their prediction is based on the assumption that as a person's material well-being increases, his or her "predilection to increase the intake of animal protein" increases.[2]

And the meat industry may be correct. The meat industry has successfully fostered the notion that only "good red meat" can supply the essential minerals and vitamins to our bodies, and so a meat-centered diet became a sign of prosperity.

It is not true, however, that *only* red meat can supply the nutritional requirements of the body. In fact, with the exception of vitamin B_{12}, which can be obtained from all dairy products,[3] non-meat sources provide a very substantial amount of the necessary vitamins and minerals. Most of our calcium is supplied by non-meat foods: good sources are plant foods such as collards, turnip greens, and lettuce. Although meat is an adequate source for potassium, the baked potato and lima bean are better. Iron can be obtained in nearly equal amounts from animal products such as eggs, milk, and cheese; various seeds and nuts contain abundant iron. For magnesium, meat is a poorer source than cocoa, nuts, soybeans, whole grains, and leafy green vegetables.[4] According to Professor Fredrick Stare, head of the Department of Nutrition at Harvard University, even vitamin A, which is a naturally-occurring substance in various animal products, could be obtained without eating meat. He asserted that "about 60% of our vitamin A intake comes from carotene, which is a pigment, out of which we make vitamin A in our bodies."[5]

To most people food is a matter of habit and taste, and is not eaten strictly for its nutritional quality. Meat is eaten partly because it tastes good; and it is the fat that gives meat its taste. Along with fat, meat supplies a large amount of cholesterol to the body. Dr. Gerald Combs, director of the Nutrition Program at NIH, indicates that both of these substances may be dangerous. He says that, "From the work that's been done so far--highly suggestive but not yet proven--there is certainly a correlation between the level of saturated fat and cholesterol in blood and heart disease."[6]

Professor Stare concurs, adding that, "Most Americans would probably be in better health if they consumed less meat. Americans probably average between 10-12 oz. of meat per day. If that meat intake was cut in half, most Americans would probably be in better health, primarily because of less saturated fat."[5]

To a vegetarian, food is more than simply habit or taste: it is a way of life. The aims of the vegetarian's lifestyle are threefold; to eliminate meat from the diet but still obtain the nutritional requirements of the body, the alleviation of the world food crisis, and the contribution to the furtherance of 'bioethics'--regarding the conservation of wild life, agriculture, and natural resources.

Vegetarian diets can be of various sorts, some wholly nutritious, others requiring specific vitamin supplement. The two main classes of vegetarian diets may be based only on plant food sources (total vegetarians, or *vegans*) or plant foods plus dairy products and eggs (*lacto-ovo-vegetarians*). Other classes of vegetarians include the lacto-vegetarian, who consumes plant foods plus milk, the fruitarian, the herbivore, and the granivore (seeds and grains).

With the elimination of meat from the diet, other sources of protein must be utilized. Only protein supplies nitrogen, sulfur, and phosphorus to the body, substances needed to build tissue fiber, and to build tissues such as hair and nails which are continually growing. Protein builds cartilage, tendons, muscles, and bone, and is the primary ingredient for basic chemical reactions in the body.

The proteins our bodies use are made of 22 amino acids. However, of these 22 only 8 cannot be synthesized directly by our bodies, so they must be obtained from outside sources. These 8 essential amino acids are leucine, tryptophan, lysine, isoleucine, valine, threnonine, methionine, and phenylalanine.

The difficulty arises in obtaining these 8 essentials. Our bodies need each of these 8 *simultaneously,* and in the right proportion. That is, if a person were to eat protein containing enough lysine to satisfy 100% of the body's requirement, and another 100% of the valine level, but only 50% of the tryptophan needed, then the body only utilizes 50% of the total protein ingested. These 8 acids, when properly combined, form a single utilizable protein unit.

Protein foods of animal origin (eggs, milk, and cheese) contain these 8 amino acids in abundant amounts. Thus, they are called "high-quality proteins." Cereal grains, however, are relatively low in lysine, though high in methionine. Thus, they provide "lower-quality proteins." In a single meal, though, if cereal grains were combined with legumes such as dried beans and peas, which contain lysine, then the 'balance' would be improved and sufficient amounts of methionine *and* lysine would be supplied.[7]

In comparing meat to plant protein, two criteria need to be considered--the *quantity* and *quality* of protein in the food. For instance, soybean flour is over 40% protein. Certain cheeses, such as Parmesan, are 36% protein. Meat is 20-30% protein. Generally, plants rank highest in *quantity* of protein.[3]

However, when the *quality* (or usability or digestibility) of those same protein foods are considered, a different story emerges. Meats, in terms of protein quality, range from 65-70%, whereas plant foods rank below meat. (Exceptions may be soybeans and whole rice, which approach or top the meat quality value.) On the average, plant foods rank around 50% "net protein utilization."[3] Therefore, in order to obtain an equal amount of the essential proteins (amino acids) from plant foods, as one would obtain from meats, a vegetarian should follow one of several alternatives: to receive an adequate amount of the 8 essential amino acids, one should eat large amounts of lower-quality protein; eat alternate animal-protein sources, such as dairy products; or eat a wide variety of plant proteins which have mutually complementary amino acid patterns.[3] The best solution would be to combine a variety of plant foods with dairy products in the same meal.

The most important nutritional safeguard for any vegetarian is variety in the diet. The greatest risk for a vegetarian comes from undue reliance on any one plant food source. Restricting the variety of foods only restricts the variety and amount of nutrients digested. If, as has been outlined, certain essential amino acids are left out of the diet, then the body's protein requirements are not met.

This has been the case with one of the more recent diet-fads, the macrobiotic diet. This diet progresses in seven stages, the elementary stages being fully nutritious. With each stage, however, certain foods are eliminated until only brown rice and tea remain. Predictably, there have been reported cases of *kwashiorkor*--a severe protein malnutrition disease native to North Africa--occurring among macrobiotic dieters and their children. In a study of the physical measurements of vegetarian infants, macrobiotic children were found to be significantly smaller in size than children of other dietary groups. Measurements included recumbent length, width, head circumference, triceps, and subscapular skinfolds.[8]

Another dangerous diet could be a single grain diet. Dr. Combs asserts that, "These are potentially very harmful. A cereal grain is seriously lacking in several things, such as vitamin C and some of the B vitamins."[6] Vitamin supplement to a single grain diet would be a necessity. Otherwise, scurvy or beriberi may occur.

For those reasons, the vegetarian is in a precarious position because he or she must know which foods contain sufficient amounts and "quality" of protein and vitamins. The vegetarian's foods must complement each other in terms of amino acids. An excellent guide, with recipes, is Frances Moore Lappe's *Diet for a Small Planet*.[3]

Like the lacto-vegetarian and the lacto-ovo-vegetarian, the vegan, or strict vegetarian, can obtain an adequate supply of protein. The vegan, however, faces a very real danger in another regard. Unlike the lacto- and lacto-ovo-vegetarian, the vegan does not eat eggs, milk, or cheese. Therefore, a vegan can not obtain vitamin B_{12}, which is found primarily in animal products, especially in kidney, liver, and various seafoods. It cannot be found in nuts or grains.[5] Consequently, a vegan must take vitamin B_{12} for vitamin supplement, or drink *fortified* soy milk.[9]

A vitamin B_{12} deficiency can damage the nervous system and cause spinal cord degeneration. This condition has been referred to as "vegan back."[10] A vitamin B_{12} deficiency can also lead to the development of pernicious anemia because B_{12} is necessary for normal blood formation.[11]

The vitamin B_{12} deficiency is especially dangerous in that it is impossible to detect until the damage has been done--and the damage is irreversible. A vitamin B_{12} deficiency may go undetected because it can be masked in the diet by the intake of folic acid. Combs comments on this problem: "Vitamin B_{12} and folic acid are both effective in curing the initial stages of the anemia problem in humans. If you have a

B_{12} deficiency and consume higher levels of folic acid you can have an apparently normal hemoglobin level, and mask the deficiency. And of course a person who eats a vegetarian diet consumes leafy green vegetables and obtains folic acid. So you can commonly have advanced B_{12} deficiencies that are masked by folic acid that result in secondary neurological lesions that you don't spot until they occur, and they are irreversible. This can be a lack of feeling in the fingers or toes. You could stick pins in a person's back and he wouldn't feel it. This is what you get in a long-term B_{12} deficiency as a first symptom. This condition is known as vegan back in the vegan diet because it's so common. You get a lot of folin but no B_{12}."[6]

Generally speaking, a vitamin B_{12} deficiency is the single danger of the vegan diet, but it need not be a problem if the proper nutritional know-how is applied. There are also special nutritional problems for a vegan child and a pregnant woman, but these can be easily resolved.

In the winter, when the child's access to sunshine is restricted, it may be necessary for the child to take a vitamin supplement to obtain an adequate amount of vitamin D.[10] The nutritional problem for the pregnant woman concerns the acquisition of enough protein. On a theoretical basis, the pregnant woman can obtain the required level if the best plant sources are utilized: peanuts, soybeans, and nuts.[6] Nevertheless, many vegans have had to resort to consuming milk and eggs to restore health, and it is likely that a vegan woman who is pregnant would need to do the same. For a lacto-ovo-vegetarian woman who is pregnant little dietary advice is needed. She will probably have an adequate supply of nutrients.[12]

Since vegetarians consume less saturated fat and cholesterol they may have a lessened chance of developing heart disease. Persons with heart problems should certainly cut their meat intake. And the *risk* of heart attacks can be reduced by sharply decreasing the consumption of foods high in saturated fats and cholesterol. These include meats, whole milk, cream, ice cream, butter, lard, heavily hydrogenated shortenings, and margarines.[13]

Vegetarians often have lower blood pressure simply because they weigh less. "The decrease in blood pressure is probably correlated more with being 10 or 15 pounds lower in weight than anything else."[5] In a Harvard study, the blood pressure and individual dietary habits of 210 men and women were observed. They lived in communal households subsisting mainly on vegetable sources. The mean blood pressure for this group (ages 16-29) was less than that usually found in Western populations. The report suggests "a relation between blood pressure levels and consumption of food from animal sources."[14]

Dr. Combs pursues this relation between food from animal sources and higher blood pressure. He comments that the correlation between a vegetarian diet and lower blood pressure "might be true on the basis of something like sodium content, because sodium content in plant material is considerably lower (than in non-plant foods). And of course sodium is one of the key nutrients that influences blood pressure. A lot of the processed foods have sodium added, salts added, so a higher plant diet would probably have reduced salt intake and probably would tend to favor normal blood pressure."[6]

Despite these benefits of the vegetarian regimen, vegetarianism continues to be viewed in the U.S. more as a fad than as a legitimate dietary alternative. Perhaps this is due to the somewhat extreme claims made in vegetarianism's behalf. One source contends that, "Intemperance which is the chief cause of pauperism and crime may be greatly discouraged by cultivation of vegetarianism."[15] Gandhi, the great Indian leader who experimented with his diet in order to observe personality development, asserted that the simplest foods (especially fresh fruits and nuts) were most beneficial for "calming of spirit and allaying animal passion."[16]

Adolf Hitler, a vegetarian, claimed that vegetarianism increased his working and intellectual capacities.[1] He constantly advocated the claims of the German composer, Richard Wagner, that a vegetarian diet had been the primeval diet of the human race. Hitler customarily entertained his associates--such as Bormann, Goring, and Himmler--at meals of vegetarian fare. After the meal, Hitler's associates often retreated to the kitchen and asked the cook for a second meal of their own choosing. This one case, however, says little about any notion that meat-eating and aggressiveness may be associated.

Perhaps these claims for vegetarianism are extreme, but they are not unusual. Strange notions about the peculiar properties of various foods have always existed. It was once popularly thought that seawater was helpful in cleaning out the digestive system. The same was later considered true of garlic. Sometimes these notions may be correct, such as the 16th century idea that by some mysterious process lemons and limes, consumed on long sea voyages, protected men from scurvy.[17]

One notion that persists until this day is the idea that fish is brain food. In the 19th century, Professor Louis Agassiz of Harvard University urged people to eat fish.[18] Fish is abundant in phosphorus, he argued, and phosphorus has been connected with thinking because certain compounds containing phosphorus are abundant in the brain. Mark Twain satirized Agassiz's assertion when he replied to an aspiring "Young Author's" letters which sought confirmation on this point.[19] Wrote Twain: "Yes, Agassiz *does* recommend authors to eat fish, because the phosphorus in it makes brains. So far you are correct. But I cannot help you to a decision about the amount you need to eat--at least, with certainty. If the specimen [writing] composition you send is about your fair, usual average, I should judge that perhaps a couple of whales would be all you would want for the present."

Fish, like the meat of land animals, consists chiefly of proteins and fat. However, the protein content of fish is generally higher than that of meat, but has a lower caloric content because of less fat and a higher water content. Fish oils are rich in vitamin D, and fish liver in vitamin A.[21]

A recent report released by the Senate Select Committee on Nutrition and Human Needs recommends significant reductions in the consumption of various foods rich in fat, sugar, and salt. Red meat, specifically, is included within the fat category. The Congressional report calls for a reduction in overall fat intake by 10 percent, replacing meat with fish or fowl.[20] The report recommends that more protein can be obtained from fish and poultry, and that these should be eaten instead of red meat. Poultry, like fish, contains less fat than red meat.

A rich supply of minerals and vitamins may also be found in shellfish. The protein content of shellfish is the same as in fish and land animals. Its main value consists in its wealth of iron, copper, and iodine. When eaten raw, oysters offer a substantial vitamin C content, and are a good substitute for fresh fruit and vegetables.[21] However, shellfish is relatively high in cholesterol.

In order to ascertain what the food-eating patterns of early man consisted of-- and what the "natural" diet of man should be today--anthropologists have studied the eating habits of our closest animal relatives, chimpanzees and gorillas. Their conclusions are neither a justification nor an explanation for the eating patterns of man. But the physical similarities between the two suggest interesting parallels. Until the 1960s, chimpanzees were considered to be complete vegetarians. But then the first-hand observations by Jane van Lawick-Goodal in Tanganyika revealed that chimpanzees occasionally eat meat. On the other hand, in Uganda in 1962 Vernon and Frances Reynolds also observed chimpanzees but failed to find any evidence of meat eating. In direct observations of gorillas in the wild, both Dian Fossey in Rwanda and George Schaller in East and Central Africa, found gorillas to be completely vegetarian in their natural habitat.[1] However, they will eat meat while confined in zoos.

These observations fail to define what the natural diet of man should be. Among anthropologists, there is a controversy as to whether primitive man was carnivorous or vegetarian. There is evidence for both views. Richard B. Lee lived for two years among the Kung Bushmen in the Kalahari Desert of Botswana. He re-ported that, by weight, 50% of the Bushmen's vegetable diet consisted of the mongongo nut. Meat is eaten only on special occasions. Besides the mongongo nut, the Bushmen's diet consisted of 84 species of edible plants, including 20 varieties of fruits, berries, and melons, and 30 types of roots and bulbs. Lee did not observe one case of nutritional deficiency,[1] suggesting that early human societies could have been vegetarian.

Robert Ardrey, author of *The Hunting Hypothesis*,[22] refutes the vegetarian hypothesis of early man. He dismisses Lee's data, claiming that the particular tribe examined was unrepresentative of Bushmen in general. Ardrey contends that primitive man was carnivorous. "Supreme, above all other reasons for rejecting the hunting hypothesis, is anthropology's will to believe in primal man happily, healthily chewing his mongongo nuts. Such an anthropological wonder can bear comparison...to the Rosseauesque image of primal innocence, primal goodness, that grips our minds."

Ardrey asserts that the Ice Age winters offer confirmation of his hunting hypothesis. Those authorities who insist that early man was dependent on plant foods, says Ardrey, forget that during the Ice Age in Europe and Asia there weren't any. To guarantee survival during these cold periods, man had to have been preadapted to a diet consisting exclusively of meat. Those modern hunting peoples such as the Eskimo, Ardrey contends, who live under ecologically comparable conditions as Ice Age man, consume a fully-nutritious diet of no more than 10% plant food.

Arctic regions provide few plants, roots, or fruits. An Eskimo diet consists of the meat of the seal, whale, narwhale, walrus, aquatic birds and their eggs, and such land animals as the bear, fox, seal, and deer. Shellfish is eaten when found in the stomach of other animals. Eskimos consume most of their meat raw. The vitamin content of meat rises when the glands, brains, entrails, and organs are consumed.[21] If properly cooked, organs and tissues can supply every vitamin and mineral needed with the exception of calcium. Raw liver contains vitamin C and A. Other organs supply elements of the vitamin B complex and vitamin D. It has been suggested by one author[21] that "the consumption of brain, heart, kidney, liver, spleen, and other organs becomes an important dietary goal of our times. By discarding these organs we throw away practically all of the animal's vitamins and minerals just as we lose the most valuable substances of vegetables by discarding the water in which they have been cooked for long periods."

Throughout history, dietary goals have played a large role in different civilizations. Vegetarianism, especially, has never been without its advocates during any period of time.[23] Most familiar in this category are Pythagoras, Buddha, Leonardo da Vinci, Montaigne, Percy Bysshe Shelley, and Benjamin Franklin, among others. Two contemporary Christian Protestant sects--the Bible Christians and the Seventh Day Adventists--require that their followers maintain a vegetarian food habit.

The largest group of vegetarians in the world today are the Hindus in India. Almost synonymous with vegetarianism and Hinduism in India is the sacred cow, which is forbidden to be killed or eaten, though younger and more liberal Indians now eat meat without regard for the established "reactionary" ways. The vegetarian basis of Hinduism is founded on the belief that the exclusion of flesh foods from the diet contributes to the principle of *ahimsa*--or non-violence. Thus, as Gandhi made known to the world, vegetarianism becomes a moral principle.

Some orthodox Jews abstain from meat eating entirely, but are commonly deemed kosher rather than vegetarian eaters. This is not to say that all Jews who eat kosher are vegetarians. The kosher laws are intended mainly to guide the observant Jew in the kosher preparation of meat. The prohibition against the consumption of blood (Leviticus 7:26-27; 17:10-14) is the basis for the process of koshering meat.[24] The purpose of the process is to draw out and drain the meat of non-veinal blood, before it is cooked. The blood can be removed either by salting the meat, or by roasting it over an open fire. The term *kasher,* or kosher, was originally used in the Bible in the sense of "fit" or "proper." From the point of view of the Jewish dietary laws all fruit and vegetables are "fit" for consumption, and do not require, as in the preparation of meat, a Rabbi's certification that a certain food has been koshered. This is based upon the first dietary directive in the Bible: "Behold I have given you every herb yielding seed which is upon the face of the earth and every tree..." (Genesis 1:29).

An ancient sect of Jews, the Essenes, lived rigid, ascetic lives in the proximity of the Dead Sea area. The Essenes cultivated and ate simple vegetarian food. Ancient historians such as Josephus and Pliny the Elder wrote about these communities.[25] The Essenes withdrew from the cities and organized society of their time (the 1st century) and formed a society of their own. There is speculation that John the Baptist was a member of the Essene community, and possibly Jesus Christ, though

Jesus was not an ascetic like John the Baptist, and Jesus ate meat.

In 1947 the American Vegetarian Party was born. In the presidential elections of 1948 a Vegetarian Party slate was nominated; its campaign motto was a diet without the flesh of meat, fish, or fowl. Symon Gould was the real force behind the Party, though it wasn't until 1960 that Gould himself actually ran for President. In 1962 he campaigned for state senator from New York against Jacob Javits, keeping vegetarianism and pacifism in the forefront of the campaign. When Gould died in 1963, the American Vegetarian Party died with him.[1]

It would be impossible to accurately count the number of vegetarians in America today. A conservative estimate may be four million persons. Most of these would be lacto- or lacto-ovo-vegetarians; there are few vegans in the U.S. In recent years, however, there appears to have been a resurgence of vegetarianism in America, especially on college campuses. One reason for this may be the financial savings in excluding meat from the diet, or it could be due to ethical beliefs of "returning to nature." Whatever the reason, an individual contemplating a vegetarian regimen should become familiar with the potential dangers. With proper knowledge and education, a vegetarian will encounter no difficulty in obtaining the full nutritional requirements. Vegetarianism is not a recent fad, but it can be an enjoyable alternate to meat, providing a sound protein diet from the abundant sources that the earth provides.

Apart from all the reasons cited above it is also argued by vegetarians that meat consumption is an unfair use of land resources to serve the rich. It requires a much larger per capita expenditure of energy and land to support a meat eating population. It is all the more ironical that the U.S. should be thought of as the world's breadbasket since we, like the Argentinians, are so meat oriented. Were we to feed less grain to animals for meat consumption we would have much more to export.

This is a very narrow view of the world's food and agricultural problems. The meat-eating habits of Americans, even if changed, will not serve the basic problems of agriculture in India, the USSR, or any other country. Certainly a drastic reduction in per capita meat consumption would be healthy.

You can support considerable intake of meat-fat and cholesterol if you match it with a strong regimen of exercise. I've never known a person who performed heavy labor who could survive without meat. Weight lifters, football players, and other athletes consume large quantities of meat without apparent damage to the cardiovascular system. It is when they stop exercising but maintain established meat-eating habits that they get into trouble.

Until some better evidence comes along the moderate, well-balanced diet is the safest course of action. Knowing how often and how easily we succumb to celebrations and feasts, we need to balance such abuse of our bodies with exercise and occasional fasting. The ideal weekly regimen for me would be a vegetarian meal on Monday, a T-Bone steak on Tuesday, a dairy-vegetarian meal on Wednesday, a seafood dinner on Thursday, a chicken dinner for Friday, and on Saturday a 12-course Chinese dinner to be shared with as many friends. On the last day I might fast, as a convenient way of watching my weight.

REFERENCES

1. **Barkas J.** *The vegetarian passion.* New York: Charles Scribner's Sons, 1975.
2. **Meeker B K.** Rising world meat consumption--and national policies. *Foreign Agriculture* 14:2-5, 15, 8 November 1976.
3. **Lappe F M.** *Diet for a small planet.* New York: Ballantine Books, 1975.
4. **Guthrie H A.** *Introduction to nutrition.* St. Louis: C.V. Mosby Co., 1967.
5. **Stare F.** Personal communication, 31 October 1976.
6. **Combs G.** Personal communication, 18 November 1976.
7. **Crosby W H.** Can a vegetarian be well nourished? *Journal of the American Medical Association* 233:898, 1975.
8. **Dwyer J T.** Physical measurements of vegetarian infants and preschool children. Paper presented at meeting of the American Society for Clinical Nutrition, Atlantic City, New Jersey, 1 May 1976. (Paper abstract in: *American Journal of Clinical Nutrition* 29:477, 1976.)
9. Committee on Nutrition Misinformation, Food and Nutrition Board, National Research Council, National Academy of Science. Vegetarian diets. *Journal of the American Dietary Association* 65:121-22, 1974.
10. **Jenkins R R.** Health implications of the vegetarian diet. *Journal of the American Collegiate Health Association* 24:68-71, 1975.
11. Introduction to anemia. *Harvard Medical School Health Letter* 1(12):2, October, 1976.
12. Dietary advice for a pregnant, vegetarian patient. *British Medical Journal* 3:689, 29 September 1973.
13. **Keys A.** The diet and plasma lipids in the etiology of coronary heart disease. In: *Coronary Heart Disease.* Edited by Russek HI & Zohman BL, Philadelphia: Lippincott Co., 1971, p. 59-75.
14. **Sacks F M.** Blood pressure in vegetarians. Paper presented at meeting of the Society for Epidemiologic Research, Berkeley, California, June 19-22, 1974. (Paper abstract in: *American Journal of Epidemiology* 100:525, 1974).
15. **Groom-Napier CO.** *Vegetarianism, a cure for intemperance.* London: William Tweedie, 1875.
16. **Gandhi M K.** *Diet and diet reform.* Ahmedabad, India: Navajivan Publishing House, 1949.
17. **Mendelssohn K.** *The secret of western domination.* New York: Praeger, 1976.
18. **Atwater W O.** How food nourishes the body. *Century Magazine* 34:50, 1887.
19. **Twain M.** Memoranda. *Galaxy* 11:159, 1871.
20. **Burros M.** Hill report asks diet changes. *Washington Post* 15 January 1977, p. A3.
21. **Graubard M.** *Man's food: its rhyme or reason.* New York: Macmillan, 1943.
22. **Ardrey R.** *The hunting hypothesis.* New York: Atheneum, 1976.
23. **Bryce A.** *World theories of diet.* London: Longmans, Green and Co., 1912.
24. **Rabinowicz H.** Dietary laws. *Encyclopaedia Judaica* (Jerusalem: Keter Publishing House Ltd., 1971) Vol. 6, p. 26-46.
25. **Flavius Josephus.** *The Jewish war.* London: William Heinemann Ltd., 1969.

The *Permuterm Subject Index:*
an Autobiographical Review*

The *Permuterm® Subject Index (PSI)* section of the *Science Citation Index®* (*SCI®*) was designed more than ten years ago and has been published both quarterly and annually since 1966. There is, however, no 'primordial' citable paper about the *PSI*. It has been described and discussed from different standpoints in a number of papers,[1,2] but none of them provides the formal description usually accorded a new bibliographic tool. This article is intended to provide such a reference point for future workers in information science.

The *PSI* was designed in 1964 at the Institute for Scientific Information® (ISI®) by myself and Irving Sher, my principal research collaborator at the time. In the subsequent development of the *PSI*, contributions were also made by others, including Arthur W. Elias, who was then in charge of production operations at ISI. In the early sixties we were too preoccupied with the task of convincing the library and information community of the value of citation indexing even to consider the idea of

publishing a word index. But it was a logical development once we added the *Source Index* containing full titles.

The value of the *PSI* as a 'natural language' index is now well recognized and exploited by its users, but this was not the original reason for its development. The *PSI* was developed as one solution to a problem commonly faced by users of the *Citation Index* section of the *Science Citation Index* (*SCI*). While the typical scientist-user could enter the *Citation Index* with a known author or paper, other users with a limited knowledge of the subject often lacked a starting point for their search. Before publication of the *PSI*, we told users whose unfamiliarity with subject matter left them doubtful about a starting point to consult an encyclopedia or the subject index of a book. If these failed, we told them to use another index, such as *Chemical Abstracts, Biological Abstracts, Physics Abstracts* or *Index Medicus*. Once the user identified a relevant older paper, it could be used to begin a search in the *Citation Index*. Users of the *SCI*—and

*Reprinted from *J. Amer. Soc. Inform. Sci.* 27(5/6):288-91, 1976.

librarians in particular — needed some tool with which a starting point, or what used to be called a target reference, could be quickly and easily identified.

In those days the information community was preoccupied with Key-Word-in-Context (KWIC) indexes. The development of the KWIC index, which was subsequently vigorously marketed by IBM, undoubtedly had an enormous impact.[3,4,5] But I was never happy with the KWIC system for a number of reasons.

First, Sher and I felt that the KWIC index was highly uneconomical for a printed index. KWIC's use of space is prodigious, and it can be extremely time-consuming to use in searches involving more than one term.

Another aspect of the KWIC system (as used for example by *Chemical Titles*) that disturbed us was its indiscriminate use of stop-lists to eliminate presumably non-significant title words. In our view, it caused considerable loss of information on many subjects of interest to some users, if not to all. Consider the effect of deleting terms like METHOD and BEHAVIOR. In order to retain much of this information, but still prevent the useless entries generated by "terms" like THE and WHICH, we developed the concept of the semi- stop list, to be used in addition to a full-stop list.

The full-stop list for the *PSI*, which contains words that are completely suppressed, was and is quite small. The semi-stop words such as METHOD, BEHAVIOR, CAUSE, REPORT and TECHNIQUE are suppressed as primary terms (main entries), but not as secondary or co-terms (subentries). In addition, certain frequently used two-word phrases, which have been identified through statistical analysis of word frequencies, are kept together and treated as a single term rather than being allowed to permute separately. Such phrases as GUINEA-PIG, NEW-YORK, ESCHERICHIA-COLI and BIRTH-CONTROL appear in the *PSI* as hyphenated terms, thus reducing look-up time in many types of searches. This is done by computer in the *PSI*, while in indexes like *Chemical Titles*, it is done by a manual process called "slash and dash."

Finally, the KWIC format was rejected because a number of studies had demonstrated that users of scientific indexes generally specify two or three terms when they use coordinate indexes. We reasoned that the optimum system would precoordinate any two terms, no matter how far apart in the title.

Over ten years of *PSI* experience has confirmed that "specificity" *per se* does not guarantee efficiency of a word as a search term. If used frequently enough, a seemingly highly specific term like DNA becomes as inefficient as more general terms that are used less frequently. The converse also holds; consider the term CREATIVITY. It is general, but because of the comparatively low frequency with which it occurs in the scientific literature, it is an efficient search term. Therefore, pairing—together with precoordination— becomes essential for high-usage terms, and merely convenient for low-usage terms. Triple coordination—and even higher-level coupling—may also be desirable if two terms occur together with a third frequently enough. But the threshold must be correlated with cost of processing and printing, not only with economies in users' time. The ideal system would handle three or more terms, but this proved too costly. We therefore settled on two terms, although recently precoordination of three terms has been built into the five-year cumulative 1965-1969 *PSI,* and an improved three-term precoordination routine will be achieved in the five-year cumulative, *PSI* for 1970-74, to be published by ISI in 1977.

The choice of name for the *Permuterm Subject Index* was quite deliberate. Ohlman suggested the term *permuted* from *cyclic permutation* used in mathematics.[6] It was in that sense appropriate to KWIC indexes. *Permuterm,* however, is a complete permutation of all title words to produce all possible pairs, including, of course, the inversion of every pair. As I and others have noted before, KWIC indexes are more appropriately called *rotated indexes.*[7,8] For example, ISI's *Rotaform Index* section of the *Index Chemicus*® is a rotated formula index. The *Chemical Substructure Index*® (*CSI*) is also a cyclic or rotated index. Using the Wiswesser Line Notation, the *CSI* rotates the line notation to create a main entry for every substantive

constituent in each notation.

For each title in the *PSI* with n title words, $n(n-1)$ word-pairs are created by permutation. After applying the full-stop list and semi-stop list, this usually produces about 40 word-pairs for the typical seven-word title. It is by no means unusual for the *PSI* to contain over 100 word-pairs for titles with 11 or more words.

In the *PSI,* every significant word in the title is permuted (not merely rotated, as in a KWIC index)[7] by computer to produce all possible pairs of terms. Every word is potentially both a primary term and a co-term. On the printed page, each permuted word-pair is arranged alphabetically by primary term. All co-terms occurring with a particular primary term are indented as subentries and listed in alphabetical order under the primary term. Dashed lines lead from the co-term to the author, whose name can be used to locate in the *Source Index* section of the *SCI* the complete bibliographic data, including the title for the article.

As part of ISI's quality-control precoordination and spelling-variance unification procedures, every incoming term—that is, every word in every title—is passed against the established *PSI* vocabulary. In this computer comparison, wrong and variant spellings are corrected and coordination tests for accepted word-pairs are applied. Terms which are truly new are selected for human review and added to the vocabulary. Naturally, many author- or ISI-produced errors are identified and corrected in this process.

From the earliest days Sher and I were aware of the enormous potential of the *PSI* vocabulary for scientific lexicography. Besides allowing very specific searches on terms that would never have appeared in thesaurus-controlled indexing systems, the use of actual title-words reflects terminological innovation long before anyone but specialists in the affected field are aware of the changes. Every year nearly two-thirds of the words *added* as primary terms to the *PSI* vocabulary are "new" in the sense that they occurred only once or not at all in titles processed the previous year.[9] This does not, of course, mean that two-thirds of each year's vocabulary is "new."

The cumulated vocabulary of the *PSI* comprises an author-generated word-index to all the significant articles of science and technology—including letters, technical notes, and proceedings of meetings. It is a pity that the *PSI* vocabulary has not yet been used by lexicographers to identify and define new scientific terms and usages.[10] A dictionary based on the *PSI*, which could be updated quarterly, would be the first current dictionary of new scientific terms based on primordial sources.

From the outset, we were aware of the shortcomings of title-word indexes: the lack of resolution of obvious (and not-so-obvious) synonyms and the unavoidable fact that morphological variations of the same primary terms, *e.g.*, CLASSIFY and CLASSIFICATION, appear separately in the index. Even the plural of a noun may be separated from its singular, *e.g.*, SUGAR and SUGARS. In Ohlman's permutation index to the proceedings of the ICSI 1958 conference, this problem was alleviated somewhat by restricting sorting of the first six characters of each term. However, use of this procedure is impractical for an index as large as the *PSI*.[3]

Such problems were of minor importance as long as the *PSI* was regarded merely as a supplement to the *Citation Index*. We found that many scientists preferred a title-word index because it enabled them to retrieve a work by a word or phrase remembered from its title, or by subject words they knew to be relevant.

It was inevitable that librarians and others would begin pressuring us to make the *PSI* a search tool in its own right. Our response began with provision of cross-references and eventually led to certain standardizations, especially in the case of spelling variations. Today the so-called source-data edit procedures at ISI are quite systematic and comprehensive,[11] and the *PSI* does stand on its own as both a current and retrospective subject index.

As early as 1969, I reported at Amsterdam on ISI's efforts to develop automatic procedures for hyphenating word-pairs into phrases, a process we called "precoordination"[12] to produce bound terms like BIRTH CONTROL. Such terms would be hyphenated automatically, provided they occurred with sufficient frequency. It was remarkable to discover that punctuation could be ignored if a given word-pair occurred above a certain very low threshold, about two or three times. One would not find too many titles in which the terms BIRTH and CONTROL were separated by a comma, such as "Season of birth, control of disease, and WHO statistics." Linguistic analysts have agonized over the problem of differentiating such items, but it is rarely a real problem.

Besides increasing the specificity and thus the informational value of the *PSI*, the main objective of precoordination is to reduce the number of permutations required. This did not prove to be as easy as we had first imagined. We have since found that precoordination is best performed by source-data edits, which requires constant monitoring of term-pair frequencies.

An important objective of permuted index display should be to minimize postcoordination by the user. For example, while BIRTH-CONTROL provides one level of precoordination, the resulting term is of such high frequency that one ought to be able to precoordinate BIRTH-CONTROL at a second level, with terms indicating drugs, devices, methods, etc., so as to narrow the focus of retrieval to less than ten articles for most searches. Obviously, the value of precoordination increases five-fold for a five-year cumulation, in which certain terms might occur dozens or even hundreds of times.

In closing this belated report on *PSI*, we should not overlook the application of the *Permuterm* concept in controlled or manual indexing systems. We first used *Permuterm* in a controlled indexing situation during the production of *Current Contents*® */Chemical Sciences.* Since then, we have used the method in producing the yearly index of the *Journal of the Electrochemical Society,* and some industrial organizations have used our *Permuterm* programs to generate their own indexes. Further, our on-line searching experience has demonstrated that *PSI* can be (and now *is*) used to facilitate searches of other data bases, such as MEDLINE, precisely because it displays term pairs that one might not think of or cannot find in thesauri such as MeSH. Otherwise, *Permuterm* indexing has had little application outside ISI.

A proper evaluation of *PSI* by the information community has yet to be published. Meanwhile, we can only report that *PSI* has been steadily gaining increasing acceptance among *SCI* subscribers. Most users today know how to optimize their use of the *SCI* with the most appropriate word index available for the time period covered in the search, whether for the period prior to 1965, when *PSI* first became available, or thereafter. Since 80 percent of *SCI* subscribers now also subscribe to *PSI*, it seems reasonable after more than ten year's development, to incorporate *PSI* into the *SCI* system. Thus in the future no user of the *SCI* will lack its complement, the *PSI.*

REFERENCES

1. **Weinstock M.** Citation indexes. In: *Encyclopedia of Library and Information Science,* 5 vols. (New York: Marcel Dekker, 1971), 5:16-40.

2. **Garfield E.** Automation of ISI services; *Science Citation Index (SCI), Permuterm Subject Index (PSI),* and *ASCA®* . In: *International Association of Agricultural Librarians and Documentalists, Fourth World Congress, Paris, 20-25 April 1970* (Paris: Institut National de la Recherche Agronomique, 1971), p. 107-12.

3. **Citron J, Hart L & Ohlman H.** *A permutation index to the preprints of the International Conference of Scientific Information.* Reprint No. SP-44, rev. ed. (Santa Monica, Ca.: Systems Development Corporation, 15 December 1959), 37 pp.

4. *Keyword-in-context index for technical literature.* Report RC 127 (New York: IBM Corp., Adv. Syst. Dev. Division, 1959). Also published in *American Documentation* 11:288-95, 1959.

5. **Stevens M E.** *Automatic indexing; a state-of-the-art report.* National Bureau of Standards Monograph 91 (Washington: Government Printing Office, 30 March 1965).

6. **Ohlman H.** Personal communication, November 1975.

7. **Garfield E.** Indexing terminology and permuted indexes. *J. Documentation* **28:** 344-45, 1972.

9. **Heumann K et al.** *The Chemical Biological Coordination Center of the National Academy of Sciences.* (Washington: National Research Council, 1954) p. 18.

9. **Weinstock M, Fenichel C & Williams M V V.** System design implications of title words of scientific journal articles in the *Permuterm Subject Index.* In: *The social impact of information retrieval; the Information Bazaar, Seventh Annual National Colloquium on Information Retrieval, 8-9 May, 1970.* (Philadelphia: College of Physicians, 1970), p. 181-200.

10. **Garfield E.** *Permuterm Subject Index,* the primordial dictionary of science. *Current Contents* No. 22, 3 June 1969, p. 5. Reprinted in: **Garfield E.** *Essays of an information scientist,* 2 vols. (Philadelphia: ISI Press, 1977), 1:39.

11. **Fenichel C.** Editing the *Permuterm Subject Index.* In: *Proceedings of the American Society for Information Science, 34th annual meeting, Denver, 7-11 November 1971;* p. 349-53.

12. **Garfield E.** Citation indexing, historio-bibliography, and the sociology of science. In: *Proceedings of the Third International Congress of Medical Librarianship, Amsterdam, 5-9 May 1969* (Amsterdam: Excerpta Medica, 1970), p. 187-204. Reprinted in: **Garfield E.** *Essays,* 1:158-74.

Highly Cited Articles. 37. Biomedical Articles
Published in the 1940s.

Number 13, March 28, 1977

In recent weeks we have listed still highly-cited articles of the 1940s from the fields of biochemistry and physics. Here we conclude our survey of the 1940s with a list of biomedical articles. Each was cited at least 150 times in the period 1961-1975. The average is about 325 times. Most were cited more than that, and are still being cited heavily after three decades. On the average each article was cited 23 times in both 1974 and 1975. This is more than ten times the citation rate for the average article cited in one year of the *Science Citation Index*®. Indeed, it is ten times the expected rate of citation for the five year *Science Citation Index* cumulative!

Figure 1 shows the 54 journals in which the articles appeared. Seven journals account for about a third: *American Journal of Physiology* (6); *Journal of Biological Chemistry* and *Proceedings of the Society for Experimental Biology and Medicine* (both 5); *Anatomical Record, Journal of Clinical Investigation, Journal of General Physiology*, and *Science* (4 each). It should be noticed that most of the journals listed in Figure 1 have impacts well above average.

Ten of the 104 articles were authored or coauthored by Nobelists: Cournand and Richards, who shared the 1956 prize for medicine (articles 9 and 39); Beadle and Tatum, who shared the prize for medicine in 1958 (article 12); A.V. Hill, 1922 laureate for medicine (article 43); A.L. Hodgkin, laureate for medicine in 1963 (articles 44 and 45); B. Katz, laureate for medicine in 1970 (article 44); G.E. Palade, laureate for medicine in 1974 (article 46); Luria and Delbruck, who shared the prize for medicine in 1969 (article 63); Sir Peter Medawar, who won the medical prize in 1960 (article 64); and Linus Pauling, laureate in chemistry in 1954 (article 73). Pauling is on the list with a medical-research paper concerning the etiology of sickle cell anemia.

The articles are listed alphabetically by first author in Figure 2. The list shows total citations for the period 1961-1975, average citations per year, and citation counts for the years 1974 and 1975. It is striking to find that about 60 of these 104 articles have citation counts for 1974 and/or 1975 that matched or exceeded their yearly

Figure 1. Journals that published the highly cited 1940s articles listed in Figure 2. A = number of articles. B = 1974 impact factor. (Present titles of journals are given in parentheses.)

A	B	Journal	A	B	Journal
1	1.042	Acta Chem. Scand.	2	3.737	J. Cell Comp. Physiology
1	1.124	Acta Med. Scand.			(J. Cell. Physiology)
2	0.809	Acta Path. Microb. Scand.	3	5.170	J. Clin. Endocrinol. Metab.
2	2.204	Acta Physiol. Scand.	4	6.992	J. Clin. Invest.
2	1.791	Amer. Heart J.	2	11.874	J. Exp. Med.
2	1.378	Amer. J. Botany	1	1.027	J. Exp. Psychology
2	1.348	Amer. J. Clin. Pathol.	1	1.412	J. Exp. Zoology
1	4.411	Amer. J. Med.	2	2.160	J. Gen. Microbiology
2	2.807	Amer. J. Pathology	4	4.308	J. Gen. Physiology
6	2.414	Amer. J. Physiology	1	5.112	J. Immunology
1	1.264	Amer. J. Psychiatry	1	2.802	J. Lab. Clin. Med.
4	2.884	Anatomical Record	3	3.289	J. Nat. Cancer Inst.
1	1.181	Ann. New York Acad. Sci.	1	4.537	J. Neurophysiology
1	2.792	Arch. Exp. Path. Pharm.	2	1.816	J. Pathol. Bacteriol.
		(Naunyn-Schmiedebergs Arch.)			(J. Pathol.; J. Med. Microbiol.)
1	1.521	Arch. Pathology	2	3.576	J. Pharmacol. Exp. Ther.
3	3.627	Biochemical Journal	2	4.495	J. Physiology
1	3.120	Biochim. Biophys. Acta	2	4.188	Medicine
1	0.813	Biometrics	1	3.636	Nature
3	3.516	Brit. J. Pharmacology	1	9.577	Pharmacol. Reviews
1	− −	Bull. Amer. Mus. Nat. Hist.	1	13.861	Physiol. Reviews
1	1.498	EEG Clin. Neurology	1	8.989	Proc. Nat. Acad. Sci. USA
3	4.337	Endocrinology	3	2.493	Proc. Roy. Soc. London B
1	5.394	Gastroenterology	5	1.471	Proc. Soc. Exp. Biol. Med.
1	2.835	Genetics	1	4.156	Psychol. Reviews
1	1.015	J. Abnormal Soc. Psychol.	4	5.412	Science
1	3.068	J. Amer. Med. Assoc.	1	− −	Trans. Ophth. Soc. Australia
1	1.284	J. Anatomy	1	1.953	Zschr. Zellforsch. Mikr. Anat.
5	5.843	J. Biol. Chemistry			

averages. The most astonishing in this respect is article 79 by G. Scatchard. This article on the attractions of proteins for molecules and ions was published in 1949. From 1961 to 1964 it was cited only 45 times. Every year thereafter it has been cited more frequently--about 40 times a year in 1965-1969; about 130 times a year in 1970-1972; and about 310 times a year 1973-1975. Its count of 352 for 1975-- almost thirty years after publication--is in fact its highest yet. Hopefully we can get the author to comment on this citation classic one day.

The most frequently cited paper

(article 61), by Litchfield and Wilcoxon, was cited 2,238 times from 1961 to 1975. Its average yearly citation rate for those years is 149. Like the paper by Scatchard, its citation rate has increased in 1974 and 1975. We recently published Litchfield's commentary on this citation classic.[1] In this week's *Citation Classics* Selye comments upon his classic paper (number 82), which I've discussed before.[2]

Current researchers in the field of biomedicine constantly refer back to these papers published over 30 years ago. Time has failed to decrease the significance of these papers, clearly reflected in their increasing citation counts. One should keep in mind, however, that often times there is a comparable if not greater failure to cite such well-known papers by those who are entitled to take them for granted as part of the common wisdom of their field. Another detail to keep in mind for a paper like number 41 (Harlow on learning sets), is that our coverage of psychology was not as complete in the early years of the *Science Citation Index.* Furthermore, there is a distinct possibility that the citation count for this paper will increase when we include data from the *Social Sciences Citation Index.* The appearance of a paper like number 85 (Simpson on classification) brings up an important point to remember. The *Bulletin of the American Museum of Natural History* is not a journal one would ordinarily expect to find on these lists. It is important to observe why.

I have observed elsewhere that the size of a particular field is not the main determinant in the average citation rate. Rather the number of references cited in the average paper is significant. But certainly the size of a field will influence the number of papers that achieve any arbitrary citation threshold. There could never have been 50,000 formal citations of the Lowry method had there not been several hundred thousand papers published on this subject. The entire literature of certain small fields may consist of only one or two thousand papers--or even less. From this it should be obvious that citation frequency is a relative measure. Thus, no comparison between any of the papers on this list is intended. Further, it is certain that other papers published in the forties, but not mentioned on this list would probably turn up were we able to have access to citation indexes for that period. It is a matter of considerable interest to science historians to know whether paper number 7 by Avery et al. was heavily cited in the forties and fifties.

REFERENCES

1. **Litchfield J T.** *Citation Classics.* A simplified method of evaluating dose-effect experiments. *Current Contents*® No. 7, 14 February 1977, p. 8.
2. **Garfield E.** Citation indexes for science. A new dimension in documentation through association of ideas. *Science* 122:108-11, 1955.

Figure 2. Highly cited articles in biological sciences and medicine published in the 1940s. A = item number. **B** = total citations 1961-1975. **C** = average yearly citations 1961-1975. **D** = citations in 1974. **E** = citations in 1975. Articles are listed alphabetically by first author

A	B	C	D	E	Bibliographic Data
1.	247	16	21	30	Abercrombie M. Estimation of nuclear population from microtome sections. Anatomical Record 94:239-47, 1946.
2.	1198	79	69	62	Ahlquist R P. A study of the adrenotropic receptors. Amer. J. Physiol. 153:586-600, 1948.
3.	163	10	12	18	Alexander R S. Tonic and reflex functions of medullary sympathetic cardiovascular centers. J. Neurophysiology 9:205-17, 1946.
4.	252	16	21	16	Anderson E H. Growth requirements of virus-resistant mutants of *Escherichia coli* strain "B". Proc. Nat. Acad. Sci. USA 32:120, 1946.
5.	214	14	10	10	Andrewes C H & Horstmann D M. The susceptibility of viruses to ethyl ether. J. Gen. Microbiology 3:290-7, 1949.
6.	157	10	16	14	Asch S E. Forming impressions of personality. J. Abnorm. Soc. Psychol. 41:258-90, 1946.
7.	242	16	12	10	Avery O T, MacLeod C & McCarty M. Studies on the chemical nature of the substance inducing transformation of pneumococcal types. J. Exp. Med. 79:137-58, 1944.
8.	224	14	16	17	Bailey K. Tropomyosin; a new asymmetric protein component of the muscle fibril. Biochem. J. 43:271-79, 1948.
9.	426	28	18	12	Baldwin E D, Cournand A & Richards D W. Pulmonary insufficiency. Medicine 27:243-78, 1948.
10.	205	13	5	17	Bargmann W. Uber die neurosekretorische Verknüpfung von Hypothalmus and Neurohypophyse (Neurosecretory linkage of hypothalamus and pituitary). Zschr. Zellforsch. Mikrosk. Anat. 34:610-34, 1949.
11.	314	20	11	13	Barr M L & Bertram E G. A morphological distinction between neurones of the male and female, and the behavior of the nucleolar satellite during accelerated nucleoprotein synthesis. Nature 163:676-77, 1949.
12.	247	16	15	8	Beadle G W & Tatum E L. *Neurospora.* 2. Methods of producing and detecting mutations concerned with nutritional requirements. Amer. J. Botany 32:678-86, 1945.
13.	257	17	14	9	Bean J W. Effects of oxygen at increased pressure. Physiol. Revs. 25:1-147, 1945.
14.	390	26	20	24	Bollman F L, Cain J C, **Grindlay J H & VanHook** E. Techniques for the collection of lymph from the liver, small intestine, or thoracic duct of the rat. J. Lab. Clin. Med. 33:1349-52, 1948.
15.	272	18	10	8	Boyle P J & Conway E J. Pottasium accumulation in muscle and associated changes. J. Physiology 100:1-63, 1941.
16.	252	16	18	17	Bradley S E, Ingelfinger F J, Bradley G P & Curry J J. The estimation of hepatic blood flow in man. **J. Clin. Invest.** 24:890-97, 1945.
17.	264	17	20	22	Bucher T. Ueber ein phosphatübertragendes Gärungsferment (On a phosphate-transporting respiratory enzyme). Biochim. Biophys. Acta 1:292-314, 1947.
18.	395	26	45	22	Bulbring E. Observations on the isolated phrenic nerve diaphragm preparation of the rat. Brit J. Pharmacology 1:38-61, 1946.
19.	354	23	33	31	Chalkey H W. Method for the quantitative morphologic analysis of tissues. J. Nat. Cancer Inst. 4:47-53, 1943.
20.	197	13	8	10	Chase M W. The cellular transfer of cutaneous hypersensitivity to tuberculin. Proc. Soc. Exp. Biol. Med. 59:134-5, 1945.

Figure 2 (cont.)

21.   207   13   6   11   Coons A H, Joner R N & Berliner E. The demonstration of pneumococcal antigen in tissues by the use of fluorescent antibody. J. Immunology 45:159-70, 1942.

22.   156   10   10   13   Dietrick J E, Whedon G D & Shorr E. Effects of immobilization upon various metabolic and physiologic functions of normal men. Amer. J. Med. 4:3-36, 1948.

23.   281   18   14   12   Duguid J B. Thrombosis as a factor in the pathogenesis of coronary atherosclerosis. J. Pathol. Bacteriol. 58:207-12, 1946.

24.   167   11   12   20   Eadie G S. The inhibition of cholinesterase by physostigmine and prostigmine. J. Biol. Chem. 146:85-93, 1942.

25.   527   35   35   34   Earle W R, Schilling E L, Stark T H, Straus N P, Brown M F & Shelton E. Production of malignancy in vitro. 4. The mouse fibroblast cultures and changes seen in the living cells. J. Nat. Cancer Inst. 4:165-212, 1943.

26.   256   17   17   13   Estes W K & Skinner B F. Some quantitative properties of anxiety. J. Exp. Psychol. 29:390-400, 1941.

27.   158   10   17   16   Everett J W. Progesterone and estrogen in the experimental control of ovulation time and other features of the estrous cycle in the rat. Endocrinology 43:389-405, 1948.

28.   195   13   13   4   Friedman M & Freed S C. Microphonic manometer for indirect determination of systolic blood pressure in the rat. Proc. Soc. Exp. Biol. Med. 70:670-72, 1949.

29.   219   14   4   6   Fulton F & Dumbell K R. The serological comparison of strains of influenza virus. J. Gen. Microbiology 3:97-111, 1949.

30.   200   13   17   18   Gall E A & Mallory T B. Malignant lymphoma; a clinicopathologic survey of 618 cases. Amer. J. Pathol. 18:381-415, 1942.

31.   520   34   41   67   Goldman D E. Potential, impedance, and rectification in membranes. J. General Physiology 27:37-59, 1943.

32.   188   12   15   13   Goldstein A. The interactions of drugs and plasma proteins. Pharmacol. Revs. 1:102-65, 1949.

33.   300   20   10   17   Gomori G. Observations with differential stains on human islets of Langerhans. Amer. J. Pathology 17:395-406, 1941.

34.   168   11   12   11   Gomori G. The distribution of phosphatase in normal organs and tissues. J. Cell. Comp. Physiol. 17:71-84, 1941.

35.   175   11   7   12   Gomori G. Distribution of acid phosphatase in the tissues under normal and under pathologic conditions. Arch. Pathol. 32:189-99, 1941.

36.   241   16   21   12   Greenspan F S. Bioassay of hypophyseal growth hormone; the tibia test. Endocrinology 45:455-63, 1949.

37.   354   23   19   18   Gregg N M. Congenital cataract following German measles in the mother. Trans. Opthalmol. Soc. Australia 3:35-46, 1941.

38.   218   14   9   9   Hahn P F. Abolishment of alimentary lipemia following injection of heparin. Science 98:19-20, 1943.

39.   189   12   6   3   Hamilton W F, Riley R L, Attyah A H, Cournand A, Fowell D M, Himmelstein A, Noble R P, Remington J W, Richards D W, Wheeler N C & Witham A C. Comparison of the Fick and dye injection methods of measuring the cardiac output in man. Amer. J. Physiol. 153:309-21, 1948.

40.   531   35   54   44   Hanks J H & Wallace R E. Relation of oxygen and temperature in the preservation of tissues by refrigeration. Proc. Soc. Exp. Biol. Med. 71:196-200, 1949.

41.   195   13   9   11   Harlow H F. The formation of learning sets. Psychol. Review 56:51-65, 1949.

42.   235   15   11   13   Hegsted D M, Mills R C, Elvehjew C A & Hart E B. Choline in the nutrition of chicks. J. Biol. Chem. 138:459-66, 1941.

43.   230   15   8   11   Hill A V. The abrupt transition from rest to activity in muscle. Proc. Roy Soc. London B 136:399-420, 1949.

Figure 2 (cont.)

44. 709 47 58 52 Hodgkin A L & Katz B. The effect of sodium ions on the electrical activity of the giant axon of the squid. **J. Physiology 108**:37-77, 1949.

45. 256 17 15 18 Hodgkin A L & Rushton W A H. The electrical constants of a crustacean nerve fiber. **Proc. Roy. Soc. London B 133**:444-79, 1946.

46. 361 24 11 18 Hogeboom G H, Schneider W C & Palade G E. Cytochemical studies of mammalian tissues. 1. Isolation of intact mitochondria from rat liver; some biochemical properties of mitochondria and submicroscopic particulate material. **J. Biol. Chem. 172**:619-36, 1948.

47. 154 10 2 10 Holmberg C G & Laurell C B. Investigations of serum copper. 2. Isolation of the copper containing protein, and a description of some of its properties. **Acta Chem. Scand. 2**:550-56, 1948.

48. 341 22 22 21 Holton P & Kennedy C R. The treatment of experimental tuberculosis with sulphetrone. **Brit. J. Pharmacology 3**:29-36, 1948.

49. 373 24 29 14 Kekwick R A. The serum proteins in multiple myelomatosis. **Biochem. J. 34**:1248-57, 1940.

50. 267 17 21 13 Kety S S. Measurement of regional circulation by the local clearance of radioactive sodium. **Amer. Heart J. 38**:321-8, 1949.

51. 228 15 13 12 Kety S S & Schmidt C F. The determination of cerebral blood flow in man by the use of nitrous oxide in low concentrations. **Amer. J. Physiology 143**:53-66, 1945.

52. 443 29 16 23 Kety S S & Schmidt C F. The effects of altered arterial tensions of carbon dioxide and oxygen on cerebral blood flow and cerebral oxygen consumption of normal young men. **J. Clin. Invest. 27**:484-92, 1948.

53. 403 26 24 26 Kety S S & Schmidt C F. The nitrous oxide method for the quantitative determination of cerebral blood blow in man; theory, procedure and normal values. **J. Clin. Invest. 27**:476-83, 1948.

54. 240 16 7 10 Klinefelter H F, Albright F & Griswold G C. Experience with a quantitative test for normal or decreased amounts of follicle-stimulating hormone in the urine in endocrinological diagnosis. **J. Clin. Endocrinology 3**:529-44, 1943.

55. 234 15 25 17 Konzett H & Rossler R. Versuchsanordnung zu Untersuchung an der Bronchialmuskulatur (Experimental procedure in studies of the bronchial musculature). **Arch. Exp. Path. Pharmakol. 195**:71-74, 1940.

56. 881 58 68 61 Kunitz M. Crystalline soybean trypsin inhibiter. 2. General properties. **J. General Physiology 30**:291-320, 1947.

57. 277 18 13 14 Leblond C P & Stevens C E. The constant renewal of the intestinal epithelium in the albino rat. **Anatomical Record 10**:357-71, 1948.

58. 156 10 17 16 Lindemann E. Symptomatology and management of grief. **Amer. J. Psychiatry 101**:141-8, 1944.

59. 255 17 10 10 Ling G & Gerard G L. The normal membrane potential of frog sartorius fibers. **J. Cell. Comp. Physiol. 34**:383-96, 1949.

60. 206 13 28 20 Litchfield J T. A method for rapid graphic solution of time-per cent effect curves. **J. Pharmacol. Exp. Ther. 97**:399-408, 1949.

61. 2238 149 190 186 Litchfield J T Jr & Wilcoxon F A. A simplified method of evaluating dose-effect experiments. **J. Pharmacol. Exp. Ther. 96**:99-113, 1949.

62. 246 16 10 6 Long C N H, Katzin B & Fry E G. The adrenal cortex and carbohydrate metabolism. **Endocrinology 26**:309-44, 1940.

63. 238 15 26 21 Luria S E & Delbruck M. Mutations of bacteria from virus sensitivity to virus resistant. **Genetics 28**:491-511, 1943.

64. 207 13 9 7 Medawar P B. The behavior and fate of skin autographs and skin homographs in rabbits. **J. Anatomy 78**:176-99, 1944.

Figure 2 (cont.)

65. 180 12. 29 20 Merlis J K. The effect of changes in the calcium content of the cerebrospinal fluid on spinal reflex activity in the dog. Amer. J. Physiology 131:67-72, 1940.

66. 487 32 49 32 Miller L C & Tainter M L. Estimation of the ED^{50} and its error by means of logarithmic-probit graph paper. Proc. Soc. Exp. Biol. Med. 57:261-4, 1944.

67. 190 12 11 6 Mirsky A E & Pollister A W. Chromosin, a desoxyribose nucleoprotein complex of the cell nucleus. J. General Physiol 30:117-47, 1946.

68. 603 40 26 45 Moruzzi G & Magoun H W. Brain strem reticular formation and activation of the EEG. Electroencephalography Clin. Neurol. 1:455-73, 1949.

69. 839 55 50 75 Ouchterlony O. Antigen-antibody reactions in gels. Acta. Path. Microb. Scand. 26:507-15, 1949.

70. 497 33 36 25 Ouchterlony O. In vitro method for testing the toxin-producing capacity of diphtheria bacteria. Acta Path. Microb. Scand. 25:186-91, 1948.

71. 183 12 10 4 Owen R D. Immunogenetic consequences of vascular anastomoses between bovine twins. Science 102:400-01, 1945.

72. 204 13 26 12 Pappenheimer J R & Soto-Rivera A. Effective osmotic pressure of the plasma and other quantities associated with the capillary circulation in the hindlimbs of cats and dogs. Amer. J. Physiology 152:471-91, 1948.

73. 279 18 19 19 Pauling L. Itano H A, Singer S J & Wells I C. Sickle cell anemia, a molecular disease. Science 110:543-48, 1949.

74. 198 13 13 8 Reifenstein E C, Albright F & Wells S L. The accumulation, interpretation, and presentation of data pertaining to metabolic balances, notably those of calcium, phosphorus, and nitrogen. J. Clin. Endocrinol. 5:367-95, 1945.

75. 197 13 10 7 Robinson J R. Some effects of glucose and calcium upon the metabolism of kidney slices from adult and newborn rats. Biochem. J. 45:68-74, 1949.

76. 289 19 11 5 Rocha e Silva M, Beraldo W T & Rosenfeld G. Bradykinin, a hypotensive and smooth muscle stimulating factor released from plasma globulin by snake venoms and by trypsin. Amer. J. Physiology 156:261-73, 1949.

77. 205 13 15 13 Sabin A B & Feldman H A. Dyes as microchemical indicators of a new immunity phenomenon affecting a protozoon parasite (Toxoplasma). Science 108:660-63, 1948.

78. 234 15 13 8 Sanford K K, Earle W R & Likely D. The growth in vitro of single isolated tissue cells. J. Nat. Cancer Inst. 9:229-46, 1948.

79. 1575 105 329 352 Scatchard G. The attractions of proteins for small molecules and ions. Ann. New York Acad. Sci. 51:660-72, 1949.

80. 270 18 24 19 Schild H O. pA, a new scale for the measurement of drug antagonism. Brit. J. Pharmacol. 2:189-206, 1947.

81. 202 13 4 2 Schwert G W, Neurath H, Kaufman S & Snoke J E. The specific esterase activity of trypsin. J. Biol. Chem. 172:221, 1948.

82. 167 11 5 6 Selye H. The general adaptation syndrome and the diseases of adaptation. J. Clin. Endocrinol. 6:117-230, 1946.

83. 289 19 30 24 Shay H, Komorov S A, Fels S S, Meranze D, Gruenstein M & Siplet H. A simple method for the uniform productions of gastric ulceration in the rat. Gastroenterology 5:43-61, 1945.

84. 209 13 18 12 Shumway W. Stages in the normal development of Rana pipiens. 1. External form. Anatomical Record 78:139-48, 1940.

85. 209 13 14 17 Simpson G G. The principles of classification and a classification of mammals. Bull. Amer. Mus. Nat. Hist. 85:1-350, 1945.

Figure 2 (cont.)

86. 352 23   7   5 Singer R B & Hastings A B. An improved clinical method for the estimation of disturbances of the acid-base balance of human blood. Medicine 27:223-42, 1948.

87. 782 52 41 39 Smith H W, Finklestein N, Aliminosa L, Crawford B & Grabar M. The renal clearances of substituted hippuric acid derivatives and other aromatic acids in dog and man. J. Clin. Invest. 24:388-404, 1945.

88. 182 12   6   9 Sokolow M & Lyon T P. The ventricular complex in left ventricular hypertrophy as obtained by unipolar precordial and limb leads. Amer. Heart J. 37:161-86, 1949.

89. 237 15 25 27 Steinbrocker O, Traeger C H & Batterman R C. Therapeutic criteria in rheumatoid arthritis. J. Amer. Med. Assoc. 140:659-62, 1949.

90. 203 13   9   6 Stetten M R. Some aspects of the metabolism of hydroxyproline studied with the aid of isotopic nitrogen. J. Biol. Chem. 181:31-37, 1949.

91. 229 15 23 13 Strom G. The influence of anoxia on lactate utilization in man after prolonged muscular work. Acta. Physiol. Scand. 17:440-51, 1949.

92. 296 19 22 18 Swift H F, Wilson A T & Lancefield R C. Typing group A hemolytic streptococci by M precipitin reactions in capillary pipettes. J. Exp. Med. 78:127-34, 1943.

93. 283 18 27 24 Taylor A C & Kollros J J. Stages in the normal development of *Rana pipiens* larvae. Anatomical Record 94:7-24, 1946.

94. 197 13 24 23 Thomas J E. An improved cannula for gastric and intestinal fistulas. Proc. Soc. Exp. Biol. Med. 46:260-61, 1941.

95. 228 15 18 15 Ussing H H. The distinction by means of tracers between active transport and diffusion; the transfer of iodide across the isolated frog skin. Acta. Physiol. Scand. 19:43-56, 1949.

96. 400 26 26 24 Verney E B. The antidiuretic hormone and factors which determine its release. Proc. Roy. Soc. London B Biol. 135:25-106, 1947.

97. 194 12   9 10 Waldenstrom J. Incipient myelomatosis or "essential" hyperglobulinemia with fibrinogenopenia; a new syndrome. Acta Med. Scand. 117:216-47, 1944.

98. 426 28 24 20 Weichselbaum T E. Studies on experimental hypertension. 12. The experimental production and pathogenesis of hypertension due to renal ischemia. Amer. J. Clin. Pathol. 10:40-72, 1946.

99. 245 16 12 20 Weichselbaum T E, Levine M G & Hoyt R E. The use of pectin and gelatin in the processing of plasma in the blood bank. Amer. J. Clin. Pathol. 16:40-44, 1946.

100. 275 18 26 19 Weiss P & Hiscoe H B. Experiments on the mechanism of nerve growth. J. Exp. Zoology 107:315-95, 1948.

101. 287 19 16 18 Westergaard M & Mitchell H K. *Neurospora*. 5. A synthetic medium favoring sexual reproduction. Amer. J. Botany 34:573-7, 1947.

102. 426 28 33 32 Wilcoxon F. Individual comparisons by ranking methods. Biometrics 1:80-3, 1945.

103. 166 11 11 12 Wright H P. The adhesiveness of blood platelets in normal subjects with varying concentrations of anticoagulants. J. Pathol. Bacteriol. 53:255-62, 1941.

104. 251 16 14 12 Zilversmit D B, Entenman C & Fishler M C. On the calculation of "turnover time" and "turnover rate" from experiments involving the use of labeling agents. J. General Physiology 26:325-32, 1943.

Proposal For a New Profession:
Scientific Reviewer

Number 14, April 4, 1977

Just a few weeks ago, Harvey Brooks, the chairman of a congressional science panel, wrote a letter to *Science*[1] in which he solicited suggestions to improve the "health of the scientific and technological enterprise" in the United States. He specifically asked, among other things, "What alternatives might and should exist to the present traditional basic research and teaching careers for scientists and engineers who are trained to the Ph.D. level primarily through research and apprenticeship?"

I would like to offer a constructive response to Dr. Brooks' invitation. The suggestion which follows will be submitted to the Office of Technology Assessment's Panel on the Health of the Scientific and Technological Enterprise.

In fact, my suggestion addresses two separate but related problems: the unemployment of Ph.D.'s and the shortage of qualified literature reviewers. Both conditions are now deteriorating, and will probably continue to worsen until some positive action is taken.

First, consider the unemployment and underemployment of people with doctoral degrees. While the situation varies from year to year and from country to country, there can be little doubt that there now exists an abundance of people with Ph.D.'s; people who were trained to perform scientific research but who, because of the current economic condition of higher education, are unable to obtain faculty positions at universities. Some of these people can be employed by industry and government, but overall their opportunities are increasingly limited.

Second, consider the dilemma of publishers of scientific journals who find it extremely difficult to hire or locate people qualified to write scientific reviews. The need for reviews is already well documented. In any given specialty, after the publication of 50 to 250 articles there is usually a need to consolidate the information into a readable, authoritative "review." Such reviews are sorely needed by administrators and science policy makers as well as by the researchers themselves.

There is ample evidence for the importance of reviews to the rapid advances in many fields. For instance, review journals achieve extremely high impact as measured in ISI® 's *Journal Citation Reports®* .[2] Also, co-citation studies have shown that a review paper can be comparable in importance to the milestone papers in the same field.[3]

In 1976 some 28,182 "review" articles were indexed for ISI's *Index to Scientific Reviews*™ .[4] Of this total, less than half were originally written as reviews--that is, for the specific purpose of consolidating the literature. In addition to these, there are perhaps 10,000 chapters in multi-authored books which are classifiable as reviews.

Those concerned with scientific recognition and professional status might be attracted by the idea of reviewing the original research of others. In fact, the "social" prospects for reviewers are very good. Scientific reviewers are well known and highly respected. Many laboratory workers in rapidly growing fields wish that they themselves could handle the task of keeping tabs on the literature. When they try, they often find that they simply can't do it.

That this kind of intellectual activity is deeply appreciated by the research community is reflected in our citation studies. Last January, in an article published in *Nature*,[5] I demonstrated the extraordinary impact and increasing importance of review journals. I found that 80 review journals had achieved an impact of two or more. This indicates that the average journal article was cited at least twice in the two previous years. Only 300 primary journals in the world--out of thousands published--achieved an equivalent or higher impact.

In the next several decades, the rate of growth of review journals can be expected to increase--while the rate of growth of primary journals will probably decrease. The world's scientific research output will continue to grow, of course, but it will be impossible for all of the research to be published in primary journals. Synopsis and other forms of publication will help slow the growth of the traditional primary journals. However, the absolute size of the literature will continue to increase significantly.

These two situations--the underutilization of Ph.D.'s and the increasing importance of reviews-- present an opportunity to create a new profession, that of the "full-time" scientific reviewer.

It is essential for a competent reviewer to have subject expertise and exposure to the research experience. In addition, reviewers must understand modern methods of information retrieval and organization. And they must be able to write clearly and concisely. Many unemployed persons with doctoral degrees have the necessary subject expertise, are trained in research methodology, and have at least a passing acquaintance with scientific communication. For those who need it, clear writing is a skill which can be taught. One wonders how anyone received a doctorate without such skill.

I have in mind a "scientific reviewer" curriculum which could be combined with a program of instruction including information retrieval and scientific writing. At present, not a single university provides this type of program. However, a dozen or so universities have information science programs easily modifiable to this curriculum. Furthermore, a few with graduate programs in scientific communication would be suitable.

Post-doctoral training of no less than one year would be essential to the creation of the new profession. Ideally, the program would be headed by a scientist who is experienced in writing reviews. Most of the candidates for program head would be drawn from the ranks of science specialties; information scientists would also qualify. The severity of unemployment among Ph.D.'s suggests that there will be no shortage of students.

In addition to courses in information sciences, the "scientific reviewer" curriculum would include courses in on-line searching techniques and in the history and sociology of science. Intensive training in science communication, with emphasis on writing, is essential. I would also stress the value of advanced reading knowledge in two or more foreign languages pertinent to the student's field of interest. This could be offered as an option, and might add an additional year of studies, preferably abroad.

Once programs like this were established, I expect that many universities could launch science review journals based on the output of their graduate students--much like law review journals.[6]

Some may argue that "scientific reviewer" is just another name for an "information scientist." But I think the distinction is real and important. In any case, the number of recent Ph.D.'s who go on to receive the Master's Degree in Information Science is trivial. And of these, many are not qualified to do reviewing--although at present they are often the best candidates we have.

For years I have been urging the National Science Foundation to help fund educational programs like that outlined above.[7] I can't understand their reluctance to attack this fundamental lack in our science education system. Programs like that proposed here could become self-sustaining after a short period, and the benefits to the research community would be significant. Hopefully, administrators would soon learn to allocate funds in their research budgets for direct purchase of reviews as well as other information tools. If not, the government might find itself subsidizing the continued employment of reviewers. Publishers and other organizations could help by supporting fellowships.

I won't attempt to spell out here how and why reviews improve the retrieval of scientific information. But it will be obvious to many that critical reviewing represents the ultimate in in-depth indexing of the primary literature. And once the size of the review literature exceeds 100,000 or more articles per year, as inevitably it must, then we can look forward to the review of reviews.

If my suggested curriculum is implemented and given government support now, it will be a small step from "scientific reviewer" to "reviewer of scientific reviews." Perhaps in the future it will be the scientific elite[8] who will be expected to produce such reviews of reviews, as an obligation both to the scientific community and to the laymen that support their efforts.

REFERENCES

1. **Brooks H.** U.S. science and technology: a prescription for "health." *Science* 195:536, 1977.

2. **Garfield E.** *Journal citation reports. A bibliometric analysis of references processed for the 1974* Science Citation Index® . Philadelphia. Institute for Scientific Information® , 1976.

3. **Small H.** A co-citation model of a scientific specialty: a longitudinal study of collagen research. *Social Studies of Science,* 1977 [in press].

4. *Index to scientific reviews: 1976 annual. An international interdisciplinary index to the review literature of science, medicine, agriculture, technology, and the behavioral sciences.* Philadelphia. Institute for Scientific Information, 1977 [in press].

5. **Garfield E.** Significant journals of science. *Nature* 264:609-15, 1976.

6. --------------. Of conferences and reviews. *Current Contents*® No. 48, 1 December 1975, p. 5-8.

7. --------------. Putting our money where our needs are. *Bulletin of the ASIS* 1:10, 32, 1974.

8. **Zuckerman H.** *Scientific elite: Nobel laureates in the United States.* New York. The Free Press, 1977.

CURRENT COMMENTS

Le Nouveau Défi Américain. I.

NUMBER 15, APRIL 11, 1977

In 1967 the Frenchman Jean-Jacques Servan-Schreiber jolted his fellow citizens by publishing *Le Défi Américain*.[1] In the past decade the book's title has become a catch-phrase for all sorts of challenges. I did not realize until recently the extent to which Servan-Schreiber stressed the importance of the information industry, but in a recent re-reading of the book's English translation I came upon this startling conclusion: "The new frontiers of human creativity in every area lie in information systems and their utilization, and the Americans themselves do not seem fully to realize this yet. We [presumably the French] must forge ahead into this area before it is taken over by others."[2]

This assertion is ironic in light of the recent *cause célèbre* in which I have been involved. For lack of a better description, I have called it "Le Noveau Defi Americain"; modesty forbids my naming it the "Garfield Challenge," since I have already named both a law[3] and a constant[4] after myself.

Last fall I published an article in *La Recherche* entitled "Is French Science Too Provincial?"[5] I said what I had to say about the French in French, but the English translation is reprinted on the following pages.

The reaction to this article has been intense. As Barbara Burke of the *Washington Post* reported from Paris just a few weeks ago, "French Scientists Resent Dominance of English"![6] One French scientist has denounced the article as "pernicious"; another accused me of "linguistic imperialism"; and still another claimed that my article "questions the existence of a civilization...." It seems that I have hit a raw nerve.

Readers of *La Recherche* have had their chance to reply to the "New American Challenge," and have certainly taken advantage of it--as I'll demonstrate at length in this space next week. In the following pages you can examine for yourself the original source of their outrage.

1. **Servan-Schreiber J J.** *Le défi américain.* Editions Denoel, 1967.
2. ---------------------------. *The American challenge.* New York: Atheneum, 1969.
3. **Garfield E.** The mystery of the transposed journal lists--wherein Bradford's law of scattering is generalized according to Garfield's law of concentration. *Current Contents*® No. 31, 4 August 1971, p. 5-6.
4. --------------. Is the ratio between number of citations and publications cited a true constant? *Current Contents* No. 6, 9 February 1976, p. 5-7.
5. --------------. La science française est-elle trop provinciale? *La Recherche* 7:757-60, 1976.
6. **Burke B.** French scientists resent dominance of English. *Washington Post* 20 March 1977, p. E6.

Translation of: **Garfield E.** La science française est-elle trop provinciale? *La Recherche* **7**: 757-60, 1976. The illustration is reproduced with permission.

by Eugene Garfield

Institute for Scientific Information

Philadelphia, Pennsylvania 19106

Is French Science Too Provincial?

■ Can one evaluate a scientific article by the number of times it's been cited? An answer to that question probably can't be attempted with too great caution. The use of quantitative data alone risks distortion of the complexity of the process of scientific publication. Indeed, one can take the position that number of citations cannot serve as even an approximate measure of scientific worth.

■ Nevertheless, some numbers and comparisons furnish food for thought. Eugene Garfield is president of the Institute for Scientific Information, which includes among its services Current Contents, well-known to most research scientists. Here Dr. Garfield examines the case of France. Are French journals cited frequently? What journals cite French authors? His findings are far from complimentary, and certainly not beyond argument. But they agree with a picture of French science that is not unique with Dr. Garfield, a picture it will be dangerous to ignore.

• About twenty years ago, I made my first visit to France. In those days I was able to read and speak French well enough to pass my doctoral language exams. As a student of linguistics, I was aware not only of the beauty of the French language but also of its vital role in the history of language, literature, diplomacy, and science. However, even 20 years ago, certain French scientists were asserting that their work was being ignored by American scientists too lazy to learn French. By the time I returned to France in 1961 these protests were increasing, and by the time I first lectured in Paris in 1965 about the then new *Science Citation Index®*, the feeling of neglect among French scientists had grown into a national mania. When French scientists first saw the *SCI®* their fears were confirmed: the data showed that their work was seldom cited by the Americans and the British. Is it a coincidence that to this day the *SCI* is used less in France than in any other country of her size?

Decline of French science?

I hope my French colleagues will forgive me for stating a painful observation: that today French science appears to be in decline. The reasons have much to do with French support for education and research, which, in comparison with that of other nations, has not been commensurate with the country's population and wealth. Surely a nation which has produced Pascal, Lavoisier, Pasteur, and Monod is capable of producing more giants of science. But it is clear that over the past three decades the conditions for fostering such giants have not been present in France. The most obvious symptom of the decline of French science is the refusal of French scientists to recognize that French is no longer a significant international language. By publishing the results of their research exclusively in the French language, French researchers prevent their findings from being casually read by the rest of the world's scientific community.

My basis for making this observation is the publication record of French scientists and French journals. This data is compiled each year in the *Science Citation Index (SCI)*, an international index to the scientific literature published by the Institute for Scientific Information®, of which I am president. Since modern science depends so heavily on the exchange of scientific information, the record of this exchange is the most comprehensive, most objective evidence on which to base an assessment of the scientific contribution of a nation, a university, a journal, or even an individual.

When one scientist cites the work of another in a published report, he or she registers an assessment of the value of the other's contribution. The aggregation of a vast number of citations comprises a consensus of the world's publishing scientists. Extensive studies have confirmed that there is a significant correlation between research performance and the number of times a scholarly article is cited in the literature.[1]

The Institute for Scientific Information recently completed a citation study of French journals.[2] In the study, 129 journals which are published in France and indexed by the *Science Citation Index* were treated as though they constituted a single journal. We then determined which journals this single French aggregate cited most frequently, and which journals published throughout the world cited the French aggregate most frequently.

Since the study covered only journal issues published in France in 1974, strictly speaking we cannot claim that the study covered all of French scientific literature--either from a linguistic or a scientific standpoint. Many French scientists publish in international or other non-French journals, and of course there are many articles written in French for journals published outside of France. Nevertheless, this group of 129 French journals probably gives us a general idea of trends in French science.

The 129 French journals represent about 5.3% of the total of 2,443 journals indexed by the *SCI* in 1974. However, these 5.3% French journals produced only 3.8% of the total source items indexed in 1974, and only 2.6% of the references. This indicates that France's journals are small in comparison with those of other nations. No matter how mediocre, larger journals tend to receive higher citation counts. While the "average" scientific article made reference to about 13 previous articles, the "average" article in French journals made only 8.6 such references. This in itself is a national peculiarity.

The French are primarily cited
by the French

The data also indicate that the French themselves are the greatest citers of the French. Of the ten journals which most frequently cited French journals in 1974, seven are themselves French. But of the ten journals most frequently cited *by* the French, only three are themselves French. Of the 50 journals most frequently cited by the French, only ten are French journals.

If the French journal literature is a characteristic segment of the international scientific literature, a list of the 50 journals most frequently cited by all French journals should correspond fairly well to a list of the 50 journals most frequently cited by the scientific literature as a whole in 1974. But in fact there are telling differences, both in ranks and in citation totals.

For example, in 1974 the most highly cited of scientific journals was the *Journal of the American Chemical Society*. All things being equal, it should appear first on a list of journals most frequently cited by French journals, and it is. Since, as noted above, the French journals contributed 2.6% of all references processed for the *SCI*, they should--all things again being equal--account for 2.6% of the citations received by the *Journal of the American Chemical Society* in 1974. As a matter of fact, the French journals account for 2555, or just about 2.6%.

But all things are not equal, and except in a few cases the journals most highly cited by the French are not identical with those most highly cited by the rest of the international scientific community. For example, in 1974 the *second* most highly cited single journal was the *Journal of Biological Chemistry* with an extremely high impact factor of 5.84. All things being equal, it should appear second on a list of journals most frequently cited by French journals. It does *not*. Instead, the journal second most highly cited by French journals was *Bulletin de la Societe Chimique de France*, with an impact factor of 0.77. It was cited by all journals 6,671 times, so the "expected" 2.6% French citation total would be 173. The actual number of French citations is 2,471. Although the *Bulletin* ranks second in French citations, it ranks ninety-fifth in worldwide citations. In fact, in every case where the ratio of French citations to worldwide citations exceeds 10%--about four times the expected rate of 2.6%--the citing journals are French journals.

The heavy citation of French journals by French journals is not wholly a matter of language, although language undoubtedly plays a part. For example, (*Nouvelle*) *Presse Medicale*, which ranks 365th when all scientific journals are listed in order of total citations received in 1974, ranks 6th on a list of journals most frequently cited by the French. Just above (*Nouvelle*) *Presse Medicale*, in fifth place on the French list, is *Lancet*--which was cited by French journals relatively more frequently than by the worldwide literature as a whole. It is clear that (*Nouvelle*) *Presse Medicale* is highly ranked by the French because it is about French medicine. *Lancet* is highly ranked by the French because it is an internationally important journal. It does not return the compliment except on rare occasions.

In another part of the same ISI® study of French journals, a listing of the 50 journals that most frequently cited French journals clearly showed that these were predominantly French journals, and that their self-citing rate was much higher than normal. This indicates that the scientific literature published in France is mainly of low impact. The French journals cite foreign literature much more heavily than their own, while their own literature is cited mainly by themselves. It is like a cosmopolitan city that is ignored by the rest of the world.

The limited dissemination of French journals.

The finding that the French scientific literature is of generally low impact has been supported in a study by F. Narin et al.[3] The study covered 492 leading journals over a time span from 1965 to 1971. Over this time period, the study found, the United States led the world in number of publications, followed at a significant distance by the U.S.S.R. Far below these two countries were the United Kingdom, Germany, Japan, and finally France. In 1972, for example, although France fared better than the Soviet Union and Japan in clinical medicine, France fared worst in engineering in the world, with only 2.1% of the total. In contrast, the United Kingdom published 11.8%, West Germany 6.8%, the Soviet Union 7.2%, and Japan 4.4%.

Measuring outside-of-country citations, the authors found that the United States is most highly cited by the outside world. The U.K. ranks next, with West Germany, Japan, and "other" countries approximately equal. France ranks significantly below them, but the Soviet Union receives the fewest citations by far from the outside world.

The most biting finding of this citation study was the very low ratio of citations to publications for France--what we call impact. The authors asserted that, "The citations/publications ratio is lower for France in every field than it is for any major country, or all the other countries combined.... Much of the low level of citations/publications for the French literature may well be due to the counting of a large number of relatively small sized articles in *Comptes Rendus*. If the articles are short, they presumably contain less material likely to be cited, and would have a relatively low number of citations per article."[3] The practice of splitting a longer article into two or three smaller parts, although raising the total publication count, results in fewer citations per publication. Multi-part articles might be better left intact.

In 1972 I examined the performance of the world-famous *Comptes Rendus* in a study of citation analysis as a tool in journal evaluation.[4] CR's performance in terms of sheer numbers of citations was quite impressive--in fact, it ranked 13th worldwide in frequency of citations, indicating that it is a major archival journal. However, its impact factor--the average number of citations per published item--was only 0.788 for 1969, and had dropped

• Journals that cited French journals in 1974 For each title the table indicates. **A** = total number of citations of other journals, **B** = total number of citations of French journals; **C** = number of self-citations. **D** = **B/A** (percentage of 'French citations' in terms of total citations; **E** = **C/A** (percentage of self-citations in terms of total citations); **F** = **C/B** (percentage of self-citations in terms of French citations') **G** = impact factor

• Journals are listed in order of the frequency with which they cited French journals; thus, it is in the *Comptes rendus de l Academie des sciences (Series D)* that one finds most references to French journals (1,952) Next, in descending order of total citations of French journals, come the *Bulletin de la Societe Chimique de France* (1,379), the *Comptes rendus de l'Academie des Sciences (Series C)* (1,151), etc

• Many of the figures seem to be significant. Thus the figure in column D for the *Comptes Rendus (Series A)* is 30 6% That means that this journal cites a large percentage of French journals But it is even more noteworthy that, eight times out of ten, this citation of French journals is self-citation . . . (very high self-citation rate, whether in terms of all citations, 24 6%, or in terms of all French citations, 80 6%). These data should be interpreted with caution. In any event, this excess of self-citation in many French journals is slightly disturbing, especially in view of the fact that the impact of these same journals on the international scientific literature is so limited

JOURNAL	A	B	C	D	E	F	G
1. C. Rend. Acad. Sci. D Nat.	11129	1952	1317	17.5	11.8	67.5	0.51
2. B. Soc. Chim. France	11102	1379	869	12.4	7.8	63.0	0.77
3. C. Rend. Acad. Sci. C Chim.	4762	1151	573	24.2	12.0	49.8	0.51
4. Semaine Hopitaux	5603	882	125	15.7	2.2	14.2	0.29
5. Nouv. Presse Medicale	4900	801	323	16.3	6.6	40.3	0.60
6. J. Organomet. Chem.	22699	655	— —	2.9	— —	— —	2.38
7. C. Rend. Acad Sci. A Math.	1924	588	474	30.6	24.6	80.6	0.20
8. J. Chim. Physique	4489	556	367	12.4	8.2	66.0	0.88
9. C. Rend. Acad. Sci. B. Phys.	2243	466	302	20.8	13.5	64.8	0.44
10. Analytical Chemistry	27658	435	— —	1.6	— —	— —	3.29
11. Tetrahedron	13059	404	— —	3.1	— —	— —	1.57
12. Ann. Chirurgie	1916	394	79	20.6	4.1	20.0	0.16
13. C. Rend. Soc. Biol.	1926	367	232	19.1	12.0	63.2	0.30
14. Lyon Medical	2771	365	49	13.2	1.8	13.4	0.24
15. Arch. Maladies Coeur	2466	358	221	14.5	9.0	61.7	0.64
16. J. Amer. Chem. Soc.	46267	343	— —	0.7	— —	— —	4.38
17. J. Chem. Soc. Perkin	20327	342	— —	1.7	— —	— —	1.34
18. J. Organic Chemistry	21976	326	— —	1.5	— —	— —	1.49
19. Revue Rhumatisme	1543	315	103	20.4	6.7	32.7	0.48
20. Tetrahedron Letters	11178	269	— —	2.4	— —	— —	1.77
21. Pathologie Biologie	2866	252	49	8.9	1.7	19.4	0.56
22. Lille Medicale	1842	249	41	13.5	2.2	16.5	0.13
23. Canad. J. Chemistry	12685	240	— —	1.9	— —	— —	1.39
24. Biochimie	4677	236	154	5.0	3.3	65.3	1.63
25. Neuro-Chirurgie	1363	230	66	16.9	4.8	28.7	0.36
26. J. Radiol. Electrol.	1264	223	65	17.6	5.1	29.1	0.21
27. Arch. Fr. Pediatrie	1642	215	72	13.1	4.4	33.5	1.01
28. J. Chirurgie	1265	215	14	17.0	1.1	6.5	0.15
29. J. Microscopie (Paris)	1634	212	129	13.0	7.9	60.8	1.60
30. Eur. J. Med. Chem.	1541	207	112	13.4	7.3	54.1	— —
31. Brain Research	19626	198	— —	1.0	— —	— —	3.10
32. Ann. Cardiol. Angeiol.	1132	192	13	17.0	1.1	6.8	0.35
33. Deut. Med. Wschr.	— —	187	— —	— —	— —	— —	— —
34. Biochim. Biophys. Acta	45366	185	— —	0.4	— —	— —	3.11
35. Coeur Med. Interne	1308	184	30	14.1	2.3	16.3	0.53
36. Physical Review B	27280	181	— —	0.7	— —	— —	2.86
37. Ann. Radiologie	1122	180	24	16.0	2.1	13.3	0.39
38. J. Urologie Nephrol.	1171	180	107	15.4	9.1	59.4	0.18

to 0.383 by 1974. In contrast, over 1500 other journals performed better. Over 300 journals had impact factors of over 2.0. The impact of the average *Comptes Rendus* article is extremely low and getting lower.

Similarly, *Presse Medicale* is widely respected among international medical journals. But its impact, which is very high relative to other French journals, ranks low in international comparison, although it rose from 0.494 in 1969 to 0.612 in 1974. France's share of the journals which excel is painfully low, especially for a country of her size and research effort.

The more distinguished French scientists published in foreign journals.

A careful examination of the citation data for many highly ranked French scientists has clearly shown that these scientists all share one characteristic: each publishes in English or in international journals outside of France. For example, most of Monod's articles were published in the *Journal of Molecular Biology*.

These highly-cited scientists wisely recognize that for the author who wishes to assure that his scientific contribution reaches the largest possible circle of readers, it is imperative to

1. 396 Thiery J P. Mise en evidence des polysaccharides sur coupes fines en micro-scopie electronique (Electron-microscopic demonstration of poly-saccharides in fine sections). *J. Microscopie* 6:987-1018, 1967.

2. 377 Mulliken R S. Quelques aspects de la theories des orbitales moleculaires (On some aspects of the molecular orbital theory).
J. Chim. Phys. 46:497-542, 1949.

3. 290 Novikoff A B & Woo-Yung Shin. The endoplasmic reticulum in the Golgi zone and its relations to microbodies, Golgi apparatus and autophagic vacuoles in rat liver cells. *J. Microscopie* 3:187-206, 1964.

4   256 Rosset R, Monier R & Julien J. Les ribosomes d'*Escherichia coli*. I. Mise en evidence d'un RNA ribosomique de faible poids moleculaire (Ribosomes of *E. coli*. I. Demonstration of a ribosomal of low molecular weight).
B. Soc. Chim. Biol. 46:87-109, 1964.

5. 213 Sussman R & Jacob F. Sur un systeme de repression thermosensible chez le bacteriophage λ d'*Escherichia coli* (On a system of heat-sensitive repres-sion in the lambda bacteriophage of *E. coli*).
C. Rend. Acad. Sci. 254:1517-1519, 1962.

6. 193 Gabe M. Sur quelques applications de la coloration par la fuchsine-paraldehyde--improved Gomori's aldehyde-fuchsin (On some applications of the fuchsin-paraldehyde stain-improved Gomoroi's aldehyde-fuchsin).
B. Micr. Appl. 3:152-162, 1953.

7. 185 Lejeune J, Gautier M & Turpin R. Etude des chromosomes somatiques de neuf enfants mongoliens (Study of somatic chromosomes in nine cases of mongolism). *C. Rend. Acad. Sci.* 248:1721-1722, 1959.

8. 184 Cohen G N & Rickenberg H V. Concentration specifique reversible des amino acides chez *Escherichia coli* (Specific reversible concentration of amino acids in *E. coli*). *Ann. Inst. Pasteur* 91:693-720, 1956.

9. 181 Gabriel P. Des categories Abeliennes (Abelian categories).
Bull. Soc. Math. France 90:323-448, 1962.

10. 167 Rickenberg H V, Cohen G N, Buttin G & Monod J. La galactoside-permease d'*Escherichia coli* (Galactoside permease in *E. coli*).
Ann. Inst. Pasteur 91:829-857, 1956.

11. 161 Dutrillaux B & Lejeune J. Sur une nouvelle technique d'analyse du caryo-type humain (A new method for analysis of human karyotypes).
C. Rend. Acad. Sci. 272:2638-2640, 1971.

12. 159 Lejeune J, Gauthier M & Turpin R. Les chromosomes humains en culture de tissus (Human chromosomes in tissue cultures).
C. Rend. Acad. Sci. 248:602-603, 1959.

13. 153 Drach P. Mue et cycle d'intermue chez les crustaces decapodes (Molting and the inter-molting cycle in decapod crustaceans).
Ann. Inst. Oceanogr. Monaco 19:103-391, 1939.

List of articles published in French journals that were cited more than 150 times in the inter-national literature during the period 1961-1975.

publish in English. But according to the results of a recent, informal ISI survey, only about 20% of French papers are published in non-French journals.

It is not linguistic imperialism that prevents English-speaking scientists from reading French articles. Indeed, many of them regularly read *La Recherche* partly in order to exercise their French. The typical American or British scientist greatly admires the French language. But while he may be content to struggle with his French on a holiday visit to France, he cannot afford this struggle in the research environment--although most *will* struggle through an important contribution. But he probably lacks the time to read all pertinent articles published in English, much less what is published in French, German, Russian, or Japanese. He also lacks the facility to scan a French contents page.

Although genuinely significant contributions will be cited no matter what language they are reported in, only the strongest motivation can cause the typical English-speaking scientist to read a French article which at first seems to be of casual interest. And yet this casual exposure is essential to the spread of ideas between disciplines. The insistence of French scientists to publish in French denies the world scientific community the opportunity to read their work casually.

At the very least, all French journals should require the publication of summaries or abstracts as well as contents pages in English. The use of English contents pages will undoubtedly cause more reprint requests; whether it causes more citations will depend on the quality and relevance of the contributions. Of a sample of 267 French-language journals covered by the *Science Citation Index* in 1974, 133 *did* contain a separate English contents page. More significant, 108 did *not*. Nineteen contained a mixed English-French contents page, and 7 used some English abstracts.

Comptes Rendus, to take just one example, should be published in an English edition. Recently, the editors reached a decision (in which the Institute for Scientific Information was instrumental) to begin using English contents pages. Whether this sensible decision will be reflected in the citation data remains to

be seen. However, I am surprised that no publisher has yet seized the opportunity to publish a cover-to-cover English translation of *Comptes Rendus*. I suspect that such a publication, which could be at least partially subsidized by foreign subscribers, might be well received. After all, if we can justify the cover-to-cover translation of many Russian journals, can't the same be done for the French? The joint publication of English and German editions of *Angewandte Chemie* is but one successful example of this type of international cooperation. But translation alone will not make up for poor quality.

The true international scientific language: English.

But it has become prohibitively expensive to maintain multilinguality. Only in the case of a few outstanding journals can we afford the luxury of cover-to-cover translations. Throughout the world, practically all prospective readers--even those who might *prefer* some other language--can immediately understand a scientific article published in English. French scientists must recognize that French is no longer *the* international language, and the adoption of English as the world language of science should be encouraged.

Today in France there is a confusion of priorities. No one denies that French scientists should have the opportunity to achieve proper international recognition. But that recognition is being sacrificed to the futile goal of preserving the French language by artificial means.

The French language will not decline because of French scientists publishing in English, Esperanto, or any other language. As long as French mothers and fathers continue to speak French to their children, French will continue to be spoken--even if their children grow up to become scientists. But in order to become contributing members of the international scientific community, French scientists cannot refuse to learn English. Neither France nor the French language will ever suffer for having encouraged the development of a strong cadre of internationally recognized bi-lingual scientists.

1. **Garfield E.** Citation indexing for studying science. *Nature* 277:669-71, 1970.
2. ------------. Journal citation studies. 23. French journals--what they cite and what cites them. *Current Contents*® No. 4, 26 January 1976, p. 5-10.
3. **Narin F & Carpenter M P.** National publication and citation comparisons. *J. Amer. Soc. Inform. Sci.* 26:80-93, 1975.
4. **Garfield E.** Citation analysis as a tool in journal evaluation. *Science* 178:471-79, 1972.

CURRENT COMMENTS

Le Nouveau Défi Américain. II.

//Number 16, April 18, 1977

Last week we presented in this space the English translation of my article, "Is French Science Too Provincial?", published originally in French in *La Recherche*. [1]

Now that the English-speaking scientific community has had a chance to examine the article, I will present some of the comments and criticisms of it by French scientists.

As I was in the process of writing the article, I did consider that I might become persona non grata in certain Francophile circles. But I never imagined that a former Prime Minister of France, Michel Debré--not to mention quite a few other distinguished Frenchmen--would make me the symbol of a new American challenge.

In his response to my article, Mr. Debré, who was Prime Minister from 1959 to 1962 and who now serves as a member of the National Assembly, claims that the current preeminence of the English language will not be eternal. Since he is a politician himself, it is not surprising that Mr. Debré views the question of language in political terms. In a reply to my article published in a subsequent issue of *La Recherche*, he says,

> It is not possible to separate the choice of scientific language from the political conceptualization one has of the future of one's own country....
> It would be a national drama with tremendous consequences to take away from French its character as a scientific language. Let's state matters as they are. If French ceases to be a scientific language, the French culture will be dealt a severe blow with the subsequent loss of a set of spiritual and moral values which, along with political and economic interests, assure the existence and permanence of the French nation. [2]

It seems that Mr. Debré has been carried away with his own argument. Does he really think that encouraging French scientists to publish in English threatens the "existence and permanence of the French nation?" But it seems that he is indeed serious, as he goes on.

> If we establish as a rule that the language of science is not in any case French, we willfully encourage an impoverishment in humanity which for a people is a detriment as serious as reduced birth rates, an impoverishment from which a people could not recover. [2]

As if the prospect of impoverishment is not gloomy enough, he warns of

> a nationalist revolt which could become, or rather will become, the
> natural attitude of young researchers if we follow Garfield. A knowledge
> of the English language, short of displacing other disciplines in our
> schools, is not within everyone's reach. To impose English is to close the
> door to scientific promotion on a number of good minds.[2]

This point is well taken, and it may indeed be necessary for English language
studies to displace some other disciplines in French schools, at least for those
students who anticipate a career in science. For such students, however, a
knowledge of English will prove quite valuable.

Mr. Debré concludes that, "The advantage of the forum by Garfield is its
function among others as a warning signal, for which we should thank him."[2] He
goes on to stress promotion and monetary support for French research and
publication.

In another letter to *La Recherche*, Jean-Marc Lévy-Leblond calls my article
"scurrilous." He points out that the Greek roots of the French language allow a
variety of linguistic nuances, concluding, "Let's carefully guard the privileged
opportunities that Greek and Latin offer us to develop words perfectly French and,
at the same time, totally comprehensible. We could not cut off these roots without
severing by the same stroke the branch on which we so comfortably sit."[3]

Still another letter came from Hubert Joly, Secretary General to the Conseil
International de la Langue Française. He says,

> First of all, I will admit to Garfield that French is no longer the inter-
> national language par excellence, and in fact it seems to me quite
> desirable that French researchers should publish the results of their work
> in several languages. The Conseil International de la Langue Française,
> on the other hand, vigorously protests the tendency of certain scientists to
> publish only in English, thus obliging French-speaking readers who were
> willing to finance the research with their taxes to assume an added
> expense or more work to secure a translation.[4]

As for my promotion of French-English bilingualism, Mr. Joly points out that
similar efforts should be made to have French scientists learn German, Russian,
Spanish, and other languages. In addition, Mr. Joly asserts that,

> one can only rejoice at knowing that scientific and technical French
> increases spontaneously each year by some 4,000 new words, not to
> mention borrowings from other languages. It is nice that French speaking
> countries can describe in French all the realities of the modern world,
> employing the work on terminology by the Conseil International and the
> monthly journal *La Clé des mots,* which locates, processes and translates

into English, German, Spanish and Russian as well as Italian and Dutch close to 2,000 new expressions each year.[4]

Still another correspondent to *La Recherche*, Professor C. Vidal of the University of Bordeaux, asserts that my article

> questions the existence of a civilization through the existence of the language which is the vehicle of its ideas.... If there is a question of quality with respect to certain French journals and if the statistics of ISI® bear this out, that is one thing. But to infer, as a result, that one should publish in English is definitely too much. Such a step must be denounced, especially since it would just add to the malaise already latent among French scientists.[5]

Professor Vidal goes on to assert that,

> French has been and still is a language perfectly adapted for the expression of scientific thought. There is no reason that it should be abandoned under the pretexts of productivity and efficiency, notions which are still disputable. If the Americans today, the Russians tomorrow and the Chinese the day after do not give proper recognition to French language publications, then it will be clearly regrettable. However, there are remedies other than that of complete abandonment advocated by E. Garfield.[5]

A more lengthy discussion was published in three different French journals,[6,7,8] by S. Bonfils, the editor of *Biologie et Gastroentérologie*, and J.J. Bernier, the editor of *Archives Françaises des Maladies de l'Appareil Digestif*, who claim that,

> Contrary to what others believe, it seems evident that continued dissemination of scientific works in French is indispensable if only for the following two practical reasons. One, it is easier to prepare manuscripts where the language employed during research corresponds to that of the paper published. Two, there is an important number of people, including colleagues, students, and followers of ideological movements, who have no desire to trouble themselves in reading an article written in a foreign language and who really resent this imposition especially by a French colleague.[6]

The authors of this paper present a practical, step-by-step guide for French authors:

1. French language publications should be included only in those journals with a constant and reliable readership. This would have the advantage of increasing the academic level of scientific journals with the subsequent attraction of more manuscripts.
2. For work in progress, the first publication considered as a prelimin-

ary report of results should be published in French and its references may be resumed systematically afterwards. In such a publication, an internationally acclaimed scientist should be presented as the first author to insure continuity of research at a high level.

3. With respect to a series of related papers, it would be a must to have at least one in French.

4. Whatever the language of publication may be, the bibliography of French papers relative to the subject matter should be as long as possible.

5. Those publications singular in their efforts to explore certain areas should be published in French provided there is a journal of a very high scientific caliber in the field concerned. In the same vein, one may suggest that techniques and general reviews should preferably be published in French, because they are almost always read regardless of the language of publication, for their convenience.[6]

French scientists certainly cannot be faulted for lack of interest in the language problem, which, as another correspondent points out, is not limited to the journal literature. Rémy Chauvin of René Descartes University points to the difficulty French scientists face when attending international scientific meetings which are conducted in English. Addressing himself to his French colleagues, he says,

It is not a matter of being able to read English fluently (we all can) or speaking it (no big problem), but you must know it perfectly and fluently in order to capture all the nuances of the discussion as in French. Most of us are not capable of doing so.

Our contributions to discussions are often lamentable, because we didn't fully understand. That, along with our accent, makes us pass for citizens of an underdeveloped country....

The solution? I don't have one on hand! I only know that the problem of communication at conventions has never undergone serious consideration; that Francophones have been the victims of a real cultural assault perpetrated by the English language (one should see all the Anglophones get up and leave the hall when a French speaker takes the floor); that the so-called international English language is rather strange in the mouth of a Japanese or certain Africans; and that their terribly harsh accent prevents communication from flowing....[9]

Mr. Chauvin's lament may cause us to feel a certain amount of embarrassment--the type of embarrassment elicited by unknowingly showing bad manners. Of course, most scientists do not mean to insult those who address scientific meetings in languages other than English. They simply do not want to waste their time becoming frustrated by their lack of comprehension. And it is positively uncivilized to denigrate a speaker because of his accent. However, I suspect that the language problem at meetings will prove even more difficult to solve than the language problem in print.

Mr. J. David, Professor of Biology at Claude Bernard University, is a pragmatist; he admits that he publishes more and more in English, but claims that he "gets no pleasure from it." In his letter to the editor of *La Recherche* he takes a cold, hard look at the publication behavior of the international scientific community, commenting,

> The morality of the scientific community is strict, at times ferocious; the acute "struggle for life" constantly persists. It is not a matter of obtaining a result and making a discovery. Authors must be recognized. Numerous examples exist of Anglo-Saxon scientists who, inspired by works in French, have more or less forgotten to indicate their sources.... One attempts to evaluate the productivity of a researcher according to the number and quality of his or her publications. We are asked to publish in "international" journals, to be recognized at an international level, etc. It is hardly possible to achieve this without publishing in English.[10]

Mr. David recognizes that economic facts--even more than national sentiment--determine the decisions of journal editors. He goes on,

> Unfortunately, foreigners, especially in Anglo-Saxon countries, tend more and more not to know our language. So in order to increase both readership and profitability of French journals, we have progressively come to the point of publishing in English.
>
> Is that to say French scientific culture is definitely condemned? Certainly not, as long as we continue to speak and teach French in laboratories and universities. But this situation itself is fragile; it requires protection, a favored status. If French science is abandoned directly to hard international competition, it will be using, before the end of the century, only the English language. If we wish to keep an important share for French and maintain privileged associations with French speaking countries (those in Africa, for example), we must be aided, particularly at the financial level.[10]

Finally, Gerard Lemaine of the Groupe d'Etudes et de Recherches sur la Science at the University of Paris has called my attention to an interesting article published in French in 1975. Lemaine remarks that the fact that I failed to mention this article in my own *La Recherche* piece "evidently confirms your results that English speaking people, i.e., Anglophones, do not read French language publications."[11]

The article itself, published in the French journal *Le Progrès Scientifique*, examines the diffusion of scientific results according to journal of publication, with the aid of the *Science Citation Index®* . The authors assert that,

Looking at the results obtained, the influence of the language of publication seems preponderant and a hasty conclusion could have lead us to the condemnation of the use of French as a scientific language, relative anyway to the criterion of diffusion.

However, their results clearly show that,

the use of the French language is not a handicap in multi-lingual international journals....

It seems, therefore, that if journals published entirely in French (and *a fortiori* in Lithuanian or Japanese) discourage the foreign reader, articles written in French in multi-lingual journals, which obviously are dominated by the English language, are diffused just as well as if they appeared in English language publications.... If one wants to reconcile the objective of conserving for the French language its international character as a scientific language with that of assuring an optimal diffusion of knowledge, it would be desirable, therefore, to recommend to French researchers not to publish in French except in multi-lingual journals with an international audience.[12]

In addition to these varied responses to my article a full-page advertisement (opposite) appeared on the back cover of the January 1977 issue of *La Recherche*.[13]

In reply to present and future critics, I categorically deny that I am anti-French, or, for that matter, pro-English. In any case, these correspondents seem to ignore my basic message. International science has always been competitive. But in the era of big science it is especially so. To compete, one must use every available resource.

If French taxpayers support French "competition" in international science, isn't it against their interests if French scientists are required to publish exclusively in the French language? Why should French scientists resent bilingualism any more than do Dutch, Scandinavian, or German scientists? However, if the French taxpayers can afford the additional expense, then by all means they should subsidize the publication of their scientists' work in two or more languages simultaneously. In fact, in my article I suggest this very possibility for the best known French journal, *Comptes Rendus*.

The best way to guarantee the improvement of the international impact of French research is to improve the quality of French research itself. The best French research is now published in English. If the authors of these articles, the most recognized of French scientists, were to publish exclusively in French, their international status gradually would be eroded. In some cases, English-speaking scientists would be forced to obtain translations of these French articles, or they would have to brush up on their French. But as I stressed in my article, the effect of serendipitous stimulation through the *casual* reading of these articles would be greatly reduced. It's true that the translated titles of these papers would be seen in *Current Contents®* and elsewhere. But once the French reprints are received and placed in the stack of dozens of other reprints, will they be read or cited?

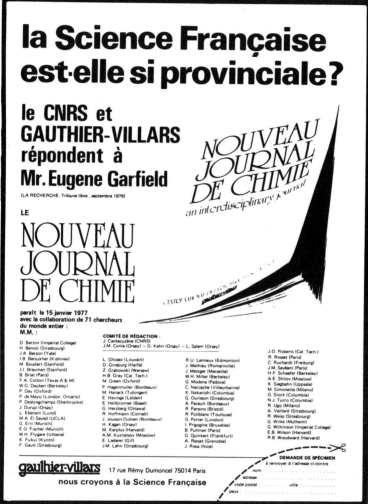

I applaud the efforts of French terminological bureaus to keep up with world-wide changes in scientific nomenclature, just as I applaud efforts to improve the overall quality of French journal articles and to improve French documentation. However, such goals can be accomplished, among other things, by improving the impoverished and deteriorated condition of French libraries. To cite just one example, among all nations France is one of the poorest users of the *Science Citation Index*.[1]

It is unfortunate that my article was interpreted by some as a denigration of French science. I tried to carefully distinguish between French research reported in French journals and that published outside France.

The ultimate solution to the provinciality of French science lies in the willingness of the French people and government to support research and graduate education on a scale that produces significant science. But even when that support is optimum it will be foolish to prevent proper recognition by archaic linguistic policies that serve only to raise the emotions.

REFERENCES

1. **Garfield E.** La science française est-elle trop provinciale? (Is French science too provincial?) *La Recherche* 7(10):757-60, September 1976.
2. **Debré M.** La langue française et la science universelle. (The French language and universal science.) *La Recherche* 7(22):956, November 1976.
3. **Lévy-Leblond J M.** Pour l'amour du grec. (For the love of Greek.) *La Recherche* 7(72):958, 1002, November 1976.
4. **Joly H.** Le français langue de communication de 230 millions de personnes. (French, the language of communication of 230 million people.) *La Recherche* 7(72):957-58, November 1976.
5. **Vidal C.** Provinciale aujourd'hui; colonisée demain? (Province today; colony tomorrow?) *La Recherche* 7(72):958, November 1976.
6. **Bonfils S & Bernier J J.** Remarques concernant l'utilisation du français comme langue de publication scientifique. (Remarks concerning the use of French as a language for scientific publications.) *Biologie et Gastro-Entérologie* 9(3):181-83, July-August 1976.
7. **Bernier J J & Bonfils S.** L'utilisation du français comme langue de publication scientifique (The use of French as a language for scientific publications.) *Archives Françaises de Pédiatrie* 33(10):1004-06, December 1976.
8. **Bonfils S & Bernier J J.** Du bon usage des publications en français. (The correct usage of French language publications.) *La Recherche* 7(72):1002, November 1976 .
9. **Chauvin R.** Francophonie et anglophonie. (The French speaking world and the English speaking world.) *La Recherche* 8(75):192-93, February 1977.
10. **David J.** Une maîtrise de sciences et techniques biomédicales à Marseille. (Graduate program in biomedical science and technology in Marseilles.) *La Recherche* 8(75):192, February 1977.
11. **Lemain G.** Personal communication, 6 September 1975.
12. **Chabbal R & Feneuille S.** La diffusion des résultats scientifiques suivant la revue de publication. (Dissemination of scientific results according to the publishing journal.) *Le Progrès Scientifique* 178:3-15, 1975.
13. *La Recherche* 8(74):107, 19 January 1977.

CURRENT COMMENTS

Citation Analysis and
The Anti-Vivisection Controversy

Number 17, April 25, 1977

Recently I was involuntarily drawn into the anti-vivisection controversy which has been raging at the American Museum of Natural History in New York City--as well as in the pages of many newspapers, magazines, and journals. The reason for my involvement was the use of *Science Citation Index®* data by a reporter to determine the scientific value of an individual's body of research.

The individual is Dr. Lester R. Aronson, Chairman and Curator of the Museum's Department of Animal Behavior since 1956 and Adjunct Professor of Biology at the City University of New York and New York University. His research involves removing glands, nerves, and brain tissue from domestic cats in order to facilitate study of animal sexual behavior.

The intense public interest in this study probably has two causes. First, the study involves cats, one of the most familiar and popular domestic species. Even those who don't own a cat invariably know someone who does. The mere thought that these friendly, furry pets are being blinded, deafened, or killed is enough to incite the anger of many sincere people.

The other factor which arouses the public's interest is sex. If the study were aimed at curing cancer, or fighting some horrible children's disease, or even at finding a cure for the common cold, it would be difficult to arouse the indignation of so many. But apparently there are many people for whom the study of sex in humans--no less in cats-- seems frivolous, unnecessary, and perhaps even a bit perverse.

The controversy began about a year ago, when a high school teacher of English named Henry Spira used the Freedom of Information Act to obtain copies of Aronson's grant application to the National Institutes of Health. The application contained much apparently routine detail which, in the hands of anti-vivisectionists, was sensationalized and widely publicized.

Picketers arrived in front of the American Museum of Natural History carrying placards with such messages as ''Castrate the Scientists,'' ''Curiosity Kills the Cats,'' and ''Close the Torture Laboratories.'' Headlines in the

National Enquirer declared, "Cats Are Tortured in Vicious Experiments at Famous N.Y.C. Museum," and the New York publication *Our Town* headlined an article, "Congress Pays for Sex Sadism at Museum." In one article, Spira claims that the experiments are merely "a way of getting government grants in exchange for animals' agony and blood." Demonstrations ensued, and accounts of the furor were carried over the national media. The museum received hate mail and bomb threats, and the lives of the researchers themselves were threatened.

In fact, according to Aronson's grant application, the researchers did intend to blind the cats, deafen them, sever nerves in the penis, cut off their testicles, destroy their sense of smell, and remove parts of their brains. All of these operations were meant to help investigate the sites of action of gonadal hormones, the role of sensory stimuli, and the role of olfaction and limbic structures in the cat's sex behavior.[1]

Aronson points out that his work is valuable because of the similarity of the cat's skull shape and nervous system to that of humans. For example, he has found that making lesions in the cat's amygdala, a part of the brain which has been associated with hypersexuality in humans, does not cause hypersexuality in cats but instead causes them to become less selective in their sexual behavior. A cat so treated may try to mount a stuffed panda or a block of wood the same size as a cat.

In his article, *Science* staff writer Nicholas Wade discusses each of the three contentions of the animal rights groups: that the cats are inhumanely treated, that the experiments are cruel, and that the experiments are unlikely to lead to any significant new knowledge.[2] The first charge Wade finds groundless since it is obvious that the experimenters were using proper, humane laboratory procedures. As for the imputed cruelty, he points out that an experimental psychologist's idea of cruelty may differ greatly from that of a pet-owner. It is in his reply to the third charge--that Aronson's cat experiments can not be expected to contribute new scientific knowledge--that Wade uses evidence based on ISI® 's *Science Citation Index*.

Although Wade is an esteemed and thorough reporter who has done excellent work--such as his report on citation analysis in 1975[3]--in this case his analysis leaves much to be desired. It is unfortunate that Wade did not consult someone familiar with citation-analysis techniques. Would he trust his own judgement to take readings from a mass-spec or an EEG?

As presumable evidence for the lack of scientific merit of Aronson's work, Wade performed his own citation analysis of Aronson's publications. He found that, "Of the 21 articles that Aronson and his colleagues have published on the cat study since 1962, 14 have never been cited in the scientific literature between 1965, when the

Science Citation Index starts, and March 1976. Because of the short citation half-life of scientific papers, it is unlikely that they ever will be cited. The seven other papers have an average 5.6 citations each over the same 11-year period."[2] It is noteworthy that Mr. Wade's assumption that the *Science Citation Index* began in 1965 is incorrect. In fact, the *SCI®* was first published in 1961; however, the first *Science Citation Index Five-Year Cumulation* covers the years 1965-1969.

I have repeatedly stated that a high citation rate probably indicates the importance or at least the utility of a contribution. But I have also repeated that we simply don't know enough about the meaning of infrequent citation. As Aronson and his associate, Madeline L. Cooper, assert in a reply to Wade's article, the *SCI* "can only serve as a valid criterion if its limitations are recognized and it is used properly."[4] Indeed, even when it *is* used properly there are some who question its validity.

In this case, Wade has failed to consider several essential matters. For one thing, he did not consider the possibility that Aronson's work may be "premature." I have often mentioned the problem of identifying "premature science."[5] This phrase is used to describe scientific advances which are ahead of their time; the classic example being the case of Gregor Mendel.

But how can we determine whether one of our contemporaries--in this case Dr. Aronson--is engaged in "premature" research? Approximately 25% of the papers published in scientific journals are never cited at all! For some low-impact journals the percentage is even higher. And Aronson's work is certainly far from uncited. Which among these papers are premature?

I am confident that the number of truly "premature" papers is small--but certainly not zero. But from such circumstantial evidence it is impossible to determine whether in fact Aronson's research is or is not premature.

Moreover, some research is "dormant," having its greatest impact years after its initial publication. Sometimes this is due simply to the small number of people working in a field. Thus, in some branches of mathematics it takes much longer for important work to make its impact than in, say, biochemistry. The same is true in some areas of descriptive biology.

This does not mean that research in biochemistry cannot also be "dormant," although the reason for this often escapes people. While there will be many more citations *from* biochemistry papers than from mathematics papers this year, it is also true that the population of biochemistry papers that can be cited is much larger than that of mathematics papers. The most critical factor in citation impact is the average number of references cited per paper. Since math papers cite 8 papers on average, while biochemistry papers cite about 20, it is to be expected that biochemistry papers generally have greater impacts than math papers.

Also, the term "field" can be deceiving. Each of us works in what we define as our own scientific "field." Some "fields" are more closely related than others. Maybe Aronson, like Mendel, happened to be working in a field where few others worked. We know that studies of animal behavior have long been artificially separated from studies of human behavior. The acceptance and recognition of ethology as a legitimate field with implications for human behavior is very recent; it is only a few years since Konrad Lorenz received the Nobel Prize. Like researchers in so many other fields, perhaps the animal behaviorists have been working in such tight compartments that they were not apt to cite one another. Maybe Aronson didn't do a good enough job of conveying his ideas to his peers in other "fields."

If Aronson's critics fail to provide convincing evidence, so do his defenders. Ms. Ann Breen, manager of the museum's Department of Development and Public Affairs, has asserted in Aronson's defense that, "The numerous and invariably favorable reports over the years is our best assurance that Dr. Aronson's research is not only important to the Museum's scientific program, but also makes an important contribution to our nation's scientific endeavor."[6] But Ms. Breen does not document the "favorable reports," nor does she explain why Aronson's work might be important to peers but not significant enough to be regularly cited.

In Wade's article, Aronson defends his record by claiming that his work on cats (which takes only about a third of his time, the rest of which is devoted to studies of fish and other animals) may have received relatively few citations because few researchers are doing this type of work. "Most of the research on reproduction is in rats and the rat people are very parochial in that they only read the rat literature and only cite rat studies, so very frequently our papers are not cited," Aronson told Wade.[2]

In his grant application, too, Aronson asserts that some problems in human sexual behavior "can only be investigated by experimentation in animals." However, he says, "The present emphasis and dependence on the physiology of sexual behavior in rodents surely presents a rather specialized and unrepresentative picture as the relatively few reports on cats, dogs, monkeys and other mammals have clearly shown." He further claims that "with the exception of our laboratory, all sex behavior research is conducted on rodents or primates with only occasional papers on other species from various laboratories."[1]

It is interesting that even before the Aronson controversy, Frank A. Beach of the University of California at Berkeley, a well-known experimental psychologist, was calling attention to the widespread use of rats among experimental psychologists. My colleague Robert K. Merton remarks in a footnote in his book *Sociological Ambivalence*, "As Frank Beach has reported...for a time more than half of American experimental psychologists had focused on one species, the rat, as their experimental organism."[7] This supports Aronson's claim that many experimenters work with only one species--the rat--and confine their interest largely to that species.

If the cat people and the rat people live in two separate worlds, then it would seem that they deserve their respective oblivion. Why would such an apparently illogical separatism exist in sexual studies?

Admittedly, determining the scientific worth of any individual's research by means of citation analysis is at best a tricky business. One must be cognizant not only of the data's implications, but also of its limitations.

First, there is the problem of defining the field in which the researcher works. The definition of fields is a fundamental problem for information scientists. But classification is our business. In order to define the field in which Aronson works I would first examine the papers that he cites. I would then examine the other papers that cited these papers as well as those that cited Aronson's work. From this I could develop clusters of papers that would define the field.

Once the field was defined, I could readily determine who in it had the greatest impact--and could test this tentative finding by asking workers in the field to name the most important workers. Judging from previous work of this kind, such informal peer review would confirm the results of the citation study.

In order to check Aronson's claim of species discrimination, I would construct similar citation clusters for other species, and then look for points of cross-over. If I found evidence of species discrimination, I would want to know if it is peculiar to Aronson or if it affects all those in this field. This mapping exercise would reveal whether he has truly been a lone wolf. Even if not, we would then have a sound basis for comparing the citation impacts within the field.

In a letter to *Science,*[8] B.D. Sachs of the University of Connecticut adds an ironic footnote to the controversy. "Ten years ago," he asserts, "*Science* rejected, without review, a report by Aronson and Cooper because the editor felt that the sex research on cats, as described in that report, would offend the sensibilities of some *Science* readers, including anti-vivisectionists. Ultimately, *Science* had the report reviewed and published a modified version (8 Apr. 1966, p. 226) with no adverse repercussions." *Science*'s publication of this letter without rebuttal by its editors suggests that the episode it describes actually occurred. If so, it is a sad commentary on the editorial practices of *Science*--at least in 1966. Surely it is ironic that a report rejected as "offensive" should a decade later become the subject of an investigative article in the journal which rejected the original report.

In their letter to *Science*,[4] Aronson and Cooper offer their own reply to Wade's citation study. "Of the 21 publications to which Wade refers," they write, "the seven full reports, each representing 3 to 5 years of continuous experimental observation, have all been cited except for one which was published in Moscow. In addition, two doctoral dissertations by former students have been cited as such, and later as journal publications. The remaining 14 publications were abstracts of reports given at scientific meetings while the work was in progress, and even a goodly number of these have been cited."

This whole unfortunate episode has caused me to reflect on some of the criticism levelled at the misuse of citation analysis, both by myself and others. I have written a general review of these criticisms which I hope will be accepted for publication in a journal of wide circulation, since it is addressed mainly to those who use citation analysis only occasionally. Perhaps that article will be reprinted in this space in the future. In addition, we plan to carry out and publish in this space the type of citation analysis of Aronson's studies outlined here.

It is increasingly clear to me that citation analysis, like any other scientific advance--whether nuclear physics, the laser, or recombinant DNA--has the potential for harm as well as for benefit. As always, the results depend upon the way the new tool is used.

1. **Aronson L R.** Behavioral effects of selected denervation. (Grant application to US Department of Health, Education and Welfare, Public Health Service) 2 January 1974.
2. **Wade N.** Animal rights: NIH cat sex study brings grief to New York museum. *Science* 194(4261):162-7, 8 October 1976.
3. **Wade N.** Citation analysis: a new tool for science administrators. *Science* 188(4187):429-32, 2 May 1975.
4. **Aronson L R & Cooper M L.** Animal welfare and scientific research. *Science* 194(4267):784-5, 19 November 1976.
5. **Lederberg J & Zuckerman H.** Discontinuities in science; the case of bacterial recombination. *Daedalus* 1977 (in press).
6. **Anonymous.** Animal rights groups demonstrate against cat research. *National Society for Medical Research Bulletin* 27:1-2, September 1976.
7. **Merton R K.** *Sociological ambivalence and other essays.* New York, The Free Press, 1976.
8. **Sachs B D.** Animal welfare and scientific research. *Science* 194(4267):786, 19 November 1976.

The ISI Grant Program

Number 18, May 2, 1977

Readers often tell me that their libraries cannot afford the *Science Citation Index®* (*SCI®*) or *Social Sciences Citation Index™* (*SSCI™*). It is surprising how often such persons are not aware that their library may be eligible for an ISI® grant. Although we have advertised this program since 1969 many people still do not know it exists. So that all *Current Contents®* readers--including those who never read the ads--can take advantage of this program, a brief recap is provided below.

Its purpose is to make the *Science Citation Index* and *Social Sciences Citation Index* available to libraries that would not have sufficient funds to purchase them at the normal price. We assume that every scientific and technical library—no matter how small or poor—wants and needs the best reference tools to support its organization's research or educational programs. For those that qualify, the ISI Grant Program provides financial help from ISI equivalent to 50% of the regular purchase price of either index. In this way it helps small libraries to function as effectively as large ones.

Most likely to qualify for grants are those libraries with severely limited acquisitions budgets, professional staffs, and journal holdings. Libraries at schools awarding doctoral degrees do not qualify. Neither do most libraries at schools awarding more than 50 master's degrees per year. However, libraries at all educational institutions which do not award graduate degrees *are* eligible for ISI grants, as are most libraries at schools and colleges of mining, veterinary science, dentistry, nursing, pharmacy, osteopathy, chiropractic, and podiatry.

Other eligible libraries include certain municipal, state, and public libraries, libraries at new medical schools, libraries at satellite schools and colleges, libraries at polytechnics and colleges of education, and the libraries of small, non-academic research organizations.

The Grant Program is also designed to help the libraries of developing nations to acquire the *SCI* and *SSCI*. Libraries in such countries as Bolivia, Colombia, El Salvador, India, Nigeria, the Philippines, Tanzania, and Thailand have already taken advantage of ISI Grants.

Even libraries which do not qualify for ISI grants under the above criteria are still eligible for second-copy grants. Many educational institutions have more than one library located on the same campus. The main library may subscribe to the *SCI* or *SSCI* at the full rate. One or more departmental or branch libraries can obtain the indexes through the grant program. For example, a grant may help place the *SSCI* in a psychology or sociology library--or the *SCI* in a chemistry or physics library. Also, libraries at hospitals affiliated with medical schools subscribing at the full rate are eligible for ISI grants.

It is surprisingly easy to find out if your library is eligible for--and to obtain--an ISI grant. Simply write to ISI's Grant Administrator (at the address given below), who will immediately send you an application form and related information, including a list of organizations which now receive ISI grants.

The application form itself is brief and uncomplicated. It allows you two options: you may indicate which years--past, present, or future--of the indexes are desired and automatically place your order if the grant is approved, or you may determine your eligibility for an ISI grant for future use. Whichever option you take, the application is quickly reviewed by our grant committee. Most of our grant decisions are made within two weeks after the receipt of a properly completed application form.

Those readers who suffer from chronic skepticism might suspect that the ISI Grant Program is nothing more than a cleverly designed scheme to increase the distribution of the *SCI* and *SSCI*. Of course, they are right!

Unfortunately, lowering the price of a product does not necessarily increase its distribution or appreciation among consumers. If by waving a magic wand I could lower the price of ISI's indexes by a third and, at the same time, triple the number of subscribers, I would gladly do it. There are precedents for charging according to a library's size, budget, amount of use, etc. And in the on-line business the user generally pays according to use. The ISI Grant Program allows us to increase distribution and use without sacrificing the high quality and comprehensiveness of our indexes.

While we do not pretend to be motivated wholly by philanthropic impulses, this year we expect to award grants totalling more than $500,000 to help almost 400 libraries improve their reference services. If your library meets the criteria mentioned above, I urge you to write to the Grant Administrator, Institute for Scientific Information® , 325 Chestnut Street, Phila., Pa. 19106, U.S.A.

CURRENT COMMENTS

Shopping for a Surgeon

Number 19, May 9, 1977

The awakening of the consumer movement in recent years has aroused interest in the quality of a variety of goods and services. Along with automobile safety, food additives, bio-degradable detergents, and the dangers of environmental carcinogens, the American public is beginning to devote its attention to the quality of medical care, especially in hospitals. The recent sharp rise in medical malpractice suits has sharply focused the interest of doctors on the same area of concern.

Unfortunately, the medical profession itself does not maintain a statistical record of the vast number of operations undergone in this country. Individual hospitals keep registries of their surgical activities, but no one gathers and disseminates this information on a national basis. Clear information with which to evaluate the performance of doctors and hospitals is scarce. However, a few researchers have studied and reported on the surgical practices of American doctors.

For example, last year a Harvard University report on surgical practices found that "far too many physicians perform surgical operations and that work loads of surgical specialists are modest."[1] In this report, Dr. Rita J. Nickerson and her colleagues suggested that the total number of operations reviewed for this study "could have been handled by a substantially smaller cadre of busier surgical specialists." They also found that some doctors who operate, including some surgical specialists, fail to perform enough operations to maintain a high level of skill. General practitioners with no special training in surgery were sometimes found to be performing such operations as appendectomies and hysterectomies.

Dr. Francis Moore, a surgeon at Harvard Medical School, called the Nickerson study "a landmark in the study of delivery of surgical care in the United States."[2] He commented that "there are too many people carrying out surgical operations in America, even though the highly trained and Board-certified surgeons could evidently carry the load easily and safely. This finding means that the current system for 'credentialing'--that is, identifying in each hospital the persons who should have the privilege and responsibility of major surgery--is much looser in the US than in comparable westernized countries. General practitioners do many operations, largely tonsillectomy, uterine dilation and curettage, and obstetric delivery." Moore also notes that "where there is a larger proportion of surgeons in the population...more operations are performed but fewer by each surgeon, and the specter of 'supplier-induced demand' is raised."

But the view that some physicians exploit their patients would seem to be contradicted in a 1974 article by Dr. John Bunker and Dr. Byron Brown, Jr. of the Stanford University School of Medicine.[3] They examined the utilization of surgical services by several West Coast professional groups including physicians, lawyers, ministers, and businessmen. Surprisingly, they found that physicians and their spouses had quite high surgical rates. "Physicians' wives tended to have more operations than wives of the other three professional groups; they underwent appendectomy and thyroidectomy significantly more often than lawyers' wives, cholecystectomy significantly more often than lawyers' and businessmen's wives, and hysterectomy significantly more often than businessmen's wives." What these results indicate, contend the authors, is that "the alleged overuse of surgical services" is not due to "a lack of consumer knowledge." On the contrary, since they assume that physicians and their spouses would be aware of the best medical procedures, the authors suggest that "as the public becomes more fully informed, the demand for surgical services will increase."

An article which appeared in *Medical World News* entitled "How Much Unnecessary Surgery?"[4] also raises some interesting points. According to the article, Harvard professor of community health Charles E. Lewis analyzed Blue Cross surgical records for 1965, finding extreme variations of surgical rates according to demographic region. Dr. Lewis sought an explanation for these variations and discovered that "those regions with the highest incidence of operations also had the higher proportion of physicians (both GP's and surgeons) who did surgery and the highest proportion of hospital beds. Dr. Lewis speculated that he might have stumbled onto a medical variation of Parkinson's Law: 'Patient admissions for surgery expand to fill beds, operating suites, and surgeons' time'."

This "law" is disputed by a Philadelphia surgeon, Dr. James Mullen, of the Hospital of the University of Pennsylvania. Mullen questions whether a high regional rate of surgery necessarily indicates lower quality of care. "A high surgical rate may mean good surgical care,"[5] he claims. Mullen points out that in England patients must often wait long periods of time to have elective surgery performed. This waiting list results in a lower surgical rate, he says, and represents a lower quality of care for the patient who is forced to wait for a needed operation.

Along with Mullen, Dr. Robert Tyson, Director of Surgery at Temple University Hospital in Philadelphia, examines the criteria which determine "quality" in surgical care.[6] It is inaccurate, he asserts, to label most surgery performed by general surgeons as either unnecessary or incompetent. General surgeons *are* surgical specialists, he says. Besides assuming the primary responsibility for teaching surgery in medical schools, general surgeons actually form the foundation of surgery. They may be even more important than the specialist. "More people need general surgeons than, say, plastic surgeons, or neurologists or urologists." Mullen adds that a general surgeon may require 5 years of training after internship, whereas some specialists, such as urologists, may require only 3 years.

Compared to specialists, general surgeons may be able to give more personal attention to the patient before and after surgery. Dr. Franz Ingelfinger, editor of *The New England Journal of Medicine*, comments that, "The care in a community hospital from everyone may be much more personal and hence much more life-sustaining than in a huge factory center of surgery. Everything counts in the outcome, not just how adroitly the surgeon wields a knife and the needle. I personally know some excellent community general surgeons who are perfectly competent to perform the type of operation most commonly carried out, even though I would not ask them to do major gastric resections, total colectomies or any major cancer operations."[7]

I myself am wary of operations performed in scientific institutes where various surgical techniques are tested under "trial" conditions. But Dr. Ingelfinger assures me that "the more scientific the institution the more likely surgeons are apt to use one or two highly specific techniques to make appropriate comparisons, the controlled trial gradually becoming practiced by surgeons as well as internists. The more 'scientific' the institution, the less chaotic ad hoc trials of all sorts of procedures.''

So it seems that it is difficult, if not impossible, to objectively determine a surgeon's ability. Doctors themselves disagree on the criteria necessary to make a choice. Dr. Mullen says that he usually receives two or three phone calls each day from people asking his opinion about various local surgeons. Their final choice of a surgeon is based largely on informal, subjective peer evaluation.

One source of statistics which people might find helpful in selecting a surgeon is not available to most of them. It is the quarterly publication *Hospital Record Study*, which contains diagnostic and surgical data on about 2,200 hospitals in the US and Canada. Since a single subscription is priced at several thousand dollars, its distribution is limited. In fact, the total subscription list, which numbers less than 25, is composed primarily of drug companies and medical and surgical manufacturers who study hospital trends with a keen eye toward new, marketable products. The *Hospital Record Study* is published jointly by the Commission on Professional and Hospital Activities of Ann Arbor, Michigan, and International Market Systems of America of Ambler, Pennsylvania.

We called these organizations to obtain a sample of their data. The Commission on Professional and Hospital Activities informed us that the information is available only to subscribers. As a matter of policy, information can be released only with the consent of the individual hospital involved. At International Market Systems of America we received a similar explanation.

However, ISI® was able to obtain a report published by the National Center for Health Statistics, entitled ''Surgical Operations in Short-Stay Hospitals.''[8] It is based on data collected by the Hospital Discharge Survey and gives estimates of the surgical operations and procedures performed during 1971 in non-Federal short-stay hospitals. Unfortunately, the data are not very current, and not specific enough to guide a consumer to a particular hospital where the surgeons have superior records for success.

In light of some of the above findings, it seems clear that those who ''shop'' for a surgeon are well advised. ''Shopping'' does not necessarily mean searching for the cheapest surgeon. As in other types of shopping, the prudent consumer considers both quality and cost.

One wonders if the newly proposed peer review system will give prospective patients a chance to examine physicians' track records. In an editorial last year the president of the *Illinois Medical Journal*, Joseph H. Skom, discussed the potential merits of the peer review system.[9] He comments that it would be effective not only in weeding out "the few charlatans and quacks in our profession," but would also enhance continuing medical education programs. Dr. Mullen, however, thinks that even if the results of the peer review system were made public, its effectiveness would not be assured. The hospitals which earnestly attempted to present accurate records, he contends, would be compared to other hospitals which might not be so eager to present self-deprecating facts.

Unfortunately, reliable information on the quality of medical care in the U.S. is sadly lacking. The available information is often contradictory. The only comprehensive data compiled on a national basis are intended solely for the use of the pharmaceutical industry. By limiting its distribution, the firms which compile and publish this data may be missing an opportunity. However, if the information is not made available to the public by these private firms, then the National Center for Health Statistics should be encouraged to do so.

Until reliable, comprehensive information on the performance of doctors and hospitals comes along, one should always seek second and third professional opinions concerning the necessity of major surgery. The life you save may be your own.

REFERENCES

1. **Nickerson R J, Colton T, Peterson O L, Bloom B S & Hauck W W.** Doctors who perform operations. A study on in-hospital surgery in four diverse geographic areas. *New England Journal of Medicine* 295:921-26, 21 October 1976.

2. **Moore F D.** Contemporary American surgery: hard data at last. *New England Journal of Medicine* 295:953-54, 21 October 1976.

3. **Bunker J P & Brown B W.** The physician-patient as an informed consumer of surgical services. *New England Journal of Medicine* 290:1051-55, 9 May 1974.

4. **Frederick L.** How much unnecessary surgery? *Medical World News* 3 May 1976, p. 50-65.

5. **Mullen J.** Personal communication, 7 April 1977.

6. **Tyson R.** Personal communication, 7 April 1977.

7. **Ingelfinger F J.** Personal communication, 21 March 1977.

8. **Blanken G E.** *Surgical operations in short-stay hospitals, United States, 1971.* Rockville, Maryland: Department of Health, Education & Welfare. Publication No. (HRH) 75-1769, November 1974.

9. **Skom J H.** Peer review. *Illinois Medical Journal* 149:548, June 1976.

CURRENT COMMENTS

Confessions of a Cab Driver

Number 20, May 16, 1977

Travelling by taxi in the U.S. must be extremely confusing for the foreign traveller. The typical experience for the foreigner is first to arrive in New York City, where taxis charge on the basis of time and distance. Then, after a train ride to Washington, the traveller finds a completely different system--this one based on arbitrary "zones"--that even the natives can't understand. A small computer might help you figure out the correct fare-- *if* you could read the arcane city "map" affixed to the back of the driver's seat in each cab.

I have long been a heavy user of taxicabs both in America and abroad. At one time I used cabs so extensively in Philadelphia that I became familiar with many of the drivers and some of the management. The Yellow Cab Company even presented me with a doorman's cab whistle.

But my interest in cabs is not only as a user. As a student at Columbia University in New York I helped support myself and my family by moonlighting as a cab driver on nights, weekends, and holidays. I could fill many pages of *Current Contents*® with stories from those days, but I'll limit this particular ego-trip to telling only a few.

Since I often brought textbooks and other reading matter with me on the job, my fellow hackies referred to me as "The Professor." In spite of this dubious distinction, I was welcomed into the "invisible college" of cab drivers located at the Horn & Hardart Automat Cafeteria at 57th Street & 7th Avenue. Seminars were usually held at 3:00 A.M. to discuss such burning topics as the 5th race at Hialeah, Babe Ruth's 1924 batting average,[1] or the up-coming All-Star football game. In those days I was not discussing how to forecast Nobel Prize winners.

The cab companies usually treated drivers like dirt. Thirty years later, the industry's labor practices are only slightly improved. As a part-time driver, one never knew from day to day whether work would be available. Like the stevedores on the New York docks as shown in the movie *On the Waterfront*, cab drivers reported to an evening "shape-up." Cabs would be doled out to part-timers according to the whims of the dispatcher. This frequently involved kickbacks or bribes, at least until one gained steady employment--and acquired a reputation as a hustler. This meant, in those days, that you turned in enough cash to please the boss. Toward the end of a slow shift, some drivers would turn on the meter in their empty cabs just to increase the amount they turned in, in order to placate the dispatcher. As a consequence, the income from tips was even more significant than passengers could ever realize.

Recently I saw Martin Scorcese's film *Taxi Driver*. You can imagine my surprise at the coincidence when Robert deNiro drove his cab into the very same garage that I had driven into on many a wintry night back in the late forties.

During a blizzard on one of those nights I stopped my cab at the sight of a woman desperately waving at me. When she entered the cab I realized she was having an asthmatic attack and could hardly breathe. Her companion asked me to rush her to Harlem Hospital. So we dashed off down the street. My cab was one of these old pre-war Checkers that had survived World War II. Most of these cabs had exceeded one million miles of use.

As I turned a corner my Checker skidded on the ice and slammed into a parked garbage truck. No one was hurt, but the cab's fender was scratched and dented. Since my passenger was near collapse I decided not to stop and quickly drove on to the hospital's emergency entrance.

When I returned to the garage that night the dispatcher noticed the dent and I was told to file an accident report. I explained why I didn't stop to take the license number of the truck. I was told that it didn't matter if the passenger died--I should have taken the license number of the other vehicle. Someone had to pay for the damage. It didn't take long for them to decide just who that "someone" would be. And I was laid off for a week as a lesson.

I've never quite understood why the taxi industry in the U.S. has re-mained so archaic. The Yellow Cab Company chain is a small fraction of what could constitute a national system, and we need one. There ought to be federal standards of safety, courtesy, and comfort, if not uniformity of prices and service.

About fifteen years ago I became conscious of the unfortunate lack of taxi service in many rural and suburban communities. At that time I was living in a town where the local commuter railroad was about a 15 minute walk downhill and 30 going up. To this day, it is impossible for anyone, including aged shoppers, to reach the town center by public transportation. This means older people, many of whom cannot afford their own autos, are almost totally dependent on others. Most suburbs and outlying towns could certainly benefit from a local taxi service. What I have in mind is a "shuttle" taxi service of the type common in many countries I have visited, including Puerto Rico, Mexico, and Israel.

One interesting idea was tried in the London suburb of Hampstead Garden, where a dial-a-bus service was put into operation. To summon the dial-a-bus, travellers phoned a control room and a small bus was dispatched to their door. Unfortunately, the system was curtailed after a year of experimental operations because it lost money.[2] The same kind of system was adopted in San Jose, California, but it, too, met an early end--because it was *too* successful. With its fare of only 25 cents it attracted so many passengers that there was a shortage of busses. Instead of a short wait for a bus, passengers often had to wait several hours.

The sorry state of the taxicab industry in the U.S. is part of the overall failure of mass transportation in American cities. As the use of railroads declined, Americans acquired even more automobiles. Besides causing traffic congestion and pollution, the ubiquitous American car has just about displaced the subway, the bus, and the taxicab as modes of transportation within and around our cities.

Although I don't know the exact figures involved, I suspect that an urban transportation system based on taxicabs and jitney-like small buses might be vastly more efficient than the present chaos of automobiles. Such a system might be worthwhile if it could just reduce the use of private automobiles containing only one person. Reducing the use of large buses, which are particularly inefficient during off-hours, would also be a bonus.

The system ought to allow for several classes of taxi service--anything from a Rolls to a VW. It is ironic that in the U.S.A. cabs are generally so low in quality. In Europe, driver comfort is a primary consideration--hence the use of many luxury cars as taxicabs.

Since operating an automobile is a skill known to most unemployed Americans, we should consider using such persons--as well as senior citizens and young adults who need part-time work--in the capacity of cab and jitney drivers. This kind of "welfare" might provide thousands of jobs while helping to solve the mass transportation problem.

In fact, the city of Los Angeles is now trying something very similar to this proposal.[3] As soon as a new ordinance goes into effect next month, almost anyone will be able to turn his private car into a taxi. What you need to become a taxi operator is the following: a taxi meter, a two-way radio, insurance, membership in one of several radio-dispatching associations, and a $250 license from the city of Los Angeles. Under the new ordinance, there will be no limit on the number of entrepreneurs who may start a taxi business.

Many cities now have "gypsy" cabs--privately owned cars illegally used as taxis. The franchise system licensed by the city governments limit the number of companies and cabs. According to the gypsies, restricting the supply keeps fares unnecessarily high. It will be interesting to see the result of Los Angeles's application of free-enterprise theory to the cab system.

In spite of my experience, I'm sure that under the right working conditions--including mutual respect and courtesy between employers and drivers--cab driving can be a rewarding experience. For one thing, there is a variety of human contacts, which involve both benefit and risk. In the world of science we are often insulated from the real world that makes our sheltered existence possible. When you drive a cab you meet, as the cliché goes, all kinds.

REFERENCES

1. Babe (George Herman) Ruth was the 1924 American Baseball League Batting Champion with an average of .378. In that same year he led the league in home runs with 46.
2. Time's up for dial-a-bus in London. *New Scientist* 69:185, January 1976.
3. **Lindsey R.** Los Angeles will allow private taxis to operate. *New York Times* April 17, 1977, p. 26.

CURRENT COMMENTS

What Some Science Students Don't Know: *Current Contents* Can Help Them During and After Their Formal Education

Number 21, May 23, 1977

We recently conducted a survey of *Current Contents*® (*CC*®) individual subscribers located in the United States. The survey was designed to let us know, among other things, when present subscribers first learned about *Current Contents* and how useful they perceived it to be at different stages of their careers. Out of 1,785 subscribers to whom the one-page questionnaire was sent, 1,042 returned it, for a response rate of 58.4 percent.

We found that over 88 percent of all respondents perceived *CC* to be either "indispensable" or "very useful" in their professional employment. Over 50 percent of the respondents, however, were not able to take advantage of *CC* until a considerate colleague told them about it--*after* they had obtained their first professional positions.

Fifty-five percent of all respondents thought that *CC* would have been "indispensable" or

"very useful" during their doctoral work. Nearly 42 percent believed that *CC* would have been at least "moderately useful" during their masters' programs; many of these felt it would be either "very useful" or "indispensable." Over twenty percent of the respondents even said that they would have subscribed to *CC* during their doctoral program--if they had known about it. Considering the financial state of most students, this is strong testimony to the value they see in *Current Contents.* Unfortunately, over half the respondents did *not* learn about *CC* during their school years.

To me, it is sadly ironic that students being trained to perform scientific research should be unaware of so important a research tool as *Current Contents.* Such students have not been prepared for their jobs as well as they might have been. But it is difficult to assess the effect of this on their future careers.

It would be interesting to see how many doctoral candidates are similarly ignorant of the existence of the *Science Citation Index®* , the *Social Sciences Citation Index™*, and other information tools. I would suspect the worst.

But ignorance of *CC* among doctoral candidates is merely indicative of a larger problem in science education: the inconsistent approach to teaching students about the use of information tools. Some colleges, of course, have excellent programs which stress the efficient use of a wide range of reference tools. But in too many colleges such programs are non-existent. Or, even if they do exist, they confine their instruction to the use of one or two indexes.

Focusing on the *Current Contents* situation, however, I'm sure it would help if we could send a free sample copy of *CC* to everyone who enters a master's or doctoral program. This would not be as beneficial to the student as classroom instruction, but it would at least be a beginning. Unfortunately, even this simple approach would be difficult because the names of such students are jealously guarded by their schools, which wish to protect them against such "intrusions" of their privacy.

Perhaps a more direct way to expose students to *CC* would be for each reader who teaches to take his or her copy to class and ask how many students recognize it. For those who don't, suggest that it would be worthwhile for them to examine your copy and, if the library has a subscription, to use its copy regularly.

Maybe our readers have some other ideas for letting graduate students know about *Current Contents*. If so, I would appreciate hearing about them.

Incidently, if you feel maligned each time your copy of *CC* is delayed by someone whose name appears before yours on the routing list, it may ease your annoyance to learn that you are not alone. According to our survey results, over 70 percent of the respondents shared a copy before subscribing to their own.

I'll present some of the other information obtained from our subscriber survey in subsequent "Current Comments."

CURRENT COMMENTS

Treating the Whole Person: The Use of Social Sciences Information in Medical Libraries

Number 22, May 30, 1977

Physicians do not treat diseases; they treat people. This simple fact, which was forgotten for a time, is just now being rediscovered. I do not denigrate the very real achievements of modern technological medicine-- the drugs, the laboratory tests, the sophisticated surgical procedures, the prostheses and life-sustaining machinery--but still it seems that something is missing in many physician-patient relationships. According to some observers, that something is an understanding and appreciation among physicians of the crucial role of psychological, social, and cultural factors in the treatment of disease.

Why don't doctors use available social sciences information? The main reason is the somatic orientation of our whole health-care system. The medical schools bear a large part of the responsibility, since they often fail to incorporate pertinent social sciences information into medical curricula. This is aggravated by the failure of many medical libraries to include relevant social science journals and books in their collections. And until recently, medical reference services have often ignored the importance of the social sciences in medical research as well as in teaching and in clinical practice.

Just a few weeks ago, in an article published in Science[1] George L. Engel, professor of psychiatry and medicine at the University of Rochester School of Medicine, called for a new medical model. "The dominant model of disease today is biomedical," he wrote, "with molecular biology its basic scientific discipline. It assumes disease to be fully accounted for by deviations from the norm of measurable biological (somatic) variables. It leaves no room within its framework for the social, psychological, and behavioral dimensions of illness." Engel goes so far as to call the biomedical model a "dogma" in the Western world.

Engel claims that, "The boundaries between health and disease, between well and sick, are far from clear and never will be clear, for they are diffused by cultural, social, and psychological considerations." He proposes a "biopsychosocial model" to replace

121

the traditional medical model of disease. "The psychobiological unity of man requires that the physician accept the responsibility to evaluate whatever problems the patient presents and recommend a course of action, including referral to other helping professions. Hence the physician's basic professional knowledge and skills must span the social, psychological, and biological, for his decisions and actions on the patient's behalf involve all three."

Physicians generally concede that their own behavior and relationship with the patient can influence the course of their patient's disease. The choice of therapy can also be strongly influenced by such factors as the social context in which the patient lives and the workings of the whole health care system. In addition, the physician must consider the effects of the behavior of others, such as the patient's family members, on the patient's seeking of medical help, reporting of symptoms, and acceptance of therapy.

Social science information can also help doctors to make ethical decisions. As Albert H. Keller, Jr., of the Medical University of South Carolina, recently pointed out, "simple adherence to a code of professional ethics is not sufficient to assure moral use of medical knowledge and skills." Keller asserts that "the social and cultural milieu in which medicine is practiced changes constantly, generating new problems unanticipated by general codes. Each physician of necessity becomes an ethicist. A grasp

of social issues, therefore, along with lucid internal norms of right and wrong, is vitally important to the practice of medicine."[2]

In addition to ethics, doctors are constantly making decisions which touch on such areas as law and religion. They may also deal with problems in rehabilitation, vocational guidance, drug addiction, criminology, health education, and individual and social psychology, to cite just a few examples of the medical use of social sciences information.

But how are doctors to become familiar with the types of social sciences information that they can use? At present their formal training rarely encompasses the social sciences. According to Halsted R. Holman, professor of medicine at the Stanford University School of Medicine, "Medical schools and centers are the pacesetters in creating the present state of affairs. It is they, not the practitioners, who emphasize technology, employ increasing numbers of drugs and tests in the name of thoroughness without adequate control, and practice institutional medicine virtually without venturing into the community where disease occurs and runs its course."[3]

However, the training of physicians is already rigorous; only the most talented and disciplined students are even admitted to medical school. Can psychology, sociology, and ethics be added to present curricula without displacing one or more equally important subjects? Even if they could, is it safe to assume that compassion, sensitivity, and morality can be taught in the classroom?

There are now signs that the "biomedical model" is changing. Some medical schools are beginning to list courses in such social science areas as medical ethics and human sexuality. And some medical libraries have supplemented their collections with social science journals and with social science reference tools. Among these tools are the American Medical Association's *Medical Socio-Economic Research Sources,* the *Hastings Center Bibliography of Society Ethics and Life Sciences,* and *Abstracts in Hospital Management Studies.* In addition, I am happy to be able to say that ISI® offers several highly useful social sciences information services.

From our social sciences data base (which now covers over 600,000 source items from the literature since 1969 as well as the nearly three million unique items cited by those source items) we offer a variety of printed and computerized services. Among these is *Current Contents® /Social and Behavioral Sciences,* (*CC® /S&BS*), which has been carefully and favorably evaluated in actual use for current awareness purposes at the Missouri Institute of Psychiatry.[4]

Most medical libraries already subscribe to the *Life Sciences* and/or *Clinical Practice* editions of *Current Contents,* but not to the *Social and Behavioral Sciences* edition. It is unfortunate that the physicians and medical researchers who use these libraries may be missing pertinent articles that could aid in diagnosis and treatment. They may also be missing enlightening articles in such areas as medical history, sociology, economics, law, and ethics. For this reason, we include a high percentage of social science items in the *ISI Press Digest,* which is contained in *every* edition of *Current Contents.*

To prepare the *ISI Press Digest,* our staff scans all six editions of *CC* plus hundreds of magazines, newspapers and books, selecting about 40 articles per week. Those readers who take a few minutes to scan the brief digests each week get a concise overview of many important--as well as merely interesting or amusing--things happening outside their specialties.

For retrospective searches ISI offers the multidisciplinary *Social Sciences Citation Index* (*SSCI*™) and our online search service, SOCIAL SCISEARCH®, in addition to the limited but still significant coverage of the social sciences in the *Science Citation Index®* (*SCI®*). Linkages between the physical, biological and social sciences in the indexes are emphasized by a new feature which will be included in the 1977 annual *SCI* and *SSCI.* A user of the *SCI* who looks up a cited item will find not only citing items from the *SCI,* but will also be alerted to citing items in the *SSCI*--and, in the same way, users of the *SSCI* will be alerted to citing items in the *SCI.*

For keeping up in highly specific subject areas, there are our selective dissemination of information (SDI) services, *ASCA®* (Automatic Subject Citation Alert) for individualized topics, and ASCATOPICS® for standardized topics.

We recently discussed the use of social sciences information with several medical reference librarians in the Philadelphia area. Ms. Loann Scarpato of the Eastern Pennsylvania Psychiatric Institute told us that she had recently filled a medical school teacher's request for background information on psychotherapy techniques for alcoholics and drug users. The teacher was planning a workshop on the subject. "Using the 1975 *Social Sciences Citation Index*," Ms. Scarpato told us, "I quickly found four articles."[5]

Other librarians told us how they had used the *SSCI* to help a graduate student who was thinking about specializing in emergency medicine, and wanted information on the development of the specialty; a nursing student writing a paper on art therapy for children; and a psychiatric resident who wanted information on behavior modification treatment for sexual disorders.

Professionals of all types can also use the *SSCI* to find out what impact their own published work has had in the social sciences. Chances are that locating and reading social sciences papers that cite your work will give you a new, interdisciplinary perspective on your own work.

In a way, ISI's various information services provide a bridge between what C.P. Snow called the two cultures. They help physical and life scientists gain access to relevant social sciences literature, just as they help social scientists find pertinent information on the physical and biological sciences.

Medical libraries can help bridge the gap by obtaining social sciences reference tools. Such tools can help practicing physicians--as well as researchers, teachers and students--to incorporate into their repertoire of medical knowledge the most recent advances in the social sciences.

REFERENCES

1. **Engel G L.** The need for a new medical model: a challenge for biomedicine. *Science* 196(4286):129-36, 8 April 1977.
2. **Keller A H.** Ethics/human values education in the family practice residency. *Journal of Medical Education* 52:107-16, Feburary 1977.
3. **Holman H R.** The "excellence" deception in medicine. *Hospital Practice* 11(4):11, 18, 21, April 1976.
4. **Matheson N W.** User reaction to *Current Contents:Behavioral, Social, and Management Sciences. Bulletin of the Medical Library Association* 59(2): 304-21, 1971.
5. **Scarpato L.** Personal communication. 27 April 1977.

CURRENT COMMENTS

Highly Cited Articles. 38. Physics and Chemistry
Papers Published in the 1950s.

Number 23, June 6, 1977

Earlier this year we presented and discussed three lists of the classic papers of the 1940s: one for biochemistry,[1] one for biomedicine,[2] and one for physics, chemistry, and mathematics.[3] Now we are moving on to the next decade. The list of highly cited physics and chemistry papers which follows is the first of three groups of classic papers published from 1950 to 1959. Later on we will list the biochemical classics and the biological, medical, and behavioral classics of the 1950s.

Overall, the 41 articles listed in Figure 1 are a remarkable group. During the period from 1961 to 1975, each was cited more than 500 times. The significance of over 500 citations in the 15-year period can be better appreciated when one considers that only 550 papers--out of a universe estimated at over 10 million items--were so highly cited during the same period.

Six items listed in Figure 1 have been cited more than 1,000 times-- a level reached by only 200 papers-- and three of these were cited more than 1,600 times: Bardeen et al. (3), Jaffe (14), and Karplus (18). Jaffe's review article, like the article by McDaniel and Brown (24), deals with the Hammett equation, widely used to determine how changes in the structure of a molecule affects its reactivity.

The other three articles in Figure 1 which were cited more than 1,000 times include an article on molecular orbital theory by Roothan (32), and a two-part article by Pariser and Parr. They developed the so-called P-P method for studying the electronic spectra of various kinds of conjugated molecules. Pariser also authored another paper (29) on this list.

The data in columns D (citations in 1974) and E (citations in 1975) of Figure 1 are general indicators of the degree of current interest in these 1950s papers. Despite the 20-year time lapse since these articles were published, six of them (3, 7, 11, 12, 15 and 24) are still attracting an increasing amount of interest. The 1974 citation count of these articles (column D) exceeded their average yearly citation rate for the years 1961-1975 (column C)--and their 1975 citation count (column E) exceeds that for 1974.

Seven of these 41 papers were authored by 11 Nobel laureates. In one article (2) three of the five

Figure 1. Highly cited articles in physics and chemistry published in the 1950s.
A = item number. B = total citations 1961-1975. C = average yearly citations 1961-1975. D = citations in 1974. E = citations in 1975. Articles are listed alphabetically by first author.

A	B	C	D	E	Bibliographic Data
1.	873	58	11	7	Ajzenberg-Selove F & Lauritsen T. Energy levels of light nuclei. VI. *Nuclear Physics* 11:1-340, 1959.
2.	740	49	34	20	Alder K, Bohr A, Huus T, Mottelson B & Winther A. Study of nuclear structure by electromagnetic excitation with accelerated ions. *Revs. Mod. Physics* 28:432-542, 1956.
3.	1662	111	95	68	Bardeen J, Cooper L N & Schrieffer J R. Theory of superconductivity. *Physical Rev.* 108:1175-1204, 1957.
4.	758	51	12	12	Berghuis J, Bertha J J, Haanappel M, Potters M, Loopstra B O, MacGillavry C H & Veenendall A L. New calculations of atomic scattering factors. *Acta Cryst.* 8:478-83, 1955.
5.	544	36	38	41	Brown H C & Okamoto Y. Electrophilic substituent constants. *J. Amer. Chem. Soc.* 80:4979, 1958.
6.	641	43	62	52	Carr H Y & Purcell E M. Effects of diffusion on free precession in nuclear magnetic resonance experiments. *Physical Rev.* 94:630-39, 1954.
7.	531	35	42	56	Dexter D L. A theory of sensitized luminescence in solids. *J. Chem. Physics* 21:836-50, 1953.
8.	770	51	31	25	Feynman R P & Gell-Mann M. Theory of the Fermi interaction. *Physical Rev.* 109:193-98, 1958.
9.	652	43	43	49	Gutowski H S & Holm C H. Rate processes and nuclear magnetic resonance spectra. II. Hindered internal rotation of amides. *J. Chem. Physics* 25:1228, 1956.
10.	525	35	41	40	Hahn E L. Spin echos. *Physical Rev.* 80:580-94, 1950.
11.	707	47	64	65	Hammond G S. A correlation of reaction rates. *J. Amer. Chem. Soc.* 77:334, 1955.
12.	748	50	64	85	Hatchard C G & Parker C A. A new sensitive chemical actinometer. II. Potassium ferrioxalate as a standard chemical actinometer. *Proc. Roy. Soc. A.* 235:518, 1956.
13.	818	55	37	33	Jacob M & Wick G C. On the general theory of collisions for particles with spin. *Ann. Physics* 7:404-28, 1959.
14.	1667	111	106	76	Jaffe H H. A reexamination of the Hammett equation. *Chem. Revs.* 53:191-261, 1953.
15.	684	46	53	57	Johnson C E Jr. & Bovey F A. Calculation of nuclear magnetic resonance spectra of aromatic hydrocarbons. *J. Chem. Physics* 29:1012, 1958.
16.	523	35	24	23	Johnston W G & Gilman J J. Dislocation velocities, dislocation densities, and plastic flow in lithium fluoride crystals. *J. Appl. Physics* 30:129-44, 1959.
17.	619	41	55	44	Kane E O. Band structure of indium antimonide. *J. Phys. Chem. Solids* 1:249-61, 1957.

Figure 1 continued

18.	1629	109	101 68	**Karplus M.** Contact electron-spin coupling of nuclear magnetic moments. *J. Chem. Physics* **30**:11-15, 1959.
19.	610	41	53 41	**Kubo R & Tomita K.** A general theory of magnetic resonance absorption. *J. Phys. Soc. Japan* **9**:888-919, 1954.
20.	947	63	88 78	**Kubo R.** Statistical-mechanical theory of irreversible process. I. General theory of simple applications to magnetic and conduction problems. *J. Phys. Soc. Japan* **12**:570-86, 1957.
21.	688	46	55 42	**Lane A M & Thomas R G.** R-matrix theory of nuclear reactions. *Rev. Mod. Physics* **30**:257-353, 1958.
22.	605	40	23 24	**Lemieux R U, Kullnig R K, Bernstein H J & Schneider W G.** Configurational effects on the proton magnetic resonance spectra of six-membered ring compounds. *J. Amer. Chem. Soc.* **80**:6098-6105, 1958.
23.	518	34	20 34	**McConnell H M & Chesnut D B.** Theory of isotropic hyperfine interactions in π-electron radicals. *J. Chem. Physics* **28**:107-17, 1958.
24.	632	42	46 47	**McDaniel D H & Brown H C.** An extended table of Hammett substituent constants based on the ionization of substituted benzoic acids. *J. Org. Chem.* **23**:420, 1958.
25.	762	51	38 42	**Mulliken R S.** Molecular compounds and their spectra. II. *J. Amer. Chem. Soc.* **74**:811-27, 1952.
26.	960	64	38 42	**Mulliken R S.** Electronic population analysis on LCAO-MO molecular wave functions. I. *J. Chem. Physics* **23**:1833-40, 1955.
27.	1090	72	77 51	**Pariser R & Parr R G.** A semi-empirical theory of the electronic spectra and electronic structure of complex unsaturated molecules. I. *J. Chem. Physics* **21**:466-71, 1953.
28.	1134	76	66 54	**Pariser R & Parr R G.** A semi-empirical theory of the electronic spectra and electronic structure of complex unsaturated molecules. *J. Chem. Physics* **21**:767-76, 1953.
29.	510	34	31 10	**Pariser R.** Theory of electronic spectra and structure of the polyacenes and of alternant hydrocarbons. *J. Chem. Physics* **24**:250-68, 1956.
30.	666	44	35 26	**Paul M A & Long F A.** H_0 and related indicator acidity functions. *Chemical Rev.* **57**:1-45, 1957.
31.	976	65	66 49	**Pople J A.** Electron interaction in unsaturated hydrocarbons. *Trans. Faraday Soc.* **49**:1375-85, 1953.
32.	1229	82	129 94	**Roothaan C C J.** New developments in molecular orbital theory. *Rev. Mod. Physics* **23**:69, 1951.
33.	652	43	49 44	**Rouse P E.** A theory of the linear viscoelastic properties of dilute solutions of coiling polymers. *J. Chem. Physics* **21**:1272-80, 1953.
34.	648	43	26 34	**Ruderman M A & Kittel C.** Indirect exchange coupling of nuclear magnetic moments by conduction electrons. *Physical Rev.* **96**:99-102, 1954.

Figure 1 continued

35. 521 35 36 28 **Shockley W & Read W T Jr.** Statistics of the recombinations of holes and electrons. *Physical Rev.* **87**:835-42, 1952.

36. 572 38 73 47 **Slater J C.** A simplification of the Hartree-Fock method *Physical Rev.* **81**:385-90, 1951.

37. 558 37 49 27 **Tanabe Y & Sugano S.** On the absorption spectra of complex ions. I. *J. Phys. Soc. Japan* **9**:753-66, 1954.

38. 582 39 35 45 **VanHove L.** Correlations in space and time and born approximation scattering in systems of interacting particles. *Physical Rev.* **95**:249-62, 1954.

39. 533 36 47 38 **Williams M L, Landel R F & Ferry J D.** The temperature dependence of relaxation mechanisms in amorphous polymers and other glass-forming liquids. *J. Amer. Chem. Soc.* **77**:3701-07, 1955.

40. 710 47 75 54 **Wolfsberg M & Helmholz L.** Spectra and electronic structure of the tetrahedral ions M_nO_4-, CrO_4. *J. Chem. Physics* **20**:837, 1952.

41. 511 34 47 40 **Zimm B H.** Dynamics of polymer molecules in dilute solution; viscoelasticity, flow birefringence and dialectic loss. *J. Chem. Physics* **24**:269-78, 1956.

authors won Nobel Prizes. Alder of Germany won the 1950 Prize in chemistry, and Bohr and Mottelson, both of Denmark, shared the 1975 Prize in physics. A. Bohr is the son of Neils Bohr, the Danish physicist who contributed to the development of quantum theory.

The remaining eight Nobel iaureates on the list are Americans. The three authors of the second most highly cited article on the list (3), Bardeen, Cooper, and Schreiffer, shared the 1972 Nobel Prize for physics. In addition, Bardeen won the 1956 Prize for physics.

Two well-known physicists, Feynman and Gell-Mann, are the authors of a paper on the Fermi interaction (8). Gell-Mann, who predicted and named the "quark" in particle physics, won the Nobel Prize for physics in 1965. Feynman, who recently helped develop the parton model of the proton--and

whose fundamental paper on quantum mechanics appeared on our 1940s list--won the Nobel Prize for physics in 1969. Purcell, the author of an article concerning nuclear magnetic resonance (6), won the Nobel Prize for physics in 1952. Mulliken, the author of two articles on the list (25, 26), won the 1966 Prize for chemistry, and Shockley won the Nobel Prize for physics in 1956.

The names of several authors of these highly cited 1950s papers also appeared on our 1940s list.[3] Mulliken (25, 26) was the sole author of two highly cited 1940s articles, and the primary author of a third 1940s article. Zimm (41) was also the sole author of two 1940s articles and primary author of a third. Four more of the authors listed in Figure 1 appeared on our 1940s list: Purcell (6), Feynman (8), Kittel (34), and Shockley (35).

Of these 41 articles of the 1950s,

one was published in 1950, two in 1951, three in 1952, six in 1953, five in 1954, four in 1955, five in 1956, four in 1957, seven in 1958, and four in 1959.

In our discussion of the 1940s classics we noted that 95% of the articles were published in English.[3]

Figure 2. Journals that published the highly cited 1950s articles listed in Figure 1, according to number of articles. A = number of articles. (Present title of journal given in parentheses).

A	Journal
12	J. Chem. Physics
8	Physical Review
5	J. Amer. Chem. Soc.
3	J. Phys. Soc. Japan
3	Rev. Mod. Physics
2	Chemical Rev.
1	Acta Crystallographica
1	Annals Physics
1	J. Appl. Physics
1	J. Organic Chem.
1	J. Phys. Chem. Solids
1	Nuclear Physics
1	Proc. Roy. Soc. London A.
1	Trans. Faraday Soc.
	(J. Chem. Soc. Faraday)

━━━━━━◆━◆━◆━━━━━━

The original language of publication of all of the 41 articles published in the 1950s was English.

In Figure 2, the journals that published the 41 articles are listed according to the number of such articles published in each. Only two journals account for almost half of the articles. Twelve of the articles were published in *Journal of Chemical Physics,* and 8 in *Physical Review.* A decade earlier, in the 1940s, the same two journals were the leading publishers of highly cited physical science articles.

Other journals which published more than one article listed in Figure 1 are *Journal of the American Chemical Society* (5 articles), *Journal of the Physical Society of Japan* (3 articles), *Reviews of Modern Physics* (3 articles), and *Chemical Reviews* (2 articles). It is significant that *two* of the top six producers of these articles--*Reviews of Modern Physics* and *Chemical Reviews*--are review journals. The importance of review journals is well-documented.[4]

A revolution in physics began in the 1950s and continues to the present. It began by overthrowing the simple concept of the atom as a nucleus composed of protons and neutrons and surrounded by orbiting electrons. This model was replaced with an examination of the internal constituents of protons and neutrons themselves, an examination which has given rise to some weird, almost mystical concepts, including quarks, charm, strangeness, and color. Many of these classic physics and chemistry papers of the 1950s helped to lay the groundwork for studying the complex subatomic world.

1. **Garfield E.** Highly cited articles. 35. Biochemistry papers published in the 1940s. *Current Contents* No. 8, 21 February 1977, p. 5-11.

2. --------------Highly cited articles. 37. Biomedical articles published in the 1940s. *Current Contents* No. 13, 28 March 1977, p. 5-12.

3. --------------Highly cited articles. 36. Physics, chemistry, and mathematics papers published in the 1940s. *Current Contents* No. 10, 7 March 1977. p. 5-11.

4. --------------Significant journals of science. *Nature* 264: 609-15, 16 December 1976.

CURRENT COMMENTS

The Significant Journals of Science

Number 24, June 13, 1977

Five years ago I published a list of the 152 most significant journals of science.[1] The impact of that list was also significant. It would be impossible to report here all the many ways in which this report on the impact of journals made its own impact.

For example, some of the most cited journals used this information, justifiably, to improve their appeals to advertisers. Dozen of libraries informed me that the list was used as justification for the addition of many journals not already in their collections. Similarly, others used the data to prune journals which they had known to be little used but which were staunchly defended as indispensable by individual patrons.

Recently, I published an up-dated and expanded version of this list.[2] It is reprinted here for the benefit of those readers who do not regularly see *Nature*. The original manuscript was unusually long for *Nature*. Since the space available was severely limited, I would now like to add a few observations.

I've often stressed the importance of limiting comparisons between journals to those in the same field. One of the simplest and best ways of locating lists of journals which are more closely related to each other than the ones listed here is to use ISI® 's *Journal Citation Reports®* (*JCR™*), for which the 1976 edition has now been published. Thus, if I am interested in comparing acoustics journals, *JCR* will tell me those journals most closely associated with any particular acoustics journal I select.[3]

As an example of the vagaries of the data presented here, consider the following examples. The impact for the *Journal of Molecular Biology* for 1974 is 7.5. This is a very high impact, but one must consider it in context. The average article in *JMB* contained a relatively high 29.4 references. Even more important, the group of journals that cited it most contained, on average, a similarly high number of references per paper. Thus, the chances of *JMB* and other biochemistry journals receiving a high average number of citations to their articles were better than for journals in some other fields. For example, *Acta Mathematica* had a 1974 impact of 2.1. But this impact must be considered in the context that the average math journal only contained approximately eight to ten references per paper.

Another factor that can affect the rankings is the time period involved. This includes not only the number of years from which the data were taken, but also the *specific years* included. For example, if impact has been calculated on the basis of five years rather than two, the average math journal would improve its impact while *JMB* and other similar journals would decline. This reflects the fact that 1975 *SCI*® citations in a hot field like biochemistry peak in 1973, while those for mathematics peak during 1970-1971.[4,5]

It is obvious, then, that if we take these other factors into consideration, we can produce a new list which may be "fairer." But that is a task for another day. So, without further ado, I present on the following pages the significant journals of science.

REFERENCES

1. **Garfield E.** Citation analysis as a tool in journal evaluation. *Science* **178**:471-79, 1972. Reprinted in: *Current Contents*® No. 6, 7 February 1973, p. 5-24.
2. ------------. Significant journals of science. *Nature* **264**:609-15, 16 December 1976.
3. **Cawkell A.** Evaluating scientific journals with *Journal Citation Reports*--a case study in acoustics. *Journal of the American Society for Information Science* (in press).
4. **Koshy G.** The life expectancy of a scientific paper. *Proceedings of the Fifth Annual Regional Conference of the American Institute for Decision Sciences* April 30-May 1, 1976, p. 224-27.
5. **Geller N L, deCani J S & Davies R E.** Lifetime-citation rates to compare scientists' work. (unpublished).

Significant journals of science*

Eugene Garfield

In 1974 the Science Citation Index® (SCI®) covered about 401,000 articles and communications in 2,443 scientific and technical journals. They cited about 3.2 million different publications an average of 1.8 times each. In this article some results of an analysis of more than 5 million citations in the references of journal articles indexed for the SCI in 1974 are presented and an attempt is made to interpret those results in the light of an earlier study of 1969 citations.

The basic information recorded in the *SCI* for citing and cited papers is a "condensed citation." It gives first author, year, journal, volume, and page. The citing—cited pairs can be sorted and subsorted in various ways, as one's interests dictate. Sorting by cited author produces the *Citation Index* section of the *SCI*. Sorting by citing and cited journals produces the two major sections of the *Journal Citation Reports* ® *(JCR™)*.

ISI® 's *Journal Citation Reports* is an index of journal-journal links based on a grouping and summation of condensed citations using journal rather than author as the primary sorting key. A preliminary *JCR*, based on an analysis of 1969 references,[1] appeared in 1972.[2] This year the *JCR* became a regular section and volume of the *SCI*.[3] It is the source of the 1974 citation data discussed here.

In this report I have used two indicators of journal significance:

total citations and impact. The first is simply the number of times a journal was cited in 1974. Impact, on the other hand, is a measure of the relationship between citations and articles published. For this report, impact was calculated by dividing the number of 1974 citations of 1972 and 1973 articles by the number of articles published in 1972 and 1973. For example, the 817 articles published in 1972 and 1973 in the *Journal of Molecular Biology* were cited 6,129 times in 1974. The impact of the journal is therefore 7.502.

Fig. 1 (*a*) lists the 206 journals most cited in 1974. Fig. 1(*b*) lists an additional 78 journals whose 1972 and 1973 articles only—rather than articles of any and all years, as in Fig. 1(*a*)—were highly cited in 1974. (The total of 284 journals in Fig. 1(*a* and *b*) corresponds to the number of journals listed in Fig. 2 (*a* and *b*), which have impacts greater than 2.) In most cases (63%)

*Reprinted from *Nature*, Vol. 264, No. 5587, pp. 609-615, December 15, 1976.

Fig. 1a, Journals most highly cited in 1974. Journals are listed in descending numerical order of total citations in the references of 1974 issues of journals processed for the *Science Citation Index*. A: rank in terms of total 1974 citations. B: rank in terms of total 1969 citations. C: total 1974 citations. D: 1974 impact. E: total 1974 citations of 1972 and 1973 articles. F: rank in terms of 1974 citations of 1972 and 1973 articles. An asterisk before a journal title indicates that counts for sections, retitled continuations, translated versions, and so on, have been combined with those for the original; the number in parentheses after the journal title indicates the number of such sections, and so on, that went into the combination, including the original. *b*, Journals whose 1972 and 1973 articles were highly cited in 1974. Journals are listed in descending numerical order of total 1974 citations of their 1972 and 1973 articles. Journals ranking higher in this respect will be found among the journals listed in Fig. 1*a*. See the legend of Fig. 1*a* for significance of the column markers. An asterisk before a journal title indicates that counts for sections, retitled continuations, translated versions, etc., have been combined with those for the original; the number in parentheses after the journal title indicates the number of such sections, etc., that went into the combination, including the original. The date of a journal's inauguration follows its title.

a

A	B	C		D	E	F
1	1	98995	J. Am. chem. Soc.	4.383	17088	3
2	2	91645	*Physical Rev. (5)	2.670	19174	1
3	3	81353	J. biol. Chem.	5.843	13685	6
4	5	75206	*Nature (3)	4.006	18924	2
5	4	66272	*J. chem. Soc. (9)	1.870	12513	7
6	6	62041	J. chem. Physics	2.918	10462	9
7	8	51491	Biochim. biophys. Acta	3.120	14129	5
8	7	47505	Science	5.412	11781	8
9	9	46917	Proc. natn. Acad. Sci. USA	8.989	15317	4
10	11	37047	Lancet	6.677	10383	10
11	10	31563	Biochem. J.	3.627	4885	23
12	12	29275	Physical Rev. Letters	5.059	10108	11
13	32	27080	Biochemistry	4.711	7325	17
14	25	26726	New Engl. J. Med.	8.364	7385	15
15	22	24768	J. clin. Invest.	6.992	5377	21
16	18	24209	J. molec. Biol.	7.502	6129	18
17	41	23220	Biochem. biophys. Res. Comm.	3.744	8110	12
18	33	22520	J. Physiol Lond	4.495	3160	46
19	33	22460	*Nuclear Physics (3)	2.514	7356	16
20	21	22245	*J. Cell Biol. (2)	6.770	3683	38
21	29	22201	Astrophys. J	4.063	7451	14
22	14	21519	Am. J. Physiol.	2.414	2412	59
23	27	20748	Brit. med. J.	3.556	4829	24
24	36	20699	J. expl Med.	11.874	5557	19
25	15	20539	J. org. Chem.	1.495	3526	40
26	16	19277	J. appl. Physics	1.558	3275	42
27	31	18375	J. Bacteriology	2.727	3809	37
28	30	18190	Analytical Chem.	3.291	4140	32
29	17	18171	Proc. Soc. expl Biol. Med	1.471	2454	58
30	23	18086	J phys. Chem.	2.031	2768	54
31	26	17211	J. Am. med. Ass.	3.068	2982	49
32	20	17201	*Proc. R. Soc. (3)	2.350	1114	185
33	13	16782	*C.r. Acad. Sci. (5)	0.529	4247	29
34	35	16509	Tetrahedron Letters	1.777	5004	22
35	38	15970	*Archs Biochem. Biophys. (2)	2.952	3050	48
36	53	15948	Endocrinology	4.337	4098	33
37	49	15826	J. Immunology	5.112	4703	26
38	34	15666	*Physics Letters (2)	2.133	7672	13
39	39	15281	J. geophys. Res	2.536	3854	36
40	24	14706	*Chem. Ber. (2)	1.506	1353	104
41	37	14668	Ann. N. Y. Acad. Sci.	1.181	1291	113
42	52	14461	Circulation	6.834	4025	34
43	50	14310	Inorg. Chem.	2.457	3589	39
44	45	13911	*Acta crystallographica (3)	1.361	2394	60
45	82	13847	*Eur. J. Biochem. (2)	3.857	4595	27
46	47	13753	J. Pharmacol. expl Ther.	3.576	2026	65
47	42	13072	Fedn Proc.	0.489	4212	30
48	58	12544	Cancer Res.	3.391	3164	45
49	69	11645	*J. clin. Endocr. Metab. (2)	5.170	3443	41

A	B	C		D	E	F
50	43	11459	*J. Physics (7)	1.689	5450	20
51	28	11421	*Zh. eksp. teor. Fiz. (2)	1.565	1607	84
52	57	11371	Virology	3.752	2949	50
53	40	11294	*J. Polym. Sci. (6)	0.964	1565	88
54	65	11127	Exp. Cell Res.	3.014	2788	53
55	48	10756	*Angew. Chem. (2)	4.140	2666	56
56	67	10231	Ann. internal Med.	4.828	2187	63
57	355	10227	Brain Res.	3.104	4522	28
58	87	10206	Analytical Biochem.	2.379	2184	64
59	46	9824	*Dokl. Akad. Nauk SSSR (7)	0.379	1681	81
60	62	9779	Am. J. Med.	4.411	1535	90
61	76	9678	J. natn. Cancer Inst.	3.289	2858	52
62	95	9497	Cancer	2.361	2056	66
63	59	9142	Can. J. Chem.	1.396	1793	73
64	707	9094	FEBS Letters	3.049	4815	25
65	74	9082	Circulation Res.	4.922	1698	79
66	108	9026	*Physica Status Sol. (3)	1.476	3201	44
67	64	8903	Tetrahedron	1.576	1913	69
68	77	8890	Am. J. Obstet. Gynec.	2.100	2236	62
69	78	8835	Plant Physiol.	2.580	1935	68
70	54	8803	*Acta chem. scand. (3)	1.042	1192	124
71	63	8798	J. Lab. clin. Med.	2.802	1132	131
72	113	8693	Gastroenterology	5.394	2260	61
73	107	8625	Appl. Physics Letters	3.220	3246	43
74	70	8619	J. appl. Physiol.	1.780	1184	125
75	481	8478	Applied Physics Letters	2.403	4205	31
76	141	8241	J. organomet. Chem.	2.392	3891	35
77	56	8183	Bull. Soc. chim. France	1.001	1492	96
78	81	7941	Bull. chem. Soc. Japan	0.932	1859	72
79	132	7928	J. Chromatography	2.173	2886	51
80	71	7922	Acta physiol. scand.	2.204	919	170
81	72	7914	J. phys. Soc. Japan	1.132	1500	95
82	61	7860	*Z. Naturforschung (3)	1.070	1503	94
83	192	7794	J. Neurochem.	3.535	2464	57
84	106	7656	*Br. J. Pharmacol.	3.516	1751	77
85	80	7459	Ann. Surgery	2.129	1060	140
86	113	7335	*Cell Tissue Res. (2)	1.961	1761	75

A	B	C		D	E	F
124	158	5197	J. Ultrastruct. Res.	2.709	837	190
125	103	5186	Revs mod. Physics	21.500	731	231
126	121	5167	J. Histochem. Cytochem.	4.005	757	224
127	102	5138	Anat. Rec.	2.884	649	265
128	235	5092	*Zh. obshch. Khim. (2)	0.808	1050	142
129	192	5063	Immunology	2.816	1118	132
130	125	5053	J. Nutrition	1.845	740	230
131	117	5038	Am. J. Roeng. Rad. Ther.	1.008	634	272
132	166	5033	J. Lipid Res.	3.525	719	238
133	134	5031	J. Urology	0.721	776	216
134	194	5000	Life Sciences	2.062	1200	121
135	177	4909	Acta endocrinologica	2.461	1383	103
136	267	4861	J. infect. Dis.	3.040	1669	82
137	75	4847	Phytopathology	1.155	789	210
138	111	4822	Physics Fluids	1.188	972	159
139	116	4801	Rev. scient. Instrum.	1.018	1001	153
140	160	4767	Can. J. Physics	1.715	1079	138
141	184	4707	Nucl. Instrum. Meth.	1.050	1420	100
142	127	4704	Z. anorg. allg. Chem.	1.019	593	286
143	159	4697	J. comp. Neurol.	3.725	771	219
144	105	4656	Can. J. Physics	1.038	774	218
145	168	4655	Lab. Investigation	2.940	932	166
146	133	4604	Hoppe-Seylers Z. physiol.Chem.	2.291	1031	146
147	211	4603	Applied Optics	1.832	1539	89
148	370	4600	Surface Science	3.340	1787	74
149	224	4511	*Comp. Biochem. Physiol. (3)	1.014	1250	116
150	247	4480	Applied Microbiology	1.292	1196	122
151	155	4479	Am. J. clin. Pathol.	1.348	663	255
152	182	4462	Am. J. Surg.	1.183	731	231
153	220	4453	Molecular Physics	2.334	1258	175
154	442	4451	*J. comp. Physiol. (2)	2.782	893	115
155	137	4416	Am. J. Dis. Child.	1.495	809	202
156	162	4393	*Archs Dermatology (3)	1.784	835	192
157	262	4369	Phytochemistry	1.103	1568	87
158	110	4356	Acta Metallurgica	1.705	583	291
159	93	4353	*J. comp. physiol. Psychol. (2)	1.230	663	256
160	140	4348	Cold Spring Harb. Symp.	2.443	623	278

87	122	7183	J. Pediatrics	2.600	1890	70
88	84	7120	Blood	4.319	1529	91
89	60	7117	Helv. chim. Acta	1.649	1034	144
90	68	7063	Philosophical Mag	1.836	876	178
91	147	7007	Biochem. Pharmacol.	2.023	1689	80
92	100	6951	Pediatrics	2.502	1346	105
93	120	6811	Am. J. Cardiol.	3.704	1889	71
94	276	6788	J. Virology	4.864	3142	47
95	149	6770	*J. Bone Jt Surg. (3)	1.358	729	234
96	73	6662	Z. Physik	1.340	864	182
97	112	6600	Experientia	0.883	1647	83
98	88	6539	J. gen. Physiol.	4.308	741	229
99	51	6362	*Fizika tverd. Tela (2)	0.762	1388	102
100	129	6307	Radiology	1.198	1320	107
101	66	6177	Annln Chemie (J. Liebig)	1.024	432	379
102	89	6066	*Archs internal Med. (2)	2.202	946	163
103	90	5994	Am. Heart J.	1.791	840	188
104	86	5885	J. opt. Soc. Am.	2.016	905	173
105	94	5849	*J. Physics Chem. Solids (2)	1.394	715	239
106	99	5761	J. inorg. nucl. Chem.	0.962	1149	128
107	156	5743	J. Endocrinology	2.919	1757	76
108	217	5683	*J. Pharmaceut. Sci. (3)	1.622	1549	92
109	92	5679	J. gen. Microbiol.	2.160	1136	129
110	115	5675	Surgery	1.559	842	187
111	378	5573	Solid St. Comm.	1.945	2768	55
112	170	5557	Clin. chim. Acta	1.669	1587	86
113	150	5556	J. Neurophysiology	4.537	676	249
114	98	5501	Methods Enzymology	1.765	547	311
115	136	5491	Archs Surgery	1.462	915	171
116	101	5486	Surgery Gynec. Obstet.	1.332	750	226
117	109	5478	J. Electrochem. Soc.	1.053	1098	136
118	55	5474	*Nuovo Cimento (3)	0.994	999	155
119	123	5428	J. acoust. Soc. Am.	1.142	830	195
120	96	5388	Am. J. Pathol.	2.807	856	184
121	91	5388	J. expl Psychol.	1.027	750	226
122	126	5363	*Spectrochim. Acta (3)	1.487	840	188
123	83	5326	Genetics	2.835	995	157

161	139	4347	Ann. Physics	2.128	598	284
162	214	4308	Planta	2.589	1261	114
163	135	4303	Archs Pathology	1.521	508	332
164	85	4277	*Proc. IEEE (2)	2.013	781	215
165	147	4253	Pflugers Arch./Eur. J. Physiol.	1.810	856	184
166	238	4208	*J. Pharmacy Pharmacol. (2)	3.140	1118	132
167	443	4180	*Zh. neorg. Khim (2)	0.523	823	198
168	199	4116	J. Anim. Sci.	1.311	1000	154
169	153	4104	Chem. Revs	11.154	580	293
170	161	4093	J. thorac. cardiovasc. Surg.	1.480	836	191
171	180	4072	*J. cell. Physiol. (2)	3.737	710	240
172	286	4068	J. Reprod. Fert.	2.357	1414	101
173	274	4054	*Transplantation (2)	2.250	1134	130
174	558	4049	Clin. expl Immunol.	4.423	1601	85
175	176	4040	Coll. Czech. chem. Comm.	0.791	831	194
176	169	4031	*Am. Rev resp. Dis. (3)	1.630	937	165
177	189	4023	Geochim. cosmochim. Acta	4.056	1160	127
178	271	4005	Analytica chim. acta	2.093	1312	110
179	157	4003	*Deut. med. Wschr. (2)	1.022	1025	149
180	148	3996	Physiol. Revs	13.861	499	334
181	138	3993	Acta med. scand.	1.124	508	331
182	195	3952	Diabetes	3.941	863	183
183	97	3932	*Zh. fiz. Khim (2)	0.331	646	266
184	194	3906	Geol. Soc. Am. Bull.	1.674	1026	147
185	364	3899	Astronomy Astrophys.	2.267	2018	67
186	172	3897	J. Dairy Sci.	0.273	569	300
187	218	3892	Neurology	2.181	796	206
188	503	3874	*Int. J. Cancer (2)	4.928	1508	93
189	367	3869	Clinical Chem.	3.195	1460	97
190	171	3864	Am. J. Ophthalmol.	1.389	792	208
190	178	3864	Progr. theor. Physics	1.421	1003	151
192	178	3858	Mon. Not. R. astr. Soc.	2.467	1036	143
193	165	3857	Archs Ophthalmology	1.293	561	302
194	154	3852	J. Fluid Mech.	1.254	617	280
195	146	3827	*Ber. Bunsenges.	1.382	532	319
196	160	3820	J. math. Physics	1.046	632	274
197	339	3777	*J. mednl Chem. (2)	1.444	1196	123

<table>
<thead>
<tr><th>A</th><th>B</th><th>C</th><th></th><th>D</th><th>E</th><th>F</th></tr>
</thead>
<tbody>
<tr><td>198</td><td>369</td><td>3726</td><td>Gut</td><td>3.336</td><td>1081</td><td>157</td></tr>
<tr><td>199</td><td>130</td><td>3710</td><td>Am. J. Botany</td><td>1.378</td><td>357</td><td>441</td></tr>
<tr><td>200</td><td>232</td><td>3701</td><td>J. Neurosurgery</td><td>1.252</td><td>636</td><td>271</td></tr>
<tr><td>201</td><td>204</td><td>3699</td><td>Scand. J. clin. Lab. Invest.</td><td>1.917</td><td>644</td><td>268</td></tr>
<tr><td>202</td><td>249</td><td>3673</td><td>•Archs Neurol. (2)</td><td>2.217</td><td>745</td><td>228</td></tr>
<tr><td>203</td><td>599</td><td>3647</td><td>•Eur. J. Pharmacol. (2)</td><td>2.537</td><td>1205</td><td>120</td></tr>
<tr><td>204</td><td>339</td><td>3633</td><td>Developmental Biol.</td><td>3.384</td><td>1242</td><td>117</td></tr>
<tr><td>205</td><td>196</td><td>3561</td><td>Arzneimittel-Forschung</td><td>0.876</td><td>833</td><td>193</td></tr>
<tr><td>206</td><td>202</td><td>3598</td><td>•Clin. Sci. mol. Med. (2)</td><td>2.474</td><td>762</td><td>223</td></tr>
</tbody>
</table>

b

<table>
<thead>
<tr><th>A</th><th>B</th><th>C</th><th></th><th>D</th><th>E</th><th>F</th></tr>
</thead>
<tbody>
<tr><td>284</td><td>—</td><td>2809</td><td>Cellular Immunol. 1970</td><td>4.848</td><td>1721</td><td>78</td></tr>
<tr><td>244</td><td>174</td><td>3164</td><td>Bull. Am. phys. Soc. 1925</td><td>0.347</td><td>1459</td><td>98</td></tr>
<tr><td>376</td><td>—</td><td>2094</td><td>Eur. J. Immunol. 1971</td><td>4.852</td><td>1441</td><td>99</td></tr>
<tr><td>348</td><td>—</td><td>2337</td><td>Infect. Immunity 1970</td><td>0.198</td><td>1335</td><td>106</td></tr>
<tr><td>272</td><td>295</td><td>2919</td><td>•Clin. Res. 1958 (2)</td><td>2.709</td><td>1516</td><td>108</td></tr>
<tr><td>307</td><td>—</td><td>2556</td><td>Transplantation Proc. 1969</td><td>5.247</td><td>1314</td><td>109</td></tr>
<tr><td>487</td><td>—</td><td>1470</td><td>Prostaglandins 1972</td><td>2.699</td><td>1296</td><td>111</td></tr>
<tr><td>281</td><td>448</td><td>2850</td><td>•Molecular gen. Genetics 1967 (2)</td><td>2.699</td><td>1293</td><td>112</td></tr>
<tr><td>242</td><td>370</td><td>3182</td><td>•J. electroanalyt. Chem. 1967 (2)</td><td>1.567</td><td>1222</td><td>118</td></tr>
<tr><td>239</td><td>744</td><td>3238</td><td>Physiol. Behavior 1966</td><td>1.678</td><td>1171</td><td>126</td></tr>
<tr><td>335</td><td>—</td><td>2406</td><td>Antimicr. Ag. Chemother. 1972</td><td>2.564</td><td>1118</td><td>132</td></tr>
<tr><td>323</td><td>507</td><td>2447</td><td>J. nucl. Med. 1960</td><td>3.040</td><td>1061</td><td>139</td></tr>
<tr><td>282</td><td>589</td><td>2831</td><td>Solar Physics 1967</td><td>1.929</td><td>1059</td><td>141</td></tr>
<tr><td>291</td><td>191</td><td>2725</td><td>NS Archs. Pharmacol. 1972</td><td>2.792</td><td>1035</td><td>145</td></tr>
<tr><td>230</td><td>319</td><td>3403</td><td>Annu. Rev. Biochem. 1932</td><td>19.358</td><td>1026</td><td>147</td></tr>
<tr><td>267</td><td>190</td><td>2946</td><td>Archs gen. Psychiatry 1960</td><td>2.475</td><td>1022</td><td>150</td></tr>
<tr><td>237</td><td>500</td><td>3279</td><td>Psychopharmacologia 1959</td><td>2.347</td><td>1002</td><td>152</td></tr>
<tr><td>352</td><td>776</td><td>2326</td><td>•Zh. analyt. Khim. 1946 (2)</td><td>1.060</td><td>996</td><td>156</td></tr>
<tr><td>370</td><td>416</td><td>2171</td><td>IEEE J. Quantum Electronics 1965</td><td>2.492</td><td>988</td><td>158</td></tr>
<tr><td>232</td><td>327</td><td>3373</td><td>Biopolymers 1963</td><td>2.492</td><td>972</td><td>159</td></tr>
<tr><td>459</td><td>—</td><td>1592</td><td>Transplantation Revs 1969</td><td>25.579</td><td>972</td><td>159</td></tr>
<tr><td>256</td><td>326</td><td>3074</td><td>Chromosoma 1939</td><td>3.875</td><td>961</td><td>162</td></tr>
<tr><td>356</td><td>—</td><td>2265</td><td>Metallurg. Trans. AIME 1970</td><td>1.054</td><td>939</td><td>164</td></tr>
<tr><td>434</td><td>—</td><td>1707</td><td>•Lettere Nuovo Cimento 1969 (2)</td><td>0.755</td><td>929</td><td>167</td></tr>
<tr><td>357</td><td>627</td><td>2258</td><td>J. gen. Virology 1967</td><td>2.501</td><td>928</td><td>168</td></tr>
</tbody>
</table>

<table>
<thead>
<tr><th>A</th><th>B</th><th>C</th><th></th><th>D</th><th>E</th><th>F</th></tr>
</thead>
<tbody>
<tr><td>349</td><td>334</td><td>2332</td><td>•Archs Microbiology 1974 (2)</td><td>1.468</td><td>684</td><td>246</td></tr>
<tr><td>281</td><td>282</td><td>2845</td><td>Metabolism 1952</td><td>2.387</td><td>678</td><td>247</td></tr>
<tr><td>828</td><td></td><td>717</td><td>Kidney International 1972</td><td>3.740</td><td>677</td><td>248</td></tr>
<tr><td>326</td><td>639</td><td>2433</td><td>Expl Brain Res. 1965</td><td>3.596</td><td>676</td><td>249</td></tr>
<tr><td>228</td><td>259</td><td>3414</td><td>J. mol. Spectroscopy 1957</td><td>1.744</td><td>675</td><td>251</td></tr>
<tr><td>371</td><td>587</td><td>2147</td><td>Vision Research 1961</td><td>1.800</td><td>675</td><td>251</td></tr>
<tr><td>353</td><td>297</td><td>2321</td><td>Planetary Space Sci. 1959</td><td>1.645</td><td>671</td><td>253</td></tr>
<tr><td>293</td><td>183</td><td>2696</td><td>Can. J. Biochem. 1964</td><td>1.671</td><td>670</td><td>254</td></tr>
<tr><td>302</td><td>472</td><td>2621</td><td>Molec. Pharmacol. 1965</td><td>3.785</td><td>670</td><td>254</td></tr>
<tr><td>238</td><td>228</td><td>3259</td><td>J. clin. Pathol. 1947</td><td>1.550</td><td>662</td><td>258</td></tr>
<tr><td>269</td><td>308</td><td>2931</td><td>J. Insect Physiol. 1957</td><td>1.505</td><td>662</td><td>258</td></tr>
<tr><td>263</td><td>308</td><td>2987</td><td>Am. J. clin. Nutrition 1954</td><td>1.714</td><td>658</td><td>260</td></tr>
<tr><td>226</td><td>185</td><td>3453</td><td>Austral. J. Chem. 1953</td><td>1.006</td><td>658</td><td>260</td></tr>
<tr><td>234</td><td>281</td><td>3321</td><td>•J. Cell Sci. 1966 (2)</td><td>2.973</td><td>657</td><td>262</td></tr>
<tr><td>317</td><td>NA</td><td>2505</td><td>J. Fish. Res. Board Can. 1938</td><td>1.053</td><td>656</td><td>263</td></tr>
<tr><td>294</td><td>230</td><td>2669</td><td>Bacteriol. Revs 1937</td><td>16.795</td><td>655</td><td>264</td></tr>
</tbody>
</table>

Fig. 2 *a*, High-impact journals in 1974 (excluding review journals). Journals are listed in descending numerical order of 1974 impact factor. *b*, High-impact review journals. A: rank in terms of 1974 impact; B: 1974 impact; C: 1969 impact; D: total 1974 citations of 1972 and 1973 articles; E: total number of 1972 and 1973 articles.

<table>
<thead>
<tr><th>A</th><th>B</th><th>C</th><th></th><th>D</th><th>E</th></tr>
</thead>
<tbody>
<tr><td>1</td><td>11.874</td><td>8.307</td><td>J. expl Med.</td><td>5557</td><td>468</td></tr>
<tr><td>2</td><td>8.989</td><td>8.566</td><td>Proc. natn. Acad Sci. USA</td><td>15317</td><td>1704</td></tr>
<tr><td>3</td><td>8.364</td><td>2.359</td><td>New Engl. J. Med</td><td>7385</td><td>883</td></tr>
<tr><td>4</td><td>7.502</td><td>8.811</td><td>J. molec. Biol.</td><td>6129</td><td>817</td></tr>
<tr><td>5</td><td>6.992</td><td>3.362</td><td>J. clin. Invest.</td><td>5377</td><td>769</td></tr>
<tr><td>6</td><td>6.834</td><td>1.214</td><td>Circulation</td><td>4025</td><td>589</td></tr>
<tr><td>7</td><td>6.770</td><td>3.386</td><td>J. Cell Biol</td><td>3683</td><td>544</td></tr>
<tr><td>8</td><td>6.677</td><td>1.485</td><td>Lancet</td><td>10383</td><td>1555</td></tr>
</tbody>
</table>

468	—	1553	Optics Communications 1969	1.551	920	169
311	345	2551	*Chest 1970 (2)	1.253	916	172
323	506	2422	Mutation Res. 1964	2.365	894	174
289	533	2738	Accts chem. Res 1968	7.403	881	177
300	394	2630	*Agric. biol. Chem. Tokyo 1961 (2)	0.982	867	179
305	470	2559	Carbohydrate Res. 1965	1.312	867	179
420	NA	1771	J. Vacuum Sci. Technol. 1964	1.472	867	179
371	539	2159	*J. chromatogr. Sci. 1969 (2)	3.196	847	186
338	512	2387	Earth planetary Sci. Letters 1966	1.802	827	196
227	268	3423	Br. J. Haematol. 1955	2.711	824	197
321	530	2449	Clin. Pharmacol. Therap. 1970	3.423	818	199
253	277	3114	Obstet. Gynecol. 1953	1.367	816	200
306	317	2557	Steroids 1963	3.189	810	201
548	—	1281	J. magn. Resonance 1969	2.082	808	203
274	248	2893	Med. J. Australia 1914	0.725	805	204
304	389	2600	Izv. Akad. Nauk SSSR Khim 1936	0.540	802	205
220	361	3530	Expl Neurology 1959	1.827	793	207
427	552	1740	J. Crystal Growth 1967	2.503	791	209
286	381	2767	*J. Obst. Gyn. Br. Comm. 1961 (2)	1.922	786	211
494	627	1453	Icarus 1962	3.489	785	212
277	343	2885	J. Catalysis 1962	1.603	784	213
428	608	1728	*Pediatric Res. 1967 (2)	4.399	783	214
384	941	2035	Macromolecules 1968	2.276	776	216
246	207	3155	Anesthesiology 1940	2.024	771	219
241	293	3186	J. agric. Food Chem. 1953	1.195	771	219
257	311	3069	*J. Atmosph. Sci. 1962 (2)	2.051	769	222
390	374	1990	*Fiz. Tekh. Poluprovodn. 1967 (2)	0.680	762	223
357	736	2261	*Zh. org. Khim. 1965 (2)	0.643	757	224
361	399	2222	Talanta 1958	1.787	731	231
267	277	2949	*Can. J. Botany 1951 (2)	1.069	729	234
251	255	3130	Archs Dis. Childhood 1926	1.901	728	236
311	320	2547	Br. J. Cancer 1947	3.232	724	237
233	164	3533	Makromolek. Chemie 1945	1.088	704	241
425	—	1755	Org. Mass Spectrometry 1968	1.088	704	241
259	235	5038	Br. Heart J. 1939	1.631	698	243
270	266	2927	*Nouv. Presse Med. 1972 (2)	0.612	696	244
387	576	2004	Toxicol. appl. Pharmacol. 1959	1.672	689	245

9	6.059	5.843	J. biol. Chem.	13685	2342
10	2.993	5.412	Science	11781	2177
11	1.147	5.394	Gastroenterology	2260	419
12		5.247	Prostaglandins	1296	247
13	3.868	5.170	J. clin. Endocr. Metab.	3443	666
14	4.121	5.112	J. Immunology	4703	920
15	4.911	5.059	Physical Rev. Letters	10108	1998
16		4.957	Scand. J. Immunology	570	115
17	2.553	4.928	Int. J. Cancer	1508	306
18	1.750	4.922	Circulation Res.	1698	945
19	5.269	4.864	J. Virolog.	3142	646
20		4.852	Eur. J. Immunology	1441	297
21		4.848	Cell. Immunology	1721	355
22	1.679	4.828	Ann. internal Med.	2187	453
23	5.694	4.711	Biochemistry	7325	1555
24	4.435	4.537	J. Neurophysiology	676	149
25	2.432	4.495	J. Physiol. Lond.	3166	703
26	3.363	4.423	Clin. expl Immunology	1601	962
27	4.516	4.411	Am. J. Med.	1535	348
28	0.680	4.399	Pediatric Res.	783	178
29	5.164	4.383	J. Am. chem. Soc.	17088	3899
30	NA	4.340	Seminars Hematology	204	47
31	2.906	4.337	Endocrinology	4098	945
32	2.219	4.319	Blood	1529	354
33	2.968	4.380	J. gen. Physiol.	741	172
34	2.925	4.140	Angew. Chemie	2666	644
35	4.661	4.063	Astrophys. J.	7451	1834
36	0.672	4.060	Arthritis Rheumatism	613	151
37	2.725	4.056	Geochim. cosmochim. Acta	1160	286
38	2.342	4.006	Nature	18924	4724
39	2.287	4.005	J. Histochem. Cytochem.	757	189
40	2.090	3.967	Cytogenet. Cell Genetics	357	90
41	2.039	3.941	Diabetes	863	219
42	2.767	3.875	Chromosoma	961	248
43	3.976	3.875	Eur. J. Biochem.	4595	1186
44		3.796	Tissue Antigens	429	113

A		B	C	D	E
45	Molecular Pharmacol.	3.785	3.916	670	177
46	Virology	3.752	4.486	2949	786
47	Biochem. biophys. Res Comm.	3.744	4.292	8110	2166
48	Kidney International	3.740		677	181
49	J. cell. Physiol.	3.737	3.488	710	190
50	Clin. Immunol. Immunopathol.	3.726		231	62
51	J. comp. Neurology	3.725	2.335	771	207
52	Am. J Cardiology	3.704	2.170	1889	510
53	Biochem. J	3.627	3.060	4885	1347
54	Expl Brain Res.	3.596	4.783	676	188
55	J. Pharmacol. expl Ther.	3.576	3.568	2060	576
56	I.E.E.J. Quantum Electronics	3.567	1.307	988	277
57	Br. med. J	3.556	0.677	4829	1358
58	J. Neurochemistry	3.535	2.884	2464	697
59	J. Lipid Res	3.525	3.876	719	204
60	Br. J. Pharmacol.	3.516	2.658	1751	498
61	Icarus	3.489	1.697	785	225
62	Br. med. Bull.	3.441	3.401	320	93
63	Clin. Pharmacol. Ther.	3.423	1.657	818	239
64	Cancer Res.	3.391	2.879	3164	933
65	Developmental Biol.	3.384	3.729	1242	367
66	Surface Science	3.340	2.629	1787	535
67	Gut	3.336	1.174	1081	324
68	Analyt. Chem.	3.291	1.605	4140	1258
69	J. natn. Cancer Inst.	3.289	4.009	2858	869
70	J. Membrane Biol.	3.266		578	177
71	Br. J. Cancer	3.232	1.670	724	224
72	Applied Physics Letters	3.220	3.545	3246	1008
73	J. Allergy clin. Immunol.	3.215	NA	463	144
74	Clin. Endocrinology	3.205		250	78
75	J. Chromatogr. Sci.	3.196	1.312	847	265
76	Clin. Chemistry	3.195	0.683	1460	457
77	Steroids	3.189	2.454	810	254
78	J. Neurobiology	3.175		200	63
79	Ann. human Genetics	3.144	1.739	283	90
80	J. Pharmacy Pharmacol.	2.140	1.256	1118	356

A		B	C	D	E
117	Planta	2.589	2.944	1261	487
118	Plant Physiol.	2.580	1.573	1935	750
119	Antimicrob. Agents Chemother	2.564		1118	436
120	Biophysical J	2.545	0.916	514	202
120	Eur. J. clin. Invest.	2.545		280	110
120	J. molecular Evolution	2.545		112	44
123	Eur. J. Pharmacol.	2.537	3.661	1205	475
124	J. grophys. Res.	2.536	3.385	3854	1520
125	Radiation Effects	2.528		493	195
125	Nuclear Physics	2.528	2.836	7356	2910
127	Thrombosis Res.	2.513		392	156
128	J. Petrology	2.512	4.965	103	41
129	J. Crystal Growth	2.503	2.277	791	316
130	Pediatrics	2.502	1.495	1346	538
131	J. gen. Virology	2.501	2.894	928	371
132	Biopolymers	2.492	2.791	972	390
133	Immunochemistry	2.484	3.232	611	246
134	In Vitro	2.481	NA	258	104
135	Archs gen. Psychiatry	2.475	1.409	1022	413
136	Clin. Sci. mol. Med.	2.474	2.732	762	223
137	Mon. Not. R. astr. Soc.	2.467	4.307	1036	420
138	Expl Hematology	2.464		69	28
139	Acta endocrinologica	2.461	1.316	1383	562
140	Inorg. Chemistry	2.457	3.188	3589	1461
141	Neuroendocrinology	2.447	2.873	438	179
142	Cold Spring Harbor Symp.	2.443	5.463	623	255
143	Neuropharmacology	2.441	1.685	554	227
144	Am. J. Physiology	2.414	3.115	2412	999
145	Hormones Behavior	2.413		193	80
146	Chem. Physics Letters	2.403	2.477	4205	1750
147	J. organomet. Chem.	2.392	3.497	3891	1627
148	Metabolism	2.387	2.088	678	284
149	Analyt. Biochem.	2.379	3.330	2184	918
150	Am. Zoologist	2.375	0.326	342	144
151	Mutation Res.	2.365	2.497	894	378

81	3.137	2.593	Am. J. human Genetics	436	139
82	3.135	1.981	Am. Naturalist	326	104
83	3.120	3.102	Biochim. biophys. Acta	14129	4529
84	3.104	3.486	Brain Res.	4522	1457
85	3.068	1.050	J. Am. med. Assoc.	2982	972
86	3.049	NA	FEBS Letters	4815	1579
87	3.048		Differentiation	64	21
88	3.040	1.000	J. infect. Dis.	1669	549
88	3.040	0.505	J. nuclear Med.	1061	349
90	3.016		Cognitive Psychology	190	63
91	3.014	2.241	Expl Cell Res.	2788	925
92	2.973	4.918	J. Cell Science	657	221
93	2.967	3.230	Arch. Biochem. Biophys.	3050	1028
94	2.940	2.008	Lab. Investigation	932	317
95	2.920		Bioinorganic Chem.	73	25
96	2.919	2.021	J. Endocrinology	1757	602
97	2.918	3.128	J. chem. Physics	10462	3585
98	2.916		Biol. Reproduction	592	203
99	2.884	0.409	Anat. Rec.	649	225
100	2.864	1.337	J. Neuropathol. expl Neurol.	232	81
101	2.846	4.057	Q. J. Med.	222	78
102	2.835	1.815	Genetics	995	351
103	2.823		J. immunol. Meth.	223	79
104	2.816	3.859	Immunology	1118	397
105	2.807	1.814	Am. J. Pathol.	856	305
106	2.802	1.702	J. Lab. clin. Med.	1132	404
107	2.792	1.266	NS Arch. Pharmacol.	1033	370
108	2.782	1.638	J. comp. Physiol.	893	321
109	2.727	3.341	J. Bacteriology	3809	1397
110	2.711	2.658	Br. J. Hematol	824	504
111	2.709	3.012	J. Ultrastruct. Res.	837	309
111	2.709		Transplantation Proc.	1314	144
113	2.704	3.596	Physical Rev.	19174	7092
114	2.699	2.880	Molecular gen. Genetics	1293	479
115	2.600		Intervirology	91	35
115	2.600	1.374	J. Pediatrics	1890	727

152	2.361	2.064	Cancer	2056	871
153	2.357	2.014	J. Reprod. Fert.	1414	600
154	2.355	NA	J. psychiat. Res.	73	31
155	2.350	3.085	Proc. R. Soc. Lond.	1114	474
156	2.349	3.662	Psychol. Bull	444	189
157	2.347	2.380	Psychopharmacologia	1002	427
158	2.337		Drug Metab. Disposition	236	101
159	2.334	2.173	Molecular Physics	1258	539
160	2.311	2.561	Faraday Disc. chem. Soc.	208	90
161	2.297	1.374	J. Verbal Learning Verbal Behav.	395	172
162	2.291	1.636	Hoppe-Seylers Z. physiol. Chem.	1031	450
163	2.286		Organic Mass Spectrometry	704	308
164	2.279		J. Neurocytology	139	61
165	2.276	2.529	Macromolecules	776	341
166	2.268	2.061	Photochem. Photobiol.	542	239
167	2.267	0.987	Astronomy Astrophysics	2018	890
167	2.267		J. Steroid Biochem.	390	172
169	2.262	0.842	Invest. Ophthalmology	579	256
170	2.250	3.164	Transplantation	1134	504
171	2.237	0.869	Gen. comp. Endocrinol.	633	283
172	2.234		Cell Tissue Kinetics	239	107
173	2.217	1.449	Archs Neurology	745	336
174	2.205	1.514	Brain	291	132
175	2.204	2.479	Acta physiol. scand	919	417
176	2.200	1.769	Archs internal Med.	946	430
177	2.199	NA	Analytical Letters	497	226
178	2.193	NA	Physics Today	182	83
179	2.181	0.868	Neurology	796	365
180	2.173	1.271	J. Chromatography	2886	1328
181	2.160	2.127	J. gen. Microbiology	1136	526
182	2.151		J. non-crystalline Solids	628	292
183	2.147	2.876	Diabetologia	307	143
184	2.134	2.359	Physics Letters	7672	3595
185	2.129	1.613	Ann. Surgery	1060	496
186	2.128	3.089	Ann. Physics	598	281

A	B	C		D	E
187	2.100	1.207	Am. J. Obstet. Gynecol.	2236	1065
188	2.096	NA	Eur. J. clin. Pharmacol.	262	125
189	2.093	0.965	Analytica chim. Acta	1312	627
190	2.090	2.027	Eur. J. Cancer	466	223
191	2.083	1.787	Acta mathematica	75	36
192	2.082	2.252	J. magnetic Resonance	808	388
193	2.073		Expl Eye Res.	537	259
194	2.071		Cell Differentiation	145	70
195	2.062	1.839	Life Sciences	1200	582
196	2.056		Contraception	368	179
197	2.054	1.643	Int. J. Radiation Biol.	456	222
198	2.051	2.016	J. Atmospheric Sci.	769	375
199	2.041	1.195	J. Antibiotics Tokyo	445	218
200	2.032		Infection Immunity	1335	657
201	2.031	2.329	J. phys. Chem.	2768	1363
202	2.024	2.040	Aesthesiology	771	381
203	2.023	1.888	Biochem. Pharmacol.	1689	835
204	2.022	1.855	Theor. chim. Acta	645	319
205	2.016	0.904	J. opt. Soc. Am.	905	449
206	2.013	1.372	Proc. Instn electl electr. Engrs	781	388

b

A	B	C		D	E
1	25.579	9.600	Transplantation Revs	972	38
2	22.643	4.317	Adv. Immunology	317	14
3	21.500	17.584	Revs mod. Physics	318	34
4	19.358	17.584	Annu. Rev. Biochem.	1026	53
5	16.795	20.615	Bacteriol. Revs	655	39
6	15.778	NA	Curr. Topics Microbiol.	142	9
7	13.861	17.333	Physiol. Revs	499	36
8	12.545	13.428	Progr. Allergy	138	11
9	11.613	8.592	Rec. Progr. Hormone Res.	360	31
10	11.154	8.160	Chem. Revs	580	52

A	B	C		D	E
46	4.339	4.685	Rev. Geophys Space Physics	269	62
47	4.300	NA	Adv. Human Genetics	43	10
48	4.188	5.000	Medicine	268	64
49	4.176	NA	Adv. microb. Physiol.	71	17
50	4.156	4.433	Psychol. Rev.	320	77
51	4.000	NA	Adv. Lipid Res.	52	13
52	3.783	5.629	Annu. Rev. nucl. Sci.	87	23
53	3.750	4.695	Coordination Chem. Revs	255	68
53	3.750	NA	Prog. med. Virol.	60	16
55	3.500	3.555	Annu. Rev. phys. Chem.	133	38
55	3.500	NA	Prog. med. Genetics	49	14
57	3.462	NA	Prog. Surf. Membrane Sci.	45	13
58	3.412	7.333	Adv. Virus Res.	58	17
59	3.000	NA	Adv. metab. Disorders	21	7
59	3.000	3.818	Botanical Rev.	66	21
59	3.000		Drug Metab. Revs.	42	14
59	3.000	NA	Essays Biochem.	27	9
59	3.000	NA	Prog. Materials Sci.	15	5
64	2.923	NA	Catalysis Revs	76	26
65	2.909	4.500	Prog. cardiovasc. Dis.	160	55
66	2.900	NA	Int. Rev expl Pathol.	29	10
67	2.844	8.296	Rep. Prog. Physics	128	45
68	2.746	4.235	Annu. Rev. Medicine	173	63
69	2.456	4.000	Adv. Enzyme Regulation	106	43
70	2.462	0.176	Q. Rev. Biology	64	26
71	2.273	5.600	Adv. Carbohydr. Chem. Biochem.	25	11
72	2.250	2.888	Harvey Lectures	36	16
73	2.200	NA	Adv. clin. Chem.	22	10
74	2.188	NA	Adv. Pharmacol	35	16
75	2.086	NA	Annu. Rev. Psychol.	73	35
76	2.079	5.485	Annu. Rev. Entomology	79	38
77	2.071	NA	Applied Spectrosc. Rev.	29	14
78	2.047	4.914	Annu. Rev. Phytopathol.	88	43

Fig. 3 Significant journals in three scientific specialities. Each list gives journal, (A) total 1974 citations, (B) impact factor, (C) total 1974 citations of 1972 and 1973 articles, (D) number of 1974 articles. Journals are listed in alphabetical order. The botany journals include all with more than 600 citations or an impact greater than 1. The astronomy/astrophysics journals include all with more than 400 citations or an impact greater than 0.8. The mathematics journals include all with more than 500 citations or an impact greater than 0.5.

BOTANY

Journal	A	B	C	D
Am. J. Botany	3710	1.378	357	127
Ann. Botany	1674	1.069	232	130
Annu. Rev. Phytopathol.	566	2.047	88	21
Annu. Rev. Plant Physiol.	1760	7.316	278	19
Bot. Review	585	3.000	66	5
Can. J. Botany	2897	1.069	729	343
J. expl Botany	1762	1.506	369	120
J. Phycology	653	1.409	193	74
Mycologia	1143	0.607	176	128
New Phytologist	1405	1.158	300	115
Physiol. Plant Pathol.	206	1.152	114	49
Physiol. Plantarum	2617	1.555	479	196
Physiol. Végét.	322	1.172	116	43
Phytochemistry	4369	1.103	1568	624
Phytopathology	4842	1.155	789	372
Plant Cell Physiol.	1223	1.164	327	115
Plant Dis. Reporter	1489	0.413	307	379
Plant Physiology	8835	2.580	1935	373
Planta	4308	2.589	1261	219
Trans. Br. Mycol. Soc.	947	0.610	186	171
Z. Pflanzenphysiol.	1008	1.340	351	180

#			Journal	C	D
11	9.700	8.888	Adv. inorganic Chem. Radiochem.	97	10
12	9.577	22.400	Pharmacol. Revs	498	52
13	9.200	3.259	Adv. chem. Physics	92	10
14	8.379	7.743	Annu. Rev. Astr. Astrophys.	243	29
15	7.875	9.176	Prog. Biophys. molec. Biol.	189	24
16	7.833	–	Curr. Topics cell. Regulation	94	12
17	7.765	20.200	Prog. nucleic Acid Res.	132	17
18	7.403	17.083	Accts chem. Res.	881	119
19	7.375	3.688	Adv. Physics	177	24
20	7.316	7.047	Annu. Rev. Plant Physiol.	278	38
21	7.143	NA	Curr. Topics dev. Biol.	50	7
22	7.000	NA	Annu. Rev. Pharmacol.	329	47
23	6.963	NA	Adv. Cancer Res.	188	27
24	6.679	NA	Annu. Rev. Genetics	187	28
25	6.636	23.000	Adv. Protein Chem.	73	11
26	6.581	4.216	Annu. Rev. Physiol.	204	31
27	6.453	9.600	Adv. Enzymology	193	30
28	6.357	3.384	Erg.physiol. biol. Chem. exp. Pharm.	89	14
29	6.133	NA	Adv. organomet. Chem.	92	15
30	6.083	18.000	Prog. phys. org. Chem.	73	12
31	6.000	NA	Topics Stereochem.	24	4
32	5.733	–	Annu. Rev. Biophys. Bioengng	172	30
33	5.689	–	Chem. Soc. Revs	256	45
34	5.500	NA	Int. Rev. Cytology	209	38
35	5.444	–	Adv. cell. molec. Biol.	49	9
36	5.214	–	Q. Rev. Biophysics	73	14
37	5.045	NA	Adv. Quantum Chem.	111	22
38	5.000	NA	Adv. Colloid Interface Sci.	25	5
38	5.000	NA	Electroanalyt. Chem.	15	3
38	5.000	NA	Vitamins Hormones	55	11
41	4.923	3.647	Adv. cyclic Nucleotide Res.	256	52
42	4.775	6.545	Annu. Rev. Microbiol.	191	40
43	4.690	5.176	Biol. Revs Cambridge Phil. Soc.	136	29
44	4.500	16.285	Solid St. Physics	45	10
45	4.375	NA	Int. Rev. Neurobiol.	35	8

ASTRONOMY/ASTROPHYSICS

Journal	A	B	C	D
Ann. Geophysique Paris	588	0.786	110	28
Annu. Rev. Astron. Astrophys.	955	8.379	243	17
Astron. Zh.	738	0.435	171	194
Astronomical J.	2383	1.953	545	182
Astronomy Astrophysics	3899	2.267	2018	497
Astrophys. J.	22201	4.063	7451	1040
Astrophys. Letters	879	1.209	347	194
Astrophysics Space Sci.	963	1.048	395	189
Earth planetary Sci. Letters	2387	1.802	827	28
EOS Trans. Am. geophys. Union	625	2.967	389	134
Geochim. cosmochim. Acta	4023	4.056	1160	150
Icarus	1453	3.489	785	211
J. atmosph. Sci.	2630	2.051	769	210
J. atmosph. terrest. Physics	1886	1.322	509	
J. geophys. Res.	15281	2.536	3854	791
J. Spacecraft Rockets	421	0.334	139	199
Mon. Not. R. astron. Soc.	3858	2.467	1036	249
Planetary Space Sci.	2321	1.645	671	155
Publ. astron. Soc. Japan	360	0.874	83	44
Publ. astron. Soc. Pacific	1191	1.081	308	161
Publ. Dominion astrophys. Observatory	136	1.250	10	2
Q.J.R. astron. Soc.	128	0.923	48	20
Solar Physics	2831	1.929	1059	282
Revs Geophys. Space Physics	872	4.359	269	40
Sov. Astronomy AJ	456	0.295	116	194
Space Sci. Revs	637	1.718	177	34
Z. Astrophysik	597			

MATHEMATICS

Journal	A	B	C	D
Acta Math.	675	2.083	75	18
Adv. Math.	137	0.647	44	50
Am. J. Math.	1064	0.474	54	88
Ann. Mathematics	1921	1.226	103	35
Bull. Am. math. Soc.	1281	0.516	221	241
Comm. pure appl. Math.	750	0.598	49	25
C.r. Acad Sci. A	845	0.210	360	688
Duke math. J.	711	0.391	70	86
Indiana Univ. math. J.	207	0.590	111	94
Inventiones math.	383	0.808	105	67
J. Algebra	834	0.775	248	213
J. differential Equations	375	0.610	111	60
J. math. Anal. Appl.	871	0.393	190	235
J. Math. pures appl.	201	0.879	29	27
Math. Annln	1190	0.381	123	145
Math. Computation	602	0.557	107	109
Math. Z.	1150	0.471	164	152
Michigan math. J.	275	0.482	40	38
Pacific J. Math.	1133	0.279	180	239
Phil. Trans. R. Soc. A	1765	1.016	188	43
Proc. Am. math. Soc.	1725	0.304	433	516
Proc. Cambridge phil. Soc.	1348	0.397	91	103
Proc. London math. Soc.	834	0.533	81	78
Q. appl. Math.	538	0.505	49	43
SIAM J. math. Analysis	107	0.467	56	93
SIAM J. num. Analysis	333	0.662	100	89
Studia math.	506	0.491	106	59
Studies appl. Math.	99	0.615	32	20
Trans. Am. math. Soc.	2622	0.488	371	340

these journals began publication in the 1960s and 70s. Older journals like the *Comptes Rendus* rank well in Fig. 1(*a*), mainly because there is so much that can be cited. Fig. 1(*b*) is a needed supplement to the list in Fig. 1(*a*), since the journals have high current citation but lack historical mass to push them up into the top of a list ranked by total citations.

Figures 2 (*a* and *b*) show the 284 journals with impacts greater than 2. Fig. 2(*a*) lists 206 primary journals. Fig. 2(*b*) lists 78 review journals; the impact of review journals is generally higher than that of primary journals.

Figure 3 lists journals that rank highest in citation and impact for three specialties: mathematics, botany, and astronomy/astrophysics. The differences in average impact and citation between the three illustrative categories indicate why comparisons between journals in different specialities may be invidious. For example, it would be foolish to conclude merely on the basis of citation counts that *Astrophysical Journal* is a "better" journal than *Annals of Mathematics,* or to hypothesize without a great deal of study which serves its own field "better."

Variation from field to field is determined by the interplay of several factors. Perhaps the most important is the average number of references per paper in the field.[4] In general, mathematicians cite less than half as many papers as do biochemists. Engineers on the other hand cite books as heavily as journals, as do social scientists. Fur-

thermore, calculation of impact based on 1972 and 1973 publications is bound to affect the impact of journals in a field like mathematics, where citation of older literature is far more common than in others. Thus, the impact of mathematics journals would be higher if calculated on the basis of 1970 and 1971 publications.

It seems necessary to point out the obvious, as I have done in preparing Fig. 3, because one shortsighted criticism of the *JCR* has been that its listings and rankings are undiscriminating. One can get from the *JCR* information on journals within disciplines for intradisciplinary comparison. None of the mathematics journals listed in Fig. 3 was cited enough to appear in Fig. 1(*a*), but the citation counts and impact factors show plainly that the two leading mathematics journals are *Transactions of the American Mathematical Society* (on the basis of total citations) and *Acta Mathematica* (on the basis of impact). In both citation and impact the average mathematics journal ranks lower than the average astronomy or botany journal.

If one wishes to add to a general-science collection the two or three leading journals of mathematics, botany, or astronomy/astrophysics, one must examine longer lists and select from them the top journals in each speciality, as I have done in preparing Fig. 3.

The remarkable stability of the significant journals of science is attested by their continued high citation and impact. Of the 206 journals most cited in 1969, 169 remain among the top 206 in 1974. One may regard the changes as the result of healthy competition. The 37 journals that dropped from the 206 most cited between 1969 and 1974 rank between 224 and 426 in the complete listing that appears in the *JCR*.[5]

Perhaps the point to be stressed in presenting these data is the bibliographic law of concentration.[6] When the *SCI* was first reviewed in *Nature* more than a decade ago,[7] the scope of its journal coverage was called into question. I believe time has shown beyond doubt that the important literature of science is encompassed by fewer than 1,000 journals. And even fewer account for the truly significant. Of some 45,000 serials of all kinds received by the British Lending Library, two-thirds are rarely, if ever, subject of request. A small core of about 5,000 accounts for almost 80% of all requests.[8]

In using the data presented here, one should be aware that we revised our definition of "source items" used to calculate impact. In 1969 we included as source items much material (editorials, non-scientific and non-technical correspondence, news notes, and so on) that does not by its very nature invite citation in scientific and technical reports. This policy worked to the disadvantage of some major journals. Our redefinition accounts in part for the changed impact in 1974 of journals like *Nature, Science, Lancet, Journal of the American Medical Association, and British Medical Journal.*

What is the significance of journal impact? By demonstrating that only 150 journals have impacts greater than 3, I believe we have established the futility of discussions based on the assumption that the average library must acquire and store thousands of journals. Since the average impact in 1974 was 1.015, any of the journals listed in the figures is likely to be a good candidate for selection.

Fig. 2(b) shows clearly the importance of review journals, confirming our earlier studies. Their extraordinary impact, along with a surge in the number of review-type articles and publications, led to ISI's decision to publish *Index to Scientific Reviews™*.[9]

Clearly, a large part of the scientific record is of low impact. Only careful study can show whether this fact supports or contradicts the idea that science is built on the accumulated results of average effort that prepare the way for breakthroughs.[10] In any event, the data seem to me to warrant an examination of the cost-effectiveness of the present publishing system. Journals devote to the mass of rarely cited papers the same resources as to the small part that citation analysis shows to be important. Less than 1% of all papers cited will be cited ten or more times in any annual *SCI*. Although more than 40 million references have been processed for the *SCI* during the past fifteen years, only 116,400 papers have been cited ten times or more in any one year.

One would hope that the availability of *Journal Citation Reports* will have a salutary effect on editorial complacency. A change in a journal's citation rate or impact rate is proper reason for editorial concern, admitting that factors beyond editorial control may be responsible. Thus, a drop in the impact of the leading Soviet journal of physics *Zhurnal Eksperimentalnoi i Teoreticheskoi Fiziki*, or a rise in the impact of *Teploenergetika* (translated as *Thermal Engineering*) may reflect a shift in interest or emphasis of research worldwide. But a change in citation rate or impact rate may just as likely reflect a change in quality of output.

Journal citation analysis can be quite complex in some cases. The problem of Soviet publications is one such case. Apart from the usual bibliographic problems encountered, one must deal with the fact that most leading Soviet journals appear in two versions, Russian and English. *Fizika i Tekhnika Poluprovodnikov* appears in English as *Soviet Physics Semiconductors*. Clearly that is not a close translation of the title, much less a transliteration. Such bibliographic casualness about titles is bad enough, but there is worse. Most of the retitled translations appear about a year after the originals. This means, if one assumes that the translation is the major stimulant of subsequent citation in Western journals, that the citable life of the Soviet literature is unfairly shortened at the outset by an overlong gestation period. And the outset is important, for if an article is going to be cited, it is most likely to be cited during the first or second year after publication. In the case of Russian journals, citations contributed by translated versions are usually out of phase with those of the rest of the literature. To assure confusion worse confounded, some of the translated versions have volume and page numbers different from the Russian originals. In our tabulations for the *JCR*, we have as far as possible compensated for these annoying vagaries.

As the data show, new journals can achieve high impact quickly. Good examples are *Cellular Immunology* (first published 1970) and *Prostaglandins* (1972). Their total 1974 citation counts were 2,809 and 1,470 respectively; their impacts, 4.848 and 5.247. Among the newer journals the 'European' journals are especially notable in this respect. *FEBS Letters* (began 1968, impact 3.049); *European Journal of Biochemistry* (began 1967, impact 3.874); *European Journal of Immunology* (began 1971, impact 4.852). We must hope that internationalization of journals will continue. I believe that Latin-American, Asian, and African journals would do well to consolidate in like manner to produce fewer but larger journals. It is clear that a large journal, even if less than first class, is more difficult to ignore than a smaller journal with equal and perhaps greater impact.

In some cases, however, consolidation is inappropriate and may be detrimental. Take, for example, *Journal of the American Chemical*

Society (*JACS*) and *Journal of the Chemical Society*. The *Journal of the Chemical Society* encompasses nine different subtitled journals. If one were to consolidate comparable journals of the American Chemical Society, their total citation count would be about 183,000, almost double the 98,995 of the *JACS*. The impact of this conglomerate would, however, be only 3.381 (respectable enough) rather than 4.383. Insistence by the Chemical Society upon corporate identity for its journals by means of an identical "main title" with repeatedly retitled sections is the source of bibliographic confusion, as well as of much tedious work in sorting out citation data. It seems to me that most commercial publishers would have refused to scrap a title as well-known as *Transactions of the Faraday Society*. In my opinion, the umbrella of a corporate main title for all a society's journals does little for their individual identities.

I have avoided commentary on the performance of specific journals, preferring to use the space granted me here for data rather than comment and speculation. And I have published many such analyses, usually on a categorical basis in *Current Contents®* . All of them have had the same purpose, and lead to the same general conclusion. Science needs objective criteria for measuring the performance of journals. Citation analysis seems to offer a sound beginning. Considering the paucity of management tools available to the average science librarian—general or specialist—and considering as well the often prejudicial role of individual scientists in journal selection (we all have our favourite journals), I feel that the *JCR* data can provide a more reliable basis for journal selection than any we have had until now.

REFERENCES

1. **Garfield E.** *Science,* **178,** 471-479 (1972).
2. *Journal Citation Reports (JCR)* 1. *Journal Ranking Package.* 2. *Source Data Package.* 3. *Reference Data Package* (Institute for Scientific Information® , Philadelphia, 1973).
3. **Garfield E.** *Journal Citation Reports: a Bibliometric Analysis of References Processed for the 1974 Science Citation Index.,* Science Citation Index 1975 Annual, 9 (Institute for Scientific Information, Philadelphia, 1976).
4. **Garfield E.** *Current Contents,* **#6,** 5-7 (1976).
5. **Garfield E.** *Journal Citation Reports,* Section 2, 2-4 (1976).
6. **Garfield E.** *Current Contents,* **#31,** 5-6 (1971).
7. **Cleverden C W.** *Nature,* **203,** 446 (1964).
8. **Line M B & Wood D N.** *J. Documentation,* **31,** 234-245 (1975).
9. *Index to Scientific Reviews 1974 Annual, an International Interdisciplinary Index to the Review Literature of Science, Medicine, Agriculture, Technology, and the Behavioral Sciences,* 2 vols (Institute for Scientific Information, Philadelphia, 1975).
10. **Cole J R & Cole S.** *Science,* **178,**368-374 (1972).

CURRENT COMMENTS

Highly Cited Articles. 39. Biochemistry Papers Published in the 1950s.

Number 25, June 20, 1977

We recently published a list of the 1950s citation classics in the physical and chemical sciences.[1] Here is the list of biochemical articles. The biological, medical, and behavioral classics will follow shortly.

Each article was cited at least 500 times in the 15 year period from 1961 to 1975. Taking the entire universe of published articles into account, only about one in 20,000--or 0.005%--receives so many citations.

In February we published a list of highly cited biochemical articles published in the 1940s.[2] That list of 89 items, like the 1930s life sciences list,[3] which was composed primarily of biochemical articles, reflected one of the basic concerns of biochemistry--the analysis of phosphorus and its physiologic compounds. Some of the 78 highly-cited biochemical articles of the 1950s, listed in Figure 1, continue to reflect the importance of research into phosphorus determination. Phosphorus is basic to the study of DNA, sugars, lipids, and other biochemical substances.

Of the 78 articles in Figure 1, 25 have received over 1,000 citations, and 13 over 2,000. The majority of these papers concern methodology. This should come as no surprise to

biochemists themselves, many of whom acknowledge that methods are the backbone of all scientific research. David Gillespie of the National Cancer Institute discussed the process by which a method paper becomes a "classic."[4] He commented that "the distinction between a classic and a quickly outmoded method lies in the ability of the investigators to see the uses to which the method will be put and evaluate particular parameters accordingly and, as importantly, to take heed of the little irregularities that lead to significant improvements."

The importance of methods papers is also emphasized by Karl Piez, Chief of the Laboratory of Biochemistry of the National Institute of Dental Research. His highly-cited 1960 paper[5] modified the methodological procedure of the 1950s paper of Spackman, Stein, and Moore (66). Piez commented that their method was "a highly developed method and one of the most important procedures in modern biochemistry...."[6] Still, Piez was compelled, for the purposes of his own biochemical investigations, to modify the procedure. This illustrates the nature of biochemical advances. Both papers have now achieved very

Figure 1. Highly cited articles in biochemistry published in the 1950s. A = item number. **B** = total citations 1961-1975. **C** = average yearly citations 1961-1975. **D** = citations in 1974. **E** = citations in 1975. Articles are listed alphabetically by first author.

A	B	C	D	E	Bibliographic Data
1.	2791	186	294	281	Bartlett G R. Phosphorus assay in column chromatography. *J. Biol. Chem.* **234**:466-68, 1959.
2.	686	46	30	25	Bennett H S & Luft J H. Collidine as a basis for buffering fixatives. *J. Biophys. Biochem. Cytol.* **6**:113-17, 1959.
3.	779	52	52	44	Bertler A, Carlsson A & Rosengren E. A method for the fluorometric determination of adrenaline and noradrenaline in tissues. *Acta Physiol. Scand.* **44**:273-92, 1958.
4.	1830	122	253	264	Bligh E G & Dyer W J. A rapid method of total lipid extraction and purification. *Canad. J. Biochem. Physiol.* **37**:911-17, 1959.
5.	1123	75	42	61	Boas N F. Method for the determination of hexosamines in tissues. *J. Biol. Chem.* **204**:553-63, 1953.
6.	506	34	35	28	Bodanszky M & duVigneaud V. A method of synthesis of long peptide chains using a synthesis of oxytocin as an example. *J. Amer. Chem. Soc.* **81**:5688-91, 1959.
7.	1203	80	69	73	Boyer P D. Spectrophotometric study of the reaction of protein sulfhydryl groups with organic mercurials. *J. Amer. Chem. Soc.* **76**:4331-37, 1954.
8.	918	61	28	24	Brown J B. A chemical method for the determination of oestriol, oestrone and oestradiol in human urine. *Biochem. J.* **60**:185-93, 1955.
9.	5037	336	541	506	Burton K. A study of the conditions and mechanism of the diphenylamine reaction for the colormetric estimation of deoxyribonucleic acid. *Biochem. J.* **62**:315-23, 1956.
10.	934	62	22	21	Bush I E. Methods of paper chromatography of steroids applicable to the study of steroids in mammalian blood and tissues. *Biochem. J.* **50**:370-78, 1952.
11.	564	38	32	16	Cahn R S, Ingold C K & Prelog V. A specification of asymmetric configuration in organic chemistry. *Experientia* **12**:81-124, 1956.
12.	506	34	34	26	Carlsson A & Waldeck S. A fluorometric method for the determination of dopamine (3-hydroxytyramine). *Acta Physiol. Scand.* **44**:293-98, 1958.
13.	1109	74	34	25	Caulfield J B. Effects of varying the vehicle for OsO_4 in tissue fixation. *J. Biophys. Biochem. Cytol.* **3**:827-29, 1957.
14.	550	37	31	53	Ceriotti G. A microchemical determination of desoxyribonucleic acid. *J. Biol. Chem.* **198**:297-303, 1952.
15.	721	48	42	47	Ceriotti G. Determination of nucleic acids in animal tissues. *J. Biol. Chem.* **214**:59-70, 1955.

Figure 1 continued

16. 1984 132 225 225 **Chen P S Jr., Toribara T Y & Warner H.** Microdetermination of phosphorus. *Analyt. Chem.* **28**:1756-58, 1956.

17. 1097 73 115 128 **Dixon M.** The determination of enzyme inhibitor constants. *Biochemical J.* **55**:170-71, 1953.

18. 2705 180 133 94 **Dole V P.** A relation between non-esterified fatty acids in plasma and the metabolism of glucose. *J. Clin. Invest.* **35**:150-54, 1956.

19. 2732 182 367 334 **Dubois M, Gilles K A, Hamilton J K, Rebers P A & Smith F.** Colorimetric method for determination of sugars and related substances. *Analyt. Chem.* **28**:350-56, 1956.

20. 2255 150 217 147 **Eagle H.** Amino acid metabolism in mammalian cell cultures. *Science* **130**:432-37, 1959.

21. 2216 148 237 262 **Ellman G L.** Tissue sulfhydryl groups. *Arch. Biochem. Biophys.* **82**:70-77, 1959.

22. 557 37 24 28 **Folch J, Ascolli I, Lees M, Meath J A & LeBaron F N.** Preparation of lipide extracts from brain tissue. *J. Biol. Chem.* **191**:833, 1951.

23. 7454 497 776 706 **Folch J, Lees M & Sloane-Stanley G H.** A simple method for the isolation and purification of total lipides from animal tissues. *J. Biol. Chem.* **226**:497-509, 1957.

24. 612 41 67 43 **Gianetto R & deDuve C.** Tissue fractionation studies. IV. Comparative study of the binding of acid phosphatase, beta-glucorinidase and cathepsin by rat-liver particles. *Biochem. J.* **59**:433-38, 1955.

25. 611 41 42 43 **Glock G E & McLean P.** Further studies on the properties and assay of glucose-6-phosphate dehydrogenase and 6-phosphogluconate dehydrogenase of rat liver. *Biochem. J.* **55**:400-08, 1953.

26. 1193 80 65 83 **Hirs C H W.** The oxidation of ribonuclease with performic acid. *J. Biol. Chem.* **219**:611-21, 1956.

27. 619 41 26 20 **Hirsch J & Anrens E J, Jr.** The separation of complex lipide mixtures by the use of silicic acid chromatography. *J. Biol. Chem.* **233**:311-20, 1958.

28. 597 40 46 49 **Hohorst H J, Kreutz F H & Bucher T.** Metabolitgehalte und Metabolitkonzentrationen in der Leber der Ratte (Metabolite content and concentration in rat liver). *Biochem. Zschr.* **332**:18-46, 1959.

29. 580 39 22 14 **Hough L, Jones J K N & Wadman W H.** Quantitative analysis of mixtures of sugars by the method of partition chromatography. V. Improved methods for the separation and detection of the sugars and their methylated derivatives on the paper chromatogram. *J. Chem. Soc.* p. 1702-6, 1950.

30. 639 43 27 20 **Huckabee W E.** Relationships of pyruvate and lactate during anaerobic metabolism. I. Effects of infusion of pyruvate or glucose and of hyperventilation. *J. Clin. Invest.* **37**:244-54, 1958.

149

Figure 1 continued

31. 768 51 57 60 **Huggett A S G & Nixon D A.** Use of glucose oxidase, peroxidase and o-dianisidine in determination of blood and urinary glucose. *Lancet* 2:368-70, 1957.

32. 767 51 27 20 **Hurlbert R E, Schmitz H, Brumm A & Patter V R.** Nucleotide metabolism. II. Chromatographic separation of acid-soluble nucleotides. *J. Biol. Chem.* **209**:23-39, 1954.

33. 619 41 29 33 **Katz A M, Dreyer W J & Anfinsen C B.** Peptide separation by two-dimensional chromatography and electrophoresis. *J. Biol. Chem.* **234**:2897-2900, 1959.

34. 896 60 92 90 **Kauzmann W.** Some factors in the interpretation of protein denaturation. *Adv. Protein Chem.* 14:1-63, 1959.

35. 766 51 30 29 **Kay E R M, Simmons N S & Dounce A L.** An improved preparation of sodium desoxyribonucleate. *J. Amer. Chem. Soc.* **74**:1724-26, 1952.

36. 776 52 52 57 **Kellenberger E, Ryter A & Sechaud J.** Electron microscope study of DNA-containing plasms. II. Vegetative and mature phase DNA as compared with normal bacterial nucleoids in different physiological states. *J. Biophys. Biochem. Cytol.* 4:671-78, 1958.

37. 672 45 20 20 **Kirby K S.** A new method for the isolation of ribonucleic acids from mammalian tissues. *Biochem. J.* **64**: 405-8, 1956

38. 805 54 102 136 **Layne E.** Spectrophotometric and turbidimetric methods for measuring proteins. I. Turbidimetric methods. *Methods Enzym.* 3:447-49, 1957.

39. 50016 3334 7075 6842 **Lowry O H, Rosebrough N J, Farr A L & Randall R J.** Protein measurement with the Folin phenol reagent. *J. Biol. Chem.* **193**:256-65, 1951.

40. 712 47 24 27 **Markert C L & Mollner F.** Multiple forms of enzymes; tissue, ontogenetic, and species specific patterns. *P. Nat. Acad. Sci. USA* **45**:753-63, 1959.

41. 585 39 21 14 **Markham R & Smith J D.** The structure of nucleic acids. I. Cyclic nucleotides produced by ribonuclease and by alkaline hydrolysis. *Biochem. J.* **52**:552-57, 1952.

42. 540 36 11 10 **Marshall J D, Eveland W C & Smith C W.** Superiority of fluorescein isothiocyanate (Riggs) for fluorescent-antibody technic with a modification of its application. *P. Soc. Exp. Biol. Med.* **98**:898-900, 1958.

43. 513 34 62 67 **McFarlane A S.** Efficient trace-labelling of proteins with iodine. *Nature* **182**:53, 1958.

44. 579 39 21 21 **Meselson M, Stahl F W & Vinograd J.** Equilibrium sedimentation of macromolecules in density gradients. *P. Nat. Acad. Sci. USA* **43**:581-83, 1957.

45. 519 35 91 69 **Miller G L.** Protein determination for large numbers of samples. *Analyt. Chemistry* **31**:964, 1959.

46. 665 44 20 16 **Moffitt W & Yang J.** The optical rotary dispersion of simple polypeptides. *P. Nat. Acad. Sci. USA* **42**:596-602, 1956.

Figure 1 continued

47. 1368 91 74 57 **Moore S & Stein W H.** A modified ninhydrin reagent for the photometric determination of amino acids and related compounds. *J. Biol. Chem.* 211:907-13, 1954.

48. 1475 98 55 65 **Moore S, Spackman D H & Stein W H.** Chromatography of amino acids on sulfonated polystyrene resins. *Analyt. Chem.* 30:1185-90, 1958.

49. 1041 69 61 47 **Nachlas M M, Tsou K, DeSousa E, Cheng C & Seligman A M.** Cytochemical demonstration of succinic dehydrogenase by the use of a new p-nitropheneyl substituted diterzole. *J. Histochem. Cytochem.* 5:420-36, 1957.

50. 706 47 124 106 **Nash T.** The colorimetric estimation of formaldehyde by means of the Hantzch reaction. *Biochem. J.* 55:416-21, 1953.

51. 570 38 16 16 **Neuman R E & Logan M A.** The determination of hydroxyproline. *J. Biol. Chem.* 184:229-306, 1950.

52. 664 44 26 16 **Ogur M & Rosen G.** The nucleic acids of plant tissues. I. The extraction and estimation of desoxypentose nucleic acid and pentose nucleic acid. *Arch. Biochem. Biophys* 25:262-76, 1950.

53. 941 63 25 14 **Peterson E A & Sober H A.** Chromatography of proteins. I. Cellulose ion-exchange adsorbents. *J. Amer. Chem. Soc.* 78:751-55, 1956.

54. 564 38 12 12 **Peterson R E, Karrer A & Guerra S L.** Evaluation of Silber-Porter procedure for determination of plasma hydrocortisone. *Analyt. Chem.* 29:144-49, 1957.

55. 1242 83 85 82 **Porter R R.** The hydrolysis of rabbit gamma-globulin and antibodies with crystalline papain. *Biochem. J.* 73:119-26, 1959.

56. 728 49 52 61 **Reissig J L, Strominger J L & Leloir L F.** A modified colorimetric method for the estimation of N-acetylamino sugars. *J. Biol. Chem.* 217:959-66, 1955.

57. 604 40 36 36 **Rondle C J M & Morgan W T J.** The determination of glucosamine and galactosamine. *Biochem. J.* 61:586-89, 1955.

58. 845 56 52 41 **Rosen H.** A modified ninhydrin colorimetric analysis for amino acids. *Arch. Biochem. Biophys.* 67:10-15, 1957.

59. 694 46 59 63 **Schwert G W & Takenaka Y.** A spectrophotometric determination of trypsin and chymotrypsin. *Biochim. Biophys. Acta.* 16:570-75, 1955.

60. 733 49 41 51 **Seifter S, Dayton S, Novic B & Muntwyler E.** The estimation of glycogen with the anthrone reagent. *Arch. Biochem. Biophys.* 25:191-200, 1950.

61. 647 43 38 27 **Sheehan J C & Hess G P.** A new method for forming peptide bonds. *J. Amer. Chem. Soc.* 77:1067-68, 1955.

62. 586 39 52 37 **Simon E J & Shemin D.** The preparation of S-succinyl coenzyme A. *J. Amer. Chem. Soc.* 75:2520, 1953.

Figure 1 continued

63. 752   50   38   31 **Skou J C.** The influence of some cations on an adenosine triphosphatase from peripheral nerves. *Biochim. Biophys. Acta* 23:394-401, 1957.

64. 2041 136 49   56 **Smithies O.** Zone electrophoresis in starch gels; group variations in the serum proteins of normal human adults. *Biochem. J.* 61:629-41, 1955.

65. 1439 96   99   81 **Somogyi M.** Notes on sugar determination. *J. Biol. Chem.* 195:19-23, 1952.

66. 5727 382 450 438 **Spackman D H, Stein W H & Moore S.** Automatic recording apparatus for use in the chromatography of amino acids. *Analyt. Chem.* 30:1190-1206, 1958.

67. 562   37   55   52 **Spizizen J.** Transformation of biochemically deficient strains of *Bacillus subtilis* by deoxyribonucleate. *P. Nat. Acad. Sci. USA* 44:1072-78, 1958.

68. 701   47   63   65 **Svennerholm L.** Quantitative estimation of sialic acids. II. A colorimetric resorcinol-hydrochloric acid method. *Biochim. Biophys. Acta* 74:604-11, 1957.

69. 561   37   54   57 **Taussky H H & Schorr E.** A microcolorimetric method for the determination of inorganic phosphorus. *J. Biol. Chem.* 202:675-85, 1953.

70. 725   48   41   36 **Tiselius A, Hjerten S & Levin O.** Protein chromatography on calcium phosphate columns. *Arch. Biochem. Biophys.* 65:132-55, 1956.

71. 2244 150 185 140 **Trevelyan W E, Procter D P & Harrison J S.** Detection of sugars on paper chromatograms. *Nature* 166:444-45, 1950.

72. 823   55   114 91 **Vogel H J.** Acetylornithinase of *Escherichia coli;* partial purification and some properties. *J. Biol. Chem.* 218:97-106, 1956.

73. 2656 177 282 293 **Warren L.** The thiobarbituric acid assay of sialic acids. *J. Biol. Chem.* 234:1971-75, 1959.

74. 552   37   19   16 **Watson J D & Crick F H C.** A structure for deoxyribose nucleic acid. *Nature* 171:737-38, 1953.

75. 2509 137 214 181 **Watson M L.** Staining of tissue sections for electron microscopy with heavy metals. *J. Biophys. Biochem. Cytol.* 4:475-79, 1958.

76. 767   51   18   10 **Wyatt G R.** The purine and pyridimine composition of deoxypentose nucleic acids. *Biochem. J.* 48:584-90, 1951.

77. 541   36   15   11 **Yarmolinsky M B & dela Haba G L.** Inhibition by puromycin of amino acid incorporation into protein. *P. Nat. Acad. Sci. USA* 45:1721-29, 1959.

78. 741   49   45   47 **Yemm E W & Cocking E C.** The determination of amino acids with ninhydrin. *Analyst* 80:209-13, 1955.

high citation rates.

On the other hand, the article by Watson and Crick (74) may be indicative of what is called the "obliteration phenomenon."[7] Many important scientific discoveries are quickly incorporated into the common wisdom of the field. Authors no longer feel compelled to cite the original discovery. Compared to the citation rates for other classics on the list, and considering the enormous amount of research in molecular biology, the Watson and Crick paper will probably soon become obliterated. In the period 1961-1975, it received only 552 citations--a yearly average of 37. In 1975 it was cited "only" 16 times. Few other papers in Figure 1 have registered such sharp decreases.

Many of the papers on this list are citation superstars--Lowry (39) with 50,016 citations; Folch (23) with 7,454; Burton (9) with 5,037; and Bartlett (1) with 2,791. All of these have 1974 and 1975 citation rates well above their yearly averages, indicating that activity in these fields has increased in recent years.

Six authors of these 1950s articles also appeared on our 1940s list with method papers: Lowry (39), Markham and Smith (41), Moore and Stein (47, 48, and 66), and Taussky (69). Those by Markham and Smith, and Moore and Stein, concerned chromatographic techniques.

Eleven of these articles have been authored by 11 Nobel laureates. Watson of the U.S. and Crick of England (74) shared the Nobel Prize for medicine in 1962. Tiselius of Sweden (70) received the 1948 Prize in chemistry for his discovery and isolation of mouse paralysis virus. In 1972 Porter of Britain (55) received the medical Prize for research on the chemical structure and nature of antibodies. The 1970 Nobel Prize for chemistry was awarded to Leloir of Argentina (56) for his discovery of sugar nucleotides and their role in the biosynthesis of carbohydrates. For his research into the inner workings of living cells, deDuve of the U.S. (24) received the 1974 Nobel Prize for medicine. The 1975 Prize for chemistry was awarded to Prelog of Switzerland (11), a native of Yugoslavia, for his research on the structure of bio-

Figure 2. Journals that published the highly cited 1950s articles listed in Figure 1, according to number of articles. A = number of articles. (Present titles of some journals are given in parenthesis.)

A	Journals
18	J. Biol. Chemistry
14	Biochemical Journal
6	Analytical Chemistry
6	J. Amer. Chem. Soc.
5	Arch. Biochem. Biophys.
5	Proc. Nat. Acad. Sci. USA
4	J. Biophys. Biochem. (J. Cell Bio.)
3	Biochim. Biophys. Acta
3	Nature
2	J. Clin. Invest.
1	Acta Physiol. Scand.
1	Adv. Protein Chem.
1	Analyst
1	Biochem. Zschr. (Eur. J. Biochemistry)
1	Canadian J. Biochem. Physiol.
1	Experientia
1	J. Chem. Soc.
1	J. Histochem. Cytochem.
1	Lancet
1	Methods Enzymol.
1	Proc. Soc. Exp. Biol. Med.
1	Science

logical molecules. In 1955 duVigneaud of the U.S. (6) received the chemistry Prize for his work on pituitary hormones. Three other Americans, Anfinsen (33), Moore and Stein (47, 48, and 66) shared the 1972 chemistry Prize for their pioneering studies on enzymes.

Figure 2 lists the 22 journals that published these articles. Just two journals published 32 of the 78 articles. The *Journal of Biological Chemistry* published 18 articles, and the *Biochemical Journal* 14. *Analytical Chemistry* and the *Journal of the American Chemical Society* published 6 each. All but 3 of the articles authored by Nobelists appeared in these four journals, which accounted for 56% (44 articles) of the papers in Figure 1.

The great majority of these 78 articles were published in the latter half of the 1950s. From 1950-1954, 23 articles were published. The remaining 55 articles appeared from 1955-1959, with increasing frequency by the years. In the late 1940s and early 1950s there was a tremendous amount of research done on the structural elements of DNA. Both Watson[8] and Crick[9] have acknowledged that at the time of their own efforts numerous other investigators were active. The success and impact of their work helps explain the flurry of activity in biochemistry in the mid to late 1950s-- with a little monetary help from our friends in Washington and elsewhere.

Much of the methodological groundwork for the 1950s biochemical research--such as chromatography and its application to nucleic acids--had been laid in previous decades. In the same way, these classic papers of the 1950s helped lay the foundation for biochemical research today. In particular, the discovery of DNA and its capacity for carrying genetic material has led science to a more complete understanding of the mysteries of life.

REFERENCES

1. **Garfield, E.** Highly cited articles. 38. Physics and chemistry papers published in the 1950s. *Current Contents®* No. 23, 6 June 1977, p. 5-9.

2. ---------------. Highly cited articles. 35. Biochemistry papers published in the 1940s. *Current Contents* No. 8, 21 February 1977, p. 5-11.

3. ---------------. Citation classics. 2. Articles from the life sciences 1930-1939. *Current Contents* No. 43, 25 October 1976, p. 5-10.

4. **Gillespie D.** *Citation classics.* A quantitative assay for DNA-RNA hybrids with DNA immobilized on a membrane. *Current Contents* No. 11, 14 March 1977, p. 14.

5. **Piez K A & Morris L.** A modified procedure for the automatic analysis of amino acid. *Analytical Biochemistry* 1:187-201, 1960.

6. **Piez K A.** Personal communication, 18 January 1977.

7. **Garfield E.** The 'obliteration phenomenon' in science, and the advantage of being obliterated. *Current Contents* No. 51/52, 22 December 1975, p. 5-7.

8. **Watson J D.** *The double helix: being a personal account of the discovery of the structure of DNA.* New York: Atheneum, 1968.

9. **Olby R.** *The path to the double helix.* Seattle: University of Washington Press, 1974.

CURRENT COMMENTS

Negative Science and "The Outlook
for the Flying Machine"

Number 26, June 27, 1977

The history of negative science has long fascinated me. There are always theoreticians around who can "prove" that almost anything can't be done. The history of heavier-than-air flying is full of such pessimistic predictions. And similar examples can probably be found in most branches of knowledge.

An often-quoted example is reprinted on page 17. "The Outlook for the Flying Machine"[1] by Simon Newcomb is a logical, rational, reasonable argument against building a flying machine. The argument is now amusingly preposterous. But given the state of aeronautics in 1903 one can easily see how Newcomb's authoritative article convinced most readers.

For many, Newcomb's prognosis for heavier-than-air flight now symbolizes the potential shortsightedness of leading establishment scientists. The example is invoked to support proponents of astrology, psychokinesis and the theories of Velikovsky.[2] If a person with Newcomb's credentials could be so wrong, why couldn't Newton, Einstein, Darwin, etc. have been equally wrong?

Newcomb was a pillar of the scientific establishment. He directed the American Nautical Almanac Office, was professor of mathematics and astronomy at Johns Hopkins University, was a founder and first president of the American Astronomical Society, and was vice-president of the National Academy of Sciences. He received numerous awards, published dozens of scholarly papers and books, and was a popularizer of astronomy and economics.

Newcomb's mathematical ideas are largely responsible for the genesis of one of the classic novels of science fiction--if not for a whole genre of science fiction which now comprises thousands of books and stories. In *The Time Machine,*[3] H.G. Wells links the idea of a fourth spatial dimension specifically with a "Professor Simon Newcomb." Apparently, Wells had read a paper in which Newcomb postulated a *spatial* dimension "at right angles to the other three."[4] Wells proposed instead that the fourth dimension is *time*--a dimension through which man can travel as easily as he travels through the three dimensions of space.

155

In the *National Observer* serialization which preceded the novel, Wells has his "Philosophical Inventor" explain that:

> ...space, as our mathematicians have it, is spoken of as having three dimensions, which one may call Length, Breadth, and Thickness, and is always definable by reference to three planes, each at right angles to the others. But some philosophical people have been asking why *three* dimensions particularly--why not another direction at right angles to the other three?--and have even tried to construct a Four-dimensional geometry. Professor Simon Newcomb was expounding this to the New York Mathematical Society only a month or so ago. You know how on a flat surface which has only two dimensions we can represent a figure of a three-dimensional solid, and similarly they think that by models of three dimensions they could represent one of four--if they could master the perspective of the thing. See?[5]

Incidentally, H.G. Wells also referred to Newcomb in a nonfiction article entitled "The Cyclic Delusion."[6]

Newcomb himself was no slouch as a philosopher. In 1898 he discussed the notion of "hyper-space"--a term which has now become a science-fiction cliché used to explain faster-than-light travel. And seven years before Einstein's special theory of relativity, Newcomb wrote,

> The laws of space are only laws of relative position.... For us the limits of space are simply the limits to which we can suppose a body to move. Hence when space itself is spoken of as having possible curvatures, hills and hollows it seems to me that this should be regarded only as a curvature if I may use the term of the laws of position of material bodies in space.[7]

The first paragraph of the reprint which follows refers to Samuel Pierpont Langley, secretary of the Smithsonian Institution and an astronomer, mathematician, inventor and optimist.[8] With a $50,000 War Department grant and five years' effort, Langley built a "man-carrying Aerodrome," which was tested by his assistant, Charles Manly, in October 1903. The result was total failure. The Aerodrome, which was launched from a catapult device mounted on a barge in the Potomac River, travelled only a few yards before falling into the water.

Two months later, on December 8, the second test failed. Although Langley blamed the failure on the launching mechanism rather than on the Aerodrome itself, he was ridiculed and abused in the press. His government funds were cut off, and he was threatened with a Congressional investigation for wasting public money. Nine days later, on December 17, 1903, the Wright brothers' "Flyer 1" rose from the sands of Kitty Hawk.

The *New York Times* and other newspapers had supported Newcomb's views. The *Times* editorial stated:

> It would serve no useful purpose to say anything which would increase the disappointment and mortification of Professor Langley at the instant and complete collapse of his airship, which broke in two and dropped into the Potomac, carrying Professor Manly to his second involuntary cold bath in that stream. The fact has established itself that Professor Langley is not a mechanician, and that his mathematics are better adapted to calculations of astronomical interest than to determining the strength of materials in mechanical constructions. Had his machine collided with a stronger and heavier machine in the launching, it might have broken its back without discrediting the formula of its inventor. But since it encountered only air, the fact that it broke in two means nothing other or different than that it was not strong enough for the work expected of it. Obviously the calculations which inspired Professor Langley with so much confidence were correct to a demonstration; probably that happened in this instance which is liable to happen in all mechanical constructions, the materials did not conform to the data on which the calculations were based. They never will. The margin of safety which the engineer allows arbitrarily for strength in excess of that which his calculations show him is sufficient is based upon experience that materials do not always, if often, do what is expected of them, and what they are theoretically capable of doing. That "there is always, somewhere, a weakest spot," is why the factor of safety is allowed. To allow it in an aeroplane would be to weight it so that it would be too heavy for its purpose.
>
> We hope that Professor Langley will not put his substantial greatness as a scientist in further peril by continuing to waste his time, and the money involved, in further airship experiments. Life is short, and he is capable of services to humanity incomparably greater than can be expected to result from trying to fly.... For students and investigators of the Langley type there are more useful employments, with fewer disappointments and mortifications than have been the portion of aerial navigators since the days of Icarus. [9]

Wilbur and Orville Wright are often thought of as semi-literate bicycle mechanics who luckily stumbled upon a workable airplane design. The fact is that the brothers were not only research scientists, but were also expert engineers and mechanics. In order to succeed in building a flying machine they had to solve many theoretical and practical problems. They did so using what is now regarded as scientific method, beginning with kites and moving on to gliders before considering the special problems of powered flight. They even began their research by requesting that the Smithsonian Institution perform a literature search on the subject of flying.

On December 17, 1903, at 10:35 a.m., Orville Wright took off at the controls of "Flyer 1," flew for 12 seconds, and landed safely--the first controlled, man-carrying mechanical-powered flight in history.

But almost five years went by before it was generally accepted that the Wright brothers had flown in their machine. After all, who were the Wright brothers to make such a claim when the most learned professors--including Professor Simon Newcomb--had "proved" that powered flight was impossible?

In fact, the first published eyewitness account of the Wright brothers' flight was published not in *Science, Nature* or the *New York Times*--but in the January 1905 issue of *Gleanings in Bee Culture*. The editor, A.I. Root, had travelled to Dayton from Medina, Ohio, to watch the flight.

Even three years after the Wrights' success, Simon Newcomb remained as adamant as ever in his conviction that man would never fly. In 1906 he wrote,

> The demonstration that no possible combination of known substances, known forms of machinery, and known forms of force can be united in a practicable machine by which men shall fly long distances through the air, seems to the writer as complete as it is possible for the demonstration of any physical fact to be.[10]

In light of the discrepancy in their forecasts for the flying machine, it is interesting to examine the later citation records of both Newcomb and the Wrights. According to *Science Citation Index®* (*SCI®*) data, in the 16 year period from 1961 to 1976, Simon Newcomb was cited 183 times. Most of the citations were made in astronomical articles on the planet Mercury. His mathematical papers on probability and statistical sampling theory were less often cited. It is a tribute to Newcomb's talents that his work is still being cited eighty years after publication. In one case, however, Newcomb was cited in a listing of ridiculous predictions.[11] Ironically, the Wright brothers, whose invention has now significantly changed our civilization, and who did publish reports of their experiences and discoveries,[12, 13] have been cited only once in the 16-year period.[14] It would be interesting to know how long it took before their work became obliterated.[15] We may learn this if we can ever compile an *SCI* for the period 1900-1960.

Of course, Simon Newcomb was not alone in his prediction of doom for the flying machine. For example, in 1888 Joseph Le Conte, Professor of Geology and Natural History at the University of California, wrote, "I am one of those who think that a flying-machine...is impossible, in spite of the testimony of the birds." Surprisingly, Le Conte admitted that "many wonderful and apparently impossible things have indeed come to pass; and that, too, in spite of the adverse predictions of some rash scientists." However, he went on to announce three "indisputable facts":

1. There is a low limit of weight, certainly not much beyond fifty pounds, beyond which it is impossible for an animal to fly. Nature has reached this limit, and with her utmost effort has failed to pass it.

2. The animal machine is far more effective than any we may hope to make; therefore the limit of the weight of a successful flying-machine can not be more than fifty pounds.

3. The weight of any machine constructed for flying, including fuel and engineer, can not be less than three or four hundred pounds.[16]

Although Le Conte later partially retracted his negative prediction,[17] in 1888 he concluded,

> A pure flying-machine is impossible. All that we can expect--all that true scientists do expect--is, by skillful combination of the balloon principle with the true flying principle, to make *aerial navigation* possible in moderately favorable weather--in other words, to make a *locomotive balloon;* or, if we choose so to call it, an *aerial swimming-machine.* That something really useful of this kind will eventually be made, there can be no reasonable doubt.[16]

Even earlier, it seems that it was fashionable to ridicule those men who were working on flying machines. In 1868 the London *Daily Telegraph* published an editorial which compared "flying philosophers" to "the proprietors of donkeys which are announced to ascend a ladder. The donkey never really goes up, and the philosopher has not yet flown."[18] (p. 64) Unfortunately, some prominent scientists tended to agree that powered flight was impossible. Lord Kelvin (William Thomsen), the engineer and physicist, commented, "I have not the smallest molecule of faith in aerial navigation other than ballooning."[18] (p. 80) The often-quoted "If God had intended that man should fly He would have given him wings" is widely attributed to the 1901 remark of George W. Melville, Chief Engineer of the United States Navy.

Even after the Wright brothers' 1903 success, some commentators hedged their bets, conceding that a heavier-than-air machine just might possibly fly, but certainly *never* would carry passengers, be used commercially, etc.

The engineer Octave Chanute said,

> This machine may even carry mail in special cases. But the useful loads will be very small. The machines will eventually be fast, they will be used in sport, but they are not to be thought of as commercial carriers.[19]

Only eleven years later the first air passenger service began in Florida. The astronomer William H. Pickering also debunked the idea of commercial, trans-Atlantic air service. He wrote,

> The popular mind often pictures gigantic flying machines speeding across the Atlantic carrying innumerable passengers. It seems safe to say that such ideas must be wholly visionary. Even if a machine could get across with one or two passengers, it would be prohibitive to any but the capitalist who could own his own yacht.[19]

Even as late as 1910, the following predictions regarding commercial aviation were made by the mechanical engineer Robert W.A. Brewer:

> One thing is certain, and that is that the future flyer will be a larger and heavier machine than it is at present--it will probably weigh at least three tons, and will be of the form of a flying yacht. It will probably have a boat body, decked in, and proper accommodation will be provided for living and sleeping.... A large area will be used for starting, and special starting and alighting grounds will be prepared throughout the civilized countries of the world. These grounds will be fitted up with large starting machines similar to enormous catapults....
>
> A trailing line will be lowered from the machine and special apparatus will be devised for picking up stores on the same lines as those adopted in railway practice for picking up mails by a passing train.
>
> It may be necessary for the machine to encircle the depot a few times for this purpose, but such manoeuvering will be an easy matter when the full area of sustentation is used. This idea can be carried out in a practical manner, and is not merely mad anticipation.[20]

It seems that at the turn of the century negative science reached a peak. Having witnessed tremendous technological changes during their own lifetimes, some scientists felt that the rate of change just had to wind down. In 1894 Albert Abraham Michelson, the co-discoverer of the speed of light, proclaimed,

> The more important fundamental laws and facts of physical science have all been discovered, and these are now so firmly established that the possibility of their ever being supplanted in consequence of new discoveries is exceedingly remote.... Our future discoveries must be looked for in the sixth place of decimals.[21]

In the nineteenth century some of the most accurate forecasters of things to come were the writers of science fiction. Over a century ago Jules Verne described voyages around the world in airships, and even postulated helicopters. In 1886 Verne wrote,

> But we must admit the possibility that continued investigation and experience will bring us ever nearer to that solemn moment, when the first man will rise from earth by means of wings, if only for a few seconds, and marks that historical moment which heralds the inauguration of a new era in our civilization.[18] (p. 72)

It is remarkable that in the thirteenth century, Roger Bacon wrote,

> It is possible to make engines for flying, a man sitting in the midst thereof, by turning only about an instrument, which moves artificial wings made to beat the air, much after the fashion of a bird's flight.[18] (p. 24)

In the seventeenth century, Robert Burton concurred,

> If the heavens then be penetrable, and no lets, it were not amiss to make wings and fly up; and some new-fangled wits, methinks, should some time or other find out.[18] (p. 24)

Greater precision was demanded by Bishop John Wilkins, who in his book *Mathematical Magick* not only conceded that man might fly, but categorized the known methods for doing so:

> There are four several ways whereby this flying in the air hath been or may be attempted. Two of them by the strength of other things, and two of them by our own strength. (1) By spirits, or angels. (2) By the help of fowls. (3) By wings fastened immediately to the body. (4) By a flying chariot.[22]

Among the many nineteenth-century engineers and inventors who considered the problem of powered flight, one of the most nearly successful was Sir George Cayley, now widely regarded as the inventor of the airplane in its present configuration. In 1809 Cayley foresaw the societal changes that the airplane would bring:

> I may be expediting the attainment of an object that will in time be found of great importance to mankind; so much so, that a new era in society will commence from the moment that aerial navigation is familiarly realised.... I feel perfectly confident, however,

that this noble art will soon be brought home to man's convenience, and that we shall be able to transport ourselves and families, and their goods and chattels, more securely by air than by water, and with a velocity of from 20 to 100 miles per hour.[18] (p. 40)

Incidentally, Cayley succeeded with a manned glider flight in 1852. The pilot for this historic flight was his coachman--who also contributed an historic comment. Upon completion of the flight, the coachman remarked, "Please, Sir George, I wish to give notice. I was hired to drive and not to fly."[23]

It is interesting that even today, almost a decade after man first set foot on the moon, a "Man Will Never Fly Memorial Society" flourishes in North Carolina. According to its founder, Dr. Ed North, it is a "bottle-in-hand, tongue-in-cheek organization" of about 5,000 people who meet each December 16 at Kitty Hawk, North Carolina. The Society contends that,

> ...deep down inside you know that no machine made of several tons of metal is going to "fly"....
>
> The Wright Brothers' alleged first flight was faked. They got their "Flyer" a few feet in the air on a windy morning just as you might get a big kite off the ground, a photographer snapped a picture of it as "proof" and people have been soaring into--and plummeting from--the skies ever since because they *believe* it can be done.
>
> But how many "unexplained" air crashes are there? And in how many of those did the pilot suddenly say to himself. "By George, The Man Will Never Fly Memorial Society is right. This thing can't possibly fly." Crash! Headlines![24]

Of course, the society is not serious--its required pledge is, "Given a choice, I will never fly, or given no choice, I will never fly sober"--but its very existence demonstrates that people still enjoy indulging in the fantasy that flying machines are impossible.

It is unfortunate that even in this century, as air travel was becoming commonplace, the naysayers were in abundant supply. Now their attention was focused on rocketry, paralleling and repeating the embarrassing mistakes of their predecessors. Since these later pessimists were probably familiar with the ridicule directed at the airplane, which had resulted in embarrassment for those who said it couldn't be done, perhaps we should admire the blind perseverence of those who continued to insist that the next step--space travel--remained impossible.

Even as commercial airmail services flourished, the *New York Times* did not learn from its previous error. Commenting on Robert Goddard's rocket research, the *Times* in 1921 remarked,

That Professor Goddard with his "chair" in Clark College and the countenancing of the Smithsonian Institution does not know the relation of action to reaction, and of the need to have something better than a vacuum against which to react--to say that would be absurd. Of course he only seems to lack the knowledge ladled out daily in high schools.[25]

In 1935 the astronomer F.R. Moulton wrote,

In all fairness to those who by training are not prepared to evaluate the fundamental difficulties of going from one planet to another, or even from the Earth to the Moon, it must be stated that there is not the slightest possibility of such journeys. [26]

And in a 1948 editorial the London *Daily Mirror* announced,

Our candid opinion is that all talk of going to the Moon...is sheer balderdash.[27]

In contrast, back in 1634 the astronomer Johannes Kepler wrote a science-fiction story in which the hero travels to the moon (towed by a flock of geese) and meets the natives.[28] In 1822 Lord Byron asserted, "I suppose we shall soon travel by air-vessels; make air instead of sea-voyages; and at length find our way to the moon, in spite of the want of atmosphere."[18] (p. 40). And between 1865 and 1870, Jules Verne's fictional forecasts verged on prophecy. His astronauts are mostly Americans; they blast off from Stony Hill, Florida (only 100 miles from Cape Canaveral); they encounter problems in space such as weightlessness; they land in the Pacific and are taken from their floating capsule by a battleship.[29]

Even a technological forecast made by the Wright brothers themselves was proved wrong only a few years later. In 1917--ironically, the year that marked the entry of the U.S. into the first World War--Orville Wright said,

When my brother and I built and flew the first man-carrying flying machine, we thought that we were introducing into the world an invention which would make further wars practically impossible.[18] (p. 40)

H.G. Wells had done better in 1902, when he predicted that by 1950 there would be heavier-than-air flying machines capable of practical use in war. However, Wells expected this view to excite "considerable ridicule."

But a decidedly modern, utilitarian attitude toward new inventions was demonstrated by Benjamin Franklin, who witnessed the first ascension of a hot-air balloon in Paris. When someone asked what good a balloon would be, Franklin is reported to have replied, "What good is a new-born baby?" Franklin went on,

> Convincing sovereigns of the folly of wars may perhaps be one effect of it, since it will be impractical for the most potent of them to guard his dominions. Five thousand balloons, capable of raising two men each, could not cost more than five ships of the line; and where is the prince who can afford so to cover his country with troops for its defense as that ten thousand men descending from the clouds might not in many places do an infinite deal of mischief before force could be brought together to repel them?[30]

Clearly, technological forecasting is a risky business. Some of the most accurate predictions, at least in the case of the flying machine, were made by science fiction writers, perhaps because they guessed so often and so wildly. In this century, between 1914 and 1935 five science fiction writers prophesied the large-scale release of nuclear energy. As Anthony R. Michaelis, editor of *Interdisciplinary Science Reviews,* has written, "It is surprising how often the trained imagination of writers, when brought to bear on scientific facts which are not yet exploited by technology, can approach the truth."[31] It is difficult to generalize about the views of scientists, either in the 19th century or today. But it is true that when asked to put their reputations on the line many scientists tend to be conservative. They are trained--quite properly--not to make categorical assertions.

As Arthur C. Clarke, the science fiction writer, has written,

> When an elderly and distinguished scientist tells you that something is impossible, he is almost certainly wrong. The expert can spot all the difficulties, but lacks the imagination or vision to see how they may be overcome. The layman's ignorant optimism turns out, in the long run--and often in the short run--to be nearer the truth.[32]

On the other hand, many gullible people with "ignorant optimism" have been conned out of their hard-earned money by those with more "imagination" and "vision."

There are an awful lot of crackpot ideas that have been popular at one time or another. Most are based on emotional, intuitive feelings rather than hard facts.

The awful truth is that hindsight is often better than foresight. How the openmindedness of a Benjamin Franklin and the closed-mindedness of a Simon Newcomb can be compared is a subject inadequately treated by philosophers and historians of science. Even the formal training of most Ph.D.'s today would not enable them to deal with the persuasiveness of a Simon Newcomb. I wonder how many of the readers of the reprint could write the appropriate rebuttal--even though all of them take flying for granted! In fact, for lack of a proper citation index, I can not determine whether anyone ever *did* publish a paper showing that Newcomb was wrong.

The important point to be made here applies equally well to the flying machine, the computer, the laser, nuclear fusion, and every other important invention ever produced. It also applies to areas of investigation at present considered by many not worthy of scientific investigation: psychokinesis, telepathy, out-of-body travel, and even pyramid power. Science is a powerful tool for discovering the truth, but in some ways it is a conservative and stabilizing tool. Those phenomena and discoveries which do not fit into the present paradigms of science are not merely discredited, but are sometimes flippantly ridiculed.

Negative scientists can avoid future embarassment by helping their antagonists design experiments that might prove or disprove the disputed scientific wisdom.

The reprint which follows should serve to remind all of us that what seems impossible, foolish, or ridiculous today may make perfect sense tomorrow. How much of today's negative science will be recognized--and perhaps reprinted--a century or two from now?

REFERENCES

1. **Newcomb S.** The outlook for the flying machine. *The Independent Magazine* 22 October 1903, p. 2508-12.
2. **Arnold L E.** To exorcise quackery. *Industrial Research* 19(2):141-45, February 1977.
3. **Wells H G.** The time machine. *The Short Stories of H.G. Wells.* (London: Ernest Benn Limited. 1948.
4. **Newcomb S.** Modern mathematical thought. *Nature* 49:325-29, 1 February 1895.
5. **Wells H G.** Time travelling. *National Observer and British Review of Politics, Economics, Literature, Science and Art* 11:446-47, 17 March 1894.
6. ------------. The cyclic delusion. *Saturday Review* 78:505-06, 10 November 1894.
7. **Newcomb S.** The philosophy of hyper-space. *Science* 7(158):1-7, 7 January 1898.
8. **Langley S P.** The possibility of mechanical flight. *The Century Illustrated Magazine* 17:783-85, September 1891, (ref. 103).
9. **Anon.** The Langley aeroplane. *New York Times* 10 December 1903, p. 8.
10. **Newcomb S.** Sidelights on astronomy. *New York: Harper, 1906.*
11. **King-Hele D G.** Truth and heresy over earth and sky. *The Observatory* 95(1004):1-12, February 1975.

12. **Wright W.** Some aeronautical experiments. *Journal of the Western Society of Engineers* December 1901. Reprinted in: *Smithsonian Institution Annual Report* Part 1., p. 133-48, 1903.

13. **Wright O.** Stability of aeroplanes. *Smithsonian Institution Annual Report* 1:209-16, 1914.

14. **Dutton J A.** Belling the cat in the sky. *Bulletin of the American Meteorological Society* 48:813, 1967.

15. **Garfield E.** The 'obliteration phenomenon' in science, and the advantages of being obliterated. *Current Contents®* No. 51/52, 22 December 1975, p. 5-7.

16. **Le Conte J.** The problem of a flying-machine. *Popular Science Monthly* 34:69-76, November 1888.

17. ―――――――. New lights on the problem of flying. *Popular Science Monthly* 44:744, April 1894.

18. **Gibbs-Smith C H.** *Flight through the ages: a complete, illustrated chronology from the dreams of early history to the age of space exploration.* New York: Thomas Y. Crowell, 1974.

19. **Berry A.** *The next ten thousand years: a vision of man's future in the universe.* New York: E.P. Dutton, 1974, p. 43.

20. **Brewer R W A.** *The art of aviation.* New York: McGraw-Hill, 1910, p. 218.

21. **Michelson A A.** Address, dedication ceremony, Ryerson Physical Laboratory, Univ. Chicago, 1894. Quoted in: **Bartlett J.** *Familiar Quotations* Boston: Little, Brown & Company, 1968, p. 827.

22. **Wilkins J.** *Mathematical Magick* 1648. Quoted in: **Ley W.** *Rockets: the future of travel beyond the stratosphere.* New York: Viking, 1944.

23. **Pritchard J L.** *Sir George Cayley.* London: Parish, 1961, p. 206.

24. **North E and Aulis J.** Birds fly--men drink. *The Man Will Never Fly Memorial Society Internationale* (P.O. Drawer 1903, Kill Devil Hills, N.C. 27948)

25. **Anon.** *New York Times* 1921. Quoted in **Weber R L.** *A random walk in science.* New York: Crane, Russak, 1973.

26. **Moulton F R.** *Consider the heavens.* New York: Doubleday, 1935, p. 107.

27. **Anon.** *Daily Mirror* (London) 18 October 1948, p. 6.

28. **Kepler J.** *The somnium.* 1634. Quoted in: **King-Hele D G.** Truth and heresy over earth and sky. *The Observatory* 95(1004):1-12, February 1975.

29. **Verne J.** *From the earth to the moon.* 1865. And *Round the moon.* 1870.

30. **Franklin B.** Quoted in: **Blanchard J P.** *The first air voyage in America: the times, the place, and the people of the Blanchard balloon voyage of January 9, 1793, Philadelphia to Woodbury.* Philadelphia: Penn Mutual Insurance Company, 1943.

31. **Michaelis A R.** How nuclear energy was foretold. *New Scientist* 13(276): 507-9, 1 March 1962.

32. **Clarke A C.** (epilogue to) **Farmer G.** *First on the moon.* London: Michael Joseph, 1970.

The Outlook for the Flying Machine*
by Professor Simon Newcomb

Mr. Secretary Langley's trial of his flying machine, which seems to have come to an abortive issue last week, strikes a sympathetic chord in the constitution of our race. Are we not the lords of creation? Have we not girdled the earth with wires through which we speak to our antipodes? Do we not journey from continent to continent over oceans that no animal can cross, and with a speed of which our ancestors would never have dreamed? Is not all the rest of the animal creation so far inferior to us in every point that the best thing it can do is to become completely subservient to our needs, dying, if need be, that its flesh may become a toothsome dish on our tables? And yet here is an insignificant little bird, from whose mind, if mind it has, all conceptions of natural law are excluded, applying the rules of aerodynamics in an application of mechanical force to an end we have never been able to reach, and this with entire ease and absence of consciousness that it is doing an extraordinary thing. **Surely our knowledge of natural laws, and that inventive genius which has enabled us to subordinate all nature to our needs, ought also to enable us to do anything that the bird can do. Therefore we must fly.** If we cannot yet do it, it is only because we have not got to the bottom of the subject. Our successors of the not distant future will surely succeed.

This is at first sight a very natural and plausible view of the case. And yet there are a number of circumstances of which we should take account before attempting a confident forecast. Our hope for the future is based on what we have done in the past. But when we draw conclusions from past successes we should not lose sight of the conditions on which success has depended. There is no advantage which has not its attendant drawbacks; no strength which has not its concomitant weakness. Wealth has its trials and health its dangers. We must expect our great superiority to the bird to be associated with conditions which would give it an advantage at some point. A little study will make these conditions clear.

We may look on the bird as a sort of flying machine complete in itself, of which a brain and nervous system are fundamentally necessary parts. No such machine can navigate the air unless guided by something having life. Apart from this, it could be of little use to us unless it carried human beings on its wings. We thus meet with a difficulty at the first step—we cannot give a brain and nervous system to our machine.

*Reprinted from *The Independent: A Weekly Magazine* 22 October 1903, pp. 2508-12.

These necessary adjuncts must be supplied by a man, who is no part of the machine, but something carried by it. The bird is a complete machine in itself. Our aerial machine must be ship plus man. Now, a man is, I believe, heavier than any bird that flies. The limit which the rarity of the air places upon its power of supporting wings, taken in connection with the combined weight of a man and a machine, make a drawback which we should not too hastily assume our ability to overcome. The example of the bird does not prove that man can fly. The hundred and fifty pounds of dead weight which the manager of the machine must add to it over and above that necessary in the bird may well prove an insurmountable obstacle to success.

I need hardly remark that the advantage possessed by the bird has its attendant drawbacks when we consider other movements than flying. Its wings are simply one pair of its legs, and the human race could not afford to abandon its arms for the most effective wings that nature or art could supply.

Another point to be considered is that the bird operates by the application of a kind of force which is peculiar to the animal creation, and no approach to which has ever been made in any mechanism. This force is that which gives rise to muscular action, of which the necessary condition is the direct action of a nervous system. We cannot have muscles or nerves for our flying machine. We have to replace them by such crude and clumsy adjuncts as steam engines and electric batteries. It may certainly seem singular if man is never to discover any combination of substances which, under the influence of some such agency as an electric current, shall expand and contract like a muscle. But, if he is ever to do so, the time is still in the future. We do not see the dawn of the age in which such a result will be brought forth.

Another consideration of a general character may be introduced. As a rule it is the unexpected that happens in invention as well as discovery. There are many problems which have fascinated mankind ever since civilization began which we have made little or no advance in solving. The only satisfaction we can feel in our treatment of the great geometrical problems of antiquity is that we have shown their solution to be impossible. **The mathematician of to-day admits that he can neither square the circle, duplicate the cube or trisect the angle. May not our mechanicians, in like manner, be ultimately forced to admit that aerial flight is one of that great class of problems with which man can never cope, and give up all attempts to grapple with it?**

I do not claim that this is a necessary conclusion from any past experience. But I do think that success must await progress of a different kind from that of invention. It is an unfortunate fact that we do not always appreciate the distinction between progress in scientific discovery and ingenious application of discovery to the wants of civilization. The name of Marconi is familiar to every ear: the names of Maxwell and Herz, who made the discoveries which rendered wireless telegraphy possible, are rarely recalled. Modern progress is the result of two factors: Discoveries of the laws of nature and of actions or possibilities in nature, and the application of such discoveries to practical purposes. The first is the work of the scientific investigator, the second that of the inventor.

In view of the scientific discoveries of the past ten years, which, after bringing about results that would have been chimerical if predicted, leading on to the extraction of a substance which seems to set the laws and limits of nature at defiance by radiating a flood of heat, even when cooled to the lowest point that science can reach—a substance, a few specks of which contain power enough to start a railway train, and seems to embody perpetual motion itself, he would be a bold prophet who would set any limit to possible discoveries in the realm of nature. We are binding the universe together by agencies which pass from sun to planet and from star to star. We are peering into the law of gravitation itself with the full hope of discovering something in its origin which may enable us to evade its action. We are determined to find out all we can about the mysterious ethereal medium which seems to fill all space, and which conveys light and heat from one heavenly body to another, but which yet evades all direct investigation. **Quite likely the twentieth century is destined to see the natural forces which will enable us to fly from continent to continent with a speed far exceeding that of the bird.**

But when we inquire whether aerial flight is possible in the present state of our knowledge; whether, with such materials as we possess, a combination of steel, cloth and wire can be made which, moved by the power of electricity or steam, shall form a successful flying machine, the outlook may be altogether different. To judge it sanely, let us bear in mind the difficulties which are encountered in any flying machine. The basic principle on which any such machine must be constructed is that of the aeroplane. This, by itself, would be the simplest of all flyers, and, therefore, the best if it could be put into operation. The principle involved may be readily comprehended by the accompanying figure. A M is the section of a flat plane surface, say, a thin sheet of metal or a cloth supported by wires. It moves through the air, the latter being represented by the horizontal rows of dots. The direction of the motion is that of the horizontal line, A P. The aeroplane has a slight inclination measured by the proportion between the perpendicular M P and the length, A P. We may raise

the edge M up or lower it at pleasure. Now the interesting point, and that on which the hopes of inventors are based, is that if we give the plane any given inclination, even one so small that the perpendicular M P is only two or three per cent of the length AM, we can also calculate a certain speed of motion through the air which, if given to the plane, will enable it to bear any required weight. A plane ten feet square, for example, would not need any great inclination, nor would it require a speed higher than a few hundred feet a second to bear a man. What is of yet more importance, the higher the speed the less the inclination required, and, if we leave out of consideration the friction of the air and the resistance arising from any object which the machine may carry, the less the horse-power expended in driving the plane.

Maxim exemplified this by experiment several years ago. He found that, with a small inclination, he could readily give his aeroplane, when it slid forward upon ways, such a speed that it would rise from the ways of itself. The whole problem of the successful flying machine is, therefore, that of arranging an aeroplane that shall move through the air with the requisite speed.

The practical difficulties in the way of realizing the movement of such an object are obvious. The aeroplane must have its propellers. These must be driven by an engine with a source of power. Weight is an essential quality of every engine. The propellers must be made of metal, which has its weakness, and which is liable to give way when its speed attains a certain limit. And, granting complete success, imagine the proud possessor of the aeroplane darting through the air at a speed of several hundred feet per second! It is the speed alone that sustains him. How is he ever going to stop? Once he slackens his speed, down he begins to fall. He may, indeed, increase the inclination of his aeroplane. Then he increases the resistance necessary to move it. Once he stops he falls a dead mass. How shall he reach the ground without destroying his delicate machinery? I do not think the most imaginative inventor has yet even put upon paper a demonstrative, successful way of meeting this difficulty. The only ray of hope is afforded by the bird. The latter does succeed in stopping and reaching the ground safely after its flight. But we have already mentioned the great advantages which the bird possesses in the power of applying force to its wings, which, in its case, form the aeroplanes. But we have already seen that there is no mechanical combination, and no way of applying force, which will give to the aeroplanes the flexibility and rapidity of movement belonging to the wings of a bird. That this difficulty is insurmountable would seem to be a very fair deduction, not only from the failure of all attempts to surmount, but from the fact that Maxim has never, so far as we are aware, followed up his seemingly successful experiment.

It may be surmounted in a way which may, at first sight, seem plausible. In order that the aeroplane may have its full sustaining power, there is no need that this motion be continuously forward. A nearly horizontal surface, swinging around in a circle, on a vertical axis, like the wings of a windmill moving horizontally, will fulfill all the conditions. In fact, we have a machine on this simple principle in the familiar toy which, set rapidly whirling, rises in the air. Why more attempts have not been made to apply this system I do not know. Were there any hopeful possibility of making any flying machine whatever, it would seem that we should look in this direction.

The difficulties which I have

pointed out are only preliminary ones, patent on the surface. A more fundamental one still, which the writer feels may prove insurmountable, is based on a law of nature which we are bound to accept. It is that when we increase the size of such a machine without changing its model we increase the weight in proportion to the cube of the linear dimensions, while the effectiveness of the supporting power of the air increases only as the square of those dimensions. For example, suppose that an inventor succeeds, as well he may, in making a machine which would go into a match case, yet complete in all its parts, able to fly around the room. It may carry a button, but nothing heavier. Elated by his success, he makes one on the same model twice as large in every dimension. The parts of the first, which are one inch in length, he increases to two inches. Every part is twice as long, twice as broad and twice as thick. The result is that his machine is eight times as heavy as before. But the sustaining surface is only four times as great. As compared with the smaller machine, its ratio of effectiveness is reduced to one-half. It may carry two or three buttons, but will not carry over four, because the total weight, machine plus buttons, can only be quadrupled, and if he more than quadruples the weight of the machine, he must less than quadruple that of the load. How many such enlargements must he make before his machine will cease to sustain itself, before it will fall as an inert mass when we seek to make it fly through the air? Is there any size at which it will be able to support a human being? We may well hesitate before we answer his question in the affirmative.

Dr. Graham Bell, with a cheery optimism very pleasant to contemplate, has pointed out that the law I have just cited may be evaded by not making a larger machine on the same model, but changing the latter in a way tantamount to increasing the number of small machines. This is quite true, and I wish it understood that, in laying down the law I have cited, I limit it to two machines of different sizes on the same model throughout. **Quite likely the most effective flying machine would be one carried by a vast number of little birds.** The veracious chronicler who escaped from a cloud of mosquitoes by crawling into an immense metal pot and then amused himself by clinching the antennae of the insects which bored through the pot until to his horror they became so numerous as to fly off with the covering, was more scientific than he supposed. Yes, a sufficient number of humming birds, if we could combine their forces, would carry an aerial excursion party of human beings through the air. If the watchmaker can make a machine which will fly through the room with a button, then, by combining ten thousand such machines he may be able to carry a man. But how shall the combined forces be supplied?

It is of interest to notice that the law is reversed in the case of a body which is not supported by the resistance of a fluid in which it is immersed, but floats in it, the ship or balloon, for example. When we double the linear dimensions of a steamship in all its parts, we increase not only her weight, but her floating power, her carrying capacity and her engine capacity eight-fold. But the resistance which she meets with when passing through the water at a given speed is only multiplied four times. Hence, the larger we build the steamship the more economical the application of the power necessary to drive it. The proportionately diminishing resistance which, in the flying machine, represents the floating power is, in the ship, something to be overcome. Thus there is a complete reversal of the law in its practical application to the two cases.

The balloon is in the same class with the ship. Practical difficulties aside, the larger it is built the more effective it will be, and the more advantageous will be the ratio of the power which is necessary to drive it and the resistance to be overcome.

If, therefore, we are ever to have aerial navigation with our present knowledge of natural capabilities, it is to the airship floating in the air, rather than the flying machine resting on the air, to which we are to look. In the light of the law which I have laid down, the subject, while not at all promising, seems worthy of more attention than it has received. It is not at all unlikely that if a skillful and experienced naval constructor, aided by an able corps of assistants, should design an airship of a diameter of not less than two hundred feet, and a length at least four or five times as great, constructed, possibly, of a textile substance impervious to gas and borne by a light framework, but, more likely, of exceedingly thin plates of steel carried by a frame fitted to secure the greatest combination of strength and lightness, he might find the result to be, ideally at least, a ship which would be driven through the air by a steam engine with a velocity far exceeding that of the fleetest Atlantic liner. Then would come the practical problem of realizing the ship by overcoming the mechanical difficulties involved in the construction of such a huge and light framework. I would not be at all surprised if the result of the exact calculation necessary to determine the question should lead to an affirmative conclusion, but I am quite unable to judge whether steel could be rolled into parts of the size and form which would be required in the mechanism.

I may, in conclusion, caution the reader on one point. I should be very sorry if this suggestion leads to the subject being taken up by any other than skillful engineers or constructors, able to grapple with all problems relating to the strength and resistance of materials. As a single example of what is to be avoided I may mention the project, which sometimes has been mooted, of making a balloon by pumping the air from a very thin, hollow receptacle. Such a project is as futile as can well be imagined; no known substance would begin to resist the necessary pressure. Our aerial ship must be filled with some substance lighter than air. Whether heated air could be made to answer the purpose, or whether we should have to use a gas, is the question for a designer.

CURRENT COMMENTS

The Agony and the Ecstasy of Publishing Your Own Book: Essays of an Information Scientist

// Number 27, July 4, 1977

The idea of collecting all my "Current Comments®" into a book was first suggested to me about four years ago by Chauncey Leake. For some very practical reasons, it was an idea that had immediate appeal.

For one thing, it seemed like a convenient way of maintaining a complete set for my own use. After fifteen years of writing "Current Comments," my files of source materials and printed copies of the essays had begun to show gaps. Some people had borrowed but often forgot to return! Also, I doubt that many libraries offer ready access to fifteen years of *Current Contents®* . Anyone wanting to refer to the earlier essays, which I often cite, would find doing so difficult or impossible. So, in 1974, we decided that ISI® would collect and publish them under the title of *Essays of an Information Scientist.*

It seemed that doing so would be easy. After all, the essays, which started appearing intermittently in 1962 and became a regular weekly feature of *Current Contents* a decade later, had already been written and published. Collecting and reprinting them did not seem complicated. Once the project got started, it became clear how mistaken I was.

First, there were seemingly endless discussions about how best to present the collection. Many alternatives involving overall format, typography, page layout, and paper stock were considered. Finally, we decided to reprint the essays just as they first appeared in *Current Contents.* Though the book will win no prizes for graphic design, the irregularities of type faces and formats reflect some of the history of the development of *Current Contents.*

Then there were questions about indexing. Although I had considered arranging the essays in subject categories, it was decided instead to reprint them in chronological order but also to include a subject-author index as well as a citation index. Additionally, the table of contents lists the full title of every essay along with its original publication date. In this way, readers can rapidly locate specific essays on topics of interest, facilitating chronological look-up as well as browsing. Incidentally, it takes 23 pages to list the 352 essays published between 1962 and 1976.

One of the serious miscalculations of the ease of publishing this book involved our ability to locate reproducible copies of the published essays. Many hours were spent searching through dusty storage shelves. A few of the columns even had to be recomposed. Nevertheless, we were able to include every line of text as well as all of the tables, figures and reprints of other articles that appeared in the original essays.

It was difficult to decide how many years of essays to include. Originally, we planned to reprint them from their inception (1962) through 1975 in one volume. As we neared completion on that plan, however, so much time had passed that it became more sensible to publish two volumes and include all the essays through 1976. In retrospect, I think it was a wise decision, but the agony of waiting to see the book finished became almost intolerable.

During the preparation of *Essays* I have also been involved in the preparation of another book—*Citation Indexing: Its Theory and Application to Science, Technology, and Humanities*, which will be published by Wiley-Interscience. These simultaneous experiences have given me what is perhaps a unique insight into the differences between self-publication and working through a commercial publisher. Neither approach is easy. While working with a commercial publisher eliminates personal involvement in the many production details, these are replaced by concerns over contracts, compatability of writing style with that of the as-signed editor, and whether you have too much or too little material for what the publisher considers to be the "right" price for your book. However, every author tends to underestimate the important role of a good publisher in promotion and distribution.

One advantage of self-publication is that we were able to keep the book's price relatively low. I am confident that *Essays*, at $25.00 for the two-volume set, is priced well below average for a technical book that contains over 1,300 pages.

Milton Van Dyke of Stanford University's School of Engineering describes an experience similar to mine in a recent letter. When the publisher let his book go out of print, he obtained the copyright and published the book himself--without having to raise the 1964 price! Van Dyke writes, "Not everyone will publish his own book, but everyone should *consider* it--and especially republishing one out of print, as I did.... Being an enthusiast, I try to encourage my colleagues, but none has tried yet."

Perhaps his colleagues understood the frustrations involved more than I did. They also may have understood the meaning of "overhead."

One outgrowth of the decision to publish the book ourselves was to establish a division within ISI to deal with book publication. The ISI Press will at least publish an annual collection of my weekly columns, as well as other ISI material.

Joshua Lederberg has written the foreword to the present collection. Dr. Lederberg, Chairman of The Department of Genetics at the Stanford

University School of Medicine, is one of the most "visible" of American scientists. His views are sought by scientific colleagues--as well as by news reporters--on subjects ranging from plasmid engineering to artificial intelligence. In his foreword Dr. Lederberg discusses the "residue of controversy" about publishing citation statistics concerning individual articles, journals, and scientists. While I won't digress into that controversy here, the statement reminded me that *Essays* includes just about every "highly cited" list ever produced at ISI. This should make the book a useful reference tool for those who are interested in the sociometrics of science.

I would be remiss to close any discussion of *Essays* without mentioning ISI's Chief Editor, Robert L. Hayne. It should be fairly obvious to most readers that many of the essays represent an effort which takes more than a few hours of research and writing. Some of my citation studies require assistance from several ISI departments. They also involve considerable bibliographic research and data analysis. Bob Hayne is notable among those who synthesize these data.

I have known Bob since 1951, when I joined the Medical Indexing Project at Johns Hopkins University. He was then the assistant editor of the *Current List of Medical Literature,* now known as the *Index Medicus.* Together we worked on the rationalization of the subject heading authority list known today as Medical Subject Headings (MeSH). Bob was well qualified. He is a Latin-Greek Scholar. What better background for an etymologist-indexer-classifier? In addition, he knows more about linguistics than I ever will, though we both received graduate training in that arcane field. I don't know where he acquired his encyclopedic knowledge of music, art, and literature. If his alma mater, Washington and Lee, is responsible, send your children there.

Bob is also the fastest typist, stenographer and indexer I ever met. When I met him he could index medical articles in at least ten languages, and recently he learned Arabic just for kicks.

After 25 years of association, Bob and I manage to disagree at least 75% of the time, but somehow eventually it all comes out okay. I push him to his limit and he does the same to me. I wish to thank him for his assistance in arranging many of the original essays and for supervising the production of *Essays of an Information Scientist.*

CURRENT COMMENTS

Robert K. Merton: Among the Giants

Number 28, July 11, 1977

"If I have seen farther, it is by standing on the shoulders of giants." The origin of this aphorism, widely attributed to Sir Isaac Newton, is the subject of Robert K. Merton's 1965 book, *On the Shoulders of Giants.*[1] If this work is not one of Merton's better known publications, it is certainly one of his most unusual. So it is not without irony that today Merton himself is widely considered one of the giants of science. Those who continue to do research in the sociology of science will stand on Merton's shoulders.

However, this intellectual giant would be among the first to moderate this tribute and apply to himself his own assertion that, "Scientists have been dehumanized by being idealized and, on occasion, idolized.... Yet an honest appreciation would see them as men, not gods, and so subject to the pressures, passions and social relations in which men inevitably find themselves."[2]

Merton's name is almost synonymous with the term sociology of science, and his sociological studies are so far-ranging that he has become widely known beyond the parameters of his own discipline. Norman Storer of Baruch College has observed, "If Robert K. Merton has not yet been publicly described as a founding father of the sociology of science, there is at least substantial agreement among those who know the field that its present strength and vitality are largely the result of his labors over the past forty years."[3]

A native Philadelphian, Merton began these "forty years labors" at Temple University. After receiving his Ph.D. from Harvard University in 1936 he joined its faculty, where he developed a theory of deviant behavior based on different types of social adaptation. Merton served on the faculty of Tulane University from 1939 to 1941. He then went to Columbia University, where he has remained for over 35 years. He was elected to the National Academy of Sciences in 1968 and its Institute of Medicine in 1973. He was elected the first President of the Society for Social Studies of Science (4S) in 1975.

Merton's titles are numerous; his achievements many. Of all his accomplishments, however, I think it is his recent election as a foreign member of the Royal Swedish Academy of Sciences--the first social scientist so honored--that is most impressive. The Swedish Academy awards the annual Nobel Prizes in physics and chemistry.

Merton was also one of three prominent social scientists who recently joined the Russell Sage Foundation in New York City. This 70-year-old foundation, named after a 19th century financier, is committed to the improvement of social conditions in the U.S. To begin in the Fall of 1977, Merton, with Nathan Glazer of Harvard University and Bernard Gifford, deputy chancellor of the New York City Board of Education, will direct a program studying New York's problems and institutions. Under their guidance, the foundation is expected to emphasize "the relationship between social science and public policy, rather than a more abstract approach to sociology that it has sometimes been described as perpetuating."[4]

The invitation extended to Merton to join this foundation is an honor which serves to acknowledge his tremendous contributions and present influence in the field of sociology. Professor Irving Horowitz of the Department of Sociology and Political Science at Rutgers University underlines these points in describing Merton as "the complete sociologist." Horowitz comments that Merton "has been the quintessential professional in sociology for most of his career. His efforts in the sociology of science, deviant behavior, and establishing 'middle range' theories that would pass pragmatic tests of workability have uniquely serviced sociology and its practitioners.... It would hardly be an exaggeration to say that this man is the most important single figure in the profession of sociology."[5]

My personal acquaintance with Bob Merton goes back about 15 years. I've often acknowledged his moral, intellectual, and personal support in developing the $SCI^®$ and especially the *Social Sciences Citation Index*™, on whose editorial advisory board he serves.[6] In recent years he has been helpful to me and ISI® in ways too numerous to list here.

An hour spent in the company of Bob Merton is a mixed blessing. Somehow you come away with a dozen ideas of your own (at least you think they're your own!) never quite realizing that what *he* said brought them about.

I have always had the kind of reaction to much of Merton's writing that I associate with a great novelist, not a great scientist. So much of what he says is so beautifully obvious--so transparently true--that one can't imagine why no one else bothered to point it out. He is a special kind of scientist: forever reminding us of the forest, while describing it tree by tree.

Merton's devotion to sociological pursuits, and the literary style by which he expresses himself, distinguishes him as a unique person. His interest in man's past, both scientific and literary, makes him a kind of classicist--or renaissance figure--concerned not only with man's past, but with how past values and perceptions may shape the future. On that subject it is appropriate to quote from Bob Merton's own extensive works. In

1957 he wondered how future historians would judge those now concerned with the sociology and history of science:

We can only guess what historians of the future will say about the condition of present-day sociology. But it seems safe to anticipate one of their observations. When the Trevelyans [a family of English historians] of 2050 come to write that history--as they well might, for this clan of historians promises to go on forever--they will doubtless find it strange that so few sociologists (and historians) of the twentieth century could bring themselves, in their work, to treat science as one of the great social institutions of the time. They will observe that long after the sociology of science became an identifiable field of inquiry, it remained little cultivated in a world where science loomed large enough to present mankind with the choice of destruction or survival.[7]

I think it is fair to attribute to scholarly modesty his erroneous speculation that the sociology of science would remain little cultivated. As a perennial optimist I can assert that owing to the enormous growth of interest in science policy studies and other branches of this field we can have hope that mankind will survive.

It has often been the case that we neglect to pay tribute to those for whom we have the greatest love and respect until it's too late for them to hear it. It is also somehow not fashionable for scientists to express such emotions publicly. When I first saw the recent festschrift[8] in honor of Bob Merton I felt excluded, but my frustration was lessened when I realized I would have an opportunity to confirm the Mertonian "law" called "the Matthew effect,"[9] by which scientific recognition is bestowed upon one who already has it. So I am delighted to pay homage to a real giant on no particular occasion but just for the pleasure in doing so.

REFERENCES

1. **Merton R K.** *On the shoulders of giants.* New York: Harcourt, Brace & World, 1965.
2. ---------------. The ambivalence of scientists. *Bulletin of the Johns Hopkins Hospital* 112(2):77-97, February 1963.
3. **Storer N.** Introduction to: **Merton R K.** *The sociology of science: theoretical and empirical investigations.* Chicago: University of Chicago Press, 1973.
4. **Quindlen A.** Sage Foundation to focus on city problems. *New York Times* 1 March 1977, p. 35.
5. **Horowitz I L.** Personal communication, 16 May 1977.
6. **Garfield E.** "Come blow your horn." Why we're proud of the *Social Sciences Citation Index. Current Contents*® No. 12, 24 March 1975, p. 5-9.
7. **Merton R K.** Priorities in scientific discovery. *American Sociological Review* 22(6):635-59, 1957.
8. **Coser L A.** Editor. *The idea of social structure. Papers in honor of Robert K. Merton.* New York: Harcourt Brace Jovanovich, 1975.
9. **Merton R K.** The Matthew effect in science. *Science* 199:55-63, 5 January 1968.

Highly Cited Articles. 40. Biomedical and
Behavioral Papers Published in the 1950s.

Number 29, July 18, 1977

We recently published lists of highly cited 1950s papers in biochemistry[1] and in physics and chemistry.[2] To conclude the discussion of that decade's scientific literature, here are the highly-cited biomedical and behavioral papers.

In Figure 1 we list the 78 articles in alphabetical order according to first author. Each article was cited at least 500 times in the 15-year period 1961-1975. Some of the authors of these articles appeared on our 1940s list:[3] Schneider (56 and 57), Hogeboom (56), Coons (13 & 14), Hodgkin (29 & 30), Ouchterlory (41 & 42), Ussing (72), Zilversmit (73), and Katz (23).

It is interesting to confirm the common wisdom that collaborative research has increased over the years. We found that 25 out of 58 classics of the 19th- and early 20th-century (43%) were collaborations.[4] On the 1940s list, 47 of 85 articles (55%) were co-authored. And in the 1950s, 55 out of 78 (70%) were collaborations.

It is well known that collaborating scientists often alternate as primary and secondary authors. And this is often true even for Nobel Prize winners. For instance, Bernard Katz of England, who won the 1970 Prize for studies of nerve impulse transmissions, is the second author of article 23. James Watson of the U.S., who won the Prize in 1962, is the second of four authors of article 71. This paper was published in the inaugural year of the *Journal of Molecular Biology*.

Other Nobelists also appear on this list. Joshua Lederberg of the U.S. (36) received the Nobel Prize in 1958 for his work in genetics. Renato Dulbecco (19), an Italian-born U.S. citizen, won the Prize in 1975 for his studies concerning the interaction between tumor viruses and genetic material in the cell. George Palade (44) and Christian deDuve (17) of the U.S. were both awarded the 1974 Prize for their studies concerning the inner workings of living cells.

The authors of article 69, William Stein and Stanford Moore of the U.S., shared the 1972 chemistry Prize for their pioneering studies in enzymes. The authors of article 29, Alan Hodgkin and Andrew Huxley of

Figure 1. Highly cited articles in biological sciences, medicine, and psychology published in the 1950s. A = item number. **B** = total citations 1961-1975. **C** = average yearly citations 1961-1975. **D** = citations in 1974. **E** = citations in 1975. Articles are listed alphabetically by first author.

A	B	C	D	E	Bibliographic Data
1.	1206	80	77	77	**Abell L L, Levy B B, Brodie B B & Kendall F E.** A simplified method for the estimation of total cholesterol in serum and demonstration of its specificity. *J. Biol. Chem.* **195**:357-66, 1952.
2.	674	45	27	33	**Astrup T & Mullertz S.** The fibrin plant method for estimating fibrinolytic activity. *Arch. Biochem Biophys* **40**:346-51, 1952.
3.	518	35	29	22	**Berson S A, Yalow R S, Bauman M, Rothschild A & Newerly K.** Insulin-I[131] metabolism in human subjects; demonstration of insulin binding globulin in the circulation of insulin treated subjects. *J. Clin. Invest.* **35**:170-90, 1956.
4.	616	41	60	48	**Blomback B & Blomback M.** Purification of human and bovine fibrinogen. *Arkiv Kemi* **10**:415-43, 1956.
5.	785	52	43	44	**Bogdanski D F, Pletscher A, Brodie B & Udenfried S.** Identification and assay of serotonin in brain. *J. Pharmacol. Exp. Ther.* **117**:82-8, 1956.
6.	1246	83	69	43	**Boyden S V.** The adsorption of proteins on erythrocytes treated with tannic acid and subsequent hemagglutination by anti-protein sera. *J. Exp. Med.* **93**:107-20, 1951.
7.	857	57	84	61	**Brecher G & Cronkite E P.** Morphology and enumeration of human blood platelets. *J. Appl. Physiol.* **3**:365-77, 1950.
8.	841	56	26	21	**Brenner S & Horne R W.** A negative staining method for high resolution electron microscopy of viruses. *Biochim. Biophys. Acta* **34**:103-10, 1959.
9.	811	54	21	21	**Burn J H & Rand M J.** The action of sympathomimetic amines in animals treated with reserpine. *J. Physiol.* **144**:314-36, 1958.
10.	870	58	72	67	**Chance B & Williams G R.** The respiratory chain and oxidative phosphorylation. *Adv. Enzymol.* **17**:65-134, 1956.
11.	606	40	51	48	**Chauveau J, Moule Y & Rouiller C H.** Isolation of pure and unaltered liver nuclei morphology and biochemical composition. *Exp. Cell Res.* **11**:317-21, 1956.
12.	1168	78	94	68	**Clarke D H & Casals J.** Techniques for hemagglutination and hemagglutination-inhibition with arthropod-borne viruses. *Amer. J. Trop. Med. Hyg.* **7**:561-73, 1958.
13.	1206	80	56	52	**Coons A H & Kaplan M H.** Localization of antigen in tissue cells. II. Improvements in a method for the detection of antigen by means of fluorescent antibody. *J. Exp. Med.* **91**:1-13, 1950.
14.	529	35	26	34	**Coons, A H, Leduc E H & Connolly J M.** Studies on antibody production. I. A method for the histochemical demonstration of specific antibody and its application to a study of the hyperimmune rabbit. *J. Exper. Med.* **102**:49-71, 1955.
15.	679	45	39	44	**Dalton A J.** A chrome-osmium fixative for electron microscopy. *Anatomical Rec.* **121**:281, 1955.

Figure 1 continued

16. 1229 82 99 99 **Davis B D & Mingioli E S.** Mutants of *Escherichia coli* requiring methionine or vitamin B$_{12}$. *J. Bacteriol.* **60**:17-28, 1950.

17. 1683 112 146 130 **deDuve C D, Pressman B C, Gianetto R, Wattiaux R & Appelmans F.** Tissue fractionation studies. 6. Intracellular distribution patterns of enzyme in rat-liver tissue. *Biochem. J.* **60**:604-12, 1955.

18. 628 42 20 27 **Dement W & Kleitman N.** Cyclic variations in EEG during sleep and their relation to eye movements, body motility, and dreaming. *EEG Clin. Neurol.* **9**:673-90, 1957.

19. 1612 107 136 127 **Dulbecco R & Vogt M.** Plaque formation and isolation of pure lines with poliomyelitis viruses. *J. Exp. Med.* **99**:167-82, 1954.

20. 3610 241 269 240 **Duncan D B.** Multiple range and multiple F tests. *Biometrics* **11**:1-42, 1955.

21. 703 47 27 25 **Eagle H.** Nutrition needs of mammalian cells in tissue culture. *Science* **122**:501-4, 1955.

22. 654 44 79 68 **Farr R S.** A quantitative immunochemical measure of the primary interaction between I*BSA and the antibody. *J. Infect. Dis.* **103**:239-62, 1958.

23. 507 34 19 36 **Fatt P & Katz B.** An analysis of the end-plate potential recorded with an intra-cellular electrode. *J. Physiol.* **115**:320-70, 1951.

24. 524 35 13 10 **Gordon R S & Cherkes A.** Unesterized fatty acid in human blood plasma. *J. Clin. Invest.* **35**:206-12, 1956.

25. 959 64 50 53 **Grabar P & Williams C A.** Methode permettant l'etude conjuguee des proprietes electrophoretiques et immunochimiques d'un melange de proteines. Application au serum sanguin. (Method permitting dual study of electrophoretic and immunochemical properties of a protein mixture. Application to blood serum.) *Biochim. Biophys. Acta* **10**:193-4, 1953.

26. 634 42 24 21 **Grabar P, Williams C A Jr. & Courcon J.** Methode immunoelectrophoretique d'analyse de melange de substances antigeniques. (Immunoelectrophoretic method for analysis of mixed antigenic substances.) *Biochim. Biophys. Acta* **17**:67-74, 1955.

27. 1015 68 118 110 **Hamburger V & Hamilton H L.** A series of normal stages in the development of the chick embryo. *J. Morphology* **88**:49-92, 1951.

28. 643 43 70 92 **Havel R J, Eder H A & Bragdon J H.** The distribution and chemical composition of ultracentrifugally separated lipoproteins in human serum. *J. Clin. Invest.* **34**:1345-53, 1955.

29. 1089 73 84 122 **Hodgkin A L & Huxley A F.** A quantitative description of membrane current and its application to conduction and excitation in nerve. *J. Physiol.* **117**:500-44, 1952.

30. 519 35 31 33 **Hodgkin A L & Horowicz P.** The influence of potassium and chloride ions on the membrane potential of single muscle fibers. *J. Physiol.* **148**:127-60, 1959.

Figure 1 continued

31. 504 34 46 29 **Hugh R & Leifson E.** The taxonomic significance of fermentative versus oxidative metabolism of carbohydrates by various gram negative bacteria. *J. Bacteriol.* **66**:24-6, 1953.

32. 548 37 39 40 **Karmen A.** A note on the spectrophotometric assay of glutamic-oxyalecetic transaminase in human serum. *J. Clin. Invest.* **34**:131-3, 1955.

33. 636 42 12 15 **Kay A W.** Effect of large doses of histamine on gastric secretion of HCl; an augmented histamine test. *Brit. Med. J.* **2**:77-80, 1953.

34. 523 35 59 54 **Kluver H & Barrera E.** A method for the combined staining of cells and fibers in the nervous system. *J. Neuropath. Exper. Neurol.* **12**:400-3, 1953.

35. 539 36 45 42 **Kramer C Y.** Extension of multiple range tests to group means with unequal numbers of replications. *Biometrics* **12**:307-10, 1956.

36. 527 35 29 19 **Lederberg J & Lederberg E M.** Replica plating and indirect selection of bacterial mutants. *J. Bacteriol.* **63**:399-406, 1952.

37. 729 49 91 68 **Lennox E S.** Transduction of linked genetic character of the host by bacteriophage P1. *Virology* **1**:190-206, 1955.

38. 538 36 37 42 **Mauzerall D & Granick S.** The occurrence and determination of δ - aminolevulinic acid and prophobilinogen in urine. *J. Biol. Chem.* **219**:435-6, 1956.

39. 704 47 78 66 **Miller G A.** The magical number seven, plus or minus two; some limits in our capacity for processing information. *Psychol. Rev.* **63**:81-97, 1956.

40. 811 54 26 27 **Morgan J F, Morton H J & Parker R C.** Nutrition of animal cells in tissue culture. I. Initial studies on a synthetic medium. *P. Soc. Exp. Biol. Med.* **73**:1-8, 1950.

41. 822 55 68 53 **Ouchterlony O.** Antigen-antibody reactions in gels. IV. Types of reactions in coordinated systems of diffusion. *Acta. Pathol. Microb. Scand.* **32**:231-40, 1953.

42. 875 58 109 121 **Ouchterlony O.** Diffusion-in-gel methods for immunological analysis. *Prog. Allergy* **5**:1-78, 1958.

43. 759 51 62 63 **Oyama B I & Eagle H.** Measurement of cell growth in tissue culture with a phenol reagent (Folin-ciocalteau). *P. Soc. Exp. Biol. Med.* **91**:305-7, 1956.

44. 2072 138 81 48 **Palade G E.** A study of fixation for electron microscopy. *J. Exp. Med.* **95**:285-97, 1952.

45. 549 37 18 18 **Porath J & Flodin P.** Gel filtration; a method for desalting and group separation. *Nature* **183**:1657-9, 1959.

46. 1203 80 49 41 **Poulik M D.** Starch gel electrophoresis in a discontinuous system of buffers. *Nature* **180**: 1477-9, 1957.

47. 516 34 24 24 **Puck T T, Marcus P I & Cieciura S J.** Clonal growth of mammalian cells in vitro. Growth characteristics of colonies from single hela cells with and without a "feeder" layer. *J. Exper. Med.* **103**:273-84, 1956.

Figure 1 continued

48.   762   51   56   54   **Quastler H & Sherman F G.** Cell population kinetics in the intestinal epithelium of the mouse. *Exp. Cell Res.* **17**:420-38, 1959.

49.   668   45   67   57   **Ratnoff O D & Menzie C.** A new method for the determination of fibrinogen in small samples of plasma. *J. Lab. Clin. Med.* **37**:306-20, 1951.

50.   1170   78   81   78   **Reitman S & Frankel S.** A colorimetric method for the determination of serum glutamic oxalacetic and glutamic pyruvic transaminases. *Amer. J. Clin. Pathol.* **28**:56-63, 1957.

51.   533   36   12   11   **Riggs J L, Seiwald R J, Burckhalter J H, Downs C M & Metcalf T G.** Isothiocyanate compounds as a fluorescent labeling agent for immune serum. *Amer. J. Pathol.* **34**:1081-98, 1958.

52.   513   34   27   25   **Saifer A & Gerstenfeld X.** The photometric microdetermination of blood glucose with glucose oxidase. *J. Lab. Clin. Med.* **51**:448-60, 1958.

53.   732   49   49   40   **Sarnoff S J, Braunwald E, Welch G H, Jr., Case R B, Stainsby W N & Macruz R.** Hemodynamic determinants of oxygen consumption of the heart with special reference to the tension-time index. *Amer. J. Physiol.* **192**:148-56, 1958.

54.   509   34   59   62   **Schachman H K.** Ultracentrifugation, diffusion, and viscometry. *Methods Enzym.* **4**:32-103, 1957.

55.   3660   244   258   202   **Scheidegger J J.** Une micro-methode de l'immuno-electrophorese. (Method for immunoelectrophoretic microanalysis.) *Internat. Arch. Allergy* **7**:103-10, 1955.

56.   947   63   59   55   **Schneider W C & Hogeboom G H.** Intracellular distribution of enzymes. V. Further studies on the distribution of cytochrome-c in rat liver homogenates. *J. Biol. Chem.* **183**:123-8, 1950.

57.   620   41   72   103   **Schneider W C.** Determination of nucleic acids in tissues by pentose analysis. *Methods Enzym.* **3**:680-4, 1957.

58.   1138   76   50   47   **Seldinger S I.** Catheter replacement of the needle in percutaneous arteriography; a new technique. *Acta Radiologica* **39**:368-76, 1953.

59.   539   36   19   20   **Shanes A M.** Electrochemical aspects of physiological and pharmacological action in excitable cells. I. The resting cell and its extrinsic factors. *Pharmacological Revs.* **10**:59-164, 1958.

60.   839   56   70   62   **Shore P A, Burkhalter A & Cohn V H Jr.** A method for the fluorometric assay of histamine in tissues. *J. Pharmacol. Exp. Ther.* **127**:182-6, 1959.

61.   1297   86   31   23   **Smithies O.** An improved procedure for starch-gel electrophoresis; further variations in the serum proteins of normal individuals. *Biochem. J.* **71**:585-7, 1959.

62.   570   38   35   25   **Silber R H, Busch R D & Oslapas R.** Practical procedure for estimation of corticosterone or hydrocortisone. *Clinical Chemistry* **4**:278-85, 1958.

63.   652   43   15   23   **Silber R H & Porter C C.** The determination of 17, 21-dihydroxy-20-ketosteroids in urine and plasma. *J. Biol. Chem.* **210**:923-32, 1954.

Figure 1 continued

64.   533   36   32   30   **Singer J M & Plotz C M.** The latex fixation test. I. Application to the serologic diagnosis of rheumatoid arthritis. *Amer. J. Med.* 21:888-92, 1956.

65.   617   41   35   32   **Singer K, Chernoff A J & Singer L.** Studies on abnormal hemoglobins. I. Their demonstration in sickle-cell anemia and other hematological disorders by means of alkali denaturation. *Blood-J. Hematology* 6:413-28, 1951.

66.   1158   77   66   39   **Sperry W M & Webb M.** A revision of the Schoenheimer-Sperry method for cholesterol determination. . *J. Biol. Chem.* 187:97-106, 1950.

67.   799   53   40   35   **Stavitsky A B.** Micromethods for the study of proteins and antibodies. I. Procedure and general applications of hemagglutination and hemagglutination-inhibition reactions with tannic acid or protein-treated red blood cells. *J. Immunol.* 72:360-75, 1954.

68.   755   50   44   23   **Steelman S L & Pohley F M.** Assay of the follicle stimulating hormone based on the augmentation with human chorionic gonadotropin. *Endocrinology* 53:604-16, 1953.

69.   571   38   30   24   **Stein W H & Moore S.** The free amino acids of human blood plasma. *J. Biol. Chem.* 211:915-26, 1954.

70.   706   47   55   45   **Taylor J A.** A personality scale of manifest anxiety. *J. Abn. Soc. Psychol.* 48:285-90, 1953.

71.   619   41   22   22   **Tissieres A, Watson J D, Schlessinger D & Hollingsworth B R.** Ribonucleoprotein particles from *Escherichia coli*. *J. Molec. Biol.* 1:221-3, 1959.

72.   855   57   56   78   **Ussing H H & Zehrahn K.** Active transport of sodium as the source of electric current in the short-circulated isolated frog skin. *Acta Physiol. Scand.* 23:110-27, 1951.

73.   1440   96   81   73   **Van Handel E & Zilversmit D B.** Micromethod for the direct determination of serum triglycerides. *J. Lab. Clin. Med.* 50:L152-7, 1957.

74.   635   42   37   29   **Vogt M.** The concentration of sympathin in different parts of the central nervous system under normal conditions and after the administration of drugs. *J. Physiol.* 123:451-81, 1954.

75.   1100   73   96   66   **Wachstein M & Meisel E.** Histochemistry of hepatic phosphatases at a physiological pH with a special reference to the demonstration of bile canaliculi. *Amer. J. Clin. Pathol.* 27:13-23, 1957.

76.   623   42   26   43   **Wilson T H & Wiseman A.** The use of sacs of everted small intestine for the study of the transference of substances from the mucosal to the serosal surface. *J. Physiol.* 123:116-25, 1954.

77.   800   53   62   58   **Wroblewski F & LaDue J S.** Lactic dehydrogenase activity in blood. *P. Soc. Exp. Biol. Med.* 90:210-13, 1955.

78.   868   58   56   60   **Zlatkis A, Zak B & Boyle A J.** A new method for the direct determination of serum cholesterol. *J. Lab. Clin. Med.* 41:486-92, 1953.

England, shared the 1963 Prize for their research on nerve cells.

The most highly-cited paper on the list is Scheidegger's "Method for Immunoelectrophoretic Microanalysis" (55), with a total citation count of 3,660. Its 15 year average citation count is 244, and in recent years its citation rate has hovered close to that figure.

Lest you jump to the erroneous conclusion that method papers are necessarily more frequently cited than other articles, I remind you that there is considerable evidence against this prevalent viewpoint. There are a number of highly cited method papers, but a large percentage achieve oblivion. One indicator of this is the impact observed for journals in analytical chemistry. Their impact is lower than what one would expect for methods journals. R.E. Davies of the University of Pennsylvania has recently reminded me of this point.[5]

These 78 highly-cited papers were

Figure 2. Journals that published the highly cited 1950s articles listed in Figure 1, according to number of articles. A = number of articles. (Present title of journal given in parentheses.)

A	Journals
6	J. Biol. Chemistry
6	J. Exp. Med.
6	J. Physiology (London)
4	J. Clin. Invest.
4	J. Lab. Clin. Med.
3	Biochim. Biophys. Acta
3	J. Bacteriol.
3	Proc. Soc. Exp. Biol. Med.
2	Acta Physiol. Scand.
2	Amer. J. Clin. Pathol.
2	Biometrics
2	Exp. Cell. Res.
2	J. Pharmacol. Exp. Ther.
2	Methods Enzymol.
2	Nature
1	Acta Pathol. Microb. Scand. (A)
1	Acta Radiologica (Diagnosis)
1	Adv. Enzymol.
1	Amer. J. Med.
1	Amer. J. Pathology
1	Amer. J. Physiology
1	Amer. J. Trop. Med. Hyg.
1	Anatomical Rec.
1	Arch. Biochem. Biophys.
1	Arkiv Kemi (Chem. Scripta)
1	Biochemical Journal
1	Blood-J. Hematology
1	Brit. Med. J.
1	Clinical Chemistry
1	EEG Clin. Neurology
1	Endocrinology
1	Internat. Arch. Allergy
1	J. Abnormal Soc. Psychol.
1	J. Appl. Physiol.
1	J. Immunology
1	J. Infect. Dis.
1	J. Molec. Biol.
1	J. Morphology
1	J. Neuropath. Exp. Neurol.
1	Pharmacological Revs.
1	Prog. Allergy
1	Psychol. Rev.
1	Science
1	Virology

published by a total of 44 journals, listed in Figure 2. Three journals published 6 articles each, accounting for 23% of all the articles: *Journal of Biological Chemistry, Journal of Experimental Medicine,* and *Journal of Physiology.* Overall, there is a wide distribution of articles by journals. Seven journals published 2 articles each, and 29 journals published 1 article.

The list of journals in Figure 2 includes two psychology journals which each published one paper: the *Journal of Abnormal Social Psychology* and *Psychological Review.* Both of the articles in these journals (39 & 70) were singly authored and have maintained 1974 and 1975 citation rates near their yearly averages. It is important to mention that in the early years of the *SCI®* our coverage of psychology was not as complete as today. However, the inclusion of data from our *Social Sciences Citation Index ™* (*SSCI ™*) has increased the citation counts for these psychology papers.

About fifteen of the papers concern hematology. This includes research into the determination of fibrinogen and fibrin in blood plasma, elements involved in blood coagulation. The data seem to confirm the assertion by Benjamin Alexander of the New York Blood Center that, "During the past decade research in coagulation, one of the vital homeostatic functions, has been in a state of intense ferment.... Knowledge has come from many disciplines--human and comparative physiology, biochemistry, physical chemistry, animal husbandry, pathology, genetics and, not least, clinical investigation--reflecting the multifaceted background required of the student of this subject."[6]

The inclusion of several papers which appeared in journals of biochemical science may be disputed. Some of these decisions were rather arbitrary in order to keep each of the three lists in the 1950s series to a manageable size. One wonders why article 4 on purification of fibrinogen was published in a chemical journal. But I suppose that if every paper appeared in the most logical journal there'd be less reason to read *Current Contents®* .

1. **Garfield E.** Highly cited articles. 39. Biochemistry papers published in the 1950s. *Current Contents* No. 26, 27 June 1977, p. 5-12.
2. --------------. Highly cited articles. 38. Physics and chemistry papers published in the 1950s. *Current Contents* No. 23, 6 June 1977, p. 5-9.
3. --------------. Highly cited articles 37. Biomedical articles published in the 1940s. *Current Contents* No. 13, 28 March 1977, p. 5-12.
4. --------------. Highly cited classics of 19th and 20th centuries. *Current Contents* No. 21, 24 May 1976, p. 5-9.
5. **Davies R E.** Personal communication, 10 June 1977.
6. **Alexander B.** Medical Progress: coagulation, hemorrhage and thrombosis. *New England Journal of Medicine* 252:432-42, 1955.

Reducing the Noise Level in Scientific Communication: How Services from ISI Aid Journal Editors and Publishers

Number 30, July 25, 1977

Have you ever madly twisted a radio dial in an attempt to hear the latest news over the static? Has a blizzard of electronic "snow" ever appeared on your television screen just at the climax of a drama? Have voices on the telephone ever sounded as if they were echoing from the bottom of a very deep well?

If you have experienced any of these inconveniences, you are familiar with what communications experts generally classify as noise. Noise creates errors or stops messages from being delivered entirely. Depending on the nature and importance of the blocked message, noise can be expensive, time-consuming, or even dangerous.

In the scientific journal literature, noise frequently occurs in the form of inconsistent, inappropriate, and outdated editorial practices. I don't mean the natural diversity in style and format that is to be expected and even encouraged, but the kind of editorial aberrations that cause time-consuming delays and prevent retrieval of vital information.

Reducing noise pollution in science communications has long been a concern at ISI®. I have written articles and letters, campaigned at scientific meetings, and bent the ears of quite a few journal editors to get them to use informative titles and more legible tables of contents. I've stressed the need to include abstracts or summaries for each article, prominently display volume and issue numbers, provide complete author addresses, and number reference citations and place them at the end of the article.

These and other noise-reducing suggestions provided the basis for a large part of a paper which I recently gave at the First International Conference of Scientific Editors in Jerusalem (April 25-29, 1977). The paper is reprinted here for those who would like to be able to judge whether the journals in which they publish are doing the best possible job to assure that all potential readers are made aware of their papers.

As the title--"How Services from ISI Aid Journal Editors and Publishers"--indicates, the paper touches areas besides how to improve the visibility of journal articles. It also deals with ways editors can help assure the quality of the papers they publish, and why it is economically beneficial to publishers to have their journals covered by secondary information services such as *Current Contents*® or *ASCA*® . There is even a discussion of why ISI's *Original Article Tear Sheet Service* (*OATS*®) actually tends to increase journal subscriptions.

In fact, according to the pricing theory of Professor W.J. Baumol of New York University, if publishers would charge a reasonable amount for reprints, libraries would be induced to order more subscriptions to some journals. High prices discourage people from requesting the reprints from libraries. If few reprint requests are received for a journal, the libraries see no reason to subscribe to it. However, reasonable charges for reprints would encourage more individuals to request them, so that eventually the library might determine that it is more economical to order another subscription to the journal.[1]

Readers who wish to help ISI in its campaign to improve science communications might send a clipping of the reprint, or a letter which reiterates some of its suggestions, to editors whose journals contribute to the noise level. After all, one can counteract noise by shouting louder than the next fellow. But the most effective way of dealing with noise is to prevent it in the first place.

REFERENCE

1. **Baumol W J.** Personal communication, 15 June 1977.

How Services From the Institute For Scientific Information (ISI) Aid Journal Editors and Publishers

Eugene Garfield, Ph.D.

President
Institute for Scientific Information
325 Chestnut Street
Philadelphia, Pennsylvania 19106

As the head of an organization that produces secondary information services, I consider ISI® to be in an active and mutually beneficial partnership with journal editors and publishers.

While I'm sure each of you, especially the publishers, readily understands how ISI benefits from the existence of your journals, past experience tells me that a good number of you are not quite so sure how you benefit from the existence of ISI and its services. The purpose of this talk is to present the basis for my belief of mutual advantage.

According to F. Peter Woodford, who used to conduct an excellent training program for scientific editors at Rockefeller University, the editor is in a position of "some power, considerable prestige and great responsibility."[1] The first responsibility Woodford identifies for the editor is to assure the *scientific worth* of the articles published in his or her journal. This involves evaluating the magnitude of each paper's scholarly contribution to an important topic, its adequacy of experimental design and methods, and the validity of its inferences and conclusions. The second responsibility is to assure the *comprehensibility* of each article; that is, the ease and accuracy with which a reader can grasp the author's thoughts. And the third responsibility is to assure the *retrievability* of each article. This includes the certainty and rapidity with which an article will reach the attention of another scientist interested in the subject, now and in the future.

Let's take the editor's first responsibility, to assure the quality of the papers accepted for publication, and see how ISI services can help.

In the reviewing process an editor frequently needs background information to support or refute referees' and authors' criticisms and claims. While most editors are attuned to the use of traditional reference tools for such purposes, many do not take full advantage of the recent innovations in information retrieval. For example, how many editors here subscribe to an SDI (selective dissemination of information) service?

By creating a profile that defines the subject scope of his or her journal, an editor can receive an SDI report at regular intervals indicating relevant articles published in other journals. In this way, the selection of manuscripts and other editorial decisions are made with more confidence.

SDI services, such as ISI's *ASCA®* and *ASCATOPICS®*, are relatively inexpensive for what they provide. *ASCA* (its full name is Automatic

Subject Citation Alert) can cover a subject area on as broad or as narrow a basis as you think necessary. *ASCA* is available with weekly reports for about $100 per year, and with monthly reports for only $50 per year. Its reports are computer-generated and they bring you lists of relevant articles published within the past few weeks. *ASCATOPICS* costs less than $100 per year and gives you broad coverage of a subject area through standard profiles.

Of course, you may argue that you can more than adequately satisfy your current awareness needs by using *Current Contents®* . And many editors do! But I think the focus of the *ASCA* services is important.

ASCA can also be used to provide an innovative service for authors that makes it more attractive for them to publish in your journal rather than with a competitor. Through *ASCA*, you can list all the current articles that cite any article *ever* published in your journal. Or you could limit the listings to citations of articles published during the past few years. This is especially useful for new journals where there is a strong chance that other journals will be the main source of citations.

Besides the constant general awareness an editor requires, specific questions must frequently be researched. Or, you may need to decide on the originality of a submitted manuscript or the completeness of the bibliography it contains. In these cases, the use of on-line search services can be quite helpful. On-line services would also make it easier to provide referees with supplementary bibliographical information. If editors used such quick-response services more often they might be able to speed up decisions and thereby earn the respect of authors who justifiably resent the time lags between submission of their articles and final publication.[2] In actuality, however, the use of on-line services by editors is astonishingly low.

Once again, the cost is minimal. With ISI's on-line services, *SCI-SEARCH®* and *SOCIAL SCI-SEARCH,* once you acquire your terminal, you pay only for the exact amount of time you are on-line and searching. There is no minimum charge for access to these data bases.

ISI can also help you assure the worth of the articles you accept in other unique ways.

In producing our information services we have created a massive, permanent record of who has published what and where in the journal literature. What's more, for about 3,500 journals, we have also recorded the references to other published work contained in each article processed. These records permit a wide range of quantitative, qualitative, and other descriptive analyses of scientific communication through journals. While some applications of these analyses, like measuring an individual's research performance, have created controversy,[3-9] other uses such as defining the history of a scientific development and measuring the activity and interaction of scientific specialties seem to be more palatable.

Citation analysis can be especially helpful to editors of new journals. By using it to identify the important people in a specific field, editors can obtain some objective input in establishing editorial advisory boards and in soliciting potential authors for review articles.

Through citation analysis one can determine those topics which are currently active.[10] And for those articles you have already published, citation analysis can help determine whether your selection criteria are corroborated by the research community.[11] Indeed, we did a study for one journal that helped evaluate the papers they had rejected.

In today's interdisciplinary world, if you are having trouble determining just where your journal fits in, citation analysis can help resolve your identity crisis. In other words, if you know which journals cite yours and which journals yours cites, you can get a clearer picture of which journals are most closely related to your field. Undoubtedly, the dozens of journal citation studies I have published in *Current Contents* have produced many surprises.[12,13]

While ISI services can help you improve and measure the scientific worth of your journal, there isn't much we can offer that directly assists you in improving *comprehension*. I've spoken out repeatedly on the need for better and clearer style in scientific writing.[14] I've even cajoled scientific authors to use a little humor now and then.[15] But, basically, you editors will have to fight this battle on your own. In this respect, the work of Woodford[16] and Debakey[17] and others is relevant.

ISI can, however, provide some important help in the third area of re-sponsibility--making your articles *retrievable*. Remember that in this context retrieval includes dissemination-- making certain that all potential readers see pertinent articles.

In my experience, this is the area where journal editors have the most problems. Many of you are still using editorial practices appropriate to another era. In the old days the typical scientist personally received all the journals he or she considered relevant and scanned them from cover to cover. Today's researchers generally use *Current Contents* or other information services to maintain their current awareness and to do retrospective searches.[18] These services supplement or even replace scanning the journals. Thus, a completely worthwhile and well presented article might be overlooked by the research community if the journal in which it appears is not covered by the various secondary information services. Even if the journal is covered, its articles can still be overlooked if certain editorial practices prevent them from being effectively abstracted and indexed.

To get a clearer picture of what I'm talking about, consider these numbers. There are nearly 30,000 subscribers to our *Current Contents* publications. Our subscriber studies indicate that over 250,000 researchers read *Current Contents* every week. This readership is matched only by a few journals like *Nature* and *Science* while the circulation of most other journals is a few thousand or even less. Obviously, then, being listed in *Current Contents* is important to the visibility of small journals. I do not know the readership figures for other services like *Chemical Abstracts* or *Biological Abstracts*, but certainly they too have significant impact on the use of small journals.

Later on I'll talk about the economic impact of having your journal covered by information services. What I would like to touch on now is the fact that even after your journal is covered, there remain many things you can do to improve retrievability. I recognize that the personalities of editors and publishers give journals much of their distinct character. But the checklist of editorial practices I am about to suggest does not infringe on your liberty or expressiveness and will help your journal immensely.

1. Use clear titles which include informative key words. A title that does not adequately identify the subject of the work reported is inexcusable.

2. For each article, include an abstract or summary that can be understood by scientists outside the particular area of specialization involved. I am delighted to note that, after years of prodding, even *Science* has now agreed to include such summaries for all of its lead articles. This is as important to those who actually scan the journal itself as to those who read the articles in the form of reprints.

3. The title of each article should be displayed on the table of contents in a bold face ahead of the author's name. Most names will not be known to the average reader, but if you insist on catering to the vanity of au-

thors, put their names in a separate column.

4. Prominently display your volume and issue number on the contents page. Too often this vital bibliographic information is too small or located in a visually obscure location.

5. Provide English titles on your contents page--even though the articles are written in another language. You can also supply the original title in parentheses, but the problem of bilinguality is probably best solved by having contents pages in separate languages. I offer this approach because the suggestion to use English exclusively may be offensive to some of you. I recently published an article in *La Recherche* in which I suggested that French scientists publish in English.[19] The reaction in France was explosive.[20]

I can only say that my stance is not one of "linguistic imperialism," as one of my critics asserted. In fact, my position is based on citation analyses of French journals which showed that articles published in French journals are infrequently cited by scientists outside France. My conclusion is that people are not browsing through these articles because of the language barrier. Even mediocre French scientists would get more attention if their articles were published in English.[21] As I stated in the article, "Throughout the world, practically all prospective readers--even those who might *prefer* some other language--can immediately understand a scientific article published in English.''

Now, to move on to a less controversial suggestion:

6. On the first page of all articles, provide the complete address (including the departmental affiliation and postal code) of each author. Ideally, the address should immediately follow the author's name.[22] You may think that this is a minor point, but at ISI we process nearly a million addresses each year and it is incredible how often addresses are incomplete. And it is often absolutely impossible to tell which address goes with which author when there are three or more authors. Since ISI publishes *Who Is Publishing In Science®* each year, our own editors know all too well the difficulties of dealing with the inconsistencies of author addresses from one journal to another as well as within individual journals. One wonders if editors and publishers are fully conscious of the importance of these addresses in promoting the sale and distribution of reprints. *Current Contents* and *ASCA,* alone, produce about 10 million reprint requests each year.

7. Finally, some advice on reference citations. Naturally, ISI has a special interest in the way you handle reference citations since we are the only

major information service currently using citation indexing. But what I suggest will reduce printing costs for your journal and avoid frustrating your readers. So, stop using archaic citation phraseology like *op. cit.* and *ibid.* And was there ever a footnote important enough to publish that could not be included in the text? Or, if some force compels you to put footnotes at the bottom of your text pages, at least separate them from the reference citations, which should be gathered together at the end of an article rather than dispersed through its pages. Naturally, the numbered or alphabetic arrangement makes it easier for ISI to process your articles. But it really is an important service to your readers, too. One of the most common things researchers do when they find an article of interest is to use its bibliography to obtain additional reading material. This is frequently done by supplying an assistant with a photocopy of the reference list so he or she can obtain the checked items. Gathering the references at the end of an article can sometimes make the difference between 20 pages of copying and just one. I will also mention, although I'm sure it will be for naught, the disservice done to readers by *Science* and other journals which omit the titles of cited articles. I have published my objections on this before, but I assure you it makes little difference to ISI in its work.[23,24]

Following these seven suggestions will help your journal's articles attain maximum exposure to the research community. You may then wish to see how well your journal is doing in terms of its relative importance. One way you can monitor this is through our *Journal Citation Reports®* , which is available as an individual publication and as a part of the *Science Citation Index®* . In *JCR™* you can observe how your journal compares with other journals in total citations, impact, immediacy, and in other measures of importance.[25-27] If you have a favorable citation analysis, you will be more likely to attract better authors. Today's more sophisticated researchers want to know in which journals their articles will be read and responded to most quickly. Most important of all, you can observe whether your journal's impact is increasing or decreasing from year to year.[28]

Until now I've dealt primarily with the concerns of journal editors. But ISI is also very much aware of the publisher's role in scientific communication.

Probably the one question most asked of me by publishers is, "Won't having my journal covered by a secondary information service reduce my total subscription level?" Such publishers are especially concerned about ISI services since they are backed up by a tear sheet service, called *OATS®* (*Original Article Tear Sheet*),which provides copies of articles from the journals we cover. Many publishers fear that users of our services will continuously order tear sheets without ever asking for the actual journal.

Realistically, economic considerations work against this happening unless you have a *very* poor journal which only infrequently publishes articles of interest. Here's why. Having your journal covered by an information service should cause an increase in the number of requests for its articles. If a library does not subscribe to your journal, copies will have to be ordered through inter-library loan. This is always slow and is now becoming quite expensive as the larger libraries increase their fees to discourage heavy use of their resources by others. Frequent purchases of articles through *OATS* at three dollars per 10-page article can quickly run up some big bills, too. So what usually happens is that librarians do some basic arithmetic and realize that it's cheaper to subscribe to a journal than to continue to buy its articles one by one.

This works on an individual basis, too. Researchers who are regularly ordering individual articles from a specific journal are going to get tired of the hassle, delay, and expense and want their own copy. This will be true whether they have been buying tear sheets or writing authors for reprints. Even a free reprint has a cost associated with it that is not trivial.

Even if a library already subscribes to your journal, having it covered by an information service may cause a second or third copy to be purchased, or influence the annual decision to renew. As more requests for articles from your journal are received, librarians are forced to do more in-house photocopying. These days nearly everyone realizes the true costs of this procedure. Furthermore, in the United States, new copyright legislation seems likely to limit the number of photocopies a librarian may legally make. The upshot of this is that most librarians will realize the economy and wisdom of buying a second copy of your journal.[29]

Of course, if your journal is really bad or of limited interest, it isn't likely that it would be covered by ISI services in the first place. In some cases this lack of exposure may well be fatal. This is not necessarily a bad thing, either, since I believe in euthanasia for poor quality journals.[30]

But why has ISI persisted in operating its *OATS* service for over 10 years in the face of publishers' strong concern that it is depriving them of subscription revenue? Basically, we do it because we want subscribers to ISI services to know that when traditional channels fail them they can get the article they want from us. I believe that even if a subscriber comes to ISI for an article just once a year, he or she must be serviced without a delay of weeks.

We also persist with *OATS* because we feel we have not done badly at all when it comes to protecting publishers' rights. Since its inception, *OATS* has been a royalty-paying service. Each *OATS* transaction is recorded and, at the end of each year, publishers receive royalty checks based on volume. Until recently that royalty was equivalent to five cents per page. Now, this amount has been doubled

and we have established a minimum payment of 50 cents per article. And we are prepared to go higher if publishers insist on it. It is their privilege and ISI supports the principle of copyright protection even when it causes ill-will with the librarians and researchers who are our customers. But if publishers insist on exorbitant royalty fees--one publisher expects to receive $3.75 per article--they will limit the effectiveness of voluntary arrangements such as the one set up by the Association of American Publishers. What they will get instead will be a compulsory licensing system similar to the one that exists for music. Under such an arrangement, publishers will be likely to receive *less* than 10 cents per page.

But despite the fears of some publishers about having their journals covered by ISI services, others are quite eager to participate. And just as an editor faces the wrath of an author when it is necessary to reject a manuscript, so it is when ISI turns down a publisher's offer to cover a new journal.

We even have some problems with editors and publishers who, once their journals are covered, try to tell us in which edition of *Current Contents* they should appear. I have in mind the editor of a botanical journal who insists that it should be in the *Life Sciences* edition instead of the *Agriculture, Biology, and Environmental Sciences* edition. We know from careful analysis, however, that the journal is of primary interest to botanists and agricultural workers. And since we can only cover a few of the *most* prestigious botanical journals in *Life*

195

Sciences--due to our absolutely comprehensive coverage of areas like biochemistry and molecular biology--our decision had to stand. I only wish that it was not necessary to make such decisions.

I now want to offer a few final suggestions on how ISI services can help publishers. For one thing, we can show you in what areas new journals are needed. A citation analysis can provide evidence that articles related to a specific subject appear in a broad range of journals. Frequently, this scattering indicates that a new journal in this emerging specialty will be well-received. Back in 1973, I published a citation analysis on pathology journals and stated that there seemed to be a field of "applied virology" developing.[31] The recent publication of the *Journal of Medical Virology* seems to have confirmed the correctness of this analysis. ISI citation analyses can also help publishers identify prospects in given specialties for mailing lists for book and journal promotions.

As I said earlier, I see ISI in a partnership with editors and publishers. I hope my talk has illuminated some of the areas in which we can work together for our mutual benefit, and I would like to continue this dialogue. For this reason, I am thinking about conducting a series of workshops at ISI that will offer more complete instruction to scientific editors and publishers on how to interface with information services. I would appreciate any comments you may have on this idea.

REFERENCES

1. **Woodford F P.** Training professional editors for scientific journals. *Scholarly Publishing* 2:41-6, 1970.
2. **Rodman H.** The moral responsibility of journal editors and referees. *The American Sociologist* 5:351-7, 1970.
3. **Wade N.** Citation analysis: a new tool for science administrators. *Science* 188:429-32, 1975.
4. **Carter G M.** Peer review, citations, and biomedical research policy: NIH grants to medical school faculty. Rand Report R-1583-HEW. Santa Monica, California: Rand Corporation, 1974.
5. **Johnson A A & Davis R B.** The research productivity of academic materials scientists. *Journal of Metals* 27:28-9, 1975.
6. **Gustafson T.** The controversy over peer review. *Science* 190:1060-6, 1975.
7. **Bayer A E & Folger J.** Some correlates of a citation measure of productivity in science. *Sociology of Education* 39:381-90, 1966.
8. **Bernier C L, Gill W N & Hunt R G.** Measures of excellence of engineering and science departments: chemical engineering example. *Chemical Engineering Education* 9:194-7, 1975.
9. **Roy R.** Comments on citation study of materials science departments. *Journal of Metals* 28:29-30, 1976.

10. **Garfield E.** Citation indexing for studying science. *Nature* 227:669-71, 1970.
11. **Margolis J.** Citation indexing and evaluation of scientific papers. *Science* 155:1213-9, 1967.
12. **Small H & Griffith B C.** The structure of scientific literatures I. Identifying and graphing specialties. *Science Studies* 4:17-40, 1974.
13. **Griffith B, Small H, Stonhill J A & Dey S.** The structure of scientific literature II. Towards a macro- and micro-structure for science. *Science Studies* 4:339-65, 1974.
14. **Garfield E.** On style in scientific writing. *Current Contents* No. 2, 10 January 1977, pp. 5-14.
15. ------------. Humor in scientific journals and journals of scientific humor. *Current Contents* No. 51, 20 December 1976, p. 664-71.
16. **Woodford F P.** *Scientific writing for graduate students.* New York : Rockefeller University Press, 1968.
17. **Debakey L & Debakey S.** Muddy medical writing--is the culprit bad grammar, technologic terminology, committee authorship, or undisciplined reasoning? *Southern Medical Journal* 69:1253-4, 1976.
18. **Garfield E.** Primary journals, current contents and the modern systems of scientific communication. *Interdisciplinary Science Reviews* (In Press).
19. ------------. La science Francaise est-elle trop provinciale? (Is French science too provincial?) *La Recherche* 7:757-60, 1976.
20. ------------. Le nouveau defi Americain. (The new American challenge.) *Current Contents* No. 16, 18 April 1977, p. 5-12.
21. ------------. Let's erect a new tower of babel. *Current Contents* No. 45, 6 November 1974, p. 507-9.
22. ------------. An address on addresses. *Current Contents* No. 28, 14 July 1975, p. 5.
23. ------------. The value of article titles in bibliographical citations. *Current Contents* No. 45, 8 November 1968, p. 7-8.
24. ------------. Citations in popular and interpretive science writing [letter to the editor of] *Science* 141:392, 1963.
25. **Virgo J A.** A statistical procedure for evaluating the importance of scientific papers. *Library Quarterly* (In Press). Dissertation, Graduate Library School of the University of Chicago, Chicago, Illinois, December 1974; 105 pp.
26. **Garfield E.** Citation statistics may help scientists choose journals in which to publish. *Current Contents* No. 7, 16 February 1972, p. 5-6.
27. **Koshy G P.** The citeability of a scientific paper. *Proceedings of Northeast Regional Conference of American Institute for Decision Sciences,* Philadelphia, Pa., April-May, 1976, p. 224-7.
28. **Garfield E.** Significant journals of science. *Nature* 264:609-15, 1976.
29. ------------. Citation studies indicate that two copies may be cheaper than one! *Current Contents* No. 23, 7 June 1972, p. 5-6.
30. ------------. Is there a future for the scientific journal? *Sci/Tech News* 29:42-4, 1976.
31. ------------. Citation analysis of pathology journals reveals need for a journal of applied virology. *Current Contents* No. 3, 17 January 1973, p. 5-8.

CURRENT COMMENTS

Hotel Horror Stories

Since most *Current Contents®* readers attend several international or national conferences each year, the following notes from my travels may interest you.

One of my many horrifying experiences occurred last year in a Swiss hotel. After registering, the reception clerk inadvertently gave me the key to the wrong room. Luckily, I didn't walk in on anyone—although that has happened to me on a few occasions. After unpacking I tried to make a few long distance telephone calls. The *same* clerk, believing I was someone who had sneaked into an unoccupied room for the purpose of making free calls, kept insisting that the lines were busy. After more than an hour of frustration, I went down to the lobby to discover the real reason why the overseas lines were so busy at midnight. But by then it was too late to place my calls.

Hospitality certainly appears to be a dying art. This doesn't mean that you can't find it--but it is usually found only in the smaller hotels and lodges. Unfortunately, international meetings need to be held in large hotels where "hospitality" is a foreign word. In such places, contrary to the popular phrase, the customer is *never* right.

For example, several years ago I made a reservation at a Sheraton Hotel in New Orleans. I arrived close to midnight, accompanied by two of my children. Even though our reservation had been confirmed only three hours earlier, I was told there was no record of it. They even denied the existence of the telephone operator whose name I quoted as having made the confirmation. The uncooperative manager of that hotel didn't find a room until I started shouting as loudly as possible that I would not leave until he found one, even if *he* had to sleep in the lobby himself. They could hear me several blocks away on Burbon Street, above the sound of several Dixieland bands. Thirty minutes later I had my room--and a very hoarse voice. This tactic reminds me of the line from the movie "Network" where the main character, Howard Beale (Peter Finch), advises the audience to go to their windows and scream out loud, "I'm mad as hell and I'm not gonna take it any more!"

In Latin countries, it is impossible to find anyone who can spell or pronounce my name--it is often filed under *Garcia*. The French pronounce it *garfeeyeld*. Given the different languages and cultures, I suppose such mistakes are to be expected. But should the same thing happen in my own country? Recently, I arrived at a posh San Francisco hotel at 11:45 p.m. The room clerk dutifully searched his reservation records, and after going through several files finally located mine under a misspelled version of my name. A victim of another clerk's bad penmanship, I was exasperated to discover that I had been filed under *Sarfied*.

Apparently hotel managers, unlike scientists, rarely travel themselves. Or if they do travel, perhaps they are so familiar with standard hotel operating procedure that they know precisely when to arrive. Just as restaurant hostesses and headwaiters save the best tables for the last to arrive, so clerks do the same with rooms--the worst always seem to go to the first to check in. If you arrive at a hotel past midnight—and they can find your reservation—you are apt to receive a three-room suite with a king-size bed. You are told, "This is all we have left." Should you arrive before noon, you will be lucky to get into your room at all, since its availability does not depend on how fatigued you may be or on how far in advance your reservation was made, but rather on the order in which the housekeeper chooses to make up the rooms. I've

slept many hours in hotel lobbies while maids chased guests out of their rooms in order to make their beds-- while my empty room went untouched.

However, I don't want to be too harsh on hotel maids. They are among the most neglected and underpaid people in the services field. And it is too easy to blame them for hotel mismanagement and disorganization. I always seek out the maid and put my tip in her hand--with much greater pleasure than with the bellhop, who expects a dollar for carrying my briefcase.

One time I arrived at one of the really posh hotels in London. It was 8:00 a.m. London time but 3:00 a.m. in Philadelphia. I was told that my room, which had been reserved since the previous day, wasn't ready because the maid couldn't prepare it. They were waiting for a guest to depart, having rented my room to him even though I had paid for it in advance. I fell asleep in the lobby and they didn't call me until after noon!

If there's one thing I've learned about hotels it is this: they are designed primarily for the benefit of the people who work there. Not only must guests fend for themselves, but they are often made to feel like intruders or outcasts. I particularly dislike the disdainful glare of the doorman who expects to be tipped for opening a cab door or lifting a bag out of your hand even though you didn't ask for the help. And then the bellhop takes over where the doorman leaves off--usually 10 yards away. This double-tipping ploy is aggravated by archaic hotel union rules. These agreements define the territorial limits of the doorman and bellhop as those boundaries which maximize tips to both. But there are wonderful exceptions. The doorman at a famous hotel in Copenhagen was delightful before he retired as a rich man. In Philadelphia the most courteous doorman in town works for Bookbinders, a restaurant near ISI® .

When in Europe, I desperately look forward to finding the *International Herald Tribune*. It is amazing how inaccessible it can be if you don't carefully plan for its purchase. Hotels never think to reserve one copy in the lobby for late arrivals.

I can't understand why hotels provide TV sets but not a daily TV guide so that you don't have to spend ten minutes scrambling through the channels in order to find something interesting. One day I expect that hotel guests will have access to Viewdata or a similar news system. Viewdata is an experimental British system for which ISI provides a science news segment. You simply dial any one of several categories in which you are interested, and Viewdata displays the most recent news reports on your TV screen. The provision of free movies via closed-circuit TV in hotels should also be encouraged.

I resent the preferential treatment given to those who drink alcohol. Are those of us who drink rarely or not at all unworthy of consideration? That some hotel would refuse to bring hot chocolate to my room but would gladly deliver a bottle of Scotch or any other alcoholic beverage seems to me to be discriminatory, as well as inconvenient. It is therefore a delight that certain hotels in Paris now have a combination bar and ice cream parlor open until 3:00 a.m.

Hotels traditionally provide soap in generous quantities. I've often wondered what happens to all those slightly used bars of soap. Do the hotels recycle them? I'd gladly accept a smaller bar of soap if only they would supply one-shot doses of shampoo and toothpaste--two items among many that the weary traveller never seems able to find when they are needed.

And is it so crazy to suggest that a pool or sauna be open as late as midnight or as early as 7:00 a.m.? I'm always arriving too early or too late for such pleasures. Even in Iceland, which is known for its natural hot-water springs and numerous swimming pools, I couldn't use the facilities because they were closed in the hours available to me after business obligations.

Too many hotel services just are not geared to the needs of the traveller. Consider the problem of laundry and dry cleaning. Hotels everywhere have yet to discover the washing machine or, as it is euphemistically referred to, automatic laundry service. Heaven forbid that a swanky, international hotel chain should install its own washing or dry cleaning machine, or even a coin-operated one that its guests could use.

Did you ever try to get clothes cleaned or pressed after 5:00 p.m. or on a Saturday or Sunday? It just isn't done. I've frequently arrived at hotels on Friday evenings, after six or seven hours in transit, and requested that a suit be pressed. The answer I've received most often is that they'd be happy to accommodate me on Monday morning.

But of course everyone knows that hotel guests are very refined. We never spill drinks on our clothes. We emerge from hours of travel without a crease or stain. And we know how to pack clothes so that they won't wrinkle. Fortunately, wrinkle-free clothes and quick-drying fabrics make the old adage work--the Lord helps those who help themselves. I often wash my own socks, underwear, and even shirts on a long journey. And I carry my own shoeshine cloth.

I remember a time when it was a beautiful European custom to leave your dull, scuffed shoes outside the door overnight and awaken to find them spotless and brilliantly shined. This was never a custom, nor is it safe to try, in an American hotel. Recently, I visited Germany and Italy and discovered that the hall porter's shoeshine has been replaced by a mechanical shoepolisher. I don't mind this so much except that the neutral polish they provide is no substitute for real shoe polish. So I carry my own supply.

These common hotel annoyances aside, my greatest agony is hotel telephones and their operators. I have lost incalculable time because of hotels' inadequate training of telephone operators. In my opinion, hotels ought to require phone operators to have degrees in information science. Considering what some graduate information specialists earn these days as librarians, they might just as well become telephone operators! The ideal telephone operator would master the local geography and be fully familiar with the neighboring restaurants, theaters, museums, athletic facilities, points of historical interest, clubs, and other places of culture and entertainment.

One solution to the problem of providing information to hotel guests might be the European concierge--almost an unknown phenomenon in America. I've had great help from the concierge in European hotels. But he or she usually can't tell you exactly what musical or other cultural events are occurring. The Hyatt Regency in New Orleans does have a concierge. She was very helpful to me during a recent visit. Hotels everywhere provide guests with little booklets that advertise the nearest striptease cabaret but rarely mention the local chamber music society or jazz club. A decent concierge would keep aware of local cultural events and maintain an accurate cinema and theater schedule. Although several cities have printed guides, they are rarely found at the hotel reception desk.

In any case, a decent concierge would enable the phone operator to concentrate on operating the telephone system. The necessity of reliable hotel phone service is illustrated by some examples.

About ten years ago I visited Portland, Oregon, to give a lecture at the Portland State College. A message containing the time and place of the lecture was to be left for me at the Hilton Hotel.

Meanwhile, I went across the river to visit some *Current Contents* readers at the Crown Zellerbach research laboratories. During my visit, I called the hotel every half hour, expecting to receive a message indicating the time and place of the agreed-upon lecture. When I came back to the hotel that afternoon, there still was no message. I called the professor involved, only to be informed that I was supposed to be there an hour earlier--that 50 students and faculty had arrived and left after waiting 30 minutes.

The hotel denied receiving the message. Later on, it turned out that a clerk had misfiled it in some other guest's key slot. My attorney informed me that the hotel was liable only for provable damages. How do you establish the worth of a lecture you haven't delivered? What is the dollar value of 50 wasted half-hours or a missed opportunity to meet some interesting people?

Such experiences lead you to organize arrangements in a less casual fashion. Your life becomes one of redundancy--always checking and re-checking to make certain there have been no slip-ups. In fact, the situation is so bad these days that I always call the hotel and ask for myself, to check if I am registered in the right room. On three separate occasions in London this year the operators denied I was registered.

I did have a very positive experience with hotel telephone operators in Copenhagen once. The hotel's manager had calculated that the audience expected for my lecture would fit comfortably into what they called a conference room. However, the ceiling was so low that we could not raise the movie screen high enough to be seen. We had to transfer the lecture to the club of the local Engineering Society. But how would we notify the audience? The operators looked up all the registered attendees' phone numbers and called as many as possible. Then we posted a bellboy at the front door and arranged to use the hotel station wagon to shuttle all of those who arrived at the hotel over to the lecture. The hotel had gotten the Engineering Society's chef to quickly arrange a fantastic display of hors d'ouevres and drinks. Everyone was kept delightfully happy during the delay.

Some hotel telephone operators try to be helpful but cannot overcome the deficiencies of an inadequately staffed switchboard. That is why I conscientiously avoid any hotel that does not have an automatic dialing system. This may deny me the pleasures and advantages of a small hotel, but I'd rather suffer the impersonal atmosphere of a large hotel and avoid frustrating delays in making calls. Many small European hotels now offer free local calls, a practice which is not widespread in the U.S.A. But many European hotels also place a scandalous surcharge on long-distance calls. In Spain one hotel refuses to place collect calls. They insist that such operator-assisted calls are delayed for hours. However, the charge for direct dialing is triple that from a public phone.

One problem I often have while travelling is beyond my diplomatic capabilities. How do you tell friends or colleagues you have just arrived in their town, after travelling 5,000 miles, but don't have time to accept *their* invitation to dinner or to visit their lab or tour their university? When I was in eastern Europe recently, I found this particularly frustrating because the opportunities to meet foreign scientists in that part of the world are less common than elsewhere. I always feel bad when I am in a friend's home town and would like to say hello but, due to other commitments, simply do not have the time to accept the friend's hospitality. As the publisher of *Current Contents,* I value the opportunity to talk to as many readers as possible. Local calls are a way of keeping in touch. So if you

receive a call one day, forgive me if I don't accept your invitation to lunch.

My complaints about hotels may seem exaggerated. Indeed, my caustic remarks may appear unkind to the many individual hotels and their employees who treat guests quite royally. After having enjoyed many pleasurable stays in certain hotels, it is fairly easy to criticize the bad experiences. One tends to forget the pleasant though uneventful visits and to remember only the horror stories.

For example, recently I was late for my departure on a flight to London. Pan Am refused to let me carry my suitcase on board, so it was sent on the following flight. When I arrived at my hotel in London the receptionist inquired about my missing baggage. Then he took a look at me and said he would contact the housekeeper, who keeps an electric razor on hand. But the hotel could not supply the other necessities that are impossible to obtain at a late hour. Always keep a spare toothbrush in your briefcase. I hesitate to carry toothpaste. The last time I did it broke open and messed up the first draft of this polemic.

I fully agree with Samuel Johnson, a literary man of wide-ranging travels, who so eloquently stated 200 years ago: "There is nothing which has yet been contrived by man by which so much happiness is produced as by a good tavern or inn."[1]

REFERENCE

1. **Boswell J.** *Life of Johnson.* 1776. Quoted in: **Bartlett J.** *Familiar Quotations.* Boston: Little, Brown, 1968. p. 432.

CURRENT COMMENTS

Will ISI's *Arts & Humanities Citation Index* Revolutionize Scholarship?

Number 32, August 8, 1977

One hears a great deal about bridging the gap between C. P. Snow's "two cultures." My respect and admiration for science notwithstanding, I have frequently felt uncomfortable among many scientific colleagues because of their awesome technical grasp of natural or physical phenomena. I have often felt equally ill-at-ease among artists, literary persons and humanities scholars when confronted with their consummate expertise. But forced to make the choice, I suspect I would favor the arts and humanities over scientific endeavors.

Fortunately, this choice is not necessary for me or for society. But ever since I entered the field of information science I have been acutely conscious of the "bias" ISI® and most similar organizations in the U.S. and abroad have towards the sciences. So it gives me special pleasure to announce that ISI will introduce in 1978 the *Arts & Humanities Citation Index (A&HCI)*.

Upon hearing about this decision, my late colleague Robert L. Hayne, ISI's Chief Editor, cautioned me to remember to mention that the history of science is replete with great scientists who combined both art and science to produce the quintessence of both. The Parthenon is but one ancient reminder of the fusion of mathematics with art, as is most great architecture. Leonardo da Vinci probably epitomizes the bridge between the two cultures, while Isaac Newton exemplifies the crossover between philosophy and scientific scholarship.

Although ISI is not the only information organization in the world covering the three major areas of research and scholarship—the sciences, the social sciences, and the arts and humanities—it is undoubtedly unique in scope, whether one thinks of the Wilson Indexes or even the Library of Congress. The processing of so many diverse journals will enable us to put at the disposal of world scholarship in all fields those occasional but significant cross-references between the two cultures. For example, if you examine either the annual *Science Citation Index®* (*SCI®*) or *Social Sciences Citation Index™* (*SSCI™*) for 1976 or 1977 you will find on almost any page an entry which reads "see *SCI* (or *SSCI*) for *n* additional citations." Similar cross-referencing is being considered for the

A&HCI. This might help preserve the elusive connective threads which are often lost when searching discipline-oriented indexes.

Of course, ISI's involvement with arts and humanities information is not totally unexpected. The wide acceptance of the *Science Citation Index,* and especially the *Social Sciences Citation Index,* has caused many librarians and scholars to ask when ISI would cover these other areas. In recent years research and scholarship in the arts and humanities have become more interdisciplinary. Investigations on such topics as the language of philosophy, the influence of women on religious art, book publishing in the Middle Ages, or even the development of protest music have become more common. According to the people who wanted ISI to become involved, no existing service provided the coverage *or* the indexing approach needed to answer such questions simply.

Quite frankly, we hesitated to enter the arts and humanities area for a number of good reasons. Nothing is more intellectually frustrating than an idea whose time has not come—to say nothing of the economic consequences of acting upon such an idea. And when we considered the large number of specialized services already available in the arts and humanities, we were concerned about unnecessary duplication.

So we undertook an intensive two-year marketing research program to determine if there was a real need. We interviewed dozens of people in North America and Europe and conducted a worldwide mail survey. We found that:

—the arts and humanities, no less than the sciences, need a large-scale index that provides multidisciplinary coverage,

—an up-to-date service issued on a current basis and cumulated annually would be welcomed, and

—there was widespread belief in the potential effectiveness of citation and title-word indexing in arts and humanities information retrieval.

Whether citation indexing and title word indexing will actually work with the literature of the arts and humanities remains to be seen. The advantages of citation indexing have often been discussed in *Current Contents®* . But in the arts and humanities the advantages over traditional indexing methods are possibly more significant than in the sciences due to the vagueness of many titles and the kinds of abstract concepts involved. Need one elaborate on the multitudinous interpretations possible in art?

It has been claimed that the arts and humanities are particularly characterized by isolated schools of thought, and that they often rely on perceptual rather than experimental evidence. Certainly the terminology of humanists lacks the precision we associate with the sciences— inconsistent as it may be. But this lack of precision in terminology does not imply a lack of careful citation. As M. S. Batts of the University of British Columbia has asserted, even though citation indexing is now restricted to the sciences and social sciences, humanities scholars "cite with equal if not greater avidity and have been doing so for hundreds of years." He states that a citation index "could, therefore, be as useful to the humanist as to the scientist."[1]

Unfortunately, it is true that the citation practices of certain journals—and even some individuals—in the arts and humanities are sometimes not as useful as they might be. And, as in the social sciences, inconsistencies of citation style in the humanities hamper the preparation of a citation index. Archaic bibliographic practices plague us and the user because of the added costs and energy involved. Articles in art, music and philosophy present special problems. They often cite literature other than journals or books, such as unpublished manuscripts and catalogs. They sometimes refer to original sources but do not cite them. Also, references and notes are often imbedded in the text. Even when they are sequentially numbered and placed at the end of the article, they can be quite involved and so require considerable effort in deciphering their meaning. Such problems may add to our processing costs, but they certainly are not insurmountable.

Unlike the *SCI* and *SSCI,* the *Arts & Humanities Citation Index* will index "implicit" citations, which occur when an article refers to and substantially discusses a specific work but does not formally cite it. Even reproduced works of art and music scores will be picked up as implicit citations, with a code indicating that the "cited" work is an illustration.

In addition to a citation index, the *A&HCI* will, like the *Science Citation Index* and *Social Sciences Citation Index,* include a permuted title word index called the *Permuterm®* *Subject Index (PSI).*[2] The *PSI* will offer rapid, highly specific searches especially when one recalls the title of an earlier work. Once retrieved, these references can be used as starting points in a search of the citation index or source index. Since subtitles are also processed for the *PSI,* it is even more likely that specific, descriptive, meaningful terms will be obtained to index each source article.

Nevertheless, we realize that we will have to deal with the problem of whimsical and other types of inadequate titles. This will be done through a title "enrichment" policy. Although titles will not be changed, an article will be indexed *as if* its title contained the name of the person, place or thing it is about. Thus, if an article about the work of Pablo Picasso does not contain the artist's name in the title, we will add it. "Picasso," along with the rest of the significant title words, will then be permuted to form a series of two-term entries or term-pairs.

There will, of course, be a source index section in the *Arts & Humanities Citation Index.* This will give

206

the full bibliographic description of each source item covered, as well as author addresses for reprint requests or other follow-up contacts. Each year's source index will be the most complete listing of arts and humanities authors ever compiled.

One of the problems addressed by our marketing research effort was that of defining the arts and humanities. From my previous experience, a pragmatic solution to this problem of definition will be found essentially in the marketplace. Starting from an obvious core of journals we will expand our boundaries as costs permit and users demand. The disciplines covered by the *A&HCI* will certainly include the traditional disciplines of literature, languages, history, philosophy, religion and classics. Other areas covered will include fine arts and architecture, music, and the performing arts of drama, dance, film, radio and television. The complete scope of our coverage of such areas as "music" will require refinement. Certainly musicology and the history of music are essential. But there are dozens of "journals" on music. Whether a jazz publication like *Downbeat* should be indexed in *A&HCI* needs to be carefully evaluated.

Arts and humanities journals contain a wide variety of items: articles, book reviews, review articles, bibliographies, letters, record and performance reviews, literary criticisms and works of fiction such as stories, plays and poems. At present, no index covers all of these diverse types of publications. The *Arts & Humanities Citation Index* will provide cover-to-cover indexing for every issue of every covered journal. Initially, over 70,000 items per year from over 1,000 journals will be covered. About half are published in the United States and half published elsewhere. As the service expands foreign coverage will be increasingly stressed.

Since long publication lag times have been a major problem with most existing arts and humanities indexes, ISI's *Arts & Humanities Citation Index* will be published on a schedule that makes it the most current tool of its size. The first softbound triannual will be issued in June, 1978, covering the journal literature published from January to April. The second triannual *A&HCI*, covering the literature from May through August, will be issued in October, 1978, and the annual *A&HCI* covering all of 1978 will appear in May, 1979. The same schedule will be followed in subsequent years. In addition, an annual *A&HCI* covering the literature published during 1977 will appear in December, 1978.

The price of the *A&HCI* will be $1500. We realize that some speciality institutions, such as small schools of art, music, dance, and religion, as well as small libraries and museums, may not be able to afford this. However, the ISI Grant Program, which provides financial help from ISI equivalent to 50% of the regular purchase price, will enable some of these institutions to purchase this new tool.[3]

We have already received many questions concerning the *Arts & Humanities Citation Index.* Will computer tapes be made available for on-line searching? Will there be a *Current Contents Arts & Humanities*? How about a *Journal Citation Reports®* for the arts and humanities? We haven't immediate answers for all these questions, but their very existence indicates a high probability of positive response. (Readers can obtain more information by sending in the coupon on the back cover of this issue.)

The computer plays an important role in the compilation of our services. Some humanists may be averse to what they see as manipulation of their scholarship by modern machines. But I cannot believe that many modern humanities scholars hold so firmly to the "Frankenstein" complex as to deny themselves the benefit of improved access to the literature of scholarship.[4]

I am reminded that when I wrote my first paper on the *SCI* I was attending library school.[5] After correcting my abysmal English, Professor Allan T. Hazen told me that, if ever applied to the humanities, citation indexing would substantially alter the quest for the doctorate. Many dissertations have consisted primarily of a search through endless bibliographies for the elusive reference to a particular literary work. In this sense, *A&HCI* could conceivably produce a revolution in literary scholarship.

Today there are many scientists who are fully conscious of the need for society to support the humanities. But far too many pursue their technical endeavors seemingly unaware, for example, that the cost of a single particle accelerator could support hundreds of painters or performing artists. Fortunately, feeling as I do that *A&HCI* will be a financial *as well as* intellectual success, it will not be necessary to justify its existence either to scientists or to the members of my Board of Directors merely on spiritual or aesthetic grounds. So I look forward to the rapid and widespread acceptance and use of ISI's new *Arts & Humanities Citation Index.* Your comments and suggestions would be appreciated.

1. **Batts M S.** Citations in the humanities. *Institute of Professional Librarians of Ontario Quarterly* 14:20-40, 1972.
2. **Garfield E.** The *Permuterm Subject Index:* an autobiographical review. *Journal of the American Society for Information Science* 27(5-6):288-91, September-October 1976.
3. --------------. The ISI grant program. *Current Contents* No. 18, 2 May 1977, p. 5-6.
4. --------------. 'Our computer goofed.' *Current Contents* No. 23, 9 June 1975, p. 5. (Reprinted in: *Essays of an Information Scientist.* Philadelphia: ISI Press, 1977. Vol. 2, p. 296.)
5. --------------. Citation indexes for science. *Science* 122(3159):108-11, 15 July 1955.

CURRENT COMMENTS

The ISI Lecturer Program:
A Pragmatic Approach to Teaching
Students About Information Services

Number 33, August 15, 1977

Earlier this year I discussed how an ISI® survey had discovered a surprising lack of awareness of *Current Contents*® among many graduate students.[1] This is symptomatic of a more general and widespread problem in science education: a shortage of effective programs to teach students about the availability and use of information tools.

Most faculty members and librarians readily agree that students need considerable information retrieval skills in order to pursue careers in science. In my opinion, the inability to convert this conviction to effective instructional programs stems largely from jurisdictional confusion. The "subject" content of most courses is the responsibility of the science faculty, while information tools are in the librarian's domain. Unfortunately, the twain never seem to meet. The questions of who should teach science students about the information tools they will need and how, where, and when this instruction should be given are largely unresolved.

Most professors have their hands full just getting through their course subject material in a semester. Since most faculty members have no formal training in the use of information

tools, they are hesitant to instruct others about them. Librarians do try to help, but their time is limited. Even a well designed library tour at the begining of a semester is not much help to a student who comes up against a real search problem two months later.

Some independent efforts to correct this situation have come to my attention. In a class given by W. R. Klemm of Texas A&M University, each student is given an older publication on a topic in physiology and told to trace in the *Science Citation Index*® the articles which have cited the older paper, articles which cited those articles, and so forth. They then write abstracts of the articles they find. According to Dr. Klemm, the class members feel that at the same time they are learning about physiology and gaining an understanding of the impact of earlier research on more recent work, they are also learning how to use an important reference tool.[2]

S. M. Plaut of the University of Maryland School of Medicine conducts seminars in research methodology that give students hands-on experience with various information services, including *Current Contents* and the *Science Citation Index.* The seminars are mandatory for certain students in child psychiatry, behavioral pediatrics, school health, and adolescent medicine and are elective for medical students, faculty, and residents. Plaut points out that once they have seen *Current Contents,* almost all of the seminar participants *ask* to be put on the routing list for it.[3]

A systematic approach to student literature searches was recently described by John MacGregor and Raymond G. McInnis of the Wilson Library, Western Washington State College.[4] In addition to discussing the efficient use of encyclopedias, reviews of research, citation indexes, abstracts, and card catalogs, their approach to teaching library research provides students with a general understanding of constructing bibliographic networks.

At the University of Arizona, all graduate students in the Department of Plant Pathology are routinely included on the routing list for *Current Contents,* according to Stanley M. Alcorn and Linda White. Further, all graduate students are encouraged to enroll in a for-credit course called "Information Sources for Agricultural Scientists." The course, which meets once a week, is designed to "orient students to current, standard science and government reference tools and to new computer-based information systems which are accessing scientific and technical information." Dr. White was kind enough to send me the course outline, and I was so impressed with its balanced and comprehensive approach that I have reproduced it here (see p. 7) as a guide for others who may wish to start similar programs.

Unfortunately, creative programs like those mentioned are the exception, not the rule. So while continuing to do its part to encourage a more general awareness of information tools and resources, ISI has also instituted a program that can provide some immediate, specific help. In late 1975, we created a new position which we called the ISI Educational Lecturer. This was in addition to our field representatives, who are also competent lecturers. Originally, the Educational Lecturer's responsibility was to instruct library and information science students in the uses of ISI services. At the time, we believed that the most pressing need was to make sure that future librarians would know how to use our services when students and faculty asked about them, or when they were confronted by search questions which our services could handle effectively. We felt this was necessary because we knew that even a few of the "better" library schools hardly gave lip service to the ISI product line—even though most of our services are now regarded as "standard" by experienced librarians and researchers.

Continuing feedback indicates that our initial thinking was correct. Later on, however, we realized that instructional help was needed in science classrooms as well as in library schools. If students don't even know that the *Science Citation Index* exists, they

Information Sources for Agricultural Scientists: Course Outline

The University of Arizona, College of Agriculture, Tucson, Arizona 85721

Week 1 INTRODUCTION
a. Growth of literature
b. Special services
c. Computers as the solution

Week 2. THE RESEARCH LIBRARY — A TRADITIONAL SOURCE
a. Interlibrary loan
b. National Union Catalog
c. The new copyright law and the library

Week 3 BASICS IN INFORMATION RETRIEVAL/ORGANIZATION
a. The citation vs. the document
b. What is a document?
c. Conventional indexing
d. Coordinate indexing
e. KWIC and KWOC indexes

Week 4 AN OVERVIEW OF PRINTED SOURCES
a. Indexes are not identical
b. Arrangement affects use
c. How to find an index in your field
d. Effect of vocabulary control
e. Recall versus precision

Week 5 INDEXES AND ABSTRACTING JOURNALS
a. Biological Abstracts
b. BioResearch Index
c. Dissertation Abstracts International and the Comprehensive Dissertation Index
d. Chemical Abstracts
e. Bibliography of Agriculture

Week 6 COMPUTER RETRIEVAL SERVICES
a. Their origin
b. Their products
c. Their access
d. Examples — CRIS, SSIE, AGRICOLA

Week 7 ABSTRACTING AND INDEXING PROCEDURES
a. Criteria for abstracts: writing and reading
b. Comparisons of abstracts
c. Subject headings vs. descriptors vs. keywords
d. The thesaurus and keyword list
e. Indexing by humans or indexing by machines

Week 8 INSTITUTE FOR SCIENTIFIC INFORMATION (ISI)
a. Science Citation Index
b. Social Sciences Citation Index
c. Index to Scientific Reviews

Week 9 DEMONSTRATION OF ON-LINE COMPUTER SYSTEM

Week 10 INFORMATION HANDLING TECHNIQUES
a. File organization
b. Indexing and coding systems
c. Information centers
d. Microform

Week 11 ALERTING SERVICES
a. Current Contents
b. Automatic Subject Citation Alerting
c. Chemical Titles
d. Hydata
e. Newsletters
f. SDI from computer bases

Week 12 GOVERNMENT DOCUMENTS
a. General documents and cataloging
b. Monthly Catalog
c. Federal Register
d. National Referral Center
e. Monthly Checklist of State Publications
f. Information Resources in U.S.
g. Acquisition and location of documents
h. Congressional Information Service indexes
i. Environmental impact statements
j. National Technical Information Service

Week 13 COMPUTER "DATA" SYSTEMS.
a. ENDEX
b. LADB
c. FAPRS

Week 14 POPULARIZED SOURCES
a. Newspapers
b. Radio-TV
c. NY Times Index
d. Extension publications

Week 15 INTERNATIONAL LITERATURE
a. FAO and UN
b. AGRINDEX
c. Translations
d. Area handbooks

Week 16 HOW TO KEEP UP AND SUMMARY
a. Systems of literature reviewing
b. Written and oral sources
c. Personal contact
d. Computer conferencing

aren't likely to ask questions about it. So at the start of 1977, we broadened the scope of the ISI lecturer's responsibilities to include instructions for science students, and we increased the number of available lecturers. We now have two full-time lecturers, with a third soon to be added.

Diane Hoffman, our lecturer for the United States and Canada, has been with the program since its beginning. A graduate of Syracuse University Library School, she served for seven years as a reference librarian, first at Syracuse and then at the State University of New York at Oswego. Karen Sandler, our lecturer in Europe, is a graduate of the Imperial College of Science and Technology at the University of London, and formerly an information officer at Beecham Medical Centre. Ms. Sandler's lectures are currently limited to the United Kingdom, Ireland, The Netherlands, and Scandinavia.

ISI lecturers tailor their presentations to fit the needs of the students to whom they are talking. They are prepared to speak on the theory of citation indexing, how to use the *Science Citation Index* and *Social Sciences Citation Index™*, how to assemble an *ASCA®* profile, and the specific applications of our indexes in different subject areas, as well as the use of citation analysis in collection management and development. They can also answer students' questions about when and how to use other types of ISI services, such as *Current Abstracts of Chemistry™*, *Index Chemicus®*, and *Chemical Substructure Index®*. The lecturers select and distribute appropriate printed literature for each audience, and usually include audio-visual aids in their presentations.

Lecturers are provided without charge. If you are interested in scheduling an ISI Educational Lecturer for the fall semester, write Ms. Hoffman at ISI in Philadelphia or Ms. Sandler at our European office.

The ISI lecturer program will not completely solve the problem of teaching science students about information tools. But when you consider that ISI lecturers and marketing representatives deliver almost 1,000 lectures each year, we think that we have taken steps in the right direction. However, our efforts cannot succeed without the help of concerned faculty members. If you teach a science course, I hope you will see that your students get the information they need about information tools.

REFERENCES

1. **Garfield E.** What some science students don't know: *Current Contents* can help them during and after their formal education. *Current Contents* No. 21, 23 May 1977, p. 5-6.
2. **Klemm W R.** Teaching physiology with citation index. *The Physiology Teacher* 5(4):8-9, 1975.
3. **Plaut S M.** Personal communication, 24 May 1977.
4. **MacGregor J & McInnis R G.** Integrating classroom instruction and library research. *Journal of Higher Education* 48(1):17-38, January-February 1977.

CURRENT COMMENTS

To Remember My Brother,
Robert L. Hayne

Number 34, August 22, 1977

It is neither fashionable nor common in the American culture to eulogize the living. This is unfortunate. We express some of the most endearing thoughts of affection for our friends and colleagues only after it is too late for them to hear. This is not entirely true of Robert L. Hayne, ISI® 's Chief Editor, who died on July 18, 1977. Bob heard me tell him—though much too late in our long "marriage"—that I loved him as much as my own brother. I would have preferred that Bob read this public tribute to him. He did confess his enjoyment at reading my recent acknowledgement of his role in my book of essays.

But while he was alive he expressly forbade me from doing this, even though I had published tributes to other ISI executives. In fact, he even went so far as to suggest that after his death the less mention of his name the better.

Since we will all achieve that eternal obscurity and oblivion soon enough, I hope he would forgive this trespass. If Bob Hayne does not want the world to know he left it a better place because of the unique person he was, certainly his children and many friends will appreciate some verbalization of their own feelings.

When I wrote about Hayne recently I erroneously confused his alma mater, William & Mary, with another well-known American college. He forgave this error when he saw it, even though he winced. But he did not question my main point: that his education had produced a person of such unique culture that he surely must have seemed an anachronism. Actually he was not only a consummate scholar, a Renaissance Man, and a man for all seasons—he was a cosmic soul. It is hard to believe that such a force does not live on in one way or another.

Part of the grief I feel for Bob is undoubtedly caused by guilt. Sometimes we take our best friends for granted, never realizing how little we know about them. Bob and I knew each other for 26 years, yet I hardly know his children. As I try to biograph him I realize that all I can remember is that he was an orphan brought up in Washington, D.C., and was later adopted as a teenager by a woman I never met.

Bob and I lived in four eras. The first was before we knew each other. We met while working on the National Library of Medicine's Subject Heading Authority List with Seymore Taine, Sanfred Larkey, Helen Field and

Williamina Himwich. We both then went through a long period of association with Smith, Kline & French Laboratories and shared a close friendship with Ted Herdegen. Finally there was our long ISI association, beginning in 1969.

While he was alive it was difficult for me to let on to other colleagues that I considered Bob as close as a brother. It may be for that reason that I often pushed him to perform incredible feats of data compilation and analysis. He worked with such amazing speed that it was hard to realize just how much was getting accomplished.

We agreed to disagree about many things. Perhaps our most recent dispute concerned an essay he drafted entitled "Leonardo in Blue Neon," about a Philadelphia artist's rendering in neon lights of DaVinci's painting, "The Last Supper." I went to look at it and told Bob I didn't like it, but I couldn't get him to agree to discuss our disagreement in *Current Contents®*

Bob was as comfortable with artistic masterpieces as with graphic design, with literary classics as with technical writing, with Mozart as with David Bowie. His intimate knowledge of ancient mythology made one think he must have lived in ancient Greece, as well as Rome and Scandinavia. He could read innumerable languages. His last request to me was to purchase an Arabic-language Bible so that he could use it for studying Arabic in the way he preferred. We both discussed many linguistically oriented projects—not the least of which is the as-yet incomplete transliterated dictionary of Russian, on which he had made considerable progress. This project will be completed in

the near future and will be a further testimony to his mark on me and on the world.

Bob's greatest failing as a manager was his difficulty in saying no. He wanted everything to get done and to get done perfectly. For years to come the essays appearing in this column will owe a large measure to Bob's ideas and contributions.

Those of you who particularly enjoy the *ISI Press Digest* should realize that it was launched under his tutelage. The same is true of *Citation Classics*. He helped train many of my ISI co-workers and numerous others elsewhere. He was habitually adopting "orphans" of one kind or another.

Those who worked for Bob considered him an ideal boss. He demanded a lot, but he recognized and appreciated work well done. And his competence was so broad that he never had to ask anyone to do something he couldn't do himself. Bob was respected by everyone at ISI, but could laugh and joke and show a genuine interest in everyone from clerks to vice- presidents. Some employees who didn't know Bob may have been intimidated by his sarcastic wit, but all of those who got close to him enjoyed his sharp, perceptive intelligence and his readiness to laugh.

Nothing can be said that can properly do justice to a person's whole life, and I would not even attempt to cover all of Bob's talents or accomplishments or character. It is certain that he will be sorely missed by all of his friends. I am confident that ISI and *Current Contents* will survive, but I am equally confident that without Bob they will never be the same.

CURRENT COMMENTS

To Cite or Not to Cite:
A Note of Annoyance

Number 35, August 29, 1977

Sociologists often talk about the "reward" system in science and scholarship. Publication of papers, especially in prestigious journals, adds to an author's credits. When an author's work contributes to your own work he is entitled to some "reward" for adding to the world's knowledge. These rewards are usually given in the form of reference citations. This is, of course, an over-simplification, but it reflects the mores or ethics of international research. Later authors "reward" the work of their predecessors, so when an author fails to cite relevant earlier work the uncited author may be justly annoyed.

This happened to me (again) recently, and has caused me to reflect once again on the citation habits of scientists. I must confess that the article in question elevated my blood pressure. But I know that this feeling is shared by many colleagues. It is, I believe, only human and natural to feel this way. However, I will not embarass the particular author concerned, who seems to have been unaware of the specific uncited work.

Ironically, the article involved concerned the citing behavior of scientists. Since citation practices are a social characteristic of science, and sociologists are interested in the analysis of such characteristics—which encompass the feelings of the individuals being studied—I will help the author in question by explicitly characterizing my feelings: *I am annoyed.*

I am annoyed because my existence has been denied, and I believe that my reaction is typical of researchers whose contributions are used but not acknowledged. Even though the author of the article clearly has studied my work; even though my contributions were essential for the development of the tools he used; even though his work would not have been possible without my contributions; he has failed to acknowledge in any way the debt he owes me. This kind of treatment helps me understand the feelings of certain "dissident" scientists whose names are erased from bibliographies.

I have been told that the failure of authors to cite my work in sociometrics is the result of the obliteration phenomenon.[1] Obliteration occurs when authors assume that the source of a previous contribution is part of the common wisdom of everyone working in the field. Thus if a physicist mentions the word *relativity* it is reasonable to assume that the reader knows it is associated with Einstein, and explicit citation of Einstein is superfluous. But if someone uses the *Science Citation Index®* (*SCI®*) or some form of citation analysis, is it equally reasonable to assume that the average sociologist, historian, or other scholar knows the papers which I or my colleagues at ISI® have published on this subject? I think not. It is a fact of life, however, that the public availability of the *SCI* and the *Social Sciences Citation Index™* (*SSCI™*) will lead to their use without explicit citation. I therefore join the ranks of those "honored" by obliteration.

Sociometrics is not yet at a stage where it can be assumed that all scholars are familiar with the primordial work in this field. But it may say something about the provinciality of some sociologists to mention that I have never published in a sociological journal. Editors and referees of such journals ought to be particularly sensitive to citation of work outside the sociology establishment. But I suppose that some either do not recall or are not aware of such work.

Reference citations are required for a variety of reasons: to help trace the development of the present contribution, provide background reading, criticize or dispute previous work, authenticate data and identify methodology. In these situations authors should be as careful about references as they are about titles, authorships, abstracts, and the substance of the data being presented. Editors and referees should insist that authors not cite too many or too few references, and that those cited be strongly relevant to the new contribution.[2] But certainly the mere quality of citations in a paper is not a guarantee of its quality.

Citations are also used as a social device for validating priority claims. Unlike such scientists as Galileo, Hooke, and Kepler, who announced their discoveries in cryptograms in order to reserve priority without helping their rivals,[3] today's researchers generally announce their significant findings as clearly and as early as possible. Priority of discovery is preserved and validated by means of the modern pattern of explicit citation to previous work, which first appeared around 1850.

An author who cites previous work formally recognizes the "property" rights of those he cites. Thus the citation is an important institutional device for coping with the imperative to communicate scientific findings freely and openly while at the same time protecting individual claims to recognition.[4]

Unfortunately, some editors, writers, and referees in all fields of science are not as concerned as they should be about the proper use of cited references. Some authors fail to cite pertinent papers, or cite for reasons which are frivolous, misleading, or dishonest. Citations may represent an author's attempt to enhance his own reputation by associating his work with greater works, or to avoid responsibility by leaning heavily on the work of others. Citations can also be intended to curry favor with influential colleagues or referees, to honor a mentor or friend, or to convey the impression of exhaustive knowledge.

Naturally, I am disappointed when I see the reward system of science abused or distorted—just as I am when citations are effectively vitiated through typographical or other errors. But it is all too easy to forget that the vast majority of citations are accurate and the vast majority of papers do properly cite the earlier literature. Unfortunately, there has never been a definitive study of this assertion. Moravcsik[5] and others have studied the reasons why people cite, but it would be a formidable task to determine, in a large enough random sample, how often papers fail to cite accurately and comprehensively.

With the advent of the *SCI* and *SSCI*, and related tools, there is an added reason why you should be cautious to include all relevant documents in your list of references. When your putative colleague elsewhere searches the *SCI* and begins by looking up where his paper has been cited, yours may be missed!

I wish that I could cite a definitive study to prove that the situation is improving. The existence of the *SCI* has increased citation consciousness because of its uses in evaluation studies, This raised consciousness seems to have led to more care in the use of the cited references. Citation practices are scrutinized when ISI evaluates new journals for inclusion in *Current Contents®* , and most conform to accepted international standards.

Apart from the annoyance we all feel when an error of omission occurs, deliberately or unwittingly, such errors are merely insignificant background noise in most statistical studies. How much does it matter in selecting citation classics if even a dozen authors wrongly cite, or fail to cite, a paper which is correctly cited 1,000 times? On the other hand, when tracing the development of a particular idea it is of significant historical interest to find that one author did or did not cite another. Without evidence to the contrary, we always assume that the uncited author was unknown to the authors who did not cite him.

Outside of the formal journal literature, of course, articles without references abound. Most newspapers and magazines—even those that purport to cover scientific and technical news—are almost completely void of references. This omission not only throws doubt on the reporter's authority and credibility, but can also be extremely frustrating to those readers with a real interest in the subject. Their curiosity is aroused but cannot be satiated. It seems like links to the primary literature sometimes are deliberately eliminated to add to the mystique of the reporter's sources. Some newspapers and magazines—notably the *New York Times* and *Science News*—usually supply at least one reference in text for major articles. It usually consists of a statement such as "in the latest issue of the *New England Journal of Medicine.*" But this amounts to little more than a token effort. There is no reason—aside perhaps from a low opinion of its readers—why the "popular" press should not supply references with articles that deal with scientific and technical material.

What newspaper and magazine editors—as well as many scientists and journal editors—don't realize is that citations are a form of communication. Like words, they can be used to mean a variety of things. They can be accurate or approximate, serious or frivolous, honest or dishonest. But in order to communicate effectively and intelligently about scientific and technical subjects, explicit citations are essential.

Perhaps that helps to explain my annoyance. Authors communicate with the entire population of working scientists, as well as with scientists of future generations. So an author who improperly cites or fails to cite does more than merely weaken his own contribution or inconvenience the readers of his paper—he retards the communication system of science, impedes information retrieval, distorts the historical network, and ignores the rights of his scientific predecessors.

REFERENCES

1. **Garfield E.** The 'obliteration phenomenon' in science—and the advantage of being obliterated! *Current Contents* No. 51-2, 22 December 1975. Reprinted in *Essays of an Information Scientist* Vol. II. Philadelphia: ISI Press, 1977. p. 396-8.

2. **Price D J D.** On the side of citations. *Agricultural Engineering* 51(2):94, February 1970.

3. ―――――――. *Little science, big science.* New York: Columbia University Press, 1963. p. 64-6.

4. **Kaplan N.** The norms of citation behavior: prolegomena to the footnote. *American Documentation* 16(3):179-84, July 1965.

5. **Moravcsik M J & Poovanalingam M.** Some results on the function and quality of citations. *Social Studies of Science* 5:86-92, February 1975.

CURRENT COMMENTS

Cremation: A Sensible Alternative

Number 36, September 5, 1977

For many, death and its aftermath is a distasteful subject; a subject to be ignored or avoided until suddenly it demands attention. Those who lose a close relative or friend are often left in a state of shock and grief. They are ill-prepared to handle arrangements for a funeral or burial or cremation—yet they often *must* attend to the myriad social and financial details.

My own mother's death last year was sudden, and—like most optimists who repress or deny even the possibility of a loved one's death—my sister, my brother, and myself were not prepared with a specific plan of action. All we knew was that—in the absence of specific instructions in her will—she had mentioned wanting her body cremated. I hope that recounting my experiences in arranging the cremation will be of some help to *CC®* readers.

In much of the world cremation is considered the only sensible form of "burial." So it is strange that it is so difficult to arrange a simple cremation in the United States. The laws concerning funeral arrangements are far from uniform in the various states, and sometimes seem to be based more on superstition than on good sense.

For example, it is not generally known that funeral laws in many states mandate that you deal with a funeral director—even though your only objective is disposal of a body through cremation. Even when a body is donated to medical research, the services of a funeral director may be required just to move it.

According to Jessica Mitford, author of *The American Way of Death,* the American funeral industry has steadfastly fought against "direct cremation."[1] This means taking the body directly to the crematorium, bypassing the need for a coffin or even an undertaker. Direct cremation is virtually impossible in the U.S. because most states require caskets for cremation.[2] Even when not required by state law, many funeral homes force those arranging cremations to purchase coffins. In one recent case, the Federal Trade Commission prohibited a funeral home chain from requiring customers to buy a coffin for immediate cremations.[3]

When my mother died, I asked the director of the hospital for the name of a reputable local funeral director. I got the name and checked the yellow pages for the telephone number. A domineering voice answered my call, and after several minutes of well-modulated condolences and circumlocution, I was told that a simple cremation would cost $400! Fifteen minutes later, this same funeral director called me back and assured me that he would never refuse to handle a needy case for $250. His eagerness to assume my burden led me back to the yellow pages, where I found a profusion of advertisements for funeral homes. Under a separate listing were the names of several crematoria. The spokesmen for these organizations were frank. I was told that the actual charge for cremation was $50 to $75, but that arrangements for pick-up and transport of the body, as well as the paperwork at the county clerk's office, added to the price.

The director of one crematorium was sympathetic to those families who preferred to conduct their own memorial services, but pointed out to me that the law required that the body be transported by a licensed person. He then gave me the name of a licensed funeral director who specialized in simple arrangements. This fellow told me that he would pick up the body, handle the paperwork, and arrange for the cremation for $175. We agreed to this. The following morning we met him at the crematorium and were asked to verify that it was indeed my mother's body—as we had done at the time of her death.

It was only at this moment that we were informed that the actual cremation would not take place immediately. The cremation was scheduled for a later time—presumably, because it would cost less

to cremate several bodies at once. A week later, I had to remind the crematorium that the ashes had not been delivered as promised.

My experience with funeral directors was hardly comforting. Some lied. One insisted that a coffin was legally required for a cremation, even though it was not. Others tried to make me feel cheap. Almost all used archaic phrases and euphemisms to describe what is really a series of simple, straightforward procedures.

I am reminded of my mother in many ways—particularly when I look at one of her paintings. At her memorial service my brother read a beautiful eulogy, which her children—and ours—will always be able to read with happy tears. A cemetery plot with an engraved stone tablet would merely be superfluous.

Interestingly, the British funeral industry has not developed in the intensely competitive way that it has in the U.S. However, even in England a coffin is a legal requirement for burial *or* cremation, and subtle pressure is exerted by funeral directors in order to sell handsome, high-priced coffins out of "respect for the dead." The British crematorium is typically set in extensive grounds and gardens. The minimum charge for a cremation is £170, or about 300 dollars. An urn costs extra.

One interesting difference between Great Britain and the United States is in the treatment of the remains of cremation. A cremated body is reduced not just to fine ashes, but to ashes and recognizable bone fragments of various sizes. It is even possible to obtain medical information from the remains of cremated bones.[4] In Great Britain the remains are usually pulverized to facilitate scattering the ashes in gardens or elsewhere. About 25% of the dead are cremated, and about 90% of the cremated remains are scattered in Britain.[1]

In the United States, however, some states prohibit scattering, and pulverizing is rare or non-existent. The reason for this cultural difference may be economic—scattering interferes with the sale of urns.

In the Soviet Union and certain Eastern European countries, cremation marks the end of a distinguished career for high-ranking government officials and other notable individuals. However, the bodies of the very highest-ranking officials are buried! There are several categories of interment, each denoting the prestige accorded to the deceased. The bodies of the most well-known and respected Soviet officials, such as Lenin, are placed in mausoleums. The next most prestigious officials are buried in the ground near the Kremlin wall. This includes foreigners such as the American John Reed, author of *Ten Days That Shook The World*.[5] Lower-ranking individuals are cremated, and their remains are placed in niches in the Kremlin wall covered by a marking plate. Ordinary citizens may opt for cremation, but there is a shortage of crematoria time due to the high demand. Getting a place in a cemetery near any large city is difficult, but it is equally difficult in the United States and elsewhere.

In the large Russian cities about 20% of bodies are cremated. The number is limited only by available capacity in the crematoria. In order to be cremated the relatives of the deceased must present letters or testimony verifying that the person deserves cremation, even though cremation costs considerably less than burial.

According to one report, the proportion of bodies cremated in the U.S. has in the last few years risen to about one in twenty.[6] In California the proportion is about one in six.[1] But even though the practice is increasing in this country it is still unusual and often complicated. What continues to puzzle me is the nonexistence, to the best of my knowledge, of some organization in the U.S. that could help make cremation a simple and inexpensive procedure.

Someone should make it easier for cremations to be arranged, and it seems appropriate that scientists take the lead in this area. In Great Britain, for example, the cremation "movement" was initiated in the 1870s mainly by physicians, scientists, and other intellectuals. Even with that kind of support, it was not until 1884 that cremation became legal in England.

There are several reasons why today's scientists should be concerned. For one thing, scientists as a group are less squeamish than others about the practical side of death. Physicians, for example, routinely deal with the realities of life and death. Life scientists of all types are intimately familiar with the processes by which we live and die, and are acutely aware of the temporary nature of all living things. Physicists and astronomers realize that our whole planet is merely a speck in

Nature's scheme, a particle of dust in the vast reaches of the Universe. Chemists know that all substances, even living bodies, are composed of parts which can be recombined in infinite variety. And engineers are trained to be pragmatic realists. For such individuals, all of whom are professional rationalists, cremation is a sensible concern.

Of course, cremation is only one option, and I would not suggest that it is appropriate for everyone. Some religions or sects forbid it, and some people, particularly in Western countries, are repelled by the idea of burning the body. Personal tastes and religious beliefs must certainly be respected.

But those of us who view cremation as a practical, sensible, dignified practice should not be forced to go through so much adversity. A cremation should be as easily arranged as a burial. A large part of the world's population accepts cremation as a commonplace, and we should do likewise.

It is a bitter and tragic irony that I discussed this very essay with my close friend and colleague, Robert L. Hayne, before his recent death. Bob had strong feelings on the subject, and it is indicative of his character that when the time came, he wanted to donate his body to medicine, to be followed by cremation.

For many people, cremation is a dignified and sensible act. It eliminates the need for many of the trappings of conventional funerals and burials, and helps to emphasize the spiritual values of life and death over the physical.

A solution to the problem of arranging cremations would have both spiritual and economical benefits. Why don't the professional societies of scientists create a Cremation Society that can deal with this problem in an intelligent fashion and set examples for the rest of society to follow? Although there is a Cremation Association of America, its members are mostly cemetery operators, so it represents the interests of those in the cremation business.[1] Most professional societies have "life" insurance plans, a euphemism if ever there was one. Why not "death" insurance plans which include a provision for simple, low-cost cremation? Your reaction to this proposal would be of interest to me.

REFERENCES

1. **Mitford J.** The American way of death. New York: Simon & Schuster, 1963, p. 161-72.
2. ----------. Should funeral homes be regulated? *US News & World Report* 10 May 1976, p. 45-6.
3. Mortuary chain agrees to refund. *New York Times* (United Press International) 10 July 1976, p. 21.
4. **Hermann B.** On histological investigations of cremated human remains. *Journal of Human Evolution* 6(2):101-3, February 1977.
5. **Reed J.** *Ten days that shook the world.* New York: Vintage, 1960.
6. **Chernow R.** F.T.C. studies the cost of dying. *New York Times* 26 September 1976, p. 29.

CURRENT COMMENTS

The Information-Conscious University and *ASCA* Software

Number 37, September 12, 1977

Universities are prodigious producers and consumers of information. But despite this day-to-day involvement with information, most universities have failed to take advantage of modern methods of *disseminating* information to faculty members and students. University libraries, for the most part, continue to play the passive role of storage depots. It is assumed that researchers designing new projects, scholars preparing articles for publication, and graduate students writing theses will learn about newly published, relevant information one way or another, such as by using abstracting publications or *Current Contents®* . But teachers faced with increasingly knowledgeable students need a more reliable way to provide awareness of current information.

One effective way of improving the flow of published information into and through a university is by the use of an automated system for selective dissemination of information (SDI). In an SDI system the user's requirements are defined by a collection of descriptors called an "interest profile." This profile is used to provide a periodic automated search of the new information added to a database. If articles or books indexed during that period specifically relate to one's profile, the computer will print out a list of those items. The key point is that the search is done

automatically and regularly, without repeated requests from the user.[1]

There are a few SDI services that can be used on a subscription basis. Biosciences Information Service offers *C.L.A.S.S.* (Current Literature Alerting Search Service) and ISI® offers *ASCA®* (Automatic Subject Citation Alert).[2,3] With these, users pay to have BIOSIS or ISI regularly search for items relevant to their profiles. Every university and many colleges, however, have enough potential users to seriously consider operating their own SDI service. While this is not a trivial undertaking, it is not as formidable nor as expensive as you may imagine.

To operate an SDI system, three components are essential: a computer, one or more relevant databases to search, and software (computer programs) capable of searching the databases. ISI is not in the hardware business, but it does provide databases and software with significant technical and economic advantages.

ISI supplies two databases on magnetic tape—the *Science Citation Index®* (*SCI®*) and the *Social Sciences Citation Index™* (*SSCI™*). Both offer multidisciplinary coverage of the journal literature. Both are extremely current (weekly). And both are formatted to allow a variety of searches. Any university which uses both these databases

223

can cover the information requirements of all its departments, with the exception of certain arts and humanities subjects. (Next year, when ISI's *Arts & Humanities Citation Index*™ is launched, even that exception may be eliminated.[4])

It is in the area of software, however, that ISI provides what may be the single most helpful item for operating an SDI system. Unlike many other database suppliers, who will sell or lease you their tapes but leave you on your own to figure out how to search them, ISI offers a complete software package capable of searching either the *SCI* or the *SSCI* database. Actually, the software we make available to tape subscribers is the same software we use to operate our own *ASCA* service. The significance of this is not small. To my knowledge, *ASCA* is the only SDI service for the journal literature that is able to exist on a fully commercial basis. It is now in its twelfth year of serving thousands of subscribers. One of the prime reasons for this success is the efficiency of the *ASCA* software.

Consider these salient facts. If necessary, the *ASCA* system is able to run on an IBM 1401 computer and requires only 16,000 bytes of core memory. A few years ago, we were even able to set up an SDI system using only 12,000 bytes. Most SDI systems operating today require core memories in excess of 500,000 bytes. I don't think I have to belabor the obvious implications of this for developing countries and smaller universities. They often cannot obtain access to anything but second generation computers with small storage capacities. And most universities with larger computers hesitate to operate a large-scale SDI system because much of the available storage is consumed by

the data processing requirements of administration and research. In these cases, the miniscule storage requirements made possible by *ASCA* software may make the difference between having and not having an SDI system on campus. And for those universities whose finances preclude the use of *any* full size computer, most minicomputers today provide sufficient storage for an SDI system.

Another important characteristic of *ASCA* software is that it can both accept an unlimited number of interest profiles and deal with a document collection of unlimited size. The system is organized so that a single pass of the database and profile tapes is all that is required to match all profiles against all documents. Most other systems require successive passes whenever the number of documents or profiles exceeds some fixed number.

The miserly storage requirements of *ASCA* software by no means imply that only crude, unsophisticated searches can be run. Quite the contrary. In addition to permitting all kinds of citation searches, *ASCA* software offers searches by words and word stems, by author, by author's organization, city or country, by language of the article, by journal, and by just about any conceivable permutation of these. In this way one could publish a weekly list of faculty publications.

Several years ago I offered to provide our databases and software free of charge to a university here in Philadelphia, provided it would do a proper sociological study to evaluate the impact of the service on university life. The university administration was unwilling to take up this challenge, fearing the cost of the work involved in preparing profiles and providing access to the journals. While one can make a profession out of profile compilation, there are also means for reducing the effort. By obtaining each faculty member's bibliography, one can use the obvious descriptors it contains (such as title words, co-authors, and the references themselves) to construct an initial profile. With this basic work done in advance, a much shorter in-person or telephone discussion with the user can refine the profile.

When an organization purchases ASCA software, ISI provides a complete training program which includes every facet of setting up and operating the SDI system at the subscriber's location. In fact, we can provide a turn-key operation. Less than a year ago, we were happy to provide this training in conjunction with the installation of an SDI system at the National University of Mexico. The system is by no means limited to the university population, which is one of the largest in the world.[5]

University administrators are sometimes concerned that providing SDI systems to make faculty members and students more aware of relevant journal items will increase subscription costs. Since the ISI databases cover over 5,000 journals, this is not a trivial considera-tion. However, it is hard to imagine a university library system that would not already receive the core of the significant journals. Furthermore, we know that academics frequently write to authors for reprints. Authors' addresses are a significant part of the SDI weekly report. What is more important is that the existing journal collection will be more effectively utilized.

One can also provide SDI service through on-line services such as SCI-SEARCH® , but I don't think they are as cost-effective as so-called batch systems when large numbers of people must be served regularly.

I am hopeful that my discussion here will put to rest a few of the misconceptions that have kept many universities from even investigating the feasibility of an on-campus SDI system. In spite of the wide availability of computers on most campuses, universities have generally been unwilling to take this step into the future. It is not enough for a university to be merely information conscious. It must also aggressively seek better ways to satisfy the real needs created by that consciousness. As I see it, SDI will only have come of age when every faculty member and student takes such a service for granted.

REFERENCES

1. **Garfield E.** "The role of man and machine in an international selective dissemination of information systems." Delivered at the International Congress of Documentation, Buenos Aires, 21-24 September 1970.

2. **Garfield E & Sher I H.** ISI's experience with *ASCA* — a selective dissemination system. *Journal of Chemical Documentation* 7:147-53, August 1967.

3. --------------. *ASCA (Automatic Subject Citation Alert).* A new personalized current awareness service for scientists. *The American Behavioral Scientist* 10:29-32, January 1967.

4. **Garfield E.** Will ISI's *Arts and Humanities Citation Index* revolutionize scholarship? *Current Contents* No. 32, 8 August 1977, p. 5-9.

5. --------------. "Universities as producers and consumers of information." Delivered at the National University of Mexico, 24 September 1976.

CURRENT COMMENTS

What This Country Needs
Is a Free Phone Call

Number 38, September 19, 1977

It is often stated that telephone service in the USA is the best in the world. By comparison with most other countries, including the United Kingdom, American phone service can seem like heaven. In Scandinavia, while the cost may be higher, the service is comparable. The ability to dial from Stockholm or Oslo to Valencia or Budapest is as technically impressive as dialing from Philadelphia to Albuquerque. And the political achievement it represents is even more impressive.

To help balance the critique which follows (after all, Ma Bell is not *all* bad), it is necessary to observe that it is the very excellence of American telephone service that has made us so dependent on it. The threat of losing it involves fundamental issues of freedom and personal security.

A fire on February 27, 1975 left a 300 block area of Manhattan without telephone service for 23 days! This affected 144,755 phones directly and the entire city indirectly. After the crisis was over interviewers talked to 600 persons who were affected. They found that the telephone was "missed pervasively and neither the exchange of letters nor the one-way flow of mass communications could be made to substitute for the *immediate interaction* provided by the telephone." To the majority of people, "The telephone proved to be a communicative mode for which no satisfactory alternative was available."[1] This is an indirect sociological commentary on the differences between Americans and those who live in Eastern Europe or other places where the telephone is not as accessible or pervasive.

Telephones do not only connect us with friends, loved ones, colleagues, and politicians. Today, the telephone provides access to reports on time and temperature, daily astrological forecasts and even hotline updates on the adventures of comic strip heroes. The Pennsylvania Hospital in Philadelphia recently initiated the TEL-MED service, as have other hospitals in the United States. TEL-MED enables you to hear tape-recorded discussions on health care topics including everything from aging to venereal disease. A number of the tapes are even recorded in Spanish. The TEL-MED service is free—with one big exception: you must pay for the cost of the phone call. As far as I'm concerned, that's the point where Ma Bell's special brand of insanity starts to get in the way of information flow.

For example, it used to be a cardinal principle of business that cash payment entitled you to something extra—not less. Yet if I call TEL-MED from a coin-operated phone, not only is the service not free, but in most parts of the U.S. it costs me more than it costs a person who calls from a private phone, where the payment is deferred until the end of the month. Since it is the poor (including many students) who depend heavily on public coin phones, their ability to use TEL-MED and other "no-cost" information services is significantly reduced. This helps to aggravate the disparities in American income levels.

While I enjoy the luxury of several touch-tone extensions at my home and office, I know that certain younger members of my family cannot afford a private telephone. For thousands of poor people even the dime phone call is a real expense. Unhappily, there are already some places in the U.S. where the phone company has succeeded in raising this price to 20 cents. I can't help but wonder how the telephone company that serves New Orleans can survive. There, you can still make a local call for a nickel.

The telephone company argues that it costs a lot to collect money through coin phones because of the personnel required to service them and because of vandalism. It is hard to assess the validity of this. The phone company also claims that coin-operated phones cost more because operators must be used to tell you how much to pay. But this is true only for toll calls. Local calls, by definition, should not require any operator assistance. So why are users of local telephone service penalized for other people's operator-assisted calls? I might add that I fail to see the logic of charging coin phone users *more*, even for a cash-payment long-distance call. Perhaps one must acknowledge the cost of vandalism and operator time without regard to the principle that cash should be king over credit.

It is true that on toll calls operators frequently must get involved, but I would like to know why the most advanced telephone system in the world does not yet have an automatic system for collecting money when the feat has been performed in Europe for years. In small towns in Spain there are now public telephones which even return change. And you can call anywhere in Europe from such phones.

If AT&T is going to insist that vandalism is a key problem, I fail to see how raising the price of a local call solves it. On the contrary, it may be time to consider making all public phones free for local use. Whatever loss of cash revenue would result from this move could be made up by eliminating those telephone operators employed to interrupt you so assiduously when three minutes have elapsed. The money collectors who apparently find nothing but empty coin boxes could also be eliminated.

Free public phones would reduce the number of unnecessary calls made from private phones to public ones in order to avoid excessive cash payments. For example, if I telephone Downingtown, just 35 miles from Philadelphia, it costs $1.05 for the first three minutes— and it is *not possible* to be charged for *less* than three minutes. If the party I'm calling, however, returns the call from a private phone it costs only 31 cents for one minute and 17 cents per minute thereafter. No matter what time of day I use a coin phone, I have to pay a *minimum* of $2.35 to call Los Angeles from Philadelphia. The same call made from a private phone at night on a weekend costs 21 cents for the first minute and 16 cents for each additional minute. With such a rate structure, it is no wonder that so many prearranged, coded messages are called in from pay phones to private phones as part of various schemes designed to beat the system.

It is not inconceivable that in this century basic telephone service, like health services, might come to be regarded as a fundamental right provided by government. While it might seem ridiculous to the AT&T economists that telephones be provided free to aged or poor people, how much paid-in-full long-distance calling by relatives and friends would this promote? Maybe this is a simplistic notion, but if AT&T ever even considers proposals like this it is keeping them secret. The lack of a more open attitude is part of the company's basic problem.

I would also like to know by what data AT&T forecasts that a call between any two points in the U.S.

will be a local call. The present distinctions of long-distance vs. local are absurd when you consider that it is often cheaper to call from Philadelphia to Los Angeles than it is from Philadelphia to a suburb just a few miles away. If the idea of a single, low charge for a phone call no matter what the distance involved seems premature, consider this. A variety of companies which offer on-line computer services already enable their customers to access their computers through the equivalent of a local phone call even though the computer may be located thousands of miles away. This is done through such communications networks as TYMESHARE. This is the same type of access ISI® provides on its incoming toll-free lines, which eliminates long-distance charges for our customers.

I also do not understand the inability of Ma Bell's computer to deal with the digital information contained in one's telephone credit card number. It would be eminently more efficient to *dial* your credit card number than to recite it like a robot—not too slow and not too fast— to an operator who is merely dialing or keying the same information you could have keyed yourself. And why can't existing technology be used to eliminate operators from collect calls? Collect calls could be preceded by a simple code. This would activate a tape recording advising the recipient that the call can be refused by simply hanging up. Most such calls would not have to be operator-assisted if one could dial in such a way that the called number would be the one charged.

And remember how long it took before Ma Bell installed telephones that do not require a coin just to reach the operator, police, or other emergency aid? For decades before this was done in the U.S., Europeans were able to reach the operator or make local calls without depositing a coin in *advance*. I find it hard to swallow the technological backwardness of the necessity of having the proper coins—and the inconvenience when one loses the coins because of an error in dialing or some peculiarity of the telephone system, which can never be perfect in its performance. In the United Kingdom you can still make a local call by depositing two pence *after* someone answers the phone. If I have to pay Ma Bell in advance, a nickel is as far as I want to go.

Despite my knowledge that the scientists at Bell Laboratories are making substantial contributions to better communications, I find it hard to believe that there are insuperable technical barriers to the implementation of completely automatic telephone service. While it is impressive to learn that 16,000 people are employed at Bell Labs, I am not impressed that the Bell system spends only one percent of its revenue on research.

William G. Sharwell, vice-president of AT&T's long-term planning, claims that costs, not lack of innovations, have impeded the pace of communications technology.[2] Others offer different reasons. Bell's monopoly is economically inefficient, according to Richard B. Long, president of the North American Telephone Asso-

ciation, a group of manufacturers, suppliers, and others who produce telephone equipment attached to AT&T lines. Long charges that lack of competition has kept Bell from developing innovations as rapidly as might be expected.[2]

When one sees how hard AT&T works at preserving its monopoly status, there is a ring of truth to Long's complaint. Early this year AT&T arranged to have a series of bills introduced in the U.S. Congress. These bills, collectively called the "Consumer Communications Reform Act," would give the telephone company virtual control over all of the country's electronic communications.[3,4] Under the proposed legislation, each state, instead of the Federal Communications Commission (FCC), would decide what devices may be connected to telephone lines. Companies providing private phone service to businesses would have to prove that they would not duplicate services that present phone companies provide or *could* provide. Private companies would also have to prove that the revenues they might drain off would not force existing phone companies to increase consumer rates, and that the private equipment would not technically impair the existing telephone network. What's more, existing phone companies would be immune to antitrust suits. Thus they could buy out the competitors driven out of business by the legislation. The stated purpose of this immunity is to "protect" the customers of competitors who might otherwise lose service.

If this act is passed the long-run consequences are even more serious, since it would eliminate choice in future telecommunications systems. The most important aspect of this for consumers would involve information terminals attached to home phone lines to allow electronic mail, checkless financial transactions, remote shopping, electronic newspapers, and much more. Explosive growth is expected in this area.

In the second quarter of 1976 alone, AT&T *reported* spending $1,040,009 to lobby for this legislation. It is no wonder, then, that 102 representatives and 9 senators have been willing to sponsor the various bills involved. It will be interesting to watch what happens when Congress resumes hearings and debate on this legislation later this year.

Our dependence on information and its transmission is becoming more crucial in our economy. Today more of the U.S. gross national product evolves in the information sector than in the production of tangible goods.[5] Economists Manley R. Irwin of the University of New Hampshire and Steven C. Johnson of the National Research Council have written that, "Policy decisions as to what information services are provided, who provides them and at what prices, go to the heart of tomorrow's economic infrastructure. The stakes, markets, and investment are incalculable. It is in this context that the public policy issues surrounding telecommunications should be considered. And it is in this context that the merits of a policy of competition and monopoly

in telecommunications should be debated and resolved."[6]

Let's return to more prosaic concerns. Ma Bell has turned a deaf ear to many consumer issues. For example, certain groups want a married woman's name listed in phone directories on an equal basis with her husband's name. The company wants to list the woman's name *instead* of her husband's or provide a separate entry for an additional fee. It claims that directories would be too expensive and bulky if additional names were included free.[7] No doubt more names will add cost and size to directories, but wouldn't such listings also increase the use of telephone service? Typically, it seems that Ma Bell has not handled this issue in a manner designed to improve service and increase its *overall* business.

The New York State Public Utilities Commission recently ordered the New York Telephone Company to tell new customers about the cheapest forms of telephone service and to allow present customers to switch to the cheaper forms without paying for the change. The order was the result of numerous complaints from consumers about the telephone company's former negligence in this matter. Before, phone company sales representatives often pushed sales of package deals of three or four phones with luxury features.[8]

With such a never-ending litany of abuses, my personal feeling is that there should be an elected panel of consumer-oriented ombudsmen to help regulate the telephone industry. The FCC and state regulatory agencies are hopelessly inadequate. It would also help if consumers were better represented on the board of directors of AT&T and the individual state telephone companies. But even Ma Bell tries to do good now and then. Last year it received so many complaints from overseas travellers overcharged by hotel keepers for trans-Atlantic phone calls that it launched a campaign called Teleplan to curb the problems. For example, travellers were charged $70 for a $17 call from Berlin to the United States, $90 for a $15 call from Paris, and $686 for $270 worth of calls from Beirut. E.E. Carr, director of overseas administration for AT&T's Long Lines Department, said one European hotel keeper admitted to earning $35,000 extra in one season by overcharging for overseas phone calls. Under Teleplan, AT&T pledges to promote travel to the countries involved and the countries are expected to charge reasonably uniform rates for overseas calls.[9] As a frequent user of overseas calls I appreciate Ma Bell's concern; but I'll be even happier when they figure out how to find me another dime when my last one has dropped into the box and I need to make another call before my train leaves.

As the country's largest corporation, AT&T undoubtedly gets a great deal of unwarranted criticism. It is difficult to understand how a company which spends so much money on public relations should have such a negative image. The PR experts at Ma Bell might tell you, off the record, that the image would be much worse without all the PR, but I fail to be impressed.

You start to wonder how bad things are when you think about T.O. Gravitt, a vice-president of Southwestern Bell Telephone Company, who killed himself in October, 1974. His suicide note said in part: "Watergate is a gnat compared to the Bell System."[3]

REFERENCES

1. **Wurtzel A L & Turner C**. What missing the telephone means. *Journal of Communications* 27:48-57, 1977.
2. **Moneyhun G**. Ma Bell bids for share of computer field. *Christian Science Monitor* 69:13, 20 January 1977.
3. **Ma Bell's consumer reform bill**. *Consumer Reports* 42:40-3, January 1977.
4. **Benjamin M R & Read W H**. Ma Bell fights for her monopoly. *New York Times Magazine* 28 November 1977, p. 33.
5. **Farber D & Baran P**. The convergence of computing and telecommunications systems. *Science* 195:1166-9, 1977.
6. **Irwin M R & Johnson S C**. The information economy and public policy. *Science* 195:1170-4, 1977.
7. **Shah D K**. Unlisted, but not by choice. *The National Observer* 11 December 1976, p. 7.
8. **Cerra F**. Commission orders New York Telephone to inform customers of cheapest service. *New York Times* 25 April 1977, p. 55.
9. **Dunphy R J**. Ma Bell acts on overseas calls. *New York Times* 7 November 1976, p. 6.

231

CURRENT COMMENTS

Restating the Fundamental Assumptions of Citation Analysis

Number 39, September 26, 1977

It is unfortunate that many people who use citation data in sociological studies fail to explicitly state their assumptions. Most of these assumptions are by now quite obvious to research workers in science policy studies. But even for those familiar with the methodology of citation analysis it is still too early in the field's development to take certain assumptions for granted. Authors who do not state their assumptions risk later criticism for their omission.

The two reprints which follow, "On the Use of Citations in Studying Scientific Achievements and Communication" by Belver C. Griffith, M. Carl Drott, and Henry G. Small,[1] and "Why I Am Not a Co-Citationist" by David Edge,[2] discuss some of the fundamental assumptions underlying citation analysis and co-citation studies.

The first article is a concise statement of the assumptions made in most citation analyses. The authors also discuss three "massive" qualifications on the use of citation data. The three qualifications concern the quality of the *Science Citation Index®* and *Social Sciences Citation Index™* files, the citation behavior of authors,[3] and the scale and pace of research activity in the discipline

being studied. This article is a thoughtful response to critics of citation studies.

Both papers take a critical view of citation analysis. The first paper exhibits a healthy, constructive skepticism. The second takes a more pessimistic view of the sociological value of studying citation relationships. But neither paper questions their validity for information retrieval.

Edge admits that his perspective "makes research more difficult than it would be under more simple-minded premises, but then I happen to believe that sociology *is* difficult." No one—least of all citation analysts—is saying that sociology is easy. But I see no reason to make it even more difficult by excluding a whole realm of valuable research work from consideration.

Edge also mentions the "relatively trivial behavior of adding citations to papers." Citation behavior may not be the most complex human behavior one could study, but even when it is abnormal, it certainly is not trivial.

Finally, Edge advances an argument that, if taken to its logical conclusion, would mean the elimination of all sciences which rely upon quantitative and statistical analyses. He claims that "citation and co-citation analysis, in striving to *accumulate and average,* destroys the evidence we need of individual variations." There is no reason that quantitative and qualitative studies should be mutually exclusive. Subjective studies of individual variations can peacefully co-exist with objective studies of aggregates.

It is strange that neither paper discusses the one fundamental assumption that I know disturbs many people—and justifiably so. It is often assumed, because of the first-author arrangement of ISI® 's citation indexes, that *all* conclusions derived from such first-author data will be wrong. There is little doubt that citation analyses based on first-author data inadequately recognize some authors who now publish mainly as "secondary" authors. This was not true for authors who published before the fifties, when single authored papers were the rule. The best way to eliminate this inadequacy is to compile data based on all co-authorships. In fact, ISI is now completing an intensive study whose aim is to eliminate the first-author artifact. When this study is completed some of the results will be published here. Meanwhile, we

will soon publish a list of the 250 most-cited first authors.[4] For this kind of study the problem of "noise" caused by errors is of minor consequence. These 250 authors are so often cited that such errors rarely have an observable effect.

Some people are also disturbed by the use of citation data to indicate areas of activity and merit in science. However, criticism which does not offer constructive alternatives has little value. Those who question the use of citation data as *"indicators"*[5] of scientific activity and accomplishment should offer alternative cost-effective means for dealing with the problem. Finding significant information about the immense world-wide scientific enterprise is not easy. There is considerable confusion in science about where the action is and where it ought to be, and citation analysis is a valuable tool for reducing the confusion.

It is in the interest of balance and fairness that these two papers are reprinted. Together they demonstrate that in citation studies—as well as in the rest of science—it is wise to take little or nothing for granted.

REFERENCES

1. **Griffith B C, Drott M C & Small H G.** On the use of citations in studying scientific achievements and communication. *Society for Social Studies of Science Newsletter* 2:9-13, Summer 1977.
2. **Edge D.** Why I am not a co-citationist. *Society for Social Studies of Science Newsletter* 2:13-9, Summer 1977.
3. **Garfield E.** To cite or not to cite: a note of annoyance. *Current Contents®* No. 34, 22 August 1977, p. 5-9.
4. -------------. And who shall occupy the 250th chair among the citation immortals? *Current Contents* No. 22, 31 May 1976, p. 5-6. (Reprinted in: *Essays of an Information Scientist.* Philadelphia: ISI Press, 1977, Vol. 2, p. 496-7.)
5. **Garfield E, Malin M V & Small H.** Citation data as science indicators. *Toward a Metric of Science.* (Elkana Y. et al., eds.) New York: Wiley, 1977. (in press).

On the Use of Citations in Studying Scientific Achievements and Communication*

Belver C. Griffith, M. Carl Drott
Graduate School of Library Science, Drexel University
Philadelphia, Pennsylvania 19104

Henry G. Small
Institute for Scientific Information
325 Chestnut Street, Philadelphia, Pennsylvania 19106

Rather than trying to reply in kind to some recent, slightly polemical, criticisms[1] of the use of citations, we will discuss the assumptions underlying the use of citations in the study of science. We shall attempt to explicate the principles underlying our work, with certain technical problems, and end with a brief panegyric on research programs and approaches to study of science and scientific communication.

Any value of citations and the restrictions on such value stems from the combined operation of several assumptions, three massive qualifications, and one critically important conjecture. The operation of these principles *differs* widely from field to field and from application to application. In discussing these principles we would note that the assumptions are very weak ones, and that their power derives from the stochastic nature of the world, laying the groundwork for true quantification only with very large files. For example, we can see a possible restriction in mathematics, where the literature base is small and each article contains few references. In such a field citations must be far more robust than in molecular biology, where the reverse holds on both dimensions.

Let's look now at four assumptions:

I. A document x cited by document y is more likely to be judged as related in content to document y than one not cited.

If we were to eponymize, this might be called the Garfield[2]-Kessler[3] Assumption, since it underlies both the remarkable *Science Citation Index®* service and the benchmark research at MIT. It's a hard assumption to gainsay.

II. If there are two documents x_1 and x_2, and x_1 is cited by document y and x_2 is not so cited, x_1 is more likely

---

Reprinted from: Society for Social Studies of Science Newsletter 2:9-13, Summer, 1977.

to have been of use in the preparation of document y than x_2.

Let's continue to honor our intellectual forebears and designate this the Gross[4]-Price[5] Assumption, after the first major user of, and the user who has extracted amazing intellectual power from this assumption. Note again the extreme modesty of this assumption.

III. If documents cite documents in common, they are more likely to be judged as related in content than documents which do not cite any document in common.[3]

IV. If documents x_1 and x_2 are cited by document y, they are more likely to be judged as related to one another in content than to document x_3, which is not so co-cited with x_1 and x_2.

This is, of course, the co-citation assumption and with a friendly, generous spirit of self-eponymization—already a tradition in this field—the first author would call this the Small[6]-Marshakova[7]-Griffith[8] Assumption, after the first "mappers" to use this assumption.

These modest assumptions lay the groundwork for quantification and introduce other considerations, in particular, a series of necessary qualifications. These qualifications are massive, and give the user of citations fair warning that use is fraught with danger. (The "conjecture" is, however, quite powerful and offers the researcher hope.)

I. Citation measures are only the by-product of a file, and their quality is directly related to the dimensions of that file and the care taken to develop the file.

II. A series of complex social, psychological and bibliographical factors intervene between any intentions of the author to acknowledge precedent work or to recognize any form of similarity.

And, less terrifying:

III. Citation measures critically reflect the scale of the literature, and slightly independently, the scale and pace of research activity, as well as norms and institutions within the specialty and discipline.

These very strong restrictive qualifications regarding the use of citation measures have been repeated as admonitions,[9] but *violated* again and again in the literature. Later, we shall argue, however, that only rather serious violations matter.

What specifically do these qualifications mean?

(1) A file that is developed by the investigator must be fully described bibliographically and its dimensions must be justified as part of the study.

(2) If *SCI®* or *SSCI™* is used, the investigator should be sensitive to the continuing improvement in coverage, particularly with regard to recent volumes of *SSCI* and, according to Derek Price, for the *SCI* prior to 1967.

(3) The difficulties encountered with developing counts for individuals have been described elsewhere,[10] and have become in certain areas of physics extremely difficult where the authorship includes 20-70 persons. For cognoscenti, we list typical considerations: homonyms, fractional authorships, self-citations, alphabetical as opposed to attributive ordering of authors, the precise relation of the citation to the content of the citing document, and multiple spellings, or arrangements, of the author(s)' name(s). (Ironically, Derek Price is a principal victim of the last. *)

(4) The investigator using *SCI* should be warned that errors normally originate in the citing document and, therefore exhibit far more creativity than typographical errors inherent in clerical operations, many of which are automatically eliminated.[11]

(5) The psychological and social factors have to do with habits, conventions, and perceptions of the scientist, his research group, his specialty, etc. Accordingly, they can be either an object of study or a bother, depending on the goals of the investigator. Also, different measures may be affected differentially. (The relative contributions to hepatic research of Baruch Blumberg and Alfred Prince, as recognized by the Nobel award to Blumberg, were reflected in total number of authorships among clustered documents on Australia Antigen, but not by number of citations to each author's most-cited article.)

(6) Bibliographical factors, alone or in conjunction with social and psychological factors, perturb citation measures. The pure case is the work of Karl Marx, where citations to a numerically small set of documents have been exploded into chaos by differently dated, different language editions (*SSCI*). Complex factors are introduced by the lack of any *necessary* correspondence between the content of dis-

---

*Derek J. DeSolla Price is often cited as Desolla P, Desolla DJ, Desollaprice D, or DJ in addition to the more logical variations on Price D, or DDS, or JDS, etc.

covery, the documents reporting the discovery, and a consensual perception of those documents by the research community. From the Australia Antigen example we can select three documents: one, a seminal finding that there may be a relation between the presence of Australia Antigen and hepatitis; the second, five years later, reporting a frequent association; and a third, slightly later, reporting 100% association within reasonable experimental error. The three taken as a group constituted the "crucial experiment" for that specialty. Citations to the first soared on appearance of the second and third papers–a formal finding only interpretable by recourse to the content of the papers. But in this case, community consensus, not the greatest credit, went to the second paper. One can easily see that any particular pattern of citing these papers might be intimately bound to the style of the citing author. The omission, or near omission, of any particular paper in citations can only be interpreted in terms of the pattern of citations and the content of related papers.

(7) Much of the above, as well as differences in scale and differences in custom of citations, renders the count of citations to an individual paper a fragile measure of the value of the paper. Instead, *the investigator should use all means at his disposal to determine the degree of consensus within the relevant community represented by a citation count and the nature of that consensus.* While the "nature" of consensus may suggest another cop-out and our rushing to content to bail out the measure, we believe it possible to turn this concept into a formally derived measure (by combining citation counts with clustering) that considers both co-citation and the total frequency of citation for each document. To give a rough idea, while papers which report standard laboratory methods in biomedicine are highly cited, they do not connect to groups of other papers and no group of new papers grows about them. On the other hand, the Nobel-award winning work of Baltimore, Blumberg, and Temin was related to existing documents and became the center of developing clusters.

(8) The scientist of science must regard his assumptions regarding the existence of a type of literature or the relevance of a particular paper to a particular literature as an *hypothesis,* which, we venture, is likely to be incorrect.

Beginning with Parker, Paisley and Garrett,[12] investigators have been guided by strong hypotheses, independent of the inherent structure of the literature. (They sought the structure of the communication research literature, and found instead sociology and psychology.) Even greater strangeness may arise through uncritical acceptance of document assignment to specialties by bibliographies.

In all the above, we hope we make clear that the measures which are likely to be the most fragile are counts for the individual document and for the individual scientist. These are the measures which create the greatest sensitivity within the scientific community; and in part, our intention in writing this piece is to argue for the development and substitution of more sophisticated approaches.

We now turn to a conjecture of great amiability. It appears strong but may resist convincing proof.

The quality and quantity of the scientific literature "channelizes." That is, a combination of social and probabilistic mechanisms ensure that most documents of a discipline, and nearly all documents of the highest quality, appear in a limited number of sources (i.e., journals in the natural sciences). Furthermore, all such important sources may be readily recognized and ranked along this quality dimension by citation counts.

This idea certainly dates from the Garfield[13]-Bourne[14] controversy over the number of scientific journals which should be covered by information services, say, 3000 ± 1000 (Garfield) as opposed to 30,000 ± 2000 (Bourne); these ideas are implicit in Price's writing, too.[15] The work of Narin on individual disciplines fully explores and supports this principle empirically.[16] However, the power of the mechanisms involved has not been emphasized sufficiently, nor has the central importance of this conjecture to citation research been indicated.

The likely truth and power of this conjecture is essential; if all journals (60,000) voted equally, research would be impossible and of course, *SCI* and *SSCI* would lose much of their usefulness as information services. Perhaps most strangely, the power of this conjecture has permitted persons, totally ill-equipped methodologically, to do valid work simply because they cannot avoid the "centers" of literatures.

This conjecture can be tested rather simply. Results of even a two-hour study within a departmental physics library—given expertise in sampling—would be sufficient for the highest ranked journals to be ordered highly reliably and with perhaps 70-80% accuracy, as compared to a full study of our best data, the *Journal Citation Reports*.[17] Our only personal misgivings about use of this conjecture focus on the difficulty of finding starting points without language or national bias.

This conjecture, which appears correct but must again be approached and used with caution, completes the set of principles which, for us, underlie citation research.

REFERENCES

1. **Edge E.** Quantitative measures of communication in science. *International Symposium on Quantitative Methods in the History of Science: Proceedings.* Berkeley, California, August 25-27, 1976.
2. **Garfield E.** Citation indexes for science. *Science* **122**:108-11, 1955.
3. **Kessler M M.** Bibliographic coupling between scientific papers. *American Documentation* **14**:10-25, 1963.
4. **Gross P L K & Gross E M.** College libraries and chemical education. *Science* **66**:385-9, 1927.
5. **Price D J D.** Networks of scientific papers. *Science* 149:510-15, 1965.
6. **Small H G.** Co-citation in the scientific literature; a new measure of the relationship between two documents. *Journal of the American Society for Information Science* 24:265-9, 1973.
7. **Marshakova I V.** Bibliographic coupling system based on cited references. *Nauchno-Tekhnicheskaya Informatsiya Seriya* 2(6):3-8, 1973.
8. **Griffith B C, Small H G, Stonehill J A & Dey S.** The structure of scientific literatures. 2. Toward a macro- and microstructure for science. *Science Studies* 4:339-65, 1974.
9. **Cole J R & Cole S.** Measuring the quality of sociological research; problems in the use of *Science Citation Index*. *American Sociologist* **6**:23-9, 1971.
10. ---------------------- . *Social stratification in science.* Chicago: University of Chicago Press, 1973.
11. **Sher I H, Garfield E & Elias A W.** Control and elimination of errors in ISI services. *Journal of Chemical Documentation* 6:132, 1966.
12. **Parker E B, Paisley W J & Garrett R.** *Bibliographic citations as unobtrusive measures of scientific communication.* Stanford, California: Stanford University Institute for Communication Research, October, 1967.
13. **Garfield E.** Significant journals of science. *Nature* **264**:609-15, 1976.
14. **Bourne C P.** The world's technical journal literature: an estimate of volume, origin, language, field, indexing, and abstracting. *American Documentation* **13**:159-68, 1962.
15. **Price D J D.** *Little science, big science.* New York: Columbia University Press, 1963.
16. **Narin F, Carpenter M P & Berlt N C.** Inter-relationships of scientific journals. *Journal of the American Society for Information Science* **23**:323-31, 1972.
17. **Garfield E.** *Journal citation reports: a bibliometric analysis of references processed for the 1975* Science Citation Index. *Science Citation Index 1976 Annual,* Vol. 9. Philadelphia: Institute for Scientific Information® , 1977.

Why I Am Not a Co-Citationist*

David Edge
*Science Studies Unit, University of Edinburgh,
Edinburgh, Scotland*

Some of us make modest use of citation analysis in our work,[1] but remain radically skeptical of the claims of those who devote more prime time and energy to the elaboration of such methods. Why do we not accept the faith? Why can we not do the proper Kuhnian thing and let the "paradigmatic achievements" of the new quantitative methods define the field for us—posing our fundamental problems, laying down agreed techniques, prefiguring acceptable answers, and unrolling a "progressive research program"? I suggest that what is at issue here is essentially a *difference of aim.* My conception of "doing the sociology of science" allows citation analysis, at best, only a very peripheral role. I will try to outline my position as succinctly as possible.

1) Let me first identify and reject a claim that seems to me to lurk, if only implicitly, behind these quantitative methods: essentially, the claim is that, in transcending the "limited, subjective and biased" perspective of individuals, and in giving some "public, aggregated, objective and unbiased" account, these measures have, as it were, "a preferred logical status". They are more "objective", more "reliable"; they can be used to *"correct"* participants' accounts; they can define "what really is (or was) the case", and can *arbitrate* between conflicting accounts; and so on. These quantitative procedures are often labelled "scientific", and the sociology (or history) to which they give rise is "scientific sociology"—as opposed, presumably, to qualitative, individualistic and "biased", "incomplete" sociology. Garfield, Sher and Torpie, for instance, in their pioneer 1964 paper, state:

> The writing of history is subject to much human error in spite of the dedication and relatively rigorous standards held by the professional historian.... Historical description must therefore fall far short of an ideal. We can only strive to develop methods that bring us somewhat closer to the truth.... The historian, in describing the progress of science, is limited by his own experience, memory, and the adequacy of the documentation available. His subjective judgment primarily determines the

Reprinted from: Society for Social Studies of Science Newsletter 2:13-19, Summer 1977.

historical picture of the development of events.[2]

And their paper concludes:

It is felt that citation analysis has been demonstrated to be a valid and valuable means of creating accurate historical descriptions of scientific fields....[3]

Small, in his most recent paper, makes a similar claim for the preferred status of co-citation analysis in preparing specialty bibliographies:

The principal difficulty...is that it is almost impossible to establish precise criteria as to what should or should not be included within the boundaries of the subject, and the temptation is to apply present-day criteria to earlier literature. [Co-citation analysis] uses a clustering algorithm to establish these boundaries; it involves no subjective decisions on what is to be included or excluded from the specialty literature.[4]

If this is so, then why bother to "validate" co-citation studies?[5] Differences between the co-citation results and those derived from other sources are only to be expected, and it is implicit in the method that preference, in such cases, should be given to the former over the latter. However, co-citation practitioners lose nerve at this point: not only do they undertake validations, but they allow *errors*. Small, for instance, says, of a paper which was missed by his computer in his study of collagen research:

The effect of thresholding was, in this case, to exclude an important and relevant item.[6]

Was the decision that this item was "important and relevant" (and therefore, presumably, that it should be included in the specialty bibliography) a "subjective" or "objective" one?
When Griffith, Drott and Small state, with emphasis, that....

...the investigator should use all means at his disposal to determine the degree of consensus within the relevant community represented by a citation count and the nature of that consensus...,

they are abandoning the notion of a preferred logical status for citation methods. We would then be *agreed* that citation and co-citation figures are just part of the range of empirical data available to the historian and sociologist—no more, and no less. Where we would still *differ* would be over the relative *weight* to be assigned to citation measures, within the context of the entire range of information.

2) The advent of the co-citation technique has involved a fundamental shift of emphasis which I welcome. Previously, the citing of B by A was taken to reflect an *influence* of B on A. Crane, for instance, claims that:

> Within a research area, frequent citation indicates that a paper contains information that has been useful to other members.[7]

And Meadows lists "two basic assumptions" in citation analyses:

> (I) that the papers selected for citation are those which have been important in an investigation; and (II) that citations are indicative of influence via the literature.[8]

However, in co-citation analysis, which is superficially so similar, the only assumption is that the citing of B and C together by A implies that, *in A's perspective, the work of B and of C are related.* In other words, co-citation "maps", strictly speaking, reflect only the *perceptions of authors.* But those using co-citation analysis act as if co-citations of B and C were evidence that *B and C are related by communication ties,* and the authors "clustered" by co-citation are *intereacting groups.* Small and Griffith, for instance, in one of the pioneer co-citation papers, talk of "the mapping of specialties, to show their internal structures and their relationships to one another", and they continue (reiterating a version of the preferred logical status claim):

> Many of the relationships we have uncovered are, of course, known to the specialists themselves, since they were established by their own citing patterns, but the perspective this method offers is far broader than can be achieved by any individual scientist. This is the crux of the method: the observed relationships are in substance those which have been established by the collective efforts and perceptions of the community of publishing scientists. Our task is to depict these relationships in ways that shed light on the structure of science.[9]

3) I, too, wish to "shed light on the structure of science", and hope to do so via an elucidation of "the collective efforts and perceptions" of the

242

scientific community. However, it is at this point that essential differences emerge.

One rationale often advanced for developing co-citation (and other quantitative) methods proceeds by analogy: until patient measurement had established the form of the gas laws (PV = RT), there was no "problem" for the kinetic theory of gases to "solve"; similarly, it is argued, quantitative studies of science are necessary to define the "problems" which sociological theory has then to solve. I reject this argument. To me, *the behavior of scientists in the conduct of their research* provides an abundance of problems of much more obvious importance than any correlations contained in a computer printout. Whenever a scientist (or a research group) decides to develop a new technique, or to pursue a fresh and unexpected phenomenon, or to adopt a perhaps unfashionable theoretical approach, there is a sociological problem: each decision brings together "cognitive" (intellectual, technical, cultural) and "social" factors, and to me, "to do the sociology of science" is to explicate such decisions, and to explore the "social grounding" of their rationality.[10]

This task starts from the "participants' perspective." Citations *could* be one relevant source of information of participants' perceptions. But every decision is *particular:* citation and co-citation analysis, in striving to *accumulate and average,* destroys the evidence we need of individual variations. It is often because individual scientists and groups *do not* share the consensus view, defined by (*inter alia*) co-citations maps, that crucial innovative decisions are made.

It is worth dwelling on the importance of *particularity* in studies in the sociology of scientific knowledge. Such is the scale of any scientific specialty, there is a limited number of researchers (and even more strikingly, of groups), who might be considered to share (roughly) similar cognitive constraints on their strategic decisions. In the early years of radio astronomy, there were only three comparable groups—Cambridge, Jodrell Bank and Sydney. In *Astronomy Transformed,* we present an analysis of the social structure of the Cambridge and Jodrell Bank groups, and attempt to relate these structures to technical developments at the two centers.[11] In "mapping" the social structures, we compiled a composite picture, melding interview material with quantitative measures—including mutual citation patterns. We found that the citation (and co-authorship) picture agreed closely with that derived from our other sources: in particular, the central influence of Ryle on the Cambridge group was clearly confirmed. Unfortunately, any attempt to repeat this approach on the Sydney group fails; Pawsey, the Sydney group leader, was, by unanimous agreement, an influence of comparable stature to Ryle at Cambridge; but there is no trace of this in the Sydney citation and co-authorship patterns. A citation analyst can brush this aside, as a mere individual variation which is swallowed up in the statistics. But, to sociologists of my ilk, experiences like this merely confirm the unreliability, and very subsidiary status, of citation measures.

4) I mentioned earlier the claim that co-citation analysis can give an "objective" decision on the composition of specialty bibliographies. I am puzzled as to why such "arbitration" is thought to be necessary. I know that the point raises considerable concern among my colleagues,[12] but I remain relatively phlegmatic. To me, the idea of a "specialty" (and of a discipline) is a *social construct*, a concept which allows actors to make transient sense of their experience, and to orient themselves accordingly.[13] I would expect related actors to have broadly similar, but *not* identical, perceptions of their collectivity. So I would expect a wide measure of agreement, but *no* detailed consensus, on the "boundaries" of the specialty. The "correct definition of a specialty" is, to me, a meaningless concept, and I have no need of anyone (computer-aided or otherwise) to provide me with it. I know that this radically sociological perspective on scientific collectivities makes research more difficult than it would be under more simple-minded premises, but then I happen to believe that sociology *is* difficult. And I am comforted by the thought of the great British "middle class": here is a social construct central to any analysis of British society, which undeniably "exists"—but which stubbornly resists the attempts of empirical researchers to "define its boundaries"! I reject any technique which appears to remove from empirical sociology this "constant-triangulation-on-shifting-sands" character, and to substitute some illusory "solid foundations."

5) One final, general objection. Citation (and many other quantitative) methods draw entirely on features of *formal scientific publications*. Griffith, Drott and Small, in their title, refer to "studying scientific achievements and communication"; yet, in their paper, they pose problems and hypotheses in terms of the properties of *literature* and *documents*—not of the *behavior of scientists*. But surely the interesting questions to sociologists of scientific knowledge (and most historians of science) concern the vast "informal" area of scientific behavior (what we might call the "soft underbelly of science"), where interpersonal influences and negotiations lead to intimate choices of theory and technique, and hence determine the precise direction of the development of scientific culture itself. Studies of communication in science emphasize the importance of informal communication, and suggest that the formal and informal areas are *different in kind*.[14] To attempt to use clues from the *formal* area (eventually) to suggest explanations applicable to the *informal* area is, I submit, to reverse the necessary explanatory logic. Explanations

of scientists' behavior in the *informal* domain should surely be extended to include within their scope aspects of "formal behavior"—including the relatively trivial behaviour of adding citations to papers.[15] But, quite apart from "explanatory logic", it is simply my *judgment* that illumination is more likely to accrue "this way round". Certainly, I cannot say that co-citation studies to date have generated any striking insights—even heuristically. But I am willing to be convinced. As Liza Doolittle (who understood epistemology profoundly) put it, in "My Fair Lady": "Show me!"

6) And one final. general point. It seems to be fashionable to say (usually with an air of rather smug satisfaction) that "the sociology of science is a self-exemplifying specialty".[16] Whether you find the insight comforting depends, of course, on the kind of sociology of science you profess: mine is reflexive, but essentially conflict-ridden, and the present debate is a "self-exemplification". To use Mannheim's terminology, the purveyors of quantitative methods seem to me to embody an "enlightenment'" (or "natural law") style of thought, while the "participants' perspective" approach is in the "conservative" (or "romantic") style.[17] Placing the respective parties in their social situations, adding positions of relative power and authority (and mutual perceptions of threat), and reflecting on the form of the rhetoric in which this debate is couched,[18] I would venture that our styles are rooted in differences too deep and incommensurable to be bridged by brief academic exchanges—however clear and rational. Since the integrity of 4S is at risk, I find this outlook disturbing. But there is one crumb of comfort: the "participants' perspective" approach generates a self-awareness which allows disputants to live with their differences. What other faith do you need?

REFERENCES

1. For confirmation, see D.O. Edge and M.J. Mulkay. *Astronomy Transformed: The Emergence of Radio Astronomy in Britain* (New York: Wiley-Interscience, 1976), Chapters 2 & 9.
2. E. Garfield, I.H. Sher and R.J. Torpie, *The Use of Citation Data in Writing the History of Science* (Philadelphia: Institute for Scientific Information, 1964), 1.
3. Ibid., 33.
4. Henry G. Small, "A Co-Citation Model of a Scientific Specialty: A Longitudinal Study of Collagen Research", *Social Studies of Science,* Vol. 7 (1977), 140.
5. For details of some recent such "validations", see *Social Studies of Science,* Vol. 7, No. 2 (May 1977).
6. Small, op.cit. note 4, 156.
7. Diana Crane, *Invisible Colleges* (Chicago: The University of Chicago Press, 1972), 19.

8. A.J. Meadows, *Communication in Science* (London: Butterworths, 1974), 171.
9. H. Small and B.C. Griffith, "The Structure of Scientific Literatures. I: Identifying and Graphing Specialties", *Science Studies*, Vol. 4, 39-40, 1974.
10. For examples of such analyses, see D.A. MacKenzie and S.B. Barnes, "Biometrician versus Mendelian: A Controversy and its Explanation", *Kölner Zeitschrift für Soziologie und Sozialpsychologie*, Vol. 18 (1975), 165-96; Jonathan Harwood, "The Race-IQ Controversy: A Sociological Approach, I: Professional factors", *Social Studies of Science*, Vol. 6 (1976), 369-404, and 11: 'External' Factors", *ibid.*, Vol. 7 (1977), 1-30. For a related approach, see H.M. Collins, "The Seven Sexes: A Study in the Sociology of a Phenomenon, or the Replication of Experiments in Physics", *Sociology*, Vol. 9, 205-24, 1975.
11. Op.cit. note 1, Chapter 9.
12. For an example of such public anguish, see S.W. Woolgar, "The Identification and Definition of Scientific Collectivities", in G. Lemaine *et al.* (eds), *Perspectives on the Emergence of Scientific Disciplines* (Paris and The Hague: Mouton, and Chicago: Aldine, 1976), 233-45.
13. On this point, Warren Hagstrom's remarks on "Sources of Resistance Among Scientists to Their Classification on the Basis of Specialty", *4S Newsletter*, Vol. 2, No. 2 (Spring 1977), 15-16, are relevant and helpful.
14. See, for example, W.D. Garvey and B.C. Griffith, "Scientific Communication: Its Role in the Conduct of Research and Creation of Knowledge", *American Psychologist*, Vol. 26, 349-62, 1971; B.C. Griffith and A.J. Miller, "Networks of Informal Communication among Scientifically Productive Scientists", in C.E. Nelson and D.K. Pollock (eds), *Communication among Scientists and Engineers* (Lexington, MA. Heath Lexington Books, 1970), 125-40; H. Menzel, "Informal Communication in Science: Its Advantages and Its Formal Analogies", in D. Bergen (ed.), *The Foundations of Access to Knowledge* (Syracuse, NY: Syracuse University Press, 1968), 153-67; and F.W. Wolek and B.C. Griffith, "Policy and Informal Communications in Applied Science and Technology", *Science Studies,* Vol. 4:411-20, 1974. (The latter contains many useful further references.)
15. See G. Nigel Gilbert, "Referencing as Persuasion", *Social Studies of Science*, Vol. 7, 113-22, 1977. The need for scientists to have some framework within which to persuade each other may account for the relatively stable and consensual perceptions of specialty boundaries—and hence for the formal properties of co-citation maps.
16. The phrase reappears in the *4S Newsletter*, Vol. 2, No. 1 (Winter 1977), 7.
17. For those unfamiliar with this approach, a succinct account is given by David Bloor, *Knowledge and Social Imagery* (London: Routledge and Kegan Paul, 1976). See also the two papers by J. Harwood cited in note 10.
18. In such disputes, claims about techniques (and, indeed, the techniques themselves) take on an *ideological status* i.e., they are claims, alleging to reflect "objective accounts of the world", which covertly advance and consolidate social interests.

CURRENT COMMENTS

ISI's New *Index to Scientific & Technical Proceedings*™ Lets You Know What Went on at a Conference Even if You Stayed at Home

Number 40, October 3, 1977

Over the last two decades the number of scientific and technical meetings held throughout the world has doubled. In 1958 about 5,000 meetings were held worldwide.[1] This year about 10,000 scientific meetings will draw participants together from almost every country in the world.[2] The formal purpose of these meetings is the exchange of research results, thoughts and ideas. Informally, the participants get the opportunity to renew old acquaintances and meet new contributors.

The names used to describe meetings vary widely. Depending on the nature of the meeting and the intentions of its organizers, a "meeting" can be called a congress, symposium, conference, colloquium, session, convention, seminar, workshop, institute, assembly, round table, clinic, teach-in, or summer school. According to Arie Manten of the Elsevier Publishing Company, "Workshop is the fashionable term of the nineteen-seventies when trying to convince funding institutions that the meeting is dynamic and worthwhile."[3]

But no matter what they are called or why they are increasing in number, more conferences mean more published material. About three out of four scientific meetings result in a published record.[2]

The "proceedings" of conferences are published under various designations including symposium, report, record—and proceedings. Many appear as multi-authored books, the titles of which do not even include the word proceedings or any of its synonyms. Others appear in society newsletters or special issues of regularly published journals. Whatever their form and title, any librarian will tell you that the conference literature is among the most difficult to search and to acquire. Consequently, I'm sure this announcement of our plans to publish the *Index to Scientific & Technical Proceedings*™ (*ISTP*™) will be appreciated by librarians and researchers all over the world.

Beginning in 1978, *ISTP* will appear monthly with semi-annual cumulations. It will be multidisciplinary, covering the proceedings literature of the life and clinical sciences (including some psychology), agriculture, biology, engineering and applied sciences, and physical and chemical sciences. Naturally it will include such important mission-oriented fields as environmental and energy sciences. In short, *ISTP* will include all the fields covered by all the *Current Contents*® editions except the social sciences. Overall, about 3,000 separate published proceedings per year will be made accessible.

ISTP is not the first reference tool to attempt to provide bibliographic control over this very elusive literature. But *ISTP* will not merely provide systematic access to overall proceedings documents; it will also index the individual papers they contain. During its first year, *ISTP* will index over 90,000 individual papers. *ISTP* will serve both as a current awareness tool (through the monthly issues) and a retrospective search tool (through the semi-annual cumulations). These distinctions are important lest *ISTP* be confused with Data Courier's *Current Programs*[4] (to be called *Conference Papers Index* in 1978) which provides information on forthcoming meetings, the British Lending Library's *Index of Conference Proceedings Received,*[5] Interdok's *Directory of Published Proceedings,* or *Proceedings in Print.*

To understand how comprehensive *ISTP* will be it is first necessary to realize that the 10,000 conferences held each year actually result in only about 7,500 published proceedings.[2] Thus, *ISTP*'s initial coverage of 3,000 proceedings per year will include nearly half of the *total* volumes published. However, as with the *Science Citation Index*® and *Current Contents*, we will use ISI® 's unique resources, with help from our Editorial Advisory Board, to identify the most significant works. Therefore, we can expect that from 75 to 90% of the important papers published in conference proceedings will be accessible through *ISTP*. I expect that Bradford's Law will apply equally to proceedings literature as it does to the journal literature. That is, most of the important material published will be contained in a relatively small core of proceedings. Of course, we plan to regularly increase *ISTP*'s coverage as its development and use permit.

ISTP will put special emphasis on coverage of proceedings literature in life sciences, technology and the applied sciences. There are two reasons for this. First, more conference proceedings are published in the life sciences and technology than in other fields. Second, technologists, engineers, and those in the applied sciences are more prone than workers in other fields to use conference proceedings. P.R. Mills of the University of Bath, England, found that of 400 conferences held in June and July of 1970, approximately 42% concerned the life sciences and 39% technology.[5] By contrast, only 18% were in the physical sciences, and 15% in the social sciences. (The percentages add up to 114% because some of the sample conferences concerned two or more subject groups.)

ISTP's coverage will reflect Mills' figures. We estimate that of *ISTP*'s total coverage the life sciences will comprise about a third. Engineering and technology together will comprise another third of *ISTP*'s total coverage. The physical and chemical sciences will comprise about 20%, clinical practice about 10%, and agriculture, biology, and the environmental sciences together about 10%.

ISTP is designed to facilitate browsing as well as specific searches. The "main entry" for each proceedings document will be presented in a table-of-contents style that will make it easy to scan the monthly issues to keep up with recently published proceedings. A multi-faceted indexing system will help users locate whatever they are looking for—whether a complete proceedings on a general topic or an individual paper dealing with a specific aspect of a narrow specialty.

In the case of proceedings published in book form, the main entry will give the title and subtitle, series title and volume, editor, publisher and publisher's address, chapter titles, authors, author addresses, and the date and site of the conference. In addition, entries for books will give the Library of Congress number and the International Standard Book Number when available. For proceedings published in journals, like the example in Figure 1, the information will include conference title, journal title, volume, issue, year, titles of papers, authors, author addresses, and the information will enable a librarian or scientist to easily acquire the book or journal from the publisher or through interlibrary loan. The inclusion of authors' addresses also facilitates reprint requests.

The indexing system includes a Permuterm® Subject Index, a Con-

ference Topic Index, a Meeting Location Index, a Sponsor Index, an Author/Editor Index, and a Corporate Index. Each of these indexes will refer the user to the main entry by means of a proceedings number.

Figure 1 contains examples of various *ISTP* entries. The main entry, designated by its proceedings number, is presented in the top half of the illustration, the indexes below it.

The Permuterm Subject Index (PSI) is based upon permutations— or pairings—of significant title words. In Figure 1, title words have been permuted from both the title of the proceedings itself and the titles of individual papers. *Ophthalmology/Contemporary* are words from the proceedings title; *Rhinoplasty/Cosmetic* and *Rhinoplasty/Structural* are title words which appear in individual papers. Beside each of these pairs the proceedings number for the main entry is given. In addition, the PSI will indicate to the user where those terms may be found within the main entry—whether in an individual paper or the proceedings title. If the subject term occurs in the proceedings title, the PSI will indicate this with a "T." If it occurs within the title of an individual paper, the page number of the title within the proceedings will be given.

Like the PSI, the Sponsor, Meeting Location, and Corporate Indexes will refer the user to the main entry via the proceedings number. The Sponsor Index will also include the geographical location of each conference. Since a single organization, such as the National Science Foun-

Figure 1. The *Index to Scientific & Technical Proceedings*™ *(ISTP*™*):* samples of various entries.

Contents Of Proceedings (Main Entry)

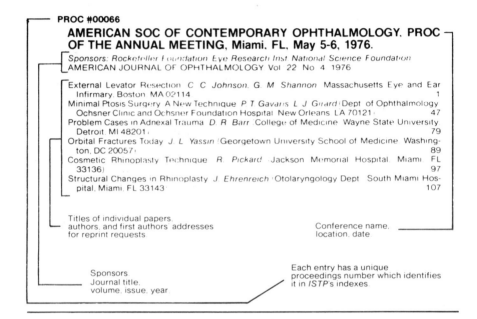

Permuterm ® Subject Index

	Proceedings #	Page	
Ophthalmology			Indicates
Contemporary	00066	T	word is in
Rhinoplasty			proceedings title
Cosmetic	00066	97	Indicates page number
Structural	00066	107	of article in proceedings

Sponsor Index

	Proceedings #
Eye Research Inst	
Miami, FL	00066
National Science Foundation	
Miami, FL	00066

Meeting Location Index

	Proceedings #
Florida	
Miami	
American Soc of Contemporary Ophthalmology,	
Proc of the Annual Meeting	00066

Corporate Index

	Proceedings #	Page
MASSACHUSETTS EYE & EAR INFIRM,		
BOSTON, MA		
Johnson CC	00066	1

dation, may sponsor several conferences a year, the conference location may help the user identify the correct meeting. The Meeting Location Index will consist of an alphabetical listing of countries, and the states and cities within them, and will supply the titles and proceedings number for conferences held in each area.

The Corporate Index lets you search by the affiliation of the author. Thus, to use the example in Figure 1, if you remembered that someone from the Massachusetts Eye and Ear Infirmary had presented a paper of interest but you didn't know the title or the author's name, you could locate not only the individual paper but the full proceedings through a single look-up in the Corporate Index.

Two other indexes not illustrated here are the Author/Editor Index and the Category Index. Both are simple to use. In the Author/Editor Index, an alphabetical look-up of the name of an author or editor will refer the user to the main entry by the proceedings number. Moreover, the index will indicate by page number, like the *PSI* and Corporate Index, where within the main entry the editor's name will be found. Editors will be designated by an "E" in the page number column.

The Category Index will organize the proceedings according to about 100 broad subject categories. Below each heading will be a listing of related conference titles and their proceedings numbers, to refer the user to the main entry.

Earlier this year I announced that the 1977 *Science Citation Index*

(*SCI*®) would include coverage of non-journal material.[6] This non-journal material presently includes published proceedings, monographic series, and multi-authored books. There will be no reduction of proceedings coverage in the *SCI* when *ISTP* comes into being. It is important to note, however, that *ISTP* will cover about 1,250 more separate proceedings volumes than the *SCI*. *ISTP* will also, with one major exception, offer a wider variety of indexing approaches to locate specific information. The exception is that the *SCI* will remain the only place you can use citation indexing to locate proceedings information. In other words, *ISTP* does not contain a citation index.

ISTP will index only proceedings literature which involves one-time outputs of scientific meetings. These should not be confused with such "proceedings" as the *Proceedings of the Society for Experimental Biology and Medicine, Proceedings of the IEEE,* and *Proceedings of the National Academy of Sciences,* which in reality are regularly published journals rather than conference proceedings. *ISTP* will not include coverage of such publications, except when special issues include the proceedings of specific, named conferences. We will be carefully screening all publications whose titles or contents suggest that they may really be one-time conference proceedings.

It is important to realize that *ISTP* will cover proceedings *only after they have been published.* Some other tools cover conference programs which may or may not develop into published proceedings.[7] Users of such tools are often frustrated trying to obtain proceedings which do not exist.

Reference librarians are often expected to act as detectives, using fragments of information to locate various items in the proceedings literature. The various indexes found in *ISTP* are vital for such detective work. And if the proceedings can be found in *ISTP*, the user can be sure that it has been published. By its very nature, therefore, *ISTP* will be an important bibliographic verification tool.

ISTP will reduce as much as possible the time lag between publication and indexing that exists with present tools. It is anticipated that the time lag between publication of a proceedings and its coverage in *ISTP* will not exceed two months. However, *ISTP* will not be able to reduce the lag time which occurs between the conference itself and publication of its proceedings. But we do find publishers most cooperative in expediting the processing of this material.

The price of *ISTP* is $500 per year. For information on ordering, please refer to the ad and order form on the back cover of this issue of *Current Contents*.

According to Helmut Drubba of the Technical Information Library in Hanover, West Germany, the proliferation of scientific conferences and their published literature has been caused by two technological developments: the jet plane and offset printing.[7] Conferences held all over the world are made possible to a large extent by jet travel, Drubba contends, and offset printing allows proceedings to be produced in large volume. This has resulted in the bibliographic nightmare that I've talked about before.[6] While *ISTP* may not end that nightmare, it will bring the handling of conference proceedings into the jet age.

When I have dicussed non-journal literature in the past, I pointed out that, unlike earlier decades, authors now seldom repeat in journals work that they have reported in full at meetings. Thus the importance of *ISTP* and non-journal coverage by *SCI* are consistent with the changed conditions of the jet-set world with its computerized typesetting and other means for making science more and more a real-time phenomenon.

1. **Murra K O.** "Futures" in international meetings. *College and Research Libraries* 19:445-50, November 1958.
2. **Short P J.** Bibliographic tools for tracing conference proceedings. *IATUL* (International Association of Technological University Libraries) *Proceedings* 6:50-3, May 1972.
3. **Manten A A.** *Symposia and Symposium publications: a guide for organizers, lecturers and editors of scientific meetings.* Amsterdam, Elsevier Scientific Publishing Company, 1976.
4. **Baum H.** A current-awareness service based on meetings—the need, the coverage, the service. *Journal of Chemical Documentation* 13:187-9, 1973.
5. **Mills P R.** Characteristics of published conference proceedings. *Journal of Documentation* 29:36-50, March 1973.
6. **Garfield E.** ISI adds "non-journal" material to the 1977 *Science Citation Index*. *Current Contents* No. 9, 28 February 1977, p. 5-6.
7. **Drubba H.** Conference documentation: general overview and survey of the present position. *Associations Internationales* 28:383-7, 1976.

CURRENT COMMENTS

Viewdata and SCITEL Bring Interactive Information Systems Into the Home

Number 41, October 10, 1977

Many Americans with cable television already enjoy the ability to receive various kinds of information on their home TV screens. But continuously displayed news headlines, weather, and stock market information is primitive in comparison to the on-line information access that many professional people have become accustomed to. That is why the imminent availability of interactive communication between citizens in their homes and computerized data banks is news of far-reaching social significance.

Since the technology already exists to convert your home television set into a computer terminal operated over regular telephone lines, ISI® has been investigating potential applications. Recently we have become involved in the development of a system called Viewdata. So far the system, operating in Britain, is in the prototype stage. But if tests planned for next year prove successful, a new era will have begun. In less than a decade more than a million private homes in Britain may have access to an array of information banks that would boggle the imagination even of H.G. Wells, creator of the World Brain.[1] Undoubtedly, once the political and other impediments are overcome, we can expect that a similar system will become available in the United States, where even more advanced technology exists.

Viewdata, developed by the British Post Office, allows subscribers to use their telephone lines to select "pages" of text for display on their home TV screens. The information now available to a small test market through Viewdata includes general news, sports, radio and TV program schedules, entertainment (film and performance schedules), holiday and travel information, stock market reports, general marketplace information, and science news. Each Viewdata "page" consists of about 1,000 characters (200 words).

What makes the system especially attractive is that the user needs no special training. To use it, you dial a number on your phone. This provides access to a local minicomputer, which can handle many inquiries simultaneously. You proceed by operating a small 10-button numeric keypad, provided by the telephone company. Once you have keyed in, the computer displays up to ten lines of information, which in effect constitutes an index to all the available information. To select one of the displayed choices, you merely press the appropriate digit. This causes a new series of choices to be displayed. By this interactive procedure you zero in on the particular page that contains the information you want.

The system is operated by the British Post Office, but data bases are provided by various other organizations. For example, ISI provides the SCITEL™ service. This is a current science news program which I will discuss later.

The Viewdata system may prove to be the most important development in decimal classification since Dewey. By a rapid keying of the right number one has access to thousands—and potentially millions—of pages. The selection path is analogous to the branch structure of a tree. Each selection made by the user results in the presentation of 10 more choices. Six successive digits select one out of one million pages. Thus a nine-digit number could select one page out of one bil-

lion! This is enough to store a vast library of information, including the *Science Citation Index®* , various encyclopedias, and a vast collection of books, journals, magazines, and newspapers.

In the British prototype of Viewdata, information is sent back along the telephone line almost immediately after a command is sent to the computer. Words are written out on the screen as fast as they can be read, and a complete page is received in a few seconds. If a viewer goes through the entire successive selection process, it may take a little while before the desired page is displayed. However, once the viewer knows the specific page number of the desired feature, the response can be almost immediate.

The minicomputers themselves perform the relatively simple task of responding to keyed commands by retrieving pages from disc memory. They also monitor the amount of time used by subscribers on specific data bases, so that the revenues received can be distributed among the network's suppliers.

Viewdata is presently in the pilot stage, with specially designed receivers available only to the British Post Office, information suppliers and manufacturers. The general public now can see Viewdata only at displays and exhibitions. However, in June 1978 the first serious marketing trial of Viewdata will begin. For this trial the Post Office ex-

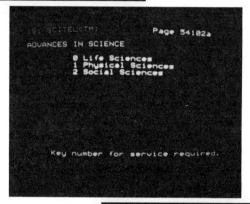

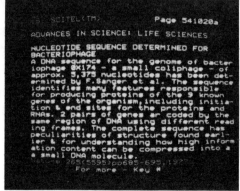

Figure 1. Viewdata sample pages as photographed from the television screen (loss of clarity due to reduction). By keying "2" and "0", the viewer goes from the SCITEL™ page at the top to the one at the bottom.

pects to sell about a thousand View-data systems in the London, Norwich and Birmingham areas.

The pilot trial will use one mini-computer with up to 70,000 pages of storage. If the trial goes well, View-data will become a public service in Britain. At that point a network of minicomputers will be needed. One machine can serve about 10,000 subscribers.

When Viewdata becomes a public service, subscribers will be provided with off-line backup. This means that they will be able to request, via a reference number punched on the keypad, specific documents related to viewed items. The requests will be forwarded from the network to the supplier, who will mail the document to the viewer. A viewer may also be able to send a message to another viewer, to be stored in the recipient's receiver until he or she comes to view it.

ISI's European branch now sup-plies the Viewdata system with a science news segment called SCITEL. SCITEL's coverage em-phasizes multidisciplinary news items in the medical and health sci-ences, chemical and physical sci-ences, technology, and the life and social sciences. In addition, SCITEL covers science policy, corporate news, recent advances in science, and news about scientists them-selves. It also provides weekly book reviews.

Let us assume that a user has ac-cessed ISI's SCITEL data base. An introductory frame explains what ISI is. The next frame presents the main routing (or index) page—a table of contents for SCITEL. The choices listed include science news, natural resources and environ-mental news, advances in science, a science book of the week, a science quarterly review, new technology, ISI activities, medicine, health and energy. If you choose "science news," a new routing page displays the following choices: headlines (items of major significance), shorts, people, company news, and science policy. Keying "advances in science" would offer choices in life sciences, physical sciences, and the social sciences. A few sample SCI-TEL "pages" photographed from the TV screen are reproduced in Figure 1.

SCITEL's coverage resembles that found in science magazines such as *New Scientist* or *Science News.* However, unlike printed magazines, the electronic medium of Viewdata allows information to reach the consumer with almost no time lag. For instance, some months ago when US scientists succeeded in isolating the cause of the "Legion-naires' Disease," we announced this news over SCITEL as soon as the story came in over the wire services. Newspapers did not carry the story until the next day. For an informa-tion scientist involved with current awareness on a day-to-day basis, the beauty of Viewdata is that it can be as current as the speed of light, the speed at which electronic signals travel through phone lines to the television receiver. But it remains to be seen whether consumers want or need access to such information so quickly.

Besides ISI, the other information suppliers for Viewdata include British Rail, the Tourist Board, the Consumers Association, Exchange Telegraph, the British Farm Produce Council, and several book and magazine publishers. Information providers are equipped with a special keyboard and modem (modulator-demodulator), enabling them to set up their material on their own display screens and, after review, to transmit it to the minicomputer data base.

There already has been speculation that the production and marketing of Viewdata equipment might cause the greatest electronics boom since color television.[2] When color television sets are modified to contain the Viewdata decoder and are manufactured in quantity, the extra cost is expected to be about $85.[3] In Britain, where most television sets are rented, this means a monthly rental increase of about $1.70. The keypad and telephone line facilities required for Viewdata can be integrated with the receiver, and also would add slightly to the cost.

The additional costs borne by the Viewdata subscriber include the price of the phone call to the network, a charge for connection time to the minicomputer, and the database charge. A 5-minute session will probably cost the user about 35 cents. One such session daily would cost the user about $120 per year.[3]

The 200-word limit per "page" might make it awkward to store the traditional page of scientific information. But if properly organized, the Viewdata system may have a significant impact on home education. How many disputes could be settled by quick perusal of the Viewdata file on sports statistics or an up-to-date almanac of facts and figures, not to mention multilingual dictionaries, encyclopedias, and reference works of all kinds?

Other systems similar, but not identical, to Viewdata have been developed for a variety of purposes. Generically, these are called "Teletext" systems. In Britain two Teletext news services known as Ceefax and Oracle have been introduced by the British Broadcasting Corporation and the Independent Broadcasting Authority, respectively.[4] These services can be viewed only on TV sets equipped with decoders. In the future, receivers will probably be equipped with combined Viewdata/Teletext decoders. Like Viewdata, Teletext information can be updated constantly. The great difference between Teletext and Viewdata is that Teletext information is broadcast continuously. It occupies a small part of the channel devoted to transmitting entertainment TV. Since there is no telephone line connection, viewer interaction with Teletext systems is limited to "capturing" a desired page by setting a control on the receiver. Also, the number of pages on Teletext systems is limited to a few hundred, while Viewdata can be made as large as required, provided sufficient memory capacity is given to the computer.

In the US several Teletext-type computer networks are already operating. In New York the British-owned Reuter news agency has financial news-on-demand available to cable-TV customers. Within the year, a Reuter general news service is expected to begin.[5]

Whether Viewdata can replace the newspaper remains to be seen. TV has already changed the role of newspapers, but they continue to thrive. In fact, the brevity of Viewdata presentations may whet the appetite for fuller coverage in newspapers, magazines and journals, as well as many types of reference books.

Viewdata can help create a new relationship between people and their television sets. The viewer, instead of passively absorbing whatever images cross the screen, can actively interact with what is being displayed, controlling the information presented on the television screen in a way never before possible. You might say that until now we have lived in the thumb-indexed era. To use a printed directory you have had to use your thumb to access randomly chosen information. Now the Viewdata keypad requires the use of your index finger. From our experience with on-line systems like SCISEARCH® we know that people prefer the simplicity and speed of the keyboard over the clumsiness of turning pages. Keying information also saves the time required to write it out. Future TV sets may even permit viewers to make a hard copy of displayed information.

There are some exciting times ahead.

1. **Garfield E.** The world brain as seen by an information entrepreneur. Presented at the American Association for the Advancement of Science Symposium on "Reorganizing information resources to improve decision-making." San Francisco, February 1975. Reprinted in: *Information for action: from knowledge to wisdom* (Kochen M., ed.). New York: Academic Press, 1975, p. 155-60.
2. Teletext to be small fry along-side Viewdata. *New Scientist* 73:586, 1977.
3. **Cawkell A E.** Developments in interactive on-line television systems and Teletext information services in the home. *On-Line Review* 1:31, 1977.
4. **Valery N.** Foot in the door for the home computer. *New Scientist* 74:63, 1977.
5. **Hoagland S.** Britons dial TV 'newspaper.' *Christian Science Monitor* 69(149):15, 1977.

CURRENT COMMENTS

A Study of Canadian Journal Data
Illustrates the Potential for Citation Analysis

Number 42, October 17, 1977

It is surprising how much of my daily correspondence comes from people seeking information on the quality of journals. Since I have published essays in this space on the journals of the French,[1] Italians,[2] New Zealanders and Australians,[3] Latin Americans,[4] Scandinavians,[5] Japanese,[6] Germans,[7] East Europeans,[8] and Russians,[9] it is natural that I would be expected to continue the exercise.

Most readers realize—I hope—that these studies are not just taken off a shelf here at ISI® . Assembling the data for each citation study takes considerable preparation and research. Sometimes new computer programs may be required. Naturally, checking and rechecking of data is mandatory before interpretation can begin. Thus, the studies you see in these pages usually represent weeks, and sometimes months, of work.

For those too impatient to wait for ISI to study the specific aspect of the journal literature of interest to them, original, interesting and valuable citation studies can certainly be done by people outside of ISI. Such studies can be accomplished through the use of the citation data which is available through ISI's *Journal Citation Reports*® (*JCR*™), *Science Citation Index*® (*SCI*®) and *Social Sciences Citation Index*™ (*SSCI*™). Or, unique data compilations can be obtained through ISI's contract research department.

An example of one study based on ISI data by Claude T. Bishop, editor-in-chief of the Canadian journals of research at the National Research Council of Canada, is reprinted here.[10] Bishop has used data from our *JCR* to support his contention that "Canadian science journals are better than some think." I have been planning to study the Canadian literature in detail, but this paper has caused me to accelerate my plans. One thing that still needs to be accomplished is a special computer run that treats all Canadian journals as though they were one large journal. As with other countries, we also need to know more about the impact of Canadian research published outside of Canada. All this information is now being compiled and analyzed at ISI.

Some important earlier citation analyses on Canadian journals were done by Herbert Inhaber of the Science Policy Branch of the Canadian Department of the Environment.[11,12] Inhaber developed a list of the 17 most highly cited Canadian journals based on 1969 *JCR* data. Of the 17, all but one appear among the top 22 journals on Bishop's list, which is based on 1974 *JCR* data. While the top Canadian journals appear to have essentially remained the same over the years, some changes in position do seem to have occurred. For example, the *Canadian Journal of Biochemistry* dropped from the third position on Inhaber's list to the fifth position on Bishop's. The *Canadian Medical Association Journal* went from fourth on Inhaber's list to third on Bishop's, and the *Canadian Journal of Botany* went from fifth on Inhaber's list to fourth on Bishop's.

It is interesting to note the different conclusions offered by Bishop and Inhaber. Both agree that there are less than two dozen Canadian journals among the world's most highly cited. However, Bishop asserts, "There are some excellent journals being published in Canada, with a significant number falling in the top 25% or so of rated journals, comparable with the best in the world." Inhaber states that "Canadian journals rank fairly low on an international scale based on citations." It seems we may have a classic case of what happens when an optimist and a pessimist view the same thing. *Current Contents®* readers will have to wait for the results of ISI's study for another opinion.

I would be delighted to see more studies like Inhaber's and Bishop's developed outside ISI. There is certainly no shortage of potential topics! Such citation studies can be national or regional in scope. In some cases, cities or individual universities could be studied. In one pioneering study, J.H. Westbrook of the General Electric Research Laboratory used citation data to rate industrial laboratories.[13]

Future researchers could also investigate the differences in impact and immediacy of letters journals or synoptic journals. There have been some interesting studies in the social sciences, but the field is essentially wide open. We have recently completed our first *JCR* for the *Social Sciences Citation Index.*

And certainly the introduction of ISI's *Arts and Humanities Citation Index* ™ in 1978 will provide scholars with some fascinating opportunities for comparative studies. The scholarly potential of the citation relationship has hardly been tapped.

1. **Garfield E.** Journal citation studies. 23. French journals — what they cite and what cites them. *Current Contents* No. 18, 26 June 1976, p. 5-10.*

2. --------------. Journal citation studies. 30. Italian journals *Current Contents* No. 4, 24 January 1977, p. 5-9.*

3. --------------. Journal citation studies. 27. Australian and New Zealand citers and citees. *Current Contents* No. 38, 20 September 1976, p. 5-10.*

4. --------------. Journal citation studies. 26. Latin-American journals. *Current Contents* No. 37, 13 September 1976, p. 5-11.*

5. --------------. Journal citation studies. 28. Scandinavian journals. *Current Contents* No. 41, 11 October 1976, p. 5-11.*

6. --------------. Journal citation studies. 24. Japanese journals — what they cite and what cites them. *Current Contents* No. 9, 1 March 1976, p. 5-10.*

7. --------------. Journal citation studies. 25. German journals — what they cite and vice versa. *Current Contents* No. 18, 3 May 1976, p. 5-11.*

8. --------------. Journal citation studies. 29. East European journals. *Current Contents* No. 45, 8 November 1976, p. 5-12.*

9. --------------. Highly cited articles. 20. Articles from Russian journals. *Current Contents* No. 45, 10 November 1975, p. 7-10.*

10. **Bishop C T.** Canadian science journals are better than some think. *Science Forum 57* 10(3):20-2, June 1977.

11. **Inhaber H.** Canadian scientific journals: Part I, coverage. *Journal of the American Society for Information Science* 26:253-7, 1975.

12. --------------. Canadian scientific journals: Part II, interaction. *Journal of the American Society for Information Science* 26:291-3, 1975.

13. **Westbrook J H.** Identifying significant research. *Science* 132:1229-34, 1960.

*Reprinted in: **Garfield E.** *Essays of an information scientist.* Philadelphia: ISI Press, 1977.

Canadian Journals
Are Better Than Some Think*

Claude T. Bishop

Editor-in-chief, Canadian Journals of Research
National Research Council of Canada
Ottawa 7, Ontario, Canada

One reason why it has been difficult to develop good scientific journals in Canada is that Canadian scientists are reluctant to publish in them. They give various reasons: that the journals are not well enough known, that they do not have high enough standards, or that they are ignored internationally.

Yet this attitude sets up a vicious circle, because no journal can become well known, have high standards, or attract international attention if it cannot publish at least some of the best work being done in the country.

What are the facts about Canadian scientific journals? Are they in fact inferior? Recent evidence suggests not. In fact, it shows that some rank relatively high in the world's scientific literature.

Until recently there has been no objective way to evaluate scientific journals. Any assessments made were, of necessity, largely subjective and were based upon such criteria as circulation, the scientific prestige of editorial boards, and the stature of authors. By these means, it was easy to identify a few of the most highly respected journals in various fields of science, but there was no quantitative measure of the impact or influence of any individual journal.

The advent of *Journal Citation Reports* (to be included on an annual basis as a separate volume of *Science Citation Index*, published by the Institute for Scientific Information, Philadelphia) now provides a quantitative measure of journal performance and may be expected to have considerable influence on journal publication.

Journal Citation Reports analyzes the 2,630 source journals of the *Science Citation Index* data base. These include all journals referred to in 4,248,065 citations contained in the reference lists of some 400,000 articles. Analysis of these citations reveals that 85% of them are from only some 2,000 or so journals. Al-

Reprinted from: Science Forum 10(3):20-22, June 1977, by permission of the author and *Science Forum.*

TABLE 1
Citation analysis of Canadian scientific journals

Journal	Citations Rank in this list	Times cited (1974)	World rank	Impact factor Rank in this list	Impact factor	World rank
Can. J. Chem. (NRC)	1	9,142	63	2	1.396	502
Can. J. Phys. (NRC)	2	4,656	147	9	1.038	718
Can. Med. Assoc. J.	3	3,115	252	3	1.249	586
Can. J. Bot. (NRC)	4	2,897	273	6	1.069	689
Can. J. Biochem. (NRC)	5	2,696	293	1	1.671	387
J. Fish. Res. Board Can.	6	2,505	317	8	1.053	711
Can. J. Microbiol. (NRC)	7	2,397	336	7	1.065	695
Can. J. Zool. (NRC)	8	1,559	466	13	0.788	936
Can. J. Physiol. Pharmacol. (NRC)	9	1,507	479	4	1.242	587
Can. Entomol.	10	1,119	613	24	0.473	1,357
Can. J. Earth Sci. (NRC)	11	1,004	657	5	1.092	676
Can. J. Genet. Cytol.	12	804	764	11	0.936	805
Can. J. Chem. Eng.	13	727	824	19	0.593	1,165
Can. J. Math.	14	649	878	27	0.366	1,685
Can. J. Psychol.	15	608	915	18	0.636	1,104
Can. J. Plant Sci.	16	601	922	26	0.341	1,629
Can. Anaesth. Soc. J.	17	432	1,114	14	0.767	954
Can. J. Anim. Sci.	18	428	1,119	17	0.701	1,033
Can. J. Comp. Med.	19	416	1,133	21	0.562	1,208
Can. J. Surg.	20	390	1,176	20	0.564	1,206
Can. J. Soil Sci.	21	358	1,235	22	0.524	1,266
Rev. Can. Biol.	22	346	1,257	16	0.723	1,008
Can. Vet. J.	23	209	1,555	30	0.301	1,727
Clin. Biochem.	23	209	1,555	15	0.757	963
Can. J. Ophthalmol.	24	198	1,590	23	0.515	1,278
Can. Met. Quart.	25	173	1,655	28	0.313	1,694
Can. J. Pub. Health	26	170	1,663	31	0.299	1,732
Can. Psychiat. Assoc. J.	27	122	1,854	35	0.095	2,184
Can. J. Pharm. Sci.	28	120	1,864	10	0.958	789
Arctic	29	110	1,911	33	0.225	1,897
Can. J. Food Sci. Tech.	30	106	1,946	37	0.061	2,260
Can. Math. B	31	94	2,023	36	0.083	2,222
Can. J. Spect.	32	65	2,154	12	0.891	840
Can. J. Behav. Sci.	33	58	2,192	25	0.351	1,610
Can. Psychol.	34	48	2,247	32	0.269	1,798
Can. J. Med. Technol.	35	30	2,359	29	0.304	1,717
J. Can. Petrol. Tech.	36	15	2,465	34	0.167	2,034
Can. Aeronaut. Space J.	37	9	2,524	38	0.051	2,279

though the fourth edition of the *World List of Scientific Journals* contains 59,961 titles, it is clear that only some 5–6% of them are being cited and that the 'core' group of 2,630 journals covered by *Journal Citation Reports* are those that participate effectively in the transfer of scientific information.

Table 1 lists those journals published in Canada that are included in *Journal Citation Reports*. The data reproduced here are limited to 'Citations' and 'Impact Factors.' The journals are listed in order of the total number of times each was cited in 1974 (middle column under Citations). The World Rank column under Citations shows the standing of the journal (by total citations in 1974) in the complete listing of all 2,630 journals covered. The Impact Factor is the ratio of the number of 1972 and 1973 items (cited in 1974 in all 2,630 source journals) published by the journal divided by the total number of articles published by that journal in 1972 and 1973. The first and third columns under Impact Factor show respectively the ranking of each journal (a) relative to the other Canadian journals listed, and (b) relative to all 2,630 journals.

To put these rankings in perspective it is necessary to look at the distribution of citations and impact factors among the total 2,630 journals. Figure 1 shows these distributions in terms of numbers of journals and figure 2 presents them on a percentage basis. Thus, from figure 1 we can see that less than 100 journals were

cited 10,000 times or more in 1974, another approximately 100 journals were cited 5–10,000 times, and, even at 1–2,000 citations there are less than 300 journals. Similarly, there are fewer than 25 journals with an impact factor higher than 10, about 50 journals with impact factors between 5 and 10, and even at impact factors of 1–2 there are only some 500 journals.

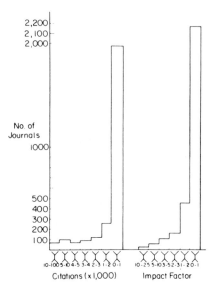

FIGURE 1

This concentration of high citation rate and high impact factor is even more apparent on a percentage basis, as shown in figure 2. Here we can see that only 25% of the journals are cited 1,000 or more times and that

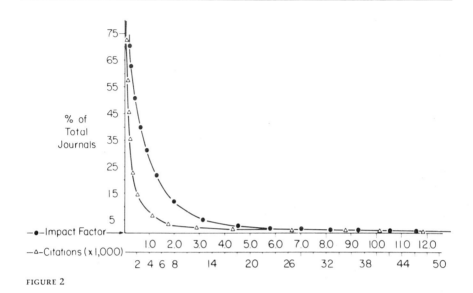

FIGURE 2

just 5% are cited 5,000 or more times. The curve of impact factor as a percentage of journals shows that 2.1% of the journals have impact factors of 5 or higher and that just 28% of them have impact factors of 1 or more.

From the data obtained and the presentations in figures 1 and 2 it is possible to see where individual Canadian journals rank in relation to the world's cited literature. E. Garfield, in his introduction to *Journal Citation Reports* (Science Citation Index, Vol. 9, 1975 Annual, Institute for Scientific Information, Philadelphia), has pointed out the limitations of these analyses for comparing journals, particularly those from different disciplines. He has also emphasized

that citation analysis cannot be the sole factor in evaluating a journal's performance.

As the National Research Council publishes the largest group of scientific journals in Canada, it was of interest to us to see how those journals rated. Other Canadian journals are included for the interest of their publishers and to provide a perspective of scientific publishing in Canada.

It is interesting to note that by citations, the first 11 journals in table 1 rank in the top 25% of the world's cited literature and that the first 22 are in the top 50%; the first 7 journals listed rank in the top 12% of all 2,630 journals covered. By impact factor, the first 5 ranked journals are in the top 25%, the first 13 ranked are in the top 35%, and the first 23 ranked journals are in the top 50% of the world's cited literature.

As indicated above, comparisons of individual journals in table 1 are neither appropriate nor meaningful. The only really valid relationship of a journal is to other similar journals in the same field. Lists of related journals have been compiled for each of the journals published by NRC and will be circulated through the appropriate scientific societies by the individual editors.

What, then, can be learned from the listing in table 1, and how could it be used? First of all, it is clear that there are some excellent journals being published in Canada, with a significant number falling in the top 25% or so of rated journals, comparable with the best in the world. This should help those editors who are trying to raise standards and improve their journals. The record shows that the vicious circle previously referred to can be broken provided that there is sufficient activity in a field and a number of good scientists who can be persuaded to support a journal by submitting papers to it.

The information available in *Journal Citation Reports* may also be useful in considering other questions about scientific publications in Canada. For example, are there too many or too few journals published in Canada for the size of our scientific community? Should some journals be combined, realigned, or eliminated, or should new ones be started? Should a journal be continued if it does not receive sufficient support (in the form of submitted papers) to make it internationally competitive? How did the highly ranked journals get that way? What steps can be taken to maintain or improve their positions and to improve others?

Finally, in times of restricted science budgets, including those for publications, there is the important question of journal economics: how many journals can we or ought we to afford? Should their management be centralized, decentralized, or somewhere in between? What is the most efficient and economical way of financing good journals? How does financing affect the performance of a journal in citation rankings?

Citation analysis *alone* will not provide answers to these questions but it does make available an objective assessment of a journal's performance among its peers. It is certainly in the best interests of the Canadian scientific community to strengthen and improve its journals wherever possible. The highly ranked journals in table 1 are circulated throughout the world, are cited heavily in the scientific literature, and reflect a credit to Canadian science that is an excellent return on the time, effort, and money spent in producing them.

CURRENT COMMENTS

To Indent Or Not To Indent? How To
Improve Journal Contents Page Formats

Number 43, October 24, 1977

Current Contents® readers scan thousands of contents pages each year. Most are aware of variations in the format of these pages. But how many realize that small changes in format can significantly increase browsing efficiency? The optimum format can save hours of scanning time and much wear and tear on the eyes.

You might assume that certain axioms of readability would be known to editors, who presumably have some expertise in communication. But most editors of scholarly journals have not had formal training in journalism—and few know much about typographic design. Even typographers leave much to be desired when it comes to arranging something as commonplace as a contents page.

One of the most important aspects of a well-designed contents page, or index for that matter, is the proper use of indentation. The failure of so many journals to use proper indentation costs you a lot of time. But if I asked readers to mention what improvements should be made in *Current Contents,* most would not even mention indentation. When is it necessary to indent? Let's say that the law of indentation for contents pages is simply as follows: when an article title is more than one line long, each remaining line should be indented. Examine any issue of *Current Contents* and you will see how often this law is violated.

Many journals put the author's name immediately after the article title. But if both the title and the author's name are printed on the same line and in the same size and style, they "blend" together. Ideally, the author's name should be placed in a column opposite the title. If this arrangement is not used, the name should be indented on a following line or printed in a style of type different from that used in the title. The article title should appear in boldface and the author's name in a lighter style.

Printing authors' names immediately after the title, instead of on a separate line, leads to another headache. The author's name is often hyphenated and continued on the next line. This should not be done, but if it is done the carryover syllable should be indented. It certainly should not appear under the first word of the title. Hyphenation should be avoided because splitting the author's name is a violation of the commandment against "widowhood."

Typographers define "widows" as very short lines at the top of a column or page. I go a step further and define widowhood to include placing last syllables where complete words or names ought to be. So, if there is not enough space to print the author's full name, print it on the next line. Do this even if you refuse to indent the second line, because the commandment against widowhood takes precedence over the law of indentation!

Many journals give authors' names the highest priority. They are printed in bold capital letters while titles are relegated to a light style. The editors of such journals might argue that within a given scientific specialty the author's name is more important than the title. Also, authors like to see their own names in boldface block letters.

But any author should be satisfied with the judicious use of both upper and lower case and the creative use of bold and light face to help the reader distinguish titles from author's names.

From the viewpoint of the average reader of *Current Contents,* I believe it is wise to put titles before authors' names. But recently the editor of one Soviet journal told me that he caters to the reader who is looking for an article by a colleague. In scientific circles it is not unusual for one to hear, "Have you read the latest article by Boggs?" But it would seem to me that this argument would lead to contents pages being arranged alphabetically by author, which creates a new set of problems. In any case, *Current Contents* readers can use the Author Address Directory to locate authors' names alphabetically.

A group of researchers at the Chaim Sheba Medical Center in Israel have determined that an ideal contents page format should satisfy three criteria: speed of scanning, ease and efficiency in finding keywords, and appeal to the reader.[1] In their study, 54 medical scientists who regularly scan *Current Contents* were instructed to scan sample contents pages for article titles. The researchers discovered that scanning for titles was easier when the titles and authors' names were typographically distinguished by type size, boldness, or order of appearance. Interestingly, although the subjects claimed to prefer that the titles *precede* authors' names, their scanning speed increased when the authors' names preceded the titles. In spite of this, I believe that the title should be listed first. It should be distinguished from the author's name by the use of both bold- and lightface type, by indentation, or by columnar arrangement.

In general, the best format for contents pages uses two columns, one for titles and the other for authors' names. This allows the reader to scan down either narrow column separately, or across both together. In the Chaim Sheba study, this format allowed the fastest scanning speed of the fourteen formats tested. It is now used by such journals as *Nature, American Scientist, Tetrahedron, Journal of Organic Chemistry, Harvard Business Review, British Journal of Psychology*, and others.

As I've stated before, our near-exact reproduction of tables of contents allows for interesting typographical variety in *Current Contents*. But some standardization of formats could help to eliminate confusion. Adjacent contents pages in *Current Contents* often have author, article title, or page number in reverse order.[2]

Another problem with some journals' formats is the placement of "degrees" next to authors' names. Besides wasting space, this has more than once led an indexer to list an author's name as "D.Phil." Within the context of a contents page, abbreviations for authors' degrees add clutter. The implicit snobbery in such a practice is particularly transparent in medical journals, and rampant in the U.K., where it is not uncommon to find four or five degrees attached to an author's name.

There are some curious practices that defy classification. The *Journal of African History*, like the *American Historical Review*, prints the word "by" in front of every author's name. I find this redundancy amusingly annoying. The word "by" occupies the normal indent spaces, cluttering up the page and adding unnecessary typesetting expense. Other journals spell out "and" between the author's names in every multiauthored article, though a comma or ampersand would suffice.

Columns which are too wide, especially when the leading (space between lines) is small, are impossible to scan rapidly. Also, when contents pages with very wide columns are reproduced for *Current Contents*, we must use reduction ratios that result in very small type. I can't understand why journals as reputable as those published by leading professional societies do not appreciate that it is very difficult to rapidly scan a column six inches wide, even if it is in large type. For twenty years I have been waging a battle against these and other editorial monstrosities.[3] Unfortunately, editors come and go, and each new generation must be taught the axioms of the past. And so even in this issue of *Current Contents* you may find a dozen or so infractions of the recommendations set down here.

But journal editors do not have a monopoly on graphic illiteracy. I've known commercial artists who could design a beautiful ad layout but were hopelessly impractical in laying out a cost-effective contents page. White space might look good, but a tighter page can contain twice as much information and cost half as much to print.

Given unlimited space in *Current Contents*, we could design beautiful contents pages with all sorts of graphic embellishments—even photographs of authors. But the use of too much space for such non-essential elements can be self-defeating. It might increase your pleasure, but could you afford the extra time required to scan those lovely diagrams, pictures, or whatever?

One might say that the different typographic policies of various journals illustrate the Matthew effect.[4] The wealthiest journals can afford the services of professional designers, but the poorest don't have the financial means to create attractive and efficient page layouts. However, I believe that there is room for improvement in most journal contents pages. Only a few achieve the ideal. Improvement must start by dealing with the "trivial" problems of indentation and widowhood, as well as typography and use of white space. If your favorite journal is guilty of unreadable contents pages, then write and tell the editor!

REFERENCES

1. **Kallner H, Modan M, Modan B & Wolman M.** Contents page format in scientific journals—effect on efficiency and ease of scanning. *Methods of Information in Medicine* 16(2):106-10, 1977.

2. **Garfield E.** ISI® cares—do you? What can *you* do about improving scientific journals as a communications medium? *Current Contents* No. 49, 5 December 1973, p. 5-6. (Reprinted in: **Garfield E.** *Essays of an information scientist.* Philadelphia: ISI Press, 1977, Vol. 1. p. 5-14).

3. --------------. Reducing the noise level in scientific communication: how services from ISI aid journal editors and publishers. *Current Contents* No. 30, 25 July 1977, p. 5-14.

4. **Merton R K.** The Matthew effect in science. *Science* 199:55-63, 5 January 1968.

CURRENT COMMENTS

Information Theory and All That Jazz:
A Lost Reference List Leads to a Pragmatic
Assignment for Students

Number 44, October 31, 1977

In 1948 Claude Shannon announced his mathematical theory of communication,[1] which has since found wide applications in fields as diverse as electronic engineering and the life sciences. Shannon's mathematical model of communications systems has been widely adopted both by information theorists, who are concerned with the fundamental limitations in the transmission of information, and by communications theorists, who mainly are concerned with the operation of communications devices.

When I first entered the field of documentation—now called "information science"—in 1951, it was quite fashionable to discuss Shannon's theory.[2] In the course of the next decade much was said about information theory—but little of practical use was accomplished in the area of information retrieval.

Back in those days, information people were preoccupied with punched cards. The bible of early

documentalists was Casey and Perry's book, *Punched Cards: Their Application to Science and Industry.*[3] It now amazes me to look back and realize that the punched card has already become obsolete as far as the information science literature is concerned. You certainly would never realize from reading professional information science journals that the punched card is still very much alive in the US and elsewhere.

I was raised and nurtured on the punched card. But by the mid-50s I was already using direct keyboard-tape input in Univac I—the first commercial electronic digital computer to use magnetic tape. I came to know the Univac well, not only through my acquaintance with John Mauchly but also because I used the machine for my doctoral dissertation.[4]

In 1959 I presented a paper on the role of information theory in the design of punched-card systems to a

271

meeting of the American Documentation Institute. The main purpose of the paper was to show how little relevance information theory had to information retrieval. Information science and information theory are quite distinct fields.

After my presentation, Herman Skolnik, who later became the first editor of the *Journal of Chemical Documentation* (now called the *Journal of Chemical Information and Computer Science*), asked me for a copy of my talk. The only copy I had was the one I'd just finished reading. Since I was so flattered by his request I gave it to him immediately. Unfortunately, the numerous references I cited were not attached or indicated in the text. Little did I realize that two years later the paper would be published verbatim—and without the missing references. Thus the foremost proponent of citation indexing became the author of a review paper without a single cited reference. To make matters worse, I lost the list of documents cited. So I never submitted a suitable correction.

The original list of references is still missing. However, I recently reconstructed it. The appropriate references are included here in the reprint of the original paper.

The loss of the references was a fortuitous blessing. As an adjunct lecturer at the University of Pennsylvania, I have used the paper as the basis of an interesting teaching exercise in documentation. In order to illustrate the variable nature of citation behavior, I have asked my students to read the paper carefully. Each student then inserts parentheses wherever he or she feels that a reference is needed. I have now performed this exercise for more than ten years. Each time the result has been the same. Although the number of references students inserted varied from about fifteen to seventy-five, they consistently averaged about forty-five. That is just about the number my original manuscript contained. In fact, the reconstructed reference list contains 41 items.

I'm convinced that many more instructors should use assignments of this type to train students in literature searching and citation consciousness. Developing a basic feel for when a reference is appropriate as well as skill in tracking down an elusive citation will serve them well during their professional careers.

Although part of the article which follows may now seem obsolete, it should be clear to most readers that the punched card remains a ubiquitous fact of life. Anyone who has ever received a government check, a phone bill, or any one of numerous computer-prepared notices should not dispute this.

But apart from the continued

relevance of punched-card technology in our lives, I cannot resist the opportunity to debunk, indirectly, the unnecessary mathematical gibberish which appears not only in journals of information science but also in the literature of other disciplines. A few years ago my old professor of chemistry, Joel Hildebrand, complained about this very problem in chemical physics.[5]

In closing, I would remind $CC^®$ readers that $ISI^®$'s director of research, A.E. Cawkell, has published some highly readable articles on information theory from the viewpoint of the information engineer.[6-8]

REFERENCES

1. **Shannon C E.** A mathematical theory of communication. *Bell System Technical Journal* 27:379, 623, 1948.
2. **Mooers C N.** Coding, information retrieval and the rapid selector. *American Documentation* 1:225, 1950.
3. **Casey R S, Perry J W, Berry M M & Kent A,** eds. *Punched cards: their application to science and industry.* New York: Reinhold, 1958.
4. **Garfield E.** Chemico-linguistics: computer translation of chemical nomenclature. *Nature* 192:192, 1961.
5. **Hildebrand J.** Operations on swollen theories with Occam's razor. *Structure-solubility relationships in polymers.* (Harris F W & Seymore R B, eds.) New York: Academic Press, 1977, p. 1-9.
6. **Cawkell A E.** Simplified information theory and data transmission. I. *Electrical Engineering* 39:212, 1967.
7. ―――――――. Simplified information theory and data transmission. II. *Electrical Engineering* 39:302, 1967.
8. ―――――――. A measure of 'efficiency factor' — communication theory applied to document selection systems. *Information Processing & Management* 11:243, 1975.

Information Theory and Other Quantitative Factors in Code Design for Document Card Systems*

Eugene Garfield

Institute for Scientific Information
325 Chestnut Street
Philadelphia, Pennsylvania 19106

In the past ten years, the field of information retrieval has witnessed the development of many new systems, devices, and theories. In particular, two opposing "schools" of thought on card indexing systems have developed. One claims that the term card (unit term) or "collating" system is the most desirable. The other advocates the document card (unit record) or "scanning" system. Dr. Whaley has noted many of the advantages and disadvantages of collating and scanning systems, and I am glad to adopt his terminology and agree with most of his comments.[1] For the record, however, I wish to remind the proponents of term card systems that theirs was no new finding. Costello[2] says Batten[3] anticipated Taube[4] by 15 years. Batten was anticipated by at least another 35 years.

One term card system began at the turn of the century at Johns Hopkins Hospital. Subsequently, it went through all the evolutionary stages which clearly demonstrate the inherent similarities between term card and document card systems. This does not mean that the rediscovery of the term card system was an insignificant development. After all, many useful ideas and inventions are rediscovered and we are grateful for these discoveries. However, when appropriate, our precursors ought to be given credit. Even the ten column posting card was anticipated by Paul Otlet, founder of the modern documentation movement.[5] Indeed, long ago, the term card system was used in several medical institutions, including Johns Hopkins Hospital and the Mayo Clinic.

Texts on medical records management demonstrate such systems.[6] These consist of one 3 x 5 card for each disease (term). Each card then lists the case history document numbers for all patients so diagnosed. Ultimately, the number of case history numbers grew larger

---

* Presented at the American Documentation Institute Annual Meeting, 22 October 1959, Lehigh University, Bethlehem, Pa.

and the time required to make any correlations between two diagnostic term cards increased to ridiculous, exponential proportions. Somewhere along the line it was decided that the document card system should be employed. At Johns Hopkins and Mayo, Hollerith cards were in use as early as the 1920's. The School of Public Health at Johns Hopkins was one of the earliest users of punched-card machines. Their equipment is still of early vintage. At Johns Hopkins, even the IBM card finally became a problem as the volume of patients grew into the hundreds of thousands. The "vicious circle" was continued when it was decided to use duplicate sets of cards—*i.e.*, rotated files, not unlike the system used at the Chemical-Biological Coordination Center (CBCC) several years ago.[7] Finally, this semi-collating,semi-scanning system was abandoned because of the high cost of storing millions of cards. The entire file was tabulated on printed sheets and the punched-cards thrown out. This printed index arrangement is very similar to the original term card arrangement. However, in a separate section, the equivalent of the document card is also printed. Thus, one is able to do a search by both methods. Depending upon the individual search either one or both may be used. Pre-coordinations were made where appropriate before printing the index.

The Mayo Clinic long ago attacked the space problem in another fashion. The storage density of the IBM card was increased by a system of binary coding.[8] These IBM methods, I believe, are still used there.

The binary coding utilizes all of the 4024 combinations possible in a 12 position punched-card column. It is understandable that a group of statisticians would discover this method. After all, statisticians work with probability data constantly. However, it is interesting that many people, including the statisticians, have been clever in finding ways of increasing the number of codes that can be crammed on a card (Wise,[9] Mooers,[10] *et al.*). However, the problem of how many times each was used was not considered as important.

This aspect first troubled me while working with the IBM 101 at the Welch Medical Library Indexing Project.[11] Some readers may recall the experimental 101 system we demonstrated in 1953 using five digit decimal codes, randomly strung along the first sixty columns of an IBM card.[12] For each subject heading or descriptor there was one five digit decimal number. Each card contained 12 such numbers. The details are described in the final report of the project. To use the same code length for all descriptors regardless of their frequency was rather inefficient in terms of space utilization, input time and searching cost. Obviously, others have arrived at similar conclusions because their coding systems *intuitively* employ a statistical approach. It is surprising, however, how many extant systems still do not make provisions for "normal distribution." A good example is the CBCC system, and the same is true of Uniterm,[13] Zatocoding[14] and others. To reiterate: they all use the same amount of coding space for each descriptor, regardless of its frequency of use.

Working with the CBCC system, and utilizing Heumann's statistical data[15] on about 25,000 chemical compounds coded with this system, it was possible to design a code which reduced significantly card space and the time and cost of searching. For the moment it is sufficient to state briefly that the statistical information available on the CBCC file was used to construct a normal distribution curve giving the frequency of use of each alphanumerical code. One then arbitrarily breaks into the frequency curves in various sections to determine the space allocations for the descriptors. If a descriptor, such as benzene, occurs in half the chemicals and the code for uranium occurs rarely, why devote the same amount of space to both. Obviously, as Wiswesser,[16] Steidle[17] and many others have found, it is quite sufficient to assign permanent card locations to frequently occurring codes. On the other hand, descriptors which occur infrequently can be assigned some coding configuration which requires, relatively, a great deal of card space. This will be of little consequence since it will crop up so rarely. These "rare" birds are treated as a class and codes are used that permit many combinations in a larger space. The Mayo system is one example; another is the Zator system, as applied by Schultz.[18] Indeed, one of the primary shortcomings of Mooers' Zator system is the indiscriminate, i.e., random assignment of an equal number of code symbols regardless of actual occurrence in the file.[19] This results in excess noise, i.e., false drops. Incidentally, I wish to point out that I am well aware of Mooers' early attempt in *American Documentation* to set Wise straight on the folly of a superimposed coding scheme for the now defunct Rapid Selector.[9,10] However, to use probability theory is one thing—to use information theory is something else. We all readily can visualize methods of utilizing card space that will *grossly* take advantage of the facts revealed by a statistical analysis of the use made of a particular descriptor dictionary or subject heading list. The theoretician, however, wants precise quantitative criteria for allocating code space to individual descriptors or groups of descriptors. Here is where Information Theory comes to the rescue. The design of the most efficient coding system does not depend upon the meaning of terms. The terms, by themselves, have no informational value. Rather, it is the frequency of use of a particular descriptor which determines its informational content. One can only measure the amount of information in the word benzene when transmitting it in English text. As a code or term in a document collection dictionary, the word has no value. It is only significant in so far as it occurs with a particular frequency. If half of the chemicals coded contain benzene then the knowledge that a particular chemical contains benzene reduces the remaining choices to one half.

Having cleared the cobwebs on what the real "coding" problem is in documentation systems it is then relatively simple to apply Shannon's basic formula for measuring informational content.[20] I might mention that it is difficult, at first, to think of the card searching problem as a transmission problem. However, if you think in terms of magnetic tape systems (Univac) or paper tape systems such as the Western Reserve Scanner, it is easier to see an analogy between "transmission" and searching. *The information content of a document file is neither the number of descriptors used, nor the number of documents which the various combinations of descriptors constitute.* The information content of a document collection is a function of the *probabilities* of the descriptors in the dictionary. *H,* the familiar thermodynamic entropy function, and Shannon's measure of information, is equal to the sum of the individual probabilities multiplied by the logarithm of the individual probabilities, ie., $H = -(P_1 \log P_1 + P_2 \log P_2 + \ldots + P_n \log P_n)$.

From this we are able to draw many interesting conclusions. For example, a document collection of 1,000 documents may contain no more information than a document collection of one million documents. This fact accounts for the intuitive decision of the Patent Office to use a "composited" card, which in certain cases is quite justifiable.[21] It also can be shown that the informational equality in two such files can be changed readily if the depth of indexing is altered. Indeed, if the informational content remains constant during such a growth one must either conclude that unnecessary cards remain in the file, new sub-dividing terms are required, or noise is present during a search. This situation is illustrated perfectly by our experience in coding steroid chemicals using the Patent Office code. In many instances a dozen different steroids were coded exactly alike. If the code dictionary is not changed, it is properly concluded that it is more economical to "composite" the 12 cards into one. However, one could increase the specificity of the coding. From the point of view of the Patent Office, with emphasis on the generic approach, the former conclusion, compositing, may appear simplest. From the point of view of the research chemist the latter approach, more specificity in coding, is more desirable. Taube's paper at the ICSI Conference implies that a term card system for the same steroid file could be used as readily as the Patent Office document card system.[22] This has a theoretical validity in view of the fact that in *both* systems no attention whatsoever is devoted to the frequency of occurrence of the various codes. (The Patent Office uses one punched hole position for each descriptor and the Uniterm system uses a 4 digit document number for each descriptor.) Indeed, from a tabulation of the coding done by the Patent Office of over 2500 U.S. patents, involving about 35,000 codes, it is no coincidence to find that seven descriptors account for over 9,200 codes, 16 additional account for another 9,100, the next 52 another 9,400 and all the remaining 359 descriptors 6,800.[23] Deciding the relative merits of working with a term card involving 1,500 document numbers (the highest frequency code) or the time to run 2,500 cards through a machine with a speed varying (according to price) from 500 to 2,000 cards per minute is meaningless. This becomes particularly ludicrous if one then considers the time required to find those chemicals containing both a 3-Hydroxy Steroid code and a 17-Hydroxy steroid which occurs with almost equal frequency (1,200 occurrences). Instead of matching numbers on Uniterm cards by eye, one can speed this up by "collating" on an IBM machine at speeds comparable to the sorting operation. Using a Ramac system or a high speed computer this can be speeded further.[24] The point is that each system, according to the circumstances, has advantages and for this reason, in certain cases, I have used a combination of both—even going so far as to maintain two independent systems. This is commonly done, but not admitted, in many installations.

Returning to the discussion of the now measurable quantity H of an information file, to explain how this measure of information is determined and used, I must resort to basic Information Theory. For that I have paraphrased Shannon's own words, to which I refer those who are not yet familiar with Information Theory.[20]

Information Theory is concerned with the discovery of mathematical laws governing systems designed to communicate or manipulate information. It sets up quantitative measures of information and the capacity to transmit, store and process information. Information is interpreted to include the messages occurring in standard communication media, computers, and even the nerve networks of animals. The signals or messages need not be meaningful in any ordinary sense. Information Theory is quite different from classical communication engineering theory, which deals with the devices used—not with that which is communicated.

I submit that most of the polemics concerning devices, *i.e.*, term card *vs.* document card systems have kept us in the dark ages of conventional engineering theory. Relatively speaking, we have paid little attention to the nature of the information itself. This led to the failure to design really efficient searching devices; anyone who rents an IBM machine knows this. The measure of information, H, is important because it determines the saving in transmission time that is possible, by proper encoding, due to the statistics of the message source. Consider a model language in which there are only four letters—A, B, C, and D. These letters have probabilities 1/2, 1/4, 1/8 and 1/8. In a long text, A will occur 1/2 the time, B one quarter, and C and D each 1/8. Suppose this language is to be encoded into binary digits, 0 or 1 as in a pulse system with two types of pulse. The most direct code is: A equal 00, B equal 01, C equal 10, and D equal 11. This code requires 2 binary digits per letter. However, a better code can be constructed, with A equal 0, B equal 10, C equal 110 and D equal 111. The number of binary digits used in this code is smaller *on the average*. It will equal 1/2 (1) + 1/4 (2) + 1/8 (3) + 1/8 (3) = 1 3/4, where the first term derives from letter A, second B, *etc.* This is just the value of H found if the probability functions are calculated.

The result verified for this special case holds generally—if the information rate of the message is H bits per letter, it is possible to encode it into binary digits using, on the average, only H binary digits per letter of text. There is no method of encoding which uses less than this amount if the original message is to be recovered without noise. An average of 1 1/4 bits is possible if the message is allowed to be noisy, *i.e.*, not a completely faithful rendition of the original message.

Before we can consider how information is to be measured it is necessary to clarify the precise meaning of "Information" to the communication engineer. In general, messages to be transmitted have "meaning," but have no bearing on the problem of transmitting the information. It is as difficult to transmit nonsense words or syllables as meaningful text (more so in fact). The significant point is that one particular message is chosen from a set of possible messages. What must be transmitted is a specification of the particular message chosen by the information source. The original message can be reconstructed at the receiving point only if such an unambiguous specification is transmitted. Thus "information" is associated with the notion of a choice of a set of possibilities. Furthermore, these choices occur with certain probabilities; some messages are more frequent than others.

The simplest type of choice is from two possibilities, each with probability 1/2, as when a coin is tossed. It is convenient, but not necessary, to use as the basic unit the binary digit or bit. *If* there are N possibilities, all equally likely, the amount of information is given by $\log_2 N$. If the probabilities are not equal, the formula is more compli-

cated. When the choices have probabilities $P_1, P_2, \ldots, P_n$, the amount of information H is given by the equation above. An information source produces a message which consists not of a single choice but of a sequence of choices, for example, the letters of a printed text or the elementary words or sounds of speech. In these cases, by an application of a generalized formula for H, the rate of production of information can be calculated. This "information" rate for English text is roughly one bit per letter, when statistical structure out to sentence length is considered (see *Bell System Tech. J.*, October 1949[25] or "Encyclopedia Britannica" article on Information Theory[26]).

The problem of applying information theory to documentation, I believe, is to be solved in properly defining the information source, which is the totality of descriptors assigned in any file. The next problem is defining the language units, *i.e.*, the descriptors and/or their components. A classification number, *e.g.*, has built into it much more information than a Uniterm. Each facet of the class number must be taken into consideration when measuring the information content of a classification system. It is then necessary to determine the probabilities of the units involved.

I will further hazard the statement that in the design of a document card of the IBM type *the most efficient space utilization will be obtained when the informational content of all card fields approach equality.* For example, in the case of the steroid file mentioned above, a card of four basic fields could be designed in which about 25% of the information was contained in each. The first "field" would consist of one column of 12 punches. The twelve most frequently occurring codes would be assigned to each of the twelve locations. The next eighteen codes would be accommodated in another column divided into six sections, each of which could accommodate three different mutually exclusive codes. You cannot have a steroid which is both an 11-keto and an 11-hydroxy compound. In actual punched-card application I suspect that one would continue to use the first five columns, at least, for direct codes covering the first 60 most frequently occurring descriptors. If not, another field could be used to accommodate the next 28 codes dividing one or more columns into 4 sections, each containing 3 punches. To accommodate the remaining 359 codes in one field would be quite simple by using all the 495 combinations (binary) of four hole punching patterns possible. The number of columns in the field would depend upon the average number of such codes possible in a single compound. Specific characteristics of existing equipment may modify this decision.

The preceding example of applying measures of information content to the design of an IBM card has been very brief and may not be entirely clear to those not familiar with IBM machines. It is important, at this point, to make clear the similarity between this simple code for an IBM card and a similar code that can be used for a variety of document card or scanning card systems. Let us take up a brief discussion of the qualitative aspects of document cards systems, particu-

larly as they relate to coding.

By document card systems, as contrasted to term card systems, we mean systems wherein all descriptors, or codes for descriptors, are retained together in the particular storage medium involved. Thus, in a punched-card document card system, i.e., McBee, E-Z Sort, IBM, Remington Rand, Underwood-Samas, etc., the holes or perforations are used to encode descriptors assigned to individual documents.[27] In a limited sense, the card is the document. Indeed, if the coding were sufficiently elaborate and detailed the card could be the document. The original Luhn Scanner employed an IBM card in which semantically factored words were stretched across the card to form an encoded telegraphic style message.[28] The IBM card employed was the standard 80 column card with a total of 960 punching positions.

Punched-card document card systems have their counterparts in film (Filmore[29] and Minicard[30]) where again all the descriptor codes are assembled together on a single piece of unitized film. The coding patterns may or may not be exactly of the type found on punched-cards. However, black or white spots correspond to perforations or the lack of perforations. The film-card (microfiche) may also contain a micro image of the original document. Similarly, an IBM card could contain the same micro image in a microfilm insert (Filmsort).[31] Similarly, the Magnacard[32] is the magnetic analog of a punched card. In this case information is coded as magnetized spots on magnetic tape.

The unit-card characteristic common to punched-cards, film cards, and magnetic cards is not only found in document-card systems. The same information found on Magna-cards can be stored on continuous magnetic tape. This is done on Univac and the IBM 700 series computers. The mechanisms employed to scan the "card" (sections of tape) are naturally somewhat different. Similarly, the defunct Rapid Selector was a continuous series of Filmorex cards strung out on one reel of film.[33] In the Benson-Lehner Flip system, the Rapid Selector system is partially revived.[34] A compromise between Filmorex and the Rapid Selector was suggested in the AMFIS system by Avakian.[35] The serial counterpart of perforated cards can be found in the Flexowriter tape used at Western Reserve where each document is represented by a series of codes exactly as in the fasion of the Luhn scanner.[36] This is no different from teletype tape except for the number of channels involved and the selector circuitry.

The Zator card is another version of the punched card.[37] The coding method employed has no basic dependence upon the card. It can be used with any type of document card system. Superimposition of codes is employed to make more efficient use of space. I mentioned earlier some of the limitations of Zator coding theory.

There are, obviously, many factors to consider in evaluating document card systems. Cost is one factor, but I believe its relative importance has been overly stressed by Taube and others.[38] Document card systems are not inherently expensive, nor small collections of

manual punched-cards. Dr. Whaley has covered more than adequately many other factors which may favor the document-card or scanning card system.[1] He particularly stressed the need, sometimes, to retain relationships between various descriptors. He did not stress adequately the advantages in terms of input convenience and cost, where it is equally advantageous to keep codes together. Preparing a single IBM card is simpler than posting a dozen or more document numbers to individual term cards. It is also simpler than duplicating the same card a dozen times, each to be filed in twelve different file locations.

At the present time, punching a really efficient IBM card is difficult because the IBM machines are not designed for retrieval purposes exclusively. However, in my own experience, preparing elaborately punched cards is not an insurmountable obstacle. Key-punching costs are not considered major problems when a file is used repeatedly. Another factor to consider is searching time for large files. This can be cut down by converting to speedier machines—if time is a problem.

The major criticism of existing document-card systems is the need to operate in a "scanning" sense, *i.e.*, each card or each unit of tape or file must physically pass by a scanning unit. When there are large volumes of records involved very high speeds may be required. This is not only costly, but it will be obvious that there is a limit to the speeds we can reach in *mechanically* transporting cards, film, *etc.* It is phenomenal how fast some sorting and scanning devices do work, and possibly these speeds will satisfy most requirements for a long time. However, these speeds are generally available only at a relatively high price. IBM machine rentals are higher in proportion to the speed at which they work, presumably because of greater maintenance and engineering cost. IBM tabulator rentals also vary according to the speed at which they are operated.

An ideal document card system would be one in which the basic advantages are retained—unit record input and storage, logical capabilities, *etc.* However, one would like to eliminate the need to scan the entire document file, in a *physical* sense, *i.e.,* by passing cards through a sorter, or magnetic tape past a reading lead, running film by a photoelectric cell. I believe such a system is possible and required particularly if we are to achieve the ultimate in access time. Such a system would be a truly random-access system and not a term card system using so-called random access. Systems such as RAMAC or AMFIS do not appear to be as energy consuming as high speed tape readers or sorters on punched cards, but their mechanical characteristics would seem to be limiting. It is comparable to solving the problem of sorting at high speeds by using a dozen sorters all at once. Similarly to use the equivalent of a dozen magnetic tape readers is no fundamental solution. In the ideal, the file will remain completely stationary and the scanning mechanism will be able to identify the existence of desired codes by scanning in a non-mechanical fashion. An approach in this direction is seen in the Bell Telephone system of routing long distance calls by use of special punched cards. Verner W. Clapp once asked me why you couldn't wave a flashlight at a file and have it throw out the answers. This is not impossible. I have been exploring a similar principle utilizing electromagnetic phenomena which I have called Radio Retrieval.

In conclusion, I have tried to show the fundamental similarities between so-called term card and document card systems by tracing the cyclical evolution of a term card system into a document card system, then into a semi-document card system employing collating methods, and finally back to a term card printed index arrangement. I maintain that the differences between term and document card systems are basically illusory. You will find vigorous proponents for each system depending upon the circumstances. If one had no indexing system at all in the first place, any system is an improvement. Once a system is adopted, thereby improving access to documents, a proposal to merely change the mechanics will not usually excite people.

An area of research which requires more fundamental work is in coding. No matter what system is used, the same amount of information is produced if one uses the same code dictionary and code frequencies.

The Patent Office Steroid Code would be, theoretically, equally efficient with a term card system as in its present document card system. From a practical point of view, it would not. Using Information Theory the coding space required in a document card system can be reduced considerably. It is possible that similar efficiencies are possible in designing term card systems, but these are not yet apparent and may be difficult to find. In other words, term card systems are inherently inefficient because they seemingly cannot take advantage of the variations in code frequencies which are inherent to *all* information systems. According to Keckley, "there is a central tendency for 90% of the activity to be concentrated within 25% of the classifications."[39] This appears to be well substantiated in the coding of 2,500 steroid compounds from the literature. Furthermore, term card space requirements may increase exponentially as the size of the collection grows. A collection of 1,000 documents requires less than 7 bits per descriptor assignment, a collection of 10,000 about 12 bits per descriptor assignment, 100,000 16 bits, and 1,000,000 20 bits.

Mooers deserves credit for recognizing the value of Information Theory for retrieval theory.[40] However, it is just as inefficient to use five punched holes for every descriptor on a document card as it is to use a five digit document number on a term card. By proper application of descriptor probabilities Information Theory can make Zato coding even more powerful.

It has been shown that one can quantitatively measure the amount of information in a document collection by the Shannon formula $H = -(P_1 \log P_1 + P_2 \log P_2 + ... P_n \log P_n)$
As a result of this expression, it is concluded that the size of a document collection is no realistic measure of its "information content." Indeed, *two collections of entirely different size contain the "same" information if they use exactly the same code or dictionary with the same percentage distribution of descriptors.* Thus, in this sense the Library of Congress Subject Catalog contains no more information than the local Public Library Catalog. This may sound startling or ridiculous to librarians. However, as long as the local Library uses the LC Subject Heading Authority List, it may even contain *more* information because it may add further refinements to the existing LC dictionary or use it with varying frequency assignments. A special library is of more use to its clientele than is the Library of Congress. *To alter the information content of a collection one must index in greater depth—not index more documents.* This point is most important in industry.

Analysis of the Patent Office steroid code frequencies illustrates in a simple case how Information Theory may be put to use.[41] A brief summary and review of Shannon's Information Theory has been presented to show that the past preoccupation of documentalists with devices is comparable to the earlier preoccupation of communication engineers with machines rather than the information they were transmitting. The main problem in applying information theory in documentation is in defining the "information source" and the "channel." A completely successful retrieval system must combine the advantages of both term and document card systems in such a way that all inertial characteristics of existing systems are removed.

REFERENCES

1. **Whaley F R.** The manipulation of nonconventional indexing systems. *American Documentation* 12:101-107, 1961. Presented at the American Documentation Institute Annual Meeting, 22 October 1959, Lehigh University, Bethlehem, Pa.

2. **Costello J C.** Uniterm indexing principles, problems and solutions. *American Documentation* 12:20, 1961.

3. **Batten W E.** Specialized files for patent searching. *Punched cards: their application to science and industry.* (Casey R S & Perry J W, eds.) New York: Reinhold, 1951, p. 169-181.

4. **Taube M. & Associates.** *Studies in coordinate indexing.* Vol. 1. Washington, D.C.: Documentation, Inc., 1953.

5. **Otlet P.** *Traité de documentation: le livre sur le livre: théorie et pratique.* Brussels: Editiones Mundaneum, Palais Mondial, 1934, p. 388.

6. **Cristina S X.** History of writing and records. *Hospital Management.* Part 1, 72:111, 1958. Part 2, 86:82, 1958.

7. **Beard R L & Heumann K F.** The chemical-biological coordination center: an experiment in documentation. *Science* 116:553, 1952.

8. **Berkson J.** A system of codification of medical diagnoses for application to punched cards with a plan of operation. *American Journal of Public Health* 26:606, 1936.

9. **Wise C S & Perry J W.** Multiple coding and the rapid selector. *American Documentation* 3:223, 1952.

10. **Mooers C N.** Coding, information retrieval and the rapid selector. *American Documentation* 1:225, 1950.

11. **Himwich W A, Garfield E, Field H G, Whittock J M & Larkey S V.** *Final report on machine methods for information searching: Welch Medical Library Indexing Project.* Baltimore: Johns Hopkins University, 1955.

12. **Garfield E.** Preliminary report on the mechanical analysis of information by use of the 101 statistical punch card machines. *American Documentation* 5:7, 1954.

13. *The uniterm system of indexing: operating manual.* Washington, D.C.: Documentation, Inc., 1955.

14. **Mooers C N.** Zatocoding applied to mechanical organization of knowledge. *American Documentation* 2:20, 1951.

15. **Heumann K F & Dale E.** *Statistical survey of chemical structure.* Presented at the American Chemical Society Meeting, 12 September 1955, Minneapolis, Minn.

16. **Wiswesser W J.** *A line-formula chemical notation.* New York: Thomas Crowell Co., 1954.

17. **Steidle W.** Possibilities of mechanical documentation in organic chemistry. *Pharmazeutische Industrie* 19:88, 1957.

18. **Schultz C K.** An application of random codes for literature searching. *Punched cards: their application to science and industry.* (Casey R S, Perry J W, Berry M M & Kent R A, eds.) New York: Reinhold, 1958, p. 232-247.

19. **Mooers C N.** Zatocoding and developments in information retrieval. *ASLIB Proceedings* 8:3, 1956.

20. **Shannon C E & Weaver W.** *The mathematical theory of communication.* Urbana: University of Illinois, 1949.

21. **Baily M E, Lanham B E & Leibowitz J.** Mechanized searching in the US Patent Office. *Journal of the Patent Office Society* 35:566, 1953.

22. **Taube M.** The Comac: an efficient punched card collating system for the storage and retrieval of information. *Proceedings of the International Conference on Scientific Information.* Vol. 2. Washington, D.C.: National Academy of Sciences/National Research Council, 1959, p. 1245-1254.

23. **Ball N T.** Searching patents by machine. *American Documentation* 6:88, 1955.

24. **Nolan J J.** Information storage and retrieval using a large scale random access memory. *American Documentation* 10:27, 1959.

25. **Shannon C E.** Communication theory of secrecy systems. *Bell System Technical Journal* 28:656, 1949.

26. ⸺⸺⸺. Information theory. *Encyclopedia Britannica* 14th edition. Vol. 12. Chicago: Encyclopedia Britannica, Inc., 1958, p. 350.

27. **Casey R S, Perry J W, Berry M M & Kent A,** eds. *Punched cards: their application to science and industry.* New York: Reinhold, 1958.

28. **Luhn H P.** The IBM universal card scanner for punched cards information searching systems. *Emerging solutions for mechanizing the storage & retrieval of information: studies in coordinate indexing.* Vol. 5. (Taube M, ed.) Washington, D.C.: Documentation, Inc., 1959, p. 112-140.

29. **Samain J.** *Filmorex. Une nouvelle technique de classement et de sélection des documents et des informations.* Paris 1952.

30. **Taube M.** The Minicard system: a case study in the application of storage and retrieval theory. *The mechanization of data retrieval: studies in coordinate indexing.* Vol. 5. (Taube M, ed.) Washington, D.C.: Documentation, Inc., 1957, p. 55-100.

31. **Rees T H.** Commercially available equipment and supplies. *Punched cards: their application to science and industry.* (Casey R S, Perry J W, Berry M M & Kent A, eds.) New York: Reinhold, 1958, p. 30-90.

32. **Hayes R M.** *The Magnacard system.* Presented at the International Conference on Information Processing, June 1959, Paris, France.

33. **Shaw R R.** The rapid selector. *Journal of Documentation* 5:164, 1949.

34. Introduction to the FLIP (film library instantaneous presentation). *American Documentation* 8:330, 1957.

35. **Avakian E & Garfield E.** AMFIS — the automatic microfilm information system. *Special Libraries* 48:145, 1957.

36. **Perry J W.** The Western Reserve University searching selector. *Tools for machine literature searching.* (Perry J W & Kent A, eds.) New York: Interscience, 1958, p. 489-579.

37. **Mooers C N.** Scientific information retrieval systems for machine operation: case studies in design. *Zator Technical Bulletin #66.* Boston: Zator Company, 1951.

38. **Taube M.** *Studies in coordinate indexing.* 5 volumes. Washington, D.C.: Documentation, Inc., 1953-1959.

39. Unidentified reference. [I would appreciate hearing from any reader who is able to supply this reference.]

40. **Mooers C N.** Information retrieval viewed as temporal signalling. *International Congress of Mathematicians, Harvard University, August 30-September 6, 1950. Proceedings.* Providence, R.I.: American Mathematical Society, 1952, p. 572-573.

41. **Andrews D D, Frome J, Koller H R, Leibowitz J & Pfeffer H.** Recent advances in patent office searching: steroid compounds and ILAS. *Advances in documentation and library science. Vol. 2. Information systems in documentation.* (Shera J H, ed.) New York: Interscience, 1957, p. 447-477.

CURRENT COMMENTS

Everything You Always Wanted To Know About ISI Data Bases But Were Afraid To Ask

Number 45, November 7, 1977

The variety of information services provided by the Institute for Scientific Information® sometimes leads to confusion. Because we offer both broad and specific information services for the sciences and social sciences, some people assume that we have several separate data bases. Others believe that ISI® has a single, monolithic data base and that we merely flip a switch to generate services for any disciplinary field.

Neither assumption is entirely correct. Whether we should be considered to have one data base or several depends on which service you are talking about and at what point in its production cycle it happens to be.

For example, the data bases for the *Science Citation Index®* and the *Social Sciences Citation Index* ™ start out in our production cycle together, but eventually they split apart. *ASCA®* and *ASCATOPICS®* are always derived from the combined single data base. The data for the *Author Address Directory* and *Weekly Subject Index* sections of the six editions of *Current Contents®* are kept together through editing and keying procedures. An extraction program later replicates and separates the addresses and index terms for use in the different

CC® editions. This process is complicated by the fact that many journals covered in *CC* are not yet covered by one of our three citation indexes. (We have gradually been working towards the elimination of this confusing distinction.)

The raw materials for the data bases—the journals themselves— are not physically segregated by subject area during their processing flow through ISI. Social science journals lie contentedly next to physics and biology journals while waiting to be processed. And the same is true in our library storage area. Our *Original Article Tear Sheet (OATS®)* service makes no disciplinary distinctions among journals.

What is this all leading to? Recently I was invited to speak at the Third Institute of Electrical and Electronics Engineers (IEEE) Conference on Scientific Journals. Although I was unable to deliver the prepared paper in person, it is reprinted on the following pages. In it, we try to answer many of the questions frequently asked about ISI's operations. While there have been other articles about ISI as an organization,[1,2] this is the first one to describe our procedures in detail. While no single article of reasonable length can describe every minute detail, this one does give a good representation of what actually happens.

The article does not include a discussion of the data base from which we produce *Current Abstracts of Chemistry and Index Chemicus*™, *Automatic New Structure Alert*®, and the *Index Chemicus Registry System*®. All of these services cover journal articles that announce new organic syntheses and compounds. For all intents and purposes, all journals, editing, keying, and data processing for this data base are handled separately from other ISI services. Descriptions have appeared in *CC* and elsewhere.[3]

Throughout the article the enormous size of the ISI operation is made clear. Over 2,000 new source items are processed each day. This requires over two million key strokes daily. I recently discussed in some detail how we use our Keysave system to cut costs and improve quality for this massive file.[4] Another example of an innovative use of the computer, not discussed in the article, is our Project ZIP. Stated simply, Project ZIP is de-signed to reduce the number of inconsistent or incomplete author addresses entered into the data base. Every organizational address processed is verified manually against an authority list of "correct" addresses. If the incoming address is not on the authority list, it is edited, assigned a number, and added to the list for future use. If an incoming address is already on the authority list, the editor writes the appropriate code number beside it. When the article is processed, the data entry operator simply keys in the code number rather than the whole address. The correct and complete address is selected later from the computer's memory and automatically entered as part of the bibliographic record for that source item.

Like much published scientific research, the article reprinted here was not completely up to date even at the time it was presented. We are making improvements all the time. And next year, when we start our *Arts & Humanities Citation Index*[5] and our *Index to Scientific & Technical Proceedings*[6], further refinements will be made.

1. **Garfield E.** The who and why of ISI. *Current Contents* No. 1, 6 January 1975, p. 5-14*

2. **Lazerow S.** Institute for Scientific Information. *Encyclopedia of Library and Information Science.* Vol. 12. (A. Kent et al., eds.) New York: Marcel Dekker, 1974, p. 89-97.

3. **Garfield E.** We've added a *Weekly Subject Index* to *Current Abstracts of Chemistry and Index Chemicus. Current Contents* No. 5, 3 February 1975, p. 5-6*

4. ——————. Project Keysave—ISI's new on-line system for keying citations corrects errors. *Current Contents* No. 7, 14 February 1977, p. 5-7.

5. ——————. Will ISI's *Arts & Humanities Citation Index* revolutionize scholarship? *Current Contents* No. 32, 8 August 1977, p. 5-9.

6. ——————. ISI's new *Index to Scientific & Technical Proceedings* lets you know what went on at a conference even if you stayed at home. *Current Contents* No. 40, 3 October 1977, p. 5-10.

*Reprinted in: **Garfield E.** *Essays of an information scientist.* Philadelphia: ISI Press, 1977.

ISI® Data-Base-Produced Information Services

E. GARFIELD, M. KOENIG, AND T. DiRENZO

Abstract—The Institute for Scientific Information® (ISI®) is a multinational corporation that provides a wide variety of information services to scientists and librarians throughout the world. Included are the *Science Citation Index®*, *Current Contents®*, and others which depend on sophisticated computer processing for timely production. This paper describes how certain information elements are extracted from each journal article and processed through the ISI system. Examples are given of how recent computer technology has been applied to keep ISI services cost-effective as well as to improve their quality.

THE Institute for Scientific Information® (ISI®) is a multinational corporation that provides a wide variety of information services to scientists and librarians throughout the world. From a functional point of view, the services for the journal literature of science and technology can be classified into the following five major groups:

- Current awareness
- Selective dissemination of information (SDI)
- Retrospective search
- Document fulfillment
- Acquisitions planning.

For broad current awareness, the *Current Contents® (CC®)*

This paper was presented by Michael Koenig at the Third IEEE Conference on Scientific Journals, May 2-4, 1977. Reston, VA.

Eugene Garfield and Thomas DiRenzo are with the Institute for Scientific Information, 325 Chestnut St., Philadelphia, PA 19106, (215) 923-3300. Dr. Garfield is President of ISI and Mr. DiRenzo is Vice-President, Communications. Michael Koenig is with the Metrek Division of Mitre Corp., 1820 Dolley Madison Blvd., McLean, VA 22102, (703) 827-6554.

services provide weekly contents-page coverage of six different disciplinary areas: life sciences; agriculture, biology, and environmental sciences; social and behavioral sciences; engineering, technology, and applied sciences; physical and chemical sciences; and clinical practice [1].

ASCA® and *ASCATOPICS*® are the Institute's SDI services. Both provide subscribers with weekly computer reports listing recent articles relevant to their specific interests. The difference between the two services is that *ASCA* uses custom, one-of-a-kind profiles to represent subscribers' interests while *ASCATOPICS* uses standard profiles [2].

For literature searches that must cover a number of years (retrospective search), the major tools ISI offers are the *Science Citation Index*® (*SCI*®) for the natural and physical sciences and *Social Sciences Citation Index*™ (*SSCI*™) for the social and behavioral sciences [3]. These large indexes are supplemented by the smaller, more specialized *Index to Scientific Reviews*™ (*ISR*™) which provides coverage limited to review articles.

To help subscribers obtain hard copies of the articles they need when they cannot get them through traditional channels, a tearsheet service, *Original Article Tearsheet Service–OATS*®, supplies items published in journals covered by ISI. This operation casts the company in the role of being a librarian's library and one of the major sources of journal material in the United States. Complementing this basic document fulfillment service is an annual directory, *Who is Publishing in Science*, which provides the names and addresses of scientists who have published during the past calendar year. Many researchers and librarians, particularly those in developing countries, have used this directory to facilitate reprint requests and other correspondence.

In the acquisitions planning area, the *Journal Citation Reports*® (*JCR*™) gives librarians and others concerned with managing journal collections a source of objective data concerning the utility of specific journals. Decisions related to which journal subscriptions should be added or deleted or how far back certain journals should be kept can now be based, at least in part, on the information provided in *JCR* [4].

Production Flow

While ISI's use of citation indexing eliminates the expensive intellectual effort associated with traditional subject-term indexing, producing a data base that grows by nearly a million items a year is a massive materials handling and information processing job. It would not be possible to diagram here all the steps involved, but Fig. 1 provides a good representation of what is required to build the ISI data base and extract various services.

The job begins with the receipt and logging in of the individual issues of journals that are covered. Immediately after the journal issues are entered into the system, their tables of contents are removed and either used as is or recomposed for use in *Current Contents*. The data for the various *CC* indexes are supplied later.

Next, the journals are sent to the editing department. There, every item must be examined to determine whether it should be covered, and everything other than minor news notices and advertisements must be marked in some way to simplify entering the information into the computer and standardizing what goes in. This process involves coding each item to show what it is; identifying the first and last pages and the references of each item; noting journals whose reference formats differ from article to article; coding titles that must be translated into English; and editing titles, authors' names, organization names and addresses, and some references.

Titles must be marked and edited to show where they begin and end, eliminate unnecessary words, add pertinent footnote annotations, and standardize punctuation, numerical expressions, and proper names. Scientific notation must be edited to meet rules of standardization and computer processing requirements.

Authors' names and addresses must be underlined, and each name must be coded to distinguish between primary and secondary authors. Authors' names must be standardized too; this includes non-English names for which the rules of standardization are quite involved. The organizational names in authors' addresses also must be standardized [5].

References interspersed throughout the text or split between the text and footnotes, and footnotes that contain multiple references, are the toughest part of the editing job. Most often found in social science journals, these types of references require extensive editing notation to identify, integrate, and complete, and may require the help of a professional translator if they involve non-English citations.

Editing time per journal varies from half an hour to three days. Journals dealing with the social sciences are generally the most time consuming because their bibliographic standards tend to be archaic and their references are frequently complex, often citing exotic types of non-journal material, such as rare documents, legislation, and laws. It is not unusual to find references scattered throughout the text of a social science journal, which means the editor must scan the entire article. Footnotes containing multiple references are common, and the format of references, regardless of where they are found, is eclectic enough to make reformating the rule rather than the exception. The impact of these problems on productivity is great enough to justify a continuing and sizeable journal-liaison effort aimed at educating editors about the reader and economic advantages to be gained from adopting simpler, more standardized format rules [6].

The next production step is putting the edited material into the computer. This job is done by 60 data-entry operators working two shifts, five days a week, on keyboard display terminals on-line (connected directly) to a central magnetic disk

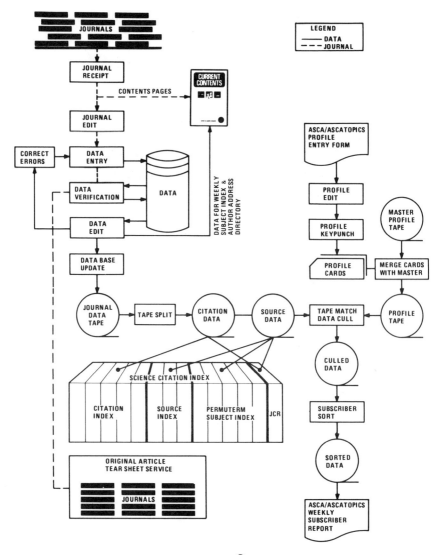

Fig. 1. Schematic of ISI® journal data flow.

memory. The journals move through this process in batches for which recording formats have been specified, and to which job control numbers have been assigned. As part of the job control procedure, individual journals are logged into the system, at the time they are assigned to a batch, by name, volume, issue, month, year, accession date, and number, and with a status-and-date statement. After that, the status-and-date statement in the system log is updated every time the journal moves from one operation to another.

Once a journal has been assigned and logged, it goes to a data-entry operator, who verifies and updates the log to let the system know what journal is being worked on and where it is. The operator then works through the journal article by article, keying the pertinent information from each into the system in a three-part sequence.

First comes the basic information that identifies the article: its type, title, page numbers, and primary author. The middle part of the data-entry sequence involves additional author information: the address of the primary author and the names and addresses of any secondary authors. The last part of the sequence deals with the references made in the article.

When all the information about all the articles in the journal has been entered into the system, the operator lets the system know the journal is finished by updating its log. Another operator then goes through the entire data-entry sequence again, character by character, to verify the work of the first operator. After data verification, the journals are filed by their ISI accession numbers and can now be used to provide tearsheets of individual articles.

Periodically, the verified records created for batches of journals are automatically transferred, under the control of someone working at a supervisory terminal, from the magnetic disk to a magnetic tape. As the records are transferred, they also are reformatted for computer processing.

The data-entry workload can be defined by a variety of numbers, all of them large. Approximately 2,000 source articles, involving some 22,000 references are processed each day. With the record length per source article averaging 1100 characters, the total number of characters entered each day is approximately one million. (If the verification operation is included, the total number of keystrokes per day is of the order of two million.)

At this point in the production cycle, the computer takes over. Despite the pains taken in the editing operation to identify, clarify, and standardize everything, and the character-by-character verification performed in data entry to assure keying accuracy, the first thing the computer must do to the tapes is edit them to make sure that all the records are complete and properly formatted. Some one percent are not and must be recycled through editing and data entry.

Besides checking the content and format of the individual records, which are organized by journal, the computer also checks the journals against a year-to-date file of the journal issues that have already been processed. Duplicates are recycled back through the journal-control people to work out the problems. Those that are not duplicates are copied onto the year-to-date file.

The tapes from data entry are edited this way on a daily basis and accumulated into a weekly data base, which is edited again to verify the daily checks of content and format. The edited weekly data base is then coded to show what journal records go into what service.

The records on the coded weekly data base are then sorted into two major data categories. The first is source data that include bibliographic descriptions (including titles) of the newly published source articles and names and addresses of the organizations with which the authors are affiliated. The second category is citation data, which are the brief bibliographic descriptions of the items referenced (including patents) in the source articles. These sorted records, except for the patent data, correspond to major sections in *SCI* and *SSCI;* the patent data are included only in *SCI*.

At this point, the data which make up the *Author Index and Address Directory* and *Weekly Subject Index* sections of the *Current Contents* publications are extracted onto tapes. This is done by a routine that organizes the material into pages and specifies formats and type fonts. The tapes are used to drive an automatic photocomposition machine, which turns out reproduction-quality page proofs from which offset negatives and plates can be made for printing. These index and directory pages will join, in the appropriate *CC* edition, their counterpart table-of-contents pages which were processed earlier in the week.

Another edit of the source data file is then done to further assure the accuracy of the title information. This is done by checking every key word in every title on the file against a key-word dictionary. Words not found in the dictionary are passed on to editors who determine whether they are misspellings of valid words or are words not yet included in the dictionary. Misspelled words are corrected; new ones that are judged to be important are validated and added to the dictionary.

After the weekly title edit, *ASCA* and *ASCATOPICS* subscriber profiles, which are stored on tape, are matched against the source and citation data elements. Whenever a match occurs, the full bibliographic description of the journal item which contained the data element is recorded on another tape. After all the profiles have passed against the source and citation data, the culled items are re-sorted by subscriber number and printed as the weekly reports which are quickly mailed to users.

The rest of the computer processing is done on quarterly, trimonthly, semiannual, and annual cycles. The quarterly cycle is concerned with preparing a three-month cumulation of items covered by the *Science Citation Index*. Here again, a computer routine reformats the material and produces tapes for photocomposition. In the last quarter of the year, the material for that quarter is consolidated with what had been published in the preceding three quarters to produce a cumulative annual index.

This same basic procedure is used to prepare the *Social Sciences Citation Index* on a four-month cycle. The *Index to Scientific Reviews* is produced on a semiannual cycle. On an annual basis, other computer routines create the tapes which produce *Who is Publishing in Science* and *Journal Citation Reports.*

In the preparation of the printed indexes there are a number of additional checks for accuracy conducted in the final stages of production. The first is a detailed check of the first statistically significant batch of pages produced by the photocomposer. The accuracy of the weekly data bases and the effectiveness of the computer routine that merges them are checked by matching a random sample of articles that should be covered in the initial pages against the page proofs. The effectiveness of other key computer programs is also checked in this initial sample by looking for discrepancies and omissions in names, cross references, and formats. If everything is correct, the rest of the pages are produced. These too are checked, but for such things as print quality, the number of columns per page, and the sequence of columns—all things that can go wrong in the photocomposition stage of production. Only then is the job released to the printer. The printer's work, too, is spot-checked for all the things that can go wrong in the printing process.

THE PROMISE OF TECHNOLOGY

Exploiting the potential of computer technology to achieve improved cost effectiveness in creating the ISI data base is a matter of continually searching for production efficiencies among the technological advances. Some of the efficiencies are built into the lower cost per unit of processing offered by succeeding generations of equipment and can be realized merely by upgrading the equipment periodically. Other, more significant efficiencies call for the ability to innovate from the improved functional base provided by the new equipment. The impact that key-to-disk data entry equipment has had on production is a case in point.

For a data entry operation as big as the one involved in the ISI data base, key-to-disk systems are more efficient than the older keypunch. Job control procedures are easier to implement; keying is done at electronic, rather than mechanical, speeds; and a lot of punched card handling is eliminated. In addition, each terminal operator has access to a central, disk memory, around which ISI has built a production innovation that increases efficiency far beyond the level made possible by the superior speed of key-to-disk systems.

The innovation consists of using the shared-disk memory to store an historical file of reference citations. The increase in efficiency comes from reducing the amount of keying necessary to enter and verify reference citations. Instead of keying the full citation, the operator keys in a 14-character code abstracted from the full citation. Each of the citations on the historical file has attached to it the same sort of coded identifier. If the code the operator enters matches one in the file, the full citation is brought up in the terminal display, where it is verified visually and entered on the disk with a single keystroke.

Every time an operator matches a reference citation against one in the historical file, the number of keystrokes required to enter the citation is reduced from an average of 70 to 14. And the keystrokes normally required for verification are eliminated completely.

The match-rate achieved depends on the number of citations in the historical file, which is limited by the size of the central disk memory available with the system. Initially, the file contained enough citations to produce a match-rate of 75 percent on the references that cited journal material. Some changes in the design of the file increased the utilization efficiency of the central memory enough to push the match-rate to 85 percent. Whether this rate can be raised still higher is uncertain, depending upon available memory capacity and how efficiently it is used.

The role of technology in the production of a data base goes beyond cost cutting into quality improvement. In some cases, the two can be combined. More often than not, however, quality improvements don't go hand in hand with cost reductions; they must be important enough to justify an increase in production cost. A computer-based system that automatically monitors the arrival of journals and tracks them through processing according to a planned schedule, for example, is more expensive than doing the same thing manually. But it does a better job, which produces the important qualitative benefit of increasing the timeliness and comprehensiveness of the data base.

Looking ahead, ISI plans to improve and expand its information services in the sciences and social sciences. Additionally, it has announced plans to offer a line of information services for the literature of the arts and humanities. To a large extent, the degree to which these plans are fulfilled depends on ISI's success in applying modern technology to building and exploiting its data base.

[1] E. Garfield, "Primary Journals, *Current Contents* and the Modern System of Scientific Communication," *Interdisciplinary Science Reviews* (in press).

[2] E. Garfield, "The Role of Man and Machine in an International Selective Dissemination of Information System," presented at the 35th Congress on Documentation of the International Federation for Documentation (FID), September 14-24, 1970, Buenos Aires, Argentina.

[3] M. Weinstock, "Citation Indexes," in *Encyclopedia of Library and Information Science.* New York: Marcel Dekker, 1971, vol. 5, pp. 16-40.

[4] E. Garfield, "Significant Journals of Science," *Nature*, vol. 264, pp. 609-15, 1976.

[5] E. Garfield, "An Address on Addresses," *Current Contents*, no. 28, p. 5, July 14, 1975.

[6] E. Garfield, "How Services from the Institute for Scientific Information Aid Journal Editors and Publishers," presented at the First International Conference of Scientific Editors, April 24-29, 1977, Jerusalem, Israel.

CURRENT COMMENTS

Sir Peter B. Medawar:
Consummate Scientific Professional,
Accomplished Literary Amateur

Number 46, November 14, 1977

I am often embarrassed by the relative poverty of my education in the classics, literature and the arts. Nevertheless, many people, especially foreigners, assume that I am able to converse on the arts and sciences with equal facility. I confess that a poem, a piece of music or a painting can bring tears to my eyes. But more often I am deeply moved by the beauty I find in the clear expression of scientific ideas, perhaps because I know how hard it is to achieve such clarity. So when remarkable lucidity and beauty of expression are combined, I am both emotionally and professionally impressed. I had this rare feeling recently while reading a book review by Sir Peter B. Medawar, the British biologist and philosopher.[1] This is not the first time I've experienced such a profound sensation while reading Medawar's work. Like Lewis Thomas,[2] the late Jacob Bronowski,[3] and a few others, Medawar combines the acumen of a scientist with the literary talent of a great writer. And lest you suspect I'm promoting a friend, I regret to report that I've never had the pleasure of meeting or even corresponding with Sir Peter.

People like Medawar, Thomas, and Bronowski provide the bridge between science and the public which is so important to a popular appreciation of science. We cannot encourage such persons enough in the pursuit of their work. Those of us who believe that basic research deserves public support should remember that one great literary or journalistic work by a scientist can do more to enhance the image of science than one hundred research projects designed to prove that basic research makes technology possible.

Medawar himself is a uniquely talented person. In 1960 he received the Nobel Prize for research on acquired immunological tolerance. But his interests are certainly not limited to medicine or biology. An examination of the select bibliography of Medawar's publications presented on the following pages indicates that his interests and expertise range from medicine to philosophy, from biology to psychology and sociology, and from the most narrow, highly specific research questions to the widest, most basic, and most urgent questions facing science.

299

Of course, years of research by a scientist like Peter Medawar don't go unnoticed. He has written over 150 articles and six books; seven of his articles and one of his books have been cited over one hundred times each. According to data from both the *Science Citation Index®* and the *Social Sciences Citation Index™*, Medawar has been cited more than 2,700 times from 1961 to 1976. On our highly-cited author list, based on total citations received by primary authors from 1961 to 1975, only about 800 names rank above Medawar's, while more than 56,000 rank below him. This does not prove the importance of his work, but surely illustrates its impact. It will be interesting to see how Medawar's citation record is affected when we complete our first all-author ranking, which will be based on citations not just to primary authors but to all co-authors. However, as Medawar himself argues in *The Uniqueness of the Individual,*[4] no single measurement or indicator can properly illuminate the whole of an individual's personality or achievements. So I will discuss some of Medawar's accomplishments and try to give readers an idea of his personality by presenting a few brief excerpts from his writings.

As an Oxford University undergraduate in zoology, Medawar did research on factors controlling growth in tissue cultures. After graduation in 1939, the outbreak of World War II caused him to focus his research on the replacement of skin lost because of severe burns, a pressing medical problem during the war. Surgeons found that most skin grafts were promptly rejected by the recipient. But why? And how could the rejection mechanism be neutralized or broken down? The British Medical Research Council supported Medawar's research on graft rejection.

In experimentation on rabbits Medawar found that the chief factor controlling acceptance or rejection of skin grafts was the genetic relationship between donor and recipient. Medawar and his research team also demonstrated that inoculation of fetal mice with living cells from a future donor made them tolerant of grafts from that donor later in life. These discoveries held enormous implications for solving the problem of tissue rejection in human beings.

Through the discovery of acquired tolerance, transplantation immunology became a major branch of experimental and clinical biology. Many people are alive today because of skin and organ transplants.

As a result of his research in tissue rejection, Medawar's scientific reputation grew rapidly. At the age of 34, the Royal Society elected him a Fellow. He became a professor of zoology, first at the University of Birmingham, and then at University College, London. In 1962 he was appointed Director of Britain's National Institute for Medical Research. In spite of a serious stroke in 1969, Medawar continued as Director until 1971. He has since made an excellent recovery, and says that his life has "picked up and has started getting good again."[5] Medawar still works for the Medical Research Council, and now has become well known as a philosopher of science, and as a student of the behavior of scientists. For example, in 1968 Medawar addressed the American Philosophical Society on the subject of what scientists really do. He said in part,

We all know in rough outline what lawyers do, or clergymen, physicians, accountants, and civil servants; we have a vague idea of the codes of practice they must abide by if they are to succeed in their professional duties, and if we were to learn more about them we should be edified, no doubt, but not surprised. But what are scientists like as professional men, and how do they set about to enlarge our understanding of the world around us? There seems to be no one answer. The layman's interpretation of scientific practice contains two elements which seem to be unrelated and all but impossible to reconcile. In the one conception the scientist is a discoverer, an innovator, an adventurer into the domain of what is not yet known or not yet understood. Such a man must be speculative, surely, at least in the sense of being able to envisage what *might* happen or what could be true. In the other conception the scientist is a critical man, a skeptic, hard to satisfy; a questioner of received beliefs. Scientists (in this second view) are men of facts and not of fancies, and science is antithetical to, perhaps even an antidote

to, imaginative activity in all its forms[6] (p. 2).

Medawar reconciled these two views by noting that

an imaginative or inspirational process enters into *all* scientific reasoning at every level: it is not confined to "great" discoveries, as the more simple-minded inductivists have supposed.

Scientists are usually too proud or too shy to speak about creativity and "creative imagination"; they feel it to be incompatible with their conception of themselves as "men of facts" and rigorous inductive judgments. The role of creativity has always been acknowledged by inventors, because inventors are often simple unpretentious people who do not give themselves airs, whose education has not been dignified by courses on scientific method. Innovators speak unaffectedly about brain waves and inspirations: and what, after all, is a mechanical invention if not a solid hypothesis, the literal embodiment of a belief or opinion of which mechanical working is the test?[6] (p. 55).

He concluded,

Imaginativeness and a critical temper are both necessary at all times, but neither is sufficient. The most imaginative scientists are by no means the most effective; at their worst, uncensored, they are cranks. Nor are the most critically minded. The man notorious for his dismissive criticisms, strenuous in the pursuit of error, is often unproductive, as if he had scared himself out of his own wits—unless indeed his critical cast of mind was the consequence rather than the cause of his infertility.[6] (p. 58).

Medawar displayed his own critical temper—and a bit of biting sarcasm as well—by distinguishing between the natural sciences and what he calls the "unnatural sciences." He wrote,

If a broad line of demarcation is drawn between the natural sciences and what can only be described as the *unnatural sciences*, it will at once be recognized as a distinguishing mark of the latter that their practitioners try most painstakingly to imitate what they believe—quite wrongly, alas for them—to be the distinctive manners and observances of the natural sciences. Among these are: (a) the belief that measurement and numeration are intrinsically praiseworthy activities (the worship, indeed, of what Ernst Gombrich calls *idola quantitatis*); (b) the whole discredited farrago of inductivism—especially the belief that *facts* are prior to ideas and that a sufficiently voluminous compilation of facts can be processed by a calculus of discovery in such a way as to yield general principles and natural-seeming laws; (c) another distinguishing mark of unnatural scientists is their faith in the efficacy of statistical formulas, particularly when processed by a computer—the use of which is in itself interpreted as a mark of scientific manhood.[1]

The tendency to quantify for the sake of quantification sometimes occurs in my own field of information science, and particularly in citation analysis. One needs a degree in mathematics to understand half the papers published in certain journals of information science. That is why one of the sensible terms associated with the quantification work going on in scientometrics these days is "indicators."[7] What I and others have been trying to stress is that citation data should not be viewed in isolation. It is useful and meaningful when its limitations are properly understood, and when it is viewed in the context of other indicators. As Medawar says, the evaluation of the individual is a complex process. And it is particularly when evaluating individual scientists that I have urged the utmost caution in using citation data.

Medawar's writings have also addressed the topic of science's impact on society. Recently, in collaboration with his wife, a botanist, he has produced a remarkable survey of modern biology and its social implications. *The Life Science*[8] is a concise and lucid look at current biological thought, in which the Medawars make some thought-provoking points about the human race.

In the following excerpt the Medawars recommend a balance between professionalism and amateurism. No one better exemplifies this type of balance than Sir Peter

Caroline Garlend

Sir Peter and Lady Medawar

Medawar himself, the consummate scientific professional, the accomplished literary amateur, and the perennial optimist.

People often wonder whether human beings are capable of further evolution. Leaving open the question of whether any such evolution will occur or not, the answer is assuredly 'Yes'. Human beings have a vast reservoir of inborn diversity and an open or 'wild type' breeding system which would make it possible for that diversity to be fully exploited; they have no extreme specialization such as the anteater's snout or the fly trap of an insectivorous plant—no specializations that commit them to one particular kind of life. Indeed, from an evolutionary point of view man is the great amateur among animals. A merely professional animal would probably have committed itself by structure or function to a bondage it could not now escape.

It is, however, very unlikely

that any major evolutionary change will come about during the future life of man on earth....

Our reasons for thinking that no major evolutionary change will occur are twofold. In the first place the exercise of any artificial selection over very many generations would require acquiescence in the rule of a long dynasty of tyrants, and although such a tyranny is not inconceivable, such consistency of policy assuredly is. In the second place ordinary or endo-somatic evolution is no longer a principal agency for securing fitness in human populations....

Another way in which human beings are amateurs in a professional world is that not all human activities have survival as their principal purpose. Even though our extra curricular activities are those that make life worth living—Mozart's piano sonatas and the paintings in the Uffizi Gallery amplify the human spirit and not human DNA—nothing will reconvert human beings from amateurs into pros more quickly than the imminence of mortal danger. In this context, being professional may imply submitting again to the tyrannical philosophy of reproductive advantage that has brought us this long way already. Clearly some compromise between the amateur and the professional is called for.

Recently, Medawar commented on the controversy surrounding genetic engineering.[9] His review of three new books on the subject contains incisive, cutting observations on the public appreciation of science and scientists. For instance, he comments,

For their excess of fearfulness, laymen have only themselves to blame and their nightmares are a judgment upon them for a deep-seated scientific illiteracy which manifests itself in two ways.

In the first place the public deserve nothing but contempt for allowing themselves to be dupes of that form of science fiction which is our modern equivalent of the Gothic romances of Mary Shelley and Mrs. Ann Radcliffe; for being taken in, that is to say, by that trusty serio-comic character, the mad scientist, who to the accompaniment of peals of maniacal laughter cries out with a strong Central European accent, "Soon ze whole vorld vill be in my power."

The second reason for their excess of fearfulness is this: That because imaginative writing is the only form of creative activity most people know, even educated laymen have no idea of the width of the gap between conception and execution in science. A writer who hits on a good idea—or even a composer who thinks of or, like Sullivan, overhears a good tune—can take up pencil and paper and write it down; he does not have to sue for bench space in a laboratory or send in five copies of an application explaining what his poem is going to be about, how many sheets of paper it will occupy, what imagery it is going to be clothed in, or how mankind will benefit by its completion.

Like the rest of his writing, Medawar's final comment on the genetic engineering controversy is clear, direct, and compelling:

I find it difficult to excuse the lack of confidence that otherwise quite sensible people have in the scientific profession, among whom sanity is much more widely diffused than seems to be generally realized. Scientists want to do good—and very often do. Short of abolishing the profession altogether no legislation can ever effectively be enforced that will seriously impede the scientists' determination to come to a deeper understanding of the material world. [9]

REFERENCES

1. **Medawar P B.** Unnatural science. *New York Review of Books* 24:13-8, 3 February 1977.
2. **Thomas L.** The lives of a cell: notes of a biology watcher. *New York: Viking Press, 1974, 180 pp.*
3. **Garfield E.** Audience of one—Jacob Bronowski. *Current Contents*® No. 41, 13 October 1975, p. 5-7. (Reprinted in Garfield E. *Essays of an information scientist.* Philadelphia: ISI® Press, 1977. Vol. 2, p. 351-3.)
4. **Medawar P B.** *The uniqueness of the individual.* New York: Basic Books, 1957, 191 pp.
5. **Gould D.** The Medawars. *New York Times Book Review,* 10 July 1977, p. 3, 32.
6. **Medawar P B.** *Induction and intuition in scientific thought: Jayne Lectures for 1968.* Philadelphia: American Philosophical Society, 1969, 62 pp.
7. **Garfield E, Malin M & Small H.** Citation data as indicators of scientific activity. *The metric of science.* (Elkana Y et al., eds.) New York: Wiley [in press].
8. **Medawar P B & Medawar J S.** *The life science: current ideas of biology.* New York: Harper & Row, 1977, p. 170-3.
9. --------------. Fear and DNA. *New York Review of Books* 24:15-20, 27 October 1977.

Peter Brian Medawar: A Select Bibliography

Books:

The uniqueness of the individual. New York: Basic Books, 1957, 191 pp.

The future of man: The BBC Reith Lectures 1959. London: Methuen, 1959, 128 pp.

The art of the soluble. London: Methuen, 1967, 160 pp.

Induction and intuition in scientific thought: Jayne Lectures for 1968. Philadelphia: American Philosophical Society, 1969, 62 pp.

The hope of progress. London: Methuen, 1972, 141 pp.

The life science: current ideas of biology. (with Medawar J S) New York: Harper & Row, 1977, 196 pp.

Articles:

Sheets of pure epidermal epithelium from human skin. *Nature* 148:783, 1941.

Peter Brian Medawar: A Select Bibliography (continued)

The behaviour and fate of skin autografts and skin homografts in rabbits. *Journal of Anatomy* 78:176-199, 1944.

A second study of the behaviour and fate of skin homografts in rabbits. *Journal of Anatomy* 79:157-176, 1945.

Size, shape, and age. *Essays on growth and form presented to D'Arcy Wentworth Thompson.* (LeGros Clark W E & Medawar P B, eds.) Oxford: Clarendon Press, 1945, p. 157-187.

Immunity to homologous grafted skin. I. The suppression of cell division in grafts transplanted to immunized animals. *British Journal of Experimental Pathology* 27:9-14, 1946.

Immunity to homologous grafted skin. II. The immunity relationship between the antigens of blood and skin. *British Journal of Experimental Pathology* 27:15-24, 1946.

Immunity to homologous grafted skin. III. The fate of skin homografts transplanted to the brain, to subcutaneous tissue, and to the anterior chamber of the eye. *British Journal of Experimental Pathology* 29:58-59, 1948.

The effects of adrenocortical hormones, adrenocorticotrophic hormone and pregnancy on skin transplantation immunity in mice. (with Sparrow E M) *Journal of Endocrinology* 14:240-256, 1956.

The Croonian Lecture. The homograft reaction. *Proceedings of the Royal Society of London. B.* 149:145-166, 1958.

The use of antigenic tissue extracts to weaken the immunological reaction against skin homografts in mice. *Transplantation* 1:21-38, 1963.

Biological effects of heterologous antilymphocyte sera. *Human Transplantation.* New York: Grune & Stratton, 1968, p. 501-509.

The future of transplantation biology and medicine. *Transplantation Proceedings* 1:666-669, March 1969.

Review Lecture. Immunosuppressive agents, with special reference to antilymphocytic serum. *Proceedings of the Royal Society of London. B.* 174:155-172, 1969.

Implications of fetal antigen theory for fetal transplantation. (with Castro J E, Hunt R & Lance E M) *Cancer Research* 34:2055-2060, 1974.

Thymus-dependent lymphocytes. (with Simpson E) *Nature* 258:106-108, 1975.

Unnatural science. *New York Review of Books* 24:13-18, 3 February 1977.

Fear and DNA. *New York Review of Books* 24:15-20, 27 October 1977.

CURRENT COMMENTS

Can Reprint Requests Serve As
A New Form of International Currency
For the Scientific Community?

Number 47, November 21, 1977

Five years ago I estimated that the costs of the international reprint exchange system were at least $10 million per year.[1,2] My estimate at that time did not fully consider the costs of printing the reprints. Today, I would at least double my original estimate. And even that would not take into account the doubling of *Current Contents®* readers—a key factor in the number of reprints requested—and the significant growth in the scientific literature.

One author claims that the cost of reprint exchange is between $1,000 and $2,000 for the "average" article.[3] Therefore, the total cost of reprints for 500,000 articles per year would be over a half-billion dollars. Obviously, this author is including many other costs of publication, since reprints would not be possible unless the articles were printed for journals in the first place. Until someone does a definitive study of the costs of the reprint system, we can only speculate. It is certainly a large-scale activity which involves many millions of dollars in real money and energy.[4]

The true cost of the system includes postage for both the request and the reply as well as the cost of printing—not only those reprints which are sent, but also those which lie unused on the shelf. A complete accounting would include the labor and materials required to send requests, to answer them, and to maintain the files of reprints requested, sent, and received.

There can be no doubt that ISI® services like *Current Contents* and *ASCA®* foster, indeed aid and abet, the reprint exchange system. To encourage this process even further, we designed the *Request-A-Print®* (*RAP*) card to make reprint exchange easier for requestors, authors, and their clerical support. *RAP* is best described as a reprint request/reply device that reduces effort and errors through a unique combination of preprinted and fill-in adhesive labels which are typewriter-compatible. The fact that we sell more than a million *Request-A-Print* cards a year indicates that they are performing a needed function. But this represents only a fraction of the world's reprint traffic.

To facilitate reprint exchange ISI has also done much to improve the accuracy and completeness of authors' addresses included in our services. We have encouraged journals to provide complete addresses,[5,6] but, though we have been somewhat successful, we still must complete thousands of partial addresses and correct many that are simply wrong.

The acceptance of the reprint exchange system is by no means universal. Some say that it is an obsolete form of communication that should be eliminated. Recently, strong criticism of the system has come from authors who bear the cost of satisfying large numbers of requests. This is not hard to understand if you happen to be someone like Jan Koch-Weser of Merrel International in Strasbourg, France, who received 3,000 requests for his article on "Binding of Drugs to Serum Albumin."[7] Estimating that it would cost $2,000 just to send regrets, he announced in the *New England Journal of Medicine* that he would send out only 300 reprints. He neglected to say on what basis he would select the lucky 300.

There are some people who would like to have Koch-Weser's "problem." Whether one has the budget for reprints or not, the psychological and other rewards of such an outpouring of interest are often priceless. Financial rewards may also be involved. Most chemists working at commercial chemical firms would undoubtedly be overjoyed to present the marketing department with 3,000 requests for an article announcing a new compound. And certainly more than a few academics facing evaluation committees have tried to establish the importance of their work by counting reprint requests received. It would be interesting to learn how often the number of reprint requests received serves as an indication of how heavily cited the article will become.

What I'm saying is that at the present time reprint exchange meets very real needs in disseminating scientific information and supporting the sociological structure of the scientific community. To discard the system entirely would be tantamount to "throwing out the baby with the bath water." What we need to do instead is devise a modification to the reprint exchange system that will keep it viable, but eliminate some of its abuses and inequities. In particular, an improved reprint exchange system should help the author who is occasionally inundated with requests.

About five years ago I proposed a system that would expedite reprint exchange by reducing the effort involved in ordering reprints.[1,2] While this system, called "Reprint Expediting Service" (REX), would have established a mechanism for delivering reprints more rapidly, it did not deal with the fundamental problem of how authors could afford to pay for them. So now, instead of Project REX, I hereby propose an ISI Reprint Exchange Stamp (RES) system. To enter the RES system you might buy 100 stamps at a cost of 25 cents each. Then, to each reprint request card you sent you would attach one or more stamps as prepayment. The stamps could be used by the recipient to request other reprints or they could be saved and eventually redeemed for cash or services.

The ISI Reprint Exchange Stamp system is a simple solution to the problem of providing an international paper currency for small payments. Since authors do not mail reprints COD (cash on delivery), they could now receive prepayments. The stamps would not be universally exchangeable, so there would be little incentive to steal them. The system would also have the kind of advantages inherent in any open marketplace subject to the laws of supply and demand. For example, under such a system, people would tend to request reprints more carefully because it would cost something to get them. Thus, the perceived value of the article involved would become a more important factor in each request.

One might think that payment for articles in this direct fashion would spur authors to produce better articles—but the prospect of payment also might encourage mediocre authors to increase their output.

The main disadvantage to my proposed stamp system is that it does not solve the problem of those authors who cannot afford or are unable to obtain "reprint currency." We then face the question of who shall be the banker or benefactor of these "impoverished" authors. Quite simply, I can't understand why the National Science Foundation, the National Institutes of Health, and other research funding agencies couldn't subsidize them in one way or another. Those scientists who have grants could simply charge the cost of the stamps to their projects. Those who do not already have grants could be allowed to apply for small grants for stamps or be issued stamps directly. After all, these agencies now pay for page charges and the reprinting of articles. So why not help pay for the ultimate use of the articles. I would also hope that internationally-minded organizations such as the Canadian International Development Research Center would support scientists in the developing nations.

If such organizations consider this problem trivial, perhaps the following literature review will enlighten all concerned as to just how widespread and complex the practice of reprint exchange really is.

For example, about 10 years ago, Warren O. Hagstrom of the University of Wisconsin found that the average number of reprints sent out varied considerably according to the author's field.[8] Data he gathered from 1,400 scientists indicated that, for each article published, over 100 reprints were sent out by 61% of experimental biologists and 56% of other biologists. Only 16% of theoretical physicists, 14% of chemists, 8% of experimental physicists, and 7% of mathematicians sent so many. In fact, 21% of mathematicians sent out no reprints. It seems likely, Hagstrom comments, "that the large number of reprint requests stems from the confused nature of specialization in biology and from the utility for clinicians of knowledge produced by a wide variety of biological research." Unfortunately, when discussing the "number of reprints sent," Hagstrom does not differentiate between those sent out automatically by the author and those requested. I suspect that the figures represent the combined totals.

In an effort to see if reprint response behavior is subject to modification, Leonard H. Epstein of Auburn University and Peter M. Miller and Diana O'Toole of the University of Mississippi Medical Center requested 216 reprints in three different ways: via standard request cards, standard cards with handwritten notes (prompts) to respond quickly, and standard cards with prompts plus praise for the article.[9] Not surprisingly, on average the "standard card" group took the longest to respond (27 days). Contrary to what people would expect, the "prompt without praise" group responded more quickly (18 days) than the "prompt plus praise" group (21 days). However, the investigators concluded that the difference between the last two groups was not significant.

William F. Harris of the University of Witwatersrand, South Africa, also examined the speed of response.[10] Selecting articles from the SDI (selective dissemination of information) reports of the Council for Scientific and Industrial Research in Pretoria (which uses *Science Citation Index*® magnetic tapes), Harris requested reprints of

3 to 4 articles of interest per week. Within six months after mailing, 70% of the requests were filled.

Roger K. Lewis of the University of Alabama School of Medicine requested reprints of 761 medical articles in American journals to test the effect the age of the article had on reprint response.[11] Articles requested immediately upon publication had the highest response rate, 77%. The response rate was 50% for year-old articles, 25% for two-year-old articles, and 21% for three-year-old articles.

To test the response rate from different geographic areas, Jan Svoboda of Czechoslovakia sent 1,000 reprint requests to scientists working in solid state physics, particularly nuclear magnetism.[12] Table 1 shows the results for countries to which at least ten requests were sent. All countries except two had a response rate greater than 85%.

The lower response rates for the USSR and India can be explained primarily on financial grounds. The cost and availability of reprints in these two countries are significant factors. And while postage is not generally a problem in the USSR, it is a significant component of cost in India. At the same time I believe the lower response rates indicate a lesser appreciation of the value of international communication by local authorities in these countries. Typically, these authorities are willing to finance scientific research through salaries and instrumentation but not through scientific information. Journals, reprints and other scientific information tools,

TABLE 1. Response rates for reprint requests (mainly in solid state physics and nuclear magnetism) sent to various countries.

Country	Number of Requests Sent	Percent of Requests Filled
Canada	68	100
Czechoslovakia	12	100
Finland	16	100
Italy	16	100
France	74	96
Federal Republic of Germany	56	93
Japan	25	92
Switzerland	37	92
Belgium	10	90
German Democratic Republic	21	90
Poland	21	90
Rumania	10	90
United States of America	381	88
Holland	40	87
England	139	86
U.S.S.R	246	57
India	12	40

Courtesy J. Svoboda

such as *Current Contents* are frequently given low priority. The situation is complicated by the fact that foreign hard currencies are in short supply.

Of course, one cannot generalize from this single study in one special field. The results might be significantly different for the earth sciences, which are given high priority in the Soviet Union, or for electrochemistry, in which the Indians do quite well.

As indicated earlier, the advent of *Current Contents, ASCA,* and other secondary information services has had a dramatic effect on reprint requests. This effect has been documented in various ways.

In 1973, E.F. Hartree reported that his article describing a modification of a method for measuring protein concentration elicited a "trickle" of reprint requests.[13] After the title appeared in *Current Contents,* however, the trickle "swelled into a torrent and passed the 2,500 mark...." By carefully examining the form of the address on requests, Hartree determined that at least 85% of them were directly attributable to the *Current Contents* listing. Five years earlier, Solomon and Jennifer Posen of Sydney Hospital studied 2,500 reprint requests for their own articles.[14] They found that about 40% of the requests came from scientists who had learned of the article through *Current Contents.*

There is still some latent resentment that anyone would request a reprint simply on the basis of reading a title in *Current Contents* or elsewhere. In 1970 a group of Cambridge physicists published a letter in *Nature* entitled, " 'Evolution'— 'development'—anatomical and cerebral features and the pathological consequences."[15] The entire text of the letter follows:

> We recently published papers in the oceanographic field which contained in their titles the words "development," "evolution," "triple junctions," and "fingers." These keywords were dispatched by computers to thousands of child psychiatrists, biologists, neurologists and medical practitioners. Hundreds have requested reprints. We are curious to know how many are going to request a reprint of the present communication on the same basis.

Other pranksters in Zambia published a letter on reprint exchange with the deliberately misleading title of "Hormones and Blood Chemistry."[16] The stated purpose of this deception was to enable the authors to further study the phenomenon of reprint requests. In their trick article the authors discussed the result of an earlier study that showed that over 70% of 188 requests for two of their earlier articles were generated by *Current Contents.*

I'm not sure what these efforts to dupe people who use secondary information services are supposed to prove. The implication is that anyone who has not seen the full text of an article should not request a reprint. Are the authors suggesting that somehow we can go back to the days when scientists could personally scan all the journals in their field? And doesn't it make sense to consider a reprint request a *redundancy* if the requestor has *already* seen the article? Actually, this last point is a bit of hyperbole on my part. There are plenty of good reasons why people want to have reprints of an article they've already read.

What these studies (both the trick ones and the straightforward ones) do show is that secondary information services can cause an unexpected strain on an author because of the magnitude of the exposure they give to an article. Escalating costs for printing and postage, not to mention the value of one's own time or the cost of clerical help, have turned the fulfillment of reprint requests into an expense that many authors cannot afford. This situation is aggravated by the fact that a relatively small percentage of the world's scientists publish a large percentage of the articles. Thus, there is a need to support a system where the requestor bears more of the financial burden. If such a system existed then we would, I believe, observe better response rates, since authors could afford to purchase larger quantities of reprints.

To implement such a system scientists and scholars would—as mentioned earlier—purchase reprint "currency" or stamps from some central source, such as ISI. These stamps would be pasted on reprint-request cards or enclosed in letters. For lengthy review articles, several stamps could be used. The author who received the currency could later use it to request reprints from other authors. Eventually the more popular authors could be expected to accumulate more currency than needed for their own requests. At that point they could use their stamps to pay for reprinting articles they publish, to purchase other types of services, or they could turn them in for cash. In some respects the system is similar to the Unesco coupon system.[17] Unesco coupons are still used by some libraries as a form of international currency, but they never had widespread support for reasons not clear to me. Unesco coupons could of course be used to purchase reprint stamps.

Obviously, someone who has no funds to buy reprint currency will have a hard time entering the system. But it would not be impossible. Some scientists would *receive* reprint currency for their own articles, even though they hadn't purchased any currency themselves. Gifts from other scientists could also get some people into the system. At present it is difficult to send money in small denominations to collaborators or colleagues in Eastern European and other countries. For such scientists, a gift of reprint currency would certainly be welcomed. Of course, those authors who are easily able to pay for the reprints they give could return reprint stamps with the reprint. They could indicate in this way that they will continue to supply them free in the future. For scientists at the beginning of their careers, it would be appropriate for their institutions to help support their needs in the same way that they support library and other services.

Until reprint currency becomes a reality, however, there are certain things that can be done to help the present situation. While it may seem degrading to some, it is not unreasonable for requestors to state briefly why their circumstances require special attention. Most authors would give priority to those who are least likely to get the information any other way.

K.P.M. Heirwegh of the Rega Institute, Leuven, Belgium, has a practical suggestion for those authors whose supply of reprints is running low.[18] Heirwegh suggests that the reply to the requestor consist of the full citation of the article, the authors' names, and a summary of the article. The summary would help those who have not seen the article to decide whether it is worth following up (in the library or through more correspondence with the author), or whether the request can be removed from the "waiting" file. Even if the summary is not included, it seems an excellent idea for authors who cannot supply reprints to include the complete citation of the article in their replies. This is far preferable to the answer, "The article you requested is no longer available"—especially when such notes are signed by secretaries or when the signature is unreadable. Such an answer makes it difficult to clear up open requests without additional correspondence.

Publishers can help by keeping the cost of reprints at reasonable levels. I believe it is a fallacy to think that reprints hurt journal sales. The more authors can afford to buy and send reprints of their articles, the less dependence there is on photocopying. Also, each reprint is an advertisement for the journal involved. When an author distributes reprints, it's a way of telling the recipient that he or she should consider publishing in and/or subscribing to that particular journal.

The custom of reprint exchange is crucial to the social process called science as it is now conducted. It is true that a few outstanding scientists receive many thousands of reprint requests and it may be impossible for such scientists to read every card. But those who complain about such problems remind me of authors who would *prefer* to be listed in the *Index Oblivionis*.[19] The fact is that most scientists *do* read reprint cards, and that their exchange does constitute an important form of scientific communication.

In my experience, reprints are not thrown away or relegated to the back shelf, but are usually filed and indexed. Thus, reprint files become important collections of scientific information. Back in 1902, a time when libraries still catalogued individual reprints (a function now performed mainly by individual scientists according to their own needs), C.D. Spivak said the following, in a letter recently republished in the *Journal of the American Medical Association:*[20]

An article in a modern periodical is like a pin in a stack of hay. That an article nowadays may make a lasting impression upon the reader, it must be an extraordinary production, indeed. The individuality and force of the majority of writings is obliterated in the "crowd." Hence, the writer unconsciously makes an attempt to rescue his production from oblivion by giving it at least the form of individuality. A reprint is an entity, a whole, not a part of a conglomerate.

There is, besides, a utilitarian reason for the existence of the reprint. It is a time-saving contrivance, since it is easier to handle and, therefore, more serviceable for purposes of reference. This is especially true in the case of long articles running through several numbers of a periodical. By using a reprint one avoids the annoyance of hunting for continuations through a maze of irrelevant literature.

REFERENCES

1. **Garfield E.** Reprint exchange. I. The multi-million dollar problem "ordinaire." *Current Contents* No. 36, 6 September 1972, p. 5-6.*
2. --------------. Reprint exchange. II. Project REX is ISI's code name for contemplated reprint expediting service. *Current Contents* No. 38, 20 September 1972, p. 5-6.*
3. **Lundh B.** Reprint requesting—time for a revision? *New England Journal of Medicine* 295:736, 1976.
4. **Bergmans L, Burgess J, Masson G, Parker C G A, Richards G F & Schroer M.** Reprint policies of scientific journals. (Personal communication to members of International Group of Scientific, Technical & Medical Publishers, Amsterdam) September 1972. 5 pp.
5. **Garfield E.** The place for an author's address is upfront—where it can be counted! *Current Contents* No. 47, 22 November 1976, p. 5-6.*
6. --------------. Reducing the noise level in scientific communication: how services from ISI aid journal editors and publishers. *Current Contents* No. 30, 25 July 1977, p. 5-15.
7. **Koch-Weser J.** Inundation by requests for costly reprints. *New England Journal of Medicine* 295:55, 1976.
8. **Hagstrom W O.** Factors related to the use of different modes of publishing research in four scientific fields. *Communication among scientists and engineers.* (Nelson C E & Pollack D K, eds.) Lexington, Massachusetts: Lexington Books, 1970, p. 85-124.
9. **Epstein L H, Miller P M & O'Toole D.** Factors influencing prompt responding to reprint requests. *Behavior Therapy* 6:414, 1975.
10. **Harris W F.** Return on reprints. *South African Journal of Science* 71:167, 1975.
11. **Lewis R K.** Responses to reprint requests. *Journal of Medical Education* 47:827, 1972.
12. **Svoboda J.** Personal communication, 23 May 1977.
13. **Hartree E F.** Reprint distribution. *Nature* 243:485, 1973.
14. **Posen S & Posen J S.** The geography of reprint requests. *Journal of Medical Education* 44:648, 1969.
15. **Davies D, McKenzie D P & Turner J S.** 'Evolution'—'development'—anatomical and cerebral features and the pathological consequences. *Nature* 225:636, 1970.
16. **Briggs M H & Briggs M.** Hormones and blood chemistry. *Nature* 240:490, 1972.
17. **Gardner A L.** Unesco coupons assist documentation services. *Unesco Bulletin for Libraries* 16:86, 1962.
18. **Heirwegh K P M.** Personal communication. 13 July 1977.
19. **Garfield E.** How *SCI®* bypasses "the road to scientific oblivion." *Current Contents* No. 56, 22 December 1971, p. 5-6.*
20. **Spivak C D.** Reprints, whence they come and whither they should go. *Journal of the American Medical Association* 237:1705, 1977.

*Reprinted in: **Garfield E.** *Essays of an Information Scientist.* Philadelphia: ISI Press, 1977.

CURRENT COMMENTS

Citation Analysis and the Anti-Vivisection
Controversy. Part II. An Assessment of
Lester R. Aronson's Citation Record

Number 48, November 28, 1977

Earlier this year I discussed the controversy surrounding animal experimentation at the American Museum of Natural History in New York City.[1] The controversy has focused mainly on the work of Lester R. Aronson, Chairman and Curator of the Museum's Department of Animal Behavior. Incidentally, Dr. Aronson is also Adjunct Professor of Biology both at the City University of New York and New York University.

I was originally drawn into the controversy because Dr. Aronson telephoned me to question the use (or abuse) of *Science Citation Index®* (*SCI®*) data in a *Science* news article written by Nicholas Wade.[2] Wade, an excellent and regular columnist for *Science,* used *SCI* data rather casually to assess Aronson's research.

The work in question involved removing certain glands and tissues from domestic cats in order to determine the effect on the cats' sexual behavior. Wade's rather superficial analysis seemed to imply that Aronson's work was unimportant. This accorded with a conclusion anti-vivisectionists had drawn in advance—that the cats were enduring mutilation for a minor or trivial gain in scientific information.

Before I report the results of our assessment of Aronson's citation record, it should be remembered that citation analysis can tell us much more about well-cited persons than it can about those who are infrequently cited. There is much mediocre and inferior research that is uncited. So it is easy to denigrate some possibly significant work that is, for other reasons, also uncited. Furthermore, superstars in very large fields are more visible than those in smaller fields because the chances are greater for their milestone papers to exceed average citation rates. Thus the superstars in biochemistry are more visible than those in a small branch of behavioral biology.

Defining and delimiting Aronson's field were important first steps in the analysis, since Aronson claims that he has been working in a small field. We began by asking Aronson to identify the articles he considered most relevant and significant for his cat research. He chose eight papers published between 1958 and 1974.[3] They are marked with an asterisk in Figure 1 on page 8. In these eight papers Aronson and his co-authors cited 226 other items in the literature written by 137 authors. Excluding self-citations, Aronson's eight cat research papers were cited in 85 papers written by 51 different authors. When duplications were eliminated, 176 individual authors were identified that either cited Aronson's papers at least once or were cited by Aronson

316

at least once. Using citation relationships as the indicator, 176 people have been involved in the field which we have, with Dr. Aronson's concurrence, named "sensory and hormonal influences on cat sexual behavior."

It could be argued, however, that a single reference is a rather weak indicator that two people are working in the same field. So we raised the citation threshold to two for those papers citing Aronson, in an attempt to identify the key papers and scientists in his field. Later these were checked against the subjective data provided by the key individuals themselves. The number of papers *citing* Aronson at least twice was 23, representing 15 unique authors.

For papers *cited by* Aronson we raised the citation threshold to three. The threshold is different for *citing* and *cited* papers because there are more references *from* a typical paper than *to* it. In general, scientific papers have about 12 to 15 references. But the average item in the *SCI* is cited only 1.87 times per year.[4] Even after five years, the average item has gained only about one more citation.

Fourteen papers by 10 authors cited Aronson at least three times. Eliminating duplicates between citing and cited authors, we created a list of 21 primary authors. These authors had either cited Aronson at least twice or had been cited by him at least three times. Thus one might say that the "invisible college" concerned with "sensory and hormonal influences on cat sexual behavior" comprises about 22 people including Aronson. To put this number in perspective, Derek deSolla Price of Yale University has estimated that the typical invisible college is composed of a "hundred or so really active and knowledgeable people in any particular part of the research

front of science."[5]

To confirm the size of the field of "sensory and hormonal influences on cat sexual behavior," we spoke with three key researchers identified by our analysis: Frank A. Beach of the University of California at Berkeley,[6] R.A. Gorski of UC/Los Angeles,[7] and B.L. Hart of UC/Davis.[8] They unanimously agreed that 15 of the 22 authors we identified had worked in the same field as Aronson. And *none of the remaining seven was disputed or unknown by all three*. They also confirmed that no important researcher in the field was omitted. Thus the field certainly is too small to sustain a specialized journal, which ordinarily requires about 100 researchers.[9]

Figure 1 is a diagram which I call an historiograph. It shows the citation connections between the 21 authors who either cited Aronson's key papers (at least twice) or were cited by him (at least three times). Each node represents a paper or group of papers by the same authors. The size of the node roughly indicates the number of papers it represents. The oldest paper is at the top; the most recent work at the bottom. Citation links are indicated by lines which connect the nodes. A line can indicate one or more citation connections.

The bibliography from which the historiograph was derived, on pages 8-9, shows that Aronson's field is multi-disciplinary. It involves the disciplines of biology, psychology, physiology, anatomy, endocrinology, zoology, urology, and biochemistry.

Having characterized Aronson's field, the next step in our analysis was to examine the relative impact of his work within that field. In his analysis Nicholas Wade stated, "Of the 21 articles that Aronson and his colleagues have published on the cat study since 1962, 14 have never been cited in the scientific literature between 1965, when the *Science Citation Index* starts, and March 1976. Because of the short citation half-life of scientific papers, it is unlikely that they ever will be cited. The seven other papers have an average 5.6 citations each over the same 11-year period."[2] Although Wade did not register an explicit assessment of Aronson's work, the reader was left with the impression that two-thirds of Aronson's articles were never cited, and that the remaining third have averaged only about half a citation per year. Is this impression accurate?

Wade made several errors. For one thing, the *Science Citation Index* started in 1961, not in 1965. (Perhaps Wade was using the five-year cumulative *SCI* for 1965-1969). In any case, we found that none of the 21 Aronson papers was cited from 1961 to 1964. However, Wade's citation count was inaccurate within the parameters he himself defined. Between 1965 and March 1976, of the 21 articles to which Wade referred, 11 (not 14, as Wade claimed) were never cited (except for self-citations) in the literature covered by the *SCI*. The remaining 10 papers were cited an average of 0.94 times in each year they could have been cited (not 0.5 times per year, as Wade implied).

In reply to Wade's analysis, Aronson claimed, "Of the 21 publications to which Wade refers, the seven full reports, each representing 3 to 5 years of continuous experimental observations, have all been cited except for one which was published in Moscow. In addition, two doctoral dissertations by former students have been cited as such, and later as journal publications. The remaining 14 publications were abstracts of reports given at scien-

tific meetings while the work was in progress, and even a goodly number of these have been cited."[10]

According to our own examination of the *SCI*, 11 of Aronson's 21 articles were never cited by anyone else. Six of these were never cited at all, and 5 were "self-cited" by Aronson or his colleague Madeline Cooper, but were cited by no one else.

However, the eight papers selected by Aronson as representing his major cat research together received 85 citations over the 15-year period from 1961 to 1975 (excluding self-citations); an average of 1.37 citations in each year that they could have been cited. To put this in perspective, consider that about one quarter of all articles covered by the *Science Citation Index* are *never cited* at all.[11] And the average number of citations to each item in a five-year cumulative *SCI* is 2.76. This is an average of 0.55 citations per year.[12] So the major papers dealing with Aronson's cat research not only have avoided "uncitedness," they are being cited at a rate that is significantly higher than average for all types of papers that do become cited in all fields of science.

For the years 1961-1975, Aronson's eight major cat papers together averaged about 10 citations yearly. When all his work, including that on species other than the cat, is considered, Aronson's average yearly citation rate rises to about 12 for the years 1961 to 1976. For each cited author in the *SCI*, the average yearly citation rate is 7.48.[4] Looked at from this perspective, Aronson's citation record as an individual author is slightly better than average. But one cannot fail to observe that 36 of the citations Aronson received were to the paper he co-authored with Rosenblatt in 1958 on

Figure 1. Historiograph based on Lester R. Aronson's research on sensory and hormonal influences on cat sexual behavior. Each node represents a paper or group of papers by the same authors; larger nodes represent more than one paper. Lines between nodes represent citations; a single line may represent multiple citations. The most recent contributions appear toward the bottom. See below for bibliographic data.

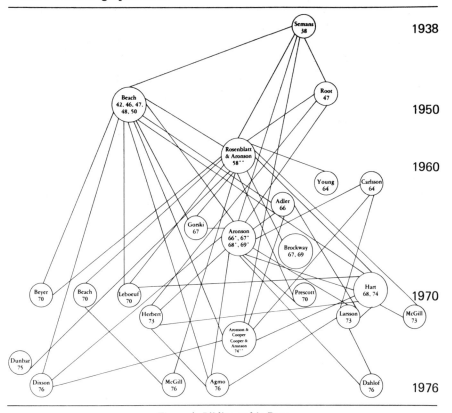

Figure 1. Bibliographic Data

Adler N & Bermant G. Sexual behavior of male rats: effects of reduced sensory feedback. *Journal of Comparative and Physiological Psychology* 61:240-3, 1966.

Agmo A. Mating in male rabbits after anesthesia of glans penis. *Physiology and Behavior* 17:435-7, 1976.

*Aronson L R & Cooper M L. Seasonal variation in mating behavior in cats after desensitization of glans penis. *Science* 152:226-30, 1966.

*------------------------------. Penile spines of the domestic cat: their endocrine-behavior relations. *Anatomical Record* 157:71-8, 1967.

*------------------------------. Desensitization of the glans penis and sexual behavior in cats. *Perspectives in reproduction and sexual behavior.* (Diamond M., ed.) Bloomington: Indiana University Press, 1968, p. 51-82.

*------------------------------. Mating behavior in sexually inexperienced cats after desensitization of the glans penis. *Animal Behaviour* 17:208-12, 1969.

*------------------------------. Olfactory deprivation and mating behavior in sexually experienced male cats. *Behavioral Biology* 11:459-80, 1974.

Beach F A. Analysis of the stimuli adequate to elicit mating behavior in the sexually inexperienced male rat. *Journal of Comparative Physiology* 33:163-207, 1942.

——————. Mating behavior in male cats castrated at various ages and injected with androgen. *Journal of Experimental Zoology* 101:91-142, 1946.

——————. A review of physiological and psychological studies of sexual behavior in mammals. *Physiological Reviews* 27:240-307, 1947.

——————. *Hormones and behaviour.* New York: PB Hoeber, 1948.

——————. Coital behavior in dogs. 6. Long term effects of castration upon mating in the male. *Journal of Comparative and Physiological Psychology Monograph* (Part 2), 70:1-32, 1970.

Beach F A & Levinson G. Effects of androgen on the glans penis and mating behavior of castrated male rats. *Journal of Experimental Zoology* 114:159-68, 1950.

Beyer C, Rivaud N & Cruz M L. Initiation of sexual behavior in prepuberally ovariectomized rabbits. *Endocrinology* 86:171, 1970.

Brockway B F. Social and experiential influences of nestbox-oriented behavior and gonadal activity of female budgerigars. *Behaviour* 29:63, 1967.

——————, Hormonal and experiential factors influencing nestbox-oriented behaviour of budgerigars. *Behaviour* 35:1, 1969.

Carlsson S G & Larsson K. Mating in male rats after local anesthetization of the glans penis. *Zeitschrift fur Tierpsychologie* 21:854-6, 1964.

*Cooper K K & Aronson L R. Effects of castration on neural afferent responses from penis of domestic cat. *Physiology and Behavior* 12:93-107, 1974.

Dahlof L G & Larsson K. Interactional effects of pudendal nerve section and social restriction on male rat sexual behavior. *Physiology and Behavior* 16:757-62, 1976.

Dixson A F. Effects of testosterone on sternal cutaneous glands and genitalia of male greater galago. *Folia Primatologica* 26:207-13, 1976.

Dunbar I F. Behavior of castrated animals. *Veterinary Record* 96:92, 1975.

Gorski R A. Localization of neural control of luteinization in feminine male rat (fale). *Anatomical Record* 157:63, 1967.

Hart B L. Alteration of quantitative aspects of sexual reflexes in spinal male dogs by testosterone. *Journal of Comparative and Physiological Psychology* 66:726-30, 1968.

——————. Gonadal androgen and sociosexual behavior of male mammals—comparative analysis. *Psychological Bulletin* 81:383-400, 1974.

Herbert J. Role of dorsal nerves of penis in sexual behavior of male rhesus monkey. *Physiology and Behavior* 10:293-300, 1973.

Larsson K & Sodersten P. Mating in male rats after section of the dorsal penile nerve. *Physiology and Behavior* 10:567-71, 1973.

Leboeuf B J. Copulatory and aggressive behavior in prepuberally castrated dog. *Hormones and Behavior* 1:127, 1970.

McGill T E & Haynes C M. Heterozygosity and retention of ejaculatory reflex after castration in male mice. *Journal of Comparative Physiology* 84:423-9, 1973.

McGill T E & Manning A. Genotype and retention of ejaculatory reflex in castrated male mice. *Animal Behaviour* 24:507-18, 1976.

Prescott R G. Mounting behavior in female cat. *Nature* 288:1106, 1970.

Root W S & Bard P. The mediation of feline erection through sympathetic pathways, with some remarks on sexual behavior after deafferentation of genitalia. *American Journal of Physiology* 151:80-90, 1947.

* Rosenblatt J S & Aronson L R. The decline of sexual behavior in male cats after castration with special reference to the role of prior sexual experience. *Behaviour* 12:285-338, 1958.

*——————. The influence of experience on the behavioral effects of androgen in prepuberally castrated male cats. *Animal Behaviour* 6:171-82, 1958.

Semans J H & Langworthy O R. Observation on the neurophysiology of sexual function in the male cat. *Journal of Urology* 40:836-46, 1938.

Young W C, Goy R W & Phoenix C H. Hormones and sexual behavior—broad relationships exist between gonadal hormones and behavior. *Science* 143:212-8, 1964.

*The eight papers selected by Lester R. Aronson as representing his most significant research on sensory and hormonal influences on cat sexual behavior.

the role of prior sexual experience in the decline of sexual behavior in male cats after castration.

Having determined Aronson's overall citation record, we then tried to gauge Aronson's importance within his own field. To do this, we ranked the 22 people involved by their first-author citation records for the years 1961-1976. They are listed in Figure 2 below. The results place Aronson eleventh in total citations received. This ranking is not

Figure 2. Authors appearing in Figure 1 ranked according to total citations from 1961 to 1976. Based on data from the *Science Citation Index®* .

Rank	Name	Total Citations 1961-1976	Average Annual Citations 1961-1976
1.	Beach FA	2424	152
2.	Young WC	1837	115
3.	Larsson K	891	56
4.	Gorski RA	797	50
5.	Beyer C	438	27
6.	Rosenblatt JS	327	23
7.	Root WS	362	23
8.	Hart BL	269	17
9.	McGill TE	213	13
10.	Herbert J	198	12
11.	Aronson LR	191	12
12.	Adler N	141	9
13.	Leboeuf BJ	124	8
14.	Brockway BF	102	6
15.	Semans JH	82	5
16.	Carlsson SG	49	3
17.	Prescott RG	26	2
18.	Agmo A	14	—
19.	Dixson AF	11	—
20.	Cooper KK	10	—
21.	Dunbar IF	1	—
22.	Dahlof LG	0	—

based just on citations to research in the field of "sensory and hormonal influences on cat sexual behavior," but includes references to Aronson's work on other species. The same is true for the others named in Figure 2.

Is Aronson a small fish in a big pond or a big fish in a small pond? According to the results of this

analysis, he seems to be neither. His work won't attract the attention of Nobel Prize committees, but he has had some influence on others whose work may.

An interesting aspect of this controversy is the claim that Aronson's cat work is not cited as much as it might be because the cat and rat people live in separate worlds. It has been claimed that rat experiments far outnumber cat experiments, and that while the rat people do not cite the cat literature, the cat people *do* cite the rat literature. Aronson himself asserts that, "the investigators of rat behavior seem to have a tradition of limiting their citations to rats (or rodents) even when they are aware of the research on other groups.... On the other hand, those working on the sex behavior of other species usually know the rat literature quite well and seem to cite it regularly. At least I do."[3] Gorski and Hart strongly support Aronson's claim of species discrimination, as does Beach, who also, after the publication of Wade's article, wrote a letter to the editor of *Science* defending the value of Aronson's research and its relevance to humans. [13] That letter was never published, so we decided to include it immediately after this essay on pages 13-14.

Robert Goy of the Wisconsin Regional Primate Research Center told us that, "Dr. Aronson works in a specialized field, and the number of other investigators working in the same field that might be likely to cite his work is relatively small.... Specifically with regard to his work on the importance of the genital sensory input, there is a lot of work going on in that area in the rat that I know of, and I think relatively few of the rat workers cite his work...."[14]

Goy pointed out that Aronson "has worked with fishes, frogs, lizards and a couple of different mammals. In other words, he has cut across all vertebral classes. His choice of mammals, I think, has been largely dictated by the fact that there were many people in this area who were working with rats, mice, hamsters, guinea pigs—common laboratory rodents—but very few people in comparative reproduction were working with species like dogs and cats."

Goy also claims that the rat people do not cite the cat people because of the restrictions journals place on bibliographies. "Today almost all leading journals require very conservative bibliographies," he said. "They don't like to give up space for comprehensive bibliographies. In fact, there are many journals that have ruled that the number of references used in an article should be limited to 20, and that if more than one reference is appropriate, to cancel them all and use a review article that cites all of the articles rather than citing each article separately. When authors are faced with restrictions like that, they don't cite primary sources as often as they should. If they did, I think Aronson's work would be more often cited."[14] I believe, however, that this contention is somewhat specious, since such practices affect the citation counts of all authors whose articles are superseded by citation of review articles.

B.L. Hart adds, "If Aronson didn't do his studies on cats there is a good chance that no one would do them. No one would do them on dogs, cats, or any intermediate species between primates and rats because of the expense and laboratory facilities needed and so forth. You cannot say that about work on rats. If someone doesn't do a study on rats, then another person is going to do it.... We really don't know how much we owe to Aronson in that respect."[8]

Of course, there is always the chance that Aronson's work has been premature,[15] or that he has produced a "stepping-stone" paper—one that helps someone else produce a classic, heavily cited paper. Perhaps Aronson illustrates the Ortega hypothesis.[16] Perhaps his contributions have been necessary to the achievement by others of more significant—and more highly cited—work. Or perhaps it is too early to tell. There is always the possibility that the citation record may change in the future, when the significance of the work is better appreciated or when other investigators are not inhibited from conducting related experiments.

In any research evaluation—and especially in analyses dealing with individual researchers—there are many caveats. The underlying assumptions and limitations must be clearly stated.[17] And the objective data obtained by counting citations must be viewed in the light of the subjective data provided by knowledgeable people. This example illustrates that a proper evaluation of an individual's work should not consist of a superficial examination of *SCI* or any other source.

The preceding analysis, which included testimony both from the *Science Citation Index* and from scientists themselves, has indicated that Lester R. Aronson's experimental work on cats has been reasonably valuable to the research community. This conclusion is important in light of recent events connected with the anti-vivisection controversy.

Over the past two years Lester Aronson has become the primary target for the outrage of a vocal group of anti-vivisectionists. On August 18, 1977, the residents of Lester Aronson's hometown received, in the mail, literature concerning his cat experiments. The literature included Dr. Aronson's home address and telephone number, and encouraged his neighbors to call him to voice their opinions of his research, as well as to write their Federal representatives and demand that their tax money "not be spent for torture of live animals in research."[18] This type of harassment of an individual scientist is unfortunate.

While it is clear that Lester Aronson's cat research does not merit the kind of furious criticism it has received, the case brings up some more fundamental issues. I am perplexed by the assertion that Aronson's work is deemed quite significant by Beach and others when their citation of his work is minimal. And I am increasingly suspicious of generalized claims that we can never know in advance (and often not even in retrospect) what value "basic" research may have in the future. In the days when there were just a few thousand people in the world doing basic research, such assertions were acceptable. But when the world's scientific population exceeds one million persons, we need something more than the bland assertions by established investigators or their peers that basic research pays off.

Finally, it is the responsibility of individuals like Aronson to do more than complain that the "rat people don't cite the cat people." In short, had Aronson done a bit of "selling" to his rat colleagues and perhaps helped to educate the public on the ramifications and value of his research, he might have prevented the unfortunate abuse heaped on him. In this respect the American Museum is equally at fault. But we should remember that most of Aronson's cat work was done when few people were questioning our medical research priorities.

REFERENCES

1. Garfield E. Citation analysis and the anti-vivisection controversy. *Current Contents* No. 17, 25 April 1977, p. 5-10.
2. Wade N. Animal rights: NIH cat sex study brings grief to New York museum. *Science* 194:162, 1976.
3. Aronson L R. Personal communication, 22 March 1977.
4. *Science Citation Index 1976 Annual Guide & Journal Lists.* Philadelphia: ISI®, 1977, p. 21.
5. Price D J D. Ethics of scientific publication. *Science* 144:655-7, 1964.
6. Beach F A. Personal communication, 26 September 1977.
7. Gorski R A. Personal communication, 26 September 1977.
8. Hart B L. Personal communication, 26 September 1977.
9. Garfield E. Is there a future for the scientific journal? *Current Contents* No. 31, 4 August 1975. Reprinted in: *Essays of an Information Scientist.* Philadelphia: ISI Press, 1977, Vol. 2, pp. 318-22.
10. Aronson L R. Animal welfare and scientific research. *Science* 194:784-5, 1976.
11. Koshy G P. The life expectancy of a scientific paper. *Fifth Annual Meeting. Northeast Regional Conference. American Institute for Decision Sciences. Proceedings.* (Naumes W, ed.) Philadelphia: AIDS, 1976, p. 224-227.
12. *Science Citation Index Five-Year Cumulation, 1970-1974.* Philadelphia: ISI, 1976, p. 17.
13. Beach F A. [Unpublished letter to the editor of *Science.*] 1 December 1976.
14. Goy R. Personal communication, 14 March 1977.
15. Lederberg J & Zuckerman H. Discontinuities in science; the case of bacterial recombination. *Daedalus* 1977 (in press).
16. Ortega y Gasset J. *The revolt of the masses.* New York: Norton, 1932, p. 84-85.
17. Garfield E. Restating the fundamental assumptions of citation analysis. *Current Contents* No. 39, 26 September 1977, p. 5-19.
18. Antivivisectionists escalate activities. *National Society for Medical Research Bulletin* 28:1, October 1977.

This letter was addressed to the editor of Science *on December 1, 1976, but was not accepted for publication. It is published here for the first time.*

December 1, 1976

Dear Sir:

Nicholas Wade's article on "animal rights" and Dr. L. R. Aronson's experiments at the American Museum of Natural History (*Science,* October 8) is of special concern to me for two reasons. First, I was Dr. Aronson's predecessor as Chairman of the Department of Animal Behavior at the Museum; and second, my own research over the past 40 years at the Museum, at Yale University and at the University of California in Berkeley has dealt with the same kind of problems with which Aronson has been dealing.

Mr. Wade's descriptions of reactions by opponents of such research indicate that these people do not understand what is being done or why. In fact I am not sure that Wade himself is entirely clear on these matters. The particular experiment chosen for the focal point of the emotional attack is a case in point. The purpose was to determine how and to what degree sensations from the penis influence sexual behavior. Anyone who has the slightest knowledge of human sexuality is aware that impotence in the male is one of the most common complaints bringing patients to the physician or sex counselor. The symptoms may consist of premature ejaculation or of inability to reach climax. Experiments on rats have demonstrated that males deprived of genital sensation exhibit predictable abnormalities of mating behavior. They are much less likely than normal males to ejaculate or achieve climax, and if they do so the time needed is much longer than normal.

If we can demonstrate similar symptoms in a number of other species, that may provide a rationale for treatment of some types of human impotence. Premature ejaculation may be delayed by decreasing penile sensitivity, and patients incapable of orgasm may be helped by increasing their genital responsiveness.

Other experiments conducted by Dr. Aronson and his associates at the Museum have already contributed importantly to our understanding of various factors that control sexual behavior in animals, and to some degree in man as well. They have shown, for example, that male cats which are altered (castrated) before acquiring mating experience are unlikely ever to achieve normal sexual performance, whereas males that have mated many times before operation are likely to retain their potency for long periods of time. Such findings have definite theoretical relevance to clinical problems of hypogonadism in men.

The fact that many studies carried out in the Department of Animal Behavior have yielded results with indirect bearing on human sexuality can be demonstrated, but this is not the major reason for supporting and encouraging such experimentation. The broader objective of achieving more complete knowledge of the ways in which any species reproduces is a central one to all of biology. Results of a given investigation may reveal similarities to human sexual psychology or they may demonstrate marked differences, and very often the differences are more illuminating than the similarities. For example, Dr. Aronson's work on the hormonal control of courtship and mating in fish fits in nicely with other experiments on amphibians, reptiles, birds and lower mammals to show that the human animal is nearly unique in a marked independence from hormonal control over sexual feelings and performance. This fact makes it easier for scientists to understand how it is possible for societies to control and redirect sexual impulses into a variety of nonreproductive but socially useful kinds of behavior. It also has bearing upon our understanding of some pressing issues such as the origins of homosexuality.

I suspect that one reason some laymen question the importance or value of studies such as the one singled out for criticism in Aronson's case is that they do not know the scientific literature well enough to see how separate studies in different laboratories fit together to provide answers to major issues in science. It takes a long time and many experiments by many scientists to arrive at a satisfactory answer to most basic problems. Any single investigation by itself may well appear pointless to a judge such as Mr. Henry Spiro, New York high school teacher and free-lance journalist who is identified by Nicholas Wade as "the chief architect" of the attack on Dr. Aronson and the American Museum of Natural History. Mr. Spiro and others of his persuasion are, of course, free to debate issues of ethics and morality, but any knowledgeable scientist must discount their judgmental assertions that experiments can just as well "use alternatives to live animals", or that particular experiments are "crude and routine and unlikely to produce any new knowledge." These are judgments that demand full familiarity with past and current research in the area under investigation as well as a grasp of theoretical issues with which nonspecialists have no acquaintance whatsoever.

One more aspect of Mr. Wade's article calls for special comment because it reflects upon Dr. Aronson's scientific reputation and indirectly involves the worthwhileness of the entire research program at the Museum. Under Dr. Aronson's leadership the Department of Animal Behavior has for nearly three decades served as a focus of original research, and a training ground for young scientists concerned with problems of behavior. Many graduate and undergraduate students have gone on from a period of apprenticeship at the Museum to take positions in major universities and research institutes and to develop their own worthwhile programs of research. This has constituted an important contribution by the American Museum to science, a contribution quite unique as museums go. Aronson's work itself is widely acknowledged to be of the highest quality. Many of his contributions are classic and have appeared in numerous reviews and textbooks on animal behavior.

Mr. Wade's critique states that the titles of some published reports from the museum do not appear in the *Science Citation Index®*, and he concludes therefore that these articles cannot have constituted important contributions to knowledge. The criterion is highly debatable since many workers, myself included, are influenced by papers we have read but have never had occasion to cite in our own publications. Research in my own laboratory certainly has been stimulated by publications of Dr. Aronson and his colleagues, and in my teaching I frequently use their experiments to illustrate important theoretical problems or useful methodological approaches; but this type of effect does not show up in the *Science Citation Index*.

Through its Director, Dr. Thomas D. Nicholson, the American Museum of Natural History has staunchly supported Dr. Aronson and his scientific work. Those of us who are committed to the importance of behavioral research, and who are aware of the important contributions which have been made by scientists working at the American Museum, hope that the lasting value of that research will continue to be recognized, and that emotional issues involved in the current teapot tempest will not exert any lasting detrimental effect on the scientific work in the Department of Animal Behavior.

Sincerely,

Frank A. Beach
Professor of Psychology
University of California
Berkeley, California 94720

CURRENT COMMENTS

The 250 Most-Cited Primary
Authors, 1961-1975. Part I.
How the Names Were Selected.

Number 49, December 5, 1977

Last year I promised to publish a list of the 250 most-cited primary authors based on data from the *Science Citation Index®* (*SCI®*).[1] I knew when I made the promise that someone would protest our failure to include author number 251. The situation would be similar to that in the French Academy, which limits membership to 40. New members can be elected only upon the death of an old member. Thus who sits waiting in the "41st chair" is a lively topic of discussion.

I certainly do *not* want to offend thousands of distinguished scientists whose names do not appear on this list. Therefore as a symbolic gesture I have omitted the final name. This list of the 250 most-cited primary authors contains only 249 names.

Since the amount of data involved is quite large, I will discuss this topic in three consecutive parts. This week's essay includes a general introduction to the list, which appears on pages 9-13. It also discusses how the list was assembled. Next week I will discuss the correlation of citedness with other forms of scientific recognition such as awards, prizes, and memberships in national academies of science. The following week I will list and discuss the most-cited publication written by each of the 250 authors.

Those unfamiliar with citation analysis may need some explanation of the mechanics of preparing a list of this type. Authors of scientific papers acknowledge prior work by citing it in their own papers. These acknowledgements, or citations, are regularly compiled in the *Science Citation Index,* enabling them to be counted and analyzed in other ways, either manually or by computer. Of course, there are many reasons why one author may cite another,[2] but in general we assume that the number of citations is positively correlated with the scientific value of the cited work. Papers which receive a large number of citations are usually found to have reported significant new scientific knowledge. And the most-cited authors are likely to be scientists who have had significant impact on the development of science.

It would have been easy to rank these authors according to their total citation counts over the 15-year period from 1961 to 1975. But we resisted the temptation to do this. Citation counts are significantly affected by many factors which

326

we did not and could not take into consideration in the time available. These factors include the author's age, the size of the author's field, the citation practices in that field, and the extent to which the field has been covered by the *SCI* since its inception in 1961. We can safely assert, however, that each of these 250 scientists has—for one reason or another—had substantial impact on the world's scientific community.

It is important to remember that this list is based only on primary-author data. A citation to a paper with three authors, for example, would be credited only to the first author. We are now working to remedy this bias by assembling a whole new data set based on citations to *all* authors. All-author data will produce a new list of highly cited authors, which can then be compared with the primary-author data. Such comparisons will tell us much about the effects of multiple authorship on citation counts. In a sense, this series of essays marks the end of the exclusive use of first-author data in compiling lists of highly cited scientists. I will elaborate on the implications of this change in Part Three.

Every author listed in Figure 1 has been cited more than 4,000 times, a yearly average of at least 266. Since the average yearly citation rate for cited authors in the *SCI* is only 7.48,[3] each of these 250 authors is clearly a citation superstar. But I hasten to add that a list of the next 1,000 most cited authors would *still* be composed exclusively of citation superstars. The difference between the group in Figure 1

and the next 250 most-cited authors is only 1,000 fewer citations over the same time period. Thus, there are 500 primary authors who were cited 3,000 or more times. And over 1,000 authors were cited 2,000 or more times in this period.

By listing authors alphabetically, rather than by citation rank, we have in effect adopted a kind of percentile ranking system. This method is similar to that used in Scholastic Aptitude Test (SAT) scores and other test results. In fact, if we assume that over one million scientists worldwide have worked over the same time period as these 250, the list in Figure 1 can be viewed as the 0.025 percentile, or the top quarter of one hundredth of one percent. The *thousand* most-cited authors would comprise the top one-tenth of one percent.

The list in Figure 1 is multidisciplinary. But similar listings based on citation counts could be developed for specific disciplines or specialties. Organic and inorganic chemistry predominate, with 81 authors (32.5% of the total). Biochemistry is represented by 42 authors (16.8%), physics including spectroscopy and mathematical physics by 40 authors (16.0%), and medicine including hematology, immunology, and pathology by 29 (11.6%). Eighteen authors are in life sciences, which include bacteriology, cytology, icthyology, microbiology, and zoology. Together, all of the disciplines mentioned above account for 84% of the 250 authors.

Of the remaining 16%, eleven authors are in physiology or histophysiology: NE Anden, DR Curtis,

JC Eccles, W Feldberg, RA Granit, B Katz, SS Kety, S Levine, H Selye, and US Von Euler. Ten authors are in mathematics or statistics: M Abramowitz, RE Bellman, N Bourbaki, S Chapman, CA Coulson, R Courant, ME Fisher, RA Fisher, A Erdelyi, and T Kato.

The list includes relatively few authors in other disciplines. However, pharmacology is represented by six authors: BB Brodie, JH Burn, A Carlsson, LS Goodman, OH Lowry, and EW Sutherland. Astrophysics and astronomy are represented by S Chandrasekhar, HL Johnson, and L Spitzer; statistics by GW Snedecor, RGD Steel, and BJ Winer; and psychology by RB Cattell, HJ Eysenck, and S Freud. Biophysics is represented by AL Hodgkin and HM McConnell. The list contains the name of only one metallurgist, M Hansen. Some fields, such as earth science, space science and botany, are not represented.

The representation on this list of given authors and disciplines is related not only to the stature of the authors but also to the amount of activity and the citation practices in their fields. For example, we know that the average number of cited references per paper differs significantly from one field to another. This can affect the average citation impact for authors in a given field. In recent years papers in biochemistry and molecular biology have contained an average of about 30 references each. Francis Narin of Computer Horizons has reported that biomedical research papers average 20 references, astronomy

and astrophysics 14, and physics 12.5.[4] But papers in general psychology average only 10 references, engineering and technology 6, and probability and statistics 5.6. Thus, the number of authors in each field who are on this list is at least roughly correlated with the average number of references per publication in the field. I would expect more authors in fields with few references to turn up in a listing of the 1,000 most cited authors.

The absence of botanists was particularly noteworthy, since the average number of references per publication in botany is about 12, which is higher than that for probability and statistics (5.6) or for engineering and technology (6), both of which *are* represented on the list. According to Dr. L. Andrew Staehelin of the Department of Molecular, Cellular and Developmental Biology at the University of Colorado, Boulder, whose education and experience are in botany, the absence of botanists from this list has two causes. "First, the lack of funding in the field has forced many of the leading botanists to leave, or to call themselves molecular biologists or cell biologists, and to center their research in these areas. This has left very few qualified scientists in the field, and in turn there are few educators to prepare future botanists. Secondly, the diversification of the field may be responsible. There are many highly specific areas in the botanical sciences; they may not be citing each other."[5]

Additional reasons for the absence of botanists from the list were advanced by Dr. Robert S. Platt,

Jr., of the Department of Botany at Ohio State University. He felt that the primary author bias was particularly significant in botany. Thus, if he is correct, the list discriminates against botanists. Whether professors of botany list their student co-authors first more often than other scientists remains to be seen. Dr. Platt also agreed with Dr. Staehelin about the narrow specialization of botanists, commenting, "Maybe there is some kind of citation barrier in botany, so that specific research in the field is only used and quoted by a limited number of other researchers in a very specific field." He went on, "There isn't a lot of cross-discipline referencing in botany. Maybe this could be turned into a real slam against botanists, that they get too narrow and don't understand anything that's going on outside their narrow field."[6] The lack of representation of agricultural disciplines might also indicate a lack of basic research in fields financed by departments of agriculture throughout the world.

In any case, it is certain that the lack of representation on this list of some scientific disciplines and specialities is an artifact of the activity and citation practices in the missing fields as well as of the limits on the length of the list we could publish. In the future we will reduce the bias of similar lists by using all-author data. We will also expand the most-cited author list to 1,000 or more names, and may list the most-cited authors in each speciality—even botany.

In Figure 1 the year of birth of each author appears in parentheses after the name. Some, of course, are now deceased. The average age overall is 63. This makes sense, since older scientists have been publishing—and therefore accumulating citations—longer than younger ones.

The list is composed mostly of those who have made their mark by continuous, usually quite prolific, contribution over the entire period from 1961 to 1975. That is why it contains the names of many scientists who are now in their 50s and 60s. Thirty-three of these 250 authors are (or would be) in their 40s, 82 in their 50s, 75 in their 60s, 34 in their 70s, 15 in their 80s and 8 in their 90s. The earliest-born scientist whose name appears on this list is Sigmund Freud, who was born in 1856 and died in 1939. The youngest is JD Bjorken, born in 1934.

For the most part, the citation rates of these 250 authors have remained static over the last two to three years. However, some have been changing, for better or worse. Although it can only be a rough indication at best, a pattern of ascending citations might help us identify those whose impact is increasing. A pattern of descending citations might help to identify those whose work was important, but is now being superseded by newer contributions.

We defined an ascending citation record as one which meets three conditions: (1) the number of cites (citations received) in 1974 is at least 10 greater than the average yearly number of cites from 1961-1975; (2) the number of cites in 1975

Figure 1. The 250 most-cited primary authors, based on *Science Citation Index*® data from 1961 to 1975. Birth date appears in parentheses after name. Ascending and descending arrows based partly on 1976 data (not shown).

	Total Citations 1961-75	Average Yearly Citations 1961-75	1974 Citations	1975 Citations	Ascending = ↑ Descending = ↓
Abragam A (1914)	6,769	451	628	608	
Abramowitz M (1915-1958)	5,108	340	720	667	
Abrikosov AA (1928)	5,429	362	407	305	
Albert A (1911)	8,664	578	586	521	
Allinger NL (1928)	4,140	276	375	323	
Allison AC (1928)	6,105	407	611	580	
Anden NE (1937)	5,147	343	884	762	
Anderson PW (1923)	6,787	452	788	600	
Andrews P (1928)	4,485	299	578	521	
Arnon DI (1910)	4,323	288	342	294	
Axelrod J (1912)	6,973	465	559	435	
Baker BR (1915)	5,395	360	230	190	↓
Bardeen J (1908)	4,788	319	365	257	
Barrer RM (1910)	5,230	349	408	279	
Bartlett PD (1907)	5,180	345	427	342	
Barton DHR (1918)	7,763	518	584	510	
Basolo F (1920)	4,083	272	394	285	
Basov NG (1922)	4,320	288	445	392	
Bates DR (1916)	6,925	462	440	340	↓
Bell RP (1907)	4,400	293	306	281	
Bellamy LJ (1916)	10,736	717	455	430	
Bellman RE (1920)	5,678	379	433	363	
Bender ML (1924)	4,924	328	341	300	
Benson SW (1918)	5,319	355	464	431	
Bergstrom S (1916)	4,473	298	348	280	
Berson SA (1918)	4,486	299	430	292	
Bethe HA (1906)	7,718	515	559	498	
Beutler E (1928)	5,636	376	481	449	
Billingham RE (1921)	6,269	418	268	248	↓
Birch AJ (1915)	4,339	289	292	231	
Bjorken JD (1934)	4,264	284	584	428	
Bloembergen N (1920)	5,234	349	318	334	
Born M (1882)	9,206	614	792	721	
Bourbaki N (——)	4,860	324	413	296	
Boyer PD (1918)	6,906	460	270	246	↓
Brachet J (1909)	5,956	397	191	119	
Braunwald E (1929)	4,980	332	390	375	
Bray GA (1931)	8,012	534	750	690	
Bridgman PW (1882-1961)	5,053	337	282	229	↓
Brodie BB (1909)	7,493	500	526	421	
Brown HC (1912)	16,623	1,108	1,257	1,153	
Brown JB (1899)	4.074	272	197	187	
Buckingham AD (1930)	4,332	289	423	372	
Budzikiewicz H (1933)	5,089	339	456	320	
Bunnett JF (1921)	4,370	291	312	294	
Burn JH (1892)	5,650	377	191	158	↓
Burnet FM (1899)	5,553	370	384	301	
Burton K (1926)	6,913	461	728	674	
Busing WR (1923)	5,066	338	518	448	

Figure 1. The 250 most-cited primary authors (continued)

	Total Citations 1961-75	Average Yearly Citations 1961-75	1974 Citations	1975 Citations	Ascending = ↑ Descending = ↓
Carlson LA (1928)	4,282	285	400	338	
Carlsson A (1923)	7,697	515	675	554	
Cattell RB (1905)	4,190	279	337	249	
Chance B (1913)	16,306	1,087	952	824	↓
Chandrasekhar S (1910)	8,179	545	724	594	
Chapman S (1888-1970)	5,235	349	326	285	↓
Chatt J (1914)	6,692	446	641	521	
Clementi E (1931)	5,684	379	637	579	
Cohen MH (1927)	4,808	321	404	389	
Conney AH (1930)	5,151	343	491	458	
Cope AC (1909)	5,269	351	281	242	↓
Corey EJ (1928)	9.901	660	1,045	1,031	
Cotton FA (1930)	12,901	860	1,416	1,493	↑
Coulson CA (1910)	6,569	438	440	362	
Courant R (1888)	4,154	277	323	255	
Cram DJ (1919)	6,148	410	391	288	↓
Cromer DT (1923)	5,148	361	933	1,029	↑
Cruickshank DWJ (1924)	4,512	301	259	258	
Cuatrecasas P (1903)	4,484	299	1,060	1,064	
Curtis DR (1927)	4,794	320	614	470	
Dacie JV (1912)	4,323	288	317	242	
Dalgarno A (1928)	5,365	358	460	395	
Davis BJ (1932)	7,074	472	1,079	989	
Dawson RMC (1924)	4,125	275	297	269	
DeDuve C (1917)	8,445	563	645	567	
DeRobertis E (1913)	4,801	320	269	205	↓
Dewar MJS (1918)	9,800	653	1,017	955	
Dische Z (1895)	7.874	525	485	367	
Dixon M (1899)	6,331	422	543	508	
Djerassi C (1923)	8,520	568	362	286	↓
Doering WVE (1917)	4,253	284	310	222	
Dole VP (1913)	5,902	393	414	342	
Duncan DB (1925)	4,153	277	311	285	
Eagle H (1905)	6,498	433	435	326	
Eccles JC (1903	10,104	674	802	545	
Eigen M (1927)	4,980	332	441	379	
Eliel EL (1921)	8,615	574	650	575	
Erdelyi A (1908)	5,978	399	390	377	
Eysenck HJ (1916)	5,241	349	379	307	
Fahey JL (1924)	4,724	315	277	235	
Falck B (1927)	4,275	285	375	290	
Farquhar MG (1928)	4,525	302	337	268	
Fawcett DW (1917)	6,236	416	505	378	
Feigl F (1891)	4,074	272	154	165	
Feldberg W (1900)	4,762	317	394	281	
Feynman RP (1918)	6,031	402	708	567	
Fieser LF (1899)	9,392	626	634	527	
Fischer EO (1918)	4,788	319	443	413	
Fisher ME (1931)	4,289	286	565	510	
Fisher RA (1890-1962)	8,336	556	672	617	

Figure 1. The 250 most-cited primary authors (continued)

	Total Citations 1961-75	Average Yearly Citations 1961-75	1974 Citations	1975 Citations	Ascending = ↑ Descending = ↓
Fiske CH (1890)	8,249	550	572	505	
Flory PJ (1910)	10,247	683	928	795	
Folch J (1917)	9,693	646	899	820	
Fraenkel-Conrat H (1910)	4,376	292	197	187	↓
Fredrickson DS (1924)	6,897	460	783	740	
Freud S (1856-1939)	8,490	566	633	530	
Friedel J (1921)	4,325	288	356	277	
Gell-Mann M (1929)	9,669	645	585	404	↓
Gilman H (1893)	7,849	523	503	435	↓
Ginzburg VL (1916)	6,834	456	530	445	
Glasstone S (1897)	5,080	339	295	289	
Gomori G (1904)	7,136	476	445	327	
Good RA (1922)	4,607	307	296	232	↓
Goodman LS (1906)	5,627	375	399	413	↑
Goodwin TW (1919)	4,727	315	243	224	↓
Gornall AG (1914)	5,921	395	532	470	
Grabar P (1898)	4,717	314	176	166	↓
Granit RA (1900)	4,629	309	245	210	↓
Green DE (1926)	4,708	314	271	163	
Gutowsky HS (1919)	4,286	286	254	223	↓
Hansen M (1921)	4,262	350	398	377	
Harned HS (1921)	4,960	331	306	276	↓
Herbert V (1927)	4,106	274	333	316	
Herzberg G (1904)	13,110	874	1,095	972	
Hirs CHW (1923)	4,578	305	322	320	
Hirschfelder JO (1911)	7,033	469	496	414	
Hodgkin AL (1914)	7,500	500	513	505	
Horner L (1911)	4,469	298	299	303	
House HO (1929)	4,393	293	484	504	↑
Hubel DH (1926)	4,640	309	562	532	
Huisgen R (1920)	9,309	621	801	772	
Huxley HE (1924)	4,073	272	300	318	
Ingold CK (1893)	4,198	280	244	171	
Jackman LM (1926)	4,927	328	325	326	
Jacob F (1920)	7,101	473	301	219	
Jaffé HH (1919)	5,106	340	344	229	
Johnson HL (1933)	4,117	274	367	337	
Jorgensen CK (1931)	6,049	403	545	472	
Kabat EA (1914)	7,529	502	450	419	↓
Karnovsky MJ (1926)	5,616	374	660	635	
Karplus M (1930)	5,770	385	415	292	
Kato T (1917)	4,138	276	597	522	
Katritzky AR (1928)	4,704	314	355	292	
Katz B (1911)	4,690	313	486	512	↑
Keilin D (1887)	4,121	275	163	131	
Kety SS (1915)	4,594	306	297	281	↓
King RB (1903	5,109	340	569	550	
Kirkwood JG (1907-1959)	4,084	272	339	291	
Kittel C (1916)	5,591	373	451	407	
Klein G (1925)	4,430	295	519	409	

Figure 1. The 250 most-cited primary authors (continued)

	Total Citations 1961-75	Average Yearly Citations 1961-75	1974 Citations	1975 Citations	Ascending = ↑ Descending = ↓
Klotz IM (1916)	4,151	277	328	292	
Kolthoff IM (1894)	9,697	646	642	511	
Kornberg A (1918)	4,548	303	240	238	
Krebs HA (1900)	7,657	510	578	539	
Kubo R (1920)	4,232	282	436	395	
Kuhn R (1900-1967)	7,488	499	401	333	
Landau LD (1908-1968)	18,888	1,259	1,767	1,533	
Lee TD (1926)	4,879	325	317	289	↓
Lehninger AL (1917)	5,507	367	410	369	
Lemieux RU (1920)	4,619	308	360	308	
Levine S (1921)	4,035	269	351	349	
Lineweaver H (1907)	5,202	347	386	325	
Löwdin PO (1916)	5,060	337	413	325	
Lowry OH (1910)	58,304	3,887	7,904	7,565	
Luft JH (1927)	8,926	595	795	671	
Marmur J (1926)	6,475	432	519	407	
McConnell HM (1927)	5,490	366	381	366	
McKusick VA (1921)	4,181	279	371	284	
Miller JFA (1931)	6,371	425	494	446	
Millonig G (1925)	4,106	274	238	209	
Mitchell P (1883)	4,086	272	455	447	
Monod J (1910)	4,791	319	383	328	
Moore S (1913)	8,167	544	560	554	
Morse PM (1903)	5,089	339	416	349	
Mott NF (1905)	10,473	698	901	885	
Muller A (1931)	4,500	300	464	344	
Müller E (1912)	4,664	311	322	249	
Mulliken RS (1896)	10,508	701	804	725	
Nakamoto K (1922)	5,132	342	492	472	
Natta G (1903)	5,735	382	246	251	
Nesmeyanov AN (1899)	6,783	452	620	457	
Newman MS (1908)	4,730	315	266	235	↓
Novikoff AB (1913)	7,662	511	500	371	↓
Olah GA (1927)	8,311	554	1,083	896	
Ouchterlony O (1914)	5,986	399	501	476	
Palade GE (1912)	5,969	398	218	216	
Pauling L (1901)	15,662	1,044	1,271	1,095	
Pearse AGE (1916)	10,522	701	879	775	
Perutz MF (1914)	4,263	284	579	533	
Pople JA (1925)	15,135	1,009	1,572	1,263	
Prigogine I (1917)	4,681	312	373	290	
Racker E (1913)	4,567	304	356	384	↑
Reed LJ (1926)	4,290	286	300	316	↑
Reynolds ES (1928)	10,115	674	1,084	903	
Roberts JD (1918)	4,501	300	251	226	
Robinson RA (1914)	5,543	370	411	419	
Rose ME (1911)	4,127	275	224	173	
Rossini FD (1899)	4,105	274	136	132	
Russell GA (1925)	5,933	396	364	275	↓
Sabatini DD (1931)	6,205	414	226	197	

Figure 1. The 250 most-cited primary authors (continued)

	Total Citations 1961-75	Average Yearly Citations 1961-75	1974 Citations	1975 Citations	Ascending = ↑ Descending = ↓
Scatchard G (1892)	4,191	279	544	511	
Scheidegger JJ (1900)	4,159	277	283	218	
Schneider WC (1919)	7,029	469	419	376	↓
Schwarzenbach G (1904)	4,618	308	309	312	
Schwinger J (1918)	4,855	324	437	367	
Seeger A (1914)	4,757	317	375	335	
Seitz F (1911)	5,396	360	130	129	
Selye H (1907)	8,928	595	480	339	
Seyferth D (1929)	4,462	297	447	368	
Sillen LG (1916)	4,375	292	583	436	
Skou JC (1918)	4,127	275	345	297	
Slater JC (1926)	7,587	506	761	650	
Smith HW (1895-1962)	5,392	359	259	387	
Smithies O (1925)	6,192	413	266	256	↓
Snedecor GW(1881-1974)	14,762	984	1,502	1,395	
Somogyi M (1883-1971)	4,465	298	262	208	
Spackman DH (1924)	6,889	459	528	495	
Spitzer L (1914)	4,238 .	283	410	417	
Stahl E (1924)	6,252	417	375	294	
Steel RGD (1917)	5,100	340	665	617	
Streitwieser A (1927)	7,511	501	557	396	
Sutherland EW (1915-1974)	5,150	343	432	384	
Taft RW (1922)	5,083	339	332	322	
Tanford C (1921)	5,934	396	534	589	↑
Udenfriend S (1918)	5,039	336	346	313	
Umbreit WW (1913)	5,229	349	297	224	
Van Slyke DD (1883)	4,282	285	147	130	
Van Vleck JH (1899)	·5,449	363	321	298	
von Euler US (1905)	8,728	582	483	375	↓
Walling C (1916)	5,590	373	349	315	↓
Warburg O (1883)	7,463	498	425	332	
Warren L (1924)	4,303	287	478	448	
Watson ML (1912)	4,176	278	282	217	
Weber G (1922)	8,319	555	534	507	↓
Weber K (1916)	5,823	388	1,409	1,481	↑
Weinberg S (1933)	6,306	420	959	734	
Weiss P (1911)	4,048	269	243	239	
Wiberg KB (1927)	5,461	364	445	387	
Wieland T (1913)	4,423	295	253	179	↓
Wigglesworth VB (1899)	4,489	299	343	319	
Wigner EP (1902)	4,948	330	366	297	
Wilson EB (1908)	5,139	342	385	357	
Winer BJ (1917)	5,145	343	667	622	
Winstein S (1912)	7,884	526	489	433	
Wittig G (1928)	6,079	405	358	304	↓
Woodward RB (1917)	7,069	471	661	497	
Zachariasen WH (1906)	4,050	270	310	310	
Zeldovich YB (1914)	4,794	320	477	473	
Ziman JM (1925)	4,499	300	379	299	
Zimmerman HE (1926)	4,217	281	457	325	

is at least 10 greater than the number in 1974; and (3) the number of cites in 1976 is at least ten greater than the number in 1975. According to this definition, only 9 of the 250 scientists have ascending citation rates. They are FA Cotton, C Tanford, K Weber, LS Goodman, DT Cromer, B Katz, E Racker, HO House, and LJ Reed.

The definition for ascending rates was inverted to define descending rates. In contrast to the relatively small number of authors with ascending citations, we identified 35 authors with descending citation rates. Although one might expect to find a difference in the ages of ascending and descending authors, we found no significant difference in the average ages of each group.

Some of the names which appeared on the original computer printout from which this list was derived proved to be homographs (the same name representing two or more individuals). While these were not difficult to detect, it was not easy to separate the publications of each person involved. For example, at first we assumed the name K Alder represented the Nobel Prize winning German chemist. However, many of the citations to K Alder were to papers published after 1958, the year the Nobel Prize winner died. Finally, we found that K Alder represented both the German chemist and a highly cited Swiss physicist.

In some cases we have retained names we know to be homographs. For instance, Henry Clay Brown III of the University of Florida has published 20 articles in organic chem-

istry. But the HC Brown on our list is Herbert Charles Brown of Purdue University, who has published 697 articles in inorganic chemistry.

Our most complex homograph problem concerned the name "E Fischer." There are *seven* Fischers with the first initial "E" listed in *World Who's Who in Science:*[7] Eric Horst Fischer, Ernst Georg Fischer, Ernst Otto Fischer, Ernst Sigismund Fischer, and *two* scientists by the name of Emil Fischer. We also found that the name "E Fischer" combined Emil Fischer, the German chemist and Nobel Prize winner born in 1852, with Emil Fischer, the Swiss physiologist born in 1868. Both were deleted from Figure 1. It is possible, although very difficult, to separate the citations received by the two Emils by carefully examining the dates of publication, journals, and titles cited. If this were done, one or both of the E Fischers might have remained on the list.

Others were eliminated from the list because they were editors, compilers, or authors of textbooks rather than reports of original research. These included SP Colowick, who was the editor of a monographic series;[8] AI Vogel, whose two textbooks account for about two thirds of his total citations;[9,10] CE Moore, who compiled a monograph on atomic energy levels;[11] RD Lillie, author of a textbook on histochemistry;[12] HU Bergmeyer, editor of a book on methods of enzymatic analysis;[13] and GEW Wolstenholme, the director of the CIBA Foundation and an editor of many CIBA studies.

However, we have decided to retain another "corporate" name on the list. Nicolas Bourbaki is the collective pseudonym for a group of French mathematicians who have written a 36-volume survey of mathematics. Although the group's membership has changed since its formation in the late 1930's, the identities of the mathematicians who have contributed to the Bourbaki books have been kept a secret.

Some readers might believe that this listing of most-cited individual scientists is simply an extension of our society's fascination with celebrities. This phenomenon is evident from the growing popularity of newspaper columns and whole magazines devoted solely to gossip. But it is absurd to compare our list of 250 most-cited scientists to a list of the most popular pop singers.

Whether the personalities behind the scientific names are charismatic or not, the publication evidence is clear that their work has been empirically important in the advance of science. These names represent, among other things, pockets of scientific creativity and activity, past and present. They may sometimes be indicators of the future.

In the next chapter of this study you can observe the high correlation between citation counts and other forms of scientific recognition. Those scientists who have been well recognized by society or their peers will not object to these listings. And if our studies call attention to the work of other individuals who, by other criteria, have not been adequately recognized, then I feel our efforts will have been well rewarded.

1. **Garfield E.** And who shall occupy the 250th chair among the citation immortals? *Current Contents®* No. 22, 31 May 1976, p. 5-6. Reprinted in *Essays of an Information Scientist* Philadelphia: ISI® Press, 1977. Vol. 2, p. 496-497.
2. ———————. To cite or not to cite. *Current Contents* No. 35, 29 August 1977, p. 5-7.
3. *Science Citation Index 1976 Annual Guide & Journal Lists.* Philadelphia: ISI, 1977, p. 21.
4. **Narin F.** *Evaluative bibliometrics: the use of publication and citation analysis in the evaluation of scientific activity.* Cherry Hill, New Jersey: Computer Horizons, Inc., 1976, p. 169-175. NTIS-PB252339/AS.
5. **Staehelin L A.** Personal communication. 8 November 1977.
6. **Platt R S Jr.** Personal communication. 8 November 1977.
7. **Debus A G.** *World Who's Who in Science.* Chicago: Marquis—Who's Who Inc., 1968, p. 569.
8. **Colowick S P & Kaplan N O.** *Methods in enzymology.* New York: Academic Press, 1955-1973. 28 Vols.
9. **Vogel A I.** *Textbook of quantitative inorganic analysis.* New York: Longman, 1972.1216 pp.
10. **Vogel A I.** *Textbook of practical organic chemistry.* New York: Halsted, 1956. Vol. 1. 1188 pp.
11. **Moore C E.** *National Bureau of Standards circular no. C467. Atomic energy levels.* Washington DC: US Government Printing Office, 1949. Vol. 1. 309 pp.
12. **Lillie R D.** *Histopathologic technic and practical histochemistry.* New York: McGraw, 1965. 715 pp.
13. **Bergmeyer H U.** *Methods of enzymatic analysis.* New York: Academic Press, 1974. 4 Vols. 2302 pp.

The 250 Most-Cited Primary Authors, 1961-1975.
Part II. The Correlation Between Citedness,
Nobel Prizes, and Academy Memberships

//Number 50, December 12, 1977

The value of citation analysis for identifying important scientific work has been amply illustrated by the many studies we have reported on highly cited papers, journals, and authors. It is less well known that a high correlation exists between citedness and other forms of scientific recognition. The purpose of this essay is to document this correlation for the 250 most-cited primary authors. Last week we explained how the names were selected.[1] This week we've added data on the most visible forms of scientific recognition: the Nobel prize and membership in a national academy of science. Next week we'll provide the most-cited publication for each of these same 250 authors.

In Figure 1 on pages 7-9 we have listed the 250 most-cited primary authors. Actually there are only 249, since one name was omitted to symbolize the lack of precision in such compilations. Each author's total citation count from 1961 to 1975 is provided, as well as memberships in national academies of science. The names of Nobel prize winners are printed in bold-face type, followed by the year the prize was awarded and a code indicating the subject area.

Our rationale for including data only on Nobel prizes and memberships in national academies of science is simply that these are the two most significant and most visible indicators of scientific status. In one study, Jonathan and Stephen Cole asked 1,278 physicists in the United States to rate 98 honorific awards in terms of visibility and prestige. The Nobel prize ranked first, followed closely by membership in national academies of science. Taken together, the Nobel and academy membership "stand out above all the rest," the Coles said.[2] (p. 47)

Our list includes 42 Nobel prize winners: 15 in physiology or medicine, 14 in physics, and 13 in chemistry. Thus, 17% of the 250 most-cited authors are Nobel laureates.

Since 1901, when the first Nobel prize was awarded, 320 persons have become laureates in the sciences. These include 121 in physiology or medicine, 109 in physics, and 90 in chemistry. A single prize can be shared by more than one individual, and a single individual can win more than one prize. Thirteen percent of *all* Nobelists appear on our list.

What about the 278 Nobel prize winners who are *not* on this list of

250 most-cited authors? Many won their prizes for work done in the late nineteenth and early twentieth centuries. While the work of such early pioneers is still cited quite often, it is not surprising that the citation rate has fallen off after so many years. Of course, many more Nobel laureates will show up when we extend our list to include the 1,000 most-cited authors. This would include authors who had been cited about 2,000 or more times. If we extend the list to the 5,000 most-cited authors, it would include all but perhaps a few Nobelists. And even 5,000 authors represent less than 1% of all publishing scientists, past and present!

I believe it is axiomatic that not all the best qualified people have received the Nobel prize. There's no shortage of deserving people. We can be thankful for this. It would be terrible indeed if the prize fell into disrepute because of a shortage of first-rate scientists. That many deserving people, including most-cited scientists, have not won the prize does not indicate a deficiency in today's criteria for selecting winners; it simply indicates an abundance of first-rate candidates.

Certainly membership in a national academy of science is a less exclusive honor than the Nobel. Nevertheless, the number of memberships in each national academy is usually strictly limited. The United States National Academy of Science (NAS) had 1,182 members in 1976. The NAS admits up to 75 new members per year. Since there were over 155,000 publishing scientists in the United States in 1976,[3] Academy members comprised an elite 0.7% of all publishing American scientists.

National academies are well represented among these 250 most cited authors. One hundred and ten —44%—have been elected to the NAS. This accounts for about 9% of the total NAS membership. Fifty-five of the 250 authors belong to the Royal Society of London—about 6% of its total membership of 836. Seven authors belong to the 226-member French Academy of Sciences. Incidentally, the latter should not be confused with the 40-member French Academy.

Seven authors belong to the 766-member Soviet Academy of Sciences. Since our counts are based on 1961-1975 data, there *may* be some underrepresentation here due to less coverage of Soviet literature in the early days of the *SCI®* .

Three authors belong to the 437-member Royal Society of Canada and 3 to the 276-member Royal Swedish Academy of Sciences. Thus, 151 of these 250 most cited authors—or over 60%—are members of at least one national academy.

There is a considerable amount of overlap between the Nobel prizes and memberships in national academies of science. Ninety-two percent of Nobel winners on the list are also members of their national academies. And over a quarter of the academy members on our list have won the Nobel prize.

Simply for lack of time and re-

Figure 1. Nobel Prizes and memberships in national academies of science among the 250 most-cited primary authors, 1961-1975. The selection of authors is based on data from the *Science Citation Index®* . Names of Nobel laureates appear in bold type, followed by year and category of prize; P = physics, C = chemistry, M = physiology or medicine. Correspondents, fellows, foreign members, and foreign associates are included as members of their respective national academies.

Name	Total Citations 1961-1975	National Academy	Name	Total Citations 1961-1975	National Academy
Abragam A	6,769	France	Brodie BB	7,493	U.S.
Abramowitz M	5,108		Brown HC	16,623	U.S.
Abrikosov AA	5,429	U.S.S.R.	Brown JB	4,074	
Albert A	8,664		Buckingham AD	4,332	U.K.
Allinger NL	4,140		Budzikiewicz H	5,089	
Allison AC	6,105		Bunnett JF	4,370	
Anden NE	5,147		Burn JH	5,650	U.K.
Anderson PW (77P)	6,787	U.S.	**Burnet FM** (60M)	5,553	U.K., U.S.
Andrews P	4,485		Burton K	6,913	U.K.
Arnon DI	4,323	U.S.	Busing WR	5,066	
Axelrod J (70M)	6,973	U.S.	Carlson LA	4,282	
Baker BR	5,395		Carlsson A	7,697	
Bardeen J (56P)	4,788	U.S., U.K.	Cattell RB	4,190	
(72P)			Chance B	16,306	U.S.
Barrer RM	5,230	U.K.	Chandrasekhar S	8,179	U.S., U.K.
Bartlett PD	5,180	U.S.	Chapman S	5,235	U.K., U.S.
Barton DHR (69C)	7,763	U.K., U.S.	Chatt J	6,692	U.K.
Basolo F	4,083		Clementi E	5,684	
Basov NG (64 P)	4,320	U.S.S.R.	Cohen MH	4,808	
Bates DR	6,925	U.K.	Conney AH	5,151	
Bell RP	4,400	U.K., U.S.	Cope AC	5,269	
Bellamy LJ	10,736		Corey EJ	9,901	U.S.
Bellman RE	5,678		Cotton FA	12,901	U.S.
Bender ML	4,924	U.S.	Coulson CA	6,569	U.K.
Benson SW	5,319		Courant R	4,154	
Bergstrom S	4,473	Sweden, U.S.	Cram DJ	6,148	U.S.
Berson SA	4,486		Cromer DT	5,418	
Bethe HA (67P)	7,718	U.S., U.K.	Cruickshank DWJ	4,512	
Beutler E	5,636	U.S.	Cuatrecasas P	4,484	
Billingham RE	6,269	U.K.	Curtis DR	4,794	
Birch AJ	4,339	U.K.	Dacie JV	4,323	U.K.
Bjorken JD	4,264	U.S.	Dalgarno A	5,365	U.K.
Bloembergen N	5,234	U.S.	Davis BJ	7,074	
Born M (54 P)	9,206	U.S.	Dawson RMC	4,125	
Bourbaki N	4,860		**DeDuve C** (74 M)	8,445	U.S., Belgium
Boyer PD	6,906	U.S.	DeRobertis E	4,801	
Brachet J	5,956	U.S., U.K.	Dewar MJS	9,800	U.K.
		France	Dische Z	7,874	U.S.
Braunwald E	4,980	U.S.	Dixon M	6,331	U.K.
Bray GA	8,012		Djerassi C	8,520	U.S.
Bridgman PW (46P)	5,053	U.S., U.K.	Doering WVE	4,253	U.S.

Figure 1. Nobel prizes and memberships in national academies of science among the 250 most-cited primary authors, 1961-1975 (continued).

Name	Total Citations 1961-1975	National Academy	Name	Total Citations 1961-1975	National Academy
Dole VP	5,902	U.S.	Hirs CHW	4,578	
Duncan DB	4,153		Hirschfelder JO	7,033	U.S.
Eagle H	6,498	U.S.	Hodgkin AL (63 M)	7,500	U.K., U.S.
Eccles J C (63M)	10,104	U.K., U.S.	Horner L	4,469	
Eigen M (67C)	4,980	U.K., U.S.	House HO	4,393	
Eliel EL	8,615	U.S.	Hubel DH	4,640	U.S.
Erdelyi A	5,978	U.K.	Huisgen R	9,309	F.R.G., G.D.R.
Eysenck HJ	5,241		Huxley HE	4,073	U.K.
Fahey JL	4,724		Ingold CK	4,198	
Falck B	4,275		Jackman LM	4,927	
Farquhar MG	4,525		Jacob F (65 M)	7,101	U.K. U.S.,
Fawcett DW	6,236	U.S.			France
Feigl F	4,074		Jaffé HH	5,106	
Feldberg W	4,762	U.K.	Johnson HL	4,117	U.S.
Feynman RP (65P)	6,031	U.S., U.K	Jorgensen CK	6,049	Denmark
Fieser LF	9,392	U.S.	Kabat EA	7,529	U.S.
Fischer EO (73C)	4,788		Karnovsky MJ	5,616	
Fisher ME	4,289	U.K.	Karplus M	5,770	U.S.
Fisher RA	8,336	U.K.	Kato T	4,138	
Fiske CH	8,249		Katritzky AR	4,704	
Flory PJ (74 C)	10,247	U.S.	Katz B (70 M)	4,690	U.K., U.S.
Folch J	9,693		Keilin D	4,121	
Fraenkel-Conrat H	4,376	U.S.	Kety SS	4,594	U.S.
Fredrickson DS	6,897	U.S.	King RB	5,109	
Freud S	8,490	U.K.	Kirkwood JG	4,084	U.S.
Friedel J	4,325	France	Kittel C	5,591	U.S.
Gell-Mann M (69 P)	9,669	U.S.	Klein G	4,430	U.S.
Gilman H	7,849	U.S., U.K.	Klotz IM	4,151	U.S.
Ginzburg VL	6,834	U.S.S.R.	Kolthoff IM	9,697	U.S.
Glasstone S	5,080		Kornberg A (59 M)	4,548	U.S., U.K.
Gomori G	7,136		Krebs HA (53 M)	7,.657	U.K., U.S.
Good RA	4,607	U.S.	Kubo R	4,232	U.S.
Goodman LS	5,627	U.S.	Kuhn R (38C)	7,488	
Goodwin TW	4,727	U.K.	Landau LD (62 P)	18,888	U.S.S.R.
Gornall AG	5,921	Canada	Lee T D (57 P)	4,879	U.S.
Grabar P	4,717		Lehninger AL	5,507	U.S.
Granit RA (67 M)	4,629	U.K., U.S.,	Lemieux RU	4,619	Canada, U.K.
		Sweden	Levine S	4,035	
Green DE	4,708	U.S.	Lineweaver H	5,202	
Gutowsky HS	4,286	U.S.	Löwdin PO	5,060	Sweden,
Hansen M	5,262	U.S.			Norway
Harned HS	4,960	U.S.	Lowry OH	58,304	U.S.
Herbert V	4,106		Luft JH	8,926	
Herzberg G (71 C)	13,110	U.S., U.K.,	Marmur J	6,475	
		Canada	McConnell HM	5,490	U.S.

Figure 1. Nobel prizes and memberships in national academies of science among the 250 most-cited primary authors, 1961-1975 (continued).

Name	Total Citations 1961-1975	National Academy	Name	Total Citations 1961-1975	National Academy
McKusick VA	4,181		Seitz F	5,396	U.S.
Miller JFA	6,371	U.K.	Selye H	8,928	Canada
Millonig G	4,106		Seyferth D	4,462	
Mitchell P	4,086	U.K.	Sillen LG	4,375	
Monod J (65 M)	4,791	U.S.	Skou JC	4,127	
Moore S (72 C)	8,167	U.S.	Slater JC	7,587	U.S.
Morse PM	5,089	U.S.	Smith HW	6,946	
Mott NF (77 P)	10,473	U.K., U.S.	Smithies O	6,192	U.S.
Muller A	4,500		Snedecor GW	14,762	
Müller E	4,664	U.S.	Somogyi M	4,465	
Mulliken RS (66 C)	10,508	U.S., U.K.	Spackman DH	6,889	
Nakamoto K	5,132		Spitzer L	4,238	U.S.
Natta G (63 C)	5,735	Italy, France, U.S.S.R.	Stahl E	6,252	
			Steel RGD	5,100	
			Streitwieser A	7,511	U.S.
Nesmeyanov AN	6,783	U.S.S.R., U.K.	Sutherland EW (71 M)	5,150	
			Taft RW	5,083	
Newman MS	4,730	U.S.	Tanford C	5,934	U.S.
Novikoff AB	7,662	U.S.	Udenfriend S	5,039	U.S.
Olah GA	8,311	U.S.	Umbreit WW	5,229	
Ouchterlony O	5,986		Van Slyke DD	4,282	
Palade GE (74 M)	5,969		Van Vleck JH (77 P)	5,449	U.S., U.K., France
Pauling L (54 C)	15,662	U.S., France, U.K., U.S.S.R.	von Euler US (70M)	8,728	U.S., U.K.
(62 Peace)			Walling C	5,590	U.S.
Pearse AGE	10,522		Warburg O (31 M)	7,463	U.K.
Perutz MF (62 C)	4,263	U.K., U.S., France	Warren L	4,303	
			Watson ML	4,176	
Pople JA	15,135	U.K.	Weber G	8,319	U.S.
Prigogine I (77C)	4,681	U.S.	Weber K	5,823	
Racker E	4,567	U.S.	Weinberg S	6,306	U.S.
Reed LJ	4,290	U.S.	Weiss P	4,048	U.S.
Reynolds ES	10,115		Wiberg KB	5,461	U.S.
Roberts JD	4,501	U.S.	Wieland T	4,423	
Robinson RA	5,543		Wigglesworth VB	4,489	U.K., U.S.
Rose ME	4,127		Wigner EP (63P)	4,948	U.S., U.K.
Rossini FD	4,105	U.S.	Wilson EB	5,139	U.S.
Russell GA	5,933		Winer BJ	5,145	
Sabatini DD	6,205		Winstein S	7,884	
Scatchard G	4,191		Wittig G	6,079	France
Scheidegger JJ	4,159		Woodward RB (65 C)	7,069	U.S., U.K.
Schneider WC	7,029		Zachariasen WH	4,050	U.S.
Schwarzenbach G	4,618		Zeldovich YB	4,794	U.S.S.R.
Schwinger J (65 P)	4,855	U.S.	Ziman JM	4,499	U.K.
Seeger A	4,757		Zimmerman HE	4,217	

sources we have not included information on other honors and awards. This does *not* mean that other prizes, awards or honors are less prestigious than the two we have discussed. There are numerous prizes, medals, awards, fellowships, and honors—some bestowed by local societies, some by national organizations, and some by international groups—which I believe are equally indicative of merit or impact. Since the prize is not awarded in such fields as engineering, mathematics, botany, and earth science, other awards are clearly *better* indicators of recognition in these fields than the Nobel prize.

The 250 listed authors have all made significant contributions to science. The citation record confirms this impact. Thus, almost all can be expected to have been recognized or honored in some way. For example, VL Ginzburg won the Lenin State Prize in Science and Technology as well as the Lomonosov Prize. RA Good received the Albert Lasker Medical Research Award. FA Cotton won the Leon H. Baekeland Award for industrial chemistry. EJ Corey has received numerous awards of the American Chemical Society. JA Pople received the American Chemical Society's Irving Langmuir Award in Chemical Physics. And EP Wigner, HA Bethe, F Seitz, B Chance, M Gell-Mann, and J Bardeen have all received the Franklin Institute's Gold Medal.

Since it is awarded only to Americans, we have not indicated which authors have received the National Medal of Science (NMS). Awarded annually in the United States since 1962, the NMS recognizes work in the physical, mathematical, biological, and engineering sciences. As of 1975, 117 scientists had received it. Twenty-six, or 10.4%, of our 250 authors have won the NMS. These 26 include nine Nobelists and 22 NAS members. E Racker, M Cohen, HS Gutowsky, and FD Rossini were among the 15 NMS winners announced as this piece went to press.

The relationship between citedness and the NMS has also been investigated by Cole and Cole. Examining citations in only one year, 1965, they found that Nobel laureates from 1955 to 1965 averaged 199 citations, while winners of the National Medal of Science averaged 154.[2] (p. 55) Both averages are, of course, very high.

The preceding discussion indicates that the 250 most-cited scientists are in turn highly recognized and honored. But are the most honored scientists also highly cited?

To answer this question we considered the citation records of all Nobel prize winners in science since 1950. The results are presented in Figure 2 on pages 12-13. Within the three subject area divisions the names of laureates are arranged chronologically by year of award. The laureate's name, country, and total citations from 1961 to 1975 are shown. The names of prize winners who also appear in Figure 1, the 250 most-cited primary authors, are in bold type.

Although the list of Nobel laureates contains 162 names, only 84 prizes in science have been awarded since 1950: one each year in physics, chemistry, and physiology or medicine. However, a single prize may be shared, as happened in 62% of the science prizes awarded since 1950. Thus, since 1950, 19 physics prizes, 11 chemistry prizes, and 22 physiology or medicine prizes have been shared.

The citation records of these 162 Nobelists range from a high of 18,888 for LD Landau to a low of 79 for JHD Jensen. Jensen, however, is an unusual case since he published only 14 papers, all in German, and all well before the advent of the *SCI* in 1961. In addition, according to EP Wigner, who shared the 1963 Nobel with Jensen and MG Mayer, ideas similar to Jensen's were proposed soon after his 1949 work on the structure of atomic nuclei, and Jensen's work may have been quickly "obliterated."[4] Overall, the average number of citations received in the period 1961 to 1975 by these 162 Nobel laureates is 2,877; the median is 1,910. The average citation total for chemistry Nobelists is 3,507; for physiology or medicine 2,882; and for physics 2,424.

These averages are extremely high when compared to typical citation rates. According to *SCI* data the average cited author now receives about 8 citations per year.[5] In the five years covered by the *SCI* cumulation for 1970-74, the average cited author received 16 citations.[6] So over a 15-year period, the average cited author could be expected to accumulate less than 50 citations!

All Nobel laureates were cited more than this average rate. Thirty-eight laureates received between 100 and 999 citations; 34 from 1,000 to 1,999; 21 from 2,000 to 2,999; 16 from 3,000 to 3,999; and *43* Nobelists—27%—received over 4,000 citations in the 15-year period.

There are two reasons why some of these Nobelists may not have been cited enough to appear on our list. First, as has already been pointed out,[1] these citation counts are based on primary-author data. Thus, a citation to a co-authored paper was credited only to the first author. Consideration of the all-author data significantly improved the citation records of the Nobelists with fewest citations. For example, DA Glaser's citations jumped from 101 to 343; SCC Ting's went from 170 to 303; FC Robbins' count rose from 126 to 584; and AR Prokhorov's count increased from 146 to 1,031. It should be noted, however, that even some highly-cited Nobelists improve dramatically when all-author data is considered. For example, D Baltimore's count rose from 2,543 to 5,270; GM Edelman's from 3,414 to 6,797; and S Ochoa's from 2,425 to 4,172. In the near future we will publish a list of most-cited authors which is based on all-author data.

Some Nobelists have relatively low citation counts which are not appreciably improved by consideration of the all-author data. These include PA Cherenkov with only 84 citations, JD Crockcroft (93), EM McMillan (97), and ETS Walton (112). But each of these authors did

Figure 2. Nobel Prize winners since 1950 in physics, chemistry, and physiology or medicine. Total citations from 1961 to 1975 based on data from the *Science Citation Index.* Names in bold type also appear in Figure 1, the 250 most-cited primary authors, 1961-1975.

PHYSICS

Name	Country*	Total Citations 1961-1975	Name	Country*	Total Citations 1961-1975
1950 Powell C	Britain	247	1964 Prokhorov AM	U.S.S.R.	1,031
1951 Crockcroft JD	Britain	93	Townes CH	U.S.	2,570
Walton E	Ireland	112	1965 **Feynman RP**	U.S.	6,031
1952 Bloch F	U.S.	2,188	**Schwinger JS**	U.S.	4,855
Purcell EM	U.S.	577	Tomonaga S	Japan	236
1953 Zernike F	Netherlands	467	1966 Kastler A	France	570
1954 **Born M**	Germany	9,206	1967 **Bethe HA**	U.S.	7,718
Bothe W	Germany	201	1968 Alvarez LW	U.S.	331
1955 Kusch P	U.S.	459	1969 **Gell-Mann M**	U.S.	9,669
Lamb WE Jr.	U.S.	1,625	1970 Alfvén HOG	Sweden	1,909
1956 **Bardeen J**	U.S.	4,788	Neel LEF	France	3,070
Brattain W	U.S.	303	1971 Gabor D	Britain	1,749
Shockley W	U.S.	3,571	1972 **Bardeen J**	U.S.	4,788
1957 **Lee TD**	U.S.	4,879	Cooper LN	U.S.	323
Yang CN	U.S.	1,728	Schrieffer JR	U.S.	1,472
1958 Cherenkov PA	U.S.S.R.	84	1973 Esaki L	Japan	747
Frank IM	U.S.S.R.	274	Giaever I	U.S.	695
Tamm IY	U.S.S.R.	1,144	Josephson B	Britain	1,265
1959 Chamberlain O	U.S.	236	1974 Hewish A	Britain	766
Segrè E	U.S.	493	Ryle M	Britain	890
1960 Glaser D	U.S.	343	1975 Bohr AN	Denmark	3,517
1961 Hofstadter R	U.S.	1,686	Mottelson BR	Denmark	1,362
Mössbauer R	Germany	436	Rainwater J	U.S.	300
1962 **Landau LD**	U.S.S.R.	18,888	1976 Richter B	U.S.	205
1963 Jensen JHD	Germany	79	Ting SCC	U.S.	303
Mayer MG	U.S.	290	1977 **Anderson PW**	U.S.	6,787
Wigner EP	U.S.	4,948	**Mott NF**	Britain	10,473
1964 **Basov NG**	U.S.S.R.	4,320	**Van Vleck JH**	U.S.	5,449

CHEMISTRY

Name	Country*	Total 1961-1975	Name	Country*	Total 1961-1975
1950 Alder K	Germany	4,450	1959 Heyrovsky J	Czech	1,418
Diels O	Germany	1,372	1960 Libby WF	U.S.	832
1951 McMillan EM	U.S.	97	1961 Calvin M	U.S.	2,713
Seaborg G	U.S.	638	1962 Kendrew JC	Britain	1,654
1952 Martin AJP	Britain	777	**Perutz MF**	Britain	4,263
Synge R	Britain	417	1963 **Natta G**	Italy	5,735
1953 Staudinger H	Germany	3,325	Ziegler K	Germany	3,258
1954 **Pauling LC**	U.S.	15,662	1964 Hodgkin DMC	Britain	359
1955 Du Vigneaud V	U.S.	1,470	1965 **Woodward RB**	U.S.	7,069
1956 Hinshelwood C	Britain	476	1966 **Mulliken RS**	U.S.	10,508
Semenov N	U.S.S.R.	1,257	1967 **Eigen M**	Germany	4,980
1957 Todd A	Britain	275	Norrish RGW	Britain	980
1958 Sanger F	Britain	3,716	Porter G	Britain	3,202

344

CHEMISTRY (continued)

Name	Country*	Total Citations 1961-1975		Name	Country*	Total Citations 1961-1975
1968 Onsager L	U.S.	3,569		1973 Fischer E	Germany	4,788
1969 Barton DHR	Britain	8,135		Wilkinson G	Britain	967
Hassel O	Norway	1,113		1974 Flory PJ	U.S.	10,247
1970 Leloir LF	Argentina	2,221		1975 Cornforth JW	Australia	2,378
1971 Herzberg G	Canada	13,110		Prelog V	Switzerland	2,229
1972 Anfinsen CB	U.S.	2,286		1976 Lipscomb WN	U.S.	1,443
Moore S	U.S.	8,167		1977 Prigogine I	Belgium	4,681
Stein WH	U.S.	1,274				

PHYSIOLOGY OR MEDICINE

Name	Country*	Total Citations 1961-1975		Name	Country*	Total Citations 1961-1975
1950 Hench PS	U.S.	316		1965 Monod J	France	4,791
Kendall EC	U.S.	179		1966 Huggins CB	U.S.	3,808
Reichstein T	Switzerland	1,178		Rous FP	U.S.	1,396
1951 Theiler M	South Africa	206		1967 Granit RA	Sweden	4,629
1952 Waksman SA	U.S.	2,291		Hartline HK	U.S.	1,183
1953 Lipmann FA	U.S.	2,038		Wald G	U.S.	3,002
Krebs HA	Britain	7,657		1968 Holley RW	U.S.	2,296
1954 Enders JF	U.S.	1,193		Khorana HG	U.S.	1,651
Robbins FC	U.S.	584		Nirenberg MW	U.S.	1,916
Weller TH	U.S.	1,972		1969 Delbruck M	U.S.	498
1955 Theorell AHT	Sweden	3,150		Hershey AD	U.S.	2,039
1956 Cournand AF	U.S.	1,263		Luria SE	U.S.	1,876
Forssmann W	Germany	637		1970 Axelrod J	U.S.	6,973
Richards D	U.S.	668		Katz B	Britain	4,690
1957 Bovet D	Italy	1,219		von Euler U	Sweden	8,728
1958 Beadle GW	U.S.	948		1971 Sutherland EW	U.S.	5,150
Lederberg J	U.S.	3,138		1972 Edelman GM	U.S.	3,414
Tatum EL	U.S.	285		Porter RR	Britain	2,528
1959 Kornberg A	U.S.	4,548		1973 von Frisch K	Germany	955
Ochoa S	U.S.	2,425		Lorenz KZ	Germany	1,560
1960 Burnet FM	Australia	5,553		Tinbergen N	Netherlands	1,205
Medawar PB	Britain	2,600		1974 DeDuve C	Belgium	8,445
1961 von Békésy G	U.S.	1,960		Claude A	U.S.	493
1962 Crick FHC	Britain	2,524		Palade GE	U.S.	5,969
Watson JD	U.S.	2,437		1975 Baltimore D	U.S.	2,543
Wilkins MHF	Britain	745		Dulbecco R	U.S.	4,005
1963 Eccles JC	Australia	10,104		Temin HM	U.S.	3,168
Hodgkin AL	Britain	7,500		1976 Blumberg BS	U.S.	3,555
Huxley AF	Britain	2,115		Gajdusek DC	U.S.	1,318
1964 Bloch K	U.S.	1,456		1977 Guillemin R	U.S.	2,395
Lynen F	Germany	3,020		Schally A	U.S.	2,985
1965 Jacob F	France	7,101		Yalow R	U.S.	3,658
Lwoff A	France	2,111				

* Citizenship of recipient at time of award.

their award-winning research well before the advent of the *Science Citation Index* in 1961.

For example, PA Cherenkov, born in 1904, discovered the "Cherenkov effect" in 1934 when he was still a student at the Institute of Physics of the USSR Academy of Sciences. In 1929, JD Cockroft, born in 1897, and ETS Walton, born in 1903, devised the accelerator that in 1931 disintegrated lithium nuclei with protons. And EM McMillan, born in 1907, isolated neptunium in 1940. Undoubtedly when we compile citation data for the pre-1961 years we will find this work heavily cited. I believe we will also observe that some of these discoveries were so profound in their impact and so quickly absorbed into the mainstream of science that they have since become obliterated.[7]

The fact is that virtually all Nobel prize winners are highly cited authors, especially in the years immediately preceding the award.[8] In *The Scientific Elite,* Harriet Zuckerman reports that, "Each year before the award, between the years 1961-1971 prospective laureates are cited 222 times on the average. This is more than twice the average of 99 citations for a random sample of American scientists about to be elected to the National Academy of Sciences during the same years and almost 40 times the average of 6.1 citations to a representative author in the *SCI*."[9] (p. 187-8).

The evidence for the correlation between citedness and Nobel awards has in fact been increasing. It is even possible to use citation analysis to forecast Nobel prize winners. I demonstrated this in 1970, when I published a list of the 50 most-cited authors for 1967.[10] Six of those 50 authors had won the Nobel previously, and *six more have won it since*. Since there have been about one million scientists who have published and could be cited, these results could hardly have been produced by a random selection.

The high citedness of Nobelists is, of course, due to the *amount* as well as the quality of the work they produce. Zuckerman found that "while still in their twenties they [Nobel laureates] published an average of 13.1 papers, strikingly more than the entire lifetime average of 3.5 pages that has been attributed to the general population of scientists."[9] (p. 145) Sher and I obtained similar results in our 1965 study of Nobel prize winners.[8]

Just a few months ago, Cole and Cole, with Leonard Rubin, again demonstrated the strong relationship between citedness and other indicators of scientific status. Writing in *Scientific American,* they characterized 1,200 scientists according to nine variables, including a ranking of the graduate departments from which they received doctorates, current academic departments and ranks, age, published works, previous grants from the National Science Foundation, and citation records. They reported, "Our results show only weak or moderate correlations between each of the nine 'social stratification' variables and the ratings received on [NSF grant] proposals.... The most highly correlated variable was the number of citations in the 1975 *Science Citation Index* of work published between 1965 and 1974."[11] Previously, Cole and Cole had asserted, "The data available indicate that straight citation counts are highly correlated with virtually every refined measure of quality."[2] (p. 35) I and those who helped in preparing this study were as surprised as any other laymen at this year's choices for the Nobel prize. But you can well understand our sense of elation in observing that four of the seven science winners were among our most cited 250. These four were the physicists, PW Anderson, JH Van Veck, and NF Mott, and the chemist, I Prigogine. The other three, R Guillemin, R Yalow, and A Schally, actually were no surprise to us. Not only would they be among the 1,000 most-cited we could list, but their rankings in all-author data show them to be among the most-cited scientists of the past decade. Schally, who has co-authored over 430 papers, was cited over 10,000 times. Similarly, Yalow's work was cited over 5,500 times, and Guillemin's over 4,000 times.

In part three of this series I will discuss the all-author data in more detail and will list the most-cited publication of each of these 250 authors.

REFERENCES

1. **Garfield E.** The 250 most cited primary authors, 1961-1975. Part I. How the names were selected. *Current Contents*® No. 49, 5 December 1977, p. 5-15.
2. **Cole J R & Cole S.** *Social stratification in science.* Chicago: University of Chicago Press, 1973. 283 pp.
3. **Price D J D & Gursey S.** Some statistical results for the numbers of authors in the states of the United States and the nations of the world. *ISI's Who is publishing in science*® *1977 annual.* Philadelphia: ISI® , 1977, p. 26-34.
4. **Wigner E P.** Personal communication. 22 November 1977.
5. *Science Citation Index. 1976 Guide & Journal Lists.* Philadelphia: ISI, 1977. p. 21.
6. *Science Citation Index Five-Year Cumulation, 1970-1974.* Philadelphia: ISI, 1976, p. 17.
7. **Garfield E.** The 'obliteration phenomenon' in science — and the advantage of being obliterated! *Current Contents* No. 51/52, 22 December 1975. Reprinted in: **Garfield, E.** *Essays of an information scientist.* Philadelphia: ISI Press, 1977. Vol. 2, p. 396-8.
8. **Sher I H & Garfield E.** New tools for improving and evaluating the effectiveness of research. *Research Program Effectiveness* (Yovits M C, Gilford D M, Wilcox R H, Stavely E & Lemer H D, eds.) Proceedings of a conference sponsored by the Office of Naval Research, Washington, D.C., July 27-29, 1965. New York: Gordon and Breach, 1966, pp. 135-146.
9. **Zuckerman H.** *Scientific elite.* New York: The Free Press, 1977. 335 pp.
10. **Garfield E.** Citation indexing for studying science. *Nature* 227:669-671, 1970. Reprinted in: **Garfield E.** *Essays of an information scientist.* Philadelphia: ISI Press, 1977. Vol. 1, p. 133-138.
11. **Cole S, Rubin L & Cole J R.** Peer review and the support of science. *Scientific American* 237:34-41, 1977.

CURRENT COMMENTS

The 250 Most-Cited Primary Authors,
1961-1975. Part III.
Each Author's Most-Cited Publication

Number 51, December 19, 1977

Previously we have listed the 250 most-cited primary authors. We have described how the names were selected.[1] And we have examined the correlation between citedness and other forms of science recognition such as the Nobel prize and membership in national academies of science.[2] In this essay, the last of three parts, we have listed each author's most-cited publication.

The list appears on pages 11-20. It contains the most-cited publication for which each author was primary author. Textbooks, manuals, reviews, and other items not considered reports of original research were excluded. About half of these publications have appeared in our previous lists of highly-cited items.

The total citation count for each item is based on *Science Citation Index*® (*SCI*®) data from 1961 to 1975, or from the year of publication if published after 1961. Since one of the 250 most-cited authors was omitted to symbolize the incompleteness of such lists, this list actually contains 249 items.

It is notable that the list contains several items which have been cited relatively few times. Every one of

the 250 most-cited authors has been cited over 4,000 times. So some readers may wonder about the paper by R M Barrer, for example, which was cited "only" 46 times. Most of the authors on this list have produced not only high-quality work, but also a large quantity of it. Barrer has published over 300 papers! His most cited publication, a 1959 textbook in physical chemistry,[3] had been cited 319 times through 1975. But we have not listed textbooks.

Over four-fifths of these papers were written in the 1950s and 1960s. Four were published in the 1920s, 8 in the 1930s, 29 in the 1940s, 103 in the 1950s, 102 in the 1960s, and 2 in the 1970s. The oldest work on the list is Freud's, which was first published in 1915. The most recent item on the list is Allison's 1971 paper on functions of thymus-derived lymphocytes in relation to autoimmunity.

Thirteen of these 250 papers have been featured in Citation Classics, the weekly *Current Contents*® (*CC*®) series in which authors comment on their classic papers. For each Citation Classic we have indicated the *CC* issue number, date and page number in brackets after the item. Undoubtedly many more of these papers will appear as Citation Classics in the future.

Just 17 journals account for over half of the articles, and less than a hundred journals account for all the articles. The *Journal of the American Chemical Society* (*JACS*) accounts for 26—over 10% of the total. The *Journal of Biological Chemistry* accounts for 15, *Biochemical Journal* 11, *Physical Review* 10, and *Journal of Chemical Physics* 6. *Angewandte Chemie, Biochimica et Biophysica Acta, Journal of Cell Biology, Journal of Molecular Biology* and *Journal of Physiology* account for 4 items each.

Several of the articles are parts of a series. The citation counts include citations only to the part listed. For instance, Seyferth's article is the second of a 79-part series on halomethyl-metal compounds. The last part was published in 1976, after which Seyferth and his colleagues ended their research in this field.

I previously discussed the fact that several scientific fields are not represented by the 250 most-cited primary authors.[1] Since botany was among the unrepresented fields, some readers may be surprised to see that D I Arnon's paper was published in *Plant Physiology*. However, Dr. Arnon assures us that he is *not* a botanist; his field is biochemistry. He explains, "At the time this article was published, there were not many chemists or biochemists interested in chloroplasts. Therefore I didn't publish it in a biochemistry journal. Today I would just as soon put it in *Biochimica et Biophysica Acta*, for example."[4]

Of course, some of these authors are well known for publications which do not appear on this list. For example, P W Bridgman is well known for his writings on the philosophy of science, which include his books *The Way Things Are*[5] and *The Logic of Modern Physics*.[6]

This list contains 40 books and 209 journal articles. Where multiple editions of a book have been published, we counted the citations to *all* editions of the book, but listed the publication date of the earliest edition. However, G W Snedecor's 1937 book on statistical methods was substantially revised and co-authored with W G Cochran in the 1956 edition.[7] This was the most-cited edition, but the citation count includes citations to all editions.

Collecting citation data on books was a bit tricky for several reasons. First, citation practices concerning books are far from uniform. Second, many of the books which appear on this list are classics which have gone through several editions.

The difficulties can be illustrated by the case of Sigmund Freud. With 8,490 citations, he is still among the most-cited authors, even though he died in 1939. In 1957 the Hogarth Press collected Freud's complete works into a multi-volume *Standard Edition*. This is often cited simply as *"Standard Edition," "S.E.,"* or

"Standard Ed." Thus, it appears in the *SCI* in all three forms. In addition, citations to Freud's work sometimes refer to the original publications. After examining the citations to all of Freud's works, it became apparent that Volume 14, concerning the history of the psychoanalytic movement, is the most-cited volume. The most-cited papers in this volume are "Instincts and their Vicissitudes," "Repression," "The Unconscious," "A Metapsychological Supplement to the Theory of Dreams," "Mourning and Melancholia," "A Case of Paranoia Running Counter to the Psycho-Analytic Theory of the Disease," "Thoughts for the Times on War and Death," and "On Transience," all written between 1915 and 1917. To simplify matters, we have listed the entire Volume 14 as Freud's most-cited work, even though he never published it as such.

Four hundred and thirty-three different authors wrote these 250 works! Eight authors are on the list both as primary and as co-authors: M Gell-Mann, C Djerassi, J Monod, L A Carlson, L D Landau, G E Palade, D H Spackman, and S Weinberg.

More than half (132) of the listed publications have only one author; 71, two authors; 29, three authors; 10, four authors; and 4, five authors. One paper has six, and two have seven authors.

During the past quarter-century the proportion of scientific papers having more than one author has in-creased significantly. Instead of working alone, as most did before World War II, many of our best scientists now work in teams.

As Derek J. De Solla Price of Yale University has reported, "Surprisingly enough, a detailed examination of the incidence of collaborative work in science shows that this is a phenomenon which has been increasing steadily and ever more rapidly since the beginning of the century.... Since that time the proportion of multi-author papers has acclerated steadily and powerfully, and it is now so large that if it continues at the present rate, by 1980 the single-author paper will be extinct."[8]

Price and others have suggested that the proportion of collaborative authorship in a field is related to the amount of economic support it receives. Price comments that "the amount of collaborative authorship measures no more than the economic value accorded to each field by society. A soft subject highly subsidized would become as collaborative as high energy physics...."[9] A recent study by Henry J. Petroski of the Argonne National Laboratory supports Price's conclusions.[10]

Although there is general consensus that collaboration is increasing, there is little agreement on how collaboration affects citation analysis. Some researchers claim that the effects are negligible, while others state that they are "intolerable."[11]

In *Social Stratification in Science,* Jonathan and Stephen Cole studied a wide range of citation data on 120 physicists. They found that, "The correlation between a straight citation count and total citations (including citations to collaborative work on which the physicist was not first author) is .96." The Coles suggest that "the omission of collaborative citations to papers on which the author was not first among collaborators does not affect substantive conclusions."[12] But this depends upon what phenomenon you are studying.

In a recent study, Duncan Lindsey of Cornell University and George Warren Brown of Washington University reached an opposite conclusion. They argued that "one of the more serious errors in empirical judgment made in the field of the sociology of science has been to measure both publications and citations with counting procedures that do not take into account multiple authorship." They explore several alternatives to the first-author dilemma, including a variety of weighting schemes such as awarding the first author of a two-author paper two-thirds credit, and the second author, one-third. However, they conclude, "Until it becomes possible to decompose the relative contribution of collaborators, it will be necessary to simply divide by the number of contributors and allocate the credit equally."[11]

Lindsey and Brown also used the *SCI* and *Social Sciences Citation Index*™ (*SSCI*™) to determine the proportion of collaborative papers in a variety of fields. Their results indicate wide variations from one field to another. For biochemistry, they found that 19% of the 155 papers sampled had one author; 46%, two; 22%, three; and 13%, four or more. For psychology (205 papers), the breakdown was 75%, one author; 21%, two; 3%, three; and only 1%, four or more. In economics, 83% of the 154 papers sampled had one author; 16%, two; 1%, three; and none had four.

In the past, there were two primary reasons for ISI® to largely ignore the first-author problem in various citation analyses. First, many of the most-cited authors did their important work in the first half of this century, when collaboration was less pervasive than at present. Second, many authors who did publish as part of a team also published many papers alone. Their "wrap-up" papers tended to be cited by others in the same way that review papers are now sometimes cited: as surrogates for groups of papers that characterize a particular research front.

The first-author "problem" in citation analysis is partly an artifact of the way *SCI* data is listed. To print the names of *all* authors of cited items would more than double the size of the *SCI—without significantly increasing its value for information retrieval.* But the data on co-authors is not lost, either in our printed indexes or on our tapes. We list only first authors in the citation indexes. But in the source indexes we include all co-authors of each item, as well as a full bibliographic description. Thus we have been able to use our own source data tapes from earlier years, in combination with citation data tapes, to compile all-author citation counts for over 4½ million source articles indexed in the *SCI* from 1961 to 1976.

This new data, which we are just now beginning to study, classifies authors in six ways. It lists authors by overall rank, by primary-author rank, by secondary-author rank, and alphabetically. A "residue" author ranking includes citations to books and journal articles published before 1961. And an alphabetic listing is provided for the "residue" authors.

There are several important differences between our new all-author data and the data which we have used in the past. First, of course, is the fact that the all-author data credits citations equally to all co-authors of a given publication, not just the first author. However, it was not feasible for us to obtain and process the names of all co-authors of material published before 1961. Citations to this material are included in the "residue" listing. Thus, for example, since Lowry's classic paper was published in 1951, his name appears only in the "residue" listing. The same is true for many Nobel laureates and other eminent scientists whose significant work was done in the forties and the fifties.

One advantage of the all-author data is that it will enable us to account for self-citations that previ-ously were difficult to detect. Through a pattern of self-citation, one large research group could build up substantial citation counts based on its own local invisible college. It would be convenient to sociologists if such groups took on pseudonyms like the famous "mathematician" Bourbaki (actually a group), who appears in this list. But the in-breeding that takes place in science is often difficult to define. When can we say that a particular scientist has severed himself from his "family" and established a truly new group? And how can we determine the true extent to which particular scientists have made an impact on families of "offspring" scientists working both at the "birthplace" and elsewhere? The all-author data can simplify finding answers to such questions.

What is the effect of using all-author data to compile a list of most-cited authors? Since this list is based only on primary-author data, we might expect some significant changes when all-author data is used. In fact, when we compared these 250 authors with the 250 most-cited authors (overall) based on all-author data, only 69 names— 28% of the total—were the same.

To conclude this series of editorials, let me remind you that our list of 250 most-cited primary authors cannot be perfect or complete. The omission of one author's name has symbolized this lack of completeness. But what is most important about this list is that we have not had to be familiar with the work of all the authors involved in order to select them. We have not had to read the authors' works or consult with their peers. Yet we have been able to produce a list of individuals who comprise a distinguished elite among scientists.

I am well aware of the possible failure of citation analysis in some cases, particularly in those of less-cited individuals. It is much easier to quarrel with the "evaluation" of a poorly-cited individual than to deny the reality of high citation impact.

Of the one million or more authors who have published between 1961 and 1975, we have looked at the top two-and-a-half hundredths of one percent. Considering the elaborate apparatus, such as peer review, needed to make selections for grants, honors, and even em-ployment and tenure, I think the method we have used to construct this list deserves further considera-tion and refinement.

Basically, I regard myself as an apolitical person. But life is politics in one form or another, and politics in science—as in other walks of life—has its own peculiar set of in-justices. Is there any way to mini-mize these injustices? The mechan-isms by which scientific recognition is achieved are certainly political. But so long as ability, insight, talent, and genius are unevenly dis-tributed among scientists, we should try to insure that the political system of science which grants re-cognition is as fair and as demo-cratic as possible. I believe that ci-tation analysis can further that ob-jective.

REFERENCES

1. **Garfield E.** The 250 most-cited primary authors. Part I. How the names were selected. *Current Contents* No. 49, 5 Dec 1977, p. 5-15.
2. --------------. The 250 most-cited primary authors. Part II. The correlation between citedness, Nobel prizes and academy memberships. *Current Contents* No. 50, 12 Dec 1977, p. 5-15.
3. **Barrer R M.** *Diffusion in and through solids.* New York: Macmillan, 1941. 464 pp.
4. **Arnon D I.** Personal communication. 30 November 1977.
5. **Bridgman P W.** *The way things are.* Cambridge: Harvard University Press, 1959. 333 pp.
6. --------------------. *The logic of modern physics.* New York: Macmillan, 1927. 228 pp.
7. **Cochran W G.** Citation Classics. *Current Contents* No. 19, 9 May 1977, p. 10.
8. **Price D J D.** *Little science, big science.* New York: Columbia University Press, 1963. 118 pp.
9. --------------. Citation measures of hard science, soft science, technology & non-science. *Communication Among Scientists and Engineers* (Nelson C E & Pollock D K, eds.) Lexington, Mass.: Heath & Co., 1970, p. 7-22.
10. **Petroski H J.** Trends in the applied mechanics literature. *Technological Fore-casting and Social Change* 10:309-18, 1977.
11. **Lindsey D & Brown G W.** Problems of measurement in the sociology of science: taking account of collaboration. [Unpublished] 1977.
12. **Cole J R & Cole S.** *Social stratification in science.* Chicago: University of Chicago Press, 1973. 283 pp.

Figure 1. Each primary author's most-cited publication. Names of the 250 most-cited primary authors, 1961-1975, appear in boldface. The listed publication is the most-cited report of original research for which the author was primary author. Total citation count based on *Science Citation Index®* data.

Total Citations 1961-1975	Primary Author's Most-Cited Publication

1. 422 **Abragam A.** *The principles of nuclear magnetism.* New York: Oxford, 1961. 599 pp.
2. 5,241 **Abramowitz M** & Stegun I. *Handbook of mathematical functions with formulas, graphs & mathematical tables.* New York: Dover, 1964. 1046 pp.
3. 851 **Abrikosov A A.** On the magnetic properties of superconductors of the second type. *Zh. Eksp. Teo.* 32:1442-52, 1952. (*Sov. Phys. JETP* 5:1174-82, 1957.)
4. 201 **Albert A,** Goldacre R & Phillips J. The strength of heterocyclic bases. *J. Chem. Soc.* p. 2240-9, 1948.
5. 167 **Allinger N L,** Hirsch J A, Miller M A, Tyminski I J & Van-Catledge F A. Conformational analysis. Part 60. Improved calculations of the structures and energies of hydrocarbons by the Westheimer method. *J. Am. Chem. S.* 1199-1210, 1968.
6. 194 **Allison A C,** Denman A M & Barnes R D. Cooperating and controlling functions of thymus-derived lymphocytes in relation to autoimmunity. *Lancet* 2:135-40, 1971.
7. 409 **Anden N E,** Dahlstrom A, Fuxe K, Larsson K, Olson L & Ungerstedt U. Ascending monoamine neurons to the telencephalon and diencephalon. *Acta. Physl. S.* 67:313-26, 1966.
8. 769 **Anderson P W.** Localized magnetic states in metals. *Phys. Rev.* 124:41-53, 1961.
9. 2,080 **Andrews P.** Estimation of the molecular weights of protein in Sephadexgel-filtration. *Biochem. J.* 91:222-33, 1964.
10. 1,806 **Arnon D I.** Copper enzymes in isolated chloroplasts; polyphenoloxidase in *Beta Vulgaris. Plant Physl.* 24:1-15, 1949.
11. 408 **Axelrod J** & Tomchick R. Enzymatic O-methylation of epinephrine and other catechols. *J. Biol. Chem.* 233:702-5, 1958.
12. 135 **Baker B R.** *Design of active-site-directed irreversible enzyme inhibitors; the organic chemistry of the enzymic active-size.* New York: Wiley, 1967. 325 pp.
13. 1,662 **Bardeen J,** Cooper, L N & Scheiffer J R. Theory of superconductivity. *Phys. Rev.* 108:1175-1204, 1957.
14. 46 **Barrer R M,** Baynham J W, Bultitude F W & Meier W M. Hydrothermal chemistry of the silicates. Part 8. Low temperature crystal growth of aluminosilicates, and some gallium and germanium analogues. *J. Chem. Soc.* p. 195-208, 1959.
15. 184 **Bartlett P D** & Hiatt R R. A series of tertiary butyl peresters showing concerted decomposition. *J. Am. Chem. S.* 80:1398-1405, 1958.
16. 267 **Barton D H R.** The stereochemistry of cyclohexane derivatives. *J. Chem. Soc.* p. 1027-40, 1953.
17. 88 **Basolo F** & Pearson R G. The transeffect in metal complexes. *Prog. Inorg. Chem.* 4:381-453, 1962.
18. 101 **Basov N G,** Grasyuk A Z, Zubarey I G, Katulin V N & Krokhin O N. Semiconductor quantum generator with two photon optical excitation. *Zh. Eksp. Teo.* 50:551-9, 1966. (*Sov. Phys. JETP* 23:366-71, 1966.)
19. 416 **Bates D R** & Damgaard A. The calculation of the absolute strengths of spectral lines. *Phi. T. Roy. A.* 242:101-22, 1949.
20. 104 **Bell R P** & Goodall D M. Kinetic hydrogen isotope effects in the ionization of some nitroparaffins. *P. Roy. Soc. A.* 294:273-97, 1966.
21. 7,300 **Bellamy L J.** *The infra-red spectra of complex molecules.* New York: Wiley, 1954. 323 pp.
22. 266 **Bellman R E.** *Introduction to matrix analysis.* New York: McGraw, 1960. 328 pp.
23. 451 **Bender M L.** Mechanism of catalysis of nucleophilic reactions of carboxylic acid derivatives. *Chem. Rev.* 60:53-113, 1960.
24. 228 **Benson S W.** Bond energies. *J. Chem. Educ.* 42:502-18, 1965.

25. 414 **Bergstrom S,** Carlson L A & Weeks J R. The prostaglandins: a family of biologically active lipids. *Pharm. Rev.* 20:1-48, 1968.

26. 518 **Berson S A,** Yalow R S, Bauman M, Rothschild A & Newerly K. Insulin-I[131]
metabolism in human subjects: demonstration of insulin binding globulin in the
circulation of insulin treated subjects. *J. Clin. Inv.* 35:170-90, 1956.

27. 545 **Bethe H A.** Zur theorie des durchgangs schneller korpuskularstrahlen durch
materie. (On the theory of the passage of corpuscular rays through matter).
Ann. Physik 5:325-400, 1930.

28. 356 **Beutler E.** The glutathione instability of drug-sensitive red cells.
J. La. Cl. Med. 49:84-95, 1957

29. 443 **Billingham R E** & Medawar P B. The technique of free skin grafting in
mammals. *J. Exp. Biol.* 28:385-402, 1951.

30. 132 **Birch A J.** The reduction of organic compounds by metal-ammonia solutions.
Q. Rev. Chem. Soc. 4:69-93, 1950.

31. 551 **Bjorken J D.** Asymptotic sum rules at infinite momentum.
Phys. Rev. D. 79:1547-53, 1969.

32. 1,145 **Bloembergen N,** Purcell E M & Pound R V. Relaxation effects in nuclear magnetic resonance absorption. *Phys. Rev.* 73:679-712, 1948.
[Citation Classics. *Current Contents®* No. 18, 2 May 1977, p. 7.]

33. 864 **Born M** & Huang K. *Dynamical theory of crystal lattices.*
New York: Oxford, 1954. 420 pp.

34. 476 **Bourbaki N.** *Algèbre commutative.* Paris: Hermann, 1961. (*Commutative algebra.*
Reading, MA: Addison-Wesley, 1972. 625 pp.)

35. 1,203 **Boyer P D.** Spectrophotometric study of the reaction of protein sulfhydryl
groups with organic mercurials. *J. Am. Chem. S.* 76:4331-7, 1954.

36. 130 **Brachet J,** Denis H & DeVitry F. The effects of antimonycin D and puromycin
on morphogenesis in amphibian eggs and *Acetabularia mediterranea.*
Develop. Bio. 9:398-434, 1964.

37. 168 **Braunwald E** & Frahm C J. Studies on Starling's law of the heart.
Circulation 24:633-42, 1961.

38. 6,952 **Bray G A.** A simple efficient liquid scintillator for counting aqueous solutions in
a liquid scintillation counter. *Analyt. Bioc.* 1:279-85, 1960.
[Citation Classics. *Current Contents* No. 2, 10 Jan 1977, p. 16.]

39. 126 **Bridgman P W.** The compression of 39 substances to 100,000 KG/CM.
P. Am. Acad. Art Sci. 76:55-70, 1948.

40. 328 **Brodie B B,** Gillette, J R & LaDu B N. Enzymatic metabolism of drugs and
other foreign compounds. *Ann. R. Bioch.* 27:427-54, 1958.

41. 544 **Brown H C** & Okamoto Y. Directive effects in aromatic substitution. Part 30.
Electrophilic substituent constants. *J. Am. Chem. S.* 80:4979-87, 1958.

42. 918 **Brown J B.** A chemical method for the determination of oestriol, oestrone, and
oestradiol in human urine. *Biochem. J.* 60:185-93, 1955.

43. 508 **Buckingham A D.** Chemical shifts in the magnetic resonance spectra of molecules
containing polar groups. *Can. J. Chem.* 38:300-7, 1960.

44. 275 **Budzikiewicz H,** Wilson J M & Djerassi C. Mass spectrometry in structural and
stereochemical problems. Part 32. Pentacyclic triterpenes.
J. Am. Chem. S. 85:3688-99, 1963.

45. 315 **Bunnett J F.** Kinetics of reactions in moderately concentrated aqueous acids. I.
Classification of reactions. *J. Am. Chem. S.* 83:4956-67, 1961.

46. 811 **Burn J H** & Rand M J. The action of sympathomimetic amines in animals
treated with reserpine. *J. Physl. Lon.* 144:314-36, 1958.

47. 175 **Burnet F M.** *The clonal selection theory of acquired immunity.*
Nashville: Vanderbilt University Press, 1959. 208 pp.

48. 5,037 **Burton K.** A study of the conditions and mechanism of the diphenylamine reac-
tion for the colorimetric estimation of deoxyribonucleic acid.
Biochem. J. 62:315-23, 1956.
[Citation Classics. *Current Contents* No. 26, 27 Jun 1977, p. 23.]

Total Citations 1961-1975		Primary Author's Most-Cited Publication

49. 448 **Busing W R,** Martin K O & Levy H A. *ORFLS, a FORTRAN crystallographic least-squares program.* Report ORNL-TM-305. Oak Ridge, Tenn.: Oak Ridge National Laboratory, 1962. 77 pp.

50. 349 **Carlson L A** & Waldeck S. Determination of serum triglycerides. *J. Atheroscl.* 3:334-6, 1963.

51. 506 **Carlsson A.** A fluorimetric method for the determination of dopamine (3-hydroxytyramine). *Acta. Physl. S.* 44:293-8, 1958.

52. 65 **Cattell R B.** The Scree test for the number of factors. *Mult. Behav. Res.* 1:245-76, 1966.

53. 870 **Chance B** & Williams G R. The respiratory chain and oxidative phosphorylation. *Adv. Enzymol.* 17:65-134, 1956.

54. 876 **Chandrasekhar S.** Stochastic problems in physics and astronomy. *Rev. M. Phys.* 15:1-89, 1943.

55. 461 **Chapman S** & Bartels J. *Geomagnetism.* Oxford: Clarendon, 1940. 2 vols.

56. 262 **Chatt J** & Duncanson L A. Olefin co-ordination compounds. Part 3. Infra-red spectra and structure: attempted preparation of acetylene complexes. *J. Chem. Soc.* p. 2939-47, 1953.

57. 948 **Clementi E.** Ab initio computations in atoms and molecules. *IBM J. Res.* 9:2-19, 1965.

58. 380 **Cohen M H** & Turnbull D. Molecular transport in liquids and glasses. *J. Chem. Phys.* 31:1164-9, 1959.

59. 1,529 **Conney A H.** Pharmacological implications of microsomal enzyme induction. *Pharmacol. Rev.* 19:317-66, 1967.

60. 108 **Cope A C.** Transannular reactions in medium sized rings. *Q. Rev. Chem. S.* 20:119-52, 1966.

61. 349 **Corey E J.** Dimethyloxosulfonium methylide [(CH$_3$) SOCH$_2$] and dimethyl-sulfonium methylide [(CH$_3$)$_2$ SCH$_2$] formation and application to organic synthesis. *J. Am. Chem. S.* 87:1353-64, 1965.

62. 266 **Cotton F A.** Vibrational spectra and bonding in metal carbonyls. 3. Force constants and assignments of CO stretching modes of various molecules; evaluation of CO bond orders. *Inorg. Chem.* 3:702-11, 1964.

63. 207 **Coulson C A** & Longuet-Higgins H C. The electronic structure of conjugated systems. 1. General theory. *P. Roy. Soc. Lond.* 191:39-60, 1947.

64. 890 **Courant R &** Hilbert D. *Methods of mathematical physics.* New York: Wiley, 1959. 2 vols.

65. 248 **Cram D J** & Elhafex F A A. Studies in stereochemistry. 10. The rule of "steric control of asymmetric induction" in the syntheses of acyclic systems. *J. Am. Chem. S.* 74:5828-35, 1952.

66. 1,780 **Cromer D T** & Waber J T. Scattering factors computed from relativistic Dirac-Slater wave functions. *Act. Cryst.* 18:104-9, 1965.

67. 394 **Cruickshank D W J.** The role of 3-d orbitals in π-bonds between (a) silicon, phosphorus, sulphur or chlorine and (b) oxygen or nitrogen. *J. Chem. Soc.* p. 5486-504, 1961.

68. 709 **Cuatrecasas P.** Protein purification by affinity chromatography; derivations of agarose and polyacrylamide beads. *J. Biol. Chem.* 245:3059-65, 1970.

69. 215 **Curtis D R** & Watkins J C. The excitation and depression of spinal neurones by structurally related amino acids. *J. Neurochem.* 6:117-41, 1960.

70. 121 **Dacie J V,** Grimes A J, Meisler A, Steingold L, Hemsted E H, Beaven G H & White J C. Hereditary heinzbody anaemia. *Br. J. Haem.* 10:388-402, 1964.

71. 282 **Dalgarno A.** Atomic polarizabilities and shielding factors. *Adv. Phys.* 11:281-315, 1962.

72. 6,342 **Davis B J.** Disc electrophoresis. 2. Method and application to human serum proteins. *Ann. NY. Acad.* 121:404-27, 1964.

73. 596 **Dawson R M C.** A hydrolytic procedure for the identification and estimation of individual phospholipids in biological samples. *Biochem. J.* 75:45-53, 1960.

74. 1,402 **DeDuve C.** Tissue fractionation studies. 6. Intracellular distribution patterns of enzymes in rat liver tissue. *Biochem. J.* 60:604-17, 1955. [Citation Classics. *Current Contents* No. 12, 21 Mar 1977, p. 11.]

75. 407 DeRobertis E, Pellegrino A D, Arnaiz G R & Salganicoff L. Cholinergic and
          non-cholinergic nerve endings in rat brain-1. *J. Neurochem.* 9:23-35, 1962.
76. 269 Dewar M J S & Schmeising H N. A re-evaluation of conjugation and hyper-
          conjugation: the effects of changes in hybridisation on carbon bonds.
          Tetrahedron 5:166-78, 1959.
77. 1,326 Dische Z. A specific new color reaction by hexuronic acids.
          J. Biol. Chem. 167:189-98, 1947.
78. 1,097 Dixon M. The determination of enzyme inhibitor constants.
          Biochem. J. 55:170-1, 1953.
79. 440 Djerassi C, Engle R R & Bowers A. The direct conversion of steroidal Δ5-
          3β-alcohols to Δ5- and Δ4-3-ketones. *J. Org. Chem.* 21:1547-9, 1956.
80. 273 Doering W V & Hoffman A K. The addition of dichlorocarbene to olefins.
          J. Am. Chem. S. 76:6162-5, 1954.
81. 2,705 Dole V P. A relation between non-esterified fatty acids in plasma and the
          metabolism of glucose. *J. Clin. Inv.* 35:150-4, 1956.
82. 3,610 Duncan D B. Multiple range and multiple F tests. *Biometrics* 11:1-42, 1955.
          [Citation Classics. *Current Contents* No. 4, 24 Jan 1977, p. 10.]
83. 2,555 Eagle H. Amino acid metabolism in mammalian cell cultures.
          Science 130:432-7, 1959.
          [Citation Classics. *Current Contents* No. 5, 31 Jan 1977, p. 13.]
84. 345 Eccles J C, Fatt P & Koketso K. Cholinergic and inhibitory synapses in a
          pathway from motor axon collaterals to motoneurons.
          J. Physl. Lon. 126:524-62, 1954.
85. 421 Eigen M. Protonenübertragung, säure-base katalyse und enzymatische
          hydrolyse. I. Elementarvorgänge. *Angew. Chem.* 75:489-515, 1963. (Proton-
          transfer, acid-base catalysis and enzymatic hydrolysis. I. Elementary
          processes. *Angew. Chem. Int.* 3:1-19, 1964.
86. 140 Eliel E L & Knoeber M C. Conformation analysis. 16. 1,3-Dioxanes.
          J. Am. Chem. S. 90:3444-58, 1968.
87. 213 Erdelyi A. *Higher transcendental functions.* Vol. 1.
          New York: McGraw-Hill, 1953. 302 pp.
88. 177 Eysenck H J. *The biological basis of personality.*
          Springfield, Ill.: Thomas, 1967. 399 pp.
89. 965 Fahey J L & McKelvey E M. Quantitative determination of serum immunoglob-
          ulins in antibody-agar plates. *J. Immunol.* 94:84-90, 1965.
90. 1,015 Falck B, Hillarp A A, Thieme G & Torp A. Fluorescence of catechol amines
          and related compounds condensed with formaldehyde.
          J. Hist. Cyto. 10:348-54, 1962.
91. 1,086 Farquhar M G & Palade G E. Junctional complexes in various epithelia.
          J. Cell Biol. 17:375-412, 1963.
92. 283 Fawcett D W. Surface specializations of absorbing cells.
          J. Hist. Cyto. 13:75-91, 1965.
93. 1,111 Feigl F. *Spot tests in organic analysis.* New York: Elsevier, 1956. 2 vols.
94. 263 Feldberg W & Lewis G P. The action of peptides on the adrenal medulla.
          Release of adrenaline by bradykinin and angiotensin.
          J. Physl. Lon. 171:98-108, 1964.
95. 770 Feynman R P & Gell-Mann M. Theory of the Fermi interaction.
          Phys. Rev. 109:193-8, 1958.
96. 133 Fieser L F. Preparation of ethylenethioketals. *J. Am. Chem. S.* 76:1945-7, 1954.
97. 116 Fischer E O & Maasbol A. Phenyl-methoxycarben-und methylmethoxycarben-
          pentacarconylchrom,-molybdan, -wolfram und -cyclopentaienyl-dicarbonyl-
          mangan. (Pentacarbonylchromium, -molybdenum, -tungsten and cyclopenta-
          dienyl-dicarbonylmanganese complexes of phenylmethoxycarbene and me-
          thylmethoxycarbene. *Chem. Ber.* 100:2445-56, 1967.
98. 623 Fischer M E. The theory of equilibrium critical phenomena.
          Rep. Pr. Phys. 30:615-730, 1967.
99. 277 Fisher R A. Dispersion on a sphere. *P. Roy Soc.A* 217:295-305, 1953.

100.	7,395	**Fiske CH** & Subbarow Y. The colorimetric determination of phosphorus. *J. Biol. Chem.* 66:375-400, 1925.
101.	407	**Flory P J.** *Principles of polymer chemistry.* Ithaca, N.Y.: Cornell University Press, 1953. 672 pp.
102.	7,454	**Folch J,** Lees, M & Sloane-Stanley G H. A simple method for the isolation and purification of total lipides from animal tissues. *J. Biol. Chem.* 226:497-509, 1957.
103.	805	**Fraenkel-Conrat H,** Harris J I & Levy A L. Recent developments in techniques for terminal and sequence studies in peptides and proteins. *Methods of biochemical analysis.* (Glick D. ed.) New York: Wiley-Interscience, 1955. Vol. 2, pp. 359-425.
104.	3,638	**Fredrickson D S,** Levy R I & Lees R S. Fat transport in lipoproteins; an integrated approach to mechanics and disorders. *N. Eng. J. Med.* 276:34-44, 94-103, 148-56, 215-25, 273-81, 1967.
105.	116	**Freud S.** *On the history of the psychoanalytic movement; papers on metapsychology; and other works.* Vol. 14 of *Standard edition of the complete psychological works of Sigmund Freud.* (Strachey J & Freud A. eds.) London: Hogarth Press, 1957. 374 pp.
106.	324	**Friedel J.** Metallic alloys. *Nuov. Ciment.* 7:287-311, 1958.
107.	1,397	**Gell-Mann M.** Symmetries of baryons and mesons. *Phys. Rev.* 125:1067-84, 1962.
108.	224	**Gilman H** & Schulze F. A qualitative color test for the Grignard reagent. *J. Am. Chem. S.* 47:2002-5, 1925.
109.	407	**Ginzburg V L** & Landau L D. On the theory of superconductivity. *Zh. Eksp. Teo.* 30:1064-82, 1950.
110.	833	**Glasstone S,** Laidler K J & Eyring H. *Theory of rate processes.* New York: McGraw-Hill, 1941. 611 pp.
111.	514	**Gomori G.** A modification of colorimetric phosphorus determination for use with the photoelectric colorimeter. *J. La. Cl. Med.* 27:955-60, 1942.
112.	184	**Good R A,** Kelly W O, Rotstein J & Varco R L. Immunological deficiency diseases. *Prog. Allerg.* 6:187-319, 1962.
113.	436	**Goodman L S** & Gilman A. *Pharmacological basis of therapeutics.* New York: Macmillan, 1941. 1383 pp.
114.	884	**Goodwin T W.** The spectrophotometric determination of tyrosine and tryptophan in proteins. *Biochem. J.* 40:628-32, 1946.
115.	5,396	**Gornall A G,** Bardawill C J & Daird M M. Determination of serum proteins by means of the biuret reaction. *J. Biol. Chem.* 78:751-66, 1949.
116.	959	**Grabar P** & Williams C A. Métbode permettant l'étude conjuguée des propriétés électrophorétiques et immunochimiques d'un mélange de protéines. Application au sérum sanguin. (Method of combined study of electrophoretic and immunochemical properties of a protein mixture. Application to blood serum.) *Bioc. Biop. A.* 10:193-4, 1953.
117.	145	**Granit R A** & Kaada B R. Influences of stimulation of central nervous structures in cat. *Act. Physl. S.* 27:130-60, 1953.
118.	250	**Green D E** & Fleisher S. The role of lipids in mitochondrial electron transfer and oxidative phosphorylation. *Bioc. Biop. A.* 70:554-82, 1963.
119.	652	**Gutowsky H S** & Holm C H. Rate processes and nuclear magnetic resonance spectra. 2. Hindered internal rotation of amides. *J. Chem. Phys.* 25:1228-34, 1956.
120.	745	**Hansen M.** *Constitution of binary alloys.* New York: McGraw-Hill, 1958. 1305 pp.
121.	1,841	**Harned H S** & Owen B B. *The physical chemistry of electrolytic solutions.* New York: Reinhold, 1943. 611 pp.
122.	659	**Herbert V,** Lau K S, Gottlieb C W & Bleicher S J. Coated charcoal immunoassay of insulin. *J. Clin. End.* 25:1375-84, 1965.
123.	479	**Herzberg G.** *Molecular spectra and molecular structure.* Vol. 1: *Spectra of diatomic molecules.* New York: Van Nostrand, 1950. 616 pp.
124.	1,193	**Hirs C H W.** The oxidation of ribonuclease with performic acid. *J. Biol. Chem.* 219:611-21, 1956.

125. 3,578   **Hirschfelder J O,** Curtis C F & Bird R B. *Molecular theory of gases and liquids.* New York: Wiley, 1954. 1219 pp.

126. 1,089   **Hodgkin A L** & Huxley A F. A quantitative description of membrane current and its application to conduction and excitation in nerve. *J. Physl. Lon.* 117:500-44, 1952.

127.   92   **Horner L** & Winkelmann E H. Neuere methoden der praparativen organischen chemie. 2. (Recently developed methods for preparatory organic chemistry. 2. *Angew. Chem.* 71:349-65, 1959.

128. 192   **House H O,** Respess W L & Whitesides G M. The chemistry of carbanions. 12. The role of copper in the conjugate addition of organometallic reagents. *J. Org. Chem.* 31:3128-41, 1966.

129. 916   **Hubel D H** & Wiesel T N. Receptive fields, binocular interaction and functional architecture in the cat's visual cortex. *J. Physl. Lon.* 160:106-54, 1952.

130. 753   **Huisgen R.** 1.3-dipolarecycloadditionen. Rückshau und ausblick. *Angew. Chem.* 75:604-37, 1963. (1,3-dipolar cycloadditions; past and future. *Angew. Chem. Inter.* 2:565-98, 1963.)

131. 650   **Huxley H E.** Electron microscope studies on the structure of natural and synthetic protein filaments from striated muscle. *J. Mol. Biol.* 7:281-308, 1963.

132. 2,011   **Ingold C K.** *Structure and mechanism in organic chemistry.* Ithaca, N.Y.: Cornell University Press, 1953. 282 pp.

133. 2,071   **Jackman L M** & Sternhell S. *Applications of nuclear magnetic resonance spectroscopy in organic chemistry.* Elmsford, N.Y.: Pergamon, 1959. 134 pp.

134. 2,227   **Jacob F** & Monod J. Genetic regulatory mechanisms in the synthesis of proteins. *J. Mol. Biol.* 3:318-56, 1961. [Citation Classics. *Current Contents* No. 33, 15 Aug 1977, p. 9.]

135. 1,667   **Jaffé H H.** A re-examination of the Hammett equation. *Chem. Rev.* 53:191-261, 1953.

136. 387   **Johnson H L** & Morgan W W. Fundamental stellar photometry for standards of spectral type on the revised system of the Yerkes spectral *Atlas. Astrophys. J.* 117:313-52, 1953.

137. 196   **Jorgensen C K.** Comparative crystal field studies of some ligands and the lowest state of paramagnetic nickel (II) complexes. *Act. Chem. S.* 9:1362-77, 1955.

138. 3,240   **Kabat E A** & Mayer M. *Experimental immunochemistry.* Springfield, Ill.: C C Thomas, 1948. 905 pp.

139. 1,689   **Karnovsky M J.** A formaldehyde-glutaraldehyde fixative of high osmolality for use in electron microscopy. *J. Cell Bio.* 27:A137-8, 1965.

140. 1,629   **Karplus M.** Contact electron spin coupling of nuclear magnetic moments. *J. Chem. Phys.* 30:11-5, 1959.

141. 759   **Kato T.** *Perturbation theory for linear operators.* New York: Springer, 1966. 592 pp.

142. 176   **Katritzky A R.** The infrared spectra of heteroaromatic compounds. *Q. Rev. Chem. Soc.* 13:353-73, 1959.

143. 216   **Katz B.** The transmission of impulses from nerve to muscle, and the subcellular unit of synaptic section. *P. Roy. Soc. B.* 155:455-77, 1962.

144. 453   **Keilin D** & Hartree E F. On the mechanism of the decomposition of hydrogen peroxide by catalese. *P. Roy. Soc. B.* 124:397-405, 1938.

145. 443   **Kety S S** & Schmidt C F. The effects of altered arterial tensions of carbon dioxide and oxygen on cerebral oxygen consumption of normal young men. *J. Clin. Inv.* 27:484-92, 1948.

146. 397   **King R B.** *Organometallic syntheses.* Vol. 1. *Transition-metal compounds.* New York: Academic Press, 1965. 186 pp.

147. 277   **Kirkwood J G** & Riseman J. The intrinsic viscosities and diffusion constants of flexible macromolecules in solution. *J. Chem. Phys.* 16:565-73, 1948.

148. 253   **Kittel C.** Physical theory of ferromagnetic domains. *Rev. M. Phys.* 21:541-83, 1949.

149. 384 **Klein G,** Sjogren H O, Kelin E & Hellstrom K E. Demonstration of resistance against methylcholanthrene-induced sarcomas in the primary autochthonous host. *Cancer Res.* 20:1561-72, 1960.

150. 216 **Klotz I M,** Walker M & Pivan R B. The binding of organic ions by proteins. *J. Am. Chem. S.* 68:1486-90, 1946.

151. 147 **Kolthoff I M,** Bruckenstein S & Chantooni K M. Acid base equilibria in acetonitrile. Spectrophotometric and conductometric determination of the dissociation of various acids. *J. Am. Chem. S.* 83:3927-35, 1961.

152. 162 **Kornberg A** & Pricer W E. Enzymatic esterification of 2-glycerophosphate by long chain fatty acids. *J. Biol. Chem.* 204:345-57, 1953.

153. 1,535 **Krebs H A** & Henseleit K. Untersuchungen über die Harnstoffbildung im Tierkörper. (Studies on urea formation in the animal organism.) *H-S Z. Physl.* 210:33-66, 1932.

154. 947 **Kubo R.** Statistical-mechanical theory of irreversible process. I. General theory of simple applications to magnetic and conduction problems. *J. Phys. Jap.* 12:570-86, 1957.

155. 412 **Kuhn R,** Trischmann H & Low I. Zur permethylierung von zuckern und glykosiden. (Permethylation of sugars and glycosides.) *Angew. Chem.* 67:32, 1955.

156. 214 **Landau L D.** The theory of superfluidity of helium II. *J. Phys. USSR.* 5:71-90, 1941.

157. 268 **Lee T D,** Weinberg S & Zumino B. Algebra of fields. *Phys. Rev. L.* 18:1029-32, 1967.

158. 412 **Lehninger A L.** Water uptake and extrusion by mitochondria in relation to oxidative phosphorylation. *Physl. Rev.* 42:467-517, 1962.

159. 605 **Lemieux R U,** Kullnig R K, Bernstein H J & Schneider W G. Configurational effects on the proton magnetic resonance spectra of six membered ring compounds. *J. Am. Chem. S.* 80:6098-6105, 1958.

160. 101 **Levine S** & Mollins R F. Hormonal influences on brain organization in infant rats. *Science* 152:1585-92, 1966.

161. 4,633 **Lineweaver H** & Burk D. The determination of enzyme dissociation constants. *J. Am. Chem. S.* 56:658-66, 1934.

162. 453 **Löwdin P O.** Quantum theory of many-particle systems. I. Physical interpretations by means of density matrices, natural spin-orbitals and convergence problems in the method of configurational interaction. *Phys. Rev.* 97:1474-89, 1955.

163. 50,016 **Lowry O H,** Rosebrough N J, Faff A L & Randall R J. Protein measurement with the folin phenol reagent. *J. Biol. Chem.* 193:256-65, 1951. [Citation Classics. *Current Contents* No. 1, 3 Jan 1977, p. 7.]

164. 6,953 **Luft J H.** Improvements in epoxy resin embedding methods. *J. Biop. Bioc.* 9:409-14, 1961. [Citation Classics. *Current Contents* No. 20, 16 May 1977, p. 8.]

165. 3,148 **Marmur J.** A procedure for the isolation of deoxyribonucleic acid from microorganisms. *J. Mol. Biol.* 3:208-18, 1961.

166. 518 **McConnell H M** & Chestnut D B. Theory of isotropic hyperfine interactions in π electron radicals. *J. Chem. Phys.* 28:107-17, 1958.

167. 887 **McKusick V A.** *Heritable disorders of connective tissue.* St. Louis: Mosby, 1956. 224 pp.

168. 669 **Miller J F A.** Immunological function of the thymus. *Lancet* 2:748-9, 1961.

169. 1,441 **Millonig G.** Advantages of a phosphate buffer for OsO_4 solutions in fixation. *J. Appl. Phys.* 32:1637, 1961.

170. 505 **Mitchell P.** Chemiosmotic coupling in oxidative and photosynthetic phosphorylation. *Biol. Rev.* 41:445-502, 1966.

171. 1,685 **Monod J.** On the nature of allosteric transitions: a plausible model. *J. Mol. Biol.* 12:88-118, 1965.

172. 1,475 **Moore S,** Spackman D H & Stein W H. Chromatography of amino acids on sulfonated polystyrene resins. *Analyt. Chem.* 30:1185-90, 1958.

173. 276 **Morse P M.** Diatomic molecules according to the wave mechanics. 2. Vibrational levels. *Phys. Rev.* 34:57-64, 1929.
174. 412 **Mott N F.** Electrons in disordered structures. *Adv. Phys.* 16:49-144, 1967.
175. 104 **Muller A & Krebs B.** Normal coordinate treatment of XY4- type molecules and ions with T_d symmetry. *J. Mol. Spect.* 24:180-97, 1967.
176.   61 **Müller E & Rundel W.** Verätherung von alkoholen mit diazomethan unter borfluorid-katalyse. (Etherification of alcohols with diazomethane under boron fluoride catalysis.) *Angew. Chem.* 70:105, 1958.
177. 960 **Mulliken R S.** Electronic population analysis on LCAO-MO molecular wave functions. I. *J. Chem. Phys.* 23:1833-40, 1955.
178. 240 **Nakamoto K,** Margoshes M & Rundle R E. Stretching frequencies as a function of distances in hydrogen bonds. *J. Am. Chem. S.* 77:6480-6, 1955.
179. 102 **Natta G.** Progress in the stereospecific polymerization. *Makrom. Chem.* 35:94-131, 1960.
180. 281 **Nesmeyanov A N.** *Davlenie para khimicheskikh elementov.* (*Vapour pressure of the elements.*) Moskow: Publishing House of the Academy of Sciences of USSR, 1961. 469 pp.
181.   84 **Newman M S & Beal P F.** An improved Wolff rearrangement in homogeneous medium. *J. Am. Chem. S.* 72:5163-5, 1950.
182. 390 **Novikoff A B,** Essner E & Quintana N. Golgi apparatus and lysosomes. *Fed. Proc.* 23:1010-22, 1964.
183. 123 **Olah G A & White A M.** Stable carbonium ions. 91. Carbon-13 nuclear magnetic resonance spectroscopic study of carbonium ions. *J. Am. Chem. S.* 91:5801-10, 1969.
184. 875 **Ouchterlony O.** Diffusion-in-gel methods for immunological analysis. *Prog. Allergy* 5:1-78, 1958.
185. 2,072 **Palade G E.** A study of fixation for electron microscopy. *J. Exp. Med.* 95:285-97, 1952.
186. 3,040 **Pauling L.** *The nature of the chemical bond and the structure of molecules and crystals; an introduction to modern structural chemistry.* Ithaca, N.Y.: Cornell University Press, 1939, 429 pp.
187. 1,256 **Pearse A G E.** *Histochemistry, theoretical and applied.* Boston: Little, Brown, 1953. 530 pp.
188. 471 **Perutz M F,** Muirhead H, Cox J M & Goaman L C G. Three dimensional Fourier synthesis of horse oxyhaemoglobin at 2.8 Å resolution: The atomic model, *Nature* 219:131-9, 1968.
189. 1,215 **Pople J A & Segal G A.** Approximate self-consistent molecular orbital theory. 3. CNDO results for AB_2 and AB_3 systems. *J. Chem. Phys.* 44:3289-96, 1966.
190. 624 **Prigogine I.** *The molecular theory of solutions.* New York: Interscience, 1957. 448 pp.
191. 358 **Racker E.** Spectrophotometric measurements of the enzymatic formation of fumaric and cisaconitic acids. *Bioc. Biop. A.* 4:211-4, 1950.
192. 3,323 **Reed L J & Meunch H.** A simple method of estimating fifty percent endpoints. *Am. J. Hyg.* 27:493-7, 1938.
193. 9,002 **Reynolds E S.** The use of lead citrate at high pH as an electron opaque stain in electron microscopy. *J. Cell Biol.* 17:208-12, 1963.
194. 206 **Roberts J D & Mazur R H.** Small-ring compounds. 4. Interconversion reactions of cyclobutyl, cyclopropylcarbinyl and allycarbinyl derivatives. *J. Am. Chem. S.* 73:2509-20, 1951.
195. 438 **Robinson R A & Stokes R H.** *Electrolyte solutions.* New York: Plenum, 1955. 559 pp.
196. 400 **Rose M E.** The analysis of angular correction and angular distribution data. *Phys. Rev.* 91:610-5, 1953.
197. 520 **Rossini F D.** *Selected values of physical and thermodynamic properties of hydrocarbons and related compounds.* Pittsburgh: Carnegie University Press, 1953. 1050 pp.
198. 307 **Russell G A,** Jazcn E G & Strom E I. Electron transfer processes. 1. The scope of the reaction between carbanions or nitranions and unsaturated electron acceptors. *J. Am. Chem. S.* 86:1807-14, 1964.

199. 4,934 **Sabatini D D.** Cytochemistry and electron microscopy: the preservation of cellular ultrastructure and enzymatic activity by aldehyde fixation. *J. Cell Biol.* 17:19-58, 1963.

200. 1,575 **Scatchard G.** The attractions of proteins for small molecules and ions. *Ann. N.Y. Acad.* 51:660-72, 1949.

201. 3,660 **Scheidegger J J.** Une micro-méthode de l'immuno-électrophase. (Immunoelectrophase micromethod.) *A. Aller.* 7:103-10, 1955.

202. 1,518 **Schneider W C.** Phosphorus compounds in animal tissues. 1. Extraction and estimation of desoxypentose nucleic acid and of pentose nucleic acid. *J. Biol. Chem.* 161:293-303, 1945.
[Citation Classics. *Current Contents* No. 8, 21 Feb 1977, p. 12.]

203. 251 **Schwarzenbach G**, Gut R & Anderegg G. Komplexone XXV. Die polarographische untersuchung von austausch-gleichgewichten. (Polarographic study on exchange equilibria.) *Helv. Chim A.* 37:937-57, 1954.

204. 245 **Schwinger J.** Field theory commutators. *Phys. Rev. L.* 3:296-7, 1959.

205. 259 **Seeger A.** The mechanism of glide and work hardening in face-centered cubic and hexagonal close-packed metals. *Dislocations and mechanical properties of crystals.* (Fisher T C, Johnston W G, Thomson R & Vreeland T, eds.) New York: Wiley, 1957, pp. 243-329.

206. 249 **Seitz F.** Color centers in alkali halide crystals. 2. *Rev. M. Phys.* 26:7-94, 1954.

207. 167 **Selye H.** The general adaptation syndrome and the diseases of adaptation. *J. Clin. End.* 6:117-230, 1946.
[Citation Classics. *Current Contents* No. 13, 28 Mar 1977, p. 13.]

208. 168 **Seyferth D**, Burlitch J M, Minasz R J, Mui J Y P, Simmons H D, Treiber A D H & Dowd S R. Halomethyl-metal compounds. 2. The preparation of *gem*-dihalocyclopropanes by the reaction of phenyl(trihalomethyl)mercury compounds with olefins. *J. Am. Chem. S.* 87:4259-70, 1950.

209. 167 **Sillen L G.** High speed computers as a supplement to graphic methods. *Act. Chem. S.* 16:159-72, 1962.

210. 752 **Skou J C.** The influence of some cations on an adenosine triphosphatase from peripheral nerves. *Bioc. Biop. A.* 23:394-401, 1957.

211. 772 **Slater J C.** Atomic shielding constants. *Phys. Rev.* 36:57-64, 1930.

212. 782 **Smith H W**, Finklestein N, Aliminosa L, Crawford B & Grabar M. The renal clearances of substituted hippuric acid derivatives and other aromatic acids in dog and man. *J. Clin. Inv.* 24:388-404, 1945.

213. 2,041 **Smithies O.** Zone electrophoresis in starch gels: group variations in the serum proteins of normal human adults. *Biochem. J.* 61:629-41, 1955.

214. 3,254 **Snedecor G W** & Cochran W G. *Statistical methods applied to experiments in agriculture and biology.* Ames, Iowa: Iowa State, 1956. 534 pp.
[Citation Classics. *Current Contents* No. 19, 9 May 1977, p. 10.]

215. 1,439 **Somogyi M.** Notes on sugar determination. *J. Biol. Chem.* 195:19-23, 1952.

216. 5,727 **Spackman D H**, Stein W H & Moore S. Automatic recording apparatus for use in the chromatography of amino acids. *Analyt. Chem.* 30:1190-1206, 1958.

217. 276 **Spitzer L.** *Physics of fully ionized gases.* New York: Interscience, 1956. 105 pp.

218. 382 **Stahl E.** Dünnschicht-chromatographie. II. Standardisierung, sichtbarmachung, dokumentation, und anwendung. (Thin layer chromatography. 2. Standardization, visualization, documentation and application.) *Chem. Zeitun.* 82:323-9, 1958.

219. 1,381 **Steel R G D & Torrie J.** *Principles and procedures of statistics, with special reference to the biological sciences.* New York: McGraw-Hill, 1960. 481 pp.
[Citation Classics. *Current Contents* No. 39, 26 Sep 1977, p. 20.]

220. 2,155 **Streitwieser A.** *Molecular orbital theory for organic chemists.* New York: Wiley, 1961. 489 pp.

221. 330 **Sutherland E W**, Cori C F, Hayes R & Olsen N. Purification of the hyperglycemic-glycogenolytic factor from insulin and from gastric mucosa. *J. Biol. Chem.* 180:825-37, 1949.

222. 331 **Taft R W.** Sigma values from reactives. *J. Phys. Chem.* 64:1805-15, 1960.

223.   356   **Tanford C.** Protein denaturation. *Adv. Protein Chem.* 23:121-282, 1968.
224.   246   **Udenfriend S,** Weissbach H & Clark C T. The estimation of 5-hydroxytryptamin (serotonia) in biological tissue. *J. Biol. Chem.* 215:337-44, 1955.
225.   916   **Umbreit W W,** Burris R H & Stauffer J F. *Manometric and biochemical techniques.* Minneapolis: Burgess, 1945. 198 pp.
226. 1,176 **Van Slyke D D** & McNeill J M. The determination of gases in blood and other solutions by vacuum extractions and manometric measurements. I. *J. Biol. Chem.* 61:523-73, 1924.
227.   907   **Van Vleck J H.** The dipolar broadening of magnetic resonance in crystals. *Phys. Rev.* 57:426-47, 1940.
228.   429   **von Euler U S** & Lishajko F. Improved technique for the fluorimetric estimation of catecholamines. *Act. Phys. S.* 51:348-56, 1961.
229.   132   **Walling C** & Thaler W. Positive halogen compounds. 3. Allylic chlorination with tert-butyl hypochlorite stereochemistry of allylic radicals. *J. Am. Chem. S.* 83:3877, 1961.
230. 2,594 **Warburg O.** Isolierung und kristallisation des gärungsferments enolase. (Isolation and crystallization of the enzyme enolase.) *Biochem. Z.* 310:384-421, 1941.
231. 2,656 **Warren L.** The thiobarbituric acid assay of sialic acids. *J. Biol. Chem.* 234:1971-5, 1959.
232. 2,509 **Watson M L.** Staining of tissue sections for electron microscopy with heavy metals. *J. Biop. Bioc.* 4:475-9, 1958.
233.   242   **Weber G.** Polarization of the fluorescence of macromolecules. 2. Fluorescent conjugates of ovalbumin and bovine serum albumin. *Biochem. J.* 51:155-67, 1952.
234. 4,586 **Weber K** & Osborn M. The reliability of molecular weight determinations by dodecyl sulfate-polyacrylamide gel electrophoresis. *J. Biol. Chem.* 244:4406-12, 1969.
235.   622   **Weinberg S.** Pion scattering lengths. *Phys. Rev. L.* 17:616-21, 1966.
236.   275   **Weiss P.** Experiments on the mechanism of nerve growth. *J. Exp. Zool.* 107:315-95, 1948.
237.   335   **Wiberg K B.** The deuterium isotope effect. *Chem. Rev.* 55:713-43, 1955.
238.   108   **Wieland T.** Poisonous principles of mushrooms of the genus amanita. *Science* 195:946-52, 1968.
239.   101   **Wigglesworth V B.** The function of the corpus allatum in the growth and reproduction of rhodnius proplexus (Hemiptera). *Q.J. Mic. Sci.* 79:91-121, 1936.
240.   386   **Wigner E P.** On unity representations of the inhomogenous Lorentz group. *Ann. Math.* 40:149-204, 1939.
241.   503   **Wilson E B.** *Molecular vibrations: theory of infra-red and raman vibrational spectra.* New York: McGraw-Hill, 1955. 388 pp.
242. 1,444 **Winer B J.** *Statistical principles in experimental design.* New York: McGraw-Hill, 1962. 672 pp.
243.   366   **Winstein S** & Holness N J. Neighboring carbon and hydrogen. 19. T-butylcyclohexl derivatives. Quantitative conformational analysis. *J. Am. Chem. S.* 77:5562-78, 1955.
244.   184   **Wittig G** & Schollkopf U. Uber triphenyl-phosphinmethylene als olefinbindende reagenzien. (Triphenyl-phosphinemethylenes as olefin-binding reagents.) *Chem. Ber.* 87:1318-30, 1954.
245.   962   **Woodward R B,** & Hoffmann R. Die erhaltung der orbitalsymmetric. (The conservation of orbital symmetry.) *Angew. Chem.* 81:797-869, 1969. (*Angew. Chem. Int.* 8:781-853, 1969.)
246.   419   **Zachariasen W H.** The secondary extinction correction. *Act. Cryst.* 16:1139-44, 1963.
247.   561   **Zeldovich Y B** & Raizer Y P. *Physics of shock waves and high temperature hydrodynamic phenomena.* New York: Academic Press, 1966. 2 vols.
248.   316   **Ziman J M.** A theory of the electrical properties of liquid metals. 1. The monovalent metals. *Philosoph. Mag.* 6:1013-34, 1961.
249.   151   **Zimmerman H E** & Schuster D I. A new approach to mechanistic organic photochemistry. 4. Photochemical rearrangements of 4,4-diphenylcyclohexadienone. *J. Am. Chem. S.* 84:4527-40, 1962.

CURRENT COMMENTS

The Computer:
Practical Tool, Ultimate Toy

Number 52, December 26, 1977

At this time of year, many adults find themselves reminiscing about the toys they wanted or received during the holiday seasons of their childhood. If you have any doubt about this, just watch parents in a toy store as they choose gifts for their children. Their attitude often seems to be,"I only had a wooden toy car you had to push around; my child is going to have an electric racer." For many adults, childhood frustrations are relieved by "hobbies" which gratify their desire to play with elaborate gadgets. Thus the electric racer often turns into a remote-control airplane not particularly appropriate for a six-year-old.

In the article reprinted on pages 8-12,[1] Mike Koenig, ISI® 's Director of Development, sees a dark side to our fondness for toys. He theorizes that we like to produce, own, and use high technology devices for the fun of it. These gadgets satisfy the unfulfilled desires of childhood. Certainly in America, many homes are littered with machines. A new home is often an investment in gadgets more than mortar and wood. We use electric can openers and toothbrushes. We buy elaborate stereophonic equipment and power tools. Many of us won't accept simply any machine; we want the newest, most powerful, most advanced model—whether lawnmower or automobile. The energy crisis has accentuated the contradictions in our predilection for power. Why do our cars have speedometers which measure up to 100 miles per hour? The speed limit in most states is 55 miles per hour.

Koenig observes that "playing with toys" is not a socially acceptable end in itself. In consequence, we have rationalized a purpose—national defense—for developing bigger and better toys. We have built a military establishment where technophiles may produce and play with enormously expensive new devices.

The danger is that these toys may

eventually be used for their avowed purpose. So Koenig suggests how the military's domination of super-toys may be diminished. He thinks we should recognize weapons for the toys they are. And the manipulation of toys should be made socially acceptable. At the same time, the entire population should be given access to toys as sophisticated as anything the military has to offer—but not as dangerous.

The one toy which now fills this need, Koenig claims, is the computer. Academia and industry already have computer systems as complex as the military's, and computers in the home are only a few years away.[2] Americans—who can't buy larger stereo speakers for fear of cracking plaster and may not legally drive their cars as fast as they will go—can put computers through their paces, making them perform any task that can be programmed.

I have no doubt that at least a few computer systems have been installed as a result of an inherent desire to possess the latest toy. At ISI, however, the computer has never been a frill. It is the central production tool which makes many of our services practical. Without the computer it would be much more difficult to produce six Weekly Subject Indexes for *Current Contents®* . And economic production of the *Science Citation Index®* would be

almost impossible.[3] But I take great pride in the fact that our ASCA® system can still be operated, if necessary, with second-generation computers.[4]

In recent years ISI has begun to use computers for administrative records. This is the purpose to which they are most often put by organizations—hence the ubiquity of punched cards, which I discussed recently.[5] Perhaps because ISI has had more experience with and understanding of computers, our use of the computer in administration has been less dramatic but more successful than that in other organizations. Of special interest are the effects of the on-line, interactive system in our subscriptions department. New subscribers are now mailed their first issue of *CC®* within days after receipt of their orders. Address changes are processed just as promptly. Similarly, subscription payments are applied to accounts within 48 hours after receipt.

The use of computers throughout ISI has led to a healthy and balanced appreciation of them among our staff. This includes many who might still consider themselves technophobes. They certainly are not technophiles. They know that *people* make most of the mistakes attributed to computers.[6] If Koenig's proposed "Toy Access Department" ever comes into being, it won't receive many calls from ISI people. They have enough contact with computers at work to want to avoid them in leisure time. Whether Koenig's highly speculative theory holds up in real life is problematic. It is somewhat simplistic to think that the solution to an entrenched military-technology establishment is merely to substitute computers for atomic weapons. The defense establishment has been playing with computers from the earliest days. You can't change the military mentality simply by sending generals to programming classes. If only the problem were that simple!

The "toy theory" certainly is not the first behavioral approach to the eternal problem of worldwide conflict resolution. But at this time of year it is especially fitting that individuals and nations reflect on these questions. While others might regard scientific competition as childish, I am naive enough to believe that worldwide commitment to basic research is crucial in helping to preserve peace on earth.

Have a happy new year!

REFERENCES

1. **Koenig M E D.** The toy theory of western history. *Bulletin of the Atomic Scientists* 23:16-8, 1977. [Reprinted in: *Chemtech* 7:595-7, 1977; and in: *The Sun* (Baltimore, Md.) 281(144):A15, 31 October 1977.]
2. **Garfield E.** Viewdata and *SCITEL*™ bring interactive information systems into the home. *Current Contents* No. 41, 10 October 1977, p. 5-10.
3. ------------. *Project Keysave*—ISI's new on-line system for keying citations corrects errors! *Current Contents* No. 7, 14 February 1977, p. 5-7.
4. ------------. The information-conscious university and *ASCA* software. *Current Contents* No. 37, 12 September 1977, p. 5-7.
5. ------------. Information theory and all that jazz. *Current Contents* No. 44, 31 October 1977, p. 5-7.
6. ------------. 'Our computer goofed.' *Current Contents* No. 23, 9 June 1975, p. 5. [Reprinted in: *Essays of an information scientist.* Philadelphia: ISI Press, 1977. Vol. 2, p. 296.]

The toy theory of western history

M. E. D. Koenig

Courtesy *The Sun*, Baltimore, Md.

The excess of militarism which has plagued Western society for the last century and a half is largely the result of a motivation which our society consistently underestimates. That motivation is very simply the desire to play with toys. The phrase "play with toys" is used here in the very broad sense of manipulating devices which are both novel and high-performance, devices which push the "state of the art."

The consequences of this seemingly harmless propensity have been extraordinarily significant and rather unfortunate. We have rationalized and built large military organizations primarily for the purpose of providing those technophiles among us with the opportunity to play with the neatest and newest toys. The military is in reality simply a gigantic communal toy-owning organization. That is its fascination and its true *raison d'être.*

The insidious nature of our predilection for toys lies not only in the consequences of the rationalizations that we have used, but in the blindness of the non-technophile to the importance that toys possess for a very major portion of our society.

The motivations of most people in the military are for the most part unrecognized, even by themselves. They are, like most of us, very unaware of their unconscious motivations. Those who are aware suppress it. Playing with toys is not perceived as a mature man-like thing to do in our society and, even if it were, the admission of it would jeopardize the military's existence by violating its rationale for existence. How many people are, on the face of it, willing to spend a vast amount of our national resources on a toy cooperative?

If the military functioned only as a toy-owning organization, its function would be innocuous enough. However, the problem is that once a military organization has been created, its momentum builds and there is a tendency to use the organization for its avowed purpose. This prob-lem arises primarily because of society's refusal to admit the importance of toys as a form of manipulation.

The military and the technophiles must find a way of rationalizing their toy coop, and the rationalization takes the all-too-familiar form of "national defense," "national preparedness," "missile gap" and so on. This rationalization has been determined in large part by the nature of technology itself. The most enjoyable toys are the most powerful, those that push the state of the art the hardest. For the last 150 years the nature of technology itself has been such that those applications which pushed the state of the art have been defensible only for the military.

A P-40 is, for example, a far more exciting toy than a DC-3; a destroyer pushing its 2,000 tons with 60,000 horsepower offers a pleasure far more visceral than a freighter using a quarter of that power to push ten times that weight. The destroyer's power-to-weight ratio is greater by more than an order of magnitude.

If one wanted to design the "hottest"—toy jargon for the fastest, most powerful, highest performance—plane one could conceive, who could possibly justify it except the military? If one wanted to build, or fly, or merely be associated with a "hot" machine, there has been essentially no alternative to the military. Admittedly, when a technology is new, there may be alternatives to military design and procurement; the national air races of the 1930s were an example of advanced high performance design in a civilian context. However, as technology grows more sophisticated, and as expenses escalate, the military tends to become the only supplier of the pleasures associated with extreme technological performance.

Democratic the military may not be, but it is in a sense a populist institution which can make available the toys of our culture to millions of people for whom they would have been otherwise unobtainable. Great personal wealth is the only alternative and not many of us are blessed with it.

Hippie Protest

The unconscious realization of this state of affairs was a major motivation behind the hippie movement, or "counterculture," of the 1960s. The hippies were saying, in effect: "Society, your goddam toys are dangerous; we want to substitute something else—love, drugs, beads." Hippies were also prisoners of our culture, and they were, unfortunately, in the main unaware of what they were really trying to say. They diluted and disguised their message with political propaganda, rationalizing their actions just as effectively as the technophiles rationalized theirs.

The irony is that while the technophiles' rationalizations continued to serve military purposes, the rationalizations of the hippies were counterproductive, alienating many of their potential supporters. For example, these unverbalized aims of the counterculture were what the policemen and the national guardsmen at the Chicago convention were responding to: the response of the child whose toy was threatened.

Despite the basic logic and relevance of the hippie protest, it was in a very real sense beside the point and after the fact. That is, new technology has been increasingly applicable directly to non-military applications. In this trend lies our hope of breaking the spiral of escalation. Toys are inevitable, and our task is to provide access to these fruits of technology *outside* the military, and to increase the opportunities for the public to participate in their pleasures.

Decreased Military Control

This trend away from military dominance of the forefront of technology is composed of three basic elements:

• One element has been the introduction of nuclear weapons. The nature of military hardware has been changed; it has been dehumanized. Destructive power has been incredibly concentrated, and the opportunity to play with the toys correspondingly lessened.

One individual ICBM in a silo in Montana contains far more destructive power than a squadron of 21, B-17s carrying ten men each, but delivers not nearly so much visceral excitement. Only a few men are directly involved, and their opportunity to "practice" with their toys is severely limited—indeed, it becomes a matter of congressional debate. This perhaps is part of the motivation for manned bombers and submarine-launched ballistic missiles—if the missiles are no longer adequate toys because practice is limited, the old standbys can be called upon and justified as new "delivery systems." In this context, the development of small "clean" nuclear warheads, and talk of limited nuclear war is a disturbing regression.

• Involvement with the military's most impressive hardware has also been limited to a select few. Increasingly, the military provides sport for spectators rather than direct participation. And the stronger this trend becomes, the greater the importance of NASA's better-quality, toy-dominated spectaculars. These spectator sports—NASA and manned-space exploration (now sadly moribund)—are the second element.

The visceral thrill, the gut-filling rumble, that a Saturn V provides is important and will be so as long as man occupies a physical self. The point is that a civilian organization, NASA, has toys the military cannot match—fascinating powerful toys that are also of relative safety to society.

• The third and most important element has been the introduction of the computer. The computer is a toy of such a vast spectrum of potential use that the military can dominate only a very small part of it. Any university computation center, or any major industrial organization, has computers of a power that are quite comparable to what the military possesses.

Computer as a Toy

A further consequence of the unique nature of the computer, and one that is equally as important, is that not only is the hardware *availa-* ble outside the military but the most interesting and satisfying opportunities to *use* that hardware are also in the non-military sector.

That is, even if the DC-3 had possessed the performance potential of a P-40, a commercial pilot, with passengers or cargo aboard, simply would never have an opportunity to "wring his plane out" in the fashion of a military pilot. But with computer technology, this position is reversed. The opportunity to put a computer through its paces is far greater in the groves of academe than in any military organization.

The computer is, in fact, a machine with an entirely new set of constraints. The most exotic use of a computer puts no more strain on any given logic circuit than does the most trivial use. The constraints are now a function of how the organization defines its role, and in this context a military rationalization becomes a constraining influence.

With pre-computer toys—aircraft, guns, motorcycles, whatever—the fascination was, in effect, with how much the toy could extend one's self—how much it could put onto you. On the other hand, with a computer the fascination is with what one puts into the toy.

At first glance, this sounds ominous, regressive: once we received from the machine; now we give to it. But now we have a toy that extends not our limbs, but our minds. When we create knowledge to impart it elsewhere, to man or machine, we have not lost but gained. A computer is a toy unique in its capacity for non-destructive manipulation—no other device can be "floorboarded" so safely.

A trend toward decreasing military control of our toys is obviously one to be encouraged. Along these lines some suggestions and ideas are herewith offered:

• We should promote the rapid acquisition of computer expertise by societies other than our own, particularly Soviet and Chinese societies, and embargoes and restricted lists should be modified. Perhaps we should give computers to the Soviet Union and to China—even parachute them in.

• We should continue with manned space exploration. There is no real need for space exploration to be a race. Indeed, it can be a very appropriate vehicle for international cooperation. However, it must be supported at a level that will allow it to maintain a technology that is substantially in advance of the military. We must also admit that an element of the spectacular is a necessary and a quite legitimate aspect of exploration. "Space spectacular" should no longer be a phrase of condescension.

• Not all of us are intrigued by computers, however, and the need to provide non-military access to "traditional" toys is of equally great importance. Given the nature of modern military weapons, the speed with which we can provide this access becomes crucial. Dare we simply wait for the slow evolution of the trends described above?

• An even more direct solution was hinted at earlier: a direct substitute for the military—a straightforward government-supported organization or agency whose explicit purpose is to provide access to toys.

Such an agency need not start with its own toys, it need only provide access—the establishment's equivalent to the *Whole Earth Catalog*.

• It has been a stock remark for years among technophiles that the government could reduce its defense budget simply by charging for access to its toys: renting brief rides in an F-4 with supersonic speeds guaranteed; holding public firepower demonstrations; selling space aboard a destroyer for a weekend of antisubmarine warfare operations.

• There is, of course, no requirement that this "toy access department" (TAD, a division of HEW) specialize in military toys. Many technophiles covet, for example, the chance to operate powerful Peterbilt's (if all the legendary prowess of Rolls Royce, Bugatti and Ferrari were combined in one automobile, that car would be to cars what Peterbilt is to trucks) or GGI's (the classic electric locomotive). What is crucial is that the hurdles obstructing non-military access to toys be drastically lowered.

* * *

The military problem has arisen not only from the nature of technology itself but also from the refusal of decision-makers and opinion leaders to legitimize toy manipulation as a socially acceptable goal, and from their maladaptive acceptance of the abstraction of "defense" as the major rationale for providing access to toys. The furtherance of toy manipulation for its own sake must be legitimized as a national goal. □

CURRENT COMMENTS

More on Cremation and Other Alternatives to Traditional Burial

Number 1, January 2, 1978

A few months ago I discussed cremation as a practical alternative to in-ground burial, and I solicited the reactions of *Current Contents*® readers to that idea.[1] I was surprised by the number of responses and by their generally positive tone.

My unfortunate experience with funeral directors was not unique. Several of my correspondents confirmed this with examples from their own experiences. Almost all agreed that cremation is preferable to burial and should not be hindered by the burial establishment.

For example, Julian B. Schorr, Director of the Tidewater Regional Red Cross Blood Program in Norfolk, wrote, "The fact that state legislatures have been 'conned' into requiring licensed 'body movers,' mandatory coffins, and the like is in about the same class of legislative activity as that which allocates money each year to tobacco growers so that more of our friends can hack themselves to death.... Taking on the vested interests requires a 'Ralph Nader' approach and per-

haps he...should be enjoined to do so."

P.H.B. Carstens of the University of Louisville Health Sciences Center, whose native country is Denmark, commented, "Most Europeans would be horrified to learn about the American practice of embalmment and showing off at the funeral homes before the burial."

Speaking from a unique perspective, W. Noel Brown, Staff Chaplain at the University of Michigan Hospitals, said, "I do take some issue with you that scientists as a group are less squeamish than others about the practical side of death. In my experience, which is primarily in university teaching centers, I see scientists as being rather like the general population, i.e., unprepared and ill-at-ease. I should add that medical physicians are often little different."

One possibly valid reservation about cremation was expressed by Joseph L. Kyner of the University of Kansas Medical Center, who asked, "Does not cremation use a significant amount of energy, chiefly, I presume, in the form of natural gas or electricity, to accomplish the final ashed product?... Perhaps the amount of energy utilized is not a big item, but if cremation was the norm it could be a significant factor."

Since the number of cremations in the U.S. is still low, the energy used per cremation is relatively high. Greater efficiency could be achieved in a variety of ways. If cremation became a routine matter, people would become less squeamish about multiple cremations. But I must confess that the images that ran through my mind when I visited a crematorium were unpleasant. I could not help recalling a visit 20 years ago to Dachau.

Of course, the energy used for a typical in-ground burial is not trivial either. Most graves are now dug by equipment powered by gasoline engines. And consider the number of automobiles that are used for wakes, funerals, and grave-site visits. Also to be considered is the energy expended in smelting, die cutting, and polishing the metal used in fancier caskets. To come up with a definitive answer to this problem, I suppose we need an operations research expert to develop a proper mathematical model. At present, I doubt that it matters much which form of body disposal is most energy-efficient.

On the subject of grave-site visits, Dr. Gunther E. Molau of Dow Chemical had this to say: "To leave a grave is, for me, not only superfluous but even somewhat harmful to my family because it ties people down to look after the grave, and today's people are mobile people."

Despite such pragmatic reasons for choosing cremation, the practice has very little acceptance in the United States. According to the 1974 edition of the *Encyclopaedia Britannica,* only 8% of those who die in the US are cremated. In Japan, where the practice was illegal a century ago, cremation now is almost universal. And in Sweden, Denmark, England and West Germany, more than 50% are cremated.[2] Telephone checks with various sources indicate that these estimates are still accurate.

Elsewhere, however, cremations sometimes carry unfavorable associations because of the Nazi atrocities in the death camps. In Lithuania, which I recently visited, there are no cremations at all. In Siberia and other parts of the U.S.S.R. that I visited there is no economic incentive to use cremation because land is plentiful. On the other hand, though they are not illegal in Israel, cremations are forbidden by Jewish religious law. Similarly, Moslems never use cremation, according to the Islamic Center in Washington, D.C.

Apparently, my call for the establishment of a cremation society was not particularly original. Several readers informed me that such organizations are already in existence. For example, I had never heard of the Continental Association of Funeral and Memorial Societies, an affiliation of some 150 local societies located throughout the United States. The individual societies are non-profit organizations that are usually founded by churches or ministerial associations. They assist members in selecting a funeral director and arranging, at the lowest price, either cremation or traditional burial. The one-time membership fees range from $5 for an individual to $20 for a family; an additional $5 charge is made at the time of death to cover record-keeping. At present, the membership of Continental's local societies totals about three-quarters of a million people. Its address and the addresses of other organizations helpful in body disposal are given on page 11.

Several readers told me about a *direct* cremation service called Telophase Society of America, which operates mainly on the West Coast. It was founded by Thomas Byrnes Weber, a biochemist, and Tom Sherrard, a lawyer, to simplify the process of direct cremation. Telophase is a for-profit organization. It has its own vehicles, personnel, storage facilities and crematory. It will file the death certificate, pick up the body, arrange the cremation, and scatter or deliver the ashes. In San Diego, where Telophase is based, cremations account for 36% of all dispositions. This rate has been increasing at the rate of 2% per year, according to Edwin H. Stivers, president of the Telophase Society. Telophase charges $15 for membership and $250 at the time of death. The same services are available to non-members for $300.

Although these amounts are far less than the $2,000 cost of an average American burial, they still seem a little higher than absolutely necessary. Previously I mentioned the funeral director who initially wanted to charge me $400 for a simple cremation.[1] Later he called me back to say he would never refuse to handle a needy case for $250. The funeral director who finally handled the cremation charged only $175 and never asked about my personal finances. So I began to wonder about the $250 figure. It was easy to understand when I learned that a Social Security death benefit of $255 is payable to the person who pays for the funeral arrangements. Most people are not aware that they are entitled to this benefit regardless of the actual cost. Incidentally, in my case, only $55 to $75 of the total cost was for the cremation itself.

A few readers urged me to publish information on how to avoid the disposal problem almost entirely by donating one's body to medical research. While many people express a desire to donate their bodies to medical research, a lack of knowledge of the procedure often prevents this wish from being fulfilled. The following explanation may be helpful to those who wish to make such a gift. I hope my foreign colleagues will understand that space and time do not permit me to elaborate on practices outside the United States.

According to the Uniform Anatomical Gift Act, anyone age eighteen or over (in a few states the age is 21) may declare himself or herself a donor by completing a Uniform Donor Card (below). A signed donor card is a legal document. As indicated on the card, donating one's body is a separate act from donating one's organs or parts. However, if only organs or parts are given, the final disposal of the body remains the responsibility of family and friends. When the entire body is given, the disposal is handled by the recipient medical school. Donors' loved ones are spared the agony which accompanies the usual funeral and burial arrangements.

Uniform Donor Cards can be obtained from all medical schools and anatomical gifts registries, the National Kidney Foundation, the American Medical Association's Transplant Committee, and the National Eye Bank Association of America. Incidentally, the Eye Bank Association has organized a nationwide ham radio network of 134 operators to make maximum use of donors by broadcasting twice a day all the needs of the 80 eye banks in the U.S.

The procedure for giving your body to medical research can be initiated by contacting the anatomy department of the nearest medical school. If there is no coordinating agency in your state, you can work directly with the school to make the gift; if there is such an agency, you will be referred to it. As a test, we actually called several medical schools in the Philadelphia area. Each of them promptly gave us the

---

UNIFORM DONOR CARD

OF_____
    Print or type name of donor

In the hope that I may help others, I hereby make this anatomical gift, if medically acceptable, to take effect upon my death. The words and marks below indicate my desires.

I give: (a) _____ any needed organs or parts
          (b) _____ only the following organs or parts

_____
        Specify the organ(s) or part(s)
for the purposes of transplantation, therapy, medical research or education;

          (c) _____ my body for anatomical study if needed.

Limitations or
special wishes, if any :_____

Signed by the donor and the following two witnesses in the presence of each other:

_____   _____
Signature of Donor   Date of Birth of Donor

_____   _____
Date Signed   City & State

_____   _____
Witness   Witness

This is a legal document under the Uniform Anatomical Gift Act or similar laws.

For further information consult your physician or

National Kidney Foundation
116 East 27th Street, New York, N.Y. 10016

The Uniform Donor Card distributed by the National Kidney Foundation. Similar cards may be obtained from other organizations.

375

number of the coordinating agency for Pennsylvania: The Humanities Gifts Registry.

The medical school or coordinating agency will send you forms to complete and return and a Uniform Donor Card to sign and keep with you. You may specify on the card which medical school is to receive the body.

The procedural steps that occur after death differ according to the state in which you live. To keep the explanation simple, I will discuss what happens in the state of Pennsylvania. It should be noted that the steps are similar in each state, but not identical, and as I will show, the differences can be very important.

When a signed donor from Pennsylvania dies, the Humanities Gifts Registry—HGR—is notified by a family member or some other person. HGR ascertains that a death certificate has been signed and sends a funeral director (paid by HGR) to transport the body—which must be unembalmed and unautopsied—to a designated medical school. The medical school then embalms the body with a special solution and stores it until research is to be performed.

Next, a letter acknowledging the thanks of HGR is sent to the family or friend of the donor. The letter includes an invitation to attend one of two memorial services arranged by HGR each year. The services are conducted in a chapel in Phila-delphia and are attended by: (1) families and friends of the donors, (2) representative medical and dental school students, and (3) a rabbi, priest, and minister, who collectively officiate the services. Very often, the memorial service takes place before medical research is performed on the donor.

If the donor had specified the taking of only certain organs or parts, a determination is made on their usefulness. (For example, kidneys are generally not taken from donors over 65 years old.) If found medically acceptable, the donated items are excised—in some cases by specially trained funeral directors—and the body is returned to the family or friend for disposal.

In cases where the entire body is donated, those that are badly burned, macerated, or contaminated with a serious communicable disease (such as tuberculosis) may be rejected. It is appropriate here to cite an important difference in the way two states handle body rejections. When HGR in Pennsylvania rejects a body, it assumes all responsibilities for final disposal. However, in the state of New Jersey—where donations are handled directly through medical schools—the final disposition of rejected bodies is left to the family or friends. Last year the Pennsylvania HGR received 527 bodies, accepted 498, rejected 21, and returned 8 to family members or friends after organs or parts were taken.

After medical research is performed on a body—a procedure taking a year or more in some cases—the remains are cremated on the school premises. The "cremains" are then placed in a small corrugated box, where they are kept until burial. HGR arranges for all cremains to be buried together in a single cemetery once a year and maintains a record of where each donor is interred.

There was some disagreement in my correspondence about whether or not there is now a shortage of cadavers. A survey of medical schools conducted in 1976 by the Continental Association of Funeral and Memorial Societies showed that there was a surplus of cadavers in some areas of the U.S., and a shortage in other areas. In general, however, more bodies are needed. In 1976, 36 schools reported an urgent need, compared to 34 in 1974 and 30 in 1972. The survey concluded that more bequeathals are needed, as well as more sharing between areas of surplus and shortage.[3]

In reflecting on my original difficulties in arranging for my mother's cremation and the responses I have received from readers, two things have become clear.

The first is that part of my original problem was caused by lack of preparation and information. At the time I needed them, I was not able to locate the Telophase Society or the Continental Association of Funeral and Memorial Societies. Certainly the phone book wouldn't have led me to them unless I already knew their names. An entry in the classified telephone directory (yellow pages) would be relevant and helpful. I could have relied more on my friends to get the information, but in a time of personal crisis, one's normal instincts are blunted. I suppose the only solution to this problem is education and promotion. I hope that future generations will not put up with the kind of nonsense I encountered.

The second point that became clear to me—and which I hope is now clear to others—is that there are indeed alternatives to "The American Way of Death."[4]

REFERENCES

1. **Garfield E.** Cremation: a sensible alternative.
   Current Contents No. 36, 5 September 1977, p. 5-8.
2. *Encyclopaedia Britannica.* (15th edition, 1974)
   Chicago: Encyclopaedia Britannica, Inc. Vol. 6, p. 740.
3. **Morgan E.** *A manual of simple burial.* (8th edition)
   Burnsville, N.C.: The Celo Press, 1977. 64 pp.
4. **Mitford J.** *The American way of death.*
   New York: Simon & Schuster, 1963. 333 pp.

For further information, readers may contact the following organizations:

Continental Association of Funeral & Memorial Societies, Inc.
Suite 1100
1828 L Street NW
Washington, D.C. 20036
(202) 293-4821

The umbrella organization for United States memorial societies. The Association will provide you with the address of the nearest memorial society. Information on simplicity in funeral arrangements and on bequeathing your body or organs, and directories of local societies are included in the booklet, A Manual of Simple Burial by Ernest Morgan, which is available from the Society for $2.00, postpaid.

Memorial Society Association of Canada
P.O. Box 96
Western, Ontario, Canada M9N 3M6
(416) 241-6274

For residents of Canada, provides information similar to that available through the Continental Association of Funeral & Memorial Societies, Inc.

The St. Francis Burial & Counseling Society
Friendship Heights Station
P.O. Box 9727
Washington, D.C. 20060
(202) 332-3797

This organization is centered in Washington D.C. but has members throughout the United States. Membership costs $12.00 yearly and includes a subscription to the St. Francis Quarterly, which publishes articles on all aspects of death and dying, burial planning, and cremation. The Society also supplies pine coffins at low cost [$160-185], and supplies designs for using coffins as bookshelves, chests, or coffee tables until needed.

The Telophase Society

200 W. Thomas St.	P.O. Box 33208	P.O. Box 4664
Seattle, WA 98119	San Diego, CA 92105	Portland, OR 97208
(206) 282-1444	(714) 299-0805	(503) 233-6852
1201 East Ball Road, Suite V	1543 W. Olympic Blvd., Suite 529,	
Anaheim, CA 92805	Los Angeles, CA 90015	
(714) 956-8340	(213) 384-2043	

A group of direct cremation service societies (not associated with the Continental Association of Funeral & Memorial Societies, Inc.) serving Pacific coastal states at the locations listed above. Membership fees are $5 for individuals, $20 for families. At the time of death, the Society will provide low-cost cremation and associated services.

The American Association of Tissue Banks
c/o Dr. Kenneth W. Sell
Scientific Director
National Institute of Allergy and Infectious Diseases
National Institutes of Health
Bethesda, MD 20014

A new, non-government-sponsored group including physicians, nurses, lawyers, technicians, and the general public. Long-range goals include setting up standards for tissue banking and establishing regional tissue banks.

National Eye Bank Association of America
3195 Maplewood Ave.
Winston-Salem, NC 27103

The governing eye bank for the United States. Local eye banks are members. The Association can provide information on eye donations, and will put you in touch with your local eye bank.

National Kidney Foundation
116 East 27th St.,
New York, NY 10016
(212) 889-2210

Provides help to kidney sufferers through research, professional education, and public information on organ donations, and by distributing the Uniform Donor Card.

CURRENT COMMENTS

Miniprint: Is It a Practical Way to Cut Publishing Costs?
or
If You Can Read This, You Can Read Miniprint!

Number 2, January 9, 1978

Back in the fifties, when I was searching for a solution to the problem of storing chemical information, I "invented" *miniprint*. Or so I thought. Later I learned that the idea of using very small print in published material is almost a century old.

Miniprint has become a generic term for any method of producing reduced-size text by printed rather than photographic methods. It is a multi-copy process designed to reduce the cost of printing full-size texts. Miniprint is usually produced on a photo-offset press by clever control of ink flow, roller pressure, etc. In general, it is from three to five times smaller than "normal" text, which is 8 to 12 point type. One point is 1/72 of an inch, or 0.31 millimeters. This essay is printed in 10 point type.

Miniprint reduces the cost of publishing primarily by reducing the amount of paper required. It also significantly reduces costs of printing plates, negatives, binding, shipping, and postage. For reference purposes, as in using a molecular formula index, I thought that miniprint might be ideal. One could easily scan boldface headings and then use a simple hand-held magnifier to "read" structural diagrams.

The main disadvantage of miniprint is that it requires an optical magnifier for reading. Only a few people can read miniprint with the naked eye for more than a few minutes. While any decent magnifier can be used to read miniprint without difficulty, there are a number of devices especially designed for the purpose. Certain reading devices designed for the partially sighted could also be used.

There is no clear dividing line between "normal" print and miniprint. In general, 8 to 12 points is considered normal for text. In Europe, however, type as small as 6 points is often used in newspapers. Type larger than 12 points is usually used for headlines. Miniprint falls in the range of 1 to 4 point type. Figure 1 shows a variety of type

379

sizes. You can determine what would be miniprint for your own eyes.

The size of the type used in the Author Address Directory of *Current Contents®* (*CC®*) is about 4 points. Thus it is just at the border of readability with the naked eye. But even a slight increase in size to 5 point type would increase space requirements significantly. Similarly, in the *Science Citation Index®* the citing line is about 3½ point type but the cited author and reference appears in about 5 point boldface.

Figure 1. Various sizes of the English typeface used in the text of this essay.

This is 12-point type

This is 11-point type

This is 10-point type

This is 9-point type

This is 8-point type

This is 7-point type

This is 6-point type

This is 5-point type

This is 4-point type

This is 3-point type

This is 2-point type

Microprint was invented by an unsung hero of documentation— Albert Boni. It is much smaller than miniprint. Microprint is the printed equivalent of *microcards.* The latter are produced by a one-at-a-time photographic process. Each micro- card is the positive version of a *microfiche.* Microprint and micro- cards require the use of viewers which enlarge the reduced image.

Special "readers" are also needed to view *microfilm* and *microfiche.* Microfilm can be 8, 16 or 35 milli- meter strips or rolls of film which contain reduced images of print or graphic material. Since typical re- duction ratios for microfilm are from 15:1 to 32:1, the actual size of the characters on the film is from 0.6 to 0.25 points. Microfiche is similar to microfilm except that it usually con- sists of 4 by 6 inch sheets of film instead of continuous rolls.

I am often surprised how difficult it is for some people to grasp the reason why miniprint and other micrographic methods produce the economies they do. If you start out with a page which is 10 by 10, the area is 100 square units. Now, if you photographically reduce the image to 2 by 2, the area is 4 square units. The reduction ratio is 1:5, but where you once had one page you can now store 25! Similarly, using a reduc- tion ratio of ten to one you can store 100 pages where you had one. The amount of space saved is much greater than one might imagine.

Over the years a variety of appli- cations have been found for very small type. In 1886 a London en- graver named Duncan C. Dallas produced a miniature edition of the Bible on pages reduced to 1 9/16 by 2 3/8 inches. In 1921, Admiral Bradley A. Fiske suggested the publication of books in reduced-size print to be read with a loupe mag- nifier. A loupe is an eyepiece mag- nifier used by jewelers and watch- makers. It enlarges an image three to four times. Around 1940, Dr. Lodewyk Bendikson of the Huntington Library of San Marino, California produced pages meant to be read with a low-powered microscope. His pages were produced on silver emulsion photographic paper. He managed to put 40 to 50 pages of a book on one 5 by 8 inch card.[1]

My deceased colleague and friend, Ralph R. Shaw, discussed the use of miniprint in the 1940's, before I had heard of it or him. From 1940 to 1954 Shaw was the Librarian of the US Department of Agriculture. Later he became President of the American Library Association, and owner of the Scarecrow Press. Shaw is known primarily for adapting scientific management and electronic methods to library service, and for the development of the "bookmobile" concept.

But Albert Boni probably thought of miniprint even before Shaw. In 1940, Boni formed the Readex Microprint Corporation. Incidentally, he is the same Boni of Boni and Liveright fame, the original publishers of James Thurber and other notables. Readex publications include *Landmarks of Science,* a collection of documents which reproduces 2½ million full-size pages on 15,000 microprint cards. *Landmarks* includes reproductions of the first editions of Newton's *Opticks,* Darwin's *Origin of Species,* and other classics. Each 6 by 9 inch microprint card contains as many as 200 reduced 8½ by 11 inch pages. They can be read easily with a

viewer sold by the company.

Of all reduced-size printing methods, miniprint is probably the most "natural." People have been reading print on pages for centuries. For most of us, gazing at an illuminated screen for more than a few minutes —as must be done to read microprint, microfilm, and microfiche— is alien and uncomfortable. Thus miniprint is better suited for the publication of original texts than are the other forms. But I think it is best used in reference works where one does not need to read the material for lengthy periods.

Recently some scientific journals have experimented with miniprint. In 1974, the *Journal of Organic Chemistry* used miniprint for the supplemental sections of 36 papers. These sections concerned peripheral or noncentral points; the major findings appeared in standard size print. According to Frederick D. Greene of MIT, *JOC*'s editor-in-chief, the journal did not save enough money to justify continuing the experiment. However, this was partly because authors did not pay the usual ACS page charges. It was dropped primarily because the editors felt, as Greene explained, "There is an esthetic drawback to miniprint."

One sarcastic reader apparently agreed. He reduced a letter to the editor to the size of a postage stamp. He then mailed it to the *JOC* with this note attached: "If you can read this, then miniprint is great."

In another experiment, the *Jour-*

Figure 2. Two frames of miniprint from the *Journal of Chemical Research* (*M*). Nine frames this size can fit on each 8¼ by 11½ inch (20.96 by 29.21 cm.) page.

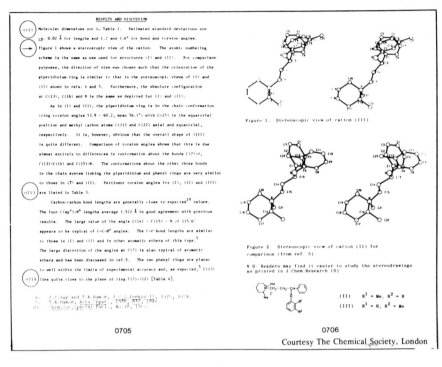

nal of Chemical Research, a synopsis journal, included complete papers in miniprint at the beginning of 1977. They plan to continue the experiment throughout 1978. I.A. Williams, its managing editor, says the journal plans to survey its readers on whether they prefer miniprint or microfiche. This journal is now available in both forms. Another part of the *Journal of Chemical Research* contains full-size synopses of articles accepted for publication in the miniprint and microfiche versions. To give you an idea of how the miniprint version

looks, Figure 2 contains a few frames from it. The print has been reduced to 3.3 points from a typewriter's 10-point type.

The most familiar example of miniprint is *The Compact Edition of the Oxford English Dictionary*.[2] It reproduces, in two miniprint volumes, the entire text of the full-size thirteen-volume set. The miniprint edition, which is 6 inches thick, requires about one-sixth as much shelf space as the 34½ inch-thick standard edition. A magnifying glass is included with the miniprint edition. Credit for this pub-

382

lishing venture, perhaps the most successful of the past decade, goes to Albert Boni, who suggested the idea. For this and his many other contributions to information science he should receive the equivalent of a Nobel or Pulitzer prize! Boni, who is 85, won the National Microfilm Association's Pioneer Medal in 1961. I hope that he will also be recognized by the Information Industry Association in the near future.

Besides the *Compact OED*, there has, to my knowledge, been only one other successful application of miniprint. In the United States, businesses often use "advertising specialties"—souvenir items such as calendars or ashtrays imprinted with the firm's logo. The manufacturers of such items need a way to reach the distributors who sell them. Advertising Specialty Institute, a division of National Business Services in Trevose, Pa., publishes an annual *Magni-File*. Using miniprint, it lists all "catalog sheets," or manufacturer's advertisements for advertising specialties. The *Magni-File* is an 8½ by 11 *inch* book, 2 inches thick. The full-size version, a "Master Catalog File," occupies an 8 x 8 x 11 *foot* filing cabinet. Apparently, a lot of people have been willing to use an inexpensive hand-held magnifier to read these reference volumes published at a 1:5 reduction ratio.

Back in the early days of *Current*

MICROPHAGIST. 414 MICROSCOPIC.

Microphagist (məikrǫ·fădʒist). [f. Gr. μικρό-ς small + φαγ-, φαγεῖν to eat + -IST.] An eater of microscopic organisms.

1853 W. SMITH *Brit. Diatom.* I. p. xxxiii, Several species [of diatoms] have been supplied in abundance by a careful dissection of the above microphagists.

Microphagocyte (məikrofæ·gǫsəit). *Phys.* [f. MICRO- + PHAGOCYTE.] = MICROPHAGE.

1896 *Allbutt's Syst. Med.* I. 79 Classifications of the varieties of leucocytes...Microphagocyte.

† **Microphily.** *Obs. rare*⁻¹. In 7 -philie. [Badly f. Gr. μικρό-ς small + φιλία friendship.] The friendship of a 'small' man with a great.

1608 D. T[UVIL] *Ess. Pol. & Mor.* 95 b, So likewise, where there is a disproportion eyther in meanes, or mindes, there can bee no other friendship, then that Microphilie, which Plato had with Dionysius the Tyrant.

Microphone (məi·krǫfǫun). [f. Gr. μικρό-ς small + φωνή sound.]

1. An instrument by which small sounds can be intensified.

1683 *Phil. Trans.* XIV. 482 Microphones or Micracousticks that is Magnifying ear instruments. 1707 in BAILEY vol. II. 1827 C. WHEATSTONE in *Q. Jrnl. Sci.* II. 69 An instrument which, from its rendering audible the weakest sounds, may with propriety be called the Microphone. 1842 BRANDE *Dict. Sci.*, etc., *Microphone*, an instrument for increasing the intensity of low sounds.

2. *spec.* An instrument (invented almost simultaneously in 1878 by Prof. Hughes and Dr. Lüdtge) by means of which the telephone is made to reproduce faint sounds with more than their original intensity.

1878 HUGHES in *Proc. Roy. Soc.* XXVII. 365, I have also devised an instrument suitable for magnifying weak sounds, which I call a *microphone*. The microphone, in its present form, consists simply of a lozenge-shaped piece of gas carbon, one inch long [etc.].

Hence **Micropho·nic** *a.*, pertaining to the microphone; *sb. pl.*, the science of magnifying sounds.

1846 BUCHANAN *Technol. Dict.*, *Microphonics*, the science of magnifying small sounds. 1878 *Jrnl. Franklin Inst.* CVI. 270 Microphonic Anticipations. 1879 *N. Eng. Hist. & Gen. Reg.* XXXIII. 158 Look at the amazing progress in telegraphic, microscopic, telephonic and microphonic arts! 1881 *Athenæum* 2 July 19/1 Dr. Moser read a paper 'On the Microphonic Action of Selenium Cells'. 1893 PREECE & STUBBS *Man. Telephony* 121 The adoption of the microphonic transmitter in any case necessitates the employment of a battery.

Microphonograph (məikrǫfǫu·nǒgraf). [f. MICRO- + PHONOGRAPH.] An instrument combining the principles of the microphone and the phonograph, designed for rendering sound audible to deaf-mutes.

this head may be included two different processes. One.. consists in copying objects on an exceedingly small scale, the photograph being intended to be viewed through a magnifier... The other.. consists in producing enlarged photographs of minute objects—that is, in fixing the images obtained in the microscope. 1867 SUTTON & DAWSON *Dict. Photogr.*, *Micro-Photography*. This term is now used to designate the reduction of negatives to a very minute size, and serves to distinguish it from the process denominated 'Photo-micrography'. 1900 *Westm. Gaz.* 12 Sept. 8/2 A letter printed in microphotography is gummed to his [a bee's] little back, and he is thrown into the air.

2. The art or process of producing by photography an enlarged image of a microscopically minute object: = PHOTOMICROGRAPHY.

1858 [see 1]. 1875 tr. *Vogel's Chem. Light* xiv. 209 Excellent results have been achieved in microphotography by Neyt at Ghent. 1889 *Anthony's Photogr. Bull.* II. 104 Examples may also be given of balloon, stellar, and microphotography.

Microphthalmia, etc.: see MICRO- 3.

Microphylline (məikrǫfi·ləin), *a.* *Bot.* [Formed as next: see -INE.] Composed of minute leaflets or scales.

1872 E. TUCKERMAN *Gen. Lichenum* 245 The foliaceous *Verrucariacei* .. passing .. into microphylline and .. into finally almost crustaceous forms.

Microphyllous: see MICRO- 4.

Microphysics, -physiography: see MICRO- b.

Microphyte (məi·krofəit). [mod. f. Gr. μικρό-ς small + φυτόν plant. Cf. F. *microphyte*.] A microscopic plant, esp. a bacterium. Hence **Microphy·tal**, **Microphy·tic** *adjs.*, pertaining to microphytes.

1863 SLACK in *Intell. Observ.* Dec. 379 In the fermentation of wheat flour he [Lémaire] observed in the course of fifteen days, *bacterium*, *vibrio*, *spirillum*, *amœba*, *monas*, and *paramecium*, after which came what he calls *microphytes*. 1867 MURCHISON *Siluria* App. O. (ed. 4) 546 The microphytes above mentioned. 1876 PAGE *Adv. Text-bk. Geol.* xx. 440 The innumerable organisms in microphytal and microzoal deposits. 1881 J. SIMON in *Nature* No. 616. 373 The microphytic origin of an important cancroid disease of horned cattle. 1896 *Allbutt's Syst. Med.* I. 210 After the rise of modern bacteriology the first attempts made were to cultivate a specific microphyte from such tumours.

Micropod (məi·krǫpǫd). *Zool.* [ad. mod.L. *Micropoda*, f. Gr. μικρό-ς small + ποδ-, πούς foot.] Any one of the *Micropoda*, in some classifications a division of bivalve molluscs including the oyster.

1854 ADAMS, etc. *Man. Nat. Hist.* 158 Micropods (Micropoda).

Micropodal (məikrǫ·pǫdăl), *a.* [f. Gr. μικρο-ποδ-, μικρόπους (f. μικρός small + ποδ-, πούς foot) + -AL.] Small-footed; esp. having the foot abnormally small though regularly developed. So **Mi-**

2. *Zool.* A special opening in a female cell for the entrance of the fertilizing cell.

1859 *Todd's Cycl. Anat.* V. [97]/2 Discoveries .. as to the existence of the micropyle in fishes. 1875 RAY LANKESTER in *Q. Jrnl. Microsc. Sci.* XV. 38 The egg-shell.. has a small hole at the narrower pole, which may be called a micropyle. 1893 TUCKEY *Amphioxus* 41 This .. explains how it is that without the formation of a micropyle the spermatozoon can force its way into the egg.

Micror(h)abd, microsclere: see MICRO- 1.

Micro-refractometer, etc.: see MICRO- 6.

Microscope (məi·krǒskǫup), *sb.* Also 7 mycroscop(e. [ad. mod.L. *microscopium*, f. Gr. μικρό-ς small + σκοπ-εῖν to look, see: see -SCOPE. Cf. F. *microscope*, Sp. *microscópio*, It. *microscopio*, G. *mikroskop*.]

1. An optical instrument, consisting of a lens or a combination of suitably adjusted lenses, (or, rarely, also of mirrors) by which objects are so magnified that details indistinct or invisible to the naked eye are clearly revealed.

1656 tr. *Hobbes' Elem. Philos.* I. IV. xxvii. 332 There are now such Microscopes .. that the things we see with them appear a hundred thousand times bigger, then they would do if we looked upon them with our bare Eyes. 1662 S. P. *New Sect Latitude-men* 21 The severall discoveries we are beholden to the new invented microscope for. 1678 *Depos. Cast. York* (Surtees) 233 Polishing glasses for prospectives, and spectackles and mycroscops. 1706 *Reflex. upon Ridicule* 244 The effects of prejudice .. are the same with those of microscopes. 1831 BREWSTER *Optics* v. 51 When such a lens is used to magnify the magnified image produced by another lens, the two lenses together constitute a compound microscope.

attrib. 1806 KIRBY & SP. *Entomol.* III. xxix. 193 Till.. they may first enter the range of the microscope-aided eye. 1875 HUXLEY & MARTIN *Elem. Biol.* (1877) 247 Microscope-needle. 1899 CAGNEY tr. *Jaksch's Clin. Diagn.* x. (ed. 4) 431 An Abbe's or other condenser adjusted movably to the microscope-stand.

b. *Lucernal, solar, oxy-hydrogen microscopes*: instruments of the nature of the magic lantern, in which the illumination employed comes from a lamp, the sun, and an oxy-hydrogen lime-light respectively.

1740 H. BAKER in *Phil. Trans.* XLI. 516 The Solar or *Camera Obscura* Microscope, and the Microscope for opake objects. 1787 G. ADAMS *Ess. Microscope* 65 This [lucernal] microscope was originally thought of, and in part executed by my father. 1797 *Encycl. Brit.* (ed. 3) XI. 725 The improved lucernal microscope. 1839 *Penny Cycl.* XV. 188/2 A few achromatic glasses for oxy-hydrogen microscopes have been made. 1845 *Encycl. Metrop.* III. 470/2 The solar microscope differs entirely .. from those above described.

2. *transf.* and *fig.*

Courtesy Oxford University Press

Figure 3. Part of a miniprint frame from the *Compact Edition of the Oxford English Dictionary.* Four 3 5/8 by 5 1/4 inch (9.21 by 13.34 cm.) frames fit on each 9 by 12 inch (22.86 by 30.48 cm.) page.

Contents, I contemplated another use of miniprint. Since its beginning, *CC* has been competing with abstract services. Even to this day some scientists insist they must have an abstract while browsing. The use of miniprint could make it possible to include abstracts in a *CC* supplement. The size of such a weekly supplement would be formidable. In the sample opposite, I've used a recent contents page from the *American Journal of Psychology* to illustrate what a contents page might look like, if it included miniprint abstracts.

As I said at the outset, I first became interested in miniprint as a way to improve the molecular formula index to new compounds listed in *Index Chemicus®* .[3] The conventional molecular formula index enables you to determine whether a particular compound has been indexed. It is easy enough to locate the empirical or molecular formula, but without the full name or structural diagram you cannot be sure which chemical has been indexed until you turn to the abstract in *Current Abstracts of Chemistry™* or *Chemical Abstracts,* whichever you are searching.

Using molecular formulas in normal-size type and structural diagrams in miniprint, I tried in the 1950's to produce a hybrid that would simplify searching. Unfortunately, there was no simple mechanical or electronic means then available to produce such an index. It would have had to be done by a completely manual procedure that was too costly. Publishing the entire index in miniprint seemed to be a reasonable way to make the inclusion of structural diagrams economically feasible.

Eventually, the Wiswesser Line Notation (WLN) was developed as an unambiguous way of describing chemical compounds with alphanumeric symbols. In theory this reduced the need for storing and reproducing structural diagrams in chemical information systems. Indeed, a molecular formula WLN index to about 1.8 million compounds reported in *CAC/IC™* from 1966-76 is available from ISI®. This molecular formula index is issued on computer output microfiche,[4] as is ISI's *Chemical Substructure Index®* *(CSI).*[5] But there can be no doubt that most chemists still prefer to scan structural diagrams. Hence the popularity of *Current Abstracts of Chemistry.* Once we have programs for converting line notations into aesthetically acceptable structural diagrams, we can use computer-activated photocomposing machines to generate miniprint molecular formula indexes.

We have also considered using miniprint in conjunction with the *Science Citation Index, Social Sciences Citation Index™,* and *Index to Scientific Reviews™.* Miniprint abstracts could be used in supplementary volumes arranged by author. The user would thus be able to move quickly from either the *Source, Citation,* or *Permuterm®*

THE AMERICAN
JOURNAL OF PSYCHOLOGY
Abstracts in English
VOL. 90 NO. 3   SEPTEMBER 1977

Louis G. Lippman and Richard W. Thompson. The effect of shock on the exploratory behavior of rats in a complex maze   363

As replication and extension of prior work, two experiments investigated the activity and exploratory behavior of rats during 10–16 days of testing in a complex environment — a +-maze with black, white, striped and checkered arms. Two measures were taken: frequency of entrance into each arm and a sampling of each animal's location within each minute of each daily 3-min trial. Results of both experiments showed consistent trends in the animals' topographies of exploratory activity and configuration of arm preference. Shock-induced fear reinstated the preferences for low-intensity and low-complexity arms exhibited at the outset of testing, thus providing evidence for the contribution of fear to exploratory activity.

Henry M. Halff. The role of opportunities for recall in learning to retrieve   383

Three theories of learning hold that test trials are equally effective on errors or successes; that test trials are effective only for successfully recalled material; or, by Restle's strategy-selection model, that presentations are effective only following failures of recall. The implications of these three theories were developed for the parameters of a two-stage Markov model of learning. An application of the model to the RTT paradigm in free recall provided support for the strategy-selection theory, as did two experiments involving error-contingent presentation. The paper concludes with a theory relating organizational aspects of free recall to the strategy-selection theory.

Charles F. Hinderliter and David C. Riccio. Long-term effects of prior experience in attenuating amnesia   407

In Experiment I, prior experience with passive-avoidance training followed by latent extinction was given 1, 3, 5, or 15 days before a noncontingent shock and an amnesic treatment. It produced nearly complete protection from retrograde amnesia at the three shorter intervals; at the longest interval, amnesia was present but less severe than in a control group without the familiarization. In Experiment II, prior experience was given 1, 5, or 15 days before a noncontingent shock and an amnesic treatment. Evidence of a reactivation of memory was obtained only at the longest interval. Thus, familiarization and reactivation seem to represent different processes. The results are interpreted as consistent with explanations stressing the disruption of retrieval in retrograde amnesia.

James W. Pellegrino and Judith Petrich. List discrimination during transfer in free recall   419

The free recall of successive partially overlapping lists was studied, using Anderson and Bower's 1972 model to derive specific predictions. All predictions were supported by the data. Specifically, items repeated across lists showed depressed recall relative to new items, particularly when repeated across multiple lists. Knowledge of the interlist relationship served only to reduce the level of negative transfer relative to an uninformed condition. The data on a test of list identification given to the experimental informed and uninformed conditions and to a control condition with nonoverlapping lists also support the model of the role of list tagging and contextual elements in the recall decision.

Robert E. Hicks, George W. Miller, Gerald Gaes, and Karen Bierman. Concurrent processing demands and the experience of time-in-passing   431

Under the prospective paradigm, judged time decreased monotonically with the increased processing demands of concurrent card sorting (Experiment I) and of concurrent verbal rehearsal (Experiment II). It was nonmonotonically related to concurrent tapping rate (Experiment III), which latter, when required during verbal rehearsal, had an identical curvilinear effect on short-term recall (Experiment IV). It is concluded that the experience of time-in-passing is an inverse function of the processing demanded by a concurrent task. An attentional model is suggested and evaluated against the literature.

James H. Neely. The effects of visual and verbal satiation on a lexical decision task   447

Immediately before a visually presented target, a string of letters that was to be quickly classified as a word or nonword, the subject saw a prime, a word either semantically related (R) or unrelated (U) to the target. Before this prime, the subject had received visual satiation (V) or both visual and verbal satiation (B) on a word either identical (I) to the prime itself or related to neither (N) the prime or target. Decision times to word targets were faster under condition R than U, but equally so under conditions VI, VN, BI, and BN. Averaged across conditions R and U, decision times to word targets were slower under condition BI than under conditions VI, VN, and BN; decision times to nonword targets under the same conditions were equal. The results are discussed in terms of the semantic-satiation hypothesis, which they fail to support.

Thomas R. Herzog and Daniel J. Weintraub. Preserving the kinesthetic aftereffect: Alternating inducing blocks day by day   461

The kinesthetic aftereffect was measured across five days by traditional wedge-adjustment procedures with wide and narrow inducing blocks alternated day by day. The results showed generally stable mean pre- and postinduction scores from day to day for both inducing blocks, a stable and significant positive mean aftereffect (post- minus preinduction) for the narrow inducing block, and a negative mean aftereffect for the wide one. Three sources of artifact in measuring the aftereffect and the problems involved in using it as an indicant of personality are discussed. Still, alternating the width of the inducing block will preserve the aftereffect, and individual differences in induction seem to lie along an augmentation/reduction dimension.

James W. Aldridge and Michael T. Farrell. Long-term recency effects in free recall   475

Although Tzeng (1973) and Bjork and Whitten (1974) have obtained positive recency effects in free recall using a procedure designed to eliminate any component of short-term storage, their procedures may not have truly cleared short-term storage. In the present experiment, subjects were presented with four lists for free recall, each list composed of seven sets of noun triples. Presentation was either visual or auditory, and subjects counted backward by sevens before and after each item. Even with short-term storage thus cleared, recency effects were obtained equally for both modalities. No effect of serial position was found in a final test of free recall.

Courtesy *American Journal of Psychology*

Figure 4. This prototype *Current Contents* page illustrates how miniprint could be used to provide abstracts in a *CC* supplement. Abstracts from the *American Journal of Psychology* were reduced 50% and combined with the journal's contents page.

indexes to the miniprint abstract. Another possibility is to include a miniprint abstract under the full-size bibliographic description of each item in the *Source Index.* The main questions are these: Would people be willing to read miniprint abstracts for retrospective searching? And would they be willing to pay for the dubious privilege? The advantages of abstracts have been described at great length. They are supposed to eliminate time spent in retrieving irrelevant papers. It is not really known whether abstracts encourage or discourage the use of original papers. I can only assume that their wide availability means editors and publishers are convinced of their value. But English-language abstracts are not yet *universally* included with original articles. So long as publishers provide abstracts, the cost of includ-

ing them in the *SCI®* might be reasonable. But to create abstracts where none exist is a formidable and expensive task, as the many existing abstracting services well know.

Many *CC* readers are concerned about the high cost of producing, storing, and distributing reprints.[6] By reducing the amounts of paper, postage, and storage space required, miniprint could help solve this problem—even at one-half to one-third the original size. And these would be readable with the naked eye.

Over the last few years more and more emphasis has been placed on conserving all types of resources. We have begun to realize that bigger is not always better. Creative applications of miniprint may thus play a large role in information handling in future years.

REFERENCES

1. **Tennant J.** Readex microprints.
   Journal of Documentary Reproduction 3:66-70, 1940.
2. *The Compact Edition of the Oxford English Dictionary.*
   New York: Oxford University Press, 1971. 2 vols.
3. **Garfield E.** ISI's chemical information system goes marching on!
   Current Contents No. 1, 5 January 1976, p. 5-6.*
4. ————. *CAC/IC* strikes again! A computer-output-microform (COM) index
   to 1.25 million new compounds.
   Current Contents No. 14, 7 April 1975, p. 5-6.*
5. ————. New *Chemical Substructure Index* is creative theoretical tool for
   molecule manipulators as well as practical system for retrieval.
   Current Contents No. 24, 16 June 1971, p. 5-6.*
6. ————. Can reprint requests serve as a new form of international currency
   for the scientific community?
   Current Contents No. 47, 21 November 1977, p. 5-13.

*Reprinted in: **Garfield E.** *Essays of an Information Scientist.*
Philadelphia: ISI Press, 1977. 2 vols.

CURRENT COMMENTS

The New Copyright Clearance Center and the Doctrine of Fair Use

Number 3, January 16, 1978

It is early Monday morning. Professor Jones of Noname University, hurrying to meet with his graduate seminar group, stops at the photocopying machine. Quickly, he sets the dial for 10 copies and begins methodically to reproduce the pages of an article from his favorite journal. Suddenly an alarm sounds and a flashing red light comes on. Jones is last seen being escorted out of the building by two burly security guards while muttering something about "fair use."

An improbable scenario? Yes. But not an impossible one in the minds of some people since January 1, 1978. That's the day the revised United States copyright law went into effect, the newly formed Copyright Clearance Center became operational, and the controversy over what constitutes "fair use" was exacerbated.

The new law (Public Law 94-553) supersedes the Copyright Act of 1908, which has remained substantially the same since its origin. The current revisions are major. They reflect the impact that technological advances of the last 68 years have had on unauthorized reproduction of copyrighted materials. I'm not a copyright lawyer so I can't speak with complete authority. But I do know that the new law is far from perfect. At least it seems to raise as many questions as it answers. However, there is no doubt that copyright infringement is now a criminal offense.

Of most concern to scientists and science librarians is the interpretation of the new law as applied to the act of photocopying journal articles. When copyrighted journal articles are photocopied beyond the "fair use" limits set by the new law, copyright holders are now entitled to collect royalty payments. Librarians have steadfastly opposed such a royalty requirement for two reasons. First, they claim that it is almost impossible to define fair use consistently. Second, even if a workable definition were possible, librarians believe that the costs of the record keeping involved in documenting and paying royalties on millions of photocopying transactions would be prohibitive.[1]

To answer the second objection and to simplify the process of collecting and distributing royalties, the Association of American Publishers (AAP) proposed the Copyright Clearance Center (CCC). Since I am on the advisory committee for the

CCC, I am aware of some of its history.

In 1975 the National Commission on New Technological Uses of Copyrighted Works (CONTU) assessed the feasibility of a single copyright payments center that would serve all U.S. publishers and libraries. As part of this work, CONTU hired the King Research Corporation to study a variety of copyright payment systems. But publishers were not waiting for CONTU's findings: they had already decided that a copyright payments system had to be operational by January 1, 1978, the effective date of the new copyright law. Early in 1976, the AAP informed CONTU that the Copyright Clearance Center would be ready by the target date.[2]

CCC is now operating as a not-for-profit corporation. Its membership includes both for-profit and not-for-profit publishers who are primarily from the United States—although other countries are represented. Ben Weil, loaned by Exxon to direct the task force that set up the CCC, estimated back in October, 1977 that there would be 2,000 publishers participating by January 1; but at present there are less than 100. At one time there were reports that publishers were being solicited for $800,000 to support CCC operations. But near the end of 1977 Weil said only $200,000 was being sought and that the operation of CCC wasn't contingent on reaching that figure before January 1.[3]

David Waite, formerly with Information Dynamics, became CCC's president, and the Finserv Computer Corporation was contracted to process all royalty transactions. Finserv's computer installation in Schenectady, New York will receive royalty information via data terminals in CCC's offices in New York City. For each fee it processes, Finserv will receive 25¢. Finserv receives no minimum annual remuneration and its income is totally dependent on the volume of transactions it handles.

Publishers register with the CCC by completing a separate form for each publication entered in the collection system. Each form includes the publication title, International Standard Serial Number (ISSN), and copying fees. All fees are set by the publishers and, starting January 1, 1978, are printed on the first page of each article for which a copying fee is desired. Included in each article's masthead is a statement that says copying fees are to be paid through the CCC. A sample statement recommended by the CCC is shown below:[4]

The appearance of the code at the bottom of the first page of an article in this journal indicates the copyright owner's consent that copies of the article may be made for personal or internal use, or for the personal or internal use of specific clients. This consent is given on the condition, however, that the copier pay the stated per-copy fee through the Copyright Clearance Center, Inc. for copying beyond that permitted by Sections 107 or 108 of the U.S. Copyright Law. This consent does not extend to other kinds of copying, such as copying for general distribution, for advertising or promotional purposes, for creating new collective works, or for resale.

Users of copyrighted materials who wish to make royalty payments through the CCC must also complete a registration form. The form includes a statement that says the user intends to comply with CCC's basic requirements. Payments are usually submitted on a monthly basis.

Publishers and royalty payers are assured that all data are completely confidential. Itemized royalty payments, receipts for payments, etc., are available only to those directly involved.

Will the CCC be successful? Will it collect enough revenues to sustain its operations? It is obvious that CCC's life depends on acceptance by librarians and the public of the principle that publishers are entitled to royalties for photocopying that exceeds the fair use limits. As I pointed out earlier, what those limits are has been an issue that has aroused heated debate between publishers and librarians for over 20 years.

Many of us know of the celebrated legal case in which the publishing firm of Williams and Wilkins in 1968 sued the U.S. government for infringement of copyright. It was public knowledge that the National Library of Medicine (NLM) and National Institutes of Health (NIH) were copying journal articles without permission—as were most other libraries.

In this *cause célèbre* many library associations expended considerable effort to file briefs as "friends of the court" in support of NLM and NIH. The Authors' League and the Association of American Publishers supported Williams and Wilkins. Trial judge James Davis said of the case that it required the "judgment of Solomon" or the "dexterity of Houdini."[5] The judge ruled in favor of Williams and Wilkins, concluding that the firm was entitled to compensation for infringement of copyright.

In 1973 the case was appealed to the U.S. Court of Claims, and in a 4-3 decision the infringement holding was reversed. In a dissenting opinion, Judge Philip Nicholas, Jr. said, "...the decision will be read that a copyright holder has no rights that a library is bound to respect."[5] The majority held that NLM and NIH photocopying practices constituted "fair use" since Williams and Wilkins could not prove "unfair use." The majority also asserted it was up to Congress to define precisely what fair use is.

In 1975 the Williams and Wilkins case reached the U.S. Supreme Court. One of the nine judges disqualified himself; the other eight voted in a 4-4 deadlock; and (adding more frustration) no opinion on the case was written. So the Supreme Court's decision in no way settled the matter—and neither will the new law.

The provisions of the new law that directly affect publishers and librarians are contained in Sections 107 and 108. Section 107 merely gives statutory recognition to the common law doctrine of fair use: the nebulous doctrine under the old law remains the same; only now it is in codified form. Section 108 specifies for libraries the circumstances under which photocopying is either permitted or proscribed.

The language and structure of

Section 108 are highly complex, however—so much so that the Special Libraries Association has told its members, "...it is not necessary to become concerned with Section 108 if the proposed photocopying is reasonably within 'fair use'." The SLA also feels that because the doctrine of fair use has been preserved, "photocopying that was permissible under the old law is permissible under the new law." Section 108 "specifically exempts a public library...from liability for the unsupervised use of reproducing equipment located on its premises provided that the reproducing equipment displays a notice that the making of a copy may be subject to copyright law. Libraries in profit making organizations do not have this exemption, and must be accountable for all uses beyond fair use as defined in Section 107."[6]

The fair use doctrine has been the crux of many court cases, and, since Congress hasn't legislated a solution, it's bound to be the basis of more disputes. According to my friend Arthur Seidel, a Philadelphia lawyer who has written extensively on copyright,[7] the doctrine of fair use was introduced in American copyright law in 1841. The case involved the use of letters written by George Washington. Since that time the doctrine has taken shape through judicial interpretation, in almost *ad hoc* fashion.[8]

"Fair use" is founded on the belief that: (1) there are certain uses of a work which one should be free to make without the consent of the copyright owner, and (2) there are limitations on the exclusive nature of the copyright itself. The doctrine has come to be an affirmative defense to a charge of infringement. The new law sets forth four criteria for determining whether or not a use of copyrighted material is fair:

1. The purpose and character of the use, whether or not it is for profit,
2. The nature of the copyrighted work,
3. The amount and substantiality of the portion used in relation to the copyrighted work as a whole,
4. the effect of the use of the copyrighted work upon the potential market for or the value of the copyrighted work.

As before, the purposes for which a fair use of copyrighted material may be made under Section 107 include, but are not limited to: criticism, comment, news reporting, teaching, and scholarship and research. There are, however, very few areas in which the fair use doctrine operates without dispute.

Whatever finally comes about from the existence of the CCC, ISI®'s *Original Article Tear Sheet* (*OATS®*) service will continue unhampered. As I stated in my recent testimony before CONTU, ISI has been voluntarily paying royalties to publishers for many years and will continue to do so through our own contractual arrangements.[9,10] We believe the publisher should get fair compensation, but we also believe the public's right to access to knowledge should be protected.

In my opinion, there are several facets to that protection. One is that publishers should charge *reasonable* fees for the right to copy their articles. How does one define what is reasonable? One of my publisher colleagues believes that a high single-copy fee will force libraries to enter subscriptions to journals which are relatively expensive by most standards. When I consulted an expert on pricing strategies, he opined that it would have the opposite effect. He believes that if reader/scientists learned that copies of articles from a given journal were very expensive, they would hestitate to ask for any articles from that journal. When the library committee got together to make subscription decisions it would never really know about the latent demand for this journal. On the other hand, publishers may justifiably fear the large-scale, systematic copying that is done at certain large centers. In England it is believed that the poor sale of scientific journals, as compared to other countries, is due to heavy use of the British Lending Library's photocopying service.

Besides charging reasonable fees, publishers should make it convenient to obtain information on copying charges and equally convenient to pay them. The CCC is a major step in that direction, but what about poor Professor Jones mentioned earlier? Even if he had wanted to pay royalties for the copies of the article he made, how would he know how much to pay? None of the publishers enrolled in CCC currently display their royalty fees for *multiple copies.* Is Jones supposed to telephone the publisher for prices every time he makes

copies of an article for his class? And is it reasonable to expect him to pay ten times the single-copy fee for ten copies of the same article? It could just as easily have been 50 copies he needed!

There can be no question that the new CCC will have its difficulties. Frankly, I doubt that a single center can fully serve the varied needs of book and journal publishers—let alone those of publishers of printed music and other copyrighted works. In the field of music, the American Society of Composers and Publishers (ASCAP), Broadcast Music, Inc. (BMI) and others have succeeded in protecting "performance" rights for composer and authors. Ironically, these organizations have never worried very much about unauthorized copying of sheet music. Perhaps music publishers thought that allowing unauthorized copying would encourage more performances! Maybe there is an analogy here. In handing out copies of a research article to students, Professor Jones is "performing" the paper. Perhaps CCC or someone else will one day figure out, as did ASCAP, how to charge for and collect reasonable fees for such performances.

Strangely enough, a comparable situation exists in the area of copyrighted musical recordings. If you want to tape-record an out-of-print record or cassette, how can you do it legally? The recording industry does nothing to make it easier for the public to satisfy specialized needs legally. Until they do, and so long as the operations of these companies are profitable, they cannot expect the public to be concerned about any revenue they may lose through unauthorized copyings. As the head of ISI—which is both a large-scale *producer* and *user* of copyrighted material—I am acutely aware of the need for those involved in this controversy to be reasonable. Perhaps if my deceased colleague Ralph Shaw were still with us he could serve as the impartial arbitrator. Ralph had the unique qualification of having been a librarian as well as the owner of a publishing firm, the Scarecrow Press.

According to Professor William Z. Nasri of the University of Pittsburgh's Graduate School of Library and Information Services, "...the publisher is the servant of the authors and their public, deserving a reward for his efforts but not to be made the master of the process by which knowledge is produced and utilized."[5] Professor Nasri's words deserve some consideration from those on both sides of the fair use issue. Most publishers are straddling the fence. Like most librarians, they are taking a "wait and see" attitude. Meanwhile, Professor Jones will continue to teach, and I will continue to tape-record favorite out-of-print saxophone solos!

REFERENCES

1. Libraries now willing to study photocopying royalty payments. *Knowledge Industry Report* 8(17): 2-3, 1975.
2. AAP spells out clearinghouse plan for photocopying at CONTU meeting. *Publishers Weekly* 211(15): 28, 1977.
3. CCC looks for 2,000 publishers to join; test scheduled for December. *BP Report* 2(44): 4-5, 1977.
4. *A handbook for serial publishers: procedures for using the programs of the Copyright Clearance Center, Inc.* AAP/TSM CCC Task Force, August 1977. 18 pp.
5. Nasri W Z. *Crisis in Copyright.* New York: Marcel Dekker, 1976, p. 75-97.
6. *Discussion of copyright clearance procedures for photocopying: information for librarians.* New York: Special Libraries Association, November 4, 1977. 18 pp.
7. Seidel A H. *What the general practitioner should know about trademarks and copyrights.* Philadelphia: American Law Institute/American Bar Association Committee on Continuing Professional Education, 1976. 254 pp.
8. Seidel A H. *Fair use of copyrighted works in a commercial context.* Paper presented at a seminar on copyright law at the American Law Institute/American Bar Association course of study: The Copyright Act of 1976. Washington, D.C., October 28-9, 1977.
9. Garfield E. *Statement on photocopying to the National Commission on New Technological Uses of Copyrighted Works (CONTU).* Washington, D.C., October 21, 1977.
10. ----------. Libraries need a copyright clearinghouse—ISI has one they can use! *Current Contents* No. 49, 8 December 1975, p. 5-7. (Reprinted in: *Essays of an Information Scientist.* Philadelphia: ISI Press. 1977. Vol. 2, p. 390-2)

CURRENT COMMENTS

ISI's Master Dictionary
Aids Scientific Etymology
And Reflects Changes in Science

Number 4, January 23, 1978

Between 1973 and 1976 *happiness, ethics,* and *self-image* increased. *Violence* doubled; *terrorism* and *soldiers* more than tripled. *Apollo* went down. *Famine* and *cannibalism* increased. But we had more *beef, chocolate, yogurt, horseradish*—and, naturally, more *garbage.*

Has *happiness* really increased? Only in an abstract sense. The fact is that from 1973 to 1976 occurrences of the word *happiness* more than doubled in article titles covered by ISI® 's data base.

One of the ways changes in the activities of scientists are reflected is by the words used in journal articles. Since ISI uses title words—as well as other bibliographic descriptors—to index each article added to our data base, we are able systematically to observe and quantify these changes. It is becoming increasingly clear that this data has practical applications in lexicography.[1]

The vocabulary of science, like that of all living languages, is constantly changing. New words are coined to describe new substances, improved processes, and previously undiscovered phenomena.[2] Extant words fall into disuse as interest wanes in the areas they describe.

In our quality-control procedures we use several manual and computer routines to verify each title word before it becomes a part of the data base.[3,4] One of these routines makes use of a machine-readable file dubbed the *Unique Word Dictionary (UWD).* Actually, the choice of this name illustrates the process by which new words are coined. No one at ISI remembers who first used the phrase "Unique Word Dictionary" to describe this particular word list. But apparently someone who worked with the list coined the name, someone else began using it, and before long "Unique Word Dictionary" had become a part of ISI's in-house jargon.

The Unique Word Dictionary can be considered a kind of subject heading authority list. It is essentially a "master list" of correctly spelled terms that have been certified as being "real" words. Real words are defined as words that have been used in the titles of pre-

393

vious journal articles and have been verified as accurate and authentic by our editors.

As we add new articles to the data base, the computer compares the words in the new titles to the words in the *UWD*. If a new word does not appear on the list, it is tagged for further evaluation. Some of the non-matching words are simply spelling errors. Some are old terms that can be found in standard reference works. Others can only be classified as valid words after our editors contact the author of the article or the editor of the journal in which it appeared. Eventually, all tagged words are either corrected or added to the dictionary.

During 1977 about 300,000 different terms were used in the titles of articles we indexed. Of these, we estimate that about 500 were used for the first time.

Some of these terms are new or unusual combinations of prefixes and suffixes with known stems. For example, *paracollege* was used in an education journal to describe an experimental satellite institution at St. Olaf's College, Minnesota. While the average reader could not know the precise meaning of *paracollege* without a proper definition or explanation, a new word like *pathobiochemical* is readily understood.

Some of the words, however, are completely new combinations of letters, such as *waxicon*. A "nonlinear waxicon" is an optical component used in lasers. It consists of a complementary pair of cone-like mir-

rors. On the other hand, *thermovision* is a temperature-controlled camera system. It's one of those words that only makes sense after you've been told what it means. *Eutonia* refers to good muscle tone, and requires no elaborate explanation. However, *ethphon,* used in horticulture, is 2-chloroethylphosphonic acid. Like many "trivial" names in chemistry, it is meaningless by itself.

A dictionary of new scientific words, assembled with the help of ISI's Unique Word Dictionary, might prove to be a valuable tool for researchers as well as for publishers of scientific books, librarians, and laymen. Such a dictionary might be updated monthly to keep up with the changing vocabulary of science.

Apart from words that occur for the first time, a dictionary of "new" scientific words should eventually take into account new uses of existing words, whether alone or in combination. One can identify such uses by examining the new contexts in which words appear. For automatic indexing and translation systems, new uses for old words probably cause even more grief than the use of idiomatic expressions, which are in fact less ambiguous. Deciphering the phrase "on the beam" is less of a problem than deciding whether the word "beam" alone refers to a beam of light or the beam of a roof!

The figure on pages 8-9 contains 172 words selected from the *UWD*. The frequency of these words has changed significantly from 1973 to 1976. When examining the list, however, it is important to keep in mind that some variations may be the result of adding and deleting new journals to the ISI data base. The size of the data base increases each year, so frequency can be expected to increase for many words. Overall, the number of source articles in the ISI data base increased by approximately 30% between 1973 and 1976. Therefore, for this highly selective list we have chosen mainly words whose change in frequency is greater than 30%.

For example, *charm* increased from 6 occurrences in 1973 to 109 in 1976. This seems to indicate increasing interest in *charm*—a property of subatomic particles. But we cannot be certain that the word *charm*—or any other word on the list—was always used as we might expect. *Charm* could have been used not only in physics titles but also in titles dealing with physical attractiveness, good luck amulets, music, or enchantment.

Another such word is *nude*, which increased from 33 occurrences in 1973 to 129 in 1976. We strongly suspect that the increase in frequency reflects increasing experimental use of the nude mouse, a hairless mutant. The nude mouse has no thymus and no cell-mediated immune system. Thus it easily accepts skin and tumor grafts. Since it was first described in 1966, the nude mouse has become increasingly popular in cancer and immunology research, according to Norman Reed of Montana State University, Bozeman. Obviously, the use of the word *nude* might also refer to people who don't wear clothes! But apparently that is not a popular area of research.

Between 1973 and 1976 *fusion* increased while *fission* decreased, as did *resistivity*. In other areas of physics, *lepton, hadron, monopole,* and *positron* all increased significantly.

The dramatic decline in the U S space program between the late sixties and early seventies is reflected in the decreasing frequency of the various Apollo designations. *Apollo 11*, the flight that landed man on the moon for the first time, took place in July 1969. *Apollo 12* occurred in 1969, *Apollo 14* and *15* in 1971, and *Apollo 16* and *17* in 1972. Altogether, the word *Apollo* with various flight numbers was used 231 times in 1973—but only 46 times in 1976. *Viking 1,* the Mars probe launched on August 20, 1975, was, of course, not mentioned in 1973; but occurred 18 times in 1976.

In medicine, such words as *cancer, mastitis, nephropathy, scurvy,* and *spasm* at least doubled in frequency. *Herpes* almost doubled, and *diabetes* significantly increased. Surprisingly, *sickle-cell* declined. *Euthanasia,* which was used only 13 times in 1973, occurred 62 times in 1976. *Cryosurgery, myeloblastic, neonate,* and *neurosurgical* at least doubled. *Histocompatibility,* which refers to the capacity of tissues to accept or reject grafts, increased from 114 to 223.

In immunology and biochemistry, *counterimmunoelectrophoresis* in-

Figure 1. Selected words from ISI's master dictionary, which includes all words used in the titles of articles covered by ISI's data base. Each word's frequency of occurrence in 1973 and 1976 is indicated.

WORD	1973	1976	WORD	1973	1976
aerosol (ized) (s)	454	630	earthquake (s)	238	407
affirmative	13	74	ethic (al) (s)	263	470
algorithm (ic) (s)	505	737	euthanasia	13	62
amniocentesis	30	46	fallout	50	31
androgyny (ous)	0	15	famine	18	55
Apollo	85	21	feminism (ist) (ists)	35	75
Apollo 11	9	0	fiber-optic (s)	55	193
Apollo 12	5	0	fission	505	423
Apollo 14	10	0	fusion	460	743
Apollo 15	23	0	garbage	4	16
Apollo 16	29	8	gene (s)	1405	930
Apollo 17	70	17	genocide	5	21
apricot (s)	10	24	grass	130	299
backache	6	14	hadron (s)	127	181
BCG (Bacillus Calmette-Guerin)	106	259	handicapped	158	289
beef	339	622	happiness	14	33
bibliography (ies)	236	556	herbicide (al) (s)	83	309
biofeedback	39	98	herpes	272	509
biopharmaceutical	2	13	hexachlorophene	68	33
biorhythm (s)	0	11	histamine	381	530
boycott (s)	2	33	histocompatibility	114	223
braille	2	16	hockey	2	25
breastfeeding	14	36	horseradish	50	147
cancer	1547	3257	insemination	43	128
cannibalism (istic)	7	22	integration	440	669
charm (ed)	6	109	invention	14	58
chocolate	11	27	kelp	8	20
clone (s) (ing) (ed) (al)	194	339	laetrile	0	19
cocaine	44	91	L- dopa	226	162
constipation	12	23	lemming (s)	4	19
copyright (s)	16	63	leprosy	100	191
counterimmunoelectrophoresis	13	38	lepton (s)	57	117
cryosurgery	22	58	linguistic (s)	167	378
cybernetic (s)	31	67	manure	67	142
deoxyribonucleic			marijuana	99	160
(ase) (ease) (s) (eate)			mastitis	63	142
(des-) (DNA)	3100	3767	microcirculation	60	128
desegregation	27	70	microsurgical	17	55
diabetic (s)(es)	1383	2140	mitogen (ic) (s)	133	225
diarrhea	188	303	monopole	27	65
dopa	75	38	morphometric	64	127
dopamine	289	620	myeloblastic	14	67

WORD	1973	1976	WORD	1973	1976
myeloid	111	259	seminar (s)	121	338
nephropathy	16	159	sexism	10	46
neonate (s)	69	148	sex-role	18	46
neurochemical	21	58	sexual	492	815
neurosurgical	23	74	sexuality	65	216
neurotoxicity	15	37	shellfish	9	33
nude	33	129	shrimp (s)	60	147
olefin	72	132	Siamese	5	20
parity	82	141	Siberia (n)	39	99
pharmacokinetic	64	157	sickle-cell	63	37
plasmid (s)	69	231	silage	78	161
positron	96	170	simplex	166	353
prostaglandin (s)	706	1661	sister (s)	43	107
quark (s)	115	219	sludge	134	282
radioimmunoassay	458	724	smog	24	61
rehabilitation	312	768	snail (s)	134	245
renal	2784	4494	snake (s)	124	220
renin	359	650	socialism (ist) (istic) (ists)	211	684
renin-angiotensin	35	61	sociobiology	0	34
renomedullary	6	24	socioeconomic	150	298
renormalization	59	124	soldier (s)	30	91
resistivity	515	361	somatomedin	20	78
reticulum	195	295	somatostatin	11	218
retinopathy	72	143	song (s)	42	97
retrograde	125	233	spasm	51	115
rheumatic (toid)	600	929	spectrin	0	23
rhizosphere	18	48	sporozoa	7	21
ribonucleic			squamous	84	143
(ease) (s) (eates) (RNA)	2388	2228	stereopsis	5	17
ringspot	43	20	sterilization	164	253
rosette	46	108	subpopulation (s)	49	267
rural	345	730	sulfobromophthalein	18	30
saccharine	9	26	terrorist (s) (ism)	10	68
sarcoplasmic	100	193	thalidomide	27	18
science	1339	2056	transactional	12	47
scientific	462	864	transcendental	15	45
scintigraphic (y)	171	416	transsexual (s, ism)	18	40
sclerosis (ing)	324	559	tumor (s)	3496	5116
scurvy	8	16	vasectomy (ies) (ized)	119	80
seawater	95	160	vasopressin	124	217
secretin	99	176	Viking 1	0	18
security	202	392	violence (violent)	143	308
segregation (ed)	169	334	winter	211	435
self-awareness	4	14	woman ('s) (en) (en's)	1139	2312
self-help	13	47	yogurt (yoghurt)	9	35
self-image	7	23	Zambia	35	83
self-sufficiency	2	25	Zen	6	25
semantic (s)	161	305			

creased from 13 occurrences in 1973 to 38 in 1976. *Radioimmunoassay*, a technique for measuring concentrations of substances developed by 1977 Nobel Prize winner Rosalyn S. Yalow, increased from 458 to 724. In 1973 the word *somatostatin*, the name of a chemical which inhibits the release of growth hormone, was used only 11 times. But in 1973 it occurred 218 times. Strangely, *dopa* and *L-dopa* decreased significantly from 1973 to 1976, but *dopamine* increased from 289 to 620! *Neurochemical*, *neurotoxicity*, and *prostaglandin* at least doubled; *renin, secretin*, and *vasopressin* almost doubled.

Looking at the drug names on the list, it is interesting to observe that *laetrile*, which did not occur at all in 1973, occurred 19 times in 1976. *Apricot*, from which laetrile is made, also more than doubled. *Biopharmaceutical* increased from 2 to 13 occurrences, and *cocaine* more than doubled. *Thalidomide*, the drug responsible for the birth defect tragedies between 1959 and 1962, decreased as a term in article titles from 27 in 1973 to 18 in 1976. *Hexachlorophene* also decreased significantly.

In genetics, *clone* almost doubled in frequency, but *DNA* "only" increased from 3100 to 3767. Surprisingly, *gene* decreased from 1405 to 930, and *RNA* decreased from 2388 to 2228.

In biology, *kelp, mitogen, rosette,* and *sporozoa* at least doubled. *Ringspot*, a plant virus, decreased by more than half.

In the area of ecology, *smog, sludge,* and *garbage* all increased dramatically.

Among words that seemed relevant mainly to the social sciences, we found that the use of the term *segregation* almost doubled, from 169 in 1973 to 334 in 1976, and *integration* increased significantly, from 440 in 1973 to 669 in 1976. Of course, these words are also used in mathematics and in other areas. The word *affirmative* increased in use from 13 to 74, possibly because of increased interest in affirmative action programs. *Feminism* increased from 35 to 75, and *sexism* from 10 to 46. *Woman* increased from 1139 to 2312, and *sister* from 43 to 107.

Socialism, genocide, violence and *terrorism* at least doubled. So did *linguistics* and *cybernetics. Bibliography* and *semantics* almost doubled. *Copyright* more than tripled, as did *fiber-optics*, a novel method for transmitting electronic signals by using clear glass fibers to conduct laser light.

According to the data presented in the figure, several of the listed words were never used at all in 1973. This is not completely accurate, however. At the end of each calendar year, words which occurred less than three times are purged, or removed, from the Unique Word Dictionary. But even if such words as *androgyny, biorhythm,* and *sociobiology* did occur once or twice in 1973, their use increased enormously by 1976.

Changes in the frequency of occurrence of a new word give us one indication of scientific activity. It is important to note, however, that the citation record of the publication in which the word was first used is often a better indicator of activity. Consider the word *quark*, which refers to the subatomic particles which constitute hadrons. From 1973 to 1976 occurrences of the word *quark* almost doubled. But even before this increase was noted, one could have determined the tremendous amount of interest in the field by examining the citation record of the primordial paper in which Murray Gell-Mann introduced the term.[5] This classic paper, with a total of 637 citations to date, was being heavily cited as early as 1965. Incidentally, Gell-Mann borrowed the term from the line, "—Three quarks for Muster Mark!" in James Joyce's *Finnegan's Wake.*[6]

If asked to name the basic "unit" of scientific communication, I think that most scientists, myself included, would mention the journal article or the book. About twenty years ago I described the article as a "micro-unit of thought" and the book as a "macro-unit of thought."[7] Somehow my use of *macro* was picked up by *Webster's Third New International Dictionary.*[8] So I suppose that by extension a word, a phrase, or even a cited reference might be regarded as submicro- or submacro-units of thought, depending upon their frequency. In any case, the communication of scientific results is accomplished mainly by the written *word.*

Scholars have long studied the evolution of words and language, not only as a joy in itself, but as a window on culture and society. In the same way, scientific etymology can help us gain a better insight on the development of science.

REFERENCES

1. **Garfield E.** Jabberwocky, the Humpty-Dumpty syndrome and the making of scientific dictionaries! *Current Contents*® No. 41, 10 October 1973, p. 5-6.*
2. --------------. On routes to immortality. *Current Contents* No. 21, 22 May 1974, p. 5-7.*
3. **Garfield E, Koenig M & DiRenzo T.** ISI data-base-produced information services. *IEEE Trans. Prof. Commun.* PC-20(2): 95-9, September 1977. Reprinted in: *Current Contents* No. 45, 7 November 1977, p. 5-17.
4. **Garfield E.** The *Permuterm*® *Subject Index:* an autobiographical review. *J. Amer. Inform. Sci.* 27(5/6):288-91, 1976. Reprinted in: *Current Contents* No. 12, 21 March 1977, p. 5-10.
5. **Gell-Mann M.** A schematic model of baryons and mesons. *Phys. Lett.* 8:214-5, 1964.
6. **Joyce J.** *Finnegan's wake.* New York: Penguin, 1967, p. 383.
7. **Garfield E.** Citation indexes for science: a new dimension in documentation through association of ideas. *Science* 122:108-11, 1955.
8. **Gove P B et al.,** eds. *Webster's third new international dictionary of the English language, unabridged.* Springfield, MA: Merriam Co., 1961, p. 1354.

*Reprinted in: **Garfield E.** *Essays of an information scientist.* Philadelphia: ISI Press, 1977. 2 vols.

CURRENT COMMENTS

IIA Hall of Fame Award Helps
Make 1977 a Good Year

Number 5, January 30, 1978

As with wines, some years in our lives are better than others. To borrow from a song made popular by Frank Sinatra, 1977 was "a very good year" for me in many ways. ISI® continued to be intellectually and financially healthy. We made the decision to launch a major tool for the literature of the arts and humanities.[1] This made ISI the only private information company involved in a large-scale way in the three major areas of scholarship—science, social science, and arts/humanities. And that ever-worrisome bottom line totalled up to what our board of directors thought it should.

Considering the difficulties faced by many universities, ISI's success may seem contradictory. But much of our new business has come from greater use of our services in budget-pinched universities all over the world—especially those in developing countries. Increasing numbers of such institutions now realize that investing in information services is not nearly as costly and frequently pays larger dividends than spending money on ever more sophisticated laboratory equipment and other types of hardware.

Much of my insight into changing budgetary priorities comes from the nearly six months I spent travelling during 1977. Besides criss-crossing North America, I travelled to Japan, Norway, Iceland, Italy, France, Lithuania, and other countries.

One trip included a lecture tour of Siberia at the invitation of the Soviet Academy of Sciences. This was preceded by a visit to the Moscow Book Fair which convinced me that there are many opportunities for publishing interesting Soviet works in English. I also presented a paper at the International Conference of Scientific and Technical Editors and Publishers in Jerusalem.[2] Subsequently, I attended the annual meeting of the International Association of Scientific, Technical, and Medical

Publishers in Frankfurt, where ISI also participated in the annual book fair.

Perhaps the most important news in 1977 for *Current Contents®* (*CC®*) readers was the ISI victory in the federal courts over the US Postal Service.[3] For the past five years we have waged a costly battle to maintain our second-class mailing privilege for *CC*. This postal class, which has substantially lower rates, is reserved for publications classified as periodicals. The post office argued that *Current Contents* is not a periodical because it does not contain primarily original material. Our attorneys convinced the court that *CC* meets so many other requirements of a periodical publication that it should be classified as one. (I will elaborate on this landmark decision in the future.) Each subscriber to *CC* can think of this victory as a New Year's present for 1978 worth $25. That is the amount we would have had to add to the cost of a subscription if we had lost. And that increase would apply to subsequent years, too.

After many delays, ISI managed to publish my first book—a two-volume compilation of these essays.[4] I am gratified not only by the steady flow of orders, but also by the friendly reviews.[5]

In October I was presented with the Information Industry Association (IIA) Hall of Fame Award.

Although I've mentioned the IIA before, many readers of these essays are probably unfamiliar with it.[6]

IIA was formed in 1967 by a half-dozen charter members; since then it has grown to over 100 corporate members. It is a trade association of for-profit organizations and individuals engaged in either the development or the application of advanced technology to meet the information demands of particular markets. The overall purpose of IIA is to promote the development of private enterprise in the information industry. IIA provides its members with a unified voice in determining national and international information policies. It also provides a necessary balance to the less market-oriented outlook of such professional societies as the American Society for Information Science.

My IIA award was presented by Herbert Brinberg, Chairman of the Board of Aspen Systems Corporation, an information subsidiary of American Can Company. Previous winners were Eugene Power, founder of University Microfilms, and Mortimer Taube, a pioneer in the field of information science.

In my acceptance speech I was asked to examine the future of the information industry. Since scholarly information plays a large role in the present and future of the information industry, I thought it would be useful to publish my talk in *Current Contents*. It appears on pages 8-11 of this issue. For those who would like to know more about IIA and its views of the future, the *Publishers Weekly* summary of the IIA's 10th annual meeting provides an excellent starting point.[7]

While there were many other pleasant events which capped off 1977, I was saddened by the deaths of my friends Robert L. Hayne, ISI's Chief Editor,[8] and Kenneth O. May, Professor of Mathematics at the University of Toronto.

Admitting to good fortune, as I have done above, seems to be tempting the fates to reverse those happy circumstances. Not being very superstitious, let me simply knock on wood, cross my fingers, and hope we can all be so fortunate during 1978.

REFERENCES

1. **Garfield E.** Will ISI's *Arts & Humanities Citation Index*™ revolutionize scholarship? *Current Contents* No. 32, 8 August 1977, p. 5-9.
2. --------------. Reducing the noise level in scientific communication: how services from ISI aid journal editors and publishers. *Current Contents* No. 30, 25 July 1977, p. 5-15.
3. *Institute for Scientific Information®, Inc. v. United States Postal Service,* 555 Fed. 2d 128 (3rd Cir., 1977).
4. **Garfield E.** The agony and ecstasy of publishing your own book: *Essays of an information scientist. Current Contents* No. 27, 4 July 1977, p. 5-7.
5. **Bennion B C.** *Essays of an information scientist* by Eugene Garfield. (Review) *Data Processing Digest* 23(12):28-9, 1977.
6. **Garfield E.** INFO-EXPO/70: the second annual meeting of the Information Industry Association. *Current Contents* No. 45, 18 March 1970, p. 5-6. (Reprinted in: *Essays of an information scientist.* Philadelphia: ISI Press, 1977. Vol. 1, p. 93-4.)
7. **Doebler P.** Ten years old, Information Industry Association grapples with far-reaching issues. *Publishers Weekly* 212(19):25-6, 1977.
8. **Garfield E.** To remember my brother, Robert L. Hayne. *Current Contents* No. 34, 22 August 1977, p. 5-6.

The Future of the Information Industry*

Eugene Garfield, President

Institute for Scientific Information
325 Chestnut Street
Philadelphia, PA 19106

I've just returned from a long trip abroad which I interrupted to get here in time to accept this award. ISI® 's Communications Director called me in Irkutsk to tell me about the award and that I was expected to talk about the future of the information industry. I had to disappoint some friends in Bangkok and Singapore, but I'm pleased to be here.

The trip itself reminded me of two old sayings. The first is that it is easier to be recognized as a "prophet" in a foreign land than in your own home town. Another version says there is more "profit" to be made in foreign lands.

Speaking of profit reminds me of a publisher who recently married a manager of an information company. Many members of the IIA and the AAP (Association of American Publishers) attended the wedding. At the proper point the minister asked if anybody had any objections to the marriage. There was the usual silence. Finally, one guy waved his hand and said, "I don't care if they get married, but would somebody like to hear about *my* information company?" Now, I'm not going to tell you about my information company. You've heard about it before. Naturally I think that our products, for those who need them, are superior.

Instead, let me tell you what I think is in store for the information industry. One can always speculate about the future. If you are wrong, who will remember? If you are right, you can always remind the historians how astute you were.

Most of my career has been devoted to "scientific" information. However, I prefer to think of the German word *Wissenschaft* or the Russian word *nauk*. Those equivalents to the word *science* are comparable to the English word *knowledge*. Neither ISI nor the IIA is limited to the area of *scientific* information, but the information industry received its early impetus in this area. That ISI is changing is indicated by the fact that we are now entering the arts and humanities. For the IIA, I foresee a rapid broadening of coverage. In particular, the information needs of the consumer will be developed and exploited in a variety of ways. The

---

*Speech given upon receipt of Information Industry Association (IIA) Hall of Fame Award, October 5, 1977, Port Chester, New York

Viewdata system, which I will discuss later, is but one example of that. This is not to say that scientific information will not continue to be a major factor in the industry. But the largest untapped opportunities lie in the consumer area.

As for science itself, I believe the basic instrument of communication is the scientific paper. I don't think anything will replace it for at least a decade. What's more, scientists will continue to publish their papers in printed journals.

Since the trend toward collaborative research is accelerating, especially in areas like particle physics, the number of research team or "groupie" papers can be expected to increase. This has happened in the last decade in the People's Republic of China. As groups of collaborators become larger and more unwieldy, perhaps there will be more authors like the famous mathematician Bourbaki. Nicolas Bourbaki, one of the most cited authors in the mathematics literature, is the pseudonym for a group of French mathematicians. However, such group identification carries its own price in anonymity for the individual scientist.

Still, the scientific process is a very personal thing. I don't think there is much chance that significant science will change its individual nature. Leonardo da Vinci and other great artists employed large teams of assistants. So do the particle accelerator people. But individual scientists will continue to point out the great new ideas of science.

My recent trip through the USSR confirmed that the pressure for individuals to publish is even greater there than it is in the US. In the Soviet Union you have to publish *before* you get your doctor's degree. Even the Russians recognize the glut that this requirement has created in their own journals. Certain journals, such as *Zhurnal Fizicheskoi Khimii,* already carry abstracts of papers placed in depositories. While Russian information hardware is still relatively primitive, they will catch up with us one of these days. The USSR's commitment to the information function is significant. In Irkutsk and Novosibirsk every lab has an information specialist assigned to it. The restrictions on travel make it all the more necessary for Soviet scientists to depend upon other means of gathering information. So I believe the USSR can become a significant market for the information industry if we try to sell them the services they require.

The competition to publish in Russia and in most other parts of the world will tend, eventually, to improve the quality of articles. Less significant reports will go into depositories or other substitute forms of publication. Hopefully, the poorest material will remain in authors' files. The publish-or-perish syndrome has a tendency to elevate the importance of publication counting. But I think that more people will begin to understand the difference between counting numbers of papers—which is a straight quantitative measure—and citation analysis, which is more of a qualitative measure.

The *percentage* of growth in the literature will continue to decline. But world-wide, the *absolute* number of articles published each year will continue to increase. This will make review articles even more important, and there will be a vast increase in the number of review journals.

As I mentioned before, the *printed* journal will, for at least 10 to 20 years, remain the principal form of scientific publication. However, we will also have various kinds of electronic data banks. In some fields we may even have totally electronic editing, switching, and distribution of manuscripts. And computerized typesetting is so commonplace today I don't really consider it futuristic. But what we take for granted in the United States is frequently something new for the rest of the world. For example, my colleagues at VINITI in Moscow demonstrated their new *Digiset* system for producing their *referativnyi zhurnaly*—or what we call abstract journals. Nevertheless, while computerized typesetting may now be an old idea, its use in the US and Western Europe, no less than in the USSR, is minuscule compared to the volume of material composed by old-fashioned methods.

If nothing else, vested interests like printers and advertisers will keep printed journals going. The inertia of the international postal system will also tend to maintain the status quo. The post office defines a journal as something printed on paper. Therefore, it isn't about to subsidize, through favorable postage rates, the distribution of journals that switch, for example, to microfilm. And even our copyright laws don't yet recognize non-print information technologies as significant. This type of thinking works against the more rapid evolution of journals into new forms of communication.

Eventually, however, I can visualize scientists using voice synthesizers to listen to papers while driving to work. Even now, one can hear some conferences on cassettes. But print substitutes like cassettes must be reduced to hard copy in order to quote the material authoritatively, and access to non-printed forms is often too slow and cumbersome for reference purposes. On-line storage of the full text of papers may overcome such difficulties.

Many of the systems that emerge will require considerable sophistication in their use. So the information industry will face a real "education" problem. This is where the National Science Foundation and other organizations can play a very important role. But the IIA is going to have to be there to prod the education establishment to get in line with the times.

In particular, universities are incredibly behind. We have very few examples in this country of what is probably the university of the future. I saw one such university, Tsukuba, in Japan. It was planned by a group completely dedicated to the information revolution. Everything in that university will be geared to whatever the information industry can do for that student body and faculty. Eventually the entire Japanese educational community will be affected. The Japanese have not left us behind yet, but many influential people in their educational system are providing them the kind of leadership necessary to make the transition.

Switching from the academic to the consumer community, I think that two-way, on-line communication between citizens and computerized data banks is now imminent. The technology already exists to convert your home television set into a computer terminal operated over your regular telephone line. In less than 10 years, more than one million private homes in Britain will have access to information banks that would boggle the imagination of H.G. Wells. Through the British Post Office system called *Viewdata,* there will be in-the-home access to potentially billions of pages of stored data. That is more than enough capacity to store a whole library, including encyclopedias, books, and journals.

A development like *Viewdata* can be expected to have far-reaching social significance. A whole new relationship between people and their television sets will be created. Instead of passively absorbing whatever images cross the screen, viewers will be able to control the information presented in a much more selective way. No longer will the average citizen live in the "thumb index" era of information retrieval. What I mean is that with printed reference tools you have to use your thumb to access randomly chosen information. The *Viewdata* system with its keyboard will make it the "index finger" era.

Whether services like *Viewdata* can replace the newspaper and other print media remains to be seen. TV has already changed their role, but they continue to survive. In fact, the brevity of *Viewdata* items may whet the appetite for the more complete accounts published in newspapers and magazines.

I am positive that these new systems will precipitate at least one reaction: an increase in the perceived need for knowledge of broader kinds. And this belief leads me to the last point that I will make in trying to project what I consider to be a very positive future for the information industry.

There is a particular economic significance to the information revolution. In our increasingly information-oriented society we are moving away from physical and toward intellectual labor. As this happens, we can observe one peculiar characteristic about the information that we generate: it is very perishable. That's just the kind of thing you need for maintaining employment. When you produce more potatoes than the population can consume, you have to start dumping them. The perishable nature of information makes it possible for you to just keep on producing it. There is no let-up. There is no end to what science can explore. There are unanswered questions that come up all the time. That's why I think that this basic ingredient of our business—the perishable commodity we produce—may prove to solve the problem posed by Marxist analysis of capitalistic society.

Thank you once again for this award. As you see, I believe that the information industry is going to thrive for many decades to come. Indeed, as Machlup and others have been trying to tell us, the information society is already here.

CURRENT COMMENTS

ISI's Who Is Publishing In Science: Why Is It An Idea Whose Time Has *Not* Come?

Number 6, February 6, 1978

For a thinking person, what is worse than an idea whose time has not arrived? While it is a rare event in publishing and in science to admit to failure, at least one of ISI® 's services can be classified as such—if success is measured in numbers of subscribers. I am referring to *WIPIS—ISI's Who Is Publishing In Science®* .[1]

Originally called *International Directory of Research & Development Scientists®* , WIPIS was created ten years ago in response to requests for an annual cumulation of the weekly author-address lists in *Current Contents®* .[2] We believed that *WIPIS* would facilitate not only reprint requests, but many other communications between publishing scientists. Yet, in spite of its scope and versatility, *WIPIS* has not achieved acceptance in the marketplace commensurate with the effort required to produce it.

Maybe we have taken *WIPIS* too much for granted. For example, although I have discussed *WIPIS/IDR&DS®* editorially, I am chagrined to note that it has never been described in a formal way in a library or information journal. In its early days it was reviewed in a few publications, but it has received

minimal publicity. Considering its size and scope, this is odd. The 1977 *WIPIS* provides the names and addresses of more than 360,000 scientific authors from about 30,000 organizations in 179 countries. These names and addresses include the first or "reprint" authors covered in all six editions of *Current Contents*. WIPIS also includes the first authors of articles in publications covered exclusively by the *Science Citation Index®* and the *Social Sciences Citation Index™* . All disciplines of the sciences and social sciences are represented. Eventually, we can easily include additional authors and scholars from the arts and humanities.[3]

The scope of *WIPIS* is well illustrated when one considers that Derek de Solla Price and others have been able to use this source as the basis for making some fascinating demographic studies of scientists.[4,5,6]

The information covered by *WIPIS* is indexed three ways, as illustrated in Figure 1. The Author Section is arranged alphabetically. It gives you the complete address for each author. You can also use this section to verify the spelling of a scientist's last name. Or, you can use *WIPIS,* like the *SCI®* , when you want to know if an author published anything during a specific year. You simply check that year's volume.

The Geographic Section is arranged by country and subdivided by state, city, and organization. The names of authors whose full addresses are found in the Author Section are listed after each organization. You can use this section to identify organizations and individuals in a specific geographical area. This might be handy if you are organizing a seminar in a particular town or country.

The Organization Section is arranged alphabetically and shows organizations which had publishing authors during the *WIPIS* coverage year. For each organization there is a list of the different cities where a branch is located. This section is really a comprehensive directory to organizations all over the world which are involved in some way with the sciences or social sciences. You can use it to locate organizations and their branches and to distinguish by location similarly named organizations.

The three indexes, as I have indicated, each function separately. But you can use them together, too. For instance, suppose you can't remem-

Organization Section	Geographic Section	Author Section

CLAYTON JR COLL
  GEORGIA MORROW
CLEARWATER CLIN LAB
  FLORIDA CLEARWATER
CLEARWATER COMMUN HOSP
  FLORIDA CLEARWATER
CLEMENS AUGUST KRANKENHAUSES
  FED REP GER BITBURG
CLEMENS HOSP
  FED REP GER MUNSTER
CLEMSON UNIV
  SOUTH CAROLINA BLACKVILLE
  SOUTH CAROLINA CLEMSON
  SOUTH CAROLINA COLUMBIA
  SOUTH CAROLINA ELGIN
CLENSOL SARL
  SWITZERLAND LUTRY
CLESA SPA
  ITALY LONIGO
CLEVELAND BOARD EDUC
  OHIO CLEVELAND
CLEVELAND BRIDGE & ENGN CO LTD
  ENGLAND CLEVELAND
CLEVELAND CLIFFS IRON CO
  OHIO CLEVELAND
CLEVELAND CLIN FDN
  OHIO CLEVELAND
CLEVELAND COLL JEWISH STUDIES
  OHIO CLEVELAND
CLEVELAND CONTROLS INC
  OHIO CLEVELAND
CLEVELAND CRYSTALS INC
  OHIO CLEVELAND
CLEVELAND CTR RES CHILD DEV
  OHIO CLEVELAND
CLEVELAND DIETETIC ASSOC
  OHIO CLEVELAND
CLEVELAND EAR NOSE & THROAT GRP
  OHIO CLEVELAND
CLEVELAND ELECT ILLUMINATING CO
  OHIO CLEVELAND
CLEVELAND FOOT CLIN
  OHIO CLEVELAND
	SOUTH CAROLINA
	CLEMSON
	  CLEMSON UNIV
	  DICKENS LL
	  DIXON GM
	  DUBOIS JA
	  DUNN BE
	  DUNN C
	  DYCK LA
	  EISIMINGER S
	  ELLICOTT AR
	  FALLAW SA
	  FANNING JC
	  FENNELL RE
	  FLOYD JA
	  FORSYTH MA
	  FOSTER DL
	  FOX RC
	  FREEMAN WL
	  FULTON JD
	  GARMON JP
	  GIMENEZ T
	  GOLDEN RM
	  GOODE H
	  GRACE JB
	  GWYTHER MJ
	  HAIR BL
	  HAMMER WB
	  HANDLIN DL
	  HAUN JR
	  HENRICKS DM
	  HENSEL JL
	  HILDERMAN RH
	  HILL JR
	  HITE J
	  HOLDER DP
	  HOLLEMAN KA
	  HOLLOWAY RL
	  HOOD CE
	  HSU JC
	  HSU JM
	  INGRAM BR
		HOLLOWAY LS
		  TEXAS TECH UNIV,SCH MED,DEPT
		  PHYSIOL
		  LUBBOCK, TX, 79409
		HOLLOWAY PAH
		  GEN HOSP HUMAN METAB
		  SOUTHAMPTON, ENGLAND
		HOLLOWAY PH
		  SANDIA LABS
		  ALBUQUERQUE, NM, 87115
		HOLLOWAY PJ
		  UNIV BRISTOL,LONG ASHTON RES
		  STN
		  BRISTOL BS18 9AF, ENGLAND
		HOLLOWAY PJ
		  UNIV MANCHESTER,DENT HLTH UNIT
		  MANCHESTER M13 9PL,
		  LANCASHIRE, ENGLAND
		HOLLOWAY PW
		  UNIV VIRGINIA,SCH MED,DEPT
		  BIOCHEM
		  CHARLOTTESVILLE, VA, 22901
		HOLLOWAY RG
		  HECHT HACKER BOLDY
		  INC
		  CHICAGO, IL
		HOLLOWAY RL
		  CLEMSON UNIV,DEPT ENTOMOL &
		  ECON ZOOL
		  CLEMSON, SC, 29631
		HOLLOWAY RL
		  COLUMBIA UNIV
		  NEW YORK, NY, 10027
		HOLLOWAY RM
		  NEW YORK CITY HLTH & HOSP
		  CORP,EMERGENCY MED SERV
		  NEW YORK, NY, 10001
		HOLLOWAY S
		  UNIV LEICESTER,DEPT PHYS
		  LEICESTER LE1 7RH, ENGLAND
		HOLLOWAY ST
		  BUR MANPOWER & EDUC
		  CHICAGO, IL, 60600

Figure 1. Sample entries from the 1977 *ISI's Who Is Publishing In Science®* (*WIPIS*). Boxed areas indicate how you would find the full address for RL Holloway if you couldn't recall the name without seeing it, but did know the author was at Clemson University. Under the Organization Section you would find the locations of the campuses of Clemson University. In the Geographic Section under South Carolina, Clemson, you would recognize the author's name. Turning to the Author section, you would find RL Holloway's full address.

ber an author's name, but can recognize it if you see it—a not unusual problem for most of us. If you know the author's organization, you can look in the Organization Section. Then in the Geographic Section you can find the list of publishing scientists and scan it for the name that has eluded you (Figure 1).

One reason why *WIPIS* works so well as a reprint-request tool lies in the fact that ISI has been crusading for the inclusion of a complete address immediately after each author's name at the beginning of all journal articles.[7,8] Many more journals now make this information available in a visible and unambiguous format. As a result, more of the addresses we put into *WIPIS* are likely to be complete and correct. Also, there is a significant amount of editorial effort expended to prevent redundancies and inconsistencies from appearing in *WIPIS*. Some authors may use six or more variations of the same address. This is not apparent in the weekly *CC*® address directory, but would be very obvious if the six versions were seen next to each other in *WIPIS*.

Another reason why *WIPIS* should be the address directory of choice is that it contains the names of younger scientists who are just beginning their careers. A biographical directory like *American Men & Women of Science* undoubtedly includes the names of those scientists who author—or co-author—a large percentage of all articles.[9] However, it is the first, and frequently the junior, authors to whom one addresses reprint requests. Their names may not get into

AM&WS for many years. (It is a mystery to me how names are selected for that work. I often wonder if they consult our *Science Citation Index*. It seems reasonable that they would, but, if so, I've never been told of it.)

AM&WS also has fewer entries than *WIPIS* (110,000 vs. 360,000), is updated irregularly, and is published in separate disciplinary sections which cost a total of $235 and do not include the social sciences. *WIPIS* is issued every year, covers the sciences and social sciences in one convenient volume, and costs only $100 per year. Of course, as a biographical directory *AM&WS* provides information not contained in *WIPIS*.

All of which leads me back to the basic, nagging question: if *WIPIS* is so good, why isn't it more successful?

It is possible that the first author limitation has a significant effect on the usefulness of *WIPIS*. I've never received a complaint on this point, but then people rarely complain. Instead, they stop using a tool which is inadequate to their needs.

Perhaps *WIPIS* would be accepted more if, like other publishers, we solicited authors to authenticate their entries and buy the directory at the same time. If we published *WIPIS* in soft cover and lowered the price to, say, $15-$20, would sales increase five-fold?

One recent suggestion is to include either a full or abbreviated version of *WIPIS* as part of each *Current Contents* subscription. This supplement could be published semi-annually or annually. I would like to hear from readers about this possibility. How often is it necessary to go through back issues of *CC* to find an author's address? Is it worth a few extra dollars per year to have this information cumulated? It might even be possible to show for each author the *CC* issue and page on which his or her article appeared. This would give you a cumulative author index to *CC* for each year—a simple way to relocate articles seen while browsing. It has also been suggested that *WIPIS* would be more useful if we provided a subject specialty code for each author. This is not so simple, but possible.

Is *WIPIS* suffering from an identity crisis? Is it mainly a librarian's tool? Do scientists know it exists? Should it be in department offices or on your personal bookshelf?

I'd like to get answers to these questions and resolve some of my speculations. So I am herewith beginning some market research to find out exactly why so many ISI subscribers have chosen to do without *WIPIS*. If you have never seen a copy of *WIPIS*, call or write ISI's Director of Communications.† He will arrange to send you a *free* copy of the 1976 annual while the supply lasts. This is not a trivial offer since we *sell* back issues. There is one hitch: I do expect you to tell me what's wrong with *WIPIS*. If you prefer, have your librarian write me. A prompt acknowledgement is assured.

Having to live with our "mistakes" is one of the more sobering human experiences. I've been living with *WIPIS* for a decade now. While this constant reminder of one's fallibility can have a salutary effect, if at all possible, I'd much rather change *WIPIS* into a success.

REFERENCES

1. **Garfield E.** *ISI's Who Is Publishing in Science (WIPIS)* offers instant access to research and research workers worldwide.
   Current Contents No. 21, 24 May 1972, p. 5-7.*
2. ——————. *IDR&DS®* , an international directory of publishing scientists.
   Current Contents No. 30, 29 July 1969, p. 4.*
3. ——————. Will ISI's *Arts & Humanities Citation Index™* revolutionize scholarship? *Current Contents* No. 32, 8 August 1977, p. 5-9.
4. **Price D J D.** Measuring the size of science.
   Proc. Israel Acad. Sci. Human. 4:98-111, 1969.
5. **Price D J D & Gursey S.** Some statistical results for the numbers of authors in the states of the United States and the nations of the world.
   ISI's Who Is Publishing In Science. Philadelphia: Institute for Scientific Information , 1977, pp. 26-34.
6. **Inhaber H.** Scientific cities. *Res. Policy* 3:182-200, 1974.
7. **Garfield E.** An address on addresses. *Current Contents* No. 28, 14 July 1975, p. 5*
8. ——————. The place for an author's address is upfront—where it can be counted!
   Current Contents No. 47, 22 November 1976, p. 5-6.*
9. **Jacques Cattell Press.** *American Men & Women of Science.*
   New York: Bowker, 1976. 7 vols.

*Reprinted in: *Essays of an information scientist.* Philadelphia: ISI Press, 1977, 2 vols.

† 325 Chestnut St., Philadelphia, PA 19106, USA. (215) 923-3300, ext. 294.

CURRENT COMMENTS

To Remember Chauncey D. Leake

Number 7, February 13, 1978

Chauncey Depew Leake, my friend and mentor, died on the day I received this last note from him, January 11, 1978. On the evening before his death he had attended "An Evening With Chauncey Leake," sponsored by San Francisco's Bohemian Club, where he and about 100 friends and colleagues read several of his poems. Chauncey collapsed while receiving an ovation and died a few hours later from a ruptured aortic aneurysm.

Chauncey Leake was so well-known to scientists throughout the world that it seems almost redundant to repeat the facts of his long and varied career. Eight years ago I paid tribute to him in this space for the many contributions he had made to the success of ISI®

411

and to my own career.[1,2,3] I cannot provide a complete biography of Chauncey in the limited space available here. I do hope some young scholar can find the time to do a complete and proper account of his life.

I first met Chauncey in 1951, when he was chairman of the advisory committee to the Johns Hopkins Welch Medical Library Indexing Project.[4] Chauncey often stressed the value of review articles, not only for integrating and synthesizing scientific accomplishments but also as a tool for information retrieval. As a result I studied the makeup of review articles very carefully and observed the peculiar similarity between the structure of indexes and the structure of sentences in reviews. In a review paper a sentence is followed by a citation. In a traditional subject index the same is true. But in a citation index the situation is reversed!

From the early days of the Welch Project and steadily thereafter Chauncey had a continuing influence on me, ISI and its products. He was chairman of the Editorial Advisory Board for *Current Contents®* /*Life Sciences* from the beginning. He also served as a member of the editorial advisory board for *Index to Scientific Reviews®* .

The encouragement to publish my recent book, *Essays of an Information Scientist,* also came directly from Chauncey. Starting almost five years ago, Chauncey urged me almost weekly to collect these essays into a book.[5]

Chauncey also contributed an occasional column to *Current Contents/Life Sciences.* Many readers probably do not realize that "Calling Attention To," which has appeared in *CC* since its inception, actually began in 1940 as a mimeographed monthly for Chauncey's friends. It was always a gold mine of information, since Chauncey's tastes were both wide-ranging and exceedingly discriminating. The "Calling Attention To" found on page 25 of the *Life Sciences* edition of this issue of *Current Contents* is, regrettably, his last.

During our 27-year friendship Chauncey and I exchanged thoughts through a voluminous correspondence. Chauncey's letters were always a source of advice, encouragement, inspiration, enthusiasm, and energy. At the top of each letter he would comment on the current weather: "Cool and windy," "Foggy, smoggy with sun breaking," and, during the recent California drought, "We had rain! Whoopee!" When conveying holiday greetings, he would invariably write "Happy Holi*daze!*" His praise for ISI and for many of my own projects was unrestrained, and his large, graceful handwriting reinforced the encouragement he always freely gave.

Chauncey was always a popularizer of science. He believed that scientists have a responsibility to communicate their findings to the public. He applauded excellent scientific journalism, writing, "Those who get knowledge across to the people are as important in our social enterprise as those who may discover it."[6] He also believed that

Elizabeth and Chauncey D. Leake in May, 1968

scientists should keep aware of the public's perception of science, and was a great fan of the ISI Press Digest.

During his lifetime Chauncey wore many hats. He was a pharmacologist, philosopher, chemist, writer, physiologist, historian, administrator, and humanist.

Chauncey was born in Elizabeth, New Jersey, on September 5, 1896. By his own account, he came from "middle class stock." His mother's family were German craftsmen, and his father, Frank W., was a coal-shipper for the Central Railroad of New Jersey. While growing up, Chauncey was "thrilled" by Mark Twain, Rudyard Kipling, Robert Louis Stevenson, and the exploits of Sherlock Holmes.[7] In high school he was on the football and track teams and was manager of the baseball team.

In 1917 Leake graduated from Princeton, where he had majored in philosophy, chemistry, and biology. Later that year he enlisted in the New Jersey National Guard. In 1918 he was transferred from a machine gun outfit to the Chemical Warfare Service, where he served in the defense effort against war gases. After the war he was asked to stay on and investigate the effects of morphine.

Chauncey thought of going into medicine, but chose instead first to get a Ph.D. and start an academic career. He never did receive an M.D., although he earned his Master's in 1920 and a Ph.D. in physiology and pharmacology in 1925 at the University of Wisconsin, where he taught for the next eight years. Later he would become one of the few non-M.D.'s to be dean of a medical school. While at Wisconsin he married Elizabeth Wilson, a microbiologist.

In 1928 Leake established the Department of Pharmacology at the University of California, San Franciso, where he was Senior Lecturer in the History and Philosophy of Medicine and Senior Lecturer in Pharmacology. From 1963 to 1966 he was Professor of Medical Jurisprudence at the Hastings College of the Law, San Francisco.

Leake's contributions to pharmacology include studies on the metabolic action of anesthetics and narcotics, the regulation of the production of red blood cells, and the biochemistry of the brain and central nervous system; studies on leprosy; and analysis of the conceptual basis of pharmacology as a scientific discipline.

He was an early believer that anesthesiology is a physiological science and not just the duty of the surgeon's assistant. He introduced divinyl ether as an anesthetic agent in 1930, developed Vioform and carbarsone in the treatment of dysentery, contributed to the development of tranquilizers, investigated the effects of pH on blood vessels, and used conceptual models of the correlation between chemical structure and biologic action which he called *biochemorphology.* Gordon Alles developed the first amphetamine drugs in Leake's laboratory. Leake always believed that a scientist should test a new drug on himself before testing it on volunteers or patients.

Chauncey was a pioneer in developing institutions, including the M.D. Anderson Hospital for cancer patients, and the Baylor Medical School in Houston. He founded, and edited from 1943 to 1955, *Texas Reports on Biology and Medicine,* and was a consulting editor for *Geriatrics, Excerpta Medica, Perspectives in Biology and Medicine,* and *Archives of International Pharmacology.* Also, for more than 15 years he wrote a column called "Review of Reviews" for the *Annual Review of Pharmacology.*

To mention his most notable honorary and administrative positions, Chauncey has been president of the American Association for the Advancement of Science (in 1960); consultant to the National Research Council, the Public Health Service, and the National Library of Medicine; chairman of the American Medical Association's Section on Pharmacology; president of the Society for Experimental Biology and Medicine; president of the American Society for Pharmacology and Experimental Therapeutics; president of the American Society for the History of Medicine; president of the History of Science Society; and president of the Ameri-

Quotations from the Writings of Chauncey D. Leake

"Let us not delude ourselves by dreaming that great achievements are imminent. Let us eschew 'breakthroughs' lest we incur frustrating breakdowns. Let us strive for equanimity for our quest for the 'truth,' remembering that whatever we call 'truth' is tentative and subject to revision as our verifiable knowledge increases, and that 'even unwelcomed truth is better than cherished error.' Let us patiently support the long-term scientific endeavor. It would be brash indeed to think that the secrets evolved over billions of years will yield overnight even with the most generous of financial backing."

Why search and research? *Journal of the American Medical Association.* 193:54-8, 1965.

"There seems to be little point in exhorting men to be good. That has been the way of the moralists for centuries and it hasn't worked with startling success. Neither fear of punishment nor hope of reward has been particularly fruitful in promoting good conduct among men."

Ethicogenesis. *The Scientific Monthly.* 60:425-53, 1945.

"Whether or not society can abolish poverty, the principal cause of frustration among the mass of people, remains a problem and may always be so. The struggle of the have-nots to get what the haves have is an ancient one, and *les miserables* are ever present. *Les misérables* can get out of their predicament and frustrations by seeking individual goals which are modest and obtainable and, having reached them, by moving along in accordance with their abilities. It is not wise to have champagne tastes when one merely has a beer pocketbook. It is wise, however, to condition oneself to work toward obtainable goals, being honest with oneself as to capability. The satisfaction coming from modest goals and purposes that have been reached may start self-generating cycles of satisfaction. This can effectively prevent dissatisfaction and its potentially disastrous psychodynamism. The sense of satisfaction, no matter how minor, is a comforting one and an encouragement to seek it again."

Human purpose, the limbic system, and the sense of satisfaction. *Zygon* 10:86-94, 1975.

"It is unwise for us to be hoping for longer lives if we do not continually strive to make them more worth the living.... Mere longevity is not a worthy goal for geriatrics: the proper social function of geriatricians is to make life more satisfying for older people. This depends neither on mechanical spare-part gadgetry nor on 'genetic intervention,' but rather on the much more difficult day-to-day psychological guidance."

Aging slowed down? What for? *Geriatrics* 21:113-4, 1966.

"Lacking directional ethics, we cannot apply our scientific knowledge to purposes we can agree upon as worthy of universal social endeavor. Our science seems to become applied chiefly to making individual and national status symbols. What gadgetry is directed toward cleanliness, comfort and convenience, is well diluted by styling for false-fronting, and the waste is monumental. What profit longer life from medical science if there is so little chance yet for living it with graciousness, dignity, self-confidence and self-reliance? What social value has our science if it is applied so successfully to the possibility of destroying us all?"

Our unbalanced biad. *Journal of the Franklin Institute.* 269:355-61, 1960.

"Science is a great adventure. It is the culminative effort on the part of peoples all over the world to get verifiable knowledge about themselves and their environment. There is nothing more important than seeking the truth about ourselves and our environment, even if we do not like it when we find it. It may take time to realize that unwelcome truth is better than cherished error, but the common experience of each one of us is testimony to the wisdom of this judgement. If we can understand that voluntary agreement constitutes the validity of scientific conclusions, then we can all realize how important science is with respect to freedom and democracy. We also may continue to appreciate how necessary freedom is for the advance of science."

Unity and communication in science and the health professions.
New York State Journal of Medicine. 60:1496-1500, 1960.

can Society of Pharmacology. He was Vice-President of the American Humanist Association in 1953 and 1954, and received its Humanist Pioneer Award in 1977.

During his active and prolific lifetime Chauncey wrote over 25 books and more than 600 articles. About ten years ago, I was planning to write a book, but just could not find the time. So I asked Chauncey how he was able to do so much writing. He wrote, "You will never *find* the time. You have to *take* it."[8]

The publications listed on pages 13-15 have been selected to indicate the breadth and depth of Chauncey's interests. The quotations reprinted on page 9 will serve as examples of his crisp, incisive writing style. He wrote on everything from pharmacology to history, from ethics to music, from travel to the limits of understanding. All of these works are characterized by Chauncey's enthusiasm, wit, and humanism. He always tried to bring a human perspective to scientific and medical subjects—and a disciplined, rational point of view to music, art, and philosophy. He also prized his honorary membership in the National Association of Science Writers.

Chauncey was also an enologist, and was particularly interested in the therapeutic uses of wine. In fact, he served as a consultant to the California Wine Growers Association, and on at least one occasion he recommended wine as an aid to restful and refreshing sleep. "Long experience has shown that wines are probably safer and more effective than any other kind of muscular relaxing and sleep-producing agent,"[9] he wrote.

Another of Chauncey's pet topics was the human life span and aging. He wrote a regular column for *Geriatrics* in which he discussed such topics as the maximum human life span, the differences in life expectancy for men and women, free radicals and aging, and the care of dying older persons.

He loved poetry, art, and drama, and enjoyed working with theatrical groups. His enthusiasms extended to music—especially opera and jazz. More than ten years ago he described with characteristic beauty and flair this scene in a New Orleans jazz hall:

The lights were dim. The benches were crowded with a motley group of swaying and clapping peoples of all kinds. The jazz group was rocking away—a little red-gartered and white-haired, wizened pianist at the dilapidated upright, the old banjoist strumming along, the trombonist "frogging," the trumpeter and clarinetist swaying their instruments to the ceiling, and the bald, grinning drummer banging it out with clicking syncopation and cymbals.[10]

Here Chauncey demonstrated his versatility. His writing style is what one might expect from an accomplished novelist, rather than from a scientist!

With all his other interests, Chauncey was a kind of international citizen. He lectured in almost every country in the world, and travelled more widely than almost anyone I've met.

In his philosophy, as in his life,

Leake was concerned with the practical affairs of day-to-day living. For example, the title of his three-volume series is *What Are We Living For? Practical Philosophy.* His books on philosophy arose out of the talks he gave to University of California Ph.D. candidates in the 1940's. Those who came to these sessions at his home near San Francisco got no academic credit, so Leake offered cookies and coffee "as bait."

Chauncey was certainly a learned and a rational man, but he was also affectionate and full of surprises. He attributed the good health he enjoyed throughout most of his life to his habit of walking up and down the hills of San Francisco. An excellent description of Chauncey appeared in *Saturday Review,* 20 years ago. The author noted,

Dr. Leake gives freely of himself with an effervescence that bubbles gaily in the mind long afterward. Met face to face, he greets the world through an imp that lives deep down in his eyes and peers out sharply through a sort of venetian blind that opens and shuts with a disconcerting speed. His Santa Claus laugh rolls gently all over a room.... Only his soap-white hair and kindly gentleman demeanor betray to strangers the scholar beneath Dr. Leake's jolly medicine-man facade.[11]

Leake was a perennial and enthusiastic optimist. For instance, in 1960 he wrote,

As our world-wide communications continue to improve, we may be sure that the traditional aspirations of people everywhere for a better life will push for the balanced triad of logics, ethics, and aesthetics: our science will become more widely understood, and as our inherent love of beauty exerts itself, our applications of scientific knowledge may be ever more wisely directed toward social welfare and the good of the people. We are witnessing a new resurgence of enthusiasm for understanding science, for achieving worthy purposes in human welfare, and in preserving the natural beauties of our world, even in our increasing industrialization.[12]

Chauncey, himself a Renaissance man, was above all a believer in broad, well-rounded education. Upon his wife's death last year, he established the Elizabeth and Chauncey Leake Fund for the Humanities at the University of Texas Medical Branch, Galveston. Its purpose is to foster well-rounded medical education by providing the community of the University of Texas Medical Branch, Galveston, with access to cultural events in the arts and humanities. The events sponsored by the Fund will include ballet, poetry readings, concerts, and lectures. Contributions may be sent to the fund's director, William B. Bean, at the Institute for Medical Humanities, University of Texas Medical Branch, Galveston, Texas, 77550.

Although I have learned that Chauncey's papers will be deposited with the National Library of Medicine, I do not know what provision, if any, has been made for his memoirs. It has often seemed to me that certain foundations might help men like Leake compile their memoirs while they are alive. Too often the papers of great scholars are collected after their death, when it is too late for their own critical evaluation. This is an unfortunate waste of brain power. Perhaps some foundation could identify such persons and set up a fellowship for graduate students to assist in writing their memoirs. This would benefit not only scholars and historians, but also would be an excellent educational experience for the students. Spending a year or so helping to write the memoirs of someone like Chauncey Leake could be vastly more worthwhile than spending a year in classes.

There is a popular song today called "You Light Up My Life." I can think of no expression that better describes the effect Chauncey Leake had on everyone who knew him. Everywhere he went he brought sunshine into the lives of all the people he touched. His outlook is amply expressed by the poem he wrote and sent to his friends on the last New Year before his death:

Greetings for a New Year

The Old Year, like an old man,
withers away, and dies;
the New Year, like a bubbling babe,
gives its puling birth cries.

What a great potential
has the New Year!
for happiness, for joy
for sorrow, for work,
for play, and for love.

Let this New Year fulfill
for you its full potential,
and come to its end
with a rainbow
arched high above.

Chauncey Leake

REFERENCES

1. **Garfield E.** Calling attention to Chauncey D. Leake — Renaissance scholar extraordinaire. *Current Contents* No. 16, 22 April 1970, p. 4-5. Reprinted in: *Essays of an information scientist.* Philadelphia: ISI Press, 1977. Vol. 1, p. 102-3.
2. ──────────. *Index to Scientific Reviews, 1974.* Philadelphia: ISI Press, 1974. Vol. 1, p. 3.
3. ──────────. Preface. *Journal Citation Reports®* . *Science Citation Index 1975 Annual.* Philadelphia: ISI, 1976. Vol. 9, p. ix.
4. **Larkey S V.** The Welch Medical Library Indexing Project. *Bull. Med. Lib. Assoc.* 41:32-40, 1953.
5. **Garfield E.** *Essays of an information scientist.* Philadelphia: ISI Press, 1977. Preface, Vol. 1, p. xix.
6. **Leake C D.** Unity and communication in science and the health professions. *N.Y. State J. Med.* 60:1496-1500, 1960.
7. ──────────. *What are we living for? Practical philosophy by Chauncey D. Leake.* Westbury, Conn: PJD Publications, 1973. Vol. 1, p. 6.
8. ──────────. Personal communication, 19 October 1967.
9. ──────────. Catnapping. *Geriatrics* 22:97-8, May 1967.
10. ──────────. Swing and feel young! *Geriatrics* 21:208-12, May 1966.
11. *Saturday Review* 41:40, 1968.
12. **Leake C D.** Our unbalanced biad. *J. Franklin Inst.* 269:355-61, 1960.

CHAUNCEY D. LEAKE: A SELECT BIBLIOGRAPHY
Books:

The action of morphine on the vomiting center in the dog.
Baltimore: Privately published, 1922.

Leukocytic reactions to morphine. Chicago: Privately published, 1922.

The loss of circulating erythrocytes in certain types of experimental pneumonia.
New York: Privately published, 1922.

Percival's medical ethics, edited by Chauncey D. Leake.
Baltimore: Williams and Wilkins Co., 1927.

1938 travelog; being an account of a European trip written for the amusement of the friends of Chauncey and Elizabeth Leake. San Francisco: Privately published, 1938. 35 pp.

Prolegomenon to current pharmacology, by Chauncey D. Leake.
Berkeley, California: University of California Press, 1938. 29 pp.

Science implies freedom.
Menasha, Wisconsin: Privately published, 1942. 320 pp.

Letheon; the cadenced story of anesthesia.
Austin, Texas: University of Texas Press, 1947. 128 pp.

Can we agree? A scientist and a philosopher argue about ethics. (with Romanell P)
Austin, Texas: University of Texas Press, 1950. 110 pp.

Yellow fever in Galveston, Republic of Texas, 1839; an account of the great epidemic. A biographical sketch of Ashbel Smith (1805-1886) and stories of the men who conquered yellow fever. Austin, Texas: University of Texas Press, 1951.

The old Egyptian medical papyri.
Lawrence, Kansas: University of Kansas Press, 1952. 108 pp.

Tissue culture cadence. Galveston, Texas: Privately published, 1954.

Impressions of physiology and other matters in the USSR.
Privately published, August, 1956. 72 pp.

The amphetamines: their actions and uses. Springfield, Illinois: C.C. Thomas, 1958. 167 pp.

Daniel Drake (1785-1852) persevering idealist.
Chicago: Privately published, 1959. 570 pp.

The Asklepian myths revalued. Columbus, Ohio: Privately published, 1960. 10 pp.

Alcoholic beverages in clinical medicine. (with Silverman M)
Cleveland: World Publishing, 1966. 160 pp.

What are we living for? Practical philosophy by Chauncey D. Leake.
Westbury, New York: PJD Publications, 1973. 3 vols. (Vol. 1: *The Ethics;* vol. 2: *The Logics;* vol. 3: *The Esthetics.*)

An historical account of pharmacology to the twentieth century.
Springfield, Illinois: C.C. Thomas, 1975. 210 pp.

CHAUNCEY D. LEAKE: A SELECT BIBLIOGRAPHY
(CONTINUED)

Articles:

A worth-while bypath in medicine. *Phi Beta Pi Q.* 18(2), 1922.
What was Kappa Lambda? *Ann. Med. Hist.* 4:192-206, 1922.
Blood reaction under morphine. (with Koehler A)
   Arch. Int. Pharmacodyn. Ther. 27:221-9, 1922.
The occurrences of citric acid in sweat. *Amer. J. Physiol.* 63:540-4, 1923.
Percival's code: a chapter in the historical development of medical ethics.
   J. Amer. Med. Ass. 81:366-71, 1923.
The historical developments of surgical anesthesia. *Scientific M.* 20:304-28, 1925.
Cooperative research: a case report. *Science* 62:251-6, 1925.
The resistance of normal human erythrocytes to hypotonic saline solutions. (with Pratt H)
   J. Amer. Med. Ass. 85:899-900, 1925.
Princeton and medicine. *Princeton Alumni W.* 26:54, 1925.
Studies in exhaustion due to lack of sleep. 2. Symptomatology in rabbits. (with Grab J A
   & Senn M J) *Amer. J. Physiol.* 82:127-30, 1927.
Medical caricature in the United States.
   Bull. Soc. Med. Hist. Chicago 4:1-29, 1928.
How is "Medical Ethics" to be taught? *Bull. Ass. Am. Med. Coll.* 3:341, 1928.
The pharmacologic evaluation of new drugs. *J. Amer. Med. Ass.* 93:1632-4, 1929.
A note on the medical books of famous printers. *Calif. Western Med.* 32(1), 1930.
Roman architectural hygiene. *Ann. Med. Hist.* 2:135-63, 1930.
The anesthetic action of divinyl oxide in animals. (with Knoefel P K & Guedel A E)
   J. Pharmacol. Exp. Ther. 47:5-16, 1933.
The role of pharmacology in the development of ideal anesthesia.
   J. Amer. Med. Ass. 102:1-4, 1934.
Chemotherapy of leprosy; clinical evaluation of antileprosy drugs.
   U. Calif. Pub. Pharmacol. 1:31-47, 1938.
Metabolic and respiratory effects of dinitrophenylmorphine. (with Abreu B E, Phatak N M,
   & Emerson G A) *U. Calif. Pub. Pharmacol.* 1:69-76, 1938.
Notes on the pharmacological action of dinitrophenylmorphine. (with Emerson G A, Klyza
   S J, & Phatak N M) *U. Calif. Pub. Pharmacol.* 1:59-67, 1938.
The toxicity of mesityl oxide. (with Hart E R & Schick A J)
   U. Calif. Pub. Pharmacol. 1:213-30, 1939.
The antiseptic efficiency of certain benzene and furan mercurials. (with Handley C & Phatak
   N M) *U. Calif. Pub. Pharmacol.* 1:175-86, 1939.
Monochloracetic acid as a food and beverage stabilizer. (with Morrison J L)
   U. Calif. Pub. Pharmacol. 1:397-421, 1941.
The toxicity of epichlorhydrin. (with Freuder E)
   U. Calif. Pub. Pharmacol. 2:66-77, 1941.
Recent books on the history of medicine. *Science* 93:424-7, 1941.
Religio scientise. *Scientific M.* 52:166-73, 1941.
Mechanism of action of ordinary war gases. (with Marsh D F) *Science* 96:194-7, 1942.
Optical illusions from train windows. *Science* 97:423-4, 1943.
Ethicogenesis. *Scientific M.* 60:245-53, 1945.
A scientific versus a metaphysical approach to ethics. *Scientific M.* 62:187-92, 1946.
Cost of hospital operation. (with Burns B I) *J. Amer. Med. Ass.* 132:238-9, 1946.
Physiological standards in adolescence. *J. Amer. Med. Ass.* 132:863, 1946.
Geriatrics and euthanasia. *Geriatrics* 1:247-8, 1946.
Gold rush doc. *Gesnerus* 8:114-23, 1951.
Short term cultures for drug assays—general considerations. (with Pomerat C M)
   Ann. N.Y. Acad. Sci. 58:1110-28, 1954.

CHAUNCEY D. LEAKE: A SELECT BIBLIOGRAPHY
(CONTINUED)

The ideals of science in relation to national security. Presented at the American Association for the Advancement of Science meeting in Berkeley, California, December 28, 1954.
Soviet physiology. *Science* 124:538-9, 1956.
What we don't know hurts us. *Sat. Rev.* 41:38-40, January 4, 1958.
Preserving our science archives. *Science* 132:158-9, 1960.
Metric system. *Pop. Mech.* 114:138, 1960.
Voluntary coordination of our expanding health. *J. Amer. Med. Ass.* 178:51-5, 1961.
Rocking chairs for pepping up oldsters. *Geriatrics* 16:260, 1961.
Political aspects of aging. *Geriatrics* 16:319, 1961.
New psychological theory on aging. *Geriatrics* 16:501, 1961.
Aging and moral judgments. *Geriatrics* 16:499, 1961.
One's body for research. *Geriatrics* 17:59-60, 1962.
Nobelist George von Bekesy. *Geriatrics* 17:57-9, 1962.
Never too late for intellectual endeavours. *Geriatrics* 18:2, 1963.
Science information. *Science* 139:1088, 1963.
Life among anesthetists: recollections of 40 years. *Anesthesiology* 25:428-35, 1964.
History of wine as therapy. *J. Lancet* 84A:12, 1964.
Library opportunities in new medical schools. *J. Med. Educ.* 40:292-3, 1965.
Interrelations of sciences with humanities and ethics. Reflections on quadricentennial of Galileo's birth. *Tex. J. Sci.* 17:5, 1965.
Enjoyment of music for old age. *Geriatrics* 20:524, 1965.
Decency and the green felt jungle. *N. Engl. J. Med.* 272:215, 1965.
Dimethyl sulfoxide. *Science* 152:1646-9, 1966.
Appraisal of Albert Schweitzer (1875-1965). *Geriatrics* 21(9):117, 1966.
Technical triumphs and moral muddles. *Ann. Intern. Med.* 67:43-50, 1967.
The role of vitamins in health maintenance. *Geriatrics* 22(8):80-2, 1967.
The retirement crisis. *Geriatrics* 22(10):103-4, 1967.
Clinical use of wine in geriatrics. (with Silverman M) *Geriatrics* 22(2):175-80, 1967.
The care of dying older persons. *Geriatrics* 22(9):91-2, 1967.
Blood sugar rises with age. *Geriatrics* 22(11):88, 1967.
Biological actions of dimethyl sulfoxide. Introductory remarks.
    Ann. N.Y. Acad. Sci. 141:1-2, 1967.
Drug information. *Science* 158:161-3, 1967.
The scope and responsibility of medicine. *Calif. Med.* 108:408-9, 1968.
The maximum human life span evaluation. *Geriatrics* 23(3):97-8, 1968.
High drug prices: a burden on the aged. *Geriatrics* 23(2):99-100, 1968.
Dance and live on. *Geriatrics* 23(6):98, 1968.
Theories of ethics and medical practice. *J. Amer. Med. Ass.* 208:842-7, 1969.
Primary journals: questionable progress and present problems. *J. Chem. Doc.* 10:27-9, 1970.
Development of primary journals and their influence on science.
    Abstr. Pap. Amer. Chem. Soc. CHO1 April, 1969.
Travelogue 1969. *Tex. Rep. Biol. Med.* 28:3-11, 1970.
Ethical theories and human experimentation. *Ann. N.Y. Acad. Sci.* 169(A2):388-96, 1970.
Percival's medical ethics—promise and problems. *Calif. Med.* 114:68-70, 1971.
Vietnam resolutions. *Science* 180:813, 1973.
Humanistic studies in United States medical education. *J. Med. Educ.* 48:878-9, 1973.
Defense of lecturing. *J. Med. Educ.* 48:193-5, 1973.
Biological actions of dimethyl-sulfoxide. Opening remarks.
    Ann. N.Y. Acad. Sci. 243:5-6, 1975.
Limits to understanding. *Science* 189:502-3, 1975.
Interactions of drugs of abuse—introductory remarks.
    Ann. N.Y. Acad. Sci. 281:R11, 1976.
Effects of hallucinogens on operant behavior. (with Harris R D, Snell D & Loh H H)
    Fed. Proc. 35:644, 1976.

CURRENT COMMENTS

To Remember My Father

Number 8, February 20, 1978

On January 23, just as I was trying to organize my thoughts on the significance in my life of Chauncey D. Leake, my father died. In referring to Chauncey I called him my friend and mentor. There can be no doubt that he was a father image for me as well. But I would not have wanted my dad to feel that he was less than an ideal father, so I left this thought unsaid.

Actually, Ernest Garofano, born May 2, 1904, was my step-father. The similarity in our surnames is purely coincidental. He married my mother when I was eleven, after they had been going together over three years. About a year after they were married, my brother Ralph was born. But even long before they were married I thought of him as my father, because he gave me the love, care and attention that my biological father did not.

My mother's marriage to Ernest Garofano after the failure of her first marriage tells in microcosm the story of thousands of American families. Not only was I the product of a broken home (a key stimulus for success, according to some sociologists), but also of an "intermarriage."

Today the marriage of black and white people is already commonplace. And the marriage of Jewish and Catholic people is quite ordinary. When I was a child, however, my mother's announcement of her plans to marry sent shock waves through both families. But my step-father, a strongly stubborn man, persisted even after the most devastating attempts by my mother's family to discourage him. Later on he became a favorite of all of them. After 40 years of marriage to my mother, few people could believe he was Italian and not Jewish.

I have rarely met a more devoted husband. He nursed my mother in her final years, until his own health declined. After she died in 1976 he became a new person. All of us then realized how much his lively personality had been smothered by my mother's illness. He was an endless source of humorous stories about the old days, and had a remarkable memory for small events. I greatly enjoyed hearing his stories and listening to his New York dialect and his heavy New York accent. In some ways he was like Archie Bunker, but the prejudices of his language never were reflected in his treatment of people.

I have often wondered what effect a good education would have had on my father. I don't think he finished grammar school. He was only 2 years old when he came to America from a small town in Italy near Naples. His father, a construction worker, was accidentally killed on the job when my dad was seven.

In America his life of poverty was not unusual for the time. He worked hard and eventually became an itinerant butcher and meat department manager for the A&P supermarket in Westchester County. There he learned to work for the super-rich who occupied the big houses in Scarsdale and similar wealthy suburbs. This experience gave him an insight into a culture vastly different from what he had lived in. Later, during the second World War, he worked with my uncle, Sam Wolf, in still another environment—the garment district of New York.

After the war he bought and operated his own taxi in New York City. His ten years as a hackie—an occupation I too worked at briefly—proved an endless source of stories he would tell us at the dinner table.

He always loved cars. I well remember riding around in the rumble seat of his Chevrolet. Sunday was always a day for a ride somewhere—often to Mt. Vernon, where he had lived, or Kensico Dam or some similar scenic spot. My dad had an instinctual love of botany, and could name most flowers and trees. I still can't tell an oak from a walnut. During the war he had a "victory garden"' just outside Montefiore Hospital in the Bronx.

He also appreciated the importance of food in our lives. He was our resident expert on meat and fish, and was always responsible for carving turkeys or roasts. But he was the slowest eater I ever met. And he never changed, even though all the rest of us ate as though food was going out of style.

Like Chauncey, my father died quite unexpectedly. Perhaps both of them could have lived many more happy and healthy years. But more years might have brought a slow and undignified end to their lives. I am thankful that neither of them suffered the agonies of a prolonged death.

My father could not, of course, provide the intellectual stimulation one finds in a Chauncey Leake. But the academic or intellectual or business life can easily become divorced from reality. Practical abilities and common sense are also necessary. You can't do much writing, abstract thinking, or anything else if the plumbing doesn't work. My dad was not artistic, but he was a "fixer" who could repair almost anything. And he had endless patience.

My father was a Rock of Gibraltar for me. He was always there when I needed him. In so many little ways I still say to myself, "Dad will take care of that." And then I realize he's gone.

CURRENT COMMENTS

Keeping Up With New Magazines

Number 9, February 27, 1978

About 2,000 popular magazines—consumer-oriented publications which accept advertising, as opposed to scholarly journals, company publications, and in-house organs—are published worldwide. Each year about 300 such magazines are born, and about 150 die. These estimates were provided by Bill Katz of the State University of New York at Albany, editor of the "Magazines" column in *Library Journal.*

Some of the new magazines that come to my attention because of the ISI® Press Digest treat topics related to science and scholarship quite substantially. What follows is a brief description of some new magazines which might interest *Current Contents® (CC®)* readers. My intent is to give you a quick impression of the major editorial thrust of each publication, not a detailed critique. Unless otherwise noted, all magazines discussed began publication during 1977. Most of them are published in the United States, but many have circulation outside the US. Subscrip-

tion information for each magazine appears on pages 13-14.

Two of the most impressive new magazines I've seen are *Human Nature* and *Quest/78.* The first issue of *Human Nature* appeared in January. Its introduction states:

Our editorial position is simple: people matter.... And so we are inviting professionals in the human sciences to discuss the topics and ideas that excite us. Each writer will describe his or her work so that you will know what effects the research could have on your life, what it explains about you, what its implications are for the rest of humanity. Such information is more than interesting—it is vital.[1]

As examples of "human sciences," *Human Nature* lists medicine and health, psychology, education, linguistics, sociology, anthropology, paleontology, genetics, ethology, biology and ecology. So far the magazine is keeping its promise to offer writing by scientists. In "Health and Creative Adaptation" Rene Dubos asserts that, "for human beings, health transcends biological fitness. It is primarily a measure of each person's ability to do what he wants to do and become what he wants to become." Michael Argyle of Oxford University discusses the social role of eye contact in "The Laws of Looking." And in "Hypnosis and Consciousness" Ernest R. Hilgard of Stanford University suggests "a division of consciousness into parallel parts instead of higher and lower levels."

One regular feature in *Human Nature*, "The Practical Cogitator," is a sort of Press Digest of the past. It contains short, thought-provoking quotes from writers like da Vinci, Francis Bacon, Emerson and Simone de Beauvoir. The magazine runs reviews not only of new books, but also of *old* books.

Unfortunately, the articles in *Human Nature*, though written by scientists, do not contain citations. However, like *Scientific American,* they do list sources "for further information," which is better than nothing at all. Too many magazines and newspapers merely mention "a paper in a recent issue of the *Journal of the American Medical Association"*—when they bother to mention the source at all! A selective bibliography at least allows readers to satisfy their curiosity.

Quest/78 (*Quest/77* last year) is described by its editor, Robert Shnayerson, as "a *New Yorker* with photographs." The purpose of *Quest,* he says, "is the dissemination of courage. Its focus is on people as they really are—and could become. Its charter is the pursuit of excellence, the search for the fully lived life.... Without being elitist or precious, it will attempt to show you the best of everything, from art to humor, science to sports ".[2] *Quest* is published by the Ambassador International Cultural Foundation. The Foundation is supported by the Worldwide Church of God, headed by TV evangelist Garner Ted Armstrong. While *Quest's* editorial policy is one of boundless optimism, Armstrong once predicted that the world would end on January 7, 1972.[3]

One *Quest* article profiles Roy Curtiss III, a microbiologist at the University of Alabama, who helped develop *chi 1776*, a strain of the bacterium *E. coli* designed to make recombinant DNA experiments safer.[4] The same issue has a story on cetologist Kenneth S. Norris of the University of Southern California. Norris' areas of interest include ecology and the possibility that dolphins and porpoises are intelligent creatures.

Two new magazines reflect growing interest in computers and electronic calculating devices. *Calculators/Computers Magazine* publishes games and exercises which can be used to teach students from elementary school through college the use of computers and hand-held calculators. Figure 1 shows a typical exercise designed to teach grade-school

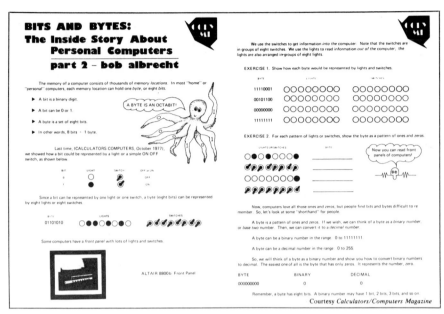

Figure 1. *Calculators/Computers Magazine* contains games and exercises students can use to learn about computers and hand-held calculators. "Bits and Bytes" is designed to teach grade-school students the fundamentals of the binary system.

children the fundamental concepts of the binary system. An explanation of bits and bytes is followed by short workbook exercises which help students understand what they have read. Later in the "lesson" the binary system is compared and contrasted with the decimal system. The "Copy Me" symbol in the upper right-hand corner encourages teachers to make photocopies and distribute them to students. Answers to problems are provided for the teacher's use.

Creative Computing, founded in 1975, is aimed at a more mature audience of computer enthusiasts. It recognizes the utility of computers as teaching tools, but also emphasizes the fun side of computers. Much space is devoted to computer games. The magazine also contains technical notes, a buyer's guide to computer equipment, and how-to articles. One article points to the possible pitfalls of banking by computer. Another protests, tongue-in-cheek, the way computers are portrayed and treated in films like *2001.*

Space travel and colonization is another area in which a new magazine has arisen to reflect growing interest. *L-5 News,* subtitled "The Latest Developments in Space Industrialization, Satellite Solar

426

Power, and Space Habitats," began in 1975 as a small newsletter and has grown into a slick 22-page magazine. It is published by the L-5 Society, a group formed to support the "space colony" concept popularized by Gerard K. O'Neill of Princeton University. L-5, incidentally, is a location in earth orbit where space colonies might be built. An object at L-5 would always remain in the same position relative to the earth and the moon (see Figure 2). The long-range goal of many members of the L-5 Society is to arrive at L-5 in person.

Articles in *L-5 News* cover topics like the space shuttle, law and industry in space, lunar colonies, mining the moon and asteroids, and pro-space lobbying of Congress. A recent article replied to Senator William Proxmire's statement that space colonization is a "nutty fantasy."[5] *L-5 News* offers a forum for discussion of such questions as: Who should exploit space, industries or government? How should "colonists" be selected? What kind of social system best fits a space station? Can satellite solar power stations be the solution to energy shortages? The magazine's tone indicates that its writers and readers believe that space will play an important part in the future of the human race.

Along with the high technology covered by magazines on computers and space exploration, several new magazines are devoted to "appropriate," or do-it-yourself, technology. Although we did not find any new publication with the wide appeal of *Popular Science* or *Science Digest,* several are aimed at readers who are also craftsmen.

One such magazine, *Telescope Making Techniques,* is aimed at the amateur astronomer. It is concern-

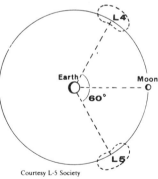

Courtesy L-5 Society

Figure 2. *L-5 News* contains articles on establishing space colonies, including the political problems involved. "'L-5' is a location in earth orbit whose position relative to earth and moon does not change.

ed with all phases of telescope making—optical and mechanical, practical and theoretical. Apparently, its readers invest a great deal of time and money in their hobby. *Telescope Making Techniques* claims to be the first magazine devoted wholly to the building of the instruments.

Mother Earth News (not to be confused with the investigative political magazine *Mother Jones*) is not really a new magazine. It was founded in 1970, but its success indicates a growing interest in alternative lifestyles. Its increased popularity might also be due to the recent energy shortages and the prevailing economic uncertainty. *Mother Earth News* presents features on more efficient ways to run a household, grow food, and build devices and structures. Recent pieces include advice on buying wood stoves, building a house from a mixture of sawdust and concrete, building a greenhouse, and raising grain. The latest issue contains an interview in which Linus Pauling discusses his controversial stand on vitamin C.

During any particular month, many magazines seem to feature stories on the same scientific subject. But *To the Point International* has demonstrated a unique ability to identify science news that one does not see elsewhere. Although it is almost four years old, it is worth mentioning here because of its excellent coverage of Africa, the Mid-East, and the rest of the world.

One new magazine should appeal to social and political scientists. *National Opinion Poll*, which began in January 1978, strives for maximum reader participation. Each issue includes a mail-in ballot for the use of readers who have previously become "registered members" of the poll. Members may also vote by phone. The editors comment, "By voting in the *National Opinion Poll*, you are really participating in a NEW DEMOCRATIC PROCESS." Geoffrey W. Dohrman, the publisher, adds, "The future of American democracy just may depend upon that participation."[6]

Actually, the premiere edition of *National Opinion Poll* contains several interesting and useful features. It lists and discusses bills before the US Congress, contains a monthly map and index to lawmakers, reports on the voting records of senators and congressmen, and summarizes legislative issues. It also features a novel, thumb-indexed contents page. It will be interesting to see whether readers support the magazine and participate in its polls.

National Opinion Poll might yield some insight on how the public views scientific topics. Questions asked in the first poll include, "Should saccharin's use be restricted?" and "Should America build more nuclear power plants?" Readers are also invited to select topics for future polls (see Figure 3). Suggested scientific topics for

When voting in the National Opinion Poll, you can help pick the issues that will appear in future polls and will be covered by the magazine.

PICK THE ISSUE

Select one of the following key issues and put the number on your mail-in ballot. If, instead, you decide to phone in your vote, give the number to the operator when asked for your choice of an issue. (See "Voting by Phone.")

You may also write in your own issue on the mail-in ballot or you may give it to the operator (no more than 15 words, please).

1. Should federal (tax) dollars be used to finance abortions?
2. Should the minimum wage be increased?
3. Should mandatory retirement be extended to age 70?
4. Should the Senate ratify the Panama Canal treaties?
5. Should Social Security taxes be raised to keep the program solvent?
6. Should we give foreign aid to countries that violate human rights?
7. Should $12 billion in Federal funds be given to the nation's aging cities?
8. Should victims of crime receive Federal aid?
9. Should we build the neutron bomb?
10. Should federal clean air standards be relaxed?
11. Should utilities be forced to burn coal rather than natural gas?
12. Should the government stop controlling the price of natural gas?
13. Should the national debt limit be raised?
14. Should the food stamp program be continued?
15. Should government prevent major oil and gas companies from buying up coal and uranium reserves?
16. Should lawmakers' outside income be limited?
17. Should tax credits be given for installing solar and wind energy equipment?
18. Should the Federal Government set efficiency standards for home appliances?
19. Should Congressional elections be financed with public (tax) dollars?
20. Should gasoline taxes be raised to reduce fuel consumption?

Courtesy *National Opinion Poll*

Figure 3. *National Opinion Poll* asks its subscribers to express their views on controversial topics by voting in its monthly poll. "Pick the Issue" allows subscribers to help select topics for future polls.

the next poll include: "Should we build the neutron bomb?" "Should federal clean air standards be relaxed?" "Should government prevent major oil and gas companies from buying up coal and uranium reserves?"

Unfortunately, the results of these polls are bound to be biased. Voting is open only to those who take out "memberships" by subscribing to the magazine. A year's subscription is $36, or $48 for households with two voters. Not everyone is willing or able to pay that amount to subscribe and the magazine cannot be purchased at newsstands. The results of the polls will have more meaning when the editors know what kind of people subscribe and vote.

Many scientists are avid readers of science fiction. *Isaac Asimov's Science Fiction Magazine,* now a little over a year old, runs short stories by veteran writers from the pulp years, as well as the work of younger writers. Asimov is the magazine's "editorial director"; he sets the policy and tone of the magazine. He also writes an editorial for each issue and regularly contributes short stories. In general, the emphasis in Asimov's magazine is on strongly plotted, traditional science fiction as opposed to the literary experiments of the last decade's "new wave."

Science fiction magazines have usually appeared in a 5½ by 7½ inch format, a size probably left over from their pulp origins. *Galileo,* founded in 1976, comes in a larger 8½ by 11 inch size. It too concentrates on fiction, but also features a regular column on sciences, "Encyclopedia Galactica," which discusses topics like space colonies or the nature of the outer planets. An article on the state of the genre by novelists Alexei and Cory Panshin asked: "Is the success of *Star Wars* an isolated phenomenon, a fluke? Or is *Star Wars* the first sign of a fundamental change?"[7] The Panshins suggest that science fiction is on the brink of unprecedented popularity, and that some day magazines devoted to it will see circulations of a million.

Science Fiction Magazine is a new French publication which places strong emphasis on artwork. The issue we examined contained, in addition to the many story illustrations, three posters. Most of these were depictions of spacecraft or alien landscapes. The magazine also runs fiction, book and film reviews, and interviews (most recently with American science fiction writer Theodore Sturgeon). So far the magazine is available only in French.

Unearth is a new science fiction magazine with a unique editorial policy. It publishes only stories by writers who have never before appeared in a science fiction magazine or anthology. Regular features include columns on writing science fiction by Harlan Ellison and Hal Clement, and reprints of first stories sold by prominent figures in the genre. The author is given a chance to tell how the story came to be written and sold, and what he thinks of it today.

Two magazines *about* science fiction also were started in 1975. *The Science Fiction Review Monthly* seems intended as a consumer guide for readers and librarians. It publishes short reviews of *all* major science fiction, including paperback originals and reprints. Richard Delap's *F&SF (Fantasy and Science Fiction) Review* does not attempt to cover the entire field, but reviews nonfiction and movies in addition to in-depth reviews of books.

Sky-Worlds, subtitled "Classics in

Science Fiction," is a quarterly devoted to reprinting old science fiction stories. The magazine does not mention when or where the stories originally appeared, but they seem to derive from the pulp magazines of the '50s. One story in the second issue, "Precedent," is by Daniel Keyes, who later wrote the excellent novel *Flowers for Algernon*. [8]

I cannot resist the temptation to mention a few new magazines devoted to a subject that interests a small but enthusiastic group of *CC* readers: jazz. *Musician, Player and Listener*, which started in 1975, seems aimed at *Downbeat's* audience. A recent issue includes a profile of jazz bassist Charles Mingus and short interviews with four jazz pianists: McCoy Tyner, George Duke, Bill Evans, and Mose Allison. Regular features include columns of advice for aspiring musicians. There is also an equipment buyers' guide.

Jazzline is a weekly six-page mimeographed newsletter published by a nonprofit group called Jazz Interactions, Inc. It is six years old, but is still little known. It lists jazz performances at clubs in New York City and surrounding areas.

The reader who is not intimately familiar with jazz may find *The Grackle*, a Brooklyn-based irregular mimeo, a good deal less accessible than *Downbeat*. Most of the articles concentrate heavily on techniques of playing and teaching jazz. *The Grackle* also views jazz largely in terms of black culture. A recent issue includes an interview with author Ralph Ellison, who discusses how jazz influenced his life.

As I've noted before, you can learn a great deal about a person by examining the list of magazines he or she reads regularly! [9] By large-scale extensions of this kind of analysis, perhaps one can characterize the changing interests of society and detect developing trends.

It is imperative that scientists remain aware, not only of what society is saying about science but also of the impact science has on society. The ISI Press Digest performs a substantial part of this alerting function, but we are well aware of the coverage limitations of an eight-page feature which digests only about 40 items per week.

For some time we have been considering a variety of ways in which ISI services might cover popular magazines on a broader scale. We soon hope to offer a new service which would announce all significant new magazines while digesting, in one form or another, the main content of the core publications in contemporary public affairs. This service would be designed to help those who would like to systematically cover such literature themselves, and would make it easy to delegate the task to others.

Producing such a service is not easy. Much of the material from magazines, like that from the arts and humanities literature,[10] is less amenable to straightforward computer processing than we would like. Considerable human intervention and intellectual enrichment of biographical records would be required to assure the retrievability of relevant items. But problems like these make the work all the more challenging.

REFERENCES

1. About *Human Nature*. *Human Nature* 1:4, January 1978.
2. **Shnayerson R.** Prologue. *Quest/77* 1:ii, March 1977.
3. Prophet of doom Armstrong tries a new gamble on the future. *People* 7:85, 11 April 1977.
4. **Durden-Smith J.** The promise of *chi 1776*. *Quest/77* 1:2-10, November/December 1977.
5. **Friedman B.** More on Proxmire. *L-5 News* 2:17, December 1977.
6. **Dohrman G.** Why a National Opinion Poll? *National Opinion Poll* 1:5, January 1978.
7. **Panshin A & Panshin C.** The end of the ghetto? *Galileo* 5:14-22, October 1977.
8. **Keyes D.** *Flowers for Algernon.* New York: Harcourt, Brace, Jovanovich, 1966. 288 pp.
9. **Garfield E.** Does the reading list make the person? *Current Contents* No. 3, 19 January 1976, p. 5-6.*
10. -------------. Citation indexes for studying science. *Nature* 227:669-71, 1970.*

*Reprinted in Garfield E. *Essays of an information scientist.* Philadelphia: ISI Press, 1977. 2 vols.

Subscription Information

Calculators/Computers Magazine
DYMAX
P.O. Box 310 Menlo Park, CA 94025
7/yr. $12; foreign $17.
started January 1977

Creative Computing
P.O. Box 789-M
Morristown, NJ 07960
6/yr. $8; 3yrs $21.
started January-February 1975

Delap's F & SF Review
11863 W. Jefferson Blvd.
Culver City, Calif. 90230
12/yr. $12; individuals $9
started 1975

Galileo
339 Newbury St.
Boston, MA 02115
4/yr. $4; $9 for 10 issues
started October 1976

Subscription Information (continued)

The Grackle
P.O. Box 244
Vanderveer Station
Brooklyn, NY 11210
Irregular, $4.50 for 3 issues
started 1976

Human Nature
P.O. Box 9110
Greenwich, CT 06830
12/yr. $15; Canada & Mexico $16.50;
elsewhere $18.
started January 1978

Isaac Asimov's Science Fiction Magazine
Box 1855 GPO
New York, NY 10001
6/yr. $5.95; elsewhere $6.97.
started winter 1977

Jazzline
527 Madison Avenue
Suite 1615
New York, NY 10022
Free copies available
at Times Square Information Center
52/yr. $15;
$10 for members of Jazz Interactions, Inc.
started 1972

L-5 News
1060 E. Elm
Tucson, AZ 85719
12/yr. $3 (included in membership dues:
$20 per year; students $10 per year)
started September 1975

Mother Earth News
P.O. Box 60
Hendersonville, NC 28739
6/yr. $12; 2 yrs. $12;
3 yrs. $33; lifetime $300.
Canada & foreign: 1 yr. $14;
2 yrs. $27; 3 yrs. $39; lifetime $350.
started 1970

Musician, Player and Listener
P.O. Box 1882
Boulder, CO 80306
8/yr. $8; 2 yrs. $15; 3 yrs. $22.
Add $1 per year outside U.S.
started December 1976

National Opinion Poll
30 North San Pedro Road
San Rafael, CA 94903
12/yr. $36; $48 per couple
started January 1978

Quest/78
P.O. Box 3700
Greenwich, CT 06830
6/yr. $12; foreign $14.
started March-April 1977

Science Fiction Magazine
18, rue Theodore-Deck
75015 Paris, France
8 francs per copy
$2.25 in U.S.
$1.50 in Canada
started 1977

The Science Fiction Review Monthly
56 Eighth Avenue
New York, NY 10014
12/yr. $11.
started 1975

Sky Worlds
100 N. Village Ave.
Rockville Centre, NY 11570
4/yr. $.75 per issue
started November 1977

Telescope Making Techniques
P.O. Box 231
Kinnelon, NJ 07405
4/yr. $12; foreign $16.
started Winter 1977

To The Point International
P.O. Box 8
2000 Antwerp 20, Belgium
US & Canadian subscriptions:
P.O. Box 697
Hightstown, NJ 08520, USA
$12/yr.
started 1974

Unearth
102 Charles St., #190
Boston, MA 02114
4/yr. $4; Canada $5; elsewhere $6.
started Winter 1977

CURRENT COMMENTS

ISI® Is Now Helping To Bridge The Three (Not Two) Cultures

Number 10, March 6, 1978

Recently I gave a talk to the Norwegian Association of Research Librarians about ISI® 's new *Arts & Humanities Citation Index*™ (*A&HCI*™).[1] My discussion stressed that *A&HCI* can become an important link between science and the arts—or between what C.P. Snow christened the "two cultures."[2]

The concept of the two cultures has received considerable attention in the many years since Snow first used the term. I am sure it is not an original idea to suggest that it is an over-simplification to divide society into just two polar cultures. Indeed, Snow himself noted that two is a very dangerous number and said that for a long time he had considered further refinements. He respected the arguments of American sociologists who had told him they "vigorously refuse to be corralled in a cultural box with people they wouldn't be seen dead with, or to be regarded as helping [artists and literary intellectuals] to produce a climate which would not permit of social hope."[2]

In any case, I believe that so far as the published literature is concerned, it is accurate to identify at least three discrete cultures: the sciences, the social sciences, and the arts and humanities. Such terms are often loosely used and variously interpreted. By *culture* I mean a particular type of intellectual development; by *sciences* branches of study based chiefly on objective quantitative hypotheses, such as biology, chemistry, or physics; by *social sciences* the study of society and individual relationships, generally regarded as including sociology, psychology, anthropology, economics, political science, and history; and by *humanities* areas of knowledge concerning the human race and its culture, such as philosophy, literature, and the fine arts. The definitions are derived from the *American Heritage Dictionary*.[3]

I am particularly conscious of the gaps between the two cultures of the sciences and social sciences when I see an article title in one edition of *Current Contents*® (*CC*®) which also ought to be listed in another. This occurs quite frequently for articles that cover the history of a science. For example, some physicists would be interested in the occasional articles on the history of physics which appear in journals like *ISIS*. Similarly, some historians would be interested in the occasional articles on the history of physics appearing in physics journals. But soaring costs won't permit us to cover *all* such articles in more than one *CC* edition. For broad current awareness, the ISI Press Digest tries to compensate for this restriction, but it can only go so far.[4]

For current awareness on a more selective basis, our *ASCA®* service already does bridge the gap between the sciences and the social sciences. It can alert you to articles appearing in any of the 5,000 journals we now cover for the six editions of *CC*. No matter whether you categorize your subject area as science or social science, *ASCA* searches through both types of journals, looking for items relevant to your profile. Thus, you are assured of being alerted to articles of interest that do not get listed in the *CC* edition you happen to read. Since January, we have been processing nearly 1,000 journals for coverage in the new *Arts & Humanities Citation Index*. When we are able to add these journals to *ASCA*, this service will bridge all *three* cultures.

Unfortunately, most *CC* readers do not use *ASCA*. I've never fully understood why this is so. I suspect that most people just don't want to be bothered preparing interest profiles. They won't believe us when we say that in 90% of the cases we can do it for them "automatically." By automatically I mean that given the smallest amount of information about your interests, our profilers can almost algorithmically expand it into an effective search profile.[5]

While *ASCA* can help bridge the cultural gap for current articles, bridges are needed for retrospective searching, too. We recently made an important improvement in our computer programming that enables us to indicate in our citation index those authors whose work is used in both the sciences and the social sciences. For example, Masters and Johnson's classic work *Human Sexual Response*[6]—which deals primarily with the physiology of sex—is cited in journals covered by both the *Science Citation Index®* and the *Social Sciences Citation Index™*. If you were to refer to the *SCI®* first, you would find that during 1977 the Masters and Johnson book was cited 22 times. You would also find a note saying that 19 additional citations would be found in the *SSCI™* from journals covered exclusively in that index. Figure 1 shows the citations to *Human Sexual Response* that would be located only in the *SCI*, only in the *SSCI*, and in both.

Of course, it is not all that surprising to find a work like *Human Sexual Response* cited in both the *SCI* and *SSCI*. That sexual response has both physical and social aspects is recognized by all modern re-

Figure 1: Papers located through a citation search of the 1977 *SCI* and *SSCI* using *Human Sexual Response* as cited item.

CITED ITEM Masters, William H & Johnson, Virginia E. *Human sexual response.* Boston, MA: Little, Brown & Co., 1966. 366 pp.

CITING ITEMS LOCATED ONLY THROUGH *SCI*

AUTHOR	JOURNAL	VOL	PG	YR
Blasco L	Fertility and Sterility	28	1133	77
Ellenberg M	Mt Sinai J of Medicine	44	495	77
Fonkalsrud EW	Annals of Surgery	186	221	77
Guharay DK	Fertility and Sterility	28	943	77
Kavanagh T	Canadian Medical Assoc J	116	1250	77
Shaw A	J of Pediatric Surgery	12	331	77

CITING ITEMS LOCATED ONLY THROUGH *SSCI*

AUTHOR	JOURNAL	VOL	PG	YR
Aldous J	Annual Review of Sociology	3	105	77
Bennett KC	Australian J of Social Issues	12	3	77
Bieber I	J of the Amer Academy of Psychoanalysis	5	195	77
Brecher J	International J of Health Services	7	89	77
Byrne D	Personality and Social Psychology Bulletin	3	3	77
Cantondutari A	Revista Latinoamericana de Psicologia	9	137	77
Coutts LM	Personality and Social Psychology Bulletin	3	519	77
Farley FH	Archives of Sexual Behavior	6	105	77
Knapp TJ	Nursing Research	26	281	77
McConnell LG	J of Marriage and Family Counseling	3	55	77
Meyer RG	J of Homosexuality	2	123	77
Mosher DL	J of Sex & Marital Therapy	3	229	77
Osborn CA	J of Sex Research	13	250	77
Sarrel PM	Archives of Sexual Behavior	6	341	77
Schlesinger B	Canadas Mental Health	25	15	77
Solnick RL	Archives of Sexual Behavior	6	1	77
Staib AR	Amer J of Clinical Hypnosis	19	201	77
Stanford D	Amer J of Nursing	77	608	77
Wiest WM	Sex Roles	3	399	77

CITING ITEMS LOCATED THROUGH EITHER *SSCI* OR *SCI*

AUTHOR	JOURNAL	VOL	PG	YR
Appel CP	Wiener Klinische Wochenschrift	89	289	77
Derogatis LR	Amer J of Psychiatry	134	385	77
Elstein M	British Medical J	1	369	77
Hecker BR	Amer J of Obstetrics & Gynecology	129	543	77
Levine SB	Annals of Internal Medicine	86	588	77
Marecek J	Psychiatry	40	323	77
Mudd JW	Amer J of Psychiatry	134	922	77
Paradowski W	Archives of Physical Medicine and Rehabilitation	58	53	77
Phoenix CH	J of Comparative and Physiological Psychology	921	697	77
Reynolds BS	Psychological Bulletin	84	1218	77
Scalzi CC	Western J of Medicine	126	237	77
Wallot H	Union Medicale du Canada	106	829	77
Weinrich JD	Behavioral Ecology and Sociobiology	2	91	77
Wilson GT	Behaviour Research and Therapy	15	239	77
Wittkower ED	Amer J of Psychotherapy	31	66	77
Zeiss AM	J of Consulting and Clinical Psychology	45	891	77

Figure 2: Papers located through a citation search of the 1977 *SSCI* and *SCI* using *Statistical Package for the Social Sciences* as cited item.

CITED ITEM   Nie N H, Hull C H, Jenkins J C, Steinbrenner K & Brent D. *Statistical package for the social sciences.* New York, NY: McGraw-Hill, 1970. 700 pp.

CITING ITEMS LOCATED ONLY THROUGH *SSCI*

AUTHOR	JOURNAL	VOL	PG	YR
Arndt J	European J of Marketing	11	13	77
Basler HD	Homo	28	35	77
Byrne DG	Australian and New Zealand J of Psychiatry	11	179	77
Cummings S	J of Negro Education	46	62	77
Fairbrother RW	Educational Research	19	92	77
Flango VE	J of Politics	39	41	77
Gibbins R	Canadian J of Political Science	10	341	77
Hirschfeld LA	Ethnology	16	147	77
Hopkins DR	Research Quarterly	48	535	77
Leece J	British J of Political Science	7	529	77
MacManus SA	Western Political Quarterly	30	263	77
Nevo B	Megamot	23	40	77
Pashley BW	Durham Research Review	8	31	77
Quinn J F	J of Human Resources	12	329	77
Sansonfisher RW	Multivariate Behavioral Research	12	357	77
Scanlan PM	Australian Geographical Studies	15	22	77
Selby J W	Personality and Social Psychology Bulletin	3	412	77
Shupe AD	Social Forces	55	613	77
Stock WP	Drug Forum	5	335	77
Thomson TL	Socio-Economic Planning Sciences	11	61	77
Travis CB	Contemporary Educational Psychology	2	373	77

CITING ITEMS LOCATED ONLY THROUGH *SCI*

AUTHOR	JOURNAL	VOL	PG	YR
Aird TJ	SIAM J on Numerical Analysis	14	296	77
Birmingham BC	Canadian J of Botany	55	1453	77
Boere CG	Ardea	64	210	76
Burns PE	Canadian Medical Assoc J	116	1131	77
Cohen E	Thrombosis Research	10	587	77
Collatz J	Monatsschrift fur Kinderheilkunde	125	594	77
Double JA	Biomedicine Express	27	11	77
Hanawalt RB	Soil Science	123	25	77
Karlberg BE	Scandinavian J of Clinical & Laboratory Investigation	37	521	77
Mamrak SA	Computer	10	32	77
McCarthy MA	Food Technology	31	86	77
Ramirez I	J of Comparative and Physiological Psychology	91	174	77
Rogers RE	Developmental Biology	55	148	77
Romkens MJM	Soil Science Society of Amer J	41	954	77
Ross ST	Copeia	1977	561	77
Ryan PM	J of the Fisheries Research Board of Canada	34	2079	77
Seveen K	J of Periodontal Research	12	340	77
Tizard IR	J of Hygiene	78	275	77
Triupp JH	Lancet	2	233	77

Figure 2 (continued)

CITING ITEMS LOCATED THROUGH EITHER *SCI* OR *SSCI*

AUTHOR	JOURNAL	VOL	PG	YR
Anonymous	New England J of Medicine	296	1185	77
Anderson RE	Amer Behavioral Scientist	20	367	77
Andrews G	Amer J Epidemiology	105	324	77
Bertinetti J F	J of Clinical Psychology	33	416	77
Carruth BR	J of the Amer Dietetic Assoc	70	42	77
Coelho AM	Amer J of Physical Anthropology	46	253	77
Feshbach S	J of Educational Psychology	69	299	77
Finlayjones RA	Psychological Medicine	7	475	77
Fischer E H	J of Nervous and Mental Disease	164	107	77
Ghodsian M	British J of Social and Clinical Psychology	16	23	77
Hewitt J K	Psychological Reports	40	183	77
Jakobovits C	J of the Amer Dietetic Assoc	71	405	77
Kern JC	J of Studies on Alcohol	38	89	77
Lifshitz M	Annals of the New York Academy of Sciences	285	338	77
Malecot A	Phonetica	34	19	77
Martin RL	Diseases of the Nervous System	38	974	77
Mueller WH	Annals of Human Biology	4	1	77
Neuwirth W	Angewandte Informatik	1977	235	77
Oldroyd R J	Psychological Reports	41	187	77
Ostrander J	J of the Amer Dietetic Assoc	70	267	77
Palmieri A	Amer J of Pharmaceutical Education	41	264	77
Richards LG	Ergonomics	20	499	77
Ronen S	J of Applied Psychology	62	582	77
Smith R J	Amer J of Physical Anthropology	47	195	77
Smith T J	Amer Review of Respiratory Disease	116	31	77
Wolck W	Amer Behavioral Scientist	20	733	77

searchers. Similarly, we would expect articles and books dealing with statistical methods to be cited by authors in both the sciences and social sciences. But even with statistics, we sometimes see unexpected applications. Nie's *Statistical Package for the Social Sciences*[7] deals with a programming language designed expressly for social sciences research. If you were to check the 1977 *SSCI* you would find that Nie's book was cited 47 times. You would also find a note telling you that it was also cited 19 times in science journals covered exclusively in *SCI*. Figure 2 shows the different citations to this book located through *SSCI* and *SCI* searches.

Another example of how *SCI/SSCI* cross-reference notes help pull together widely scattered citations involves an article on the population problem published in *Science*.[8] In "The Tragedy of the Commons," noted biologist Garrett Hardin of Stanford University says that the solution to the population problem is moral and not technical. During 1977 this article was cited 10 times in journals exclusively covered by the *SSCI* and 3 times in journals exclusively covered by the *SCI*.

Last June, in the *American Journal of Psychiatry*, Herbert

438

Wagemaker of the University of Louisville School of Medicine and Robert Cade of the University of Florida School of Medicine reported some work showing that schizophrenia could be physiologically based.[9] A female schizophrenic suffering a kidney disorder was treated with dialysis, and unexpectedly her schizophrenic symptoms disappeared. Four other schizophrenics were dialyzed and they experienced similar remissions. If further studies confirm these highly tentative results, the Wagemaker-Cade article is likely to be cited both by scientists investigating the biochemistry of the illness and by psychotherapists reporting on their use of dialysis as a treatment.

During the first year of the *Arts & Humanities Citation Index* we will not provide comparable cross-overs between it and the *SCI* and *SSCI*. I have no doubt, however, that once *A&HCI* is fully operational we can implement a similar cross-reference feature. How many such relationships will we see? More than a few, I'm sure. I recently read of a master's program in art conservation which requires a student to "combine the skills of an organic chemist with those of a studio artist and art historian."[10] And the impact of electronics on music is apparent to anyone who turns on a radio.

I admit that I am quite excited about the prospect of soon seeing the *Arts & Humanities Citation Index* join the *Science Citation Index* and *Social Sciences Citation Index* upon my bookshelf. I firmly believe that when this happens the combination will help to establish a genuine pattern of cross-cultural communication—a goal that ISI has persistently and patiently pursued.

REFERENCES

1. **Garfield E.** Will ISI's *Arts & Humanities Citation Index* revolutionize scholarship? *Current Contents* No. 32, 8 August 1977, p. 5-9.
2. **Snow C P.** *The two cultures and the scientific revolution—the Rede lecture, 1959.* London: Cambridge University Press, 1959. 52 pp.
3. **Morris W, ed.** *The American Heritage Dictionary.* New York: American Heritage Publishing Co., Inc., 1969. 1550 pp.
4. **Garfield E.** ISI's Press Digest helps narrow the gap between the scientist and the layman. *Current Contents* No. 20, 16 May 1973, p. 5-6. Reprinted in *Essays of an information scientist.* Philadelphia: ISI Press, 1977, Vol. 1, p. 448-9.
5. -------------. The information-conscious university and *ASCA* software. *Current Contents* No. 37, 12 September 1977, p. 5-7.
6. **Masters W H & Johnson V E.** *Human sexual response.* Boston: Little, Brown & Co., 1966. 366pp.
7. **Nie N H, Hull C H, Jenkins J C, Steinbrenner K & Bent D.** *Statistical package for the social sciences.* New York: McGraw-Hill, 1970. 700 pp.
8. **Hardin G.** The tragedy of the commons. *Science* 162:1243-8, 1968.
9. **Wagemaker H & Cade R.** Use of hemodialysis in chronic schizophrenia. *American Journal of Psychiatry* 134:684-5, 1977.
10. **Spencer I.** Vigor is restored to masters in art preservation. *Philadelphia Inquirer,* 27 November 1977, p. 8-B.

CURRENT COMMENTS

Style in Cited References

Number 11, March 13, 1978

In most matters related to journal format and presentation, diversity and idiosyncrasy are desirable. For example, journals can be easily distinguished from one another by creative typography and design. However, certain aspects of journal publication are amenable to international standardization. Such things as contents page format, authors' addresses, and cited reference style are easily standardized. And their standardization would offer significant benefits to readers and authors alike. Having suggested guidelines for contents page format[1] and authors' addresses[2] earlier, I've been acutely aware that a discussion of references was long overdue.

A cited reference should contain enough information to enable the reader to understand why it is being cited. This means it ought to contain the title of the cited work. References ought to be complete enough so that one can retrieve the document with minimum stress. These two objectives are rather straightforward. Consequently, one might think that the format and style of cited references would be fairly standardized by now. But this is far from the reality.

The reference styles used by scientific journals—even those in the same discipline—vary widely. In the social sciences, the main differences between competing journals are often apparent in their obsession with style rather than content. Even the many so-called "standard" style guides are quite diverse in recommended reference styles.

Consider authors' names, for example. Most style manuals recommend full *last* names, and first and middle initials. Some, like the Harvard University Press manual,[3] allow full first names *or* first initials. But the Modern Language Association's *MLA Style Sheet*[4] recommends full *first* names. Even those styles that insist on first initials instead of full first names present the initials in various ways. The University of Chicago Press *Manual of Style* recommends placing initials before the last name.[5] But the European Life Science Editors (ELSE) recommend that initials be placed *after* the surname.[6]

The treatment of cited references

with multiple authors is also inconsistent. For example, the *Journal of the American Medical Association (JAMA)* separates the names of different authors with commas. But *JAMA* omits the period after authors' initials. *Nature* and many other journals use a period after each initial, and use an ampersand to separate the name of the last of several authors.

All such matters may seem like trivialities, but scientists and their assistants spend an inordinate amount of time dealing with such vagaries. And inconsistencies inevitably lead to errors and wasted time and money.

Journals disagree on where to cite the year of publication. A good case can be made for each of the two most common practices. *The Journal of the American Chemical Society (JACS)* places the year in parentheses at the end of the reference. Thus a typical reference in *JACS* looks like this:

J.A. Berson, L.D. Pedersen, and B.K. Carpenter, *J. Am. Chem. Soc.* **98**, 122 (1976).

However, *Proceedings of the National Academy of Sciences (PNAS)* and most biochemistry journals place the cited year immediately after the authors' names:

Blume, A. J., Dalton, C. & Sheppard, H. (1973) *Proc. Nat'l Acad. Sci. USA* **70**, 3099-3102.

In fact, the American Chemical Society's *Handbook for Authors* recommends *both* these styles for various ACS journals.[7] ISI® also

uses both these methods. In the *Citation Index* section of the *Science Citation Index® (SCI®)* the year of publication follows the cited author's name. But in the *Source Index* we place the year at the end of the full citation. To my knowledge this has not caused confusion to users; rather it helps distinguish the cited from the citing entry.

One can also find significant variations in the treatment of pagination. *Nature* gives the inclusive page numbers:

Wheeler, A.M. & Hartley, M.R. *Nature* **257**, 66-67 (1975).

However, *Physical Review* and many others provide only the first page:

R. P. Feynman and M. Gell-Mann, Phys. Rev. 1<u>09</u>, 193 (1958).

Since this practice is so widespread, we have been forced to use the first page only in our *Citation Indexes,* but in the *Source Indexes* full pagination is provided.

Unless boldface or underlining is used to distinguish the volume or year from the cited page, they are frequently confused with one another. Four-digit page numbers beginning with 19 are often confused with the year of publication. This problem is compounded by those journals which do not use a volume number at all. Yet another variation is to cite the volume followed by the year and then the page! While life scientists or physicists may not encounter this format very often, it is not unusual in social science journals.

Clearly an international standard for reference formats would benefit everyone involved in scientific and scholarly communication. If such a standard were universally adopted, authors would no longer need to change their reference style for each journal they publish in. Manuscripts could be submitted or re-submitted to different journals without extensive revisions. Readers would benefit by a uniform style, and librarians could save countless hours in tracking down elusive references. There is no doubt that the work of ISI and other information processing organizations would also be simplified.[8,9] These efficiencies could then be translated into real user benefits.

One group has produced a viable reference standard. The American National Standards Institute (ANSI) is a nonprofit organization of 1025 members representing US government agencies, trade associations, technical societies, consumer groups, and industry. ANSI serves as a national clearinghouse for voluntary safety, engineering, and industrial standards, including definitions, terminologies, symbols, and abbreviations. It recently published a booklet called *American National Standard for Bibliographic References,*[10] which recommends reference style for a variety of print and nonprint materials.

Lest we be accused of scientific imperialism, I can assure our non-US readers that ANSI is affiliated with the International Organization for Standardization (ISO). Unfortunately, the ISO last proposed an international reference standard for serials and monographs in 1968.[11] This outdated standard, which is now being revised, differs from the new ANSI standard mainly in the location of the date of the cited item. Although ISO placed the date of a serial *between* the volume and paging, ANSI more sensibly places the date *after* the volume, issue, and page numbers. In addition to its similarity to the ISO's standard, the ANSI standard for bibliographic references also encompasses many of the concepts being developed by groups such as the International Federation of Library Associations and UNESCO.

The American Society for Information Science adopted ANSI's style for all ASIS publications in January 1978. The American Chemical Society and the Council of Biology Editors also plan to adopt this style, with some minor variations.

ANSI has produced two formats for references. The *abbreviated* form contains only the shortened journal title, volume, first page number, and year of publication.

ANSI recommends the use of its abbreviated style only when saving space is a major concern. In my opinion it is an unacceptable condensed form in *any* situation, mainly because it omits authors' names. From the librarian's viewpoint there are numerous occasions when two or more items start on the same page in a journal. This applies to letters, editorials and other brief communications. It is folly to leave out the author's name, because this information is critical to even a minimal evaluation of the reference. Its omission forces the citing author to mention the author's name in the text. One might not even recognize one's *own* work if cited simply by journal!

ANSI's *comprehensive* form comes closer to an ideal reference style for journal articles. It includes the author's name and article title along with all the other key bibliographic elements. For serials, either the full journal title or a condensed title may be used. There are also some superfluous, or "optional" elements. For a typical journal article, the ANSI format looks like this:

> Downer, Nancy W; Englander, S. Walter. Hydrogen exchange study of membrane-bound rhodopsin. Journal of Biological Chemistry 252 (22): 8101 - 1804; 1977 November 25.

ANSI's comprehensive reference style for journal articles and books is similar to the style now used in the references in these essays. There are some differences, however, which deserve explanation.

ANSI permits the use of the author's first name when it is given in the original work, but we prefer to use first and middle initials. This saves space on both the printed page and on computer tape. Some readers complain that initials are not enough. Sometimes their use creates a homograph problem. But even "Smith J," if combined with other information in the citation, is invariably enough to uniquely identify a document.[12]

The universal use of first names would, however, resolve most homograph problems in large-scale compendia such as the *Science Citation Index*. The homograph problem does not occur when one is simply interested in learning who has cited a particular paper. Rather, homographs are a problem when one wants to ascertain quickly how often a particular author has been cited. The full bibliography of the author is often needed to differentiate two or more authors with the same last name and initials.

Most of our other modifications of the ANSI standard are also meant to save space. ANSI repeats digits when indicating inclusive pagination (193-198), but we eliminate repetitive digits (193-8). ANSI writes a date as 1978 March 13, but we write 13 March 1978. In this respect, we use the European rather than the American convention. Since the year is the most important part of the date, placing it at the end gives it added emphasis and visibility. ANSI also recommends that the journal issue number (in parentheses) immediately follow the journal volume number. We follow this practice in the *SCI*, but in *Current Contents®* *(CC®)* essays we only use issue numbers when the journal is being cited in the same year it appeared, or if its pages are not continuously numbered throughout a volume, as, for example, in *Chemical & Engineering News*.

Finally, there is a unique reason for our failure to use volume numbers when we cite *Current Contents* essays. There are six different editions of *CC*. Each carries a different volume number because they were started at different times. However, the weekly issue numbers are the same for all editions of *Current Contents*. Therefore, in referring to these essays only the issue number, in parentheses, is used. Some readers are not aware that the weekly essay and ISI Press Digest are printed in all six editions.

As indicated previously, some journals, such as the British *Journal of the Chemical Society (JCS)* and *Tetrahedron Letters,* don't *have* volume numbers. A citation in *JCS* to an earlier article in that journal might read as follows:

J. Smith, *J. Chem. Soc.,* 1971, 1972.

Which is the year and which is the page? According to ANSI, 1971 should be the page. But in *JCS* 1971 is the year. I hope that the few journals which still create this irritating source of ambiguity adopt volume numbers very soon. If not, the use of *inclusive* pagination would eliminate most confusing situations. This would also tell the reader how long the article is.

One of the most important style elements recommended by ANSI concerns the article title. That so many reputable journals persist in dropping article titles in references is frustrating indeed. *Science* and *Nature* are well-known offenders, but there are many others. It is true that this saves space. But editors should realize that a significant cost is passed on to the reader in the form of inconvenience, incomprehension, and wasted time. We are all forced to complete the citation for one reason or another. And eventually librarians suffer the most. Without the title the reader can never be sure of the specific subject matter of the cited article.[13] Titles are also useful for many interlibrary loan requests.

Lest readers think that inclusion of titles benefits ISI, remember that we do not use or need titles to prepare the *Citation Index* section of the *Science Citation Index*. In fact, titles get in the way of processing citations, so their use adds to our costs. (Titles for the *Source Index* are picked up when we process the original papers—not from cited references.) Nevertheless, we recommend that titles always be used in references.

For books, the ANSI abbreviated form includes author's name, title, place of publication, publisher and year of publication. The only item the comprehensive form adds to the abbreviated form is the number of pages. Including the number of pages gives the reader a rough idea of the scope and size of the work. It aids librarians enormously.

Incidentally, some readers may wonder why some journal and book titles are not italicized in the examples given above. For the sake of simplicity, ANSI recommends a single typeface for all bibliographic elements, but does not object to the use of italics, boldface, or underscoring.

Figure 1 shows examples of ANSI's comprehensive style for selected types of materials. In addition to the examples shown, ANSI also suggests specific styles for referring to trade and serial catalogs, brochures, unpublished supplemental materials, maps, motion pictures, slides, videorecordings, pictures, computer programs, magnetic tapes, computer data bases, and even antique cylinder sound recordings. The ANSI booklet does not specify where the references should be placed. I think they belong in a single list at the end of the article.[14] References should be indicated with a superscript or a number in parentheses in the text. The full reference list should be placed at the end of the article in numerical order. This makes it easier to locate relevant passages.

ANSI also does not specify whether titles in references should be translated from the original language. The most important consideration here is precision. Since translation of bibliographic elements can lead to uncertainties in the translated form, references

Figure 1. The following examples illustrate the American National Standard Institute's (ANSI's) comprehensive style (minus optional elements) for bibliographic references.

Journal Article:
Silverberg, Michael; Marchesi, Vincent T. The anomalous electrophoretic behavior of the major sialoglycoprotein from the human erythrocyte. Journal of Biological Chemistry 253(1):95-98; 1978 January 10.

Monograph:
Heilbrun, James. Urban economics and public policy. New York: St. Martin's Press; 1974. 380 p.

Book Chapter:
King, J.S. Neutron scattering from polymers. Allen, G.; Petrie, S.E.B., eds. Physical structure of the amorphous state. New York: M. Dekker, Inc.; 1976:13-25.

Conference Proceedings:
Fraser, R.D.B. The structure of fibrous proteins. Walton, A.G., ed. Proceedings of the first Cleveland symposium on macromolecules; 1976 October 11-15; Cleveland, OH. Amsterdam: Elsevier Scientific Publishing Co;1977:1-21.

Report:
Robert, D.A. Review of recent developments in the technology of nickel-base and cobalt-base alloys. Columbus, OH: Battelle Memorial Institute, Defense Metals Information Center; 1961 August 4; DMIC memorandum 122. 2 p. Available from: NTIS, Springfield, VA; AD 261292.

should always be in the language of the original work. But for the sake of convenience, an English translation may be provided in brackets.

In a multi-authored book a single chapter is analogous to an article in a journal. It ought to be cited separately, as ANSI recommends (see Figure 1).

When repeated reference to a book or article is required, terms like " ibid." or "op. cit." should be avoided. They are frequently ambiguous and take up a lot of space. If a book or an article is cited several times you should list the work once in the bibliography but cite the specific page numbers in parentheses within the text. I think this would be a great time-saver, especially in chemical libraries. A particular page of an article can be legitimately cited for a datum like a melting point. Unfortunately, this is often done without giving the complete pagination of the article cited. Thus one can not be sure how to order a copy of the article from the library.

Placing notes, comments, or additional explanations in cited references is usually confusing,

---

Figure 1 (continued)

Unpublished Paper:
Feast, M.W.; Garton, W.R.S. The Schumann-Runge bands of O_2 in emission and absorption in the quartz ultraviolet region. 1950. Unpublished draft supplied to author by W.R.S. Garton.

Dissertation or Thesis:
Cairns, R.B. Infrared spectroscopic studies of solid oxygen. Berkeley, CA: Univ. of California; 1965. 156 p. Dissertation.

Newspaper Article:
Robinson, Eugene. A report on new vaccines for 3 diseases. San Francisco Chronicle. 1978 January 20:20.

Letter:
DeRussy, R.E., Lieut. Col. [Letter to Brevet Gen. J.G. Totten]. 1853 May 15. 1 leaf. Located at: National Archives, Washington, DC; Record Group 77.

Patent Document:
Harred, John F; Knight, Allan R; McIntyre, John S., inventors; Dow Chemical Co., assignee. Epoxidation process. U.S. patent 3,654,317. 1972 April 4. 2 p.

Photograph:
Haas, Ernst. A man-made span [Photograph]. The best of Life. New York: Time-Life Books, ©1973: [p. 150]; 35 × 27 cm.

Printed Music:
Tchaikovsky, Peter Ilich. The swan lake ballet: op 20 [Score]. New York: Broude Brothers; [1951] (B.B. 59). vi. 685 p.

time-consuming and costly. References should only include works cited. In most cases I have found that extensive footnotes could just as easily be part of the text.[15] If not they should become true footnotes at the bottom of the page.

Almost everyone agrees on the value of good style in scientific writing.[16] But we should remember that the characteristics of clear writing also apply to clear references. The adoption of ANSI's style, with or without *Current Contents'* modifications, would benefit all concerned. A summary of the ANSI style recently appeared in the *Journal of the American Society for Information Science.*[17] Or you can get a copy of the *American National Standard for Bibliographic References* (ANSI-Z39.20-1977) for $11.50 from ANSI, Inc., 1430 Broadway, New York, NY 10016; (212) 354-3300.

REFERENCES

1. **Garfield E.** To indent or not to indent? How to improve journal contents page formats. *Current Contents* (43):5-8, 24 October 1977.
2. ------------. An address on addresses. *Current Contents* (28):5, 14 July 1977.*
3. *Mostly for authors.* Cambridge, MA: Harvard University Press, 1972. 37 p.
4. Modern Language Association of America. *The MLA style sheet.* New York: Modern Language Association of America, 1970. 48 p.
5. The University of Chicago Press. *A manual of style.* Chicago: University of Chicago Press, 1969. 546 p.
6. **O'Connor M & Woodford F P.** *Writing scientific papers in English: An ELSE-Ciba Foundation guide for authors.* New York: American Elsevier, 1976. 108 p.
7. *Handbook for authors of papers in the journals of the American Chemical Society.* Washington, D.C.: ACS Publications, 1967, p. 70.
8. **Garfield E, Koenig M & DiRenzo T.** ISI data-base-produced information services. *Current Contents* (45): 7-17, 7 November 1977.
9. **Garfield E.** Reducing the noise level in scientific communication: How services from ISI aid journal editors and publishers. *Current Contents* (30):5-15, 25 July 1977.
10. American National Standards Institute. *American national standard for bibliographic references.* New York: American National Standard Institute, 1977. 92 p.
11. *International standard bibliographic references—essential and supplementary elements.* Geneva: International Organization for Standardization, 1968. ISOR690-1968(E). 16 p.
12. **Garfield E.** Why initials instead of first names in ISI's indexes? *Current Contents* (32):5-6, 11 August 1975.*
13. ------------. Uniformity of editorial policy on titles in citations will aid referees, librarians and authors. *Current Contents* (8):5-6, 24 February 1975.*
14. ------------. Numerical vs. alphabetic order for cited references. *Current Contents* (44):5, 13 December 1968.*
15. **Inglis B.** Vanished footnotes. *New Scientist* 77(1089):384, 9 February 1978.
16. **Garfield E.** On style in scientific writing. *Current Contents* (2):6, 13 January 1977.
17. **Mount E.** A national standard for bibliographic reference. *J. Amer. Soc. Info. Sci.* 28:3-13, January 1977.

*Reprinted in Garfield E. *Essays of an information scientist.* Philadelphia: ISI Press, 1977. 2 vols.

CURRENT COMMENTS

Information Science and Technology Have Come of Age— Organizational Names Should Show It

Number 12, March 20, 1978

The National Science Foundation (NSF) organized a task force in 1976 to recommend the roles and responsibilities of NSF for science information in the 1980's. The task force report, released last year, recommended (among other things) the abolition of NSF's Division of Science Information and the creation of a Division of Information Science with a research program equal to those of the established scientific disciplines.[1] Recently NSF carried out this recommendation by setting up a new Division of Information Science & Technology. They are now looking for a person to head the division.

The distinction between science information and information science is not trivial. The change at NSF can one day mean significant funding for basic and applied research in information science. More important, the new division certifies to the public, the government, and the scientific community that the field of information science has come of age.

Names *are*, indeed, very important. Many people do not seem to grasp this fact. What a group is called affects the way outsiders and its members respond to it.

That is one reason I worked in the fifties and sixties to change the name of the American Documentation Institute to the American Society for Information Science. To someone outside the field, this effort may not mean much, but to those involved it was an important alteration.

Back in the 1930's when ADI began, "documentation" was an avant-garde term in library and archival circles. Microfilm was seen as the wave of the future. Watson Davis, the founder of *Science News*, helped establish the American Documentation Institute mainly to promote this medium. By the late 1950's, however, "documentation" had out-moded connotations. Computers, far more than microfilm, were revolutionizing scientific information processing and retrieval. Members of the American Documentation Institute were already creating computer programs and mathematical models for information systems. But the name of the organization did not suggest the nature of their endeavors. Worse, the old name failed to indicate that ADI was a vital professional organization. Many of us foresaw an explosive expansion of information science in the decades ahead. We realized that the use of the term "information science" in the title of our professional society would convey an image of an organization in tune with the times.

Eventually the effort to change the name proved successful. But the exertion required was enervating to say the least. I was subjected to considerable abuse by members of the old guard, many of whom seemed to have a vested interest in the word "documentation." In 1968 ADI was finally changed to American Society for Information Science (ASIS). But by that time it was already apparent that this change was not enough. While there has been considerable theoretical work in information science, much more growth has taken place in the area of information technology.

By omitting any mention of information technology from its title, ASIS seems to discourage membership by an essential and growing segment of its constituency that needs and wants a forum for airing their interests and problems. So in 1972 I began to suggest that ASIS change its name to American Society for Information Science & Technology (ASIST). Although the

then president of ASIS told me that many other information scientists had shown considerable interest in this change,[2] no action has been taken.

My concern with organizational names developed from some early personal experiences.

In 1954 I set up practice as a documentation consultant. By 1956 I had incorporated the company as DocuMation, Inc. This caused some consternation to Mortimer Taube who had formed Documentation, Inc. in 1953. Later on, at the urging of a public relations person, I changed this to Eugene Garfield Associates—Information Engineers. Shortly thereafter, I received a letter from the Pennsylvania Society of Professional Engineers informing me that it was illegal to call myself an engineer. Apparently in Pennsylvania any idiot can call himself a scientist but only a select group are entitled to be called engineers.

The issue became moot when, in 1960, I decided to change the name of the company to the Institute for Scientific Information® . Undoubtedly we were inspired by establishment in the USSR of the All Union Institute for Scientific & Technical Information. Furthermore, for many people the word "institute" connoted a non-profit organization. In those days many of my colleagues and customers had antipathetic feelings about for-profit organizations in the information field. Probably some still do.

Figure 1. Organizations affiliated with the American Association for the Advancement of Science Section T, which is concerned with information science, communications, and computing.

American Anthropological
  Association
American Chemical Society
American Institute of Aeronautics
  and Astronautics
American Institute of Biological
  Sciences
American Institute of Physics
American Library Association
American Medical Writers'
  Association
American Meteorological Society
American Microscopical Society
American Physical Society
American Society of Animal Science
American Society for Cybernetics
American Society for Information
  Science
American Society for Metals
American Statistical Association
Association for Computing
  Machinery
Conference Board of the
  Mathematical Sciences

Council of Biology Editors
Human Factors Society
Institute of Electrical and
  Electronics Engineers
Institute of Mathematical Statistics
International Communication
  Association
Mathematical Association of
  America
Medical Library Association
National Association of Science
  Writers
National Association of Social
  Workers
National Federation of Abstracting
  and Indexing Services
Oak Ridge Associated Universities
Speech Communication Association
Society for Industrial and Applied
  Mathematics
Society for Technical
  Communication

Strangely enough this was most often the case among people in private industry. They worshipped as sacred cows the non-profit organizations which produced *Chemical Abstracts, Biological Abstracts, Index Medicus,* etc. And, in fact, at one time I really considered establishing ISI® as a non-profit organization. In 1961 the infamous Fountain Committee, which was investigating NIH's procurement policies, caused NIH to terminate research grants to all commercial firms. By converting to non-profit status, we would have remained eligible for NIH grants. But my experience with NSF, NIH, and other government agencies convinced me that I did not want to make the switch. As it turned out, we were eventually able to continue research through an NSF *contract.*

My continuing interest in names of organizations related to the information field leads me to mention that I have recently assumed the chairmanship of Section T of the American Association for the Advancement of Science, which is concerned with information science, communications, and computing. The variety of organizations affiliated with Section T are shown in Figure 1.

The organizations concerned

with information are, of course, not limited to these groups. However, the diversity of their titles indicates why there may be an identity crisis for many information people whose professional activities span the boundaries of several groups.

Members of Section T will be getting together early in May to discuss its *raison d'etre* and perhaps the necessity of finding a new name which better identifies our interests. We hope to use the public broadcasting system to conduct a multi-city teleconference experiment so that members of Section T and all concerned can contribute to a discussion of "Whither Information Science?"

Although the typical layman still responds with a blank expression when you identify yourself as an information scientist, I think the average scientist today does recognize the term. And as society's preoccupation with computers and electronic communications grows, so will its need for and awareness of information scientists. Information science and technology have indeed come of age!

REFERENCES

1. A report to the Director of the National Science Foundation. Science Information Activities Task Force, NSF. Washington, D.C.: National Science Foundation, 1977. 18p.
2. Kyle R J. Private communication. 22 August 1972.

CURRENT COMMENTS

The Gordian Knot of Journal Coverage: Why We Can't Put All the Journals You Want into the *Current Contents* Edition You Read

Number 13, March 27, 1978

When you publish an information service like *CC®* with six disciplinary editions, there is no way you can please all of the people all of the time. I cannot think of a problem about which there is more disagreement than journal coverage. We can't please the editor of a botany journal who is slighted because his "obviously life science" journal is not covered in *CC/Life Sciences.* Nor can we satisfy the engineer who thinks all applied physics journals should be in *CC/Engineering, Technology & Applied Sciences.*

I am well aware of these journal coverage problems because I meet so many *CC* readers in my travels. I also receive hundreds of letters each year and survey readers by mail and phone. A recent letter expressed a common criticism of *CC* coverage:

"My chief complaint would be that CC/Agriculture, Biology & Environmental Sciences *is treated as a poor second cousin of* CC/Life Sciences. *This year you dropped* Nature *and* Science *from* CC/AB&ES. *Why? Do you think 'agriculture' scientists don't need such first-rate journals or is it (as it seems) a scheme to get some of us to subscribe to both issues?*

"...Why don't you do a survey of the subscribers to CC/AB&ES *to see what journals, now covered in* CC/LS, *would be useful additions to* CC/AB&ES? *If a lot of subscribers are like me (those in the fields of ecology, etc.), my guess is that there are relatively few (in my case about 20) journals that, if added to* CC/AB&ES, *would make* CC/LS *unnecessary. Much of* CC/LS *is now noise for me."*

I answered this person with a letter, but his questions are quite typical. So the main points of my response should interest most *CC* subscribers, but especially those who read *CC/AB&ES, CC/Clinical Practice,* and *CC/ET&AS.*

It is true that *CC/AB&ES* is treated differently than *CC/Life Sciences.* But from ISI® 's viewpoint it is treated more like a preferred youngest brother or sister than a poor cousin. *CC/Life*

452

Sciences and *CC/Physical & Chemical Sciences,* the big brother editions with the largest number of subscribers, actually subsidize the costs of producing other *CC* editions.

For example, if there were no *CC/LS, CC/AB&ES* would indeed be difficult to justify financially. This is because the audience for applied biology is much smaller than that for the life sciences generally. J. Levitt of the Carnegie Institution of Washington explained the problem when he pointed out that botanists cite basic life and physical science literature, but basic scientists don't cite botanists.[1] Botany journals have few outside readers. This was reflected in our citation study of the journals in this discipline.[2] For these reasons botanists doing basic research usually subscribe to *CC/LS.*

We do, however, cover the top botany journals in *CC/LS* for the benefit of non-botanists who just want an overview of what is going on in that field. But it would be too costly and of little help to most *CC/LS* readers to attempt to be *comprehensive* in botany, or in agriculture and environmental science—two other areas that may be of minor interest to *CC/LS* readers.

The deletion of *Science, Nature,* and other journals from *CC/AB&ES* is not a scheme to make two editions of *CC* necessary. Rather it is a response to reality. Over 50% of *CC/AB&ES* readers cover these journals by reading

CC/Life Sciences. By minimizing the overlap between the two editions, half of *CC/AB&ES* buyers do not have to pay twice for the same information. Deletion of these two very large journals enabled us to cover many less accessible journals.

Suppose we published *CC/AB&ES* as though *CC/Life Sciences* didn't exist. We would have to add to it hundreds of journals now covered in *CC/LS.* This was clearly proven when we did a study of the literature cited by agriculture scientists.[3] While one subscriber may assert he or she needs only 20 more journals, the total number reaches the hundreds when other readers' needs are considered.

And suppose we disregarded al other costs of duplicating this coverage. Just the paper and printing of these extra pages would be a significant added expense. Although some agriculture-oriented subscribers to *CC/Life Sciences* would *switch* to the new *CC/AB&ES,* we would probably gain very few *new* subscribers. There is no evidence that there is a large number of applied biologists out there waiting for a self-sufficient *CC/AB&ES.* However, such a change could result in a significant cost and price increase for both editions.

The harsh truth is that *CC/Agriculture, Biology & Environmental Sciences is* a supplement to *CC/Life Sciences.* It is in effect the *applied biology* section of

CC/LS. Similarly *CC/Clinical Practice* is the *applied medicine* supplement to *CC/LS* and *CC/ET&AS* is the *applied science* supplement to *CC/P&CS*.

Actually, this will be no surprise to those who have used *CC/AB&ES* since its first issue. I stated then that "many life scientists in agriculture, biology and environmental sciences...need [the] supplemental coverage [available in *CC/AB&ES*]."[4]

In *CC/Life Sciences* there is a section covering the core clinical journals which is found in *CC/Clinical Practice* as well. Thus, *CC/LS* is useful to many clinical people who are also involved in research. Unfortunately this solution is not possible for applied biology. But it would be possible to create a new section, consisting of all those applied biology journals not now covered by *CC/LS*, which could be substituted for the clinical section. *CC/Life Sciences* subscribers would have the option of receiving their edition with either the clinical section or the new *AB&ES* section. I can't help thinking of the dilemma this solution would pose for those doing veterinary research. But this approach could eliminate much duplicate coverage.

Optimizing journal coverage is not an easy task. We are always under great pressure from publishers, editors, and readers to cover more. At the same time we must try to exert quality as well as financial control. But if you are dissatisfied with coverage or any other facet of an ISI service, complain.[5] We can't satisfy everyone completely. But we do react to all constructive suggestions.

The viability of an ISI printed service depends upon our ability to sell it to a relatively large number of people. Hence, we are always looking for economical ways to improve our products' acceptance. Marketing strategy is designed to optimize not only producer profit, but also user benefit.

REFERENCES

1. **Levitt J.** Personal communication. December 14, 1977.
2. **Garfield E.** Journal citation studies. 18. Highly cited botany journals. *Current Contents* (2):5-9, 13 January 1975.*
3. --------------. Journal citation studies. 20. Agriculture journals and the agricultural literature. *Current Contents* (20):5-11, 19 May 1975.*
4. --------------. How can you separate agriculture, biology, and environmental sciences from life sciences (if you must)? *Current Contents* (33):5-8, 16 August 1972.*
5. --------------. Don't kill us with kindness—COMPLAIN! *Current Contents* (6):5-6, 10 February 1975.*

*Reprinted in: *Essays of an information scientist.* Philadelphia: ISI Press, 1977. 2 vols.

CURRENT COMMENTS

Creative Philanthropy. I.
Is It Necessary to be Non-Profit
to be Philanthropic?

Number 14, April 3, 1978

Several years ago my dear friend Jacob Gershon-Cohen,[1] the late distinguished radiologist, told me he was in a quandary over how to bequeath his life savings. A childless widower, he had considered leaving the money to his local medical society to improve the dissemination of medical information. But he felt that the society was inadequate to the task. He wondered if there was some way ISI® and the College of Physicians of Philadelphia could work together toward his objective. But although ISI and the College had many common goals regarding the dissemination of information, there was a serious stumbling block which ultimately precluded mutual effort. The College was a non-profit organization, while ISI was a for-profit corporation.

Gershon-Cohen was trying to be creative in disposing of his wealth. He wanted to use his money to aid the flow of medical information and saw that ISI's activities would help fulfill his desire. But he was discouraged by archaic tax laws which make it difficult or impossible for for-profit firms to accept philanthropy or even to work with non-profit organizations.

People of wealth often want to see their money put to good social use or to further scientific research. While the initial motivation of such persons as Andrew Carnegie, John D. Rockefeller, and Henry Ford may not have been entirely for this reason, there can be little doubt that the organizations which immortalize them have accomplished a great deal. In order to carry out their personal goals, which included maintaining family power, they established non-profit foundations. In this way they prevented the government from confiscating their wealth through inheritance taxes. Today we are still benefiting from foundations established to retain power and wealth. By being independent, these institutions have often been ahead of the government in pioneering social changes and reforms of one kind or another.

The "success" of the foundation idea is indicated by their proliferation during the past century. It has been estimated that there are well over 125,000 in the world—about 32,000 in the Netherlands, 26,000 in the United States, 20,000 in Switzerland, 10,000 in Great Britain, 10,000 in Denmark, 4,500 in Spain, 4,000 in Germany, 4,000 in Italy, 1,400 in Canada, 800 in Latin America, 660 in Austria, and 260 in France.[2-6]

While these numerous non-profit organizations provided billions for philanthropic purposes, only a fraction went for research. In the United States, foundations gave about $125 million to support research in 1976. In comparison, the taxpayer-supported National Science Foundation provided $625 million for research in 1976.[7] The National Institutes of Health gave more than $75 million for intramural research, nearly $1½ billion in research grants, and over $386 million in research and development contracts during the same year.[8] Similar comparisons in other countries would be interesting but not particularly necessary to my main theme. And in the socialist countries such comparisons may be pointless.

Many US foundations gave money to support international programs. According to Patrick W. Kennedy, editor of *Foundation News*, about three cents of every dollar given by US foundations goes abroad.[9] And some foreign foundations contribute to American organizations. For example, the British Rhodes Trust annually selects 32 American college students to study at Oxford; the British Wellcome Trust gives medical research grants to Americans; and the German Volkswagen Foundation sponsors projects to promote international scientific cooperation.

The numbers and wealth of foundations have necessitated the creation in the United States of the Foundation Center, a foundation-supported information clearinghouse, which disseminates information about foundations and their grants.[10]

Too often, however, foundations do not really reflect the objectives, vitality, and creativity of their originators. J. Paul Getty perceiv- the implicit irony in establishing these institutions when he refused to set up one of his own:

It always works against the grain to see these foundations so opposed to what I know was the philosophy of the founder [he said]. You can't tell me that ninety percent of what the Ford Foundation is doing would have been approved by Henry Ford.[11]

In spite of this he left many millions of dollars to the J. Paul Getty Museum (of art) in Malibu, California, which he had started in 1953. He obviously had ambivalent feelings on this subject. I have observed that the "meanest" for-profit businessman is often favorably disposed towards non-profit enterprises outside of his own field.

Henry Ford II, in a letter that echoed Getty's feelings about foundations, resigned last year as a trustee of the Ford Foundation, leaving it beyond the control of the family. He noted that "the foundation is a creature of capitalism—a statement that, I'm sure, would be shocking to many professional staff people in the field of philanthropy."[12]

George G. Kirstein, former *Nation* editor and head of several foundations, notes that spokesmen for foundations like to stress their innovative role in providing "seed money" for research:

> They cite Rockefeller's early support to Dr. Jonas Salk's research on polio and the Guggenheim Foundation's aid to Dr. Charles Goddard in rocket research.... However, the truth is that these "seed money" ventures are the rare exception rather than the rule.... The role that foundations really play is to sustain already established institutions, not to create new ones.... Almost without exception, those who constitute the governing boards of the big foundations tend toward conservatism in their political philosophies and prefer maintaining the status quo.[13]

Furthermore, foundations are often established for emotional reasons which may ultimately conflict with the goal of the endower. People set up foundations for research on a disease which has killed a family member. The result is that many foundations duplicate efforts. There is often no simple way for them to combine endowments and facilities. And their charters often forbid any obscuring of the name they are supposed to immortalize.

Foundations devoted solely to research can play a vital role, especially when they identify areas of research neglected by NSF and the other granting agencies like NIH. However, potential endowers and existing philanthropic organizations could aid science in other ways.

For instance, if you donate $1 million to investigate a particular disease, you can easily calculate what that $1 million will buy in labor, equipment, etc. But if you give $1 million to fund a lobbyist, your donation may eventually result in $1 *billion* in government grants. This is what I call "creative philanthropy"—getting more for your money or "more bang for the buck."

One way to give money for lobbying purposes is to donate it to scientific associations like the American Association for the Advancement of Science (AAAS). And there are plenty of them around. Such non-profit organizations in the United States are permitted to lobby, although their expenditures in this area are limited. Under the Tax Reform Act of 1976, non-profit organizations which spend $500,000 or more per year may use no more than 20% of that money for lobbying. The overall limit is $1 million for lobbying, and to spend that much, a non-profit group would have to spend a yearly total of $17 million. Congress also set a spending limit of 25% for "grassroots" lobbying, or taking one's case directly to the public rather than to the legislature.[14] Previous laws regulating lobbying by non-profit organizations had been so vague that few institutions were willing to use this means of furthering their interests.[15] Under the new law, this may change. If it does, it could mean more lobbying for research.

One small informal organization of researchers is now lobbying for a 10% increase in the National Institutes of Health budget.[16] And I myself have discussed the formation of a biomedical lobby.[17]

Foundations in the United States, which have plenty of money to use for worthy purposes, have not been permitted to lobby since passage of the Tax Reform Act of 1969. Congressman Wright Patman, architect of the law, believed that foundations were simply perpetuating the influence of the moneyed elite.[18]

However, foundations which want to aid scientific research through a lobbyist have a few alternatives. I know of at least one family-run research foundation whose benefactor also supports a lobbyist from personal funds. This, of course, is not tax-deductible.

Foundations, however, may give money to non-profit organizations which *can* lobby for research. The foundation's contributions may not be used *directly* for lobbying. By increasing a non-profit organization's assets, the donor foundation indirectly increases the amount that can be spent on lobbying.

Another example of "creative philanthropy" involves the political sphere. Several foundations and other organizations already sponsor programs which bring scientists into the legislative branch of government. The Foundation for Microbiology and the American Society for Microbiology (ASM) Foundation co-sponsor the ASM Congressional Fellowship which each year enables a postdoctoral or mid-career microbiologist to spend a year on a congressional staff or committee. The Fellow acts as both a legislative assistant and a science advisor. This fellowship is modeled on the AAAS Congressional Science Fellows Program. The AAAS works closely with both the ASM and the American Physical Society (APS), which also has a Fellows program.

So far the AAAS and the APS have sent about 50 scientists to work on congressional staffs. About half of them were physical scientists; the rest included biologists, social scientists, and engineers. Richard A. Scribner of the AAAS and Mary L. Shoaf of the APS evaluate the need for the program this way:

> Because a scientifically trained person in the Congressional staff brings a unique professional training and perspective, the significance of that person's role is perhaps greater than that of just one more competent staff person. We think these scientific skills and viewpoints are especially needed in Washington.... Aside from augmenting the scientifically trained Congressional staff, we see substantial impact of the Fellow on legislative issues. Not the kind of impact that replaces or in any way subverts the legislative process and the legitimate decision role of the legislators, but rather the impact on the complete staff work that often benefits from a unique perspective and application of a "scientific" methodology aimed at uncovering pertinent facts.[19]

Apparently the science fellowships have resulted in considerable interaction between scientists and politicians. In 1976 Congress passed a resolution praising the program. Ten of the seventeen physicists who were APS Fellows have taken permanent staff positions.

Another form of creative philanthropy might involve funding a political action group to support candidates amenable to the advancement of scientific research.

I don't think any such group now exists in the US, but the idea is similar to that of the late physicist Leo Szilard when he founded the Council for a Livable World in 1962. As a scientist, Szilard was concerned about the escalating arms race and wished to set up an organization which could work effectively for disarmament. Today the Council for a Livable World spends about $200,000 a year on United States Senate campaign contributions. Donations to this organization, however, are not taxdeductable. The Council concentrates on the Senate because, next to the President, a single senator has more influence on the issue of world peace than any other elected official. It usually allocates its resources on Senate campaigns in the smaller states where its contributions are likely to be most effective.[20] According to the Council's president, William von E. Doering of the Harvard University Chemistry Department, about one-third of the Senate's present members were supported by the Council.

About 3,000 of the Council's 10,000 members are scientists, Doering estimates. The Council lobbies on defense-related issues. It supported the appointment of Paul Warnke as head of the Arms Control and Disarmament Agency. It also played a major role in the fight against the antiballistic missile. But the Council does not lobby for scientific research. Some members, Doering says, might consider that a conflict of interest.

Szilard's impulse in founding the Council for a Livable World was similar to that of Alfred Nobel. The inventor of dynamite and other explosives, Nobel wanted to stimulate research that would benefit humanity. The considerable money value of the awards he set up in 1896 was meant to help finance the winners' future research. This has occurred indirectly, since so many more recent Nobel winners were students of previous winners. Only a few winners do further work of Nobel caliber after receiving the awards.[21] But the prizes are creative in a way that Nobel may not have foreseen. The announcement of the prizes each year creates a public awareness of the benefits of basic research.

The subject of non-profit organizations and private philanthropy is one which is of deep personal interest to me. On the one hand, I have observed the stultifying effect of entrenched bureaucracies in many such organizations, not unlike that observed in government. But in a democratic society, there is presumably ultimate recourse to reform through the political system (including lobbying). On the other hand, I am very concerned that my own wealth, present or future, not be left to be used by mediocrities who could not recognize a new or original idea under any circumstance. I propose to continue the discussion of this topic next week and several times again in the future.

REFERENCES

1. **Garfield E.** Jacob Gershon-Cohen, M.D., D.Sc. In memoriam. *Current Contents* (11):4-5, 17 March 1971.*
2. Continental European foundations put at 90,000. *Foundation News* 12:242, 1971.
3. **Buckman T R.** US foundations: a statistical survey. *Foundation News* 16(3):17-28, 1975.
4. European foundations and research. *Foundation News* 7:45-7, 1966.
5. **Arlett A,** ed. *Canadian directory to foundations.* Ottawa, Canada: Association of Universities and Colleges of Canada, 1973. 161 p.
6. **Stromberg A,** ed. *Philanthropic foundations in Latin America.* New York: Russell Sage Foundation, 1968. 215 p.
7. **Haskins C P.** Public and private science. *American Scientist* 65:493-9, 1976.
8. **Gardner F.** Chief, Budget Presentation & Formulation Branch of the Division of Financial Management of the Office of the Director of the National Institutes of Health. Personal communication. 16 March 1978.
9. **Kennedy P W.** International grant making and US foundations. *Foundation News* 18(6):40-7, 1977.
10. **Margolin J B.** The Foundation Center. *Special Libraries* 67:568-73, 1976.
11. **White V P.** *Grants: How to find out about them and what to do next.* New York: Plenum Press, 1975. 354 p.
12. **Carroll M.** Henry Ford 2nd quits foundation, urges appreciation for capitalism. *The New York Times* 12 January 1977: 1, B6.
13. **Kirstein G G.** *Better giving: the new needs of American philanthropy.* Boston: Houghton Mifflin Company, 1975. 196 p.
14. **Stahr E J.** Lobbying is coming out of the shadows. *Council on Foundations Reporter Supplement* 5:1977.
15. **Walsh J.** Lobbying rules for nonprofits: new option sets specific limits. *Science* 196:40-2, 1977.
16. **Lyons R D.** Scientists plunge into lobbying for more medical research aid. *The New York Times* 19 January 1978: 38.
17. **Garfield E.** Biomedical and health care systems research should be financed from social security and health insurance funds. A permanent lobby could swing it. *Current Contents* (3):5-7, 16 January 1974.*
18. **Nielsen W A.** *The big foundations.* New York: Columbia University Press, 1972. 475 p.
19. **Scribner R A & Shoaf M L.** Four years of Congressional Science Fellows. *Physics Today* 30:36-40, 1977.
20. **Williams R M.** Hard cash from tender minds. *World* 2(5):32-5, 1973.
21. **Zuckerman H.** *Scientific elite: Nobel laureates in the United States.* New York: The Free Press, 1977. 335 p.

*Reprinted in: **Garfield E.** *Essays of an Information Scientist.* Philadelphia: ISI Press, 1977. 2 vols.

CURRENT COMMENTS

Creative Philanthropy. II.
Getting More Bang for the Buck!

Number 15, April 10, 1978

Last week's discussion of creative philanthropy began by noting the problems inherent in the present foundation system of funding research. Apart from duplication of effort by numerous small foundations, many projects are unimaginative and often run counter to the philosophy of the founder. I suggested that scientific research might be better aided in indirect ways which would make better use of the donors' money. Lobbies and political action groups were two alternatives, because they could repay the donor's investment by stimulating government research grants worth many times the original contribution.[1]

Finally, it was noted that the most creative aspect of the Nobel prize has turned out to be the publicity it generates to increase public awareness and (by inference) public support for basic research.

One of the newest creative awards is the National Academy of Science's James Murray Luck Award for Excellence in Scientific Reviewing. Co-sponsored by ISI®

and Annual Reviews, Inc., the non-profit publisher of *Annual Reviews,* the award, consisting of a scroll and $5,000, will be given annually, starting next year, to an author of a particularly meritorious scientific review.

Although it is agreed that good reviews are an important aid to scientists, getting people to write them has always been difficult.[2] Those best qualified to do the work are also most likely to be involved in original research. To write reviews, they must put aside their research efforts and expend a great deal of time and intellectual effort in analyzing, synthesizing, and evaluating information in a limited subject area. In return, they have received very small financial recompense. The new award will provide for fine reviewers not only financial rewards but also the recognition they deserve. More importantly, the award will symbolize the debt we owe reviewers. We hope that it will also encourage other qualified persons to write excellent reviews.

461

Just as there is a need for competent scientific reviewers, so there is a need for popular science writers. The $2,000 James T. Grady Award for Interpreting Chemistry to the Public, given by the American Chemical Society,[3] recognizes that the public must understand and take an interest in science if scientists are to expect wide support for research. Winners, including Isaac Asimov (1965) and Walter Sullivan (1969), have through their writing helped the cause of science.

Grants, too, may sometimes be examples of creative philanthropy. For instance, the Teacher-Scholar Grant Program of the Camille and Henry Dreyfus Foundation is designed to keep teachers most qualified to train researchers in university classrooms. Recipients are given a great deal of freedom in how to spend the money, but the foundation specifies that the grant should not take the teacher away from classes and that it should promote better contact with students. Instead of supporting one person's research, the award permits excellent training of many students and helps insure the quality of science graduates from our universities.

Another Dreyfus Foundation program, Innovations in Education in Chemistry, provides funds to universities to help encourage new ways of teaching chemistry. The foundation does not recommend changes in the educational process, but expects colleges and universities to develop their own innovations. Among the projects the foundation is now funding is a series of seminars designed to make students at the University of Nebraska more aware of current trends in chemistry and to help them plan their careers accordingly. Another is a course in the history of science and technology at Franklin and Marshall College. According to Dreyfus Foundation director William L. Evers, the Innovation in Education grants are intended to help students broaden their intellectual awareness and strengthen their feelings of social responsibility. "This is a counter-move to the criticism that scientific and technically-trained people do not have a broad intellectual base, that they are too highly specialized," he says.

Both Dreyfus programs are far-sighted, creative endeavors because they are aimed at helping, not a few science researchers of the moment, but the many scientists of the future.

One effort to aid technological progress is the Research Corporation's Inventions Evaluation program. The Corporation—actually a foundation—was founded in 1912 by Frederick Gardner Cottrell, who was *not* a multi-millionaire. His endowment consisted solely of the patent rights to his inventions. The most successful of these, which helped the foundation really get underway, was the electrostatic precipitator, which removes some pollutants from industrial smoke-stacks. The foundation evaluates 500 inventions a year from the 300 universities and other scientific institutions it works closely with. According to James Fulleylove, director of the program, among the inventions the Corporation supported are vitamin B_1, the maser, and a drug for curing fungus infections.

When an invention is successfully marketed, about 15% of the royalties are given to the inventor. The rest is divided between the Corporation and the inventor's home institution, to be used for more research. The Corporation takes credit for stimulating academic research early in this century, before industry realized its value and the academic world cared much about marketing its discoveries. It claims that its program helps industry locate new technology while saving the inventor legal expenses. "The value of the first outside recognition of a young researcher, the upgrading of a whole science department, the salvage of a worthwhile piece of research that otherwise might not be done, all are effects that can be described but not measured," according to the foundation.[4]

Clearly then, foundations and other nonprofit organizations can make good use of their money and accomplish a great deal—when they use their imagination. Unfortunately, many do not seem to have the creativity necessary.

The stultifying effect of some nonprofit organizations was brought home to me when I visited in Pittsburgh several years ago the Carnegie Museum—a veritable mausoleum. As I walked through it, I wondered if Carnegie might not have done better by leaving his money to P. T. Barnum or Walt Disney to create and run a museum for him. So what if they received 10% of the action, and so what if the government got its fair (or unfair) share in taxes? The museum would not have been a lifeless shrine, but a living, dynamic reminder of its founder.

There *are* many ways to benefit society other than by setting up a nonprofit organization. Possibly the most creative thing a wealthy person can do with money is to invest it in corporations whose objectives coincide with the donor's. This could be done by establishing a foundation whose funds would be invested in new enterprises—even a venture capital group. Such organizations would earn money for further investment in a way not entirely dissimilar to that of the Research Corporation. And they would be "philanthropic" because they would help society by creating new jobs and industries.

In the United States and elsewhere, anachronistic tax laws are helping to create a society of nonprofit organizations designed to prevent the government from swallowing the fruits of lifetimes of creative endeavor. But a "for-profit foundation" might have the mandate simply to see that the founder's goals in life are actively pursued after his or her death, provided that such purposes remained relevant to society's needs.

It remains to be seen whether the increased efficiency, responsiveness, and incentives of a for-profit enterprise would make up for the loss of tax-free nonprofit status. Our corporate tax laws might require extensive revision if "for-profit philanthropy" caught on. But if immortality is the goal that benefactors seek—and I believe that in part it is—then for-profit foundations could provide equally lasting memorials.

While we should discuss new directions for philanthropy, one should not forget that, under the existing system, foundations could be doing more than they are doing today. Dr. Paul N. Ylvisaker of Harvard University notes that dur-ing the "cold war" United States Senator Joseph McCarthy wondered if foundations represented the interests of Communists or radicals. Now, Ylvisaker says, the question in the minds of Congressmen and the public is "not why are you so radical, but so completely the opposite?... Why aren't you being creative? Why aren't you doing much more interesting things with your money...?"[5]

Undoubtedly many of my ideas about for-profit philanthropy are not original, but I have reason to believe that there are hundreds if not thousands of wealthy people who are looking for more creative ways to use their money to help society. Perhaps these essays will serve to open up a public discussion of these problems. Your comments are welcome and if appropriate will be incorporated into a later essay.

REFERENCES

1. **Garfield E.** Creative philanthropy. I. Is it necessary to be non-profit to be philanthropic? *Current Contents* (13):5-10, 3 April 1978.
2. ⸻. So you wanted more review articles—ISI's new *Index to Scientific Reviews (ISR)* will help you find them.
   Current Contents (44):5-6, 30 October 1974. (Reprinted in:
   Garfield E. *Essays of an information scientist.*
   Philadelphia: ISI Press, 1976. Vol. 2, p. 170-1.)
3. American Chemical Society. *Awards administered by the American Chemical Society.* Washington: The American Chemical Society, 1978. 32 p.
4. Research Corporation. *Science invention and society.*
   New York: The Research Corporation, 1972. 40 p.
5. Call for more enterprise in philanthropy.
   Council on Foundations Reporter 5:1, 1976.

CURRENT COMMENTS

Chemical Information for the Man Who Has Everything

Number 16, April 17, 1978

Most *Current Contents®* readers would be surprised to learn that chemical information retrieval was, so to speak, my first love. Many associate me exclusively with *CC®* or the *Science Citation Index®* and do not know that I have long been preoccupied with problems of chemical documentation. Indeed, in a sense, ISI® has been "competing" with *Chemical Abstracts* for almost twenty years.

This may help explain the mixed emotions I felt about the Herman Skolnik award I received about a year ago. This award is presented annually by the American Chemical Society's Division of Chemical Information for "outstanding and sustained service to chemical information." While I'm pleased to have this recognition, I'm sure that those who are not chemical information "insiders" believe the award reflects only my work on *CC* and the *SCI®*. On the other hand, chemical information specialists have never fully appreciated the importance of *CC*!

ISI has been building its chemical data base since 1960.[1] It was originally designed primarily to alert chemists to new organic compounds reported in the journal literature. Later on, new reactions and new syntheses were also covered. About 150,000 new compounds are added to the data base each year. This is estimated to include 90% of all the new compounds reported in the literature since 1960. Although neither ISI's nor any other system available is absolutely complete, I doubt that much of *significance* is missing.

Over the years, the ISI chemical data base has been continually improved and made available in an increasing variety of formats. It is now accessible through print and microform publications, computer-generated reports, and magnetic tapes—all of which are functionally integrated and cross-referenced to each other. This flexibility means that a wide variety of organizations, ranging from national institutions to multi-national companies to comparatively small institutes, are able to make use of the data base in the form best suited to their needs.

One of the problems we have in promoting the data base is dealing with the names of the different services we extract from it. The names tend to be long, not self-explanatory, and easily mistaken for other services produced by ISI and other organizations. We made things even more complicated by twice changing the name of one service. So, here for the first time in one place in *CC* are the correct names of our chemical information services with very brief explanations of what they do.

Current Abstracts of Chemistry™ *(CAC*™*)* is a weekly printed service that contains graphic abstracts of the articles reporting new compounds (including intermediates), reactions, or syntheses. Emphasis is on ease of browsing, through liberal use of structural diagrams, and rapid coverage of the literature. Most compounds are reported in *CAC* within 45 days after their initial appearance in the journal literature.

Index Chemicus® *(IC*®*)* is now the index section to the abstracts. It was the original title of the entire service. *IC* is included as part of the weekly *CAC*. It is also issued separately in quarterly and annual cumulations. *IC* provides a variety of ways to search the file of abstracts—by molecular formula, author, journal, organization, and subject term searches. The quarterly and annual cumulations also include a rotated molecular formula index.

The next three services I will describe involve the use of Wiswesser Line-Notation (WLN).[2] We have pioneered in the use of this linear notation since 1968. WLN describes compounds unambiguously. It also shows how the substituents are arranged in relation to each other. Since WLN uses standard alpha-numeric characters, it is ideal for input to computerized "substructure searching" systems. It is also compatible with manual searching. A substructure search enables you to locate all compounds reported that contain a specific molecular substructure or fragment.

Chemical Substructure Index® *(CSI)* is another index to the compounds reported in *CAC*. *CSI* is an alphabetic list of permuted WLN descriptions of compounds.[3] Issued monthly with a semi-annual and annual cumulation, *CSI* has been in microfilm format since 1976. The years 1966-1975 are covered by printed indexes. It is shocking how few chemists make use of this incredibly simple and useful tool covering over a million compounds.

Automatic New Structure Alert® *(ANSA*®*)* is a computerized personal alerting service similar to our *ASCA*® system.[4] *ANSA* automatically selects those articles reporting new compounds that match a pre-established interest profile. In addition to the familiar types of profile terms which can be used (e.g., authors, key words, molecular formulas, etc.), WLN descriptions of substructures can also be employed. Subscribers receive a printout once a month providing the bibliographic descriptions of articles reporting the compounds matching the profile. Substructure searching is done by direct computer scanning of the linear WLN notations and/or by scanning connectivity tables generated from the WLN.

Index Chemicus Registry System® *(ICRS)* is the complete chemical data base supplied on magnetic tape.[5] Issued monthly with an annual cumulation, the tapes can be used for current awareness or retrospective searching. In addition to WLN descriptions of compounds, *ICRS* tapes contain, as an option, fragment code descriptions based on the so-called Ring Code of the *Pharmadokumentationsring* group of companies.[6] A subscription to *ICRS* includes search software at no extra cost.[7].

The reprint of "Where is Chemical Information Going," which appears on the following pages, is the acceptance talk I gave when I received the ACS award.[8] I originally entitled the talk, "For the Man Who Has Everything." This was my way of acknowledging the irony of receiving such an award from the American Chemical Society—an organization with which my disagreements have been long and loud. But if the man who has everything could *really* have his way, he would want ISI's chemical services to come out from under the shadow of their more famous siblings, *Current Contents* and the *Science Citation Index.*

In closing I might add that while they are a small and select group, those chemists and pharmacologists who do make use of *Current Abstracts of Chemistry and Index Chemicus*™ are as strongly addicted to it as most of you are to *CC*. This is partly because they realize that searching *Index Chemicus* for current information is a logical step before or after using *Chemical Abstracts* or *Beilstein.* They also know that a search of the *SCI* is an important way to supplement searches done with the other tools.

In the near future ISI is going to make a concerted effort to expand the use of our chemical services. We hope to accomplish this through substantive changes that will make the services better able to meet the increased need for the retrieval of specific chemical data.

REFERENCES

1. **Garfield E.** ISI's chemical information system goes marching on!
   Current Contents (1):5-6, 5 January 1976.*
2. **Gibson G W & Granito C E.** Wiswesser chemical line-notation.
   Amer. Lab. 14:27-37, 1972.
3. **Granito C E & Rosenberg M D.** *Chemical Substructure Index (CSI).* A new research tool. *J. Chem. Doc.* 11(4):251-6, 1971.
4. **Garfield E.** Introducing ANSA—ISI's Automatic New Structure Alert—a compound-retrieval service for people more interested in compounds than retrieval!
   Current Contents (19):5-10, 9 May 1973.*
5. **Garfield E & Sim M.** The *Index Chemicus Registry System* —past, present and future. *Pure Appl. Chem.* 49:1803-5, 1977.
6. **Garfield E.** ISI's *CHEMTRAN* 'compatibilizes' files of encoded chemical structures.
   Current Contents (46):5-6, 15 November 1972.*
7. --------------. The retrieval and dissemination of chemical information. 4. *ICRS RADIICAL* software. *Current Contents* (31):M1-2, 5 August 1970.*
8. --------------Where is chemical information going?
   J. Chem. Inform. Comput. Sci. 18(1):1-4, 1978.

*Reprinted in: *Essays of an Information Scientist.* Philadelphia: ISI Press, 1977. 2 vols.

Where is Chemical Information Science Going? [†]

Eugene Garfield

Institute for Scientific Information
325 Chestnut Street
Philadelphia, Pennsylvania 19106

Professor Robert K. Merton of Columbia University is a genius when it comes to naming social phenomena. Several years ago, in *Science*,[1] he created the term the "Matthew effect". I thought about this when I selected the title for my talk today: "For the Man Who Has Everything". Merton's term is based on a quotation in the New Testament. In Matthew, Chapter 13, Verse 12, we find:

> "For whosoever hath, to him shall be given, and he shall have more abundance: but whosoever hath not, from him shall be taken away even that he hath."

Well, I suppose it is only natural that after receiving the ASIS Award of Merit—delivered and presented to me, ironically enough, by Dale Baker of *Chemical Abstracts*—the man who has everything should get an American Chemical Society award. I begin to wonder what the future has in store.

It is interesting that the very next verse in Matthew describes my feelings about the Establishment 25 years ago; by Establishment I mean *Chemical Abstracts*, the National Science Foundation, and other entrenched fortress mentalities:

> "Therefore speak I to them in parables: because they seeing see not; and hearing they hear not, neither do they understand."

Some of you may recall that two years ago in Philadelphia I was the luncheon speaker at the ACS Division of Chemical Information. There, I spoke about some seemingly unrelated topics, such as "The Entrepreneur as a Doctoral Candidate", in which I described the agony and the ecstasy of obtaining a Ph.D. in chemical linguistics.[2] So why have you asked me to come back so soon? Is it possible your awards committee figured as follows: If we give Garfield this award he will have nothing to say, having covered everything he could imagine last time?

When the subject of nothing to say comes up I always think of the story about the wedding of the librarian and the information scientist. When asked if anyone had any objection to their marriage, an ASIS member in the audience waved his hand and said, "I have no objection to the wedding but would anyone like to hear about my information retrieval system?" I suppose an ACS member would have proposed discussing a new method for manipulating connectivity tables.

As you can see, I was somewhat desperate for a topic. I've spoken to you so many times in the past and write so much in *Current Contents*® and elsewhere that it is often difficult to be original. So I wrote to Peter Sorter out of desperation and asked him to suggest a topic. Pete is concerned about the climate for chemical information

[†]Presented before the Division of Chemical Information, 173rd National Meeting of the American Chemical Society, New Orleans, La., 21 March 1977.

Reprinted by permission of the *Journal of Chemical Information and Computer Sciences* 18:1-4, 1961. Copyright © 1978 by the American Chemical Society.

science during the next five to ten years. He is also concerned about the role of the Division of Chemical Information and what its members can expect in the always uncertain future.

After all, there is good evidence that the rate of growth of chemical and scientific information has decreased in recent years. However, the absolute growth of scientific information each year is still substantial. Even if the literature were simply to grow at an arithmetic rate, the existing quantity of information is already so large that new methods of dealing with it are needed more than ever. If we needed *Beilstein* when the literature was "small" how do we manage without it or its equivalent when the literature is "large?" Thus, the need for information scientists is assured.

Certainly the need to extract chemical and physical data from the literature, as contrasted with bibliographic information, will increase. The new breed of chemical information specialists will not only have to be trained in information storage and retrieval but also in writing and digesting information—what is otherwise called reviewing. We are in the era of the critical review. I believed this when ISI® launched the *Index to Scientific Reviews*™ (ISR™). I believed it even more when we began including multiauthored books as source material for the *Science Citation Index*® (*SCI*) this year and in *Current Book Contents* a few years ago.

Where are all the new chemical information specialists going to come from? Many of them will be people who start out in a career path in information science. But most will be Ph.D. chemists who will turn to information science as an alternative career in a tough job market. They will be no different than the many chemists who wound up as chemical marketing specialists back in the depression.

Recently, I wrote a proposal to Dean Harvey Brooks of Harvard University entitled "Alternatives to Research and Teaching for Unemployed Ph.D.'s".[3] I suggested that the oversupply of Ph.D.'s could be usefully directed into a new profession of scientific reviewing. The program would comprise postdoctoral training of no less than one year and could be established at selected information science departments. Preferably we would create new information science programs at every leading university. I hope to push these ideas further as the chairman-elect of Section T of the American Association for Advancement of Science

(AAAS). I hope the ACS will evaluate this notion in the Division of Chemical Education and here in the Division of Chemical Information. I also hope that the National Science Foundation (NSF) will begin to pay serious attention to the proposal as originally outlined in the *Bulletin of the American Society for Information Science*.[5]

But what are the real prospects for scientific reviewers? The research in hard science fronts moves forward in quanta of 50 to 250 papers. In other fields, like descriptive biology, the number may be much larger. In any case, someone has to digest the information and present it in a synthesized, readable form. Keeping tabs on the literature, especially in rapidly growing fields, is a task which many laboratory investigators wish they could handle. For a variety of reasons—temperamental and otherwise—they usually cannot do this successfully. Scientific reviewing is thus an intellectual activity that is deeply appreciated. Its impact is reflected in the citation data we have compiled at ISI.

In December 1977 I published an article in *Nature*[6] which listed 80 different review journals that achieved an impact higher than two. Consider that only 300 scientific journals, out of the thousands published throughout the world, achieved a similar or higher impact. The average journal in our file had an impact score of 1.015. Impact tells us how often the average article was cited in the two years prior to the year under study. For example, *Chemical Reviews* had an impact of 8.1. Its articles for 1973 and 1974 were cited 530 times in 1975. And it ranked among the 50 most-cited journals of science, with 11,000 citations. We also know that review articles have a high immediacy. Some review journals are cited heavily within months of publication because, among other reasons, they become surrogates for the literature they digest. Thus, chemists can cite the previous research literature by a single reference to a review article. Incidentally, Angela Mazella at ISI is studying the characteristics of the review literature under an NSF grant.[7] Tony Woodward of ASLIB also has made some important contributions.[8]

Another way we have learned of the importance of review journals is through co-citation analysis. In these studies Henry Small and others have drawn cluster maps showing the most cited papers in certain specialties. Quite frequently, the papers that turn up in these co-citation maps are review papers.

All of this evidence indicates that chemists should not be reluctant to write reviews if they are interested in promoting their visibility among their peers. It is almost as good as being a journal editor—maybe better. In the past, people like Herman Skolnik realized, instinctively or otherwise, that another form of reviewing—section editing for CA—provided a similar visibility. I might point out that my proposal in no way denigrates the valuable service performed by such persons. Someone must agree with this—why else am I receiving the Skolnik award?

Our citation studies have shown that one must be careful to distinguish the various reasons why highly cited papers are heavily cited. The contribution of a reviewer is important, indeed essential to the progress of science. This view may or may not support the Ortega hypothesis.[9,10] But this is different from the importance and significance of breakthrough papers which report new phenomena or new theoretical insights—or the much maligned new methods. Recently we started a new feature in Current Contents called Citation Classics.[11] These autobiographical accounts of how and why certain highly cited papers were written have provided new insight into the role of new methods in science.

Of course reviews are not of uniform style. Many of them are speculative and stimulate needed research. In this connection, it is interesting how citation indexes and reviews are associated. The SCI was an outgrowth of my detailed analysis of review articles as suggested by Chauncey D. Leake. Later, Professor Joshua Lederberg mentioned the importance of citation indexes to help in his own review activities. He needed to know where and by whom his speculations (e.g., on exobiology) had been taken up by others. And review papers provide an important source for a posteriori indexing entries in the Citation Index. The average review article contains in excess of 150 references and provides an equal number of indexing terms in the SCI and ISR.

Many years ago in CC® I published a piece entitled, "Who are the Information Scientists?".[12] I said then that in the future it would be more and more difficult to distinguish (ordinary) laboratory scientists from information specialists, as we then knew them. This is one of my few correct predictions. I think the evidence is quite clear. Today we have in the ACS not only a Division of Chemical Information, but also a Division of Computers in Chemistry. And it is not surprising that the programs of these two divisions overlap significantly. Nor is it any more surprising to find further overlap here in New Orleans. Consider the program in the Division of Physical Chemistry concerning computer analysis of reaction mechanisms.

One can argue that it is primarily the impact of the computer that has accelerated the transition of the laboratory chemist into the information chemist. Sociological and behavioral changes of this kind are not easy to measure. However, in addition to computer consciousness I believe the average working scientist today is far more information conscious than his counterpart 25 years ago.

We used to have long discussions about the presumed importance of information retrieval. Many argued it was a waste of time and actually stifled creativity. The research administrator who encourages his staff to ignore the literature today does so at his organization's economic peril. One doesn't hear the old song about the literature discouraging creativity quite so often any more, but the melody lingers on. The evidence is clear that our most creative scientists are those who use and help create the literature that others would like to avoid. At one time scientists had a legitimate excuse to ignore the literature. But today they have a large variety of mechanisms to help them keep up. It is now much easier to avoid the worst possible kind of duplication so prevalent just 20 years ago. I don't know how often one can cite examples of unwitting duplication of effort. It would be interesting for NSF to support a repetition of John Martyn's survey to see if the situation has improved or deteriorated.[13]

I think by now I should have made Pete Sorter happy. He can count on being employable for at least another ten years. Even Herman Skolnik won't be replaced by a computer, and somehow Chemical Abstracts will survive the synopsis journals designed to eliminate secondary services. With your future secure, and without stirring up any emotions, I've managed to get this far without really saying too much. But let me pursue my theme, "For the Man Who Has Everything", a little further.

In publishing Citation Classics we have learned from many authors that their most cited work is not necessarily the work they consider to be their most significant contributions. Sometimes we pay tribute to those accomplishments which have a certain intellectual elegance. But they are not necessarily those that have had the greatest social or scientific impact. In my opinion, that is why the method paper is regarded in less esteem than it ought to be. Let me carry this notion a bit further in a more personal way. There is a certain irony in my receipt of the Skolnik award when you consider the interesting paper Herman published concerning milestones in chemical information science.[14] In his very comprehensive review of milestones since 1943, he most graciously mentioned *Index Chemicus®*, *Rotaform Index®*, and *Science Citation Index*. I used the word "graciously" because Herman has never really used any of these tools in his shop but respects them as intellectual achievements.

However, it is most significant to me that Herman *didn't* mention *Current Contents*, which I am sure he also never uses. Nevertheless, thousands of scientists throughout the world, who couldn't care less about information science, consider *Current Contents* a milestone of far greater significance than *Index Chemicus* or *SCI*. You see, my friends, beauty is in the eyes of the beholder. *CC* is a methodology so simple that I have never been able to publish a paper about it.

But it was as editor and publisher of *Current Contents* that I was invited three years ago to publish an article in the French equivalent of *Scientific American—La Recherche*. The editor of that journal knew how important *Current Contents* had been in calling his new journal to the attention of the world scientific community. He also knew my views on English as the "lingua franca" of science.[15] So I published an article in *La Recherche* entitled "Is French Science Too Provincial?"[16] For those of you who don't have time to read it in French, the English version of this article was published in *Current Contents*.[17] In this article I provide rather conclusive data showing that French language journals today have very little impact on international science. Even more interesting, I showed that even French scientists do not cite French journals very much.

The data confirmed what a large number of French scientists knew better than I: the quality of the French scientific press had declined significantly in the past three decades. The publication of this article sent reverberations throughout the French scientific community. My article prompted a critical response from no less than a former Prime Minister of France.[18] I didn't realize at the time that a large number of French language journals receive government subsidies. Possibly as a response to my article, and as a result of subsequent deliberations, the French National Center for Scientific Research (CNRS), the equivalent to NSF, decided to launch a new journal in chemistry called *Nouveau Journal de Chimie*. Although the new journal is published primarily in English, it is understandable that CNRS was not so bold as to give this journal an English title.

The linguistic issue in France, as in Canada and Belgium, is politically sensitive. Having recommended the use of English by French scientists, I was falsely accused of cultural imperialism. In fact, I was trying to do a service to the French scientific community. It deserves better treatment for its efforts. Perhaps the most remarkable outcome of this incident is illustrated by the advertisement that appeared in a recent issue of *La Recherche*. Even if you don't read French, I think you will comprehend the simple message (see Figure 1).

Since *Nouveau Journal de Chimie* is probably a response to my article, this may be the first time in the history of science that a new journal was started in response to a challenge from an individual. I wouldn't be categorical about this claim because jour-

Figure 1. Advertisement announcing new French chemical journal with articles published in English.

471

nals have been founded for a variety of reasons. It may well be that some other journal found its beginning in a similar way. At least it illustrates that an individual is not *entirely* powerless in this world. But we rarely have the opportunity to see the results of our efforts so directly and so quickly.

I have a feeling that something similar is going to happen in Italy. I recently prepared some similar data regarding Italian journals.[19] Subsequently, I participated in a conference of Italian Scientific Editors in Rome.[20] I would not be surprised if we see the establishment one day soon of a new *Italian Journal of Science* published in English on a prompt publication schedule. Consider that there are over 500 biomedical journals published in Italy, 95% of which are rarely consulted by anyone.

The importance of the role played by *Current Contents* in these transformations is indicated by the fact that the editor of *Nouveau Journal de Chimie* was quite upset that it was not immediately covered in CC. He knows his journal will get immediate recognition from the French scientific community when it is listed in CC. It is an awesome responsibility to realize that so many newer journals are dependent upon CC for survival. It is also true that many of the most important journals of the world would survive quite well without us. But even for established publishers the difference of 5 to 10% in revenue or profit performance can make or break a journal. Consider that *Current Contents* is directly or indirectly responsible for 50 to 80% of the reprint requests received by many authors. Publishers often derive that needed extra margin of profit from the sale of reprints. The number of photocopies made in response to CC listings is miniscule when compared to reprint requests. For every tear sheet or photocopy we provide, 50 to 100 reprint requests are sent out by readers. In fact, we sell over 1,000,000 Request-A-Print® Cards per year! And now that a payment clearinghouse will be established, the real cost of photocopying will, I believe, provide greater incentives for using reprints.

In closing, I not only want to thank you for this award, but also want to mention a few people who were very important in my professional life—especially here in the ACS. Though we never actually worked together, I met Jim Perry at the 1951 ACS meeting in New York. I think that was the Diamond Jubilee meeting. Somehow I walked in there and heard a few papers and knew that I was in the right place. I walked up to him and asked: "How does one get a job in this racket?" Later on he came to my house in the Bronx and ate my mother's cooking. Still later, he introduced me to Sanford V. Larkey at Johns Hopkins. Then, at the Welch Library, I met most of the leaders of the profession. This was a lucky opportunity for a young upstart. But most of the people I met had been upstarts at one time themselves; these included Ralph Shaw, Mort Taube, and Pete Luhn.

Through the Welch project I met E.J. Crane and Charles Bernier. At the CBCC I met Karl Heumann and Isaac Welt. I also first met Ted Herdgen in Baltimore. Later he hired me as a consultant to Smith Kline & French Co. (now Smithkline Corp.) and became one of my closest friends; the first issue of *Index Chemicus* was dedicated to his memory. I was always encouraged by Madeline Berry, Hannah Friedenstein, Aaron Addelston, Al Gelberg, Bill Longenecker, and other Division members too numerous to mention. I was going to mention more names but as I reviewed some old correspondence, I realized how fallible my memory is. For example, if I were to name one member of the CNA I would have to name a dozen or more. But certainly Bill Wiswesser and Al Smith have played a key role in the development and use of WLN by ISI. So did Howard Bonnett.

As many of you know, the *Index Chemicus* was started with the support of approximately twelve drug companies. Joe Clark of Lederle, Bill Sullivan of Hoffman-La Roche, and Alex Moore of Parke-Davis were especially helpful to me. Others who helped IC® were Walt Southern of Abbott Labs., Howard Nutting of Dow, George McCarthy of Geigy, Charles Rice at Lilly, Evelyn Armstrong and Bob Harte at Merck, Rita Goodemote at Schering, Max Gordon at Smithkline, Doug Remsen at Squibb, Fred Bassett of Upjohn, Eliot Steinberg and Lee Starker at Warner-Lambert, and Ernie Hyde of Imperial Chemical Industries.

My own co-workers at ISI, including Gaby Revesz, Bonnie Lawlor, and Charlie Granito, have made it possible for some of these ideas to persevere in the face of tremendous odds. Not the least of my friends have come from the ranks of CA. I will not embarrass those who still work there by naming them. But for the man who has everything, it is perhaps most gratifying of all to have respected competitors as friends.

REFERENCES

1. **Merton R K.** The Matthew effect in science: the reward and communications systems of science are considered. *Science* 199:55, 1968.
2. **Garfield E.** Citation analyses, mechanical translation of chemical nomenclature, and the macrostructure of science. *J. Chem. Inform. Comput. Sci.* 15:153, 1975.
3. --------------. Proposal for a new profession: scientific reviewer.
   Current Contents (14):5-8, 4 April 1977.
4. **Brooks H.** U.S. science and technology: a prescription for 'health'. *Science* 195:536, 1977.
5. **Garfield E.** Putting our money where our needs are.
   Bull. Amer. Soc. Inform. Sci. 1:10, 32, 1974.
6. --------------. Significant journals of science. *Nature* 264:609, 1976.
7. **Mazella A.** Bibliometric study of the review literature. Final report to the National Science Foundation on Grant No. DSI-76-0534. Philadelphia: Institute for Scientific Information, 1977.
8. **Woodard A M.** Review literature: characteristics, sources and output in 1972.
   ASLIB Proc. 26:367, 1974.
9. **Cole J & Cole S.** The Ortega hypothesis. *Science* 178:368, 1972.
10. **Turner S T & Chubin D.** Another appraisal of Ortega, the Coles, and science policy: the Ecclesiastes hypothesis. *Soc. Sci. Inform.* 15:657, 1976.
11. **Garfield E.** Introducing Citation Classics: the human side of scientific reports.
    Current Contents (1):5-6, 3 January 1977.
12. --------------. Who are the information scientists? *Current Contents* (5):32, 7 August 1962.*
13. **Martyn J.** Unintentional duplication of research. *New Sci.* 21:388, 1964.
14. **Skolnik H.** Milestones in chemical information science.
    J. Chem. Inform. Comput. Sci. 16:187, 1976.
15. **Garfield E.** Let's erect a new Tower of Babel. *Current Contents* (45):5-7, 6 November 1974.*
16. --------------. La science francaise est-elle si provinciale? (Is French science too provincial?).
    Recherche 7:757-60, 1976.
17. --------------. Le nouveau défi américain I. *Current Contents* (15):5-11, 11 April 1977.
18. **Debre M.** La langue francaise et la science universelle (The French language and universal science). *Recherche* 7:956, 1976.
19. **Garfield E.** Highly cited articles. 33. Articles from Italian journals and from Italian laboratories. *Current Contents* (6):5-12, 7 February 1977.
20. --------------. Can Italian biomedical journals survive? Presented at the First Conference of the Biomedical Press in Italy. Rome, 16 February 1976.

*Reprinted in: **Garfield E.** *Essays of an information scientist.* Philadelphia: ISI Press, 1977.
2 vols.

CURRENT COMMENTS

National Science Foundation Stimulates Sociometric, Science Policy Studies Through Innovative Contract With ISI

Number 17, April 24, 1978

By now it is not particularly newsworthy when a government agency uses the *Science Citation Index®* data base on magnetic tape to provide computer-assisted literature search services. However, it *is* news when a US government agency makes the data base available to stimulate science policy and other sociometric studies.

Under a recent agreement with ISI ® the National Science Foundation is making the *SCI®* data base available to its staff, contractors, and grantees for use in such bibliometrically based studies. NSF hopes this program will encourage researchers to carry out more studies designed to gain insight into scientific communication and the history and sociology of science. Previous studies have shown that bibliometric data and citation analyses can provide indicators of science activity, productivity, and impact.

The main feature of the agreement is that persons authorized by NSF can use the data base without paying an access fee. Normally, this fee is $5,000 for each year of data used and must be paid in addition to charges for special programming and computer time. Now, only the latter charges must be paid by the researcher.

Scholars have used bibliometric data to study science activities for over half a century. But the literature has become so large that simple studies as well as large-scale data analyses are beyond the financial resources of most researchers. The NSF contract puts these studies once again within the reach of many by making accessible the *SCI* file of machine-readable bibliographic descriptions of over 5 million source articles published from 1961 through 1977. Also included are the nearly 50 million reference citations which these source articles contain.

The file enables you to perform an infinite variety of analyses. Chronological comparisons, ranked lists, frequency distributions, growth and decay studies, impact measurements, etc., are just a few that come to mind. More specifically, you could determine how many articles were published in specified languages in one or more categories of journals. Word or phrase frequency studies are possible, as is quantification of the growth of multi-authored papers in a specific field.

A large variety of citation studies is also possible. Literally hundreds of them have already been done. For example, one study compared citation frequencies of groups which had received funding with those of groups which had not in order to test the effectiveness of an NSF program.[1] In another study, citation analyses of NSF grantees and of those who did not receive grants helped to determine the efficacy of the NSF's peer review system.[2] Citation patterns were also studied as part of a project to identify the role of the review literature in science.[3]

NSF has also supported research on co-citation frequency (how often two documents are cited together). "Clusters" of co-cited papers identify new and emerging scientific specialties quite rapidly.[4] For this reason, science policy makers can use "cluster maps" to obtain indications of science activity—where it exists and where it doesn't. In this way funds may be allocated to stimulate needed research or sustain it in breakthrough areas. Historians and sociologists of science can use these maps to trace the growth and decline of specific fields or specialties.

This unique agreement could be especially useful to information scientists. With the very recent inception of NSF's new Division of Information Science & Technology, it is likely that more information scientists will be funded for basic research efforts.[5,6] Bibliometric data are essential for testing basic "laws" in information science.

While sociologists and information scientists in the US may be the most obvious users of this data base, they are by no means the only ones who could use the bibliometric data in the *SCI* file. *Current Contents®* readers include editors and editorial board members of thousands of journals. They should use this unique opportunity to apply for NSF research grants to pinpoint important new trends in the disciplines their journals serve. They could also study citation data to help evaluate journal performance, to learn which other journals cite theirs most often.

Scientists outside the United States who are interested in this program should contact the appropriate agencies in their country. We have negotiated similar agreements in other countries but nothing on such an extensive scale as the NSF contract.

If you are in the US and you think that the *SCI* data base would be helpful in a study you are planning, you should include the computer-time costs as line items in your budget proposal to NSF. You can determine the cost and whether special programming is needed by contacting Dr. Morton Malin, Vice President, Professional Relations and Contract Research, at 800-523-1850. You can also write to him at 325 Chestnut St., Philadelphia, PA. 19106, USA.

REFERENCES

1. **Wilson M K.** The top 20 and the rest: big chemistry and little funding. *Annu. Rev. Phys. Chem.* 26:1-16, 1975.
2. **Cole S, Rubin L & Cole J R.** Peer review and the support of science. *Sci. Amer.* 237:34-41, October 1977.
3. **Mazella A.** Bibliometric study of the review literature. Final Report to the National Science Foundation on Grant No. DS1-76-0534. Philadelphia: Institute for Scientific Information, 1977. 94 p.
4. **Garfield E.** ISI is studying the structure of science through co-citation analysis. *Current Contents* (7):5-6, 13 February 1974. (Reprinted in: *Essays of an information scientist.* Philadelphia: ISI Press, 1977. Vol. 2, p. 26-31.)
5. ------------. Information science and technology have come of age—organizational names should show it. *Current Contents* (12):5-8, 20 March 1978.
6. **Lepkowski W.** NSF revamps science information office. *Chem. Eng. News* 56(11):18-9, 13 March 1978.

CURRENT COMMENTS

Social Sciences Information—A Vital Link Between the Law and Our Evolving Society

Number 18, May 1, 1978

I have often mentioned the cultural gap between the sciences and the arts.[1-2] Even within the sciences there are gaps—between the clinical practitioner and the researcher and between the teacher and the researcher. Lawyers also live in their own little world. (If you consider that there are over a million of them around the globe, it may not be so little after all.) As a result lawyers are isolated from a resource of potential value: social sciences information.

It is the pioneers of law that we remember, and in most instances the pioneers were willing to listen to scholars.

In 1916, Supreme Court Justice Louis Brandeis wrote, "A lawyer who has not studied economics and sociology is very apt to become a public enemy."[3] His statement may have been an exaggeration. But his firm belief in the value of social sciences information to lawyers was manifested in his work. As early as 1908 he cited studies by social scientists on the deleterious effects of excessively long working hours on the health of women.[4] He was arguing to uphold an Oregon law which made it a misdemeanor to employ women in factories for more than 10 hours a day.

Some people (and especially lawyers) question the need for social sciences information in the practice of law. They say that the job of the attorney is simply to "argue the law"—to base cases on the principle of *stare decisis,* of following the legal precedents which spell out the "letter of the law." However, this is not always possible. On the frontiers of law—as in cases involving civil rights, environmental protection, data banks and individual privacy—there are few if any earlier cases to cite. In these areas the law is not clearly delineated and legal precedent will be established by the decisions made. In these situations it may be necessary to support an argument with an academic treatise such as an article in a sociology journal.

For example, US Public Law 94-142 states that mentally-retarded, brain-damaged, and gifted children must receive an education "appropriate" to their needs. But what is an "appropriate" education for a brain-damaged child? A lawyer bringing suit on behalf of such a child must become an "instant expert" on the psychological and educational issues involved. To argue the client's interests persuasively, he or she must be familiar with the "state of the art"; that is, the literature.

The vital importance of social sciences information was demonstrated in one of the most widely discussed cases of this century—*Brown* v *Board of Education of Topeka* (1954). This unanimous opinion of the Supreme Court outlawed racial segregation in public schools. Chief Justice Earl Warren wrote that to separate children "from others of similar age

---

Figure 1. The six social sciences works cited in Footnote Eleven of the Supreme Court opinion in *Brown* v *Board of Education of Topeka* (1954).

---

1. **Clark K B.** Effect of prejudice and discrimination on personality development. *Personality in the making: the fact finding report of the Mid-Century White House Conference on Children and Youth, 1950.* (Witmer H L & Kotinsky R, eds.) New York: Harper & Brothers, 1952, p. 135-58.

2. **Deutscher M, Chein I & Sadigur N.** The psychological effects of enforced segregation: a survey of social science opinion. *J. Psychol.* 26:259-87, 1948.

3. **Chein I.** What are the psychological effects of segregation under conditions of equal facilities? *Int. J. Opinion & Attitude Res.* 3:229-34, 1949.

4. **Brameld T.** Education costs. *Discrimination and National Welfare: a series of addresses and discussions.* (MacIver R M, ed.) New York: Institute for Religious & Social Studies, Jewish Theological Seminary of America, 1949, p. 44-8.

5. **Frazier E F.** *The Negro in the United States.* New York: Macmillan, 1949, p. 674-81.

6. **Myrdal G.** *An American dilemma, the Negro problem and modern democracy.* New York: Harper and Brothers, 1944. 2 vols.

and qualifications solely because of their race generates a feeling of inferiority as to their status in the community that may affect their hearts and minds in a way unlikely ever to be undone."[5] The famous "Footnote Eleven" that supported this statement cited six social science works which dealt with the psychology and sociology of black Americans. The works cited are listed in Figure 1.

Social sciences information can also be used by attorneys for other purposes than as arguments to support legal briefs. Trial lawyers, for instance, can use the conclusions of many psychology articles which examine the reactions of various social groups to the sex, race, social status, or physical attractiveness of a defendant. By selecting jurors more likely to favor a particular type of defendant, the lawyer can influence the outcome of a case.

Thomas E. Salisbury of the Oklahoma firm, R.M. Mook, drew on results from such studies to provide advice to attorneys on jury selection:

> Since the general public image of a criminal is male, the female defendant is an anomaly within the criminal justice system.... Women are more punitive toward other women than are men; salesmen and office workers are less punitive toward women than are other occupational groups; people in lower income groups, making less than $5,000, tend to be more punitive toward women than other income groups; people of upper middle class income, making between $10,000 and $15,000, are more likely to be punitive toward an unmarried defendant than other income groups. Defense counsel could easily elicit this type of information during voir dire [the screening of jurors] and rank prospective jurors accordingly....
> If the defendant is black, defense counsel should attempt to impanel a jury which is generally young, above-average occupational status, above-average income, well-educated, politically liberal, not identified with organized religion or regular church attendance, and single....
> When the defendant is poor, defense counsel should follow the same principles as when the defendant is black, except that persons of high income and education should be excluded from the jury....[6]

Lawyers can also use social sciences information in dealing with clients. People involved in law suits are usually under stress.[7] Just as a doctor's patient is not merely a collection of symptoms, the legal client is not just a bundle of legalities. Like doctors, lawyers need to "treat" the "whole client."[8]

Since it is fairly obvious that social sciences information is critical to attorneys and judges, why don't they use it more often? The answer lies, I think, in the legal education system. Unlike their medical or scientific counterparts, most law schools make courses in legal research mandatory. Law students learn how to search the literature. Such legal reference tools as *Shepard's Citations, LEXIS* (the on-line legal data base), *Wilson's Guide to Legal Periodicals,* and *West Digest System* are essential tools of the trade. Law students also traditionally serve as clerks for lawyers or judges. Legal research is a significant part of clerking. Consequently, most young attorneys know from firsthand experience the reference tools of the profession.

However, there is one weakness in this system. This is the lack of exposure to research tools which are not specifically designed for legal work. The result is that many legal researchers are like chemists who never got beyond *Beilstein* or psychologists who think a search of *Psychological Abstracts* is all one needs. This situation is of course aggravated by the fragmentation of university library systems. For example, the *Social Sciences Citation Index*™, like other extralegal reference tools, is found in relatively few law school libraries. But often it is in another library on campus where it remains unknown to law students.

It is ironic that lawyers, the one professional group most familiar with the citation indexing concept, are almost totally ignorant of the *SSCI*™. Both *Shepard's Law Review Citations* and the *SSCI* cover a large number of legal periodicals. However, the *SSCI* also covers the interface between the social sciences and the law.

At the Georgetown University Law Center Library, which subscribes to the *SSCI*, reference librarian Bill Maxon reports, "It is not being used as much as it should be." He thinks this may be because the index is a relatively new tool and students are unfamiliar with it. However, instruction in using the *SSCI* will be included in the first-year course in legal research at Georgetown this year. But in most instances lawyers are still limited in their exposure to non-legal sources.

For example, though we cover most important legal journals in *Current Contents*® */Social & Behavioral Sciences,* very few professors of law make use of this resource. *CC*® should be of special value to them. Not only would it permit them to locate articles on particular topics appearing in these legal journals, it would also give them needed exposure to the ideas reported in the non-legal press. *CC/S&BS* provides a broad perspective on sociology, psychology, economics, and the interfaces between science and law such as forensic science.

According to Philip Selznick, "Legal reasoning cannot but accept the authority of scientifically validated conclusions regarding the nature of man and his institutions. Therefore, inevitably, sociology and every other social science must have a part in the legal order."9

Social sciences information is no substitute for a well-prepared argument based on the law. In some cases it merely demonstrates the erudition of the attorneys involved and may even alienate less literate judges. But in cases where its introduction is appropriate, social sciences information is essential for lawyers and judges alike. In an age of accelerating social change, we can expect and should demand greater use of relevant social sciences information by the legal profession. By the same token all of us should have greater access to legal information. If an educated patient can search *Medline* or *Scisearch*® for his or her doctor, so can the knowledgeable client search *LEXIS* or information banks of the social sciences like *Social Scisearch* ® to "help" his or her attorney. This is one of the ways in which we as clients can make up for the deficiencies of the legal and medical education systems. In this way we can help practitioners bridge the gaps that seem to exist everywhere between all fields of specialization.

REFERENCES

1. **Garfield E.** Will ISI's *Arts & Humanities Citation Index* revolutionize scholarship? *Current Contents* (32):5-9, 8 August 1977.
2. --------------. ISI is now helping to bridge the three (not two) cultures. *Current Contents* (10):5-10, 6 March 1978.
3. **Brandeis L D.** The living law. *Ill. Law Rev.* 10:461-71, 1916.
4. 208 US 412 (1908).
5. 347 US 483 (1954), p. 494-5.
6. **Salisbury T E.** Forensic sociology and psychology: new tools for the defense attorney. *Univ. Tulsa Law J.* 12:274-92, 1976.
7. **Foster L M.** Training lawyers in behavioral science and its applications. *J. Psychiat. Law* 4:403-13, 1976.
8. **Garfield E.** Treating the whole person: the use of social sciences information in medical libraries. *Current Contents* (22):5-8, 30 May 1977.
9. **Selznick P.** The sociology of law. *Law and the Behavioral Sciences.* (Friedman L M & Macaulay S, eds.) New York: The Bobbs-Merrill Company, 1969. 1059 p.

CURRENT COMMENTS

In Recognition of Journals
Which Prove that Change *Is* Possible

Number 19, May 8, 1978

I have often used this space to exhort journal publishers and editors to make their journals meet international standards of excellence.[1-2] And, of course, their tables of contents are particularly important to *Current Contents®*. I'd now like to acknowledge here a group of journals that have, in one way or another, made significant changes. By doing so, they have not only made the production of *Current Contents* a little easier. They have also facilitated scientific communication. If nothing else, their own readers have benefited.

Current Contents is intentionally *designed* to be simple. This simplicity hides the fact that far more is involved in producing *Current Contents* than photographing tables of contents. For example, a large staff of commercial artists enhances every contents page in several ways. They add that line of information just below the journal title which tells you the languages used in its articles and abstracts. The artists also obtain special, computer-composed volume, issue number, and date elements for each

issue, and place this information in the same conspicuous location for all journals. Our "paste-up" specialists also add the ISI® accession number which appears in an oval to the left of the journal title. These numbers greatly simplify the ordering of tearsheets through our *OATS®* service and the retrieval of journals from our stacks.

I have great admiration for the skill involved in the variety of "cut and paste" tasks our artists perform. They routinely excise extralarge mastheads, extensive statements of journal sponsorship, other extraneous text, and excess white space to make better use of the space in *Current Contents*. It is always amazing to me how they manage to keep the lines of information evenly spaced.

However, there are many journals whose formats present problems that defy remedy even by extensive graphic rearrangement. These contents pages must be completely recomposed. Naturally this extra production step adds to our costs and may delay coverage by a week or more. In some cases recomposition is done manually on a small photocomposition machine. Most often, however, the contents page is generated by one of several computer programs which extracts the information from the master ISI data base, and then activates a phototypesetter. Contents pages must be reset for many reasons. The following categories cover the most commonly encountered problems.

Non-English Text. Almost every contents page in *Current Contents* appears completely in English—no matter what its original language. Most publishers now realize that an English contents page is essential if non-English language journals are to be noted by our readers. Thus it is no longer a rarity to see two contents pages in each issue—one in English and the other in the language of the journal. Other publishers send us translations of their contents pages for use in *Current Contents* even though they do not actually publish them in their journals. But some journals do not cooperate. When we have to translate the titles in specialized journals, significant delays can occur. We need time not only for the translation but also to photocompose the contents page.

Oversized Formats. Since the basic printing process involved is "photo-offset," we must photograph each contents page. If the page's column width is too wide in relation to the type size, then photoreduction produces a final type size that is too small to be legible in *CC*. I cannot understand why

so many journals fail to realize that such formats are hard to scan even in the original version.

Undersized Format. For similar reasons, if the type size of the original is too small, we may have to enlarge it. This can only be done if the column width is appropriate.

Poor Print Quality. Some printers do not exercise proper quality control. For example, if the printer has applied too much ink, it smears. If too little, then the letters may not be legible. Poor camera work can also result in a bad offset negative. Or smearing may occur in the bindery, especially if the pages have not been properly dried. Smears may also occur through mishandling in the post office.

Use of Color. When a journal prints the contents page in black on dark-colored (red, orange, etc.) paper or tinted background, the camera work becomes difficult. Since we photograph several pages at a time, it is not practical to use color filters. Text printed on pastel-colored paper may also require additional time and labor since we now microfilm each page by a special photographic technique. And the use of non-black inks for the text itself may present special problems even though the paper is white. Obviously, this depends upon the spectral response of the film we are using.

Omission of Important Information. Some journals actually omit from their contents pages such essential elements as the names of authors or the titles of some of the substantive items which appear in

Figure 1. Journals in which improvements to tables of contents in 1977-78 eliminated need for recomposition prior to publication in *Current Contents.* Information is presented in the following sequence: name of journal (in boldface type); changes made; name of publisher (in italics).

AAPG Bulletin—American Association of Petroleum Geologists: Changed color.
American Association of Petroleum Geologists

Acustica: Added separate English contents page.
S. Hirzel Verlag

American Psychologist: Changed format.
American Psychological Association

Angewandte Informatik: Changed format.
Friedrich Vieweg & Son

Annales de l'Anésthesiologie Francaise: Enlarged type size for English contents page.
Association des Anesthésiologistes Francais

Annals of Otology, Rhinology and Laryngology: Changed format.
Annals Publishing Co.

Archives Francaises de Pédiatrie: Providing English contents page.
Doin Editeurs

Archiv für Elektrotechnik: Added English contents page.
Springer Verlag

Archiv für Geflügelkunde: Added English contents page.
Verlag Eugen Ulmer

Arizona Medicine: Added authors to contents page.
Arizona Medical Association

Berichte der Bunsen Gesellschaft für Physikalische Chemie: Changed format.
Verlag Chemie International

Botaniska Notiser: Changed color.
Liberlaeromedel

Bulletin d'Ecologie: Providing English contents page.
Masson Editeur

Bulletin de l'Académie Vétérinaire de France: Added English contents page.
Académie Vétérinaire de France

Bulletin of the British Psychological Society: Changed color.
British Psychological Society

Clinical Chemistry: Changed format.
American Association of Clinical Chemists

Contributions to Mineralogy and Petrology: Changed color.
Springer Verlag

Differentiation: Changed color.
Springer Verlag

Drug Therapy: Changed format.
Biomedical Information Corp.

European Journal of Cardiology: Changed format.
Elsevier/North Holland Biomedical Press

Herz Kreislauf: Providing advance proof in English.
Verlag Gerhard Witzstrock GmbH

Indian Journal of Chest Diseases & Allied Sciences: Improved print quality.
Indian Association for Chest Diseases

Ingenieur Archiv: Added English contents page.
Springer Verlag

Figure 1 (continued). Journals that improved their contents pages in 1977-78.

Innere Medizin: Providing advance proof in English.
Verlag Gerhard Witzstrock GmbH

International Journal of Clinical Pharmacology and Biopharmacy: Changed format.
Urban & Schwarzenberg

Journal for the Theory of Social Behaviour: Added separate black and white contents page.
Basil Blackwell & Mott

Journal of Chemical Engineering of Japan: Improved print quality.
Society of Chemical Engineers—Japan

Journal of Clinical Chemistry and Clinical Biochemistry: Added English contents page.
Walter de Gruyter & Co.

Journal of Embryology and Experimental Morphology: Added separate black and white contents page.
Cambridge University Press

Journal of Personality Assessment: Changed color.
Society for Personality Assessment, Inc.

Journal of the American College Health Association: Changed format.
American College Health Association

Khimiya Prirodnykh Soedinenii: Added English contents page.
Akademiya Nauk Uzbekskoi S.S.R.

Laboratory Animals: Eliminated color.
Laboratory Animals Ltd.

Leber Magen Darm: Providing proof in English.
Verlag Gerhard Witzstrock GmbH

Local Government Studies: Changed color.
Charles Knight & Co. Ltd.

Marine Technology Society Journal: Changed format.
Marine Technology Society

Medical Group Management: Eliminated color.
Medical Group Management Association

Medicina—Buenos Aires: Added English contents page.
Instituto de Investigaciones Medicas

Medikon: Added English contents page.
European Press

Mikroskopie: Added separate English contents page.
Verlag Georg Fromme & Co.

Monatsschrift für Brauerei: Changed format.
Versuchs und Lehranstalt für Brauerei, Berlin

NEC (Nippon Electric Company) Research & Development: Changed format.
Nippon Electric Co. Ltd.

Operative Dentistry: Providing advance black and white proof.
University of Washington

Oxford Bulletin of Economics and Statistics: Changed color.
Basil Blackwell & Mott

Phytopathology: Providing specially formatted contents page.
American Phytopathological Society

Photosynthetica: Eliminated addresses on contents page.
Publishing House of the Czechoslovak Academy of Sciences

Plastics and Rubber International: Changed format.
Plastics Institute

Postgraduate Medicine: Changed format.
McGraw-Hill

Quarterly Journal of Mathematics: Changed color.
Oxford University Press

Revista Brasileira de Medicina: Changed format.
Editora Medica Brasileira, Ltd.

Social Behavior and Personality: Improved print quality.
Society for Personality Research

Stärke: Added English contents page.
Verlag Chemie International

Stroke: Changed format.
American Heart Association

Texas Agricultural Progress: Added authors to contents page.
Texas Agricultural Experiment Station

Thrombosis Research: Changed format.
Pergamon Press

Wärme und Stoffübertragung: Added English contents page.
Springer Verlag

Werkstoffe und Korrosion: Added English contents page.
Verlag Chemie International

World Oil: Added authors to contents page.
Gulf Publishing Co.

Zeitschrift für Ernährungswissenschaft: Providing English contents page.
Dr. Dietrich Steinkopff Verlag

Zeitschrift für Gerontologie: Added English contents page.
Dr. Dietrich Steinkopff Verlag

Zeitschrift für Kardiologie: Added English contents page.
Dr. Deitrich Steinkopff Verlag

Zeitschrift für Naturforschung Part A—Physik, Physikalische Chemie, Kosmophysik: Enlarged type size.
Verlag der Zeitschrift für Naturforschung

Zeitschrift für Naturforschung Part C—Biosciences: Enlarged type size.
Verlag der Zeitschrift für Naturforschung

Zeitschrift für Pflanzenkrankheiten und Pflanzenschutz: Added English contents page.
Verlag Eugen Ulmer

Zeitschrift für Rheumatologie: Added separate English contents page.
Dr. Dietrich Steinkopff Verlag

Zeitschrift für Sozialpsychologie: Providing advance proof in English.
Verlag Hans Huber

Zuchthygiene: Added English contents page.
Verlag Paul Parey

the issue. We must add this information if their contents pages are to be complete both for scanning and reference purposes. The titles of letters to the editor are also frequently omitted. It is ironic to me that library and information science journals are the worst offenders.

We constantly urge publishers to adopt formats that facilitate rapid scanning. I have often asked that the title be given priority over the author because the average reader is not familiar with the authors' names. Often, the first author is an unknown junior collaborator, especially when the senior author is well-known. The best solution in my opinion is to clearly separate these two elements of information. This can be done by using a two column format or by contrasting typefaces.

Each year we send hundreds of letters to publishers and editors requesting modifications. It is very gratifying to me that these efforts have had some concrete results. During the past year or so, many journals improved their contents pages in a way that enabled us to print them in *Current Contents* without recomposing them. The names of 67 journals appear in Figure 1, together with the names of their publishers and brief descriptions of the changes which were made. A few of these journals may not have made their alterations at our request, but whatever their motive I applaud them. Not included in the list are many journals that made changes in policies regarding the treatment and placement of author addresses[3] or the treatment of cited references.[4]

If you are affiliated with any of the journals listed—through editorial boards, membership in the sponsoring society, etc.—you should be pleased that the journal's management is showing concern for better international communication. A note of acknowledgement would be a good way to indicate your support for this kind of responsible leadership. On the other hand, many journals still have a long way to go and any help you can render will be appreciated not only by us but by every reader who benefits from the improvements.

REFERENCES

1. **Garfield E.** Reducing the noise level in scientific communication: how services from ISI aid journal editors and publishers. *Current Contents* (30):5-15, 25 July 1977.
2. ⸻. To indent or not to indent? How to improve journal contents page formats. *Current Contents* (43):5-8, 24 October 1977.
3. ⸻. An address on addresses. *Current Contents* (28):5, 14 July 1975. (Reprinted in: **Garfield E.** *Essays of an information scientist.* Philadelphia: ISI Press, 1977. Vol. 2, p. 310.)
4. ⸻. Style in cited references.*Current Contents* (11):5-12, 13 March 1978.

CURRENT COMMENTS

False Publication Dates and Other Rip-Offs

Number 20, May 15, 1978

It is remarkable how scientists and librarians tolerate publishing practices by scholarly journals which they would find intolerable or unacceptable in "popular" magazines. If you entered a subscription to the *New Yorker*, the *New Scientist* or any other magazine and discovered you would not receive your January issue until June, you would be outraged—and rightly so. Yet the scholarly community docilely accepts this treatment from many journal publishers. Numerous journals of sufficiently high scientific or scholarly value to be listed in *Current Contents®* are issued late as a matter of course.

Some of the culprits are not the least bit coy or shy about continuing this practice. Scan any issue of *CC®* and you will find examples. They are easy to recognize. Look for the qualifying statement: "This is the latest issue of this journal. The cover date does not correspond to the actual date of publication."

We don't add this blurb to every late issue. Hundreds of journals appear one or two numbers late. And occasionally journals are lost in the mail or unavoidably delayed despite the best efforts of the publisher. We reserve our qualifying statement for only those journals that consistently arrive three or more months after the "publication date" listed on their covers.

I've mentioned the problems associated with false publication dates before.[1-2] They are especially frustrating to us at ISI® because our reputation is based in part on timeliness. Journals that appear with misleading publication dates make it seem that *CC* is not current. In fact, most time lags you may notice are caused by the journals themselves. You can judge our almost obsessive concern for timeliness by observing our treatment of weekly journals with regular and timely schedules. We have an elaborate priority system, based on frequency and *known* importance, that assures prompt coverage of the most significant and timely material.

Our indexes, too, suffer when journals bear false publication dates. It is our policy to index all issues that actually arrive at ISI during the period on the index's cover. The *Science Citation Index®* *(SCI®)* quarterly for January to March 1977, for example, contains information on the journal issues that came into our offices during those months. Due to the vagaries of mail strikes, etc., you would expect a small percentage of the items in the index to bear 1976 publication dates. Unfortunately, a disproportionate number do so. The abundance of 1976 dates makes it seem as though our indexing is lagging behind when, in fact, it is not. Rather, it is the late journals that make it impossible to produce a perfectly complete calendar-year index.

But we are certainly not the only victims of these publishing practices. Subscribers are often led to believe by the time lapses that their copies were lost in the mail. They then begin a usually futile but time-consuming correspondence with the publishers or innocent subscription agents. Librarians and agents spend inordinate amounts of time claiming "missing" issues which in reality have never been published.

Intentionally or not, some publishers are devious about publication dates. They incompletely identify journal issues by putting nothing more specific than the volume, issue number, and year on the cover. This practice gives the impression of currency except in obvious cases, such as a monthly. If issue No.12 arrives in June, then something is obviously wrong.

Consider a horrible example we covered in *CC/Life Sciences* No. 8 (20 February 1978). This particular issue had "Vol. 10, No. 5, 1977" on its cover. If the journal is a monthly, then No. 5 is the May 1977 issue—nine months late. Or perhaps the journal is a bimonthly. Then No. 5 would be the September-October 1977 issue. Even if by chance it was the last issue for 1977, the journal arrived late because it was received in February, 1978.

Another deplorable practice followed by some publishers is their refusal to correlate a volume number with a calendar year. A volume should consist of journal issues published during a specified calendar year only. It should not begin in July and end the following June. Scholars and librarians should always be able to correlate a particular volume number with a single year.

The volume-year correspondence is a century-old tradition that should not be mindlessly ignored or changed at will. It provides the added degree of redundancy which reduces the possibility of errors and mitigates the effects of an error should one occur in writing a citation.[3]

Volume numbers were created to simplify the librarian's task in binding journals in "volumes" of manageable size. Without them libraries would never know when to bind a group of journal issues. In my experience the lack of volume numbers invariably results in oversized, unmanageable volumes such as those of the journals published by the Chemical Society (London) and other publishers who refuse to use a volume number. Why the publisher of *Tetrahedron Letters* follows this practice for that journal and not for its many other excellent journals is a policy I'll never understand.

However, non-correspondence of volume and year is most inexcusable in a new journal whose first issue is dated November or December. The publisher could easily have waited and started the journal and the volume in January.

I've urged journal publishers to correct these practices and I am gratified that some have made significant changes, especially in publication dates. However, most of the journals guilty of the practices I have mentioned would quickly find a way to publish on time if they were required to do so by law. It is remarkable what legislation can accomplish when voluntary action fails. Look, for ex-

ample, at the many journals which suddenly found it possible to place a unique bibliographic citation on the first page of each article when the new US Copyright Act took effect. For decades, most publishers ignored our pleas that each article's citation should be included on its first page. In that way one could cite a reprint without having to go to the original journal or an index for the necessary bibliographic information. But as soon as the new law permitted journal publishers to collect royalties for photocopies, dozens of publishers suddenly found it possible to include the citation so that payments could be made through the Copyright Clearance Center.[4] *Science* took the lead when it announced earlier this year that it was signing up with the Center. I only wish that *Science* could now find a way to number its editorial page!

Is there an alternative to legislative restrictions on journals which refuse to meet minimum international standards? Perhaps the American Association for the Advancement of Science and other professional societies should establish watchdog committees similar to science courts. Maybe publishers of journals should get together through STM (International Scientific, Technical, and Medical Publishers Association) and support the appointment of ombudsmen to regulate journal practices. Members could be rotated periodically and appointed by organizations of publishers, scholars, and librarians. Friendly persuasion can go a long way, but I feel that the clout represented by such a group could provide the regulation that is so desperately needed. The International Council of Scientific Unions (ICSU) could also play a constructive role, not unlike that of the International Standards Organization. But neither ICSU nor ISO has the influence that industry ombudsmen could exercise over recalcitrant journals.

Fortunately most of the journals we cover in the *SCI* or *CC* do adhere to high standards. But it is remarkable how many of the most significant journals of science, no less than the mediocre ones, refuse to modify archaic or idiosyncratic policies which work against the best interest of science. Many of these practices involve "trivialities" by any reasonable standard. But it is the accumulated burden of such trivialities which eventually leads to radical solutions unless wisdom prevails.

REFERENCES

1. **Garfield E.** Publication dates—realities or promises.
   Current Contents (34):4, 22 August 1967.*
2. --------------. ISI cares—do you? What can you do about improving scientific journals as a communications medium?
   Current Contents (49):5-6, 5 December 1973.*
3. --------------. Incomplete citations and other sources of bibliographic chaos.
   Current Contents (24):5, 17 June 1969.*
4. --------------. The new copyright clearance center and the doctrine of fair use.
   Current Contents (3):5-10, 16 January 1978.

*Reprinted in **Garfield E.** *Essays of an information scientist.* Philadelphia, ISI Press, 1977, 2 vols.

CURRENT COMMENTS

So Who's Perfect? Corrections and Additions to the 250 Most-Cited Authors List

Number 21, May 22, 1978

Last December we published three essays in *Current Contents*® on the 250 most-cited primary authors, 1961-1975.[1-3] Based on data from the *Science Citation Index*® for 1961-1975, the studies gave the number of citations each author received during that time period, and correlated high citation frequency with authors' ages, memberships in national academies, and Nobel prizes. A list of the authors' most-cited publications was also supplied.

As a number of readers have noted, several errors were made in the lists. After more than a little additional effort, we are now able to supply the corrections which appear in Figure 1.

Since there was no "logical" reason to cut off the original lists at 249 or 250 names, we have taken this opportunity to list (in Figure 2) those authors who were cited 4,000 or more times, but did not make the top 249. Were space unlimited, I would be pleased to go much further, since we know that most authors who have been highly cited have distinguished themselves in

one way or another. I hope we can expand these lists in the future.

The preparation of the original 250 most-cited authors list last year was in some ways a unique experience for us. Although we had done many citation studies before, most dealt with *journals* or *articles.* While these studies are not simple, they are easier to complete than ones that deal with *authors* and give as much information as we did. The reason for this is that much of the bibliographic information we need to deal with journals and articles is contained in our own files. Personal information on authors, such as birthdates and academy memberships, has to be obtained from other sources. This is one reason that even the few studies on authors we did in the past were limited. For the most part, we simply listed their names and their citation counts.

To obtain biographical information on our 250 authors, we checked two biographical dictionaries: *World Who's Who in Science* and *American Men and Women in Science (AMWS).* All but about 40 of the original 250 authors were

Figure 1: Corrections to the lists of the 250 most-cited authors, 1961-1975, which appeared in *Current Contents* Nos. 49, 50, and 51 in 1977.

1. *Birth and Death Dates*

Allison A C:
born in 1925, not 1928
Born M:
1882-1970 (death date omitted)
Cuatrecasas P:
born in 1936, not 1903
Hansen M:
born in 1901, not 1921
King R B: born in 1938, not 1903, making him the youngest author on the list

Reed L J:
1886-1956, not born in 1926
Seeger A:
born in 1927, not 1914
Slater J C:
born in 1900, not 1926
Weber K:
born in 1936, not 1916

2. *Academy Memberships*
  Many memberships in national science academies were originally omitted because the information was not available. However, many individuals and some academies have since alerted us to memberships that were missing. The following is not necessarily complete, but it does indicate the additional information we have received. Academy memberships which were not on the original list are in boldface type.

Name	National Academy	Name	National Academy
Arnon D I	**Sweden,** U.S.	Fisher R A	U.K., **U.S.***
Berson S A	U.S.*	Friedel J	France, **Sweden**
Burnet F M	**Australia, Sweden,** U.K., U.S.	Hodgkin A L	**Sweden,** U.K., U.S.
Carlsson A	**Sweden**	Ouchterlony O	**Sweden**
Chance B	**Sweden,** U.S.	Smith H W	U.S.*
Chandrasekhar S	**Sweden,** U.K., U.S.*	Sutherland E W	U.S.*
		Van Slyke D D	U.S.*
Cope A C	U.S.*	Van Vleck J H	France, **Sweden,** U.K., U.S.
Courant R	U.S.*		
DeRobertis E	**Argentina**	von Euler U S	**Sweden,** U.K., U.S.
Djerassi C	**Sweden,** U.S.		
Eccles J C	**Australia,** U.K., U.S.	Winstein S	U.S.*

*Former (deceased) members.

3. *Corrections to the list of most-cited research publications by the 250 authors*
  The publications given on the original list for L.S. Goodman and M. Hansen were, respectively, a textbook and a reference book, rather than reports of original research. The publication attributed to A.N. Nesmeyanov was a work by his brother. The most-cited research publications by these authors are:

Goodman L S, Grewal M S, Brown W C & Swinyard E A. Comparison of maximal seizures evoked by pentylenetetrazol (metrazol) and electroshock in mice, and their modification by anticonvulsants.
J. Pharmacol. Exp. Ther. **108**:168-97, 1953.
[This article was cited 62 times from 1961 to 1975.]

Figure 1. Corrections to the 250 most-cited authors list (continued).

Hansen M & Smith A L. Studies on the mechanism of oxidative phosphorylation. 7. Preparation of submitochondrial particle (ETP$_H$), which is capable of fully coupled oxidative phosphorylation.
Biochim. Biophys. Acta **81**:214-22, 1964.
[This article was cited 162 times from 1964 to 1975.]

Nesmeyanov A N & Sokolik R A. *Metody elemento-organicheskoi khimii. Bor, aliuminii, gallii, indii, talii. (Methods of elemento-organic chemistry. Boron, aluminum, gallium, indium and thallium.)* Moscow: Nauka, 1964.
[This publication was cited 101 times from 1964 to 1975.]

---

4. Replacements on the list

The names "E. Muller" and "S. Levine," which were each treated as one person on the original lists, proved to be homographs representing several persons, none of whom had received enough citations to make the list. M. Abramowitz was on the list because of a handbook, rather than reports of original research.

These three names have therefore been deleted from the list and replaced with the following authors:

Hill A V (1886-1977)
Total times cited 1961-1975: **4,032**
Yearly average: **269**
Times cited in 1974: **250**
Times cited in 1975: **255**
Prizes: **Nobel Prize in Physiology or Medicine, 1922**
Membership in national academies: **U.S., U.K.**
Most-cited publication:
Hill A V. The heat of shortening and the dynamic constants of muscle.
Proc. Roy. Soc. London Ser. B. **126**:138-95, 1938.
[This article was cited 517 times from 1961 to 1975.]

Rouser G (1923)
Total times cited 1961-1975: **4,032**
Yearly average: **269**
Times cited in 1974: **341**
Times cited in 1975: **243**
Most-cited publication:
Rouser G, Kritchevsky G, Heller D & Lieber E. Lipid composition of beef brain, beef liver & sea anemone. 2. Approaches to quantitative fractionation of complex lipid mixtures.
J. Amer. Oil Chem. Soc. **40**:425-54, 1963.
[This article was cited 749 times from 1963 to 1975.]

Wurtman R J (1936)
Total times cited 1961-1975: **4,030**
Yearly average: **269**
Times cited in 1974: **443**
Times cited in 1975: **385**
Most-cited publication:
Wurtman R J & Axelrod J. A sensitive and specific assay for the estimation of monoamine oxidase.
Biochem. Pharmacol. **12**:1439-41, 1963.
[This article was cited 283 times from 1963 to 1975.]

Figure 2. Authors who did not make the original 250 most-cited author lists, but who received 4,000 or more citations, 1961-1975.

Dauben W G (1919)
Total times cited 1961-1975: **4,028**
Yearly average: **269**
Times cited in 1974: **303**
Times cited in 1975: **324**
Membership in national academies: **U.S.**

Most-cited publication:
Dauben W G, Fonken G J & Noyce D S.
Stereochemistry of hydride reductions.
J. Amer. Chem. Soc. **78**:2579-82, 1956.
[This article was cited 224 times from 1961 to 1975.]

Dulbecco R (1914)
Total times cited 1961-1975: **4,005**
Yearly average: **267**
Times cited in 1974: **334**
Times cited in 1975: **282**
Membership in national academies:
U.S., U.K.

Most-cited publication:
Dulbecco R & Vogt M. Plaque formation and isolation of pure lines with polio-myelitis viruses.
J. Exp. Med. **99**:167-82, 1954.
[This article was cited 1,612 times from 1961 to 1975.]

Kunkel H G (1916)
Total times cited 1961-1975: **4,026**
Yearly average: **268**
Times cited in 1974: **198**
Times cited in 1975: **138**
Membership in national academies: **U.S.**

Most-cited publication:
Kunkel H G & Slater R J. Zone electro-phoresis in a starch supporting medium.
Proc. Soc. Exp. Biol. Med. **80**:42-4, 1952.
[This article was cited 164 times from 1961 to 1975.]

Leonard N J (1916)
Total times cited 1961-1975: **4,013**
Yearly average: **267**
Times cited in 1974: **227**
Times cited in 1975: **237**
Membership in national academies:
U.S., Poland

Most-cited publication:
Leonard N J & Johnson C R. Periodic oxidation of sulfides to sulfoxide: scope of the reaction.
J. Org. Chem. **27**:282, 1962. [This article was cited 125 times from 1962 to 1975.]

Nelson N (1910)
Total times cited 1961-1975: **4,016**
Yearly average: **267**
Times cited in 1974: **270**
Times cited in 1975: **307**

Most-cited publication:
Nelson N. Photometric adaptation of the Somogyi method for the determination of glucose.
J. Biol. Chem. **153**:375-80, 1944.
[This article was cited 3,265 times from 1961 to 1975.]

Porter K R (1912)
Total times cited 1961-1975: **4,003**
Yearly average: **266**
Times cited in 1974: **197**
Times cited in 1975: **288**
Membership in national academies: **U.S.**

Most-cited publication:
Porter K R & Palade G E. Studies in the endoplasmic reticulum. 3. Its form and distribution in striated muscle cells.
J. Biophys. Biochem. Cytol. **3**:269, 1957.
[This article was cited 313 times from 1961 to 1975.]

Smith I (1926)
Total times cited 1961-1975: **4,025**
Yearly average: **268**
Times cited in 1974: **258**
Times cited in 1975: **208**

Most-cited publication:
Smith I. Colour reactions to paper chro-matograms by a dipping technique.
Nature **171**:43-4, 1953. [This article was cited 183 times from 1961 to 1975.]

located in these sources. Getting information about these last 40 was more of a challenge. Since birth dates for authors of books are listed on the index cards in card catalogs, we consulted the National Union Catalog at a local university library and got correct birth dates for many of those who had published books. But we were still left with a number of authors for whom we had no personal data at all—people who were still just names on our printouts.

By consulting *ISI's Who is Publishing in Science*® or by obtaining journal articles by these remaining authors, we were able to find their addresses. The US National Academy of Sciences provided us with birth dates for its members, and we phoned other authors living in the US. Embassies were contacted for information on authors living outside the US.

Determining whether authors were members of national science academies was a difficult process. Although academy memberships were listed for the people we found in *World Who's Who in Science* and *AMWS*, the most recent editions of both these references are several years old. Thus, we had to write to national academies throughout the world for their current membership lists. Some academies responded, but many did not. So we were forced to omit many academy memberships.

After the essays had been published, we also discovered that we should not have limited our request to *current* membership information. For example, the list of members of the US National Academy of Sciences which we requested did not include deceased members. That's why we failed to mention that a few of the deceased authors on our list had been Academy members.

To create the bibliography containing the most-cited publication for each author, we first relied on the *SCI*® 's *Source Index*. However, since so many of the articles were published before 1961, we usually consulted the original journals in local libraries.

While we were gathering these data, we found that some of the most-cited publications were in fact textbooks or handbooks. This suggested, as we had expected from previous studies, that some people on the list had achieved high impact because of their work as editors. When a text or a handbook was the most-cited item, we checked the author's second most-cited publication. If this was a report of original research, it was used. If a person proved not to have written significant research articles, his or her name was deleted from the list.

Among the more difficult jobs in assembling the list of 250 authors was the identification of homographs (names that represent two or more authors). The *SCI* provides initials only, and not first names of cited authors. Works by two or more people with the same surname and initials are of necessity listed under one entry.

Homograph consciousness might best describe the care we gave to this problem. Whenever we consulted a biographical dictionary, we checked for other scientists with the same last name and similar initials. Academy membership lists were always checked for people with the same surnames. In a few cases, the highly cited publication was a tip-off. If the biographical index had given us information about a physicist, but the item was a biochemistry paper, we knew we probably had a homograph problem.

We then had to separate the citations—those belonging to physicist J. Doe, those received by biochemist J. Doe, etc. If none of these people had received enough citations to make the list, the name was dropped. We added the next person's name to the list and began to gather personal information about him or her.

When the lists were approaching completion, we sent them to seven eminent scientists for review. They made many helpful comments and alerted us to some errors at that stage of the work.

Despite all our efforts, a few mistakes remained undetected. I apologize for these errors, especially to those who were personally affected by any of them. Nevertheless, I hope it is obvious that the number of errors is relatively small if the full size and scope of the study is considered. In all, it took approximately 500 hours to complete the work.

We were breaking new ground with this study and in the process we learned a great deal. For example, we have developed a better procedure for identifying homographs. We have also learned the necessity of contacting authors to verify their own personal data.

In the next few months we will be publishing two very important citation studies. One will deal with frequently cited authors in science. For the first time, however, this study will not be restricted to "first" authors. There will also be a study of frequently cited social scientists.

We will continue to make every reasonable effort to assure accuracy in these studies. The magnitude of the work involved seems to ensure that a few factual errors will occur. But with your help we can keep these to a minimum. If you believe we have committed the most serious error of all—that of omitting a highly cited author—please contact me. We will provide the citation data for any single author. You can, of course, obtain this information yourself by consulting the *Science Citation Index* directly.

REFERENCES

1. **Garfield E.** The 250 most-cited primary authors, 1961-1975. 1. How the names were selected. *Current Contents* (49):5-15, 5 December 1977.
2. --------------. The 250 most-cited primary authors, 1961-1975. 2. The correlation between citedness, Nobel prizes, and academy memberships. *Current Contents* (50):5-15, 12 December 1977.
3. --------------. The 250 most-cited primary authors, 1961-1975. 3. Each author's most-cited publication. *Current Contents* (51):5-20, 19 December 1977.

CURRENT COMMENTS

Do French Scientists Who Publish Outside of France and/or in English Do Better Research?

Number 22, May 29, 1978

Last year I reported to you the *cause célèbre* which developed from my assertions about the poor quality of French journals and the need of French scientists to publish in English.[1-2]

A major question which could not be answered at that time concerned the impact of French-authored articles published outside of France—especially those in English. It had already been demonstrated that the impact of the average article published in French journals was significantly lower than that of articles published in journals of any other major country except the Soviet Union.[3-4]

The major problem we faced was how to identify articles by French authors in other than French journals, and to determine the language of those articles. Once we had this information, we could use our citation files to measure the impact of the articles.

Fortunately, the ISI® tape files contain addresses for *all* the authors of articles indexed in the *Science Citation Index®*. Even though it was only last year that we added addresses to the printed *Source Index* section of *SCI®*, we have processed and retained this information in our computer files since 1961. In addition, the record for each article in the file contains a language indicator.

In order to limit the size of the study, we searched only our 1973 *Source Index* files. We learned that there were 17,376 articles which had *at least one* author with a French address. Of these, 10,112 were articles published in French journals. The remaining 7,264 articles (42% of the total) appeared in international multilingual or other primarily English journals. We confirmed that 61% of these 7,264 articles were, in fact, published in English.

In order to measure the impact of all the articles by French authors, we matched the 1973 *Source Index* file against the 1973 to 1976 *Citation Index* section of our *SCI* tape file to see how many times the 1973 articles were cited. Of the 17,376 articles by French authors, 9,723 were cited 43,181 times. This is an average of 4.44 citations per cited article. This figure is significantly lower than the 5.68 citations received by the average 1973 article which was cited during 1973-76.

Of the 9,723 French-authored articles that were cited, 5,151 were

498

published in journals from France, while 4,572 were published in journals from other countries. Thus, 49% of the 10,112 articles published in France were not cited; only 37% of the 7,264 articles published in other countries remained uncited. This is the preliminary indicator of the impact of scientific publication in France. Now comes the clincher! The 4,572 cited articles published outside France received 28,951 citations—an average of 6.33. The 5,151 cited articles published in France's own journals received 14,230—an average of 2.76. The difference in impact is 2.3 to 1!

The dramatic difference in impact of the two groups was confirmed by constructing a special list of most-cited 1973 articles by French authors. This was arranged so that we could identify the most-cited articles published in France and outside France. Here again, the group which published outside France was outstanding. Of these articles, 248 were cited over 20 times, while only 22 articles published in France achieved this citation frequency. Of the 270 articles which were cited 20 times or more, 240 (89%) were published in English. In Figure 1 we have listed the five most-cited articles published "inside" France. Ironically, the most highly cited article was published in English. In Figure 2, we have listed the 15 most-cited articles from the "outside" group. Only one of these was published in French.

Next we examined the effect of language of publication on the im-

pact of French-authored articles. We found that of 12,593 articles published in French, only 6,075 were cited. This leaves 52% of the French language group uncited. By contrast, of the 4,724 articles published in English, 3,547 were cited. Only 25% of the articles published in English were uncited during the years studied. The impact of the average English article was 7.45, while that for the French group was only 2.95! These are even more dramatic differences than the figures for the "inside-outside" comparison.

It is important to note, however, that similar differences will be observed for other bilingual comparisons, such as Spanish-English, German-English, or Russian-English. In the case of Spain, the average article published in English is cited 2.4 times as often as one published in Spanish. More than half the articles published in Spanish were not cited, while over 60% of those in English were. Incidentally, only 773 articles were published by Spanish authors in our 1973 file.

One interesting by-product of this study has been the observation that articles covered by the *SCI* were cited with significantly higher frequency than the average cited item in our files. Experience shows that the average cited item tends to be cited 2.5 times over a *five-year* period. We have shown above that when the file is limited to items covered by the *SCI*, the average cited item achieved a citation rate of 5.7 over only a *four-year* period. The citation rate per cited item

Citations 1973-1976	Author/Affiliation	Article	Language
65	Faye G, Fukuhara H, Grandchamp C, Lazowska J, Michel F, Casey J, Getz O S, Locker J, Rabinowitz M, Bolotin-Fukuhara M, Coen D, Deutsch J, Dujon B, Netter P, Slonimski, P P. *Centre de Génét. Moléc. (CNRS). Gif-sur-Yvette*	Mitochondrial nucleic acids in the petite colonie mutants: deletions and repetitions of genes. *Biochimie* **55**:779-92, 1973.	EN
60	Leonardelli J, Barry J, Dubois M P. *Lab. de Zoologie (CNRS). Besançon*	Neuro-endocrinologie - Mise en évidence par immuno-fluorescence d'un constituant immunologiquement apparente au LH-RF dans l'hypothalamus et l'émin-ance médiane chez les mammifères. (Immuno-fluorescent presentation of component immuno-logically related to LH-RF in hypothalamus and eminentia medialis in mammals.) *C.R. Acad. Sci. Ser. D.* **276**:2043-9, 1973.	FR
58	Dutrillaux B, Laurent C, Couturier J, Lejeune J. *Inst. de Progenèse, Paris*	Cytogénétique-coloration des chromosomes humains par l'acridine orange après traitement par le 5-bromodéoxyuridine. (Coloration of human chromo-somes by acridine-orange after treatment with 5-bromodeoxyuridine.) *C.R. Acad. Sci. Ser. D.* **276**:3179-81, 1973.	FR
51	Barry J, Dubois M P, Poulain P, Leonardelli J. *Lab. d'Histologie (CNRS). Faculté de Médicine, Lille*	Neuroendocrinologie - Caracterisation et topographie des neurones hypothalamiques immunoréactifs avec des anticorps anti-LRF de synthèse. (Characteriza-tion and topography of immunoreactive hypo-thalamic neurons with synthetic anti-LRF anti-bodies.) *C.R. Acad. Sci. Ser. D.* **276**:3191-3, 1973.	FR
46	Cagnac B, Grynberg C, Biraben F. *Lab. de Spectroscopie Hertzienne de l'ENS (CNRS). Paris*	Spectroscopie d'absorption multiphotonique sans effet Doppler. (Multiphotonic absorption spectro-scopy without Doppler broadening.) *J. Phys.-Paris* **34**:845-58, 1973.	FR

Figure 1. Most-cited articles by French authors published *in* France during 1973 (Note: in all cases, the affiliation is that of the first author)

Figure 2. Most-cited articles by French authors published *outside* France during 1973
(Note: in all cases, the affiliation is that of the first author)

Citations 1973-1976	Author/Affiliation	Article	Language
158	Gerschenfeld H. *Lab. de Neurobiologie, Ecole Normale Supérieure, Paris*	Chemical transmission in invertebrate central nervous systems and neuromuscular junctions. *Physiol. Rev.* **53**:1-119, 1973	EN
103	Comes R, Lambert M, Launois H, Zeller H R. *Lab. de Physique des Solides, Université Paris-Sud, Orsay*	Evidence for a Peierls distortion or a Kohn anomaly in one-dimensional conductor of the type $K_2Pt(CN)_4Br_{0.30} \times H_2O$. *Phys. Rev. B-Solid State* **8**:571-5, 1973.	EN
99	Brouet J C, Flandrin G, Seligmann M. *Inst. de Recherche sur les Maladies de Sang, Hôpital St.-Louis, Paris*	Indications of the thymus derived nature of the proliferating cells in six patients with Sezary's Syndrome. *N. Engl. J. Med.* **289**:341-7, 1973.	EN
88	DeVries R M. *Département de Physique Nucléaire a Moyenne Energie, Centre d'Etudes Nucléaires de Saclay, Gif-sur-Yvette*	Recoil effects in single-nucleon-transfer heavy-ion reactions. *Phys. Rev. C-Nucl. Phys.* **8**:951-60, 1973.	EN
73	Tardieu A, Luzzati V, Reman F C. *Centre de Génét. Moléc. (CNRS), Gif-sur-Yvette*	Structure and polymorphism of the hydrocarbon chains of lipids. A study of lecithin-water phases. *J. Mol. Biol.* **75**:711-33, 1973.	EN
72	Thiérry A M, Stinus L, Blanc G, Glowinski J. *INSERM. Lab. de Biologie Moléc.. Collège de France, Paris*	Some evidence for the existence of dopaminergic neurons in the rat cortex. *Brain Res.* **50**:230-9, 1973.	EN
64	Dutrillaux B. *Chaire de Génétique Fondamentale, Inst. de Progenèse, Paris*	Nouveau système de marquage chromosomique: Les bandes T. (New system of chromosome banding—T-bands.) *Chromosoma* **41**:395-402, 1973.	FR

Figure 2. Most-cited articles by French authors published *outside* France during 1973 (continued)

Citations 1973-1976	Author/Affiliation	Article	Language
63	Mathé G, Kamel M, Dezfulian M, Panneko O H, Bourut C. *Hôpital Paul Brousse, Inst. Cancer, Villejuif*	An experimental screening for systemic adjuvants of immunity applicable in cancer immunotherapy. *Cancer Res.* **33**:1987-97, 1973.	EN
62	LeClerc J C, Gomard E, Plata F, Levy J P. *Lab. d'Immunologie des Tumeurs, Hôpital Saint-Louis, Paris*	Cell-mediated immune reaction against tumors induced by oncornaviruses. 2. Nature of the effector cells in tumor-cell cytolysis. *Int. J. Cancer* **11**:426-32, 1973.	EN
61	Artzt K, Dubois P, Bennett D, Condamine H, Babinet C, Jacob F. *Lab. de Génét. Cellulaire, Inst. Pasteur et Collège de France, Paris.*	Surface antigens common to mouse cleavage embryos and primitive teratocarcinoma cells in culture. *Proc. Nat. Acad. Sci. US* **70**:2988-92, 1973.	EN
60	Vargaftig B B, Zirinis P. *Merrell Int'l. Research Center, Strasbourg*	Failure to produce cell-free lymphotoxin. *Nature New Biol.* **244**:114-6, 1973.	EN
59	Barojas J, Lévesque D, Quentrec B. *Lab. de Physique Théorique et Haute Energie, Faculté des Sciences, Orsay*	Simulation of diatomic homonuclear liquids. *Phys. Rev. A-Gen. Phys.* **7**:1092-105, 1973.	EN
57	Bach J F, Dardenne M, Salomon J C. *Hôpital Necker, Paris*	Studies on thymus products. 4. Absence of serum "thymic activity" in adult NZB and (NZB x NZW) F 1 mice. *Clin. Exp. Immunol.* **14**:247-56, 1973.	EN
57	Reeves H, Audouze J, Fowler W A. *SEP, CEN Saclay, and Inst. d'Astrophysique, Paris*	On the origin of light elements. *Astrophys. J.* **179**:909-30, 1973.	EN
57	Thiérry A M, Blanc G, Sobel A, Stinus L, Glowinski J. *Groupe de Neuropharmacologie Biochimique, Collège de France, Paris*	Dopaminergic terminals in the rat cortex. *Science* **182**:499-501, 1973.	EN

would be considerably higher if we eliminated from the calculations those items which are not substantive articles (e.g., letters, editorials, corrections). These items tend, when cited at all, to be cited only once.

It is of course necessary to consider whether the French-authored articles discussed above will become more heavily cited if one waits a few more years. The so-called half-life of articles in certain fields may be higher. It is possible that French science is more heavily committed to slower moving fields—such as mathematics. But clearly in the life sciences there can be little doubt about the difference in impact.

There is also the possibility that the papers published during 1973 are not typical of those published during other years. After all, if there can be vintage years for French wines, why not for French research, too?

Nevertheless, it does seem obvious that, with certain exceptions, the best of French research is published outside of France and in English. Unfortunately, we do not have a definitive answer to the question of how much publication in French affects the citation rate of a truly high quality paper. But for the reasons I've stated many times, scientists risk oblivion when they avoid the reality of English as the international language of science. As future reports will demonstrate, this applies not only to our French colleagues but equally, if not more so, to scientists who speak and publish in German, Spanish, Italian, Japanese, or Russian.

REFERENCES

1. **Garfield E.** Le nouveau défi américain. I. *Current Contents* (15):5-11, 11 April 1977.
2. ⸻. Le nouveau défi américain. II. *Current Contents* (16):5-12, 18 April 1977.
3. ⸻. Journal citation studies. 23. French journals—what they cite and what cites them. *Current Contents* (4):5-10, 26 January 1976.
4. **Narin F & Carpenter M P.** National publication and citation comparisons. *J. Amer. Soc. Inform. Sci.* 26:80-93, 1975.

To Remember Ralph Shaw

Number 23, June 5, 1978

In 1954, I was under consideration for a job teaching at the Graduate School of Library Services at Rutgers University. There was only one slot open. The Dean, Lowell Martin, told me I had the position if my friend Ralph Shaw—who was already an eminent librarian, inventor and publisher—did not accept it. He did, and my career as a full-time academic came to an end before it began. This was probably the best thing that ever happened to me. I went on to establish ISI ®, and Ralph went on to have ten innovative years at Rutgers and a brilliant teaching career, until his life was cut short by cancer in 1972.

Before he died, Ralph compiled an impressive list of credentials and accomplishments that left his mark on librarianship and information science and on those of us who knew and admired him.

From his first library-related job as a page in the Cleveland Public Library in 1923 to his last as Professor and Dean of Library Activities at the University of Hawaii from 1964 to 1968, Ralph aggressively initiated creative programs, invented and applied systems to better serve library patrons, stimulated students to turn out a body of directed research and prodded stodgy institutions into action.[1] An intensely political man, Ralph could confound any opponent on a public platform. His unique knack for demolishing an antagonist with a few succinct (but not necessarily relevant) remarks was unnerving.

In his relationships with colleagues, students and friends, Ralph demonstrated his marvelous sense of humor. I experienced his ability to turn a phrase in 1953 when I arranged a documentation seminar and buffet luncheon at Johns Hopkins University, which Shaw attended.[2] After the meeting, he wrote me a note that said: "Garfield, as a documentalist you make a great caterer." Other Shaw aphorisms are quoted on page 9.[3]

I first met Ralph Shaw when he attended a meeting of the committee of consultants that supervised the work of the Welch Medical Library Indexing Project at Johns Hopkins. Ralph was instrumental in my receiving the first Grolier Society fellowship at Columbia University, since Frank B. Rogers (National Library of Medicine), Verner Clapp (Library of Congress), and he were my "references."

Ralph was born May 18, 1907, in Detroit and received his B.A. from Western Reserve (now Case Western Reserve) University in Ohio. He then moved to New York, first landing his B.S. from Columbia University's School of Library Services in 1929 and then an M.S. in 1931. During his years in New York he was employed as Senior Assistant Chief Bibliographer of the Engineering Societies Library, a post he held until 1936.

Throughout his long career, Ralph was responsible for many innovations and inventions in the library field. One of his well-known contributions during his tenure as chief librarian of the Gary, Indiana Public Library from 1936 to 1940 was the trailer bookmobile concept. Ralph's version of the bookmobile used a single motorized cab to haul three different book trailers to their destinations. It was less costly than using individual bookmobiles with their own engines.[3]

While at Gary, Ralph also made an important innovation in the way libraries record circulation information. In the 1930's the prevailing method of book charging involved stamping the "date due" and writing the borrower's name or identification number on a card. When the book was returned, the card had to be retrieved from a file and replaced in the book before the volume could be shelved. A librarian with overdue notices to write had to go through the entire file of cards to find which books were late.[4]

Ralph conceived "transaction card charging" to simplify this process. In transaction card charging, the librarian uses due date cards, each numbered in serial order. A due date card, a card identifying the book, and the borrower's identification card are photocopied at the charge desk. The due date card is put into a pocket in the book. When the book is returned, the card is removed, and the book is immediately reshelved.

The returned due date cards may be quickly sorted in serial order. If the books issued on, for example, June 1 used cards 1-1000 and all cards have been returned, the librarian knows that there are no overdue books to be called in. If numbers are missing, a clerk can turn to the copies of those transactions and write overdue notices. This system or some variation of it is used today in many libraries throughout the world. As an integral part of his system, Ralph invented the Photoclerk, a small photostat machine (since superseded by more sophisticated copiers).[3]

During his next fourteen years

(1940 to 1954) as Director of the US Department of Agriculture Libraries in Washington, D.C., Ralph helped pioneer the development of miniprint. Later, he published some of his students' dissertations in the reduced-size print format, to demonstrate the effectiveness of the concept. Miniprint is still under discussion as a way to cut publishing costs.[5]

In 1942, Ralph planned and produced the first *Bibliography of Agriculture,* which consolidated into one source bibliographies of botany, irrigation, entomology, forestry, agriculture economics and plant science literature. To those topics, Ralph added animal husbandry and food processing. The first *Bibliography of Agriculture* was produced by photocopying the original index cards.[3] Still published today, the present version is produced from computer tapes and appears monthly, indexing about 150,000 articles a year.

Also in the 1940's, Ralph developed the Rapid Selector, a device of which he was particularly proud. Before the machine's existence, there had been no fast way to search a reel of microfilm for a specific bit of information. With the Rapid Selector, microfilm could be electronically scanned at the rate of over 10,000 frames per minute. When the desired frame of text was located, a camera would automatically photograph it. The Rapid Selector received a great deal of fanfare and was described as an

Courtesy *Library Journal.*

Ralph R. Shaw

"electronic marvel" which could "revolutionize the whole science of bibliography."[6]

Ralph credited the basic electronic principles applied in his Rapid Selector to Dr. Vannevar Bush, who had produced an earlier version at MIT. With Dr. Bush's permission, Ralph used his concepts to develop a more effective and commercially viable machine.[7]

For the Rapid Selector, a code of dots describing the frame's content was placed beside each frame of microfilm. When a library patron needed specific information, a clerk input a card punched with the appropriate code. Using a photocell, the Rapid Selector searched each frame and compared dots on the microfilm with the holes in the card until the correct frame was found. The matched dots tripped a flash lamp and camera shutter, making a copy of the text frame.[8]

Nothing ever came of the Rapid

Selector. But I was intensely interested in it for many reasons. In the early fifties Jacques Samain developed a system called Filmorex which, I felt, solved some of the basic problems of the Rapid Selector. Had it not been for the inventor's lackadaisical attitude about marketing his invention, I might today be a Filmorex salesman. Filmorex was a combination of punched-card technology and microfilm—a hybrid of the punched-card and Ralph's Rapid Selector.

As an eminent educator, Ralph was extremely controversial and frequently dogmatic, to both the delight and chagrin of his colleagues and students. In his work with doctoral candidates, for example, Ralph gave far more guidance than some members of the faculty liked. He would map out a field to be studied and assign various parts of it to the students in order to expand the body of knowledge in that area. These studies have been credited, however, with creating new insights into information science.

Ralph was also a curriculum innovator. At Rutgers, during his tenure as Dean of the School of Library Services from 1959 to 1964, he began the first regular class in scientific management in a library school.[9]

While he was still in Washington, Ralph put on his publisher's hat and founded the Scarecrow Press in 1950. Scarecrow was a specialized low-overhead publication house, begun in the basement of his Georgetown home and expanded to a multi-million dollar enterprise.[3] The books published by Scarecrow in those days were offset from typewritten pages, a method that did not make them aesthetically pleasing. Ralph vociferously defended this method, however, and several observers have noted that Scarecrow made available many reference works that otherwise might have gone unpublished. Ralph relinquished all interest in Scarecrow in 1968. It is now a subsidiary of Grolier Educational Corporation.

A prolific writer, Ralph published at least eight books plus a twenty-two-volume *American Bibliography, 1801-1819,* and many articles. For his last work, he translated and edited Richard Muther's *German Book Illustration of the Gothic Period and the Early Renaissance (1460-1530).* So prolific a writer was he that a complete bibliography of his works has yet to be compiled. Linda Leff, Ralph's grandniece and candidate for a master's in library science at the University of Hawaii, is in the process of doing just that. A selected bibliography which she prepared accompanies this essay.

A man of many facets, Ralph enthusiastically threw himself into the work of the American Library Association from the beginning of his career. He even became the organization's president in 1956-

APHORISMS OF RALPH SHAW

Every time we don't think a job through and do it right, we think up a new name for it.

Our basic task, regardless of the kinds of libraries in which we work, deals with books for people.

The shortest distance between two points is around all the angles.

Why do efficiently something that doesn't need to be done at all?

Each person under you should be smarter and abler than you about what he does.

Parkinson's Law is what happens in the absence of good personnel administration.

We often substitute cooperation for thinking through the whole problem.

Anything beyond the copyright notice itself is bullying.

There is no way for a person to commune with a computer tape to find things he is not looking for. Giving a person profiles of stuff he knows he's looking for is only about 50 percent of the job.

Reprinted by permission from *Essays for Ralph Shaw*. (Norman D. Stevens, ed.) Metuchen, N.J.: Scarecrow Press, 1975. Copyright © 1975 by Norman D. Stevens.

1957, despite his dislike of the association's bureaucracy.

Ralph's unique combination of interests as an inventor, librarian, and publisher brought him face to face with copyright issues, and so he became an expert in the field. His doctoral thesis, submitted to the University of Chicago in 1950, was entitled *Literary Property and the Scholar*. In his last year Ralph published a brilliant analysis of the celebrated Williams & Wilkins copyright case in *American Libraries*.[10]

People were often hard pressed

to understand Ralph's attitude towards computers in the library. Although he adapted and invented machines to do library work, he frequently and vociferously denounced library applications of the computer. When he went to the University of Hawaii as head of its new library school and of its university library, Ralph unceremoniously threw out a brand-new IBM circulation record system and replaced it with an efficient manual system he designed.[11] But he was not against computers *per se.* He was anxious to be shown improvements that would result only from their installation. He liked to tell a story about a library that analyzed its operations in order to put in a computer. The analysis resulted in such a massive clean-up of bad procedures that the computer was found to be unnecessary.[3]

A pioneer, a courageous advocate of controversial causes, a distinguished professor, internationally known librarian, inventor, information scientist, copyright law expert—all these and more was Ralph Shaw. Ralph was dedicated to keeping librarianship a service occupation. All of his inventions were service-oriented ideas to make the library system work better for patrons. He was fond of asking, "Why do we have a dichotomy between what's good for people and what's good for the library?"

His concern for people carried over into his personal life. Though we were not close personal friends, Ralph visited my son in a hospital in Hawaii after he was wounded in Vietnam. Ralph not only cheered Stefan up but, in his typical takeover fashion, made certain that he was getting the best care possible. Ralph was a person who enriched the lives of those who knew him, and I am happy to have had this opportunity to pay homage to him.

REFERENCES

1. **McDonough R H.** Ralph R. Shaw, 1907-1972. *Libr. J.* 97:3952, 1972.
2. **Hyslop M R.** Documentalists consider machine techniques. *Spec. Libr.* 44:196-8, 1953.
3. **Stevens N, ed.** *Essays for Ralph Shaw.* Metuchen, N.J.: The Scarecrow Press, 1975. 212 p.
4. **Kirkwood L H.** Charging systems. *The state of the library art.* (Shaw R R, ed.) New Brunswick, NJ: Rutgers University Press, 1961. Vol. 2, part 3.
5. **Garfield E.** Miniprint: is it a practical way to cut publishing costs? *Current Contents* (2):5-7, 9 January 1978.
6. **Downs R B.** Foreword. *Bibliography in an age of science.* (Ridenour L N, Shaw R R & Hill A G, eds.) Urbana: University of Illinois Press, 1951, p. 1-4.
7. **Shaw R R.** The rapid selector. *J. Doc.* 5:165-71, 1949.
8. *Report for the microfilm rapid selector.* St. Paul, MI: Engineering Research Association, Inc., 1949. 30 p.

REFERENCES (continued)

9. **Gaver M U.** Ralph Shaw at Rutgers. *Wilson Libr. Bull.* 47:478-80, 1973.
10. **Shaw R R.** Williams & Wilkins v. the U.S: a review of the commissioner's report. *Amer. Libr.* 3:987-99, 1972.
11. **West S L.** Ralph R. Shaw: the Hawaiian years. *Hawaiian Libr. Assn. J.* 30:47-50, 1977.

Ralph Shaw: A Select Bibliography

Muther R. *German book illustration of the Gothic period and the early Renaissance (1360-1530).*
(Shaw R R, trans.) Metuchen, NJ: Scarecrow Press, 1972. 233 p.

Schneider G. *Theory and history of bibliography.*
(Shaw R R, trans.) New York: Columbia University Press, 1934. 306 p.

Shaw R R. Form and the substance: Address, 1964. *Libr. J.* 90:567-71, 1965.

------------. From fright to Frankenstein. *DC Libraries* 24:6-10, 1953.

------------. Integrated bibliography. *Libr. J.* 90:819-22, 1965.

------------. *Libraries of metropolitan Toronto: a study of the library service prepared for the Library Trustees' Council of Toronto and district.*
Toronto: Library Trustees' Council, 1960. 98 p.

------------. *Literary property and the scholar.* Chicago, University of Chicago, 1950. 335 p. Dissertation. (Revised edition published with title *Literary property in the United States.* Metuchen, NJ: Scarecrow Press, 1950. 277 p.)

------------. Management, machines and the bibliographic problems of the twentieth century. (Shera J H & Egan M E, eds.) *Bibliographic organization.*
Chicago: University of Chicago Press, 1951, p. 200-25.

------------. *Pilot study on the use of scientific literature by scientists.*
Metuchen, NJ: Scarecrow Press, 1971. 139 p.

------------. Introduction. (Shaw R R, issue ed.) Scientific management of libraries. *Libr. Trends* 2:359-60, 1954.

------------, ed. *The state of the library art.*
New Brunswick, NJ: Rutgers University Press, 1960-61. 2 vols.

------------. *The use of photography for clerical routines: A report to the American Council of Learned Societies.* Washington, DC: American Council of Learned Societies, 1953. 85 p.

------------. Williams & Wilkins v. the U.S : a review of the commissioner's report. *Amer. Libr.* 3:987-99, 1972.

------------ & Shoemaker R. *American bibliography: A preliminary checklist, 1801-1819.* Metuchen, NJ: Scarecrow Press, 1958-63. 22 vols.

Courtesy of Linda Leff

CURRENT COMMENTS

The Scientist in the Courtroom:
A Heady Experience with Many Dangers

Number 24, June 12, 1978

Social sciences information has become increasingly important to lawyers throughout this century.[1] Therefore, it is not surprising that social scientists themselves have become involved in the legal process through their professional assistance to attorneys. Scientists from many other disciplines as well are called upon to act as expert witnesses in cases dealing with such diverse issues as environmental pollution, computer crime, trademark litigation and medical malpractice.

Conducting research for an attorney or giving expert testimony can be an ego-building experience for a scientist. It can also satisfy a desire to contribute to the public good. However, euphoria may be shortlived when the expert witness is attacked by the opposing attorney. And scientists, trained to seek truth, may find themselves uncomfortable cooperating with attorneys who, in adversary situations, are more interested in proving their clients' cases than in obtaining a scientific analysis or expert opinion which is unbiased.

Over the past decade in the US, social scientists have stirred controversy by aiding lawyers in jury selection. For example, a team of five social scientists worked with the defense in the "Harrisburg Seven" trial, in which seven antiwar activists were charged with conspiring to destroy draft records, kidnap presidential advisor Henry Kissinger, and blow up heating tunnels in Washington, D.C.

The trial took place in Harrisburg, Pennsylvania, a small, politically conservative city. The social scientists conducted a survey of people in the area from which jurors would be drawn, and obtained demographic data on the type of person most likely to be sympathetic to the defendants. From these data they developed five characteristics for a good *defense* juror:

1. Under 30; the closer to 18, the better.

2. Black.

3. Possessing elements of a counter-culture style of life.

511

4. Showing opposition to the Vietnam war.

5. Having a close male relative who was of or near to draft age.[2]

Of the 12 jurors, the defense team was able to pick seven with one or more of these characteristics. Potential jurors with any were so few that the defense had to choose five who had none of these characteristics.

The jury convicted two of the defendants on minor charges, but deadlocked on the conspiracy charges. Ten jurors voted for acquittal. The two who voted for conviction were "second-choice" jurors. "The jury's decision was more favorable to the defendants than almost anyone would have predicted," the social scientists stated.[2] The government dropped charges instead of asking for a new trial.

Social scientists have also aided the defense in other highly-publicized "political" trials. Sociologist Jeffry M. Paige conducted a telephone survey to provide evidence that the Angela Davis trial should be moved to another district. Also, four psychologists evaluated prospective jurors in that case. Davis was acquitted of the conspiracy charges against her.[3]

Psychologist June L. Tapp helped the defense select jurors in the 1975 trial of two leaders of the American Indian Movement (AIM) involved in the 71-day seizure of Wounded Knee, South Dakota in 1973. The trial ended in a hung jury. Social scientists also helped select jurors in the trial of Watergate figures John Mitchell and Maurice Stans, who were accused of obstructing justice in return for a large political contribution. Both men were acquitted.[3]

However, social scientists' jury-selecting activities raised some ethical questions. It is normal for a lawyer to be an advocate, but the role is an unusual one for a scientist. Some of the social scientists involved in court cases found that to some extent they had to compromise their professional code of conduct to serve the client.

The scientists involved in the Harrisburg case did not tell the people questioned in their surveys that the information given might be used to help the defendants, "since we feared that to do so would seriously bias our results."[2] Instead they told respondents that the survey was being made simply because Harrisburg was to be the site of an important trial. "This...clearly violated the principle that research subjects should know the uses to which their data will be put," the team admitted. "We went ahead with the deception only after we had concluded that it was extremely unlikely that our procedure could harm the respondents."[2]

The efforts of social scientists to help impanel "friendly" juries may be detrimental to the cause of justice. This may be especially true if only one side has the resources to employ them.

Lawyers are finding many other uses for social science techniques. In Britain "a growing band of specialists who call themselves forensic psychologists...are carrying out experiments to see whether evidence presented in a court case is credible or not." So says Arthur Smith, science reporter for the London *Daily Mirror* writing in *Science Forum.* Lionel Haward of Surrey University, for example, has conducted experiments to determine the validity of testimony in the courtroom.[4]

In one case, a policeman testified that he took down the license number of a speeding motorcycle. Haward, working for the defense, conducted a study using 100 trained observers who tried to duplicate the sighting. None could do it. This does not mean the policeman lied, Haward said, but that he genuinely *thought* he saw what he *said* he saw.

Another case, a civil suit, involved a dispute between two competing manufacturers. The plaintiff claimed that a new label on the competitor's product was copied from the plaintiff's label, and that customers in supermarkets were mistaking the defendant's product for the plaintiff's. Haward's team observed supermarket customers' reactions to the labels and later asked them which they thought they had purchased. In most cases like this, Smith notes, the jury would have had to decide if customers *could* be misled. Haward's results showed that they actually *were* being misled. His work helped the plaintiff win the case.

Haward notes that "forensic psychologists" have usually helped private defense attorneys. He

thinks that the prosecution should also take advantage of "forensic psychology." But this is unlikely to happen in England, according to Smith, "because of the fear that the prosecution might be accused of being unfair if it set up elaborate and costly experiments to test defense evidence in advance."[4]

Perhaps that is just as well. Haward also advocates the use of voiceprints or hidden heartbeat-monitoring devices for determining if witnesses are telling the truth. It might have been interesting to test this method in cases like those of Sacco-Vanzetti or the Rosenbergs. However, using machines to extract the truth from people is reminiscent of Orwell's *1984.*

Besides forensic psychologists, there are many other forensic scientists—pathologists, toxicologists, chemists, psychiatrists, dentists—who run tests for lawyers or the courts. However, scientists in the US who testify in court need not be familiar with the law or judicial system. "Expert witnesses" need only to be qualified in their fields. As a result, the first-time expert witness may feel as though he or she has entered a mine field rather than a courtroom.

The scientist faces a serious communication problem in dealing with friendly as well as opposing attorneys. Trained to be objective, the scientist is careful to weigh all the complex facts. But he or she soon finds that neither lawyer wants to hear the whole story. As partisans, the attorneys want to avoid opinions which do not support their clients' positions. Both want unambiguous testimony simply phrased so that it may be easily understood by jurors. In this situation, the scientist may feel uncomfortable making statements without the qualifications normal in scholarly discussions.

Another problem makes communication difficult: legal definitions of certain concepts sometimes differ from and are simpler than scientific definitions.

For example, the medical definition of "causation" is more complex than the legal definition. Consider the remarks of Boston attorney Douglas Danner and Harvard physician Elliot L. Sagall:

> Medical practitioners tend to be concerned with *all* possible causes of the patient's current medical condition, whereas legal practitioners in personal injury cases generally focus on a particular event as possibly precipitating, hastening or aggravating a particular aspect of the patient's condition to the extent that the event in question is, in legal language, the "proximate cause" of an injurious result.[5]

Danner and Sagall use the analogy of "the straw that broke the camel's back." A physician will tend to say that the cumulative weight of all the straws on the overburdened camel broke its back. But a lawyer may try to prove that the last solitary straw was responsible for the damage done. The danger is that doctors and lawyers may misunderstand each other when talking about causation. Thus, Danner and Sagall note:

When the medical expert is asked the classic question, "Doctor, do you have an opinion, with reasonable medical certainty, as to whether the conduct of the defendant proximately caused the injury and damage to the plaintiff?" his answer will be incorrect unless he fully understands the meaning of legal causation.

Many expert witnesses are called to the stand to testify about causation (of a physical condition, a polluted river, a defective machine, etc.) when there is no definitive scientific test which can clearly prove the cause. In such cases, authorities may disagree. It is not unusual to see expert witnesses called to the stand by both the defense and the prosecution.

Naturally, each attorney tries to attack the credibility of the other side's witness. For the scientist on the stand, this can be a shocking experience. The advice New York attorney Charles Kramer offers to other lawyers on handling a medical expert sums up what all expert witnesses can expect:

> The fundamental concept of the cross-examination of any witness applies to the medical expert—that is, you can attack the witness, his story, or both the witness and his story. If you choose to attack the witness, you can show any possible bias, prejudice or interest.... Some lawyers may view this kind of attack with disdain as superficial and avoiding the issues. Maybe so, but I consider it the *best* kind of cross-examination and the kind that jurors understand. It is far more effective than an esoteric

analysis of medicine. Of course, the ideal is to couple this with the medical attack.[6]

Kramer's emphasis on attacks "that jurors understand" points out another pitfall of giving expert testimony. A scientist's appearance, manner of speaking, and coolness under fire can make as great an impression on jurors as the content of the testimony. Exeter F. Bell, Jr., superintendent of the Central State Psychiatric Hospital in Nashville, Tennessee, notes, "Unfortunately, *who* is testifying often is more important than what is said."[7]

Lawyers who call expert witnesses do not want them to fail on the stand, and usually discuss potential problems with them in advance. Morgan P. Ames, formerly an officer of the American Trial Lawyers Association, advises lawyers on the "care and feeding of the expert witness." According to Ames, the witness:

> ...should simply answer the questions put, clearly and firmly and not volunteer any extraneous matter.
>
> Further, the lawyer might warn the prospective witness that his entire prior life, and especially all his earlier professional career, may be subjected to intense, outside investigation, and in-court interrogation, so that he should reveal to the attorney calling him any earlier associations or experiences that might be invoked in an effort to discredit him on the stand.
>
> The witness should be reminded of Harry Truman's oft-quoted remark, "If you can't stand the heat, stay out of the kitchen." The witness stand is no place for the faint-hearted, however brilliant they may be, and however valid may be their opinions on the subject at hand.[8]

Some scientists may consider the pressures placed upon expert witnesses as good reason to avoid courtroom proceedings. Physicians and psychiatrists may also refuse to testify because it takes up a lot of time and energy that might be better (or more lucratively) spent in their own private practices. I think most scientists feel that if their knowledge can be useful in the court of law, it is their duty to society and to the individuals involved to testify.

As more scientific issues become legal problems, we can probably expect to see more scientists working closely with lawyers and judges. Undoubtedly, recombinant DNA technology will bring about "forensic biochemistry."

Dozens of other special aspects of forensic science may develop. Since the increased application of social science or science and technology is inevitable in certain types of cases, it is possible that the legal system may one day permit scientists to participate in a manner more compatible with their training and professional standard.

Presumably the legal system and science are ultimately (but in different ways) dedicated to the pursuit of truth. However, if lawyers and scientists are to cooperate in the emerging scientific-legal areas, both groups will have to learn more about each other's work and attitudes. Certainly, better communication and more interdisciplinary knowledge will be necessary if the two professions are to work well together.

We can expect in the future that it will not be unusual for a scientist to take a law degree or for a lawyer to specialize in one or more of the sciences.

Perhaps if some law students took pre-med instead of political science undergraduate training, we might develop some interesting legal talent. We already have scientists trained as patent lawyers. Why should it stop there?

REFERENCES

1. **Garfield E.** Social sciences information—a vital link between the law and our evolving society. *Current Contents* (18):5-9, 1 May 1978.
2. **Schulman J, Shaver P, Colman R, Enrich B & Christie R.** Recipe for a jury. *Psychol. Today* 6(12):77-84, 1973.
3. **Bermant G.** Juries and justice: "The notion of conspiracy is not tasty to Americans." *Psychol. Today* 8(12):60-7, 1975.
4. **Smith A.** Exploiting psychology in the name of the law: what benefits, what dangers? *Science Forum* 57:25-7, June 1977.
5. **Danner D & Sagall E L.** Medicolegal causation: a source of professional misunderstanding. *Amer. J. Law Med.* 3(3):303-8, 1977.
6. **Kramer C.** Cross-examination of the medical expert. *Trial* 13(12):26-7, 1977.
7. **Bell E F, Jr.** How to be an expert witness. *J. Legal Med.* 4(9):17-9, 1976.
8. **Ames M P.** Preparation of the expert witness. *Trial* 13(8):20-8, 1977.

CURRENT COMMENTS

Radio: The Neglected Medium for Scientific Communication

Number 25, June 19, 1978

It is 8:30 AM. You have just reached your office. First you order some coffee. Then you turn on the radio. As you begin to go through the morning mail, there is a little Beethoven, Bach, or Basie. Then the news broadcast begins. Instead of the usual fire, tornado, or accident report the announcer tells you about a bill in Congress that may make your present research illegal. A few minutes of music and he introduces an interdisciplinary panel to discuss the waste disposal problems faced by your city. After more music there is a report on the meeting of the American Association for the Advancement of Science you couldn't attend. Finally, the announcer gives a brief summary of some recently published papers. The hour-long broadcast is over before you know it. If you came in a little late, you are informed that the broadcast will be repeated several times that day.

This scenario is fictional. It ought not to be. The potential value of radio as a means of scientific communication has been underestimated and certainly underutilized.

The amount of science programming on US radio is amazingly small. In other nations it is probably more extensive. But in no country is it used to serve the specific needs of the scientific community. This is unfortunate because radio is a particularly appropriate medium for much scientific communication.

For one thing, radio is an almost painless way to be exposed to information. You don't have to devote your attention exclusively to it as you do with TV and print. You can listen while you are looking through papers, moving about, or setting up equipment in the lab. Even as you drive to work or sit on the beach, you could be keeping up with the latest scientific information. And it can also be a shared experience, during a coffee break or in the classroom.

A radio is an inexpensive purchase. It is easy to operate and maintain. You can take a small, battery-powered model virtually anywhere. By using an earphone, you can listen without disturbing others. Even the morning newspaper is more intrusive. Did you ever sit beside someone on a train who is leafing through the *New York Times* or *Wall Street Journal*?

Radio offers several more advantages over other media as a means of scientific communication. Radio can transmit the latest news more quickly than print. It can provide the listener with all the energy and emotion of "live" discussion. Such human qualities are often lost in a printed transcript.

Radio is often more appropriate for science broadcasting than television because many programs of interest to scientists do not require video. Science news, discussions, talks by individual scientists, even educational courses often lose little or nothing by being aired on radio.

Moreover, the requirements of radio program production and transmission are less distracting to the participants than TV. For example, if a discussion at a conference is being aired, the members of the panel do not have to worry about makeup or to be subjected to hot lights. The broadcast equipment involved is not so cumbersome that it separates the panel from the audience. TV cameras necessarily do this.

With radio, scientists throughout the world could participate in a program merely by sending in audio cassettes of their talks. This would avoid the travel expenses and loss of time incurred by the need to appear in person at a TV studio. Even when an on-site broadcast is necessary, the cost of sending a radio crew is far less than the cost for a TV crew.

I have often wondered why the "simple" solution offered by radio is not used more often for communicating scientific information. However, on further investigation I found that there are very real difficulties facing anyone wanting to operate an "all-science" station or network.

Using a commercial radio station in the US for this purpose would be out of the question except in a very few localities. All commercial stations are governed by a complex set of regulations, outlined by the Federal Communications Commission (FCC).[1] These regulations require commercial stations to meet the needs of the local communities they serve. This geographic limitation most likely means that a science-oriented station would only be sanctioned in an area with a high percentage of scientists. Among the few communities which might qualify are Bethesda, Maryland; Cambridge, Massachusetts; or Palo Alto, California.

Commercial stations, of course, do carry short science programs designed for lay audiences, since these programs are deemed in the public interest. The American Chemical Society sponsors one such program called *Man and*

Molecules. The ACS distributes tapes to over 500 stations in the US and other countries. But this type of programming is designed for the public, not the professional scientist.

Public radio could carry programming aimed at scientists.[2] Stations run by colleges, universities, and public school districts fall into this category. Sometimes known as educational radio, public radio stations provide instructional programming to teachers and students, as well as cultural, informational, public affairs and entertainment programs to the general public.

Unlike ordinary AM and FM, public radio stations carry no advertising and may be licensed only to non-profit organizations with an educational purpose. They are supported by funding from their parent institutions, state or local governments, foundations, private firms, or contributions from the listening audience.

Science programming for the professional would be a possibility on public radio only if it could be provided cheaply enough to fit public radio stations' budgets. I do not know if any large corporations have considered funding such programming. While they might be willing to support an occasional program, the costliness of a regular feature—without the chance to advertise—has probably deterred them.

With commercial or public radio seemingly beyond consideration, I did find one viable method for broadcasting science programs and one organization that has had the initiative to do so. The organization is the Physicians Radio Network (PRN), a New York based group that transmits news, short courses, live call-in shows, and reports from various medical associations to doctors.

PRN is a for-profit enterprise, financed by drug company advertising. It is permitted to broadcast its special-interest programs over Subsidiary Communications Authorization (SCA) sidebands. Ordinary FM broadcasting uses a main channel and two sidebands. However, in 1955, the FCC granted FM stations permission to sell the use of their SCA sidebands to those who wished to transmit programs of interest to a limited segment of the general public—such as a professional group. Broadcasts over SCA bands can be picked up only by a special receiver tuned to the SCA frequency. Ordinary FM radios filter out the broadcasts that are transmitted over these bands.

PRN distributes these special receivers to physicians within the 35-mile radius of their signal in 33 cities. About 75,000 doctors are now listening to the network. Certainly as many or more scientists in both university and industrial positions would listen to all-science stations.

A science radio network patterned after PRN could distribute receivers free of charge to qualified scientists. Revenue would be received from program sponsors. Certain advertisers should be eager to reach a guaranteed audience of scientists. Scientific and technical journal, book, and magazine publishers might be interested. They could attract new readers to their publications through commercials on an all-science station. Industry is also a potential sponsor. Science-oriented companies could attract new employees through appropriate spot announcements. Manufacturers of scientific instruments, too, might find radio an attractive supplement to journal and direct mail advertising. Of course, separation of advertising from editorial content would have to be strictly maintained.

PRN uses medical journalists to write and edit the material it presents. An all-science network would also require the services of senior science journalists able to report science news events in proper perspective. Short courses would be prepared by researchers and educators in the field, and most programs would have to be reviewed by qualified scientists.

In my opinion, one drawback to PRN is that doctors cannot as yet listen to these programs in their cars. The network has considered putting receivers in automobiles. The idea was dismissed because the task of installing them proved too difficult. The special receivers must be hooked up in addition to or in place of the regular car radio. Each installation job is different because each car maker has different specifications for installing the equipment. An individual listener, who was willing to go to the expense and fuss of having the radio installed, could do so. PRN is considering the use of portable receivers that doctors could take with them in their cars, but an appropriate antenna needs to be devised.

PRN has been successful by aiming its programming at practicing clinical physicians. These doctors face a wide variety of medical problems and make decisions based on current information. The counterpart to the clinician in science is the engineer. In some ways engineers might benefit even more than pure scientists from a science radio network. The engineer is an applied scientist. His or her need for continuing science education is perhaps greater than that of the academic scientist doing research.

If no one else is interested in starting the network, I suppose this might be another job for ISI® . Our basic objective is to communicate scientific information effectively through any appropriate medium. Radio will not replace print. But it can help us do a better job of digesting and communicating the results of research. I can even see the various media supplementing each other. For example, additional instructional materials for short courses via radio as well as programming schedules could be included in *Current Contents®* . I can also envision people using our TV-based SCITEL™ service to peruse the radio schedule for the day.[3] An ISI radio network could, of course, provide me with a new opportunity for ego gratification. I don't know whether my essays would be as well-received were I to read them over the air. But I am sure that items in our Press Digest could be interesting "hearing."

Perhaps the Science Radio Network can only be realized through a collaborative effort involving several organizations: government (National Science Foundation and/or National Institutes of Health), societies (American Association for the Advancement of Science), and private enterprise (ISI and other science-oriented corporations). Anyone out there listening?

REFERENCES

1. **Federal Communications Commission.** Broadcast services. *FCC Information Bulletin Number 3.* Washington, DC: FCC, 1977. 39 p.
2. --. Educational radio. *FCC Information Bulletin Number 17.* Washington, DC: FCC, 1977. 18 p.
3. **Garfield E.** Viewdata and SCITEL bring interactive information systems into the home. *Current Contents* (41):5-10, 10 October 1977.

CURRENT COMMENTS

Money Exchange—The Traveler's Dilemma

Number 26, June 26, 1978

This year, about 23 million Americans will travel abroad; about 20 million visitors will come to the United States.[1] Millions will cross other international borders. Most of these people will be either vacationing or traveling for business reasons. Consequently, they will stay in one or more countries for just a short period of time. For this reason they usually need to exchange only small quantities of foreign currency. Unfortunately, most of these travelers will be subjected to "small" rip-offs each time.

Obviously, rates of exchange are dependent upon the currency exchange market. Rates vary from day to day, but usually there is an "official" rate. However, not all banks give you this official rate. While practices vary from country to country, you can't be certain without shopping around which bank gives the best rate.

In most countries the government is usually more than glad to have you convert your money into local currency. If nothing else, it increases the chances that you will spend money there. But in countries where the banks are privately owned, this likelihood is an insufficient incentive. Private banks expect to make a profit, one way or another, on the individual transaction. Since there is paperwork, even of the most minute kind, something must be charged to cover the overhead. Depending upon the efficiency (or the greed) of the bank, you may find considerable variation in the service charges involved. Perhaps the most absurd service charge is the fixed fee, which can mean that as much as 90¢ will be charged—to change one dollar.

Another peculiar money exchange policy hurts the tourist who is traveling rapidly through several countries. Let's assume that you are waiting at Stockholm airport for a flight to Switzerland. You decide to use the time to buy Swiss francs. You present your pounds at the airport bank. The clerk proceeds to convert pounds to Swedish kronor first and then exchanges the kronor for francs. You pay twice for the privilege of exchanging your money.

I realize that the person conducting the transaction is a clerk working with an exchange chart that only lists rates for the local currency. But why can't countries publish multi-currency forms—at least for those foreign currencies most likely to be exchanged? There must be enough tourists in Sweden carrying British pounds to warrant a chart showing the direct exchange rate for all the major European currencies.

Like other unscrupulous shopkeepers, some money exchangers will do anything to attract your business. In London you will frequently see an exchange rate posted in the window that looks exceptionally good. It may be the "official" rate. So you wander in, only to learn that a 4 or 5% commission is charged.

Hotels are similarly usurious. Thus if you exchange money in a London hotel, you will forfeit $1.00 for every $20 bill you change. Hotel managers no doubt will argue that their exchange charges are a necessary source of income—like any other hotel service. (One wonders if you will be charged next for maid service.) However, if you go around the corner to the nearest bank, should it be open, you won't do much better unless you can change amounts in excess of $100—and in some places these days the amount must be higher to get the better exchange rate.

However, if you do exchange even $200 or $300, you may find at the end of your stay that you are stuck with unused money which must be reconverted—at the same low rate you would have received had you only changed a small amount in the first place.

Even if you try to be frugal, it is difficult to avoid small rip-offs that are especially frustrating. Suppose you are passing through Norway, having just come from London. At the airport newsstand you buy the *International Herald Tribune* and *Time* magazine. The total cost is 9.5 Norwegian kroner. You hand the clerk a one-pound note. For change, you get back a piece of adding-machine paper and a friendly smile. According to the official exchange rates, you were entitled to 9.96 kroner for one pound. Somewhere you lost almost half a krone. This is a 5% commission. You realize you've been had when you see the rate quoted at the airport bank, 20 yards away.

Consider the tourist who is about to catch a plane back to the US. He arrives at Heathrow airport in London with about ten pounds in his wallet. He figures he has bought all the presents he requires. So he converts his pounds to dollars at a cost of at least 2.5%. However, after emerging from passport control, our traveler finds himself in the "never-never land" of the "duty-free" shop. He decides to buy a bottle of perfume at the bargain "tax-free" rates. In fact, the merchandise is no less expensive than in most London shops. At the checkout stand, a clerk tells him he can pay in dollars. As the clerk makes change, the tourist reads an inconspicuous sign on the wall which announces that dollars are exchanged at a rate that is at least 10% less than the rate he just received at the airport bank.

Once on board the airplane our hypothetical tourist still must be on the lookout for small hustles. For example, at one point the airlines offered headsets, to allow passengers to listen to the movie soundtrack, for $2.50 or one British pound. That price was fine when the two amounts were equivalent. But when the pound fell in value to $2, those who paid for the earphones in dollars were ripped off. Of course, if you paid in pounds you got a bargain. I have never quite understood how flight attendants are able to prove to management how many persons pay in dollars. I resent being taken in such situations. After all, you really have little choice. Airline officials are in a position to do something about the various little rip-offs, but most of them choose not to. Lest you doubt this, consider the case of the recent flap at British airlines. Flight attendants were going on strike because management wanted to control the sale of alcohol more closely. It seems that drinks were being "shorted" so that attendants could sell a few to their own benefit.

Attempting to exchange *coins* can be an almost insurmountable problem for the traveler. For example, I recently tried to exchange some Dutch coins for pounds at London airport. I was shocked to be offered just 50% of the official rate. So I refused. When I walked into the tax-free shop, beyond

passport control, the clerks there were happy to take my Dutch coins—albeit at the excessive rates they charge for bills. Why is it that a duty-free shop knows what to do with those coins, but not a bank which exchanges money all day long? Airline attendants are equally happy to accept your coins.

But the situation in London with respect to exchanging coins is good in comparison to that in Copenhagen! There you can't exchange foreign coins for anything at the airport bank. The post office next door, ironically, will gladly accept your coins in payment for postage or telephone calls. This policy was only recently implemented. In the past it was first necessary to exchange bills at the bank and then purchase stamps with local currency.

Since foreign coins usually cannot be easily exchanged once borders are crossed, many countries provide charity boxes at airports where travelers can deposit their change.[2] At least worthy causes benefit from those otherwise all but useless coins.

Lest any of my foreign friends think I am exhibiting my American bias by saying all of the above, let me be the first to point out how difficult it is to exchange currency of any kind in the average American city. The tourist who needs to convert foreign currency to the American dollar must find either a bank with a foreign exchange department or a broker who will accept his or her money.

In Philadelphia, for example, the only money-exchange broker listed in the telephone book is the airport exchange facility operated by Fidelity Bank. Area banks which have international divisions will exchange currency for tourists. However, most will do so only at designated branches—invariably located in the center of the city. The traveler who ventures out into the suburbs or country can have a difficult time of it. In addition, few hotels will exchange foreign currency, even that of our Canadian neighbors. In Philadelphia neither the Sheraton nor the Hilton hotel will exchange foreign money or travelers' checks. Most tourists from other countries, of course, have been forewarned and carry travelers' checks for American dollars, which are acceptable.

The major international airports in the US, of course, have booths where tourists can exchange their money as they enter or leave the country. But the rates at these places, in my experience, have always been usurious compared to the rates available in the comparable foreign city. Thus if you are on your way to France, don't buy francs at JFK airport in New York, but wait until you get to DeGaulle airport.

Following this advice is not without risks, however. Assured that most foreign airports have 24-hour banks for money exchange,[3] I once arrived at DeGaulle airport with no French money. It was 11:15 p.m. when I arrived in the baggage area. As I waited for my baggage, I noticed that there was a bank in the area with counters on both sides of the customs barrier. So I decided to change my dollars before my luggage arrived. When I went to the bank counter, the clerk signalled me to come around to the other side, after my baggage arrived. The bags came at 11:29. At precisely 11:30, I arrived at the counter only to have the window closed in my face. The clerk ignored my loud bilingual protestations. I was infuriated and searched for an Air France official. After ten minutes, I finally located one. I told him what had happened. He suggested that I take a taxi to my hotel and ask the driver to wait, meter running, while I exchanged my money there, at high hotel rates. That solution seemed unacceptable to me. For one thing, I know how abusive Paris cab drivers can be when asked to wait outside a hotel for any reason. After another 15 minutes of loud exchanges, the official finally went to a safe and exchanged ten dollars for me.

When I arrived home, I wrote Air France about the experience and suggested that the bursar on each transatlantic plane be prepared to exchange $20 for francs on all flights arriving after banking hours. Although I received a polite reply to my letter, the airline stated that such a service would put it in competition with banks, something it had no intention of doing. Since the banks seem to be unmindful of the needs of arriving passengers, I don't see why the airlines shouldn't step in. If the airlines provided a money-exchange service on board, passengers would no longer have to wait in long lines at the airport.

It is almost impossible for the traveler to avoid rip-offs on his journey. However, in an effort to do so, some travelers pay for their major purchases with credit cards. Credit cards enable you to carry less cash, but the cards are not without their problems.[4] Sometimes travelers are in for a big surprise when they get their bills at home.

Let's take our typical tourist again. He goes into a London shop and purchases a £10 Wedgwood candy-dish as a gift. At the time of the purchase, the gift costs $20 because each pound is worth $2. The sale takes place on Thursday, but the shopkeeper waits until the following Tuesday to deliver the credit slip to the card company. By the time the slip arrives at the company, the value of the pound has increased to $2.10. Thus when the charge appears on our traveler's bill, it is $21, not $20, or 5% more than he expected to pay. This rip-off happens all the time, and the traveler is the loser. But of course if the shopkeeper does this when the pound is going down in value, you should be the gainer.

One of the bankcard companies, BankAmericard (VISA) is attempting to cope with the problem by standardizing rates. When the com-pany receives the credit slips from the participating merchant, it converts the charges at "interbank rates," or rates banks use among themselves for very large transactions. To this they add 0.5%. This method of conversion reportedly gives the bankcard's users better rates than they would have received with cash.[5] Yet the rate of exchange is still dependent on the date the credit slip reaches the processing center.

Of course, credit-card holders who feel excessively ripped off may appeal the bill to the company. You have to show proof-of-purchase data along with the exchange rate of the day. BankAmericard and American Express both promise "good faith" review of these complaints. But few travelers keep dated receipts or want to become enbroiled in a billing dispute with a credit-card company.

Americans are not alone in being ripped off by quickly changing exchange rates. Foreign tourists are often plagued by the fluctuations of our dollar. Earlier this year, *Newsweek* reported on the plight of one British tourist. While planning a trip to New York, he exchanged £200 at $1.87 per pound. When he had to cancel his trip a week later, the tourist tried to exchange his money, only to find that the value of the pound had increased to $1.94. He lost 6 pounds without ever leaving Britain.[6]

Some sources say that travelers can avoid some money-exchange rip-offs by using travelers' checks. Foreign exchange bureaus sometimes keep excess dollars until they can be used in another transaction. These dollars do not earn interest until exchanged. For this reason, the traveler sometimes gets a better rate if exchanging travelers'checks. Travelers' checks may be deposited immediately, allowing the exchanger to apply the funds at once to an interest-earning account. In some cases, you can expect to get 2% more for travelers' checks than for US currency. Since most travelers' checks cost 1% of their face value, the tourist makes 1% on the transaction.[7]

Another way tourists can try to stay one step ahead of the money-exchange hustlers is to buy currency for countries like Italy or those in South America before leaving home. Traditionally, banks in these "soft" currency countries give you the least favorable rates. But the tourist must be very careful when trying to beat the system this way. Foreign-exchange brokers, of course, charge a commission to provide their services. Also, many countries impose restrictions on the amount of money that can be taken into and out of the country. A traveler could be stuck at a border trying to get into the country with too much local currency. And of course, you are subject to arrest if you are caught "smuggling" money. Travelers in these countries should exchange all of their local currency for dollars before leaving.

Once across the border the "soft" currency drops in value. The tourist returning from Italy today will probably get much less for lire in another country.

In an effort to avoid those long lines at money-exchange counters at most airports, some travelers buy tipping packs—packets of coins and paper money that can be used for tipping, taxi fare, and telephone calls—in each currency they plan to use. However, the dealers who sell these packs here get about a 10% commission for their service. For travelers willing to pay such a high price, the packets can bring peace of mind and eliminate the risk of being caught without cash in a strange country.

Frequent travelers to Europe sometimes get around currency problems by opening Eurocheck accounts. These accounts enable you to write checks for amounts in the local currency.

Those of us who travel often for professional or business reasons, must live with the inconsistencies, irritations, and hustles associated with international travel. Surely I am not the only person who resents being robbed even though only a little bit at a time. Something ought to be done to standardize regulations, prevent shops—especially at airport or train terminals—from charging unreasonable rates to tourists, and to provide convenient methods of exchanging currency. Tourists and business travelers represent far too much money for most countries to ignore their complaints. Changing these policies, whether official or unofficial, is in the economic interest of the countries involved. A happy tourist will part with his money much faster than an unhappy one. And a disgruntled tourist may decide never to return.

REFERENCES

1. U.S. business. *U.S. News World Rep.* 83(24):62, 12 December 1977.
2. **Sloane L.** Money-wise: foreign currency: should you buy it here, or when abroad? *Moneysworth* 6(12):8, 12 June 1976.
3. **Fielding T.** *Fielding's travel guide to Europe.* New York: Fielding Publications, 1977. 1204 p.
4. **Ferri J.** It's in the cards: travel by credit. *Holiday* 57(4):22, 70, 80, June/July/August 1976.
5. Corporation affairs: BankAmericard's units billing by computer. *The New York Times* 15 April 1977, Section 4, p. 11.
6. Saving the sick dollar. *Newsweek* 91(3):63, 16 January 1978.
7. **Rondthaler E.** *Traveler's instant money converter.* New York: Grosset & Dunlap, 1976. 62 p.

CURRENT COMMENTS

Chiropractic: Still Controversial After Nearly 100 Years

Number 27, July 3, 1978

Whenever a journal article on chiropractic appears, there is a good chance it will bear a title similar to the one in the September 13, 1974 issue of *Science*—"Chiropractic: Healing or Hokum?"[1] Since 1895, when Daniel David Palmer, a Davenport, Iowa tradesman, founded the profession that advocates healing through spinal manipulation, chiropractic has been in the center of controversy. On one side are the chiropractors who say that millions of patients have found relief through chiropractic. On the other is the medical establishment, which advocates the view advanced in a 1968 report to Congress, *Independent Practitioners Under Medicare*, submitted by then Health, Education and Welfare secretary Wilbur J. Cohen, an eminent educator. The report concluded that "Chiropractic theory and practice are not based upon the body of basic knowledge related to health, disease and health care that has been widely accepted by the scientific community."[2] Yet, in spite of its lack of a scientific basis,

chiropractic is making increasing inroads into American health care.

According to *Dorland's Illustrated Medical Dictionary*, chiropractic is a system of therapy based on the belief that all disease is caused by the abnormal functioning of the nervous system.[3] Chiropractic attempts to restore the normal functioning of the nervous system by manipulation and treatment of the structures of the human body, especially the spinal column. The word chiropractic is derived from the Greek and means "done by hand."[4]

Each year chiropractors see about 5 million patients, who come to them with a variety of complaints ranging from infectious diseases and physical handicaps to back ailments. A high percentage of patients is seen for musculoskeletal problems.[5] When a patient visits a chiropractor, he or she usually receives a spinal X ray and examination.[6] After the analysis of the problem has been completed, the chiropractor makes an "adjustment" to the patient's spine. This is accomplished through what chiropractors call a "dynamic thrust," a quick movement that usually produces a "click" sound in the joint manipulated. Spinal manipulation is performed to adjust a subluxation or misalignment of the vertebrae. Practitioners believe that correcting the subluxation will cure the disease or condition being treated.

When chiropractic was introduced at the end of the 19th century, the health care professions in the United States, especially in the midwest and west, were relatively unregulated.[4] There were several theories of healing, based on different philosophies of disease.[5] Homeopaths, for example, followed the teaching of Samuel Hahnemann of Leipzig. In 1810 he originated a system of treatment that involved the administration of small doses of drugs whose effects resembled the effects of the disease being treated.

Shortly before chiropractic was established, Andrew Taylor Still founded osteopathic medicine.[4,7,8] Still believed that the way drugs were used and surgery performed in his day did more harm than good. His school of thought placed emphasis on recognizing and correcting structural problems and advocated manipulative therapy as well as other types of treatment. Allopaths, or conventional medical doctors, made up the major group of practitioners. These doctors sometimes got their training in university medical schools, some-times through apprenticeship to other doctors. In addition, magnetic healing, which combined the "laying on of the hands" with a form of hypnotherapy, and naturopathy, or drugless healing, were popular forms of health care.

Out of this unregulated environment, chiropractic emerged. By most accounts, D. D. Palmer, who started chiropractic, was a former grocer and fishmonger who felt he had a gift for healing.[8,9] He operated a magnetic healing studio in Davenport at the time of his "discovery." One of Palmer's patients was Harvey Lillard, a janitor who had been deaf for some 17 years. Discouraged that magnetic healing was not helping Lillard, Palmer examined his patient and found a protruding painful area on his back near his spine. He decided that attempting to reduce the bump might bring the janitor some relief. Giving Lillard an adjustive thrust, Palmer reportedly properly aligned the patient's vertebrae and restored his hearing.

Scientists, however, object to the assertion that spinal manipulation cured Lillard's hearing. According to William M. Keane, a neuro-otologist at Philadelphia's Pennsylvania Hospital, Department of Otorhinolaryngology, nerves controlling hearing are self-contained in the skull and inaccessible to manipulation. Manipulation of the vertebrae might help some kinds of dizziness, but not hearing loss. Nevertheless, from his treatment of Lillard, Palmer developed the theory of chiropractic and began teaching others his methods. Among his students was a son, Bartlett Joshua Palmer, who is now called the "Developer" of chiropractic medicine.

Like many other fields, chiropractic's early history was marked by dissent and factionalism from within. Shortly after its founding, a rift developed between father and son, prompting them to have separate practices for a time and causing the development of separate schools of chiropractic.[9] Some of the early students—who happened to be medical doctors—rejected the notion that chiropractic methods were a panacea. A. L. Foster, M.D., for example, wrote, "Other methods of treatment have shown their effectiveness in different diseases, and should therefore be used. Spinal adjustment is not to be regarded as all in all in the treatment of disease and other measures which are of proven value should be considered."[5] Several of these doctors also formed their own schools of chiropractic medicine.

Particularly disturbing to some members of the chiropractic community were the methods used by B. J. Palmer to promote the profession.[5, 8] These methods brought criticism from outside of chiropractic as well. For example, in 1924, Palmer introduced a machine called the neurocalometer, which supposedly located the pinched nerves that were the cause of disease. He leased the machines to chiropractor graduates of his school. Immediately after the ten-year lease ran out, Palmer came up with another device for chiropractors to use in their practice. Introduction of the devices angered graduates of other chiropractic schools, as well as members of the public and medical doctors, who denounced the machines as moneymaking schemes and claimed that they did not do what they were supposed to do.

There are still factions in modern chiropractic, but these are consolidated into two major groups. The International Chiropractors Association represents about 30% of the chiropractors and includes those practitioners who confine their treatments to manipulation. The other faction, which includes the majority of chiropractors, is the "mixers." Associated with the American Chiropractic Association, these professionals use manipulation along with other therapies to cure patients. ACA members, for example, might use vitamin and mineral therapies, exercise programs, ultrasound treatments and traction as methods of treating a patient.[5] Neither group of chiropractors prescribes drugs or performs surgery, since both believe that disease is caused by nervous system disturbances that can be corrected by manipulation.

Since its inception, chiropractic has faced opposition, which has continued to this day. Physicians reject what they see as a one cause-one cure profession and assert that there is no scientific evidence to support the profession's teachings. In addition, they attack the chiropractor's claim of being an entry point into the health care system comparable to the general practice physician. Until recently, opponents say, chiropractic education has been in such a shambles that graduates were hardly prepared to produce an adequate diagnosis and so not enough patients were referred to other members of the health care professions. Chiropractic treatment also delays the patient from seeking appropriate medical care, thus causing consequences that otherwise might have been avoided, they state. Far too many X rays are given as part of chiropractic diagnosis, critics continue, exposing patients to unnecessary levels of radiation. Manipulative therapy can sometimes be painful and is not without its hazards, they add.[10]

Despite the criticism, chiropractic has made steady gains throughout this century. Even as the health care professions came under state licensure (with regulations favoring medical doctors), chiropractic survived while alternative health care systems like "magnetic healing" died. In 1913, Kansas became the first state to legally recognize chiropractors. Several states followed suit, but not before many chiropractors were arrested for practicing medicine without a license.[9] In 1925, in an attempt to raise the quality of health care in their respective states, both Connecticut and Wisconsin passed "basic science" laws that required all practitioners to take exams in anatomy, bacteriology, chemistry and other sciences before they could apply to take their board examinations. Medical authorities hoped, and many chiropractors thought, that chiropractic was doomed to extinction by the stringent requirements.[8] In fact, few chiropractors were licensed in those states immediately following the implementation of the boards. But basic science boards were not adopted by other states until much later, and so chiropractic flourished. By 1931, chiropractors were legally recognized in 39 states. Many of the states changed their laws and regulations regarding chiropractic through the years, often raising standards for licensing or wavering between the philosophies of the "straight" chiropractors and the "mixers."

By 1974, chiropractic had won licensure in Louisiana and Mississippi, the last two states to thus recognize the practice. At present, about 17,000 people practice chiropractic in the US and another 4,000 practice it in other countries. Switzerland, West Germany, New Zealand, South Africa and Bolivia all regulate chiropractic.[5] In Britain, the practice of chiropractic is unlicensed, but it is not illegal.

Belgian chiropractors practice at the pleasure of the crown and French practitioners are unregulated. In Italy, a chiropractor must work under a licensed allopath. Nine Canadian provinces and one Australian province license the practice as well. From informal inquiries I have learned that chiropractic is not unknown in the USSR. It enjoyed a vogue in the past. The Soviet government does not license chiropractors. It would seem that chiropractic is tolerated, however.

Once the states accepted the profession, chiropractic turned its attention to the problems of federal recognition. In response to a seven-year effort by chiropractors and supporters, who lodged a vigorous mail campaign,[10] Congress, in 1972, passed a law (PL 92-603) that said in part that Medicare payments could go to chiropractors for manual manipulation of the spine to correct a subluxation that appeared on an X ray. The coverage under Medicare was gained despite opposition by medical physicians and some senior citizens' groups.

Another victory came in 1974 when the US Commissioner of Education granted the Council of Chiropractic Education (CCE) the right to accredit chiropractic colleges as institutions of higher learning. The CCE is an autonomous corporation sponsored by the ACA and the Federation of Chiropractic Licensing Boards of the various states.[5] The commissioner's action made chiropractic colleges that were accredited eligible for federal funding. The American Medical Association contested chiropractic's recognition but was told that the Commissioner does not have to express an opinion on the usefulness or legitimacy of the field of training. Accredited institutions simply meet educational standards.[11]

The CCE set up standards for chiropractic schools.[5] For example, students admitted to an accredited school must have completed two years of a science curriculum in a college. A course of study that includes at least 1840 hours of basic science (anatomy, physiology, chemistry, pathology and hygiene) and 2080 hours of clinical science, including diagnosis, gynecology and obstetrics, principles of chiropractic and other such subjects, must be followed. Eighty hours in requirements selected by the college and 200 more hours in optional electives must also be taken, bringing the total number of hours required to 4,200 for the four-year course. The chiropractic profession feels that the upgrading of educational standards and formal accreditation of its colleges have done much to invalidate some criticisms by its opponents. However, it is still possible to question the value of an education based on an unproven theory.

At present there are four chiropractic colleges in the US that are accredited.[5] They are the Los

Angeles College of Chiropractic in Glendale, California; the National College of Chiropractic in Lombard, Illinois; Northwestern College of Chiropractic in St. Paul, Minnesota; and Texas Chiropractic College in Pasadena, Texas. Four more colleges in the US have achieved status as recognized candidates for accreditation. Three foreign colleges are also affiliated with CCE.

Besides qualifying for Medicare payments and federal funding for their accredited colleges, chiropractors have been eligible since 1974 for the National Institutes of Health grants for research into spinal manipulation.

Lack of research has indeed been a resounding criticism against the profession. Chiropractors have responded that prejudice kept them out of the running for government grants, which support much of the medical community's research. Now chiropractors have at least a potential source of funding. Yet neither of the two grants awarded by NIH for research into spinal manipulative therapy has gone to a chiropractor.

The profession's stated concern with research is indicated by its establishment of the Foundation for Chiropractic Education and Research. This nonprofit institution makes grants for research and has supported projects at the University of Colorado at Boulder and the Rensselaer Polytechnic Institute in Troy, N.Y.[5] In addition, chiropractic colleges are conducting their own research projects.

The chiropractic community publishes its findings in a body of journal literature that is largely unknown to health care professionals in other disciplines. There are at least two major US chiropractic journals representing the two chiropractic factions: the *ACA Journal of Chiropractic* and the *International Review of Chiropractic*. In addition, almost every state and five Canadian provincial associations sponsor their own journals. Foreign journals of chiropractic are published in Australia, Britain, New Zealand, and Africa.

Chiropractic journals are not covered in the major indexing services, including *Index Medicus* and ISI®'s *Science Citation Index®*. Neither are they covered in *Current Contents®*. At ISI, we have not purposely excluded these journals. They have never been covered for several reasons. Lack of demand for their inclusion is but one. The primary reason is their lack of scholarly content. For example, the *International Review of Chiropractic* is little more than a newsletter. The *ACA Journal of Chiropractic* contains one or two "professional papers" in each issue, but none that I saw documented original research.

Despite the strides made by their profession, chiropractors feel they still have several stumbling blocks to overcome. The majority of chiropractors who are "mixers" note that all "usual and customary" chiropractic services are covered by most private health insurance plans, but that Medicare and Blue Cross plans only pay for spinal manipulative therapy and not for the other types of treatment they prescribe. They are also continually fighting against legislation that would limit their practice to spinal manipulation only.

Chiropractors also regularly face opposition from journalists and consumer advocates. For example, in 1976, the practitioners were dealt a blow by a *Consumer Reports* study. The study concluded that chiropractic is a "significant hazard to many patients." It decried the "aura of legitimacy" licensing laws have lent to the practice. The report also urged government to restrict the chiropractors' scope of practice to musculoskeletal complaints. In addition, it recommended that chiropractors be prohibited from treating children.[11]

After urging readers to reconsider before going to a chiropractor, the report then listed some pointers, offered by chiropractors, to those who would go anyway. Readers were told to avoid practitioners who make claims about cures, ask the patient to sign a contract for services, advertise free X rays, want advance payments or charge for extra units of treatment, or who talk of irreversible damage if treatment isn't started right away.

Moreover, Professor Edmund Crelin of the Yale-New Haven Medical Center warns of potentially lethal devices which many chiropractors use. He has reported that one such device, called the specific adjustment machine, could, "without exceeding pressures recommended for use on humans...put a nail through a half-inch board." He states that "if the compressor gauge or part of the control mechanism becomes defective, the device could maim or kill the 'patient.' "[12]

Beyond all of this, chiropractors say that people who visit them do get well and point to case histories to support their assertions.[5] The claim is supported by social science research as well. The chiropractor "often succeeds in treatment when other practitioners have failed," according to a study by psychiatrist Gregory Firman and sociologist Michael S. Goldstein.[13] "Whether this success is due in fact to greater professional skill and knowledge (particularly in the musculoskeletal area), to more positive feeling engendered in the patient by the 'patient' orientation of the practitioner, as opposed to the 'illness' orientation of the physician, or to the placebo effect of the 'laying on of the hands' is unclear."[13] According to chiropractors, the practitioners succeed because they treat the whole patient, not just part of one.

Palmer's theory of vertebral subluxations causing pressure on spinal nerves has been found erroneous in a scientific test.[14] And you would think that any schoolchild who has had a course in hygiene would be suspicious of anyone claiming to cure tuberculosis by spinal manipulation. Yet chiropractic rolls on, attracting more patients each year.

Perhaps spinal manipulation therapy is efficacious for a certain small group of physical conditions. If so, the onus is on the chiropractors to prove it. But, according to Dr. H. Thomas Ballantine, Jr., of Massachusetts General Hospital, "the chiropractors and their proponents have challenged the medical profession and the biologic scientists to disprove the theory and efficacy of chiropractic."[15] It is time that chiropractors produced their own body of documented research as scientific evidence. Their inability or unwillingness to do so does much to invalidate their claims.

Of course, the chiropractic associations have begun to fund research which is relevant to chiropractic. So far, work at the University of Colorado, which was supported in part by these funds, has led to the publication of papers in such mainstream journals as *Brain Research, Mathematical Biosciences,* and *Experimental Neurology.* Several of these papers have concerned models of neuron networks, neuron configurations, and nerve compression.[16-19] Other work reported a method of precision analysis of spinal X rays, which would enable researchers to record more accurate data on the exact positions of tissues of the spinal column.[20] Research findings have also

been published on changes in neural proteins after nerve damage.[21] While I cannot comment on the merits of this research, it is still far from the clinical testing that chiropractors themselves could do. I suppose, if any clinical research based on chiropractic theory were to satisfy the standards of leading medical journals, it would be published in one of them. I have not seen such an article yet.

What we don't know about chiropractors is the number of backs they have literally broken or the nerve damage they have caused. But then we really don't know how often physicians make bad diagnoses, or perform poor or unnecessary operations. Medical science still has a long way to go before it will be able to cure the myriads of diseases and physical conditions. One might argue that the state of medical science and the inadequacy of some of its practitioners have enabled chiropractic to thrive. Human beings have the eternally optimistic belief that somewhere, somehow, something will provide a cure.

Lest there be any doubt about my opinion on this subject, let me reiterate. Much chiropractic, especially that which claims a cure for cancer or heart disease, is a palpable and dangerous fraud. The only controversy concerns the other possibly legitimate applications of spinal manipulation.

REFERENCES

1. Chiropractic: healing or hokum? HEW is looking for the answers. *Science* 185:922-3, 1974.
2. U.S. Dept. of Health, Education and Welfare. *Independent practitioners under Medicare: A report to Congress.* Washington, D.C.: HEW, 1969. 84 p.
3. *Dorland's illustrated medical dictionary.* Philadelphia: W.B. Saunders, 1974. 1748 p.
4. **Gibbons R W.** Chiropractic in America: the historical conflicts of cultism and science. *J. Pop. Culture* 10:720-31, 1977.
5. **Schafer R C, ed.** *Chiropractic health care.* Des Moines, IA: The Foundation for Chiropractic Education and Research, 1977. 118 p.
6. **Chimes M.** The healing art of chiropractic. *40 for the Chief Exec. Officer* 3(1):30-2, January/February 1978.
7. **Northrup G W.** History of the development of osteopathic concepts; osteopathic terminology. (Goldstein M, ed.) *The research status of spinal manipulative therapy: A workshop held at the National Institutes of Health, February 2-4, 1975.* Washington, D.C.: United States Department of Health, Education and Welfare, 1975. DHEW Publication No. (NIH) 76-998, p. 43-52.
8. **Homola S.** *Bonesetting, chiropractic, and cultism.* Panama City, FL: Critique Books, 1963. 281 p.
9. **Maynard J E.** *Healing hands: The story of the Palmer family, discoverers and developers of chiropractic.* New York: Jonorm Publishing, 1959, 365 p.
10. Chiropractors: healers or quacks? Part 1: The 80-year war with science. Part 2: How chiropractors can help—or harm. *Consumer Rep.* 40:542-7; 606-10, 1975.
11. **Ballantine H T, Jr.** Federal recognition of chiropractic: a double standard. *Ann. Intern. Med.* 82:712-3, 1975.
12. **Crelin E.** A lethal chiropractic device. *Yale Scientific* 49:8-11, 1975.
13. **Firman G J & Goldstein M S.** The future of chiropractic: a psychosocial view. *N. Engl. J. Med.* 293:639-42, 1975.
14. **Crelin E.** A scientific test of the chiropractic theory. *Amer. Sci.* 61:574-80, 1973.
15. **Ballantine H T, Jr.** Will the delivery of health care be improved by the use of chiropractic services? *N. Engl. J. Med.* 286:237-42, 1972.
16. **MacGregor R J.** A model for reticular-like networks: ladder nets, recruitment fuses, and sustained responses. *Brain Res.* 41:345-634, 1972.
17. --------------------. Intrinsic oscillations in neural networks: a linear model for parallel, single-unit pathways. *Math. Biosci.* 17:121-35, 1973.
18. --------------------, **Sharpless S K & Luttges M W.** A pressure vessel model for nerve compression. *J. Neurol. Sci.* 24:299-304, 1975.
19. -------------------- **& Oliver R M.** A general-purpose electronic model for arbitrary configurations of neurons. *J. Theor. Biol.* 38:527-38, 1973.
20. **Suh C H.** The fundamentals of computer aided x-ray analysis of the spine. *J. Biomech.* 7:161-9, 1974.
21. **Luttges M W, Kelly P T & Gerren R A.** Degenerative changes in mouse sciatic nerves: electrophoretic and electrophysiologic characterizations. *Exper. Neurol.* 50:706-33, 1976.

The 300 Most-Cited Authors, 1961-1976,
Including Co-Authors at Last.
1. How the Names Were Selected

Number 28, July 10, 1978

Recently we listed and analyzed the 250 most-cited primary authors.[1-4] In compiling these "most-cited" lists, we tested the assumption that frequent citation is an indication of significance in science. Of course, capricious or ill-chosen references may account for some citations. And sometimes papers are cited in order to criticize them. But if an author is consistently cited, indeed thousands of times over a number of years, this record indicates (with occasional exceptions) that he or she has made a significant impact on science.

Our assumption was borne out in our study of primary authors. By analyzing their various academy memberships and awards, we showed that their citation ranking correlated fairly well with peer recognition. The scientists on the primary-author list are members of an elite group, past and present, who have had a great effect on science through their research publications.

But no matter how far we might have extended our list—even to the first several thousand names—we could be seriously criticized for omissions, due to a convention involved in compiling the *Citation Index* section of the *Science Citation Index®*. In this section we record only the names of the first authors of cited items. Co-authors' names are included only in our *Source Index*.

Co-authorship was less frequent in the early part of this century. But it has increased significantly since the 1950s. It was inevitable that the "primary author" approach would overlook many important authors who have published significant work as co-authors in the last twenty years.

Therefore, we felt it imperative to produce data that would include the citations scientists had received as co-authors. I hope that those who have felt slighted by our earlier studies will appreciate how difficult it has been to do this.

Recently we ran the ISI® computer day and night for about a month to collect data for our first "all-author" study. Over 10 million *Source Index* author entries in our *Science Citation Index* data base were matched against millions of citations in the *Citation Index*. The source file consists of all the articles published during the period 1961-1976 which were covered by the *SCI*® . The "citation" file consists of all the references made by these articles in the same period.

To obtain this all-author information, we had to make certain compromises. The *Source Index* file of the *Science Citation Index* data base contains the names of all authors of source items covered by *SCI* from 1961 on. Thus, our "all-author" analysis is only as complete and reliable as that file.

Since our *Source Index* file begins with 1961, citations to papers published prior to that year are excluded. Out of 56 million citations, 24 million were thus excluded. This chronological bias distorts rankings for those scientists who published their most important papers prior to 1961. Also, obviously, authors who have been publishing steadily since 1961 fare better in this analysis than, say, those who started in 1971.

However, this bias will shift as we produce similar reports from year to year.

Since the analysis was limited to articles appearing in journals indexed by *SCI,* authors who published in journals which were not covered would not be treated evenly. Fortunately, our original selection of journals included all but a few of those most frequently cited. This original group of periodicals still receives over 75% of all citations. However, in our earlier files, certain fields such as botany and mathematics were not covered as comprehensively as they are today. But for the basic life and physical sciences, the file is essentially complete.

Finally, by limiting our "data bank" for this study to the items covered by *SCI,* we restricted the cited items to journal articles. The *SCI* indexed only the journal literature until 1977, when it began to cover books.

It is important to remember these compromises when you scan the list of most-cited authors based on "all-author" data which begins on page 7.

It is also essential to realize that this list and the earlier "250 most-cited primary authors" list are very different, because the all-author list includes only citations to papers published 1961-1976. For example, L. D. Landau, who was a highly cited *primary* author (with over 18,000 citations), is not on the "all-author" list because his highly cited work was done prior to 1961. However, his early papers continue to be heavily cited.

Scientists on the primary-author list who received most of their citations for books or other reports not published in journals do not appear on this list either. The "all-author" list is limited to those who were primary and co-authors of highly cited journal articles which were published 1961-1976 and covered by the *SCI* during that time period.

Only 77 authors from the "250 most-cited primary authors" list appear on the "all-author" list. Each is identified by an asterisk which precedes his or her name. As the

Figure 1: The 300 authors whose articles published 1961-1976 were most-cited during that time period. Based on *Science Citation Index®* data, the list shows citations for *co-authored* as well as primary-authored articles. An asterisk before a name indicates that the author also appeared in the 250 most-cited *primary* authors list.

Author (Birthdate)	Total Citations	Total Papers	Citations as 1st Author	1st Author Papers	Citations as Co-Author	Co-Author Papers

Organic & Inorganic Chemistry

Author (Birthdate)	Total Citations	Total Papers	Citations as 1st Author	1st Author Papers	Citations as Co-Author	Co-Author Papers
*Bender ML (1924)	5,131	148	3,029	69	2,102	79
*Benson SW (1918)	4,359	157	2,239	52	2,120	105
*Brown HC (1912)	10,288	400	8,337	289	1,951	111
*Clementi E (1931)	5,440	92	4,819	61	621	31
*Corey EJ (1928)	8,500	247	7,646	229	854	18
*Cotton FA (1930)	10,292	350	7,664	250	2,628	100
*Cram DJ (1919)	3,827	164	2,057	58	1,770	106
Davidson ER (1936)	3,757	60	436	24	3,321	36
*Dewar MJS (1918)	6,635	224	4,805	168	1,830	56
*Djerassi C (1923)	11,027	431	2,118	77	8,909	354
Drago RS (1928)	4,178	165	984	38	3,194	127
*Flory PJ (1910)	5,538	133	2,079	49	3,459	84
Grant DM (1931)	3,869	90	896	12	2,973	78
Gray HB (1935)	4,526	175	988	20	3,538	155
Hammond GS (1921)	5,129	141	1,859	38	3,270	103
Hoffmann R (1937)	7,969	125	5,761	61	2,208	64
*Huisgen R (1920)	4,996	242	3,965	166	1,031	76
Ibers JA (1930)	6,452	209	919	29	5,533	180
Jortner J (1933)	4,821	197	1,144	42	3,677	155
*Karplus M (1930)	6,193	128	3,063	25	3,130	103
Khorana HG (1922)	6,620	174	770	12	5,850	162
*King RB (1938)	4,583	252	3,656	207	927	45
Kochi JK (1928)	3,919	159	2,151	55	1,768	104
Li CH (1913)	3,908	248	1,212	65	2,696	183
Lipscomb WN (1919)	6,364	218	495	20	5,869	198
Muetterties EL (1927)	3,883	128	2,193	58	1,690	70
Nemethy G (1934)	3,927	43	2,214	17	1,713	26
*Olah GA (1927)	7,451	380	6,683	346	768	34
Paquette LA (1934)	3,819	270	3,448	235	371	35
*Pople JA (1925)	10,479	121	6,287	33	4,192	88
*Roberts JD (1918)	6,088	196	118	6	5,970	190
Robins RK (1926)	4,239	247	167	6	4,072	241
Samuelsson B (1934)	5,849	148	1,019	27	4,830	121
Scherage HA (1921)	9,232	280	315	14	8,917	266
Schleyer PV (1930)	5,806	169	1,484	29	4,322	140
Sörm F (1913)	5,858	492	261	17	5,597	475
Stewart RF (1936)	3,894	52	3,219	42	675	10
Sweeley CC (1930)	4,424	85	2,124	14	2,300	71
*Tanford C (1921)	5,888	107	1,638	28	4,250	79
*Winstein S (1912-69)	4,522	162	1,302	26	3,220	136
Witkop B (1917)	4,341	194	70	5	4,271	189
*Woodward RB (1917)	4,044	48	2,292	24	1,752	24

Figure 1. The 300 most-cited authors, 1961-1976.

Author (Birthdate)	Total Citations	Total Papers	Citations as 1st Author	1st Author Papers	Citations as Co-Author	Co-Author Papers
Biochemistry						
Allfrey VG (1921)	6,069	79	1,461	15	4,608	64
Ames BN (1928)	6,689	69	1,925	19	4,764	50
*Andrews P (1928)	4,606	50	4,385	27	221	23
Anfinsen CB (1916)	4,942	119	452	14	4,490	105
Brady RO (1923)	3,744	143	1,758	51	1,986	92
Cleland WW (1930)	4,652	63	3,421	15	1,231	48
*Cuatrecasas P (1936)	6,777	142	4,932	62	1,845	80
*DeDuve C (1917)	4,178	50	1,754	15	2,424	35
Deluca HF (1930)	8,622	275	825	31	7,797	244
Doty P (1920)	7,422	86	38	4	7,384	82
Edelman GM (1929)	6,797	127	2,934	29	3,863	98
Estabrook RW (1926)	4,546	109	818	23	3,728	86
Hales CN (1935)	3,936	67	2,479	18	1,457	49
Harris H (1919)	4,326	117	909	25	3,417	92
Horecker BL (1914)	4,529	154	334	13	4,195	141
Jencks WP (1927)	4,299	126	932	25	3,367	101
Kaplan NO (1917)	7,248	180	660	11	6,588	169
*Kornberg A (1918)	6,706	115	424	8	6,282	107
Koshland DE (1920)	5,136	120	1,495	19	3,641	101
Krebs EG (1918)	4,043	63	353	2	3,690	61
*Krebs HA (1900)	5,146	93	1,607	33	3,539	60
Lardy HA (1917)	4,954	131	761	11	4,193	120
*Lehninger AL (1917)	4,651	119	1,286	23	3,365	96
Lipmann F (1899)	5,019	75	203	7	4,816	68
*Moore S (1913)	5,619	121	1,646	36	3,973	85
Morris HP (1900)	4,319	282	68	5	4,251	277
Ochoa S (1905)	4,172	95	267	8	3,905	87
Passonneau JV (1924)	4,034	61	821	9	3,213	52
Piez KA (1924)	4,302	61	1,399	20	2,903	41
Prockop DJ (1929)	5,187	142	1,064	23	4,123	119
Randle PJ (1926)	6,442	92	897	9	5,545	83
Reich E (1927)	4,996	87	1,929	17	3,067	70
Rodbell M (1925)	4,037	47	2,478	23	1,559	24
Roseman S (1921)	4,068	105	765	7	3,303	98
Rutter WJ (1928)	4,147	85	536	8	3,611	77
Seegmiller JE (1920)	4,690	166	1,121	23	3,569	143
Smith EL (1911)	3,861	113	466	16	3,395	97
Tappel AL (1926)	4,665	158	483	15	4,182	143
*Udenfriend S (1918)	10,507	200	1,180	15	9,327	185
Umezawa H (1914)	5,781	501	1,319	53	4,462	448
Vallee BL (1919)	5,527	179	714	18	4,813	161
Van Deenen LL (1928)	6,873	214	521	13	6,352	201
Immunology						
Austen KF (1928)	6,023	253	554	24	5,469	229
Benacerraf B (1920)	9,197	239	1,359	26	7,838	213
Cooper MD (1945)	3,905	108	1,663	33	2,242	75
*Fahey JL (1924)	6,482	140	3,494	47	2,988	93

Figure 1. The 300 most-cited authors, 1961-1976.

Author (Birthdate)	Total Citations	Total Papers	Citations as 1st Author	1st Author Papers	Citations as Co-Author	Co-Author Papers
Immunology (continued)						
Finland M (1902)	4,082	165	323	29	3,759	136
Franklin EC (1928)	4,358	175	981	49	3,377	126
Fudenberg HH (1928)	7,523	332	707	30	6,816	302
*Good RA (1922)	17,641	694	680	36	16,961	658
Grey HM (1932)	3,788	86	1,511	34	2,277	52
Haber E (1932)	4,638	153	1,338	27	3,300	126
Hirschhorn K (1926)	4,548	193	1,608	31	2,940	162
Ishizaka K (1925)	4,947	190	2,348	66	2,599	124
*Kunkel HG (1916)	9,031	200	942	26	8,089	174
Merrill JP (1917)	5,262	235	464	29	4,798	206
Moller G (1936)	4,383	109	1,961	51	2,422	58
Muller-Eberhard HJ (1927)	5,924	144	1,089	16	4,835	128
Nossal GJV (1931)	3,985	99	2,374	54	1,611	45
Paul WE (1936)	4,189	126	592	27	3,597	99
Pressman D (1916)	3,726	240	127	10	3,599	230
Reisfeld RA (1926)	4,559	109	2,052	21	2,507	88
Roitt IM (1927)	3,902	103	513	11	3,389	92
Rosen FS (1930)	4,149	148	779	29	3,370	119
Sela M (1924)	4,987	238	841	24	4,146	214
Terasaki PI (1929)	5,174	176	1,076	26	4,098	150
Waksman BH (1919)	4,730	145	1,143	34	3,587	111
Wigzell H (1938)	4,046	85	719	16	3,327	69
Endocrinology						
Aurbach GD (1927)	3,887	100	375	14	3,512	86
Bartter FC (1914)	3,736	176	756	25	2,980	151
*Berson SA (1918-72)	5,474	64	1,930	27	3,544	37
Conn JW (1907)	3,938	108	1,527	27	2,411	81
Daughaday WH (1918)	3,731	101	676	20	3,055	81
Greenwood FC (1927)	5,572	42	2,732	8	2,840	34
Guillemin R (1924)	4,200	128	632	25	3,568	103
Hunter WM (1929)	5,214	64	2,537	24	2,677	40
Kastin AJ (1934)	3,852	166	1,437	54	2,415	112
Kipnis DM (1927)	4,805	111	345	8	4,460	103
Laragh JH (1924)	4,763	134	1,263	38	3,500	96
Lever AF (1929)	3,884	127	326	7	3,558	120
Liddle GW (1921)	4,483	105	538	15	3,945	90
Lipsett MB (1921)	3,912	112	661	30	3,251	82
Midgley AR (1933)	5,108	101	1,540	21	3,568	80
Pastan I (1931)	5,997	145	1,644	41	4,353	104
Potts JT (1932)	4,148	148	568	13	3,580	135
Rasmussen H (1925)	4,489	133	2,128	49	2,361	84
Roth J (1934)	5,647	159	1,635	50	4,012	109
Schally AV (1926)	10,386	430	2,378	80	8,008	350
Unger RH (1924)	4,623	124	1,997	36	2,626	88
Wilson JD (1932)	4,140	147	1,745	72	2,395	75
*Wurtman RJ (1936)	6,170	223	3,175	74	2,995	149
Yalow RS (1921)	5,595	82	1,569	27	4,026	55

Figure 1. The 300 most-cited authors, 1961-1976.

Author (Birthdate)	Total Citations	Total Papers	Citations as 1st Author	1st Author Papers	Citations as Co-Author	Co-Author Papers
Molecular Biology						
Baltimore D (1938)	5,270	111	2,505	32	2,765	79
Berg P (1926)	5,307	111	645	15	4,662	96
Bonner J (1910)	7,096	121	1,523	21	5,573	100
Changeux JP (1936)	6,208	109	1,841	27	4,367	82
Gros F (1925)	3,712	104	743	8	2,969	96
Hurwitz J (1928)	4,873	102	1,318	16	3,555	86
*Jacob F (1920)	10,383	115	4,990	21	5,393	94
Leder P (1934)	3,892	70	683	20	3,209	50
Maizel JV (1934)	4,807	50	1,076	12	3,731	38
*Marmur J (1926)	10,254	87	5,856	23	4,398	64
*Monod J (1910-76)	6,945	33	3,079	7	3,866	26
Nomura M (1927)	5,100	147	2,089	49	3,011	98
*Perutz MF (1914)	4,734	61	3,475	37	1,259	24
*Racker E (1913)	4,876	141	997	33	3,879	108
Rich A (1924)	6,075	168	784	20	5,291	148
Schimke RT (1932)	4,816	76	2,254	22	2,562	54
Singer SJ (1924)	4,422	83	1,964	12	2,458	71
Szybalski W (1921)	3,753	84	499	10	3,254	74
Tomkins GM (1926-75)	6,157	135	1,171	20	4,986	115
Vinograd J (1913-76)	4,956	75	1,240	10	3,716	65
Weissbach H (1932)	4,112	163	685	31	3,427	132
Pharmacology						
*Anden NE (1937)	4,475	95	4,172	84	303	11
*Axelrod J (1912)	15,769	308	2,633	50	13,136	258
*Brodie BB (1909)	6,246	152	1,400	40	4,846	112
*Carlsson A (1923)	4,786	117	3,971	80	815	37
*Conney AH (1930)	6,366	143	3,098	32	3,268	111
Corrodi H (1929-74)	4,366	76	2,536	38	1,830	38
Costa E (1924)	3,994	184	543	22	3,451	162
*Curtis DR (1927)	3,728	88	2,985	65	743	23
Fuxe K (1938)	8,888	203	1,456	52	7,432	151
Gillette JR (1928)	3,869	136	594	25	3,275	111
Glowinski J (1936)	4,502	117	1,935	17	2,567	100
Greengard P (1925)	4,916	104	445	21	4,471	83
Iversen LL (1937)	5,833	128	2,608	60	3,225	68
Kopin IJ (1929)	6,694	217	1,790	29	4,904	188
Levy G (1928)	3,898	255	2,213	136	1,685	119
*Lowry OH (1910)	4,867	81	2,299	19	2,568	62
Robison GA (1934)	4,051	48	1,744	15	2,307	33
Sjoerdsma A (1924)	6,479	156	500	13	5,979	143
Snyder SH (1938)	6,687	211	2,131	59	4,556	152
*Sutherland EW (1915-74)	11,644	92	2,158	10	9,486	82
Vane JR (1927)	6,292	138	1,573	17	4,719	121

Figure 1. The 300 most-cited authors, 1961-1976.

Author (Birthdate)	Total Citations	Total Papers	Citations as 1st Author	1st Author Papers	Citations as Co-Author	Co-Author Papers
Cell Biology						
Aaronson SA (1942)	3,821	113	1,782	33	2,039	80
*Allison AC (1925)	5,807	187	3,434	86	2,373	101
Barrnett RJ (1920)	5,945	100	178	6	5,767	94
Brenner S (1927)	6,334	78	1,364	19	4,970	59
Busch H (1923)	4,736	256	420	29	4,316	227
*Davis BJ (1932)	7,602	13	7,436	1	166	12
Ernster L (1920)	5,884	120	1,651	21	4,233	99
*Farquhar MG (1928)	5,149	48	3,106	15	2,043	33
*Green DE (1910)	5,482	161	2,265	69	3,217	92
Green H (1925)	4,338	89	642	19	3,696	70
Leblond CP (1910)	5,165	90	119	5	5,046	85
McCulloch EA (1926)	4,417	82	603	11	3,814	71
*Palade GE (1912)	11,242	104	478	7	10,764	97
Penman S (1930)	7,124	101	2,278	15	4,846	86
*Porter KR (1912)	4,221	65	523	19	3,698	46
*Sabatini DD (1931)	4,649	23	4,164	8	485	15
Sachs L (1924)	5,982	176	333	14	5,649	162
Sandberg AA (1921)	4,489	171	1,467	40	3,022	131
Weissmann G (1930)	5,210	164	2,975	80	2,235	84
Physiology						
Arimura A (1923)	5,278	210	934	41	4,344	169
Brown JJ (1928)	3,892	148	2,797	85	1,095	63
Butcher RW (1930)	6,875	48	3,020	13	3,855	35
*Carlson LA (1928)	4,002	146	2,316	89	1,686	57
*Eccles JC (1903)	4,579	108	3,238	84	1,341	24
*Fredrickson DS (1924)	7,871	128	4,929	28	2,942	100
*Hubel DH (1926)	4,474	35	3,572	24	902	11
Lassen NA (1926)	4,004	121	1,715	40	2,289	81
McCann SM (1925)	4,956	176	657	15	4,299	161
Meites J (1913)	4,665	183	599	15	4,066	168
Mirsky AE (1900-74)	5,083	61	206	8	4,877	53
Munro HN (1915)	4,414	143	809	32	3,605	111
Odell WD (1929)	3,720	109	1,505	28	2,215	81
Page IH (1901)	5,161	178	728	52	4,433	126
Park CR (1916)	3,763	72	55	3	3,708	69
Robertson JI (1928)	3,705	135	83	3	3,622	132
Starzl TE (1926)	4,901	190	2,354	75	2,547	115
Waldmann TA (1930)	4,088	111	1,657	31	2,431	80
Wiesel TN (1924)	4,605	34	872	7	3,733	27
Microbiology & Virology						
Blumberg BS (1925)	6,029	173	2,850	63	3,179	110
Chanock RM (1924)	7,659	219	1,807	19	5,852	200
Darnell JE (1930)	9,091	83	1,654	11	7,437	72
Henle G (1912)	5,261	93	1,740	14	3,521	79

Figure 1. The 300 most-cited authors, 1961-1976.

Author (Birthdate)	Total Citations	Total Papers	Citations as 1st Author	1st Author Papers	Citations as Co-Author	Co-Author Papers
Microbiology & Virology (continued)						
Henle W (1910)	4,908	100	1,024	23	3,884	77
Hilleman MR (1919)	4,871	180	713	37	4,158	143
Huebner RJ (1914)	8,418	237	2,319	16	6,099	221
Koprowski H (1916)	4,419	195	797	17	3,622	178
McCarthy BJ (1934)	4,625	102	1,176	23	3,449	79
Melnick JL (1914)	7,466	341	868	54	6,598	287
Rapp F (1929)	3,729	174	1,299	52	2,430	122
Rapp HJ (1923)	3,762	118	325	11	3,437	107
Rowe WP (1926)	7,183	130	1,344	27	5,839	103
Sever JL (1932)	4,599	179	2,350	48	2,249	131
Spiegelman S (1914)	9,712	149	1,233	26	8,479	123
Strominger JL (1925)	5,854	212	567	15	5,287	197
Uhr JW (1927)	4,567	110	1,904	23	2,663	87
Yanofsky C (1925)	4,640	145	937	19	3,703	126
Physics & Biophysics						
*Anderson PW (1923)	3,838	77	2,750	45	1,088	32
*Chance B (1913)	7,981	320	4,370	150	3,611	170
*Cromer DT (1923)	5,587	48	4,910	21	677	27
*Dalgarno A (1928)	3,712	186	1,831	77	1,881	109
*Fisher ME (1931)	5,164	109	3,509	63	1,655	46
Franklin RM (1930)	3,917	89	802	19	3,115	70
*Gell-Mann M (1929)	4,912	23	3,902	15	1,010	8
Mandel P (1942)	3,881	395	418	43	3,463	352
*McConnell HM (1927)	4,309	103	391	19	3,918	84
Miledi R (1927)	4,111	93	1,339	31	2,772	62
Osborn M (1940)	6,618	21	199	7	6,419	14
Rice SA (1932)	4,034	189	312	13	3,722	176
Setlow RB (1921)	3,777	74	2,166	25	1,611	49
Sinsheimer RL (1920)	5,332	132	183	8	5,149	124
Till JE (1931)	5,109	92	1,600	17	3,509	75
*Weber K (1936)	8,517	98	6,784	35	1,733	63
*Weinberg S (1933)	7,349	85	5,467	57	1,882	28
Wyman J (1901)	4,208	91	288	12	3,920	79
Histology & Oncology						
Boyse EA (1923)	8,239	169	1,424	25	6,815	144
Carbone PP (1931)	4,413	136	697	20	3,716	116
*Falck B (1927)	4,088	101	1,934	29	2,154	72
Heidelberger C (1920)	3,981	145	691	21	3,290	124
Hellstrom I (1932)	5,219	100	3,482	56	1,737	44
Hellstrom KE (1934)	4,985	101	811	21	4,174	80
Hokfelt T (1940)	4,553	127	1,592	53	2,961	74
Klein E (1925)	4,650	239	1,268	80	3,382	159
*Klein G (1925)	7,393	300	2,808	93	4,585	207
*Luft JH (1927)	8,902	21	8,446	12	456	9
Moore GE (1920)	4,026	247	1,746	101	2,280	146

Figure 1. The 300 most-cited authors, 1961-1976.

Author (Birthdate)	Total Citations	Total Papers	Citations as 1st Author	1st Author Papers	Citations as Co-Author	Co-Author Papers
Histology & Oncology (continued)						
Old LJ (1933)	8,457	146	2,614	24	5,843	122
*Pearse AGE (1916)	4,415	173	1,746	44	2,669	129
Todaro GJ (1937)	6,936	135	2,466	37	4,470	98
*Weber G (1932)	4,744	272	2,463	125	2,281	147
Pathology						
Benditt EP (1916)	3,755	117	317	22	3,438	95
Bensch K (1928)	3,775	19	164	4	3,611	15
Dixon FJ (1920)	6,590	169	1,163	23	5,427	146
Edwards JE (1911)	3,828	270	234	18	3,594	252
Fasman GD (1925)	4,149	98	951	21	3,198	77
*Karnovsky MJ (1926)	10,114	116	4,601	17	5,513	99
Metcalf D (1929)	3,904	130	1,750	78	2,154	52
*Miller JFA (1931)	4,432	54	2,346	32	2,086	22
*Novikoff AB (1913)	5,101	91	2,841	48	2,260	43
Popper H (1903)	3,795	168	788	50	3,007	118
*Reynolds ES (1928)	10,453	46	10,078	30	375	16
Trump BF (1932)	3,973	152	1,963	41	2,010	111
Weiss L (1928)	4,072	254	2,326	149	1,746	105
Miscellaneous Medical Disciplines						
(Cardiology, Hematology, Gastroenterology & Radiology)						
*Beutler E (1928)	4,537	239	3,117	133	1,420	106
*Braunwald E (1929)	15,040	422	2,255	68	12,785	354
Epstein SE (1935)	3,948	198	1,157	35	2,791	163
Frei E (1924)	4,167	173	861	46	3,306	127
Freireich EJ (1927)	3,998	179	417	14	3,581	165
Gorlin R (1926)	5,697	227	732	26	4,965	201
Grossman MI (1919)	6,096	236	864	57	5,232	179
*Herbert V (1927)	5,739	169	3,107	70	2,632	99
Hofmann AF (1931)	4,254	154	2,127	36	2,127	118
Isselbacher KJ (1925)	5,027	202	1,024	19	4,003	183
Kaplan HS (1918)	4,187	170	1,415	51	2,772	119
Lees RS (1934)	5,667	61	803	19	4,864	42
Levy RI (1937)	8,227	156	814	31	7,413	125
Lieber CS (1931)	4,432	154	2,039	59	2,393	95
Mason DT (1932)	4,232	311	1,534	59	2,698	252
Morrow AG (1922)	5,308	239	587	32	4,721	207
Mustard JF (1927)	4,852	198	1,668	53	3,184	145
Ross J (1928)	7,207	220	1,337	38	5,870	182
Sherlock S (1918)	5,421	243	931	51	4,490	192
Sonnenblick EH (1932)	8,540	237	2,800	44	5,740	193
Wagner HN (1927)	4,951	288	1,200	38	3,751	250
Wallach DFH (1926)	3,835	102	1,104	34	2,731	68

lists are not fully comparable, it would be rash to attribute this relatively small number solely to the effect of co-author citation data. It would have been interesting to produce a directly comparable list, but that will not be possible until we go back to compile source data for pre-1961 material.

In Figure 1, the authors are listed alphabetically under their disciplines. The alphabetical ordering is intended to avoid the connotation that absolute frequency of citation indicates the greater or lesser merit of an author's work. The grouping by discipline will obviate invidious comparisons across disciplines.

Each author's discipline was identified by checking a number of biographical indexes, including *American Men & Women of Science* and *World Who's Who in Science*. However, many of the authors are involved in interdisciplinary work. Thus, some may feel that they have been slightly misclassified.

The representation within disciplines is of course related to citation practices in various fields. Thus, the number of authors in a field like biochemistry, which now averages 30 references per article, is expected to be significantly higher than that for physics, where papers have an average of 12.5 citations.[5]

While the bio-medical disciplines dominate the list overall, the two largest groups are organic and inorganic chemistry and biochemistry, each with 14% of the total. Of the 42 authors in chemistry, 29 are organic chemists and 13 are inorganic chemists. Immunology is represented by 26 authors (8.7%); endocrinology by 24 (8.0%).

Molecular biology and pharmacology, with 21 authors apiece, each account for 7.0% of the total. Physiology and cell biology are both represented by 19 authors (6.3%); physics and biophysics by 18 (6.0%). There are also nine microbiologists and nine virologists on the list, who together account for 6.0% of the total. Pathology is represented by 13 (4.3%) authors, oncology by ten (3.3%), and cardiology also by ten.

Five authors (1.7%) are in gastroenterology. And another five are in histology. Hematology is represented by four authors (1.3%). And there are three radiologists (1.0%).

No mathematicians *per se* appear on the list. However, M.E. Fisher, a mathematical physicist, is in the top 300. Engineers do not appear on the list either. This may be due to the fact that engineering and technology papers average only 6 citations and tend to cite handbooks and textbooks rather than engineering papers.[6]

In the past it was claimed by Dr. Robert S. Platt, Jr., of the Department of Botany, Ohio State University, that botanists were particularly slighted by the first-author phenomenon.[7] Yet no botanists appeared on this "all-author" list. The most-cited botanist is F. Skoog, who ranked 489th with 3,141 citations. The absence of botanists in the top 300 can be attributed to many causes. Dr. L. Andrew Staehelin of the University of Colorado, Boulder has suggested that many botanists call themselves molecular or cell biologists these days.[8]

J. Levitt of the Carnegie Institution of Washington points out that botanists cite the life and physical sciences literature, but that the reverse is not true for chemists and other basic scientists.[9] This would suggest that botany is primarily descriptive and applied, and is no longer a "basic" science.

In any case, it is certain that the lack of representation on this list of some scientific disciplines and specialties is an artifact of the activity and citation practices in the missing fields, as well as of the limits on the length of the list we could publish. We may expand the most-cited "all-author" list to 1,000 or more names in the future. Hopefully, the most-cited authors in all specialties would be represented—even botany, earth sciences, and other poorly represented fields.

In Figure 1, we have also shown the total number of citations received and the total number of papers written by each author, 1961-1976. Following this is a breakdown of the citations to papers on which the person was the primary author, the number of papers on which the person was the primary author, citations to co-authored papers, and the number of papers on which the person was co-author.

These data give a more accurate picture of the accomplishments of many authors. For example, Carl Djerassi would have ranked in the top 200 authors if we had only counted citations to publications on which he was primary author. When the papers he co-authored are taken into account, he ranks as the *sixth* most-cited author.

The reason for this great discrepancy is simple. Between 1961 and 1976, he was first author of 77 papers. However, he was a co-author on 354 papers.

Anyone familiar with the work of this genius, who helped develop the first successful birth-control pill, knows that this citation record accurately reflects his formidable impact on science during the past few decades—no less than his remarkable and continuing productivity.

An even more extreme example is Nobelist H.G. Khorana. By primary-author count alone, he would not have ranked in the top 2,000 authors. But the inclusion of citations to papers he co-authored puts him into the top 300.

Every author on this list has been cited at least 3,700 times. The average number of citations is 5,496. The average number of citations for primary-authored papers is 1,794; for co-authored papers, 3,791. Incidentally, there are another 1,150 authors who were cited 2,000 or more times in this period.

In Figure 1, the year of birth of each author appears in parentheses after the name. A few authors are deceased. The average age is 54.

It is not surprising that only one author, F. Lipmann, was born before 1900. The citation counts on which this study is based are only to papers published, 1961-1976. Only 4% (12) of the authors were born 1900-1909; 21% (63), 1910-1919. Almost half (142) were born in the 1920's and one fourth in the 30's. Of the five authors born in the 40's, M.D. Cooper (1945) appears to be the youngest.

Some readers may criticize the methodology adopted here. After all, if ten people co-author one paper, why should each author be treated equally with those who have written a paper alone? I think the data will show that "junior" technicians and authors rank poorly unless they have consistently co-authored papers with a senior author like Khorana. For example, none of Djerassi's co-authors appears on this list. Khorana's three co-authors on the list—Kornberg, Racker, and Roseman—were all professors at the time they authored papers with him. Roseman, for example, was a "visiting professor" when he and Khorana worked together.[10]

The present list does include some scientist-administrators who are inclined to place their names on hundreds of papers, as secondary authors. The list may also include certain academicians, who have not achieved great distinction but have co-authored dozens of papers with graduate students. I have observed that long series of papers by such "groups" tend to be displaced by "review" papers written by the

"senior" scientists on the team. That's why first-author data identified so many scientists who had also been secondary authors on many papers.

As always, we have tried to avoid errors due to homographs (names which represent more than one person). While these were not difficult to detect, it was not easy to separate the publications of each person involved. In some cases, homographs were removed from our original list because none of the people had 3,700 or more citations. In others, one of the persons did have enough citations to remain in the top 300. We have adjusted the number of citations and papers attributed to him or her. A good example of our method is E. Klein, which proved to be a homograph representing several scientists: Edmund Klein, Eva Klein, Elias Klein, and others. We separated the citations belonging to each and discovered that Eva Klein was the only one who had enough citations to remain on the list. We then adjusted the number of citations and papers attributed to her.

For the majority of authors, however, the figures were not changed. Some of the authors who scan the list may find a few more papers attributed to them than they wrote. We considered homographs with just a few papers and citations insignificant "noise."

Now that we have compiled this all-author file, we can better study patterns of self-citation. Indeed, we are in a position to measure degrees of "incestuous citation," or citation among teams of researchers. Previously, with only first-author data available, a person's self-citations could only be identified when the person was the *first* author of a cited work. Now we can identify citations to publications on which a person was a co-author. We might use this new capability to explore the inbreeding patterns of certain groups who tend to cite each other. Indeed, such incestuous citation might be characteristic of some milestone developments. If such enclaves exist, we need to know more about them, and why they remain isolated.

Now that we have begun to compile this kind of information, we will need to produce new reports every year or two, eliminating as we go the oldest years of our data. This will reduce the rankings of those scientists who published high-impact works in earlier years.

As each year passes, our data will become ever more comprehensive, because of the rapid growth of the *SCI* files in the sixties. I would expect, therefore, that our future studies will be more comprehensive and accurate than the present one.

As always, your comments are invited. If you think we have made an error, please do not hesitate to contact us. From our earlier experience, we have reason to expect correction notes from a few authors.

As we have done in the past, we will soon publish a list of each author's most-cited work, as well as academy memberships and awards.

ERRATUM:
During the computer run for the 300 authors list, a few names which should have been on the list were not picked up. I apologize to W.C. Hamilton and G.R. Satchler for their omission from the list. The computer problem has now been corrected, and these scientists will appear in our upcoming study of the 1,000 most-cited authors.

REFERENCES

1. **Garfield E.** The 250 most-cited primary authors, 1961-1975. 1. How the names were selected. *Current Contents* (49):5-15, 5 December 1977.
2. ------------. The 250 most-cited primary authors, 1961-1975. 2. The correlation between citedness, Nobel prizes, and academy memberships. *Current Contents* (50):5-15, 12 December 1977.
3. ------------. The 250 most-cited primary authors, 1961-1975. 3. Each author's most-cited publication. *Current Contents* (51):5-20, 19 December 1977.
4. ------------. So who's perfect? Corrections and additions to the 250 most-cited authors list. *Current Contents* (21):5-10, 22 May 1978.
5. **Narin F.** Evaluative bibliometrics: the use of publication and citation analysis in the evaluation of scientific activity. Cherry Hill, NJ: Computer Horizons, Inc., 1976, p. 171. NTIS-PB252339/AS.
6. **Garfield E.** Characteristics of highly cited publications in the engineering sciences. *Current Contents* (12):5-10, 22 March 1976.
7. **Platt R S, Jr.** Personal communication. 8 November 1977.
8. **Staehelin L S.** Personal communication. 8 November 1977.
9. **Levitt J.** Personal communication. 14 December 1977.
10. **Livesey E.** Personal communication. 19 June 1978.

Introducing PRIMATE™
—*Personal Retrieval of Information*
by *Microcomputer* And *Terminal* Ensemble

Number 29, July 17, 1978

On several occasions I've suggested that the rapid decrease in cost of minicomputers would have a great impact on all existing methods of retrieving information,[1-2] including on-line systems like *Scisearch*® and Medline.

A. E. Cawkell, ISI® 's Director of Research,[3] has been working on a microcomputer retrieval system called PRIMATE. The essay which follows is an effort on my part to do some market research for him. We would like to know if there is any serious interest in personal search systems.

After you scan *Current Contents*® each week, you write for reprints, make photocopies in your library, or order tear sheets from ISI. When the reprints arrive, you scan most of them quickly. Then, if you are like most readers, you "file" them. Or you may just note the article in the library and file an abstract.

I've said a great deal about reprints in the past. But I've avoided a discussion of methods of retrieving or storing reprints.

The literature is overloaded with articles on all sorts of filing systems.

It is precisely because of this that I am not citing any of them here.

Some people have undoubtedly succeeded in setting up and maintaining elaborate filing systems. Perhaps one of the most elaborate is the system established by Hans Selye in Montreal.[4] And I have seen many large indexed files of reprints collected by individual scientists. Some of these were developed over a 40-50 year period.

Many teachers maintain file folders of broad general categories corresponding to lectures they give. Reprints are added to these folders as acquired. They are reviewed when the appropriate lecture has to be prepared.

But while there are numerous well-organized reprint collections, most scientists lose their initial enthusiasm. They wind up filing reprints alphabetically by author. Still other scientists and especially physicians start out with the best intentions, but in the hustle and bustle of everyday research or clinical practice, they abandon any attempt to be systematic. They never seem to put their reprints into any kind of file. Their reprint "files" cover their bookcases, labs, desktops, and window sills. I am always impressed when they are able to find anything in this seeming chaos.

Those of us who have a less than effective filing arrangement know we have a problem. We put up with it partly out of inertia and partly because we believe that there is no simple alternative. We prefer not to evaluate the consequences of information delayed, lost, or never used by reason of ineffective retrieval.

Frequently when we try to find information in our own files, we wind up relying first on the library. The many published indexes often enable us to identify papers that already exist in our files. I have on occasion dreamt about personalized editions of the *Science Citation Index*® that would tell the reader which articles were in his or her reprint file.

ISI is trying to find a solution to the seemingly hopeless problem of personal filing systems. We are now studying the feasibility of desktop information storage and retrieval systems. One prototype is PRIMATE—*P*ersonal *R*etrieval of *I*nformation by *M*icrocomputer *A*nd *T*erminal *E*nsemble.

PRIMATE hardware would consist of a microcomputer with at least a 16K-byte CPU (Central Processing Unit), 9″ CRT (Cathode Ray Tube) display, double-density dual "floppy" magnetic disc, mass storage device, and a keyboard. It would be able to store information on 10,000 papers, indexed by up to ten terms per paper.

But the key to an effective PRIMATE system is software. I use

this term to include not only the computer programs necessary to operate the microcomputer, but also the indexing systems used to characterize the documents.

In the PRIMATE system, each incoming paper is assigned a serial number. For each new paper, you'd enter this serial number, a complete bibliographic description, and set of indexing terms. You add information for a group of papers every week, perhaps after reading *Current Contents* or as reprints arrive.

The indexing information is entered into PRIMATE and automatically added to the computer's memory. The reprints are filed in numerical order in filing cabinets or loose-leaf binders. If you prefer, a system based on using authors' names instead of serial numbers could be employed. But the serial number system maintains the chronological integrity of your file. It also facilitates the use of microfilm, holographic or video files.

When you needed to retrieve papers, you would command PRIMATE to display citations for articles filed under particlar terms. Using the CRT display, you could peruse the titles retrieved, check the serial numbers, and examine them in the loose-leaf binders.

Alternatively, you could command PRIMATE to display an indexing term along with the number of articles you have stored under it. If you have used authors' names as indexing terms, you could learn whether the file includes papers by a particular author and if so, how many. You could then display the records for these papers and locate them in your binders.

PRIMATE is a rather straightforward, simple system of personal information retrieval. But it could provide several sophisticated functions which are needed for an effective and convenient system.

For example, suppose you display the indexing term "virus". You find out there are 35 papers indexed under this term. When you put the first virus-related paper in your file, "virus" was an adequate indexing term. But now it is too general for your needs. So you review the 35 titles on the CRT screen and assign more specific terms, such as adenovirus, RNA virus, etc. To do this, you simply type in the new indexing terms. PRIMATE reorganizes itself so that your next search can be more specific. Since they are filed by number (or by author), the papers themselves do not need refiling.

Searches could be very specific, both as to subject matter and chronology. For example, you could ask to see adenovirus papers published after or before 1977.

We are also considering an optional updating service called ASCAMATE. This would help keep you aware of new articles pertaining to your interests. You give us a profile (made up of key words, citations, authors' names, etc.). ISI's computer will match the profile against our weekly file of new articles.

As we do in our *ASCA®* service now, we would periodically send you descriptions of pertinent current articles. But instead of print-outs we would send you a "floppy disc." You plug the disc into PRIMATE, observe the records on the screen, and place those of interest in temporary store. You can then obtain the reprints of the articles you want by writing authors. Or you may obtain them from your local library or from our *OATS®* library service. When the reprints arrive, you would number them serially and file them in numerical order. You would then recall the appropriate records from computer store, add your indexing terms, and send them automatically to main storage.

Although I have discussed PRIMATE in terms of retrieving *articles,* it is probably apparent that you can use it for filing books, letters, drawings, etc. And if your collection of information includes many different types of documents located in different places, you can create a numbering system which will tell you where and what something is. For instance, the numbers 1-3000 could be reserved for reprints, 3000-4000 might indicate books in the department library, and 4000-5000 would be correspondence, etc.

Undoubtedly many readers will think that PRIMATE is a fine idea. But from experience they realize that effective indexing can be a problem. How would a computerized system overcome that difficulty? The answer is that the system may not but an ISI information specialist can.

At the time of the system's delivery, one of our specialists would call upon you to describe

PRIMATE's operation. After discussing your retrieval needs, the specialist would recommend appropriate indexing procedures. I could suggest that the simplest title-word indexing would be as effective as most controlled vocabulary systems in existence. Most of you would not believe me. And yet that is precisely what we do with our Permuterm® system. On the other hand, title-word indexing can be easily augmented by "enrichment." We do this for the humanities literature. Or you might prefer to use author-assigned indexing terms, as emphasized by such journals as *Proceedings of the National Academy of Sciences* or *Tetrahedron*. The subtleties of indexing are the subject of thousands of papers in the literature of information science. Eventually, if you would use a system like PRIMATE, you would have to select *some* indexing system. That may be the hardest decision of all. I remember the dozens of scientists who were interested in our *ASCA* system, but were never willing to prepare a profile.

Once you do decide on a preferred indexing philosophy, you would enter a limited number of papers into the system. Retrieval on this small file would be tested to identify peculiarities or problems. When you decided the system was working effectively, you could begin to enter information regularly. Or we could train your assistant to do the same.

Some readers may feel that such a system could help retrieve the information buried in their reprint files. But where does one find time to put hundreds or thousands of older papers into the system? We would also offer to index your backfiles. Since this is *your* personal system, you would be consulted at the initial indexing stage. But once that's done, you could have a complete backfile organized and easily retrievable.

The cost of a PRIMATE system is still somewhat uncertain. However, based on present equipment costs, the rental charges would be in the range of $100-$150 per month including installation and software.

The ASCAMATE updating service might run $400 per year for weekly updates or $250 per year for less frequent monthly updates. The backfile service, of course, would be subject to quotation, depending on the state and size of the files. This could easily involve a few thousand dollars, unless you get student assistants to do the work.

If you compare these costs to the price of a *Current Contents* subscription, then you may be in a state of shock. You may in fact be forced to re-evaluate your own existing manual system. You may be surprised by what it is really costing you to maintain and use it. Most people will not have any way to compare since they have no existing system at all.

PRIMATE hardware and software will not be absolutely unique. I fully expect that microcomputer manufacturers will design software packages that handle most everyday retrieval problems. Even the maintenance of an up-to-date address file is an important retrieval problem in every lab. But I recall myriad personal indexing systems—including those based on edge-notched cards, peek-a-boo, delta cards, etc.—that are now defunct. So, I am convinced that microcomputers will only be successful when the software and indexing system are adequate to the task.

If you have any interest in PRIMATE or other personal information systems, please write to me in Philadelphia or to Mr. A. E. Cawkell, Director of Research, ISI, 132 High St., Uxbridge, Middlesex, England UB8 1DP.

REFERENCES

1. **Garfield E.** The information-conscious university and ASCA software. *Current Contents* (37):5-7, 12 September 1977.
2. -------------. Mini-computer or on-line access? *MEDOK* 1975(2):7-11, 1975.
3. -------------. A. E. Cawkell, information detective—and ISI's man in the U.K. *Current Contents* (40):5-6, October 1971.
   [Reprinted in: **Garfield E.** *Essays of an Information Scientist.* Philadelphia: ISI Press, 1977. 2 vols.]
4. **Selye H & Ember G.** *Symbolic shorthand system for physiology and medicine.* Montréal: Université de Montréal, 1964. 238 p.

CURRENT COMMENTS

Announcing *Current Contents/Arts & Humanities:* **in 1979 our** *Current Contents* **series will cover virtually every academic discipline**

Number 30, July 24, 1978

When ISI® launched the *Arts & Humanities Citation Index*™ this year,[1] we reversed a pattern that had been established by the *Science Citation Index*® and the *Social Sciences Citation Index*™. *SCI*® was introduced eight years *after* we published the first issue of *Current Contents*® */Life Sciences* and four years after the earliest version of *CC*® */Physical & Chemical Sciences*. *SSCI*™ was introduced nearly 20 years *after* the first version of *Current Contents* for the social sciences (now entitled *Current Contents/Social & Behavioral Sciences*). But in the arts and humanities, we have produced a comprehensive citation index *before* starting the corresponding *Current Contents* edition.

There probably is no reasonable logic to this progress of events. We were uncertain about the needs of scholars in the arts and humanities. But the publication of *A&HCI*™ has been received with such enthusiasm by scholars and librarians that we now feel that *Current Contents/Arts & Humanities* will be equally well accepted. In my contacts with humanities scholars, both young and old, I have not found attitudes towards information problems significantly different from those of their counterparts in the sciences.

The new *Current Contents* edition will be a unique tool in the arts and humanities. I am not aware of any other weekly current awareness publication covering these disciplines. For scholars working on books or articles, or students writing master's or doctoral theses, *CC/A&H* will be invaluable for learning about the most recent scholarship on their subjects.

Scheduled for introduction in January, 1979, *CC/A&H* will be published weekly like the six other editions of *CC*. It will cover over 900 journals from the fields of literature, music, art and architecture, history, philosophy, theology and religion, classics, dance, film, TV and radio, folklore, linguistics and philology, and theater.

The format of the new *CC* edition will look much the same as that of the existing editions. But there will be a major difference in its indexing philosophy. Unlike most scientific or even social sciences titles, the titles of arts and humanities articles can sometimes be hopelessly nonspecific. For this reason, we will adopt a policy of title enrichment.

For example, if you scanned the contents page of a humanities journal and saw an article entitled "A Portrait in Black," you would be little the wiser. However, in *CC/A&H* you will see, with the title, the name of the person, place, or thing which was the subject of the article. For "Portrait in Black" this might be Franz Kafka. Our staff will enrich each nonspecific title by adding appropriate terms. Thus readers will be able to identify articles relevant to their interests—even for titles that do not adequately describe the subject matter.

Terms added by title enrichment will of course be included in *CC/A&H's Weekly Subject Index.* This will enable users of *WSI* to locate articles which otherwise would not be retrievable. There will be other indexing policies which will preserve the integrity of phrases or names that require "invisible" hyphenation. Thus, *War and Peace* would appear as a single term.

Another enhancement to contents pages in *CC/A&H* will be the listing in full of all books reviewed in each issue. Arts and humanities journals include numerous reviews, but they often fail to print this information in their tables of contents. Instead they list only the title of the section, i.e., *Book Reviews, Reviews in Brief,* etc. When this is the case, we will add the title and author of each book as well as the reviewer.

These enhancements to the contents pages are much greater than those we provide for other editions of *Current Contents.* For this reason, we are planning to photocompose most of the contents pages instead of cutting, pasting, and photographing the originals. This will enable us to use formats that we believe to be most efficient for rapid scanning. Many contents pages will lose their original format but not necessarily their individuality. Style will be varied as much as possible. Our arts edition of *CC* should retain all the esthetic benefits to be derived from variations in type style.

Like other editions of *CC, CC/A&H* will provide a weekly author-address directory and a journal publisher directory three times per year. Readers will be able to order tear sheets of articles from our *OATS® (Original Article Tear Sheet)* service. This may be particularly relevant for articles containing color photos or plates. On the other hand, this may also mean we can less often supply a photocopy in lieu of the original when our supply of tear sheets is exhausted. If there is sufficient demand we could use a color copier, but in most cases I believe the publishers will have original copies still in stock.

Following our policy with other *CC*s, we will include the Press Digest and *Current Comments®*. We will not include Citation Classics until the second year of publication. By then we will have had a chance to analyze our files of *A&HCI* to identify highly cited works in appropriate fields of the arts and humanities.

Selecting arts and humanities 'citation classics' will certainly present some interesting problems.

Undoubtedly we will be more interested in identifying interpreters of certain well-cited works in the humanities. It would not seem particularly appropriate for us to ask Aristotle or Plato why their works were heavily cited last year. We have on occasion had this same problem in the sciences.

However, we could annually prepare lists of highly cited or discussed philosophers, writers, artists, etc., for publication in *Current Comments*. Over a period of time these lists would give us insights into the waxing and waning fashionability of various works among scholars.

CC/A&H will also contain a significant *Current Book Contents*® section. Using data from *A&HCI*, we can identify those books most frequently reviewed and perhaps publish a "review of reviews" for those works that warrant such treatment.

With the introduction of *CC/A&H* we will complete our coverage of most types of journal literature received in most university libraries and comparable institutions.

Yet there is one category that is not yet encompassed by a *CC* edition. It can best be described as contemporary and public affairs. I hope that by 1980, we will be ready to launch a *CC* edition covering this area. Some of the journals it would include—*Scientific American, Psychology Today,* etc.—already appear in various editions of *CC*. However, some publications, like *Time,* or *Newsweek,* which would be appropriate for this edition, are not covered by any of our existing *CC*s. The edition would also include an enlarged Press Digest. It might also contain a section announcing significant new magazines, as I suggested in an earlier essay.[2]

With the launching of *CC/Arts & Humanities* in 1979 and *CC/Contemporary & Public Affairs* in 1980, we will cover the full range of periodicals available to the potential reader.

One of the main reasons for the existence of *CC* is to counter the feeling of inadequacy described by Eugene Wigner,[3] among others, when confronted with the always growing mass of publications in science and elsewhere. At least *CC* enables you to see what is published and to select what is important for your immediate interests. But perhaps *CC* has a more important function. It facilitates the process whereby the more perceptive scholar discovers a relationship between two ideas that otherwise seemed unrelated. In the final analysis one might say that's what creative work is all about.

REFERENCES

1. **Garfield E.** Will ISI's *Arts & Humanities Citation Index* revolutionize scholarship? *Current Contents* (32):5-9, 8 August 1977.
2. --------------. Keeping up with new magazines. *Current Contents* (9):5-14, 27 February 1978.
3. **Wigner EP.** *Symmetries and reflections.* Bloomington Indiana University Press, 1967. As cited in: Weinberg A M. The limits of science and trans-science. *Interdisciplinary Science Reviews* 2:337-42, 1977.

CURRENT COMMENTS

The Endless Quest for Timeliness— A Fourth Quarterly *Science Citation Index*

Number 31, July 31, 1978

Timeliness is an ISI® characteristic in which we take special pride. Back in 1964 when the first commercial version of the *Science Citation Index®* was launched, the up-to-date coverage of *SCI®*'s quarterly and annual indexes was considered remarkable. By then we had been publishing *Current Contents®* on a *weekly* schedule for eight years, so this did not seem especially remarkable to us.

The size of the indexing job involved, however, has quadrupled in the 14 years since *SCI* started. In 1964 a typical quarterly index included 35,000 source articles. In 1979 *SCI* quarterlies will each cover about 135,000 source items per issue. And the number of references per source article has also increased significantly. For example, in biochemistry the average number of references per paper has increased 50%. Quarterly *SCI Citation* and *Source Indexes* now cover more than an annual did 14 years ago! Also, *SCI* did not have a *Permuterm® Subject Index* in 1964.[1] The size of a typical quarterly *SCI*, therefore, is now almost ten times what it was in the early 60's.

Furthermore, we have always guaranteed to index 95% of all journal issues which have publication dates falling within the period indexed in each annual cumulation. *SCI* is supposed to be a *calendar-year* index. The 5% not in the annual are published so late that we have to include them in the next year's index. However, covering 95% means we must delay our closeout until late January or early February in order to accommodate late journals. Some rather important journals appear a month or so late on a regular basis. There are also inevitable postal delays even with air delivery.

The resultant delay in publishing *SCI* then gives rise to complaints from librarians and users for whom the timeliness of the index is one of its most valuable features. This situation is further complicated by the fact that many users misinterpret the date on the cover (which shows the indexing period) as the publication date of the index. They ask why we don't practice what we preach about the necessity for publishing on time.[2]

One reason that subscribers are more concerned these days with "lateness" is the advent of SCISEARCH® and other on-line information facilities. These services have changed the user's perception of "up-to-date coverage." The immediate access to information which SCISEARCH now provides makes the frequent user conscious of and therefore impatient with the necessary delay between the end of an indexing period and the publication of the printed index.

The result of this is that by May or June (when we ordinarily publish the *SCI* annual) it *seems* like forever to our subscribers since they received anything. After all, they received the last (July-September) quarterly in November or December.

Therefore, for the 1979 *SCI*, ISI is taking important steps to provide more timely service for its clients. As a first step we are going to publish a fourth quarterly covering the October-December period formerly absorbed by the annual index. This quarterly will appear in late February or early March.

We had considered publishing a fourth quarterly in the past. But so long as we could deliver the annual within a month or so after the fourth quarterly would have appeared, the quarterly would have wasted money. Now, as we face the increasing time requirements of processing a larger and larger *SCI*, there is no doubt that a fourth quarterly can be delivered to users at least 90 days before the annual.

There are several reasons for this. The quarterlies are "perfect" bound in stiff paper, whereas cloth binding is required for the more permanent annuals. The time required to perform this laborious task is very significant. Apart from the fact that the annual is four times as large, the handling of our special lightweight paper is very involved. Besides this labor of binding, a lot of computer and photocomposer work is required before the annual is printed. And if you add to this the extra editing we do for an annual, there is no question that we would sacrifice quality if we rushed to get the annual out much earlier.

As a second step, we will modify our cutoff dates for the new fourth quarterly. Those journals will be included which are received by the end of the indexing period. We will no longer wait for the tardy journals. Their issues will be indexed in the next quarterly covering January-March receipts. On the other hand, the annual will be published later, in June or July of each year. This additional time to compose the annual will permit us to improve manual and machine editing procedures to raise its quality. It will also enable us to step up our quality control procedures.

The third step will be the use of a publication date (similar to that on a journal issue) on every *SCI* quarterly and annual. Subscribers can then judge our promptness in delivering our indexes by this standard.

As a final step to improve the timeliness of our services, we are reevaluating our present shipping methods, especially to overseas locations. We will no longer use slow-boats to anywhere, even though the weight of our annual *SCI* shipments is enough to fill a sizable cargo vessel. Air shipment will be the general rule or, alternatively, an optimal combination of air-cargo and surface facilities such as we use for *Current Contents* each week.

A special advantage to our users is the effective reduction in cost of *SCI* which addition of a fourth quarterly makes possible. Since the annual will not cover any more material than the quarterly indexes, the four separate quarterlies can then be used as a second set for satellite or departmental libraries. However, the annual indexes do contain considerable editing improvements and corrections, as well as the annual *Journal Citation Reports®* and reader guides.

In effect, the consumer will receive two indexes for the price of one. Although it is not so fast or convenient to search four quarterlies as it is to use an annual cumulation, it is better than doing an incomplete search. Since we supplied only three quarterlies in the past, most libraries discarded their quarterlies when the annual arrived. However, when they receive their 1979 annual, they will be able to put this extra set to good use.

Of course, the last word on timeliness for *SCI* has not yet been said. The next step "obviously" is to issue *SCI* every two months, or six times per year. While this would mean searching more issues by the time the annual appears, it is certainly more timely. Indeed, why stop there? Why not a monthly *SCI*? One could push this argument all the way towards daily publication. Indeed, I made such a proposal to the

National Science Foundation once, in conjunction with the idea of a daily newspaper of science.[3] The on-line availability of SCISEARCH might seem to obviate the need for more frequent issues of *SCI*. But why should users be forced to use an on-line system? In some parts of the world such systems may not be available for at least a decade.

Another way to give quick and easy access to the recent literature is to cumulate the *Weekly Subject Indexes (WSI)* to *Current Contents* on a monthly basis. Now that these appear in all six editions of *CC®* and are being used by many readers, there is considerable interest in such a cumulation. We are evaluating the possibility, especially for *CC/Life Sciences,* the largest of our six editions.

However, before a monthly cumulation of *WSI* would be feasible, ISI would need to devise better methods for controlling the specificity of the indexing procedures used. In a weekly issue you may not object to finding five or six entries under a particular indexing term. In a monthly issue you might not be so happy to find twenty-five, unless they were subdivided somehow. This problem is avoided in *SCI*'s *Permuterm Indexes* by the pairing of title-words to make two-level indexing entries. But this requires an amount of space difficult to justify in a weekly *CC* or even a monthly cumulation of the *WSI*.

We are now in the process of modifying our vocabulary control procedures so we can watch on a *daily* basis for phrases in titles that should be treated in the *Weekly*

Subject Index as single hyphenated terms. This improves specificity in searching.

Thus, while timeliness is our major preoccupation at ISI, we have to keep in mind other factors which may slow the user down. It does no good for us to turn out our indexes faster if it takes you forever to use them. I have no doubt that in the future readers will expect articles to be indexed and accessible on a daily basis—a real-time system as it were. At that point the quest for timeliness may take on a different dimension. I hope our fast performance in indexing will set an example for journals to process manuscripts faster and reduce further the lag between research and the public's access to information.

REFERENCES

1. **Garfield E.** The Permuterm Subject Index: an autobiographical review.
   J. Amer. Soc. Inform. Sci. 27:288-91, 1976.
   (Reprinted in: *Current Contents* (12):5-10, 21 March 1977.)
2. --------------. False publication dates and other rip-offs.
   Current Contents (20):5-8, 15 May 1978.
3. --------------. Ever think of *Current Contents* as a newspaper?
   Current Contents (40):5-6, 6 October 1975. (Reprinted in:
   Garfield E. *Essays of an information scientist.*
   Philadelphia: ISI Press, 1977. Vol. 2, p. 349-50.)

Current Comments

The 100 Articles Most Cited by Social Scientists, 1969-1977

Number 32, August 7, 1978

This week we are publishing the first in a series of studies on the literature and authors most cited by social scientists. The studies are based on data from the *Social Sciences Citation Index* ™ *(SSCI* ™*)*. For years we have been producing citation studies in the natural and physical sciences. But this is the first time we are publishing in *Current Contents*® *(CC*® *)* a citation study taken from the *SSCI* data base. We have, however, used the *SSCI* to produce cluster studies.[1]

In this week's essay we will present the 100 articles cited most frequently during the period 1969-1977. This is, of course, the period for which we have published *SSCI* to date.

Five of these 100 articles have been featured in Citation Classics, the weekly *CC* series in which the authors themselves tell us why their papers were heavily cited. For each "classic" we have indicated the appropriate *CC* issue number, date, and page number. Undoubtedly more of the papers on this list will appear in Citation Classics in the future.

Those unfamiliar with citation analysis may need some explanation of the mechanics of preparing lists of this type. Social scientists, like all other scholars, acknowledge prior publications by citing (or referencing) them in their own papers. These acknowledgements, or citations, are regularly compiled in the *SSCI*. This enables us to count and analyze them, either manually or by computer.

There are many reasons why one author may cite another.[2] We assume that the number of citations is a measure of the relative impact of the cited work. Papers which receive a large number of citations are usually found to have reported significant new knowledge or to have had a significant effect on a field.

Although it would have been easy to rank the papers by total citations, we resisted the temptation to do so. The list of articles which begins on page 8 is in alphabetical order. We wanted to avoid the assumption that frequency of citation indicates lesser or greater absolute merit. This assumption would be particularly absurd when comparing articles from different fields.

The papers on this list have been cited a minimum of 186 times. The average number of citations was 279. Compare this to the 10.6 citations the average cited item received, 1969-1977. The most-cited articles received an average 31.2 citations per year, while all cited items averaged only 1.33 per year. Thus, the papers on our list must be considered superstars—or unusual, to say the least.

To say that psychology dominates the disciplines represented on the list would be an understatement. Seventy-seven of the articles are in psychology. Of these, 12 were published in psychiatry journals. Of the psychology articles 16, or 21%, are in the subfield of learning and memory; eight, or 10% in research methodology; eight, or 11%, in social psychology; seven, or 9%, in conditioned learning, and the same number in motivation and behavior. Psychometrics accounted for 7 of the articles (9%), cognition five (6.5%), personality three (4%).

The reason why psychology papers predominate is fairly obvious. While psychology papers only contain an average of 9.4 references per article,[3] there is a substantial volume of psychology papers published each year. From our *SSCI Journal Citation Reports*® we can count the numbers of articles published in each journal. Psychology dominates this list because it is the largest of the social science research fields; as I have said for fields like biochemistry, the size of the field increases the chances for superstar papers. It is unlikely that you will find papers that are cited 200 or more times in disciplines that produce only a few thousand papers.

To offset the overshadowing effect of psychology in this list of social sciences articles, we will in the future list articles by each of the leading disciplines. Thus we might list the 50 most-cited articles in sociology, or economics, or law.

Indeed, only six of the articles on this list are in sociology, five in law, and four in economics. Three are in statistics. Political science and education are each represented by one article.

Two physiology articles, both by D.H. Hubel and T.N. Weisel, deal with the eye. The only biochemistry paper is Oliver Lowry's paper on protein determination. The presence of these three articles on the *SSCI* list may be in part attributed to citations in articles from such journals as *Brain Research, Vision Research*, etc., which were concerned with the physiological bases of perception.

The articles that appear on the *SSCI* most-cited list have publication dates that span five decades. The oldest paper on the list is a 1935 review article, J. R. Stroop's "Studies of Interference in Serial Verbal Reactions." The most recent article is H. H. Clark's 1973 paper, "Language-as-Fixed-Effect Fallacy: A Critique of Language Statistics in Psychological Research."

Clark's paper is the only one on the list five years old, and Stroop's the only one more than 37 years old. Twenty-two percent of the papers are six to ten years old, 31% 11 to 15 years old, 24% 16 to 20 years old, and 12% 21 to 25 years old. Only 5% of the articles are 26 to 30 years old, and 4% between 31 and 40 years old.

The 100 most-cited items appeared in 43 journals. Four of the journals—*Psychological Review, Psychological Bulletin, Psychometrika* and *Journal of Abnormal and Social Psychology*—account for over a third of the articles on the list. Seventeen of the most highly cited articles appeared in *Psychological Review*. Other journals that published more than one of the highly cited papers are: *American Journal of Psychiatry, American Psychologist, American Sociological Review, Archives of General Psychiatry, Harvard Law Review, Journal of Physiology—London, Journal of Experimental Psychology, Journal of Verbal Learning and Verbal Behavior, Journal of the Experimental Analysis of Behavior, Journal of Consulting and Clinical Psychology, Journal of Applied Behavior Analy-*
sis, *Psychological Monographs, Psychological Reports,* and *Science.*

Eleven of the authors appear twice on the most-cited article list. They are: A. Amsel, D. T. Campbell, L. J. Cronbach, D. H. Hubel, T. N. Wiesel, J. B. Kruskal, A. Paivio, R. N. Shepard, G. Sperling, S. Sternberg and E. Tulving. In all, 138 different authors were responsible for the 100 papers. Sixty-seven of the papers were the work of an individual author, and 25 the work of two; three of the papers had three authors, three had four, one had five and another six.

Most of the articles on the list will be recognized by social scientists as having some importance for their fields. They are highly cited for a number of reasons. Some are seminal papers, presenting a new finding that stimulated a body of research. Others are comprehensive review papers. Still others present research methods and procedures and are cited primarily by others using those methodologies. At least one of the articles is highly cited because it is controversial.

This article is Arthur Jensen's "How Much Can We Boost IQ and Scholastic Achievement?" The paper, which appeared in the *Harvard Educational Review* in the Winter 1969 issue, received 579 citations, 1969-1977. Some people claim that many of these citations are critical of the paper's content. In the article, Jensen argued that genetic factors may be involved in

Figure 1. The 100 most-cited articles, based on *Social Sciences Citation Index* data from 1969 to 1977.

Total Citations	Bibliographic Data
350	**Amsel A.** The role of frustrative nonreward in noncontinuous reward situations. *Psychol. Bull.* **55**:102-19, 1958.
230	**Amsel A.** Frustrative nonreward in partial reinforcement and discrimination learning: some recent history and a theoretical extension. *Psychol. Rev.* **69**:306-28, 1962.
211	**Anderson N H.** Likableness ratings of 555 personality-trait words. *J. Pers. Soc. Psychol.* **9**:272-9, 1968.
219	**Archer E J.** Reevaluation of the meaningfulness of all possible CVC trigrams. *Psychol. Monogr.* **74**:1-23, 1960.
203	**Argyle M & Dean J.** Eye-contact, distance and affiliation. *Sociometry* **28**:289-304, 1965.
217	**Asch S E.** Forming impressions of personality. *J. Abnormal Psychol.* **41**:258-90, 1946.
258	**Baer D M, Wolf M M & Risley T R.** Some current dimensions of applied behavior analysis. *J. Appl. Behav. Anal.* **1**:91-7, 1968.
196	**Bandura A, Ross D & Ross S A.** Imitation of film-mediated aggressive models. *J. Abnormal Psychol.* **66**:3-11, 1963.
255	**Bateson G, Jackson D D, Harley J & Weakland J.** Toward a theory of schizophrenia. *Behav. Sci.* **1**:251-64, 1956.
210	**Becker G S.** A theory of the allocation of time. *Econ. J.* **75**:493-517, 1965.
268	**Bem D J.** Self-perception: an alternative interpretation of cognitive dissonance phenomena. *Psychol. Rev.* **74**:183-200, 1967.
219	**Bolles R C.** Species-specific defense reactions and avoidance learning. *Psychol. Rev.* **77**:32-48, 1970. (Citation Classics. *Current Contents* (31):9, 31 July 1978).
186	**Bousfield A K & Bousfield W A.** Measurements of clustering and of sequential constancies in repeated free recall. *Psychol. Rep.* **19**:935-42, 1966.
204	**Broverman I K, Broverman D M, Clarkson F E, Rosencrantz P S & Vogel S R.** Sex-role stereotypes and clinical judgments of mental health. *J. Consult. Clin. Psychol.* **34**:1-7, 1970.
220	**Brown P L & Jenkins H M.** Auto-shaping of the pigeon's key-peck. *J. Exp. Anal. Behav.* **11**:1-8, 1968.
200	**Byrne D.** Interpersonal attraction and attitude similarity. *J. Abnormal Psychol.* **62**:713-5, 1961.
229	**Campbell D T.** Reforms as experiments. *Amer. Psychol.* **24**:409-29, 1969.
592	**Campbell D T & Fiske D W.** Convergent and discriminant validation by the multitrait-multimethod matrix. *Psychol. Bull.* **56**:81-105, 1959.
186	**Clark H H.** Language-as-fixed-effect fallacy: a critique of language statistics in psychological research. *J. Verb. Learn. Verb. Behav.* **12**:335-59, 1973.

Figure 1. The 100 most-cited social science articles (continued)

Figure 1. The 100 most-cited social science articles (continued)

Total Citations	Bibliographic Data
204	**Hamilton M.** A rating scale for depression. *J. Neurol. Neurosurg. Psychiat.* **23**:56-62, 1960.
194	**Hardin G.** Tragedy of the commons. *Science* **162**:1243-7, 1968.
232	**Hebb D O.** Drives and the C.N.S. (Conceptual Nervous System). *Psychol. Rev.* **62**:243-54, 1955.
298	**Holmes T H & Rahe R H.** The social readjustment rating scale. *J. Psychosom. Res.* **11**:213-8, 1967.
203	**Hubel D H & Wiesel T N.** Receptive fields and functional architecture of monkey striate cortex. *J. Physiol. London* **195**:215-43, 1968.
297	**Hubel D H & Wiesel T N.** Receptive fields, binocular interactions and functional architecture in the cat's visual cortex. *J. Physiol. London* **160**:106-54, 1962.
579	**Jensen A R.** How much can we boost IQ and scholastic achievement? *Harvard Educ. Rev.* **39**:1-123, 1969.
311	**Johnson S C.** Hierarchical clustering schemes. *Psychometrika* **32**:241-54, 1967.
498	**Kaiser H F.** The varimax criterion for analytic rotation in factor analysis. *Psychometrika* **23**:187-200, 1958.
229	**Kanner L.** Autistic disturbances of affective contact. *Nerv. Child.* **2**:217-50, 1943.
197	**Keller F S.** Good-bye, teacher. *J. Appl. Behav. Anal.* **1**:79-89, 1968.
233	**Kendler H H & Kendler T S.** Vertical and horizontal processes in problem solving. *Psychol. Rev.* **69**:1-16, 1962. (Citation Classics. *Current Contents* (9):15, 27 February 1978.)
186	**Kimble D P.** Hippocampus and internal inhibition. *Psychol. Bull.* **70**:285-95, 1968.
200	**Kimura D.** Cerebral dominance and the perception of verbal stimuli. *Can. J. Psychol.* **15**:166-71, 1961.
450	**Kruskal J B.** Multidimensional scaling by optimizing goodness of fit to a nonmetric hypothesis. *Psychometrika* **29**:1-27, 1964.
262	**Kruskal J B.** Nonmetric multidimensional scaling: a numerical method. *Psychometrika* **29**:115-29, 1964.
283	**Lefcourt H M.** Internal versus external control of reinforcements: a review. *Psychol. Bull.* **65**:206-20, 1966.
298	**Liberman A M, Cooper F S, Schankweiler D P & Studdert-Kennedy M.** Perception of the speech code. *Psychol. Rev.* **74**:431-61, 1967.
243	**Lindemann E.** Symptomatology and management of acute grief. *Amer. J. Psychiat.* **101**:141-8, 1944.
438	**Lowry O H, Rosebrough N J, Farr A L & Randall R J.** Protein measurement with the folin phenol reagent. *J. Biol. Chem.* **193**:265-75, 1951. (Citation Classics. *Current Contents* (1):7, 3 January 1977.)

Figure 1. The 100 most-cited social science articles (continued)

Total Citations	Bibliographic Data
193	**Mandler G & Sarason S B.** A study of anxiety and learning. *J. Abnormal and Social Ps.* **47**:166-73, 1952.
655	**Miller G A.** The magical number seven, plus or minus two: some limits on our capacity for processing information. *Psychol. Rev.* **63**:81-97, 1956.
240	**Miller N E.** Learning of visceral and glandular responses. *Science* **163**:434-45, 1969.
595	**Orne M T.** On the social psychology of the psychological experiment: with particular reference to demand characteristics and their implications. *Amer. Psychol.* **17**:776-83, 1962.
218	**Osgood C E & Tannenbaum P H.** The principle of congruity in the prediction of attitude change. *Psychol. Rev.* **62**:42-55, 1955.
443	**Overall J E & Gorham D R.** The brief psychiatric rating scale. *Psychol. Rep.* **10**:799-812, 1962.
321	**Paivio A.** Mental imagery in associative learning and memory. *Psychol. Rev.* **76**:241-63, 1969.
274	**Paivio A & Madigan S A.** Imagery and association value in paired-associate learning. *J. Exp. Psychol.* **76**:35-9, 1968.
359	**Peterson L R & Peterson M J.** Short-term retention of individual verbal items. *J. Exp. Psychol.* **58**:193-8, 1959.
203	**Pratt J W.** Risk aversion in the small and in the large. *Econometrica* **32**:122-36, 1964.
202	**Reich C A.** The new property. *Yale Law J.* **73**:733-87, 1964.
194	**Rescorla R A.** Pavlovian conditioning and its proper control procedures. *Psychol. Rev.* **74**:71-80, 1967.
199	**Reynolds G S.** Behavioral contrast. *J. Exp. Anal. Behav.* **4**:57-71, 1961.
200	**Robinson W S.** Ecological correlations and the behavior of individuals. *Amer. Sociol. Rev.* **15**:351-57, 1950.
1345	**Rotter J B.** Generalized expectancies for internal versus external control of reinforcement. *Psychol. Monogr.* **80**:1-28, 1966.
206	**Samuelson P A.** The pure theory of public expenditure. *Rev. Econ. Statist.* **36**:387-9, 1954.
347	**Schachter S & Singer J E.** Cognitive, social, and physiological determinants of emotional state. *Psychol. Rev.* **69**:379-99, 1962.
311	**Schildkraut J J.** The catecholamine hypothesis of affective disorders: a review of supporting evidence. *Amer. J. Psychiat.* **122**:509-22, 1965.
212	**Schou M.** Lithium in psychiatric therapy and prophylaxis. *J. Psychiat. Res.* **6**:67-95, 1968.
215	**Seeman M.** On the meaning of alienation. *Amer. Sociol. Rev.* **24**:783-91, 1959.

Figure 1. The 100 most-cited social science articles (continued)

Total Citations	Bibliographic Data
238	**Sharpe W F.** Capital asset prices: a theory of market equilibrium under conditions of risk. *J. Finan.* **19**:425-42, 1964.
264	**Shepard R N.** The analysis of proximities: multidimensional scaling with an unknown distance function. 1. *Psychometrika* **27**:125-40, 1962.
186	**Shepard R N.** The analysis of proximities: multidimensional scaling with an unknown distance function. 2. *Psychometrika* **27**:219-46, 1962.
236	**Sperling G.** A model for visual memory tasks. *Hum. Factors* **5**:19-31, 1963.
291	**Sperling G.** The information available in brief visual presentations. *Psychol. Monogr.* **74**:1-29, 1960.
228	**Srole L.** Social integration and certain corollaries: an exploratory study. *Amer. Sociol. Rev.* **21**:709-16, 1956.
302	**Sternberg S.** High-speed scanning in human memory. *Science* **153**:652-4, 1966.
216	**Sternberg S.** Memory-scanning: mental processes revealed by reaction-time experiments. *Amer. Sci.* **57**:421-57, 1969.
254	**Stevens S S.** On the psychophysical law. *Psychol. Rev.* **64**:153-81, 1957.
234	**Stroop J R.** Studies of interference in serial verbal reactions. *J. Exp. Psychol.* **18**:643-62, 1935.
540	**Taylor J A.** A personality scale of manifest anxiety. *J. Abnormal and Social Ps.* **48**:285-90, 1953.
191	**Thompson R F & Spencer W A.** Habituation: a model phenomenon for the study of neuronal substrates of behavior. *Psychol. Rev.* **73**:16-43, 1966.
191	**Tulving E.** Subjective organization in free recall of "unrelated" words. *Psychol. Rev.* **69**:344-54, 1962.
218	**Tulving E & Pearlstone Z.** Availability versus accessibility of information in memory for words. *J. Verb. Learn. Verb. Behav.* **5**:381-91, 1966.
198	**Tussman J & ten Broek J.** The equal protection of the laws. *Calif. Law Rev.* **37**:341-81, 1949.
213	**Van Alstyne W W.** The demise of the right-privilege distinction in constitutional laws. *Harvard Law Rev.* **81**:1439-64, 1968.
359	**Waugh N C & Norman D A.** Primary memory. *Psychol. Rev.* **72**:89-104, 1965.
190	**Wechsler H.** Toward neutral principles of constitutional law. *Harvard Law Rev.* **73**:1-35, 1959.
344	**White R W.** Motivation reconsidered: the concept of competence. *Psychol. Rev.* **66**:297-333, 1959.
194	**Wickens D D.** Encoding categories of words: an empirical approach to meaning. *Psychol. Rev.* **77**:1-15, 1970.
228	**Zajonc R B.** Social facilitation. *Science* **149**:269-74, 1965.
252	**Zung W W K.** A self-rating depression scale. *Arch. Gen. Psychiat.* **12**:63-70, 1965.

the one-standard-deviation IQ difference (15 IQ points) between blacks and whites. The Jensen article is lengthy—123 pages. It presents many opportunities for citation. Without further analysis we do not know whether these citations are critical or not. We are investigating this and in a future essay I will report on our findings.

Some of the papers on the list have imprecise titles that really do not describe the information or ideas contained in the paper. One such article is Garret Hardin's "Tragedy of the Commons." In it, Hardin draws an analogy between the overuse of common land by herdsmen in 18th-century Britain and the world population problem. The herdsmen, in order to increase their profits, added animals to their herds at the expense of the overgrazed land. The land then could not support all the animals. According to Hardin, the world's people, too, have children at an unlimited rate in a limited world. "No technical solution can rescue us from the misery of overpopulation," he concludes. "Freedom to breed will bring misery to all."[4]

Another "soft"-titled paper is Fred Keller's "Good-bye, Teacher..." which deals with a method of personalized individual instruction. He and his colleagues devised the method for an introductory course in general psychology. He also reviews methods developed by others. Of the method Keller says: "The teacher of tomor-row will not, I think, continue to be satisfied with 10% efficiency (at best).... No longer will he need to live, like Ichabod Crane, in a world that increasingly begrudges providing him room and lodging for a doubtful service to its young. A new kind of teacher is in the making. To the old kind, I, for one, will be glad to say, 'Good-bye!' "[5]

The title of a third article may give some readers pause. It is D. O. Hebb's "Drives and the C.N.S. (Conceptual Nervous System)." Since C.N.S. usually stands for Central Nervous System, many readers may wonder if "conceptual" is a typographical error.

According to Dr. Hebb, the title "was a little joke. B. F. Skinner had said that in psychology C.N.S. stands for 'conceptual' nervous system (instead of 'central'). True enough—we're still far from an adequate understanding of the brain's activity—but we have to use what conceptions are available. The moral is to make them as good as possible, so I proposed to bring Skinner's CNS, and mine, up to date."[6] Hebb's article is a review of the then-new conceptions of brain function which were changing psychologists' ideas about behavior.

One article on the list, noteworthy for its 1345 citations, is Julian B. Rotter's "Generalized Expectancies for Internal versus External Control of Reinforcement." A seminal paper, the article describes investigations into whether people perceive that rewards are contingent upon their own behavior or whether they feel that rewards are controlled by forces outside themselves. According to Rotter, the 1966 paper, which included a test for these internal and external control factors, presented a classic example of test development. However, the article may have received so much attention for another reason. As Rotter states in a soon-to-be-published book, the body of research which cited his article is due in part to "the Vietnam War, the student revolution, the black riots, the political scandals of Watergate and the assassinations.... Certainly these events have brought home to many both their inability to control events and the lack of predictability of events which are important in their lives." The interests of social scientists "often reflect what is happening out there in the real world."[7]

In an upcoming essay we will take a look at the 100 most-cited *SSCI* books. In a later essay we will list highly cited authors as well. While many of them will have appeared as authors of highly cited articles or books, there will be some who have not.

Unfortunately, for the reasons given, we do not get a complete or rounded picture of the social sciences from this list. We can only attain this by extending the analysis further and subdividing by journals or some other criterion so that all disciplines are adequately represented.

REFERENCES

1. **Garfield E.** Social Sciences Citation Index clusters. *Current Contents* (27):5-11, 5 July 1976. (Reprinted in: **Garfield E.** *Essays of an Information Scientist.* Philadelphia: ISI Press, 1977, Vol. 2, p. 509-15.)
2. --------------. To cite or not to cite. *Current Contents* (35):5-7, 29 August 1977.
3. **Narin F.** *Evaluative bibliometrics: the use of publication and citation analysis in the evaluation of scientific activity.* Cherry Hill, NJ: Computer Horizons, Inc., 1976, p. 140. NTIS-PB252339/AS.
4. **Hardin G.** Tragedy of the commons. *Science* 162:1243-7, 1968.
5. **Keller F S.** Good-bye, teacher. *J. Appl. Behav. Anal.* 1:79-89, 1968.
6. **Hebb D O.** Citation Classics. *Current Contents* (in press).
7. **Rotter J B.** Comments on the effects of individual differences on perceived control (Perlmuter LC & Monty RA eds.) *Choice and Perceived Control.* Hillsdale, N.J.: Lawrence Earlbaum Associates (in press).

Current Comments

Introducing *Index to Social Sciences & Humanities Proceedings* — **More Help in Locating and Acquiring Proceedings**

Number 33   August 14, 1978

Helmut Drubba of the Technical Information Library in Hannover playfully ended his fine survey of conference documentation by paraphrasing Irving Berlin—"There's no literature like conference literature."[1] Certainly conference literature presents unique bibliographic problems for both librarians and researchers.

ISI® recognized this fact when we introduced our *Index to Scientific & Technical Proceedings™*.[2] *ISTP™* covers about 3,000 proceedings each year in the physical, natural, and engineering sciences. Its rapid acceptance in its first year testifies to the need it serves. *ISTP* seems to have filled a vacuum in university, industrial, public, and government libraries. We have reason to believe that the enthusiastic reception of *ISTP* will be matched in 1979 by the response to our new *Index to Social Sciences & Humanities Proceedings™ (ISSHP™)*.

We expect *ISSHP* to be welcomed because conference proceedings have been difficult to locate and acquire in the past.[3]

Finding individual papers delivered at a conference was even more time-consuming.

The difficulties posed by the conference literature arise from several sources. One of the biggest problems is the time lag that develops between the date of the conference and the actual date of proceedings publication. According to P. R. Mills of the University of Bath, this time lag is especially long for the social sciences.[4] Librarians sometimes find they are spending time on fruitless searches for literature that has not yet been published.

Another problem is that proceedings may be included in an issue of a society's journal or they may be published as multi-authored, hardbound books.[4]

Finally, proceedings (especially those in book form) may appear under titles that do not adequately describe their contents. For example, the title of a book may be *Language and Mother-Child Interaction*. Only in the preface is it revealed that the contents are all papers delivered at a conference on the psychology of language.

We think that *Index to Social Sciences & Humanities Proceedings* will help overcome these problems. *ISSHP*'s four quarterly issues and annual cumulation will cover published proceedings in psychology, sociology, anthropology, economics, and political science. In addition, proceedings in law, literature, public health, women's studies, education, linguistics, history, international affairs, urban studies, criminology, alcoholism and drug addiction, management science, business, and religion will be included.

In its first year *ISSHP* will provide access to some 20,000 published papers delivered at 1,000 social sciences and humanities meetings. This coverage will be expanded in the future as resources permit.

The number of proceedings covered by *ISSHP* is lower than that covered by *ISTP* for a good reason: there are fewer proceedings published in the social sciences and the humanities. According to Christopher Watson of the British Library Lending Division at Boston Spa, the Library received 13,828 proceedings last year. From a sampling, he estimates that approximately 87% were in science and technology, 11% in social science, and 2% in the humanities. This means that only about 1,800 were social sciences or humanities proceedings.[5] P. R. Mills has also estimated that approximately 2,000 proceedings each year are from the social sciences.[4] As stated before, at least 1,000 published proceedings

will be indexed in *ISSHP* in 1979. If Bradford's law holds for this literature, then we will certainly be covering most of the significant papers published.

The proceedings to be included in *ISSHP* will be selected with the help of our Editorial Advisory Board. We also have regular contact with most publishers of proceedings. Although we cannot prevent the time lag between conferences and the publication of proceedings, we will be in touch with conference sponsors before meetings to insure that new proceedings are received at ISI and indexed as quickly as possible after publication.

Other reference tools have attempted to handle the social sciences and humanities proceedings literature. However, *ISSHP*'s depth of indexing is unique. It will not merely provide access to overall proceedings documents as most of these tools do; it will also index the individual papers they contain. Thus, *ISSHP* will go way beyond the scope of the *Interdok Directory of Published Proceedings in Print.* Nor should *ISSHP* be confused with *World Meetings: United States and Canada* which gives information on meetings scheduled up to two years ahead, not the published proceedings.

ISSHP is suitable for browsing as well as for specific searches. Each proceedings will have a "main entry" giving its table of contents. This is similar to the presentation in *Current Contents®* . The multifaceted indexing system allows users to search at the level of the specific paper as well as the overall proceedings document.

To appreciate the problems librarians faced in the past, consider a not unusual situation. You remember that your colleague presented a paper somewhere on X. You think it might have been within the past two years. You certainly can't remember, if you ever heard it, the name or sponsor of the conference. However, with just this brief information you or your librarian can now use *ISSHP* to quickly find not only the paper itself but also the publisher, etc. If it isn't already in your library, you have enough information to order it from the publisher or from some other library or the individual himself.

For proceedings published in book form, *ISSHP*'s main entry will give the conference title, book's title and subtitle, series title and volume, editor, publisher and publisher's address, chapter titles, beginning page numbers, all authors' names, primary authors' addresses, price, date and place of the conference, and sponsor. In addition, the Library of Congress number and the International Standard Book Number, when available, will be given. (See the main entry example in Figure 1.) For proceedings published in journals, the main entry will include conference title, location, sponsors, journal title, volume, issue, year, titles of papers, authors, and primary authors' addresses. Using this information, librarians or researchers can easily purchase the journal issue from the publisher or consult it in the library. Of course, the inclusion of authors' addresses facilitates reprint requests when only individual papers are needed.

Each proceedings in the main entry section is given a proceedings number which appears in the upper lefthand corner of the entry. This number identifies the proceedings in the indexes of *ISSHP*.

Conference proceedings will be indexed in six different ways. A *Permuterm® Subject Index, Category Index, Meeting Location Index, Sponsor Index, Author/Editor Index* and *Corporate Index* provide numerous access routes to simplify searching. Each of these indexes refers you to the appropriate main entry by means of its proceedings number.

The *Permuterm Subject Index (PSI)* is based on pairings of significant title words. In the figure, title words have been permuted from both the title of the proceedings itself and the titles of individual papers. For example, "influenza/history" is a word-pair generated from the title of a conference. Influenza/children is a pair devised from the title of an individual paper. Next to each word-pair, the number for the main entry is given.

The *PSI* entry also indicates whether the term came from the main title or the title of a specific paper. A "T" indicates that the subject term occurs in the proceedings title. If it occurs within the title of an individual paper, the specific page number is given.

Figure 1. Entries in the *Index to Social Sciences & Humanities Proceedings™ (ISSHP™)*.

MAIN ENTRY

PROC#
02648
7th ANNUAL INTERNATIONAL INTERDISCIPLINARY UNIVERSITY AFFILIATED
PROJECT CONF ON PIAGETIAN THEORY AND ITS IMPLICATIONS FOR
THE HELPING PROFESSIONS, LOS ANGELES, CA, JAN, 1977
Sponsors: Childrens Hosp Los Angeles, Univ Affiliated Program Univ So Calif, Sch Social Work, Univ So Calif
Sch Educ
PIAGETIAN THEORY AND ITS IMPLICATIONS FOR THE HELPING PROFESSIONS:
EMPHASIS: SOCIAL WORK AND PSYCHOLOGICAL SERVICES
EDS: R. WEIZMANN, R. BROWN, P.J. LEVINSON, P.A. TAYLOR
Univ Affiliated Program Childrens Hosp of Los Angeles, Los Angeles, 1978, 432 pp., 6 chaps, $12.00 softbound
PREPAYMENT REQUIRED WITH ORDER
USC SPECIAL ORDER DEPT & BOOKSTORE UNIVERSITY PARK LOS ANGELES CA 90007
PIAGETIAN PRINCIPLES APPLIED TO BEGINNING PHASE IN PROFESSIONAL HELPING, H.W. Maier
  (Univ Washington Seattle WA 98195). 1
ROOTS OF PROSOCIAL BEHAVIOR IN CHILDREN, P. Mussen (Univ Calif Berkeley Inst Human Dev
  Berkeley CA 94720). 14
CONCEPT OF FUNCTIONAL REGRESSION—ITS VALUE FOR PIAGETIAN THEORY AND ITS CLINICAL
  APPLICATION, S.J. Friedland, R.B. Shilkret (Farmington Youth Guidance Ctr Farmington MA
  01701). 130
MORAL DEVELOPMENT AND PLAY OF CHILD WITH MINIMAL BRAIN DYSFUNCTION—
  OCCUPATIONAL THERAPY CASE, F. Gold (Univ So Calif Los Angeles CA 90007) 145
PROVERBS, PROPORTIONS AND PIAGET, M.H. Holden (Calif State Coll Dominguez Hills
  Dominguez CA 90747) 182
REASONING ABILITIES OF LEARNING DISABLED BOYS, L.T. Grossi (Boston Univ Boston
  MA 02215). 244

Chapter title, author, address of first author

Book title & subtitle, editors

Sponsors

Conference name, date, location

Each entry will have a unique identification number.

PERMUTERM®SUBJECT INDEX
(to book titles & subtitles, conference names & individual papers)

	PROC #	PAGE
INFLUENZA		
AMERICA	02506	T
CHILDREN	03902	61
HISTORY	02506	T

Indicates word is in title of a proceedings

Figure 1. (continued)

SPONSOR INDEX

PROC #

AMERICAN ASSOC FOR THE HISTORY OF MEDICINE
MADISON, WI, USA   02506

CHILDREN'S HOSP, LOS ANGELES, CA, USA
┌─────── LOS ANGELES, CA, USA   02648

│

└─── Location of meeting

MEETING LOCATION INDEX

PROC #

U.S.A.
CALIFORNIA
Los Angeles
7th Annual International Conf on
Piagetian Theory and its Implications
for the Helping Professions   02648

CORPORATE INDEX

PROC #   PAGE

CALIFORNIA STATE COLLEGE, DOMINGUEZ
HILLS, DOMINGUEZ, CA 90747, USA
HOLDEN MH   02648   182

AUTHOR/EDITOR INDEX

	PROC #	PAGE
HOLDEN MH	02648	182
MAIER HW	02648	1
MILLAR JD	02506	15
MUSSEN P	02648	14
OSBORN JE	02506	E ──┐

Indicates editor of proceedings ─┘

CATEGORY INDEX

SOCIAL PSYCHOLOGY
7th ANNUAL INTERNATIONAL CONF ON
PIAGETIAN THEORY AND ITS IMPLICATIONS
FOR THE HELPING PROFESSIONS   02648

The *Sponsor Index* will provide the name of the sponsoring organization and the geographical location of each conference it sponsored. Since a single organization may sponsor several conferences in a year, the location can help the user identify the particular meeting in which he or she is interested.

The *Meeting Location Index* will include an alphabetical listing of titles arranged by country, state, and city where the meeting took place. The *Corporate Index* will list institutional affiliations of the authors. Suppose you remember that someone from the Center for Disease Control in Atlanta spoke at a conference. You can't remember the author's name, or the title of the paper. You can still find it through the *Corporate Index.*

The *Author/Editor Index* is an alphabetical listing of authors and editors of proceedings and papers. Editors are indicated by an "E" in the page number column. The *Category Index* organizes proceedings according to broad topic areas. Under each category there is a listing of the relevant conference titles. The proceedings number refers you to the main entry. A proceedings will be listed under a maximum of five categories.

As indicated earlier *ISSHP* can also be used for current awareness. By scanning each quarterly issue researchers can keep up with the published conference literature. Librarians can scan the quarterly issues to select proceedings pertinent to their specific collections.

The index will also appeal to those who wish to perform retrospective searches of the social sciences and humanities conference literature. Annual cumulations will simplify searches of proceedings published over several years.

In the past, conference proceedings presented one of the largest bibliographic headaches to librarians and one of the most frequent sources of frustration to researchers.[6] With the introduction of the *ISSHP* and the continuing success of the *ISTP,* we hope to alleviate most of those headaches. At the same time we hope that there will be greater utilization of published conference literature.

The price of the *ISSHP* will be $250 per year. For information on ordering, please refer to the ad and order form on the back cover of this issue of *Current Contents.*

REFERENCES

1. **Drubba H.** Conference documentation: general overview and survey of the present position. *Associations Internationales* 28:383-7, 1976.
2. **Garfield E.** ISI's new *Index to Scientific and Technical Proceedings*™ lets you know what went on even if you stayed home. *Current Contents* (40):5-10, 3 October 1977.
3. **Short P J.** Bibliographic tools for tracing conference proceedings. *IATUL (International Association of Technological University Libraries) Proceedings* 6:50-3, 1972.
4. **Mills P R.** Characteristics of published conference proceedings. *J. Doc.* 29:36-50, 1973.
5. **Watson C.** Personal communication. 23 June 1978.
6. **Garfield E.** ISI adds "non-journal" material to the 1977 *Science Citation Index*®. *Current Contents* (9):5-6, 28 February 1977.

Current Comments

Science Journalism: You've Come a
Long Way Baby, But . . . !

Number 34,   August 21, 1978

Most of the public's knowledge of science, technology, and medicine comes from the mass media. Since so many social, political, and economic issues revolve around scientific questions, you might expect significant science coverage. The sad fact is that science reporting is minimal.

In 1975 only about 5% of American newspaper stories was devoted to science and medicine—the *same* figure reported for 1958 (p. 455).[1] Up-to-date figures on science news are difficult to find. We called several major newspapers to ask for estimates. The *New York Times* and *Washington Post* told us they did not keep track of such information. Robert C. Cowen, science editor of the *Christian Science Monitor*, estimates that one page per week goes to natural science.

I believe that European newspapers do a much better job of covering science. However, this coverage is difficult to quantify. Dr. Bernard Dixon, editor of *New Scientist*, estimates that the space allocated for science and technology in Britain's six national dailies

"is so small as to be negligible—certainly less than one percent."[2] Dr. Greta Jones and Professor A.J. Meadows of the University of Leicester's Primary Communications Research Centre in England reported that the London *Daily Telegraph*'s amount of science coverage has actually been declining. In 1968, they say, the paper published 515 items relating to science; in 1969, 409; in 1971, 396; and in 1973, 290.[3] But from informal inquiries I have learned that Russian newspapers devote roughly 5 to 10% of their space to science, and that many news stories include more technical detail than American readers are accustomed to getting. I do know that the German *Frankfurter Allemeine Zeitung* has a large full time staff of science writers. They subscribe to *Current Contents®* and use it regularly.

Popular magazines deal with a wide variety of specialties. It is difficult to make generalizations about the amount or quality of science writing in these magazines as they are aimed at so many different audiences. Bill Katz of the State

University of New York at Albany, editor of the "Magazines" column in *Library Journal,* estimates there are about 2,000 of them published in the world today.[4] *Time* and *Newsweek,* America's two best known weekly news magazines, have circulations of about five and three million, respectively. Both regularly publish short features on science, medicine, and the social and behavioral sciences, although they rarely do an in-depth cover story (of 5 or 6 pages) on a science topic.

My friends at ISI® who regularly watch television tell me that only a small fraction of American TV is devoted to science. It was not easy to get relevant data. The research department at the American Broadcasting Company (ABC) said one to two percent of the network's news coverage goes to science. The National Broadcasting Company (NBC) and the Columbia Broadcasting System (CBS) couldn't give us exact figures, but the amount is probably roughly the same. So much for science on the commercial networks.

The Public Broadcasting Service (PBS), however, estimated that about 11% of their daytime hours devoted to instructional programs cover science. Unfortunately, these programs reach a relatively small part of the total viewing audience.

The only weekly American TV program which deals with general science is PBS's *Nova.* PBS tells us that in February of this year *Nova* reached 4.88 million households, or only about 5.7% of the homes in the US.

The BBC, sometimes helped by American co-sponsors, does better. Their *Horizon* programs give a comprehensive treatment to different areas of current scientific research. They have also produced such outstanding two-hour epics as "The Restless Earth." This covered plate tectonics for the informed layman.

National Public Radio, which, like PBS, is funded by the Corporation for Public Broadcasting and private donations, tells us that roughly 5% of the material sent over its 180 stations deals with science. However, as I mentioned in an earlier essay, the American Chemical Society's *Man and Molecules,* a science program aimed at the lay audience, is broadcast by 500 commercial stations in the US and other countries.[5]

Of course, none of these estimates takes into account science-oriented entertainment programs. For example, *Marcus Welby, M.D.* would not be classified as science reporting. But this program (now in reruns) does indeed convey a considerable amount of authentic medical information. All medical data was checked with qualified consultants. Unfortunately, the program gives a syrupy and grossly distorted view of the present-day American family doctor. If every doctor spent as much time with each patient as Welby does, we'd need at least five times as many doctors. Maybe we do, but we don't have them now!

David Perlman, science editor of the *San Francisco Chronicle,* asserts that there is "virtually no biology, no behavioral science, no physical science on everyday television."[6] But commercial TV will drop everything to cover a manned flight to the moon. Carl Sagan claims that "in all three [commercial] network news departments there is not a single person whose job includes scanning *Science* or *Nature* each week for newsworthy material."[7]

Apart from the abysmally small quantity of science reporting in newspapers or radio and TV, what about the quality?

One good example of a highly publicized story was the 1976-77 swine-flu vaccination program. The scientific aspects had grave implications for society. In 1976, the US government launched a $135 million program to innoculate the American people against an epidemic that never materialized. Several elderly people in Pittsburgh, Pennsylvania died shortly after receiving the shot. This led to fears that the vaccine itself was dangerous.

Unlike many science projects, which don't affect members of the public personally, this one affected everybody. In the face of apparent confusion and incompetence on the part of the government, every American had to weigh the risks of catching swine flu against the risks of taking the shot.

Dixon asserts that the coverage of the swine flu vaccine debacle by major US newspapers is a model of science journalism. "Instead of blow-by-blow accounts of every minor twist in the plot," he writes, "news features were used to convey in a balanced and informative fashion principal shifts in the argument."[2]

However, David Rubin and Val Hendy of the New York University School of Journalism claim that coverage by papers such as the *New York Times, Washington Post, Los Angeles Times,* and *Miami Herald* were exceptions to otherwise mediocre coverage.

They studied swine-flu stories in 19 daily newspapers. They also studied the evening news shows of the three commercial television networks. And they looked at coverage by the two major syndicated American wire services, Associated Press and United Press International. (Associated Press serves 1,300 newspapers and radio and TV stations in the US and over 100,000 abroad. For United Press International the figures are 1,150 and 2,250.) Rubin and Hendy focused on the week of October 11-17, 1976, "the week the [immunization] program began in earnest, the week a number of elderly people died after receiving the shot."

They conclude that, "while most press coverage was unoriginal, predictable, [and] superficial...it was not misleading, sensational or inaccurate except in a couple of instances." They complain that *most* of the coverage consisted of body counts and the detailing of the byzantine twists and turns of the *political* side of the story. Coverage, they say, "faithfully reflected the confusion among public health officials."[8]

Thus, their agreement with Dixon was qualified somewhat. Dixon complains that balanced, comprehensive science reporting is all too rare in Britain. Rubin and Hendy argue that, at least in the swine-flu case, it was rare except in the case of major US newspapers.

The question is, how typical is this particular story? The quality of science reporting in newspapers has, on the average, increased greatly since the 1920s. Dr. Rae Goodell teaches science writing at the Massachusetts Institute of Technology. She noted that many journalists classify science reporting from early in this century as "gee-whiz" reporting—the kind that concentrates on the sensational side of science. The '40s and '50s saw "conveyor belt" reporting. Such science stories may clearly explain the technical aspects of a discovery to the reader. But they do not examine the larger social, economic or political repercussions of the story.

"Gee-whiz" and "conveyor belt" reporting are still with us today. But Goodell and other observers see the rise, in the last decade or so, of "science policy reporting." This type of science journalism tells readers what new developments and discoveries *really* mean, and how they affect their lives (p. 127-8).[9]

Science reporting on TV generally has not reached this stage of maturity. Rubin and Hendy, in their study of the swine-flu story, singled out television for especially severe criticism. No network, they assert, preempted regular programming to cover the swine-flu case. Nor did any of them try to answer questions like "What is swine-flu?" or "What is the risk of inoculation?" The networks offered only "typical correspondent-on-the-scene coverage." Rubin and Hendy comment: "It was a sad performance by television, on which 36% of Americans say they rely exclusively for their news."[8]

Other observers have criticized television for excessive coverage of the paranormal and "pseudoscience." NBC in particular has been censured for lavishing attention on the dubious "ancient astronaut" question. And on October 30, 1977, NBC aired "Exploring the Unknown," a program on "psychokinesis," or the ability to move objects by psychic power. The Committee for the Scientific Investigation of the Claims of the Paranormal (CSICP) condemned the program for giving the impression that the existence of such psychic powers has been scientifically validated. Its complaint to the Federal Communications Commission was recently published in *The Humanist,* which CSICP chairman Paul Kurtz edits. Speaking for CSICP, Kurtz said

NBC should provide equal time and funding for a program to present "the critical scientific viewpoint."[10]

CSICP's aim—to keep the public skeptical of occult or paranormal reports—is laudable. Telepathy, UFOs, ancient astronauts, biorhythms, astrology, and the Bermuda triangle are all topics which excite the imagination, even if they carry with them questionable scientific validity. Many find it more fun to believe in them than to disbelieve in them. In the minds of many editors and TV programmers (and readers and viewers), stories about such alleged phenomena make better entertainment than the rebuttals.

However, Carl Sagan has managed to remain quite popular on TV even though he debunks such theories. He has also performed this valuable service in books such as *The Dragons of Eden*, where he writes:

> ...There is today in the West...a resurgent interest in vague, anecodotal and often demonstrably erroneous doctrines that, if true, would betoken at least a more interesting universe, but that, if false, imply an intellectual carelessness, an absence of toughmindedness, and a diversion of energies not very promising for our survival.... It may be that there are kernels of truth in a few of these doctrines, but their widespread acceptance betokens a lack of intellectual rigor, an absence of skepticism, and a need to replace experiments by desires.[11] (p. 247-8)

Much can be done to improve the treatment of science in newspapers and television. But both scientists and reporters need to reach a better understanding of each others' professional concerns.

For example, scientists must realize that reporters are under severe deadline pressures which usually prevent print or TV journalists from doing much research on their own.

Space is also at a premium in newspapers. A story may have to be cut, sometimes by copy editors who may not realize that an important clarification or explanation is being sacrificed. Walter Sullivan of the *New York Times* had 30% of a story on quarks cut. The result was that through no fault of his, only one scientist's name was mentioned, but not the names of others who contributed significantly to the discovery (p. 124).[9]

Reporters' stories face another peril at the copy desk: headline writers may give items titles that are short, snappy and attention-grabbing—but not completely accurate. Sagan has a headline horror story. He gave a press conference where he spoke of the possibility that organic molecules might exist in the atmosphere of Jupiter. He says he made it very clear that he was talking about organic molecules, not life. Yet the following day a San Francisco headline declared: "Life on Jupiter, scientist says." (p. 173)[9]

Television reporters, too, are allotted only a few minutes on the air to tell their stories. Tapes must be edited and valuable information dropped from an interview. And of course, the reporter has no control over the way the anchorperson (the broadcaster who coordinates the news program) will lead into the story.

Reporters have the obligation to understand scientists' problems and professional concerns. If a scientist takes the care to qualify a statement, that qualification should get a prominent place in the story. Also, depending on the size of the news operation and reporters' schedules, it is possible for reporters to help write headlines and edit stories, to avoid inaccuracies and distortions.

Also, scientists should realize that, as Perlman puts it, reporters "are in business to report on the activities of the house of science, not to protect it, just as political writers report on politics and politicians."[6] Scientists cannot expect reporters to act as public relations agents, even though the great majority of science writers probably have a favorable attitude towards science and scientists.

The best popular science writers strive to learn what they can about science. In their swine-flu study, Rubin and Hendy assert that reporters' science backgrounds made the biggest difference in the quality of the coverage. Lawrence K. Altman of the *New York Times,* for example, is an MD.[8] Yet many reporters begin without a scientific specialty or a strong general science background.

Perlman asserts that this is not an entirely bad thing; that on-the-job training has worked for some. He writes that Walter Sullivan is "virtually a card-carrying geophysicist by now, he has written so often on the subject." Perlman, himself without formal science training, describes his job as "a full-time, perpetual fellowship to a graduate school with a varied and endlessly challenging curriculum."[6]

You don't need a Ph.D. to be a good popular science writer. And perhaps it doesn't matter whether reporters get their science training in or out of universities, though more formal training might be called for.

Relatively few journalism schools offer courses in science *writing.* A *Directory of Science Communication Courses and Programs* lists 34 programs and 105 courses in 58 colleges and universities in the US.[12] Since science writing carries with it special problems not faced by reporters of politics, business or sports, more formal training might be needed here.

Some organizations are trying to improve science news by making scientists in certain fields available for interviews by reporters. The public relations office of Drexel University in Philadelphia operates a "Deadline Doctors" program. It is designed to help reporters who need a qualified source on a scientific topic. Calls are referred to an appropriate faculty member.

The Society for Neuroscience, a group of 4700 scientists who have done research relating to the nervous system, plans to introduce a similar service this fall. The Bethesda, Maryland-based group, publisher of the quarterly *Neuroscience Newsletter* and the annual *Neuroscience Proceedings*, will publish a directory of scientists who expressed willingness to talk to reporters in need of a clear explanation or quotable source.

The American Cancer Society invites science writers to attend its annual meetings. This gives writers a chance to hear the latest developments in cancer research. The Federation of American Societies for Experimental Biology publishes a newsletter called *FASEB Feature Service*. This monthly publication is distributed without charge to about 400 newspapers. It explains new developments in the laity's language.

Some organizations have grown up with the specific aim to improve science writing. The National Association of Science Writers, Box H, Sea Cliff, New York 11579, is a group of about 1,000 science writers and editors. It holds seminars on science writing at the annual American Association for the Advancement of Science meeting. Participants discuss the problems of communicating science-related information through the various media. Both journalists and scientists attend these seminars.

The Council for the Advancement of Science Writing, 618 N. Elmwood Oak Park, Illinois 60302, is a group of 26 writers, editors, television executives, scientists and physicians. The group tries to upgrade the quality of science writing, and improve the relationship between scientists and the media. CASW holds annual press briefings on new horizons in science and the social and behavioral sciences as well.

One of CASW's special programs provides on-the-job training to journalists. Journalists who can't take time off from work for special training are supplied with textbooks and journal subscriptions. Also, CASW members provide guidance on how to deal with scientist-sources, and how to cover scientific meetings.

Another CASW program brings journalists directly into laboratories or field studies. Journalists spend weeks or months with scientists to get a better idea of how research is actually conducted.

Other journalism or scientific societies could try offering services similar to these. The fact that some groups are already trying to improve the system by opening communications is cause for optimism.

Calls for cooperation between various professions go out constantly. Yet between journalism and the sciences, cooperation is especially important. Journalists and scientists both have a stake in raising the quality of science reporting. Science is at least as important as politics, sports, or the personal lives of movie and TV stars. And the less the public knows about what is going on in science, the less likely it is to hold intelligent opinions about the directions research should take and the amount of funding it should receive.

Science journalism has come a long way from the "gee-whiz" days but it still has a long way to go. Advances in television technology may lead to improvements in the quality of information that the public gets via the small screen. I have described elsewhere how the British "Prestel" (formerly Viewdata), operated by the British Post Office, may revolutionize the dissemination of scientific information.[13] ISI's European branch supplies the Prestel system with a science news segment called SCITEL™.[14] However, the problem with the commercial networks does not seem to be lagging technology but lagging will. The networks could be doing a far better job of reporting science with the resources they already have.

Journalism itself leaves much to be desired but the investigative reporting typified by Bernstein and Woodward in the Watergate case signalled a new era.[15] Just this sort of thorough investigative reporting is what we need in the mass media. They would do well to emulate the excellent job done by *Science* in its "News and Comment" Section.

That the public is ready for more science I have no doubt. The AAAS is studying the feasibility of a science magazine geared to a mass audience. And the publishers of *Penthouse* and *Viva* have announced a new science magazine, *Omni*, to be launched in September. All in all I think we can say about science journalism, as they do in the ads: "You've come a long way baby." but you've still got a way to go!

REFERENCES

1. **Sandman P M, Rubin D M & Sachsman D B.** *Media: an introductory analysis of mass communications.* Englewood Cliffs, NJ: Prentice-Hall, Inc., 1976. 483 p.
2. **Dixon B.** Medicine and the media: popular science. *Brit. J. Hosp. Med.* 18:497, 1977.
3. **Jones G & Meadows A J.** Public understanding of science—British experience. *Social Innovation* (2):A7-13, 1976.
4. **Garfield E.** Keeping up with new magazines. *Current Contents* (9):5-13, 27 February 1978.
5. ----------. Radio: the neglected medium for scientific communications. *Current Contents* (25):5-9, 19 June 1978.
6. **Perlman D.** Science and the mass media. (Holton G & Blanpied W A, eds.) *Science and its public: the changing relationship.* Boston: D. Reidel Publishing Company, 1976.
7. **Sagan C.** There's no hint of the joys of science. *TV Guide* (26):6-8, 4 February 1978.
8. **Rubin D M & Hendy V.** Swine influenza and the news media. *Ann. Intern. Med.* 87:769-74, 1977.
9. **Goodell R.** *The visible scientists.* Boston: Little, Brown and Company, 1977. 242 p.
10. **Kurtz P.** Complaint to FCC against NBC. *The Humanist* 38(1):5, January/February 1978.
11. **Sagan C.** *The dragons of Eden.* New York: Ballantine Books, 1977. 271 p.
12. **Friedman M S, Goodell R, & Verbit L.** Directory of science communication courses and programs. Binghamton, NY: State University of New York at Binghamton, 1978. 46 p.
13. **Hawkes N.** Science in Europe/British may use telephone, TV's, to tap data banks. *Science* 201(4350):33-4, 7 July 1978.
14. **Garfield E.** Viewdata and SCITEL bring interactive information systems into the home. *Current Contents* (41):5-10, 10 October 1977.
15. **Bernstein C & Woodward B.** *All the president's men.* New York: Simon and Schuster, 1974. 349 p.

Current Comments

The 300 Most-Cited Authors, 1961-1976, Including Co-Authors. Part 2. The Relationship Between Citedness, Awards, and Academy Memberships

Number 35　　　　　　　　　　　　　　　　August 28, 1978

In our 1977 study of primary authors we provided information on the relationship between citedness and other forms of recognition.[1] In this second part of our "all-author" study, we will document the same relationship.

Our new study is based on citation counts for both primary and secondary authorships. To obtain these data, we had to make certain compromises which I discussed in the first part of this "all-author" study.[2] In brief the 300 authors on this list are those who published—from 1961 to 1976—journal articles which were indexed by the *Science Citation Index®* . The chronological bias and the restriction to the journal literature should be kept in mind. Authors who published important research in books or in conference proceedings may have been missed.

The list of the 300 most-cited authors, the number of citations they received, and their memberships, honors, and awards appear in Figure 1 which begins on page 9. Authors are listed alphabetically under their disciplines.

To obtain data on the awards and memberships in honorific academies, we consulted several biographical directories. Our chief sources were Marquis' *World Who's Who in Science* and *American Men & Women of Science*. Unfortunately, the most recent editions of these directories are out of date. For example, *World Who's Who in Science* was last published in 1968. As a result, some of the scientists on our list did not appear in either directory. And entries for many others were incomplete. So we wrote to the 300 authors involved for an up-to-date list of their prizes and/or memberships. Most responded and gave us a complete list of their awards. Some listed only a few, but added that they had "many others," without naming them.

Since we were interested in listing only honors received for scientific research, we deleted all those given for nonscientific achievement, e.g., public service awards. We also omitted awards given by local organizations. Of course, there are some awards for scientific research which do not appear here, but we feel that the 57 which are shown in the figure are an *indication* of the recognition the authors have received.

Naturally, the Nobel Prize was included on our list because it is still the single most visible and prestigious award in science.[3] The relationship between citedness and winning a Nobel has already been demonstrated.[4-5]

It was not surprising that twenty-six of the 300 authors are Nobel laureates: two in physics, six in chemistry, and 18 in physiology or medicine.

However, eleven Nobelists, who did not make our earlier most-cited *primary* author list, appear in this "all-author" study. Winners in chemistry who make their first appearance here are C.B. Anfinsen and W.N. Lipscomb. Winners in physiology or medicine are F.A. Lipmann, S. Ochoa, H.G. Khorana, G.M. Edelman, D. Baltimore, B.S. Blumberg, R. Guillemin, A. Schally, and R. Yalow.

What about the Nobel prize winners who are not on this list? Many won the prize for work done prior to 1961. Although their research may still be highly cited, it was excluded from this study. Others, like A. Hewish and M. Ryle, the first astronomers to win the Nobel in physics, are from small fields. Thus, it would be very difficult for them to amass enough citations to appear on this list. Of course, many other Nobel laureates would show up if we extended our list to include the 1,000 most-cited authors. You must remember that the top 300 is an in-

finitesimally small percentage of the scientists who published between 1961-1976. That is why we want to expand these lists in the future.

The other prizes included on the list cover most of the honors mentioned by the authors themselves. One hundred seventy-seven (about 59%) of the authors won at least one of these prizes, awards, or honors. Many of the authors have won several. (A note at the end of the figure gives the full name of each award, the organization which presents it, and its purpose.)

In each discipline except one, over half of the authors have won at least one award. In pharmacology only about one-third have won. An informal survey of pharmacologists resulted in one possible reason for this phenomenon: there are fewer awards specifically for scientists in this field than in other disciplines like chemistry and physics.

We also included membership in national academies because such memberships are strictly limited, and are indeed comparable in prestige to awards.

For example, the US National Academy of Sciences (NAS) had only 1,182 members in 1976. It has been estimated that there were approximately 150,000 publishing scientists in the US that year.[6] The NAS admits as many as 75 new members per year; still Academy members make up less than 0.7% of all American publishing scientists.

One hundred fifteen of the authors on our list, or 39%, are members of the US National Academy of Science. They account for nearly 10% of the total NAS membership. This is another indication why it would be desirable to extend this analysis to at least the 1,000 most-cited scientists.

Twenty-one authors are members of the United Kingdom's equivalent to the NAS, the Royal Society of London. Twenty-five belong to the Deutsche Akademie Naturforscher Leopoldina, the 300-year-old organization which functions as the national academy of science for the Federal Republic of Germany, the German Democratic Republic, and other German-speaking nations. The national academies of Denmark and Sweden each have seven members on the list.

Australia's national academy of science is represented by six authors; India's and Canada's by four each. The Netherlands, USSR, France, and Israel each have three members of their academies of science on the list. The academies of Brazil, Italy, and Poland are represented by two members each. Other academies which have one each on the list are: Chile, Mexico, Yugoslavia, Republic of China (Taiwan), Hungary, Rumania, Japan, Ireland, Belgium, Czechoslovakia, Spain, and Austria.

Twenty-nine authors on the list are members of national academies of medicine. Thirteen belong to the US Institute of Medicine, nine to the UK's Royal Society of Medicine. Belgium's academy of medicine is represented by three authors; Argentina's by two. The academies of medicine of Mexico, France, and Brazil each have one member on the list.

The list also includes 112 members of the American Academy of Arts & Sciences. Founded in 1780, the Academy honors men and women (both US and non-US citizens) for their attainments in the mathematical and physical sciences, biological sciences, social arts and sciences, and the humanities. There are currently more than 3,000 members. Approximately 1,800 are from the sciences.

One hundred sixty of the authors on this list are members of at least one academy. Sixty-seven of them are also members of a second academy, 26 of three, 12 of four. H.A. Krebs and C.R. deDuve are members of 5 academies; S. Ochoa is a member of six. C.D. Djerassi, and M.F. Perutz hold seven memberships; R.B. Woodward and J.C. Eccles eight, and F. Sorm, nine. Incidentally, all Nobelists on the list are also members of national academies. This is not always true. Nobel prize winners are often elected to national academies after they get the prize, which seems to say something about the politics of local science bodies.

The American Philosophical Society is also on our list, although it is not, strictly speaking, an academy. Founded in 1767 by Benjamin Franklin, the Society now elects to its membership outstanding contributors to the mathematical and physical sciences, geological and biological sciences, social sciences, and humanities. Membership is limited to 500 US citizens and 100 non-US citizens. Twenty authors on our list are members of the American Philosophical Society. All of them belong to at least one national academy, and twelve have won Nobel Prizes. Members of the APS tend to be much older than the academy membership.

In all, 220, or 73%, of the authors have received recognition in the form of honors and honorific memberships we have listed. But we may also inquire into the reasons why 80 authors on the list have not been so recognized. One of the authors stated, "Since I am not a joiner of societies, I do not receive any prizes." I doubt that this is a universal factor. There are too many people who are joiners who don't receive recognition either. Knowledgeable persons involved in the politics of science would agree that for every member of an academy, there is at least one person equally deserving. The interesting question is whether the existing selection procedures are overly subjective. And yet we know from certain studies that subjective peer judgments correlate well with citation analysis.[7,8] If it works for grants, why not for awards and academy elections?

Those of you who serve on awards committees may find some names here worthy of consideration. It should be obvious that we have identified many scientists whose work has had significant impact. But for reasons known best to others, they have not yet received formal recognition commensurate with that impact.

REFERENCES

1. **Garfield E.** The 250 most-cited primary authors, 1961-1975. Part II. The correlation between citedness, Nobel prizes, and academy memberships.
   Current Contents (50):5-15, 12 December 1977.
2. -------------. The 300 most-cited authors, 1961-1976, including co-authors at last. Part I. How the names were selected.
   Current Contents (28):5-17, 10 July 1978.
3. **Cole J R & Cole S.** *Social stratification in science.*
   Chicago: University of Chicago Press, 1973. 283 p.
4. **Zuckerman H.** *Scientific elite.* New York: The Free Press, 1977. 335 p.
5. **Garfield E.** Citation indexing for studying science. *Nature* 227:669-71, 1970.
   (Reprinted in: Garfield E. *Essays of an information scientist.*
   Philadelphia: ISI Press, 1977. Vol. 1, p. 133-8.)
6. **Price D J D & Gursey S.** Some statistical results for the numbers of authors in the states of the United States and the nations of the world.
   ISI's Who is publishing in science® 1977 annual.
   Philadelphia: Institute for Scientific Information® , 1977. p. 26-34.
7. **Carter G M.** *Peer review, citations, and biomedical research policy: NIH grants to medical school faculty.*
   Rand Corporation: Santa Monica: CA, 1974. 90 p. (Rand Report number: R-1583-HEW).
8. **Cole S, Rubin L, & Cole J R.** Peer review and the support of sciences.
   Scientific American 237(4):34-41, 1977.

Figure 1. The 300 most-cited authors, including co-authors, 1961-1976, listed with their total citations, 1961-1976, honorific academy memberships, and awards and honors. A key to the full names of academies and awards follows the figure. The honors shown do not represent a complete list of awards won by each author. They are meant to give some indication of the recognition these authors have received.

Organic & Inorganic Chemistry

Name	Total Citations 1961-1976	National Academy	Awards & Prizes
Bender ML	5,131	US	Sloan (Chem)/59-63
Benson SW	4,359		Guggenheim/50-1; Petroleum Chem./77
Brown HC	10,288	Am. Acad. Arts/Sci.; India; US	Howe/53; Nichols/59; Synth. Org..Chem./60; Pauling/68; NMS/69; Adams/71
Clementi E	5,440		
Corey EJ	8,500	Am. Acad. Arts/Sci.; US	Sloan (Chem)/55-9; Guggenheim/56, 68; Pure Chem./59; Guenther/68; Howe/70; Pauling/73; Cope/76
Cotton FA	10,292	Am. Acad. Arts/Sci.; Denmark; US	Guggenheim/56; Sloan (Chem.)/60-4; Inorganic Chem./62; Baekeland/63; Dist. Service/74; Nichols/75; Howe/75; Pauling/76
Cram DJ	3,827	Am. Acad. Arts/Sci.; US	Guggenheim/54-5; Synth. Org. Chem./65; Cope/74
Davidson ER	3,757		Sloan (Chem.)/67-9; Guggenheim/74
Dewar MJS	6,635	Am. Acad. Arts/Sci.; UK	Howe/61
Djerassi C	11,027	Am. Acad. Arts/Sci.; Brazil; Leop.; Mexico; Sweden; US; US/Med.	Pure Chem./58; Baekeland/59; Guenther/60; Creative Invention/73; NMS/73; Wolf/78
Drago RS	4,178		Inorganic Chem./69; Guggenheim/73
Flory PJ	5,538	Am. Acad. Arts/Sci.; APS; US	Guggenheim/54; Nichols/62; NMS/74; Nobel/C/74; Priestley/74; Weizmann/76
Grant DM	3,869		

Figure 1. (cont'd.)

Name	Total Citations 1961-1976	National Academy	Awards & Prizes

Organic & Inorganic Chemistry (cont'd.)

Name	Total Citations 1961-1976	National Academy	Awards & Prizes
Gray HB	4,526	Denmark; US	Sloan (Chem.)/64-6; Pure Chem./70; Howe/72; Guggenheim/72; Inorganic Chem./78
Hammond GS	5,129	Am. Acad. Arts/Sci.; US	Guggenheim/55; Petroleum Chem./61; Norris/68; Priestley/76;
Hoffmann R	7,969	Am. Acad. Arts/Sci.; US	Sloan (Chem.)/66-8; Pure Chem./69; Howe/69; Cope/73; Pauling/74
Huisgen R	4,996	Am. Acad. Arts/Sci.; Leop.; Spain	Adams/75
Ibers JA	6,452		
Jortner J	4,821	Israel	Weizmann/73
Karplus M	6,193	Am. Acad. Arts/Sci.; US	Sloan (Chem.)/59-63; Howe/67
Khorana HG	6,620	Am. Acad. Arts/Sci.; APS; India; Leop.; US	Lasker/BR/68; Nobel/M or P/68; Synth. Org. Chem./69
King RB	4,583		Sloan (Chem.)/67-9; Pure Chem./71
Kochi JK	3,919		
Li CH	3,908	Am. Acad. Arts/Sci.; Chile; Republic of China; US	Oppenheimer/47; Guggenheim/48; Lasker/BR/62
Lipscomb WN	6,364	Am. Acad. Arts/Sci.; Netherlands; US	Guggenheim/54-72; Howe/58; Dist. Service/68; Nobel/C/76
Muetterties EL	3,883	Am. Acad. Arts/Sci.; US	Inorganic Chem./65
Nemethy G	3,927		Pius XI/72
Olah GA	7,451	US	Petroleum Chem./56; Baekeland/67; Morley/70; Guggenheim/72

Name		Organizations	Awards
Paquette LA	3,819		
Pople JA	10,479	Am. Acad. Arts/Sci.; UK; US	Sloan (Chem.)/65-7; Morley/71; Guggenheim/71 Langmuir/70; Howe/71; Pauling/77
Roberts JD	6,088	Am. Acad. Arts/Sci.; APS; US	Guggenheim/52, 54; Pure Chem./54; Howe/57; Adams/67; Nichols/72, Morley/76
Robins RK	4,239		
Samuelsson B	5,849		Lasker/BR/77
Scheraga HA	9,232	Am. Acad. Arts/Sci.; US	Guggenheim/56, 62; Lilly/57; Nichols/74
Schleyer PV	5,860	Am. Acad. Arts/Sci.;	Sloan (Chem.)/62-6; Guggenheim/64
Sorm F	5,858	Czechoslovakia; Denmark; Hungary; Leop.; Poland; Rumania; US; USSR	Guenther/59
Stewart RF	3,894		Sloan (Chem.)/70-2
Sweeley CC	4,424	Am. Acad. Arts/Sci.; US	Guggenheim/70
Tanford C	5,888		Guggenheim/56
Winstein S	4,522	Am. Acad. Arts/Sci.; US	Pure Chem./48; Norris/67; NMS/70
Witkop B	4,341	Leop.; US	
Woodward RB	4,044	Am. Acad. Arts/Sci; APS; Australia; Ireland; India; Leop.; UK; US; USSR	Baekeland/55; Nichols/56; Synth. Org. Chem./57; Adams/61; Pius XI/61; NMS/64; Nobel/C/65; Weizmann/69; Cope/73

Biochemistry

Name		Organizations	Awards
Allfrey VG	6,069		
Ames BN	6,689	Am. Acad. Arts/Sci.; US	Lilly/64
Andrews P	4,606		

Figure 1. (cont'd.)

Biochemistry (cont'd.)

Name	Total Citations 1961-1976	National Academy	Awards & Prizes
Anfinsen CB	4,942	APS; Denmark; US	Guggenheim/57; NIH Lecture/64; Weizmann/69; Nobel/C/72
Brady RO	3,744	Argentina/Med.; US	Gairdner/73; NIH Lecture/70; Modern Med./76
Cleland WW	4,652	Am. Acad. Arts/Sci.	
Cuatrecasas P	6,777		Abel/72; Lilly (Diabetes)/75
deDuve CR	4,178	Am. Acad. Arts/Sci.; Belgium; Belgium/Med.; US	Pfizer/57; Gairdner/67; Nobel/M or P/74
DeLuca HF	8,622	Am. Acad. Arts/Sci.	Lichwitz/69; Gairdner/74
Doty P	7,422	Am. Acad. Arts/Sci.; APS; US	Guggenheim/50; Pure Chem./56
Edelman GM	6,797	Am. Acad. Arts/Sci.; US	Lilly/65; Nobel/M or P/72; NIH Lecture/76
Estabrook RW	4,546	US/Med.	
Fasman GD	4,149		Guggenheim/74
Hales CN	3,936		
Harris H	4,326	UK; US	
Horecker BL	4,529	Am. Acad. Arts/Sci.; Leop.; US	Pfizer/52; NIH Lecture/70
Jencks WP	4,299	Am. Acad. Arts/Sci.; US	Lilly /62; Guggenheim/73
Kaplan NO	7,248	Am. Acad. Arts/Sci.; US	Lilly/53; Guggenheim/64, 74
Kornberg A	6,706	Am. Acad. Arts/Sci.; APS; Leop.; UK; US	Pfizer/51; Nobel/M or P/59; NIH Lecture/59; Weizmann/65; Borden/68; Guggenheim/69
Koshland DE	5,136	Am. Acad. Arts/Sci.; US	Guggenheim/71; Jones/77

Name	Number	Memberships	Awards/Honors
Krebs EG	4,043	Am. Acad. Arts/Sci.; US	Guggenheim/59, 66
Krebs HA	5,146	Am. Acad. Arts/Sci.; APS; France/Med.; Leop.; UK; US	Nobel/M or P/53; Lasker (APHA)/53
Lardy HA	4,954	Am. Acad. Arts/Sci.; APS; UK	Pfizer/49
Lehninger AL	4,651	Am. Acad. Arts/Sci.; APS; Leop.; US; US/Med.	Pfizer/48; Guggenheim/51, 62
Lipmann F	5,019	APS; Denmark; Leop.; UK; US	Nobel/M or P/53; NMS/66
Moore S	5,619	Am. Acad. Arts/Sci.; Belgium/Med.; US	Chromatography/64; Nobel/C/72
Morris HP	4,319		
Ochoa S	4,172	Am. Acad. Arts/Sci.; APS; Leop.; Poland; UK; US; USSR	Borden/58; Nobel/M or P/59; Virchow/63
Passonneau JV	4,034		
Piez KA	4,302		Borden/66
Prockop DJ	5,187		Jones/70; NIH Lecture/75
Randle PJ	6,442		
Reich E	4,996	Am. Acad. Arts/Sci.	Waksman/64; Guggenheim/74
Rodbell M	4,037	US	
Roseman S	4,068	US	
Rutter WJ	4,147		Guggenheim/62; Pfizer/68
Seegmiller JE	4,690	US	Gairdner/68
Smith EI	3,861	Am. Acad. Arts/Sci.; APS; US	Guggenheim/38-9
Tappel AL	4,665		Guggenheim/65; Borden/73
Udenfriend S	10,507	Am. Acad. Arts/Sci.; US	Gairdner/67; Sollmann/75
Umezawa H	5,781	Am. Acad. Arts/Sci.; Japan; Leop.	
Vallee BL	5,527	Am. Acad. Arts/Sci.; Denmark; US	
Van Deenen LL	6,873	Netherlands	

Figure 1. (cont'd.)

Immunology

Name	Total Citations 1961-1976	National Academy	Awards & Prizes
Austen KF	6,023	Am. Acad. Arts/Sci.; US	Gairdner/77
Benacerraf B	9,197	Am. Acad. Arts/Sci.; US	Jones/76
Cooper MD	3,905		
Fahey JL	6,482		
Finland M	4,082	Am. Acad. Arts/Sci.; US	
Franklin EC	4,358	UK/Med.	
Fudenberg HH	7,523	Am. Acad. Arts/Sci.; US; US/Med.	Lasker/CR/70; Gairdner/70; Borden/70; Virchow/75
Good RA	17,641		
Grey HM	3,788		
Haber E	4,638	Am. Acad. Arts/Sci.; UK/Med.	Virchow/74
Hirschhorn K	4,548		Gairdner/73
Ishizaka K	4,947	Am. Acad. Arts/Sci.; US	Gairdner/62; Jones/74; Lasker/BR/75
Kunkel HG	9,031	Am. Acad. Arts/Sci.	Modern Med./65; Gairdner/69
Merrill JP	5,262		Jahre/76
Moller G	4,383	UK/Med.; US	Jones/71; Modern Med./74; Gairdner/74
Muller-Eberhard HJ	5,924	Am. Acad. Arts/Sci.; Australia	
Nossal GJV	3,985		
Paul WE	4,189		

Pressman D	3,726		Morley/67
Reisfeld RA	4,559		
Roitt IM	3,902		Van Meter/57; Gairdner/64
Rosen FS	4,149		Guggenheim/74
Sela M	4,987	Am. Acad. Arts/Sci.; Israel; US	NIH Lecture/73
Terasaki PI	5,174		Modern Med./71
Waksman BH	4,730		
Wigzell H	4,046		

Endocrinology

Aurbach GD	3,887		Lichwitz/68
Bartter FC	3,736		Modern Med./77
Berson SA	5,474	UK/Med.; US	Lilly (Diabetes)/57; Middleton/60; Gairdner/71
Conn JW	3,938	Argentina/Med.; US; US/Med.	Gairdner/65; CIBA-Stouffer/69
Daughaday WH	3,731		Modern Med./77
Greenwood FC	5,572		
Guillemin R	4,200	Am. Acad. Arts/Sci.; US	NIH Lecture/73; Gairdner/74; Lasker/BR/75; NMS/76; Borden/76; Nobel/M or P/77
Hunter WM	5,214		
Kastin AJ	3,852		Tyler/75
Kipnis DM	4,805	Am. Acad. Arts/Sci.; US/Med.	Lilly (Diabetes)/67; Oppenheimer/67
Laragh JH	4,763		CIBA-Stouffer/69
Lever AF	3,884		
Liddle GW	4,483		
Lipsett MB	3,912		Sloan/55
Midgley AR	5,108		

Figure 1. (cont'd.)

Name	Total Citations 1961-1976	National Academy	Awards & Prizes
Endocrinology (cont'd.)			
Pastan I	5,997		Van Meter/71; NIH Lecture/73
Potts JT	4,148		Oppenheimer/68; Lichwitz/68
Rasmussen H	4,489		Lichwitz/71
Roth J	5,647		Oppenheimer/74; Lilly (Diabetes)/74
Schally AV	10,386	Am. Acad. Arts/Sci.; Mexico/Med.; US	Van Meter/69; Middleton/70; Gairdner/74; Borden/75; Lasker/BR/75; Tyler/75; Nobel/M or P/77
Unger RH	4,623		Lilly (Diabetes)/64; Middleton/69
Wilson JD	4,140		Oppenheimer/72
Wurtman RJ	6,170		Abel/68; Oppenheimer/73
Yalow RS	5,595	Am. Acad. Arts/Sci.; US	Middleton/60; Lilly (Diabetes)/61; Gairdner/71; Modern Med./76; Lasker/BR/76; Nobel/M or P/77; Virchow/78
Molecular Biology			
Baltimore D	5,270	Am. Acad. Arts/Sci.; US	Lilly (Microbiology)/71; Gairdner/74; Nobel/M or P/75
Berg P	5,307	Am. Acad. Arts/Sci.; US	Lilly/59; NIH Lecture/76
Bonner J	7,096	Am. Acad. Arts/Sci.; APS; Leop.; US	Waksman/56
Changeaux JP	6,208	Leop.	

Name	Number	Memberships	Awards
Gros F	3,712	Am. Acad. Arts/Sci.; France	Pius XI/64
Hurwitz J	4,873	Am. Acad. Arts/Sci.; US	Lilly/62; Guggenheim/68
Jacob F	10,383	Am. Acad. Arts/Sci.; APS; France; UK; US	Nobel/M or P/65
Leder P	3,892		NIH Lecture/77; CIBA-GEIGY Drew/78
Maizel JV	4,807		
Marmur J	10,254		Waksman/62
Monod J	6,945	APS; Leop.; US	NIH Lecture/64; Nobel/M or P/65
Nomura M	5,100	Am. Acad. Arts/Sci.; Denmark	
Perutz MF	4,734	Am. Acad. Arts/Sci.; APS; Austria; France; Leop.; Netherlands; UK; US	Weizmann/61; Nobel/C/62
Racker E	4,876	Am. Acad. Arts/Sci.; US	NIH Lecture/75; NMS/76
Rich A	6,075	Am. Acad. Arts/Sci.; US	Gairdner/60; Guggenheim/63
Schimke RT	4,816	Am. Acad. Arts/Sci.; US	Pfizer/69
Singer SJ	4,422	Am. Acad. Arts/Sci.; US	Guggenheim/59
Szybalski W	3,753		
Tomkins GM	6,157		
Vinograd J	4,956	Am. Acad. Arts/Sci.; US	Jones/72
Weisbach H	4,112		Pfizer/70

Pharmacology

Name	Number	Memberships	Awards
Anden NE	4,475		
Axelrod J	15,769	Am. Acad. Arts/Sci.; US	NIH Lecture/67; Gairdner/67; Nobel/M or P/70; Virchow//71; Sollmann/73

Figure 1. (cont'd.)

Name	Total Citations 1961-1976	National Academy	Awards & Prizes
Pharmacology (cont'd.)			
Brodie BB	6,246	Am. Acad. Arts/Sci.; US; US/Med.	Sollmann/63; Modern Med./64; Lasker/BR/67; NMS/68; Hunter/70
Carlsson A	4,786	Sweden	Jahre/74
Conney AH	6,366		
Corrodi H	4,366		
Costa E	3,994		
Curtis DR	3,728	Australia; UK	
Fuxe K	8,888		
Gillette JR	3,869		
Glowinski J	4,502		
Greengard P	4,916	Am. Acad. Arts/Sci.; US	
Iversen LL	5,833		
Kopin IJ	6,694		
Levy G	3,898		
Lowry OH	4,867	Am. Acad. Arts/Sci.; US	Borden/66
Robison GA	4,051		
Sjoerdsma A	6,479		
Snyder SH	6,687	US	Abel/70
Sutherland EW	11,644		Guggenheim/55; Gairdner/69; Sollmann/69;Lasker/BR/70; Nobel/M or P/72; NMS/73
Vane JR	6,292	UK	Lasker/BR/77

Cell Biology

Name	Number	Affiliation	Awards
Aaronson SA	3,821		
Allison AC	5,807		
Barrnett RJ	5,945		
Brenner S	6,334	Am. Acad. Arts/Sci.; Leop.; US; UK	Lasker/BR/71
Busch H	4,736		
Davis BJ	7,602		
Ernster L	5,884	Sweden	
Farquhar MG	5,149		
Green DE	5,482	Am. Acad. Arts/Sci.; US	Pfizer/46
Green H	4,338	Am. Acad. Arts/Sci.	
Leblond CP	5,165	Am. Acad. Arts/Sci.; Canada; UK	Gairdner/65
McCulloch EA	4,417	Canada	Gairdner/69
Palade GE	11,242	Am. Acad. Arts/Sci.; Belgium/Med.; US; US/Med.	Lasker/BR/66; Gairdner/67; NIH Lecture/67; Nobel/M or P/74
Penman S	7,124	Am. Acad. Arts/Sci.	
Porter KR	4,221	Am. Acad. Arts/Sci.; US	Gairdner/64; Guggenheim/67-8; NMS/76
Sabatini DD	4,649		
Sachs L	5,982	Israel	
Sandberg AA	4,489		
Weissmann G	5,210		Guggenheim/73

Physiology

Name	Number
Arimura A	5,278
Brown JJ	3,892

Figure 1. (cont'd.)

Name	Total Citations 1961-1976	National Academy	Awards & Prizes
Physiology (cont'd.)			
Butcher RW	6,875		
Carlson LA	4,002	Sweden	
Eccles JC	4,579	Am. Acad. Arts/Sci.; APS; Australia; Belgium; India; Italy; Leop.; UK; US	Nobel/M or P/63
Fredrickson DS	7,871	Am. Acad. Arts/Sci.; US; US/Med.	McCollum/71; Modern Med./71
Hubel DH	4,474	Am. Acad. Arts/Sci.; Leop.; US	
Lassen NA	4,004		Jahre/77
McCann SM	4,956		Oppenheimer/66
Meites J	4,665		
Mirsky AE	5,083	APS; US	
Munro HN	4,414	US	Borden/78
Odell WD	3,720		
Page IH	5,161	Am. Acad. Arts/Sci.; Brazil; Sweden; US	Modern Med./56; Lasker/AHA/59; Gairdner/63; Hunter/66; CIBA—Stouffer/70
Park CR	3,763		
Robertson JI	3,705		
Starzl TE	4,901	Am. Acad. Arts/Sci.	Middleton/68; Eppinger/70
Waldmann TA	4,088		
Wiesel TN	4,605	Am. Acad. Arts/Sci.	NIH Lecture/75

Microbiology & Virology

Name	Number	Memberships	Awards
Blumberg BS	6,029	US	Eppinger/73; Modern Med./75; Gairdner/75; Nobel/M or P/76
Chanock RM	7,659	US	
Darnell JE	9,091	Am. Acad. Arts/Sci.; US	
Henle G	5,261	US	
Henle W	4,908	Am. Acad. Arts/Sci.	
Hilleman MR	4,871	US	NIH Lecture/61; NMS/69; Adams/75
Huebner RJ	8,418	US	
Koprowski H	4,419	Am. Acad. Arts/Sci.; US; Yugoslavia	
McCarthy BJ	4,625		Lilly (Microbiology)/68
Melnick JL	7,466		Modern Med./65
Rapp F	3,729		CIBA-GEIGY Drew/77
Rapp HJ	3,762		
Rowe WP	7,183	US	Lilly (Diabetes)/60; NIH Lecture/73
Sever JL	4,599		Borden/57
Spiegelman S	9,712	Am. Acad. Arts/Sci.; Brazil/Med.; Leop.; US	Lasker/BR/74
Strominger JL	5,854	Am. Acad. Arts/Sci.; US; US/Med.	Abel/60; Pfizer/62; Guggenheim/74
Uhr JW	4,567		
Yanofsky C	4,640	Am. Acad. Arts/Sci.; Leop.; US	Lilly (Microbiology)/59; Lasker/BR/71

Physics & Biophysics

Name	Number	Memberships	Awards
Anderson PW	3,838	Am. Acad. Arts/Sci.; US	Heineman/75; Nobel/Physics/77; Guthrie/78
Chance B	7,981	Am. Acad. Arts/Sci.; APS; Leop.; Sweden; US	Guggenheim/45, 47; Pfizer/50; Howe/66; Franklin/66; Nichols/69; Gairdner/72; NMS/74

Figure 1. (cont'd.)

Physics & Biophysics (cont'd.)

Name	Total Citations 1961-1976	National Academy	Awards & Prizes
Cromer DT	5,587		Lawrence/69
Dalgarno A	3,712	Am. Acad. Arts/Sci.; UK	Hodgkins/78
Fisher ME	5,164	UK	Guggenheim/70; Langmuir/71
Franklin RM	3,917		
Gell-Mann M	4,912	Am. Acad. Arts/Sci.; US; US/Med.	Sloan (Physics)/57-61; Heineman/59; Franklin/67; Nobel/Physics/69; Guggenheim/71
Mandel P	3,881		
McConnell HM	4,309	Am. Acad. Arts/Sci.; US	Pure Chem./62; Howe/68; Langmuir/72
Miledi R	4,111	UK	
Osborn M	6,618		
Rice SA	4,034	Am. Acad. Arts/Sci.; Denmark; US	Sloan (Chem.)/58-62; Guggenheim/59; Pure Chem./63; Baekeland/71
Setlow RB	3,777	Am. Acad. Arts/Sci.; US	
Sinsheimer RL	5,332	Am. Acad. Arts/Sci.; US	NIH Lecture/72
Till JE	5,109	Canada	Gairdner/69
Weber K	8,517		
Weinberg S	7,349	Am. Acad. Arts/Sci.; US	Sloan (Physics)/61-5; Oppenheimer/73; Heineman/77
Wyman J	4,208	Am. Acad. Arts/Sci.; Italy; US	

Histology & Oncology

Boyse EA	8,239	Am. Acad. Arts/Sci.; UK	
Carbone PP	4,413		Lasker/CR/72
Falck B	4,088		
Heidelberger C	3,981		National (Am. Cancer Soc.)/74
Hellstrom I	5,219		National (Am. Cancer Soc.)/74
Hellstrom KE	4,985		National (Am. Cancer Soc.)/74
Hokfelt T	4,553		
Klein E	4,650		
Klein G	7,393	Am. Acad. Arts/Sci.; Sweden; US	National (Am. Cancer Soc.)/73; Gairdner/76
Luft JH	8,902		
Moore GE	4,026		Modern Med./62
Old LJ	8,457	Am. Acad. Arts/Sci.; US/Med.	Sloan/62
Pearse AGE	4,415	Leop.	
Todaro GJ	6,936		
Weber G	4,744	UK/Med; US	

Pathology

Benditt EP	3,755	US	
Bensch K	3,755		
Dixon FJ	6,590	US	Modern Med./61; Gairdner/69; Lasker/BR/75
Edwards JE	3,828		Modern Med./65

Figure 1. (cont'd.)

Pathology (cont'd.)

Name	Total Citations 1961-1976	National Academy	Awards & Prizes
Karnovsky MJ	10,114	Am. Acad. Arts/Sci.	
Metcalf D	3,904	Australia	
Miller JFA	4,432	Australia; Belgium/Med.; UK; UK/Med.	Gairdner/66
Novikoff AB	5,101	US	
Popper H	3,795	Am. Acad. Arts/Sci.; Leop.; US	Modern Med./77
Reynolds ES	10,452		
Trump BF	3,973		
Weiss L	4,072		

Miscellaneous Medical Disciplines (Cardiology, Hematology, Gastroenterology & Radiology)

Name	Total Citations 1961-1976	National Academy	Awards & Prizes
Beutler E	4,537	Am. Acad. Arts/Sci.; US	Gairdner/75
Braunwald E	15,040	Am. Acad. Arts/Sci.; US; US/Med	Able/65; Modern Med./68
Epstein SE	3,948		
Frei E	4,167		Lasker/CR/72
Freireich EJ	3,998		Lasker/CR/72
Gorlin R	5,697	UK/Med.	
Grossman MI	6,096		Modern Med.
Herbert V	5,739	UK/Med.	McCollum/72

Hofmann AF	4,254		Eppinger/76
Isselbacher KJ	5,027	Am. Acad. Arts/Sci.; US	
Kaplan HS	4,187	Am. Acad. Arts/Sci.; US	
Lees RS	5,667		
Levy RI	8,227		
Lieber CS	4,432		McCollum/73; Middleton/77
Mason DT	4,232		
Morrow AG	5,308		
Mustard JF	4,852	Canada	Gairdner/67
Ross J	7,207		
Sherlock S	5,421	UK/Med.	
Sonnenblick EH	8,540		
Wagner HN	4,951		
Wallach DFH	3,835		Guggenheim/70

Key to Abbreviations in Figure 1

Academies

Memberships in national academies of sciences are indicated by country abbreviations. Memberships in national academies of medicine are indicated by "country/med."

Exceptions:
Am. Acad. Arts/Sci. = American Academy of Arts and Sciences
APS = American Philosophical Society
Leop. = Deutsche Akademie der Naturforscher LEOPOLDINA, which serves as the national academy of sciences for the Federal Republic of Germany, the German Democratic Republic, and the other German-speaking countries.

Awards and Prizes

Name	Description
Abel	John Jacob Abel Award—given by the American Society for Pharmacology & Experimental Therapeutics—for outstanding research in pharmacology-toxicology.
Adams	Roger Adams Award—in Organic Chemistry—given by the American Chemical Society (ACS) and sponsored by Organic Reactions, Inc. and Organic Synthesis, Inc.—for outstanding contributions to research in organic chemistry.
Baekeland	Baekeland Award—awarded by North Jersey section of ACS and supported by Union Carbide Plastics Company—to recognize accomplishments in pure or industrial chemistry.
Borden	Borden Award in Medical Science—awarded by Association of American Medical Colleges—for faculty members of AAMC schools who have done outstanding research.
Chromatography	Chromatography Award—given by ACS, sponsored by SUPELCO, Inc.—to recognize outstanding contributions to the fields of chromatography.
CIBA-GEIGY Drew	CIBA-GEIGY Drew Award in Biomedical Research—given by CIBA Pharmaceuticals Divisions—to stimulate new concepts for research in the overlapping disciplines of biology, chemistry, and medicine.
CIBA—Stouffer	Stouffer Award—superseded by CIBA Award—given by CIBA Pharmaceuticals Division—for research in high blood pressure and arteriosclerosis.
Cope	Arthur C. Cope Award—given by ACS—for outstanding achievement in the field of organic chemistry, the significance of which has become apparent within the 5 years preceeding the year in which the award will be considered.

Abbreviations (cont'd.)

Creative Invention	ACS Award for Creative Invention—sponsored by the ACS Committee on Corporation Associates—to recognize individual inventors for successful applications of research in chemistry and/or chemical engineering which contribute to the material prosperity and happiness of people.
Dist. Service	ACS Award for Distinguished Service in the Advancement of Inorganic Chemistry—sponsored by Mallinkrodt, Inc.—for distinguished service in the advancement of inorganic chemistry.
Eppinger	Eppinger Prize—given by Herbert Falck Company—for research in liver pathology.
Franklin	Franklin Medal—given by Franklin Institute—for those workers in physical science or technology, without regard to country, who have done the most to advance a knowledge of physical science or its appreciation.
Gairdner	Gairdner Foundation Award—given by Gairdner Foundation of Toronto—for outstanding medical research.
Guenther	Ernest Guenther Award in the Chemistry of Essential Oils and Related Products—given by ACS and sponsored by Fritzsche, Dodge, and Olcott, Inc.—to recognize and encourage outstanding achievements in analysis, structure elucidation, chemistry synthesis of essential oils, isolates, and related substances.
Guggenheim	Guggenheim Fellowship—given by John Simon Guggenheim Memorial Foundation—grants to foster research and provide for the cause of better international understanding.
Guthrie	Guthrie Medal and Prize—awarded by Institute of Physics, London—for contributions to physics by a physicist of international reputation.
Heineman	Dannie Heineman Prize—awarded jointly by the American Physical Society and the American Institute of Physics—for the outstanding publication in the field of mathematical physics.
Hodgkins	Hodgkins Medal and Prize—given by Smithsonian Institute—for recognition of significant contributions in atmospheric science.
Howe	Harrison Howe Award—given by Rochester section of ACS—to recognize outstanding achievement in chemistry, particularly in opening new areas of knowledge important to the future of chemistry.
Hunter	Oscar B. Hunter Award—given by American Society for Clinical Pharmacology & Therapeutics—for research which advances the science of human pharmacology and therapeutics.

Abbreviations (cont'd.)

Inorganic Chem.   ACS Award in Inorganic Chemistry—sponsored by Monsanto Company—to recognize and encourage fundamental research in the field of inorganic chemistry.

Jahre   Anders Jahre Endowment for Advancement of Science—to individuals for distinguished work or significant findings in Scandinavian medicine.

Jones   T. Duckett Jones Memorial Award—given by Helen Hay Whitney Foundation—in recognition of outstanding accomplishments in research on connective tissues.

Langmuir   Irving Langmuir Award in Chemical Physics—given by ACS, and American Physical Society. Sponsored by G.E. Foundation—to recognize and encourage outstanding interdisciplinary research in chemistry and physics.

Lasker/BR
Lasker/CR
Lasker/AHA
Lasker/APHA   Albert & Mary Lasker Foundation Awards—sponsored by Lasker Foundation—to recognize those who have made significant contributions to research in the diseases which are the main cause of death and disability. BR = basic research award given by Lasker Foundation. CR = clinical research award given by Lasker Foundation. AHA = basic research award given through American Heart Association. APHA = basic research award given through American Public Health Association.

Lawrence   E.O. Lawrence Memorial Award—given by US Atomic Energy Commission—for recognition of young scientists who have made recent, meritorious contributions to the development, use or control of atomic energy.

Lichwitz   Andre Lichwitz Prize—given by the French National Institute of Health and Medical Research—for research in calcium and phosphorous compounds.

Lilly   Eli Lilly Award—given by Division of Biological Chemisry of ACS—to stimulate fundamental research in biological chemistry.

Lilly (Diabetes)   Eli Lilly Award—given by American Diabetes Association—for outstanding medical research.

Lilly (Microbiology)   Eli Lilly Award—awarded by American Society for Microbiology, American Association of Immunologists and American Society for Experimental Pathology—for outstanding fundamental research in microbiology or immunology research.

McCollum   McCollum Award—established by National Dairy Council, awarded by American Society for Clinical Nutrition—for outstanding research in clinical nutrition.

Middleton   William S. Middleton Award—given by US Veterans Administration—for recognition of outstanding achievements in medical research by clinical investigators who are employed by the Vet. Administration.

Modern Medicine

Modern Medicine Award for Distinguished Achievement—given by Modern Medicine Publications—for recognition of great discoveries and practical applications in medical science.

Morley

Morley Award—given by Cleveland section of ACS—to recognize outstanding contributions to chemistry.

National (Am. Cancer Soc.)

National Award of the American Cancer Society—given by American Cancer Society—the society's highest award—in recognition of outstanding contributions in the field of oncology.

Nichols

William H. Nichols Medal—given by N.Y. section of ACS—for recognition of outstanding contributions to physical organic chemistry.

NIH Lecture

National Institutes of Health Lectureship—given by NIH-for recognition of outstanding scientific accomplishment.

NMS

National Medal of Science—given by National Science Foundation—for recognition of outstanding contributions in the physical, biological, mathematical and engineering sciences. Individuals are nominated by NMS Committee and then selected by President of US.

Nobel/C
Nobel/Physics
Nobel/M or P

Nobel Prizes given by Nobel Foundation — a) *in Chemistry* — b) *in Physics*—presented and administered by the Royal Swedish Academy—given to persons who have made the most important discovery or improvement in chemistry or physics c) *in Medicine/Physiology*—presented and administered by Karolinska Institute Faculty of Medicine, Stockholm for most important discovery or improvement in the field of medicine/physiology.

Norris

James Flack Norris Award in Physical Organic Chemistry—sponsored by Northeast Section of ACS—for outstanding contribution to physical organic chemistry.

Oppenheimer

Ernst Oppenheimer Award—awarded by Endocrine Society and sponsored by CIBA-GEIGY Corp.—for recognition of meritorious accomplishments in basic clinical endocrinology.

Pauling

Linus Pauling Award—given jointly by Oregon and Puget Sound Sections of ACS—for outstanding contributions to chemistry of a character that has merited national and international recognition.

Petroleum Chem.

ACS Award in Petroleum Chemistry—sponsored by Lubrizol Corp.—to recognize, encourage, and stimulate outstanding achievements in the field of petroleum chemistry in US and Canada.

Pfizer	Pfizer Award—also called ACS Award in Enzyme Chemistry, superseded the Paul-Lewis Labs Award—to recognize outstanding fundamental research in enzyme chemistry.
Pius XI	Pius XI Gold Medal—given by Pontifical Academy of Science—to reward a young scientist having reached international reputation due to his research activity.
Priestley	Priestley Medal—given by ACS-to recognize distinguished services to chemistry in any nation.
Pure Chem.	ACS Award in Pure Chemistry—sponsored by Alpha Chi Sigma Fraternity—to recognize and encourage fundamental research in pure chemistry.
Sloan	Alfred P. Sloan Award for Cancer Research—awarded by Sloan-Kettering Institute—for outstanding work in cancer research.
Sloan (math) *Sloan (physics)* *Sloan (chem.)* *Sloan (neuroscience)*	Sloan Fellowships—awarded by Sloan Foundation of the Sloan-Kettering Institute for Cancer Research—funding for continued research in math, physics, chemistry, and neuroscience.
Sollmann	Torald Sollmann Award—given by American Society for Pharmacology & Experimental Therapeutics—for outstanding pharmacological research.
Synth. Org. Chem.	ACS Award for Creative Work in Synthetic Organic Chemistry—sponsored by the Aldrich Chemical Company, Inc.—to recognize and encourage creative work in synthetic organic chemistry.
Tyler	E.T. Tyler Fertility Award—given by International Fertility Society—for outstanding research in the medical/endocrinology field.
Van Meter	Van Meter Prize Award—given by American Thyroid Association—to acknowledge investigators doing outstanding research in thyroid physiology or pathology.
Virchow	Rudolph Virchow Medal—given by Virchow-Pirquet Medical Society—for outstanding research in medicine and/or pathology.
Waksman	Waksman Award—given by Institute of Microbiology at Rutgers University—for outstanding contributions to microbiological research.
Weizmann	Weizmann Fellowship—awarded by the Weizmann Institute of Science in Israel—to eminent scientists and public figures.
Wolf	Wolf Prize—given by Wolf Foundation in Israel—for outstanding scientific research.

Current Comments

Scientists' Image in Movies and TV Programs

Number 36   September 4, 1978

When the *Philadelphia Inquirer* ran a page one story about an experiment in which a few human chromosomes were inserted into mice, the paper made it clear that the mice were "not anything like monsters." And the caption under a picture of two of the experimenters, Drs. Hilary Koprowski and Carl Croce of Philadelphia's Wistar Institute, pointed out that they were "no mad scientists."[1]

In a similar vein, a *New Times* article on brain transplant research with monkeys asserts that Dr. Robert White, director of Cleveland's Brain Research Laboratories, "is certainly no mad scientist out to create a Frankenstein monster."[2] The fact that the paper and the magazine felt the need to add these disclaimers to their stories says something about the popular image of the scientist.

"Without a doubt, Dr. Frankenstein is better known in America today than any other scientist, living or dead," writes George Basalla, a University of Delaware historian who specializes in the study of the social implications of science and technology.[3] Panelists at a symposium at this year's annual meeting of the American Association for the Advancement of Science (AAAS) agreed that the popular image of scientists is remarkably bad, and that the mass media bear a great deal of the responsibility for that. Thomas H. Maugh II, who covered the meeting for *Science,* reports that panelists agreed that movies and television portray scientists as "frequently foolish, inept, or even villainous," and that the image is "eroding public support for science and may be turning away potential Einsteins, Paulings and Pasteurs before they mature enough to appreciate the joys and the wonders of science."[4]

I must confess I am a bit skeptical of the effects of these portrayals on children and adults. Ask typical working-class parents if they would approve of their child becoming a scientist. I think they would be delighted that one of their children had enough intelligence to do so. But how their attitude affects the child's career choice is another issue. Teachers are probably a more potent force in career choices. Unless parents present a career model they would prefer, teachers make the most significant impact.

However, it is probably true that many persons who might otherwise pursue a scientific career are turned off to science at an early age for a multitude of reasons, perhaps including the negative portrayals of scientists on TV and in movies.

There are about 130 million television sets in use in the US alone,[5] many of them tuned to the popular reruns of *Star Trek* and *Twilight Zone* which are shown in most major American cities. The many science fiction films of the past few decades are also viewed on TV again and again on Saturday afternoons and late at night. In contrast to science news and documentaries which get relatively little air time on TV,[6] fictionalized portrayals of scientists are available to the public at almost any hour.

Add to all this TV viewing the fact that *Star Wars,* the highest-grossing film of all time, so far has made over $225 million in the US and Canada alone.[7] If the average admission price is $3, that means over 75 million tickets were sold. And another recent science fiction film, *Close Encounters of the Third Kind,* has grossed $115 million in just over seven months, having sold approximately 38 million tickets.[8]

With science fiction movies and TV programs reaching such large audiences, it is obvious that these media have the potential to affect the public's perceptions of science and scientists. Some believe that what the public is seeing on TV sets and movie screens should cause disquiet in the scientific community.

Most often the scientist is seen as a dangerous character—especially in the horror films of the 1930s and '40s, and the science fiction films of the '50s. But as film director and critic Susan Sontag points out, this presentation of scientists as dangerous is nothing new. She asserts that Shakespeare's Prospero (in *The Tempest*), "the overdetached scholar forcibly retired from society to a desert island, only partly in control of the magic forces in which he dabbles," remains one of the oldest images of the scientist.[9]

Scientists often appear as satanists or Faust-like figures in the movies, and Sontag sees this as an extension of attitudes that have been with us for a long time. The link between past and present images is clearly illustrated by a film deliberately modelled on *The Tempest.* In *Forbidden Planet,* directed by Fred Wilcox in 1956, Morbius, an overdetached futuristic Prospero, is marooned on a desert planet and only partly in control of a vanished race's magic-like technology.

Like Dr. Frankenstein (who is best known today through James Whale's 1931 film *Frankenstein*), Morbius unleashes a monster not through malevolence but through irresponsibility. Like Dr. Frankenstein he watches the monster menace his loved ones, repents, and is killed by the creature. This is what scientists get for tampering with "things man was not meant to know." Both characters are typical of the scientists who appeared in the B-movies, and are not especially different from those who are seen on screen today.

Scientists in the movies of the

'30s and '40s have a number of easily recognizable characteristics. The scientist is usually an elderly white male. He may be insane or evil. But since the 1950s, the cackling madman hatching plots to rule the world has more or less vanished from the screen (though he remains a favorite prop in comic strips and comic books).[3]

More often in the films of the last 25 years, the scientist (still a white male) is well-meaning but obsessed with the pursuit of knowledge. Amoral rather than immoral, he will stop at nothing to find out what he wants to know. He will not let human sensitivities or sympathies stand in his way.

He displays his insensitivity in small ways. If the scientist has a family, he usually neglects it. More often, scientists in the movies are shown as bachelors or widowers; they are rarely shown as being sexually or emotionally involved. The audience may hear his beautiful daughter or assistant say that he is married to his test tubes and has no time for socializing.

But the scientist's capacity for destruction on a large scale is the major recurring theme in the films. Sontag notes, "Science fiction films are not about science. They are about disaster, which is one of the oldest subjects of art. In science fiction films disaster...is always extensive."[9] She notes also that somewhere between the film *Frankenstein* and the period that produced *Forbidden Planet*, the scientist's capacity for causing disaster increased. In the horror films of the '30s, Sontag suggests, the worst scientists could do was lay a small Bavarian village to waste. But later they had the power to imperil the world, even many worlds.

Note that the scientist most often wreaks havoc by building or creating something. The process of scientific research is rarely distinguished from the process of technological application; usually they are one and the same.

Sontag notes that the B-films of the '50s reflected the fears of the time: nuclear war, political subversion, dehumanization, and mass conformity. She suggests that the films represent, at least in part, attempts to exorcise those fears by treating them symbolically. Thus many of the film disasters were brought about by the atomic bomb or its after effects. Prehistoric monsters awakened by nuclear testing were easier for audiences to pretend to deal with than the complex issues surrounding disarmament.[9] Scientists, of course, were often seen as responsible for the sudden appearance of monsters.

Scientists also played an important role in the many alien invasions or infiltrations portrayed on film in the '50s. The aliens, cold and implacably hostile, either brought ruin to the world with flying saucers and ray guns, or took over the minds of humans by remote control. In *The Thing from Another World*, a hostile alien threatened an arctic research base staffed by scientists and soldiers. The foolish scientist wanted to communicate with the hostile invader; the military men wisely saw the menace and tried to destroy the creature. In films where the aliens turned humans into mindless robots who did their bidding by remote control, scientists were often the first to submit. These themes are important if seen in the context of the Cold War, when many real scientists and intellectuals were accused of being dupes of subversives. Scientists, in the movies, were always to be distrusted, and they were especially suspect in that paranoid atmosphere.

Has the situation improved since the '50s? While recent screen science fiction is more visually satisfying than ever, the stereotype of scientists, with a few exceptions, remains much the same. Television certainly hasn't changed it much. In *Space: 1999* a scientist developed a spacecraft propulsion method which, for reasons not made clear to the viewer, destroyed several inhabited planets. The responsibility for this catastrophe fell on the shoulders of the scientist who, like Dr. Frankenstein, repented and ended up dead.

Carl Sagan points to a Saturday morning cartoon program for children in which a "Dr. Nerdnik" has to be told that "the people of Earth will not appreciate being shrunk down to 3 inches high, even if it *will* save space...."[10] And the weekly series *Man from Atlantis* features as a recurring character a scientist villian who is always trying to do things like melt the icecaps.[11]

In an episode of the popular American series *Star Trek*, a scientist developed a computer that could think for itself. True to the conventions of video science fic-

tion, this made it dangerous. The machine was put in command of a test flight of the spaceship *Enterprise,* promptly ran amok, and had to be destroyed. The problem, it turned out, was a flaw in the programming. The scientist, in bestowing a personality on the computer, gave it *his* personality. This scientist got off easy; he merely had a nervous breakdown.

If you look hard enough, you can find a few exceptions to the stereotype. In *Star Trek,* Leonard Nimoy played the *Enterprise*'s "Science Officer," one Mr. Spock from the planet Vulcan. The inhabitants of Vulcan had no emotions, and for much of the series, Mr. Spock was a relentlessly rational, typically heartless scientist. He was only half-alien, however; his mother was terrestrial. Carl Sagan calls this "about as likely as successful mating between a man and a petunia,"[12] but it allowed for occasional dramatic conflicts between Spock's Vulcan nature and his human one. He was thus a sympathetic character, and this characterization accounts for much of *Star Trek*'s popularity.

A few recent science fiction movies have also broken the scientist stereotype. Robert Wise's 1971 film, *The Andromeda Strain,* shows us a scientist with a conscience. The story is about a team of scientists who try to contain a deadly micro-organism brought to earth by a malfunctioning satellite. They learn that the accident resulted from a secret military attempt to use the organism as a biological weapon. Kate Reid, in a refreshing departure from the amoral, uncaring (male) scientist, plays the scientist who condemns the military project. She serves as the story's moral voice. Also, Nelson Gidding's screenplay, based on Michael Crichton's novel,[13] emphasizes the difference between pure science and its applications. We see a discovery misused, not by an irresponsible scientist, but by irresponsible militarists. It was interesting, for a change, to see scientists trying to save the world from disaster that was someone else's fault.

Jaws, the 1976 blockbuster, also gave us an unstereotyped scientist. Instead of unleashing a monster, the young marine biologist in the movie helped destroy the white shark which had been preying on swimmers at a beach resort.

And what of last year's science fiction films? In George Lucas' *Star Wars* and Steven Speilberg's *Close Encounters of the Third Kind,* the image of a scientist, if not entirely favorable, is at least ambiguous. Both films contain spectacular special effects and provide little more than escapist entertainment. *Star Wars* has no scientists in it at all (except for one brief scene), but is worth mentioning here because it seems to contain certain tacit assumptions about technology. But there is wide disagreement on what those assumptions are.

The universe in *Star Wars* is one in which scientific discoveries and their applications have supplied the characters with a host of devices most viewers would be delighted to have—notably fast-moving hover crafts and robots to handle every-day drudgery. Harvard University sociologist Nathan Keyfitz says the film shows a favorable attitude towards the promise of science and technology. But, he complains, the most spectacular technology is shown in the service of war, and the film seems to approve of that.[14]

One could argue, however, that a more complex inference could be drawn from the film. The large-scale war technology of the villains is overcome by the relatively small-scale technology (small spacecraft and swords with blades of deadly light) of the heroes. And the film's most sympathetic characters, two robots, are unswervingly loyal and helpful to the human heroes. They seem to suggest that humans may make a technological advance without it necessarily turning into a Frankenstein monster.

On the other hand, Ben Bova, editor of *Analog,* asserts that the film is anti-science and technology because during a crucial space battle, the film's hero shuts off his ship's computer and relies instead on "The Force."[15] "The Force," the film explains, is a "mystical energy field" that can be harnessed to deliver miracles. "The Force" is the film's *deus ex machina;* it serves the heroes of *Star Wars* in much the same way as the good witch of the north periodically aided Dorothy in *The Wizard of Oz.* Bova considers this anti-science because it compromises human rationality.

Bova, like other observers, sees an anti-intellectual attitude in *Close Encounters,* a film about contact with UFOs.[15] Why, he asks, do creatures capable of building a mountain-sized interstellar vessel ignore the scientists and engineers who come to greet them? Instead, the aliens wish to deal with the film's "Everyman" protagonist. Bova's point is reasonable, but the film seems to have a few saving graces. It displays curiosity towards the unknown, rather than the paranoia of the '50s. Also, the closest thing in the film to a scientist, a UFOlogist played by Francois Truffaut, is portrayed sympathetically. Like Reid's character in *The Andromeda Strain,* he acts as the film's conscience, opposing the government's cover-up of the truth about flying saucers.

This image can be seen as an improvement over much of what has been offered. But in the minds of many filmmakers, scientists are still nothing but trouble. In the recent film *Capricorn One,* Hal Holbrook plays a formerly idealistic NASA scientist who worked for years to send a manned flight to Mars. But a contractor delivered a "faulty life support system," forcing the agency to scrub the flight.

To keep the space program alive, the scientist supervises a faked flight to Mars, filmed in a TV studio. The scientist commits everything up to and including blackmail, kidnapping, and murder to keep the secret covered up. The message is not new: a scientist will walk over his grandmother for the sake of his project.

Why do the media present such a poor image of scientists? Various reasons have been suggested. Bova asserts that American cinema has a wide anti-intellectual streak: "The

'natural' farmer always outsmarts the city slicker. Rural values always prevail over urban values."[15] He suggests that this attitude is naturally carried over to story lines in which scientists represent the intellectual city slickers.

Bova also suggests that another reason scientists are inaccurately portrayed is because most Americans have never met a scientist.[4] George Basalla of the University of Delaware suggests a similar reason: the public really doesn't have a clear idea of what goes on in a research institution. Basalla contrasts this with the favorable treatment of physicians in televised drama. Physicians' work is tangible; it is therefore widely appreciated.[3]

This may be changing. Although the family physician, sentimentally portrayed on TV, is still with us, successful movies have mirrored public dissatisfaction with large health care establishments. *The Hospital* (1974) was a black comedy in which the staff and patients were easily murdered by a madman in the confusion and depersonalized environment of a big city hospital. In this year's film *Coma,* an unscrupulous director of another large hospital runs a black market in heart, kidney, and lung transplants. With a recent Harris poll showing public confidence in physicians at a twelve-year low,[16] one wonders if doctors will soon face the same negative media treatment as scientists.

Basalla also asserts that the confusion between science and technology so apparent on screen is at least partly the fault of scientists.

He writes: "By overemphasizing the practical results of his work, especially when seeking public funds, [the scientist] contributes to the existing national confusion between science and technological application and opens himself to criticism that might be better directed against engineers, managers, and industrialists."[3] He further argues that scientists cultivate the image of the cold, distant, humorless individual, leading others to caricature that image.

Does the media image of scientists mold the public's image? Or does it reflect perceptions that already exist? Basalla writes of a "feedback loop between widely held American ideas of science and their popular artistic representation." He argues that "by presenting these attitudes in a popular medium...the creators of popular culture perpetuate and strengthen them."[3]

What can be done to improve the situation? Science fiction novelist and screenwriter David Gerrold, as well as other panelists at the AAAS symposium on the scientists' image, noted that blacks, women, chican-os, and gays have protested to networks when they have seen inaccurate or degrading portraits of themselves. The protests have been so effective, Gerrold said, that sometimes the networks ask feminist and minority groups to screen scripts in advance, to help guard against stereotypes. Gerrold asserted that similar pressure by scientists could yield similar results. He said, "When people tell a network, 'This is wrong,' they appoint a vice president to listen to you. They don't want anybody to make waves. All they want is to see the money rolling in."[4] Presumably similar values prevail in the motion picture industry.

If, as Sagan warns,[10] TV and films are leaving children (and many adults) with the impression that science is always dangerous and never beneficial, then scientists could not make the situation worse by making their views known. Scientists are a minority group in society, but groups that suffer discrimination must defend themselves before they win the sympathy and support of intelligent outsiders.

REFERENCES

1. **Shurkin J N.** In a Philadelphia lab, creating a mouse with human genes. *Philadelphia Inquirer* 3 April 1978, p. 1A-2A.
2. **Hardigree P.** Put your head on my shoulder. *New Times* 10(9):78, 1 May 1978.
3. **Basalla G.** Pop science: the depiction of science in popular culture. (Holton G & Blanpied W A, eds.) *Science and its public: the changing relationship.* Boston: D. Reidel Publishing Company, 1976, p. 261-78.
4. **Maugh T H.** The media: the image of the scientist is bad. *Science* 200(4337):37, 7 April 1978.
5. **Dolmatch T B, ed.** *Information please almanac 1978.* New York: Information Please Publishing, Inc., 1977. p. 606.

REFERENCES (continued)

6. **Garfield E.** Science journalism: you've come a long way baby, but . . . !
   Current Contents (34):5-12, 21 August 1978.
7. **DeWolf R.** What's a wookie to do?
   Evening Bulletin (Philadelphia) 17 July 1978, p. 15.
8. 'Encounters' at $115-mil. *Variety* 291(11):6, 19 July 1978.
9. **Sontag S.** The imagination of disaster. (Denby D, ed.) *Awake in the dark: an anthology of American film criticism, 1915 to the present.*
   New York: Vintage Books, 1977. p. 263-78.
10. **Sagan C.** 'There's no hint of the joys of science.'
    TV Guide 26(5):6-8, 4 February 1978.
11. **Asimov I.** If it's good science fiction...
    TV Guide 25(52):17-9, 24 December 1977.
12. **Sagan C.** Growing up with science fiction.
    New York Times Magazine 28 May 1978, p. 24, 28-31.
13. **Crichton M.** *The Andromeda strain.*
    New York: Dell Publishing Company, Inc., 1969. p. 294.
14. **Keyfitz N.** Science: the bad image. *Science* 200(4341):486, 5 May 1978.
15. **Bova B.** 'Trust the Force.'
    Analog Science Fiction/Science Fact 98(6):5-10, June 1978.
16. Doctors' public image hits a 12-year low.
    Medical World News 19(3):8-13, 26 June 1978.

Current Comments

The 100 Books Most Cited by Social Scientists, 1969-1977

Number 37   September 11, 1978

Recently we presented the 100 articles most cited by social scientists from 1969 to 1977.[1] Now we have compiled a list of the 100 books most cited in the journals covered by the *Social Sciences Citation Index™ (SSCI™)*, 1969-1977.

The articles were listed alphabetically by author, while books are listed by discipline. This may obviate invidious comparisons across fields. Since psychology (including psychoanalytic theory) dominates the list, we have created subdisciplinary categories for this field.

We have also avoided ranking the books by total citations in order to avoid the suggestion that absolute frequency of citation indicates greater or lesser merit. Perhaps more than anything else, it indicates activity in the field involved.

Obtaining citation data on books is a much more complex undertaking than getting citation counts on articles. This is because authors may cite books in a wide variety of ways. For example, some authors may cite the whole work while others reference particular pages or chapters. Translations cause more problems, since different authors may cite English, German, and French versions of the same book. "Unifying" the citations of a book is therefore tricky. There is no doubt, however, that the books on the list received enough citations to appear in the top 100.

It is quite possible that for a multi-authored work in which there is a different author for each chapter, citations to such chapters are not counted in the total. Thus, the work by Rokeach had separate chapters by J. M. Levy, C. G. Kemp, and B. Mikol. During 1969-1977 Levy's chapter was cited four times, Kemp's twice, and the chapter by Mikol twelve times. These 18 citations to individual chapters were not included in the total number of citations shown for Rokeach's book in Figure 1.

Providing bibliographic information about books also presents problems because of the multiplicity of editions involved. Should we give the earliest publication date or the most recent? We compromised by showing two dates when applicable. The first date listed represents the currently available edition. The second date, in parentheses, indicates the year the book was first published to the best of our knowledge. This will indicate how long the work has been available to be cited.

Our data indicate the relatively greater importance of books to social scientists as compared with other scientists. The 100 most-cited articles averaged 281 citations. The books on our most-cited list average 761 citations. Also, the least cited article on the articles list received 186 citations. In contrast, the last item on this book list received 434 citations.

Psychology dominates the most-cited books list but not to the extent it dominated the articles list. While 77 of the 100 most-cited articles were in psychology, only 51 of the 100 books are. Of these, 11 are in social psychology and motivation theory, nine are in behavioral theory (operant and classical), six in organizational and management psychology. These three categories represent over a quarter of the books on the list. In order to give a more balanced presentation of the other fields in the social sciences, we may publish the 50 most-cited books in individual disciplines in the future.

Eleven of the books on the list are in sociology; seven in economics and econometrics; five in education; three in linguistics; two in philosophy and history of science; and one in law.

Twenty titles concern statistics and research methodology. It is ob-vious that social science research requires the frequent use of statistical methods and theories—perhaps more than the "hard" sciences. Why people select one statistical textbook over another is probably due to such prosaic factors as which text they used as undergraduates.

The oldest book on the list is Karl Marx's *Das Kapital* published in 1867. The most recent book is *Inequality: a reassessment of the effect of family and schooling in America* (See C. Jencks et al.), published in 1972. The ages of the books are shown in Table 1.

Only seven of the authors appear on both the most-cited books and articles list: A. Bandura, L. Festinger, D. O. Hebb, G. A. Miller, C. E. Osgood, A. Paivio and P. A. Samuelson.

Eleven authors wrote more than one of the books listed. A. Bandura, J. S. Bruner, E. Goffman, A. B. Hollingshead, D. C. McClelland and R. Rosenthal each authored two books. N. Chomsky, J. P. Guilford, and J. Wolpe authored three. B. F. Skinner authored two by himself and co-authored one with C. B. Ferster. R. R. Carkhuff authored one alone, and another with C. B. Truax.

Most of the books on the list have a single author. This is significant and one of the reasons why citation analyses based on primary author data are not nearly as biased in the social sciences as they prove to be

Table 1: Age of Books		Table 2: Number of books with one or more authors.	
Ages of Books	**No. of Books**	**Authors Per Book**	**No. of Books**
5-10 yrs. old	9	1	71
11-20 yrs. old	44	2	17
21-30 yrs. old	30	3	5
31-40 yrs. old	8	4	2
41-50 yrs. old	7	7	1
64 yrs. old	1	8	1
111 yrs. old	1	12	1
		23	1
		28	1

in the "hard" sciences. Table 2 presents a breakdown of the books by number of authors.

The open and closed mind: investigations into the nature of belief systems and personality systems, with 23 authors, is actually a collection of articles Milton Rokeach wrote in collaboration with 22 co-authors. *Explorations in personality: a clinical and experimental study of fifty men of college age* by H. A. Murray and the workers at the Harvard Psychological Clinic lists all 28 authors who participated in the study.

In an unpublished paper, Henry Small of ISI® and Belver C. Griffith of Drexel University examined some of our data on most-cited *SSCI* books.[2] They found that there is no consistent pattern. Some of the works present specific methods. For instance, C. E. Osgood and A. B. Hollingshead deal with the semantic differential and a social class index respectively. Thorndike's *Teachers' word book of thirty thousand words* is a tool for teachers to use to determine at what point in the educational cycle certain words should be introduced to children. However, a large number are major conceptual works. Several present both a specific method and a distinctive theoretical approach. For instance, *The authoritarian personality* by T. W. Adorno et al. presents an authoritarianism scale and deals with theory and experiments in personality psychology.

One of the more surprising items on the list is Alvin Toffler's *Future shock.* It seems clear that this work, aimed at a non-scientific audience, has had a major impact on social scientists as well. The popular bestseller described the "shattering stress and disorientation that we induce in individuals by subjecting them to too much change in too short a time."[3] According to Toffler, the book had been cited in scholarly journals for a number of reasons. The term "future shock" provided a conceptual handle for a phenomenon that until the book's publication in 1970 "had been widely experienced but as yet unnamed." The book also cut across disciplinary boundaries, challenged orthodox assumptions held by social scientists, and "in a time of heavy accent on refined empirical analysis, it offered a broad theoretical synthesis." The method of presentation, in everyday English, also may have had something to do with the large number of citations it received, Toffler said.[4]

As with the articles list, several books appear to have been cited often because of their controversial nature. For example, the J. S. Coleman study of *Equality of educational opportunity,* cited 1042 times, reaped both critical and supportive citations. According to Coleman, the report gained attention for three reasons. It found a lack of relation between traditional input measures and school achievement, "a result that disturbed conventional wisdom." It also showed that the backgrounds of fellow students in school were related to achievement. This finding helped in the "growing push toward affirmative racial integration of the schools." In addition, the report represented an "early example of a new genre of research on a large scale directed to issues of social policy."[5] In that way it attracted the attention of practitioners of social research, Coleman said.

Another book, *Pygmalion in the classroom,* by R. Rosenthal and L.

Jacobson also falls into the "controversial" category. *Pygmalion* deals with self-fulfilling prophecy or "how one person's expectation for another person's behavior can quite unwittingly become a more accurate prediction simply for its having been made."[6] The researchers presented the results of a study in which 20% of the children in an elementary school, selected randomly, were identified to their teachers as having great potential for intellectual work. "Eight months later these unusual or 'magic' children showed significantly greater gains in IQ than did the others." The researchers attributed this change in IQ to teachers' change in expectation. Some social scientists have, however, questioned the methodology used in the book. For example, Stanford's Lee Chronbach said, "In my view, *Pygmalion in the classroom* merits no consideration as research. The 'experimental manipulation' of teacher belief was unbelievably casual— one sheet of paper added to the teacher's in-basket."[7] Nevertheless, the Rosenthal work had far reaching impact with its implication that one cannot study anything without changing it. It would be interesting to know if Rosenthal had ever heard of the Heisenberg Uncertainty Principle. If he had, why was he so surprised at this discovery?

It is hard for me to believe it has taken so long to publish these data. But now that we have, I can see that the list does not go far enough, not only because of the heavy emphasis on psychology, but also because there are still so many other books that have made significant impact. For example, over 260 social science books were cited over 200 times in this period. Perhaps there are more surprises to be found than in this list of "obvious" classics.

Snedecor and Cochran's *Statistical methods* has been covered in Citation Classics, the weekly *Current Contents® (CC®)* series in which authors explain why they believe their classic papers were heavily cited. Several additional titles on this list will be in Citation Classics in the near future.

We can only devote so much space in *CC* to lists of these books. However, it is becoming increasingly obvious to me that we have to move ahead to publish such data on a more comprehensive basis for each of the main fields of the social and behavioral sciences.

REFERENCES

1. **Garfield E.** The 100 articles most cited by social scientists, 1969-1977. *Current Contents* (32):5-14, 7 August 1978.
2. **Griffith B C & Small H G.** *The structure of the social and behavioral sciences' literature.* Unpublished paper presented at the first annual meeting of the Society for the Social Study of Science. October, 1976, Cornell University, Ithaca, New York.
3. **Toffler A.** *Future shock.* New York: Random House, 1970. 505 p.
4. -----------. Citation classics. *Current Contents* (in press).
5. **Coleman J S.** Citation classics. *Current Contents* (in press).
6. **Rosenthal R & Jacobson L.** *Pygmalion in the classroom: teacher expectation and pupil's intellectual development.* New York: Holt, Rinehart & Winston, 1968. 240 p.
7. **Cronbach L J.** Five decades of public controversy over mental testing. *Amer. Psychol.* 30:1-14, 1975.

Figure 1: The 100 books, most cited by social scientists, 1969-1977, based on data from the *Social Sciences Citation Index*™ . Bibliographic data are for current editions. Dates in parentheses are the years of first publication.

Total
Citations
1969-1977   Bibliographic Data

PSYCHOLOGY

Social Psychology & Motivation Theory

579   **Bandura A & Walters R H.** *Social learning and personality development.*
New York: Holt, Rinehart & Winston, 1963. 329 p.

440   **Brown R.** *Social psychology.*
New York: Free Press, 1965. 785 p.

1140   **Festinger L.** *A theory of cognitive dissonance.*
Stanford, CA: Stanford Univ. Press, 1962 (1957). 291 p.

612   **Goffman E.** *The presentation of self in everyday life.*
New York: Doubleday, 1974 (1956). 255 p.

437   **Hall E T.** *The hidden dimension.*
New York: Doubleday, 1969 (1966). 217 p.

942   **Heider F.** *The psychology of interpersonal relations.*
New York: Wiley, 1958. 322 p.

674   **Homans G C.** *Social behavior; its elementary forms.*
New York: Harcourt Brace Jovanovich, 1961. 404 p.

635   **McClelland D C.** *The achieving society.*
New York: Irvington, 1976 (1961). 512 p.

454   **McClelland D C & Atkinson J W.** *The achievement motive.*
New York: Irvington, 1976 (1953). 384 p.

615   **Mead G H.** *Mind, self & society: from the standpoint of a social behaviorist.*
Chicago: Univ. of Chicago Press, 1934. 400 p.

537   **Thibaut J W & Kelley H H.** *The social psychology of groups.*
New York: Wiley, 1959. 313 p.

Behavior Theory (Operant & Classical)

612   **Berlyne D E.** *Conflict, arousal and curiosity.*
New York: McGraw-Hill, 1960. 350 p.

542   **Broadbent D E.** *Perception and communication.*
Elmsford, NY: Pergamon, 1958. 338 p.

478   **Hull C L.** *Principles of behavior: an introduction to behavior theory.*
Englewood Cliffs, NJ: Prentice-Hall, 1966 (1943). 422 p.

630   **Ferster C B & Skinner B F.** *Schedules of reinforcement.*
Englewood Cliffs, NJ: Prentice-Hall, 1957. 741 p.

434   **Skinner B F.** *Behavior of organisms: an experimental analysis.*
Englewood Cliffs, NJ: Prentice-Hall, 1966 (1938). 457 p.

587   **Skinner B F.** *Science and human behavior.*
New York: MacMillan, 1953. 461 p.

PSYCHOLOGY (continued)

Behavior Theory (Operant & Classical) (continued)

856   **Wolpe J.** *Psychotherapy by reciprocal inhibition.*
      Stanford, CA: Stanford Univ. Press, 1958. 239 p.

533   **Wolpe J.** *The practice of behavior therapy.*
      Elmsford, NY: Pergamon, 1974 (1969). 318 p.

434   **Wolpe J & Lazarus A A.** *Behavior therapy techniques: a guide to the treatment of neuroses.* Elmsford, NY: Pergamon, 1966. 198 p.

Organizational & Management Psychology

542   **Cyert R M & March J G.** *A behavioral theory of the firm.*
      Englewood Cliffs, NJ: Prentice-Hall, 1963. 332 p.

540   **Katz D & Kahn R L.** *The social psychology of organizations.*
      New York: Wiley, 1966. 498 p.

446   **Likert R.** *New patterns of management.*
      New York: McGraw Hill, 1961. 279 p.

594   **March J G & Simon H A.** *Organizations.* New York: Wiley, 1958. 262 p.

487   **Thompson J D.** *Organizations in action; social science bases of administrative theory.* New York: McGraw-Hill, 1967. 192 p.

586   **Vroom V H.** *Work and motivation.* New York: Wiley, 1964. 331 p.

Cognitive Psychology

438   **Bruner J S, Olver R R, Greenfield P M, Hornsby J R, Kenney H J, Maccoby M, Modiano N, Mosher F A, Olsen O R, Potter M C, Reich L C & Sonstroen A M.** *Studies in cognitive growth; a collaboration at the center for cognitive studies.* New York: Wiley, 1966. 343 p.

450   **Bruner J S, Goodnow J J & Austin G A.** *A study of thinking.*
      Huntington, NY: Krieger, 1977 (1956). 330 p.

623   **Green D M & Swets J A.** *Signal detection theory and psychophysics.*
      Huntington, NY: Krieger, 1974 (1966). 479 p.

486   **Miller G A, Galanter E & Pribram K H.** *Plans and the structure of behavior.* New York: Holt, Rinehart & Winston, 1960. 226 p.

1060 **Neisser U.** *Cognitive psychology.*
      Englewood Cliffs, NJ: Prentice-Hall, 1967. 351 p.

1770 **Osgood C E, Suci G & Tannenbaum P.** *The measurement of meaning.*
      Urbana, IL: Univ. of Illinois Press, 1967 (1957). 346 p.

455   **Paivio A.** *Imagery and verbal processes.*
      New York: Holt, Rinehart & Winston, 1971. 596 p.

Figure 1. (continued)

Total
Citations
1969-1977   **Bibliographic Data**

PSYCHOLOGY (continued)

Developmental & Child Psychology

514   **Bowlby J.** *Attachment and loss.*
New York: Basic Books, 1977 (1969). 2 vols.

1211   **Erikson E H.** *Childhood and society.*
New York: Norton, 1964 (1950). 397 p.

482   **Flavell J H.** *The developmental psychology of Jean Piaget.*
New York: Van Nostrand, 1973 (1963). 472 p.

451   **Guilford J P.** *The nature of human intelligence.*
New York: McGraw-Hill, 1967. 538 p.

475   **Piaget J.** *La naissance de l'intelligence chez l'enfant. (Origins of intelligence
in children.)* New York: International Univ. Press, 1966 (1936). 449 p.

Personality

861   **Adorno T W, Frenkel-Brunswik E, Levinson D J & Sanford R N.**
The authoritarian personality.
New York: Norton, 1969 (1950). 990 p.

796   **Maslow A H.** *Motivation and personality.*
New York: Harper & Row, 1970 (1954). 369 p.

500   **Mischel W.** *Personality and assessment.* New York: Wiley, 1968. 365 p.

434   **Murray H A, Barret W G, Langer W C, Morgan C D, Homburger E,
Mekeel H S, White R W, Diven K, Frank J D, Jones E C,
Mackinnon D W, Rosenzweig S, Sanford R N, Wheeler D R, Beck S J,
Christenson J A, Cobb E A, Inglis E, Kunze K R, Moore M,
Rickers-Ovsiankina M, Peterson R T, Sears R N, Shevach B J, Smith C E,
Trowbridge E H, Whitman E M and Wolf R E.** (The workers
at the Harvard Psychological Clinic.) *Explorations in personality: a
clinical and experimental study of fifty men of college age.*
New York: Oxford Univ. Press, 1938. 761 p.

895   **Rokeach M, Bonier R, Cheek G, Denny M R, Evans R I, Geierhaas F,
Gladin L, Kemp C G, Laffey J J, Levy J M, Matheson F,
McGovney W C, Mikol B, Oram A, Restle F, Rottman T, Smith P W,
Swanson T S, Toch H H, Trumbo D A, Vidulich R N, Zlotowski M
& Zlotowski S.** *The open and closed mind; investigations into the nature
of belief systems and personality systems.*
New York: Basic Books, 1960. 447 p.

Clinical Psychology

1157   **Bandura A.** *Principles of behavior modification.*
New York: Holt, Rinehart & Winston, 1969. 677 p.

536   **Carkhuff R R.** *Helping and human relations; a primer for lay and professional helpers.* New York: Holt, Rinehart & Winston, 1969. 2 vols.

PSYCHOLOGY (continued)

Clinical Psychology (continued)

674   **Kelly G A.** *The psychology of personal constructs.*
New York: Norton, 1955. 2 vols.

516   **Truax C B & Carkhuff R R.** *Toward effective counseling and psychotherapy: training and practice.*
Chicago: Aldine, 1967. 416 p.

651   **Fenichel O.** *The psychoanalytic theory of neurosis.*
New York: Norton, 1945. 703 p.

647   **Freud S.** *Zur Geschichte der psychoanalytischen Bewegung. (On the history
of the psychoanalytic movement; papers on metapsychology; and other
works.)* London: Hogarth Press, 1957 (1914). 374 p.

Genetic Psychology

748   **Witkin H A, Dyk R B, Faterson H F, Goodenough D R & Karp S A.**
Psychological differentiation: studies of development. New York:
Halsted Press, 1974 (1962). 418 p.

Neuro-Psychology

599   **Hebb D O.** *The organization of behavior; a neuropsychological theory.*
New York: Wiley, 1949. 355 p.

STATISTICS & RESEARCH METHODOLOGY

609   **Anderson T W.** *An introduction to multivariate statistical analysis.*
New York: Wiley, 1958. 374 p.

732   **Blalock H M.** *Social statistics.* (Edwards D M, ed.)
New York: McGraw-Hill, 1972 (1960). 465 p.

861   **Edwards A L.** *Experimental design in psychological research.*
New York: Holt, Rinehart & Winston, 1972 (1950). 446 p.

683   **Guilford J P.** *Psychometric methods.*
New York: McGraw-Hill, 1954 (1936). 597 p.

761   **Guilford J P & Fruchter B.** *Fundamental statistics in psychology and
education.* New York: McGraw-Hill, 1973 (1942). 546 p.

1063   **Harman H H.** *Modern factor analysis.*
Chicago: Univ. of Chicago Press, 1976 (1960). 487 p.

Figure 1. (continued)

Total
Citations
1969-1977   Bibliographic Data

STATISTICS & RESEARCH METHODOLOGY (continued)

1167   **Hays W L.** *Statistics for psychologists.*
       New York: Holt, Rinehart & Winston, 1963. 719 p.

846   **Kendall M G & Stuart A.** *The advance theory of statistics.*
       New York: Hafner, 1969 (1958). 3 vols.

915   **Kirk R E.** *Experimental design: procedures for the behavioral sciences.*
       Belmont, CA: Brooks/Cole, 1968. 577 p.

717   **Lindquist E F.** *Design and analysis of experiments in psychology and
       education.* Boston: Houghton Mifflin, 1956 (1953). 393 p.

820   **McNemar Q.** *Psychological statistics.*
       New York: Wiley, 1969 (1949). 529 p.

517   **Nunnally J C.** *Psychometric theory.*
       New York: McGraw-Hill, 1967. 640 p.

591   **Rao C R.** *Linear statistical inference and its applications.*
       New York: Wiley, 1973 (1965). 625 p.

660   **Rosenthal R.** *Experimenter effects in behavior research.*
       New York: Irvington, 1976 (1966). 500 p.

552   **Scheffe H.** *The analysis of variance.* New York: Wiley, 1959. 477 p.

3414   **Siegel S.** *Nonparametric statistics for the behavioral sciences.*
       New York: McGraw-Hill, 1956. 312 p.

631   **Snedecor G W & Cochran W G.** *Statistical methods.*
       Ames: Iowa State Univ. Press, 1967 (1937). 593 p.
       [Citation Classics. *Current Contents* (19):10, 9 May 1977.]

523   **Torgerson W S.** *Theory and method of scaling.*
       New York: Wiley, 1958. 460 p.

474   **Wechsler D & Matarazzo J D.** *Die Messung der Intelligenz Erwachsener:
       Textband zum Hamburg-Wechsler-Intelligenztest fur Erwachsene.
       (Wechsler's measurement and appraisal of adult intelligence.)*
       Baltimore: Williams & Wilkins, 1972 (1944). 297 p.

5279   **Winer B J.** *Statistical principles in experimental design.*
       New York: McGraw-Hill, 1971 (1962). 907 p.

SOCIOLOGY

672   **Becker H S.** *Outsiders: studies in the sociology of deviance.*
       New York: Free Press, 1963. 179 p.

565   **Blau P M, Duncan O D & Tyree A.** *The American occupational
       structure.* New York: Wiley, 1967. 520 p.

543   **Campbell A, Converse P E, Miller W E & Stokes D E.** *The
       American voter.* Chicago: Univ. of Chicago Press, 1976 (1960). 573 p.

895   **Goffman E.** *Asylums: essays on the social situation of mental patients
       and other inmates.* Garden City, NY: Anchor Books, 1961. 386 p.

513   **Hollingshead A B.** *Two-factor index of social position.*
       New Haven: Published privately by Author, 1957. 11 p.

630

Figure 1. (continued)

Total
Citations
1969-1977   **Bibliographic Data**

SOCIOLOGY (continued)

1114   **Hollingshead A B & Redlich F C.** *Social class and mental illness; a community study.* New York: Wiley, 1958. 442 p.

687   **Lipset S M.** *Political man: essays on the sociology of democracy.* New York: Doubleday, 1959. 432 p.

1179   **Merton R K.** *Social theory and social structure; toward the codification of theory and research.* New York: Free Press, 1968 (1949). 702 p.

335   **Myrdal G, Sterner R & Rose A.** *An American dilemma: the negro problem and modern democracy.* New York: Pantheon, 1975 (1944). 2 vols.

751   **Parsons T.** *The social system.* New York: Free Press, 1964 (1951). 575 p.

569   **Toffler A.** *Future shock.* New York: Random House, 1970. 505 p.

ECONOMICS & ECONOMETRICS

543   **Arrow K J.** *Social choice and individual values.* New York: Norton, 1970 (1951). 99 p.

562   **Galbraith J K.** *The new industrial state.* Boston: Houghton Mifflin, 1971 (1967). 423 p.

449   **Goldberger A S.** *Econometric theory.* New York: Wiley, 1964. 339 p.

780   **Johnston J.** *Econometric methods.* New York: McGraw-Hill, 1971 (1963). 437 p.

511   **Samuelson P A.** *Foundations of economic analysis.* Cambridge: Harvard Univ. Press, 1947. 447 p.

1462   **Marx K.** *Das Kapital. (Capital.)* New York: Modern Library, 1936 (1867). 479 p.

471   **Weber M.** *The theory of social and economic organization.* (Henderson A R & Parsons T, trans.). New York: Oxford Univ. Press, 1947. 404 p.

EDUCATION

530   **Bloom B S, ed.** *Taxonomy of educational objectives: the classification of educational goals. Handbook 1: the cognitive domain.* New York: Longmans, Green Inc., 1956. 207 p.

1042   **Coleman J S, Campbell E Q, Hobson C J, McPartland J, Mood A M, Weinfeld F D & York R L.** *Equality of educational opportunity.* Washington, DC: US Dept. of Health, Education and Welfare, Office of Education, GPO. 1966. 548 p.

Figure 1. (continued)

EDUCATION (continued)

595   **Jencks C, Smith M, Acland H, Bane M J, Cohen D, Gintis H, Heyns B & Michelson S.** *Inequality; a reassessment of the effect of family and schooling in America.* New York: Basic Books, 1972. 399 p.

544   **Rosenthal R & Jacobson L.** *Pygmalion in the classroom: teacher expectation and pupil's intellectual development.* New York: Holt, Rinehart & Winston, 1968. 240 p.

1111   **Thorndike E L & Lorge I.** *Teachers' word book of thirty thousand words.* New York: Teachers College, Columbia Univ. Press, 1944. 274. p.

LINGUISTICS

1124   **Chomsky N.** *Aspects of the theory of syntax.* Cambridge, MA: MIT Press, 1965. 251 p.

556   **Chomsky N.** *Syntactic structures.* Atlantic Highlands, NJ: Humanities Press, 1957. 116 p.

579   **Chomsky N & Halle M.** *The sound pattern of English.* New York: Harper & Row, 1968. 470 p.

PHILOSOPHY & HISTORY OF SCIENCE

1645   **Kuhn T S.** *The structure of scientific revolutions.* Chicago: Univ. of Chicago Press, 1970 (1962). 210 p.

498   **Popper K R.** *Logik der Forschung zur Erkenntnis Theorie der modernen Naturwissenschaft. (Logic of scientific discovery.)* New York: Basic Books, 1959 (1935). 479 p.

LAW

539   **Rawls J.** *A theory of justice.* Cambridge, MA: Belknap Press, 1971. 607 p.

Current Comments

The 100 Most-Cited *SSCI*
Authors, 1969-1977.
1. How the Names Were Selected

Number 38   September 18, 1978

As promised previously[1-2] here is the list of authors most cited by social scientists. This list is based on data taken from our *Social Sciences Citation Index™ (SSCI™)* from 1969 to 1977. We have arranged the list by discipline. Psychology (including psychoanalytic theory) is by far the largest field and is thus subdivided into specialties.

Arranging the list categorically should prevent invidious comparisons across disciplines. In a few cases, however, authors involved in interdisciplinary research may feel they have been misclassified by our system.

For each name we have also provided the birthdate, the total number of citations, and the average number of citations from 1969-77. In addition, the citation counts for 1976 and 1977 are also provided. This gives an idea of the continuing interest in the areas involved.

For those readers unfamiliar with citation analysis, let me recapitulate the selection procedure. Authors of scholarly papers acknowl-edge the work of other authors through citations. To compile the *SSCI*, we created an entry for each of these explicit citations. For the period 1969-1977, we processed nearly 8 million citations appearing in 800,000 source items.

Once the basic *SSCI* is compiled, we sort the file by number of citations received by each author. The list shown in Figure 1 is the tip of an enormous iceberg of cited scholars. Limiting the list to 100 authors is arbitrary and based on cost and the lack of space and energy.

It is important to point out that this list is based on primary author data. In this study, citations to a publication with two or more authors are credited only to the first author. Readers familiar with our recent study of the 300 most-cited scientists will appreciate the potential shortcomings of a list that doesn't account for co-authors.[3]

However, as seen in the earlier parts of this study, co-authorship in the social sciences is by no means as significant as in the hard sciences. Nevertheless, in the future we will try to apply the programs we developed for the *Science Citation Index®* to our *SSCI* data base. The average number of citations for those primary authors listed here is 2,548 or 283 citations per year for the nine-year period, 1969-1977. Clearly these authors are in a special "superstar" category. But the same is probably true for the next hundred authors who received an average of 1,260 citations; that is, 140 per year. One would at least want to examine the 1,000 most-cited authors. The 1,000th most-cited name received 497 citations.

There are 55 psychologists on the list along with 15 sociologists. Twelve authors are in statistics or psychometrics; eleven in economics or econometrics; three in the history of science and philosophy; two in anthropology; one in linguistics; and one in political philosophy. We may present the 50 most-cited authors in each social science field in future essays.

Of those authors in psychology, ten are in social psychology and motivation theory, eight are involved with behavior theory, seven are in cognitive psychology, and seven in developmental and child psychology. Six of the authors are in personality and five in clinical psychology. There are three authors each in educational psychology and in neuro-psychology, two each in psychoanalytic theory and

organizational psychology, and one each in genetic psychology and mathematical psychology.

As with similar studies of scientists in which we made no age limitations, the average age is especially high. Classical authors like Marx and Freud continue to be heavily cited, but the age of living authors averaged 62. One might have expected this to be even higher considering that older scholars have published much more that could have been cited than their young colleagues.

The list contains 35 authors in their 50s, born between 1919 and 1928, and 24 in their 60s, born between 1909 and 1918. Ten authors are in their 40s.

About 31, or almost a third are (or would be) over 70. Fifteen are (or would be) in their 70s, eight in their 80s, and eight would be over 100 if they were still alive. Jung, Thorndike, and Lenin would be between 100 and 110; Weber and Dewey between 110 and 119; S. Freud and Durkheim between 120 and 129; and Marx would be 160. In contrast, the youngest author to appear on the list was Posner, born in 1936.

It is interesting to note that many of the authors on this list did not publish a Citation Classic or highly-cited article or book. However, it is usually possible to identify, for each author, his or her most significant work. Thus, Allport did not have an item on the lists of most-cited articles or books. But his most-cited work was *The nature of prejudice* which received 194 citations during the nine-year period.

The most-cited author was Sigmund Freud. The 12,319 citations to his various works, as with other classical authors like Marx, are not exactly equatable to citations to current articles or books. There is a tendency to cite chapter and verse in greater detail with these authors. Thus, six specific passages in a single work by Freud might each be cited in a paper. This would give Freud six citations. You would get significantly different counts if you counted each cited author for each citing work. Freud would then receive only one citation no matter

how often a single paper cited his works.

The appearance of controversial authors such as Eysenck, Rosenthal, and Jensen may cast suspicion on the methodology. But it is impact we are measuring. It turns out that this is *usually* associated with significance. You must judge the results. To help you do this, we intend to analyze the recognition these authors have received. Those social scientists who have been well recognized by awards and other honors should not object to the corroboration of citation analysis. But more importantly, if our studies call attention to the work of those who have not been adequately recognized, the effort will have been rewarded.

REFERENCES

1. **Garfield E.** The 100 articles most cited by social scientists, 1969-1977. *Current Contents* (32):5-14, 7 August 1978.
2. -------------. The 100 books most cited by social scientists, 1969-1977. *Current Contents* (37):5-16, 11 September 1978.
3. -------------. The 300 most-cited authors, 1961-1976, including co-authors at last. 1. How the names were selected. *Current Contents* (28):5-17, 10 July 1978.

Figure 1: The 100 most-cited authors, based on data from the *Social Sciences Citation Index™*, 1969-1977.

Name (Birthdate)	Total Citations 1969-1977	Average Citations 1969-1977	1976 Citations	1977 Citations
PSYCHOLOGY				
Social Psychology & Motivation Theory				
Bandura A (1925)	5,050	561	763	554
Berkowitz L (1926)	1,992	221	233	186
Brown R (1925)	2,158	240	311	255
Deutsch M (1920)	2,019	224	217	178
Festinger L (1919)	2,888	321	362	271
Jones EE (1926)	1,564	174	272	183
McClelland DC (1917)	1,960	218	251	205
Rokeach M (1918)	2,370	263	273	250
Rosenthal R (1933)	2,466	274	294	221
Schacter S (1922)	1,703	189	248	221
Behavioral Theory (Operant & Classical)				
Anderson NH (1925)	2,139	238	285	263
Berlyne DE (1924-1976)	2,186	243	311	210
Broadbent DE (1926)	1,810	201	245	212
Eysenck HJ (1916)	5,370	597	634	582
Posner MI (1936)	1,523	169	243	198
Skinner BF (1904)	3,672	408	589	367
Underwood BJ (1915)	2,156	240	200	127
Wolpe J (1915)	2,617	291	290	276
Cognitive Psychology				
Bruner JS (1915)	2,692	299	339	272
Miller GA (1920)	2,843	316	348	295
Neisser U (1928)	1,594	177	184	174
Osgood CE (1916)	3,412	379	388	283
Paivio A (1925)	2,363	263	340	297
Postman L (1918)	1,523	169	153	109
Tulving E (1927)	2,018	224	305	277
Developmental & Child Psychology				
Bowlby J (1907)	1,602	178	224	194
Erikson EH (1902)	2,566	285	341	245

Name (Birthdate)	Total Citations 1969-1977	Average Citations 1969-1977	1976 Citations	1977 Citations
Developmental & Child Psychology (continued)				
Freud A (1895)	1,864	207	239	210
Kagan J (1929)	2,444	272	372	288
Kohlberg L (1927)	1,924	214	355	368
Piaget J (1896)	7,572	841	1,231	1,007
Rutter M (1933)	1,821	202	346	339
Personality				
Allport GW (1897-1967)	1,766	196	227	162
Byrne D (1931)	2,614	290	257	226
Cattell RB (1905)	4,282	476	554	412
Maslow AH (1908-1970)	1,954	217	253	238
Mischel W (1930)	1,759	195	352	287
Rogers CR (1902)	2,128	236	260	225
Clinical Psychology				
Carkhuff RR (1934)	1,563	174	203	213
Cohen J (1923)	2,184	243	310	313
Gough HG (1921)	1,652	184	177	213
Lewin K (1890-1947)	1,793	199	233	211
Rotter JB (1916)	2,615	291	350	352
Educational Psychology				
Cronbach LJ (1916)	2,748	305	397	332
Jensen AR (1923)	2,177	242	267	182
Thorndike EL (1874-1949)	1,787	199	220	189
Neuro-Psychology				
Hebb DO (1904)	1,516	168	172	141
Miller NE (1909)	1,606	178	213	174
Stevens SS (1906-1973)	2,252	250	244	233
Psychoanalytic Theory				
Freud S (1856-1939)	12,319	1,369	1,880	1,439
Jung CG (1875-1961)	1,720	191	316	254
Organizational & Management Psychology				
Campbell DT (1916)	3,337	371	567	479
Simon HA (1916)	2,160	240	320	263

Figure 1. (continued)

Name (Birthdate)	Total Citations 1969-1977	Average Citations 1969-1977	1976 Citations	1977 Citations
Genetic Psychology				
Witkin HA (1916)	2,147	239	271	280
Mathematical Psychology				
Rapoport A (1911)	1,580	176	169	140

STATISTICS & PSYCHOMETRICS

Anderson TW (1918)	1,591	177	259	202
Box GEP (1919)	1,832	204	316	290
Edwards AL (1914)	2,389	265	249	203
Fisher RA (1890-1962)	1,605	178	243	195
Goodman LA (1928)	1,704	189	270	267
Guilford JP (1897)	3,413	379	383	329
Kendall MG (1907)	1,863	207	255	204
Rao CR (1920)	1,639	182	202	172
Shepard RN (1929)	1,582	176	239	197
Siegel S (1916-1961)	4,038	449	584	482
Wechsler D (1896)	1,788	199	256	273
Winer BJ (1917)	5,233	581	739	584

SOCIOLOGY

Argyris C (1923)	1,674	186	262	183
Becker HS (1928)	1,588	176	198	191
Blalock HM (1926)	2,188	243	305	277
Blau PM (1918)	2,134	237	279	265
Campbell A (1910)	1,808	201	269	222
Coleman JS (1926)	2,963	329	419	302
Duncan OD (1921)	2,238	249	325	313
Durkheim E (1858-1917)	2,337	260	327	285
Etzioni A (1929)	2,018	224	305	187
Goffman E (1922)	3,473	386	506	480
Habermas J (1929)	1,542	171	301	304
Hollingshead AB (1907)	1,831	203	216	192

Name (Birthdate)	Total Citations 1969-1977	Average Citations 1969-1977	1976 Citations	1977 Citations

SOCIOLOGY (continued)

Name (Birthdate)	Total Citations 1969-1977	Average Citations 1969-1977	1976 Citations	1977 Citations
Lipset SM (1922)	2,923	325	317	253
Merton RK (1910)	3,030	337	385	313
Parsons T (1902)	5,600	622	749	517

ECONOMICS & ECONOMETRICS

Name (Birthdate)	Total Citations 1969-1977	Average Citations 1969-1977	1976 Citations	1977 Citations
Arrow KJ (1921)	3,013	335	494	401
Baumol WJ (1922)	1,744	194	281	207
Friedman M (1912)	3,879	431	612	579
Galbraith JK (1908)	1,612	179	207	147
Johnson HG (1923-1977)	1,923	214	288	201
Marx K (1818-1883)	6,807	756	1,431	1,126
Myrdal G (1898)	1,885	209	241	184
Samuelson PA (1915)	3,431	381	531	414
Theil H (1924)	1,739	193	272	249
Tobin J (1918)	1,569	174	240	210
Weber M (1864-1920)	3,627	403	568	460

HISTORY OF SCIENCE & PHILOSOPHY

Name (Birthdate)	Total Citations 1969-1977	Average Citations 1969-1977	1976 Citations	1977 Citations
Dewey J (1859-1952)	2,042	227	274	262
Kuhn TS (1922)	1,765	196	332	242
Popper KR (1902)	1,543	171	255	186

ANTHROPOLOGY

Name (Birthdate)	Total Citations 1969-1977	Average Citations 1969-1977	1976 Citations	1977 Citations
Levi-Strauss C (1908)	2,270	252	321	230
Mead M (1901)	1,588	176	200	175

LINGUISTICS

Name (Birthdate)	Total Citations 1969-1977	Average Citations 1969-1977	1976 Citations	1977 Citations
Chomsky N (1928)	4,584	509	658	467

POLITICAL PHILOSOPHY

Name (Birthdate)	Total Citations 1969-1977	Average Citations 1969-1977	1976 Citations	1977 Citations
Lenin VI (1870-1924)	2,219	247	507	409

Current Comments

ASCA Can Help You Monitor
Publication in Your Organization
or Country

Number 39   September 25, 1978

If we could justify the space required to publish a geographic and/or organizational index for each issue of *Current Contents®* , I have no doubt that many readers would find it useful. For example, a science administrator in Nigeria might be interested to learn which articles, or how many, had been published by Nigerian scientists each week. Similarly, other *Current Contents* readers might want to follow the publishing activities of particular institutions or individual laboratories.

The mere suggestion of this new index may now require a serious investigation of its financial viability by ISI® 's product enhancement committee. Actually, this same information retrieval capability exists in an old established ISI service. Alas, this service, to my chagrin, has been insufficiently exploited by the scientific community. Indeed, I have stated elsewhere[1] that selective dissemination of information (SDI) has proved to be a great disappointment. After more than a dozen years it is, relatively speaking, used by only a fraction of the scientific and scholarly community.

Although this is not the place for us to explore the reasons for SDI's lack of success, I need to refresh your memory about ISI's SDI service called *ASCA® (Automatic Subject Citation Alert)*. This is necessary in order to elaborate on a particular facet of the service that can be of special help to administrators or others who keep tabs on scholarly publication occurring in their own organizations or elsewhere.

ASCA is a personalized current awareness service designed to help keep you informed of new articles relevant to topics specified in a customized profile. Many readers use *ASCA* as "awareness" insurance—to make sure they don't miss anything important, especially when they don't have time to browse through *Current Contents*.[2] In fact, we designed a special low-cost *ASCA* service for *Current Contents* readers. The response to this particular service has been dismal. However, *ASCA* continues to be used by several thousand subscribers for current awareness. But, its use for other purposes, mainly by librarians, sociologists of science, or administrators, is the main point of this piece.

An *ASCA* profile usually contains a list of words or phrases likely to appear in relevant titles. It may also include names of authors who have written on the subject or specific publications likely to be cited by pertinent new articles.[3] This "interest profile" is matched by computer against 10,000 articles published each week in more than 5,200 science and social sciences journals in the ISI data base. Each subscriber gets a weekly printout of all new articles which match his or her profile.

Since we record authors' addresses you can include any organization in a profile. Thus, one primatologist subscriber uses "Yerkes Primate Center" as one of the descriptors in her profile. This produces a list of the articles published by anyone affiliated with Yerkes. Such an "organizational" question is generic—it saves one the trouble of specifying the names of all individuals affiliated with that organization.

ASCA's ability to search by organization was originally conceived as a way to retrieve articles on specific topics. But administrators have increasingly used it to monitor new publications by scientists in their own organizations.

Roberta Kolman, head of the reference department at the University of Connecticut Health Center Library in Farmington, calls *ASCA* "a lifesaver." Kolman is in charge of maintaining the Center's medical archives. For years she has been trying to identify every article published by the faculty. But most faculty members are too busy or too

forgetful to inform her of recently published papers.

Obviously, it would be impossible for her to monitor over 5,000 journals for faculty publications. But by using "University of Connecticut Health Center" as the descriptor in her *ASCA* profile, Kolman receives a weekly report that alerts her to all new articles by authors at the Center.

The Louisiana State University Medical Center at Shrevesport also uses *ASCA* to find out about recent faculty publications so they can be listed in the university's quarterly faculty newsletter. And the staff of a well-known corporation uses *ASCA* to locate recent employee publications. A list of the new articles appears in each issue of the company's journal.

I can also envision invidious applications of *ASCA* by university administrators who like to count publications. Obviously, *ASCA* makes it easy to play the 'publish-or-perish' game. But I do believe it is important that administrators know *what* their faculty staffs are publishing. It would later be more relevant for them to use citation analysis to determine the impact of these publications.[4]

A few publicity-minded universities or corporations also use *ASCA* to keep an eye on interesting developments worthy of a press release.

We have had the organizational search capability since *ASCA* began in 1965. I had always assumed that you could search by each element of an organization's address. But in fact I had never tried to include a city or a country in my own profile. However, a request by Dr. Regina Morel, a social scientist at the Institute of Research of Rio de Janeiro, Brazil, made me realize how wrong my assumption was. Morel wanted an *ASCA* report based on her country. She uses this information for studies of the publication productivity of Brazilian science. She recently published her first data.[5] In this study she compares the output of Brazilian scientists to that of other countries. She also provides a breakdown by regions, institutions, etc.

In response to Morel's requirements, we made "country" searches available through *ASCA* in 1977.

Since then a number of national science libraries have also expressed interest in maintaining complete archives of articles published by native scientists. *ASCA* can simplify this task considerably.

Costs of individual *ASCA* subscriptions vary. However, the minimum fee for a year of service is $115 in the US and Canada, $125 elsewhere. Like words or phrases, the frequency of publication within countries varies considerably. Most countries of the world can be covered by the minimum fee, but the more frequent publishers are listed in Table 1. The prices were calculated on the basis of 1977 data and will be modified from time to

Table 1: Annual *ASCA*® subscription prices for locating articles by authors in the countries listed. An *ASCA* subscription for a country not listed here is $115 per year in US and Canada, $125 per year elsewhere. Divisions of the UK (Wales, England, Scotland, and Northern Ireland) and republics of the USSR may be searched individually. Write to ISI® for rates.

Annual Price	Country	Annual Price	Country
$ 674	Australia	$ 812	India
204	Austria	354	Israel
300	Belgium	700	Italy
126	Brazil	1,584	Japan
1,618	Canada	434	Netherlands
340	Czechoslovakia	168	New Zealand
226	Denmark	164	Norway
2,176	Federal Republic of Germany	328	Poland
146	Finland	176	South Africa
1,808	France	206	Spain
456	German Democratic Republic	430	Sweden
206	Hungary	476	Switzerland
		3,278	United Kingdom
		2,406	USSR

time as is necessary with high frequency words.

If the price for monitoring the Soviet literature seems low in comparison to other countries listed, keep in mind that even in the hard sciences our coverage of Soviet literature, while quite extensive, is selective and not comprehensive.

We have omitted the US from the list because anyone prepared to receive such an enormous printout would probably acquire our tapes. A purely statistical report could be prepared on request if our published data are not current enough.

If you are interested in *ASCA* for organizational or country searches (or for the many other types of searches available), please contact Mr. James Hofstaedter, Institute for Scientific Information®, 325 Chestnut Street, Philadelphia, PA. 19106.

REFERENCES

1. **Garfield E.** The information-conscious university and *ASCA* software. *Current Contents* (37):5-7, 12 September 1977.
2. -------------. *Current Contents*—All inclusive or personalized? Using *ASCA* is a reasonable compromise! *Current Contents* 36:5, 8 September 1975.*
3. -------------. "The role of man and machine in an international selective dissemination of information system." Delivered at the International Congress of Documentation, Buenos Aires, 21-24 September 1970.
4. -------------. Publication counting vs citation counting in evaluating research. *Current Contents* (22):5-7, 2 June 1971.*
5. **Morel R L & Morel C M.** Un estudo sobre a producao cientifica *Brasileira*, segundo os dados do Institute for Scientific Information (ISI). (A study on Brazilian scientific productivity based on data of the Institute for Scientific Information.) *Ciencia d Informacao (Rio de Janeiro)* 6:99-109, 1977.

*Reprinted in: Garfield E. *Essays of an information scientist.* Philadelphia: ISI Press, 1977. 2 vols.

Lord Kelvin is reputed to have published about 660 scientific papers in his working lifetime—almost one excellent paper every five weeks for a period of 67 years.[1] With typewriters and computers, not to mention laboratory technicians, why shouldn't we expect at least a few of our modern geniuses to be as prolific?

I say this because a number of readers expressed a certain skepticism about our recent data on most-cited authors.[2] R. A. Good, for example, was the author of at least 694 journal articles, 1961-1976. Since we excluded conference proceedings, books, reports, etc., from our analysis, certain authors may have written much more than our figures indicate. Sir Gustav Nossal was listed as the author of 99 journal articles, but we know that he was the author of at least twice this number of publications during the period.[3] However, it seems reasonable to expect that few modern authors are as prolific as Kelvin.

Figures, however, may be distorted by national customs. Professor Nossal, Director of the Hall Institute in Melbourne, points out that there is a great cultural difference between the British and American traditions of authorship: "In the United States it is virtually obligatory for the head of a group to put his name on a paper, even if he hasn't done much or perhaps any of the relevant laboratory work.... In the United Kingdom, on the other hand, it would be quite common for younger people, even postdoctoral fellows, to publish under their own names and only give an acknowledgement to their 'boss' by way of a footnote at the end of a paper."[3]

An institutional approach to citation analysis may solve some of the problems created by "cultural" differences. About one-third of the authors on our most-cited list were affiliated with about 5 universities or well-known institutes. (A complete table of affiliations will appear in a future essay.) But team research, however it is handled, raises important ethical questions about scientific authorship.

The dictum that "one should give credit where credit is due" is simplistic, to say the least. For example, there is no sure method for assigning credit when one author is the "major" contributor and two authors are "minor" contributors. Is the major author the one who originated the basic idea while his "minor" collaborators merely did the laboratory work? And how major is the role of the person who did the writing job? Ghost-writing is not unknown in the scientific community. Indeed, the role of the technical reports writer is critical in scientific and technical communication. Brilliance in science is not always accompanied by literary talent.

Should authorship also be extended to administrators? And what about librarians or others who help collect data? Indeed, what about the colleague who was called in for professional advice?

In the days when most papers were written by one author, attribution of credit was not a problem. But the trend to multiple authorship has increased the importance of these ethical questions. Back in 1963 Derek de Solla Price noted in *Little science, big science* that the number of papers with three authors was already increasing faster than those with two. And four-author papers were increasing even more quickly than those with three.[4] More recent studies have substantiated the growth in multiple authorship.[5,6] A quick scan of *Current Contents®* attests to the preponderance of multiple-author papers, especially in the "hard" sciences.

Scientists have come up with many schemes for arranging the order of author by-lines to indicate the magnitude of each author's contribution. Sociologist Harriet Zuckerman has reported on several

of these methods. One "logical" technique involves a display of names in descending order of contribution. Thus, the first author contributed most, the last author least.

Another method is to place all other co-authors in alphabetical order, while the most significant contributor's name is placed first or last.[7] This is often done by an individual who has already received widespread recognition. And sometimes the most important contributor is designated as the reprint author.[8]

Certain research teams make no attempt to designate a single major contributor. The equality of all members is indicated by rotating names, alphabetically or otherwise, on a series of papers.[7] I believe this method also tends to increase the number of papers. Findings published in a series often could be published in one paper. This practice artificially inflates the cost of publication and indexing.

Some might argue that the best solution to this problem is to eliminate real names entirely. Thus, a group of mathematicians adopted the pseudonym "Bourbaki." The elimination of authors' real names was characteristic of Chinese publications in the days of the cultural revolution. But now we see in Chinese publications a return to papers on which the names of the authors are specified.

Many times the solution adopted is really no solution at all. For example, a wide practice, especially in the United Kingdom, is for authors simply to list their names in alphabetical order. Thus, the reader has no idea which author was the major contributor, if there was one.

From the above mentioned practices it becomes evident that the use of so many different ordering patterns by journals only adds to the confusion. How is one to know from one article or journal to another which system is in operation? The problem is further complicated by other factors which militate against the usefulness of name-order patterns.

Price claimed that "new information-handling methods have a heavy impact on the intuitive ethic, such as it is, that governs the awarding of credit by deciding who is listed as first author in multiple authorship.... There is now at least ten times as much value in being listed first on the by-line as there is in being anywhere else on the rapidly growing list."[9] In most circumstances, it is claimed, the first author's name will be remembered and credited with the work if none of the authors is well known. In the *Science Citation Index*® this problem is accentuated because we use the first author's name as a simple means of abbreviating the citing and cited work.

No matter what order is adopted, the "Matthew Effect," a phenomenon described by Robert K. Merton, will cause misallocation of credit. Merton adopted the term "Matthew Effect" from a Bible verse: "For unto everyone that hath shall be given, and he shall have abundance; but from him that hath not shall be taken away even that which he hath"[10] (Gospel according to St. Matthew). In other words, the work will be associated with the best-known person in the group.

Zuckerman noted that the "Matthew Effect" occurs frequently among Nobel laureates.[11] Although Nobelists frequently exercise *noblesse oblige* and give primary authorship to junior colleagues,[12] the work is usually attributed to the Nobelists by the scientific community.

Another factor working against name-order patterns is the policy of some *journals* of placing authors' names in alphabetical order — no matter how the authors would have arranged them themselves.

Alphabetizing names gives rise to the "second author syndrome," the semi-serious belief by co-authors that they are the victims of a subtle but vicious form of discrimination by the alphabetizers.[13] This is a variant on the "alphabetic disorder" described by Weston.[14]

Some people think that a journal's alphabetic arrangement of author names is of minor importance. But two psychologists provided evidence that this policy significantly influenced the content of one journal. They found that researchers whose surnames began with the letters P-Z avoided publication in the journal to a statistically significant degree.[15]

Probably no single pattern of name-ordering will ever be acceptable to everyone. But there is no reason why authors must rely on name-order alone to indicate their contributions.

A 1970 study conducted by Don Spiegel (Brentwood Hospital, Los Angeles) and Patricia Keith-Spiegel (San Fernando Valley State College) surveyed 746 psychologists from a cross-section of specialties on the problems and ethics of assigning credit to authors.[16] Many of the respondents said the ideal solution to the multiple-author problem would be to explain each author's contribution in a footnote, thus eliminating ambiguities created by a particular ordering system.

Herbert Dardik, a fellow of the American College of Surgeons, supports this idea by suggesting that science follow the example set by the arts and music, where the contributions of many are clearly defined.[6] For example, in a theatrical production the director, set designer, stage manager, as well as the actors are clearly credited in the play bill. The members of the audience can judge for themselves the major and minor contributions to the production because they are aware of the value of each role. Unfortunately, the roles are not always that clear-cut in science. However, it would be refreshing to see an admission in print that "the following paper is based on an idea I heard at a party."

The convention of explaining contributions in a separate paragraph can help alleviate the problem of allocating authorship credit. Actually, there are two aspects to this problem. One is the problem of the non-contributor who should not get co-authorship status, but obtains it by virtue of his or her power. The other is the problem of the real contributor who does *not* receive co-authorship status when in fact it is warranted.

In their book *Ethics in social and behavioral research,* Edward Diener (University of Illinois) and Rick Crandall (Texas Christian University) write that "little has been written on the guidelines that govern publication credit. Yet, publication issues often come before professional ethics committees."[17]

An informal survey of selected professional societies revealed that the ethics committees of these organizations acknowledge the existence of the problem. But they say they rarely, if ever, receive complaints.

Only the American Psychological Association reported that complaints about unfair assignment of authorship credit are received on a regular basis, perhaps five to ten a year. Maybe this is because APA is one of the few professional societies that has issued guidelines about authorship.

However, in a letter to the editor of *Drug Intelligence and Clinical Pharmacy,* three anonymous authors attacked the practice of superiors receiving authorship status for work performed completely by their subordinates.

"This is not only an act of egomania, but a means by which non-achievers fabricate achievement," the letter states. "A non-achiever could actually obtain a job over the achiever, simply because he has more publications listed on his curriculum vitae, thereby appearing to be more accomplished.... If the person(s) did not intend to use the false-authorship for further self-benefit, then why is it so important that they demand their name(s) be included? The reasons are obvious."[18]

Since the authors wished to remain anonymous, it is unlikely that we will ever know all the facts of their case. Stories of graduate students and others who are denied authorship credit are also difficult to substantiate.

What we do know from such letters and stories is that some members of the scientific community feel that the ethics of publication have not been defined clearly enough to meet the problems encountered today.

In my own experience I suspect that my mentor and colleagues at the time were more than generous in giving me credit as a co-author.[19] Under other circumstances I might have received a note in the last paragraph thanking me for preparing the chemicals involved or for confining all explosions to my side

of the laboratory. But in another instance I had to fight the resistance of my former boss when I tried to publish my first paper in a documentation journal.[20]

The Spiegel survey probed these problems, and the authors were able to draw some conclusions from psychologists' responses about the ethical determination of authorship status. They state: "It is unethical to give co-authorship to someone of higher status in one's organization unless he makes a substantial contribution to the project.... The results [of the survey] suggest that neither power nor status should be determinants of credit assignment."[16] By "substantial contribution" they mean actual work on the project.

Diener and Crandall concur: "The general principle governing publication credit is that authorship is assigned to individuals according to the magnitude of their scientific contribution to the study."[17] They define scientific contributions as the concept and design of the study and the writing of the report.

These general statements are less than definitive answers to the ethical questions of multiple authorship. Individual cases do not lend themselves to "prepackaged" solutions. However, general criteria are necessary so that decision-making on specific cases may operate within some broad standards.

Diener and Crandall also address a related problem: students who put professors' names on their papers—not at the professors' behest — but because they are grateful to their teachers or feel their work will receive greater recognition if the higher-status individual's name appears along with their own. "Authorships should never be given out of gratitude or deference to persons of higher status," Diener and Crandall assert.[17] Again, the rule of thumb is the measure of significant contribution.

The Spiegel survey also elicited responses from psychologists on the rights of sub-doctoral-level workers and of scientists only tangentially involved in a project.

The Spiegel report concluded that paid personnel below the doctoral level who are part of the research team are entitled to the same credit as doctoral-level participants, if they make similar contributions. However, activities that do not affect the scientific character of the study do not deserve publication credit.[16] Diener and Crandall mention typing the report, computer programming for data analysis, and clerical work as activities within this category. These individuals, however, may deserve footnote credit.[17]

They add, "A person who only analyzes the results of a study usually does not deserve authorship unless the analysis represents an important contribution to understanding or rethinking the study. A person who only collects data usually should not be an author, whereas a person whose contribution also includes planning the study or writing it up will deserve authorship."[17]

When the idea for the project comes from a colleague not part of a research team, respondents in the Spiegel survey suggested giving credit in a footnote to the originator. However, some respondents also noted that before work has begun, the originator of the idea should be invited to collaborate on the project.[16]

When a colleague provides assistance for a small portion of the study which requires his professional skill, recognition should be indicated in a footnote, according to respondents.[16]

To avoid the conflict over assigning credit after the project has been completed, Spiegel and Keith-Spiegel recommend a thorough discussion of assignment of responsibility and subsequent credit *before* work has begun. They caution to maintain flexibility, however, so that if individuals do not fulfill their responsibilities, adjustments in credit can be made. If all else fails, a neutral third party should be chosen to serve as an arbitrator.[16]

The conclusions of Diener and Crandall and Spiegel and Keith-Spiegel are drawn from the attitudes and circumstances of researchers in the behavioral sciences. Perhaps the professional societies of other disciplines should run their own surveys and create guidelines appropriate to the work in those fields. If strict guidelines were adopted, they might deter the powerful from using their influence to get their names on papers to which they did not contribute. With guidelines, workers below the doctoral level and colleagues tangentially involved in the work would be apprised of their rights. They would feel less at the mercy of the persons running the project.

However, Spiegel and Keith-Spiegel conclude that guidelines, however fair and comprehensive they may be, will still not guarantee an equitable distribution of credit if the decision is left to a manipulative, egotistical, or unethical individual: "Unfortunately, it is the person with the most status and power who usually makes the ultimate credit determination. The lower status individual, if dependent on the higher status individual for his job, may be reluctant to even bring up the issue of credit."[16]

One of the problems with scientific journals is that they do not provide enough of an outlet for administrators. They should be encouraged to write periodic review papers in which they can demonstrate their role, if any, in the work reported.

In the absence of specific guidelines or other restraints, Dardik's words may serve as a strong warning and a general guideline: "Publications serve as the concrete art form for the scientist. It is his *modus operandi*. Authorship is akin to success and achievement. It cannot and should not deteriorate into a bargaining tool or commodity."[6]

Just as authorship can be abused so can citation practices. Referees have a right, indeed an obligation, to verify the claims of authorship just as they ought to insist on the proper and adequate selection of works to be cited. Only the most outrageous and persistent egomaniac could put his name on papers that were not his. But it is even more improbable that this same individual would be cited with a frequency that would distort the perception of his peers as to his real contribution to science.

REFERENCES

1. **Price D J D.** *Science since Babylon.* Enlarged edition.
   New Haven: Yale University Press, 1976. 215 p.
2. **Garfield E.** The 300 most-cited authors, 1961-1976, including co-authors at last. 1. How the names were selected.
   Current Contents (28):5-17, 10 July 1978.

REFERENCES (continued)

3. **Nossal G J V.** Personal communication. 26 July 1978.
4. **Price D J D.** *Little science, big science.*
   New York: Columbia University Press, 1963. 118 p.
5. **Strub R L & Black F W.** Multiple authorship. (Letter to the editor).
   Lancet 2:1090-1, 1976.
6. **Dardik H.** Multiple authorship. *Surg. Gynecol. & Obstet.* 145:418, 1977.
7. **Zuckerman H A.** Patterns of name-ordering among authors of scientific papers: a study of social symbolism and its ambiguity.
   Am. J. Sociol. 74:276-91, 1968.
8. **Crandall R & Diener E.** Determining authorships of scientific papers (Letter to the editor). *Drug Intell. & Clin. Pharm.* 12:375, June 1978.
9. **Price D J D.** Ethics of scientific publication: rules for authors and editorials may depend on something more than taste and convention.
   Science 144:655-7, 1964.
10. **Merton R K.** The Matthew Effect in science. *Science* 159:56-63, 1968.
11. **Zuckerman H A.** *Scientific elite: Nobel laureates in the United States.*
    New York: Free Press, 1977. 335 p.
12. ------------------. Deviant behavior and social control in science. (Sagarin E, ed.)
    Deviance and social change.
    Beverly Hills: Sage Publications, 1977, p. 87-138.
13. **Garfield E.** Does ISI's international directory of R&D authors and organizations perpetrate alphabetic discrimination?
    Current Contents (1):4-5, 6 January 1971. (Reprinted in: Garfield E. *Essays of an Information Scientist.* Philadelphia: ISI Press, 1977.
    Vol. 1, p. 146-7.)
14. **Weston T.** The alphabetic disorder. *Medical News* (168):5, 24 December 1965.
15. **Over R & Smallman S.** (Letter to the editor). *Nature* 228:1357, 1970.
16. **Spiegel D & Keith-Spiegel P.** Assignment of publication credits: ethics and practices of psychologists. *Amer. Psychol.* 25:738-47, 1970.
17. **Diener E & Crandall R.** *Ethics in social and behavioral research.*
    Chicago: University of Chicago Press, 1978. 266 p.
18. **Anonymous.** Author plagiarism. (Letter to the editor).
    Drug Intell. & Clin. Pharm. 11:244, 1977.
19. **Bernhard S A, Garfield E & Hammett L P.** Special effects in acid catalysis by ion exchange resins. III. Some observations on the effects of polyvalent cations. *J. Am. Chem. Soc.* 76:991-2, 1954.
20. **Garfield E.** The preparation of subject heading lists by automatic punch-card techniques. *J. Doc.* 10:1-10, 1954.

Current Comments

Great science, whose importance is recognized, always has high impact. But not all high impact science is great science.

No other statement about citation analysis needs as much repetition. However, only on rare occasions can we identify specific examples of high impact papers that have a large percentage of critical or negative citations. The reason for this is simple. Scientists generally disregard the obviously erroneous or the trivial. Yet in the case of Arthur Jensen's 123-page work, "How much can we boost IQ and scholastic achievement?"[1] they did not disregard it. Perhaps scientists felt they *could not* disregard it.

To appreciate the impact of Jensen's article in the 1969 *Harvard Educational Review* one only has to look at the large number of citations it has received. The *Science Citation Index® (SCI®)* and the *Social Sciences Citation Index™ (SSCI™)* indicate it was cited 638 times between 1969 and 1977. The data for each year are as follows: 1969, 20 times; 1970, 62 times; 1971, 103 times; 1972, 74 times; 1973, 110 times; 1974, 67 times; 1975, 75

times; 1976, 66 times and 1977, 61 times. Many of these citations, 101 to be exact, appeared in letters, notes and editorials in journals. The rest, 537, were references in articles. We are unable to report in how many books it was cited.

Since Jensen's article was cited so often it proved to be one of the papers on our list of 100 most-cited *SSCI* articles.[2] Consequently we wrote to Jensen asking him to write a commentary on his article for *Citation Classics*. We are publishing that commentary in this issue.

As I promised in the essay accompanying the *SSCI* 100 most-cited articles list, we have conducted an investigation into why the Jensen article was so frequently cited. Later in this editorial I will present the results of that investigation.

Arthur Jensen was born August 24, 1923 in San Diego, California.[3] He has a BA in psychology from the University of California, Berkeley (1945); MA in psychology from San Diego State College (1952) and a Ph.D. from Teachers College of Columbia University (1956). Jensen's dissertation was entitled "Aggression in fantasy and overt behavior." After graduation, Jensen worked for a time with Hans Eysenck, whose views on genetic determination of intelligence were expressed in his 1971 book *The IQ argument*.[4] His views seem to closely parallel Jensen's.[5] At the time he wrote his controversial article, Jensen was a member of the faculty of the University of California at Berkeley and of the Institute of Learning, where he still works.

According to Stanford University education professor Lee Cronbach, Jensen's article was prepared in relative haste.[6] In his preface to *Genetics and education*[7] Jensen himself notes that the article grew out of two lectures he gave. One was on "Social class, race, and genetics: implications for education" and dealt with the question of educating children of differing learning abilities. The other, on intelligence testing, presented Jensen's findings on the interaction among social class, intelligence, and rote learning ability. The graduate student editors of the *Harvard Educational Review* asked Jensen to synthesize the lectures into one statement of views conforming to an outline they presented. He did so. Cronbach points out that Jensen let other work crowd his schedule "until mid-September and then put together 50,000 words in two months."[6]

The Jensen article[1] covers a lot of territory. Some of its main points are listed below. In the article Jensen:

1. Argued that the failure of compensatory education efforts to produce lasting changes in the IQs of disadvantaged children meant that the programs should be reevaluated.
2. Questioned the prevailing idea that IQ differences are the result of environmental factors.
3. Discussed the nature of intelligence and gave a history of IQ testing.
4. Correlated occupation with intelligence.
5. Using evidence presented by Sir Cyril Burt, showed how IQ can be viewed as nearly normally distributed throughout a population. He then provided a variance model to explain how IQ could be broken into its genetic and environmental components.
6. Discussed heritability — a statistical tool used to assess the degree to which differences in intelligence within a population are due to genetic factors. Backed by kinship studies by Burt and others, Jensen proposed that there is a .8 heritability factor. This means that 80% of the variance of intelligence in the observed population can be attributed to genetic factors.
7. Said that some environmental factors such as prenatal care can influence intelligence. However, he asserted that social class and racial variations in intelligence (such as the one standard deviation, 15 point IQ difference between groups

of blacks and groups of whites) cannot be accounted for by environmental factors.

8. Argued that a deprived environment can keep a child from performing up to his genetic potential, but that an enriched educational program cannot push the child above that potential.

9. Presented his own theory that people are endowed with two kinds of learning ability, associative or Level I and cognitive or Level II. According to Jensen, disadvantaged children do better on Level I tasks and not as well as advantaged children on Level II tasks. Level I tasks include rote learning and selective trial and error learning with feedback for correct responses. Level II tasks include concept learning and problem solving. He concluded that education should be changed. "Diversity rather than uniformity of approaches would seem to be the key to making education rewarding for children with different patterns of ability."

From a quick reading of the above highlights it is easy to see that many of Jensen's conclusions were likely to provoke controversy. So sure of this were the editors of *Harvard Educational Review* that they "arranged for a panel to provide comments" on the work, Cronbach said.[6] Those comments were later published in book form.[8] Subsequent comments on the Jensen paper were also gathered together in book form.[9]

To examine the nature of the Jensen controversy we decided to do an in-depth citation study at ISI®. Using both the *SSCI* and the *SCI* we randomly selected 60 articles, (every 9th article) or about 10% of the items that cited the 1969 Jensen work, to see why the authors did so.

Of the 60 papers in our sample, 29 cited Jensen's article negatively. This number includes articles that took exception to almost every point presented in the paper. It also includes those in which the authors debated specific points Jensen made. Eight of the articles cited Jensen's paper as an example of a controversy. Eight more used the article as a background reference. Only fifteen of the articles cited Jensen in agreement with his positions, and seven of them only on minor points. Further readings have confirmed that our sample is typical of the way authors have cited the Jensen work.

Fourteen of the 60 papers cited Jensen's article as part of the continuing "gene vs. environment" controversy. This familiar argument, sometimes known as the nature/nurture debate, pits those who believe in environmental determination of IQ or other traits against those who believe that these traits are genetically determined. Of the 14 papers, five were clearly against Jensen's stand that genetic factors, more than environmental factors, account for differences in

IQ between individuals and between racial and cultural groups. Four of the papers supported his stand. Five more used Jensen's article as an example of a study embroiled in the controversy.

Eleven of the articles we selected called into question Jensen's use of data. None of them specifically supported his methodology. One of the articles attacking Jensen's use of data was by David Layzer of the Harvard College Observatory.[10] In the article, called "Science or superstition (a physical scientist looks at the IQ controversy)," Layzer "analyzes the implicit assumptions underlying Jensen's theoretical analysis and demonstrates that they are untenable." He points out that the IQ measurements do not satisfy certain formal requirements needed to make them reliable and meaningful. Thus, according to Layzer, the estimates of heritability given by Jensen are meaningless. He also says that the data Jensen provides do not support his view that children with low IQs or children of parents with low IQs have limited capacity for acquiring cognitive skills.

Another of these articles on Jensen's use of data, this one by M. Golden and W. Bridger,[11] "A refutation of Jensen's position on intelligence, race, social class and heredity," attacked his use of statistics. The researchers flatly said, "Jensen's fundamental error lies in his misuse of statistics to make unwarranted statistical or logical inferences from one set of data or facts to another set of facts." Golden and Bridger note that mean IQ differences and the correlations between any two sets of measures are completely independent of one another. There is no statistical basis "for predicting one on the basis of knowledge of the other," as Jensen seems to do in his article.

Eight of the papers in the sample specifically mentioned Jensen's use of IQ measurements. Six of the eight expressed opposition to the way the measurements were used. M. W. Feldman and biologist R. C. Lewontin, for example, discussed Jensen's use of a variance model to measure IQ populations in "The heritability hang-up."[12] The analysis of variance cannot really "separate variation that is a result of environmental fluctuation from variation that is a result of genetic segregation," the authors said. The two articles not negatively citing this aspect of Jensen's work referenced the article as part of the debate over using IQ measurements.

Eleven of the articles referred to Jensen's correlation between race and genetic inferiority. Nine of these attacked Jensen's conclusions, one agreed with them and one cited Jensen's work as an example of an idea involved in the controversy. A typical article in this group was Richard Wienke's on racial differences in educability which presents evidence "that black students learn as well as white."[13]

Seven of the papers on the list referenced Jensen's remarks on the failure of compensatory education. Three of them agreed that these programs had failed and four did not agree. One paper that agreed with Jensen's views was "Compensatory education and contemporary liberalism in the United States: sociological view" by D. C. Morton and D. R. Watson. The authors cited Jensen to counter the liberal argument that working-class groups are in need of "compensation" at school.[14] On the other hand, Martin Deutsch presented data to support his argument that Jensen "prematurely classified compensatory education as a failure."[15] In the article "Happenings on the way back to the forum: social science, IQ and race differences revisited," Deutsch concluded that "continuous and carefully planned intervention procedures" could have a positive influence on the performance of disadvantaged children.

The remainder of the papers in our sample cited Jensen for reasons ranging from disagreement with his definition of intelligence to observations about the lack of new data presented in the work. The authors claimed that Jensen just rearranged existing data from studies done by others, relying on the previous data as accurate.

We end our citation study here. But in order to further understand the impact of the Jensen paper we did some additional research. We found that Jensen's reliance on the original work of others to make his case has brought much vocal criticism from educators, psychologists, scientists and others. Probably the most outspoken of the experts who attacked Jensen's use of data developed by others is psychologist Leon Kamin of Princeton University. Kamin, who wrote a book and has delivered lectures on the sub-

ject, closely examined Jensen's sources to see if their work really backed his conclusions.[16] Although he found many instances where Jensen seemingly misused the data that others reported, he also found some startling inconsistencies in the work of one of Jensen's primary sources.

To back much of his line of reasoning, Jensen relied on the data assembled by Sir Cyril Burt, the late British psychologist. Burt's kinship studies had been looked upon as standards for the scholarly community. Jensen particularly leaned on Burt's studies of separated identical twins to draw his conclusions. According to Kamin, with support from others who have now closely examined Burt's data, the numbers Burt supplied are unusable.

For three of the twin studies, which included 21 pairs, "over" 30 pairs and 53 pairs of twins respectively, the correlation between the IQ scores of the separated twins, given by Burt, was .771. This correlation remained the same through three studies of unequal size. Not only did that particular correlation remain constant over the different sample sizes but the IQ correlations between identical twins reared together also stayed the same over three sample sizes.

Kamin also charged that Burt's papers "are often remarkably lacking in precise descriptions of the procedures and methods that he employed."[16] Items such as the children's ages, sexes, name of the test administered and how and when the tests were given are often missing from the data supplied in the published version. When these findings began to cast some doubt on Burt's work, others began to investigate. Out of these investigations came further charges, well-reported in the science press,[17] that Burt may even have "invented" the data and "made-up" the co-workers he said collaborated with him on some of his studies.

Some researchers have pointed out that the discrediting of Burt's data does not remove the "underpinnings of the view that intelligence has a large genetic component."[18] According to Bernard Rimland of the Naval Electronics Laboratory and Harry Munsinger of the Department of Psychology of the University of California at San Diego, "Such a conclusion is unwarranted." In a letter to *Science,* the two researchers presented a chart of correlation coefficients for "intelligence" test scores from 52 studies. They asserted that "the deletion of Burt's data would have no appreciable effect on the overall picture." The data "demonstrating the heavy dependence of IQ on genetic factors are far too solid to be shaken by the rejection of the work of any single investigator — even Sir Cyril Burt."[18]

The validity of the IQ test itself to give accurate measures of the capabilities of a group of people has been questioned by many critics. Kamin in *The science and politics of IQ*[16] pointed out that IQ tests administered in the early part of this century "proved" the inferiority of certain immigrants to the US. No reputable scientist today would, for example, agree with Henry God-dard's assessment that "83 percent of Jewish immigrants were feeble-minded." Yet many are willing to agree with Jensen when he states that "on the average, Negroes test about 1 standard deviation (15 IQ points) below the average of the white population" and draws his conclusions as to what this test score means.

In the chapter "IQ, heritability and inequality," in *The IQ controversy,* N. J. Block and Gerald Dworkin attack, among other aspects of the Jensen article, the correlations he drew between IQ and job categories. According to the researchers, "Even if the number of hairs in a person's nose correlated with success in the same way IQ does, no one would be entitled to conclude that a certain level of nose hair numerosity is a requirement or a condition of eligibility for any level of success" (p. 414).[5]

Of course, not all those who found fault with the Jensen article were as vehement as those mentioned above. The early reaction of Lee Cronbach, for example, in his 1969 paper "Heredity, environment and educational policy" was to disagree with several aspects of the Jensen article.[8] Nevertheless he said, "Professor Jensen is among the most capable of today's educational psychologists. His research is energetic and imaginative." Cronbach called the Jensen paper "an impressive example of [Jensen's] thoroughness." He added, "Dr. Jensen has girded himself for a holy war against 'environmentalists' and his zeal leads him into overstatements and misstatements.'' Cronbach went on to say, ''Because learning abilities are plural, they are not adequately conceptualized by Jensen's Level I–Level II systems.'' He also disagreed with Jensen on the implications of his findings for educational policy.

In a subsequent article that appeared in *American Psychologist* in 1975, Cronbach analyzed the controversies over mental testing that have developed in the last five decades. He noted, ''Our scholars chose to play advocate when they went before the public, and they abandoned scholarly consistency ....The academic needs writing skills of an entirely unaccustomed order if he is to make sure that no unwanted implication will be drawn from a buried sentence ...''[6]

Jensen had his unabashed supporters within the scientific community. For example, Harvard psychologist Richard Herrnstein in his 1971 *Atlantic* article argued that American society is heading for a meritocracy based on heredity and IQ differences.[19] According to Herrnstein, society in the future will be socially stratified by inborn differences. Social standing will be given to groups with higher IQs. Herrnstein's arguments have been called the popularization of Jensen.

Nobel laureate physicist William Shockley shared Jensen's views as well. According to Lewontin,[5] in ''Race and intelligence'' reprinted in *The IQ controversy,* Shockley distributed Jensen's paper to every member of the National Academy of Sciences soon after it was pub-

lished. He did so ''as part of his continuing campaign to have the Academy study the effects of interracial mating'' (p. 78).[5] Shockley also wrote several papers defending the Jensen article. In his 1971 article ''Models, mathematics and the moral obligation to diagnose the origin of Negro IQ deficits'' Shockley concluded that ''nature has color-coded groups of individuals so that statistically reliable predictions of their adaptability to intellectually rewarding and effective lives can easily be made. ... If those members of our black minority with the least percentage of Caucasian genes are both the most prolific and the least intelligent, then a form of genetic enslavement is the destiny of their next generation.''[20]

Many of Jensen's supporters say that those who oppose them seek to restrict free scientific inquiry. The result, according to Edward O. Wilson in his article ''The attempt to suppress human behavioral genetics,'' has been that ''studies on the genetics of cognitive abilities including intelligence have been inhibited.''[21] While many scientists would support Wilson's call to depoliticize science, some will point out that science does not exist in a vacuum. Sensitive subjects can be approached, but the data at least should be accurate, the methodology sound and the conclusions logical.

During the nine years since the publication of his article, Jensen has replied repeatedly to his critics in letters and articles.[22-33] The first major work in response was ''Reducing the heredity-environment uncertainty'' which appeared along-side several critical articles in the book *Environment, heredity and intelligence.* In this article, Jensen noted that many of his critics agreed with his major stands but disagreed with him on minor points. He added, ''If there are weaknesses in the methods and evidence I have presented, and of course there inevitably are at this stage, we would do well to note them as a basis for seeking more refined research methods and more and better data, rather than as a basis for minimizing the ... importance of these questions.''[8]

In some of his responding works, Jensen refuted his critics point by point, prompting counter responses. For example, after Layzer wrote his critical article,[10] Jensen replied with a 26-page detailed work[30] that explains why IQ scores can be viewed as fitting an interval scale and why the concept of heritability could be used to understand human differences, among other things. Layzer, in turn, counterattacked with a 19–page article entitled ''Jensen's reply: the sounds of silence,'' in which he accused Jensen of serious omissions and irrelevancies.[34] This type of exchange was carried on several times with others, as the debate continued and remained unresolved.

After the publication of his 1969 article, Jensen wrote three books. *Genetics and education* (1972) was his first. In his preface he called this work a ''book-length treatment of those parts of my HER article which were generally regarded as the most controversial ...''[7] Included in *Genetics and education* was a reprint of the 1969 article. The second book, *Educational differences* (1973) was a collection of articles dealing with ''the psychology of mental abilities.''[35] Topics such as the heritability of intelligence, individual differences in learning and culture-fair testing were covered in the book. *Educability and group differences,* also published in 1973, dealt ''with the fact that various subpopulations (social and ethnic groups) ... show marked differences in the distributions of those mental abilities most importantly related to educability and its occupational and socioeconomic correlates.''[36] All three of the works supported the 1969 article.

Jensen has continued to perform work in the field of genetics and education. Since 1969 he has published well over twenty articles that expanded on or clarified the points made in the 1969 article or represented new research in this field. His recent studies have led him to perform a cautious about–face on his stand that IQ is primarily genetically determined.[37]

In his 1977 article ''Cumulative deficit in IQ of blacks in the rural south'' Jensen studied 1,479 children in a very poor area of Georgia. He compared IQ test scores of pairs of black siblings and white siblings to test the hypothesis that environmental factors cause IQ scores to decline. The black children showed a decline in IQ scores between the ages of 5 and 18 while the white children did not. He compared results with those from another study of more affluent blacks in California which he also conducted, and concluded that the Georgia study "would seem to favor an environmental interpretation of the progressive decrement phenomenon .... It appears that a cumulative deficit due to poor environment has contributed, at least in part, to the relatively low IQ in the present sample."[37]

Jensen's recent work on the IQ controversy appeared in the March 1978 *Australian Psychologist*.[38] In it, he reviewed the current status of the debate, analyzing several general areas still under discussion by scientists. These include the nature and measurement of intelligence; the heritability of IQ within culturally homogeneous populations; the genetic components in IQ differences between groups and the social and educational implications of a genetic component in IQ variance. The article attempts to place the controversy in perspective some nine years after the publication of the *Harvard Educational Review* piece.

Jensen's role in the IQ controversy continues even as this essay goes to press. An article in the September 9 issue of *Science News* reported a study presented by Jensen at the recent American Psychological Association meeting in Toronto that indicated that IQ "has a definite 'biological basis.'"[39]

According to the article, "the cornerstone of his latest work involves reaction time (RT), as measured on a rather simplistic panel consisting of sets of ... lights. RT is measured by how long it takes a person to lift his finger off a central pushbutton and move it to the button under the light that has just flashed on ..." Jensen "found that reaction times of the more than 400 subjects correlated 'across the board' with their performances on a variety of verbal and non–verbal intelligence measures.... Although he found no sex differences in performance, Jensen says he did detect 'black-white difference at the junior college level,' with blacks exhibiting somewhat slower reaction times...." According to the *Science News* article, Jensen emphasizes "that these results do 'not at all' alter his previous conclusions that environment contributes to intelligence at some level. 'I'm not putting any stress on the racial aspects,' he says of his latest research. 'That would be kind of a red herring and detract from the use of reaction time' as an indicator of intelligence."

Usually when a researcher presents mediocre or inferior work to the scholarly community that work elicits no response. But when an article is published in a highly visible and reputable journal such as the *Harvard Educational Review*, as was Jensen's article, even if it didn't have methodological problems, it was inevitable that it would not be ignored. Furthermore, scientists of reputation felt compelled to rebut the article after popular versions of it appeared in the lay press. After all, how many lay people, who would be making the decisions regarding education in this country, would wade through the 123-page study? And if they did, how many would recognize the problems with the research if not pointed out by scientists? Very few, I'm afraid. The Jensen article is certainly a high impact article. But contemporary scientists must classify it as important but questionable science. Since most high impact science proves to be great science, the Jensen case is an exception that illustrates one must be cautious in using citation data. But clearly it is the extreme of science. The citation data and the realities on which they are based show that Jensen's work is a milestone event in the history of social science.

REFERENCES

1. **Jensen A R.** How much can we boost IQ and scholastic achievement? *Harvard Educ. Rev.* 39:1-123, 1969.
2. **Garfield E.** The 100 articles most cited by social scientists, 1969-1977. *Current Contents* (32):5-14, 7 August 1978.
3. *Current biography, 34th annual cumulation – 1973.* New York: H. W. Wilson Co., 1974. 481 p.
4. **Eysenck H.** *The IQ argument.* Freeport, NY: Library Press, 1971. 155 p.
5. **Block N J & Dworkin G, eds.** *The IQ controversy.* New York: Pantheon Books, 1976. 557 p.
6. **Cronbach L J.** Five decades of public controversy over mental testing. *Amer. Psychol.* 30:1-14, 1975.
7. **Jensen A R.** *Genetics and education.* New York: Harper & Row, 1972. 378 p.
8. **Harvard Educational Review** . *Environment, heredity and intelligence.* Cambridge: HER, 1969. 246 p.
9. **Harvard Educational Review**. *Science, heritability and IQ.* Cambridge: HER, 1969. 97 p.
10. **Layzer D.** Science or superstition. (A physical scientist looks at the IQ controversy). *Cognition* 1:265-300, 1972.
11. **Golden M & Bridger W.** A refutation of Jensen's position on intelligence, race, social class, and heredity. *Mental Hyg.* 53:648-53, 1969.
12. **Feldman M W & Lewontin R C.** The heritability hang-up. *Science* 190:1163-8, 1975.
13. **Wienke R.** Are there racial differences in educability? *J. Hum. Relat.* 18:1190-203, 1970.

REFERENCES (continued)

14. **Morton D C & Watson D R.** Compensatory education and contemporary liberalism in the United States: a sociological view. *Int. Rev. Ed.* 17:289-307, 1971.
15. **Deutsch M.** Happenings on the way back to the forum: social science, IQ, and race differences revisited. *Harvard Educ. Rev.* 39:523-57, 1969.
16. **Kamin L.** *The science and politics of IQ.* New York: Wiley, 1974. 179 p.
17. **Wade N.** IQ and heredity: suspicion of fraud beclouds classic experiment. *Science* 194:916-9, 1976.
18. **Rimland B & Munsinger R.** Letter to the editor. *Science* 195:248, 1977.
19. **Herrnstein R.** IQ. *Atlantic* 228(3):43-58, 63-4, 1971.
20. **Shockley W.** Model, mathematics, and the moral obligation to diagnose the origin of Negro IQ differences. *Rev. of Educ. Res.* 41:369-77, 1971.
21. **Wilson E O.** The attempt to suppress human behavioral genetics. *J. Gen. Educ.* 29(4):277-87, 1978.
22. **Jensen A R.** Criticism or propaganda? *Am. Psychol.* 24:1040-41, 1969.
23. _____. A reply to Danielian. *Contemp. Psychol.* 14:682, 1969.
24. _____. Jensen's theory of intelligence: a reply. *J. Educ. Psychol.* 60:427-31, 1969.
25. _____. Rejoinder: promotion of dogmatism. *J. Soc. Issues* 25:212-7, 1969.
26. _____. Counter response. *J. Soc. Issues* 25:219-22, 1969.
27. _____. Hebb's confusion about heritability. *Am. Psychol.* 26:394-5, 1971.
28. _____. The ethical issues. *Humanist* 32(1):5-6, 1972.
29. _____. Interpretation of heritability. *Am. Psychol.* 27:973-5, 1972.
30. _____. The IQ controversy: a reply to Layzer. *Cognition* 1:427-52, 1972.
31. _____. The differences are real. *Psychol. Today* 7:80-6, 1973.
32. _____. The strange case of Dr. Jensen & Mr. Hyde? *Am. Psychol.* 29:467-8, 1974.
33. _____. Heritability of IQ. *Science* 194:6; 8, 1976.
34. **Layzer D.** Jensen's reply: the sounds of silence. *Cognition* 1:453-73, 1972.
35. **Jensen A R.** *Educational differences.* London: Methuen & Co., 1973. 462 p.
36. _____. *Educability and group differences.* New York: Harper & Row, 1973. 407 p.
37. _____. Cumulative deficit in IQ of blacks in the rural south. *Develop. Psychol.* 13:184-91, 1977.
38. _____. The current status of the IQ controversy. *Australian Psychol.* 13(1):7-27, March 1978.
39. Jensen: Intelligence a 'biological rhythm'. *Science News* 114(11):181, 9 September 1978.

Current Comments

Is *Current Contents* a Periodical?
The Landmark Case of *ISI* v. *US Postal Service*

Number 42   October 16, 1978

On May 14, 1971, I thought the earth stood still. That was the day the US Postal Service revoked *Current Contents*® ' second-class mailings permit. But then on May 5, 1977, ISI® won a landmark case against the Postal Service heard before the US Court of Appeals for the Third Circuit.[1] The appellate court ruled that the Postal Service had wrongfully revoked ISI's second-class mailing privileges. The court's decision affected not only every subscriber to *Current Contents* but also the producers and users of all other information services that go through the US mails.

When the US Postal Service notified ISI that it was revoking second-class mailing privileges for *CC*®, it was a heavy blow for us. In the US, second-class mail is much less expensive than first-class. For example, it presently costs less than a dime to mail a copy of *CC/Life Sciences* at second-class rates in the US. (This rate does not apply to foreign subscribers.) It would cost $.80 to mail the same copy first-class—over $40 per year at current postal rates. Had the Postal Service succeeded in revoking our second-class privileges, we would have had

to mail *CC* first-class in order to maintain all-important timely delivery. This would have meant a significant increase in subscription rates.

According to the *Postal Service Manual*, "Only newspapers and other periodical publications...may be mailed at the second-class rates" (p. 132.2).[2] Postal authorities in 1971 disqualified *CC* because, they asserted, it was not a periodical. This reasoning was based on a 1904 Supreme Court decision, *Houghton v. Payne*.[3] In that case the Court decided that a series of reprints of famous works (analogous to today's book clubs) did not qualify as periodical literature. For the purposes of the case, the Supreme Court described "periodical" as follows:

A periodical, as ordinarily understood, is a publication appearing at stated intervals, each number of which contains a variety of original articles by different authors, devoted either to some branch of learning or to a special class of subjects. Ordinarily each number is incomplete in itself, and indicates a relation with prior or subsequent numbers of the same series.

The Postal Service interpreted the *Houghton* decision to require that a periodical contain "a variety of original articles." According to this reasoning, *CC* could not be a periodical and could not be entitled to second-class rates.

The Postal Service has used the "original articles" phrase many times in the past seven years in order to revoke or deny second-class privileges of information services on the grounds that they are not periodicals. Standard Rate and Data Service, American Chemical Society (ACS), American Bibliographic Center, H. W. Wilson Company, and McGraw-Hill, Inc. are among the publishers who have had second-class privileges revoked or denied during the 1970s.[4] In some cases the services involved had been accepted as periodicals for over 50 years. In the case of *Current Contents,* we had enjoyed second-class classification for some editions for about 14 years.

These impingements on the effective dissemination of information came in the wake of the reorganization of the Postal Service into a semi-private, semi-governmental organization. In 1970, Congress enacted the change to encourage more cost-effective mail delivery.[5] Among several approaches to reduce costs to the US Treasury, the Postal Service began reviewing many publications, and applied the presumed *Houghton* rule to them.

One might ask how, out of the thousands of periodicals published in the US, the Postal Service was able to find out that *CC* existed. It was another publisher's difficulties with the Postal Service that led to ours. When the American Chemical Society applied for a second-class permit for one of its publications, *Single Article Announcement,* the application was denied. The Postal Service argued that this publication contains only contents pages of ACS journals, and no original articles. Hence, it is not a periodical. When ACS appealed this decision, it argued that if *Single Article Announcement* isn't a periodical, what about *Current Contents?* ACS lost its appeal and did not appeal again. The stakes were not high enough since ACS's primary journals were not threatened.

ISI was the first organization to seriously challenge the Postal Service's campaign to deny second-class privileges to information services. As soon as we were informed that we were being denied second-class mailing privileges, we contacted our legal counsel, Kimber Vought of the Washington office of Schnader, Harrison, Segal, and Lewis. Vought is also a member of ISI's Board of Directors. Our attorneys obtained immediate relief for us pending appeal. (In the interim we were permitted to mail *CC* third-class while still enjoying more rapid second-class service. Third-class is a more expensive rate than second-class, but less costly than first-class.)

We appealed the arbitrary action before the Postal Service's administrative law judge. The administrative hearing is the first of two levels of appeal in the Postal Service. The administrative law judge upheld the Postal Service's decision on May 22, 1975. At the second level of appeal, the Postal Service's judicial officer did the same on October 2, 1975.

Throughout the proceedings, the Postal Service argued that *CC* is not a periodical because it does not contain "a variety of original articles."

ISI's attorneys (Vought, Irving R. Segal, and John E. McKeever) argued that the Postal Service was interpreting the *Houghton* case narrowly and improperly. They contended that "a variety of original articles" is not the only factor defining a periodical. They stressed that the Postal Service was ignoring another aspect of *Houghton:* that each issue of a periodical is incomplete in itself, that continuity or periodicity is also a characteristic of a periodical.

During the Postal Service administrative hearing, several *CC* subscribers testified on this point. They were Leonard Stoloff and Milton Stephenson of the Food and Drug Administration, Edward G. Feldmann of the American Pharmaceutical Association, and Charles Scanio, formerly of the Groton, Connecticut branch of the pharmaceutical company, Pfizer, Inc. and now with the New Haven, Connecticut branch of the Upjohn Company. Their testimony supported the contention that a single

issue of *Current Contents* is essentially useless—that only the continuous weekly availability of *Current Contents* makes it a valuable service. As we expected, this argument did not persuade the administrative law judge or the judicial officer at hearings within the Postal System itself.

In 1975 ISI took its case to the US District Court for the Eastern District of Pennsylvania. This court also upheld the Postal Service's decision. But in May 1977 the US Court of Appeals for the Third Circuit ruled that *Current Contents* was entitled to second-class privileges.[1]

Circuit Judges Ruggero J. Aldisert and James Hunter III accepted ISI's position that the "original articles" requirement was just one factor to be considered in granting or revoking second-class privileges. It was not an "absolute litmus test." The court also ruled that to qualify for second-class privileges, "periodicity," or continuity, is the important factor. (Chief Judge Collins J. Seitz dissented from the majority opinion.)

This did not end our problems. Subsequently, the Postal Service tried to convince the US Department of Justice to take the case to the Supreme Court. But the Justice Department declined, and the deadline for appeal passed on June 4, 1977. So ISI's 6-year, $35,000 legal battle was ended. However, the Court of Appeals' ruling governs, technically, only in the states of Pennsylvania, New Jersey, and Delaware. It does not apply directly to publishers in other parts of the country. However, it has encouraged others to take the Postal Service to court themselves.

In *H. W. Wilson, v. US Postal Service,*[6] decided July 7, 1978, the US Court of Appeals for the Second Circuit said the Postal Service was wrong in revoking the second-class privileges of eight Wilson information services, including *Readers' Guide to Periodical Literature, Social Sciences & Humanities Index,* and *Applied Science & Technology Index.* Citing the *ISI* decision, the court held that "the 'variety of original articles' standard is erroneous and unworkable, is not mandated by *Houghton,* and has not been consistently applied by the Postal Service."

In *Standard Rate and Data Service, Inc. v. US Postal Service,*[7] decided July 14, 1978, the US Court of Appeals for the District of Columbia Circuit held that the Postal Service has not been consistent in applying the *Houghton* standard. This court also cited the *ISI* case.

It sent this case back to the Postal Service, to give it "an opportunity to develop, or at least articulate, a more consistent, and perhaps a more purposeful, policy with respect to entry into the second-class mails." At present, Standard Rate and Data Service is mailing its seven publications second-class. These publications, including *Business Publications Rates and Data* and *Newspaper Rates and Data,* keep advertising agencies informed of print and broadcast advertising rates.

This year the Postal Service tried to revoke the second-class privileges of *Management Contents* (*MC*), published by John D. Kuranz in Skokie, Illinois. A bi-weekly, *MC* is a periodical quite similar to *Current Contents.* It reproduces the contents pages of management and business journals. This May the Postal Service told Kuranz that *MC* was not a periodical under the principles of the *Houghton* case. Kuranz tells us that Management Contents, Inc. is a small publishing house, with a full-time staff of three. Thus, Kuranz says, he could not afford to sue. All he could do was complain to the Postal Service and Illinois' two senators. After consulting ISI, he argued that, as a result of the *ISI* decision, the Postal Service had no right to revoke his second-class privileges.

The Postal Service told Kuranz that it is deferring further action on its decision. Now Kuranz is mailing *MC* at the more expensive third-class rates, and will be reimbursed if the Postal Service decides in his favor.

Until now, publishers have had to defend themselves individually. But the Information Industry Association (IIA), among others, is trying to initiate organized action. A Postal Affairs Task Force, chaired by Peter Aborn, ISI's vice president of administrative services, is now being formed. This group will establish cooperative efforts with the Magazine Publishers Association and others. It will also keep

IIA members informed of events affecting mail distribution of their publications. Right now the Task Force is trying to start discussion among concerned groups about what sort of action is needed. Also, it is attempting to keep groups up-to-date on recent developments.

As the matter stands today, the Postal Service may well take the advice of Circuit Judge Harold Leventhal in the *Standard Rate and Data Service* case and develop a more consistent policy on second-class mail. The danger is that the policy may not be in the public interest. But the 1970 postal law never intended that the Postal Service may arbitrarily exclude one type of periodical from second-class privileges. Rather than say that information services like *CC* are not periodicals, it would be easier for the Postal Service to argue that magazines like *The New Yorker* or *Reader's Digest* are not. A single issue of one of these could probably be used purposefully. But the continuity of secondary information services is indeed critical to their use.

The decisions the courts have handed down so far have been favorable to the companies involved. But as the *Management Contents* incident shows, the Postal Service has not stopped trying to deprive information services of fast, inexpensive delivery. The final decision may have to come from the Supreme Court or an act of Congress. There is no guarantee that decision will be favorable. Thus, the outcome depends largely on how well, and how quickly, all those involved in the production and use of information services act. Included here are not only for-profit organizations in the IIA but also members of the National Federation of Abstracting and Indexing Services as well as other publishers not in either. At the very least, they should inform their representatives in Congress that information services should be entitled to the same treatment as other periodicals.

REFERENCES

1. *Institute for Scientific Information, Inc. v. United States Postal Service*, 555 F.2d 128 (3d Cir. 1977).
2. United States Postal Service. *Postal Service manual.* Washington, DC: US Government Printing Office, 1977.
3. *Houghton v. Payne*, 194 U.S. 88 (1904).
4. Data services win on second-class mail. *Business Week* 18 July 1977, p. 23.
5. American Enterprise Institute for Public Policy Research. *Postal Service legislative proposals.* Washington, DC: American Enterprise Institute for Public Policy Research, 6 October 1977, 36 p.
6. *H. W. Wilson Co. v. United States Postal Service*, No. 78-6013 (2nd Cir. July 7, 1978).
7. *Standard Rate and Data Service, Inc. v. United States Postal Service, et al.*, No. 77-1848 (D.C. Cir. July 14, 1978).

Making Contacts at Conferences—
A Problem for the Young Scientist

Number 43   October 23, 1978

Most scientists or scholars attend conferences as part of their professional lives. Conferences, whether they are called symposia, meetings, congresses, jamborees, or workshops, are supposed to "provide opportunities for conferees to exchange information, evaluate proposed ideas, cross-pollinate views and extend knowledge."[1] One of the best ways to accomplish these goals is through meeting other scientists with similar interests.[2] But young professionals, graduate students, and other newcomers often have difficulties making contacts at conferences.[3] My personal experience and a review of the recent literature confirm this view. And because of rising expenses, young people especially have difficulties getting to conferences.[4] So it is important for them to get the most out of those they can attend.

Whether a conference is large or small it often seems to present some serious stumbling blocks to young scientists. In fact, one of the major criticisms of large international or national meetings is that they are less valuable to the young than they

should be.[5] One reason for this is that they are often held in large metropolitan areas. Attendees with little money—students or young professionals—usually must travel to the conference at their own expense. Once there, they must pay a registration fee which many feel is rising beyond the means of the young.

Accommodations present another problem. In order to get an inexpensive room, the young attendee is often forced to stay miles away from the conference proper. This segregation inhibits interaction between the young and the more established professionals staying close to the meeting site.[6] As H. Gutfreund of the University of Bristol pointed out, "Interaction between all ages and interests must be made inevitable by accommodation in close proximity and joint eating facilities."[5]

Isaac Welt, professor of information science at American University, comments that societies can help solve this problem by scheduling meetings in hotels that give differential rates to young people or in inexpensive hotels.[7] Organizations should also gear conference registration fees to the young professional's income in the same way some membership rates are now determined. Many professional societies have student membership rates. These price reductions could be extended to student registration fees at society conferences.

If larger meetings inhibit young scientists from making contacts, one would think that smaller meetings would be the solution. Unfortunately, small meetings restrict attendance. Often only "invited" speakers can participate. These are usually senior people. This practice locks out others who might be interested in attending. One solution to this problem is to organize sessions devoted to "contributed" papers. Speaking on this issue recently, Herbert A. Laitinen, editor of *Analytical Chemistry*, pointed out that these "open" sessions sometimes represent the only mechanism by which the young investigator may penetrate the inner circle. Nevertheless, these open sessions can be less than satisfactory. He recommends "more critical evaluation of openly contributed papers to screen out those of a routine character, whose main reason seems to be to justify attendance." He adds, "If meeting attendance were not conditional upon presentation of a paper, the results would be an improvement in the meetings."[8]

One idea advanced by Welt is that small meetings should have a quota for first-time attendees.[7] If a certain number of the participants were required to be novices, the conference could be prevented from becoming the breeding ground for a self-perpetuating elite.

Another problem with small meetings is that it is difficult to cover the expenses required to bring eminent scholars there. Given a choice, the young scientist will go to the larger meeting if it increases the chance for encounters with scientists in the forefront of research. Small meetings afford little opportunity to meet people outside a narrow specialty. Large meetings can bring together people with diverse interests.

In an article entitled "Meeting failure and participant frustration", Anthony Judge agrees that a frequent source of frustration for many participants is lack of adequate contact between attendees. Since it is well-documented that establishing contacts is one of the major reasons young as well as established professionals attend conferences, this frustration can be acute.[3]

Robert Freedman adds that attending a meeting allows conference goers to "strike up a casual conversation in the lunch queue and hear about a technique which will solve their problems, to track down a Romanian who published a rather interesting paper last year, to steel themselves to approach a legendary figure to ask if they may come to his lab."[6] Judge points out that "more experienced participants select sessions and parts of sessions and spend the remainder of their time in the hallways talking to the eminent people seated at strategic spots to receive them." The most eminent people, however, are "found outside the conference centre in a bar arranging the next conference."[3]

If the established professionals are not actually at the conference sessions, how then can the newcomer really break into their inner circle? In a previous essay, I pointed out how difficult it is for people to introduce themselves to strangers at conferences.[9] At that time, I proposed that the first day of any conference be devoted to information encounter groups. Each attendee would be assigned to a small group of about 30 persons. In the morning each person would speak for about five minutes, providing biographical information and discussing the problems he or she hoped the meeting would help him or her solve. In the afternoon, a follow-up discussion would allow participants to make suggestions or ask clarifying questions. This method allows both the established professionals and the young conference goers to make contacts and also gives them some information upon which to base a later approach. Such meetings, however, require a strong group leader to guide the discussions.

A variation on this theme would be to organize informal discussion groups led by well-known scientists or scholars. Participation could be limited to 30 to 50 people who had applied in advance. Priority in selection could be based on age, research interests, or other considerations.

Established professionals need to be reminded that it is their responsibility to make sure their charges meet the right people at conferences. I agree with Welt when he says that it is the duty of the young professional's mentor, professor, or job supervisor to help the young scientist meet not only senior people but each other.[7] Senior people should act as "people-to-people catalysts," he says.

The American Chemical Society (ACS), has grappled with the problems of young chemists in their Younger Chemists Committee (YCC). During national and regional meetings, young professionals can stop by the YCC booth and meet the members of the committee.[10] At national meetings, ACS sponsors an Industrial Forum. Several invited industrial chemists speak for a few minutes and then answer questions from the young audience. In that way, students can get to know working scientists.

Several of my colleagues have pointed out that the problem of making contacts at conferences applies even to experienced professionals if they wish to attend conferences outside their field. For example, a person with a Ph.D. in biology who has just gotten a job in publishing feels "lost" at a publishing conference. People trying to expand their interdisciplinary horizons should be given a chance to mingle with the "in-groups." The same applies to people who go to school while they work and have no time to go to conferences. When they've finally completed their studies and can attend the meetings, they feel isolated. They are older than the students, but far less experienced in conferences than others their age.

Professional conference organizers see great hope in the future use of computers to facilitate making contacts at conferences.[11] This new technology can help both the young and the more established scientist find people with similar interests. Future conference participants will preregister their specific areas of interest and indicate their preferences for meeting in small groups or on a one-to-one basis. Each participant will also indicate the time he or she will be available. The computer would then match parties with the same interests and schedule contacts.

Conferences can be computerized by using a message processing system. Groups of terminals could be set up at the conference site with assistants available to help participants use them. To retrieve your messages, you would simply type your name and registration number. All messages for you would either appear on the terminal's screen or be printed out. Simple messages like "you left your coat in my car" could be stored. But more importantly, a graduate student could ask, for example, if anyone at the conference would like to discuss his or her thesis topic. Or you could ask a question of a particular speaker that you didn't have a chance to ask during the session. The speaker could answer the question some time later. You would find the answer when you interrogated the terminal the next day. This could help young scientists participate more fully since they are often reluctant to ask questions from the conference floor.

An extensive article on this method of making contacts at conferences appeared recently in *Associations Transnationales,* published by the Belgium-based Union of International Associations. The article listed the almost endless possible uses that could be made of computers at conferences. "Each person should leave with the belief that he or she has been provided with an environment which made possible the optimum number of useful contacts under the circumstances," it concluded.[11]

Surely the use of computers will enhance conferences, especially for the young attendee. More young professionals will travel to the large gatherings if they have better chances of making beneficial contacts. But the day of the computerized conference, although on the horizon, has not yet arrived. For young scientists, many successful contacts are still too often made by chance. They deserve some special attention from conference organizers to make sure the established and the not-so-established meet and share experiences.

Perhaps what is needed is for some of the professional societies to set up a conference on the problem of making contacts at conferences. Professional conference organizers have already taken up the question at their meetings. But the scientific information and communication societies, which are most affected by the problem, should devote more attention to it.

In the meantime, young scientists should try to discard their assumptions that eminent people are unapproachable. In my experience, I have always found that leading scientists were willing to talk for at least a few minutes. If our interests coincided, there was always a way to find more time. I remember my first professional society meeting in 1951—the American Chemical Society's annual meeting in New York City. I wandered into the session given by the Division of Chemical Literature. After I heard the chairman, James W. Perry, speak, I walked up to him and said, "How do you get into this racket?" A few days later he was eating dinner at my parents' apartment in the Bronx.

REFERENCES

1. **Kindler H S.** *Organizing the technical conference.*
   New York: Reinhold, 1960. 139 p.
2. **Manten A A.** *Symposia and symposium publications.*
   Amsterdam: Elsevier Scientific 1976. 153 p.
3. **Judge A J N.** Meeting failure and participant frustration.
   Assoc. Internat. 1:34-7, 1976.
4. **Whelan W J.** A return to the simple life. *Trends Biochem. Sci.* 1:25-6, 1976.
5. **Gutfreund H.** Discussion forum: are international congresses an expensive waste of time? *Trends Biochem. Sci.* 1:198-9, 1976.
6. **Freedman R.** Specialist jamborees—who benefits?
   New Sci. 76:98-9, 1977.
7. **Welt I.** Personal communication 13 September 1978.
8. **Laitinen H.** On scientific meetings. *Analyt. Chem.* 50(7):833, June 1978.
9. **Garfield E.** Information encounter groups.
   Current Contents (23):5-6, 7 June 1976. (Reprinted in:
   Garfield E. *Essays of an information scientist.*
   Philadelphia: ISI Press, 1977. Vol. 2, p. 498-9.)
10. **Bonds W.** Contacts: the neglected variable in getting a job.
    Forum 2(1):1, April 1978.
11. Enhancing communications at a large conference festival.
    Assoc. Transnat. 12:532-40, 1977.

Current Comments

The Incredible INFOROMETER

Number 44   October 30, 1978

"Quantifying the intangible" is a phrase often used by A. E. Cawkell, ISI® 's research director. This is how he describes the problem of defining the value of information services.[1] Producers and users of information services often have trouble explaining the value of such services to administrators. Research administrators willingly allocate funds for expensive electron microscopes, particle accelerators, or other scientific instruments. But often they are reluctant to spend money for information services.[2,3,4]

What is the source of this kind of bias? An electron microscope, spectrograph, gas chromatograph, or colorimeter is a shiny, metallic, conspicuous, scientific-looking sort of thing. If someone asks, "What's it for?", you can always explain what it does, regardless of whether it is necessary.

In contrast, a copy of *Current Contents®* is rather unobtrusive. The layman often thinks it is a scientific version of *TV Guide*. It certainly doesn't look scientific, metallic, or expensive. Of course, if you let a few years' worth of *CC®* accumulate you have an impressive volume of paper. Perhaps it is not as impressive as a five-year cumula-

tion of the *Science Citation Index®* *(SCI®)* or *Chemical Abstracts*. In any case, paper does not impress administrators. They are up to their ears in it already.

I've often wondered about a new approach to the problem. Is it a matter of semantics? Maybe we should call *Current Contents* an "Inforometer." That ought to impress any self-respecting purchasing agent! Or maybe we should call the *SCI* a "SCItometer" — that is much more impressive than *Science Citation Index*. A "SCItometer" sounds like something every scientist ought to have.

Recently, I told you about our plans for PRIMATE—*Personal Retrieval of Information by Minicomputer And Terminal Ensemble*.[5] The unusual thing about PRIMATE is that it involves a piece of hardware. Never in the entire history of *CC* have I received so many letters about an editorial. The response surpasses anything I've ever written on sex, Nobel Prizes, or motherhood.

You may recall that in talking about PRIMATE I mentioned the possibility that we could deliver your *CC* in the form of a floppy disc. That would be tantamount to

673

a shipment of test tubes or petri dishes every week. It would be very conspicuous. Your shipping department would have a package to receive each week, instead of this silly little magazine that comes in with the junk mail. Even the security guards would be happy. Who wants to investigate someone for stealing a copy of *Current Contents*? But if someone steals your floppy disc, they'll never hear the end of it.

We could start to deliver *Current Contents* in a metal or plastic box. It wouldn't be as cheap, or as convenient, as the paper version. I don't know how you would read it on the train or in the john. But I suppose some readers might sacrifice these conveniences for the status conveyed by owning a Mark IV Inforometer. Even if it were the size of a pocket calculator few people would question its value, as long as it looked scientific. If an administrator asks you, "What's it for?", you can say, "It's an information generator." If that doesn't impress him then simply say it is an ISI Inforometer. By that time he will have seen our four-color ads in all the trade journals and won't dare ask how, or if, it works.

REFERENCES

1. **Cawkell A E.** Quantifying the intangible — in what terms can information be evaluated? Paper presented at Institute of Information Scientists 1978 Annual Conference: Selling information to the organization, 13-15 April 1978, Loughborough, England.
2. **Garfield E.** Is the *SCI* a Rolls Royce in your budget? *Current Contents* (30):5-7, 28 July 1975.*
3. --------------. Are information services worth the money? *Current Contents* (34):5-12, 25 August 1975.*
4. **Cawkell A E & Garfield E.** The cost-effectiveness and cost benefits of commercial information services. *Current Contents* (34):5-12, 25 August 1975.*
5. **Garfield E.** Introducing PRIMATE — *P*ersonal *R*etrieval of *I*nformation by *M*icrocomputer *A*nd *T*erminal *E*nsemble. *Current Contents* (29):5-9, 17 July 1978.

*Reprinted in: **Garfield E.** *Essays of an information scientist.* Philadelphia: ISI Press, 1977, 2 vols.

Current Comments

The 100 Most-Cited *SSCI* Authors. 2. A Catalog of Their Awards and Academy Memberships.

Number 45   November 6, 1978

Following up on our recent study of most-cited social scientists, I want to catalog the awards and other forms of recognition these authors have received.[1] In this way, we can once again illustrate the impact made by *most* highly-cited authors as reflected in positive peer judgments.

I have already discussed in some detail how the individuals listed became eligible.[2] Out of the thousands cited, these 100 authors were cited 1500 or more times, 1969-1977. The data were extracted from the *Social Sciences Citation Index™ (SSCI ™)* for that period. It is quite possible that some of these authors, especially in experimental psychology and statistics, might have even higher counts were we to include data from the *Science Citation Index®* .

In Figure 1 the authors are listed by discipline. Psychology has been further sub-divided into well-known specialties because of its size. Next to each name we have indicated the number of citations the author received, memberships in national academies, and awards or prizes, if any.

To gather the data, we examined several biographical directories. *Who's Who in America, World Who's Who in Science,* and *American Men and Women of Science* were our primary sources. Unfortunately, the most recent editions of these last two directories are somewhat out of date. So we wrote to all the living authors, most of whom sent a current list of their awards.

Since we were interested in listing only honors received for research in the social sciences, we deleted all those given for other achievements such as public service awards. In fact, we limited this analysis to 14 national or other significant awards. These awards are sufficient to provide a good *indication* of the recognition these authors have received. A key which follows Figure 1 gives the full name of the award, the organization that presents it, and its purpose.

In our recent study of most-cited authors in the "hard" sciences, we showed that most of those authors had received significant awards or prizes.[2] The social sciences, however, are relatively young. There are fewer prestigious awards given to social scientists than to researchers in the "hard" sciences. Furthermore, most social sciences

Figure 1: The most-cited *SSCI* ® authors, 1969-1977, listed with their total citations, 1969-1977, honorific academy memberships, awards and honors. A key to the full names of academies and awards follows the figure. The honors shown do not represent a complete list of awards won by each author. They are meant to give an indication of the recognition these authors have received.

Name	Total Citations 1969-1977	National Academies	Awards

PSYCHOLOGY

Social Psychology & Motivation Theory

Name	Total Citations 1969-1977	National Academies	Awards
Bandura A	5,050		Guggenheim/72
Berkowitz L	1,992		CASBS/70-1
Brown R	2,158	Am. Acad. Arts/Sci.; NAS	Guggenheim/65; DSC/APA/71; Hall/73
Deutsch M	2,019		
Festinger L	2,888	Am. Acad. Arts/Sci.; NAS	DSC/APA/59
Jones EE	1,564		CASBS/63-4; DSC/APA/77
McClelland DC	1,960	Am. Acad. Arts/Sci.	Guggenheim/58
Rokeach M	2,370		CASBS/61-2
Rosenthal R	2,466		Guggenheim/73
Schachter S	1,703	Am. Acad. Arts/Sci.	Guggenheim/67; DSC/APA/69

Behavioral Theory (Operant & Classical)

Name	Total Citations 1969-1977	National Academies	Awards
Anderson NH	2,139		
Berlyne DE	2,186		CASBS/56-7
Broadbent DE	1,810	NAS; RS/London	DSC/APA/75
Eysenck HJ	5,370		
Posner MI	1,523		
Skinner BF	3,672	Am. Acad. Arts/Sci.; Am. Phil. Soc.; NAS	Guggenheim/42, DSC/APA/58; NIH/68; NMS/68
Underwood BJ	2,156	NAS	Warren/64; DSC/APA/73
Wolpe J	2,617		CASBS/56-7

Cognitive Psychology

Name	Total Citations 1969-1977	National Academies	Awards
Bruner JS	2,692	Am. Acad. Arts/Sci.; NA Educ.	Guggenheim/55; DSC/APA/62
Miller GA	2,843	Am. Acad. Arts/Sci.; Am. Phil. Soc.; NAS	CASBS/58-9; DSC/APA/63
Neisser U	1,594	Am. Acad. Arts/Sci.	CASBS/73-4
Osgood CE	3,412	Am. Acad. Arts/Sci.; NAS	Guggenheim/55, 72; DSC/APA/60; CASBS/65
Paivio A	2,363	Canada	
Postman L	1,523	NAS	
Tulving E	2,018		CASBS/72-3

Developmental & Child Psychology

Name	Total Citations 1969-1977	National Academies	Awards
Bowlby J	1,602		Hall/74
Erikson EH	2,566	Am. Acad. Arts/Sci.; NA Educ.	

676

PSYCHOLOGY (continued)

Developmental & Child Psychology (continued)

Freud A	1,864	Am. Acad. Arts/Sci.; NA Educ.	
Kagan J	2,444	Am. Acad. Arts/Sci.	
Kohlberg L	1,924		CASBS/61-2
Piaget J	7,572	Am. Acad. Arts/Sci.; Belgium; NA Educ.; NAS	DSC/APA/69
Rutter M	1,821	RS/Med (London)	

Personality

Allport GW	1,766		DSC/APA/64
Byrne D	2,614		
Cattell RB	4,282		
Maslow AH	1,954		
Mischel W	1,759		
Rogers CR	2,128	Am. Acad. Arts/Sci.	DSC/APA/56

Clinical Psychology

Carkhuff RR	1,563		
Cohen J	2,184	Am. Acad. Arts/Sci.	
Gough HG	1,642		Guggenheim/65
Lewin K	1,793		
Rotter JB	2,615		

Educational Psychology

Cronbach LJ	2,748	Am. Acad. Arts/Sci.; Am. Phil. Soc.; NA Educ.; NAS	CASBS/63-4; Guggenheim/71; DSC/APA/73
Jensen AR	2,177		Guggenheim/64; CASBS/66-7
Thorndike EL	1,787	Am. Phil. Soc.; NAS	

Neuro-Psychology

Hebb DO	1,516	Am. Acad. Arts/Sci.; Canada; RS/London	Warren/58; DSC/APA/61
Miller NE	1,606	Am. Acad. Arts/Sci.; Am. Phil. Soc.; NAS	Warren/54; DSC/APA/59; NMS/64
Stevens SS	2,252	Am. Acad. Arts/Sci.; Am. Phil. Soc.; NAS	Warren/43; DSC/APA/60

Psychoanalytic Theory

Freud S	12,319	RS/London	
Jung CG	1,720	RS/Med (London)	

Figure 1 (continued)

PSYCHOLOGY (continued)

Organizational & Management Psychology

Campbell DT	3,337	Am. Acad. Arts/Sci.; NAS	CASBS/65-6; DSC/APA/70
Simon HA	2,160	Am. Acad. Arts/Sci.; Am. Phil. Soc.; NAS	DSC/APA/69; Nobel/E/78

Genetic Psychology

Witkin HA	2,147		Guggenheim/63

Mathematical Psychology

Rapoport A	1,580	Am.Acad. Arts/Sci.	CASBS/54-5

STATISTICS & PSYCHOMETRICS

Anderson TW	1,591	Am. Acad. Arts/Sci.; NAS	Guggenheim/46
Box GEP	1,832	Am. Acad. Arts/Sci.	Guy-Silver/64
Edwards AL	2,389		Guggenheim/59
Fisher RA	1,605	Am. Phil. Soc.; India; NAS; RS/London	Guy-Gold/46
Goodman LA	1,704	Am. Acad. Arts/Sci.; Am. Phil. Soc.; NAS	Guggenheim/59; Stouffer/74
Guilford JP	3,413	NAS	DSC/APA/64
Kendall MG	1,863		Guy-Silver/45; Guy-Gold/68
Rao CR	1,639	Am. Acad. Arts/Sci.; India; RS/London	Guy-Silver/65
Shepard RN	1,582	NAS	Guggenheim/71; DSC/APA/76
Siegel S	4,038		
Wechsler D	1,788		
Winer BJ	5,233		

SOCIOLOGY

Argyris C	1,674		
Becker HS	1,588		
Blalock HM	2,188	Am. Acad. Arts/Sci.; NAS	Stouffer/73
Blau PM	2,134	Am. Acad. Arts/Sci.	CASBS/62-3; Sorokin/68
Campbell A	1,808	Am. Acad. Arts/Sci.	DSC/APA/74
Coleman JS	2,963	Am. Acad. Arts/Sci.; Am. Phil. Soc.; NA Educ.; NAS	CASBS/55-6; Guggenheim/66; Stouffer/75
Duncan OD	2,238	Am. Acad. Arts/Sci.; Am. Phil. Soc.; NAS	Sorokin/68; Stouffer/74, 77
Durkheim E	2,337		
Etzioni AW	2,018	Am. Acad. Arts/Sci.	CASBS/65-6; Guggenheim/68
Goffman E	3,473	Am. Acad. Arts/Sci.	MacIver/61
Habermas J	1,542		
Hollingshead AB	1,831		MacIver/59

SOCIOLOGY (continued)

Lipset SM	2,923	Am. Acad. Arts/Sci.; NA Educ.; NAS	MacIver/62; Guggenheim/71
Merton RK	3,030	Am. Acad. Arts/Sci.; Am. Phil. Soc.; NA Educ.; NAS Sweden	Guggenheim/62; NIH/64
Parsons T	5,600	Am. Acad. Arts/Sci.; Am. Phil. Soc.	CASBS/57-8; Guggenheim/66

ECONOMICS & ECONOMETRICS

Arrow KJ	3,013	Am. Acad. Arts/Sci.; Am. Phil. Soc.; NAS	CASBS/56-7; Clark/56; Nobel/E/72; Guggenheim/72
Baumol WJ	1,744	Am. Acad. Arts/Sci.; Am. Phil. Soc.	Guggenheim/56
Friedman M	3,879	Am. Phil. Soc.; NAS	Clark/51; Nobel/E/76
Galbraith JK	1,612	Am. Acad. Arts/Sci.; Belgium	Guggenheim/55
Johnson HG	1,923	Am. Acad. Arts/Sci.; Canada	
Marx K	6,807		
Myrdal G	1,885	Am. Acad. Arts/Sci.; Hungary; Sweden	Nobel/E/74
Samuelson PA	3,431	Am. Acad. Arts/Sci.; Am. Phil. Soc.; NAS	Clark/47; Guggenheim/48; Nobel/E/70
Theil H	1,739	Am. Acad. Arts/Sci.	
Tobin J	1,569	Am. Acad. Arts/Sci.; Am. Phil. Soc.; NAS	Clark/55
Weber M	3,627		

HISTORY OF SCIENCE & PHILOSOPHY

Dewey J	2,042	Am. Phil. Soc.; NAS	
Kuhn TS	1,765	Am. Acad. Arts/Sci.	Guggenheim/54; CASBS/58-9
Popper KR	1,543	Am. Acad. Arts/Sci.; Belgium; France; New Zealand RS/London	

ANTHROPOLOGY

Lévi-Strauss C	2,270	Am. Acad. Arts/Sci.; Am. Phil. Soc.; France; NAS; Norway; Netherlands	Viking/66
Mead M	1,588	Am. Acad. Arts/Sci.; NA Educ.; NAS	Viking/57

LINGUISTICS

Chomsky N	4,584	Am. Acad. Arts/Sci.; NAS	Guggenheim/71

POLITICAL PHILOSOPHY

Lenin VI	2,219	

Key to Abbreviations in Figure 1

Academies

Memberships in national academies of sciences are indicated by country abbreviations. Exceptions:

Am.Acad.Arts/Sci. = American Academy of Arts and Sciences
NA Educ. = National Academy of Education (United States)
NAS = National Academy of Sciences (United States)
RS = Royal Society
Am. Phil. Soc. = American Philosophical Society

Awards and Prizes

CASBS	=	Center for Advanced Study in the Behavioral Sciences—provides 53 postdoctoral fellowships annually to scientists and scholars in the behavioral science fields.
Clark	=	J.B. Clark Medal—given by the American Economic Association—for an American economist under the age of 40 for significant contribution to economic thought.
DSC/APA	=	Distinguished Scientific Contribution—given by the American Psychological Association—for distinguished theoretical or empirical contributions to scientific psychology.
Guggenheim	=	Guggenheim Fellowship—given by John Simon Guggenheim Memorial Foundation—grants to foster research and provide for the cause of better international understanding.
Guy	=	Guy Medals (gold, silver and bronze)—given by the Royal Statistical Society (London)—for outstanding contributions to the field of statistics.
Hall	=	G. Stanley Hall Award—given by Division 7 of the American Psychological Association—for distinguished contributions to developmental psychology.
MacIver	=	MacIver Award—given by the American Sociological Association—for an outstanding publication in sociology. Discontinued in 1968.
NIH	=	National Institutes of Health Lectureship—granted by NIH—for recognition of outstanding scientific accomplishment.
NMS	=	National Medal of Science—given by the National Science Foundation—for recognition of outstanding contributions in the physical, biological, mathematical, and engineering sciences. Individuals are nominated by NMS Committee and then selected by the President of the US.
Nobel/E	=	Nobel Prize in Economics—given by the Nobel Foundation and presented by the Royal Swedish Academy of Sciences—for contributions to the field of economic science.
Stouffer	=	S.A. Stouffer award—given by the American Sociological Association—for a work or series of works published during the past five years, advancing the methodology of sociological research.
Sorokin	=	Sorokin Award—given by the American Sociological Association—for a publication (theoretical essay or empirical report, book, or article) during the two preceding years which makes an outstanding contribution to the progress of sociology.
Viking	=	Viking Fund Medal—given by the Wenner-Gren Foundation for Anthropological Research—for outstanding achievement in the sciences of man.
Warren	=	Howard Crosby Warren Medal—given by the Society of Experimental Psychologists—for recognition of outstanding research contributions in experimental psychology.

awards have been instituted relatively recently, while some science awards have a long history. For instance, the most prestigious award in science, the Nobel Prize, has been given for over 75 years to researchers in chemistry, physics, and medicine or physiology. Until less than ten years ago no social scientists were recognized by a Nobel Prize. However, in 1969 the committee began granting prizes in economics. Five authors on our list — G. Myrdal, M. Friedman, K.J. Arrow, P. Samuelson, and H.A. Simon — have won Nobels in economics. The Swedish Academy of Sciences announced that H.A. Simon had received the 1978 economics prize just as we were going to press. Simon, a professor of computer science and psychology at Carnegie-Mellon University (Pittsburgh), was cited "for his pioneering research into the decision-making process within economic organizations."

Even though most social sciences awards are relatively new, 65 authors on the list have received at least one. Seven authors on the list did their work in the nineteenth century or in the first three decades of this century. This was long before the inception of most social sciences awards. One could say that people like Sigmund Freud, Carl Jung, Emile Durkheim, Max Weber, Karl Marx, V. I. Lenin, and John Dewey have achieved far greater recognition than any award could bestow. How one would quantify this statement is another matter. Perhaps one ought to count the number of biographies written about them. Or should we count the number of copies of their works sold?

In the specialties of personality and clinical psychology, very few of the authors listed have won awards, or are members of academies. An informal survey of psychologists revealed a possible reason for this. One of the most-cited authors noted that the awards that are around have only been established within the last 15 years, and are given sparingly. Few awards exist for young social scientists in these fields, he added.

Sixty-three authors on the list are members of national academies. Almost half, 49, are members of the American Academy of Arts and Sciences. Founded in 1780, the Academy honors both US and non-US citizens for their accomplishments in the mathematical and physical sciences, biological sciences, social arts and sciences, and the humanities. There are currently more than 3,000 members, about 800 of them in the social sciences.

Thirty-three authors are members of the US National Academy of Sciences (NAS), which currently has 1468 members. Of these, only 139 are in the social sciences. It will be interesting to see how far we will have to extend our list to include most of the social scientists already in NAS.

Several authors on the list are members of one or more foreign academies of science. Three belong to the Royal Academy of Belgium. The national academies of Sweden and India are each represented by two members. The academies of

Hungary, the Netherlands, New Zealand, and Norway are each represented by one. Six authors are members of the Royal Society of London. Three more belong to the Royal Society of Canada. Two of those on the list, M. Rutter and C.J. Jung, are members of the UK's Royal Society of Medicine. C. Levi-Strauss is a member of the Academie Francaise; Sir Karl Popper is a corresponding member of the Institut de France.

Nine authors are members of the US National Academy of Education, founded in 1965 to parallel "in general purposes, programmes and prestige of the National Academy of Sciences." Most of the members are from the behavioral sciences, the humanities, or education. The Academy currently has 76 members.

Of those who are members of national academies, 26 belong to a single academy, 24 to two, and eight to three. J. Piaget and R. K. Merton list memberships in four national academies. K. R. Popper and C. Levi-Strauss have memberships in five. The five Nobelists in economics each belong to at least one national academy.

Although it is not, strictly speaking, a national academy, we have also included the American Philosophical Society on our list. Twenty social scientists on our list have attained membership in the Society, which was founded in 1767 by Benjamin Franklin. The Society elects outstanding contributors to the social sciences, the hard sciences, and the humanities. Membership is limited to 500 US and 100 foreign scholars. All of the authors listed who are members of the American Philosophical Society are members of at least one national academy. Fifteen are members of two academies.

Seventy-nine authors on the list have been recognized with either academy memberships or prizes. It is interesting that a little over 20% of the high-impact authors on our list have not been formally recognized.

In similar compilations we have usually indicated each author's most-cited publication. However, the most-cited works for 66 of the authors appeared recently on the lists of most-cited social science books and articles.[3,4] So we have simply provided in Figure 2, which follows this essay, a list of the most-cited publications for authors not represented on these lists.

The publications in Figure 2 were highly-cited, but not enough to qualify among the most-cited books or articles. Thus, the authors involved amassed large numbers of citations for several works.

Of particular interest is the most-cited publication of V. I. Lenin. Lenin's works have been published in many editions and languages and are thus cited under different titles. Unifying English, Russian, and German citations to the same work was therefore a time-consuming problem. We finally determined that volume 29 of his complete works, containing speeches, essays, and reports, March to August 1919, was his single most-cited publication. This volume was probably most-cited because it covers the period immediately following Lenin's founding of the Third International. The volume includes several essays on the Third International as well as reports and speeches given at the Eighth Congress of the Russian Communist Party and Lenin's lecture on "The State" which delineates the Marxist-Leninist doctrines of the origin and nature of the state.

This essay concludes our first series of studies based on the *SSCI* data base. As I have said before, we hope to publish additional studies of the individual disciplines within the social sciences. We also plan to produce lists that take into account secondary authorships. While multiple authorship is generally not as significant in the social sciences as in the hard sciences, there are some specialties where it may be important.

To obtain the names of co-authors we would have to search our *SSCI Source Index* tapes which contain the names of all authors of articles indexed by the *SSCI*. We would use these tapes in combination with citation data tapes to compile "all-author" counts for the source articles indexed by *SSCI* from 1969 to 1977.

These new data would differ in several ways from the data we have already presented. They would give citation counts for only those authors who published since 1969 in journals covered by *SSCI*. Since monographs are extremely important in the social sciences, a study based only on citations to journal articles would produce results vastly different from those of the current study. And by limiting the study's chronological scope to articles published after 1968 we would eliminate a large number of classical authors. On the other hand, an "all-author" study would recognize the work of contemporary contributors to the social sciences.

REFERENCES

1. **Garfield E.** The 100 most cited *SSCI* authors, 1969-1977. 1. How the names were selected. *Current Contents* (38):5-11, 18 September 1978.
2. ------------. The 300 most-cited authors, 1961-1976 including co-authors. 2. The relationship between citedness, awards and academy memberships. *Current Contents* (35):5-30, 28 August 1978.
3. ------------. The 100 articles most cited by social scientists, 1969-1977. *Current Contents* (32):5-14, 7 August 1978.
4. ------------. The 100 books most cited by social scientists, 1969-1977. *Current Contents* (37):5-16, 11 September 1978.

Figure 2: The most-cited publications of those most-cited authors who did not have a publication on the most-cited books or articles list. Bibliographic data are for current editions of books. Dates in parentheses are the years of first publication.

Total Citations	Bibliographic Data

397 **Allport G W.** *The nature of prejudice.*
Cambridge, MA: Addison-Wesley, 1954. 537 p.

249 **Argyris C.** *Integrating the individual and the organization.*
New York: Wiley, 1964. 330 p.

176 **Baumol W J.** *Business behavior: value and growth.*
New York: Harcourt, Brace & World, 1967 (1959). 159 p.

258 **Berkowitz L.** *Aggression: a social psychological analysis.*
New York: McGraw Hill, 1962. 361 p.

394 **Box G E P** & Jenkins G M. *Time series analysis, forecasting and control.*
San Francisco: Holden-Day, 1976 (1970). 575 p.

336 **Cattell R B,** Eber H W & Tatsuoka M M. *Handbook for the sixteen personality factor questionnaire (16PF) in clinical, educational, industrial, and research psychology, for use with all forms of the test.*
Champaign, IL: Institute for Personality and Ability Testing, 1970. 388 p.

132 **Deutsch M** & Gerard H B. A study of normative and informational social influences upon individual judgment.
J. Abnorm. Psychol. 51:629-36, 1955.

247 **Dewey J.** *Democracy and education: an introduction to the philosophy of education.* New York: Free Press, 1966 (1916). 378 p.

389 **Durkheim E.** *Suicide: a study in sociology. (Le Suicide.)*
New York: Free Press, 1951 (1897). 405 p.

354 **Etzioni A W.** *A comparative analysis of complex organizations, on power, involvements, and their correlates.*
New York: Free Press, 1975 (1961). 366 p.

354 **Eysenck H J** & Eysenck S B G. *Manual of the Eysenck personality inventory.* London: University of London Press, 1964. 24 p.

288 **Fisher R A.** *Statistical methods for research workers.*
New York: Hafner, 1973 (1925). 362 p.

384 **Freud A.** *The ego and the mechanisms of defense.*
New York: International University Press, 1967 (1937). 191 p.

297 **Friedman M.** *A theory of the consumption function.*
New York: National Bureau of Economic Research, 1957. 243 p.
Princeton University Press.

310 **Gough H G.** (California University. Institute of Personality Assessment and Research.) *Adjective check list analyses of a number of selected psychometric and assessment variables.* Maxwell A F B, AL: Officer Education Research Laboratory, Air Force Personnel and Training Research Center, Air Force Personnel and Development Command, 1955. 95 p.

247 **Habermas J.** *Knowledge and human interests. (Erkenntnis und Interresse.)* Boston: Beacon Press, 1971 (1968). 356 p.

119 **Johnson H G.** *International trade and economic growth: studies in pure theory.* Cambridge: Harvard University Press, 1958. 204 p.

241 **Jones E E** & Davis K E. From acts to dispositions. The attribution process in person perception. *Adv. Exp. Soc. Psychol.* 2:219-66, 1965.

145 **Jung C G.** *Psychological types (Psycholigische Typen.)*
Princeton: Princeton University Press, 1976 (1921). 617 p.

212 **Kagan J** & Moss H A. *Birth to maturity: a study in psychological development.* New York: Wiley, 1962. 381 p.

Figure 2 (continued)

Total Citations	Bibliographic Data
310	**Kohlberg L.** Stage and sequence: the cognitive-developmental approach to socialization. (Goslin D A, ed.) *Handbook of socialization theory and research.* Chicago: Rand McNally, 1969, p. 347-480.
109	**Lenin V I.** *Polnoe Sobranie Sochinenii (Complete works).* Vol. 29 (March 1919 - August 1919). Moscow: Progress Publishers, 1974 (1941). 599 p.
322	**Levi-Strauss C.** *Structural anthropology (Anthropologie structurale.)* New York: Basic Books, 1963 (1958). 410 p.
299	**Lewin K.** *Field theory in social science; selected thematical papers.* Westport: Greenwood, 1975 (1951). 346 p.
129	**Mead M.** *Culture and commitment.* New York: Natural History, 1970. 91 p.
103	**Postman L,** Stark K & Fraser J. Temporal changes in interference. *J. Verb. Learn. Verb. Behav.* 7:672-94, 1968.
151	**Posner M I** & Mitchell R F. Chronometric analysis of classification. *Psychol. Rev.* 74:392-409, 1967.
163	**Rapoport A** & Chammah A M. *Prisoner's dilemma, a study in conflict and cooperation.* Ann Arbor: University of Michigan Press, 1965. 258 p.
400	**Rogers C R.** *Client centered therapy.* Boston, MA: Houghton Mifflin, 1951. 560 p.
209	**Rutter M.** *Education, health and behaviour: psychological and medical study of childhood development.* New York: Wiley, 1970. 474 p.
432	**Simon H A.** *Administrative behavior: a study of decision making processes in administrative organization.* New York: Free Press, 1976 (1945). 259 p.
342	**Theil H.** *Principles of econometrics.* New York: Wiley, 1971. 736 p.
153	**Tobin J.** Liquidity preference as behavior towards risk. *Rev. Econ. Stud.* 25:65-86, 1958.
410	**Underwood B J** & Schulz R W. *Meaningfulness and verbal learning.* Chicago: Lippincott, 1960. 430 p.

Current Comments

**Beverly Bartolomeo
and 20 Years of *Current Contents***

Number 46   November 13, 1978

In July 1958, I placed an ad for a secretary in the Philadelphia newspapers. It was time for Eugene Garfield Associates, as ISI® was then called, to hire its first full-time employee. I had just started publishing a current awareness service under the title *Current Contents® /Pharmaco-Medical & Life Sciences.* I was also working under contract to Bell Laboratories to produce a service called *Survey of Current Management Literature,* the precursor of *Current Contents/Social & Behavioral Sciences.*[1] My office was located in a broken-down tenement at 1523 Spring Garden Street in Philadelphia. That location had been selected because it was across the street from Smith, Kline and French Labs, where I still worked part-time as a consultant in pharmaceutical documentation.

In answer to my ad, the Pennsylvania State Employment Agency sent Beverly Bartolomeo, a young woman just out of high school, whom I interviewed and hired immediately. Beverly and I just celebrated our 20th anniversary together. We had dinner at a quiet and elegant French restaurant and reminisced about the old days.

Beverly, who is now Director of *Current Contents,* has a very good memory of those early days — much better than mine.

I can imagine what Beverly's first impression must have been as she and her father arrived at that shabby looking building with its freshly painted red door. Beverly remembers that her father had arranged to drop her off for the interview on his way to work that day. But when he pulled up in front of the three-story ghetto building, he decided to wait for her. Beverly, however, was intrepid. She had been advised by a high school teacher to look for a job with a new company with potential so she could grow with that company. ISI was indeed a new company, but perhaps a little newer than her teacher had in mind.

In those first few years Beverly did a little of everything. She logged in the journals, pasted up the contents pages, and performed secretarial and bookkeeping duties. Since there was no maintenance crew, Beverly's job also included sweeping the floor and cleaning the bathroom.

In time I needed someone to perform secretarial duties full-time. Before I hired another employee I gave Beverly the choice: become my full-time secretary or continue to work on *Current Contents*. Of course she chose the latter and has remained effectively *CC®'s* managing editor.[2]

Beverly has reminded me that when I interviewed applicants for secretarial jobs in those days, I used real correspondence. When letters were typed, I wrote in corrections and sent them out. You could get quite a few letters out that way, even if they weren't perfect. In fact, I found most people appreciated a letter that had the personal touch of handwritten corrections.

In those early days Beverly had to overcome the obstacles of out-of-date office equipment, poor facilities, and inadequate help. We had not yet discovered the straight-edge, so Beverly "eyeballed" the contents pages she had pasted up. Since we had no camera or photocopy machine, she had to give elaborate instructions to the printer. This was especially the case for journals that had the text of their tables of contents on both sides of the cover or used odd color combinations. When the issue was ready, the printer would deliver the "blueline" proof to her apartment at 10 p.m. Then she could make sure he had followed her instructions correctly.

Back at the office we contended with such "amenities" as an unreliable furnace. When it occasionally broke down, we sat around in sweaters and mufflers. Sometimes it actually got too cold to work.

Beverly Bartolomeo

Beverly and I share a common cultural heritage: her father is Italian and her mother, Jewish. I don't remember if I discovered this during her employment interview, but it probably accounts for a special comprehension of each other we shared almost immediately.

As my close co-worker for many years, Beverly has naturally been exposed to some of my family problems. One day in 1960, Beverly, my brother Ralph (who was then working at ISI), and I were all working late. So we decided to take Beverly out to a late dinner. At the same time, I was very upset because my son Stefan had not shown up at school that day. It was not the first time he played hooky. Since no one could find him, I contemplated calling the police. Bev and Ralph convinced me to wait. When we walked to my car, we found Stefan hiding in the back seat. Being the strict disciplinarian that I am, I took him along to the restaurant.

Beverly giggled all night as I kept reminding Stefan that the dinner was a treat for *Beverly* and not meant to reward *him* for his disruptive and outrageous behavior.

As ISI grew, Beverly's career blossomed. As we added new products and services, Beverly was charged with the responsibility of managing many of them. For example, when we began our *Original Article Tear Sheet (OATS®)* service, it was under her direction. That service is now handled by an entire department. Journal acquisition, one of Beverly's initial jobs when she joined the company, is also now handled by an entire department.

Inevitably Beverly became a supervisor. First we needed one additional paste-up artist, then two and now ten. Beverly later rose to manager. Now she is the director of *Current Contents* with 28 people reporting to her. She is ultimately responsible for all six — seven in 1979 — editions of *Current Contents*. She also coordinates the activities of her department with those of the computer, data entry, and other departments of the company. While the computer is very important at ISI, it takes people like Beverly to make sure it is used effectively.

As part of her job, Beverly must judge which journals use space efficiently and if or how they should be photocomposed rather than photographed. She maintains excellent and important relations with our printer. The production of *CC* involves an amazing amount of detail.[3] It is performed under constant pressure of weekly and daily deadlines. There are of course separate but integrated deadlines for the weekly subject indexes, the address directories, Press Digest, and other *CC* features.

In many ways Beverly's professional development parallels the development of the company over the past 20 years. As the company grew, the complexities of management also increased. Beverly was able to do much better than merely cope. She provided effective management and guidance to others. I like to think that her success is an important "role model" for other ISI employees. When I consider how much Beverly Bartolomeo has changed, I can only look forward to the next twenty years with the greatest sense of exciting anticipation. Happy anniversary, Beverly!

REFERENCES

1. **Lazerow S.** Institute for Scientific Information. In: *Encyclopedia of library and information science.* (A. Kent et al. eds) New York: Marcel Dekker, 1974 Vol. 12 p. 89-97.*
2. **Garfield E.** *Current Contents* — ninth anniversary. *Current Contents* (8):4-8, 21 February 1967.*
3. ------------. In recognition of journals which prove that change is possible. *Current Contents* (19):5-10, 8 May 1978.

*Reprinted in: **Garfield E.** *Essays of an information scientist.* Philadelphia: ISI Press, 1977. 2 vols.

Current Comments

The 300 Most-Cited Authors, 1961-1976,
Including Co-Authors. 3A.
Their Most- Cited Papers — Introduction
and Journal Analysis

Number 47   November 20, 1978

In earlier essays on the 300 most-cited authors we explained how the names were selected.[1] We also showed the relationship between citedness, awards, and academy memberships.[2] In this and the next two editorials, we will list the authors' most-cited publications. Approximately 100 articles will be listed in each essay.

In earlier portions of this study we arranged authors' names by their disciplines. However, we soon realized that it would be absurd to list publications by the authors' disciplines. Many of the authors work on interdisciplinary research. Thus, publications are often in fields other than those indicated by the authors' disciplines. For example, the author may be a biochemist, but his or her most-cited paper could be in physiology, endocrinology, etc. Consequently, we have categorized the papers by subject matter rather than the authors' discipline.

Categorizing papers in this way may be quite arbitrary, too. For instance, G. Klein's article on tumor antigens could be categorized under oncology or immunology. In cases like this, we used the journal in which the article was published

and/or the author's organization to make a judgment. Nevertheless, some authors may feel that their papers have been misclassified.

The group of papers presented this week cover the fields of biochemistry, endocrinology, pharmacology, and physiology.

For each discipline, the papers are listed alphabetically by the most-cited author whose name is shown in bold face. Following the bibliographic data for each article is the affiliation of the author at the time the paper was published. Some of the papers on the list have been described in the *Citation Classics* section of *Current Contents®*. This is noted below the affiliation.

As we were compiling this list we discovered that several pairs of authors shared the same most-cited publication. In these cases, we have shown for the second author his or her second most-cited publication. A "see" cross-reference directs the reader to the most-cited article.

In this first portion of the list, the following authors shared the same most-cited publication: D. S. Fredrickson and R. S. Lees, O.H. Lowry and J. V. Passoneau, C. N. Hales and P. J. Randle, A. Sjoerdsma and S. Udenfriend, F. C. Greenwood

Figure 1: Part 1 of the list of the 300 most-cited authors' most-cited publications, 1961-1976. Publications are listed by discipline, then alphabetically by most-cited author in bold-face type. Authors' affiliations at the time the papers were written are included in parentheses.

Total
Citations
1961-1976   Bibliographic Data

BIOCHEMISTRY

495 **Allfrey V G**, Littau V C & Mirsky A E. On the role of histones in regulating ribonucleic acid synthesis in the cell nucleus.
Proc. Nat. Acad. Sci. US. 49:414-21, 1963.
(Rockefeller Inst. (University), New York, NY 10021)

3,024 Martin R G & **Ames B N.** A method of determining the sedimentation behavior of enzymes: application to protein mixtures.
J. Biol. Chem. 236:1372-9, 1961. (NIH, NIAMDD, Bethesda, MD 20014)

2,321 **Andrews P.** Estimation of the molecular weights of proteins by sephadex gel-filtration. *Biochem. J.* 91:222-33, 1964.
(Nat. Inst. Res. Dairying, Shinfield, Reading RG2 9AT, Berkshire, England)

576 Cuatrecasas P, Wilchek M & **Anfinsen C B.** Selective enzyme purification by affinity chromatography.
Proc. Nat. Acad. Sci. US. 61:636-43, 1968.
(NIH, NIAMDD, Lab. Chem. Biol. Bethesda, MD 20014)

336 Matsuo H, Baba Y, Nair R M G, **Arimura A** & Schally A V. Structure of the porcine LH- and FSH-releasing hormone. I. The proposed amino acid sequence. *Biochem. Biophys. Res. Commun.* 43:1334-9, 1971.
(VA Hospital, New Orleans, LA 70118)

187 Steele W J, Okamura N & **Busch H.** Effects of thioacetamide on the composition and biosynthesis of nucleolar and nuclear ribonucleic acid in rat liver. *J. Biol. Chem.* 240:1742-9, 1965.
(Baylor Univ. Coll. Med., Dept. Pharmacol., Houston, TX 77025)

942 **Cleland W W.** The kinetics of enzyme-catalyzed reactions with two or more substrates or products. 1. Nomenclature and rate equations.
Biochim. Biophys. Acta 67:104-37, 1963.
(Univ. Wisconsin, Coll. Agriculture, Madison, WI 53706)
[Citation Classic. *Current Contents* (28):8, 11 July 1977.]

923 **Cuatrecasas P.** Protein purification by affinity chromatography. Derivations of agarose and polyacrylamide beads. *J. Biol. Chem.* 245:3059-65, 1970.
(NIH, NIAMDD, Lab. Chem. Biol., Bethesda, MD 20014)

259 Blunt J W, **DeLuca H F** & Schnoes H K. 25-hydroxycholecalciferol. A biologically active metabolite of vitamin D_3.
Biochemistry USA 7:3317-22, 1968. (Univ. Wisconsin, Dept. Biochem., Madison, WI 53706)

1,042 Marmur J & **Doty P.** Determination of the base composition of deoxyribonucleic acid from its thermal denaturation temperature.
J. Mol. Biol. 5:109-18, 1962. (Harvard Univ., Dept. Chem., Cambridge, MA 02138)

415 **Edelman G M** & Poulik M D. Studies on structural units of the γ -globulins.
J. Exp. Med. 113:861-84, 1961. (Rockefeller Inst. (University) New York, NY 10021)

433 Greenfield N & **Fasman G D.** Computed circular dichroism spectra for the evaluation of protein conformation.
Biochemistry USA 8:4108-26, 1969.
(Brandeis Univ., Grad. Dept. Biochem., Waltham, MA 02154)

278 **Green D E** & Fleischer S. The role of lipids in mitochondrial electron transfer and oxidative phosphorylation.
Biochim. Biophys. Acta 70:554-82, 1963.
(Univ. Wisconsin, Inst. Enzyme Res., Madison, WI 53706)

387 Kuo J F & **Greengard P.** Cyclic nucleotide-dependent protein kinases. 4. Widespread occurrence of adenosine 3', 5'-monophosphate-dependent protein kinase in various tissues and phyla of the animal kingdom. *Proc. Nat. Acad. Sci. US.* 64:1349-55, 1969.
(Yale Univ. Sch. Med., Dept. Pharmacol., New Haven, CT 06510)

1,667 **Hales C N** & Randle P J. Immunoassay of insulin with insulin-antibody precipitate. *Biochem. J.* 88:137-46, 1963.
(Univ. Cambridge, Dept. Biochem., Cambridge CB2 2QR, England)

312 Spencer N, Hopkinson D A & **Harris H.** Phosphoglucomutase polymorphism in man. *Nature* 204:742-5, 1964.
(Dept. Biochem., King's College, London W.C.2, England)

239 Hartmann K U & **Heidelberger C.** Studies on fluorinated pyrimidines. 13. Inhibition of thymidylate synthetase. *J. Biol. Chem.* 236:3006-13, 1961.
(Univ. of Wisconsin, Med School, McArdle Mem. Lab., Madison, WI 53706)

173 Avigad G, Amaral D, Asensio C & **Horecker B L.** The d-galactose oxidase of *polyporus circinatus. J. Biol. Chem.* 237:2736-43, 1962.
(New York Univ. Sch. Med., New York, NY 10016)

737 Cahn R D, **Kaplan N O,** Levine L & Zwilling E. Nature and development of lactic dehydrogenases. *Science* 136:962-9, 1962.
(Brandeis Univ., Grad. Dept. Biochem., Waltham, MA 02154)

324 Steiner A L, **Kipnis D M,** Utiger R & Parker C. Radioimmunoassay for the measurement of adenosine 3',5'-cyclic phosphate. *Proc. Nat. Acad. Sci. U.S.* 64:367-73, 1969.
(Washington Univ. Sch. Med., Metabolism Div. St. Louis, MO 63110)

390 Josse J, Kaiser A D & **Kornberg A.** Enzymatic synthesis of deoxyribonucleic acid. 8. Frequencies of nearest neighbor base sequences in deoxyribonucleic acid. *J. Biol. Chem.* 236:864-75, 1961.
(Stanford Univ. Sch. Med., Dept. Biochem., Palo Alto, CA 94305)

612 **Koshland D E,** Nemethy G & Filmer D. Comparison of experimental binding data and theoretical models in proteins containing subunits. *Biochemistry USA* 5:365-87, 1966.
(Brookhaven Nat. Laboratory, Biol. Dept., Upton, NY. 11973)

458 Walsh D A, Perkins J P & **Krebs E G.** An adenosine 3', 5'-monophosphate-dependant protein kinase from rabbit skeletal muscle. *J. Biol. Chem.* 243:3763-5, 1968. (Univ. Washington, Dept. Biochem., Seattle, WA 98195)

440 Williamson D H, Mellanby J & **Krebs H A.** Enzymic determination of d(—)- β -hydroxybutryric acid and acetoacetic acid in blood. *Biochem. J.* 82:90-6, 1962.
(Univ. Oxford, Med. Res. Council Unit, Dept. Biochem., Oxford, England)

263 Shrago E, **Lardy H A,** Nordlie R C & Foster D O. Metabolic and hormonal control of phosphoenolpyruvate carboxykinase and malic enzyme in rat liver. *J. Biol. Chem.* 238:3188-92, 1963.
(Univ. Wisconsin, Inst. Enzyme Res., Madison, WI 53706)

471 **Lees R S** & Hatch F T. Sharper separation of lipoprotein species by paper electrophoresis in albumin-containing buffer. *J. Lab. Clin. Med.* 61:518-28, 1963.
(Mass. Gen. Hosp. Med. Services, Arteriosclerosis Unit, Boston, MA 02114)
(See Fredrickson D S in Physiology)

199 Brown J J, Davies D L, **Lever A F,** Robertson J I S & Tree M. The estimation of renin in human plasma. *Biochem. J.* 93:594-600, 1964.
(St. Mary's Hospital, Med. Unit, London W.C. 2, England) (See Brown J J in Physiology)

105 **Li C H,** Liu W K & Dixon J S. Human pituitary growth hormone. 12. The amino acid sequence of the hormone. *J. Amer. Chem. Soc.* 88:2050-1, 1966.
(Univ. California, Hormone Res. Lab., Berkeley, CA 94720)

Figure 1 (continued)
BIOCHEMISTRY (continued)

489 Nathans D & **Lipmann F.** Amino acid transfer from aminoacyl-ribonucleic acids to proteins on ribosomes of *Escherichia coli.* *Proc. Nat. Acad. Sci. US.* 47:497-504, 1961.
(Rockefeller Inst. (University), New York, NY 10021)

1,041 **Lowry O H,** Passonneau J V, Hasselberger F X & Schultz D W. Effect of ischemia on known substrates and cofactors of the glycolytic pathway in brain. *J. Biol. Chem.* 239:18-30, 1964.
(Washington Univ. Sch. Med., Dept. Pharmacol., St. Louis, MO 63110)

2,142 Shapiro A L, Vinuela E & **Maizel J V.** Molecular weight estimation of poly-peptide chains by electrophoresis in SDS-polyacrylamide gels. *Biochem. Biophys. Res. Commun.* 28:815-26, 1967.
(Albert Einstein Coll. Med., Dept. Cell Biol., Bronx, NY 10461)

105 Chambon P, Weill J D, Dolly J, Strosser M T & **Mandel P.** On the formation of a novel adenylic compound by enzymatic extracts of liver nuclei. *Biochem. Biophys. Res. Commun.* 25:638-43, 1966.
(CNRS, Centre de Neurochimie, Strasbourg, France)

1,297 **Moore S.** On the determination of cystine as cysteic acid.
J. Biol. Chem. 238:235-7, 1963. (Rockefeller Inst. (University), New York, NY 10021)

653 Fleck A & **Munro H N.** The precision of ultraviolet absorbtion measurements in the Schmidt-Thannhauser Procedure for nucleic acid estimation. *Biochim. Biophys. Acta* 55:571-83, 1962.
(Univ. Glasgow, Dept. Biochem., Glasgow, Scotland)

211 Stanley W M, Salas M, Wahba A J & **Ochoa S.** Translation of the genetic message: factors involved in the initiation of protein synthesis. *Proc. Nat. Acad. Sci. US.* 56:290-5, 1966.
(New York Univ. Sch. Med., Dept. Biochem., New York, NY 10016)

379 Morgan H E, Henderson M J, Regen D M & **Park C R.** Regulation of glucose uptake in muscle. 1. The effects of insulin and anoxia on glucose transport and phosphorylation in the isolated, perfused heart of normal rats. *J. Biol. Chem.* 236:253-61, 1961.
(Vanderbilt Univ. Sch. Med., Nashville, TN 37203)

405 **Passonneau J V** & Lowry O H. Phosphofructokinase and the Pasteur effect. *Biochem. Biophys. Res. Commun.* 7:10-5, 1962.
(Washington Univ. Sch. Med., Dept. Pharmacol., St. Louis, MO 63110) (See Lowry O H)

494 **Piez K A,** Eigner E A & Lewis M S. The chromatographic separation and amino acid composition of the subunits of several collagens. *Biochemistry USA* 2:58-66, 1963.
(NIH, NIDR, Biochem. Lab., Bethesda, MD 20014)

279 Kivirikko K I, Laitinen O & **Prockop D J.** Modifications of a specific assay for hydroxyproline in urine. *Anal. Biochem.* 19:249-55, 1967.
(Univ. Penn., Depts. Med. & Biochem., Phila., PA 19104)

181 Vambutas V K & **Racker E.** Partial resolution of the enzymes catalyzing photophosphorylation. 1. Stimulation of photophosphorylation by a preparation of a latent, Ca^{++} dependent adenosine triphosphate from chloroplasts. *J. Biol. Chem.* 240:2660-7, 1965.
(Pub. Health Res. Inst., Dept. Biochem., New York, NY 10009)

568 **Randle P J,** Garland P B, Hales C N & Newsholme E A. The glucose fatty-acid cycle: its role in insulin sensitivity and the metabolic disturbances of diabetes mellitus. *Lancet* 1:785-9, 1963.
(Univ. Cambridge, Dept. Biochem., Cambridge, England) (See Hales C N)

564 Warner J R, Knopf P M & **Rich A.** A multiple ribosomal structure in protein synthesis. *Proc. Nat. Acad. Sci. US.* 49:122-9, 1963.
(MIT, Dept. Biol., Cambridge, MA 02139)
[Citation Classics. *Current Contents* (41):11, 10 October 1977.]

1,303 **Reisfeld R A,** Lewis U J & Williams D E. Disk electrophoresis of basic proteins and peptides on polyacrylamide gels. *Nature* 195:281-3, 1962.
(Merck, Sharp & Dohme Res. Lab., Rahway, NJ 07065)

846 **Robison G A,** Butcher R W & Sutherland E W. Cyclic AMP. *Annu. Rev. Biochem.* 37:149-74, 1968.
(Vanderbilt Univ., Dept. Pharmacol. & Physiol., Nashville, TN 37235)

979 **Rodbell M.** Metabolism of isolated fat cells. 1. Effects of hormones on glucose metabolism and lipolysis. *J. Biol. Chem.* 239:375-80, 1964.
(NIH, NIAMDD, Lab. Nutrit. & Endocrin., Bethesda, MD 20014)

318 **Roseman S.** The synthesis of complex carbohydrates by multiglycosyl-transferase systems and their potential function in intercellular adhesion. *Chem. Phys. Lipids* 5:270-97, 1970. (Johns Hopkins Univ., Dept. Biol., Baltimore, MD 21218)

465 Roeder R G & **Rutter W J.** Multiple forms of DNA-dependent RNA polymerase in eukaryotic organisms. *Nature* 224:234-7, 1969.
(Univ. Washington, Dept. Biochem., Seattle, WA 98105)

353 Green K & **Samuelsson B.** Prostaglandins and related factors. 19. Thin-layer chromatography of prostaglandins. *J. Lipid Res.* 5:117-37, 1964. (Karolinska Inst., Dept. Chem., 104 01, Stockholm, Sweden)

372 **Schimke R T,** Sweeney E W & Berlin C M. The roles of synthesis and degradation in the control of rat liver tryptophan pyrrolase. *J. Biol. Chem.* 240:322-31, 1965. (NIH, NIAMDD, Bethesda, MD 20014)

437 **Seegmiller J E,** Rosenbloom F M & Kelley W N. Enzyme defect associated with a sex-linked human neurological disorder and excessive purine synthesis. *Science* 155:1682-4, 1967.
(NIH, NIAMDD, Sect. Human Biochem. Genet., Bethesda, MD 20014)

288 DeLange R J, Fambrough D M, **Smith E L** & Bonner J. Calf and pea histone 4. 2. The complete amino acid sequence of calf thymus histone 4; presence of ϵ-N-acetyllysine. *J. Biol. Chem.* 224:319-34, 1969.
(UCLA Sch. Med., Dept. Biol. Chem., Los Angeles, CA 90024)

354 Fish W W, Mann K G & **Tanford C.** The estimation of polypeptide chain molecular weights by gel filtration in 6 M guanidine hydrochloride. *J. Biol. Chem.* 244:4989-94, 1969.
(Duke Univ. Med. Ctr., Dept. Biochem., Durham, NC 27706)

172 Shibko S & **Tappel A L.** Rat-kidney lysosomes: isolation and properties. *Biochem. J.* 95:731-41, 1965. (Univ. California, Dept. Food Sci. & Tech., Davis, CA 95616)

540 Nagatsu T, Levitt M & **Udenfriend S.** Tyrosine hydroxylase: the initial step in norepinephrine biosynthesis. *J. Biol. Chem.* 239:2910-7, 1964.
(NIH, NHLI, Lab. Clin. Biochem., Bethesda, MD 20014) (See Sjoerdsma A in Pharmacology)

279 Sokolovsky M, Riordan J F & **Vallee B L.** Tetranitromethane. A reagent for the nitration of tyrosyl residues in proteins. *Biochemistry USA* 5:3582-9, 1966.
(Harvard Univ. Sch. Med., Dept. Biol. Chem., Boston, MA 02115)

145 Demel R A, **Van Deenen L L M** & Pethica B A. Monolayer interactions of phospholipids and cholesterol. *Biochim. Biophys. Acta* 135:11-9, 1967.
(Rijks Univ., Organ. Chem. Lab., Utrecht, Netherlands)

1,272 Fairbanks G, Steck T L, & **Wallach D F H.** Electrophoretic analysis of the major polypeptides of the human erythrocyte membrane. *Biochemistry USA* 10:2606-17, 1971.(Mass. Gen. Hosp., Biochem Res. Lab., Boston, MA 02114)

6,097 **Weber K** & Osborn M. The reliability of molecular weight determination by dodecyl sulfate-polyacrylamide gel electrophoresis. *J. Biol. Chem.* 244:4406-12, 1969. (Harvard Univ., Biol. Labs., Cambridge, MA 02138)

372 Lovenberg W, **Weissbach H** & Udenfriend S. Aromatic L-amino acid decarboxylase. *J. Biol. Chem.* 237:89-93, 1962.
(NIH, NHLI, Lab. Clin. Biochem. & Exper. Therapeut. Branch, Bethesda, MD 20014)

Figure 1 (continued)

BIOCHEMISTRY (continued)

438   Gross E & **Witkop B**. Nonenzymatic cleavage of peptide bonds: the methionine residues in bovine pancreatic ribonuclease. *J. Biol. Chem.* 237:1856-60, 1962.
(NIH, NIAMDD, Chem. Lab., Bethesda, MD 20014)

364   **Wurtman R J** & Axelrod J. A sensitive and specific assay for the estimation of monoamine oxidase. *Biochem. Pharmacol.* 12:1439-40, 1963.
(NIH, NIMH, Lab. Clin. Sci. Bethesda, MD 20014)

ENDOCRINOLOGY

276   Chase L R & **Aurbach G D**. Renal adenyl cyclase: anatomically separate sites for parathyroid hormone and vasopressin. *Science* 159:545-7, 1968. (NIH, NIAMDD, Sect. Mineral Metabolism, Bethesda, MD 20014)

219   **Bartter F C** & Schwartz W B. The syndrome of inappropriate secretion of antidiuretic hormone. *Amer. J. Med.* 42:790-806, 1967.
(NIH, NHLI, Clin. Endocrinol. Branch, Bethesda, MD 20014)

365   Roth J, Glick S M, Yalow R S & **Berson S**. Secretion of human growth hormone. Physiologic and experimental modification. *Metabolism* 12:577-9, 1963. (VA Hospital, Radioisotope Service, New York, NY 10068) (See Roth J)

274   **Conn J W**, Cohen E L & Rovner D R. Suppression of plasma renin activity in primary aldosteronism. *J. Amer. Med. Ass.* 190:213-21, 1964.
(Univ. Michigan, Dept. Internal Med., Ann Arbor, MI 48104)

223   Takahashi Y, Kipnis D M & **Daughaday W H**. Growth hormone secretion during sleep. *J. Clin. Invest.* 47:2079-90, 1968.
(Washington Univ. Sch. Med., St. Louis, MO 63110)

2,153   **Greenwood F C,** Hunter W M & Glover J S. The preparation of ^{131}I-labelled human growth hormone of high specific radioactivity. *Biochem. J.* 89:114-23, 1963.
(Imperial Cancer Res. Fund, Div. Chem. Biochem., London W.C.2, England)
[Citation Classics, *Current Contents* (15):12, 11 Ap 1977.]

293   Brazeau P, Vale W, Burgus R, Ling N, Butcher M, Rivier J & **Guillemin R**. Hypothalamic polypeptide that inhibits the secretion of immunoreactive pituitary growth hormone. *Science* 179:77-9, 1973.
(Salk Inst. Neuroendocrin. Lab., La Jolla, CA 92037)

899   **Herbert V,** Lau K S, Gottlieb C W & Bleicher S J. Coated charcoal immunoassay of insulin. *J. Clin. Endocrinol. Metab.* 25:1375-84, 1965.
(Mt. Sinai Hospital, Dept. Hematol., New York, NY 10029)

1,582   **Hunter W M** & Greenwood F C. Preparation of iodine^{131} labelled human growth hormone of high specific activity. *Nature* 194:495-6, 1962.
(Imperial Cancer Res. Fund, Div. Chem. & Biochem., London W.C.2 England) (See Greenwood F C)

209   Schally A V, Arimura A, **Kastin A J,** Matsuo H, Baba Y, Redding T W, Nair R M G & Debeljuk L. Gonadotropin-releasing hormone: one polypeptide regulates secretion of luteinizing and follicle-stimulating hormone. *Science* 173:1036-8, 1971. (VA Hospital, New Orleans, LA 70146)

218   Gordon R D, Kuchel O, **Liddle G W** & Island D P. Role of the sympathetic nervous system in regulating renin and aldosterone production in man. *J. Clin. Invest.* 46:599-605, 1967.
(Vanderbilt Univ. Sch. Med., Dept. Med., Nashville, TN 37203)

626   Niswender G D, **Midgley A R,** Monroe S E & Reichert L E. Radioimmunoassay for rat luteinizing hormone with antiovine LH serum and ovine LH-^{131} I. *Proc. Soc. Exp. Biol. Med.* 128:807-18, 1968.
(Univ. Michigan Med. Sch., Dept. Pathol., Ann Arbor, MI 48104)

179 **McCann S M** & Porter J C. Hypothalamic pituitary stimulating and inhibiting
hormones. *Physiol. Rev.* 49:240-84, 1969.
(Univ. Texas S.W. Med. Sch., Dept. Physiol., Dallas, TX 75235)

258 Odell W D, Wilber J F & **Paul W E.** Radioimmunoassay of thyrotropin
in human serum. *J. Clin. Endocrinol. Metab.* 25:1179-95, 1965.
(NIH, NCI, Endocrinol. Branch, Bethesda, MD 20014)

249 Berson S A, Yalow R S, Aurbach G D & **Potts J T.** Immunoassay of
bovine and human parathyroid hormone.
Proc. Nat. Acad. Sci. US. 49:613-7, 1963. (NIH, NHLI, Bethesda, MD 20014)

543 **Rasmussen H.** Cell communication, calcium ion, & cyclic adenosine
monophosphate. *Science* 170:404-12, 1970.
(Univ. Penn., Sch. Med., Philadelphia, PA 19104)

463 **Roth J,** Glick S M, Yalow R S & Berson S A. Hypoglycemia:
a potent stimulus to secretion of growth hormone. *Science* 140:987-8, 1963.
(VA Hospital, Radioisotope Service, New York, NY 10068)

201 **Schally A V,** Arimura A, Baba Y, Nair R M G, Matsuo H, Redding T W,
Debeljuk L & White W F. Isolation and properties of the FSH and
LH-releasing hormone. *Biochem. Biophys. Res. Commun.* 43:393-9, 1971.
(VA Hospital, New Orleans, LA 70112) (See Arimura A in Biochemistry)

256 **Unger R H,** Aguilar-Parada E, Muller W A & Eisentraut A M. Studies of
pancreatic Alpha cell function in normal and diabetic subjects.
J. Clin. Invest. 49:837-48, 1970. (Univ. Texas S.W. Med. Sch., Dept. Int. Med., Dallas, TX 75235)

496 Bruchovsky N & **Wilson J D.** The conversion of testosterone to
5α androstan-17 β -ol-3-one by rat prostate *in vivo* and *in vitro.*
J. Biol. Chem. 243:2012-21, 1968.
(Univ. Texas S.W. Med. Sch., Dept. Int. Med., Dallas, TX 75235)

429 Glick S M, Roth J, **Yalow R S** & Berson S A. Immunoassay of human
growth hormone in plasma. *Nature* 199:784-7, 1963.
(VA Hospital, Radioisotope Service, New York NY 10068) (See Roth J)

PHARMACOLOGY

477 Whitby L G, **Axelrod J** & Weil-Malherbe H. The fate of H^3-norepinephrine
in animals. *J. Pharmacol. Exp. Ther.* 132:193-201, 1961.
(NIH, NIMH, Lab. Clin. Sci. & Neuropharmacol. Res. Center, Bethesda, MD 20014)

876 Krishna G, Weiss B & **Brodie B B.** A simple, sensitive method for the
assay of adenyl cyclase. *J. Pharmacol. Exp. Ther.* 163:379-85, 1968.
(NIH, NHLI, Lab. Chem. Pharmacol., Bethesda, MD 20014)

499 **Carlsson A** & Lindqvist M. *In-vivo* decarboxylation of α -methyl DOPA and
α-methyl metatyrosine. *Acta Physiol. Scand.* 54:87-94, 1962.
(Univ. Göteborg, Dept. Pharmacol., Fack, S-400, 33, Göteborg, Sweden)

1,749 **Conney A H.** Pharmacological implications of microsomal enzyme induction.
Pharmacol. Rev. 19:317-66, 1967.
(Burroughs Wellcome & Co., Wellcome Res. Lab., Tuckahoe, NY 10707)

243 Bloom F E, Algeri S, Groppetti A, Revuelta A & **Costa E.** Lesions of
central norepinephrine terminals with 6-OH-dopamine: biochemistry and
fine structure. *Science* 166:1284-6, 1969.
(NIH, NIMH Lab. Neuropharmacol. & Preclin. Pharmacol., Washington, DC 20032)

222 **Curtis D R** & Watkins J C. The pharmacology of amino acids related to
gamma-aminobutyric acid. *Pharmacol. Rev.* 17:347-91, 1965.
(Australian Nat. Univ., Dept. Physiol., Canberra, Australia)

257 **Eccles J C,** Schmidt R & Willis W D. Pharmacological studies on
presynaptic inhibition. *J. Physiol. London* 168:500-30, 1963.
(Australian Nat. Univ., Dept. Physiol., Canberra, Australia)

Figure 1 (continued)

PHARMACOLOGY (continued)

574 Schenkman J B, Remmer H & **Estabrook R W.** Spectral studies of drug interaction with hepatic microsomal cytochrome. *Mol. Pharmacol.* 3:113-23, 1967.
(Univ. Pennsylvania, Johnson Res. Foundation, Phila., PA 19104)

431 Andén N E, Butcher S G, Corrodi H, **Fuxe K** & Ungerstedt U. Receptor activity and turnover of dopamine and noradrenaline after neuroleptics. *Eur. J. Pharmacol.* 11:303-14, 1970.
(Karolinska Inst., Dept. Histol, 104 01 Stockholm, Sweden)   (See Anden N E in Physiology)

357 Kato R & **Gillette J R.** Effect of starvation on NADPH-dependent enzymes in liver microsomes of male and female rats. *J. Pharmacol. Exp. Ther.* 150:279-84, 1965.
(NIH, NHLI, Lab. Chem. Pharm., Bethesda, MD 20014)

514 **Glowinski J** & Iversen L L. Regional studies of catecholamines in the rat brain. 1. The disposition of (^{3}H)norepinephrine, (^{3}H)dopamine and (^{3}H)dopa in various regions of the brain. *J. Neurochem.* 13:655-9, 1966.
(NIH, NIMH, Lab. Clin. Sci., Bethesda, MD 20014)

406 Anden N E, Rubenson A, Fuxe K & **Hokfelt T.** Evidence for dopamine receptor stimulation by apomorphine. *J. Pharm. Pharmacol.* 19:627-9, 1967.
(Karolinska Inst., Dept. Histol., 104 01 Stockholm, Sweden)

330 Uretsky N J & **Iversen L L.** Effects of 6-hydroxydopamine on catecholamine containing neurones in the rat brain. *J. Neurochem.* 17:269-78, 1970.
(Univ. Cambridge, Dept. Pharmacol., Cambridge, England)   (See Glowinski J)

238 **Kopin I J.** Storage and metabolism of catecholamines: the role of monoamine oxidase. *Pharmacol. Rev.* 16:179-91, 1964.
(NIH, NIMH, Lab. Clin, Sci., Bethesda, MD 20014)

286 Buhler F R, **Laragh J H,** Baer L, Vaughan E D & Brunner H R. Propranolol inhibition of renin secretion. A specific approach to diagnosis and treatment of renin-dependent hypertensive diseases. *N. Engl. J. Med.* 287:1209-14, 1972.
(Columbia Univ. College of Physicians, Dept. Med., New York, NY 10032)

181 Yaffe S J, **Levy G,** Matsuzawa T & Baliah T. Enhancement of glucuronide-conjugating capacity in a hyperbilirubinemic infant due to apparent enzyme induction by phenobarbital. *N. Engl. J. Med.* 275:1461-71, 1966.
(State Univ. New York at Buffalo, Sch. Pharm. Amherst, NY 14260)

580 Spector S, **Sjoerdsma A** & Udenfriend S. Blockade of endogenous norepinephrine synthesis by α-methyl-tyrosine, an inhibitor of tyrosine hydroxylase. *J. Pharmacol. Exp. Ther.* 147:86-95, 1965.
(NIH, NHLI, Exp. Therapeut. & Lab. Clin. Biochem., Bethesda, MD 20014)

350 **Synder S H,** Axelrod J & Zweig M. A sensitive and specific fluorescence assay for tissue serotonin. *Biochem. Pharmacol.* 14:831-5, 1965.
(NIH, NIMH, Lab. Clin. Sci., Bethesda, MD 20014)

975 **Vane J R.** Inhibition of prostaglandin synthesis as a mechanism of action for aspirin-like drugs. *Nature N. Biol.* 231:232-5, 1971.
(Royal Coll. Surgeons, Dept. Pharmacol., Lincoln's Inn Fields, London W.C.2 England)

PHYSIOLOGY

499 **Andén N E,** Dahlström A, Fuxe K, Larsson L, Olson L & Ungerstedt U. Ascending monoamine neurons to the telencephalon and diencephalon. *Acta Physiol. Scand.* 67:313-26, 1966.
(Univ. Göteborg, Dept. Pharm., Fack, S-400, 33, Göteborg, Sweden)

261 **Brown J J,** Davies D L, Lever A F & Robertson J I S. Variations in plasma renin concentration in several physiological and pathological states. *Can. Med. Ass. J.* 90:201-6, 1964.
(St. Mary's Hospital, Med. Unit, London W.C. 2, England)

1,280 **Butcher R W** & Sutherland E W. Adenosine 3', 5'-phosphate in biological materials. 1. Purification and properties of cyclic 3', 5'-nucleotide phosphodiesterase and use of this enzyme to characterize adenosine 3', 5'-phosphate in human urine. *J. Biol. Chem.* 237:1244-50, 1962.
(Case Western Reserve Univ., Sch. Med., Dept. Pharm., Cleveland, OH 44106)

480 Bergström S, **Carlson L A** & Weeks J R. The prostaglandins: a family of biologically active lipids. *Pharmacol. Rev.* 20:1-48, 1968.
(Karolinska Hospital, King Gustav Res. Inst., Dept. Int. Med., Stockholm, Sweden)

1,014 **deDuve C** & Wattiaux R. Functions of lysosomes. *Annu. Rev. Physiol.* 28:435-92, 1966. (Rockefeller Univ., New York, NY 10021)

894 **Frederickson D S,** Levy R I & Lees R S. Fat transport in lipoproteins—an integrated approach to mechanism and disorders. *N. Engl. J. Med.* 276:148-56, 1967. (NIH, NHLI, Lab. Mol. Dis., Bethesda, MD 20014)
[Citation Classics. *Current Contents* (3):11, 16 January 1978]

617 **Haber E,** Koerner T, Page L B, Kliman B & Purnode A. Application of a radioimmunoassay for angiotensin I to the physiologic measurements of plasma renin activity in normal human subjects. *J. Clin. Endocrinol. Metab.* 29:1349-55, 1969.
(Mass. Gen. Hosp., Cardiac Unit, Boston, MA 02114)

1,051 **Hubel D H** & Wiesel T N. Receptive fields, binocular interaction and functional architecture in the cat's visual cortex. *J. Physiol. London* 160:106-54. 1962. (Harvard Med. Sch., Dept. Pharm., Boston, MA 02115)

276 **Lassen N A,** Lindbjerg J & Munck O. Measurement of blood-flow through skeletal muscle by intramuscular injection of Xenon-133. *Lancet* 1:686-9, 1964. (Bispebjerg Hospital, Dept. Clin. Physiol., DK-2400, Copenhagen, Denmark)

438 **Lehninger A L.** Water uptake and extrusion by mitochondria in relation to oxidative phosphorylation. *Physiol. Rev.* 42:467-517, 1962.
(Johns Hopkins Univ. Sch. Med., Dept. Physiol. Chem., Baltimore, MD 21205)

244 **Meites J** & Nicoll C S. Adenohypophysis: prolactin. *Annu. Rev. Physiol.* 28:57-88, 1966. (Michigan State Univ., Dept. Physiol., E. Lansing, MI 48823)

350 **Odell W D,** Ross G T & Rayford P L. Radioimmunoassay for luteinizing hormone in human plasma or serum: physiological studies. *J. Clin. Invest.* 46:248-55, 1967.
(NIH, NICHHD, Endocrinol. & Metabolism Branch, Bethesda, MD 20014)

312 Pickens P T, Bumpus F M, Lloyd A M, Smeby R R & **Page I H.** Measurement of renin activity in human plasma. *Circ. Res.* 17:438-48, 1965.
(Cleveland Clin. Found., Res. Div., Cleveland, OH 44106)

124 Lever A F, **Robertson J I S,** Tree M. The estimation of renin in plasma by an enzyme kinetic technique. *Biochem. J.* 91:346-52, 1964.
(St. Mary's Hospital, Med. Unit, London W.C.2, England) (See Brown J J)

665 **Sutherland E W,** Robison G A & Butcher R W. Some aspects of the biological role of adenosine 3',5'-monophosphate (cyclic AMP). *Circulation* 37:279-306, 1968.
(Vanderbilt Univ., Dept. Physiol. & Pharmacol., Nashville TN 37235) (See Butcher RW)

588 Hubel D H, **Wiesel T N.** Receptive fields and functional architecture in two nonstriate visual areas (18 and 19) of the cat. *J. Neurophysiol.* 28:229-89, 1965.
(Harvard Med. Sch., Dept. Pharmacol., Neurophysiol. Lab., Boston, MA 02115)
(See Hubel D H)

and W. M. Hunter, A. V. Schally and A. Arimura, N. E. Anden and K. Fuxe, J. Glowinski and L. L. Iversen, R. W. Butcher and E.W. Sutherland, D. H. Hubel and T. N. Wiesel. J. Roth, R. Yalow, and S. Berson — three authors on the list—shared one most-cited article. J. J. Brown, A. F. Lever, and J.I.S. Robertson also shared a single most-cited paper.

In eight of these twelve cases, both authors also appeared on the second most-cited paper. This is not surprising since the research team is a common phenomenon. We expected the "all-author" data to include members of teams, since each author was given equal treatment just as though he or she had been the first author.

However, we sometimes ran into trouble assigning each of our 300 authors a unique paper. For example, Arimura and Schally shared a most-cited paper. But Schally's second most-cited paper was the *most-cited* article by another author on the list, A. J. Kastin. So we had to go to Schally's third most-cited paper. The purpose of all this was to have an equal number of highly cited papers and authors.

As you look over the list, you will observe a considerable "overlap" in authorship. For example, P. Cuatrecasas appears in the list for his paper on protein purification by affinity chromatography. But he was co-author on C. B. Anfinsen's most-cited paper. Many of these 300 most-cited authors have worked together, but not necessarily on the same most-cited article listed.

Since this is the first of three installments it may be well to discuss the list as a whole.

All 300 publications on the list are journal articles. This is because the data bank used for this study was the source material covered by the *Science Citation Index®*, 1961-1976. From 1961-1976 the *SCI®* indexed only journal literature. In most cases, the most-cited journal article shown is in fact the author's most-cited publication from the time period. But in some instances an author's book (not on the list) may be more highly cited than the article shown. For example, C. Tanford's most-cited article received 354 citations. But his 1961 book, *Physical chemistry of macromolecules*, received 1,283 citations during the same time period. Since it was not a source publication in the 1961 *SCI*, it does not appear on the list.

Some readers may be surprised by the relatively low number of citations certain papers received. After all, on the average these 300 authors were each cited 5,000 times. These 1,500,000 citations constitute a substantial percentage of the entire file. Yet many items on this list received "only" a few hundred citations. The reason is that most of the 300 authors published a large number of papers during the time period studied. For example, F. Sorm's most-cited publication received only 86 citations. But

Sorm published 509 papers, 492 as first author, 17 as co-author.

Since the data bank for the study included only information on papers published between 1961-1976, it is not surprising that most of the 300 articles are from the early '60s. In fact, over half the articles were published prior to 1966, three-quarters before 1969. Next year, we plan to publish a list of the most-cited authors, 1965-1978. We can expect to see some significant changes. If certain fields were under-represented in our files from 1961 to 1964 then their *relative* status should improve significantly.

The 300 articles appeared in 86 journals. Five journals accounted for more than one-third of the articles, ten for about half. These journals appear in Figure 2. They emphasize the bio-medical bias of the list. This bias can be corrected only by compiling lists based on categories.

The average number of authors per paper is three. This is *very*

Figure 2: The 10 journals which accounted for about half the most-cited articles.

Proceedings of the National Academy of Sciences - USA	26
Journal of Biological Chemistry	23
Journal of the American Chemical Society	23
Science	16
Journal of Experimental Medicine	15
Nature	11
Journal of Cell Biology	9
Journal of Molecular Biology	9
New England Journal of Medicine	9
Journal of Clinical Investigation	8

significant since our methodology gives equal weight to all co-authors. Only 35 papers out of the 300 are authored by one person. Figure 3 shows the number of authors per paper. On a little over half the papers the most-cited author was *not* the first author. This emphasizes the need to take into account all-author citations data when doing evaluations.

Figure 3: The number of authors on most-cited papers.

Number of Authors	Number of Papers
1	35
2	110
3	78
4	42
5	19
6	8
7	2
8	3
9	1
10	1
11	1

It is of interest to note that one of the 1978 Nobelists in physiology or medicine, D. Nathans, appears as the primary author on F. Lipmann's most-cited paper in the biochemistry section. If we had extended our all-author list to the first *500* authors, Nathans and another winner in physiology of medicine, H. O. Smith, would have appeared on the list. If we extended our list to the top 700 authors, P. Mitchell, the 1978 Nobelist in chemistry, would have also been included. (Mitchell did appear on our earlier list of the 250 most-cited primary authors.[3]) Again, it is apparent that in the future we must publish lists of at least the 1,000 most-cited authors.

The choice of two of the 1978 winners in physics — A. Penzias and R. Wilson — underlines the need which I have mentioned before for lists of the most-cited authors in various disciplines. Penzias and Wilson do not appear even among the top 1,000. This is not expected because the field of radio astronomy is relatively small. We checked our "cluster" data for this field and verified that their respective citation counts of 1235 and 1412 are quite high.

W. Arber, who shared the prize in medicine, and P. L. Kapitsa, who shared the physics award, probably do not appear on our list for another reason. Much of Arber's work was done in the late 1950s; Kapitsa's in the 1930s. Since our data are based on articles published since 1961, citations to their earlier work were not counted.

In the second part of this study we will list 100 most-cited papers in immunology, molecular biology, cell biology, oncology, histology, pathology, as well as physics and biophysics.

REFERENCES

1. **Garfield E.** The 300 most-cited authors, 1961-1976, including co-authors at last. 1. How the names were selected. *Current Contents* (28):5-17, 10 July 1978.
2. -------------. The 300 most-cited authors, 1961-1976, including co-authors. Part 2. The relationship between citedness, awards, and academy memberships. *Current Contents* (35):5-30, 28 Aug 1978.
3. -------------. The 250 most-cited authors, 1961-1975. Part I. How the names were selected. *Current Contents* (49):5-15, 5 Dec 1977.

Current Comments

Last week we began presenting the most-cited articles by the 300 most-cited authors, 1961-1976. In that essay I explained the format and conventions of the list.[1] This week we will present about 100 more articles. They appear in Figure 1 and cover the fields of immunology, molecular biology, cell biology, oncology and cancer research, physics and biophysics, histology, and pathology.

In looking over this portion of the list, you will notice several husband and wife teams. Kark Eric Hellström and Ingegerd Hellström share the same most-cited article. Mary Osborn's second most-cited article appears this week because she, too, shares her most cited article with her husband, Klaus Weber. (That article appeared last week in the biochemistry section.) Another husband and wife are listed with different most-cited publications. Eva Klein's most-cited publication is "A microassay for cell-mediated immunity," while George Klein's paper, "Tumor antigens" also appears on the list. A further examination of our citation data shows that the two do work together on some projects.

Eva Klein's second most-cited article "Antigenic properties of lymphomas induced by the Moloney agent" lists George Klein as co-author. Gertrude and Werner Henle, who appear in the portion of the list to be published next week, also work together on their projects.

I wish to mention here that there were some errors on our earlier lists of names.[2-3] One name was discovered to be a homograph. We have, therefore, added a new author to the list, J. L. Gowans. His most-cited publication appears in the immunology section of the list this week. Complete citations for Gowans as well as his prizes and academy memberships appear in Figure 2 along with other corrections.

We would like to thank the readers who brought these errors to our attention. We also apologize for the errors, especially to those who were personally affected by them. I hope that it is obvious that the number of errors discovered to date is relatively small in comparison to the full size and scope of the study.

Next week we will present the final group of most-cited articles for the fields of organic and inorganic chemistry, microbiology and virology, cardiology, hematology and gastroenterology. There will also be a table of affiliations of the most-cited authors.

REFERENCES

1. **Garfield E.** The 300 most-cited authors, 1961-1976, including co-authors. 3A. Their most-cited papers — introduction and journal analysis. *Current Contents* (47):5-16, 20 November 1978.
2. ------------. The 300 most-cited authors, 1961-1976, including co-authors at last. 1. How the names were selected. *Current Contents* (28):5-17, 10 July 1978.
3. ------------. The 300 most-cited authors, 1961-1976. 2. The relationship between citedness, awards, and academy memberships. *Current Contents* (35):5-30, 28 August 1978.

Figure 1. Part 2 of the list of the 300 most-cited authors' most-cited publications, 1961-1976. Publications are listed by discipline, then alphabetically by most-cited author in bold-face type. Authors' affiliations at the time the papers were written are included in parentheses.

Total Citations 1961-1976 **Bibliographic Data**

IMMUNOLOGY

289 **Allison A C,** Denman A M & Barnes R D. Cooperating and controlling functions of thymus-derived lymphocytes in relation to auto-immunity. *Lancet* 2:135-40, 1971.
(Clin. Res. Ctr., Watford Rd., Harrow, Middlesex HA1 3UJ, England)

123 Ruddy S, Gigli I & **Austen K F.** The complement system of man. Part I. *N. Engl. J. Med.* 287:489-95, 1972.
(Robert Bent Brigham Hosp., Dept. Med. & Dermatol., Boston, MA 02120)

421 **Benacerraf B** & McDevitt H O. Histocompatibility-linked immune response genes. *Science* 172:273-9, 1972. (Harvard Med. Sch., Dept. Pathol., Boston, MA 02115)

455 **Cooper M D,** Peterson R D A, South M A & Good R A. The functions of the thymus system and the bursa system in the chicken. *J. Exp. Med.* 123:75-102, 1966.
(Univ. Minn., Variety Club Heart Hosp., Ped. Res. Lab., Minneapolis, MN 55455)

892 McConahey P J & **Dixon F J.** A method of trace iodination of proteins for immunologic studies. *Int. Arch. Allergy Appl. Immunol.* 29:185-9, 1966.
(Scripps Clinic & Res. Found., Dept. Exper. Pathol., La Jolla, CA 92037)

1,069 **Fahey J L** & McKelvey E M. Quantitative determination of serum immunoglobulins in antibody-agar plates. *J. Immunol.* 94:84-90, 1965.
(NIH, NCI, Immunol. & Med. Branch, Metabolism Service, Bethesda, MD 20014)

296 Benacerraf B, Ovary Z, Bloch K J & **Franklin E C.** Properties of guinea pig 7S antibodies. 1. Electrophoretic separation of two types of guinea pig 7S antibodies. *J. Exp. Med.* 117:937-64, 1963.
(N.Y.U. Sch. Med., Dept. Med. & Pathol., New York, NY 10016)

367 Stiehm E R & **Fudenberg H H.** Serum levels of immune globulins in health and disease: a survey. *Pediatrics* 37:715-27, 1966.
(Univ. Calif. Sch. Med., Dept. Ped. & Hematol., San Francisco, CA 94122)

355 **Good R A,** Delmasso A P, Martinez C, Archer O K, Pierce J C & Papermaster B W. The role of the thymus in development of immunologic capacity in rabbits and mice. *J. Exp. Med.* 116:773-95, 1962.
(Univ. Minn., Variety Club Heart Hosp., Ped. Res. Lab., Minneapolis, MN 55455)

510 **Gowans J L** & Knight E J. The route of re-circulation of lymphocytes in the rat. *Proc. Roy. Soc. London Ser.B.* 159:257-82, 1964.
(Univ. Oxford, W. Dunn School of Pathology, Oxford, England)

401 Rabellino E, Colon S, **Grey H M** & Unanue E R. Immunoglobulins on the surface of lymphocytes. 1. Distribution and quantitation. *J. Exp. Med.* 133:156-67, 1971. (National Jewish Hosp. & Res. Ctr., Denver, CO 80206)

412 Sjögren H O, Hellström I, Bansal S C & **Hellström K E.** Suggestive evidence that the "blocking antibodies" of tumor-bearing individuals may be antigen-antibody complexes. *Proc. Nat. Acad. Sci. US.* 68:1372-5, 1971.
(Univ. Washington Med. Sch., Depts. Microbiol. & Path., Seattle, WA 98105)
(See Hellström I in Oncology & Cancer Research).

412 **Hirschhorn K,** Bach F, Kolodny R L, Firschein L & Hashem N. Immune response and mitosis of human peripheral blood lymphcoytes *in vitro.* *Science* 142:1185-7, 1963. (N.Y.U. Sch. Med., Dept. Med., New York, NY 10016)

206 **Ishizaka K,** Ishizaka T & Hornbrook M M. Physicochemical properties of reaginic antibody. 5. Correlation of reaginic activity with γ E-globulin antibody. *J. Immunol.* 97:840-53, 1966.
(Children's Asthma Res. Inst. & Hosp., Denver, CO 80204)

315 Takasugi M & **Klein E.** A microassay for cell-mediated immunity. *Transplant* 9:219-27, 1970.
(Karolinska Inst., Med. Sch., Dept. Tumor Biol., 104 01 Stockholm Sweden)

362 Koffler D, Schur P H & **Kunkel H G.** Immunological studies concerning the nephritis of systemic lupus erythematosus. *J. Exp. Med.* 126:607-23, 1967.
(Rockefeller Univ., Dept. Immunol., New York, NY 10021)

471 Mitchell G F & **Miller J F A P.** Cell to cell interaction in the immune response. 2. The source of hemolysin-forming cells in irradiated mice given bone marrow and thymus or thoracic duct lymphocytes. *J. Exp. Med.* 128:821-37, 1968.
(Royal Melbourne Hosp, Walter & Eliza Hall Inst. Med. Res., Melbourne 3050, Victoria, Australia)

226 Purcell R H., Holland P V., Walsh J H, Wong D C, **Morrow A G** & Chanock R M. A complement-fixation test for measuring Australia antigen and antibody. *J. Infec. Dis.* 120:383-6, 1969.
(NIH, NHLI, Lab. Infectious Dis., Bethesda, MD 20014)

227 **Möller G** & Wigzel H. Antibody synthesis at the cellular level. Antibody-induced suppression of 19S and 7S antibody response. *J. Exp. Med.* 121:969-89, 1965.
(Karolinska Inst. Med. Sch., Dept. Tumor Biol., 104 01 Stockholm, Sweden)

278 Nilsson U R & **Muller-Eberhard H J.** Isolation of β -1F-globulin from human serum and its characterization as the fifth component of complement. *J. Exp. Med.* 122:277-98, 1965.
(Scripps Clinic & Res. Found., Div. Exper. Pathol., La Jolla, CA 92037)

150 Yagi Y, Maier P, **Pressman D,** Arbesman C E & Reisman R E. The presence of the ragweed-binding antibodies in the β -2A- and β -2M- and γ -globulins of the sensitive individuals. *J. Immunol.* 91:83-9, 1963.
(Roswell Park Mem. Inst., Dept. Biochem., Res., Buffalo, NY 14203)

320 **Roitt I M,** Torrigiani G, Greaves M F, Brostoff J & Playfair J H L. The cellular basis of immunological responses. A synthesis of some current views. *Lancet* 2:367-71, 1969.
(Middlesex Hosp., Med. Sch., Dept. Immunol., London W1P 9PG, England)

171 Fudenberg H, Good R A, Goodman H C, Hitzig W, Kunkel H G, Roitt I M, **Rosen F S,** Rowe D S, Seligmann M & Soothill J R. Primary immunodeficiencies. Report of a World Health Organization Committee. *Pediatrics* 47:927-46, 1971.
(Harvard Med. Sch., Dept. Ped., Lab. Immunol., Boston, MA 02115)

Figure 1 (continued)

IMMUNOLOGY (continued)

212 McDevitt H O & **Sela M.** Genetic control of the antibody response.
1. Demonstration of determinant-specific differences in response to
synthetic polypeptide antigens in two strains of inbred mice.
J. Exp. Med. 122:517-31, 1965.
(Weizmann Inst. of Science. Dept. Chem., Rehovot, Israel)

205 Dudley F J, Fox R A & **Sherlock S.** Cellular immunity and hepatitis-
associated Australia antigen liver disease. *Lancet* 1:723-6, 1972.
(Royal Free Hospital, Dept. Med., London W.C. 1, England)

207 **Starzl T E,** Marchioro T L, Porter K A, Iwasaki Y & Cerilli G J. The
use of heterologous antilymphoid agents in canine renal and liver
homotransplantation and in human renal homotransplantation.
Surg. Gynecol. Obstet 124:301-18, 1967.
(Univ. Colorado Sch. Med., Dept. Surg., Denver, CO 80220)

518 Mittal K K, Mickey M R, Singal D P & **Terasaki P I.** Serotyping
for homotransplantation. 18. Refinement of microdroplet lymphocyte
cytotoxicity test. *Transplant* 6:913-27, 1968.
(UCLA Sch. Med., Dept. of Surg., Los Angeles, CA 90024)

398 **Uhr J W** & Finkelstein M S. Antibody formation. 4. Formation of
rapidly and slowly sedimenting antibodies and immunological memory to
bacteriophage ϕ X 174. *J. Exp. Med.* 117:457-77, 1963.
(N.Y.U Sch. of Med., Dept. Med., New York, NY 10016)

311 Jankovic̃ B D, **Waksman B H** & Arnason B G. Role of the thymus in immune reactions in rats. 1. The immunologic response to bovine serum
albumin (antibody formation, arthus reactivity, and delayed hypersensi-
tivity) in rats thymectomized or splenectomized at various times after
birth. *J. Exp. Med.* 116:159-75, 1962.
(Harvard Med. Sch., Dept. Bact. & Immunol., Boston, MA 02115)

841 Jondal M, Holm G & **Wigzell H.** Surface markers on human T and B
lymphocytes. 1. A large population of lymphocytes forming nonimmune
rosettes with sheep red blood cells. *J. Exp. Med.* 136:207-15, 1972.
(Karolinska Inst. Dept. Tumor Biol. 104 01 Stockholm, Sweden)

MOLECULAR BIOLOGY

691 **Baltimore D.** Viral RNA-dependent DNA polymerase.
Nature 226:1209-11, 1970. (MIT, Dept. Biol., Cambridge, MA 02139)

923 Chamberlin M & **Berg P.** Deoxyribonucleic acid-directed synthesis of
ribonucleic acid by an enzyme from *Escherichia coli.*
Proc. Nat. Acad. Sci. US. 48:81-94, 1962.
(Stanford Univ., Sch. Med., Dept. Biochem. Stanford, CA 94305)

695 Huang R C & **Bonner J.** Histone, a suppressor of chromosomal RNA
synthesis. *Proc. Nat. Acad. Sci. US.* 48:1216-30, 1962.
(Calif. Inst. Technol., Div. Biol., Pasadena, CA 91109)
[Citation Classics. *Current Contents* (12):9, 20 March 1978]

774 Jacob F, **Brenner S** & Cuzin F. On the regulation of DNA replication in
bacteria. *Cold Spring Harbor Symp.* 28:329-47, 1963.
(Medical Res. Council, Lab. Mol. Biol., Cambridge, England)

897 Monod J, **Changeux J P** & Jacob F. Allosteric proteins and cellular control
systems. *J. Mol. Biol.* 6:306-29, 1963.
(Institut Pasteur, Unite de Neurobiol. Mol., Service de Biochem. Cell., Paris, France)
(See Wyman J)

828 Scherrer K & **Darnell J E**. Sedimentation characteristics of rapidly labelled RNA from HeLa cells. *Biochem. Biophys. Res. Commun.* 7:486-90, 1962.
(MIT, Dept. Biol., Cambridge, MA 02139)

397 **Gros F**, Hiatt H, Gilbert W, Kurland C G, Risebrough R W & Watson J D. Unstable ribonucleic acid revealed by pulse labelling of *Escherichia coli. Nature* 90:581-5, 1961.
(Institut Pasteur, Dept. Mol. Biol., Paris, France)

625 **Hurwitz J**, Furth J J, Malamy M & Alexander M. The role of deoxyribonucleic acid in ribonucleic acid synthesis. 3. The inhibition of the enzymatic synthesis of ribonucleic acid and deoxyribonucleic acid by actinomycin D and proflavin. *Proc. Nat. Acad. Sci. US.* 48:1222-30, 1962.
(N.Y.U. Sch. Med., Dept. Microbiol., New York, NY 10016)

2,338 **Jacob F** & Monod J. Genetic regulatory mechanism in the synthesis of proteins. *J. Mol. Biol.* 3:318-66, 1961.
(Institut Pasteur, Serv. de Genetique Microbienne et de Biochimie Cell., Paris, France)

922 Nirenberg M & **Leder P**. RNA codewords and protein synthesis. *Science* 145:1399-1407, 1964. (NIH, NHLI, Sect. Biochem. Genet. Bethesda, MD 20014)

3,431 **Marmur J**. A procedure for the isolation of deoxyribonucleic acid from micro-organisms. *J. Mol. Biol.* 3:208-18, 1961.
(Harvard Univ., Dept. Chem., Cambridge, MA 02138)

224 Bolton E T & **McCarthy B J**. A general method for the isolation of RNA complementary to DNA. *Proc. Nat. Acad. Sci. US.* 48:1390-7, 1962.
(Carnegie Inst. of Washington, 1590 P St. NW, Washington, DC 20005)

501 Jacob F & **Monod J**. On regulation of gene activity.
Cold Spring Harbor Symp. 26:193-209, 1961.
(Institut Pasteur, Serv. de Genetique Microbienne et de Biochem. Cell., Paris, France)
(See Jacob F)

78 Mathews M B & **Osborn M**. Translation of globin messenger RNA in a heterologous cell-free system. *Nature N. Biol.* 233:206-9, 1971.
(Medical Res. Council, Lab. Mol. Biol., Hills Road, Cambridge, England)
(See Weber K in Biochemistry : *Current Contents* (47):5-16, 20 November 1978) ·

307 Levan A. Fredga K & **Sandberg A A**. Nomenclature for centromeric position on chromosomes. *Hereditas* 52:201-20, 1964.
(Roswell Park Mem. Inst., Buffalo, NY 14203)

663 **Setlow R B** & Carrier W L. The disappearance of thymine dimers from DNA: an error-correcting mechanism.
Proc. Nat. Acad. Sci. US. 51:226-31, 1964.
(Oak Ridge Nat. Lab., Biol. Div., Oak Ridge, TN 37830)

271 Strauss J H & **Sinsheimer R L**. Purification and properties of bacteriophage MS2 and of its ribonucleic acid. *J. Mol. Biol.* 7:43-53, 1963.
(Calif. Inst. Technol., Div. Biol., Pasadena, CA 91125)

1,346 Gillespie D & **Spiegelman S**. A quantitative assay for DNA-RNA hybrids with DNA immobilized on a membrane. *J. Mol. Biol.* 12:829-42, 1965.
(Univ. Illinois, Dept. Microbiol., Urbana, IL 61801)
[Citation Classics. *Current Contents* (11):14, 14 March 1977.]

275 Iyer V N & **Szybalski W**. A molecular mechanism of mitomycin action: linking of complementary DNA strands.
Proc. Nat. Acad. Sci. US. 50:355-62, 1963.
(Univ. Wisconsin, McArdle Mem. Lab., Madison, WI 53706)

323 **Tomkins G M**, Gelehrter T D, Granner D, Martin D, Samuels H H & Thompson E B. Control of specific gene expression in higher organisms. *Science* 166:1474-80, 1969.
(Univ. Cal., San Francisco, Med. Ctr., Dept. Biochem. & Biophys., San Francisco, CA 94122)

705

Figure 1 (continued)
MOLECULAR BIOLOGY (continued)

620 Radloff R, Bauer W & **Vinograd J.** A dye-buoyant-density method for the detection and isolation of closed circular duplex DNA: the closed circular DNA in HeLa cells. *Proc. Nat. Acad. Sci. US* 57:1514-21, 1967.
(Calif. Inst. Technol., Norman W. Church Lab. Chem. Biol., Pasadena, CA 91125)

1,882 Monod J, **Wyman J** & Changeux J P. On the nature of allosteric transitions: a plausible model. *J. Mol. Biol.* 12:88-118, 1965
(Intitutio Regina Elena per lo Studio e la Cura dei Tumori, Rome, Italy)

184 **Yanofsky C** & Junetsu I. Nonsense codons and polarity in the tryptophan operon. *J. Mol. Biol.* 21:313-34, 1966.
(Stanford Univ., Dept. Biol. Sci., Stanford, CA 94305)

CELL BIOLOGY

277 **Aaronson S A,** Todaro G J & Scolnick E M. Induction of murine C-type viruses from clonal lines of virus-free BALB/3T3 cells. *Science* 174:157-9, 1971.
(NIH, NCI, Viral Leukemia & Lymphoma Branch, Bethesda, MD 20014)

300 Smuckler E A, Iseri O A & **Benditt E P.** An intracellular defect in protein synthesis induced by carbon tetrachloride.
J. Exp. Med. 116:55-72, 1962. (Univ. Washington, Dept. Pathol., Seattle, WA 98195)
(See Trump B F in Histology)

545 Sottocasa G L, Kuylenstierna B, **Ernster L** & Bergstrand A. An electron-transport system associated with the outer membrane of liver mitochondria. *J. Cell Biol.* 32:415-38, 1967.
(Univ. Stockholm, Wenner-Gren Inst., S-106 91 Stockholm, Sweden)

1,185 **Farquhar M G** & Palade G E. Junctional complexes in various epithelia.
J. Cell Biol. 17:375-412, 1963. (Rockefeller Inst. (Univ.), New York, NY 10021)

503 Reich E, **Franklin R M,** Shatkin A J & Tatum E L. Effect of actinomycin D on cellular nucleic acid synthesis and virus production.
Science 134:556-7, 1961.
(Rockefeller Inst. (Univ.), New York, NY 10021) (See Reich E)

351 Todaro G J, Lazar G K & **Green H.** The initiation of cell division in a contact-inhibited mammalian cell line.
J. Cell Comp. Physiol. 66:325-34, 1965.
(N.Y.U. Sch. Med., Dept. Pathol., New York, NY. 10016)
(See Todaro G J)

210 Becker A J, **McCulloch E A** & Till J E. Cytological demonstration of the clonal nature of spleen colonies derived from transplanted mouse marrow cells. *Nature* 197:452-4, 1963.
(Univ. Toronto, Dept. Med. Biophys., Toronto, Ontario, Canada)
(See Till J E in Physics & Biophysics)

461 Bradley T R & **Metcalf D.** The growth of mouse bone marrow cells *in vitro. Aust. J. Exp. Biol. Med. Sci.* 44:287-99, 1966.
(Royal Melbourne Hosp., Melbourne 3050, Victoria, Australia)

495 Allfrey V G, Littau V C & **Mirsky A E.** On the role of histones in regulating ribonucleic acid synthesis in the cell nucleus.
Proc. Nat. Acad. Sci. US. 49:414-21, 1963.
(Rockefeller Inst. (Univ.), New York, NY 10021)

462 **Novikoff A B** & Goldfischer S. Nucleosidiphosphatase activity in the Golgi apparatus and its usefulness for cytological studies.
Proc. Nat. Acad. Sci. US. 47:802-10, 1961.
(Albert Einstein Coll. Med., Dept. Pathol., New York, NY 10461)

581 Caro L G & **Palade G E.** Protein synthesis, storage, and discharge in the pancreatic exocrine cell. *J. Cell Biol.* 20:473-95, 1964.
(Rockefeller Inst. (Univ.), New York, NY 10021) (See Farquhar M G)

301 **Pearse A G E.** The cytochemistry and ultrastucture of polypeptide hormone-producing cells of the APUD series and the embryologic, physiologic and pathologic implications of the concept.
J. Histochem. Cytochem. 17:303-13, 1969.
(Royal Postgraduate Med. Sch., London, England)

782 **Penman S.** RNA metabolism in the HeLa cell nucleus.
J. Mol. Biol. 17:117-309, 1966. (Albert Einstein Coll. Med., New York, NY 10461)

469 Roth T F & **Porter K R.** Yolk protein uptake in the oocyte of the mosquito *Aedes aegypti*, L. *J. Cell Biol.* 20:313-32, 1964.
(Harvard Univ., Biol. Labs., Cambridge, MA 02138)

581 **Reich E,** Franklin R M, Shatkin A J & Tatum E L. Action of actinomycin D on animal cells and viruses. *Proc. Nat. Acad. Sci. US.* 48:1238-45, 1962.
(Rockefeller Inst., (Univ.), Lab. Biochem. Genetics, New York, NY 10021)

3,389 **Sabatini D D.** Bensch K & Barrnett R J. Cytochemistry and electron microscopy. The preservation of cellular ultrastructure and enzymatic activity by aldehyde fixation.
J. Cell Biol. 17:19-86, 1963.
(Yale Sch. Med., Dept. Anat., New Haven, CT 06510)

476 Inbar M & **Sachs L.** Interaction of the carbohydrate-binding protein concanavalin A with normal and transformed cells.
Proc. Nat. Acad. Sci. US. 63:1418-25, 1969.
(Weizmann Inst. of Science, Dept. Genet., Rehovot, Israel)

1,233 **Singer S J** & Nicholson G L. The fluid mosaic model of the structure of cell membranes. *Science* 175:720-31, 1972.
(Univ. Cal., San Diego, Dept. Biol., Box 109, La Jolla, CA 92037)
[Citation Classics. *Current Contents* (46):13, 14 November 1977]

487 **Todaro G J** & Green H. Quantitative studies of the growth of mouse embryo cells in culture and their development into established lines.
J. Cell Biol. 17:299-313, 1963. (N.Y.U. Sch. Med., Dept. Pathol., New York, NY 10016)
(See Huebner R J in Oncology & Cancer Research)

185 Sutton J S & **Weiss L.** Transformation of monocytes in tissue culture into macrophages, epithelioid cells, and multinucleated giant cells. An electron microscope study. *J. Cell Biol.* 28:303-30, 1966.
(Johns Hopkins Univ. Sch. Med., Dept. Anat., Baltimore, MD 20014)

311 **Weissmann G** & Thomas L. Studies on lysosomes. 1. The effects of endotoxin, endotoxin tolerance, and cortisone on the release of acid hydrolases from a granular fraction of rabbit liver.
J. Exp. Med. 116:433-50, 1962. (N.YU. Sch. Med., New York, NY 10016)

ONCOLOGY & CANCER RESEARCH

500 **Blumberg B S,** Alter H J & Visnich S. A "new" antigen in leukemia sera. *J. Amer. Med. Ass.* 191:101-12, 1965.
(Inst. Cancer Res., 7701 Burholme Ave., Phila., PA 19111)

370 Old L J, **Boyse E A,** Clark D A & Carswell E A. Part II. Antigens of tumor cells. Antigenic properties of chemically induced tumors.
Ann. NY Acad. Sci. 101:80-106, 1962.
(Sloan Kettering Inst. Cancer Res., New York, NY 10021) (See Old L J)

334 DeVita V T, Serpick A A & **Carbone P P.** Combination chemotherapy in the treatment of advanced Hodgkin's Disease. *Ann. Intern. Med.* 73:881-900, 1970.
(NIH, NCI, Bethesda, MD 20014)

Figure 1 (continued)

ONCOLOGY & CANCER RESEARCH (continued)

188 Hersh E M, Bodey G P, Nies B A & **Freireich E J.** Causes of
death in acute leukemia. A 10-year study of 414 patients from
1954-1963. *J. Amer. Med. Ass.* 193:105-9, 1965.
(NIH, NCI, Acute Leukemia Serv., Bethesda, MD 20014)

470 **Hellström I,** Hellström K E, Sjögren H O & Warner G A. Demonstration
of cell-mediated immunity to human neoplasms of various histological
types. *Int. J. Cancer* 7:1-16, 1971.
(Univ. Washington Med. Sch., Depts. Microbiol. & Pathol., Seattle, WA 98105)

525 **Huebner R J** & Todaro G J. Oncogenes of RNA tumor viruses as
determinants of cancer. *Proc. Nat. Acad. Sci. US.* 64:1087-94, 1969.
(NIH, NCI, Viral Carcinogenesis Branch, Bethesda, MD 210014)

257 Carbone P P, **Kaplan H S,** Musshoff K, Smithers D W & Tubiana M.
Report of the Committee on Hodgkin's disease staging classificaiton.
Cancer Res. 31:1860-1, 1971. (Stanford Univ., Stanford, CA 94305)

338 **Klein G.** tumor antigens. *Annu. Rev. Microbiol.* 20:223-52, 1966.
(Karolinska Inst., Med. Sch., Dept. Tumor Biol., 104 01 Stockholm Sweden)

167 Hertz R, Lewis J & **Lipsett M B.** Five year's experience with chemotherapy
of metastatic choriocarcinoma and related trophoblastic tumors in women.
Amer. J. Ob. Gynecol. 82:631-45, 1961.
(NIH, NCI, Endocrin. Branch, MD 20014)

227 Pitot H C, Potter V R & **Morris H P.** Metabolic adaptations in rat
hepatomas. 1. The effect of dietary protein on some inducible enzymes in
liver and heaptoma 5123. *Cancer Res.* 21:1001-14, 1961.
(NIH, NCI, Bethesda, MD 20014)

386 **Old L J** & Boyse E A. Immunology of experimental tumors.
Annu. Rev. Med. 15:167-86, 1964.
(Sloan Kettering Inst. Cancer Res., New York, NY 10021)

369 Johnson G S, Friedman R M & **Pastan I.** Restoration of several
morphological characteristics of normal fibroblasts in sarcoma cells
treated with adenosine-3':5'-cyclic monophosphate and its derivatives.
Proc. Nat. Acad. Sci. US. 68:425-9, 1971.
(NIH, NCI, Molecular Biol. Lab., Bethesda, MD 20014)

409 Huebner R J, **Rowe W P,** Turner H C & Lane W T. Specific
adenovirus complement-fixing antigens in virus-free hamster and rat
tumors. *Proc. Nat. Acad. Sci. US.* 50:379-89, 1963.
(NIH, NIAID, Lab. Infectious Dis., Bethesda, MD 20014)

PHYSICS & BIOPHYSICS

852 **Anderson P W.** Localized magnetic states in metals.
Phys. Rev. 124:41-53, 1961. (Bell Telephone Labs., Murray Hill, NJ)

319 **Chance B.** The energy-linked reaction of calcium with mitochondria.
J. Biol. Chem. 240:2729-48, 1965.
(Univ. Penn. Sch. Med., Johnson Res. Found., Philadelphia, PA 19104)

2,167 **Cromer D T** & Waber J T. Scattering factors computed from relativistic
Dirac-Slater wave functions. *Acta Crystallogr.* 18:104-9, 1965.
(Univ. Calif., Los Alamos Science Lab., Los Alamos, NM 87544)

144 **Dalgarno A** & McCray R A. Heating and ionization of HI regions.
Annu. Rev. Astron. Astrophys. 10:375-426, 1972.
(Harvard Coll. Observatory, Smithsonian Astrophys. Ctr., Cambridge, MA 02138)

718 **Fisher M E.** The theory of equilibrium critical phenomena.
Rep. Progr. Phys. 30:615-730, 1967. (Cornell Univ., Baker Lab., Ithaca, NY 14850)

1,435 **Gell-Mann M.** Symmetries of baryons and mesons.
Phys. Rev. 125:1067-84, 1962. (Calif. Inst. Technol., Pasadena, CA 01125)

414 Hubbell W L & **McConnell H M.** Molecular motion in spin-labeled
phospholipids and membranes. *J. Amer. Chem. Soc.* 93:314-33, 1971.
(Stanford Univ., Stauffer Lab. Phys. Chem., Stanford, CA 94305)

217 **Miledi R,** Molinoff P & Potter L T. Isolation of the cholinergic
receptor protein of *Torpedo* electric tissue. *Nature* 229:554-7, 1971.
(Univ. Coll., Dept. Biophys., London, England)

156 Jortner J, **Rice S A,** Katz J L & Choi S I. Triplet excitons in
crystals of aromatic molecules. *J. Chem. Phys.* 42:309-23, 1965.
(Univ. Chicago, Dept. Chem. & Inst. for Study of Metals, Chicago, IL 60637)

1,013 **Till J E** & McCulloch E A. A direct measurement of the radiation
sensitivity of normal mouse bone marrow cells.
Radiat. Res. 14:213-22, 1961.
(Ontario Cancer Inst., Div. Biol. Res. & Phys., Toronto M4X 1K9, Ontario, Canada)

769 **Weinberg S.** A model of leptons. *Phys. Rev. Lett.* 19:1264-6, 1967.
(MIT. Lab. Nuclear Science & Phys. Dept., Cambridge, MA 02138)

HISTOLOGY

168 Sabatini D D, Miller F & **Barrnett R J.** Aldehyde fixation for
morphological and enzyme histochemical
studies with the electron microscope.
J. Histochem. Cytochem. 12:57-71, 1964.
(Yale Sch. Med., Dept. Anat., New Haven, CT 06510)
(See Sabatini D D in Cell Biology)

476 **Corrodi H** & Jonsson G. The formaldehyde fluorescence method for the
histochemical demonstration of biogenic monoamines: a review on the
methodology. *J. Histochem. Cytochem.* 15:65-78, 1967.
(A B Hässle, Biochem., Res. Lab., Göteborg, Sweden)

1,146 **Falck B,** Hillarp N A, Thieme G & Torp A. Fluorescence of catechol
amines and related compounds condensed with formaldehyde.
J. Histochem. Cytochem. 10:348-54, 1962.
(Univ. Lund, Dept. Histol., Biskopsgatan 5, Lund, Sweden)

2,005 **Karnovsky M J.** A formaldehyde-glutaraldehyde fixative of high osmolality
for use in electron microscopy.
J. Cell Biol. 27:137A-8A, 1965. (Harvard Med. Sch., Dept. Pathol., Boston, MA 02115)

603 Kopriwa B M & **Leblond C P.** Improvements in the coating technique of
radioautography. *J. Histochem. Cytochem.* 10:269-84, 1962.
(McGill Univ., Dept. Anat., Montreal, P.Q., Canada)

7,440 **Luft J H.** Improvements in epoxy resin embedding methods.
J. Biophys. Biochem. Cytol. 9:409-14, 1971.
(Univ. Washington, Dept. Anat., Seattle, WA 98195)
[Citation Classics. *Current Contents* (20):8, 16 May 1977]

340 **Moore G E.,** Gerner R E & Franklin H A. Culture of normal human
leukocytes. *J. Amer. Med. Ass.* 199:519-24, 1967.
(Roswell Park Mem. Inst., Buffalo, NY 14263)

9,396 **Reynolds E S.** The use of lead citrate at high pH as an electron-
opaque stain in electron microscopy. *J. Cell Biol.* 17:208-12, 1963.
(Harvard Med. Sch., Dept. Anat., Boston, MA 02115)

641 **Trump B F,** Smuckler E A & Benditt E P. A method for staining epoxy
sections for light microscopy. *J. Ultrastruct. Res.* 5:343-8, 1961.
(Univ. Washington, Dept. Pathol., Seattle, WA 98105)

Figure 1 (continued)
PATHOLOGY

123 **Bensch K,** Schaefer K & Avery M E. Granular pneumocytes:
electron microscopic evidence of their exocrinic function.
Science 145:1318-9, 1964.
(Yale Sch. Med., Dept. Pathol., New Haven, CT 06510)
(See Sabatini D D in Cell Biology)

208 **Brady R O,** Gal A E, Bradley R M, Martensson E, Warshaw A L
& Laster L. Enzymatic defect in Fabry's disease: ceramidetrihexosidase
deficiency. *N. Engl. J. Med.* 276:1163-7, 1967.
(NIH, NINDS, Lab. Neurochemistry, Bethesda, MD 20014)

133 Eickhoff T C, Klein J O, Daly A K, Ingall D & **Finland M.**
Neonatal sepsis and other infections due to group B beta-hemolytic
streptococci. N. Engl. J. Med. 271:1221-8, 1964.
(Harvard Med. Sch., Boston, MA 02115)

208 Hollenberg N K, Epstein M, Rosen S M, Basch R I, Oken D E
& **Merrill J P.** Acute oliguric renal failure in man: evidence for pre-
ferential renal cortical ischemia. *Medicine* 47:455-74, 1968.
(Peter Bent Brigham Hosp., Cardiorenal Div., Boston, MA 02115)

227 deGroote J, Desmet V J, Gedigk P, Korb G, **Popper H,** Poulsen H,
Schever P J, Schmidt M, Thaler H & Uehlinger E. A
classification of chronic hepatitis. *Lancet* 2:626-8, 1968.
(Mt. Sinai Sch. Med., Stratton Lab. Liver Disease, New York, NY 10029)

Figure 2: Corrections to the list of the 300 most-cited authors, 1961-1976.

1. Birth Dates
We erroneously reported Max D. Cooper to be the youngest author on the list with a
birth date of 1945. Dr. Cooper was born in 1933. Stuart A. Aaronson, born in 1942, is the
youngest author.

Paul Mandel was not born in 1942 as we originally reported, but in 1908.

2. Disciplines
Gerald D. Fasman is a biochemist, not a pathologist,

Paul Mandel is in cell biology rather than biophysics, H.N. Munro is a biochemist rather
than a physiologist, and K. Weber is in biochemistry, not biophysics.

3. Awards
The Waksman Award is given by the Theobald Smith Society, New Jersey branch of
the American Society for Microbiology.

4. Replacement
The name "G. Weber" proved to be a homograph, representing several people, none of
whom received enough citations to make the list. The name has therefore been deleted
and replaced with the following:

Gowans J L (1924) in Immunology

Total citations:	3702	Total papers: 37
Citations as 1st author:	1891	1st author papers: 11
Citations as co-author:	1811	Co-author papers: 26
Awards: Gairdner/68		Academy: UK

Gowans' most-cited paper appears in Figure 1 in the Immunology section.

Current Comments

The 300 Most-Cited Authors, 1961-1976, Including Co-Authors. 3C. Their Most- Cited Papers and Affiliation Data

Number 49   **December 4, 1978**

This is the last part of the series of essays listing the most-cited journal articles of the 300 most-cited authors.[1,2] This week's list, which appears in Figure 1, covers papers from the fields of organic, inorganic, and physical chemistry, chemical physics, microbiology and virology, cardiology, hematology, and gastroenterology. The format and conventions of the list were explained in the first part of this series.

Along with the remainder of the most-cited authors' most-cited publications, we are also including a table of affiliations for the authors. The table, in Figure 2, includes the names of the institutions with which the authors were affiliated at the time their papers were written. The number of most-cited papers from each institution is also given. Previously, I noted that nearly a third of the authors on our most-cited list are affiliated with about five universities or well-known institutes.[3]

A glance at this list shows that by far the largest employer was the US government. Forty-five of the authors were affiliated with the Na-tional Institutes of Health when they wrote their papers.

That nearly a sixth of all the papers on this list were written while their authors were associated with NIH is significant but not surprising. In a recent study, Francis Narin and Stephen B. Keith of Computer Horizons, Inc. examined data from the *SCI®* from 1973 to 1975.[4] They found that "investigations at the NIH produce more biomedical research papers per year than any other group in the US, accounting for approximately 3.4% of all US biomedical research papers." When the investigators looked at "the 20 journals that have the highest influence per paper rating," they found the NIH fraction to be over 5%. "In the 12 biomedical review journals covered by the *SCI*, 7.5% of the authors are NIH scientists."

Two Veterans Administration Hospitals appear on this list and account for six papers. Thus 51 of the 300 papers were written while their authors were employees of the US government. Of course, a number of the other institutions on this list received US government contracts and much of the work performed was underwritten by US government grants.

Nineteen of the authors worked at Harvard University when they wrote their most-cited papers. Ten of these were associated with the medical school there. The University of California system accounts for 13 authors. Five were affiliated with the University of California, Los Angeles (UCLA).

Most of the authors listed are affiliated with organizations in the US. However, 60 of the authors were affiliated with institutions in 13 other countries. Australia, Canada, France, Czechoslovakia, Denmark, Sweden, England, Italy, Japan, West Germany, the Netherlands, Israel, and Scotland appear on the list. Twenty-one of the authors were associated with English institutions at the time they wrote their most-cited papers, 14 with Swedish institutions.

Although much of the research to produce these papers went on in universities, hospitals, and research institutions, some took place in private industry. Thus such companies as IBM, Merck, Sharp & Dohme, and E. I. DuPont appear on the list.

That a large amount of most-cited research is conducted in a small number of institutions comes as no surprise to most of those who follow these kinds of studies. Perhaps the names of these organizations will surprise some. Yet, more than 110 universities, research organizations, companies, and hospitals appear on the list. This diversity makes it clear that excellent research can be and is conducted in many different kinds of organizations — not just a few elite laboratories.

This concludes our study of the 300 most-cited author's most-cited publications. In the future we will be expanding these studies. We will change the period studied to 1965-1978. This will enable you to see the authors who have had significant impact in more recent years. We also need to expand our list to include at least the 1,000 most-cited authors. This will not only allow us to report on the many others who are doing significant work in science but also overcome the biases of the data base. We need to pay particular attention to "small" fields which we hope to identify through our cluster analyses.

REFERENCES

1. **Garfield E.** The 300 most-cited authors, 1961-1976, including co-authors. 3A. Their most-cited papers — introduction and journal analysis. *Current Contents* (47):5-16, 20 November 1978.
2. -------------. The 300 most-cited authors, 1961-1976, including co-authors. 3B. Their most-cited papers and a correction note. *Current Contents* (48):5-14, 27 November 1978.
3. -------------. The ethics of scientific publication. *Current Contents* (40):5-12, 2 October 1978.
4. **Narin F & Keith S B.** The intramural role of the NIH as a biomedical research institute. *Federation Proc.* 47:2120-3, 1978.

Figure 1: Part 3 of a list of the 300 most-cited authors' most-cited publications, 1961-1976. Publications are listed by discipline, then alphabetically by most cited author in bold-face type. Authors' affiliations at the time the paper was written are included in parentheses.

Total
Citations
1961-1976   Bibliographic Data

ORGANIC & INORGANIC CHEMISTRY

355 **Bender M L** & Kézdy F J. Mechanism of action of proteolytic enzymes. *Annu. Rev. Biochem.* 34:49-76, 1965.
(Northwestern Univ., Dept. of Chemistry, Evanston, IL 60201)

265 **Benson S W,** Cruickshank F R, Golden D M, Haugen G R, O'Neal H E, Rodgers A S, Shaw R & Walsh R. Additivity rules for the estimation of thermochemical properties. *Chem. Rev.* 69:279-324, 1969.
(Stanford Res. Inst., Dept. Thermochem. & Chem. Kinetics, Menlo Pk., CA, 94025)

316 **Brown H C** & Garg C P. A simple procedure for the chromic acid oxidation of alcohols to ketones of high purity. *J. Amer. Chem. Soc.* 83:2952-3, 1961.
(Purdue Univ., R.B. Wetherill Lab., W. Lafayette, IN, 47907)

406 **Corey E J** & Chaykovsky M. Dimethyloxosulfonium methylide ($(CH_3)_2SOCH_2$) and dimethylsulfonium methylide ($(CH_3)_2SCH_2$). Formation and application to organic synthesis. *J. Amer. Chem. Soc.* 87:1353-64, 1965.
(Harvard Univ., Converse Lab., Cambridge, MA, 02138)

456 **Cotton F A** & Kraihanzel C S. Vibrational spectra and bonding in metal carbonyls. 1. Infrared spectra of phosphine-substituted group VI carbonyls in the CO stretching region. *J. Amer. Chem. Soc.* 84:4432-41, 1962.
(MIT, Dept. Chem. & Lab. of Chem. & Solid State Physics, Cambridge, MA, 02139)

134 **Cram D J,** Rickborn B, Kingsbury C A & Haberfield P. Electrophilic substitution at saturated carbon. 13. Solvent control of rate of acid-base reactions that involve the carbon-hydrogen bond. *J. Amer. Chem. Soc.* 83:3678-87, 1961.
(Univ. California, Dept. Chem., Los Angeles, CA, 90024)

506 Moffitt W, Woodward R B, Moscowitz A, Klyne W & **Djerassi C.** Structure and the optical rotatory dispersion of saturated ketones. *J. Amer. Chem. Soc.* 83:4013-8, 1961.
(Stanford Univ., Dept. Chem., Stanford, CA, 94305)

139 Joesten M D & **Drago R S.** The validity of frequency shift-enthalpy correlations. 1. Adducts of phenol with nitrogen and oxygen donors. *J. Amer. Chem. Soc.* 84:3817-21, 1962. (Univ. Illinois, Noyes Lab., Urbana, IL 61820)

259 Brant D A & **Flory P J.** The configuration of random polypeptide chains. 2. Theory. *J. Amer. Chem. Soc.* 87:2791-2, 1965.
(Stanford Univ., Dept. Chem., Stanford, CA, 94305)

293 **Grant D M** & Paul E G. Carbon-13 magnetic resonance. 2. Chemical shift data for the alkanes. *J. Amer. Chem. Soc.* 86:2984-90, 1964.
(Univ. Utah, Dept. Chem., Salt Lake City, UT 84112)

408 **Hammond G S,** Saltiel J, Lamola A A, Turro N J, Bradshaw J S, Cowan D O, Counsell R C, Vogt V & Dalton C. Mechanisms of photochemical reactions in solution. 22. Photochemical *cis-trans* isomerization. *J. Amer. Chem. Soc.* 86:3197-3217, 1964.
(Calif. Inst. Tech., Gates & Crellin Lab. Chem., Pasedena, CA 91125)

Figure 1 (continued)

ORGANIC & INORGANIC CHEMISTRY (continued)

375 **Huisgen R.** 1.3-dipolare Cycloadditionen; Rückshau und Ausblick. (1,3-di-
polar cycloadditions; past and future). *Angew. Chem.* 75:604-37, 1963.
(Univ. Munich, Inst. Organic Chem., D-8000 Munich 2, FRG)

493 Corfield P W R, Doedens R J & **Ibers J A.** Studies of metal-
nitrogen multiple bonds. 1. The crystal and molecular structure of
nitridodichlorotris (diethylphenylphosphine) rhenium(V), ReNCl$_2$
(P(C$_2$H$_5$)$_2$C$_6$H$_5$)$_3$. *Inorg. Chem.* 6:197-210, 1967.
(Northwestern Univ., Dept. Chem., Evanston, IL 60201)

183 **Jencks W P** & Gilchrist M. Nonlinear structure—reactivity correlations.
The reactivity of nucleophilic reagents toward esters.
J. Amer. Chem. Soc. 90:2622-37, 1968.
(Brandeis Univ., Grad. Dept. Biochem., Waltham, MA 02154)

1,035 **Karplus M.** Vicinal proton coupling in nuclear magnetic resonance.
J. Amer. Chem. Soc. 85:2870-1, 1963.
(Columbia Univ., Dept. Chem., New York, NY 10025)

301 Moffatt J G & **Khorana H G.** Nucleoside polyphosphates. 10. The synthesis
and some reactions of nucleoside-5' phosphoromorpholidates and related
compounds. Improved methods for the preparation of nucleoside-5'
polyphosphates. *J. Amer. Chem. Soc.* 83:649-63, 1961.
(British Columbia Res. Council, Chem. Div., Vancouver, Canada)

121 **King R B.** Complexes of trivalent phosphorus derivatives. 2. Metal carbonyl
complexes of tris-(dimethylamino)-phosphine. *Inorg. Chem.* 2:936-44, 1963.
(Mellon Inst., Pittsburgh, PA 15213)

116 Krusic P J & **Kochi J K.** Conformational effects of sulfur, silicon,
germanium, and tin on alkyl radicals. An electron spin resonance
study of the barriers to internal rotation.
J. Amer. Chem. Soc. 93:846-60, 1971.
(Indiana Univ., Dept. Chem., Bloomington, IN 47401)

349 **Muetterties E L** & Schunn R A. Pentaco-ordination. *Quart. Rev.* 20:245-99, 1966.
(E. I. Du Pont de Nemours & Co., Central Res. Dept., Wilmington, DE 19801)

155 **Olah G A** & White A M. Stable carbonium ions. 91. Carbon-13
nuclear magnetic resonance spectroscopic study of carbonium ions.
J. Amer. Chem. Soc. 91:5801-10, 1969.
(Case Western Reserve Univ., Dept. Chem., Cleveland, OH 44106)

84 **Paquette L A.** Catalysis of strained σ -bond rearrangements by silver(I)
ion. *Account. Chem. Res.* 4:280-7, 1971.
(Ohio State Univ., Dept. Chem., Columbus, OH 43210)

210 Patel D J, Howden M E H & **Roberts J D.** Nuclear magnetic
resonance spectroscopy. Cyclopropane derivatives.
J. Amer. Chem. Soc. 85:3218-23, 1963.
(Calif. Inst. Tech. Gates & Crellin Lab., Pasadena, CA 91125)

208 Jones J W & **Robins R K.** Purine nucleosides. 3. Methylation studies of
certain naturally occurring purine nucleosides.
J. Amer. Chem. Soc. 85:193-201, 1963.
(Arizona State Univ., Dept. Chem., Tempe, AZ 85281)

342 Laszlo P & **Schleyer P V R.** Analysis of the nuclear magnetic
resonance spectra of norbornene derivatives.
J. Amer. Chem. Soc. 86:1171-9, 1964.
(Princeton Univ., Frick Chem. Lab., Princeton, NJ 08540)

86   Piskala A & Šorm F. Nucleic acids components and their analogues. 51. Synthesis of 1-glycosyl derivatives of 5-azauracil and 5-azacytosine. *Collect. Czech. Chem. Commun.* 29:2060-76, 1964.
(Czechoslovak Acad. Sciences, Inst. Organ. Chem. & Biochem., Prague, Czechoslovakia)

1,364   **Sweeley C C**, Bentley R, Makita M & Wells W W. Gas-liquid chromatography of trimethylsilyl derivatives of sugars and related substances. *J. Amer. Chem. Soc.* 85:2497-507, 1963.
(Univ. Pittsburgh Sch. Med., Depts. Biochem. & Nutrit., Pittsburgh, PA 15261)
[Citation Classics. *Current Contents* (43):11, 24 October 1977.]

157   **Winstein S** & Sonnenberg J. Homoconjugation and homoaromaticity. 3. The 3-bicyclo[3.1.0]hexyl system. *J. Amer. Chem. Soc.* 83:3235-44, 1961.
(Univ. California, Dept. Chem., Los Angeles, CA 90024)

725   **Woodward R B** & Hoffmann R. The conservation of orbital symmetry. *Angew. Chem.* 8:781-853, 1969. (Harvard Univ., Dept. Chem., Cambridge, MA 02138)

PHYSICAL CHEMISTRY & CHEMICAL PHYSICS

1,090   **Clementi E.** *Ab initio* computations in atoms and molecules. *IBM J. Res. Develop.* 9:2-19, 1965. (IBM Res. Lab., San Jose, CA, 95113)

150   Bender C F & **Davidson E R**. A natural orbital based energy calculation for helium hydride and lithium hydride. *J. Phys. Chem.* 70:2675-85, 1966. (Univ. Washington, Seattle, WA 98105)
(See Stewart R F)

257   **Dewar M J S** & Haselbach E. Ground states of σ-bonded molecules. 9. The MINDO/2 method. *J. Amer. Chem. Soc.* 92:590-8, 1970.
(Univ. Texas, Dept. Chem., Austin, TX 78712)

226   **Gray H B** & Ballhausen C J. A molecular orbital theory for square planar metal complexes. *J. Amer. Chem. Soc.* 85:260-5, 1963.
(Columbia Univ., Dept. Chem., New York, NY 10027)

1,511   **Hoffmann R.** An extended Hückel theory. 1. Hydrocarbons. *J. Chem. Phys.* 38:1397-412, 1963. (Harvard Univ., Chem. Dept., Cambridge, MA 02138)

267   Bixon M & **Jortner J.** Intramolecular radiationless transitions. *J. Chem. Phys.* 48:715-26, 1968. (Tel-Aviv Univ., Dept. Chem., Tel-Aviv, Israel)

275   Hoffmann R & **Lipscomb W N.** Theory of polyhedral molecules. 1. Physical factorizations of the secular equation. *J. Chem. Phys.* 36:2179-89, 1962. (Harvard Univ., Dept. Chem., Cambridge, MA 02138)

621   **Nemethy G** & Scheraga H A. Structure of water and hydrophobic bonding in proteins. 1. A model for the thermodynamic properties of liquid water. *J. Chem. Phys.* 36:3382-400, 1962.
(Cornell Univ., Dept. Chem., Ithaca, NY 14853)
[Citation Classics. *Current Contents* (22):11, 29 May 1978.]

1,358   **Pople J A** & Segal G A. Approximate self-consistent molecular orbital theory. 3. CNDO results for AB_2 and AB_3 systems. *J. Chem. Phys.* 44:3289-96, 1966.
(Carnegie-Mellon Univ., Dept. Chem., Pittsburgh, PA 15213)

559   Nemethy G & **Scheraga H A.** The structure of water and hydrophobic bonding in proteins. 3. The thermodynamic properties of hydrophobic bonds in proteins. *J. Phys. Chem.* 66:1773-89, 1962.
(Cornell Univ., Dept. Chem., Ithaca, NY 14853) (See Nemethy G)

2,497   **Stewart R F,** Davidson E R & Simpson W T. Coherent X-ray scattering for the hydrogen atom in the hydrogen molecule. *J. Chem. Phys.* 42:3175-87, 1965. (Univ. Washington, Dept. Chem., Seattle, WA 98195)
[Citation Classics. *Current Contents* (48):15, 28 November 1977.]

Figure 1 (continued)

MICROBIOLOGY & VIROLOGY

576 **Chanock R M,** Hayflick L & Barile M F. Growth on artificial medium of an agent associated with atypical pneumonia and its identification as a PPLO. *Proc. Nat. Acad. Sci. US* 48:41-9, 1962.
(NIH, NIAID, Lab. Infectious Dis., Bethesda, MD 20014)

611 **Henle G** & Henle W. Immunofluorescence in cells derived from Burkitt's lymphoma. *J. Bacteriol.* 91:1248-56, 1966.
(Children's Hospital, Virus Lab., Phila., PA 19146)

488 Henle G, **Henle W** & Diehl V. Relation of Burkitt's tumor-associated Herpes-type virus to infectious mononucleosis. *Proc. Nat. Acad. Sci. Wash.* 59:94-101, 1968.
(Children's Hospital, Virus Lab., Phila. PA 19146) (See Henle G)

420 Field A K, Tytell A A, Lampson G P & **Hilleman M R.** Inducers of interferon and host resistance. 2. Multistranded synthetic poly-nucleotide complexes. *Proc. Nat. Acad. Sci. US* 58:1004-10, 1967.
(Merck Inst. Therapeutic Res., Div. Virus & Cell Biol., West Point, PA 19486)

242 **Koprowski H,** Ponten J A, Jensen F, Ravdin R G, Moorhead P & Saksela E. Transformation of cultures of human tissue infected with simian virus SV_{40}. *J. Cell. Compar. Physiol.* 59:281-92, 1962.
(Univ. Pennsylvania, Wistar Inst. Anat. & Biol., Philadelphia, PA 19104)

158 Rawls W E, Tompkins W A F & **Melnick J L.** The association of herpesvirus type 2 and carcinoma of the uterine cervix. *Amer. J. Epidemiol.* 89:547-54, 1969.
(Baylor Univ. Coll. Med., Dept. Virol. & Epidemiol., Houston, TX 77025)

238 Ozaki M, Mizushima S & **Nomura M.** Identification and functional characterization of the protein controlled by the streptomycin-resistant locus in *E. coli. Nature* 222:333-9, 1969.
(Univ. Wisconsin, Lab. Genet., Madison, WI 53706)

155 Duff R & **Rapp F.** Properties of hamster embryo fibroblasts transformed *in vitro* after exposure to ultraviolet-irradiated herpes simplex virus type 2. *J. Virology* 8:469-77, 1971.
(Penn. State Univ., Coll. Med., Dept. Microbiol., Hershey, PA 17033)

201 Zbar B, Berstein I D & **Rapp H J.** Suppression of tumor growth at the site of infection with living bacillus Calmette-Guérin. *J. Nat. Cancer Inst.* 46:831-9, 1971. (NIH, NCI, Biol. Branch, Bethesda, MD 20014)

1,477 **Sever J L.** Application of a microtechnique to viral serological investigations. *J. Immunol.* 88:320-9, 1962. (NIH, NINDS, Bethesda, MD 20014)

230 Tipper D J & **Strominger J L.** Mechanism of action of penicillins: a proposal based on their structural similarity to acyl-D-alanyl-D-alanine. *Proc. Nat. Acad. Sci. US* 54:1133-41, 1965.
(Univ. Wisconsin Med. Sch., Dept. Pharmacol., Madison, WI 53706)

185 **Umezawa H,** Maeda K, Takeuchi T & Okami Y. New antibiotics, bleomycin A and B. *J. Antibiot.* 19:200-9, 1966. (Nat. Inst. Health, Tokyo, Japan)

CARDIOLOGY

242 Gleason W L & **Braunwald E.** Studies on the first derivative of the ventricular pressure pulse in man. *J. Clin. Invest.* 41:80-91, 1971.
(NIH, NHLI, Cardiol. Branch, Bethesda, MD 20014)
(See Ross J)

85 Shone J D, Sellers R D, Anderson R C, Adams P, Lillehei C W & **Edwards J E**. The developmental complex of "parachute mitral valve," supravalvular ring of left atrium, subaortic stenosis, and coarctation of aorta. *Amer. J. Cardiol.* 11:714-25, 1963.
(Charles T. Miller Hosp., Dept. Pathol., St. Paul MN 55102)

249 **Epstein S E**, Robinson B F, Kahler R L & Braunwald E. Effects of beta-adrenergic blockade on the cardiac response to maximal and submaximal exercise in man. *J. Clin. Invest.* 44:1745-53, 1965.
(NIH, NHLI, Cardiol. Branch, Bethesda, MD 20014)

254 Herman M V, Heinle R A, Klein M D & **Gorlin R**. Localized disorders in myocardial contraction. Asynergy and its role in congestive heart failure. *N. Engl. J. Med.* 277:222-32, 1967.
(Peter Bent Brigham Hospital, Cardiovascular Unit, Boston, MA 02115)

160 Heinle R A, **Levy R I**, Frederickson D S & Gorlin R. Lipid and carbohydrate abnormalities in patients with angiographically documented coronary artery disease. *Amer. J. Cardiol.* 24:178-86, 1969.
(NIH, NHLI, Lab. Mol. Dis., Bethesda, MD 20014)
(See Frederickson D S in Physiology)

219 **Mason D T**. Usefulness and limitations of the rate of rise of intraventricular pressure (dp/dt) in the evaluation of myocardial contractility in man. *Amer. J. Cardiol.* 23:516-27, 1969.
(Univ. California Sch. Med., Dept. Med., Davis, CA 95616)

418 Maroko P R, Kjekshus J K, Sobel B E, Watanabe T, Covell J W, **Ross J** & Braunwald E. Factors influencing infarct size following experimental coronary artery occlusions. *Circulation* 43:67-82, 1971.
(Univ. California, Sch. Med., La Jolla, CA 92037)

532 **Sonnenblick E H**. Force-velocity relations in mammalian heart muscle. *Amer. J. Physiol.* 202:931-9, 1962.
(NIH, NHLI, Lab. Cardiovascular Physiol., Bethesda, MD 20014)

225 **Wagner H N**, Sabiston D C, McAfee J G, Tow D & Stern H S. Diagnosis of massive pulmonary embolism in man by radioisotope scanning. *N. Engl. J. Med.* 271:377-84, 1964.
(Johns Hopkins Univ.Sch. Med., Dept. Med. & Radiol., Baltimore, MD 21218)

HEMATOLOGY

441 **Beutler E**, Duron O & Kelly B M. Improved method for the determination of blood glutathione. *J. Lab. Clin. Med.* 61:882-92, 1963.
(City Hope Med. Ctr., Dept. Med., Duarte, CA 91010)

7,401 **Davis B J**. Disc electrophoresis. 2. Method and application to human serum proteins. *Ann. NY Acad. Sci.* 121:404-27, 1964.
(Mt. Sinai Hosp., Dept. Hematol., Cell. Res. Lab., New York, NY 10029)

236 Fallon H J, **Frei E**, Davidson J D, Trier J S & Burk D. Leukocyte preparations from human blood: evaluation of their morphologic and metabolic state. *J. Lab. Clin. Med.* 59:779-91, 1962.
(NIH, NCI, Bethesda, MD 20014)

359 **Mustard J F** & Packham M A. Factors influencing platelet function: adhesion, release, and aggregation. *Pharmacol. Rev.* 22:97-187, 1970.
(McMaster Univ., Dept. Pathol., Hamilton, Ontario, Canada)

318 Wilson J D & **Nossal G J V**. Identification of human T and B lymphocytes in normal peripheral blood and in chronic lymphocytic leukaemia. *Lancet* 2:788-91, 1971.
(Royal Melbourne Hosp., Walter & Eliza Hall Inst. Med. Res., Victoria, Australia)

Figure 1 (continued)

HEMATOLOGY (continued)

710 **Perutz M F.** Stereochemistry of cooperative effects in haemoglobin.
Nature 228:726-34, 1970.
(Medical Res. Council, Mol. Biol. Lab., Cambridge, CB2 2QH, England)

GASTROENTEROLOGY

162 Jacobson E D, Linford R H & **Grossman M I.** Gastric secretion in
relation to mucosal blood flow studied by a clearance technique.
J. Clin. Invest. 45:1-13, 1966.
(Univ. California, Dept. Physiol., Los Angeles, CA 90073)

251 **Hofmann A F** & Borgström B. Physico-chemical state of lipids in intestinal
content during their digestion and absorption.
Fed. Proc. 21:43-50, 1962. (Univ. Lund, Dept. Physiol. Chem., Lund, Sweden)

203 **Isselbacher K J** & Greenberger N J. Metabolic effects of alcohol on the
liver. *N. Engl. J. Med.* 270:351-6, 1964.
(Mass. Gen. Hospital, Gastrointestinal Unit, Boston, MA 02114)

200 **Lieber C S** & Schmid R. The effect of ethanol on fatty acid metabolism:
stimulation of hepatic fatty acid synthesis *in vitro.*
J. Clin. Invest. 40:394-407, 1961. (Harvard Med. Sch., Dept. Medicine, Boston, MA 02115)

193 **Waldmann T A,** Steinfeld J L, Dutcher T F, Davidson J D & Gordon R S.
The role of the gastrointestinal system in "idiopathic hypoproteinemia."
Gastroenterology 41:197-214, 1961. (NIH, NCI, Bethesda, MD 20014)

Figure 2: Affiliations of the 300 most-cited authors at the time of publication of their most-cited articles. The number of papers from each institution is listed.

Number of Papers	Institute
45	National Institutes of Health, Bethesda, MD
	National Cancer Institute (12)
	National Heart & Lung Institute (14)
	National Institute of Allergy & Infectious Diseases (2)
	National Institute of Arthritis, Metabolism & Digestive Diseases (8)
	National Institute of Child Health & Human Development (1)
	National Institute of Dental Research (1)
	National Institute of Mental Health (5)
	National Institute of Neurological Diseases & Strokes (2)
19	Harvard University, Cambridge, MA
	Biological Laboratories (2)
	Converse Laboratory (1)
	Dept. Chemistry (5)
	Harvard College/Smithsonian Astrophysics Observatory (1)
	Medical School (10)
11	Rockefeller University, New York, NY
	Dept. unspecified (9)
	Dept. Immunology (1)
	Laboratory of Biochemical Genetics (1)
9	New York University School of Medicine, New York, NY

9 University of Washington, Seattle, WA
  Dept. unspecified (1)
  Dept. Anatomy (1)
  Dept. Biochemistry (2)
  Dept. Chemistry (1)
  Dept. Microbiology & Pathology (1)
  Dept. Pathology (2)
  Medical School (1)
8 Karolinska Institute, Stockholm, Sweden
  Dept. Chemistry (1)
  Dept. Histology (2)
  Dept. Tumor Biology (1)
  King Gustav V Research Institute (1)
  Medical School (3)
8 University of Wisconsin, Madison, WI
  College of Agriculture (1)
  Dept. Biochemistry (1)
  Institute for Enzyme Research (2)
  Laboratory of Genetics (1)
  McArdle Mem. Laboratory (1)
  Medical School (2)
7 Stanford University, Stanford, CA
  Dept. unspecified (1)
  Dept. Biological Science (1)
  Dept. Chemistry (2)
  School of Medicine (2)
  Stauffer Laboratories of Physical Chemistry (1)
6 California Institute of Technology, Pasadena, CA
  Dept. unspecified (1)
  Division of Biology (2)
  Gates & Crellin Laboratory of Chemistry (2)
  Norman W. Church Laboratory of Chemical Biology (1)
5 Massachusetts Institute of Technology, Cambridge, MA
  Dept. Biology (3)
  Dept. Chemistry (1)
  Laboratory for Nuclear Science & Dept. Physics (1)
5 University of California, Los Angeles, CA
  Dept. Chemistry (2)
  School of Medicine (2)
  Veterans Administration Center (1)
5 University of Pennsylvania, Philadelphia, PA
  Dept. Biochemistry & Medicine (1)
  Johnson Research Foundation (1)
  School of Medicine (2)
  Wistar Institute (1)
4 Institut Pasteur, Paris, France
4 Johns Hopkins University, Baltimore, MD
  Dept. Biology (1)
  School of Medicine (3)
4 Massachusetts General Hospital, Boston, MA
  Arteriosclerosis Unit (1)
  Biochemistry Research Laboratory (1)
  Cardiac Unit (1)
  Gastrointestinal Unit (1)
4 Vanderbilt University, Nashville, TN
  Dept. Pharmacology & Physiology (2)
  School of Medicine (2)
4 Washington University School of Medicine, St. Louis, MO
  Dept. unspecified (1)
  Dept. Pharmacology (2)
  Metabolism Division (1)

Figure 2 (continued)

4 Yale School of Medicine, New Haven, CT
Dept. Anatomy (2)
Dept. Pathology (1)
Dept. Pharmacology (1)

3 Brandeis University, Graduate Dept. Biochemistry, Waltham, MA

3 Columbia University, New York, NY
College of Physicians (1)
Dept. Chemistry (2)

3 Cornell University, Ithaca, NY
Baker Laboratory (1)
Dept. Chemistry (2)

3 Albert Einstein College of Medicine, New York, NY
Dept. unspecified (1)
Dept. Cellular Biology (1)
Dept. Pathology (1)

3 Medical Research Council, Molecular Biology Laboratory, Cambridge, England

3 Mt. Sinai School of Medicine, New York, NY
Dept. Hematology (2)
Stratton Laboratory of Liver Disease (1)

3 Roswell Park Memorial Institute, Buffalo, NY
Dept. unspecified (2)
Dept. Biochemistry Research (1)

3 Royal Melbourne Hospital, Walter & Eliza Hall Institute for Medical Research, Cancer Research Unit, Victoria, Australia

3 St. Mary's Hospital, Medical Unit, London, England

3 University of Cambridge, Cambridge, England
Dept. Biochemistry (2)
Dept. Pharmacology (1)

3 University of Texas, Southwestern Medical School, Dallas, TX

3 Veterans Administration Hospital, Endocrinology Section, New Orleans, LA

3 Veterans Administration Hospital, Radioisotope Service, New York, NY

2 Australian National University, Dept. Physiology, Canberra, Australia

2 Baylor University College of Medicine, Houston, TX
Dept. Pharmacology (1)
Dept. Virology and Epidemiology (1)

2 Peter Bent Brigham Hospital, Boston, MA
Cardiorenal Unit (1)
Cardiovascular Unit (1)

2 Case Western Reserve University, Cleveland, OH
Dept. Chemistry (1)
School of Medicine (1)

2 Children's Hospital, Virus Laboratory, Philadelphia, PA

2 Imperial Cancer Research Fund, Division of Chemistry & Biochemistry, London, England

2 Northwestern University, Dept. Chemistry, Evanston, IL

2 Scripps Clinic & Research Foundation, Division of Experimental Pathology, La Jolla, CA

2 Sloan-Kettering Institute for Cancer Research, New York, NY

2 University of California, Davis, CA
Dept. Food Science & Technology (1)
School of Medicine (1)

2 University of California, San Diego, La Jolla, CA
Dept. Biology (1)
School of Medicine (1)

2 University of California School of Medicine, San Francisco, CA
2 University of Göteborg, Dept. Pharmacology, Fack, 33, Göteborg, Sweden
2 University of Illinois, Urbana, IL
  Dept. Microbiology (1)
  Noyes Laboratory (1)
2 University of Lund, Lund, Sweden
  Dept. Histology (1)
  Dept. Physiological Chemistry (1)
2 University of Michigan, Ann Arbor, MI
  University Hospital, Dept. Internal Medicine (1)
  Medical School (1)
2 University of Minnesota Variety Club Heart Hospital, Pediatric Research Laboratories, Minneapolis, MN
2 University of Oxford, Oxford, England
  Dept. Biochemistry (1)
  W. Dunn School of Pathology (1)
2 Weizmann Institute of Science, Rehovoth, Israel
  Dept. Chemistry (1)
  Dept. Genetics (1)
1 Arizona State University, Dept. Chemistry, Tempe, AZ
1 Bell Telephone Laboratories, Murray Hill, NJ
1 Bispebjerg Hospital, Dept. Clinical Physiology, Copenhagen, Denmark
1 Robert Bent Brigham Hospital, Dept. Medicine & Dermatology, Boston, MA
1 British Columbia Research Council, Chemistry Division, Vancouver, Canada
1 Brookhaven National Laboratory, Biology Dept., Upton, NY
1 Burroughs Wellcome & Co., Wellcome Research Laboratory, Tuchahoe, NY
1 Carnegie Institute of Washington, Washington, DC
1 Carnegie-Mellon University, Dept. Chemistry, Pittsburgh, PA
1 Centre National Recherche Scientifique, Centre de Neurochimie, Strasburg, France
1 Children's Asthma Research Institute & Hospital, Denver, CO
1 City of Hope Medical Center, Dept. Medicine, Duarte, CA
1 Cleveland Clinic Foundation Research Division, Cleveland, OH
1 Clinical Research Center, Harrow, Middlesex, England
1 Czechoslovak Academy of Sciences, Institute of Organic Chemistry & Biochemistry, Prague, Czechoslovakia
1 Duke University Medical Center, Dept. Biochemistry, Durham, NC
1 E. I. Du Pont de Nemours & Co., Central Research Dept., Wilmington, DE
1 A. B. Hässle, Biochemical Research Laboratory, Göteborg, Sweden
1 Indiana University, Dept. Chemistry, Bloomington, IN
1 Institute for Cancer Research, Philadelphia, PA
1 International Business Machines Corporation, Research Laboratory San Jose, CA
1 Istituto Regina Elena per lo Studio la Cura dei Tumori, Rome, Italy
1 King's College, Dept. Biochemistry, London, England
1 McGill University, Dept. Anatomy, Montreal, Canada
1 McMaster University, Dept. Pathology, Hamilton, Ontario, Canada
1 Mellon Institute, Pittsburgh, PA
1 Merck Institute for Therapeutic Research, Division of Virus and Cell Biology Research, West Point, PA
1 Merck, Sharp & Dohme, Research Laboratory, Rahway, NJ
1 Michigan State University, Dept. Physiology, East Lansing, MI

Figure 2 (continued)

1 Middlesex Hospital Medical School, Dept. Immunology, London, England
1 Charles T. Miller Hospital, Dept. Pathology, St. Paul, MN
1 National Institute for Research in Dairying, Shinfield, Berkshire, England
1 National Institute of Health, Tokyo, Japan
1 National Institute of Mental Health, Laboratories of Neuropharmacology and Preclinical Pharmacology, Washington, DC
1 National Jewish Hospital & Research Center, Denver, CO
1 Oak Ridge National Laboratory, Biology Division, Oak Ridge, TN
1 Ohio State University, Dept. Chemistry, Colombus, OH
1 Ontario Cancer Institute, Divisions of Biological Research & Physics, Toronto, Ontario, Canada
1 Pennsylvania State University College of Medicine, Hershey, PA
1 Princeton University, Frick Chemical Laboratory, Princeton, NJ
1 Public Health Research Institute of the City of New York, Dept. Biochemistry, New York, NY
1 Purdue University, R. B. Wetherill Laboratory, West Lafayette, IN
1 Rijks University, Organic Chemistry Laboratory, Utrecht, Netherlands
1 Royal College of Surgeons, Dept. Pharmacology, London, England
1 Royal Free Hospital, Dept. Medicine, London, England
1 Royal Postgraduate Medical School, London, England
1 Salk Institute, Neuroendocrinology Laboratory, La Jolla, CA
1 Stanford Research Institute, Dept. Thermochemistry & Chemical Kinetics, Menlo Park, CA
1 State University of New York, School of Pharmacy, Amherst, NY
1 Tel-Aviv University, Dept. Chemistry, Ramat-Aviv, Tel-Aviv, Israel
1 University College, Dept. Biophysics, London, England
1 University of California, Hormone Research Laboratory, Berkeley, CA
1 University of California, Los Alamos Science Laboratory, Los Alamos, NM
1 University of Chicago, Dept. Chemistry & Institute for Study of Metals, Chicago, IL
1 University of Colorado School of Medicine, Dept. Surgery, Denver, CO
1 University of Glasgow, Dept. Biochemistry, Glasgow, Scotland
1 University of Munich, Institute for Organic Chemistry, Munich, Federal Republic of Germany
1 University of Pittsburgh Graduate School of Medicine, Dept. of Biochemistry & Nutrition, Pittsburgh, PA
1 University of Stockholm, Wenner-Gren Institute, Stockholm, Sweden
1 University of Texas, Dept. Chemistry, Austin, TX
1 University of Toronto, Dept. Medical Biophysics, Toronto, Ontario, Canada
1 University of Utah, Dept. Chemistry, Salt Lake City, UT

Current Comments

Additional History and Sociology of
Science Coverage in *Current Contents*

Number 50   December 11, 1978

For some time we have covered history and sociology of science journals in *Current Contents® /Social & Behavioral Sciences*. Beginning in 1979, we are extending our coverage to other editions of *CC®* , and to other ISI® information services. Figure 1 shows how coverage will be extended.

Considering my own interest in the field, I'm surprised I took so long to broaden *CC*'s coverage of this subject. Early in my career in information science, I almost became a historian of science myself. When I was the young upstart member of the Johns Hopkins University Welch Medical Library Indexing Project, my boss was Dr. Sanford V. Larkey.[1] He had been trained in medicine, but became fascinated by Elizabethan medicine and wrote several papers on it.[2,3,4] My friend and mentor Chauncey Leake was one of the project's advisors.[5] Chauncey was one of the rare individuals who was interested in the history of science while he was still doing scientific research. During my tenure on the project, I often attended Oswei Temkin's and Richard Shryock's lectures on the history of

medicine.[6] During that time I also met Estelle Brodman, the only person who ever succeeded in getting a Ph.D. awarded jointly by the history and anatomy departments and the school of library service at Columbia University.[7]

Obviously we have weightier reasons for extending our coverage than to allow me to pursue an interest. When Robert Merton recommended that we cover the history of science in our new *Arts & Humanities Citation Index™ (A&HCI ™)*, I realized we had not taken this step for the *Science Citation Index® (SCI®)*. From there it became obvious that we had neglected to do this for *CC*. Some of the historians we talked to gave us their opinions on how knowledge of the history of science can benefit scientists.

Robert Multhauf, who is retiring this year as editor of *Isis*, says it can open the scientist's mind and illuminate the process of discovery. Multhauf states that "in order to discover anything, a scientist has to deviate from the things that he was taught in school....The ordinary student who takes a course in science never hears that there are any wrong answers because the

Figure 1: History, philosophy, and sociology of science journals that will be covered in *Current Contents®* and other ISI services. The line in bold-face indicates services to which the journals will be added in 1979. The line in parentheses indicates which services already cover the journals.

Annals of Science
CC® /LS, CC/P&CS, SCI®
(CC/S&BS, SSCI™, A&HCI™, ASCA®)

Archives for History of Exact Sciences
(CC/S&BS, CC/P&CS, SCI, ASCA)

British Journal for the
History of Science
CC/LS, CC/P&CS, SCI
(CC/S&BS, SSCI, A&HCI, ASCA)

British Journal for the
Philosophy of Science
CC/LS, CC/P&CS, SCI
(CC/S&BS, SSCI, A&HCI, ASCA)

Bulletin of the History of Medicine
CC/LS, SCI, SSCI, ASCA

Centaurus
CC/LS, CC/P&CS, SCI
(CC/S&BS, SSCI, A&HCI, ASCA)

Isis
CC/LS, CC/P&CS, SCI
(CC/S&BS, SSCI, A&HCI, ASCA)

Journal of the History of Medicine
and Applied Sciences
CC/LS, CC/CP, SCI, SSCI, ASCA

Journal of the History of the
Behavioral Sciences
CC/LS, CC/CP, SCI
(CC/S&BS, SSCI, ASCA)

Medical History
CC/LS, CC/CP, SCI, SSCI, ASCA

Philosophy of Science
CC/LS, CC/P&CS
(CC/S&BS, SCI, SSCI, A&HCI, ASCA)

Scientia
CC/LS, CC/P&CS, SCI
(CC/S&BS, SSCI, A&HCI, ASCA)

Social Studies of Science
CC/LS, CC/P&CS
(CC/S&BS, SCI, SSCI, A&HCI, ASCA)

Studies in History & Philosophy of Science
CC/LS, CC/P&CS, SCI
(CC/S&BS, SSCI, A&HCI, ASCA)

Synthesis - Cambridge
CC/LS, CC/P&CS, SCI
(SSCI, A&HCI, ASCA)

Technology and Culture
CC/P&CS
(CC/ET&AS, CC/S&BS, SSCI, A&HCI, ASCA)

textbook only has right answers; that is, answers that are considered right at the time the textbook is written. He is likely to come out of school not having any idea of what is involved in the act of discovery, but this is something you can learn from the history of science."

Estelle Brodman, now librarian and professor of history at Washington University in St. Louis, Missouri, points out another advantage that a historical perspective can give: "It's useful to see some of the things that *didn't* work out, to find out what made things successful....It gives a little humility to a group that thinks it knows everything about everything and should be allowed to make all the decisions for everybody in the world."

Alexander Vucinich of the University of Pennsylvania Department of the History and Sociology of Science notes that some historians do not concentrate solely on the study of scientific progress. They also take note of science in a social, economic, and political context. Their work can therefore help scientists explore the relationship between science and society.

For these reasons, you might expect scientists to be keenly interested in the history of science. Yet many historians of science believe they are not. Multhauf states that before 1900, scientists received some general science history as part of their education. This is no longer true. One reason, he suggests, is that scientists are being forced to absorb more and more technical information. Thus, they are pressed for time and reluctant to spend it studying history. Another reason, Multhauf adds, is that "scientists have been very prosperous for the last generation, and prosperous people tend to become narrow-minded."

One historian of science here at ISI, Henry Small, editor of the Society for Social Studies of Science's *4S Newsletter*, says another reason is that scientists are forward-looking individuals. They are interested in what is happening now, or what is going to happen tomorrow. The scientists who take an interest in history usually do so after their careers have peaked, when they have the leisure time to study the past and the inclination to do so.

Stephen G. Brush of the University of Maryland's Department of History and Institute for Physical Sciences and Technology says many scientists are still unaware that the history of science exists as an independent, established discipline. However, Derek de Solla Price estimates that in the US there are about 40 universities which teach history of science courses, and about 25 that give Ph.D.s in the history of science "or in some combination of it with the philosophy of science."[8] Genevieve Miller, director of the Howard Diettrick Museum of the History of Medicine in Cleveland, Ohio, estimates that there are about 40 medical schools which offer electives in the history of medicine.

Arnold Thackray, also with the University of Pennsylvania Department of the History and Sociology of Science and the new editor of *Isis,* estimates that there are about 100 to 200 Ph.D.s in the history of science in the US, and about 30 each in Great Britain, France, and West Germany. He also estimates that there are about a hundred historians of science in the USSR. He blames scientists' lack of interest in the history of science on specialization, but cautions against exaggerating that lack of interest. Thackray thinks that though the percentage of interested scientists is relatively small, the number of interested *individuals* may be quite large.

Despite the benefits that our coverage should bring, some readers of the editions affected may be puzzled to find history of science journals in *Current Contents.* Others might object to this change and point to a few specialty journals that their editions of *CC* do not yet cover. However, I expect that

725

readers will find much useful or interesting material in them that they would have missed otherwise.

Our extended coverage should also please the publishers of the journals themselves. I'm sure they can use the additional exposure and subscription support that our coverage may stimulate. However, I must point out that many journals in this field adhere to archaic editorial and bibliographic styles.

We hope that the inevitable new contacts with *CC* readers will lead them to change them.

More importantly, we think our extended coverage will help increase interdisciplinary contact between scientists, sociologists, and historians of science—groups which, common sense tells us, ought to have a lot to say to each other.

REFERENCES

1. **Larkey S V**. The Army Medical Library Research project at the Welch Medical Library. *Bull. Med. Libr. Ass.* 37:121-4, 1949.
2. ------------. Childbirth in the days of Queen Elizabeth.
   Amer. J. Obstet. Gynecol. 27:303-8, 1934.
3. ------------. Public health in Tudor England.
   Amer. J. Public Health 24:912-3, 1934.
4. ------------. Public health in Tudor England.
   Amer. J. Public Health 24:1099-1102, 1934.
5. **Garfield E**. To remember Chauncey D. Leake.
   Current Contents (8):5-15, 13 February 1978.
6. **Shryock R**. *The development of modern medicine.*
   Philadelphia: University of Pennsylvania Press, 1936. 442 p.
7. **Brodman E**. *The development of medical bibliography.*
   Baltimore, MD: Waverly Press, 1954. 226 p.
8. **Price D J D**. *Science since Babylon. Enlarged edition.*
   New Haven, CT: Yale University Press, 1976. 215 p.

Current Comments

**Five Years of *Current Book Contents*
and Multi-Authored Book Indexing**

Number 51   December 18, 1978

It's hard to believe it has been five years since ISI® first started covering multi-authored books in *Current Contents*® *(CC*® *)*. When we began *Current Book Contents*® *(CBC™)* in the latter part of 1973 we looked on it as an experiment. As I reported to you before, that experiment was a resounding success.[1] At first we listed books only in the *Life Sciences* edition of *CC*. Now books are covered in every *CC* edition including our new *CC/Arts & Humanities*.[2]

Scientists and publishers may not be aware of this — although librarians surely are—but our treatment of books in *CBC* is revolutionary.[1] Libraries and other organizations traditionally catalog books. But they do not often catalog or index books at the chapter level. We treat each chapter as if it were a journal article, indexing title words and authors. Thus, we give readers access points to single chapters which had not been available before.

By the end of 1978, we will have covered 330 multi-authored books in *CC/Life Sciences*. Over 300 books, most of them multi-authored, will also be listed in 1978 in each of three other editions—

CC/Social & Behavioral Sciences, CC/Physical & Chemical Sciences, and *CC/Agriculture, Biology & Environmental Sciences.* Over 400 multi-authored books will be covered each in *CC/Engineering, Technology & Applied Sciences* and *CC/Clinical Practice.* We expect this growth to continue.

In 1979, some editions will list up to 600 books — about one dozen per week. As you might expect, there is some overlap between editions just as there is with journals. Nevertheless, the number of unique multi-authored book titles we will cover is in excess of 2,000.

There is an indexing fee for books listed in *CC/Life Sciences.* These fees are based on the number of chapters in the books. To date we have covered over 1,600 books in *CC/Life Sciences* alone. Over 70 different publishers were represented.

For the *CBC* sections of other editions of *Current Contents* no indexing fees are charged. We use several methods to locate books of potential interest to readers. Our staff examines publishers' catalogs, book announcements, and even the backs of book jackets for recent books of interest. Conference listings in journals are examined for proceedings published as books. We then request copies of these books from the publishers. We have also built a close working relationship with many publishers who automatically send us books which they feel our readership might find valuable.

After we receive the books, we go through a further selection process before they can be covered in *CBC*. Since information about the contents of *multi-authored* works is poorly disseminated and inadequately indexed, priority is given to these books.

About 95% of the materials we handle in *CBC* are multi-authored works. Of that number, more than half are conference or symposium proceedings. This makes it easier for you to keep up-to-date on this rather elusive literature. Many of these are works in a series. We generally cover all volumes in major series, including review series.

To make information about *CBC* entries even more accessible to *CC* users, we include title words or phrases from book and chapter titles in the *Weekly Subject Index*. We also include the addresses (when provided) of first authors of chapters in the author-address directory.

From the beginning of *CBC*, ISI has provided a special coupon for readers who want to save time or consolidate their book orders by "ordering" through ISI. Having read the contents page you can simply circle the *CBC* number and just mail the coupon to us. ISI forwards these orders to the publishers as a free service to readers and publishers. From past surveys we know that for every order we receive at ISI there are an additional nine or ten sent through other channels. Most of our readers use their institutional libraries or purchasing departments to order books. Nevertheless, from 1973 to 1977 we forwarded almost 29,000 orders to publishers. During the first 10 months of 1978 we forwarded another 4,500 orders.

We thought it might interest you to know which books generated the most orders during the last five years. In Figure 1 the number of orders we received and the book's citation count are listed. The citation data were obtained from the *Science Citation Index®* *(SCI®)* and the *Social Sciences Citation Index™*. Some of the books have been well-cited in the one or two years since their publication. But considering the number of papers these books contain, the number of citations most received is not yet so impressive. Their impact may not be noticed for several more years.

Two of the books on the list seem to be of general interest to scientists—books they might want for their private collections. *The excitement and fascination of science* is a collection of autobiographical and philosophical essays written by scientists. A possible reason for its popularity: Annual Reviews, Inc. offered it to our readers (and still does) at a minimal charge of $1.50.

The books which generated the most orders forwarded to publishers by ISI® through *CBC*™ from 1974 to the present.

Number of Orders	Books	Total Citations to Date
365	*The excitement and fascination of science. A collection of autobiographical and philosophical essays by contemporary scientists.* Palo Alto, CA: Annual Reviews, Inc., 1965. 566 p. $1.50 (35 papers)	62
147	Bloom B R & David J R, eds. *In vitro methods in cell-mediated and tumor immunity.* New York: Academic Press, 1976. 748 p. $34.50 (58 papers)	186
131	Smith J R & Smith L G, eds. *Beyond monogamy — recent studies of sexual alternatives in marriage.* Baltimore: Johns Hopkins University Press, 1974. 336 p. $15.00 (16 papers)	54
122	Mendoza E, ed. *A random walk in science. An anthology compiled by R.L. Weber.* New York: Crane, Russak & Co., 1974. 206 p. $12.50 (100 papers)	18
90	Travis J C. *Fundamentals of RIA (radioimmunoassay) and other ligand assays. A programmed text.* Anaheim: Scientific Newsletters, Inc., 1977. 168 p. $25.00	—
67	Bergmeyer H U, ed. *Principles of enzymatic analysis.* Weinheim: Verlag Chemie, 1978. 260 p. $19.60 (20 papers)	1
63	Bach F H & Good R A, eds. *Clinical immunobiology. Vol. 3.* New York: Academic Press, 1976. 422 p. $24.50 (21 papers)	25
61	National Cancer Institute. *Modern concepts in brain tumor therapy: laboratory and clinical investigations. National Cancer Institute monographs. Vol. 46.* Bethesda: National Cancer Institute, 1977. 250 p. $8.00 (32 papers)	9
61	Mulvihill J J, Miller R W & Fraumeni J F, eds. *Genetics of human cancer. Progress in cancer research and therapy. Vol. 3.* New York: Raven Press, 1977. 519 p. $19.00 (47 papers)	48
60	Nierlich D P, Rutter W J & Fox C F, eds. *Molecular mechanisms in the control of gene expression.* New York: Academic Press, 1976. 655 p. $28.50 (65 papers)	78

Another general interest book, *A random walk in science,* is an anthology of both amusing and serious pieces written about science and scientists. It sold for $12.50.

Most of the other items on the list seem to reflect highly active areas in scientific research. Several deal with cancer. For example, *In vitro methods in cell-mediated and tumor immunity* has been cited 186 times since its publication in 1976. *Molecular mechanisms in the control of gene expression* deals with another area that has been much talked about of late — cloning. It has received 78 citations since it was published in 1976. Both were published by Academic Press.

Several of the books cover methods. One of these was actually a programmed text. Although few texts appear in *CBC*, we are pleased this one piqued our readers' interests.

Encouraged by the success of *CBC*, we expanded our book coverage in 1977 to the *Science Citation Index*, again indexing at the chapter level. For the *SCI*, we create an indexing entry for every author and every significant title word. In addition, we index every cited reference, making the chapter retrievable through the *Citation Index* section of *SCI*. Most books covered in *SCI* have also appeared in *Current Book Contents*. This year we further expanded our book coverage at the chapter level by introducing *Index to Scientific &*

Technical Proceedings™. In 1979, we will add books to the *Social Sciences Citation Index* and the *Arts & Humanities Citation Index*™ and we will introduce a new service which will also cover books, the *Index to Social Sciences & Humanities Proceedings*™.

CBC was thus an important beginning for us. But we must go on to more comprehensive book coverage in our services. How we will do this is the subject of another essay. Perhaps we will be able to use citation methods to select books for retrospective indexing. Any well-cited book ought to become one of our source publications.

In the meantime, I hope that editors of books and authors of chapters will appreciate the significance of our decision to select their books. On the other hand, we hope that editors and authors of books which we do not select will understand that there are economic limitations to our coverage of books as there are to our journal coverage.

REFERENCES

1. **Garfield E.** *Current Book Contents* settles in; progress report on a resoundingly successful experiment! *Current Contents* (34):5-6, 21 August 1974. (Reprinted in: Garfield E. *Essays of an information scientist.* Philadelphia: ISI Press, 1977. Vol 2, p. 118-9).
2. ------------. Announcing *Current Contents/Arts & Humanities:* in 1979 our *Current Contents* series will cover virtually every academic discipline. *Current Contents* (30):5-7, 24 July 1978.

Current Comments

Reflections on 1978; Looking Forward to 1979

Number 52   December 25, 1978

For ISI® , 1978 was a very good year indeed. There is every reason to believe 1979 may prove to be even better.

It was a big year for us in several ways. We initiated an important change in the *Science Citation Index® (SCI®)*. Earlier this year I announced that we would publish four *SCI* quarterlies (instead of three) in 1979.[1] However, we decided to accelerate our schedule and modify our decision. Rather than wait until 1979 we will publish in 1978 a fourth softbound issue of *SCI* covering October and November. In this way articles indexed in that period will be retrievable at least four months earlier than before. We are also accelerating our printing schedule for the 1978 annual which covers the December material.

Beginning in 1979 subscribers will receive six bi-monthly *SCI* issues. With accelerated printing and delivery, *SCI* information will be available, on average, at least two months earlier than in the past. The six bi-monthly issues will constitute a second set of *SCI* which can be used in branch libraries of the large institutions that use *SCI* the most.

Next year we will also be investigating a possible need and preference for semiannual rather than annual cumulations.

In 1979 we will make significant changes in *Current Contents® (CC®)*. We will eliminate the "C" section which appeared in the center of *CC/Life Sciences* and *CC/Clinical Practice*. We are *not* eliminating coverage of clinical journals which appeared in "C"—only the section itself which was common to the two editions. Having the "C" section in both editions represented a significant savings in preparation and printing. But its elimination will save *CC* readers valuable time. We can now arrange journals in *CC/LS* and *CC/CP* in a more logical and consistent manner. In *CC/LS* clinical journals will no longer be artificially located in the middle of the section devoted to pre-clinical subjects. And in the clinical edition we can place leading general medical journals at the beginning, followed by those devoted to medical specialties. The elimination of the "C" section will also do away with the annoying "C" pagination in our weekly indexes.

We will also be changing the title of the physical science edition of CC to *Current Contents/Physical, Chemical & Earth Sciences.* We will be adding significantly to our coverage of the earth sciences. We have had good coverage all along, but increased interest in this area recently led us to re-examine our coverage. My trip to the Soviet Union and the Far East last year convinced me that we should not only take this step, but plan for a large scale retrospective *Earth Sciences Citation Index.*

In 1978 we also took a first step in providing information services for scholars in the arts and humanities by introducing the *Arts & Humanities Citation Index* ™ *(A&HCI* ™*).* As I pointed out before, for a company largely concerned with the natural, physical, and social sciences, this was a giant step.[2] We always knew that the information needs of scholars in the arts and humanities were as great, if not greater, than those in the sciences and social sciences. But modern tools to help them with ever increasing amounts of information were slow in coming for a variety of reasons. I had often discussed this problem with Robert Hayne, ISI's chief editor.[3] The joy of publishing our first annual volume of *A&HCI* covering 1977 literature is diminished considerably by his absence. However, that volume is dedicated to his memory. I was also thinking about Bob Hayne when I was recently presented with the annual award of the American Society for Information Science for the best information science book of 1977.[4]

We will extend our arts and humanities information services in 1979 by producing *Current Contents/Arts & Humanities.*[5] This edition of *Current Contents* is designed for scholars in such disciplines as music, literature, art, linguistics, etc. It should prove especially useful to those who want to have a broad multi-disciplinary overview of the arts and humanities. We will also launch the *Index to Social Sciences & Humanities Proceedings* ™.[6]

Other changes scheduled for 1979 include improvements in *CCs* Author Address Directory which will benefit users of all editions of *Current Contents.* In past years, the Directory has included only the names of first authors whose addresses were given in the article. Now all first authors will be listed so that the Directory is at least a complete index to first authors.

Another improvement in the Directory will be the inclusion of the reprint author's address directly under the name of first author. Formerly, users looked up the name of the first author and were directed by a "see" cross-reference to the names of the reprint author. Our new format eliminates this second step.

An even more important improvement will be introduced, and welcomed, especially by secretaries and others who have to prepare reprint requests. The type size of the Directory will be increased significantly early in 1979. Another improvement will please our Canadian authors and readers alike. Postal zones will appear at the end of the addresses to conform with Canadian postal regulations.

In 1979 we will also introduce a product designed to alert organic chemists to new and newly modified reactions and syntheses described in the journal literature. *Current Chemical Reactions™ (CCR™)* will be appreciated by chemists who need information about reactions that produce better yields or who need to duplicate certain reactions or find faster and cleaner methods. I will describe *CCR* more fully in a future essay.

All of the above are important changes. But by far the most important decision we made in 1978 was to leave our present headquarters. ISI has been located at 325 Chestnut Street, about a block from Independence Hall, for ten years now. However, the steady growth of the company has made our present quarters exceedingly cramped. Desks and people are crammed into every conceivable working area. Since this situation would have continued as ISI kept growing, we felt it necessary to find larger quarters.

Once the decision to move had been reached, we were faced with a number of alternatives. We could lease more space in a larger office building, lease an entire building, buy an already existing building, or construct our own. We opted for the latter choice for a variety of reasons. By building our own head-

quarters we can have offices that uniquely fit this company's needs. We especially need flexibility in adapting to a stream of new products and services.

I am often asked why ISI is located in Philadelphia. That is an accident of history which has been described recently in a local magazine.[7] Undoubtedly, ISI could function in California, New York, or some other place. Without claiming sentimentality we are content to remain in Philadelphia.

Our new building will be located in the heart of the University City Science Center. The Science Center can best be described as an urban research park. Its primary asset is its close proximity to the University of Pennsylvania and Drexel University (formerly Drexel Institute of Technology). Our neighbors will be science-oriented companies with whom we can share the joint resources of the Science Center. The Center will also include an international conference facility.

Our new building, shown in Figure 1, will also provide a pleasant and spacious working area. Designed by the award-winning architectural firm of Venturi & Rauch, it will offer 130 thousand square feet in four stories—enough space to meet our projected needs for at least ten years. However, additional land is available for another building.

In cooperation with the University City Science Center, ISI is also planning to provide a child care center for ISI employees on or near

Figure 1: *An artist's rendering of the new ISI building.*

the new site. Since I was raised by a working mother, I can appreciate how important an adequate and convenient child care facility is to working parents.

The construction of our building is in some ways ironic. When I originally conceived many of the information services we now produce, I tried to design them so that machines rather than people would do most of the work. I wanted to limit the number of employees I would need to yours truly. That's proven to be an elusive ideal.

We do have our share of machines today—our computer runs constantly. But we also have nearly 500 employees. And we will be expanding to nearly 1,000 people over the next ten years unless technology or world conditions prove me wrong. I suspect, however, that what we may not need in production we will need in marketing! Both the history and

future of ISI show that automation does not necessarily mean unemployment.

At the groundbreaking ceremony for our new building in October, I took the opportunity to say a few words of thanks to the people who have helped make ISI a success. Reprinted on the following pages is the text of my speech. In it I thank various groups, including our subscribers. But most of all it concerns ISI employees.

The past year has been, as you have seen, a good one for me professionally. Unfortunately, 1978 was a sad year for me personally. In rapid succession I lost two people who were very important in my life.[8,9] But as they would have observed, life must go on. And so it does at ISI as elsewhere. I hope that 1979 will be a happy and productive year for all of ISI's friends, subscribers, readers, and employees.

REFERENCES

1. **Garfield E.** The endless quest for timeliness—a fourth quarterly *Science Citation Index. Current Contents* (31):5-8, 31 July 1978.
2. ------------. Will ISI's *Arts & Humanities Citation Index* revolutionize scholarship? *Current Contents* (32):5-9, 8 August 1977.
3. ------------. To remember my brother Robert L. Hayne. *Current Contents* (34):5-6, 22 August 1977.
4. ------------. *Essays of an information scientist.* Philadelphia: ISI Press, 1977. 2 vols.
5. ------------. Announcing *Current Contents/Arts & Humanities:* in 1979 our *Current Contents* series will cover virtually every academic discipline. *Current Contents* (30):5-7, 24 July 1978.
6. ------------. Introducing *Index to Social Sciences & Humanities Proceedings*—more help in locating and acquiring proceedings. *Current Contents* (33):5-10, 14 August 1978.
7. Man on his own: Gene Garfield takes on the world. *Focus (Philadelphia)* (530):20-1, 25 October 1978.
8. **Garfield E.** To remember Chauncey D. Leake. *Current Contents* (7):5-13, 13 February 1978.
9. ------------. To remember my father. *Current Contents* (8):5-6, 20 February 1978.

Remarks of

Eugene Garfield, Ph.D.

President

Institute for Scientific Information® (ISI®)

Corporate Headquarters Groundbreaking Ceremony
October 17, 1978

Over 20 years ago, when I had just started *Current Contents®* , I could honestly identify with the comedian, Rodney Dangerfield. His famous complaint, of course, is, "I don't get no respect."

I certainly didn't get no respect then either. Not only was I a one-man operation, but I was a *for-profit* one-man operation in a field in which commercial organizations were virtually nonexistent.

In those days, my company was called Eugene Garfield Associates. So I figured that if "Eugene Garfield" couldn't get no respect, perhaps the Institute for Scientific Information could. That's why I changed the name. And, quite frankly, I really think it helped.

As the first ISI employee, I'm in a unique position to see how far we've really come since then. And, when I look back, I realize how many people in how many professions I need to thank.

Certainly, I need to acknowledge our customers who now include researchers and librarians working in the sciences, social sciences, and the arts and humanities. And I should mention the editors and publishers of the primary journals which are, in effect, ISI's raw materials. Of course, the suppliers who provide ISI with printing, composition, office supplies, computer hardware, and the million other things that are needed to operate our business shouldn't be forgotten. And neither should those in the financial community who have looked after ISI's money matters. Without the advice and support of all of the people I have mentioned, ISI could never have become a success.

But today I want to pay special tribute to the group I have depended on the most—the people who work at ISI.

Now, I'm not going to stand up here and say that ISI is one big happy family. That would be a lot of sentimental rubbish. We are, like many other successful organizations, able to work reasonably well as a team. After a while, an organization has a momentum of its own. Each of you contributes to the vigor, productivity, and prestige of ISI. In a very real sense, this new building is as much yours as it is mine.

My late friend Chauncey Leake clarified my feelings quite well when he told me that "self interest must merge with community interests." I like to believe that at ISI the company's interests have largely merged with employees' interests. But ultimately each employee must decide whether that is really true in his or her own case. We cannot be all things to all of you.

ISI wants to provide the good working conditions this new building will offer because it realizes that the effectiveness of each employee is crucial to ISI's overall effectiveness. If an issue of *Current Contents* leaves the mailroom late, the customer gets it late. If the wrong tearsheet is sent, the customer may not be able to complete a project on time. If a data-entry operator misspells an author's name, then for all intents and purposes that author ceases to exist. To the extent that things like inadequate space, poor lighting, uneven heating and cooling, and excessive noise can increase these kinds of errors, it is in the interest of ISI to improve those conditions.

But even under present working conditions, which are far inferior to those we will have at our new building, mistakes like the ones I just mentioned don't happen very often. If they did, ISI's products would never receive the wide acceptance that they have today.

Our customers are among the most educated and demanding individuals in the world. They have exceedingly sophisticated information needs. Yet the renewal rate for our products is incredibly high. This is a fact that ISI employees can be proud of. You are, in the final analysis, the ones who satisfy the customers. And, ISI's employees are obviously doing their jobs well.

ISI is playing a valuable role in making research more effective and productive. All of the people who make up ISI can therefore take pride in the work we've done thus far. This new building symbolizes our commitment to continue the work we've begun. But it also gives us an occasion to look back with satisfaction on how far we've come, and how well we've already done.

CITED-AUTHOR INDEX
Volumes 1, 2 & 3

This index lists the names of all authors of items cited in the references of the essays and in the references of the reprints which some of the essays introduce. Cited anonymous items are alphabetically listed according to source—either publication or organization. Citations of E. Garfield have not been included.

Authors are listed alphabetically along with a volume, page and reference number. Thus, the following entry

Chagas C   2:583r5

indicates that in Volume 2, on page 583,

the fifth reference is to author C. Chagas. A page number followed by no reference number indicates an unnumbered item listed alphabetically on that page. (Volume numerals for Vol. 3 are in boldface.)

Readers doing name searches should also consult the Subject Index and the Index to Authors in Most-Cited Lists.

Aarons M W 2:150r38	Artandi J 1:90r6
Aaronson S 2:96r2, 285r1, 314r8	Arutyunov N B 1:526r7
Abbott M T J 1:62r2, 218r9	Ashby D E T F 2:486r10
Abelson P H 1:22r5, 216, 437r3	*Ashby Report* 2:337r2
Ackoff R L 2:303r7	Asimov I 2:149r11; **3:**620r11
Adair W C	Asselin T H 2:149r26
Amer. Doc, 1955 1:214r6; 2:204r4, 682r4	*Associations Transnationales* **3:**672r11
Amer. Doc, 1963 1:46r25	Atherton P 1:215r18
Albritton E C 1:437r3	Atwater W O **3:**69r18
Alexander B **3:**186r6	Auerbach C 1:119r2
Allen G 1:46r5, 46r21, 138r10(a)	Aulis J **3:**166r24
Allison S K 2:406r2	Avakian E 2:645r5; **3:**285r35
Alt F L 1:214r12	Avery O T 1:269r8
Altschuler M D 2:486r9, 486r11	Avias J 2:682r13
Ambos M 1:174r20	
American Chemical Society **3:**447r7, 464r3	
American Documentation **3:**75r4, 285r34	
American Enterprise Institute for Public Policy Research **3:**667r5	**B**
American Library Association 2:244r6	
American Men and Women of Science, (Cattell) **3:**410r9	Bachman C H 1:323r4
American National Standards Institute (ANSI) **3:**447r10	Bailey M E **3:**284r21
	Baker D 1:447r4; 2:418r18, 466r7
Ames M P **3:**516r8	Ball N T **3:**285r23
Amick D J 2:46r2	Ballantine H T, Jr. **3:**537r11, 537r15
Anderla G 2:67r2	Ballhausen C J 2:228r3
Anderson H E 2:149r22	Baltimore D 2:337r1, 337r3
Andrews D D **3:**285r41	*Baltimore Sun* 1:503r6
Ardrey R **3:**69r22	Banner B **3:**21r5
Arends T 2:583r7, 583r8	Bannur B B 1:108r1, 129r5
Argyle E 2:486r6	Baran P **3:**231r5
Arlett A **3:**460r5	Barber B 1:267r1
Arnett E M 1:218r7	Barkas J **3:**69r1
Arnold L E **3:**165r2	Barkla J 1:130r1, 218r8
Arnon D I **3:**353r4	Barlup J 1:215r29
Aronson L R **3:**108r1, 108r4, 323r3, 323r10	Barnett S A 1:490r1

Burros M   **3:**69r20

Burstall R M   2:150r34

Bush V   1:174; 2:639r6

Business Week   **3:**667r4

Butcher R W   1:218r2

Butler D D   2:149r12

Butler S   2:381r1

Byck R   1:174r20, 174r21

C

Cabe P A   1:22r2

Cade C M   2:486r5

Cade R   **3:**439r9

Calder R   1:490r1

Calderon M M   1:313r5; 2:204r14

Campbell W   2:334r1

Carpenter M P   **3:**503r4, 94r3, 239r16

Carroll M   **3:**460r12

Carter G M   **3:**196r4, 590r7

Cartter A M   1:157r9

Case P W   2:150r29

Casey R S   **3:**273r3, 285r27

Cashel M   1:383r2, 383r3

Caskey D L   2:150r28

Casper R   1:123r2

Cavalli-Sforza L   1:46r5

Cawkell A E

  Aslib Proc., 1968   1:62r3

  Brit. J. Anaesth., 1970   1:244r4

  Chem. Inf. Sys., 1975   2:327r3

  Comp. Based Inf. Ret. Sys., 1968   1:48r2,
    141r4, 214r15, 220r5, 244;   2:31r8, 191r4

  Current Contents, 1971 1;331r5, 355r1

  Current Contents, 1975   **3:**674r4

  Elect. Eng., 1967 3;273r6, 273r7

  Inf. Process. Manage., 1975   **3:**273r8

  Inf. Scientist, 1976   2:542r1

  ISI Sci. 1978 Annual Conf.   **3:**674r1

  J. Amer. Soc. Inf. Sci., 1970   2:334r7

  J. Amer. Soc. Inf. Sci., 1974   2:194r3,
    549r8

  J. Amer. Soc. Inf. Sci., 1978   **3:**131r3

  J. Document., 1968   2:421r4

  J. Document., 1971   2:334r35

  Nature, 1970   1:143r7, 156r5, 282r7

  New Scientist, 1968   1:26r3, 141r3

  On-Line Rev., 1977   **3:**258r3

  Pers. Commun., 1976   2:486r4

  Radio Electron. Eng., 1968   1:216

Cerra F   **3:**231r8

Ceshner R A   2:150r30

Chabbal R   **3:**102r12

Chagas C   2:583r5

Chapman A J   2:385r6

Charman N   2:486r8

Chauvin R   **3:**102r9

Chedd G   1:174, 495r3

Chemical & Engineering News

  1969   1:125r2; 2:418r19, 534r1

  1973   1:476r1; 2:67r1

  1974   2:76r5, 79r3

  1976   2:437r2

Chen C C   2:157r4

Chernow R   **3:**222r6

Cheryni A I   1:542r13

Childs N   2:317r1

Chimes M   **3:**537r6

China Reconstruction   2:280r6

Choueka Y   1:480r3

Christie R   **3:**516r2

Chubin D   **3:**473r10

Citron J   **3:**75r3

Clark A K   **3:**15r21

Clark K E   2:534r4

Clark R   1:380r2

Clarke A C   **3:**166r32

Cleverden C W   **3:**146r7

Cleverdon C W

  Aslib Proc., 1967   1:299r5

  Conference 1970   2:334r17

  Nature, 1964   1:174r3

  Nature, 1965   2:59r2

  Nature, 1970   1:282r5

  Pers. Commun., 1970   1:220r6

Cochran W G   1:510r5; **3:**353r7

Cohen M   1:480r3

Cohen S N   2:337r1

Coile R C   1:223r4

Cole D E   1:490r6

Cole J R

  Am. Soc. Rev., 1967   1:138r14, 157r10,
    216r37, 470r4

  Am. Soc. Rev., 1968   1:121r6, 157r7, 174

  Am. Sociol., 1971   **3:**239r9

  Science, 1972   2:27r2, 418r6; **3:**146r2,
    473r9

  Science, 1974   2:27r4, 549r3

  Sci. Am., 1977   **3:**347r11, 476r2, 590r8

  Soc. Strat. Sci., 1973   2:549r4; **3:**239r10,
    347r2, 353r2, 590r3

Cole S

  Am. Soc. Rev., 1967   1:138r14, 157r10,
    216r37, 470r4

  Am. Soc. Rev., 1968   1:121r6, 157r7, 174

  Am. Sociol., 1971   **3:**239r9

  Science, 1972   2:27r2, 418r6; **3:**146r2,
    473r9

  Science, 1974   2:27r4, 549r3

  Sci. Am., 1977   **3:**347r11, 476r2, 590r8

  Soc. Strat. Sci., 1973   2:549r4; **3:**239r10,
    347r2, 353r2, 590r3

Coleman J S   **3:**625r5

Coler M A   1:120

Collart P   1:353r4

F

G

Gilmer

Cited Author Index

Henry N L   2:36r1

Hermann B   **3:**222r4

Herner S   1:394r1; 2:645r12

Herodotus   1:155r1

Herrnstein R   **3:**662r19

Herschman A   2:437r5

Heumann K F   **3:**75r8, 284r7, 284r15

Hiatt R B   1:462r6

Hildebrand J   **3:**273r5

Hill E L   2:486r7

Hillinger C   1:271r9

Himwich W A   1:103r2, 441r3, 441r6; **3:**284r11

Hoagland S   **3:**258r5

Hodge M H Jr   1:181r2

Hodgson G   1:503r2

Hoffman R   2:228r3

Hofmann A F   1:11r1

Hogness D S   2:337r1

Holden C   **3:**14r2

Holden J C   2:670r7

Holman N W   **3:**124r3

Homola S   **3:**537r8

Horowitz I L   **3:**178r5

Houghton V. Payne   **3:**667r3

Howard R A   2:334r30

Hubert P   2:486r18

Huidodro F   2:583r6

Huisgen R   2:228r3

Hull C H   **3:**439r7

Hull R   2:34r2

Human Nature   **3:**432r1

Hungiville M   2:113r7

Hunt P R   2:113r5

Hunt R G   **3:**196r8

Hunter I S   1:62r2

Huxley A   2:373r4

H. W. Wilson Co. v. US Postal Service
   3:667r6

Hyslop M R   2:334r31; **3:**509r2

I

IEEE Transactions   1:518r4

Ingelfinger F J   2:109r5; **3:**115r7

Inglis B   **3:**447r15

Inhaber H   2:157r1; **3:**261r11, 261r12, 410r6

Institute for Scientific Information
   Index Sci. Rev., 1974   **3:**146r9
   Index Sci. Rev., 1976   **3:**87r4
   J. Cit. Rep., 1973   **3:**146r2
   SCI, Cumulation 1970-74   **3:**323r12, 347r6
   SCI Guide & Journal List, 1976   **3:**336r3, 347r5
   SCI Guide & Journal List, 1979   **3:**323r4

*Institute for Scientific Information, Inc. v.
   U.S. Postal Service*   **3:**402r3, 667r1

International Organization for Standardization
   3:447r11

Irwin M R   **3:**231r6

Isenberg A C   2:418r14

IUB Commission of Editors of Biochemical
   Journals   2:230r3

J

Jacobs F   2:451r1

Jacobs G   1:249r1, 250r1

Jacobson L   **3:**625r9

James W   **3:**13r19

Janke N C   2:27r3, 106r3

Jenkins J C   **3:**439r7

Jenkins R R   69r10

Jensen A R   **3:**661r1, 661r7, 662r22-33, 662r35-38

Jewell W S   2:149r24

Johansen R   2:645r10

Johnson A A   **3:**196r5

Johnson S C   **3:**231r6

Johnson V E   **3:**439r6

Joly H   **3:**102r4

Journal Citation Reports   **3:**146r2

Journal of American Dietary Association
   3:69r9

Journal of Biological Chemistry   1:220r4

Journal of Heredity   1:46r2

Journal of the American Medical Association
   1:147r2

Joyce J   **3:**399r6

Judge A J N   **3:**672r3

K

Kahn A B   1:46r19

Kaitz M J   2:150r27

Kalbacher B   1:383r3

Kallner H   **3:**270r1

Kamin L   **3:**662r16

Kanz E   1:353r1

Kapitsa P L   2:486r15, 486r16

Kaplan M   1:468r1

Kaplan N   **3:**218r4

Kaplan N O   1:225r1; **3:**336r8

Kash D E   1:323r1

Kassab J L   2:534r5

Katz S   2:150r32

Kaye M   2:670r16

Keenan S   1:215r18

Keith S B   **3:**712r4

Keith-Spiegel P   **3:**651r16

Keller

Price

Wilkinson

Z

SUBJECT INDEX
Volumes 1, 2 & 3

Numbers following each subject entry direct the reader to the volume and then to the first page of the essay in which reference to the subject occurs. Thus, 3:608 refers the reader to page 608 in Vol. 3. (Volume numerals for Vol. 3 entries are in boldface.)

Some essays introduce reprints, which are listed in the Subject Index under their authors' names. For example

Edge, David, reprint **3:240**

Mention or discussion of individuals in an essay often includes reference to one or more of that person's published papers. Therefore, readers doing name searches should also consult the Cited-Author Index and the Index to Authors in Most-Cited Lists.

addresses

Annals of Otology, Rhinology and Laryngology **3:**484

Annals Rheumatic Diseases 1:340

Annual Review of Pharmacology **3:**414

Annual Reviews **3:**461, 728

anonymous publication 2:438, 506

ANSA 1:442; **3:**287, 466

ANSI **3:**442

anthropology
most-cited authors **3:**639, 679

anti-science 1:494

anti-vivisectionists **3:**103, 316

aphorisms of Ralph Shaw **3:**508

Apollo space flights **3:**395

applied biology journals **3:**454

applied chemistry articles 2:184

applied research 1:242

apricots **3:**398

Arber, W. **3:**700

Archiv fur Elektrotechnik **3:**484

Archiv fur Geflugelkunde **3:**484

Archives Francaises de Pediatrie **3:**484

Archives Francaises des Maladies de l'Appareil Digestif **3:**97

Archives Italiennes de Biologie **3:**22

Ardrey, Robert **3:**66

Argyle, Michael **3:**425

Armstrong, Evelyn **3:**472

Armstrong, Garner Ted **3:**425

Aronson, Lester R. **3:**103, 316

art and science, cultural gap **3:**204, 434, 477

art, article title enrichment in A&HCI **3:**206

Arthritis and Rheumatism 1:340

Arthur C. Cope Award **3:**608

article(s)

see also most-cited articles; review articles, and each of the individual journal titles

arts **3:**206

citation networking 1:139

half life **3:**503

humanities **3:**206

impact
see journal(s), impact

language
see science, language

method **3:**1, 147, 185

milestone articles 1:139

music and philosophy **3:**206

review
see review articles

title, abbreviations 1:381

title enrichment **3:**206, 556

titles in bibliographic references 1:25, 231; 2:229; **3:**444

titles in journal contents pages **3:**267

arts and humanities and the culture gap **3:**434

Arts & Humanities Citation Index
announcement of publication, introduction and description **3:**204, 556, 732

book coverage in 1979 **3:**730

history of science coverage **3:**723

link between science and the arts **3:**434

Arts & Humanities/Current Contents **3:**556

ASCA
ASCA IV, introduction and description 1:38

ASCAmatic 1:22

citation analysis 1:268; **3:**640

computers **3:**365

cost of individual subscription **3:**642

current awareness 1:28

Current Contents readers 1:28; 2:342

cyclic AMP research 1:217

data base **3:**286

evaluation by UK Office of Scientific and Technical Information 1:130

high-frequency list 1:368

international contacts 1:100

Multi-ASCA 1:279, 336

multidisciplinary specialties **3:**28

nation, searching by **3:**640

organization monitoring **3:**640

personalized journal 1:22, 336

publicity **3:**640

'publish or perish' syndrome **3:**640

reprints **3:**307

search strategy 1:50

services available **3:**189

software **3:**223

three cultures **3:**435

ASCAMATE **3:**553

ASCAP **3:**391

ASCATOPICS
cost **3:**189

cyclic AMP research 1:217

data base **3:**286

personalized 1:278

Asimov, Isaac **3:**430, 462

ASIS
see American Society for Information Science

Aspen Systems Corporation **3:**401

assembly(ies)
see conference(s)

Associated Press **3:**581

Association of American Publishers **3:**387, 389, 403

astronauts **3:**163

astronomy
most-cited authors **3:**328, 337
their most-cited articles **3:**348
most-cited journals 1974 **3:**130

Astrophysical Journal 2:120

astrophysics
most-cited articles 2:120
most-cited journals 1974 **3:**133
250 most-cited authors **3:**326, 337
their most-cited articles **3:**348

AT&T 2:245; **3:**226

Subject Index

Atlas

Atlas of Science   2:311, 496

Australia, regulation of chiropractic   **3**:533

Australian and New Zealand journals   2:584, 593

author(s)

  see also   homographs; multiple authorship

  address directory and *CBC*   **3**:728

  author-assigned indexing terms   **3**:554

  author-journals   1:6

  cited more than 4,000 times, 1961-75   **3**:492

  co-citation analysis   **3**:232

  corporate   2:438

  cultural differences   **3**:644

  fees   1:411

  most-cited   1:488, 2:496

  most-cited in 1967   1:170

  100 most-cited *SSCI* 1969-1977   **3**:633, 675

  300 most-cited *SCI* 1961-1976   **3**:538, 587, 689, 701, 711

  250 most-cited *SCI* 1961-75   **3**:326, 337, 348

  250 most-cited *SCI* 1961-75 (corrections)   **3**:492

The authoritarian personality   **3**:623

authority list   **3**:393

authors' addresses

  see also   *International Directory of Research and Development Scientists; Who is Publishing in Science*

  in *ASCA*   **3**:225; **3**:641

  in *Current Contents*   1:4, 148; **3**:268, 380, 557

  directory of   1:4; **3**:286, 407, 728

  entry into data base   **3**:287

  in journals   **3**:387

  placement in journal articles   2:636

  reprints   2:310; **3**:194, 307

  in *Science Citation Index*   **3**:498

  style of   **3**:440

  300 most-cited authors, 1961-1976   **3**:711

  ZIP codes in   1:17

Author's League   **3**:389

authors' names

  see also   homographs; multiple authorship

  bibliographic references   **3**:443

  contents page formats   **3**:267

  initials   1:77; 2:323

  transliteration problems   1:314

authorship

  see also   multiple authorship

  anonymity   2:438, 506

  ethics   **3**:644

Automatic New Structure Alert   1:442; **3**:287, 466

Automatic Subject Citation Alert

  see   *ASCA, ASCATOPICS*

automation

  citation indexing   1:83, 98

  classification of articles in science   2:356

  criticism and documentation   1:83, 98

awards and prizes

  forecasting Nobel Prize recipients   1:132, 487

  James Murray Luck Award   **3**:461

awards and prizes   (cont'd)

  100 most-cited *SSCI* authors 1969-1977   **3**:675

  300 most-cited *SCI* authors 1961-76   **3**:587

  250 most-cited *SCI* authors, 1961-1975   **3**:337

B

Bacon, Roger   **3**:161

bacteriology

  250 most-cited authors   **3**:327, 337

  their most-cited articles   **3**:348

Baekeland Award   **3**:608

ball lightning   2:479

BankAmericard   **3**:526

banks and currency exchange   **3**:522

Bartolomeo, Beverly   1:15; **3**:686

Basalla, G.   **3**:613, 618

basic research   1:242; 2:61, 297; **3**:448

basic science laws   **3**:532

Bauman Amendment   2:269

Baylor Medical School   **3**:414

BBC   **3**:257

Beach, Frank A.   **3**:106

behavior and psychology

  most-cited journals   2:231, 262

behavioral sciences

  most-cited articles, 1950s   **3**:179

  most-cited articles, 1940s   **3**:76

behavioral theory

  most-cited articles   **3**:563

  most-cited authors   **3**:633, 675

  most-cited books   **3**:626

Belgium, legality of chiropractic   **3**:533

Bell, G.   **3**:171

Bell Telephone System   2:245; **3**:226, 282

Beltran, Sergio   2:540

Bendikson, Dr. Lodewyk   **3**:381

Berichte der Bunsen Gesellschaft fur Physikalische Chemie   **3**:484

Berlin, Irving   **3**:573

Bernhard, Silke   2:387

Bernier, J.J.   **3**:97

Beyond Monogamy   **3**:729

bibliographic chaos   1:40

bibliographic coupling   1:46, 124

  see also   co-citation analysis; co-citation clusters

bibliographic descriptors and ISI's *Unique Word Dictionary*   **3**:393

bibliographic information in *Source Index*   2:190

bibliographic records in ISI databases   **3**:287

bibliographic references

  see   references

Subject Index

bibliographic research
  see information science; literature searches
bibliography(ies)
  see also citation(s); literature searches; references
  article titles in 1:25
  preparation of 1:60
Bibliography of Agriculture **3:**506
bibliometrics 2:70
bilingualism **3:**96
Biochemistry, journals most cited by 1:265
biochemistry
  core literature 1:262, 274
  most-cited articles, 1950s **3:**147
  most-cited articles, 1940s **3:**45
  most-cited journals 1:262, 274
  300 most-cited authors **3:**690; 701
    their most-cited articles **3:**713
  250 most-cited authors **3:**327, 337
    their most-cited articles **3:**348
biochemorphology **3:**414
bioethics of vegetarianism **3:**62
biographical directories
  see also *American Men and Women of Science, Who is Publishing in Science* and *World Who's Who in Science*
Biological Abstracts
  see BIOSIS
biological sciences
  most-cited articles, 1950s **3:**179
  most-cited articles, 1940s **3:**76
Biologie Gastroenterologie **3:**97
biology, applied biology journals **3:**454
biomedical information 1:425; 2:10; **3:**121
biomedicine
  most-cited articles, 1950s **3:**179
  most-cited articles, 1940s **3:**76
biophysics
  300 most-cited authors **3:**689, 708
    their most-cited articles **3:**711
  250 most-cited authors **3:**328, 337
    their most-cited articles **3:**348
BIOSIS **3:**223, 450
bird as flying machine **3:**167
Bishop, C.T. reprint **3:**262
Bliss classification 1:95
Bliss, Henry E. 1:95; 2:250
Block, N.J. **3:**657
blood research and C. D. Leake **3:**414
Blue Cross 2:10; **3:**112, 535
BMI **3:**391
bodies, donation for medical research **3:**374
body scanner 2:429
Bohemian Club, San Francisco **3:**411
Bohr, Neils **3:**128
Bolletino della Societa Italiana di Biologia Sperimentale **3:**23
Bond, James 2:501

Bonfils, S. **3:**97
Boni, Albert **3:**380
book indexing 2:82; **3:**173
Bookbinders Restaurant, Philadelphia, PA **3:**200
bookmobiles **3:**381, 505
books
  see also *Current Book Contents*
  coverage in *SCI* & *SSCI* 2:82
  most-cited by applied chemists 2:184
  most-cited, engineering 2:441
  most-cited, mathematics 1:504
  most-cited 1961-1972 2:1
  most-cited 1967 1:224
  multi-authored
    see multiple authorship
  100 most-cited in *SSCI,* 1969-1977 **3:**621
  ordering through *Current Book Contents* **3:**728
  textbook errors 1:233
  250 most-cited *SCI*
    primary authors **3:**348
Borden Award **3:**608
Botaniska Notiser **3:**484
botany
  journals in *Current Contents* **3:**453
  most-cited articles, from botanical journals 2:216
  most-cited articles, from plant physiology journals 2:210
  most-cited authors **3:**328, 547
  most-cited journals, 1974 **3:**142
  most-cited journals, 1969 2:205
Bourbaki, Nicolas 2:440; **3:**336, 404, 645
Bova, B. **3:**617
Bradford's Law 1:222, 247; 2:301; **3:**248, 574
brain biochemistry, and C. D. Leake **3:**414
Brain Research, publication of chiropractic research **3:**536
Brain, Towards a World 1:8; 2:638
Brandeis, Justice Louis **3:**477
Breen, Ann **3:**106
bridging the culture gaps **3:**204, 434, 477
Brinberg, Herbert **3:**401
Britain, legality of chiropractic **3:**532
British airlines **3:**524
British Broadcasting Company **3:**257
British Library, Lending Division **3:**391, 574
British Post Office **3:**253, 406
Broadcast Music, Inc. **3:**391
Bronowski, Jacob 2:351; **3:**299
Brown, H.C., homograph **3:**125, 335
Brown v. Board of Education of Topeka **3:**478
Brown, W. Noel **3:**372
Buchwald, Art 2:72, 502
Bulletin d'Ecologie **3:**484
Bulletin de l'Academie Veterinaire de France **3:**484
Bulletin de la Societe Chimique de France **3:**91

Subject Index

Bulletin

Subject Index

citation

citation networks (cont'd)
 duplication of research 1:220
 electromagnetic flowmeters 1:140
 explosive welding 1:354
 forms of display 2:145
 history and sociology of science 1:43, 139;
  2:543
 Mendel's work 1:136
 milestone articles 1:139
 nucleic acids 1:135, 167; 2:138
 particle physics, 1971 2:28
 pertubation of ion transport 1:242
 UFO's 1:142
citation/publication ratio
 see journal(s), impact
Cited Author Index to *Essays*, V.1 & 2 2:689
cited references
 see references
Clapp, Verner W. 1:438; **3:**505
Clark, Joe **3:**472
Clark, Kenneth F. 2:289
C.L.A.S.S. **3:**223
classification
 algorithmic 2:356
 artificial language 1:479
 automatic classification in science 2:356
 Bliss classification 1:95
 co-citation analysis 2:354
 mechanical 2:684
La Cle des Mots **3:**96
Cleveland Public Library **3:**504
climate-control systems 1:352
clinic **3:**247
 see also conference(s)
Clinica Chimica Acta 2:179
Clinical Chemistry 2:179; **3:**484
clinical psychology
 most-cited authors **3:**634, 677
 most-cited books **3:**681
cloning **3:**730
Close Encounters of the Third Kind **3:**614,
  617
cluster data
 see co-citation analysis
co-authorship of articles
 see multiple authorship
co-citation analysis
 Atlas of Science 2:311, 496; **3:**vii
 classification 2:354; **3:**vii
 controversy **3:**232, 234, 240
 description, by Aaronson S. 2:286
 description, by Cawkell, A. E. 2:543
 description, by Garfield, E. 2:26
 description, by Small H. 2:28
 engineering sciences 2:441
 immortality 2:71
 mapping scientific specialties 2:60, 311; **3:**vi
 Mendel, Gregor 1:70
 multiple authorship **3:**232

co-citation analysis (cont'd)
 and natural order of science **3:**vii
 public interest 1:285
 scientific research 2:26
 social sciences 2:509
co-citation clusters
 see co-citation analysis
coding systems **3:**274
cognitive psychology
 most-cited articles **3:**563
 most-cited authors **3:**633, 675
 most-cited books **3:**621
Cohen, R., reprint **3:**15
coins, currency exchange **3:**522
Coleman, Earl 1:334; 2:417
Coleman, J. S. **3:**624
collaborators
 see multiple authorship
*Collection of Czechoslovak Chemical
  Communications* 2:629
college education as job requirement 2:238
College of Physicians, Philadelphia **3:**455
colloquium **3:**247
 see also conference(s)
Coltrane, John 2:466
Columbia Broadcasting System **3:**580
Columbia University **3:**505, 723
Coma **3:**618
Combs, Gerald **3:**61
Commission on Professional and Hospital
  Activities **3:**114
Committee for Biomedical Research 2:271
Committee for the Scientific Investigation of
  the Claims of the Paranormal **3:**582
communication, theory of **3:**271
 see also science, communication
compensatory education **3:**655
complaints, individual and corporate
  responsibility 1:465; 2:223
Comptes Rendus **3:**91, 100, 143
computer(s)
 associations and organizations **3:**448, 450
 arts and humanities **3:**208
 computer output microform (COM) 2:248
 conferencing **3:**451
 errors 2:296
 and information retrieval **3:**253, 286, 404,
  448, 551, 640, 673
 ISI **3:**286, 365, 538, 551, 673
 magazines **3:**425
 making contacts at conferences **3:**671
 music 2:94
 potential **3:**vi
 toys **3:**364
concierges in hotels **3:**201
conditioned learning
 most-cited articles **3:**564
conference(s)
 accommodations and expenses **3:**198, 668

Current

cytology
  250 most-cited authors   **3:**327, 337
    their most-cited articles   **3:**348

D

Dachau   **3:**373

Dahlem Conferences   2:387

Daily Scientist   2:349

Daily Telegraph   **3:**579

Dallas, Duncan C.   **3:**380

Dangerfield, Rodney   **3:**735

Darwin, Charles   1:246

data bases   **3:**223, 286, 405

data, definition   2:47

David, J   **3:**99

Davis, Angela   **3:**512

Davis, James   **3:**389

Davis, Watson   **3:**448

DC-3, destroyer   **3:**368

Deadline Doctors program at Drexel University   **3:**584

death and burial   1:196, 229; **3:**219, 372

death camps   **3:**373

deathless world   1:196

Debre, Michel   **3:**95

Le Defi Americain   **3:**viii, 88, 95

degrees and employment practices   2:238

Dehart, Charles   2:168

Delap's *Fantasy and Science Fiction Review*   **3:**430, 432

Democratic Convention- Chicago, 1968   **3:**369

Deutch, Martin   **3:**656

Deutsche Akademie Naturforscher Leopoldina   **3:**589

developing countries, use of *CC*   1:108, 128

developmental psychology
  most-cited authors   **3:**636, 676
  most-cited books   **3:**628

Dewey Decimal System   2:252

Dictionary of Primordial Citations   1:163

dictionary(ies)
  Transliterated Dictionary of the Russian Language   2:280
  scientific   1:489
  Unique Word Dictionary   **3:**393

Diener, Edward   **3:**647

diet and vegetarianism   **3:**61

Diet for a Small Planet   **3:**63

Differentiation   **3:**484

Digiset system   **3:**405

Dinnerstein, Michael   2:325

Directory of Published Proceedings (Interdok)   **3:**248

Directory of Science Communication Courses and Programs   **3:**584

discrimination by alphabetization
  see   multiple authorship

disease, treatment of whole person   **3:**121

dissemination of French journals   **3:**91

dissemination of information   **3:**223

dissertations
  author fee for *CC* coverage of   1:411
  review articles as   2:175
  unanswered questions of science as source of topics for   2:75
  uncited papers as source   1:291

Distinguished Scientific Contribution   **3:**680

Distinguished Service Award, American Chemical Society   **3:**609

Dixon, Bernard   **3:**579

DNA, citation network   1:168; 2:142

DNA, recombinant   2:335; **3:**154, 304, 516

doctors
  see   physicians

DocuMation, Inc.   **3:**449

document card systems   **3:**274

documentation, and Claude Shannon   **3:**271

documentation of research papers   1:83

Doering, William von E.   **3:**459

dogs   2:382

Dohrman, Geoffrey W.   **3:**428

doomsday philosophers   1:458

dormant research and science   **3:**105

The Double Helix   1:133

Downbeat   **3:**431

Dragons of Eden   **3:**583

Drexel University, Deadline Doctors program   **3:**584

Dreyfus Foundation, grant programs   **3:**462

Drott, M. Carl, reprint   **3:**234

Drubba, Helmut   **3:**573

Drug Therapy   **3:**484

Dubos, Rene, article in *Human Nature*   **3:**425

duplication of research   1:219

Dworkin, Gerald   **3:**657

dysentery, treatment of   **3:**414

E

East Germany
  see   Germany

Eastern Europe
  most-cited articles   2:631
  most-cited journals   2:623

economics and econometrics
  most-cited articles   **3:**563
  most-cited authors   **3:**639, 679
  most-cited books   **3:**631
  of information revolution   1:475, 2:65
  of publishing journals   1:23

Subject Index

Edge

Edge, David, reprint **3**:240

editors, as most-cited authors **3**:496

editors of scientific journals **3**:187, 216, 424

Edizione Scientifica **3**:23

education

advertising's role 1:330

breadth vs. depth 1:95

compensatory **3**:655

effects **3**:423

grading 1:450

information science

see information science, education

law **3**:479

medicine **3**:121

most-cited articles **3**:564

most-cited books **3**:631

purpose and goals 2:110

scientific reviewing **3**:84

use of information tools and services

see information science, education

educational psychology

most-cited authors **3**:637, 677

educational television **3**:580

Einstein, Albert 1:45, 258

Elias, Arthur W. and *PSI* **3**:70

Elizabethan medicine **3**:723

Ellison, Ralph **3**:431

Elsevier/North Holland **3**:53

EMI scanner 2:429

employment 2:66, 238; **3**:84

encounter groups at conferences 2:498

endocrinology

300 most-cited authors **3**:542, 597

their most-cited articles **3**:694

energy crisis **3**:364

engineering

definition of 2:304

most-cited articles 2:441

most-cited books 2:441

most-cited journals 2:304, 441

Engineering Societies Library and Ralph Shaw **3**:505

engineering-technology and *Current Contents* 1:67

England

see United Kingdom

English as international language of science

see science, language

enology 1:460; **3**:416

enrichment policy of *A&HCI* **3**:206

environmental sciences, journals **3**:453

Equality of Educational Opportunity **3**:624

errors and correction notes

computer 2:296

contents pages 2:80

core literature of chemistry study 1:274

Frankfurter Allemeine Zeitung **3**:726

IEEE Transactions on Professional Communications **3**:306

errors and correction notes (cont'd)

ISI products and services 2:81

Italian article study **3**:41

textbook 1:233

250 most-cited authors **3**:492

Eskimo diet **3**:66

Essays of an Information Scientist **3**:173, 412

Essenes **3**:67

ethics in medical practice **3**:121

ethics of scientific publication **3**:644

Ethiopia, small pox eradication program **3**:27

ethology **3**:106

ethphon and ISI's *Unique Word Dictionary* **3**:394

etymology

see science, language

Etzioni, Amitai **3**:17

Eugene Garfield Associates 1:13, 438; **3**:449, 686, 735

euphenics 1:209

European Association of Advertising 1:332

European Journal of Cardiology **3**:484

European Life Science Editors **3**:440

European telephone service **3**:226

eutonia and ISI's *Unique Word Dictionary* **3**:394

evangelists **3**:14

Evers, William L. (Dreyfus Foundation) **3**:462

exchange of currency **3**:522

The Excitement and Fascination of Science **3**:728

Experimental Neurology, publication of chiropractic research **3**:536

explosive welding 1:354

eye banks **3**:375

Eysenck, Hans **3**:653

F

facts, definition 2:47

Fair Use Doctrine **3**:387

false publication dates **3**:488

Fantasy and Science Fiction Review **3**:430, 432

Il Farmaco **3**:23

FASEB Feature Service **3**:585

fasting **3**:68

Federal Communications Commission **3**:229, 518, 582

Federal Republic of Germany

see Germany

Federation of American Scientists 2:270

Federation of American Societies for Experimental Biology **3**:585

Federation of Chiropractic Licensing Boards **3**:533

Feldmann, Edward G. **3**:665

Subject Index

Garfield

fiber-optics and ISI's *Unique Word Dictionary*   **3:**398

Field, Helen   **3:**213

filing systems, personal   **3:**551

film, *Putting Scientific Information to Work* 1:324, 2:49

Filmorex   **3:**507

films, science fiction   **3:**614

Finnegan's Wake   **3:**399

Finserv Computer Corporation   **3:**388

'first author' problems
  see multiple authorship

Fischer, E. (homograph)   **3:**335

Fiske, Admiral Bradley A.   **3:**380

floppy discs
  Current Contents   **3:**673
  PRIMATE   **3:**553

flowmeters, electromagnetic   1:25, 51, 140

flying machines   **3:**155

Forbidden Planet   **3:**614

Ford Foundation   **3:**456

Ford, Henry, philanthropist   **3:**456

Ford, Henry II, Chairman of Ford Foundation **3:**456

foreign languages
  see language(s)

forensic science   **3:**480, 513

Fossey, Dian   **3:**66

Foster, Al   **3:**531

Foundation Center   **3:**456

Foundation for Microbiology, Congressional Fellowship   **3:**458

Foundation News   **3:**456

Foundation of Chiropractic Education and Research   **3:**534

foundations, non-profit, proliferation and statistics   **3:**455, 461

Fountain Committee, and NIH grant policy   **3:**450

4S Newsletter   **3:**vi, 725

Fraenkel, A.S.   1:479

France
  journals   2:409; **3:**88, 95, 471
  legality of chiropractic   **3:**532
  science and language   2:409; **3:**viii, 88, 95, 192, 471, 498

Frankenstein   **3:**614

Frankfurter Allemeine Zeitung   **3:**579, 726

Franklin Medal   **3:**609

French telephone   2:245

Freud, Sigmund   **3:**328, 635

friendship, loyalty and ISI   2:168

full-stop words
  see stopwords

full-text searching systems   1:479

Fuller, Buckminster   **3:**17

Fulleylove, James   **3:**463

Fundamentals of RIA and Other Ligand Assays **3:**729

funerals, burial and cremation   **3:**219, 613

Future Shock   **3:**623

G

G. Stanley Hall Award   **3:**680

Gairdner Foundation Award   **3:**609

Galileo   **3:**430, 432

games scientists play   2:107

Garfield, Eugene
  biography   2:32, 45, 415, 590; **3:**v, 271, 422
  cab driver   **3:**116
  citation indexes   1:191
  forecasting Nobel Prize recipients   2:289
  foundation of ISI   **3:**504
  Garfield-Bourne Controversy   **3:**238
  Garfield Challenge   **3:**88, 95
  Garfield-Kessler Assumption   **3:**234
  Garfield's axiom of economics   2:590
  Garfield's constant   1:289; 2:419
  Garfield's law of concentration   1:222
  Grolier Society Fellowship   **3:**505
  jazz afficionado   2:393, 461; **3:**431
  Hayne, Robert L.   **3:**213
  Le Nouveau Journal de Chimie controversy **3:**101, 471
  publishing *Essays of an Information Scientist*   **3:**173, 412
  reading habits   2:407
  travel   **3:**198

Garfield, E., reprints
  American Documentation 1963   1:43
  Bull. Amer. Soc. Inform. Sci., 1974   2:151
  Chem. Eng. News, 1966   1:120
  Chemistry in Britain, 1969   1:126
  CHEMTECH, 1976   2:525
  Corporate Headquarters Groundbreaking Ceremony, 1978 (speech)   **3:**735
  IEEE Conference on Scientific Journals, 1977 (speech)   **3:**288
  Information for Action, 1975   2:640
  Information Industry Association Hall of Fame Award, 1977 (speech)   **3:**403
  International Conference of Scientific Editors; Jerusalem, 1977 (Speech)   **3:**189
  J. Amer. Med. Assoc., 1971   1:249
  J. Amer. Soc. Inform. Sci., 1971   1:236
  J. Chem. Documentation 1961   **3:**274
  J. Chem. Inform. & Comp. Sci., 1975   2:415
  J. Chem. Inform. & Comp. Sci., 1978   **3:**468
  J. Indian Inst. Science, 1975   2:356
  J. Library History, 1970   1:139
  Journal Citation Reports 1976   2:558
  Karger Gazette, 1966   1:33
  Nature,
    1969   1:77
    1970   1:133
    1973   1:443, 487
    1976   **3:**132

Subject Index

Garfield

Garfield, E., reprints (cont'd)
New Scientist,
  1968 **1**:27
  1970 **1**:71
Pathology Annual 1976 **2**:646, 658
Proceedings of the International Conference on Scientific Information, 1959 **2**:674
Proceedings of the Third International Congress of Medical Librarianship, 1970 **1**:158
La Recherche 1976 **3**:89
Science 1972 **1**:527
Sci-tech News 1975 **2**:318
Statistical Association Methods for Mechanized Documentation, Symposium Proceedings, 1964 **1**:84
Toward a Theory of Librarianship; Papers in Honor of Jesse Hawk Shera, 1960 **2**:136
Wilson Library Bull., 1974 **2**:250
Garfield, Stefan **3**:687
Garofano, Edith Wolf **2**:535; **3**:422
Garofano, Ernest **3**:422
GASP **1**:415
gastroenterology
  300 most-cited authors **3**:546, 606
  their most-cited articles **3**:718
gatekeepers in science **2**:404
Gazzetta Chimica Italiana **3**:23
Gell-Mann, Murray **3**:128, 399
generation gap **2**:325
genetic engineering
  see DNA, recombinant
genetic psychology
  most-cited authors **3**:638, 678
  most-cited books **3**:629
Genetics and education **3**:653
Genetics Citation Index **1**:192; **2**:189
Genetics of Human Cancer **3**:729
geology and geophysics
  most-cited journals **2**:102, 114
Geriatrics **3**:414, 416
German Book Illustration of the Gothic Period and the Early Renaissance 1460-1530 **3**:507
Germany **2**:467, 516; **3**:91, 373, 532, 589
Gerrold, David **3**:619
Gershon-Cohen, Jacob **1**:152; **3**:455
Getty, J. Paul **3**:456
ghost-writing in science **3**:645
Giant Steps **2**:462
Gifford, Bernard **3**:177
Glazer, Nathan **3**:177
Gleanings in Bee Culture **3**:158
Goddard, Henry **3**:657
Goldstein, Lester **2**:506
Good, R. A. **3**:644
Goodell, Rae **3**:582
gordian knot of journal coverage **3**:452
Gordon Research Conferences **2**:388

government subsidy
  cancer information **1**:391
  information science **2**:151
  medical information **1**:372
The Grackle **3**:431, 433
Granito, C., reprint **1**:304
Grant Program of the Institute for Scientific Information
  see Institute for Scientific Information, Grant Program
grants
  see research, grants
Gravitt, T.O. **3**:231
Great Britain
  see United Kingdom
Greene, Frederick D. **3**:381
Griffith, B. C. **3**:vi
  reprint **3**:234
Grolier Society Fellowship **3**:505
Gross-Price Assumption and co-citation analysis **3**:235
groundbreaking ceremony, ISI new building **3**:735
Gruman, Gerald J. **1**:229
Guenther Award **3**:609
Guggenheim Foundation **3**:457, 609, 680
Guthrie Medal and Prize **3**:609
Guy Medals **3**:680

H

H.C. Warren Medal **3**:680
H.W. Wilson Co. and second class mail **3**:664
Hahnemann, Samuel **3**:530
half-life of articles **3**:503
Halford, Ralph **3**:56
Hall of Fame Award
  see Information Industry Association
Hammett equation **3**:125
Handbook for Authors of Papers in the Journals of the American Chemical Society **3**:441
handbooks and textbooks **3**:496
happiness and ISI's *Unique Word Dictionary* **3**:393
Hardin, Garrett **3**:438, 571
hardware
  see computer(s)
Harris, Richard M. **1**:300
Harris, Zellig **2**:415
Harrisburg Seven trial **3**:511
Harte, Robert **3**:472
Harvard Educational Review **3**:652
Haward, Lionel **3**:513
Hayne, Robert L.
  biography **3**:175, 213
  bridging the two cultures of art and science **3**:204
  eulogy **3**:213, 732

Subject Index

IIS

Subject Index

Subject Index

ISI

ISI Press

   see   Institute for Scientific Information - ISI Press

ISIS **3:**435, 723, 725

Islamic law and cremation **3:**373

ISO

   see   International Organization for Standardization

ISSHP

   see   *Index to Social Sciences & Humanities Proceedings*

ISSN **3:**388

Italy

  most-cited journals **3:**22, 34

  regulation of chiropractic **3:**533

  science in **3:**22, 34, 472

J

J.B. Clark Medal **3:**680

J.M. Luck Awards **3:**461

J. Paul Getty Museum **3:**456

jabberwocky 1:489

Jahre Endowment **3:**610

James T. Grady Award for Interpreting Chemistry to the Public **3:**462

Japan, journal citation study 2:430

jargon in scientific writing 1:489; **3:**3

Jaws **3:**617

jazz magazines **3:**431

jazz transcriptions 2:393, 461

Jazzline **3:**431, 433

Jensen, Arthur **3:**565, 652

Jewish law and cremation **3:**373

jitney service **3:**118

Johns Hopkins University, Welch Medical Library Indexing Project

   see   Welch Medical Library Indexing Project

journal(s)

   see also   contents pages; most-cited articles; and each of the individual journal titles

  acquisitions 1:21, 417, 475; **3:**130

  arts **3:**206, 556

  astronomy/astrophysics **3:**141

  author-journals 1:6

  authors' addresses in **3:**487

  biochemistry 1:262

  botany **3:**142

  Canadian **3:**259

  choosing where to publish 1:268

  citation by association 1:452

  core journal collections 1:247; 2:300

  core journals and Bradford's law 1:222

  cost/benefit analysis in libraries 1:247

  coverage in *SCI*

   see   *Science Citation Index*, coverage

  coverage in *SSCI*

   see   Social Sciences Citation Index, coverage

journal(s) (cont'd)

  coverage in various *Current Contents* editions

   see   *Current Contents*, coverage

  cover-to-cover translation 1:104, 334, 523

  definition 1:6, 376; **3:**663

  design and format **3:**267, 482

  duplicate copies for subscribers 1:320

  editorial policies **3:**488

  editors **3:**187, 216, 482

  evaluation with citation analysis

   see   most-cited journals; *Journal Citation Reports*

  for-profit and non-profit 2:226

  French **3:**88, 95

  future evolution 1:6; 2:318; **3:**405

  gatekeepers in science 2:404

  humanities **3:**204

  humorous 2:664

  impact

    of Canadian journals **3:**259

    citation by association 1:452

    50 important science journals 1:270

    French journals **3:**91

    of *JCR* on publication 1:473

    journal significance 1:106; **3:**130

  keysave **3:**43

  most-cited articles 1:485

    1969 journals 1:270, 527

  improvement 1:514; **3:**267, 482

  Italian **3:**22, 34

  language of 1:445; **3:**88, 95, 498

  late publication **3:**488

  mathematics **3:**142

  'minor' journals as burial grounds 1:126

  names 2:378

  page-charges 2:226

  personalized 1:22, 336

  preparation for *Current Contents* **3:**483

  print quality **3:**483

  printed vs. other formats **3:**405

  publication dates 1:16; 2:236, 286; **3:**488

  publication of most-cited articles 1:485

  publication quality 1:417

  publication readability **3:**267

  publication time-lags 1:452; 2:236

  publishers 1:417; **3:**187, 482

  readability **3:**267

  reference style **3:**440, 487, 490

  science **3:**130

  scientists' reading lists 2:407

  selection

   see   journal(s), acquisitions

  significance

   see   journal(s), impact

  Soviet **3:**145

  subscriptions and second copies 1:320

  subscriptions to *CC* **3:**27

  subscriptions, correspondence about 1:23

  subscriptions, need for prompt payment 1:23; 2:590

  tear-sheet copies 1:320

Subject Index

journal(s) (cont'd)
titles of 2:378
titles, translations of 3:145
transposed lists 1:222
use of color 3:483
volume numbers 3:489
Journal Citation Index 1:289, 292, 417;
2:357
see also *Journal Citation Reports*
Journal Citation Reports
see also *Journal Citation Index*
Canadian journals 3:259
inauguration 1:473
introduction 2:556, 558
journal publishers 3:194
journal selection for *CC* 1:475
library acquisition 3:289
library weeding 2:300
significant science journals 3:130
Journal Citation Reports for the *Social
Sciences Citation Index* 3:564
journal citation studies
see most-cited journals
Journal of African History 3:269
Journal of Applied Virology 1:400
Journal of Bacteriology and Project
Keysave 3:43
Journal of Biological Chemistry 3:154
Journal of Chemical Education 1:233
Journal of Chemical Physics 1:274, 3:129
Journal of Chemical Research 3:382
Journal of Clinical Investigation 2:13
Journal of Experimental Medicine 1:326
Journal of Geophysical Research 2:115
Journal of Immunology 1:326
Journal of Insignificant Research 2:669
Journal of Irreproducible Results 2:664
Journal of Molecular Biology 3:130
Journal of Molecular Biology and Project
Keysave 3:43
Journal of Organic Chemistry 3:381
Journal of Pharmaceutical Sciences 1:435
Journal of Submicroscopic Cytology 3:22
Journal of the American Chemical Society
journals most-cited by 1:264
correction 1:274
most-cited by French journals 3:90
most-cited 1950s articles 3:129, 154
reference style 3:441, 444
"typical" chemistry journal 1:262
Journal of the American Medical Association
2:17; 3:314, 441
*Journal of the American Society for
Information Science* 3:447
Journal of the Electrochemical Society,
yearly index 3:74
Journal of the Physical Society of Japan
3:129
Journal of Really Important Papers 2:301

Journal of Virology and Project *Keysave*
3:43
journalism, coverage of science
see science, public image
Joyce, James, *Finnegan's Wake* 3:399
junior members of research team
see multiple authorship
jury selection 3:479, 511

K

Kamin, Leon 3:656
Kansas, legal recognition of chiropractors 3:532
Das Kapital 3:622
Katz, Bill 3:424
Keane, William M. 3:530
Key-word-in-context indexes 3:71
Keysave
see Project *Keysave*
Khorana, Hargovind G. 1:132, 281; 3:548
kidney donations 3:375
Klein, E., homograph 3:549, 701
Koenig, M.E.D. reprint 3:367
Koprowski, H. 3:613
Korea 3:16
Kosher diet 3:67
Kuranz, John D. 3:666
kwashiorkor in vegetarians 3:63
KWIC indexes 3:71
Kyner, Joseph L. 3:372

L

L-5 Society 3:427
laetrile 3:398
Lancet 3:91
Landmarks of Science 3:381
Langmuir Award 3:610
language(s)
see also linguistic(s); science, language;
translation(s)
article titles 1:381
artificial 2:174
barriers 1:150
English as international language of science
see science, language of
imperialism 3:89
information science 3:150, 393
journals
see journals, language of
most-cited authors 3:639, 679
most-cited books 3:632
Permuterm Subject Index as natural
language index 3:70
problems at international conferences 3:98

771

language

Subject Index

Mendel

Mendel, Gregor   1:69, 135, 246; **3:**105

Merton, Robert K.

see also   the Cited Author Index, *Essays,*
V.3

A&HCI, influence on   **3:**723

biography   **3:**176

Matthew Effect   **3:**646

scientists' behavior patterns   2:60

SSCI, on the use of   2:244

metallurgy

250 most-cited authors   **3:**328

their most-cited articles   **3:**348

methodology articles

see   article(s), method

Mexico, National University of   **3:**225

Miami Herald   **3:**581

microbiology

300 most-cited authors   **3:**544, 603

their most-cited articles   **3:**716

250 most-cited authors   **3:**327, 337

their most-cited articles   **3:**348

microform   **3:**380

Middletown Award   **3:**610

milestone papers   1:139

see also   *Citation Classics;* most-cited
articles

military establishment and high technology
devices   **3:**364

Minerva (Italian medical journal series)
3:26

minicomputers   **3:**551

miniprint   **3:**379, 506

'minor' journals   1:126

Mitchell, Charlotte S.   1:13

MLA Style Sheet   **3:**440

Modern Concepts in Brain Tumor Therapy   **3:**729

Modern Language Association   **3:**440

Modern Medicine Award   **3:**611

Molau, Gunther E.   **3:**373

molecular biology

300 most-cited authors   **3:**543, 598

their most-cited articles   **3:**704

molecular formula index of *Index Chemicus*
3:384

*Molecular Mechanisms in the Control of Gene
Expression*   **3:**730

money

collection   2:590

exchange rates   **3:**522

Monod, Jacques   **3:**93

monographic series, coverage in *SCI*   **3:**52

Moon, Rev. Sun Myung   **3:**14

Moore, Alex   **3:**472

Morley Award   **3:**611

morphine, effects of   **3:**413

Moscow Book Fair   **3:**400

Moslem law and cremation   **3:**373

most-cited articles

by year of study, *see* first page of index

see also   article(s), impact; *Citation
Classics*

animal behavior   2:257

astrophysics   2:120

Australia and New Zealand   2:584, 593

behavior   2:262

behavioral science, 1950s   **3:**179

behavioral sciences, 1940s   **3:**76

behavioral theory   **3:**563

biochemistry, 1950s   **3:**147

biochemistry, 1940s   **3:**45

biological sciences, 1950s   **3:**179

biological sciences, 1940s   **3:**76

biomedicine, 1950s   **3:**179

biomedicine, 1940s   **3:**76

botany, from botanical journals   2:216

botany, from plant physiology journals   2:210

cancer   2:160

chemistry, from *Acta Crystallographica*
2:128

chemistry, 1950s   **3:**125

chemistry, 1940s   **3:**54

chemistry, 1972   2:37

cognitive psychology   **3:**563

conditioned learning   **3:**563

crystallography   2:128

Eastern Europe   2:631

economics and econometrics   **3:**563

education   **3:**563

engineering   2:441

France   2:409; **3:**88, 95, 498

geophysics   2:114

Germany   2:516

Italy   **3:**34

Japan   2:430

journals publishing   1:485

law   **3:**563

life sciences, 1930s   2:611

mathematics, 1940s   **3:**54

mathematics, 1961-1972   1:504, 509

medicine, 1950s   **3:**179

medicine, 1940s   **3:**76

medicine, 1961-1972   2:86

method articles   **3:**147

motivation theory   **3:**563

New Zealand and Australia   2:584, 593

Nineteenth Century   2:491

pathology   2:658

pediatrics   2:97

personality   **3:**564

physical sciences, 1975   2:457

physical sciences, 1930s   2:617

physics, 1950s   **3:**125

physics, 1940s   **3:**54

physiologic psychology   2:257

physiology   **3:**564

plant physiology   2:210, 216

political science   **3:**563

psychology   2:257, 262, **3:**564

psychology, 1950s   **3:**179

multidisciplinary

multiple

multiple authorship
  alphabetic syndrome 1:146, 280; **3:**351, 538, 644
  books 1:477; 2:386; **3:**84, 621
  citation analysis 1:280; **3:**179, 348, 644
  co-citation analysis **3:**232
  competition in science 2:60; **3:**644
  conference papers and publications **3:**247
  husband and wife research teams **3:**701
  Matthew Effect **3:**646
  Nobel laureates **3:**646
  primary authors **3:**317
  SCI citation study **3:**539
  Spiegel Survey **3:**649
music
  articles **3:**206
  computer 2:94
  jazz 2:393, 461
  journals **3:**431, 433
Musician, Player and Listener **3:**431, 433

N

narcotics, metabolic action **3:**414
NASA **3:**370
Nasri, William Z. **3:**392
Nation **3:**457
National Academy of Science **3:**461, 492, 588
National Association of Science Writers **3:**416, 585
National Award of the American Cancer Society **3:**611
National Broadcasting Company **3:**580
National Business Services **3:**383
National Center for Health Statistics **3:**114
National College of Chiropractic **3:**534
National Commission on New Technological Uses of Copyrighted Works **3:**388
National Enquirer **3:**104
National Eye Bank Association of America **3:**375
National Federation of Abstracting and Indexing Services **3:**667
National Foundation for Biomedical Research 1:420
National Guard **3:**369
National Information Funding Authority 1:373
National Institutes of Health
  copyright **3:**389
  funding of chiropractic research **3:**534
  lectureship **3:**611, 680
  nutrition program **3:**61
  reprint stamps **3:**309
  research funds and grants **3:**309, 450, 456
National Kidney Foundation **3:**375
National Lending Library 1:108
National Library of Medicine **3:**389, 414, 417
National Library of Medicine's Subject Heading Authority List **3:**213

National Medal of Science **3:**342, 611, 680
National Microfilm Association, Pioneer Medal **3:**383
National Opinion Poll **3:**428, 433
National Public Radio **3:**580
National Research Council of Canada **3:**259
National Science Foundation
  congressional approval of grants 2:269
  education programs **3:**86
  history of science research **3:**474
  ISI databases **3:**474
  reprint currency **3:**86
  research funds **3:**456
  science information **3:**v, 405, 448
National Union Catalog **3:**496
National University of Mexico **3:**225
Nature
  CC/AB&ES coverage **3:**453
  and network news science coverage **3:**581
  reference style **3:**441, 444
nature/nurture debate **3:**654
naturopathy **3:**530
Nazi atrocities **3:**373
NEC (Nippon Electric Company) Research & Development **3:**485
negative science **3:**155
negative search results 1:117
neologism and immortality 2:70
Network (film) **3:**198
Neurath, Otto 2:638
neurological journals, Italian **3:**35
Neuro-Psychology
  most-cited authors **3:**637, 677
  most-cited books **3:**629
Neuroscience Newsletter **3:**585
Neuroscience Proceedings **3:**585
The new American challenge **3:**viii, 88, 95
New England Journal of Medicine 2:13, 17
New Jersey National Guard **3:**413
New Scientist **3:**488, 579
New Times **3:**613
New Year's greetings **3:**27
New York State Public Utilities Commission **3:**230
New York Telephone Company **3:**230
New York Times **3:**157, 162, 218, 579
New York University, School of Journalism **3:**581
New Yorker **3:**425, 488
New Zealand and Australian most-cited journals 2:584, 593
New Zealand, regulation of chiropractic **3:**532
Newcomb, Simon, reprint **3:**167
news, science 1:7; 2:349, 537; **3:**218, 253, 517, 579
newspaper of science 2:349
Newsweek **3:**526, 580
Newton, Sir Isaac **3:**176
NFAIS **3:**667

Subject Index

patent

patent lawyers   **3:**516

patent royalties   **3:**462

patents in *SCI*   2:52

Pathologie Biologie   1:402

pathology
  most-cited articles and journals   1:400; 2:646, 658
  300 most-cited authors   **3:**546, 605
    their most-cited articles   **3:**710
  250 most-cited authors   **3:**327, 337
    their most-cited articles   **3:**348

patient-doctor relationship   1:425

Patrick, Ted   **3:**20

Pauling, Linus   2:299; **3:**428

pay telephone   **3:**227

pediatrics
  most-cited articles   2:97

peer review   **3:**114

Pennsylvania Society of Professional Engineers   **3:**449

Penthouse   **3:**586

performance rights   **3:**391

periodicals and the US Postal Service   **3:**663

Permuterm Subject Index
  A&HCI   **3:**206
  description   **3:**70
  ISSHP   **3:**575
  primordial dictionary of science   1:39, 163

Perry, Jim   **3:**472

Personal Retrieval of Information by Microcomputer and Terminal Ensemble (PRIMATE)   **3:**551, 673

personality
  most-cited articles   **3:**564
  most-cited authors   **3:**634, 677
  most-cited books   **3:**628

personalized journal   1:22

Perspectives in Biology and Medicine   **3:**414

Perutz, M.F.   **3:**589

Peterbilt trucks   **3:**371

Petroleum Chemistry Award   **3:**611

Pfizer Award   **3:**612

pharmacists as information-workers   1:284

pharmacology
  Leake C.D.'s contribution   **3:**413
  300 most-cited authors   **3:**538, 587
    their most-cited articles   **3:**689
  250 most-cited authors   **3:**326, 337
    their most-cited articles   **3:**348

Philadelphia and the US bicentennial   2:572

Philadelphia College of Physicians   **3:**455

Philadelphia, currency exchange   **3:**522

Philadelphia Inquirer   **3:**613

philanthropy
  anachronistic tax laws   **3:**463
  creative   **3:**455, 461
  venture capital   **3:**463

philosophy
  A&HCI   **3:**204
  most-cited authors   **3:**633, 675
  most-cited books   **3:**632

photo-offset press   **3:**397

Photoclerk   **3:**505

photocopying   1:431, 523; 2:55; **3:**387, 450
  see also   copyright

photographic paper & silver emulsion   **3:**381

Photosynthetica   **3:**486

physical chemistry
  300 most-cited authors' most-cited articles   **3:**711

Physical Review, most-cited 1950's articles   **3:**129

physical sciences
  journals   **3:**453
  most-cited articles, 1975   2:457
  most-cited articles, 1930's   2:617
  problem of overlap   1:67

physicians
  see also   medicine
  doctor-patient relationship   1:425, 448, 502
  Physicians Radio Network   **3:**519
  social science information   **3:**121
  surgery   **3:**111

physicists
  employment   1:177
  reprint requests   **3:**309

physics
  Italian journals   **3:**23
  most-cited articles, 1950s   **3:**125
  most-cited articles, 1940s   **3:**54
  most-cited journals   2:154
  300 most-cited authors   **3:**545, 603
    their most-cited articles   **3:**708
  250 most-cited authors   **3:**327, 337
    their most-cited articles   **3:**348

physiologic psychology
  most-cited articles   2:257

physiology
  most-cited articles   **3:**564
  300 most-cited authors   **3:**544, 601
    their most-cited articles   **3:**701
  250 most-cited authors   **3:**327, 337
    their most-cited articles   **3:**348

Phytopathology   1:401; **3:**486

pi, history   2:396

Pickering, W.H.   **3:**160

pioneer medal   **3:**383

Pius XI Gold Medal   **3:**612

Planet of the Apes   2:297

plant physiology
  most-cited articles   2:210, 216

Plastics and Rubber International   **3:**486

police   **3:**369

political philosophy
  most-cited authors   **3:**639, 679

political science
  most-cited articles   **3:**564
politics
  and citations   2:58
  and science   1:418; 2:158, 297
  and taxes   1:380
Pony Express   1:154
popular press and scientific news
  see   news, science
Popular Science   **3:**427
popular science writing
  see   science, writing
postage costs   **3:**401, 663
Postal Affairs Task Force   **3:**666
Postgraduate Medicine   **3:**486
power   1:266
Power, Eugene   **3:**401
premature research and science   **3:**105, 155
presidents   1:380
Press Digest
  announcement and introduction   1:448
  CC/A&H   **3:**557
  CC/BS&ES   1:456
  CC/S&BS   2:73
  description and purpose   2:371
  Hayne, Robert L., his influence   **3:**214
  history of science coverage   **3:**435
  irate readers   **3:**28
  Leake, C. D., his interest   **3:**413
  Lederberg, Joshua, his comments   **3:**29
  mass media and scientists   1:448; 2:371; **3:**28, 579, 613
  new magazines   **3:**424, 431
  reader survey   1:481
  social science items   **3:**123
Presse Medicale   **3:**91
Prestel   **3:**253, 586
Price, Derek de Solla
  see also   the Cited Author Index, *Essays*, V.3
  citation analysis   2:291
  Foreword, *Essays*, V.3   **3:**v
  multiple authorship   **3:**645
  Project *Keysave*   **3:**42
  WIPIS   **3:**407
  World Brain   2:638, 643
Priestly Medal   **3:**612
primary authorship
  see   multiple authorship
PRIMATE   **3:**551, 673
primordial dictionary of science   1:39
Princeton University   **3:**413
Principles of Enzymatic Analysis   **3:**729
printing paper, shortages   1:483
printing, reduced size   **3:**381
priority claims, scientific   **3:**216
PRN   **3:**519

proceedings
  see   conference papers and publications
Proceedings in Print   **3:**248
Proceedings of the National Academy of Sciences   **3:**441, 554
product guarantees   2:223
Le Progres Scientifique   **3:**99
Project *Keysave*   **3:**viii, 42, 287
Project *REX*   1:359, 363; **3:**308
Project *ZIP*   **3:**287
prolongevity   1:229
Prospero   **3:**614
protein in vegetarian diet   **3:**62
provincialism of French journals   **3:**88, 95
proximate cause   **3:**514
Proxmire, Senator William   **3:**427
pseudoscience   **3:**582
PSI
  see   *Permuterm Subject Index*
psychoanalytic theory
  most-cited authors   **3:**633, 675
psychology
  most-cited articles   2:257, 262; **3:**564
  most-cited articles, 1950s   **3:**179
  most-cited authors, 1969-1977 *SSCI*   **3:**636
  most-cited books   **3:**626
  most-cited journals   2:231, 262
psychometrics
  most-cited articles   **3:**564
  most-cited authors   **3:**638, 678
Public Broadcasting Service   **3:**580
Public Health Service   **3:**414
public image of science
  see   science, public image
Public Law 94-553   **3:**387
public telephones   **3:**227
public transportation   **3:**116
publication counting vs citation counting   1:179
publication dates   1:16, 287; **3:**488
publication outlets   1:268
publish-or-perish   **3:**404
publishers of journals   **3:**482, 490, 726
Publishers Weekly   **3:**402
publishing, costs of   1:23; **3:**144, 379
publishing, ISI Press   **3:**174
punched cards   **3:**271
Pure Chemistry Award   **3:**612
Putting Scientific Information to Work (film)   1:324; 2:49
Pygmalion in the Classroom   **3:**624

Q

quantifying the intangible   **3:**673
quarks and ISI's *Unique Word Dictionary*   **3:**399

Subject Index

Quarterly

science

science

Subject Index

social

social sciences

  see also *Current Contents/Behavioral, Social & Educational Sciences;* research; science; *Social Sciences Citation Index;* Social *SCISEARCH*

  citation indexing 1:397

  co-citation analysis 2:509; **3:**232

  conference proceedings **3:**573

  culture gap **3:**434

  Current Contents 1:516

  future information systems 1:516

  grants

    see research, funding; research, grants

  information problems 1:516

  ISI's information systems for 1:397, 500

  literature 2:550

  most-cited authors **3:**675

  most-cited articles **3:**563, 682

  most-cited books 1969-1977 **3:**621, 682

Social Sciences Citation Index

  announcement and introduction 1:317

  author addresses **3:**407

  citation abstracts 2:190

  citation consciousness **3:**216

  citation data on most ordered books **3:**728

  co-citation analysis 2:509; **3:**232

  cost

    see *Science Citation Index,* cost; ISI Grant Program

  coverage 1:318; 2:550; **3:**730

  cross references **3:**204, 435

  culture gap 1:397

  data base **3:**683

  history and description 1:317, 471; 2:240

  Journal Citation Reports **3:**564

  magnetic tape **3:**223

  medical sciences information **3:**123

  Merton, R.K. **3:**177

  miniprint **3:**384

  most-cited articles **3:**563

  most-cited authors **3:**633, 675

  most-cited books **3:**621

  quality **3:**232

  Source Index 2:190

  use by legal profession **3:**480

social sciences information and medical care **3:**121

social sciences information, use by legal profession **3:**477

social scientists

  most cited, 1969-1977 **3:**633, 675

Social *SCISEARCH* **3:**123, 481

Social Security death benefit **3:**374

Society for Neuroscience **3:**584

Society for Social Studies of Science **3:**vi, 725

Society of Experimental Psychologists **3:**680

sociology

  most-cited articles **3:**563

  most-cited authors **3:**633, 675

  most-cited books **3:**630

sociology of science 1:42, 156; **3:**176, 216, 233, 474, 723

  see also history of science

socio-political magazines **3:**428

solid state physics and reprints **3:**310

Sollmann Award **3:**612

somatostatin and ISI's *Unique Word Dictionary* **3:**398

Somogyi method for determination of glucose **3:**46

Sontag, S. **3:**614

Sopinsky, Phil **3:**42

Sorokin Award **3:**680

South Africa

  regulation of chiropractic **3:**532

Southern, Walt **3:**472

Southwestern Bell Telephone Company **3:**231

space magazines **3:**426

Space: 1999 **3:**616

space-travel **3:**162, 371

Spanish language in scientific publication **3:**499

Special Libraries Association **3:**390

specialty mapping

  see citation analysis; co-citation analysis

spectroscopy

  250 most-cited authors **3:**327, 333

    their most-cited articles **3:**348

Spiegel survey and multiple authorship **3:**648

Spiegelman, Sol 1:418

Spin-offs 1:467

spinal manipulation **3:**529

Spira, Henry **3:**103

Sponsor Index, for *ISSHP* **3:**575

SPSS **3:**437

SSCI

  see *Social Sciences Citation Index*

Standard Rate and Data Service and second-class mail **3:**664

standards

  bibliographic references 1:27, 40; 2:229; **3:**43, 440

  International Standard Book Number **3:**575

  International Standard Serial Number **3:**388

  journal publication **3:**482, 490

Stans, Maurice **3:**512

Star Trek **3:**614, 616

Star Wars **3:**614, 617

stare decisis **3:**477

Starke **3:**486

Starker, Lee **3:**472

statistical methods **3:**625

Statistical Package for the Social Sciences **3:**437

statistics

  most-cited articles **3:**563

  most-cited books **3:**629

  250 most-cited authors **3:**328, 633, 675

    their most-cited articles **3:**348

Steinberg, Eliot **3:**472

Tragedy

word-phrases

LIST OF ESSAY TITLES
Volumes 1, 2 & 3

The titles of all the essays appear here in alphabetical order, usually according to the first significant word in each title. The entry for each title refers the reader to the volume and page number. (Volume numerals for Vol. 3 entries are in boldface.) Thus, the entry

The proper study of mankind is . . . whose? or, *Planet of the Apes* revisited   2:297

means that the essay with the title shown begins on page 297 of Vol. 2. The entry

Canadian journals are better than some think (reprint)   **3:**262

means that the item with the title shown

begins on page 262 of Vol. 3. The word "reprint" in parentheses identifies items originally published elsewhere.

Additional history and sociology of science coverage in *Current Contents*   **3:**723

Addresses and ZIP codes   1:17

Advertising, education, and marketing of information services   1:330

A. E. Cawkell, information detective—and ISI's man in the UK   1:245

Aesthetics in scientific communication   1:5

All the I's at ISI   2:399

An address on addresses   2:310

The agony and the ecstasy of publishing your own book: *Essays of an Information Scientist*   **3:**173

And who shall occupy the 250th chair among the citation immortals?   2:496

Announcing *Current Contents/Arts & Humanities:* in 1979 our *Current Contents* series will cover virtually every academic discipline   **3:**556

Anonymity in refereeing? Maybe—but anonymity in authorship? No   2:438

Anonymous publication by 1984?   2:506

Are information services worth the money?   2:327

Are you ready for chemical linguistics? chemical semantics? chemical semiotics? or, why WLN?   1:386

ASCA, ASCATOPICS, and cyclic AMP   1:217

ASCA can help you monitor publication in your organization or country   **3:**640

ASCA—insurance for *CC* readers   1:28

ASCA plus *OATS* equals the 'repackaged' or 'personalized' journal   1:336

ASCAmatic—the personalized journal   1:22

ASIS national convention and the information-conscious society   1:96

Audience of one—Jacob Bronowski   2:351

B

A basic journal collection—ISI lists the fifty most-cited scientific and technical journals   1:255

Beverly Bartolomeo and 20 years of *Current Contents*   **3:**686

Bibliographies, citations, and citation abstracts   2:190

Biomedical and health care systems research should be financed from social security and health insurance funds. A permanent lobby could swing it   2:10

Bought term papers: symptom or challenge, or using term papers to teach   2:110

Bradford's law (reprint)   1:247; 2:303

British quest for uniqueness versus American egocentrism (reprint)   1:77

C

CAC/IC strikes again. A computer-output-microform (COM) index to 1.25 million new compounds   2:248

Calling attention to Chauncey D. Leake—Renaissance scholar *extraordinaire*   1:102

Can citation indexing be automated? (reprint)   1:84

Can criticism and documentation of research papers be automated?   1:83

Can reprint requests serve as a new form of international currency for the scientific community?   **3:**307

Canadian journals are better than some think (reprint)   **3:**262

CC's new computer composed author address directory   1:148

CC's Weekly Subject Indexes can help you complete the incomplete in references, bibliographies and journal coverage   2:347

List of Essays

List of Essays

I

List of Essays

List of Essays

List of Essays

List of Essays

List of Essays

List of Essays

INDEX TO ILLUSTRATIONS
Volumes 1, 2 & 3

This is a subject index to the various charts, tables, lists, figures, etc. contained in the essays. Each entry leads the reader to a volume number and a page number. (Volume numerals for Vol. 3 entries are in boldface.) Thus, the entry

articles, most cited
Acta Crystallographica 2:130

means that on page 130 in Vol. 2 there is a list of the most-cited articles published in *Acta Crystallographica.*

authors

S

T

U

V

W

INDEX TO AUTHORS IN MOST-CITED LISTS

Volumes 1, 2 & 3

This index enables the reader to determine whether a specific author is included in one or more of the "most-cited" lists contained in some of the essays. Authors are listed alphabetically, along with a P or an S to indicate whether each qualified for a most-cited list as a primary or secondary author. Also given are the date, volume, and page of the essay in which the author appeared in a most-cited list. Thus, the entry

Adams P   S Dec. 4, 1978   **3:**717

indicates that an essay published December 4, 1978 contains a most-cited list which includes P. Adams as a secondary author. The essay appears in Vol. 3 and begins on page 717. (Volume numerals for Vol. 3 entries are in boldface.)

Readers doing name searches should also consult the Cited-Author Index and the Subject Index.

Aaronson S A	P Jul. 10, 1978	**3:**544	**Abrikosov A A**	(cont'd)		
	P Aug. 28, 1978	**3:**601		P Nov. 10, 1975	2:376
	P Nov. 27, 1978	**3:**706		P Dec. 5, 1977	**3:**330
Aas K	S Oct. 18, 1976	2:609		P Dec. 12, 1977	**3:**339
Abarbanel H D I	P Oct. 31, 1973	1:499		P Dec. 19, 1977	**3:**354
Abbot A	S Oct. 4, 1976	2:595	**Abulhaj S K**	S Dec. 13, 1976	2:661
Abbott W S	P May. 24, 1976	2:493	**Achong B G**	S Jul. 3, 1974	2:92
Abeles F B	P Jan. 20, 1975	2:212	**Acland H**	S Sep. 11, 1978	**3:**632
Abelev G I	P Oct. 16, 1974	2:167	**Ada G L**	P Oct. 4, 1976	2:595
Abell L L	P Feb. 6, 1974	2:24		S Oct. 4, 1976	2:596
	P Jul. 18, 1977	**3:**180		P Oct. 4, 1976	2:598
Abelson J	S Apr. 12, 1976	2:454	**Adair G S**	P May. 24, 1976	2:493
Abercrombie M	P Oct. 16, 1974	2:165	**Adams C W M**	P Dec. 13, 1976	2:661
	P Mar. 28, 1977	**3:**79	**Adams D D**	P Oct. 4, 1976	2:597
Abragam A	P Aug. 11, 1971	1:227	**Adams J M**	P Apr. 14, 1971	1:173
	P Oct. 3, 1973	1:488		P Apr. 12, 1976	2:456
	P Jan. 2, 1974	2:2	**Adams M H**	P Jan. 2, 1974	2:4
	P Dec. 5, 1977	**3:**330	**Adams P**	S Dec. 4, 1978	**3:**717
	P Dec. 12, 1977	**3:**339	**Adams R D**	S Dec. 13, 1976	2:663
	P Dec. 19, 1977	**3:**354	**Adams T F**	S Aug. 28, 1974	2:123
Abraham D	S Nov. 27, 1974	2:183	**Addicott F T**	P Jan. 20, 1975	2:215
Abraham G	P Apr. 12, 1976	2:456	**Adkinson N F**	S Feb. 23, 1976	2:428
Abrahamson G R	P Aug. 30, 1972	1:355	**Adler N**	P Nov. 29, 1977	**3:**321
Abramowitz M	P Aug. 11, 1971	1:227		P Nov. 29, 1977	**3:**319
	P Nov. 28, 1973	1:511	**Adler R**	P Mar. 22, 1976	2:446
	P Jan. 2, 1974	2:5	**Adorno T W**	P Sep. 11, 1978	**3:**628
	P Mar. 22, 1976	2:443	**Afkham J**	S Oct. 16, 1974	2:165
	P Dec. 5, 1977	**3:**330		S Jul. 12, 1976	2:519
	P Dec. 12, 1977	**3:**339	**Agmo A**	P Nov. 29, 1977	**3:**321
	P Dec. 19, 1977	**3:**354		P Nov. 29, 1977	**3:**319
Abrams	P Apr. 19, 1976	2:460	**Agmon S**	P Nov. 21, 1973	1:508
Abrams C A L	S Jul. 17, 1974	2:101	**Aguilar-Parada E**	S Nov. 20, 1978	**3:**695
Abrams G S	S Apr. 19, 1976	2:459	**Aharonov A**	S Apr. 12, 1976	2:453
Abramsky O	P Apr. 12, 1976	2:453	**Ahkong Q F**	P Apr. 12, 1976	2:453
Abrikosov A A	P Jan. 2, 1974	2:3	**Ahlquist R P**	P Apr. 14, 1971	1:161
	P Nov. 10, 1975	2:375			

Ahlquist

Batterman

Bangham A D	P Sep. 22, 1971	1:243	Barrnett R J	(cont'd)		
	S Sep. 22, 1971	1:243		P Jul. 10, 1978	3:544
Bansal S C	S Nov. 27, 1978	3:703		P Aug. 28, 1978	3:601
Barbaro-Galtieri A	S Apr. 14, 1971	1:172		S Nov. 27, 1978	3:707
Barbeau A	P Jul. 3, 1974	2:93		S Nov. 27, 1978	3:709
Bard P	S Nov. 29, 1977	3:320	Barron F	P May. 5, 1975	2:264
Bardawill C J	S Apr. 14, 1971	1:171	Barrow E M	S Dec. 13, 1976	2:663
	S Jan. 9, 1974	2:7	Barrs H D	P Oct. 4, 1976	2:597
	S Feb. 21, 1977	3:49	Barry J	P May. 29, 1978	3:500
	S Dec. 19, 1977	3:358		S May. 29, 1978	3:500
Bardeen J	P Apr. 14, 1971	1:161	Barry J D	P May. 17, 1976	2:487
	P Apr. 14, 1971	1:172	Bartel W	S Feb. 16, 1976	2:423
	P Jan. 9, 1974	2:8	Bartels J	S Dec. 19, 1977	3:356
	S Feb. 23, 1976	2:427	Bartlett G R	P Apr. 14, 1971	1:161
	P Jun. 6, 1977	3:126		P Apr. 14, 1971	1:172
	P Dec. 5, 1977	3:330		P Jan. 9, 1974	2:8
	P Dec. 12, 1977	3:339		P Jun. 20, 1977	3:148
	P Dec. 12, 1977	3:344			
	P Dec. 19, 1977	3:354	Bartlett P D	P Dec. 5, 1977	3:330
Bardeen W A	P Apr. 19, 1976	2:460		P Dec. 12, 1977	3:339
Barfield M	P Mar. 6, 1974	2:43		P Dec. 19, 1977	3:354
Bargmann V	P Nov. 21, 1973	1:507	Barton D H R	P Oct. 3, 1973	1:488
	P Nov. 28, 1973	1:512		P Dec. 5, 1977	3:330
	P Mar. 7, 1977	3:57		P Dec. 12, 1977	3:339
Bargmann W	P Mar. 28, 1977	3:79		P Dec. 12, 1977	3:345
Barile M F	S Dec. 4, 1978	3:716		P Dec. 19, 1977	3:354
Barka T	P Jan. 2, 1974	2:4	Bartter F C	S Jul. 3, 1974	2:90
Barker J A	P Oct. 4, 1976	2:596		P Jul. 10, 1978	3:542
Barker N W	S Jul. 3, 1974	2:88		P Aug. 28, 1978	3:597
	S Oct. 25, 1976	2:615		P Nov. 20, 1978	3:694
Barker S B	P Apr. 14, 1971	1:161	Baryakhtar V G	S Nov. 10, 1975	2:376
	P Apr. 14, 1971	1:172	Basch R I	S Nov. 27, 1978	3:710
	P Jan. 9, 1974	2:8	Baserga R	P Oct. 16, 1974	2:166
	P Feb. 21, 1977	3:48	Basinski Z S	P Oct. 4, 1976	2:598
Barnes C S	P Oct. 4, 1976	2:595	Basolo F	P Dec. 5, 1977	3:330
Barnes J M	S Oct. 16, 1974	2:166		P Dec. 12, 1977	3:339
	P May. 5, 1975	2:265		P Dec. 19, 1977	3:354
Barnes M W	S Jul. 3, 1974	2:90	Basov N G	P Dec. 5, 1977	3:330
Barnes R D	S Dec. 19, 1977	3:354		P Dec. 12, 1977	3:339
	S Nov. 27, 1978	3:702		P Dec. 12, 1977	3:344
				P Dec. 19, 1977	3:354
Barnes W M	S Apr. 12, 1976	2:454	Bass H	P Nov. 21, 1973	1:507
Barnett R M	P Apr. 19, 1976	2:458	Bassham J A	S Jan. 27, 1975	2:217
Barojas J	P May. 29, 1978	3:501	Basten A	P May. 10, 1976	2:475
Baron S	S Oct. 16, 1974	2:166	Bateman D F	P Jan. 27, 1975	2:220
Barr M L	P Mar. 28, 1977	3:79	Bates D H	S Jan. 27, 1975	2:218
Barr Y M	S Jul. 3, 1974	2:92	Bates D R	P Oct. 3, 1973	1:488
Barrer R M	P Dec. 5, 1977	3:330		P Mar. 7, 1977	3:57
	P Dec. 12, 1977	3:339		P Dec. 5, 1977	3:330
	P Dec. 19, 1977	3:354		P Dec. 12, 1977	3:339
Barrera F	S Dec. 13, 1976	2:660		P Dec. 19, 1977	3:354
	S Jul. 18, 1977	3:182	Bateson G	P May. 5, 1975	2:264
Barret W G	S Sep. 11, 1978	3:628		P Aug. 7, 1978	3:566
Barrnett R J	S Apr. 14, 1971	1:171	Batini C	P Feb. 7, 1977	3:36
	S Jan. 9, 1974	2:7	Battaille J	S Jan. 27, 1975	2:220
	P Oct. 16, 1974	2:167	Batterman R C	S Mar. 28, 1977	3:83

Bianchi

Boyse

Burnet

Burnet F M   (cont'd)

	P Oct. 4, 1976	2:598
	P Dec. 5, 1977	**3:330**
	P Dec. 12, 1977	**3:339**
	P Dec. 12, 1977	**3:345**
	P Dec. 19, 1977	**3:355**
	P May. 22, 1978	**3:493**
Burnett H	S Dec. 13, 1976	2:660
Burnett J P	S Oct. 16, 1974	2:167
Burns R C	S Jan. 20, 1975	2:214
Burny A	S Dec. 19, 1973	1:522
Burr G O	S Jan. 20, 1975	2:213
Burris R H	S Aug. 11, 1971	1:226
	S Jan. 2, 1974	2:4
	S Dec. 19, 1977	**3:363**
Burrows J H	S Oct. 31, 1973	1:499
Burstone M S	P Oct. 16, 1974	2:165
	P Oct. 16, 1974	2:166
Burton K	P Apr. 14, 1971	1:161
	P Apr. 14, 1971	1:171
	P Oct. 3, 1973	1:488
	P Jan. 9, 1974	2:8
	P Jun. 20, 1977	**3:148**
	P Dec. 5, 1977	**3:330**
	P Dec. 12, 1977	**3:339**
	P Dec. 19, 1977	**3:355**
Busch H	P Oct. 16, 1974	2:167
	S Oct. 16, 1974	2:167
	P Jul. 10, 1978	**3:544**
	P Aug. 28, 1978	**3:601**
	S Nov. 20, 1978	**3:690**
Busch R D	S Nov. 27, 1974	2:183
	S Jul. 18, 1977	**3:183**
Bush I E	P Feb. 6, 1974	2:25
	P Jun. 20, 1977	**3:148**
Busing W R	P Mar. 6, 1974	2:40
	P Mar. 6, 1974	2:41
	P Sep. 11, 1974	2:131
	P Oct. 18, 1976	2:609
	P Oct. 18, 1976	2:610
	P Dec. 5, 1977	**3:330**
	P Dec. 12, 1977	**3:339**
	P Dec. 19, 1977	**3:356**
Buss A H	P May. 5, 1975	2:267
	S May. 5, 1975	2:267
Bussolati G	P Feb. 7, 1977	**3:39**
Butcher M	S Feb. 16, 1976	2:424
	S Nov. 20, 1978	**3:694**
Butcher R W	P Jul. 10, 1978	**3:544**
	P Aug. 28, 1978	**3:602**
	S Nov. 20, 1978	**3:693**
	P Nov. 20, 1978	**3:697**
	S Nov. 20, 1978	**3:697**
Butcher S G	S Nov. 20, 1978	**3:696**
Butler J J	S Oct. 16, 1974	2:167
Butler W L	P Jan. 20, 1975	2:212
	S Jan. 20, 1975	2:215

Butterworth M	S Jul. 17, 1974	2:101
Buttin G	S Jan. 26, 1976	2:413
Byram E T	S Aug. 28, 1974	2:124
Byrne D	P May. 5, 1975	2:266
	P Aug. 7, 1978	**3:541**
	P Sep. 18, 1978	**3:637**
	P Nov. 6, 1978	**3:677**
Byrne J P	P Oct. 4, 1976	2:597
Byvoet P	S Oct. 16, 1974	2:167

C

Cabaud P G	P Dec. 13, 1976	2:661
Cabibbo N	P Feb. 7, 1977	**3:39**
Cade C M	P May. 17, 1976	2:487
Cade J F J	P Oct. 4, 1976	2:595
Cagnac B	S Feb. 23, 1976	2:428
	P May. 29, 1978	**3:500**
Cahill L J	P Aug. 14, 1974	2:116
Cahn R D	P Nov. 20, 1978	**3:691**
Cahn R S	P Jul. 12, 1976	2:518
	P Jun. 20, 1977	**3:148**
Cain D L	S Feb. 23, 1976	2:428
Cain J C	S Aug. 14, 1974	2:116
	S Mar. 28, 1977	**3:79**
Cairns J	S Feb. 7, 1977	**3:39**
Calderon A P	P Nov. 15, 1976	2:633
Callahan R	S Jul. 3, 1974	2:91
Callan C G	P Apr. 19, 1976	2:458
Callow N H	P Oct. 25, 1976	2:613
Callow R K	S Oct. 25, 1976	2:613
Calvary E	S Dec. 13, 1976	2:661
	S Feb. 21, 1977	**3:51**
Calvert J G	P Aug. 11, 1971	1:228
Calvin M	S Jan. 27, 1975	2:217
	P Mar. 7, 1977	**3:57**
	P Dec. 12, 1977	**3:355**
Cameron G R	P Oct. 25, 1976	2:613
Campbell A	P Sep. 11, 1978	**3:630**
	P Sep. 18, 1978	**3:638**
	P Nov. 6, 1978	**3:678**
Campbell B A	P Apr. 28, 1975	2:260
Campbell D T	P May. 5, 1975	2:265
	P Aug. 7, 1978	**3:566**
	P Sep. 18, 1978	**3:637**
	P Nov. 6, 1978	**3:678**
Campbell E Q	S Sep. 11, 1978	**3:631**
Campbell M	S Aug. 14, 1974	2:116
Candia O	S Feb. 7, 1977	**3:37**
Cantor H	P Apr. 12, 1976	2:453
Capecchi M R	S Apr. 14, 1971	1:173
Capiluppi P	S Oct. 17, 1973	1:493
Carafoli E	S Feb. 7, 1977	**3:39**
Carbonara A O	S Jan. 9, 1974	2:9

Chandrasekhar

Chandrasekhar S	P Oct. 3, 1973	1:488
	P Jan. 2, 1974	2:3
	P Aug. 28, 1974	2:124
	P Mar. 7, 1977	3:57
	P Dec. 5, 1977	3:331
	P Dec. 12, 1977	3:339
	P Dec. 19, 1977	3:356
	P May. 22, 1978	3:493
Chaney A L	P Nov. 27, 1974	2:183
Chang K J	S Feb. 23, 1976	2:427
Chang P	S Dec. 4, 1974	2:186
Changeux J P	S Apr. 14, 1971	1:172
	S Feb. 6, 1974	2:23
	P Jul. 10, 1978	3:543
	P Aug. 28, 1978	3:598
	S Nov. 27, 1978	3:704
	S Nov. 27, 1978	3:706
Chanock R M	P Jul. 10, 1978	3:544
	P Aug. 28, 1978	3:603
	S Nov. 27, 1978	3:703
	P Dec. 4, 1978	3:716
Chanowitz M S	S Apr. 19, 1976	2:460
Chantler S	S Feb. 16, 1976	2:423
Chantooni K M	S Dec. 19, 1977	3:360
Chapman D	S Sep. 22, 1971	1:243
Chapman S	P Dec. 5, 1977	3:331
	P Dec. 12, 1977	3:339
	P Dec. 19, 1977	3:356
Chappel C I	S Dec. 13, 1976	2:661
Chappell J B	P Jul. 3, 1974	2:93
Chargaff E	P Aug. 11, 1971	1:226
Charlton G	P May. 10, 1976	2:476
Charman W N	P May. 17, 1976	2:487
	P May. 17, 1976	2:488
Charney J	S Oct. 31, 1973	1:499
Chase L R	P Nov. 20, 1978	3:694
Chase M W	P Mar. 28, 1977	3:79
Chasson A L	P Dec. 13, 1976	2:663
Chaston S H H	P Oct. 4, 1976	2:595
Chatt J	P Oct. 3, 1973	1:488
	S Mar. 6, 1974	2:44
	P Dec. 5, 1977	3:331
	P Dec. 12, 1977	3:339
	P Dec. 19, 1977	3:356
Chattock A P	P May. 17, 1976	2:488
Chaudhuri N K	P Oct. 16, 1974	2:167
Chauveau J	P Jul. 18, 1977	3:180
Chaykovsky M	S Dec. 4, 1978	3:713
Cheek G	S Sep. 11, 1978	3:628
Chem P	S Oct. 4, 1976	2:596
Chen P S	P Jan. 9, 1974	2:9
	P Jun. 20, 1977	3:149
Cheng C	S Jun. 20, 1977	3:151
Cheng D C	S Feb. 23, 1976	2:427
Cherenkov P A	P Dec. 12, 1977	3:344

Cherkes A	S Jul. 18, 1977	3:181
Cherney P J	S Dec. 13, 1976	2:660
Chernoff A J	S Jul. 18, 1977	3:184
Cherry R J	P Sep. 22, 1971	1:243
Chesnut D B	S Jun. 6, 1977	3:127
Chestnut D B	S Dec. 19, 1977	3:360
Cheung I K	S Mar. 22, 1976	2:443
Chew G F	S Oct. 31, 1973	1:499
	P Feb. 16, 1976	2:424
	P Feb. 7, 1977	3:37
Chiancone E	S Feb. 7, 1977	3:41
Chideckel E	S Feb. 23, 1976	2:428
Child J J	P Apr. 12, 1976	2:454
Chir B	S Jul. 3, 1974	2:93
Chladek S	S Nov. 15, 1976	2:635
Choi S I	S Nov. 27, 1978	3:709
Chomsky N	P Sep. 11, 1978	3:632
	P Sep. 18, 1978	3:639
	P Nov. 6, 1978	3:679
Chorover S L	P Apr. 28, 1975	2:261
Chou P Y	P Feb. 23, 1976	2:427
	P Feb. 23, 1976	2:428
Chrispeels M J	P Jan. 20, 1975	2:214
Christenson J A	S Sep. 11, 1978	3:628
Christian J W	S Oct. 4, 1976	2:598
Christian W	S Apr. 14, 1971	1:172
	S Jan. 9, 1974	2:8
	S Jul. 12, 1976	2:518
	S Feb. 21, 1977	3:51
Christy R F	P Aug. 28, 1974	2:123
Chu J	P Jul. 17, 1974	2:101
Churchill W H	S Feb. 16, 1976	2:424
Churg J	P Dec. 13, 1976	2:662
Chused T M	S Apr. 12, 1976	2:454
Ciampolini M	P Feb. 7, 1977	3:39
Cieciura S J	S Jul. 18, 1977	3:182
Ciocalteu V	S May. 24, 1976	2:494
Claman H N	P Oct. 18, 1976	2:610
Clapham W F	S Jul. 3, 1974	2:91
Clare B G	S Jan. 20, 1975	2:213
Clark B F C	P Apr. 14, 1971	1:173
Clark B G	P Aug. 28, 1974	2:124
Clark C T	S Dec. 19, 1977	3:363
Clark D A	S Nov. 27, 1978	3:707
Clark E P	P May. 24, 1976	2:493
Clark G W	P Aug. 28, 1974	2:124
Clark H H	P Aug. 7, 1978	3:566
Clark R B	S Jan. 20, 1975	2:212
Clarke D A	S Oct. 16, 1974	2:166
Clarke D H	P Feb. 6, 1974	2:25
	P Jul. 18, 1977	3:180
Clarke J S	P Feb. 16, 1976	2:424

Cook

Cook L J	S Oct. 4, 1976	2:597	Costa E	(cont'd)		
Cooke R E	S Jul. 17, 1974	2:100			P Aug. 28, 1978	3:600
Cool R L	P Feb. 7, 1977	**3:39**			S Nov. 20, 1978	**3:695**
	P Feb. 7, 1977	**3:40**	Cottam G		P Jan. 27, 1975	2:217
Cooley J W	P Nov. 28, 1973	1:511	Cottingham W N		S Feb. 7, 1977	**3:37**
	P Mar. 22, 1976	2:445	Cotton E		S Jul. 17, 1974	2:101
Cooley W W	P Nov. 28, 1973	1:513	Cotton F A		P Oct. 3, 1973	1:488
Coombs R R A	P Oct. 16, 1974	2:167			P Dec. 5, 1977	**3:331**
	P Dec. 13, 1976	2:662			P Dec. 12, 1977	**3:339**
Coons A H	P Feb. 6, 1974	2:23			P Dec. 19, 1977	**3:356**
	P Mar. 28, 1977	**3:80**			P Jul. 10, 1978	**3:540**
	P Jul. 18, 1977	**3:180**			P Aug. 28, 1978	**3:591**
Cooper A	S Oct. 31, 1973	1:498			P Dec. 4, 1978	**3:713**
Cooper F S	S May. 5, 1975	2:268	Cottrell A H		P Mar. 7, 1977	**3:57**
	S Aug. 7, 1978	**3:568**	Cotzias G C		P Jul. 3, 1974	2:93
Cooper G R	S Feb. 21, 1977	**3:51**	Couch A		P May. 5, 1975	2:265
Cooper K K	P Nov. 29, 1977	**3:320**	Couchman K G		S Jul. 3, 1974	2:91
	P Nov. 29, 1977	**3:321**			S Dec. 13, 1976	2:661
Cooper L N	S Apr. 14, 1971	1:172	Coulson C A		P Mar. 7, 1977	**3:57**
	S Jan. 9, 1974	2:8			P Dec. 5, 1977	**3:331**
	S Jun. 6, 1977	**3:126**			P Dec. 12, 1977	**3:339**
	P Dec. 12, 1977	**3:344**			P Dec. 19, 1977	**3:356**
	S Dec. 19, 1977	**3:354**			S Dec. 4, 1978	**3:713**
Cooper M D	S Jul. 3, 1974	2:92	Counsell R C			
	P Jul. 10, 1978	**3:541**	Courant R		P Aug. 11, 1971	1:227
	P Aug. 28, 1978	**3:596**			P Nov. 21, 1973	1:506
	P Nov. 27, 1978	**3:702**			P Nov. 21, 1973	1:508
Cooper M L	S Nov. 29, 1977	**3:319**			P Jan. 2, 1974	2:3
Cope A C	P Dec. 5, 1977	**3:331**			P Dec. 5, 1977	**3:331**
	P Dec. 12, 1977	**3:339**			P Dec. 12, 1977	**3:339**
	P Dec. 19, 1977	**3:356**			P Dec. 19, 1977	**3:356**
	P May. 22, 1978	**3:493**			P May. 22, 1978	**3:493**
Coppens P	P Sep. 11, 1974	2:132	Courcon J		S Jul. 18, 1977	**3:181**
Coppo A	S Feb. 7, 1977	**3:41**	Cournand A		S Mar. 28, 1977	**3:79**
Coraboeuf E	S Jul. 12, 1976	2:523			S Mar. 28, 1977	**3:80**
Corey E J	P Oct. 3, 1973	1:488	Cournand A C		S Jul. 3, 1974	2:89
	P Dec. 5, 1977	**3:331**	Cournand A F		P Dec. 12, 1977	**3:345**
	P Dec. 12, 1977	**3:339**	Courtbrown W M		S Jul. 3, 1974	2:91
	P Dec. 19, 1977	**3:356**	Couturier J		S May. 29, 1978	**3:500**
	P Jul. 10, 1978	**3:540**	Covell J W		S Dec. 4, 1978	**3:717**
	P Aug. 28, 1978	**3:591**	Covington A E		P May. 17, 1976	2:488
	P Dec. 4, 1978	**3:713**	Cowan D O		S Feb. 16, 1976	2:424
Corfield P W R	P Mar. 6, 1974	2:41			S Dec. 4, 1978	**3:713**
	P Dec. 4, 1978	**3:714**	Cowan G R		P Aug. 30, 1972	1:355
Cori C F	S Feb. 21, 1977	**3:51**			P Aug. 30, 1972	1:357
	S Dec. 19, 1977	**3:362**	Cowan W M		P May. 10, 1976	2:477
Corliss C H	P Aug. 28, 1974	2:123	Cowgill W		P May. 17, 1976	2:488
Corneo G	P Feb. 7, 1977	**3:40**	Cox D P		P Aug. 28, 1974	2:124
Cornforth J W	P Dec. 12, 1977	**3:345**	Cox G M		S Nov. 28, 1973	1:511
Cornsweet T N	P May. 5, 1975	2:266			S Jan. 2, 1974	2:5
Corrodi H	P Jul. 10, 1978	**3:543**	Cox J M		S Feb. 7, 1977	**3:39**
	P Aug. 28, 1978	**3:600**			S Dec. 19, 1977	**3:361**
	S Nov. 20, 1978	**3:696**	Craig J M		S Jul. 17, 1974	2:100
	P Nov. 27, 1978	**3:709**			S Jul. 17, 1974	2:101
Cory S	S Apr. 12, 1976	2:456	Craik F I M		P Aug. 7, 1978	**3:567**
Costa E	P Jul. 10, 1978	**3:543**	Cram D J		P Dec. 5, 1977	**3:331**

Dahlstrom

Dahlstrom A	P Oct. 18, 1976	2:608
	S Oct. 18, 1976	2:609
	S Dec. 19, 1977	**3:354**
	S Nov. 20, 1978	**3:696**
Dailey B P	S Mar. 7, 1977	**3:60**
Dainty J	P Jan. 20, 1975	2:211
	P Jan. 27, 1975	2:218
Daird M M	S Dec. 19, 1977	**3:358**
Dairman W	S May. 10, 1976	2:476
Dakin J T	S Apr. 19, 1976	2:459
Dale H H	P May. 24, 1976	2:492
Dalgarno A	P Dec. 5, 1977	**3:331**
	P Dec. 12, 1977	**3:339**
	P Dec. 19, 1977	**3:356**
	P Jul. 10, 1978	**3:545**
	P Aug. 28, 1978	**3:604**
	P Nov. 27, 1978	**3:708**
Dalton A J	P Oct. 16, 1974	2:166
	P Jul. 18, 1977	**3:180**
Dalton C	S Dec. 4, 1978	**3:713**
Daly A K	S Nov. 27, 1978	**3:710**
Damgaard A	S Mar. 7, 1977	**3:57**
	S Dec. 19, 1977	**3:354**
Danckwerts P V	P Dec. 4, 1974	2:186
Danielli J F	P Oct. 25, 1976	2:613
Danzinger R G	P Oct. 17, 1973	1:493
	P May. 10, 1976	2:477
Dardenne M	S May. 29, 1978	**3:501**
Darken L S	S Mar. 7, 1977	**3:57**
Darnell J E	P Oct. 31, 1973	1:499
	P Jul. 10, 1978	**3:544**
	P Aug. 28, 1978	**3:603**
	S Nov. 27, 1978	**3:705**
Darrell J H	P Dec. 13, 1976	2:662
Dartnall H J A	P Jul. 3, 1974	2:89
Das M R	S Dec. 19, 1973	1:522
Dassu G	P Aug. 30, 1972	1:356
Dauben C H	P Sep. 11, 1974	2:130
	P Oct. 18, 1976	2:609
Dauben W G	P May. 22, 1978	**3:495**
Daughaday W H	P Jul. 10, 1978	**3:542**
	P Aug. 28, 1978	**3:597**
	S Nov. 20, 1978	**3:694**
David C S	S Apr. 12, 1976	2:456
David M M	S Apr. 14, 1971	1:171
	S Jan. 9, 1974	2:7
	S Feb. 21, 1977	**3:49**
Davidson D G	S Jul. 3, 1974	2:90
Davidson E R	S Mar. 6, 1974	2:38
	P Jul. 10, 1978	**3:540**
	P Aug. 28, 1978	**3:591**
	S Dec. 4, 1978	**3:715**
Davidson G P	P Apr. 12, 1976	2:455
Davidson J	S Aug. 11, 1971	1:226
Davidson J D	S Dec. 4, 1978	**3:717**

Davidson J D (cont'd)		
	S Dec. 4, 1978	**3:718**
Davidson J N	P Aug. 11, 1971	1:227
Davidson K	P Feb. 16, 1976	2:423
Davidson N	S Apr. 12, 1976	2:455
Davidson W M	P Jul. 3, 1974	2:89
Davies C W	P Nov. 1, 1976	2:620
Davies D L	S Nov. 20, 1978	**3:691**
	S Nov. 20, 1978	**3:697**
Davies D W	P May. 17, 1976	2:488
Davies H E F	S Jul. 3, 1974	2:90
Davies N R	S Mar. 6, 1974	2:44
Davies P C W	P May. 17, 1976	2:488
Davies P L	S Jul. 3, 1974	2:92
Davis B D	P Feb. 6, 1974	2:25
	P Jul. 18, 1977	**3:181**
Davis B J	P Apr. 14, 1971	1:161
	P Apr. 14, 1971	1:171
	P Oct. 3, 1973	1:488
	P Jan. 9, 1974	2:8
	P Mar. 6, 1974	2:40
	P Dec. 5, 1977	**3:331**
	P Dec. 12, 1977	**3:339**
	P Dec. 19, 1977	**3:356**
	P Jul. 10, 1978	**3:544**
	P Aug. 28, 1978	**3:601**
	P Dec. 4, 1978	**3:717**
Davis K E	S Nov. 6, 1978	**3:684**
Davis K R	S Feb. 23, 1976	2:428
Davis L	S Aug. 28, 1974	2:123
	S Feb. 23, 1976	2:427
Davis N C	S Jul. 17, 1974	2:101
Davis P J	P Nov. 28, 1973	1:512
Davis R W	S Apr. 12, 1976	2:454
Davison G C	P May. 5, 1975	2:268
Davson H	S Oct. 25, 1976	2:613
Davydov B I	P Nov. 10, 1975	2:375
Dawson A B	P May. 24, 1976	2:494
Dawson B	P Sep. 11, 1974	2:132
Dawson G A	P May. 17, 1976	2:488
Dawson R M C	P Dec. 5, 1977	**3:331**
	P Dec. 12, 1977	**3:339**
	P Dec. 19, 1977	**3:356**
Day G A	P Oct. 4, 1976	2:596
Dayton S	S Jun. 20, 1977	**3:151**
Deak B D	S Feb. 23, 1976	2:428
Dealfaro V	P Feb. 7, 1977	**3:38**
Dean J	S Aug. 7, 1978	**3:566**
Debeljuk L	S Nov. 20, 1978	**3:694**
	S Nov. 20, 1978	**3:695**
Debye P	P May. 24, 1976	2:493
	P Mar. 7, 1977	**3:57**
Deduve C	P Apr. 14, 1971	1:161

INDEX TO AUTHORS IN MOST CITED LISTS

Graev

Gollub L R	S Apr. 28, 1975	2:260
Gomard E	S May. 29, 1978	3:501
Gomori G	P Aug. 11, 1971	1:227
	P Oct. 3, 1973	1:488
	P Jan. 2, 1974	2:4
	P Oct. 25, 1976	2:614
	P Dec. 13, 1976	2:660
	P Dec. 13, 1976	2:661
	P Feb. 21, 1977	3:49
	P Mar. 28, 1977	3:80
	P Dec. 5, 1977	3:332
	P Dec. 12, 1977	3:340
	P Dec. 19, 1977	3:358
Gonatas J	S Dec. 13, 1976	2:661
Gonatas N K	P Dec. 13, 1976	2:661
Good C A	P Oct. 25, 1976	2:614
Good R A	P Aug. 11, 1971	1:227
	S Jul. 3, 1974	2:92
	P Jul. 17, 1974	2:100
	P Dec. 5, 1977	3:332
	P Dec. 12, 1977	3:340
	P Dec. 19, 1977	3:358
	P Jul. 10, 1978	3:542
	P Aug. 28, 1978	3:596
	P Nov. 27, 1978	3:702
	S Nov. 27, 1978	3:702
	S Nov. 27, 1978	3:703
Goodale T C	S Jan. 27, 1975	2:217
Goodall D M	S Dec. 19, 1977	3:354
Goodenough D R	S Sep. 11, 1978	3:629
Goodier J N	S Mar. 22, 1976	2:443
Gooding R	S May. 17, 1976	2:490
Goodlet B L	P May. 17, 1976	2:488
Goodman H C	S Nov. 27, 1978	3:703
Goodman L A	P Aug. 7, 1978	3:567
	P Sep. 18, 1978	3:638
	P Nov. 6, 1978	3:678
Goodman L S	P Aug. 11, 1971	1:226
	P Jan. 2, 1974	2:4
	P Dec. 5, 1977	3:332
	P Dec. 12, 1977	3:340
	P Dec. 19, 1977	3:358
	P May. 22, 1978	3:493
Goodner C J	S Feb. 23, 1976	2:428
Goodnow J J	S Sep. 11, 1978	3:627
Goodwin T W	P Oct. 3, 1973	1:488
	P Feb. 21, 1977	3:49
	P Dec. 5, 1977	3:332
	P Dec. 12, 1977	3:340
	P Dec. 19, 1977	3:358
Gordon A H	P May. 17, 1976	2:488
	S Feb. 21, 1977	3:48
Gordon J E	S Jul. 3, 1974	2:90
Gordon M	S Mar. 6, 1974	2:41
	S Feb. 7, 1977	3:38
Gordon R D	P Nov. 20, 1978	3:694
Gordon R S	P Jul. 18, 1977	3:181

Gordon R S (cont'd)		
	S Dec. 4, 1978	3:718
Gordon S A	P Jan. 20, 1975	2:211
Gordy W	P Mar. 7, 1977	3:58
Gorenstein D	P Nov. 21, 1973	1:507
Gorer P A	P Oct. 16, 1974	2:165
Gorham D R	S May. 5, 1975	2:266
	S Aug. 7, 1978	3:569
Gorkov L P	P Nov. 10, 1975	2:375
	S Nov. 10, 1975	2:376
Gorlin R	P Jul. 10, 1978	3:546
	P Aug. 28, 1978	3:596
	S Dec. 4, 1978	3:717
Gorman M	S Oct. 16, 1974	2:167
Gornall A G	P Apr. 14, 1971	1:161
	P Apr. 14, 1971	1:171
	P Jan. 9, 1974	2:7
	P Feb. 21, 1977	3:49
	P Dec. 5, 1977	3:332
	P Dec. 12, 1977	3:340
	P Dec. 19, 1977	3:358
Gorski R A	P Nov. 29, 1977	3:320
	P Nov. 29, 1977	3:321
Goss W M	P Aug. 28, 1974	2:124
Gottfried K	S Apr. 19, 1976	2:459
	P Feb. 7, 1977	3:35
Gottlieb C W	S Dec. 19, 1977	3:358
	S Nov. 20, 1978	3:694
Gottlieb D I	S May. 10, 1976	2:477
Gough H G	P Sep. 18, 1978	3:637
	P Nov. 6, 1978	3:673
	P Nov. 6, 1978	3:684
Gould R J	S Aug. 28, 1974	2:124
Gouldner A W	P Aug. 7, 1978	3:567
Gourdin M	P Feb. 7, 1977	3:36
	P Feb. 7, 1977	3:37
Govan D E	S Jul. 3, 1974	2:93
Gowans J L	S Oct. 16, 1974	2:166
	S Dec. 13, 1976	2:660
	P Nov. 27, 1978	3:703
Goy R W	S Apr. 28, 1975	2:260
	S Apr. 28, 1975	2:261
	S Nov. 29, 1977	3:320
Grabar M	S Mar. 28, 1977	3:83
	S Dec. 19, 1977	3:362
Grabar P	P Jul. 18, 1977	3:181
	P Dec. 5, 1977	3:332
	P Dec. 12, 1977	3:340
	P Dec. 19, 1977	3:358
Grace J T	S Jul. 3, 1974	2:92
Grad H	P Nov. 28, 1973	1:512
Gradshteyn I S	P Nov. 21, 1973	1:506
	P Jan. 2, 1974	2:5
Grady H J	S Dec. 13, 1976	2:663
Graev M I	S Nov. 21, 1973	1:507

835

Graham

Graham D	S Jan. 27, 1975	2:220	Greenwood F C	P Jul. 10, 1978	**3:**542
Graham F K	P Apr. 28, 1975	2:261		P Aug. 28, 1978	**3:**597
	P Aug. 7, 1978	**3:**567		P Nov. 20, 1978	**3:**694
Graham J B	S Dec. 13, 1976	2:663		S Nov. 20, 1978	**3:**694
Grahame D C	P Mar. 7, 1977	**3:**58	Greer J	S Feb. 7, 1977	**3:**41
Grandchamp C	S May. 29, 1978	**3:**500	Gregg N M	P Mar. 28, 1977	**3:**80
Granick S	S Jul. 18, 1977	**3:**182	Grewal M S	S May. 22, 1978	**3:**493
Granit R A	P Dec. 5, 1977	**3:**332	Grey H M	S Oct. 31, 1973	1:498
	P Dec. 12, 1977	**3:**340		S Feb. 16, 1976	2:424
	P Dec. 12, 1977	**3:**345		P Jul. 10, 1978	**3:**542
	P Dec. 19, 1977	**3:**358		P Aug. 28, 1978	**3:**596
				S Nov. 27, 1978	**3:**703
Granner D	S Nov. 27, 1978	**3:**705	Greytak T J	S Feb. 16, 1976	2:423
Grannis P	S Feb. 16, 1976	2:423	Gribov V N	P Nov. 10, 1975	2:377
Grant D A	P May. 5, 1975	2:265	Griem H	P Jan. 2, 1974	2:3
Grant D M	P Jul. 10, 1978	**3:**540	Grieshaber E	S Jan. 27, 1975	2:219
	P Aug. 28, 1978	**3:**591	Grieve A	S Jan. 27, 1975	2:220
	P Dec. 4, 1978	**3:**713	Griffing B	P Oct. 4, 1976	2:595
Grant P M	S Apr. 19, 1976	2:459	Griffith A A	P May. 24, 1976	2:493
Grasyuk A Z	S Dec. 19, 1977	**3:**354	Griffith J D	P Apr. 12, 1976	2:456
Graves M	S Apr. 12, 1976	2:454	Griffiths R B	P Feb. 16, 1976	2:424
Gray H B	P Jul. 10, 1978	**3:**540		P Feb. 7, 1977	**3:**40
	P Aug. 28, 1978	**3:**592			
	P Dec. 4, 1978	**3:**715	Grillo M A	P Feb. 7, 1977	**3:**39
Greaves M F	P May. 10, 1976	2:476	Grimby G	S Jul. 3, 1974	2:91
	P Feb. 7, 1977	**3:**40	Grimes A J	S Dec. 19, 1977	**3:**356
	S Nov. 27, 1978	**3:**703	Grindlay J H	S Mar. 28, 1977	**3:**79
Green D	S Feb. 16, 1976	2:423	Grisham J W	P Oct. 16, 1974	2:167
Green D E	P Dec. 5, 1977	**3:**332	Griswold G C	S Mar. 28, 1977	**3:**81
	P Dec. 12, 1977	**3:**340	Grof P	S Jul. 12, 1976	2:522
	P Dec. 19, 1977	**3:**358		S Oct. 25, 1976	2:615
	P Jul. 10, 1978	**3:**544			
	P Aug. 28, 1978	**3:**601	Groliman J H	S Nov. 25, 1970	1:141
	P Nov. 20, 1978	**3:**690	Gronau M	P Feb. 16, 1976	2:424
Green D H	P Jul. 12, 1976	2:520	Groppetti A	S Feb. 7, 1977	**3:**40
Green D M	P Sep. 11, 1978	**3:**627		S Nov. 20, 1978	**3:**695
Green H	P Jul. 10, 1978	**3:**544	Gros F	P Jul. 10, 1978	**3:**543
	P Aug. 28, 1978	**3:**601		P Aug. 28, 1978	**3:**599
	S Nov. 27, 1978	**3:**706		P Nov. 27, 1978	**3:**705
	S Nov. 27, 1978	**3:**707	Gross C	P Jul. 12, 1976	2:521
Green H D	S Nov. 25, 1970	1:141	Gross D J	P Feb. 23, 1976	2:427
Green K	P Nov. 20, 1978	**3:**693	Gross E	P Nov. 20, 1978	**3:**694
Greenberg J R	S May. 10, 1976	2:476	Gross-Bellard M	S Apr. 12, 1976	2:456
Greenberger N J	S Dec. 4, 1978	**3:**718	Grossman L I	S Feb. 7, 1977	**3:**40
Greene R L	P Apr. 19, 1976	2:459	Grossman M I	P Jul. 10, 1978	**3:**546
Greenfield N	P Nov. 20, 1978	**3:**690		P Aug. 28, 1978	**3:**606
Greenfield P M	S Sep. 11, 1978	**3:**627		S Dec. 4, 1978	**3:**718
Greengard P	S May. 10, 1976	2:476	Grubb R	P Dec. 13, 1976	2:661
	P Jul. 10, 1978	**3:**543	Grubisic Z	P Dec. 4, 1974	2:187
	P Aug. 28, 1978	**3:**600	Gruenstein M	S Mar. 28, 1977	**3:**82
	S Nov. 20, 1978	**3:**691	Gruenwald P	P Jul. 17, 1974	2:101
Greenspan F S	P Mar. 28, 1977	**3:**80	Grumbach M M	S Jul. 17, 1974	2:101
Greenspon S A	S Dec. 13, 1976	2:662	Grun F	S Mar. 7, 1977	**3:**59
Greenstein J L	P Aug. 28, 1974	2:122	Grunwald E	P Mar. 7, 1977	**3:**58
	S Aug. 28, 1974	2:123	Grynberg C	S May. 29, 1978	**3:**500

Hamilton

Hamilton W C (cont'd)				**Harlow H F**	P Apr. 28, 1975	2:259
	P Sep. 11, 1974	2:132			P Mar. 28, 1977	**3:80**
	S Sep. 11, 1974	2:132		**Harm R**	S Aug. 28, 1974	2:124
	P Sep. 11, 1974	2:133		**Harman H H**	P Nov. 28, 1973	1:513
	P Oct. 18, 1976	2:607			P Sep. 11, 1978	**3:629**
Hamilton W F	S May. 24, 1976	2:494		**Harnden D G**	S Jul. 3, 1974	2:91
	P Oct. 25, 1976	2:614			P Oct. 16, 1974	2:166
	P Mar. 28, 1977	**3:80**			P Dec. 13, 1976	2:660
Hammerling G J	P Feb. 23, 1976	2:428		**Harned H S**	P Aug. 11, 1971	1:226
Hammerling U	S Feb. 23, 1976	2:428			P Jan. 2, 1974	2:3
Hammett L P	P Nov. 1, 1976	2:621			P Dec. 5, 1977	**3:332**
Hammond G S	P Mar. 6, 1974	2:40			P Dec. 12, 1977	**3:340**
	P Jun. 6, 1977	**3:126**			P Dec. 19, 1977	**3:358**
	P Jul. 10, 1978	**3:540**		**Harold F M**	P May. 10, 1976	2:477
	P Aug. 28, 1978	**3:592**		**Harper C M**	S Jul. 3, 1974	2:91
	P Dec. 4, 1978	**3:713**		**Harrington B J**	P Apr. 19, 1976	2:459
Hammond J	S Jul. 3, 1974	2:93		**Harrington R F**	P Nov. 28, 1973	1:513
Hamprecht B	S Apr. 12, 1976	2:455		**Harris C S**	P May. 5, 1975	2:267
Hamzi H Q	S Jan. 27, 1975	2:220		**Harris H**	P Jul. 10, 1978	**3:541**
Handel P H	P May. 17, 1976	2:488			P Aug. 28, 1978	**3:594**
Hanes C S	P Feb. 6, 1974	2:23			S Nov. 20, 1978	**3:691**
	P Feb. 21, 1977	**3:49**		**Harris H K**	S Aug. 14, 1974	2:117
Hanks J H	P Mar. 28, 1977	**3:80**		**Harris J I**	S Dec. 19, 1977	**3:358**
Hannig K	P Nov. 27, 1974	2:183		**Harris T E**	P Nov. 21, 1973	1:508
Hansen M	P Aug. 11, 1971	1:226		**Harrison J S**	S Apr. 14, 1971	1:172
	P Jan. 2, 1974	2:2			S Jan. 9, 1974	2:8
	P Mar. 22, 1976	2:443			S Jun. 20, 1977	**3:152**
	P Dec. 5, 1977	**3:332**		**Harrison W A**	P Jan. 2, 1974	2:3
	P Dec. 12, 1977	**3:340**		**Hart B L**	P Nov. 29, 1977	**3:320**
	P Dec. 19, 1977	**3:358**			P Nov. 29, 1977	**3:321**
	P May. 22, 1978	**3:493**		**Hart E B**	S Mar. 28, 1977	**3:80**
	P May. 22, 1978	**3:494**		**Harting D**	P Feb. 7, 1977	**3:36**
Hanshaw J B	S Jul. 3, 1974	2:91		**Hartley H O**	P Nov. 28, 1973	1:513
Hansman C	S Jul. 17, 1974	2:101		**Hartline H K**	P Dec. 12, 1977	**3:345**
Hanson H M	P Apr. 28, 1975	2:260		**Hartman P**	P Nov. 21, 1973	1:507
Hanson H P	P Mar. 6, 1974	2:39		**Hartmann H A**	S Oct. 16, 1974	2:166
	P Sep. 11, 1974	2:130		**Hartmann K U**	P Nov. 20, 1978	**3:691**
	P Oct. 18, 1976	2:607		**Hartree E F**	S Oct. 25, 1976	2:615
Hanzal R F	S Oct. 25, 1976	2:614			S Dec. 19, 1977	**3:359**
Hara T	S Feb. 7, 1977	**3:37**		**Hartroft P**	S Dec. 13, 1976	2:663
Harari H	P Oct. 31, 1973	1:499		**Hartt C E**	S Jan. 20, 1975	2:213
	P Feb. 16, 1976	2:423		**Harvey A M**	P Jul. 3, 1974	2:89
Harary F	P Nov. 21, 1973	1:508		**Harvey E N**	S Apr. 28, 1975	2:259
Harbers E	S Oct. 16, 1974	2:166		**Harvey J**	S Apr. 19, 1976	2:458
Harboe M	P Dec. 13, 1976	2:662		**Harvey J A**	P Apr. 28, 1975	2:261
	P Dec. 13, 1976	2:663		**Haselbach E**	S Dec. 4, 1978	**3:715**
Hardebeck H E	S Aug. 28, 1974	2:124		**Hashem N**	S Nov. 27, 1978	**3:703**
Hardin G	P Aug. 7, 1978	**3:568**		**Hassel O**	P Dec. 12, 1977	**3:345**
Hardwicke J	S Jul. 3, 1974	2:90		**Hasselbach W**	P Jul. 12, 1976	2:519
Hardy G H	P Nov. 28, 1973	1:513			P Jul. 12, 1976	2:523
Hardy R W F	P Jan. 20, 1975	2:214		**Hasselberger F X**	S Nov. 20, 1978	**3:692**
Hare A T	P May. 17, 1976	2:488		**Hasting A B**	S Mar. 28, 1977	**3:83**
Harkins W D	P May. 24, 1976	2:493		**Hastings A B**	S Jul. 3, 1974	2:89
Harley J	S Aug. 7, 1978	**3:566**				

Hirschhorn K	(cont'd)			Hokfelt T	(cont'd)		
	P Aug. 28, 1978	3:696			S Nov. 20, 1978	3:696	
	P Nov. 27, 1978	3:703		Holden H T	S Apr. 12, 1976	2:454	
Hirsh J	S Feb. 16, 1976	2:424		Holland M G	S Mar. 22, 1976	2:445	
Hirst A E	P Jul. 3, 1974	2:90		Holland N H	S Jul. 17, 1974	2:101	
Hirth L	S Jan. 27, 1975	2:220		Holland P V	S Nov. 27, 1978	3:703	
Hiscoe H B	S Mar. 28, 1977	3:83		Hollenberg N K	P Nov. 27, 1978	3:710	
Hitzig W	S Nov. 27, 1978	3:703		Holley R W	P Dec. 12, 1977	3:345	
Hjerten S	S Jun. 20, 1977	3:152		Holling H E	S Jul. 3, 1974	2:91	
Ho Y C	S Mar. 22, 1976	2:443		Hollingshead A B	P Jan. 2, 1974	2:4	
Hobart G A	S Apr. 28, 1975	2:259			P Sep. 11, 1978	3:630	
Hobson C J	S Sep. 11, 1978	3:631			P Sep. 11, 1978	3:631	
Hodgkin A L	P Mar. 28, 1977	3:81			P Sep. 18, 1978	3:638	
	P Jul. 18, 1977	3:181			P Nov. 6, 1978	3:678	
	P Dec. 5, 1977	3:332		Hollingsworth B R	S Jul. 18, 1977	3:184	
	P Dec. 12, 1977	3:345		Holm C H	S Mar. 6, 1974	2:44	
	P Dec. 12, 1977	3:340			S Jun. 6, 1977	3:126	
	P Dec. 19, 1977	3:359			S Dec. 19, 1977	3:358	
	P May. 22, 1978	3:493		Holm G	S May. 10, 1976	2:475	
Hodgkin D M C	P Dec. 12, 1977	3:344			S Nov. 27, 1978	3:709	
Hoffbrand A V	P Dec. 13, 1976	2:661		Holmberg C G	P Mar. 28, 1977	3:81	
Hoffman A K	S Dec. 19, 1977	3:357		Holmes I H	S Apr. 12, 1976	2:455	
Hoffman B	P Jan. 2, 1974	2:4		Holmes T H	P Aug. 7, 1978	3:568	
Hoffman K	P Nov. 21, 1973	1:508		Holmgren P	S Jan. 20, 1975	2:212	
Hoffman R	P Mar. 6, 1974	2:43			P Jan. 20, 1975	2:213	
	S Mar. 6, 1974	2:43		Holmsen H	S Jul. 12, 1976	2:523	
	S Dec. 4, 1974	2:186		Holness N J	S Dec. 19, 1977	3:363	
Hoffman W S	P Feb. 6, 1974	2:23		Holstein T	P Mar. 7, 1977	3:58	
	P Oct. 25, 1976	2:614		Holsten R D	S Jan. 20, 1975	2:214	
Hoffmann R	P Oct. 3, 1973	1:488			S Jan. 27, 1975	2:219	
	P Feb. 6, 1974	2:24		Holton P	P Mar. 28, 1977	3:81	
	S Mar. 6, 1974	2:38		Holy A	S Nov. 15, 1976	2:635	
	P Mar. 6, 1974	2:39		Holzer R E	P Aug. 14, 1974	2:117	
	P Mar. 6, 1974	2:42		Homans G C	P Sep. 11, 1978	3:626	
	S Jul. 12, 1976	2:518		Homburger E	S Sep. 11, 1978	3:628	
	S Dec. 19, 1977	3:363		Hones E W	S Aug. 14, 1974	2:116	
	P Jul. 10, 1978	3:540			S Aug. 14, 1974	2:117	
	P Aug. 28, 1978	3:592		Honzl J	P Nov. 15, 1976	2:633	
	P Dec. 4, 1978	3:715		Hood W B	S Jul. 3, 1974	2:93	
	S Dec. 4, 1978	3:715		Hooke R	P Nov. 28, 1973	1:512	
Hofmann A F	S Oct. 17, 1973	1:493		Hoopes J J	S Apr. 28, 1975	2:261	
	P Jul. 3, 1974	2:93		Hope A B	P Oct. 4, 1976	2:598	
	S May. 10, 1976	2:477		Hopkinson D A	S Nov. 20, 1978	3:691	
	P Jul. 10, 1978	3:546		Hopp A G	S Jul. 3, 1974	2:93	
	P Aug. 28, 1978	3:607		Hopper J	S Dec. 13, 1976	2:663	
	P Dec. 4, 1978	3:718		Horecker B L	P Feb. 21, 1977	3:49	
Hofstadter R	P Dec. 12, 1977	3:344			P Jul. 10, 1978	3:541	
Hogeboom G H	P Mar. 28, 1977	3:81			P Aug. 28, 1978	3:594	
	S Jul. 18, 1977	3:183			S Nov. 20, 1978	3:691	
Hoglund B	S Aug. 28, 1974	2:123		Horhammer L	S Jul. 12, 1976	2:519	
Hognestad H	P Nov. 25, 1970	1:141		Hornbrook M M	S Nov. 27, 1978	3:703	
Hohorst H J	P Jul. 12, 1976	2:518		Horne R W	S Jul. 18, 1977	3:180	
	P Jun. 20, 1977	3:149					
Hokfelt T	P Jul. 12, 1976	2:523					
	P Jul. 10, 1978	3:545					
	P Aug. 28, 1978	3:605					

Horner

Horner L	P Dec. 5, 1977	3:332
	P Dec. 12, 1977	3:340
	P Dec. 19, 1977	3:359
Hornig D F	P Mar. 7, 1977	3:58
Horning E S	S Oct. 16, 1974	2:166
Hornsby J R	S Sep. 11, 1978	3:627
Hornykiewicz O	S Jul. 3, 1974	2:90
	S Jul. 12, 1976	2:519
Horowicz P	S Jul. 18, 1977	3:181
Horstmann D M	S Mar. 28, 1977	3:79
Horton A A	S Jan. 27, 1975	2:218
Hotchkiss R D	P Feb. 21, 1977	3:49
Hough L	P Jun. 20, 1977	3:149
Houghton A	S Apr. 19, 1976	2:459
House H O	P Dec. 5, 1977	3:332
	P Dec. 12, 1977	3:340
	P Dec. 19, 1977	3:359
Hovig T	P Jul. 12, 1976	2:523
Howard J G	P Apr. 12, 1976	2:456
Howden M E H	S Dec. 4, 1978	3:714
Howells E R	P Sep. 11, 1974	2:131
	P Oct. 18, 1976	2:609
Howie J	S Oct. 4, 1976	2:595
Howitt G	S Jul. 3, 1974	2:92
Howley P	S Apr. 12, 1976	2:455
Hoyle F	S Aug. 28, 1974	2:122
Hoyt R E	S Mar. 28, 1977	3:83
Hozier J C	S Apr. 12, 1976	2:455
Hruban Z	P Dec. 13, 1976	2:660
Hsien W	S May. 24, 1976	2:493
Hsu T C	S Oct. 31, 1973	1:498
	P Oct. 16, 1974	2:167
Huang K	S Aug. 11, 1971	1:227
	S Jan. 2, 1974	2:2
	S Dec. 19, 1977	3:355
Huang M L	P Mar. 7, 1977	3:58
Huang R C	P Nov. 27, 1978	3:704
Hubbell J P	S Jul. 17, 1974	2:100
Hubbell R B	P Oct. 25, 1976	2:615
Hubbell W L	P Oct. 31, 1973	1:499
	P Nov. 27, 1978	3:709
Hubel D H	P Dec. 5, 1977	3:332
	P Dec. 12, 1977	3:340
	P Dec. 19, 1977	3:359
	P Jul. 10, 1978	3:544
	P Aug. 7, 1978	3:568
	P Aug. 28, 1978	3:602
	P Nov. 20, 1978	3:697
Hubert P	S May. 17, 1976	2:488
Huckabee W E	P Jun. 20, 1977	3:149
Huckel E	S May. 24, 1976	2:493
	P Jul. 12, 1976	2:521
	P Nov. 1, 1976	2:621
Hudecki S M	S Feb. 16, 1976	2:424

Hudson B	P Oct. 4, 1976	2:597
Hudson C S	P May. 24, 1976	2:492
Huebner R J	S May. 10, 1976	2:477
	P Jul. 10, 1978	3:545
	P Aug. 28, 1978	3:603
	P Nov. 27, 1978	3:708
Huggett A S G	P Jul. 3, 1974	2:90
	P Jun. 20, 1977	3:150
Huggins C	S Feb. 21, 1977	3:51
Huggins C B	P Dec. 12, 1977	3:345
Huggins M L	P Mar. 7, 1977	3:58
Hugh R	P Jul. 18, 1977	3:182
Hughes B P	P Nov. 27, 1974	2:183
Hughes D E	P Oct. 16, 1974	2:165
	P Dec. 13, 1976	2:660
Hughes E W	P Mar. 6, 1974	2:42
	P Feb. 21, 1977	3:49
Hughes J	P Apr. 12, 1976	2:456
Hughes S J	P Jan. 27, 1975	2:217
Hughes W L	S Feb. 21, 1977	3:48
Huijing F	P Mar. 1, 1976	2:434
Huisgen R	P Oct. 3, 1973	1:488
	P Mar. 6, 1974	2:41
	P Mar. 6, 1974	2:42
	P Jul. 12, 1976	2:518
	P Jul. 12, 1976	2:519
	P Dec. 5, 1977	3:332
	P Dec. 12, 1977	3:340
	P Dec. 19, 1977	3:359
	P Jul. 10, 1978	3:540
	P Aug. 28, 1978	3:592
	P Dec. 4, 1978	3:714
Hull C L	P Sep. 11, 1978	3:626
Hulse R A	P Apr. 19, 1976	2:459
Hultgren R	P Jan. 2, 1974	2:3
Humphreys W J	P May. 17, 1976	2:488
Hungerford D A	S Apr. 14, 1971	1:171
	S Jan. 9, 1974	2:8
	S Oct. 16, 1974	2:165
	S Oct. 16, 1974	2:167
Hunneman M E	P May. 17, 1976	2:488
Hunt H F	S Apr. 28, 1975	2:261
Hunt J N	P Aug. 30, 1972	1:356
Hunter W M	P Jul. 10, 1978	3:542
	P Aug. 28, 1978	3:597
	P Nov. 20, 1978	3:694
	S Nov. 20, 1978	3:694
Huppert B	P Nov. 21, 1973	1:508
Hurlbert R E	P Jun. 20, 1977	3:150
Hursh J B	P Oct. 25, 1976	2:615
Hurst P L	S Jul. 17, 1974	2:100
Hurwitz J	P Jul. 10, 1978	3:543
	P Aug. 28, 1978	3:599
	P Nov. 27, 1978	3:705
Huus T	S Jun. 6, 1977	3:126

Kende H	P Jan. 20, 1975	2:212	Kimble D P	P Apr. 28, 1975	2:261
	S Jan. 20, 1975	2:212		P Aug. 7, 1978	**3**:567
	P Jan. 27, 1975	2:219	Kimura D	P May. 5, 1975	2:266
Kendler H H	P May. 5, 1975	2:266		P Aug. 7, 1978	**3**:567
	P Aug. 7, 1978	**3**:568	Kincaid-Smith P	P Oct. 4, 1976	2:598
Kendler T S	S May. 5, 1975	2:266	Kind P R N	P Dec. 13, 1976	2:660
	S Aug. 7, 1978	**3**:568	King E J	P Jul. 3, 1974	2:88
Kendrew J C	S Feb. 7, 1977	**3**:39		P Oct. 25, 1976	2:615
	S Feb. 7, 1977	**3**:40		S Dec. 13, 1976	2:660
	P Dec. 12, 1977	**3**:344	King M J	S Jul. 3, 1974	2:91
Keniston K	S May. 5, 1975	2:265	King R B	P Dec. 5, 1977	**3**:332
Kennedy C R	S Mar. 28, 1977	**3**:81		P Dec. 12, 1977	**3**:340
Kennedy G C	P Aug. 14, 1974	2:117		P Dec. 19, 1977	**3**:359
Kennel C F	P Aug. 14, 1974	2:115		P May. 22, 1978	**3**:493
	P Feb. 7, 1977	**3**:39		P Jul. 10, 1978	**3**:540
Kenney H J	S Sep. 11, 1978	**3**:627		P Aug. 28, 1978	**3**:592
Kent A E	S Jan. 27, 1975	2:219		P Dec. 4, 1978	**3**:714
Keppel G	P May. 5, 1975	2:266	King T E	P Aug. 11, 1971	1:227
Kerr J A	P Mar. 6, 1974	2:42	Kingsbury C A	S Dec. 4, 1978	**3**:713
Kervaire M A	P Nov. 21, 1973	1:507	Kingsley R L	S Apr. 19, 1976	2:458
Kessler G	P Nov. 27, 1974	2:183	Kinmonth J B	P Jul. 3, 1974	2:89
Kessler H	P Dec. 19, 1973	1:522	Kinoshita T	S Apr. 19, 1976	2:459
	P Mar. 6, 1974	2:41	Kinsman J M	P May. 24, 1976	2:494
	P Jul. 12, 1976	2:520		S Oct. 25, 1976	2:614
Kessler J T	S Dec. 19, 1973	1:522	Kipnis D M	P Jul. 10, 1978	**3**:542
Kestin J	S Mar. 22, 1976	2:443		P Aug. 28, 1978	**3**:597
Kety S S	P Mar. 28, 1977	**3**:81		S Nov. 20, 1978	**3**:691
	P Dec. 5, 1977	**3**:332		S Nov. 20, 1978	**3**:694
	P Dec. 12, 1977	**3**:340	Kiraly Z	S Jan. 27, 1975	2:218
	P Dec. 19, 1977	**3**:359	Kirby K S	P Jun. 20, 1977	**3**:150
Key J L	P Jan. 20, 1975	2:212	Kirby W M M	S Dec. 13, 1976	2:659
	P Jan. 20, 1975	2:213	Kirchner H	P Apr. 12, 1976	2:454
	P Jan. 20, 1975	2:215	Kirk J T O	P Jan. 20, 1975	2:214
	P Jan. 27, 1975	2:219	Kirk R E	P Sep. 11, 1978	**3**:630
Keydar J	S Dec. 19, 1973	1:522	Kirkwood J G	P Nov. 1, 1976	2:621
Keys A	S Nov. 27, 1974	2:183		P Mar. 7, 1977	**3**:59
Kezdy F J	S Dec. 4, 1978	**3**:713		P Dec. 5, 1977	**3**:332
Khokhlov R V	S Nov. 10, 1975	2:377		P Dec. 12, 1977	**3**:340
Khorana H G	S Apr. 14, 1971	1:173		P Dec. 19, 1977	**3**:359
	S Apr. 14, 1971	1:174	Kirsch E	S Dec. 13, 1976	2:662
	P Dec. 12, 1977	**3**:345	Kisaki T	S Jan. 20, 1975	2:215
	P Jul. 10, 1978	**3**:540	Kister A T	S Mar. 7, 1977	**3**:60
	P Aug. 28, 1978	**3**:592	Kittel C	P Mar. 7, 1977	**3**:59
	S Dec. 4, 1978	**3**:714		S Jun. 6, 1977	**3**:127
Khoury G	P Apr. 12, 1976	2:455		P Dec. 5, 1977	**3**:332
Kielland J	P Nov. 1, 1976	2:621		P Dec. 12, 1977	**3**:340
Kikkawa Y	P Dec. 13, 1976	2:662		P Dec. 19, 1977	**3**:359
Kilmartin J V	S Feb. 7, 1977	**3**:41	Kivirikko K I	P Nov. 20, 1978	**3**:692
Kilmer V J	P Feb. 21, 1977	**3**:49	Kjekshus J K	S Dec. 4, 1978	**3**:717
Kilpatrick J E	P Mar. 7, 1977	**3**:58	Kjellmer I	S Jul. 3, 1974	2:91
Kim J J	S Feb. 16, 1976	2:423	Klatzo I	P Dec. 13, 1976	2:663
	S Feb. 23, 1976	2:428	Klaus M H	S Jul. 17, 1974	2:101
Kim S H	P Feb. 16, 1976	2:423	Klee W A	S Apr. 12, 1976	2:456
	S Feb. 23, 1976	2:428	Kleeman C R	P Jul. 3, 1974	2:90

Kleihauer

LaDu

LaDu B N	S Dec. 19, 1977	3:355
LaDue J S	S Jul. 18, 1977	3:184
Laemmli U K	P Dec. 19, 1973	1:521
Laetsch W M	P Jan. 27, 1975	2:220
Laffey J J	S Sep. 11, 1978	3:628
Lahey M E	S Jul. 17, 1974	2:101
Lai M C M	P Oct. 17, 1973	1:493
Laidler K J	S Dec. 19, 1977	3:358
Laitinen O	S Nov. 20, 1978	3:692
Lamb G A	S Jul. 3, 1974	2:93
Lamb H	P Aug. 11, 1971	1:227
	P Jan. 2, 1974	2:3
Lamb W E	P Dec. 12, 1977	3:344
Lambek J	P Nov. 21, 1973	1:508
Lambert M	S May. 29, 1978	3:502
Lamberti A	S Feb. 7, 1977	3:41
Lamola A A	S Dec. 4, 1978	3:713
Lamori P N	S Aug. 14, 1974	2:117
Lamper J O	S Jul. 12, 1976	2:521
Lampert P W	P Dec. 13, 1976	2:662
Lampson G P	S Dec. 4, 1978	3:716
Lancefield R C	P Oct. 25, 1976	2:615
	S Mar. 28, 1977	3:83
Landau L	P Nov. 10, 1975	2:375
	P Nov. 1, 1976	2:621
	S Mar. 7, 1977	3:58
	P Mar. 7, 1977	3:59
Landau L D	P Oct. 3, 1973	1:488
	P Jan. 2, 1974	2:3
	P Nov. 10, 1975	2:375
	P Mar. 7, 1977	3:59
	P Dec. 5, 1977	3:333
	P Dec. 12, 1977	3:340
	P Dec. 12, 1977	3:344
	S Dec. 19, 1977	3:358
	P Dec. 19, 1977	3:360
Landel R F	S Dec. 4, 1974	2:186
	S Jun. 6, 1977	3:128
Landing B H	P Jul. 17, 1974	2:101
	S Jul. 17, 1974	2:101
Lane A M	P Jun. 6, 1977	3:127
Lane H C	S Jan. 20, 1975	2:212
Lane K D	S Apr. 19, 1976	2:459
Lane W T	S Nov. 27, 1978	3:708
Lang A	S Jan. 20, 1975	2:212
	S Jan. 27, 1975	2:219
Lang A R	P Sep. 11, 1974	2:132
Lang H	S Sep. 22, 1971	1:244
Lang P J	P May. 5, 1975	2:267
	S May. 5, 1975	2:267
Langer W C	S Sep. 11, 1978	3:628
Langmuir I	P May. 24, 1976	2:493
	S May. 24, 1976	2:494
Langues J	S Nov. 1, 1976	2:620

Langworthy O R	S Nov. 29, 1977	3:320
LaPlaca S J	P Sep. 11, 1974	2:132
Laragh J H	S Jul. 3, 1974	2:90
	P Jul. 3, 1974	2:91
	S May. 10, 1976	2:475
	P Jul. 10, 1978	3:542
	P Aug. 28, 1978	3:597
	S Nov. 20, 1978	3:696
Lardy H	S Aug. 11, 1971	1:226
Lardy H A	P Jul. 10, 1978	3:542
	P Aug. 28, 1978	3:695
	S Nov. 20, 1978	3:691
Larigan G R	S Aug. 14, 1974	2:116
Lark K G	P Oct. 17, 1973	1:493
Larkin A I	S Nov. 10, 1975	2:377
Larsson K	S Oct. 18, 1976	2:609
	P Nov. 29, 1977	3:320
	P Nov. 29, 1977	3:321
	S Dec. 19, 1977	3:354
Larsson L	S Nov. 20, 1978	3:696
Lasfargues E Y	S Oct. 31, 1973	1:499
Lassen N A	P Jul. 10, 1978	3:695
	P Aug. 28, 1978	3:602
	P Nov. 20, 1978	3:697
Last J A	S Apr. 14, 1971	1:173
	P Apr. 14, 1971	1:174
Laster L	S Nov. 27, 1978	3:710
Laszlo P	P Dec. 4, 1978	3:714
Laties G G	S Jan. 20, 1975	2:213
	P Jan. 20, 1975	2:215
Latimer W M	P Jan. 2, 1974	2:3
Latner A L	P Sep. 22, 1971	1:243
Latorre J	S May. 10, 1976	2:476
Latter R	S Aug. 28, 1974	2:123
Latzin S	S Apr. 12, 1976	2:455
Lau K S	S Dec. 19, 1977	3:358
	S Nov. 20, 1978	3:694
Launois H	S May. 29, 1978	3:502
Laurell A B	S Dec. 13, 1976	2:661
Laurell C B	S Mar. 28, 1977	3:81
Laurelli P	S Feb. 16, 1976	2:423
Laurent C	S May. 29, 1978	3:500
Lauridse P	P Nov. 25, 1970	1:141
Lauritsen T	S Jun. 6, 1977	3:126
Laver M B	S Jul. 3, 1974	2:91
Laver M C	S Oct. 4, 1976	2:598
Law L W	S Oct. 16, 1974	2:166
Law M E	S Feb. 23, 1976	2:427
Layne E	P Jun. 20, 1977	3:150
Lazar G K	S Nov. 27, 1978	3:706
Lazarides M	P May. 17, 1976	2:489
Lazarus A A	S Sep. 11, 1978	3:627
Lazarus H	S Oct. 16, 1974	2:167

Lubchenco

Lubchenco L O	P Jul. 17, 1974	2:101
Lucas-lenard J	P Apr. 14, 1971	1:173
Lucky R W	P Mar. 22, 1976	2:443
Lucy J A	S Apr. 12, 1976	2:453
Luderitz O	S Jul. 12, 1976	2:518
	S Jul. 12, 1976	2:521
Luduena M A	S Oct. 31, 1973	1:498
Luft J H	P Apr. 14, 1971	1:161
	P Apr. 14, 1971	1:171
	P Oct. 3, 1973	1:488
	P Jan. 9, 1974	2:7
	S Jun. 20, 1977	3:148
	P Dec. 5, 1977	3:333
	P Dec. 12, 1977	3:340
	P Dec. 19, 1977	3:360
	P Jul. 10, 1978	3:545
	P Aug. 28, 1978	3:605
	P Nov. 27, 1978	3:709
Luhrs C E	S Jul. 17, 1974	2:101
Lukes R J	P Oct. 16, 1974	2:167
	P Apr. 12, 1976	2:454
Lumachi B	S Oct. 17, 1973	1:493
Lundberg A	S Feb. 7, 1977	3:36
Lundby A	S Feb. 7, 1977	3:39
Lundevall J	S Dec. 13, 1976	2:662
Lundgren C	S Sep. 22, 1971	1:243
Luria S E	P Mar. 28, 1977	3:81
	P Dec. 12, 1977	3:345
Lurie D	S Feb. 7, 1977	3:37
Luzzati V	S May. 29, 1978	3:496
Lwoff A	P Dec. 12, 1977	3:345
Lycette R R	S Jul. 3, 1974	2:92
Lyddane R H	P Mar. 7, 1977	3:59
Lynch J	S Oct. 25, 1976	2:614
Lynen F	P Dec. 12, 1977	3:345
Lyon J L	S Jan. 20, 1975	2:215
Lyon T P	S Mar. 28, 1977	3:83

M

Ma T S	P Mar. 7, 1977	3:59
Maaloe O	S Jul. 12, 1976	2:519
Maasbol A	S Dec. 19, 1977	3:357
MacArthur R H	P Jan. 27, 1975	2:219
Maccoby M	S Sep. 11, 1978	3:627
MacDiarmid A G	S Apr. 19, 1976	2:458
MacFadyen D A	P Feb. 21, 1977	3:50
MacGillavry C H	S Jun. 6, 1977	3:126
MacGregor T N	S Jul. 3, 1974	2:91
Machado R D	S Jan. 27, 1975	2:218
MacKey G W	P Nov. 21, 1973	1:508
Mackey M B	S Oct. 4, 1976	2:596
Mackinney G	P Feb. 21, 1977	3:50
Mackinnon D W	S Sep. 11, 1978	3:628

Mackintosh N J	P Apr. 28, 1975	2:261
MacLachlan E A	S Jul. 17, 1974	2:100
MacLean N	S Jul. 3, 1974	2:91
MacLeod C	S Mar. 28, 1977	3:79
Macmahon B	P Oct. 16, 1974	2:167
MacRobbie E A C	P Oct. 4, 1976	2:597
Macruz R	S Jul. 18, 1977	3:183
Madden R P	P Aug. 28, 1974	2:123
Madigan S A	S May. 5, 1975	2:268
	S Aug. 7, 1978	3:569
Maeda K	S Dec. 4, 1978	3:716
MaGee P N	P Oct. 16, 1974	2:166
Magoun H W	S Mar. 28, 1977	3:82
Mahajan S	S Apr. 19, 1976	2:460
Maia I G	S Nov. 25, 1970	1:141
Maier P	S Nov. 27, 1978	3:703
Main J M	S Oct. 16, 1974	2:165
Main P	S Oct. 18, 1976	2:609
Maizel J V	S Feb. 6, 1974	2:23
	P Jul. 10, 1978	3:543
	P Aug. 28, 1978	3:599
	S Nov. 20, 1978	3:692
Makinose M	S Jul. 12, 1976	2:519
	S Jul. 12, 1976	2:523
Makita M	S Feb. 6, 1974	2:24
	S Mar. 6, 1974	2:43
	S Dec. 4, 1978	3:715
Maksimov L	S Nov. 10, 1975	2:376
Malamy M	S Nov. 27, 1978	3:705
Malin M V	P Sep. 22, 1971	1:244
Mallory T B	S Dec. 13, 1976	2:660
	S Mar. 28, 1977	3:80
Malloy H T	S Oct. 25, 1976	2:614
	P Oct. 25, 1976	2:615
Malmfors T	P Oct. 18, 1976	2:610
Malmo R B	P Apr. 28, 1975	2:260
Maloney J R	S Jul. 17, 1974	2:101
Man E B	S Jul. 3, 1974	2:91
Manaker R A	S Oct. 16, 1974	2:166
Mancini G	P Jan. 9, 1974	2:9
Mandel J L	S Dec. 19, 1973	1:522
Mandel P	P Jul. 10, 1978	3:545
	P Aug. 28, 1978	3:607
	S Nov. 20, 1978	3:692
Mandelkern L	P Dec. 4, 1974	2:186
Mandell J D	P Apr. 14, 1971	1:161
	P Apr. 14, 1971	1:172
	P Jan. 9, 1974	2:9
Mandelstam S	P Feb. 7, 1977	3:35
	P Feb. 7, 1977	3:36
	S Feb. 7, 1977	3:37
Mandler G	P May. 5, 1975	2:264
	P Aug. 7, 1978	3:569

Mason

Metcalf

Metcalf T G (cont'd)		
	S Jul. 18, 1977	3:183
Meunch H	S Dec. 19, 1977	**3:361**
Meyer D B	S Dec. 13, 1976	2:663
Meyer H M	S Jul. 3, 1974	2:93
Meyer-Arendt E	S Jul. 12, 1976	2:518
Meyer-Bertenrath T	S Jan. 20, 1975	2:213
Mezger P G	P Aug. 28, 1974	2:123
	S Aug. 28, 1974	2:123
Michaelis L	P May. 24, 1976	2:492
	P Oct. 25, 1976	2:616
Michel D	S Feb. 21, 1977	**3:48**
Michel F	S May. 29, 1978	**3:500**
Michel H O	P Feb. 21, 1977	**3:50**
Michelson S	S Sep. 11, 1978	**3:632**
Michin G M	P May. 17, 1976	2:489
Mickey M R	S Nov. 27, 1978	**3:704**
Middleton D	P Nov. 28, 1973	1:512
Midgley A R	P Jul. 10, 1978	**3:542**
	P Aug. 28, 1978	**3:597**
	S Nov. 20, 1978	**3:694**
Mie G	P Mar. 22, 1976	2:445
	P May. 24, 1976	2:492
Miettinen H I	S Feb. 16, 1976	2:424
Migdal A A	S Nov. 10, 1975	2:377
Migdal A B	P Nov. 10, 1975	2:375
Mihalas D	P Aug. 28, 1974	2:122
	P Aug. 28, 1974	2:123
Mikol B	S Sep. 11, 1978	**3:628**
Mikulska Z B	S Oct. 16, 1974	2:165
Mikulski C M	S Apr. 19, 1976	2:458
Milborrow B V	P Jan. 20, 1975	2:214
Milch R A	P Oct. 16, 1974	2:166
Miledi R	P Oct. 31, 1973	1:499
	P Jul. 10, 1978	**3:545**
	P Aug. 28, 1978	**3:604**
	P Nov. 27, 1978	**3:709**
Miles A A	P Oct. 25, 1976	2:616
Milic-Emili J	P Feb. 7, 1977	**3:39**
Millar R L	S Jan. 27, 1975	2:220
Millar W J	P May. 17, 1976	2:489
Miller B E	S Jul. 17, 1974	2:101
Miller C O	P Jan. 27, 1975	2:217
	S Jan. 27, 1975	2:218
Miller E	S Oct. 16, 1974	2:166
Miller E C	S Oct. 16, 1974	2:165
	P Oct. 16, 1974	2:166
	S Oct. 16, 1974	2:167
Miller F	S Nov. 27, 1978	**3:709**
Miller G	P Feb. 16, 1976	2:423
Miller G A	P May. 5, 1975	2:265
	P Jul. 18, 1977	**3:182**
	P Aug. 7, 1978	**3:569**

Miller G A (cont'd)		
	P Sep. 11, 1978	**3:627**
	P Sep. 18, 1978	**3:636**
	P Nov. 6, 1978	**3:676**
Miller G L	P Jun. 20, 1977	**3:150**
Miller H	S Nov. 27, 1974	2:183
Miller J A	S Oct. 16, 1974	2:165
	S Oct. 16, 1974	2:166
	P Oct. 16, 1974	2:167
Miller J F A	P Oct. 3, 1973	1:488
	P Jul. 3, 1974	2:91
	P Oct. 16, 1974	2:166
	S May. 10, 1976	2:475
	P Oct. 18, 1976	2:609
	P Dec. 5, 1977	**3:333**
	P Dec. 12, 1977	**3:339**
	P Dec. 19, 1977	**3:360**
	P Jul. 10, 1978	**3:546**
	P Aug. 28, 1978	**3:606**
	S Nov. 27, 1978	**3:703**
Miller L C	P Mar. 28, 1977	**3:82**
Miller M A	S Dec. 19, 1977	**3:354**
Miller M J	S Apr. 14, 1971	1:174
Miller N	S Sep. 22, 1971	1:243
Miller N E	P Apr. 28, 1975	2:259
	P Apr. 28, 1975	2:261
	P Aug. 7, 1978	**3:569**
	P Sep. 18, 1978	**3:637**
	P Nov. 6, 1978	**3:677**
Miller S L	P Sep. 22, 1971	1:243
Miller W E	S Sep. 11, 1978	**3:630**
Miller W J	S Apr. 12, 1976	2:455
Millonig G	P Apr. 14, 1971	1:161
	P Apr. 14, 1971	1:172
	P Feb. 6, 1974	2:23
	P Dec. 5, 1977	**3:333**
	P Dec. 12, 1977	**3:339**
	P Dec. 19, 1977	**3:360**
Mills A A	P May. 17, 1976	2:489
Mills B Y	P Oct. 4, 1976	2:597
Mills C J	P Nov. 25, 1970	1:141
Mills I H	S Jul. 3, 1974	2:91
Mills J A	S Oct. 4, 1976	2:597
Mills R C	S Mar. 28, 1977	**3:80**
Milne D K	P Oct. 4, 1976	2:595
Milne M D	P Jul. 3, 1974	2:90
Milner P	S Apr. 28, 1975	2:259
Milstead K L	S Jul. 17, 1974	2:101
Mimno H R	P May. 17, 1976	2:489
Minasz R J	S Dec. 19, 1977	**3:362**
Minden J H	S Feb. 16, 1976	2:424
Mingioli E S	S Feb. 6, 1974	2:25
	S Jul. 18, 1977	**3:181**
Minis D H	S Jan. 27, 1975	2:219
Minobe K	S Feb. 7, 1977	**3:37**

Moore

Moore S (cont'd)

	S Dec. 4, 1974	2:186
	P Feb. 21, 1977	**3:**50
	P Jun. 20, 1977	**3:**151
	S Jun. 20, 1977	**3:**152
	S Jul. 18, 1977	**3:**184
	P Dec. 5, 1977	**3:**333
	P Dec. 12, 1977	**3:**339
	P Dec. 12, 1977	**3:**345
	P Dec. 19, 1977	**3:**360
	S Dec. 19, 1977	**3:**362
	P Jul. 10, 1978	**3:**591
	P Aug. 28, 1978	**3:**595
	P Nov. 20, 1978	**3:**692
Moorhead P	S Dec. 4, 1978	**3:**716
Moorhead P S	P Apr. 14, 1971	1:161
	P Apr. 14, 1971	1:171
	P Jan. 9, 1974	2:8
Morgan A R	P Apr. 14, 1971	1:173
	S Apr. 14, 1971	1:174
Morgan C D	S Sep. 11, 1978	**3:**628
Morgan H E	P Nov. 20, 1978	**3:**692
Morgan J F	P Jul. 18, 1977	**3:**182
Morgan M	S Apr. 12, 1976	2:454
Morgan W J	P Aug. 14, 1974	2:115
Morgan W T J	S Oct. 25, 1976	2:614
	S Jun. 20, 1977	**3:**151
Morgan W W	S Aug. 28, 1974	2:122
	S Dec. 19, 1977	**3:**359
Mori H	P Mar. 1, 1976	2:434
Morre D J	S Jan. 20, 1975	2:213
Morris D L	P Feb. 21, 1977	**3:**50
Morris G	S Apr. 19, 1976	2:460
Morris H P	P Jul. 10, 1978	**3:**541
	P Aug. 28, 1978	**3:**595
	S Nov. 27, 1978	**3:**708
Morrison D F	P Nov. 28, 1973	1:513
Morrison M	S Aug. 11, 1971	1:227
Morrison P	S Aug. 28, 1974	2:123
Morrow A G	P Jul. 10, 1978	**3:**546
	P Aug. 28, 1978	**3:**607
	S Nov. 27, 1978	**3:**703
Morse P M	P Jan. 2, 1974	2:3
	P Mar. 22, 1976	2:443
	P May. 24, 1976	2:494
	P Dec. 5, 1977	**3:**186
	P Dec. 12, 1977	**3:**339
	P Dec. 19, 1977	**3:**361
Morton D C	P Aug. 28, 1974	2:123
Morton H J	S Jul. 18, 1977	**3:**182
Morton R A	S Feb. 21, 1977	**3:**49
Moruzzi G	S Feb. 7, 1977	**3:**36
	P Mar. 28, 1977	**3:**82
Moscowitz A	S Dec. 4, 1978	**3:**713
Mosher F A	S Sep. 11, 1978	**3:**627

Moss B	S Apr. 12, 1976	2:455
	S Apr. 12, 1976	2:456
Moss H A	S Nov. 6, 1978	**3:**684
Mossbauer R	P Dec. 12, 1977	**3:**344
Motoyama E K	S Dec. 13, 1976	2:662
Mott F T	P May. 17, 1976	2:489
Mott N F	P Oct. 3, 1973	1:488
	P Nov. 1, 1976	2:622
	P Dec. 5, 1977	**3:**333
	P Dec. 12, 1977	**3:**339
	P Dec. 12, 1977	**3:**344
	P Dec. 19, 1977	**3:**361
Mottelson B	S Jun. 6, 1977	**3:**126
Mottelson B R	P Dec. 12, 1977	**3:**344
Moule Y	S Jul. 18, 1977	**3:**180
Mourant A E	S Oct. 16, 1974	2:167
	S Dec. 13, 1976	2:662
	P Dec. 13, 1976	2:663
Movat H Z	S Apr. 12, 1976	2:454
Muchmore A V	P Dec. 19, 1973	1:521
Mueller A H	S Oct. 16, 1974	2:165
Mueller G C	P Oct. 16, 1974	2:166
Muench H	S Apr. 14, 1971	1:171
	S Jan. 9, 1974	2:8
	S Oct. 25, 1976	2:616
Muetterties E L	P Jul. 10, 1978	**3:**540
	P Aug. 28, 1978	**3:**592
	P Dec. 4, 1978	**3:**714
Muhlethaler K	P Jan. 20, 1975	2:213
	S Jan. 27, 1975	2:218
	S Jan. 27, 1975	2:219
Mui J Y P	S Dec. 19, 1977	**3:**362
Muirhead H	P Feb. 7, 1977	**3:**39
	S Feb. 7, 1977	**3:**41
	S Dec. 19, 1977	**3:**361
Muldrew D B	P Aug. 14, 1974	2:116
Mulford D J	S Feb. 21, 1977	**3:**48
Muliken R S	P Oct. 3, 1973	1:488
Muller A	P Dec. 5, 1977	**3:**333
	P Dec. 12, 1977	**3:**339
	P Dec. 19, 1977	**3:**361
Muller E	P Dec. 5, 1977	**3:**333
	P Dec. 12, 1977	**3:**339
	P Dec. 19, 1977	**3:**361
	P May. 22, 1978	**3:**494
Muller E A	S Aug. 28, 1974	2:122
Muller M	S Oct. 16, 1974	2:165
	S Jul. 12, 1976	2:519
Muller W A	S Nov. 20, 1978	**3:**695
Muller-Eberhard H J	P Jul. 10, 1978	**3:**542
	P Aug. 28, 1978	**3:**596
	S Nov. 27, 1978	**3:**703
Mullertz S	S Jul. 18, 1977	**3:**180
Mulliken R S	P Oct. 3, 1973	1:488
	P Mar. 6, 1974	2:39

Nesmeyanov

Nesmeyanov

Orci

Novikoff A B (cont'd)
| | P Aug. 28, 1978 | 3:606 |
| | P Nov. 27, 1978 | 3:706 |

Nowell P C
	S Apr. 14, 1971	1:171
	S Jan. 9, 1974	2:8
	P Oct. 16, 1974	2:165
	P Oct. 16, 1974	2:167

Noyes R W — S Aug. 28, 1974 — 2:123
Nozieres P — P Feb. 7, 1977 — **3:37**
Nuckolls J — P May. 10, 1976 — 2:477
Nunnally J C — P Sep. 11, 1978 — **3:630**
Nyhan W L — S Jul. 3, 1974 — 2:92

O

O'Brien B J — P Aug. 14, 1974 — 2:116
O'Brien J K — S Jul. 17, 1974 — 2:101
O'Brien J R
| | P Dec. 13, 1976 | 2:661 |
| | P Dec. 13, 1976 | 2:663 |

O'Brien J S — P Jul. 17, 1974 — 2:101
O'Brien S E — S Feb. 16, 1976 — 2:424
O'Brien T P — S Jan. 27, 1975 — 2:220
Occolowitz J L — S Oct. 4, 1976 — 2:595
Ochkur V I — P Nov. 10, 1975 — 2:376
Ochoa S
	S Apr. 14, 1971	1:173
	S Apr. 14, 1971	1:174
	P Dec. 12, 1977	**3:345**
	P Jul. 10, 1978	**3:541**
	P Aug. 28, 1978	**3:595**
	S Nov. 20, 1978	**3:692**

O'Conor G T
| | S Oct. 16, 1974 | 2:166 |
| | S Oct. 16, 1974 | 2:167 |

Odell C R — P Aug. 28, 1974 — 2:124
Odell G B — P Jul. 17, 1974 — 2:100
Odell W D
	P Jul. 10, 1978	**3:544**
	P Aug. 28, 1978	**3:602**
	P Nov. 20, 1978	**3:695**
	P Nov. 20, 1978	**3:697**

Odland G F — S Dec. 13, 1976 — 2:663
Oeser A
| | S Jan. 20, 1975 | 2:215 |
| | S Jan. 27, 1975 | 2:220 |

O'Gallagher J J — S Feb. 23, 1976 — 2:428
Ogsbury J S — S Dec. 19, 1973 — 1:522
Ogston A G — S Mar. 7, 1977 — **3:58**
Ogur M — P Jun. 20, 1977 — **3:151**
Ohno K — S Mar. 1, 1976 — 2:434
Ohtsuka E — S Apr. 14, 1971 — 1:173
Okami Y — S Dec. 4, 1978 — **3:716**
Okamoto Y
	S Mar. 6, 1974	2:42
	S Jun. 6, 1977	**3:126**
	S Dec. 19, 1977	**3:355**

Okamura N — S Nov. 20, 1978 — **3:690**
Okazaki R — S May. 10, 1976 — 2:476
Oke J B
| | P Aug. 28, 1974 | 2:122 |
| | P Aug. 28, 1974 | 2:123 |

Oke J B (cont'd)
| | P Aug. 28, 1974 | 2:124 |

O'Keefe E — S Apr. 12, 1976 — 2:453
Oken D E — S Nov. 27, 1978 — **3:710**
Okubo S
	P Mar. 1, 1976	2:434
	S Apr. 19, 1976	2:458
	P Apr. 19, 1976	2:459

Okumura F S — S Jan. 27, 1975 — 2:217
Olah G A
	P Oct. 3, 1973	1:488
	P Oct. 17, 1973	1:493
	P Dec. 5, 1977	**3:333**
	P Dec. 12, 1977	**3:339**
	P Dec. 19, 1977	**3:361**
	P Jul. 10, 1978	**3:540**
	P Aug. 28, 1978	**3:592**
	P Dec. 4, 1978	**3:714**

Olbrisch R R — S Sep. 22, 1971 — 1:244
Old L J
	P Jul. 3, 1974	2:92
	P Oct. 16, 1974	2:166
	P Oct. 16, 1974	2:167
	P Jul. 10, 1978	**3:546**
	P Aug. 28, 1978	**3:605**
	P Nov. 27, 1978	**3:707**
	P Nov. 27, 1978	**3:708**

Olds J
| | P Apr. 28, 1975 | 2:259 |
| | P Apr. 28, 1975 | 2:260 |

Olesen P — S May. 10, 1976 — 2:477
Olins A L — S Apr. 12, 1976 — 2:454
Olins D E — S Apr. 12, 1976 — 2:454
Oliver J
| | S Aug. 14, 1974 | 2:115 |
| | P Aug. 14, 1974 | 2:116 |

Olsen N
| | S Feb. 21, 1977 | **3:51** |
| | S Dec. 19, 1977 | **3:362** |

Olsen O R — S Sep. 11, 1978 — **3:627**
Olson J M — S Jan. 20, 1975 — 2:214
Olson L
	S Oct. 18, 1976	2:609
	S Dec. 19, 1977	**3:354**
	S Nov. 20, 1978	**3:696**

Olson L C — S Jul. 17, 1974 — 2:101
Olver R R — S Sep. 11, 1978 — **3:627**
O'Malley B W — P Feb. 23, 1976 — 2:427
Omnes R — P Feb. 7, 1977 — **3:36**
O'Neal C — S Apr. 14, 1971 — 1:173
O'Neal H E — S Dec. 4, 1978 — **3:713**
Onsager L
	P Mar. 6, 1974	2:44
	P Nov. 1, 1976	2:622
	P Mar. 7, 1977	**3:59**
	P Dec. 12, 1977	**3:345**

Oort J
| | P Oct. 16, 1974 | 2:167 |
| | P Dec. 13, 1976 | 2:662 |

Oosterhof D K — P Apr. 12, 1976 — 2:455
Oppenheimer G D — S Oct. 25, 1976 — 2:613
Oppenheimer R — S May. 24, 1976 — 2:494
Oram A — S Sep. 11, 1978 — **3:628**
Orci L — S Apr. 12, 1976 — 2:455

Perutz

Park C R	P Jul. 10, 1978	3:544	Pearlstone Z (cont'd)			
	P Aug. 28, 1978	3:602		S Aug. 7, 1978	3:570	
	S Nov. 20, 1978	3:692	Pearmain G	P Jul. 3, 1974	2:92	
Park J T	P Feb. 21, 1977	3:50	Pearse A G E	P Aug. 11, 1971	1:226	
Park S V	S Apr. 19, 1976	2:459		P Oct. 3, 1973	1:488	
Parker A J	P Mar. 6, 1974	2:43		P Jan. 2, 1974	2:4	
Parker C	S Nov. 20, 1978	3:691		S Feb. 7, 1977	3:39	
Parker C A	S Mar. 6, 1974	2:40		P Dec. 5, 1977	3:333	
	S Jun. 6, 1977	3:126		P Dec. 12, 1977	3:339	
Parker E N	P Aug. 28, 1974	2:122		P Dec. 19, 1977	3:361	
Parker F	P Dec. 13, 1976	2:663		P Jul. 10, 1978	3:546	
Parker R C	S Jul. 18, 1977	3:182		P Aug. 28, 1978	3:605	
Parkman P D	S Jul. 3, 1974	2:93		P Nov. 27, 1978	3:707	
Parr R G	S Feb. 6, 1974	2:24	Pearson P L	P Dec. 19, 1973	1:521	
	S Mar. 6, 1974	2:39	Pearson R G	P Mar. 6, 1974	2:41	
	S Jun. 6, 1977	3:127		S Dec. 19, 1977	3:354	
Parsons E M	S May. 10, 1976	2:475	Peccei R D	S Feb. 16, 1976	2:424	
Parsons T	P Sep. 11, 1978	3:631	Pedersen K O	S Jan. 2, 1974	2:4	
	P Sep. 18, 1978	3:639	Peebles P J E	S Aug. 28, 1974	2:122	
	P Nov. 6, 1978	3:679		P Aug. 28, 1974	2:124	
Partridge S M	P Feb. 21, 1977	3:50	Peirson A G	S Nov. 28, 1973	1:513	
Passonneau J V	P Jul. 10, 1978	3:541	Pelczynski A	S Nov. 15, 1976	2:633	
	P Aug. 28, 1978	3:595		P Nov. 15, 1976	2:634	
	P Nov. 20, 1978	3:692		S Nov. 15, 1976	2:634	
	S Nov. 20, 1978	3:692	Pellegrino A D	S Dec. 19, 1977	3:357	
Pastan I	S Oct. 31, 1973	1:498	Penman S	P Feb. 7, 1977	3:38	
	P Jul. 10, 1978	3:542		S Feb. 7, 1977	3:41	
	P Aug. 28, 1978	3:598		P Jul. 10, 1978	3:544	
	S Nov. 27, 1978	3:708		P Aug. 28, 1978	3:601	
Patau K	P Jul. 3, 1974	2:91		P Nov. 27, 1978	3:707	
	S Jul. 17, 1974	2:100	Penrose R	P Nov. 28, 1973	1:512	
	S Jul. 17, 1974	2:101	Penzias A A	P Aug. 28, 1974	2:122	
	P Jul. 12, 1976	2:522	Perevodchikova N I	S Oct. 16, 1974	2:167	
Patel D J	P Dec. 4, 1978	3:714	Perkins J P	S Nov. 20, 1978	3:691	
Patter V R	S Jun. 20, 1977	3:150	Perkins M	S Feb. 23, 1976	2:428	
Paul E G	S Dec. 4, 1978	3:713	Perlmann H	S May. 10, 1976	2:477	
Paul M A	P Mar. 6, 1974	2:44	Perlmann P	P May. 10, 1976	2:477	
	P Jun. 6, 1977	3:127	Perlstein J H	S Feb. 16, 1976	2:424	
Paul W E	S May. 10, 1976	2:475	Pernis B	P Dec. 19, 1973	1:522	
	P Jul. 10, 1978	3:542		S May. 10, 1976	2:476	
	P Aug. 28, 1978	3:596		P Feb. 7, 1977	3:40	
	S Nov. 20, 1978	3:695	Perova S D	S Oct. 16, 1974	2:167	
Pauling L	P Aug. 11, 1971	1:226	Perrin D D	P Oct. 4, 1976	2:597	
	P Oct. 3, 1973	1:488	Perrin F	P Nov. 1, 1976	2:622	
	P Jan. 2, 1974	2:2	Perry J H	P Dec. 4, 1974	2:186	
	P Dec. 4, 1974	2:186	Perry R P	P Apr. 12, 1976	2:456	
	P Mar. 28, 1977	3:82		P May. 10, 1976	2:476	
	P Dec. 5, 1977	3:333	Perutz M F	P Dec. 19, 1973	1:521	
	P Dec. 12, 1977	3:339		S Feb. 7, 1977	3:39	
	P Dec. 12, 1977	3:344		P Feb. 7, 1977	3:41	
	P Dec. 19, 1977	3:361		P Dec. 5, 1977	3:333	
Pauliny-Toth I I K	P Aug. 28, 1974	2:124		P Dec. 12, 1977	3:339	
Paupoulis A	P Mar. 22, 1976	2:443		P Dec. 12, 1977	3:344	
Paymaster J C	S Oct. 31, 1973	1:499		P Dec. 19, 1977	3:361	
Peaceman D W	P Nov. 28, 1973	1:512		P Jul. 10, 1978	3:543	
Pearlstone Z	S May. 5, 1975	2:268				

Perutz

Perutz M F (cont'd)		
	P Aug. 28, 1978	3:599
	P Dec. 4, 1978	3:718
Petersen F E	P Dec. 4, 1974	2:187
Peterson E A	P Feb. 6, 1974	2:25
	P Jun. 20, 1977	3:151
Peterson L R	P May. 5, 1975	2:265
	P Aug. 7, 1978	3:569
Peterson M J	S May. 5, 1975	2:265
	S Aug. 7, 1978	3:569
Peterson P A	P Feb. 23, 1976	2:427
Peterson P L	S Nov. 25, 1970	1:141
Peterson R D A	P Jul. 3, 1974	2:92
	S Nov. 27, 1978	3:702
Peterson R E	P Jun. 20, 1977	3:151
Peterson R T	S Sep. 11, 1978	3:628
Peterson S W	P Sep. 11, 1974	2:132
Peterson W W	P Nov. 21, 1973	1:507
	P Mar. 22, 1976	2:443
Pethica B A	S Nov. 20, 1978	3:693
Petrinovich L F	S Apr. 28, 1975	2:261
Petropoulos P	S Oct. 16, 1974	2:165
	S Jul. 12, 1976	2:519
Petrzilk V A	P May. 17, 1976	2:489
Petschek H E	S Aug. 14, 1974	2:115
	S Aug. 14, 1974	2:116
	S Feb. 7, 1977	3:39
Petzold G L	S May. 10, 1976	2:476
Pfleiderer G	S Jul. 12, 1976	2:518
Phillips C H	S Jul. 3, 1974	2:92
Phillips D C	P Sep. 11, 1974	2:131
	S Sep. 11, 1974	2:131
	S Oct. 18, 1976	2:609
Phillips G E	S Nov. 27, 1974	2:183
Phillips J	S Mar. 7, 1977	3:57
	S Dec. 19, 1977	3:354
Phillips M J	S Dec. 13, 1976	2:662
Philpot G R	S Jul. 3, 1974	2:91
Phoenix C H	P Apr. 28, 1975	2:260
	S Apr. 28, 1975	2:261
	S Nov. 29, 1977	3:320
Piaget J	P Sep. 11, 1978	3:628
	P Sep. 18, 1978	3:637
	P Nov. 6, 1978	3:677
Piccioni R L	S Feb. 23, 1976	2:427
Pickens P T	P Nov. 20, 1978	3:697
Pickles V A	S Oct. 4, 1976	2:595
Pierce J C	S Nov. 27, 1978	3:702
Piessens W F	P Feb. 16, 1976	2:424
Pietra G	P Oct. 16, 1974	2:167
Piez K A	P Jul. 10, 1978	3:541
	P Aug. 28, 1978	3:595
	P Nov. 20, 1978	3:692

Pilcher J	S Feb. 23, 1976	2:427
Pilkuhn H	S Feb. 7, 1977	3:36
Pimentel G C	P Aug. 11, 1971	1:227
	P Jan. 2, 1974	2:2
Pines D	S Feb. 7, 1977	3:37
Pings W	P Sep. 22, 1971	1:244
Pinsky S S	S Feb. 16, 1976	2:424
Pirila P	S Apr. 19, 1976	2:459
Pisano J J	P Nov. 27, 1974	2:183
Piskala A	P Dec. 4, 1978	3:715
Pitcock J A	P Dec. 13, 1976	2:663
Pitman M G	P Oct. 4, 1976	2:597
Pitman W C	S Aug. 14, 1974	2:115
	P Aug. 14, 1974	2:117
Pitot H C	P Nov. 27, 1978	3:708
Pittendrigh C S	P Jan. 20, 1975	2:213
	P Jan. 27, 1975	2:218
	P Jan. 27, 1975	2:219
Pitts J N	S Aug. 11, 1971	1:228
Pitzer K S	S Mar. 7, 1977	3:58
Pivan R B	S Feb. 21, 1977	3:49
	S Dec. 19, 1977	3:360
Plata F	S May. 29, 1978	3:501
Platt J R	P Mar. 7, 1977	3:59
	S Mar. 7, 1977	3:59
Playfair J H	S Feb. 7, 1977	3:40
	S Nov. 27, 1978	3:703
Pletscher A	S Jul. 18, 1977	3:180
Plotz C M	S Jul. 3, 1974	2:89
	S Jul. 18, 1977	3:184
Plunkett G T	P May. 17, 1976	2:489
Pocalyko A	P Aug. 30, 1972	1:356
Podolsky W J	S Apr. 14, 1971	1:172
Pohley F M	S Jul. 18, 1977	3:184
Polder D	S Mar. 7, 1977	3:57
Politzer H D	S Feb. 23, 1976	2:427
	S Apr. 19, 1976	2:458
	S Apr. 19, 1976	2:459
Poljakoff-Mayber A	S Jan. 20, 1975	2:211
Polley M J	S Feb. 16, 1976	2:424
Pollister A W	S Mar. 28, 1977	3:82
Pomeranchuk I Y	P Nov. 10, 1975	2:375
Pompe A	S Oct. 4, 1976	2:596
Pon N G	S Jan. 20, 1975	2:212
Ponten J A	S Dec. 4, 1978	3:716
Pontoppidan H	S Jul. 3, 1974	2:93
Pontryagin L S	P Nov. 21, 1973	1:506
	P Mar. 22, 1976	2:443
Poon C H	S Oct. 17, 1973	1:493
Pople J A	P Oct. 3, 1973	1:488
	P Jan. 2, 1974	2:3
	P Mar. 6, 1974	2:39
	P Mar. 6, 1974	2:40

Rich

Shanks

Shanks R G	S Jul. 3, 1974	2:92	Sherwood T K	S Dec. 4, 1974	2:186
Shankweiler D P	S May. 5, 1975	2:268	Shettles L B	S Feb. 21, 1977	**3:48**
Shannon C E	P Nov. 21, 1973	1:506	Shevach B J	S Sep. 11, 1978	**3:628**
	P Nov. 28, 1973	1:513	Shibko S	P Nov. 20, 1978	**3:693**
	P Mar. 7, 1977	**3:60**	Shillingford J P	S Nov. 25, 1970	1:141
Shannon J C	S Jan. 20, 1975	2:212	Shilov G E	S Nov. 21, 1973	1:507
Shannon J E	S Oct. 16, 1974	2:167	Shimmins A J	S Oct. 4, 1976	2:596
Shannon J S	S Jan. 27, 1975	2:219		S Oct. 4, 1976	2:598
	S Oct. 4, 1976	2:595	Shockley W	P Mar. 22, 1976	2:445
	P Oct. 4, 1976	2:597		P Mar. 7, 1977	**3:60**
Shannon R D	P Mar. 6, 1974	2:41		P Jun. 6, 1977	**3:128**
	P Sep. 11, 1974	2:131		P Dec. 12, 1977	**3:344**
	P Oct. 18, 1976	2:608	Shoenrich E H	S Jul. 3, 1974	2:89
Shapiro A L	P Feb. 6, 1974	2:23	Shone J D	P Dec. 4, 1978	**3:717**
	P Nov. 20, 1978	**3:692**	Shonk C E	P Oct. 16, 1974	2:167
Shapiro B	S Dec. 13, 1976	2:660	Shore P A	P Jul. 18, 1977	**3:183**
Shapiro P O	S Nov. 27, 1974	2:183	Shortman K	P Oct. 4, 1976	2:596
Shapland C	S Jul. 3, 1974	2:91	Shpolskii E V	P Nov. 10, 1975	2:376
Sharma S K	P Apr. 12, 1976	2:456	Shrago E	P Nov. 20, 1978	**3:691**
Sharon N	P May. 10, 1976	2:475	Shreffler D C	P Apr. 12, 1976	2:456
Sharp L E	S Aug. 28, 1974	2:124	Shu F H	S Aug. 28, 1974	2:124
Sharpe W F	P Aug. 7, 1978	**3:570**	Shubic P	S Oct. 16, 1974	2:167
Sharpless S	P Aug. 28, 1974	2:124	Shulman L E	S Jul. 3, 1974	2:89
Shatkin A J	S Apr. 12, 1976	2:454	Shumway W	P Mar. 28, 1977	**3:82**
	S Apr. 12, 1976	2:455	Shurrocks V M	S Jan. 27, 1975	2:218
	S Apr. 12, 1976	2:456	Sibley J A	P Feb. 21, 1977	**3:51**
	S Nov. 27, 1978	**3:706**	Sica V	S Feb. 23, 1976	2:427
	S Nov. 27, 1978	**3:707**	Siddall T H	S Mar. 6, 1974	2:43
Shaw M	P Jan. 27, 1975	2:219	Sidman M	P Apr. 28, 1975	2:259
Shaw R	S Dec. 4, 1978	**3:713**	Siegbahn K	P Aug. 11, 1971	1:227
Shay H	P Mar. 28, 1977	**3:82**	Siegel S	P Aug. 11, 1971	1:226
Shearer G M	S Feb. 23, 1976	2:427		P Oct. 3, 1973	1:488
Sheehan J C	P Apr. 14, 1971	1:172		P Nov. 28, 1973	1:511
	P Jun. 20, 1977	**3:151**		P Jan. 2, 1974	2:5
Sheldon R	P Oct. 17, 1973	1:493		P Sep. 11, 1978	**3:630**
	P May. 10, 1976	2:476		P Sep. 18, 1978	**3:638**
Shelley H J	P Jul. 3, 1974	2:91		P Nov. 6, 1978	**3:678**
Shelton E	S Oct. 16, 1974	2:165	Siegelman H W	S Jan. 20, 1975	2:212
	S Mar. 28, 1977	**3:80**	Sierra M F	S Feb. 16, 1976	2:424
Shemin D	S Jun. 20, 1977	**3:151**	Sievers R E	S Oct. 31, 1973	1:498
Shepard C U	P May. 17, 1976	2:489		S Mar. 6, 1974	2:41
Shepard R N	P Nov. 21, 1973	1:507	Sifferd R H	P Oct. 25, 1976	2:616
	P May. 5, 1975	2:266	Siggaard-Andersen O	P Oct. 18, 1976	2:609
	P Aug. 7, 1978	**3:570**	Sikes M P	S Oct. 16, 1974	2:166
	P Sep. 18, 1978	**3:638**	Silber R	S Apr. 12, 1976	2:454
	P Nov. 6, 1978	**3:678**	Silber R H	P Nov. 27, 1974	2:183
Sheppard J R	P May. 10, 1976	2:475		P Jul. 18, 1977	**3:183**
Shercliff J A	P Nov. 25, 1970	1:141	Silberg P A	P May. 17, 1976	2:489
Sherlock S	P Jul. 10, 1978	3:28-13	Silengo L	S Feb. 7, 1977	**3:40**
	P Aug. 28, 1978	**3:607**	Silin V P	P Nov. 10, 1975	2:377
	S Nov. 27, 1978	**3:704**	Sillen L G	P Dec. 5, 1977	**3:334**
Sherman F G	S Jul. 18, 1977	**3:183**		P Dec. 12, 1977	**3:339**
Sherr E	S Mar. 28, 1977	**3:80**		P Dec. 19, 1977	**3:362**
Sherris J C	S Dec. 13, 1976	2:659			

Smillie

Silva R W	S Aug. 14, 1974	2:117	Sjogren H O	(cont'd)		
Silver W K	S Oct. 16, 1974	2:166			S Nov. 27, 1978	3:708
Silverman D	S Oct. 17, 1973	1:493	Skeggs L T		P Dec. 13, 1976	2:660
Silverman F N	S Jul. 17, 1974	2:101	Skillman S		S Mar. 6, 1974	2:39
Silverman J	P May. 5, 1975	2:267			S Sep. 11, 1974	2:130
Silverman W A	P Jul. 17, 1974	2:100			S Oct. 18, 1976	2:607
Simha R	P Mar. 7, 1977	3:60	Skillman T L		S Aug. 14, 1974	2:116
Simmons H D	S Dec. 19, 1977	3:362	Skinner B F		S Jan. 2, 1974	2:4
Simmons N S	S Jun. 20, 1977	3:150			S Apr. 28, 1975	2:259
Simon E J	P Jun. 20, 1977	3:151			S Mar. 28, 1977	3:80
Simon G	S Dec. 13, 1976	2:661			S Aug. 7, 1978	3:567
Simon G W	S Aug. 28, 1974	2:123			P Sep. 11, 1978	3:626
Simon H A	S Sep. 11, 1978	3:627			S Sep. 11, 1978	3:626
	P Sep. 18, 1978	3:637			P Sep. 18, 1978	3:636
	P Nov. 6, 1978	3:678			P Nov. 6, 1978	3:676
	P Nov. 6, 1978	3:685	Skipper H E		P Oct. 16, 1974	2:167
Simpson E	S Apr. 12, 1976	2:453	Sklar A L		S Nov. 1, 1976	2:621
Simpson G G	P Mar. 28, 1977	3:82	Skobov V G		S Nov. 10, 1975	2:376
Simpson J A	P Feb. 23, 1976	2:428	Skoog F		S Jan. 20, 1975	2:211
Simpson W T	S Mar. 6, 1974	2:38			S Jan. 20, 1975	2:213
	S Dec. 4, 1978	3:715			S Jan. 27, 1975	2:217
Singal D P	S Nov. 27, 1978	3:704			P Jan. 27, 1975	2:218
Singer J E	S Apr. 28, 1975	2:260			P Jan. 27, 1975	2:220
	S Aug. 7, 1978	3:569			S Oct. 18, 1976	2:608
Singer J M	P Jul. 3, 1974	2:89			S Oct. 18, 1976	2:610
	P Jul. 18, 1977	3:184	Skou J C		P Jun. 20, 1977	3:152
Singer K	P Jul. 18, 1977	3:184			P Dec. 5, 1977	3:334
Singer L	S Jul. 18, 1977	3:184			P Dec. 12, 1977	3:339
Singer R B	P Jul. 3, 1974	2:89			P Dec. 19, 1977	3:362
	P Mar. 28, 1977	3:83	Slack C R		S Jan. 20, 1975	2:215
Singer S	P May. 17, 1976	2:489			P Jan. 27, 1975	2:220
Singer S J	P Oct. 17, 1973	1:493			S Jan. 27, 1975	2:220
	S Feb. 23, 1976	2:428	Slansky R		S Oct. 17, 1973	1:493
	P May. 10, 1976	2:475	Slater E C		S Mar. 1, 1976	2:434
	S Mar. 28, 1977	3:82	Slater J C		P Oct. 3, 1973	1:488
	P Jul. 10, 1978	3:543			P Nov. 1, 1976	2:622
	P Aug. 28, 1978	3:599			P Jun. 6, 1977	3:128
	P Nov. 27, 1978	3:707			P Dec. 5, 1977	3:334
Sinsheimer R L	P Jul. 10, 1978	3:545			P Dec. 12, 1977	3:339
	P Aug. 28, 1978	3:604			P Dec. 19, 1977	3:362
	S Nov. 27, 1978	3:705			P May. 22, 1978	3:493
Siplet H	S Mar. 28, 1977	3:82	Slattery P		P Feb. 16, 1976	2:423
Sirsat S M	S Oct. 31, 1973	1:499	Slee O B		S Oct. 4, 1976	2:597
Siscoe G L	S Aug. 14, 1974	2:116	Slepian D		P Nov. 28, 1973	1:512
Sjoberg O	S May. 10, 1976	2:477	Slepian J		S Nov. 25, 1970	1:141
Sjoerdsma A	P Jul. 10, 1978	3:543	Sloane-Stanley G H		S Apr. 14, 1971	1:171
	P Aug. 28, 1978	3:600			S Jan. 9, 1974	2:7
	S Nov. 20, 1978	3:696			S Mar. 6, 1974	2:42
Sjogren H O	S Oct. 31, 1973	1:499			S Jun. 20, 1977	3:149
	P Oct. 16, 1974	2:165			S Dec. 19, 1977	3:358
	S Oct. 16, 1974	2:165	Slonimski P P		S May. 29, 1978	3:500
	P Oct. 16, 1974	2:166	Small D M		S Jul. 3, 1974	2:93
	S Oct. 16, 1974	2:166	Small P A		P Dec. 4, 1974	2:186
	S Dec. 19, 1977	3:360	Smeby R R		S Nov. 20, 1978	3:697
	P Nov. 27, 1978	3:703	Smetana K		S Oct. 16, 1974	2:167
			Smillie R M		P Jan. 27, 1975	2:218

Van

Watson

Watson M L (cont'd)	P Dec. 19, 1977	3:363
Watson R E	P Sep. 11, 1974	2:132
Watson R H	S Oct. 4, 1976	2:598
Wattiaux R	S Apr. 14, 1971	1:172
	S Feb. 6, 1974	2:23
	S Jul. 18, 1977	3:181
	S Nov. 20, 1978	3:697
Waugh N C	P May. 5, 1975	2:267
	P Aug. 7, 1978	3:570
Waymouth C	P Oct. 16, 1974	2:166
Weakland J	S May. 5, 1975	2:264
	S Aug. 7, 1978	3:566
Weatherley P E	P Jan. 27, 1975	2:217
	S Oct. 4, 1976	2:597
Weaver W	S Nov. 28, 1973	1:513
Webb C	S Apr. 12, 1976	2:453
Webb E C	S Aug. 11, 1971	1:226
	S Jan. 2, 1974	2:4
Webb J	S Jul. 3, 1974	2:90
Webb M	S Feb. 6, 1974	2:24
	S Jul. 18, 1977	3:184
Webb R A	P Feb. 16, 1976	2:423
Webber W R	S Aug. 14, 1974	2:116
Weber E J	P Aug. 28, 1974	2:123
Weber G	P Oct. 3, 1973	1:488
	P Dec. 5, 1977	3:334
	P Dec. 12, 1977	3:339
	P Dec. 19, 1977	3:363
	P Jul. 10, 1978	3:546
	P Aug. 28, 1978	3:605
Weber K	P Jan. 9, 1974	2:9
	P Dec. 5, 1977	3:334
	P Dec. 12, 1977	3:339
	P Dec. 19, 1977	3:363
	P May. 22, 1978	3:493
	P Jul. 10, 1978	3:545
	P Aug. 28, 1978	3:604
	P Nov. 20, 1978	3:693
Weber M	P Sep. 11, 1978	3:630
	P Sep. 18, 1978	3:639
	P Nov. 6, 1978	3:679
Weber R P	S Jan. 20, 1975	2:211
Webster B L	S Oct. 17, 1973	1:493
Webster H D F	P Dec. 13, 1976	2:663
Webster R E	P Apr. 14, 1971	1:173
Wechsler D	P Sep. 11, 1978	3:629
	P Sep. 18, 1978	3:638
	P Nov. 6, 1978	3:678
Wechsler H	P Aug. 7, 1978	3:570
Weedon B C L	S Feb. 6, 1974	2:24
	S Mar. 6, 1974	2:41
	S Mar. 7, 1977	3:57
Weeks J R	S Dec. 19, 1977	3:355
	S Nov. 20, 1978	3:697

Wei C M	P Apr. 12, 1976	2:455
	P Apr. 12, 1976	2:456
Weichselbaum T E	P Dec. 13, 1976	2:659
	P Mar. 28, 1977	3:83
Weigele M	S May. 10, 1976	2:476
Weijers H A	P Jul. 17, 1974	2:100
Weil-Malherbe H	S Nov. 20, 1978	3:695
Weill J D	S Nov. 20, 1978	3:692
Weinberg S	P May. 10, 1976	2:476
	P Dec. 5, 1977	3:334
	P Dec. 12, 1977	3:339
	S Dec. 19, 1977	3:360
	P Dec. 19, 1977	3:363
	P Jul. 10, 1978	3:545
	P Aug. 28, 1978	3:604
	P Nov. 27, 1978	3:709
Weinfeld F D	S Sep. 11, 1978	3:628
Weinstein M	S Apr. 19, 1976	2:460
Weinstein V	S Feb. 23, 1976	2:427
Weinzierl J	S Feb. 16, 1976	2:423
Weis J H	S Oct. 31, 1973	1:498
Weisbach H	P Aug. 28, 1978	3:599
Weisenberg R C	P May. 10, 1976	2:476
Weiss B	S Nov. 20, 1978	3:695
Weiss B Z	P Aug. 30, 1972	1:357
Weiss J F	P Feb. 7, 1977	3:39
Weiss L	P Jul. 10, 1978	3:546
	P Aug. 28, 1978	3:606
	S Nov. 27, 1978	3:707
Weiss M	S Dec. 13, 1976	2:661
Weiss P	P Mar. 28, 1977	3:83
	P Dec. 5, 1977	3:334
	P Dec. 12, 1977	3:339
	P Dec. 19, 1977	3:363
Weissbach H	S Apr. 14, 1971	1:173
	S Dec. 19, 1977	3:363
	P Jul. 10, 1978	3:544
	S Nov. 20, 1978	3:693
Weisskopf V	P Nov. 1, 1976	2:622
Weissmann G	P Jul. 10, 1978	3:545
	P Aug. 28, 1978	3:601
	P Nov. 27, 1978	3:707
Welch G H	S Jul. 18, 1977	3:183
Weldon E J	P Nov. 21, 1973	1:507
	S Mar. 22, 1976	2:443
Weller T H	P Jul. 3, 1974	2:91
	P Dec. 12, 1977	3:345
Wells I C	S Mar. 28, 1977	3:82
Wells M	S Sep. 11, 1974	2:131
Wells R D	S Apr. 14, 1971	1:173
Wells S L	S Mar. 28, 1977	3:82
Wells W W	S Feb. 6, 1974	2:24
	S Mar. 6, 1974	2:43
	S Dec. 4, 1978	3:715
Wen W Y	S Mar. 6, 1974	2:43

Wilkinson

Wilkinson J H	P Nov. 21, 1973	1:507
	P Mar. 22, 1976	2:443
Willard H H	P Nov. 1, 1976	2:622
Williams C A	S Jul. 18, 1977	**3:**181
	S Dec. 19, 1977	**3:**358
Williams D	S Apr. 19, 1976	2:459
Williams D E	S Nov. 20, 1978	**3:**693
Williams D H	S Aug. 11, 1971	1:227
	S Oct. 31, 1973	1:498
	S Dec. 19, 1973	1:521
	S Mar. 6, 1974	2:39
	S Mar. 6, 1974	2:40
Williams D J	P Aug. 14, 1974	2:116
Williams E	P Nov. 25, 1970	1:141
Williams E D	P Dec. 13, 1976	2:663
Williams G R	S Jul. 18, 1977	**3:**180
	S Dec. 19, 1977	**3:**356
Williams J	S Sep. 22, 1971	1:244
Williams M L	P Dec. 4, 1974	2:186
	P Jun. 6, 1977	**3:**128
Williams P A R	S Nov. 27, 1974	2:183
Williams P J S	S Aug. 28, 1974	2:122
Williamson D H	P Nov. 20, 1978	**3:**691
Willins R	S Dec. 13, 1976	2:662
Willis A L	S Oct. 31, 1973	1:499
Willis W D	S Nov. 20, 1978	**3:**695
Willis W J	S Apr. 14, 1971	1:172
Wilson A J C	P Mar. 6, 1974	2:40
	P Mar. 7, 1977	**3:**60
Wilson A T	S Mar. 28, 1977	**3:**83
Wilson E B	P Jan. 2, 1974	2:2
	P Nov. 1, 1976	2:622
	P Mar. 7, 1977	**3:**60
	P Dec. 5, 1977	**3:**334
	P Dec. 12, 1977	**3:**339
	P Dec. 19, 1977	**3:**363
Wilson J A	P Apr. 19, 1976	2:460
Wilson J D	P Jul. 10, 1978	**3:**542
	P Aug. 28, 1978	**3:**598
	S Nov. 20, 1978	**3:**695
	P Dec. 4, 1978	**3:**717
Wilson J M	S Dec. 19, 1977	**3:**355
Wilson K B	S Nov. 28, 1973	1:513
Wilson K G	P Oct. 17, 1973	1:493
	P May. 10, 1976	2:475
Wilson K W	S Mar. 7, 1977	**3:**57
Wilson M P W	P Aug. 30, 1972	1:357
Wilson O C	P Aug. 28, 1974	2:124
Wilson R	S Feb. 23, 1976	2:427
Wilson R W	S Aug. 28, 1974	2:122
Wilson T H	P Jul. 18, 1977	**3:**184
Winer B J	P Aug. 11, 1971	1:226
	P Nov. 28, 1973	1:511
	P Jan. 2, 1974	2:5

Winer B J (cont'd)		
	P Dec. 5, 1977	**3:**334
	P Dec. 12, 1977	**3:**339
	P Dec. 19, 1977	**3:**363
	P Sep. 11, 1978	**3:**630
	P Sep. 18, 1978	**3:**638
	P Nov. 6, 1978	**3:**678
Winkelmann E H	S Dec. 19, 1977	**3:**359
Winokur G	S May. 10, 1976	2:477
	S Aug. 7, 1978	**3:**567
Winstein S	P Oct. 3, 1973	1:488
	S Mar. 7, 1977	**3:**58
	P Dec. 5, 1977	**3:**334
	P Dec. 12, 1977	**3:**339
	P Dec. 19, 1977	**3:**363
	P May. 22, 1978	**3:**493
	P Jul. 10, 1978	**3:**540
	P Aug. 28, 1978	**3:**593
	P Dec. 4, 1978	**3:**715
Winston P W	P Jan. 27, 1975	2:218
Winther A	S Jun. 6, 1977	**3:**126
Wintour M	S Oct. 4, 1976	2:597
Wintrobe M M	P Aug. 11, 1971	1:227
	P Jan. 2, 1974	2:4
Winzler R J	P Feb. 21, 1977	**3:**60
Wirtz E O	S Jul. 17, 1974	2:101
Wiseman A	S Jul. 18, 1977	**3:**184
Wiskich J T	P Jan. 20, 1975	2:212
Wissler R W	S Dec. 13, 1976	2:660
Witham A C	S Mar. 28, 1977	**3:**80
Witkin H A	P May. 5, 1975	2:264
	P May. 5, 1975	2:267
	P Sep. 11, 1978	**3:**629
	P Sep. 18, 1978	**3:**638
	P Nov. 6, 1978	**3:**678
Witkop B	P Jul. 10, 1978	**3:**540
	P Aug. 28, 1978	**3:**593
	S Nov. 20, 1978	**3:**694
Wittig G	P Dec. 5, 1977	**3:**334
	P Dec. 12, 1977	**3:**339
	P Dec. 19, 1977	**3:**363
Wittman R H	P Aug. 30, 1972	1:356
Wittmann A	P May. 17, 1976	2:490
Wofsy S C	P Apr. 19, 1976	2:459
Wohl C G	S Apr. 14, 1971	1:172
Wolanski B S	S Apr. 12, 1976	2:455
Wolf E	S Aug. 11, 1971	1:226
	S Aug. 11, 1971	1:227
	S Jan. 2, 1974	2:2
Wolf K	P May. 17, 1976	2:490
Wolf M M	S Aug. 7, 1978	**3:**566
Wolf R E	S Sep. 11, 1978	**3:**628
Wolfe J H	P Aug. 14, 1974	2:117
Wolff J	P Feb. 16, 1976	2:424
Wolff P	S Jul. 12, 1976	2:519

NOTES

NOTES

NOTES

NOTES